SOCIOLOGY IN AMERICA

D1500709

SOCIOLOGY *in* AMERICA

A History

EDITED BY CRAIG CALHOUN

An ASA Centennial Publication

The University of Chicago Press :: CHICAGO AND LONDON

CRAIG CALHOUN is president of the Social Science Research Council and
professor of sociology and history at New York University. He is the editor or
coeditor of several volumes and author of *Nationalism* and *Neither Gods nor
Emperors*.

The University of Chicago Press, Chicago 60637
The University of Chicago Press, Ltd., London
© 2007 by The American Sociological Association
All rights reserved. Published 2007
Printed in the United States of America
16 15 14 13 12 11 10 09 08 07   1 2 3 4 5

The University of Chicago Press gratefully acknowledges the financial assistance
of the American Sociological Association in defraying publication costs.

ISBN-13 (cloth): 978-0-226-09094-8
ISBN-13 (paper): 978-0-226-09095-5
ISBN-10 (cloth): 0-226-09094-9
ISBN-10 (paper): 0-226-09095-7

Library of Congress Cataloging-in-Publication Data

Sociology in America : a history / edited by Craig Calhoun.
    p.   cm.
    Includes bibliographical references and index.
    ISBN-13: 978-0-226-09094-8 (cloth : alk. paper)
    ISBN-13: 978-0-226-09095-5 (pbk : alk. paper)
    ISBN-10: 0-226-09094-9 (cloth : alk. paper)
    ISBN-10: 0-226-09095-7 (pbk : alk. paper)
    1. Sociology—United States—History. I. Calhoun, Craig J., 1952–
HM477.U6S63 2007
301.0973—dc22

                                                      2006013213

CONTENTS

In 1932, Helen Irene McCobb of the University of North Carolina sought to derive a definition of sociology from the titles of courses. It was a quixotic project. She surveyed forty universities around the United States. Two did not teach sociology at all, but the remaining thirty-eight offered 803 separate courses; only four of these were offered at as many as nine institutions: social problems, social progress, social institutions, race and nationality. "When all the offerings in the subject are considered," McCobb was forced to conclude, "sociology appears to be some kind of glorified Irish stew in which are found liberal amounts of the usual ingredients and also a surprising conglomeration of other materials to give it variety and a spice to suit anyone's taste" (1932, 357).

McCobb wrote a few years before a major dispute in the discipline led to the 1936 founding of the *American Sociological Review* (*ASR*) and a sustained effort at professionalization. Disciplinary unity was one of the goals; it was sought in an internal hierarchy tied to quality of scientific research, a growing emphasis on statistics, and the promotion of functionalism as a broad theoretical orientation. Sociology's boundaries with other disciplines were never entirely clear and settled; while some sought such demarcations, others sought to situate sociology within an interdisciplinary social science (famously in Harvard's Department of Social Relations). The relation of "general sociology" to what in the discipline's early years were called the various "special sociologies" or subfields—from race to crime to family to community—was always uncertain and often contested. When the ASA later divided into a growing range of sections, this rupture renewed the controversy, which has recurrently focused also on whether the *ASR* adequately represents the field as a whole (or in its diversity). In *The Impossible Science*, Stephen and Jonathan Turner remark that "the proliferation of sections of the ASA also has provided some organizational structures with some of the ambiance of a smaller organization, and sometimes the sections serve as an organizational base for a heterodox movement or specialty distant from the 'mainstream' that nevertheless wishes to preserve its claim on legitimacy as a part of sociology" (1990, 156). The professionalizers of the mid-twentieth century, however, sought a whole clearly greater than its parts (or at least dominant over them). They sought a hierarchy rooted in demonstrated achievements in scientific research. They resisted identification of sociology with social reform and even more with socialism; most sought distance from applied fields, including especially social work. They invested in a vision of science as incremental progress toward the goal of greater positivist truth.

In the course of all this, the mid-twentieth-century professionalizers of sociology rewrote the history of the discipline. Talcott Parsons (along with Edward Shils and other collaborators) was instrumental in claiming a new pedigree and canon that emphasized European theory, displacing much of the work that had oriented American sociology before. Robert Merton introduced a distinction between the history and systematics of sociological theory (supported by Alfred North Whitehead's aphorism that "a science which hesitates to forget its founders is lost") that made the past more foreign to the present. Many of the American founders were literally forgotten. A variety of self-styled hardheaded behaviorists derided what had gone before as "speculative."

The professionalizers did not win a total victory. Grass roots resistance remained strong. Many sociologists emphasized concrete social problems rather than abstract social systems. The teaching of sociology revealed a different field from that seen in articles published in the *ASR*. Eventually, the 1960s happened, with sociologists (though not the professionalizers) in the vanguard. The period of professionalization was also a period of considerable achievement—both in the institutional advancement of sociology and in its intellectual work —but it disrupted the discipline's grasp of its own past and trajectory.

In any event, from its nineteenth-century origins to its twenty-first-century present, American sociology has derived vitality from its diversity but seldom attained clarity of definition. The intellectual projects that recruit and excite sociologists are many and varied; so too the subfields, theory groups, methodological orientations, and analytic perspectives into which the discipline divides. These make the field's history all the more interesting but significantly harder to write. I should have thought of that three years ago.

I was present at the 2002 meeting of the American Sociological Association's council when realization dawned that the association's centennial was imminent. The ASA, after all, had been born in 1905, though it was then called the American Sociological Society. The part of sociology most aware of disciplinary history is perhaps not the part most committed to predictive science. Still, one might have thought this could have been foreseen sooner. And one might have thought I could anticipate the consequences of speaking up at the next meeting, as plans began to be made for the centennial celebration, when someone called for a book. "Not just a book on the history of the ASA," I said, "surely we want one on the history of sociology in America." A committee was formed.

Seeing where this was headed, I began to produce reasons why I could not be involved. Still, it had the ring of inevitability when then president-elect Michael Burawoy showed up in my office in 2003 to press me to edit the centennial history of sociology in America. Whether I was wise or foolish to accept the charge, it is clear that I was wildly unrealistic to think I might manage to get the book out in time for the 2005 centennial meeting of the association. Even to be a year late has meant pressing contributors relentlessly (and losing a couple along the way). I do not apologize, but I am very grateful to all who wrote and revised such strong pieces under the pressure imposed by a late start.

An exceptional range of sociologists has joined the project. They include past presidents of the association with fifty years of distinguished work behind them and assistant professors from whom comparable achievements are likely in coming decades. Contributors are diverse in background, subdiscipline, and intellectual orientation but are joined by a deep engagement with the past of the field and its implications for the future, and by the intellectual strength they bring to the project. Most are not, however, primarily specialists in the history of sociology. They approach their subjects as sociologists who see historical understanding as a part of contemporary intellectual reflexivity. I have encouraged all to write in their own voices and in lively and accessible prose, and to offer critical engagement with the history of sociology, not only celebration of its accomplishments.

Most histories of sociology have centered on its early years and on its history in Europe. But it was in the United States that sociology grew most dramatically and that the strongest traditions joining theory to empirical research were forged. American sociology is the largest "national" branch of the discipline and is disproportionately influential throughout the world. Yet there exists no strong, recent book-length history of sociology in America. We can only wish for a study of sociology comparable to Peter Novick's magisterial *That Noble Dream: The "Objectivity Question" and the American Historical Profession* or Joseph Schumpeter's much earlier and broader *History of Economic Analysis*. The present volume only partially meets this need, but I hope it will stimulate more research on the history of sociology.

There is good research to build on, much of it by historians. Robert Banister, Mary Furner, Thomas Haskell, and Dorothy Ross have all written major works on sociology or on social science with sociology prominent. Many others have looked at the place of sociology in specific periods, for example, James Kloppenberg in his study of the Progressive Era. And of course sociologists as well as historians have written on particular departments, schools of thought, conflicts, and fields (as well as prominent individuals). Studies of the University of Chicago's sociologists figure especially prominently, from Robert Faris to Gary Alan Fine, J. David Lewis and Richard L. Smith, Mary Jo Deegan and Andrew Abbott. In the present volume, in a chapter on the historiography of sociology, Alan Sica describes how, in an earlier generation, systematic examination of the genesis of sociology was part of the way the field defined its disciplinary identity. A bibliographic essay by Alton Phillips and Jonathan VanAntwerpen is included in this volume as a further guide to the literature, so I will say little here.

Most existing general histories of sociology are primarily histories of sociological theory, many intended to double as textbooks. Some are very good, like Lewis Coser's classic *Masters of Sociological Thought*. This, however, is *not* the genre taken up here. Most of these books are summaries of the key ideas and sometimes the lives of important individual sociologists. Emphasizing iconic theorists, they give less coverage to collective efforts and subfields that those theorists have neglected (gender, for example, and criminology). They tell us little about shifts in research methods, for example, or major research projects that reshaped the discipline in important ways (like the *American Soldier* studies of the mid-twentieth century). They typically focus disproportionately on the European founders of sociology and tend to represent only Americans who fit a similar model (e.g., Talcott Parsons).

This imbalance is even true for the most part of the otherwise valuable collection *A History of Sociological Analysis*, edited twenty-five years ago by Tom Bottomore and Robert Nisbet. The collection is organized mostly by schools of thought rather than individuals (although an exception is made for Durkheim) and therefore contains chapters on conservatism, theories of social action, and structuralism. One of these, "American Trends," although a nice chapter, is organized as brief accounts of a series of individuals presented mainly as theorists: Sumner, Ward, Ross, Veblen, Cooley, Mead, Thomas, and Park. The result is that one of the most prominent histories of sociological analysis has no discussion of the rise of quantitative methods, the growing prominence of women in the discipline, or studies of race other than those by the Chicago school (and they are mentioned only in passing).

Even James Coleman, in the chapter "Sociological Analysis and Social Policy," devotes more attention to Marx and Weber than to any modern or American studies—though he does provide the book with its only discussion of Paul Lazarsfeld, *The American Soldier*, survey research, or applied sociology. The chapter "Social Stratification," remarkably, does not mention Blau and Duncan's *The American Occupational Structure* (at one time the most-cited book written by any living sociologists) or the industry of survey-based stratification and mobility research that it shaped. On the other hand, three and a half pages in the stratification chapter constitute the book's only dealings with gender.

Among the best recent studies of the history of sociology is Donald Levine's *Visions of Sociological Tradition*, which is distinctive for also offering an analysis of how the history of sociology is itself conceptualized and claimed as part of disciplinary projects. Indeed, the first section of that volume, on different forms of disciplinary narratives, is an important intellectual resource. Levine shares concerns with the Turners, including the problem of fragmentation. Like them, and indeed in a more sustained way, he links his examination of history to an argument about how the discipline can advance now. But Levine's account is about sociology in general; American sociology is only one thread in his fabric. And he, like most of sociology's historians, is concerned mainly with the history of sociological theory.

Jonathan Turner and Stephen Turner in *The Impossible Science* (1990) are among the few sociologists who attempt a broader history. They explain the institutional history of American sociology largely in terms of a variety of historical accidents and contingent effects, including the deployment of foundation funding. On the basis of this institutional history, they explain why the field is so diverse and loosely structured in terms of both theory and research, and why (as they see it) sociology has relatively little institutional force inside universities or in policymaking. Their book offers a compact, integrated narrative, but although it describes and seeks to explain the diversity of the field, it does not offer much depth on such topics as its diverse branches or its changing demography.

The present book is not organized as a history of great men or women or schools of thought, nor as a history of departments. These are of course discussed, but in the context of various analytic questions. Likewise, "coverage" was not a paramount goal in planning the book but only one among many. I preferred a broad and diverse range of contributions to an effort at exhaustive documentation or narrative integration. And I knew that there was no way to cover everything. Even important fields would inevitably be slighted, and all the more so if there was a pretense to thoroughness. Indeed, there is not as much coverage here as ideally there should be of rural sociology, or for that matter of urban, of ethnicity as distinct from race, or of immigration, medical sociology, relations to other disciplines, and the history of teaching of sociology. That said, there is a lot here.

This volume is a *sociological* history in three senses: it has been written by sociologists; its focus is on understanding the development of the discipline more than its implications for broader national or intellectual history; and it focuses largely on institutional patterns shaping the field. It is thus not a historians' history of sociology—though it is informed by the work of historians and I hope will be useful to historians. Equally, it is not the sort of naïve history of thinkers and ideas that sociologists too often write of their own field.

I am grateful, most of the time, to the ASA for entrusting me with this task and providing its support. I am grateful all of the time to the contributors and to the five distinguished sociologists who served as an editorial advisory committee: Andrew Abbott, Troy Duster, Barbara Laslett, Alan Sica, and Margaret Somers.

Most remarkably of all, despite how much I learned during this project about sociology's recurrent divisions and struggles, I find myself at the end all the more convinced of its value and optimistic about its future. I hope readers will feel the same.

[ONE] Sociology in America: An Introduction

Craig Calhoun

The word *sociology* was invented (in its French spelling) by Auguste Comte in the 1830s. One of America's first great sociologists, William Graham Sumner, found the compound of Latin and Greek so inelegant that he tried to replace it with the more etymologically consistent *societology*.[1] Had he succeeded, perhaps Americans could have claimed the field originated in the United States. But terminological origins are not much to go by. In intellectual terms it would make at least as much sense to say that sociology is much older—as old as systematic inquiry into the nature of social life or, at minimum, as old as the early modern interest in what besides political rule knit together distinctive peoples or nations. In institutional terms it would make equal sense to say that sociology is somewhat newer—that it dates from the formation of an academic discipline in the late nineteenth century.

On the latter account, the United States was in the forefront. Sociology grew in prominence as the new PhD-granting research university developed in the late nineteenth century. Its first great institutional base was at the University of Chicago, itself a new institution receptive to new approaches to knowledge. Indeed, the heterogeneity as well as the growth of U.S. academic institutions facilitated the formation of a new discipline. Sociology gained a disciplinary basis at Chicago in 1892 and at Columbia in 1893, some twenty years before Durkheim succeeded in transforming a chair of education into a chair of sociology in Paris.

Of course to privilege only the institutional and not the intellectual would be senseless. Sociology could become a discipline in Chicago and New York—and in Paris and Berlin and for that matter in Lawrence, Kansas, and New Haven, Connecticut (other claimants to the pioneering role in America)—because it could draw on a wealth of intellectual resources established in previous generations. It drew, of course, on social thought and

---

1. Sumner and Keller, *Science of Society;* Sumner wrote early drafts and partial texts for this posthumously completed magnum opus under the title "Societology." On Comte's coinage, see Levine, *Visions of the Sociological Tradition,* 14.

philosophical inquiries into the nature of human relationships, groups, communities, publics, and polities that stretch back into the ancient world. But it also drew on a number of protean thinkers who helped to establish distinctively sociological reasoning as part of their rebellions against or innovations in other lines of work. Thomas Hobbes, John Locke, Baron de Montesquieu, Jean-Jacques Rousseau—and for that matter Thomas Paine and Mary Wollstonecraft—all appealed to accounts of social life in order to resolve problems in political philosophy. Adam Ferguson and Adam Smith pioneered the notion of self-organizing civil society and developed a sociological approach to key issues in political economy (and Smith would presumably be recognized more clearly as a central figure in the sociological tradition if he were not so emphatically claimed by economics). Both Smith and Jeremy Bentham sought what might be seen as sociological solutions to problems of moral philosophy, an approach that would influence Hegel among many others. Edmund Burke and Joseph De Maistre helped create modern conservatism by appealing not only to tradition but to more organic social processes that underpinned it.

In the wake of the French Revolution and in response to industrialization, a variety of Europeans examined social institutions, conditions, and change in new ways. By the time Auguste Comte first used the word *sociology* in 1839, utopian socialists, social reformers, and conservative social critics were all contributing to the rise of a notion of society and social organization as distinct from government. This distinction was prominent in explorations of natural law, pivotal to histories of civil society, and influentially linked to the development of nationalism. Alexis de Tocqueville's *Democracy in America* and the *Old Regime and the French Revolution* were among the highlights. Conceptualizations like Ferdinand Tönnies's distinction of *gemeinschaft* and *gesellschaft* were efforts to understand this change in relation to the nature of social order. From contrasting ideological perspectives, both Marx's critique of political economy and Le Play's social economics helped to establish "the social" as a concern for economic as well as political debate. By the mid-nineteenth century a variety of organizations focused the attention of less radical and less conservative—and for the most part less famous—thinkers on the practical pursuit of a scientific approach to social policy.

Sociology was from the outset marked by both an engagement with projects of social reform and an understanding of society as quasi-natural, even organic—and by the tension between the two. This grew more pronounced during the nineteenth century. New inequalities, industrialization, the squalor associated with rapid urbanization, intensified fear of immigrants, crime, and challenges to idealized family life all brought forth privately organized ameliorative projects, incipient welfare states, and challenging social movements. Sociology took shape trying to inform each in America as in Europe. Anxieties over immigration loomed larger in the United States, and concern over race was enduringly prominent. Religion loomed larger in the United States, shaping approaches to social problems as well as to social order.

And concern for social order—the social whole—was enduringly central. Attempts to reestablish social order after revolutionary disruptions were basic in Europe. In the United States, social science grew in the wake of the Civil War and in a context of economic booms and recessions. Rural to urban migration, black migration from South to North, and the westward movement of the U.S. population all figured alongside international migration as sociological concerns. Rural sociology was initially and until World War II one of the field's largest branches. Thinking about social order was shaped less than in Europe by ideas of tradition and focused more on the achievement of community. But in the United States as in Europe, concern for both social order and social change flowed into the deep channels of evolutionary theory—which formed in social thought as in biology. Herbert Spencer was a key influence. In the 1850s, indeed, Spencer addressed these topics in *Social Statics* (launching his long-term engagement with social morphology) and, famously, *Progress: Its Law and Cause*. And through the rest of the nineteenth century, American sociology would be deeply engaged with both social organization (and disorganization) and with progress.

Progress was a fundamental theme for the emerging field of sociology and the broader social context of its reception. In the United States, if anything, it was more central than social order (though the two were closely related in most formulations).[2] In Europe, the problem of order was focused centrally on political stability (versus revolution) and clashing economic interests. Class conflict, and indeed socialism, figured more prominently for early American sociologists than is sometimes thought. But in the United

2. For a compelling study of the idea of progress (and its critics) in America, see Lasch, *True and Only Heaven*. See also Robert Nisbet's critique of confounding historical change with development, *Social Change and History*. Nisbet's critique was rooted in the arguments of his teacher, Frederick J. Teggart, a very sociological historian who had founded a department of social institutions at Berkeley and resisted the founding of a sociology department (which Dorothy Swaine Thomas had been hired to develop). The tendency of sociology to erase actual history in favor of either developmentalism or research contemporary issues abstracted from the historical contexts was one of his reasons. On the resistance to sociology at Berkeley and its eventual transcendence, see VanAntwerpen, "Resisting Sociology's Seductive Name."

States, the problem of order became to a large extent the problem of integration—how to assimilate immigrants, how to overcome (or at least deal with) racial division, and how to nurture self-improvement and strong families among the poor. For many sociologists, these became matters of psychological "adjustment" as well as social change. At the same time, when the term *social integration* came to indicate a general theoretical concern with questions of social cohesion, it became to some extent abstracted from the concrete questions about race, immigrants, political minorities, the working class, and the rights of women that preoccupied reform-oriented sociologists.

Social Change and Evolution

Evolutionary and "progressive" thought dominated in the nineteenth-century context of early U.S. sociology. Some American sociologists embraced evolutionary accounts enthusiastically, engaged them deeply, and made contributions to them. Others drew on the common rhetorical framework they provided for discussing social change without an equally close grappling with specifics. Spencerian arguments that sociology was part of a holistic, evolutionary natural science commanded widespread tacit acceptance.[3] The prestige of the biological sciences added to the attraction of an evolutionary synthesis (though this was still resisted by many religious thinkers). Like Spencer himself, Lester Frank Ward—the first great American sociologist—contributed to biology as well as sociology (not to mention what were then called "cosmic" theories of the general evolution of everything).[4] Franklin H. Giddings and William Graham Sumner too offered evolutionary syntheses. But this revealed also that evolution was a broad framework. Sumner followed Spencer more closely, not only in matters of evolutionary theory proper but in advocating laissez-faire; he was the original social Darwinist.[5] Giddings, by contrast, stressed social organization rather more and biological determinism much less, and was more liberal and supportive of state action than was Sumner.

Not everyone was equally convinced of progress or evolution. Indeed,

3. See Breslau, chap. 2, in this volume, for more on the American Spencerians.

4. Ward, *Dynamic Sociology*.

5. Through most of his career, Sumner was more influential as an essayist and especially a teacher at Yale than as an author of big books (and his books were largely on economic subjects). In 1906 he published *Folkways*, his most influential study. His evolutionary synthesis had to wait for posthumous publication, with considerable assistance from Albert Keller; see Sumner and Keller, *Science of Society*.

the word *sociology* was first used in the United States in 1854 by George Fitzhugh and Henry Hughes. Both were Southerners who found a Comtean version of sociology—in Hughes's case augmented by Fourier—helpful in giving an account of an organic society threatened by socioeconomic change and the growing abolitionist movement.[6] Fitzhugh was not alone in defending local community and more organic understandings of society against liberal economics and industrial transformation. Similar ideas informed other sociologists of different ideological commitments, including several influenced by utopian socialism.[7] In general, though, Comte did not catch on as fast in the United States as did Spencer, and most American sociologists shared the pervasive individualism of their national context.

Sumner married evolutionary theory to economic liberalism and arguments for a minimal state, and thus contributed to the popular stereotype of social Darwinism as a rationalization for the market competition of the Gilded Age. But Sumner's major work *Folkways* focused more on cultural evolution. He approached folkways as habits and customs developed by individuals in order to meet needs and reproduced in social relations and social learning mainly where they proved effective in doing so. By *mores* he intended the elevation of folkways to the status of beliefs and practices held to be not merely convenient but good and/or true and thus the objects of religious or philosophical commitments. Note that the units of selection are not, in the first instance, persons or groups but practices and ideas. Folkways and mores may be mistaken, though the more firmly they are woven into a fabric of cultural commitments, the harder they are to replace.

Sumner experienced something of this phenomenon personally when he assigned Spencer's *The Study of Sociology* as an undergraduate text and suffered a sharp attack from Yale's president, Noah Porter, for doing so.[8]

6. Fitzhugh, *Sociology for the South*; Hughes, *Treatise on Sociology*. See also Bernard, "Henry Hughes, First American Sociologist." Bernard published several other articles on southern sociology and repeatedly praised Hughes as a pioneer.

7. Fourier and St. Simon are familiar European exemplars. Less well-known American counterparts included Albert Brisbane, one of Fourier's most influential followers, and Lewis Masquerier, who sought a pure democracy partly through redistribution of land. The subtitle of Masquerier's 1877 book, *Sociology*, is representative of the genre: *Or, the Reconstruction of Society, Government, and Property, upon the Principles of Equality, the Perpetuity, and the Individuality of the Private Ownership of Life, person, Government, Homestead and the Whole Product of Labor, by Organizing all Nations into Townships of Self-Governed Homestead democracies—Self-Employed in Farming and Mechanism, Giving All the Liberty and Happiness to Be Found on Earth*. See the discussion in Bernard and Bernard, *Origins of American Sociology*.

8. See Bannister, *Sociology and Scientism*. The *New York Times* coverage of the matter referred to Spencer as the "White Czar of Agnosticism." Thorstein Veblen, as it happens, did his

Though in other contexts evolutionary sociology drew prestige from biology, teaching evolution meant taking up a controversial new perspective that existed in tension with the still powerful if no longer completely dominant clerical leadership in academia. The issue was not only evolution but the claim to move beyond theology in putting science on positivist foundations. Sumner's turn to sociology was deeply influenced by Darwin and Spencer, but it was also broader. As he wrote in the middle of the controversy, "four or five years ago my studies led me to the conviction that sociology was about to do for the social sciences what scientific method has done for the natural and physical sciences, viz: rescue them from arbitrary dogmatism and confusion."[9]

Neither social Darwinism nor liberal doctrines were unique to Sumner, who was simply one of their strongest proponents. A wide range of sociologists (and others) in the late nineteenth century took up these themes, not simply to describe competition but to explain progress. At the center of their concern were large-scale and disruptive processes of social change; the social Darwinists were at the center of interpreting these processes as necessary to social improvements—that is, to progress. In this they drew on Spencer's famous essay, *Progress: Its Law and Cause,* which was published in 1857—two years before Darwin's *On the Origin of Species.*[10]

The importance of evolutionary theories for nineteenth-century American sociology lay partially in establishing the idea that sociology could be a science in the same sense as the natural sciences—since evolutionary theory was potentially a unified theory. It is instructive, for example, that Robert Merton's classic (1942) account of the ethos of science references Sumner for the idea of "ethos."[11] Sumner saw an ethos as the totality of cultural traits that individualized a group and its members and differentiated them from other groups. Merton was interested in what rendered science and scientists distinctive. But Sumner and Merton were also interested in what connected tradition to progress—in the case of science, for example, in what connected the learning of accumulated knowledge to innovative breaks with such tradition in the production of new knowledge. Sumner

---

PhD at Yale during this controversy. Porter was his primary adviser, but Veblen found himself drawn to Sumner, whom he admired both as a scientist and as a combative individualist, though he did not share Sumner's conservative political-economic views.

9. Quoted in Marsden, "God and Man at Yale (1880)," 40.

10. This "progressivist" orientation is, of course, quite different from the gloomier projections of the social scientist who stimulated Darwin's thinking about the struggle for survival— Thomas Malthus, who argued that population would inevitably outstrip food supply.

11. Merton, "Normative Structure of Science."

himself was greatly interested in the balance between tradition and inno-vation and saw science as crucial, since it combined a method that had proven highly productive with an ethos of its own, a specifically profes-sional ethos of discipline, denial, and detachment—which produced the equivalent of public virtue (without depending as heavily as moral teaching typically did on appeals to individual character).

Sumner, in other words, engaged science in general and evolutionary theory in particular in order to pursue virtue. His goals were not altogether different from what they had been when he was the rector of an Episcopal parish.[12] Sumner shared a strongly religious—and indeed clerical—back-ground with many other sociologists of his era. But whereas he was drawn to scientific positivism, and the bundle of doctrines associated with social Darwinism and laisser-faire economics, this was not equally the story of all. Other leading sociologists were evolutionists and indebted to Spencer, but they were also moralists—a stance Sumner sharply rejected. Although they shared a version of individualism with Sumner, they were far more concerned with the motivation and capacity for autonomous judgment.

Despite Sumner, most leading nineteenth-century sociologists chal-lenged laissez-faire doctrine. They did this as individualists convinced that Spencer's (and Sumner's) account was too deterministic to do justice to in-dividuals and their potential; in this most drew on religious vocabularies of interior life (whether or not they remained active Christians). Most also saw a greater role for human intelligence in shaping the course of social change.

Lester Frank Ward, perhaps the most influential of nineteenth-century U.S. sociologists and near the end of his life the first president of the Amer-ican Sociological Society, was exemplary in this regard. His first career was that of a paleobotanist, and he worked for many years for the U.S. Geologi-cal Survey. He thought it contradictory to assert the virtues of human con-trol over nature by means of science and at the same time to suggest that human affairs should be governed by the blind necessity of nature. Rather, he suggested, biology gave human beings intelligence, which in turn offered them the capacity to shape nature to their own purposes. Where Spencer approached biological and human "association" without distinction of kind, Ward emphasized the centrality of purpose to human social life. This notion informed the strong interest in social psychology that was charac-

---

12. Sumner remained an Episcopal priest all his life but famously lost commitment to his earlier beliefs during the 1870s and 1880s, the same period during which he took up sociology and evolution. As he famously wrote, "I never consciously gave up a religious belief. It was as if I had put my beliefs into a drawer, and when I opened it, there was nothing there at all." See Marsden, "God and Man at Yale."

teristic of much early American sociology and also established the limits of a completely naturalistic theory of human evolution. "My thesis," wrote Ward, "is that the subject matter of sociology is human achievement. It is not what men are but what they do. It is not the structure but the function."[13]

Though an evolutionist, Ward was also deeply concerned with problems of motivation and will. Human beings are creatures of subjective desires and feelings; individuals act on desire, while nature selects those acts that are congruent with the survival of the race. Subjective desire thus gives rise to objective social forces. Ward saw human freedom as a basic good, but one that could only be achieved through social organization and rational control of the irrational and impulsive side of human behavior. Social disorder, he saw, was as much an enemy to freedom as overly rigid order. Part of his success was the result of his capacity to avoid extremes and bridge (though not overcome) these dualisms.[14] Over the course of his long career, his early emphasis on subjective desire faded in favor of greater focus on social control—a central concern for American sociologists. One of his greatest disciples (and the husband of his niece) was the economist Edward A. Ross, who became a sociologist and social psychologist precisely to focus on this subject.[15] Yet ultimately Ward's engagement was with a liberal project of progress. He moved away from more radical positions but remained committed to the view that most social problems could be addressed by reform of social institutions. He followed a somewhat racist account of Negroes' primitive traits with the suggestion that if blacks had the same opportunities as whites, they too would become civilized. Ambivalence regarding race—as well as outright racism—was widespread in early sociology. Charlotte Perkins Gilman, a self-professed disciple of Ward's, was among the most important pioneers of feminism, yet she thought Jews and African Americans examples of arrested evolution.[16] Sociology developed in a

13. Ward, *Pure Sociology*, 15. Ward influentially distinguished "pure" from "applied" sociology and focused on the second in a 1904 book.

14. As Bannister has argued in *Sociology and Scientism*, 22.

15. See E. Ross, *Social Control*, which addresses the ways in which personalities are molded by institutions (for better or worse, depending on how institutions are structured) and how this shapes the balance of individual freedom and social stability in a liberal society.

16. Gilman for a time embraced Nationalism, a utopian socialist movement inspired by Edward Bellamy, and her racial and ethnic intolerance was linked to this vision of a scientifically engineered, ethnically homogeneous, and eugenically advanced society. To it she brought an account of the ills wrought by patriarchy and a vision of the benefits that emphasizing motherhood could bring. She moved out of New York at one point, saying she found its multiracial tumult annoying. Perhaps ironically, she was a grandniece of Harriet Beecher Stowe. See Lane, *To "Herland" and Beyond*; Seitler, "Unnatural Selection"; and Doskow, introduction to *Gilman's Utopian Novels*.

period when such views were common; they are not so much indicators of conservatism as of the limits of liberalism and of the epoch.[17]

Franklin H. Giddings, remembered most today as a pioneering advocate for quantitative research (and founder of the Columbia University sociology department), was also centrally an evolutionary theorist and historical sociologist. Staking a position between Ward and Sumner, he emphasized that mere gregariousness among animals was not the same as human association because it was not mediated by speech and consciousness of kind. This latter concept, central to his work, was influenced by Adam Smith's notion of reflexive sympathy (from *The Theory of Moral Sentiments*). Using it, Giddings elaborated an account of the history of civil society in which purposive associations complemented communities formed by incident of birth. History manifested growth in organization (though sometimes also its collapse), not merely structural differentiation. Organization is produced by intelligent action on nature as well as by evolutionary history. "Society," Giddings wrote, "is a means to a definite end—namely, the survival and improvement of men through a continuing selection of intelligence and sympathy."[18] This end was accomplished, he stressed, by both cooperation within and competition among social groups. Social control matters alongside natural selection in that it shapes group formation (although internal heterogeneity makes for stronger, more adaptive groups). The state is the most important organization for producing civil society, but it "could not exist in a free or republican form, were there not voluntary and private political associations."[19] Political associations are not merely governmental in nature, therefore, but organizations for mutual aid and coordination of social action—including economic activity.

Like most early sociologists, Giddings advocated social science as a means to social improvement.[20] Indeed, it was on this basis that he was hired by Columbia: he was to provide a scientific background for education

17. See Stanfield, "Historical Considerations."

18. Giddings, *Studies in the Theory of Human Society*, 246.

19. Giddings, *Inductive Sociology*, 217.

20. I have stressed Giddings because he was considerably more important and influential in his time than he is prominent in histories of sociology. This is due to several factors, including perhaps the fact that he didn't knit together a systematic summation of his work (though other founding fathers' lack of systematicity has not blocked their recognition). As important, I think, is the fact that when a Chicago school emerged in the mid-twentieth century, it actively sought to claim the heritage of the founders of the University of Chicago department and the *American Journal of Sociology* (including Albion Small, who was considerably less systematic than Giddings). By contrast, when Robert Merton and Paul Lazarsfeld developed the most prominent Columbia school, they represented their approach as a break with what had gone before (and indeed, they both arrived as outsiders rather than as returning students).

in practical action and administration, notably of charities. This practical focus reflects the second main current in the formation of American sociology, ameliorative social reform—pronounced even in one of the era's leading advocates of sociology as science. Sociology grew in the context of a predisciplinary movement to put "social science" to work in improving laws, public policy, and private action—most notably in regard to poverty, but also race, immigration, and family.[21] Making charity and public "benevolence" more effective was a primary goal. These were largely religious projects, and the development of sociology was deeply influenced by Christianity. Sociology was not simply an extension of theology, however, but the development of a project of "this-worldly" (and in that sense, secular) efforts at practical reform. Rooted in religion, it reached beyond it, eventually in ways that proved problematic for believing sociologists and more sharply so for their external critics. It was largely because of attempts to answer questions they initially framed in religious terms that many nineteenth-century sociologists turned to—and developed—the new field.[22]

Social Reform

Sociology developed in the context of dramatic social change and widespread debates over what constituted progress and how progress could be attained more surely and rapidly. It took shape in the eras American historians describe as the Gilded Age and the Progressive Era. If the Gospel of wealth preached by Andrew Carnegie is one iconic reflection of the time, so is the Social Gospel propounded by Walter Rauschenbusch (who, unlike Carnegie, published in the *American Journal of Sociology* [*AJS*]). At least as many early sociologists were drawn to socialism and social democracy as to social Darwinism, and the socialism was usually a variant of Christian socialism.

Nineteenth-century social science engaged intellectuals, advocates, and administrators on the basis of a broadly shared concern with social problems and social change. Theirs was not first and foremost an interest in research or knowledge for its own sake but instead for dealing with social (and sometimes personal) problems. Once the disciplinary project launched, however, advancing sociology became more often an end in itself. This did

21. Luther and Jessie Bernard emphasized the "movement" character of early social science in *Origins of American Sociology*.

22. Sociology was part of a more general process of secularization in American higher education. See Smith, "Secularizing American Higher Education"; and more generally, see Marsden, *Soul of the American University*.

not go uncontested. The tension between achieving intellectual authority and being publicly engaged has been present throughout the discipline's history. Many academic sociologists articulated a commitment to science intended both to claim authority over and to secure independence from extra-academic reformers.

Sociology drew its specifically scientific claims at first largely from evolutionary theory and then increasingly from empirical research, including the development of statistics (though it is worth noting that insofar as the latter offered empirical generalizations without deductive demonstrations, their scientific standing was disputed). Economics and sociology both emerged as disciplines within this broad context, with many members minimally engaged with scientific theory and maximally engaged with social reform. If "liberal" market theory would eventually become clearly dominant in economics, this destiny was by no means obvious in the late nineteenth century. And sociology, in any case, would remain enduringly divided over the primacy of scientific pursuit of generalizable, lawlike knowledge versus engagement with social problems and social change. Its dominant elites would more often make the discipline's claims in the language of incremental improvements to a store of positive scientific knowledge, but its recruitment of students, teachers, and researchers would be heavily influenced by the desire to make direct contributions to understanding—or better, solving—social problems and advancing human welfare.

Through the last third of the nineteenth century, concerned citizens advocated a more "scientific" approach to addressing social problems and understanding social change. Initially, this advocacy was largely nonacademic, the pursuit of ministers and administrators of aid to the poor. It gained an organizational vehicle in the American Social Science Association (ASSA), founded in 1865.[23] The members of the association were generally not professional social scientists. Many were serious scholars, but at the outset few earned their living as full-time researchers or even university professors. In addition to ministers, there were lawyers, educators, physicians, and gentlemen of independent means. The founder, Frank Sanborn, was one of many engaged in the administration of social welfare efforts. As he wrote in the letter that invited participants to the organizational meeting that led to the ASSA:

> Our attention has lately been called to the importance of some organization in the United States, both local and national, whose object shall be discussions of

23. See Bernard and Bernard, *Origins of American Sociology;* and especially Haskell, *Emergence of Professional Social Science.*

those questions relating to the Sanitary Condition of the People, the Relief, Employment, and Education of the Poor, the Prevention of Crime, the Amelioration of Criminal Law, the Discipline of Prisons, the Remedial treatment of the Insane, and those numerous matters of statistical and philanthropic interest which are included under the general head of "Social Science."[24]

The organizational meeting was sponsored by the Massachusetts Board of Charities, one of the most influential of such bodies. The board was long a base for Sanborn, and he was long the key leader of the ASSA.

The new organization drew its model from the British National Association for the Promotion of Social Science (founded in 1857), a largely Benthamite effort to combine the production of scientific knowledge with its distillation into specific legislation and expert advice to government. The association's American counterpart was less effective politically; it also reflected a national context in which government action on social issues was decentralized into efforts within the separate states as well as a context in which nongovernmental action was more prominent. The association engaged to make useful knowledge available to all those who sought to improve social conditions, especially private philanthropists.

This project necessarily entailed sharing existing knowledge, gained in practical experience and refined in reflection, but also producing new knowledge. Many of the members were engaged in "social surveys," sometimes massive efforts to document conditions among the poor or other groups. *Survey* did not yet connote systematic sampling but rather a rationally organized overview, not unlike the work of a land surveyor who documents the contours and boundaries of a terrain. Surveys were often designed as much to prove the need for action to political and other powers as to gain greater precision in scientific understanding. Indeed, the distinction between the two agendas was initially vague if it was recognized at all. W. E. B. DuBois's pioneering study *The Philadelphia Negro* was at once an intellectual effort at understanding and a political project of persuasive documentation—conducted at the invitation of Philadelphia city officials as well as the University of Pennsylvania.[25] The work of Jane Addams and her associates at Hull House included surveys designed both to improve the management of settlement houses and to call attention to the ills they sought to address. They also advised a Pittsburgh team that undertook the largest and most influential of such reform-oriented surveys.[26] Addams and

24. Cited in Haskell, *Emergence of Professional Social Science,* 97–98.

25. DuBois, *Philadelphia Negro.* Also Katz and Sugrue, *DuBois, Race, and the City.*

26. Bulmer, Bales, and Sklar, *Social Survey in Historical Perspective;* Turner, "World of the Academic Quantifiers"; Gordon, "Social Survey Movement."

her associates, especially Florence Kelley, also developed mapping as a strategy to relate survey data to urban areas (later carried on by the Chicago school of urban sociologists).[27]

Gradually there were improvements in both data gathering and analytic techniques. Centrally, perhaps, there was a shift from identifying a common tendency—a mean that was sometimes then presented as a type—toward analyzing patterns of variation. Early sociologists, including Lester Frank Ward, who worked for many years as a government statistician, drew primarily on numerical tabulations; he saw statistics less as tools for analyzing variation than as demonstrations of the regularities of natural law. Eventually, toward the end of the nineteenth century, partly under the influence of work on heredity and evolution pioneered by Francis Galton and refined by Karl Pearson and George Yule, scientific statistics took its modern shape through its proponents' focus on the analysis of probabilities.[28] It was not until the 1920s, however, that this "new statistics" became prominent in American sociology.[29] And then it was contested, notably by sociologists from the Chicago school, who decried its emphasis on tracking correlations rather than testing hypotheses. Although the Chicago sociologists are remembered often as "qualitative," this label is misleading. They commonly used a mixture of methods but advocated separation of the scientific use of data from the general documentation of social ills typical of earlier social surveys—conducted by those whom they called "social politicians."[30]

Indeed, the ASSA membership overlapped that of the American Statistical Society, which was founded in 1839 and may justly claim to be the country's oldest social science society, though at its origin it was not a specifically academic or professional society. And the place of statistics can exemplify a larger pattern: as the nineteenth century progressed, there was more differentiation between the effort to produce authoritative knowledge

27. *Hull-House Maps and Papers*; Deegan, *Jane Addams and the Men of the Chicago School.* The *Hull-House Maps and Papers* were published collectively by "Residents of Hull House, a Social Settlement." They had been associated especially with Addams, who was indeed central, but her fame overshadowed the core contributions of a number of others, including notably Florence Kelley, the American translator of Engels' writings (and thus a link to his proto-evolutionary, proto-ecological view of the city), and the Chicago sociology PhD's Sophonisba Breckinridge and Edith Abbott.

28. Francis Galton and Karl Pearson developed the ideas of Quételet into modern social statistics, but they also were followers of Gobineau, who focused on inherited racial differences and innate inequalities. In the United States, Franklin Giddings championed their statistics and took on a similar racialist project.

29. Porter, *Rise of Statistical;* Oberschall, "Two Empirical Roots of Social Theory."

30. See Bulmer, Bales, and Sklar, *Social Survey in Historical Perspective;* and Abbott, *Department and Discipline.*

and the effort to put it to use. Skilled specialists emerged, and these derived their standing in large part from the regard of other skilled specialists. These specialist communities would eventually develop into academic disciplines within the context of the transformed, increasingly research-oriented university.

The demand for social science knowledge was fueled in the late nineteenth century by the growing interdependence of social life and large-scale social organization. This theme, perhaps most familiar to sociologists today in Durkheim's contrast of mechanical to organic solidarity, was pervasive among the members of the ASSA as it was among their European counterparts. Perhaps ironically, the complexity this interdependence created was a basis for the development of quasi-independent academic disciplines that explored it from different vantage points, with different techniques, and frequently contested notions of a division of labor. Comte's assertion that sociology was the "queen of the sciences" (precisely because it was the most integrative) was not always accepted. In this context, those who would assert sociology as a specific social science—as distinct from social science in general—would necessarily confront boundary questions and employ distinctions from other disciplines to define their own.[31] Durkheim famously opposed sociology to psychology. This contrast resonated very little in the United States, where early sociology embraced the study of personality as a core concern and developed social psychology as a central field. Demarcations from history, economics, philosophy, and the emerging professional field of social work were more significant.[32]

Both reformism and concern for social integration were evident at the University of Chicago, but the Chicago sociologists' engagements were less with progress than with social problems and processes.[33] Indeed, America's single most influential sociology department was among those least closely

31. For a general account of academic disciplines and fields as products of ecological organization and competition, see Abbott, *Chaos of Disciplines*.

32. On sociology's relation to philosophy, see Gross, chap. 6, in this volume.

33. Both Park and especially Thomas were close to George Herbert Mead, who was himself more active in social reform than common representations among his declared followers suggest. Mead was active in philosophy and psychology as well as sociology, and of course a key member of the pragmatist circle. A strand in his work was later claimed by the symbolic interactionist tradition in sociology, which integrated his influence with that of Thomas and of Michigan's Charles Horton Cooley to form the most influential microsociological research tradition. Cooley was reclusive in a way that Mead was not, but he contributed not only famous concepts such as "primary group" but perhaps the most sustained treatment of the individual and society of any early sociologist, *Human Nature and the Social Order*. How close the relations among Mead, Thomas, and Cooley were can be traced not only in their references to each

shaped by evolutionary synthesis. The University of Chicago sociologists did not eschew theory or deny evolutionary thought but did shift the emphasis. Albion Small considered himself broadly Spencerian, as a follower of Gustav Ratzenhofer and Lester Frank Ward, but the Chicago sociologists were never fully engaged in the same project of evolutionary synthesis, and they more readily absorbed the critique of evolution offered by Franz Boas and other cultural anthropologists.[34] Small was active in bringing Simmel, Ratzenhofer, and other key German thinkers to attention through publication in the *AJS*. Small's main synthetic work, *General Sociology*, assumed evolution as a general framework but focused on the social process of group formation, social conflict, and the resolution of conflicts through adjustment and innovation.[35] The concrete acting group, a vessel of organized interests, became a core focus in Chicago and in American sociology more generally.

Almost all the early Chicago sociologists were active in a range of reform organizations. Most wrote on problems of social action and contemporary social problems. W. I. Thomas was a key influence and the most important bridge from early Chicago sociology to Robert Park and the later

---

other's work (Mead wrote the preface to Cooley's book) but in Cooley's independent formulation of almost the same principle that Robert Merton would later call the Thomas theorem. Cooley wrote: "The imaginations people have of one another are the solid facts of society" (ix). The phrase *symbolic interactionist* has often been used to denote a more or less atheoretical orientation to direct description of face-to-face social life. For attempts to establish more clearly its theoretical provenance and engagements, see Blumer, *Symbolic Interactionism;* and Fine, *Second Chicago School.*

34. Many early American sociologists, including of course the evolutionists, were considerably influenced by and engaged with anthropology. The sociology department at Chicago was, however, from early on especially close to anthropology and connected by approaches to practical work—including ethnographic fieldwork—as well as intellectual syntheses. The influence of A. R. Radcliffe-Brown and Bronislaw Malinowski was large on Chicago anthropology and encouraged a more "sociological" style of analysis than was typical of German-influenced American cultural anthropology. W. I. Thomas published several ethnological studies and explicitly saw the study of primitive behavior as crucial to sociology. Later W. Lloyd Warner shared an appointment in sociology and anthropology and did pioneering work on American community life (the Yankee City studies) as well as on Australian kinship. Through much of the twentieth century, sociology and anthropology developed as parallel specializations within joint departments.

35. Roscoe Hinkle's generally useful *Founding Theory of American Sociology* misleadingly presents Small (and Sumner) as "anti-evolutionary." For evidence of how the idea of progress remained central in American sociology even after the collapse of nineteenth-century evolutionism, see Luther L. Bernard's three 1925 articles on the concept of progress, in *Social Forces* 3(2): 207–12; 3(4): 617–212; 4(1): 36–43—one each for theological, metaphysical, and scientific phases (in classic Comtean formulation).

fieldwork tradition. His place in the canon is secured by *The Polish Peasant in Europe and America*. This massive study, a collaboration with Florian Znaniecki and probably the preeminent American sociological study of its era, gained its "center" from immigration, but it was also a study of the life of peasants, the nature of the family, social psychology, the influence of social contexts on individual behavior and attitudes, and the ways in which people manage transitions in their lives.[36] In it, theorizing was closely related to the attempt to understand concrete social phenomena and act on social problems. Thomas also pioneered work on gender, youth, and childhood, and again was much concerned with the ways in which his studies might inform social action.[37] Of course it was partly his activism—and his wife's nationally prominent pacifism—that made him a target of attacks and led to his dismissal from the University of Chicago in 1918.

Even more important in social reform was Jane Addams, whose Hull House was part of the social and intellectual fabric of early Chicago sociology. Hull House was the most important of a wave of "settlements" founded in the late nineteenth century to facilitate projects of practical philanthropy and self-improvement among the poor.[38] More than four hundred were in operation by World War I. Hull House—like most—was at once a "commune" of professional women who devoted themselves to practical reform efforts, a center for educational activities and political and intellectual discussion, a vehicle for transforming a specific community, and a self-conscious part of a movement for societal transformation. Both Hull House specifically and the settlement movement more generally have been claimed primarily for histories of social work, but they figure integrally in late nineteenth-century sociology. Indeed, what was to become the separate professional field of social work was largely extra-academic in the nineteenth century, but participants commonly considered themselves sociolo-

36. Originally published in five volumes, the study is more commonly read in an abridged version today. The latest includes a useful introduction by Eli Zaretsky; Thomas and Znaniecki, *Polish Peasant in Europe and America*. Znaniecki was an aristocratic Polish nationalist, which may be a source of some of the tensions in the book. After his collaboration with Thomas, he returned to Poland where he was a key intellectual figure. Visiting the United States in the late 1930s to give a series of lectures at Columbia, he was trapped in the United States by the outbreak of World War II and went on to help develop sociology at the University of Illinois.

37. See Thomas, *Unadjusted Girl;* and Thomas and Thomas, *Child in America*). It is in the latter volume that the famous Thomas theorem ("If men define situations as real they are real in their consequences" [572]) is stated, though versions of the idea informed his work earlier. See Merton, "Self-Fulfilling Prophecy."

38. Lengermann and Niebrugge-Brantley, "Back to the Future."

gists, and the more intellectual and research-oriented among them—like many residents of Hull House—were active in academic sociology.[39] Addams published five articles in the *AJS*, and her books were regularly reviewed there.[40]

Albion Small, George Herbert Mead, W. I. Thomas, Charles Henderson, and other early Chicago sociologists were all active at Hull House. The ideas that drew them to both sociology and the settlement house were not dissimilar to those that led Washington Gladden to urge workers to seek unity in Christianity or William Dwight Porter Bliss to work with the Knights of Labor and the Socialist Party. Addams, Thomas, and for the most part their generation were less religious. Small, Henderson, and others of the first generation, though, were drawn to sociology (and often socialism) through, not instead of, Christianity. Small offered a recurrent lecture at Hull House titled "The Social Philosophy of Jesus."[41] Work with immigrants and the poor at Hull House and other settlement houses was only one manifestation of an engagement with moral reform that also shaped movements for temperance, women's suffrage, and civil rights for former slaves. Activist engagements with these movements were linked to the pursuit of scientific knowledge by the desire to produce a "rational benevolence" and to find a link between personal and social ethics.[42] Andrew Carnegie's vision of acquiring wealth by hard work, individual effort, and competition and then disposing of it on the basis of "scientific philanthropy" was part of the same broad ethical milieu as that of the Christian reformers and early sociologists who questioned whether hard work, individual effort, and competition gave everyone an equal chance or constituted adequate explanations for their success, and who saw the best marriage of science and philanthropy as leading to active engagement in changing the way society was organized.

Elite sociologists like Small and Giddings took up academic positions defined in part as providing the scientific basis for philanthropy. They promoted a division of labor in which the "general" occupied the high ground. Small focused less on Lester Frank Ward's distinction of "pure" from "ap-

39. See Lengermann and Niebrugge, chap. 3, in this volume; also see Lengermann and Niebrugge-Brantley, *Women Founders;* and see especially Lengermann and Niebrugge-Brantley, "Back to the Future."

40. See Deegan, *Jane Addams and the Men of the Chicago School,* an examination of both Addams's (and her Hull House colleagues') influence on early Chicago sociology and the partial erasure of that influence by a more professionalizing later generation. On Addams herself, see Elshtain, *Jane Addams and the Dream of American Democracy.*

41. Deegan, *Jane Addams and the Men of the Chicago School,* 82.

42. See Kloppenberg, *Uncertain Victory.*

plied" sociology than on the relationship between general sociology and the various "special sociologies" of race relations, immigration, neighborhoods, families, and the like. In all of these, however, both expected "application"—not merely in the sense of expert advice to policymakers but also in the sense of informed contributions to public debate. George Vincent was the son of the founder of the Chautauqua movement, with which he was himself involved. At Chicago and as president of the University of Minnesota and then of the Rockefeller Foundation, he pursued this vision of putting science to work for the public. Yet this was also a vision that rationalized a hierarchy, with the most elite university faculty responsible for general knowledge, while many teachers and certainly those engaged in applied social work outside the academy focused on "special sociologies."[43]

The effort to achieve scientific authority was basic to the ASSA, and struggles over scientific authority were crucial reasons for the development of specific disciplinary interests within it and eventually the founding of separate professional societies. When the American Association for the Advancement of Science was founded in 1847 (with geologists and naturalists in the lead), it was assumed that all science would advance more or less in unity. By the 1870s, not only were disciplines beginning to differentiate, but the broad division of arts and science faculties into the natural and physical sciences, the social sciences, and the humanities was becoming institutionalized. Concern to separate inquiry into religion and values from more "objective" or "positivist" pursuits (and tactics of verification) was one of the key bases for the division.[44] In the same late nineteenth- and early twentieth-century period, universities developed professional schools for the pursuit of practical or applied subjects, in many cases transforming the

43. The hierarchy was also gendered, especially with regard to social work (as Lengermann and Niebrugge demonstrate in chap. 3, in this volume). L. L. Bernard edited a prominent anthology, *The Fields and Methods of Sociology*, with chapters such as "The Functions and Limits of Social Work as Viewed by a Sociologist," "The Functions and Limits of Social Work as Viewed by a Social Worker," and "Methods of Defining the Sphere, Problems and Effective Procedures of Social Work." This suggests something of the way the relationship to social work troubled "scientific" sociologists—since in no other instance were "limits" stressed, and other fields were approached under titles addressing either "the field and problems" or "the sources and methods" of the specific domain. The first of these three articles (204-17), by James H. S. Bossard of the University of Pennsylvania begins: "To the union of social-mindedness and social sympathy, two children were born. The older one, a daughter, became 'outgoing' in her emotional adjustments and insisted on doing something about it; the second, a son, developed into an 'ingoing' child, and its introjective behavior took the form of scientific analysis. The daughter was called social work; the son rejoices in the name of sociologist" (204).

44. See Reuben, *Shaping of the Modern University*.

place of older theological faculties and drawing into the academic folds the training systems that had developed outside universities in fields like law.

In the late nineteenth century, sociology was less an emerging specialization than a central intellectual perspective for the social sciences in general (and the social sciences included applied social reform and philanthropy). For some it was the synthesis, for some the foundation. As Franklin Giddings put the case for the latter perspective, "to teach ethnology, the philosophy of history, political economy, and the theory of the state to men who have not learned the first principles of sociology, is like teaching astronomy or thermodynamics to men who have not learned the Newtonian laws of motion."[45]

Institutional Context

In the 1870s, a transformation of American universities created an opening for a more academic sociology. Johns Hopkins University, founded initially as an exclusively graduate institution, pioneered the PhD degree. The degree was an import from Germany, where educational reform had been on the agenda for decades and was linked closely to both the rise of scientific research and state demands for technical expertise of various kinds. In the United States, the rise of a university focused more on new research than on mastery of existing knowledge; a university more open to new subjects was shaped also by the Civil War—and the recognition of how technological capacity was central to military power as well as economic development. MIT and Cornell were pioneers in this turn toward a more practically oriented university. The Morrill Act of 1862 launched a system of federal land grants to create state universities focused on practical subjects and the education of leaders outside the traditional elite. Sociology would eventually prosper disproportionately in these and other state universities.

The older classical curriculum gave way not only to more "practical" subjects but also to the growth of PhD programs and the invention of the undergraduate major. This change affected not only technical subjects or the sciences but fields such as history. At Johns Hopkins, history was an important focus, and it was transformed by ideas of "original" scientific research and professional expertise. Many of the leaders of the ASSA saw their intellectual roots in the field of history and expected sociology to develop alongside it, perhaps even at Johns Hopkins. In fact, Hopkins would be one of the last major American universities to open a sociology depart-

45. Quoted in Northcott, "Sociological Theories of Giddings," 744-75.

ment—nearly a century after it began to offer PhD's in history. Part of the reason is that the late nineteenth-century sociologists were less professional, more strongly committed to social reform agendas than were the Hopkins historians. The development of the university involved a redefinition of loyalties as much as a debate over the internal organization of knowledge. As researchers earned and offered PhD degrees, they affirmed a commitment to academic knowledge and a new normative distinction between academic fields and broader public concerns. Of course this was not hard and fast but it did set the stage for an issue that would run through the history of sociology (perhaps even more acutely than through the rest of the university): uncertainty and contest over how much the field should serve to inform public debates and practical social services, and how much it should pursue autonomy and knowledge for its own sake.[46]

Sociology emerged as a discipline more at the University of Chicago than anywhere else. There it combined, also perhaps more than anywhere else, philosophy and the history of social thought with a close relationship to social reform, Christian socialism, and ideals of ethically informed action in the city. It became less politically engaged and activist as it became more disciplinary and professional—and as a new generation led by Robert Park and Ernest Burgess distinguished themselves from their founding predecessors.

The key founder was Albion Small, and the key catalyst was the creation of the new University of Chicago itself. The two were brought together by Chicago's founding president, William Rainey Harper, who thought that nurturing new scientific fields was a good way for a new university to prosper. Harper called Small to Chicago from Colby College in his native Maine, where he was president as well as a professor of history. Small was one of nine college presidents recruited to the new university, lured in part by its emphasis on graduate education. He had also trained as a Baptist minister, which was key, since John D. Rockefeller had established the University of Chicago on a firm Baptist basis (as well as with funds from his Standard Oil Company). The early university would tread a careful line, trying to balance its moral stance (which for some faculty extended to Christian Socialism) with its close ties not only to capitalism but to specific capitalists (including Chicago leaders and donors as well as Rockefeller).

At Colby, Small had replaced the standard moral philosophy course for undergraduates with an introduction to sociology. In 1890 he published a textbook—the first sociology textbook—with this course in mind. At Chi-

46. See Furner, *Advocacy and Objectivity.*

cago, Small replicated the course and, with George Vincent, published a new version of the textbook in 1894. Both course and text helped shape the discipline.[47] But the course's origins as a replacement for moral philosophy were significant. Sociology was to provide a needed scientific, rather than speculative, approach to understanding human beings' obligations to each other. And it would be useful at once through practical (applied) sociology, through interventions in the public sphere, and through advice to philanthropic organizations.[48]

Small was centrally active as an organizer and institutionalizer—at Chicago and on the national level. In addition to founding the Department of Sociology, he was for many years dean of the university's graduate school. He was instrumental in shaping the careers of numerous Chicago PhD's, finding them jobs throughout the Midwest especially, but also beyond. He founded the *American Journal of Sociology* and worked tirelessly to secure material for it, writing much himself. And he was instrumental in the founding of the American Sociological Society.

The notion of a Chicago school is the result of later claims on the Chicago traditions in sociology and has been both promulgated and contested for decades. There is no single principle to which its followers all subscribed; certainly Small did not offer that kind of founding orientation. If anything, it was the Chicago sociologists of the interwar years—most prominently Robert Park and later Louis Wirth and Herbert Blumer—who constituted a "school" in relation to other versions of sociology.[49] Even then, it would be more accurate to see it as a style or characteristic set of concerns. In Andrew Abbott's summary:

> It is often about the city and, if so, nearly always about Chicago. It is processual—examining organization and disorganization, conflict and accommodation, social movements and cultural change. It imagines society in terms of

47. Small and Vincent, *Introduction to the Science of Society.*

48. The next phase of sociology's development in the United States would indeed be closely tied to "professional" philanthropy, with Rockefeller funding important and organizations like the Social Science Research Council providing a bridge between the academics and the philanthropists. See Turner and Turner, *Impossible Science,* for an account of sociology's development that "follows the money."

49. In many ways it was the claims of their students on a distinctive Chicago identity that were crucial. The construction of symbolic interactionism and of human ecology as sociological fields involved tracing a lineage to Chicago (although with more fealty in the former case). For a review of the relatively large literature on the Chicago school, see Abbott, *Department and Discipline,* chap. 1. The classic text codifying the notion of a Chicago school centered on Park was Faris, *Chicago Sociology.*

groups and interaction rather than in terms of independent individuals with varying characteristics. Methodologically, it is quite diverse, but it always has a certain empirical, even observational flavor, whether it is counting psychotics in neighborhoods, reading immigrants' letters to the old country, or watching the languid luxuries of the taxi-dance hall.[50]

Roots of these ideas were evident in the late nineteenth- and early twentieth-century origins of the department. All reflected, in some degree, the engagement with practical reform, and usually with practical reform at a relatively local level. Chicago sociology was less engaged with the state and high politics and with structural economic questions; it was more engaged with locally acting groups—including the press, machine politics, and clashes over trade unions.

The Chicago sociologists of the late nineteenth and early twentieth centuries were invested in being specifically sociologists (rather than using sociology in a larger, interdisciplinary undertaking such as political economy). They, and especially Small, took on the labor of knitting together the growing band of researchers and teachers who identified sociology as their major pursuit. The *AJS* began a practice, for example, of announcing all the dissertations in sociology each year. And indeed, the field did grow.

In the nineteenth century, American sociology grew in closest relationship to economics. Economists and sociologists together had hived off from the American Historical Association. Both history and political science were conservative disciplines, and both had more establishment roots in elite universities. Economics and sociology both grew out of the extra-academic social reform movements as much as inside universities. Both came of age, alongside the Knights of Labor, the populist movement, and the IWW, with a concern for exploitation and inequality, and with the consideration that socialism was a real possibility, whether they individually favored it or not.[51]

Indeed, many leading sociologists were recognized more or less equally as economists. Sumner was among the last of the prominent classical economists, and some of his Yale students made careers as distinguished economists. Edward A. Ross did his PhD in economics under Richard T. Ely and taught economics at Stanford together with Thorstein Veblen—before both

50. Abbott, *Department and Discipline,* 6.

51. Many early sociologists were "Christian socialists"; few were Marxists. It is not clear that many were radical enough to vote for the Socialist Party of America, but Eugene Debs was a contemporary of Ward, Small, Giddings, and Sumner—and he polled nearly a million votes in 1912.

were dismissed for their pro-labor sympathies.[52] Giddings coauthored a prominent book with John Bates Clark, the most influential American leader of the marginalist revolution in economics. In the end, though, marginalism was the most decisive intellectual force separating economists from sociologists. It provided the basis for a view of "the economy" as a self-subsistent system and a framework for continuing mathematicization. This in turn enabled economists to present their work more clearly as a set of tools for analyzing the economy as it existed, rather than as a program for changing it. It also underwrote a successful project of professionalization.

It was not evident in advance that this should be so. The American Economics Association (AEA) was launched in a rebellion against an older, more conservative economics—personified by the same William Graham Sumner who is remembered as one of sociology's founders and a one-time radical for teaching Spencer. The younger economists held that historical change had rendered classical political economy obsolete and called for a fully historical approach to economics, inspired (like many early American sociologists) by the German historical school. A young John Bates Clark wrote that "present institutions contain in themselves the germs of a progress that shall ultimately break the limits of the existing system" and that there is "an undercurrent flowing calmly and resistlessly in the direction of a truer socialism . . . directed by the Providence which presides over all history."[53] In a similar spirit, Richard T. Ely proposed organizing a professional association "to combat the influence of the Sumner crowd."[54] Both Clark and Ely were appalled by inequality and the use of political power to support business interests. They found it natural to include sociologists in their new association.

Ironically, the AEA itself played a role in the deradicalization of economics, and this in turn helped precipitate the eventual departure of soci-

---

52. The firings were pivotal events in the history of academic freedom and the development of the institution of tenure. Another prominent economics professor (and later ASS president) George Elliott Howard was fired for protesting the dismissal of Ross. See Haskell, "Justifying the Rights of Academic." Several other faculty members resigned in protest. If the Stanford firings were the most egregious, Chicago also repeatedly disciplined faculty who became too radical—firing or forcing resignations from some. The new universities created by "robber baron" fortunes produced opportunities for sociology to flourish but also disciplined the new discipline. Chicago was built largely with Standard Oil money; Stanford's wealth was based on the Union Pacific Railroad (hence its sensitivity on Chinese labor questions).

53. Clark, "Nature and Progress of True Socialism," 571, as quoted in Ross, *Origins of American Social Science*, 107.

54. Quoted in Ross, *Origins of American Social Science*, 110. See more detailed discussion in Furner, *Advocacy and Objectivity*, chap. 3.

ology. Clark and his colleagues noted the conservative political attacks that led many universities to dismiss reformers in the 1880s and 1890s.[55] During this period economists learned not to take internecine feuds into public debates but rather to preserve the appearance of professional solidarity. At the same time, they also found in marginalist theory a justification for the competitive market and capital accumulation. The market gave "to every agent of production the amount of wealth which that agent creates."[56] Where the historical school had departed from classical economics in seeking a more historically specific understanding of the institutions that shaped economic life—including capitalism—the neoclassical marginalists were able to dispense with history (save as a source of "distortions") and for the most part with institutions.

Institutionalism would survive as a minority current in economics—famously with Veblen. But institutions were central to sociologists. Giddings and Clark shared a vision of liberal market society, but they recognized a disciplinary division of labor. For other sociologists, the turn away from historical and institutional economics and toward neoclassical marginalist individualism at turn of the century was something to be regretted, even attacked. Not least, especially for religiously rooted sociologists like Albion Small, the new economics removed the ethics from social science. Sociology was also shaped by concern simultaneously for voluntary action against determinist models and for the situation of economic action in relation to its noneconomic contexts and conditions. This would, in the 1930s, be central to the conversion of the twentieth century's single most influential sociologist, Talcott Parsons, from his previous career as an economist.[57]

The actual 1905 secession of sociologists from the AEA was a culmination of growing divergence in intellectual perspective as well as extra-academic engagements. It was also shaped by straightforward academic aspirations for autonomy and prosperity as a discipline. Not surprisingly, Albion Small was in the forefront along with E. A. Ross, Lester Frank Ward, William Graham Sumner, Franklin Giddings, and other prominent figures. The initiative, however, was started by the less well-known C. W. A. Veditz

55. Again, see Furner, *Advocacy and Objectivity.*

56. Clark, *Distribution of Wealth,* v.

57. Indeed, when Parsons established his canon of European theorists in the 1930s, his interest in precisely these problems drew him to the otherwise odd mix of Weber, Durkheim, Pareto, and Marshall. Weber was the most important for a variety of reasons, but not least as a link to the institutional analysis of historical economics. Parsons, *Structure of Social Action;* see also Parsons and Smelser, *Economy and Society.* See also Camic, "Making of a Method"; and idem, "Structure after 50 Years."

of George Washington University. The first planning meeting was chaired by William Davenport of Hamilton College. This is a reminder of the dangers of trying to grasp the history of sociology as though it were only a matter of dominant departments, such as those of Columbia and Chicago, and of the sort of individual "stars" who would be elected presidents of the American Sociological Association. Sociology had already spread to a wide range of institutions.[58] And faculty, from small liberal arts colleges to the different sorts of larger universities, all felt incentives to express an autonomous collective identity (and perhaps to have more opportunities for participation and leadership). Frank W. Blackmar of the University of Kansas (one of the earliest sociology departments) called for "a separate and independent organization" because "to make it a part of one of the associations named would give it a subordinate position, and, what is worse, would seem to indicate that sociology is a branch of either history, political science, economics, or anthropology." E. A. Ross, then at the University of Nebraska, concurred: "For three or four years I have thought the time was ripe for American sociologists to come together and thresh out their differences. . . . I should thereafter heartily welcome the project for some sort of national association and believe that such an association could do a great deal to clarify our minds, acquaint us with one another's opinions, and exalt the dignity of sociology in the public eye."[59]

Nonacademic sociologists seemed to agree. Anna Garlin Spencer of the New York School of Philanthropy wrote of her "keen interest in any effort to consolidate and make more effective the labors of those who are trying to solve social problems and initiate social movements by the light of science. I am very desirous that there shall be a `clearing-house' in the field of sociology, especially that which has focused into practical effort."[60] But when the draft constitution for the ASS was presented at the end of 1905, there were worries that its statement of purpose for the new organization

58. A favorite genre of early *AJS* and *Social Forces* articles documented the proliferation of sociology courses and departments. Such major sociologists as Luther Bernard were active contributors. See, e.g., Bernard, "Teaching of Sociology in the United States." During its first decades the *AJS* was also full of reviews of proposed standard courses, and efforts to synthesize the history of the field in a way that gave form to its current flourishing (and leadership to the sociologists who did the synthesizing). Albion Small mastered this genre with a nine-article series titled "The Scope of Sociology" in 1900-1904, and a twenty-three-article series titled "Contributions to the History of Sociology" in 1923-24.

59. Quoted in Rhodes, *History of the American Sociological Association.* On sociology at Kansas and Nebraska, respectively, see Sica, "Sociology at the University of Kansas"; and Deegan, "Sociology at Nebraska."

60. Rhodes, *History of the American Sociological Association,* 41.

appeared to exclude or at least neglect "practical" sociologists. The stated purpose was "the encouragement of sociological research and discussion, and the promotion of intercourse between persons engaged in the scientific study of society." Giddings among others suggested it was ample enough to include all with legitimate interests in sociology. It remained intact. Likewise, there was debate as to how the constitution should prevent members posing "any resolution approving or disapproving specific sociological doctrines or specific schemes for social betterment." On both fronts, the early debate reflected tensions between academic and public agendas that have generated recurrent conflicts.[61]

The first 1905 meeting discussed simply organizing a more formal section with the AEA but quickly turned to planning for a new association—the American Sociological Society (ASS) (which, when acronyms later gained prominence, eventually changed its name to the American Sociological Association [ASA]). This was launched the next year. Lester Frank Ward became its first president.

Albion Small secured a relationship to the University of Chicago—already institutionally central to the new discipline—not least by having the University of Chicago Press publish the *Papers and Proceedings* of the ASS's annual meetings and also by positioning the *AJS* as the association's de facto journal. "More will be said, and more definitely, and with more confident emphasis, from and about the sociological point of view" because the ASS had provided sociology with a "corporate form," Small wrote in 1907 in the first volume of *Papers and Proceedings*.[62]

Over the next fifty years, departments and journals proliferated, and the PhD degree became more standard. Sociology continued to be shaped by efforts to synthesize the history of social thought, by new empirical inquiries, and by sociologists' engagements in projects of social reform. But professionalization now had the upper hand over engagements in extra-academic reform movements. Robert Park's peculiar dual career suggests something of this. Park initially thought of a career in philosophy, then became a journalist—by his own account a muckraker—and later secretary to Booker T. Washington at the Tuskegee Institute—before becoming a professor at Chicago. He retained an engagement in social reform but kept this distinct (at least in principle) from his academic work and insisted vehemently that there was no room in sociology for "moralism."[63]

61. See Lengermann and Niebrugge, chap. 3, in this volume, for an analysis of how these tensions figured in the separation of sociology and social work.

62. American Sociological Society, Papers and Proceedings, Volume I (May 1907), pp. 1-2.

63. On Park, see Matthews, *Quest for an American Sociology*; and Ross, *Origins of American Social Science*.

At Chicago, Park continued and amplified the effort of W. I. Thomas (who initially brought him there) to turn sociology from social philosophy toward empirical research. His circle of contacts included Dewey and Mead, and he sought to integrate pragmatism and social psychology with human ecology. His strongest interests and those most definitive of the Chicago "school" to which he helped give rise were in cities and relations among groups, especially race relations. The *Introduction to the Science of Society* that Park edited with Ernest W. Burgess in 1921 became at once a widely used textbook and a sort of manual for students who subscribed to the Chicago approach—the "green bible" many called it.[64] His students took on a host of projects, most involving an ethnographic component and the study of specific, socially located communities. Herbert Blumer and Everett Hughes (as well as Burgess) would complement Park in shaping the classic Chicago sociology of the era.

On the one hand, Park was deeply engaged with issues of race relations. On the other hand, he was party to the tacit agreement of leading American sociologists to focus on what they regarded as proper and practical approaches—exemplified by Booker T. Washington—to the exclusion of engagement with the more critical and more sociological work of W. E. B. DuBois.[65] Although American sociology was distinctively concerned with race and immigration, it was not consistently egalitarian. Many early soci-

64. The structure of the book combined substantial texts by Park and Burgess with selections from contemporary writings. These ranged from Simmel, Durkheim, and Cooley to Dewey, Thomas, and Gumplowicz. There were several excerpts from Charles Darwin and a number from psychologists, including Edward L. Thorndike. The format was drawn significantly from Thomas's 1908 *Sourcebook for Social Origins: Ethnological Materials, Psychological Standpoint, Classified and Annotated Bibliographies for the Interpretation of Savage Societies.* The title, however, was a direct replication of that used by Small and Vincent for their earlier, leading textbook.

65. See Morris, chap. 15, in this volume. There were also, of course, more conformist figures than Washington and more radical figures than DuBois. Among the few relatively early sociologists who did pay closer attention to DuBois (from the 1920s on) were E. Franklin Frazier, of Fisk and then Howard University, and Guy B. Johnson of the University of North Carolina. In 1937, Johnson summed up the condition of "Negro movements" in the United States: "So far only two significant Negro philosophies have crystallized. One was personified in Booker T. Washington, who preached patience and good will and was as much a leader of white as of Negro opinion. His rise to power helped to solidify an opposition group represented by the National Association for the Advancement of Colored People, an upper-class Negro movement, under the leadership of W. E. B. DuBois, based upon the idea of militant legal tactics to enforce the recognition of the legal rights of Negroes. Increasing class consciousness and economic stress are bringing about a realignment of Negro leadership. The stage is now set for the emergence of a third great movement, based upon the united efforts of black and white workers to change the economic order" (Johnson, "Negro Racial Movements and Leadership in the United States," 57).

ologists were systematic racists, and both evolutionary theory and the rise of social statistics were shaped by racialist projects.[66] Similarly, although reform projects were central to nineteenth-century sociology, they were from early on contested. Many academic sociologists articulated a commitment to science intended both to claim authority and to secure independence from extra-academic reformers. The division that grew between Jane Addams and her colleagues in the settlement house movement and the University of Chicago department of sociology in the era of Robert Park reflects this (as well as the politics of gender, which have recurrently been correlated with distinctions of "pure" versus "applied" and employment in academic versus nonacademic positions).[67] But it is worth noting that Addams and many of her colleagues contested the division of labor. They did not merely aspire to higher status for the practical—the professionalization of social work, for example. They aspired to an alternative kind of intellectual and practical life in which science and action would not be severed from each other (and indeed, in which both would be full-time commitments, not merely jobs or careers).

Although Chicago retained a leading role, Columbia exerted a comparable (though less corporate) influence. Indeed, into the 1930s, Columbia produced even more PhD's than Chicago did. At its origin in the 1890s, Columbia's department was at least as concerned with social reform as Chicago's was. Under Giddings's leadership, it was distinctive partly for a much stronger relationship to and concern with state-centered politics (including what is sometimes called "macrosociology" or the comparative study of social institutions). It is instructive that Giddings's most prominent public engagement was his advocacy for imperialism in the pursuit of democracy and progress at the time of the Spanish-American War.[68] After Giddings, macrosociology remained an interest, but so did intermediate levels of social organization. Robert McIver wrote an enormous tome on the idea of community, while Robert and Helen Lynd wrote the classic *Middletown* studies. These were designed in part to study "normal" American social organization rather than the disorganization and change of urbanization in the Chicago model. The Lynds were, however, active in the labor and civil

66. On the long history of sociological analyses of race, see Winant, chap. 16, in this volume.

67. Deegan, *Jane Addams and the Men of the Chicago School*; and idem, *Race, Hull-House, and the University of Chicago*.

68. See Giddings, *Democracy and Empire*. Giddings was, of course, a liberal progressive. The conservative William Graham Sumner took the opposite side, arguing forcefully against imperialism.

rights movements. One should not exaggerate the Chicago–Columbia divergence. Giddings promoted statistics more than his Chicago contemporaries such as Small did, but one of his best-known students, William Fielding Ogburn, became an integral part of Chicago sociology through the first half of the twentieth century. There he pioneered quantitative research as well as the study of social change more generally.[69] For the most part, the Columbia-trained quantifiers backed the also elitist University of Chicago faculty in intradisciplinary struggles in the 1930s.

In 1936, after five years of conflict and jockeying for position, the ASA severed what had once been a close relationship with the University of Chicago and the *American Journal of Sociology* to launch the *American Sociological Review*.[70] The quarrel had several dimensions, but a central one had to do with sociology's response—or failure to produce a concerted response— to the Great Depression.[71] Sociology lost prestige, influence, and jobs. Between 1929 and 1932, the ASS lost as much as a quarter of its membership. This setback concerned the Chicago–Columbia elites, but it much more directly affected those without comparably secure and well-paid positions. The rebels against Chicago control responded to intellectual deficiencies in the model of sociology that Robert Park and his colleagues, such as Ernest Burgess, put forward. But they also tried to create a new model of engagement in social issues. The split simply reflected a loss of cohesion following internal differentiation

Despite the leading roles of Chicago and Columbia, whose PhD's staffed colleges and universities around the country, sociology grew disproportionately in state universities. Rural sociology was especially prominent at land grant institutions and was long a major branch of the field, although the urban studies of the Chicago school were destined to be better remembered, partly because urbanization was such a strong social trend. By the 1920s there were already major departments at Michigan, Wisconsin, Mis-

69. Other Giddings students included Howard Odum and F. Stuart Chapin. They were perhaps not a "school" (and they did not constitute themselves as a school by claiming a particular tradition of Columbia sociology the way symbolic interactionists laid claim to an ostensible Chicago school. They were nonetheless influential in establishing core quantitative-empirical traditions in American sociology.

70. See Lengermann, "Founding of the *American Sociological Review*."

71. See Camic, chap. 7, in this volume. Sociology had seemed to be surging forward in the late 1920s and early 1930s. President Hoover's appointment of a Research Committee on Social Trends symbolized this surge, but by the time the committee reported (1933), the Depression had struck and President Roosevelt had come to power. The New Deal privileged other disciplines, notably economics, and ivy league faculty members. It was also led by liberals concerned to minimize their connections to an older style of radicals more common in sociology.

souri, and North Carolina (though efforts to launch a department of sociology at Berkeley were resisted until after World War II).[72] A 1925 poll by Raymond Hughes (one of the earliest comparative rankings in American higher education) ranked the top ten sociology departments in desirability for graduate work as follows: (1) Chicago; (2) Columbia; (3) Wisconsin; (4) Minnesota; (5) Michigan; (6) Harvard; (7) Missouri; (8) Pennsylvania; (9) North Carolina; and (10) Yale. The rankings would change over the ensuing decades, of course. Missouri seems to have been the biggest loser.[73] Berkeley and UCLA were the most important new entrants. But perhaps more telling than the positional struggle among the elite was a decline in the percentage of PhD's produced by the discipline's most prestigious departments. In the 1930s, nearly 70 percent of PhD's were awarded by a "top-ten" department. Out of the 156 PhD's awarded, Chicago and Columbia accounted for 46. But by the 1990s, top-ten departments accounted for less than 30 percent of the total.[74] An ever-narrower Michelsian oligarchy—or caste system—was arguably being created as the discipline grew, since the elite did (and do) tend to circulate graduate student job-market entrants among themselves.[75] At the same time, however, the diversity of institutional bases was—and remains—mirrored in a diversity of approaches.

Visions and Divisions

By the 1920s, American sociology's founders were fading from the scene. William Graham Sumner had died in 1910, Lester Frank Ward in 1913; Albion Small would follow in 1926, and Franklin Giddings in 1931. At Chicago, Robert Park was ascendant (the 1920s were the heyday of his version of the Chicago school); at Columbia, MacIver and the Lynds were in the leadership. Edward Ross lived until 1951, chairing the Wisconsin department until 1937 and helping to secure its rise to prominence in the field—and in effect spanning two of sociology's early generations. But as

72. See Turner, chap. 4, in this volume, on Charles Ellwood, for an account of a major sociologist who worked outside the dominant departments and had a large influence on teaching but has a minimal place in the enduring sociological canon. Canonical disciplinary histories tend to be Whig histories; they are also disproportionately histories of "schools of thought" with which authors and readers can identify. On Berkeley, see VanAntwerpen, "Resisting Sociology's Seductive Name"; and Murray, "Resistance to Sociology at Berkeley."

73. Missouri's early prominence figures in the story of Charles Ellwood, as told by Turner, chap. 4, in this volume.

74. This calculation is based on unpublished research I conducted with Alton Phillips and Jonathan VanAntwerpen.

75. Burris, "Academic Caste System."

the example of Ross's Wisconsin suggests, a range of other departments were gaining influence. Charles Horton Cooley, part of the founding generation, died in 1929 but left behind a University of Michigan department that would remain among the central influences in the field. Minnesota was particularly prominent, with not just George Vincent (a professor as well as president) but Pitirim Sorokin (who taught at Minnesota through most of the 1920s), Luther Bernard, and the department's long-term guiding influence, Giddings's student F. Stuart Chapin.

Bernard was an illuminating figure, a man of strong personal contradictions who participated in some of the central conflicts of the field.[76] He was a charismatic teacher who placed the highest value on empirical research without producing much of it (unless his important studies of sociology itself counted). He was a volatile, often angry individualist who vehemently praised objectivism as the standard for sociology. He was a critic of the "new woman" (and a notorious philanderer) who married and collaborated with one of sociology's most important early feminists, Jessie Bernard. Bernard was uncompromising in his distaste for charity sociology—he feared that even the science-oriented quantifier Chapin was tainted by an association with social work. Yet the "scientific" sociologists pursued the authority of objective research in part to legitimate critical analyses of social conditions. It was Luther Bernard who nominated W. I. Thomas to become president of the ASA seven years after he was forced to resign from the University of Chicago (and it was sociology's old guard "moralists" who opposed Thomas).

Sorokin too was a major influence. He had done important sociological research in Russia, before serving as Alexander Kerensky's secretary and fleeing in the wake of the Bolshevik Revolution. When he was appointed at Minnesota, there was anxiety that he was still too revolutionary—even if a Menshevik rather than a Bolshevik. Over his long career he pursued a wide range of research projects from one of the first studies of social mobility to the massive attempt to theorize all of history in an oscillation of ideational, sensate, and idealistic systems of culture.[77] Late in his life, he criticized both the typical quantitative empiricism of American sociology and the functionalism of Parsons, and called for a sociology more engaged with public issues and shaped by the pursuit of "creative altruism."

A range of other founders left a legacy measured less on PhD programs than in public engagements, both through their writings and their work in

---

76. There is a good account of Bernard in Bannister, *Sociology and Scientism*, chaps. 8 and 9.
77. Sorokin, *Social Mobility*; idem, *Social and Cultural Dynamics*.

social movements. Jane Addams was preeminent, as we have already seen. But W. E. B. Dubois was also a major sociologist of the founding generations, though without founding influence on a major department of sociology. After gaining his PhD at Harvard (where his main training was in philosophy under William James and George Santayana, though he also studied history and sociology), Dubois, like many others among the early American sociologists, went to Germany. He was engaged by the epistemological crisis of the late nineteenth century, but his inquiries into knowledge were repeatedly challenged by "the truth in the world" and "the most immediate face of this 'truth' was 'the problems of racial and social contacts.'"[78] DuBois published his classics, *The Philadelphia Negro* and *The Souls of Black Folk*, in 1898 and 1903, respectively—pioneering works of empirical investigation rivaling anything produced by the Chicago or Columbia sociologists of the era (complete with a positivist defense of scientific objectivity), followed by a philosophical, almost metaphysical exploration of the meaning of African American life. Here in one author were two sides of American sociology (a double consciousness of another sort). But the methodological doubling was met with a consistent (if frequently rethought) integration of practical engagement in reform with more abstract intellectual pursuits. DuBois taught from 1897 to 1910 at Atlanta University, but then for twenty-four years worked at the NAACP, editing its journal, *The Crisis*, as well as serving as a key administrator in the organization he helped to found. In 1934 he returned to Atlanta and in 1940 founded the race relations journal *Phylon*. His engagement with academic sociology and sociological research was long but for the most part ignored by the dominant currents of disciplinary sociology—both Park's Chicago school and their "radical" critics.[79]

The founders did not have a clearly unified vision of the field, but they joined in a more or less cohesive debate framed by questions such as the extent to which evolution and broad patterns in historical change should be

78. DuBois, *Dusk of Dawn*, quoted in Zamir, *Dark Voices*. See also Lewis, *DuBois: Biography of a Race*.

79. DuBois was not completely ignored; an *AJS* review by Theophilus Bolden Stewart praised *Souls of Black Folk* for approaching "the many-sided Negro question with the confidence and conviction of a master, and with the grace and beauty of a poet" (136–37). By the 1920s and 1930s there would be a bit more attention to his work. Nonetheless, there was little serious engagement with DuBois's sociology. See Morris, chap. 15, in this volume, for speculation on how the history of American sociology might have been different had sociologists engaged more seriously with DuBois. DuBois stayed at Atlanta until 1944, when he returned to the NAACP before becoming more actively engaged in politics, first in the United States and then as a Pan-Africanist in postcolonial Ghana.

emphasized, ways to relate the organic wholeness of society to individual freedom and action, and the extent to which inequalities of power and economic position could be mitigated by social reform. Many of the enduring lines of tension and division had already been established as well. The relationship between science and social action, for example, has remained an enduring question for sociologists since the discipline's founding. But many sociologists truly desired to achieve both scientific authority and influence in social reform. Sociology has developed since in a recurrent interplay of visions of sociology's potential and divisions over how to pursue it.

In this introduction, I have traced the story only into the very early twentieth-century period of sociology's institutionalization. Certainly competing visions and consequent divisions continued. In the wake of the 1936 conflict, for example, a disciplinary elite founded the Sociological Research Association to consecrate itself. This invitation-only body essentially claimed (and to some extent still claims) to control the apex of sociology's pyramid and at least implicitly affirms the unity of the field as well as the dominance of "science."[80] With more practical effect, the interdisciplinary Social Science Research Council (SSRC) mobilized similar elites from sociology and other disciplines in pursuit of an integrated—and scientific—research agenda. Primary initial support came from the Rockefeller Foundation (whose president, George Vincent, was a former Chicago and Minnesota sociologist). Chicago and Columbia social scientists were central to the creation of the SSRC (though other key figures such as Stuart Chapin and Howard Odum were also involved in the Council's early work).

As always, both unity and boundaries were in question as sociology overlapped a number of other more or less distinct fields: social work, rural sociology, criminology, marriage and family studies, and anthropology. Indeed, many fields have been founded largely within sociology and then "spun off."[81] For all the push toward a more scientific sociology, and the association of science with quantification, sociologists remained committed to field research as well as quantitative, especially survey methods.[82] Field studies, such as William Foote Whyte's 1943 classic *Street Corner Society,* often reached enormous publics. Quantitative research more often gained

---

80. For decades, though, the SRA has been little more than an honorary society networking at an annual dinner.

81. See Short (criminology), chap. 18, and Walters (sociology of education), chap. 19, in this volume, on fields of research and teaching that have had an ambiguous, often arm's-length relationship with disciplinary sociology. Also see Lengermann and Niebrugge, chap. 3, on sociology's separation from social work.

82. See DeVault, chap. 5, in this volume.

influence with policymakers; for example, William Fielding Ogburn not only pioneered techniques but chaired the President's Research Committee on Social Trends in the early 1930s, and later James Coleman shaped Supreme Court decisions on desegregation with his studies of schools.

Although sociologists advanced new theories and vocabularies, none bridged disciplines or the growing borders between academic science and reform movements the way evolution and progressive thought had earlier. Sociology itself became less cohesive, partly because it grew larger, and specialization became the order of the day. Sociologists recurrently bemoaned it but nonetheless joined in. A new unifying perspective would not appear until functionalism provided a common conceptual framework and vocabulary, and multivariate statistics a common analytic strategy—both mainly after World War II. Sociology then entered what has often been seen as a "golden age." Rapid growth (based partly on expansion of the university system and the passage of the GI bill) coincided with renewed prestige. Professionalism was ascendant.

The growth of large-scale, substantially financed research projects—especially with foundation funding but also corporate and government support—encouraged one version of professionalization, epitomized by Paul Lazarsfeld's and Robert Merton's leadership at Columbia, with its Bureau of Applied Social Research and enormously successful graduate training program throughout the postwar era. Foundation support—notably from Rockefeller and Ford—was also pivotal in establishing demographic and survey research.[83] Quantitative methods were widely seen as linked to professionalizing projects.

Both statistical analysis and functionalism were often challenged, however, by field researchers, specialists on social problems, those carrying on the reform traditions, and critical theorists. Especially important was a long, mostly Midwestern, and in many ways populist tradition anchored in the Society for the Study of Social Problems. Its journal, *Social Problems,* was more widely read but less professionally prestigious (an indicator of division between sociology as taught most widely and as pursued in the best-funded research departments). The contrast in styles was apparent in the very titles of two classic, almost simultaneous studies of medical education, *Boys in White* by Howard S. Becker et al., and *The Student Physician* by Robert K. Merton et al. Many of the Social Problems researchers resisted the hegemony of quantitative research methods and functionalist theory. The Social

---

83. Turner and Turner, in *The Impossible Science,* see this shift as a basic turn away from earlier theoretical projects, and see foundation money as determinative.

Problems researchers were not always politically engaged but frequently irreverent toward established hierarchies and institutions.

Theory had its own professionalizer in Talcott Parsons, who used his base at Harvard to promote a standard canon of sociological texts and his own synthetic theoretical framework. This professionalism flourished, but in tension with more critical perspectives. Parsons' functionalist theory would by the 1960s provide one of the dominant images of a disciplinary mainstream (in all senses of the term *disciplinary*).[84] Formal analyses of survey data would offer another. The 1960s was not only an era of radicalism but of major advances in quantitative research, including especially a growing use of multivariate statistics—exemplified by the introduction of path analysis by Otis Dudley Duncan and the enormously influential study *The American Occupational Structure*, which he coauthored with Peter Blau in 1967.

C. Wright Mills both analyzed and satirized the complementary pairing of "grand theory" and "abstracted empiricism" in *The Sociological Imagination*. His point was how this dualism obscured lack of critical attention to public problems. In a range of books through the 1950s he had pursued intellectual analyses that could also reach broad publics, with *Power Elite* the most prominent.[85] Alvin Gouldner took up a similar theme in *The Coming Crisis of Western Sociology*. Mills's book appeared in 1959 and would shape the rise of the New Left; Gouldner's appeared in the 1970s and marked the crest of a wave of campus politics in which sociology was centrally involved. But in between, a range of other critics challenged sociology's conventional structure and advocated for—or simply exemplified—more public engagement. Daniel Bell, for example, saw himself (like his friend Mills) as a marginal man in elite academia.[86] Ambivalent about standing firmly either inside or outside the university, Mills and Bell responded to trends in social science that were shaped not only by ideas but by the expansion of the university system and a narrowing of the space for extra-academic "public intellectuals."[87] A socialist intellectual from the 1930s, Bell attended graduate school at Columbia and served a stint as an instructor at Chicago before becoming the labor editor at *Fortune* magazine in 1948 (while at the same time editing the socialist theory journal *Modern Review*—on which future ASA president Lewis Coser worked as an associate editor). Bell's trajectory was taking him away from the Left as Mills moved more

84. See Calhoun and VanAntwerpen, chap. 10, in this volume.

85. Mills, *Power Elite*.

86. See Brick, *Daniel Bell and the Decline of Intellectual Radicalism*.

87. See Jacoby, *Last Intellectuals*.

firmly into the New Left. But despite differences from Mills's political orientation and analysis, Bell's *The End of Ideology,* published in 1960, was in a similar structural relationship to conventional academic sociology.

Growth in sociology wasn't just a matter of foundation funding or professional projects. It was shaped by engagements in government during the New Deal and World War II, and by the GI bill afterward.[88] The growth of universities during the 1950s and 1960s brought the founding of new sociology departments—especially in the West—and rapid expansion of the field nationally. Sociology was prominent in analyzing and addressing domestic issues such as race and poverty. It was central—especially in the work of Edward Shils and Talcott Parsons—to the rise of modernization theory as an understanding of global social change. Perhaps no discipline was shaped more by these boom years or contributed more to the student movements of the 1960s. The Port Huron Statement was greatly influenced by the writings of C. Wright Mills (and its authors included several sociology students); several of the early leaders of the Students for a Democratic Society (including one president, Todd Gitlin) became prominent sociologists.

But the legacy of the boom years was broader. Sociology became a dramatically more inclusive discipline during the course of its expansion, building on the gains of the civil rights movement as well as a long tradition of sociological research on questions of race and ethnicity. Women grew more numerous in the field, though also frustrated at continued male dominance of it—and to this day, even as women make up the majority of the field, they are underrepresented in many of the most prestigious departments.[89] In 1970 Sociologists for Women in Society was founded, with implications not just for internal participation in the discipline but also for the study of gender. Meeting resistance from the ASA, it launched *Gender and Society* as an autonomous journal. A more or less parallel movement led to the founding of the Caucus of Black Sociologists.[90] The intersections among questions of race, gender, and class came to the foreground as matters of debate and research as well as of a perspective that shapes teaching and a good deal of research.

Efforts to promote diversity contended with an extremely tight job market during the 1970s and 1980s. Graduate students attracted to the field by the social engagements of the late 1960s and early 1970s found it hard to

88. See Camic, chap. 7, and Abbott and Sparrow, chap. 8, in this volume.

89. See Ferree, Khan, and Morimoto, chap. 13, in this volume.

90. This later became, more formally, the Association of Black Sociologists. See Dickerson, "Blooming in the Noise of the Whirlwind."

make a career. This was an era of tight funding for higher education generally. It was also an era in which sociology had to compete for students and resources with growing business schools and other fields that catered to students concerned about job and career prospects.

Sociologists were prominent in several of the growing professional fields. Criminology and medical sociology were among the largest branches of the discipline, for example, although increasingly distinct in their work. As had long been the case with social work, in fields like the sociology of education there was an ambivalent relationship between disciplinary departments and professional schools.[91] Enrollments often grew faster in "applied" fields rather than in those shaped by the research emphases of the most prestigious departments. Indeed, tenure decisions at many leading departments placed a positive value on many of the characteristics of the "mainstream" derided by the 1960s critics—from publication in the *ASR* to externally funded research. And there were transformative improvements in research techniques and data sets. The late 1970s, however, ushered in an era in which the elite departments and journals largely pursued agendas only loosely connected to either of the main sources of undergraduate interest—the social problems tradition and the new professional fields. This was especially true, perhaps, of work based on ever more sophisticated quantitative techniques, but also of much macrohistorical inquiry into large-scale social transformations.

This trend began to shift in the 1990s, partly because of the development of some prestigious research fields such as economic sociology, which forged closer relations to professional schools. At the same time, if business seemed to rule the roost, the 1990s was also a watershed for interest in civil society and nongovernmental organizations. Sociologists not only studied these developments—on themes as diverse as the environment, the arts, and human rights; they also put their research skills to work on problems confronted by social movements and civil society organizations. Globalization shaped the growing internationalization of sociology.[92] Soaring numbers of immigrants pushed sociologists to return to classic issues about assimilation and ethnic identities, discrimination and access to opportunity—as did continuing struggles of American minority groups for equal rights. Sociology contributed the idea of social capital to public debates over citizenship and participation as well as to research on class and social mobility.

91. See, in this volume, Lengermann and Niebrugge, chap. 3; Short, chap. 18; and Walters, chap. 19.

92. See Kennedy and Centeno, chap. 20 (who find the glass of internationalization at most half full).

As importantly, undergraduate enrollment started to increase again, and job market prospects for new PhD's improved. An increasing number now turn to jobs outside the academy, but by choice not only necessity, and partly because of the centrality of sociological issues to both corporations and nongovernmental organizations. In recent years sociologists have celebrated their public mission, and membership in the ASA and attendance at annual meetings hit new highs for the first time since the 1970s.[93]

Both "professional" and more "public" visions of sociology are prospering, growing from roots in nineteenth-century evolutionary research and social reform activism. Perhaps they are less in tension with each other now than at some earlier times. But, of course, sociology remains heterogeneous. The chapters in the present book reveal a field that derives vitality from its diversity but that also sometimes frustrates its members. The chapters here don't begin to exhaust the diversity, nor does this book provide the thorough history that the field deserves. The chapters do suggest how rich the history of sociology is and how instructive exploring that history can be. If science aspires to transcend the limits of surface observation and prejudice, historical understanding of the conditions and trajectories of scientific work can be as valuable as theoretical frameworks and research methods.

---

93. See Burawoy, "For Public Sociology," and the wide range of commentary and discussion provoked by Burawoy's address and more generally the 2004 annual meeting of the ASA.

[TWO] The American Spencerians: Theorizing a New Science

Daniel Breslau

Anyone studying the founders of academic sociology in the United States has the advantage of always finding the treatises written by these figures exactly where they belong on the library shelves. The works of Franklin Giddings, Albion Small, William Graham Sumner, and Lester Ward—the first four presidents of the American Sociological Association—are infrequently cited in works on the history of sociology and almost never for their sociological insights.[1] And no one has stepped forward as a champion of these founders, protesting the neglect of their contributions and calling for their reinsertion into the canon. Their verbose works seem to be couched at a level of generality too remote from objects of sociological research, and they use much more space proposing and justifying the new science than they do actually realizing it. Their (Lamarckian) evolutionary naturalism (Stocking 1962) seems quaint and hardly relevant to a field that has almost universally adopted the Durkheimian view of society as fully emergent from and discontinuous with biology. Although most of the nineteenth-century social theorists in the United States were opposed to social Darwinism, it does not help that they generally viewed social hierarchy as the result of natural differences in intellectual endowments (Phelan 1989). When not neglected, the founders and their worldview are more likely to be used as a foil against which to define an adequate sociology. When Talcott Parsons announced, on the first page of *The Structure of Social Action,* that Spencer was dead, he was referring not only to Spencer himself but to these American Spencerians (Parsons 1968).

It is not my intention in this chapter to revive the reputations of these

---

1. This is a minimal listing of the founders of academic sociology in the United States. They were recognized by others at the time, and by one another, as the core of the discipline. To this quartet one might add Edward Allsworth Ross and Charles Horton Cooley (although Cooley himself refused the disciplinary identity of sociologist). These two emphasized the psychological dimensions of social order but adhered to an evolutionary naturalist definition of society and sociology.

neglected figures. Their importance is not in the value of their works as a canon for sociology but in their effects on the field that persist into the present. The neglect of their works as theoretical source material should not lead to a forgetting of the social origins of sociology, and of its object of study and legitimate research practices. Thus, the features of the founders' sociology that seems most dated and irrelevant, including their Spencerianism, may be simply the most repressed features of the discipline as it exists today.

This chapter therefore examines the social sources of Spencerian sociology and the practices of research and discipline-building that it contains. By Spencerianism, I mean the founders' adoption of Herbert Spencer's definition of society, and their adoption of his definition of sociology as the science that takes society as its object. Spencer's society is an integrated whole that is naturally occurring, continuous with the natural world, and subject to transhistorical laws of evolution. Sociology is therefore, by this definition, a holistic, naturalistic, and evolutionary science of society. Notwithstanding their disagreements, some quite radical, on theoretical particulars (Ross 1991, 122–38; Stern 1932), the founders unanimously accepted this constitution for their discipline, just as sociologists today, with perhaps slightly less unanimity, would reject it.

Histories of Ideas

Institutional histories and intellectual histories of the formative years of sociology in the United States have been pursued quite separately. Studies of the intellectual content of the theories have tended to treat the theoretical corpus of each sociologist as a timeless system, to be classified, contrasted, and evaluated in relation to other systems. Such works exemplify a tendency described by Bourdieu in which "the work as it presents itself, that is, as an *opus operatum*, totalized and canonized in the form of a corpus of 'complete works' torn from the time of its composition and capable of being run through in all directions, obscures the work in the process of construction and above all the *modus operandi* of which it is the product" (Bourdieu 2000, 53). Hinkle's study of the "founding theory," in its preoccupation with constructing a coherent system of each of these figures and resolving all the apparent inconsistencies their works, misses the ways that those inconsistencies arise from the changing practical challenges of establishing a sociology under different conditions, before different audiences, and on different questions (Hinkle 1980). A thoroughgoing evolutionist like Sumner, who made a few statements against the literal application of some

Darwinian principles to society, is therefore spuriously classified as an anti-evolutionist and contrasted with the others on that basis. The result is a multiplication of fine shadings of difference among these theorists, who in practice were not engaged in writing down complete and self-consistent theories but in constructing a discipline and its object of study.

Studies that venture to relate the works of the early sociologists to their social context exhibit an interesting divide as a result of their opposed ways of conceiving of the context for those works. Echoing the division between critical ("reflection") studies and the "production of culture approach" in the sociology of culture (Griswold 1981) is the opposition between studies that relate sociological works to class interests and features of the society as a whole, and studies that place works in the more immediate context of the institutional setting of sociology. In an example of the first type of study, Schwendinger and Schwendinger argue that the academic sociologists at the turn of the twentieth century elaborated an ideology of corporate liberalism. The "sociologists of the chair" were critical of laissez-faire capitalism, but largely for the social unrest and disintegration it seemed to cause, not for its inherent social domination and inequality. They were not social Darwinists, except perhaps for Sumner, in that they did not believe that a natural evolutionary process could be counted on to perpetually improve the human condition, or that it was impossible for deliberate intervention to improve on the course of evolution. Nonetheless, they were what the Schwendingers call "reform Darwinists," believing in a continued evolutionary improvement based on scientifically informed reforms. They were "liberal syndicalists," calling for coordination among the conflicting interest groups, coordinated by the enlightened liberal state and its sociologists. The "radicalism" of even those who were censured for their views did not contain radical proposals for transforming the social order (Schwendinger and Schwendinger 1974).

To the Schwendingers' credit, they relate the ideological position of the founders to the founders' social position, particularly at the institutions that supported them and their work. Yet the interests of the sociologists seem to collapse entirely into those of the monopoly capitalists. Clearly, the works of the American Spencerian sociologists, in calling for a harmonized social order that was more than unfettered competition but less than state coordination or socialism, an organized capitalism, supported what was becoming the new social order. But class interest does not account for their "evolutionary naturalism," to which most of their work was devoted. This was not a vision for capitalist society but for sociology and its object of study. The sociologists were not primarily agents for a monopoly fraction of the capitalist class but had interests of their own in securing their cultural authority and a market for their research and teaching.

Perhaps the most familiar of the second type of study, relating the works of sociologists to the immediate institutional context in which they worked, are works that treat the intellectual content of sociology, and other social sciences, as strategically oriented to a discipline-building project. According to this argument, the nascent disciplines were faced with a struggle for legitimation. Economics and sociology, in particular, needed to draw models and methods from the natural sciences in order to establish their legitimacy and their rightful place among the university disciplines (Camic 1995; Camic and Xie 1994; Mirowski 1989). The social sciences faced special problems of legitimation, and their very presence in the new universities was by no means certain. They therefore imitated the established natural sciences in order to appear "scientific." One way of doing this was to adopt research methods that had proven their utility in the natural sciences, such as statistics (Camic and Xie 1994). Another way of drawing on the natural sciences was through the transfer of conceptual systems as metaphors, for instance, the way that marginalist economics was invented by metaphorically applying the nineteenth-century physics of energy to the social world (Mirowski 1989). This type of borrowing is germane to the founders of sociology in the United States, who, following Herbert Spencer, argued that the analogy between society and a living organism justified applying to the former those modes of analysis developed in studying the latter. We might wonder whether sociology may have been to biology what neoclassical economics was to physics.

The use of metaphors as conduits through which to adapt natural science methods to the social world is easily observed in the cases just mentioned, as well as in the evolutionary naturalism of the founding sociologists in the United States. But this use does not warrant the argument that the adoption of those metaphors and methods is the result of the need to draw on the legitimacy of the established sciences. The argument suggests that the discipline-building project was prior to the adoption of a natural science orientation. Any historical investigation will show that sociology began as the effort to apply natural science methods to the social world and only late became less dependent on its natural science sources. For Auguste Comte, Herbert Spencer, and their American followers, sociology was nothing if not the application of natural science methods to society, even if, as in the case of Comte, that application would have to take into account the greater complexity of the queen of the sciences. The early sociologists were not interested in a sociology that looked like the natural sciences but in a natural science about society. They did not begin with a discipline-building project and then cast about for theories and methods that would lend them an air of scientific legitimacy. As I suggest in the following discussion, the discipline was not an end but a means to secure an institutional home for a new form of cultural authority.

The legitimation arguments also imply an unwarranted asymmetry between the social sciences and their natural science sources. The development of scientific methods, field theories of energetics, and statistical techniques in the natural sciences is assumed to be the result of an autonomous logic of inquiry. There is no suggestion that physics or the newer life sciences were adopting methods and metaphors in order to appear scientific. Rather, their methods are presumably a response to the demands of producing reliable knowledge about their objects of study. The social sciences, it is argued, contain a different logic of theory selection and methodological innovation, driven not by the autonomous course of discovery and dispute within their fields but by the need for the legitimacy already enjoyed by the natural sciences. A further implication is that social scientists would have adopted *whatever* method or conceptual framework the natural sciences had consecrated, regardless of its suitability for studying the social (Breslau 2003). Indeed, Mirowski's criticisms of economics are premised on the unsuitability of a framework adapted from physics for understanding economic reality and the implication that the same practices are somehow more suitable to their source domain in physics.

Science and Cultural Authority

This chapter explains the specific content of the works of the founding sociologists as social practice, but in terms of a social context that is broader than the intra-academic search for disciplinary legitimacy. The founders were engaged in a struggle for authority regarding social problems and modes of intervention outside of markets, and their work can be understood as a strategy in such a struggle. They did not carry on this struggle as a self-contained and homogeneous intellectual community but as occupants of a distinct position among many other positions in this struggle. In particular, they were part of a broader field of sociology that included practical workers in charities, public administration, applied research, and reform. Their presence in university departments would be justified by their role as trainers, credentialers, and theoretical unifiers for this much more numerous group of "practical sociologists."

From the early years of the nineteenth century, the professions of medicine, law, and the clergy were exposed to a quickening erosion of their authority and market. The growth of population and of proprietary professional training threatened to swamp the elite professionals with an unregulated mass of practitioners. Degrees of medicine or law corresponded to no standard training, and the honorifics Dr. and Professor were adopted by anyone making a claim of expertise (Bledstein 1976, 21). Elite professionals felt their own repute was being damaged by the many disreputable practitioners. A series of campaigns to raise professional standards were debilitated by the absence of translocal structures. Moreover, elite professions were losing the political and legal struggle to maintain their privilege, and official sanction of professions was withdrawn a number of states.

The challenges to authority and the intense competition among professional groups set in motion a cognitive transformation of professions. Thomas Haskell has argued that the increasing social interdependence, with an increasing geographic scope, was experienced as a "recession of causation" in which events could no longer be explained in terms of local causes but had to be related to a broader and unseen web of interdependencies. Like contemporary arguments about globalization, Haskell's arguments are surely incorrect in positing a qualitative increase in the extent to which local events were dependent on remote causes (Fligstein 2001, 301–6; Haskell 1977). Economic historians have given us many studies that show how local events were dramatically and fatefully tied to remote, even global, causes, long before the social sciences described such ties. Causal recession was not the result of a quantum leap in the degree of interdependence of society but an easily demonstrated leap in the intensity of competition for authority. It was driven by a search for distant causes, and thus more stable and universal causal accounts, not a transformation of the reality in which causal knowledge was sought. The more local and superficial a causal attribution, the more it was subject to challenge. Social science was part of a general drive toward abstraction and technicalization of knowledge, which, as a response to the erosion of professional authority, preceded the awareness of this impulse as "scientific." As with challenges to professional authority in general, elite professions respond to these challenges by building networks that extend farther and become increasingly abstract at their cores.

Social science was one of the supreme stakes of this competition. As unrestricted competition among middle-class claimants to authority undermined the traditional sources of authority, claims to authority and to substantive knowledge were increasingly grounded in nature. Many groups within the growing ranks of middle-class cultural producers were working to achieve natural-scientific grounding. Social movements, whether trans-formative or reformist, sought to connect their claims to science, conceived as a unified natural history. These movements included socialists, economic reformers such as Henry George, anarchists such as those of the Philadel-phia Social Science Club following Kropotkin's qualified endorsement of Spencer, and the temperance movement, whose members insisted that their moral claims were based on an objective study of evolution (Gusfield 1981; Kropotkin 1908).

Accompanying these movements, and with overlapping personnel, was the effort to base authority for administering the "dependent population" on scientific knowledge. In 1865, the American Social Science Association (ASSA) was formed as a way of making all forms of ameliorative social work scientific. The term *social science* unambiguously meant the application of scientific methods to a catalogue of problems, involving what Foucault has called the "excess population,"

> [to] aid the development of social science, and to guide the public mind to the best practical means of promoting the Amendment of Laws, the Advancement of Education, the Prevention and Repression of Crime, the Reformation of criminals, and the progress of Public Morality, the adoption of Sanitary Regu-lations, and the diffusion of sound principles on questions of Economy, Trade, and Finance. It will give attention to Pauperism, and the topics related thereto, including the responsibility of the well-endowed and successful, the wise and the educated, the honest and respectable, for the failures of others. It will aim to bring together the various societies and individuals now interested in these ob-jects for the purpose of obtaining by discussion the real elements of Truth; by which doubts are removed, conflicting opinions harmonized, and a common ground afforded for treating wisely the great social problems of the day. (ASSA 1866, 3)

The term "social science" is here used to transform personalistic and reli-gious authority into a technocratic and universalistic expertise. The ASSA founders were upper-class professionals, capitalists, and their wives and daughters. The conception of their jurisdiction as a catalogue of social prob-lems reflects the membership of the association, composed of administra-tors and practical workers in "charities and corrections." If there is a social theory embedded in this statement of purpose, it is the commonsense the-ory of the responsibility of the better-off for "the failures of others." The theory of knowledge adopted by the members of the ASSA, often explicitly, was Baconian empiricism, with its confidence that the accumulation of facts will lead to the establishment of valid scientific generalizations in each of these areas of applied knowledge.

The reforms in the civil service and universities created new positions for aspirants without dominant class ties, who were able to seek careers in the government bureaucracy first, and then in the new university positions as well (Veysey 1965). These positions created secure institutional locations for those who made up the first generation of academic sociologists. Lacking the class origins and social ties of the ASSA founders, they often possessed a high degree of cultural capital, derived from their and their families' origins in the clergy. Some of them gained positions that were not dependent on ongoing practical work in charities, corrections, and churches. Among these were the founders of the discipline of sociology, who proceeded to construct a social science, its object and its institutional home, that would allow them to secure a monopoly of authority on the social problems of the day. Themselves the products of the new positions afforded by institutional reforms, they became agents of further reform, particularly in the reconstructed American universities.

In the works of Comte and Spencer, the sociologists found symbolic resources that could be adapted to the American scene. Comte, in his *Cours de philosophie positive,* developed the paired notions of sociology and society. One was to be the most general and complex of the sciences, the latter its unified and organismlike object. The two were mutually reinforcing, since the more unified and total the object, the more the science had to be distinct and irreducible to any special category of facts or professional expertise. Comte defined the discipline by defining the object, and each implied the other (Comte and Andreski 1974). Comte's collectivism was of less interest to these sociologists, who did not insist that the functioning of the social organism required the degree of moral integration that Comte demanded.

Spencer's Sociology

In pronouncing Spencer dead, Parsons (after Crane Brinton) acknowledged the pervasive presence of the preeminent Victorian philosopher in the works of the earlier generation of sociologists (Parsons 1968). It is beyond dispute that Herbert Spencer was the most influential source for nineteenth-century sociology in the United States. Charles Horton Cooley later remarked that "nearly all of us who took up sociology between 1870, say, and 1890 did so at the instigation of Spencer" (Cooley 1920, 129). Spencer's following in the United States was enormous, and he was regarded by many American intellectuals as the most important living philosopher (Hofstadter 1959, 31–50). But the familiar term *influence* fails to describe the full importance of Spencerianism for the founders of the discipline in North America.

The name of Herbert Spencer is associated today, as it was in the nineteenth century, with radical laissez-faire liberalism and principled hostility to state-directed social reform. Spencer will always be linked with social Darwinism in the United States, for which his work was a major inspiration. His first work, *Social Statics,* published in 1850, is an extended derivation and elaboration of the principle that every man (or woman) has the right to do "all that he wills, provided he infringes not the equal freedom of any other man" (Spencer 1892, 55). The work is largely devoted to debunking Benthamite ideas of social amelioration through the use of the state's power and challenging well-intentioned distinctions between benevolent state intervention and despotism. In it, Spencer staked out his well-known positions against the poor laws, state-provided education, and tariffs, and justified them on putatively scientific grounds. Spencer revised utilitarianism by making it transgenerational and evolutionary: adhering to the strictest definition of liberal freedoms in the short run would promise utilitarian goals in the glacial temporal scale of evolution. Seeking the greatest human happiness in the present could only backfire. This side of Spencer's thought was appealing to conservatives in the late nineteenth-century United States and could be used to justify any social hierarchy as a hierarchy of evolutionary fitness (Hofstadter 1959, 31–50).

The characterization of Spencer as a conservative social Darwinist, which was so important for his loss of currency during the Progressive Era, does not account for much of his enormous appeal to the postbellum intellectuals, and indeed to the broad literate public. During the years 1870 to 1890, Spencer was probably more widely read and discussed in the United States than any other living philosopher. His works were known and debated throughout the literate population, and he enjoyed a vogue that has not been known by any philosopher before or since (Carneiro 1974; Hofstadter 1959). He became the emblem of what was referred to as the "scientific spirit," an unbounded confidence in the power of systematic observation to advance any and all utilitarian goals, and to replace other forms of knowledge from other sources. Spencer's positivism was unified not only in method but in substance, so that the "scientific spirit" encompassed not only Baconian virtues but the unifying framework of evolution.

Other than William Graham Sumner, the Spencerian sociologists had no difficulty separating the method of *The Study of Sociology* from the objectionable moral and political philosophy of *Social Statics* and Spencer's many essays against social reform. They did not read Spencer as a social Darwinist but as a philosopher and architect of a new science that was not necessarily attached to any particular program of action. Although *The Study of Sociology* contained reminders of the conclusions Spencer claimed could be readily drawn from his method, such as the effect of the poorhouse, of "helping the worthless to multiply at the expense of the worthy," its method could be applied by those who would draw opposed practical implications (Spencer 1929, 94). Unlike *Social Statics,* and to some extent the later *Principles of Sociology,* the book did not present a completed system. Nor was it a methodological handbook describing specific research techniques. It fit into university teaching as a kind of moral philosophy for the sociologist, describing the qualities, habits of mind, temperament, and abilities requisite to "the social science." Social science requires an "equilibrium of feeling" that is free of biases introduced by patriotism, class, political interests, and religion.

Spencer's sociology was not an outgrowth or extension of his overall evolutionary framework but was its centerpiece. He retained Comte's paired social-sociological holism but added an evolutionary framework and a structural-functionalist understanding of the anatomy of society (Spencer 1975). His evolutionary scheme was derived from a physical principle that he had argued was a fundamental principle of all phenomena—suborganic, organic, and superorganic. Entities differentiated into interdependent parts were more adaptable to their environment than homogeneous ones. Coupled with the conception of society as an organism, Spencer could extend a scheme of evolution as a process of differentiation and integration to society.

Spencer's importance to sociology is magnified if his work is not understood as a theoretical system but as a practical model for a new discipline. It was—to use appropriately an often-misused word—a paradigm, a set of practical exemplars to coordinate the production of knowledge. In the course of insisting on his evolutionary naturalism of social wholes, Spencer specified, sometimes explicitly, how the new science is to be implemented. His hierarchies of categories were also social hierarchies of knowers, with the functionally integrated social whole corresponding to the work of integration carried out by the sociologist. Spencer's two substantive sociological works, *The Principles of Sociology* and *Descriptive Sociology,* exemplified the role of his evolutionary naturalism in coordinating the social process of social research. Consistent with the overall methodology of his *Synthetic Philosophy,* Spencer's evolutionary scheme supplied the classificatory means for organizing knowledge. It followed from Spencer's evolutionism that the scientific laws that were the raison d'être of sociology, and of the synthetic philosophy as a whole, could only be derived by relating empirical data to the social whole. The case studies of *Descriptive Sociology* were therefore classified in terms of their position in a progression of evolutionary stages (Spencer et al. 1873).

The American sociologists are often described as opponents of Spencer, or in terms of their objections to Spencer's radical laissez-faire liberalism. But their rejection of some details of Spencer's thought should not obscure the fact that their very milieu was thoroughly Spencerian. They did not approach Spencer's sociology as a body of ideas to be considered among other sources and selectively drawn on or critiqued. Spencer's sociology was Sociology, providing the only institutionalized definition of their discipline, within which they were obliged to work. Sociology was paradigmatic as it has not been since, and its paradigm was Spencer. For instance, Albion Small spent years during the 1880s studying in Germany, at the feet of some of the leading historians and historical school economists. He incorporated the works of figures of the German historical school he had encountered, such as Gumplewitz and Shafflë. But his key German source was the most Spencerian of the German historians, namely, Ratzenhofer, whose writings on social evolution, conflict, and reintegration could be incorporated within Spencerian evolutionary naturalism (Small 1905b).

The first sociological treatise published in the United States, Lester Ward's *Dynamic Sociology,* shows that even a work formulated in opposition to Spencer's political and economic philosophy was thoroughly circumscribed by the universe of Spencer's sociology (Ward 1968). Ward's exposition of sociology and his justification of the natural science of society begin on the most general level imaginable. He reviews and states his own position on the fundamentals of natural science, beginning with the nature of the basic concepts of force, matter, time, and space, as they describe the physical universe. Like Spencer, Ward is interested in describing universal features of natural processes, which will prevail in all scientific fields and will establish sociology as a natural science. For Ward, like Spencer, the universal process is an evolution from a homogeneous and undifferentiated state toward greater heterogeneity. Although Spencer describes this process as one of internal differentiation and integration, for Ward it is characterized by aggregation, and further aggregation of aggregates. His book includes extended passages on the nature of celestial nebulae, the solar system, and the chemical composition of the earth's crust. Yet these passages are not incidental to the sociology Ward wants to construct. The evolution of matter from the more homogeneous nebulae, to the great heterogeneity of the earth, "in strict conformity with the laws of evolution in general," is something more than a metaphor for the evolution of human societies

(Ward 1968, 283). Through an evolutionary process that encompasses not only organisms but all aggregates of matter, only those that resist disintegration survive. Although Ward is known as a severe critic of Spencer's laissez-faire stance, he is perhaps the most Spencerian of the American sociologists in his insistence on an integrated and causally monist evolutionary scheme, culminating in human societies. Ward has been characterized as a Comtean, favoring the reconstruction of collective life around enlightened scientific knowledge through educational institutions. But the method by which Ward reached these Comtean recommendations was the Spencerian approach of tracing a monistic process of evolution.

The Social Conditions for Sociology

For the founders of academic sociology in the United States, collectively, the intellectual strategy of evolutionary naturalist holism was matched with a narrow range of social positions within the new middle class. The first academic sociologists in the United States were without exception members of the new, upwardly mobile, middle class, whose positions were owed to their own or their families' investments in education. In this section I briefly sketch the social origins and trajectories of the four figures most active in the writing of textbooks and the establishment of training programs in sociology during the last years of the nineteenth century.

William Graham Sumner was the child of a blacksmith mechanic who immigrated from Lancashire in 1836. Though the family struggled economically through several failed real estate partnerships, they managed to secure assistance to send Sumner to Yale, from which he graduated in 1863. With a loan from the family of a wealthy classmate, Sumner bought exemption from service in the Union Army, and traveled to England and then Germany, where he studied philology, theology, and philosophy at Göttingen. He returned to tutor at Yale, while serving as an Episcopal minister and then an ordained priest. In 1872 he was awarded the chair of political and social science at Yale, where he remained until his death in 1910. Notorious for his social Darwinist views, he adopted much of Spencer's social philosophy. His was a radical social liberalism, adamantly opposed to conservative sentimentalism as well as all forms of social engineering. From his chair at Yale, Sumner published very little but was famous for his lectures. His lecturing style was described by more than one observer as "preaching," and the prime target of his preaching was anything that smacked of naïve philanthropy. Late in life, he published *Folkways*, his major sociological statement and most important work (Barnes 1948b; Fuhrman 1980).

Sumner's position, then, was defined by scholarly cultural capital and the new positions available to those with such holdings, the result of reforms in higher education. The Spencerianism that he vigorously adopted— he was the first to use Spencer's *Study of Sociology* as a textbook and was a key figure in the introduction of Spencer's writing to North Americans— made an epistemological virtue of this position. Spencer's evolutionary naturalism placed theoretical knowledge above practical knowledge, scholarly distance over direct experience, knowledge of the social whole over expertise regarding part of society.

In *Folkways* Sumner took what he called the *mores* to define the level of analysis proper to the new science. The mores, and the folkways that they supported, belong to a level of collective regulation, social control, that is intermediate between purely self-seeking utilitarianism, or the unchecked play of "social forces," and that of legislation. The mores, despite individualistic drives, support a collective adaptation to environmental conditions. But they are prior to any legal codification, to which they never fully correspond. Society is neither the simple equilibration of individual drives, as in utilitarian thought, nor the product of legislation. It emerges historically without the conscious participation of individuals or the legal establishment (Sumner 1940). Sumner, more than his contemporaries, emphasized the formation of an "ideological community," to use Therborn's term, which turns a functionally differentiated society into an integrated whole (Therborn 1976, 219–315). The preoccupations of Sumner's *Folkways* were less of a departure from Spencerian sociology as is often supposed and amount to a change in emphasis from broad evolutionary processes to adaptation of cultures to their evolutionary conditions. As such, it carries forth themes that Spencer developed in *The Principles of Psychology* (Spencer 1896).

Sumner took exception to some major elements of Spencer's philosophy and style, and was somewhat repelled by the dogmatism and premature systematicity he detected in Spencer's evolutionary framework. But the science that Spencer proposed, as set out in his small book, *The Study of Sociology,* was eagerly adopted by Sumner as his own practical program, despite his divergence from certain details of Spencer's philosophy. He describes his encounter with this work as a self-affirming epiphany: "The conception of society, of social forces, and of the science of society there offered was just the one which I had been groping after but had not been able to reduce for myself" (quoted in Bledstein 1974, 343).

Like Sumner, Lester Ward was the son of a skilled tradesman who struggled and never managed to move the family out of economic hardship. But unlike Sumner, Ward had no chance of attending an elite college. His scholarly career was not supported by faculty positions but by a series of positions in the federal bureaucracy, with increasingly scholarly components. His first and only academic appointment was to the chair in sociology at Brown University, in 1906, at the age of sixty-five. He was a tireless autodidact, and while employed in the government he acquired degrees in law and medicine, and mastered modern and classical languages. Although the importance of his contributions to natural science, particularly paleobotany, have been disputed, there is no question that he was at least a competent professional in this field, as well as in botany and geology.

The possibility of a Lester Ward, an agent whose position is derived solely from scholarly scientific accomplishments, was created by the reforms in the civil service and the increasing use of scientific information by federal government. His government trajectory is testimony to the new scientific capacity and universalistic legitimation of the liberal state: he worked for the Smithsonian Institution, as geologist and paleontologist in the U.S. Geological Survey, and as librarian of the Bureau of Immigration (Scott 1976).

Ward was a critic of Spencer and of Sumner in that he strongly objected to social Darwinism and to their insistence that deliberate intervention could not improve on the natural course of social evolution. Nonetheless, his work should be regarded as a Spencerian critique of Spencer in that he insisted Spencer erred in concluding that his evolutionism justified his strong opposition to deliberate social intervention. Ward's two-volume treatise, *Dynamic Sociology,* traced the genesis of society, the organism, through the evolution from suborganic, to organic, to supraorganic. Following Spencer's precedent, Ward put forth this unified evolutionary scheme as a framework for coordinating observations on all societies at all stages of evolution. But he argued that evolution itself had created the possibility of "telic" processes by which societies could consciously and deliberately improve their own functioning (Finlay 1999). He thereby used a Spencerian procedure to bring back the Comtean themes of enlightened social technology that Spencer himself had excluded. The second volume of *Dynamic Sociology* detailed how evolution itself brings into existence a "sociocracy," where legislation is crafted by those with the epistemological privilege of seeing and knowing society as a whole (Ward 1968; Ward and Commager 1967).

Franklin Giddings was born into a highly religious family, with a father who was a successful and prominent Congregationalist minister. Like Ward, Giddings initially supported himself and his sociological writing outside of universities, through his work for the Massachusetts Bureau of Labor Statistics under Carrol Wright. On the basis of his published work, Giddings was appointed to succeed Woodrow Wilson as lecturer on politics at Bryn Mawr in 1888. Initially appointed to teach courses on scientific approaches to charities, social services, and corrections, he pursued writing and eventually teaching in theoretical sociology of the reigning Spencerian variety. He was appointed to the country's second full-time chair of sociology, at Columbia, in 1894, based on the idea that a scientific sociological theorist should direct the university's administration and training in settlement and charity work (Gillin 1927b).

At Columbia, Giddings was responsible for the fullest realization of the Spencerian vision for sociology: systematic empirical inquiry guided and coordinated by the scientist who would assemble the data in a way that would represent the whole social organism and its evolution. He revised the Spencerian constitution, however, by promoting statistical methods (Camic and Xie 1994). Within the Spencerian universe, he was distinctive as a theorist for his subjectivist, even intellectualist, construction of the sociological object of study. Sociology is the study of the interaction among minds, which form patterns of association and conflict based on elaborations of a fundamental "consciousness of kind" (Giddings 1896).

Albion Small, like Giddings, was the son of a successful clergyman. He was preparing himself for the calling as well, having studied divinity at Colby College and then at Newton Theological Institution, where he graduated as an ordained Baptist minister in 1879. He traveled to Germany, where he studied history and German-school historical economics at Leipzig and Berlin. In 1892, he was appointed head professor of social science at the University of Chicago, under circumstances similar to those of Giddings's appointment at Columbia two years later. The university's president, William Rainey Harper, was committed to a range of graduate programs with a practical bent and was convinced that the coordinator of the training of practical experts in "charities and corrections," and the administration of the university's charitable enterprises, should be a scientific, theoretical sociologist. Although he did not launch an ambitious research project, as did Giddings, Small structured the new Department of Sociology and Anthropology at Chicago as a hierarchical division between theoretical and practical sociology. Courses were divided between these two areas, with the practical side providing a required foundation for practical electives. The same conception of the discipline was embedded in Small's tireless discipline-building work in helping to establish the American Sociological Society (1905) and almost single-handedly founding the *American Journal of Sociology* (1895) (Bulmer 1984a).

Small's theoretical writings are often treated as comprising a system to be compared with the systems of his contemporaries and theorists of other eras. But his works were not intended as such. Rather, they are defenses and elaborations of the Spencerian understanding of sociology, as part of a strategic effort to establish it as the general coordinator and dispenser of authority to speak about and administer social problems. To a greater extent than the others, Small developed the theme of wholism. Society had to be understood as a whole. In its totalizing epistemology, sociology was thereby differentiated from practical social reformers, whose perspective on the social world was partial and fragmentary, and from political ideologues, whose perspective was incomplete as a result of the limitations of their own interests (Small 1905b; Small and Vincent 1894).

The founding sociologists faced a twofold competition in establishing a natural science of the social. First, within the university, they were engaged in a struggle to redefine pedagogical values in a way that would assign the greatest value to scientific knowledge, based on empirical research and principles of material causality, while devaluing cultural capital based on traditional learning in humanities. Outside the confines of academe, they were in competition with various proponents of "social science" for the claim to offer a scientific basis for acting on social problems.

Herbert Spencer's sociology, having emerged out of a homologous set of struggles in the English intellectual context, was a comprehensive and systematic set of discursive resources for this dual task. Spencer's reflexive heretical attitude toward traditional academic values, with their definition of *culture* based in classics and philosophy, was appealing to these figures, who, though in some cases more "cultured" than Spencer himself, were at a distinct disadvantage in terms of traditional erudition. Sumner's dispute with Noah Porter, the president of Yale, over the adoption of Spencer's *Study of Sociology* as a textbook, was a dispute over clashing understandings of the purpose of university teaching. Superficially, the argument, which ended with Sumner eventually dropping the book from his course, concerned the perceived atheistic nature of Spencer's writings. When the *New York Times* picked up the story, the paper framed it as a confrontation of science and religion. Yet, as Porter made clear, and as Sumner perceived the dispute as well, the target was not atheism, an offense of which Spencer was innocent, but the prospect of basing instruction in the philosophy of society and history purely on natural forces, to the exclusion religious teachings (Bledstein 1974, 345). Here, the book in question was unequivocal in substituting science for traditional learning as the source of valid knowledge about the social world. Sumner would adopt Spencer's hostility toward the established humanities in an 1884 essay titled "Colleges before our Country," in which he compared the education dispensed at American colleges to the long fingernails of a "belle in Siam," which are cultivated to the point where "she cannot even dress herself. And everyone who sees her knows that she is helpless and elegant" (Sumner 1919). Sumner's advocacy of practical, science-based education was echoed by the other founders and supported by Spencer's writings.

With respect to social science understood as the science of social amelioration, the Spencerian constitution gave the founding sociologists a rationale for valuing the rationalist labor of the coordinator and systematizer over the Baconian empiricism of nonacademic investigators. The rationale contained a social classification in which all particular classes of phenomena were meaningful only in terms of the relation to the functioning of the whole, and a disciplinary classification in which sociology was the general and synthesizing social science. Knowledge or experience of any fragment of the organism was worthless, even misleading, until it was inserted into a comprehensive knowledge of the organism as a whole.

Thus, one should not exaggerate, as many intellectual histories have (e.g., Hofstadter 1959), the differences between what we might call the "right" Spencerians, such as Sumner, and the "left" Spencerians, exemplified by Ward and Small. Those who shared the English philosopher's pessimism regarding the potential of reform programs and those who reserved a role for deliberate guidance of social evolution were allies in the struggle over the basis of sociological authority. In their efforts to establish human science over and against traditional humanism, Ward and Sumner were comparably fervent and comparably energized by their encounters with Spencer, especially his *Study of Sociology*. Spencer's method, laid out in that book, was also a method of intellectual positioning, defining a consistently argued stance in opposition to traditional humanistic studies.

The sociologists were successful to the extent that they found powerful allies in a broader movement that was sympathetic to their dual goals of reforming curricula along scientific and practical lines, and giving practical work in social services and corrections an academic, scientific basis. After Sumner, the first courses in sociology were taught by Albion Small at Colby College and by Franklin Giddings at Bryn Mawr, both in 1890. By 1894, Small was leading the first sociology department in the country, at the University of Chicago, and Giddings held the first chair in sociology at Columbia. Both positions were sponsored by vigorous academic and social service reformers. At Chicago, William Rainey Harper's approach went further

than that of any university innovator at the time in reducing the elite ac-
culturation function of higher education to a minimum (Bulmer 1984a, 15).
By the time Giddings was hired at Columbia, leading universities were already feeling competitive pressure from institutional innovators such as
Cornell, Johns Hopkins, Chicago, and Harvard to incorporate the full range
of natural and social scientific disciplines (Geiger 1986).

The Two Sociologies

The Spencerian definition of sociology was used by the founding theorists
to simultaneously *exclude* the many nonacademic researchers and social
service workers from dominant positions in the discipline and *incorporate*
them as its subordinate, applied wing. The social scientists of the ASSA,
with their responsibility for specific institutions and social problems, promoted a capital of practical expertise (Haskell 1977). Science meant the scientific perfection of methods of charity, correction, and sanitation. The
founders of academic sociology, to the contrary, used the metaphor of the
social organism to systematically subordinate any such practical expertise
to the competence of coordinating theorists. What had been "social science"
to the ASSA was now pejoratively termed "practical sociology" and was distinguished from their own "general sociology," or, more often, simply "sociology." In his treatise *The Elements of Sociology*, Franklin Giddings summed
up the lineage of Comte, Spencer, and Ward:

> "Sociology," then, in the view of all these scholars, is the descriptive, historical,
> and explanatory science of society. It is not a study of some one special group of
> social facts: it examines the relations of all groups to each other and to the
> whole. It is not philanthropy: it is the scientific groundwork on which a true
> philanthropy must build. (Giddings 1898)

Spencer's evolutionism served the founding sociologists by setting empirical observation in the broadest imaginable temporal context. It demanded
that society be studied in the slowly unfolding time frame of natural history.
Spencer contrasted this time awareness with that of the layperson:

> Even true appreciation of the successive facts which an individual life presents,
> is generally hindered by inability to grasp the gradual processes by which ulti-
> mate effects are produced; as we may see in the foolish mother who, yielding to
> her perverse child, gains the immediate benefit of peace, and cannot foresee
> the evil of chronic dissension which her policy will hereafter bring about. And
> in the life of a nation, which, if of high type, lasts at least a hundred individual
> lives, correct estimation of results I still more hindered by this immense dura-

tion of the actions through which antecedents bring their consequents. (Spencer 1929, 93)

This parable distinguishes between the time orientation of the practical worker with that of the academic scientists. Evolution could be used to place human social phenomena in the context of the broadest contours of natural history. Sociology, as outlined by Spencer, was not Durkheim's study of an emergent domain that was characterized by emergent processes and laws. Social science was not distinguished from natural science by the independence of its object from nature but was a branch of natural science as a result of the evolutionary continuity between nature and society.

The two eldest of the founders, Lester Ward and William Graham Sumner, who are generally thought to represent two opposing poles of early sociology, were in agreement on naturalism and holism, and the division of sociological labor they entailed. Ward is described as a Comtean who was interested ultimately in sociology as a "telic" science, a guide to deliberate social reform, while Sumner adopted the most adamant position of social laissez-faire, echoing Spencer's warnings against tampering with the benign natural growth of the social organism. But the difference between these two poles of the small universe of general sociology was one of degree. Both rejected action based on anything short of knowledge of the social organism as a whole, and even Sumner acknowledged the possibility, though indefinitely deferred, of guiding social intervention on the basis of sociological knowledge of the natural social laws. Both adhered to slightly modified Spencerian schemes of social evolution, and both insisted that knowledge of society as a whole was the only truly scientific sociology.

The practical link between the social position of the founders and their Spencerian holism was a methodology of comparative-historical compilation. This methodology was also a straightforward adherence to the model that Spencer had set out. In *Descriptive Sociology,* Spencer had outlined an enormous scheme for systematizing all social knowledge and had begun commissioning collection of data from a range of societies representing each evolutionary stage (Spencer et al. 1873). When they transposed Spencer's method onto their own institutional setting, the American Spencerians saw themselves as the coordinators of the ongoing investigations of social problems. Their relationship to the practical sociologists corresponded to the Spencerian relationship of the social whole to its constituent parts. As Albion Small and George Vincent wrote in the first college textbook in sociology:

> [Sociology] is a work of combination which will be performed most judicially, not by experts in the processes of investigation peculiar to the special social sci-

ences, but by men trained to be experts in codifying the results of the special social sciences, and in organizing these groups of scientific data into a coherent
social philosophy. (Small and Vincent 1894, 76)

In *Dynamic Sociology* Ward made more specific and pointed reference to the
practical sociologists, turning their Baconian understanding of scientific
method into their greatest liability:

> So, with the social science, there are even now those claiming to be its votaries
> who imagine that it consists of a chaotic mass of incoherent and independent
> facts of a highly complex order, and that the pursuit and investigation of this
> science consist of the gathering in and storing away in vast volumes (usually
> without indexes) of these bewildering details. (Ward 1968, 457)

In practice, the general sociologists encouraged empirical investigation,
while subordinating it to their own work within the division of sociological
labor.

Although there were other proposed sciences of society that featured a
foundational holism, notably Marxism and Hegelian historiography, Spencerian evolutionary naturalism was especially well suited to the social and
intellectual project of the founding sociologists. On one hand, evolutionary
theory served them as it had Spencer, in understanding existing social arrangements as the outcome of a natural, and therefore necessary, process.
Naturalism could thereby be used as a scientized version of Burkean ro-
manticism—to expose the folly of rationalist utopias designed in ignorance
of the natural laws of society. But the analogy to the organism, as well as
Spencer's well-known evolutionary logic of differentiation and integration,
introduced new justifications for scientific/moral intervention. It contains
the normative principle of the healthy functioning of the organism, which,
when applied to society, calls for the harmonious integration of groups and
institutions. Within the Spencerian universe, therefore, the social problem
was conflict and dis-integration of the social whole, rather than any inherent feature or tendency of the whole itself. This definition of society could
therefore include the existing definitions of social groups, charities, public
agencies, and problems, which the practical sociologists adopted as a matter of practical necessity, but assign to the theorist competence to study
their relationship to the social whole. The smooth functioning of the social
organism mirrored and justified the normative standard of the smooth,
bureaucratic integration of social knowledge and intervention, with the
academic sociologists at the nerve center.

During the late decades of the nineteenth century and the early twentieth century, when sociology was gaining acceptance and an institutional

foothold in the new universities, it encompassed both the Spencerian holistic sociological theory and the practice of ameliorative reform and service. University sociology departments included courses in both theoretical (or general) sociology and practical sociology. Surveys of sociology teaching at the time show that practitioners and teachers of practical sociology were by far more numerous than the general sociologists, who were found in a small number of elite universities (Bernard 1909). Typical graduate departments included a single professor of theoretical sociology and a number of part-time practical sociologists, with curricula combining general theoretical courses with courses such as Methods of Social Amelioration, Charities and Corrections, and Preventive Philanthropy. Programs that did not include graduate study were even more focused on training for practical work, and these were often the departmental home of university training in charity and social service work (Breslau 1990b, 428; Tolman 1902c). All indications are that it was the demand for instruction in practical matters, rather than a demand for academic research, that drove the growth of the discipline in those decades.

The professional literature also reflected this symbiosis between theory at the most general level and discussions of practical work. The quaint assortment of topical articles found in the *American Journal of Sociology* in its early years did not simply reflect the field's professional underdevelopment but reflected this division of labor as well (Phelan 1989). Serialized theoretical treatises, such as E. A. Ross's *Social Control* (1898), were included next to serialized textbooks in administration of social services, such as *The Law Relating to the Relief and Care of Dependents,* by H. A. Millis (1898). Reports on social institutions, such as R. C. Bates's description of job training and parole in the New York State Reformatory, were not framed as sociological analyses but were couched entirely in the everyday language of administrators (Bates 1898).

Andrew Abbott has used the term "professional regression" to describe a process typical of fields "where a small, but very elite, core maintains intellectual control over a much wider jurisdiction" (1988, 238). Unlike the cases that Abbott examines, however, the sociologists did not regress to a more abstract or mathematical form of knowledge but to a knowledge that was pure in its monism and holism. The object of the theoretical sociologists was society as a whole, governed by a homogeneous set of causal principles or, in the case of Franklin Giddings, a single universal principle of causation that defines the social. What standard histories of the discipline have described as a lack of interest in empirical research among the founders can be attributed to the requirement of maintaining the purity of the discipline's academic center and thereby maintaining their position relative to the many practical sociologists.

Gender Exclusion

The definition of sociology instituted by the founders provided symbolic reinforcement for the exclusion of women from the discipline's leadership (Breslau 1990a). Its mapping of the intellectual terrain assured the virtual invisibility of the writings and research of women in the canon and the curriculum by including them in the intellectually subordinate specialty of practical sociology. Women were overrepresented among the middle-class reformers and social service workers that the academic sociologists sought to annex as their discipline's applied wing. Social science had been referred to as "the feminine side of political economy," since its practitioners tended to be women and its focus the limited public domains that extended women's traditional domestic roles (Leach 1980). Women who conducted research and theorized about society were excluded from full-time faculty positions in universities and were therefore attached to practically oriented social services as a condition of their professional work. Women such as Jane Addams and Charlotte Perkins Gilman, whose works have since been rediscovered for their historical and sociological importance, were well known by the founding, male sociologists, but their scholarly work was rendered invisible by the division between theoretical and practical sociology (Deegan 1990; Gilman 1998). The Spencerian constitution attached an epistemological privilege to scholarly distance from practical necessities of the social world and therefore to those who had access to such distance, namely, educated men.

Conclusions

Histories of American sociology often treat the discipline's nineteenth-century founders as actors in a kind of prehistory, since they did not actively engage in research but are known solely for their detached, scholarly, theoretical tomes. But, as I have suggested, the notion of sociological theory that they institutionalized was not detached from social research. In its very substance, it presupposed a particular division of social scientific labor and a way of organizing research. Theories such as evolutionary naturalism, with its metaphor of the organism, serve to legitimate particular sociological regimes. The organism was a way of establishing the theorist as the coordinator of prescientific empirical labors, so that the structure of the organism was a kind of totemic representation of the discipline's social structure.

After the first decade of the twentieth century, the weakness of the sociological constitution became apparent as professional training in social work and public administration offered credentials and a body of knowledge that were much closer than sociology to the practical requirements of work with the "dependent classes" (Ehrenreich 1985). The Chicago School of Civics and Philanthropy, founded in 1904, became increasingly independent of the Chicago sociologists as it elaborated its own curriculum and definition of professional competence, becoming the school of Social Service Administration in 1920 (Lubove 1965). The loss of its applied wing and its role as the credentialing discipline for practical sociologists may have prompted the shift in academic sociology from social wholes to social processes and the conferral of scientific status to empirical work within university departments (Ross 1991, 346–71).

The use of some elements of Spencerian naturalism remained a part of sociology well into the twentieth century, however. Robert Park and Ernest Burgess, in elaborating Chicago-school human ecology, explicitly used the Spencerian analogy to the organism, though transposing it into geographical terms, to describe the city as an organism (Park 1915). The city evolved and underwent a process of differentiation and integration that formed the neighborhoods, institutions, and occupations that were the topics of the empirical research of the Chicago school. Park and Burgess were explicit in declaring that the many empirical investigations of neighborhoods, institutions, and immigrant groups were only elevated to scientific status by the theoretical work of inserting them into the city as a whole. In terms that were clearly informed by the founding sociologists, they distinguished science from philanthropy on this basis (Breslau 1990b). Years after declaring Spencer's death, Parsons elaborated a structural functionalism that may have owed more to Spencer than to Durkheim and Weber (Turner 1985). And for Parsons, the evolutionary functionalist scheme had the same role it had played for the nineteenth-century sociologists: positing the differentiated and harmoniously integrated functioning society as the normative standard for identifying social health and pathology. It also mediated between empirical studies of specific institutions and groups, and an abstract theoretical "core," embedding the division of sociological labor in the definition of sociology's object of study.

The works of the founding sociologists, like any sociological writings, are not simply theories about a static sociological object but are acts of construction of their object. Regardless of the value of these works for our theorizing today, the object they constructed was a new one, and its creation occurred at a crucial moment in the history of the construction of society as an object of knowledge and intervention. In constructing that object, the founders were also constructing a new kind of expertise, of authority, regarding the social world. The scientific-liberal regime in the Western industrialized nations, which eventually encompassed most of the world, is premised on the taken-for-granted existence of a number of key objects and institutions. Along with its institutions of the liberal state, citizenship, and economy is the society, a nationally bounded population differentiated into groups and institutions with functional as well as competitive relationships. The state's intervention cannot be formulated or justified in terms of a partial perspective of a particular group but must be couched in terms of an external perspective on this object, described in theoretical and statistical terms.

[THREE] Thrice Told: Narratives of Sociology's Relation to Social Work

Patricia Lengermann & Gillian Niebrugge

There are three narratives of the relation of sociology to social work: a natural history, a social history, and a critical history. These stories are told by sociologists, historians of social science, and social workers, but the division among them is not by discipline but by interpretation. This chapter concerns both the content of these narratives and the fact of their coexistence. Our thesis is that an interpretation of these three stories can be used to link the first decades of sociology in the United States to the form of the profession in America today.

Our claim that there are three narratives is not meant to suggest that there is no empirically knowable history of the relation of sociology to social work. Rather, the narratives function like transparencies which, placed one on top of the other, build a picture of the significance of sociology's relation to social work in the shaping of the discipline. Some of the key events composing that picture are presented in chronological order in table 3.1. What that picture reveals is that sociology and social work began not as distinct fields but as part of a general impulse for social science that emerged out of the reform activism of the mid-nineteenth century. What we today take for granted as the "natural" division of social science into separate disciplines, including sociology and social work, was a decades-long development out of that original impulse. The emerging fields of sociology and social work continued to draw energy from reform activism through the Progressive movement of the early twentieth century, particularly as that movement was expressed in the social settlement. Both fields, at the same time, felt the counterpressure to "professionalize," a pressure that grew with U.S. industrialization and urbanization and with the modern university system. In response to this pressure, each discipline defined itself in part by distinguishing itself from the other, while each at various moments attempted closer relations with the other. This history is a summation of the actions of individuals who frequently had allegiances to both fields and conflicting views about how the fields should relate. The competing narratives of sociology's relation to social work rest on the complexity of these negotiations and the politics they gave rise to.

Table 3.1 Key events in the development and relation of sociology and social work in the United States

Years	Events
1836–37	U.S. edition of Harriet Martineau's sociological study *Society in America* is published in two volumes.
1843	Ideas of Auguste Comte are introduced into the United States through J. S. Mill's *System of Logic*.
1853	Martineau's English edition of Comte's *Positive Philosophy* is widely discussed in northeastern United States.
1858	First social science course in the United States is offered at Oberlin College.
1860s–70s	Spencer's sociology becomes a topic of common discussion.
1861	Massachusetts Board of State Charities is organized; it helps found the ASSA.
1865	American Social Science Association (ASSA) is established.
1872	National Conference of Charities and Corrections (NCCC) is established as an offshoot of the ASSA.
1875	The word *sociology* is introduced into a course title by William Graham Sumner at Yale.
1876	Johns Hopkins University is founded—the first of new wave research universities emphasizing graduate education and the production of knowledge.
1878	First Charity Organization Society (COS) is established in Buffalo, New York.
1884	American Historical Association is organized out of the ASSA.
	ASSA secretary Frank Sanborn is invited to teach the first social science course at Cornell, focusing on "what is broadly termed sociology."
1885	American Economics Association (AEA) is organized under the auspices of the AHA, meeting concurrently with the ASSA; sociologists meet and participate under aegis of the AEA.
1886	First U.S. settlement—known as the Neighborhood Guild—is founded on the Lower East Side of Manhattan by Stanton Coit.
1889	Jane Addams and Ellen Gates Starr start Hull House settlement in Chicago.

Table 3.1 continued

1892	First graduate program in sociology is established at the University of Chicago.
	Jane Addams lays out the mission of settlement sociology in a speech, "On the Subjective Necessity of Social Settlements," at the School of Applied Ethics in Plymouth, Massachusetts.
1893	Anna Dawes calls for formal training of social workers at the annual meeting of NCCC.
1895	*American Journal of Sociology* is established at the University of Chicago.
1897	Mary Richmond of the Baltimore COS repeats a call for formal training in social work, at the NCCC annual meeting.
1898	First formal program for social work education is established by New York City COS.
1902	Charles Horton Cooley's *Human Nature and the Social Order* describes sociology's subject matter as the science of social interaction.
1904	American Political Science Association is founded at the ASSA annual meeting—about one-third of members are not academics.
1905	American Sociological Society (ASS) differentiates out of the AEA at a concurrent annual meeting of the AEA, ASSA, and APSA; key debate is in formation over the role of applied sociologists.
1909	ASSA formally dissolves itself.
1910	A total of 413 social settlements are active in the United States; academic sociologists are among participants.
1917	National Social Workers Exchange (later American Association of Social Workers) is organized.
	Mary Richmond publishes *Social Diagnosis*, a basic methodological text for social work education.
1921	Robert E. Park and Ernest Burgess publish *The Science of Sociology*, foundational work on sociology as a separate and distinct scientific discipline.
1927	ASS forms the section Sociology and Social Work.
1928	About 14 percent of ASS members also hold memberships in social work organizations.

Continued

Table 3.1 continued

1929	*Social Work Yearbook* lists nine sociologists who established schools of social work—four of whom serve as presidents of the ASS.
2004	National Association of Social Workers has over 150,000 members; ASA has 13,712
	Michael Burawoy, as president of the ASA, calls for "public sociology," at the ASA annual meeting; the meeting draws the largest attendance in ASA history.
	Frances Fox Piven becomes president-elect of ASA; she features prominently in current revisionist histories of social work as political activism.

In our focus on the three narratives of this history—the natural, the social, and the critical—we assume, following Levine (1995) interpreting Halbwachs (1992), that narratives function as collective memory in an intellectual community, and that "collective memories form a focus for group solidarity" (Levine 1995, 10). We argue that the existence of these multiple narratives shows us much about sociology's still contested and divided identity and purpose.

Levine's thesis is supported in our research. These narrative accounts show that the issue of sociology's relation to social work (or "practical sociology" as it was sometimes called) was a central problematic in sociological discourse from about 1880 to 1920, the decades when academic sociology professionalized. Since that time this problematic has intermittently reappeared as a topic of interest to sociologists in their reflective attempts to define the nature of their discipline. For the term *social work* frequently stands in this discourse for a number of issues that affect sociology's sense of itself: the meanings of professionalization; the tension between objectivity and advocacy as part of that undertaking; the importance to be accorded to theory—especially to grand theory; the place of quantitative research methodology and of substantive interest in fields like medicine or crime, in a discipline that tells its history as the history of its theories; the relation to persons doing sociology outside the academy; the historical significance of a number of public intellectuals and activists; and the gender makeup of the profession. An examination of the relation between sociology and social work allows us to set sociology in a broad perspective on American life, understand its relation to social reform in the United States, and appreciate the range of people who identified as and were identified by others as sociologists. (It is important to keep in mind that the definition of a person as "sociologist" was as diffuse as the field itself in this early period and was applied liberally to anyone who showed an interest in the questions that concerned the social science community.)

Our focus is on what these competing narratives tells us about sociology—though we suggest what they tell us about social work. Our primary data are the narratives that sociologists have offered about the relation of sociology to social work, starting with Albion Small's 1916 account, "Fifty Years of Sociology in the United States (1865–1916)," and continuing on to accounts written in our own time, for example, Jonathan Turner and Stephen Turner's *The Impossible Science* (1990), Mary Jo Deegan's voluminous body of work beginning with *Jane Addams and the Men of the Chicago School* (1988) and continuing to *Race, Hull-House, and the University of Chicago* (2002), and our work *The Women Founders* (1998) and "Back to the Future: Settlement Sociology, 1885–1930" (2002). We also draw on the original source material of these narratives and on accounts by professional historians whose body of work on the history of social science is daunting in size, perhaps because, as Mary Furner has said in *Advocacy and Objectivity:* "Attempts to probe the working of the social science profession have a special significance, for professional social scientists, through their extensive control over formal education and publication in the social sciences, have developed the power to influence the content and extent of social criticism in the United States" (1975, ix).

These three narratives may be seen in the following relation to each other: the natural history is a product of the social processes described in the social history; the critical history is an extension and revision of that social history to show how an outcome other than the one presented by the natural history might have been possible. Our motive for this examination is similar to that of Dorothy Ross, though we problematize things she does not, "that by demonstrating the extent to which social scientific choices were rooted in history, [we] suggest those choices are open to reexamination" (1991, xxi).

The Natural History Narrative

The narrative we call a natural history is the ascendant reconstruction of sociology's past, a story so taken for granted that it can be described briefly and schematically. To a degree, this story serves as a foil in our analysis, a base that the social and critical narratives in various ways augment and correct. But the natural history is not a fiction; it reflects an image of and an aspiration for sociology that was present from the earliest discourses on the possibilities of such a field.

The natural history presents sociology and social work as developing separately, each growing in stage—like phases out of its own internal logic. For sociology, that logic is said to be an intellectual and theoretical concern with how to make truth claims about the nature of the social, a concern that by the early nineteenth century had situated its quest in the processes of scientific inquiry. In this telling, the work of Comte and Spencer is typically named as the critical moment when sociology is born and social philosophies of earlier periods relinquished. The internal logic of social work is said to be a practical concern with effectively administering aid to society's needy in a social world where the phenomenon of need is increasingly complex and demanding. This concern, whose origins predate history, began to assume modern form with public administration of the British Poor Laws in the sixteenth century. The transfer of the central concern from Europe to the United States is presented as nonproblematic (and is, therefore, underexplored), apparently occurring seamlessly, and, in the case of sociology, continuing through the twentieth century as the ideas of now canonized European thinkers—notably Simmel, Durkheim, and Weber—are absorbed into American discourse about sociology. Indeed, *discourse* may be an inappropriate word, for it suggests human actors in communication, but ideal-typically the natural history of sociology underemphasizes human actors in communication and negotiation, focusing instead on the ideas and intellectual concerns of important thinkers. Along parallel lines the natural history of modern social work is told as the increasing realization of the need for professional expertise in the administration of aid and an expanding classification of the needy or dysfunctional. The development of expertise centers around an increasing sophistication of the diagnosis and the remedy of maladjustment using therapeutic skills. By the 1920s these became the dominant histories of the two worlds of sociology and social work.

A landmark in the presentation of the natural history is Albion Small's "Fifty Years of Sociology in the United States (1865–1915)," a 150-page essay published in the *American Journal of Sociology* in 1916. This article is significant in part because Small, who, at the time of the essay, has lived through the social construction of academic sociology and is a prime maker of the story of the natural history, cannot quite let go of his awareness of sociology as a made object. He begins by engagingly—and daringly, in terms of the academic mores of his day—putting himself directly in the story:

No excuses will be offered for rather liberal transgression of the conventionalities of impersonal writing. The years I have spent in studying the social scientists of the last four centuries have lodged in my mind one indelible impression, viz., that . . . [i]f each writer in the field of social science had also been a Pepys, or if he had been shadowed by a Boswell, the reasons why thinking in social science had meandered in the precise courses which it has followed might be much more evident than they are. (Small 1916, 721–22)

In these introductory remarks, sociology emerges as a social construction that has "meandered" to its current state—an awareness Small shows on occasion throughout the article in revealing first-person accounts. But overall, he seeks to explain how sociology arrived at what he sees as its natural home in the academy. After a brief acknowledgment of the early origins of American social science, he moves without formal transition to a history of the teaching of sociology in the United States. This unproblematized identification of sociology with academic location and expression is strategic to the natural history Small is establishing. He maintains this focus on the growth of academic sociology for much of the article, selecting cases that present a clear emergence of sociology courses. He is, however, aware enough of the confusions that surrounded even the naming of sociology programs, including the University of Chicago department, which was first called the Department of Social Science and Anthropology until the faculty complained to the Board of Trustees, saying that the name was "analogous . . . with 'mathematics and algebra' and the Trustees at once authorized the change of designation to 'Sociology and Anthropology' . . . the official title since 1893" (Small 1916, 766). When he turns to sociological theory, he notes that Lester Ward was not, at the time of writing *Dynamic Sociology* (1883), an academic sociologist but "a museum investigator," while "the other prominent American sociologists, as just now observed, have all been academic teachers" (1916, 752). Small leaves the academy only briefly in section 6, "Extra-Academic Organization for Promotion of Social Science," in which he lists some fifty associations, such as the National Conference of Charities and Corrections, the National Prison Association, the National Education Association, and the National Consumers' League. Segregating these groups acknowledges their existence in the history of social science and, by extension, sociology, but does not interfere with the narrative of sociology's natural home in the academy: "The sociologists have been more or less conscious of interests in common with those of these organizations. . . . The obvious fact . . . is that American sociology has been one expression among many of a movement in the whole realm of social science and social practice" (Small 1916, 773–74).

Less than a decade later even this sense of commonality had disappeared. Ernest Burgess, of the Chicago sociology faculty and coauthor with Robert E. Park of *Introduction to the Science of Sociology* (1921), spoke with the authority those accomplishments conferred when he wrote in the first volume of *Social Forces* the following description of the relation of sociology and social work:

> It is a fallacy, widely current, that social work has been, and is, applied sociology. As things are, nothing could be farther from the truth. The origins of sociology and social work go back to different motives, they have pursued independent paths, each has upon occasion been indifferent, hostile, or even contemptuous of the other. . . . The beginnings of sociology are to be found in the philosophy of history. Comte, Spencer and Ward, three pioneers in sociology, were social philosophers rather than social scientists. *General works on sociology preceded investigation of social problems.* Indeed, the earliest sociological research seems to have been concerned with ethnographical data, rather than with materials drawn from contemporary social life. (1923, 366; our italics)

Burgess is certainly right to say "as things are," for the efforts of academic sociology in the 1920s were pointed toward establishing the kind of history Burgess goes on to give—a history of ideas that grew up independent of practical applications to social problems. And Burgess saying it helps to make this history become true.

For the social work side, in 1928 Sydnor Walker of the Rockefeller Foundation attempted to capture social workers' understandings of their history and their relation to sociology:

> Probably the independent development of social work and of the social sciences explains to a large extent the gap in thinking between those who promote social welfare and those who study the phenomena of social behavior. Social work has passed through many stages of development, each characterized by different objectives and a different philosophy. The period at which the social group first recognized the need of charity towards weaker members antedates history itself. (1928, 177)

Walker then briefly puts social work in historic context beginning with the Middle Ages—a vision with which Burgess would probably have agreed, although his social work history begins with the "attempts to organize and systematize the giving of relief" in the nineteenth century (Burgess 1923, 362).

Thus, by the 1920s, the natural history narratives of sociology and social work had defined the fields as fundamentally and historically separate projects. From then on, each would exist in the other's narrative typically as an absence, unseen and unreflected upon, and sociology would maintain as its main narrative "the development of sociological theory" (see Levine [1995] for a detailed discussion of key works in this tradition).

As with any definition of a situation, this narrative has become more true as it has been repeated over time, becoming central to sociologists' identity and shaping interpretations by historians of the social sciences. For example, Ross begins *The Origins of American Social Science* by stating: "The social sciences began in America by importing and adapting models of political economy, political science, and sociology developed in Europe in the early eighteenth and nineteenth centuries" (1991, 3); she then moves to an account of social science as fundamentally a history of ideas located in the academy. Although not unaware of extra-academic influences, Ross chooses this approach in order to "to capture a central line of development in American social science" (xviii), restricting her account primarily to battles within the academy. She neither problematizes sociology's location in the academy nor considers its relation to social work.

This natural narrative is the chief account of the discipline's history, used to socialize its new recruits in the introductory course and in the social theory course at both the graduate and undergraduate levels. This approach is one that most sociologists so take for granted that the establishment of the American Sociological Association section History of Sociology did not take place until 1999, amid protests, which still dog its efforts, that the discussion of sociology's past was already appropriately housed in the Theory section. Even today, the major texts in the history of sociology are its texts in sociological theory (e.g., Collins and Makowsky 1998; Coser 1971/1977; Ritzer and Goodman 2004; Turner, Beeghley, and Powers 2002). The point here is not to censure these texts as *theory* texts but to call attention to the fact that sociologists have allowed the history of the discipline and profession to be taught solely as a history of the field's ascendant ideas; they have failed to construct a sociological history of sociology.

There are costs to the sociological community of so great a reliance on this natural history, for it produces a profound incoherence in the relationship of the discipline's identity to its routine practices. The natural history omits any account of methodological invention, of the role of sociology in the society, of the societal impact of major empirical studies, and of the origin and significance of its substantive areas of inquiry as represented by the ASA's largest sections—Medicine; Sex and Gender; Organizations; Occupations; Education; Community; Urban Life; Aging; Labor; and Crime,

Law, and Deviance.[1] To begin to build an understanding of the origins of these central areas of sociological inquiry, one would have to go back to the history of the relation between sociology and social work—and to the second narrative about that relation, the social history.

The Social History Narrative

The social history narrative treats the relation between sociology and social work as an ongoing social construction, created not by the autonomous development of abstract theoretical systems but out of the actions, relationships, negotiations and associational inventions of individual social actors in multiple social settings, of which the academy is only one. The story is told, usually as part of a larger narrative, by historians (e.g., Furner 1975; Haskell 1977/2000; Leach 1980; Trattner 1979), social workers (e.g., Bruno 1957; Leighninger 1987; Popple and Reid 1999), and sociologists (e.g., Bernard and Bernard 1943; Oberschall 1972; Schwendinger and Schwendinger 1974; Turner and Turner 1990), and there are, understandably, differences in interpretation of individual events.

The version of the story we follow here is framed by Luther and Jessie Bernard's underappreciated 1943 study, *The Origins of American Sociology*, whose thesis is that the history of sociology (and, by extension, social work) lies in a broadly democratic movement of nineteenth-century America that they name the Social Science Movement. The Bernards are, of course, themselves located in history; the history shaping their telling is that of World War II; their interpretation, thus, emphasizes the basis of American social science in the intellectual traditions of British and French democratic thought (rather than in what they see as the authoritarian German tradition) and in American democratic practice—most especially social movement activity. They set the Social Science Movement in the grand tradition of the struggle for human betterment:

1. By membership count of the ASA as of December 31, 2003, the leading ASA sections were as follows: Sex and Gender, 989 members; Sociology of Culture, 895; Organizations, Occupations, and Work, 861; Medical Sociology, 860; Race, Gender, Class, 731; Sociology of the Family, 655; Community and Urban Sociology, 640; and Racial and Ethnic Minorities, 629. Theory, a section in which sociology understood as a history of major ideas would have its base, ranked about ninth, with 627 members. Conversely, Sociological Practice, perhaps the heir to applied sociology and to earlier efforts to create a Social Work division, had only 205 members. And sadly, for an understanding of the profession, the History of Sociology was one of the two smallest sections with 168 members.

we are concerned with a great historic movement, almost heroic in its aspirations. The last men who participated in the endeavor have now passed off the stage and . . . their efforts to construct a single body of scientific knowledge which would be used as the basis of an intellectual and scientific solution of the welfare problems of mankind is almost forgotten. . . . Our generation of scholars and men of affairs look[s] askance at large scale programs of human betterment . . . suspecting that they are Utopistic and impractical. . . . [Yet] [s]carcely a generation has passed since the academic scene and the world of practical affairs were in daily contact [through] outstanding leaders of the Social Science Movement. (Bernard and Bernard 1943, 3-4)

In the Bernards' presentation of the social history narrative, the story begins in the United States in the decades immediately preceding and following the U.S. Civil War. In that period, American social science in general, and sociology and social work in particular, was produced out of a mobilization by individuals seeking to use scientific method to solve the social problems generated by American industrialization—in effect, out of a social movement for progressive reform. The first and chief social science products of this mobilization were in the areas of research techniques and substantive analyses of issues such as poverty and urban life, crime and deviance, health, education, work and recreation—issues the social narrative shows to be foundational interests of sociology and social work, their common concerns, even after their professional separation. There are three chapters, or stages, in the telling of this story: common beginnings, a "hiving off" or differentiation into separate professions, and an ongoing process of reconsidering the relation between the two professions.

A COMMON BEGINNING

Although the Bernards offer no formal definition of a social movement, the social science activism in which their narrative locates the origins of sociology had most of the qualities sociologists assign to a social movement: a focus on a perceived problem, a belief that human agency can correct that problem, a belief system that guides the effort at correction, and the development of organizations, outside the institutionalized power structures, to promulgate those ideas, mobilize resources, and develop strategies for change.

The preconditions of the Social Science Movement included the following: Americans' engagement with Comte's theories of Positivism through the works of J. S. Mill and Harriet Martineau; the high level of social activist mobilization around abolition, the women's rights movement, and the demands of the Civil War; and the acceleration of social problems during the post-Civil War industrialization. The movement itself may be dated from 1865 to 1909, years that mark the life course of its primary organization, the American Social Science Association (ASSA).[2] The workings of the ASSA may serve as a lens for viewing how sociology and social work related within the Social Science Movement.

The ASSA was created out of the convergence of two lines of activity: the Massachusetts Board of State Charities (MSBC) organized in 1861 to bring order to the disparate and uncoordinated charity work in the state, and the initiative by a group of influential Boston citizens to create a parallel organization to the National Association for the Promotion of Social Science established in Britain in 1856. A major actor in this latter group was Mrs. Caroline Healey Dall, Unitarian reformer, women's rights advocate, editor, author, and public speaker. The arguments of this group resonated with the perceptions of MSBC head Dr. Samuel Gridley Howe (husband of Julia Ward Howe) that his agency needed "*first,* a 'Knowledge of the fact.' The statistics now gathered and published by the Secretary of State are valuable as far as they go, but they do not go far enough. . . . *Second,* a board . . . to collect and diffuse knowledge . . . and to establish . . . a uniform and wise system of treatment of pauperism over the Commonwealth" (as quoted in Bernard and Bernard 1943, 531–32). Together these groups proposed a meeting that in October 1865 established the American Association for the Promotion of Social Science on the relatively democratic principle that the only requirements for membership be a yearly dues of three dollars (though this amount would certainly have stopped many persons and reflects the class of the participants). The constitution of the ASSA made clear its wish to link investigation, advocacy, and reform:

> Its objects are, to aid the development of Social Science, and to guide the public mind to the best practical means of promoting the Amendment of Laws, the Advancement of Education, the Prevention and Repression of Crime, the Reformation of Criminals, and the Progress of Public Morality, the adoption of Sanitary Regulations, and the diffusion of sound principles of Economy, Trade, and Finance. It will give attention to Pauperism, and the topics related thereto; . . . obtaining by discussion the real elements of Truth; by which doubts are removed, conflicting opinions harmonized, and a common ground afforded for

2. Small's "Fifty Years of Sociology" in fact achieves a fifty-year history only by starting in 1865 with the founding of the ASSA, even while he seeks to establish sociology's theoretical origins by somewhat trivializing the ASSA and its activities.

treating wisely the great social problems of the day. (As quoted in Haskell 1977/
2000, 100–101)

The ASSA undertook a wide range of investigation and social reform under
the rubric "social science."[3] In the social history narrative, sociology and social work took form, cojoined, in this enterprise and in the wider mobilization it represented. This intertwining is reflected in the accomplishments of
and debates within the ASSA.

The vision of social science (and of sociology and social work as that terminology began to appear in movement communications by the 1880s) as a
dynamic mixture of research, grounded theories, social problem analyses,
and activism to redress those problems was visible in the practices of the
various reform groups that proliferated in the movement. The ASSA established local chapters, or perhaps, more accurately, stimulated grass roots
organization of analogous groups in the excitement that was part of the
general movement. Local chapters sprang up in Boston, Quincy, New York
City, New Haven, Philadelphia, Detroit, Cincinnati, St. Louis, Chicago, Indianapolis, San Francisco, Nashville, and Galveston, along with state associations in Pennsylvania, Ohio, Iowa, Wisconsin, Illinois, Indiana, and Kansas.
The Philadelphia local was the most successful, eventually organizing itself,
with the aid of the University of Pennsylvania, as the American Academy of
Political and Social Science—whose *Annals* in the 1890s regularly included
articles on "sociology."

Around the ASSA swirled a vast network of other reform groups—for
women's rights, temperance, education for African Americans, urban sanitation, community social services, abolition of sweatshops and child labor,

3. The ASSA divided its work into four departments: Education, Public Health, Social
Economy, and Jurisprudence. Jurisprudence was to serve as "the final resort of the other
three," which as they determined by investigation the universal societal laws underlying their
respective subjects would turn to Jurisprudence to have these laws of social science incorporated into government. Haskell (1977/2000, 107) raises the pertinent question of why the
ASSA divided departments as it did: "is there some circuitous path of evolution from the ASSA
departments to the modern disciplines, or are we dealing with two irreconcilable modes of dividing up the task of social inquiry?" He suggests that the departments reflected "the existing
pattern of specialization within the professional class: lawyers handled the Department of
Jurisprudence; doctors, Public Health; college teachers, Education." The department without
a corresponding professional class was Social Economy, whose duties, the Bernards note, were
outlined by Mrs. Dall to include pauperism, hours of labor, women's employment, public
libraries and museums, debt, and tariff. This department became unmanageable and was
divided in 1874 into two separate ones, Trade and Finance, and Social Economy. Haskell (108)
characterizes Trade and Finance as conservative and Social Economy as liberal.

and care for the indigent, the orphan, the elderly, the disabled, the incarcerated. Some of the reform groups pursuing these ends had organizationally spun out of the ASSA structure, notably the National Prison Association begun in 1872 and the National Conference of Charities and Corrections (NCCC) begun 1874. The ASSA also interacted with other associations in the movement, such as the Association for the Advancement of Women (which had begun as the Ladies' Social Science Association in 1873) and the Woman's Christian Temperance Union, under Frances Willard the largest organization of women in the world (Leach 1980, 86, 317).

Besides this network of organizations, the ASSA also spelled out its mission to members and the public in the papers formally presented at semi-annual national meetings and published in its official periodical, the *Journal of Social Science (JSS)*.[4] Within *JSS* readers would have found abstract statements of social science philosophy or social theory mingled with a jostling throng of statements about the political issues and social problems of the day and with activists' accounts of their programs and successes in addressing those problems—from house drainage to inebriety to new methods of historical research and the Dewey decimal system. Readers would have seen social science as a democratic undertaking, with contributions coming from men and women, whites and blacks, amateurs, public intellectuals, activists, academics, and professionals, including lawyers, ministers, doctors, college and university presidents, and administrators from governmental and nongovernmental agencies.

The *JSS* had frequent discussions on the central question for social science practitioners—the issue of the balance among scientific investigation, social advocacy, and reform activism. Formal statements issued on behalf of the ASSA tilted firmly toward science, as in the opening statement in the first issue of the *JSS* (1869):

> Social Science, or the Science of Society, treats of man as a social being. It fufils its functions just as other sciences fulfil theirs, by collecting facts, applying principles, and reaching the general laws which govern the social relations. . . . The subjects it embraces [include] Education, Health, Economy and Jurisprudence. . . . [T]his science is to be carefully distinguished from some other movements, with which it is apt to be confounded. Social Science is not Socialism [which] deals with Society destructively, . . . Social Science differs also from Philanthropy [which] . . . seeks for the remedy rather than the prevention, of

4. The *JSS* from 1869 to 1901 is available online through ProQuest's American Periodicals series. Haskell in the 2000 edition of *Professional Social Science* lists all the articles published between 1869 and 1901.

ills. . . . Social Science . . . acts from convictions based upon enquiry, as well as enduring principle. (1-2)

This view, repeated frequently by ASSA officeholders, was given forceful expression in the 1880 ASSA presidential address by Daniel Coit Gilman (also president of Johns Hopkins University): "The aim of this Association is . . . [to discover] those laws of cooperation which will secure to every individual his highest development. . . . [The Association is] not a society for the promotion of reform, nor an assembly whose object is charity; but its object is the promotion of science, the ascertainment of principles and laws" (as quoted in Haskell 1977/2000, 158). But other members had different ideas. Elizabeth Boynton Harbert, of the Illinois State Social Science Association argued that "experience demonstrates to me that the pioneer work of the social scientist is to arouse the people to the suffering and oppression, the starvation and crime which are direct results of the *bad methods* now universally employed" (as quoted in Bernard and Bernard 1943, 567).

The essence of the original dream was perhaps caught in the definition given by the second ASSA president, Samuel Eliot, in 1866: social science is "emphatically the science of reform" (as quoted in Bernard and Bernard 1943, 573).

The Social Science Movement's attempts at a science of reform were nowhere more tested than in efforts to combat poverty. Two related organizations grew up within the movement—the NCCC, named earlier, and the local Charity Organization Societies (COS). Both confronted the existing chaos of welfare services throughout the country—in Philadelphia alone, in 1878, it is estimated that there were over 800 different organizations dispensing relief, and in many cities the directories of aid ran to over 100 pages (Trattner 1979, 79). The COS began in Buffalo in 1877 in imitation of the established British Charity Organization Society and with a program that called not simply for aid to the poor but for "scientific charity" (Popple and Reid 1999). The COS idea became popular across the United States: by 1883, about twenty-five cities had a COS, and by 1900 there 138 such groups.

Scientific charity emphasized systematic investigation and assessment of the type and the validity of need before aid was given. The investigations were done by volunteer "friendly visitors" who were expected both to evaluate the conditions of aid applicants and to provide "moral uplift," and there was frequently a small paid office staff to keep records. Underlying scientific charity was the untested hypothesis that the problems of poverty were the result of character. Yet despite this methodological weakness, the charity organizations are an impressive triumph of empiricism. For instance, Mrs. Josephine Shaw Lowell, a founder of the New York Charity Organization Society, began her work firmly against the principle of giving money to the poor: "No human being . . . will work to provide the means of living for himself if he can get a living in any other manner agreeable to himself" (as quoted in Trattner 1979, 83). But by 1889, Mrs. Lowell had turned her efforts to preventing poverty, and in the early twentieth century she became a socialist (Reisch and Andrews 2001, 23). At the 1886 meeting of the National Conference of Charities and Corrections, George Buzelle, the general secretary for the Brooklyn Bureau, summed up what was being learned: "Once some of us would have undertaken to arrange all the human family according to intellectual development, merit, and demerit, in accurate divisions and subdivisions, each with a label, ready for indexing and filing away. . . . [But we have learned that] the poor . . . have not in common any type of physical, intellectual, or moral development which would warrant an attempt to group them as a class" (as quoted in Trattner 1979, 87).

The Social Science Movement also established a sphere of influence in American colleges and universities. The Bernards locate the first social science course at Oberlin in 1858 (an honor still claimed today on its sociology department Web site). They link the development of social science curricula to changes in the "internal organization" of colleges during the 1870s and 1880s, as "departments" were established under which the proliferating set of college courses could be grouped and organized. By 1890 the Bernards estimate—drawing on a study of 231 college and university catalogues—that some thirty schools offered courses with Social Science in the title, while every school had a course like Social Problems, or Practical or Applied or Christian Ethics. Attempting to encourage this trend, the ASSA did a survey (1885) of social science offerings, which revealed a wild diversity, perhaps to the point of eccentricity (and suggesting that the beginnings of sociology are not so clear as Small suggested in 1916).

Insight into the nature of the courses and the way that the ASSA and the Social Science Movement affected curriculum is offered by looking at experiences at Harvard and Cornell. Harvard professor of philosophy F. G. Peabody, in an issue of the *JSS* in 1886, told of his efforts teaching a course titled Practical Ethics: "As a teacher of ethics I became aware of the chasm which exists between such abstract study and the practical application of moral ideals; and it seemed to me possible to approach the theory of ethics inductively through the analyses of great moral movements." He assigned the class to study such practical social problems as "Charity, Divorce, the Indians, the Labor Question, Intemperance" and required "[e]ach student [to make] written reports of personal observation of some institutions of charity or reform; and from these data . . . I endeavored in each case to draw out the ethical principles involved" (as quoted in Bernard and Bernard 1943, 615-16). Writing of Peabody's class from the perspective of social work, Bruno (1957) notes that in the period between 1885 and 1893 the Peabody class at Harvard turned out four presidents of the NCCC, a pioneer in child welfare, a leader of the Boston Provident Association, and a Boston juvenile court judge.

At Cornell instruction in social science was begun by its first president, Andrew White, who wrote in an 1890 *JSS* of the role the ASSA had played in forming his commitment to social science: "as a member of the Senate of the State of New York, I had had frequent occasion to regret want of knowledge in various departments, not only in myself, but in most, if not all, of my colleagues. . . . [I] welcomed the early meetings of this Association of Social Science [and] the papers read by Henry Villard, Goldwin Smith and others who then came together in the little room at Albany" (as quoted in Bernard and Bernard 1943, 618). As president of Cornell, White invited Frank Sanborn, the ASSA general secretary to teach the university's first course in social science. Sanborn's course involved students in fieldwork by visiting a county jail, a poorhouse, a state prison, and an asylum. Sanborn, under what he attributes as White's guidance, began "the new department neither with ethics nor economics but with what is broadly termed sociology, with practical lectures on the treatment of the public dependents." Sanborn did not see the course simply as fieldwork but tried to provide a measure of "theory," requiring careful definitions and classifications from his students (as quoted in Bernard and Bernard 1943, 619-21).

HIVINGS OFF

The second chapter in the social history narrative of the relation of sociology and social work covers the years 1890 to 1921. During that period the community of social workers completed a move that had begun in 1874 with the founding of the NCCC: they established a formal professional organization, the American Association of Social Workers (later the National Association of Social Workers). And in 1921 the community of academic sociologists acquired its most influential textbook, Robert E. Park and Ernest Burgess's *Introduction to the Science of Sociology.* Known as "the green bible," this volume gave sociology a defining statement of its subject matter as distinct from that of social work: "Sociology, so far as it can be regarded as a *fundamental science* and not mere congeries of social-welfare programs and practices, may be described as the science of collective behavior" (Park and Burgess 1921, 42; our italics). It also provided a natural history narrative of sociology's development as a fundamental science: "The . . . periods in the history of the science [are] . . . (1) the period of Comte and Spencer . . . a philosophy of history . . . (2) the period of the 'schools'; sociological thought . . . absorbed in an effort to define its point of view . . . (3) the period of investigation and research, the period into which sociology is now entering" (Park and Burgess 1921, 44).

The story of how sociology and social work evolved from their intertwined existence in the Social Science Movement to a place where they existed as separate disciplines can be told from two standpoints: from a standpoint in the Social Science Movement, and from the standpoint in the two disciplines as they understood themselves in 1921. We look briefly at the first and then in more detail at the second.

Within the Social Science Movement, the separation of sociology and social work was unremarkable, a part of a bigger pattern, a measure among many of the success of the movement—a success that simultaneously elaborated and dissolved it. By the 1890s the movement's reform ethic, its collective energy for social amelioration, was absorbed into the multiple reform groups and projects of Progressivism. By 1905, ASSA, the movement's organizational core, had spun off a host of separate disciplinary associations that claimed the loyalties of sections of the social science community: the NCCC in 1874, the American Historical Association (AHA) in 1884, the American Economic Association (AEA) in 1885, the American Political Science Association (APSA) in 1904, and the American Sociological Society (ASS) in 1905. In 1909 the ASSA acknowledged this fragmentation into specialized social science disciplines by suspending operations. Over the years, the groups born out of the ASSA chose variously among its multiple goals of science, advocacy, and activism. From this standpoint the paths followed by the disciplines of social work and sociology were not so much a separation from each other as choices made among possibilities within the Social Science Movement.

From within either discipline, the story of the period 1890–1921 is built around one major theme, professionalization—which is how historians, sociologists, and social workers themselves have typified it. That explanation hinges on an understanding of professionalization based on three things: (1) an ideology of expertise to be placed at the service of a wider public; (2) an interest in securing income and prestige for its practitioners; and (3) a location—a social space—with which the professional group could be identified as it pursued the first and second goals. The ideological explanation is the one most frequently offered by social scientists themselves. Making the claim that professionalization is an essential feature of a highly differentiated industrialized society, Talcott Parsons (1959b, 547), for example, defines a profession as "a category of occupational role which is organized about the mastery of and fiduciary responsibility for any important segment of a society's cultural tradition." Similarly Goode and Huntington claim that "if one extracts from the most commonly cited definitions . . . all the items which characterize a profession, . . . a commendable unanimity is disclosed. . . . The two . . . core characteristics are a prolonged specialized training in a body of abstract knowledge, and a service orientation" (Goode 1960, 903). Haskell, drawing on sociology, explains professionalization as "the transit of authority from laymen and amateurs to professionals . . . in an urbanizing, industrializing society that made some people receptive to expert advice about human affairs and gave others the confidence to offer such advice" (1977/2000, 27).

The criticism can be made that in this account "professionalization" becomes a deus ex machina used to explain just about everything that happened in the institutionalization of social science in the period 1890–1921 (Silva and Slaughter 1980; Stricker 1988). Although this criticism does not necessarily obviate the thesis, it alerts us to the need not to focus solely on the lofty theoretical issues involved in professionalization but to heed the bread and butter interests that are also part of the story. As Stricker argues,

> In all that has been written about the professions, little has been done to analyze the social and economic history of individual professions or to test the linkages between professionalization and material success. . . . But social science and common sense supported an alternative view. It was always unrealistic to assume that professionals, even academics, were free of concerns about money; income and consumption are important not only in themselves but as symbols of status. (1988, 231–32)

The members of a professionalizing community are, as embodied subjects, affected by the dictum articulated in John Grisham's novel about homelessness, *Street Lawyer:* "Everyone has to be some place." This image may serve as a metaphor for understanding the separation that occurred between sociology and social work. In the high mobilization phase, members of a social movement participate while sustaining themselves in a variety of social locations; as the mobilization gives way to reinstitutionalization, however, its members have to create sites from which to continue the pursuit of movement ideals. Part of the project between 1890 and 1921 for persons whom we now identify as sociologists and social workers was to settle on a place to be—a more problematic issue in sociology than social work. During that period social workers reconfirmed their primary base in public and private social service agencies, and sociologists established themselves in the academy. These sites would profoundly affect the subsequent form of each profession.

SOCIAL WORK PROFESSIONALIZATION

The professionalization of social work seems to have had a clearer trajectory than did that of sociology, at least as the history is told in social work accounts (e.g., Bruno 1957; P. Klein 1968; Popple and Reid 1999; Trattner 1979). In part this is so because social work practitioners had always had two of the prerequisites for professional practice: a location from which to work—the array of governmental and private relief agencies, and a clientele—the persons served by those agencies who were dependent on the social worker for mediation of the relief process. What social workers had to do was establish their claim to the authority of the expert and increase their status and income. The way they did that is a classic illustration of the sociological proposition that professionalization is a characteristic of industrializing societies. There were four sources of change in social work professionalization: the impacts of industrialization, urbanization, and immigration; generational shifts; social invention; and struggles over definitions of the situation.

By the 1890s in the United States, industrialization, urbanization, and immigration had caused an enormous increase in social problems and the numbers of persons requiring aid. That aid was still distributed through the old system of a small paid clerical office staff and a larger group of volunteer "friendly visitors" who collected information, suggested what clients should do, and made possible their clients' formal access to help. But now need was far outstripping the supply and skill of volunteers, and a gradual shift occurred in which the visitors became the paid staff and volunteers did the office work of keeping records.

At the same time, two important generational shifts were also taking place. First, a generation of relief volunteers was aging. The NCCC had been founded in 1874, and by 1893 at its annual meeting, longtime worker Anna Dawes delivered a paper, "The Need for Training Schools for a New Profession," suggesting that experienced charity workers needed to find some formal way to transmit their knowledge to new persons joining the work. Further, a new generation of potential workers was coming into being with the increase in the number of women college graduates seeking employment rather than volunteer activity.

Two inventions transformed these trends into an emergent profession: the invention of training programs and of formal professional organization. At the 1897 NCCC, Mary Richmond, a leader of the Baltimore COS, repeated the call for specialized training in her paper "The Need of a Training School in Applied Philanthropy." Richmond's paper reveals the fledgling state of the profession as she struggled for a name, arguing that potential aid workers "surely . . . have a right to demand from the profession of applied philanthropy (*we really do not have even a name for it*) that which they have a right to demand from any other profession—further opportunities for education and development and, incidentally, the opportunity to earn a living" (as quoted in Popple and Reid 1999, 13; our italics). In 1898 the New York City COS established a Summer School of Philanthropy, which by 1904 had expanded to a full-year course as the New York School of Philanthropy. Similar schools were established in Boston, Chicago, St. Louis, and Philadelphia.

In 1911 women college graduates established their own employment agency, the Intercollegiate Bureau of Occupations, which had so many requests for social work employment that it set up a separate department, which in 1917 became an independent agency, the National Social Workers' Exchange (Popple and Reid 1999; Trattner 1979). By 1921, meeting with the NCCC, the Exchange changed its name to the American Association of Social Workers. The AASW, unlike the NCCC, took as its primary responsibility the development of the profession on behalf of the practitioners— through accreditation of educational programs, licensing of practitioners, and the establishment of professional journals, local chapters, and a central office for both organizing and lobbying.

In the midst of all this there occurred an important act of definition at the 1915 NCCC when Abraham Flexner, a noted educator, answered his title question, "Is Social Work a Profession?" with a resounding no. Flexner argued that social work lacked "an educationally communicable technique and practitioners assuming a large degree of individual responsibility" (Popple and Reid 1999, 15–16). The social work audience seemed to accept with concern Flexner's reasoning—though as Bruno points out, Anna Dawes in 1893 had had no doubt that she had a communicable technique to pass on. In 1917, two years later, Richmond provided an answer to Flexner in her book *Social Diagnosis,* which pronounced the method of social work to be casework: "The effort to get the essential facts bearing upon a man's social difficulties has commonly been called 'an investigation,' but the term here adopted as substitute—social diagnosis—has the advantage that from the first step it fixes the mind of the case worker upon the end in view. The primary purpose of the writer, in attempting an examination of the initial process of social case work, is to make some advance toward a professional standard" (Richmond 1917, 26).

The casework approach proved a stroke of genius for social work. *Social diagnosis* as a term had the advantage of the weight of medical analogy; as ideology, it gave specific, educationally communicable steps to the old method of COS investigation and status to the caseworker as the trained evaluator of human need. It would lead social workers to positions as counselors, often of middle-class and upper-middle-class persons experiencing difficulties in social relationships. And this "expertise" was acceptable to U.S. society, threatening neither its economic system nor its ideology, for it located the social problem in the individual client, who could be reincorporated into society by the caseworker.

The path the social work profession took toward professional expertise, that is, the centrality of a casework method, affected the relationship between social work and sociology. The more social work tended toward casework study of the individual, the less interest it would have in sociology; on the other hand, an alliance with sociology departments might have moved both toward fuller professionalization as experts in social policy about public welfare. Instead, the freestanding schools of social work in which this methodology was established were incorporated into the university on terms that varied widely according to the particular circumstances of the school and local social work leaders. But whatever the path, these schools and departments of social work all had one thing in common—they were beachheads in the academy for a woman-dominated profession. The politics of gender in that academy would help to ensure the separation of the two fields.

While they acknowledged that "mass betterment and individual betterment are interdependent . . . social reform and social work of necessity progressing together" (Richmond 1917, 3), social workers had found their place as professional practitioners of casework-based therapies in a society whose economic system would guarantee a permanent clientele and, secondarily, as teachers and trainers of such caseworkers.

PROFESSIONALIZATION OF SOCIOLOGY

The story of sociology's professionalization is more complex than that of social work, for in 1890 sociologists lacked all the attributes of a profession:

a particular location they could call theirs, a clientele, a particular claim to expertise, and thus a particular profile of income and status.[5] These attributes of professionalization would be acquired between 1890 and 1920, sometimes by collective effort but often by happenstance.

As part of the Social Science Movement, sociology in 1890 was practiced in multiple locations—universities and colleges, government agencies, Charity Organization Societies, theological centers, social settlements, labor unions—and by both public intellectuals and ordinary citizens, as shown by the contributors to the *JSS*. In this section, which draws primarily on the narrative of the Bernards (1943) and Furner (1975), we trace how professional sociology established the academy as its base, what the consequences for sociology were of an academic base, and how that move affected its relations to social work. We argue that, from the perspective of the social history narrative, in the 1890s a combination of opportunity and competition moved academic sociologists to secure and expand their base.

Opportunity was provided by an expansion of and change in American universities. A key factor in this change was Americans traveling aboard to study at German universities; Metzger (1961, 93) estimates that "more than nine thousand Americans studied at German universities in the nineteenth century." These German-trained PhD's brought back to the United States a sense of the university as a research institution, where previously in America the term had seemed to mean a college with a least one professional school, or a state-controlled institution of higher education, or any school with grand aspirations (Metzger 1961, 95). This shift—to an emphasis on universities as producers of new knowledge rather than as teachers of a classical curriculum—professionalized the academic disciplines, impacting established universities like Columbia and Yale and leading to the founding of new ones, such as Johns Hopkins, Stanford, and the University of Chicago. It expanded opportunities for the growth of relatively new fields, notably for the social sciences. In 1876 Johns Hopkins University opened as the first American school based on the German model; its president, Daniel Coit Gilman (who would also be an ASSA president), saw its purpose as "the encouragement of research; . . . and the advancement of individual scholars, who by their excellence will advance the sciences they pursue, and the society where they dwell" (as quoted in Metzger 1961, 103). An academic

---

5. An interesting comparison can be made between this description of sociology from around 1890 and Halliday's apt contemporary description of "sociology's fragile professionalism" (Halliday and Janowitz 1992).

discipline, in this understanding, was to function as both a discipline and a profession: as a discipline its purpose was knowledge; as a profession its purpose was service to society.

In this milieu of expanding opportunity, academic sociologists, or rather those academic social scientists and social theorists who thought of themselves as sociologists, found themselves in competition with other social science practitioners. To grasp this situation, we must realize how fluid were the boundaries around sociology and how underdefined it was: no one claiming to be an academic sociologist had a graduate degree in sociology; no consensus existed about the field's subject matter or its method; no textbooks were available for the training of new sociologists; and except perhaps for the work of Comte, Spencer, Sumner, and Ward, there were no commonly accepted theoretical works. What sociology did have was its designation as the logical successor to the more general idea of social science. Tracing the changes in courses titles between 1858 and about 1901, the Bernards found that the term *sociology* increasingly replaced that of *social science* so that by 1891 the balance had shifted in favor of *sociology* (Bernard and Bernard 1943, 639-40). The Bernards (1943, 666, 656) conclude that although "there was no single and specific discipline called Social Science, recognizable to everyone . . . sociology was . . . the subject into which Social Science was most commonly merged or reorganized." That this emerging consensus lacked any specific content was shown in an 1894 survey by Ira Howerth, a student of Small's, who wrote to forty schools asking their opinion on the subject matter of sociology. He found a "chaotic condition of social thought": there was little agreement about what sociology was or how it related to other fields, but three-quarters of the respondents believed that sociology was becoming a science (Howerth 1894, 260-69).

To secure the new academic opportunities, sociologists, no matter how underdeveloped their discipline, had to enter into competition for academic recognition with other more established social sciences. To compete successfully they had to demonstrate three qualities: (1) that sociology would not encroach on the existing territory of other social science disciplines; (2) that sociology could contribute useful knowledge; and (3), that that useful knowledge did not threaten the interests of those who made the university possible, whether private donors, state legislators, and trustees.

Territorial battles with other disciplines took place on two levels, one of which was in organizational politics at individual colleges and universities. Here happenstance sometimes worked for sociology. For example, at the newly founded University of Chicago, President Harper's friendship with Small and his commitment to sociology led to a graduate department in sociology in 1892, the capacity to award PhD's (the first in 1895), and, through the casual transfer of funds by Harper from one publication idea to another, to the founding of the *American Journal of Sociology* in 1895. All this occurred before sociologists had any clear idea of either subject matter or method.

The second level of territorial negotiation occurred at the national level as sociologists officially debated the status of their discipline with other social scientists, chiefly with those in economics, their most mobilized rivals and critics. In these debates, sociologists began to move to consensus on their subject matter. A classic moment in this process occurred at the 1894 meeting of the AEA, following the establishment of the University of Chicago sociology department. Called on to define what was sufficiently unique about their discipline to warrant formal academic recognition, sociologists participating in the meeting arrived at two answers—neither of which were likely to, nor did they, please the economists. Small claimed that sociology was the synthesizing social science that patterned the findings of the other social sciences. Franklin Giddings of Columbia expanded on the thesis he was then developing that sociology was the fundamental social science in that it engaged in the study of human association as the process basic to society and culture. While the economists successfully refuted the sociologists, who could not agree among themselves, and sociology continued as part of the AEA for the next ten years, academic sociologists began to understand their project as the scientific study of the processes of human interaction, or association, or people in groups. In 1902, the publication of Cooley's *Human Nature and the Social Order* helped crystallize sociologists' understanding of their subject as that of human relationships or the social group (Cravens 1971; Furner 1975; Reiss 1968).

As they moved to codify their subject, they also had to consider the substantive relation of the discipline to the concerns of social work, which was still very present in their own minds and the public's. In Howerth's 1894 survey, the last question asked about "the importance of social pathology or the treatment of the dependent, defective and delinquent classes, as a branch of sociology." Here there was agreement. Giddings's reply, endorsed by Stuart Chapin and Charles Henderson, was that "social pathology has for the sociologist the same importance that physical or mental abnormality . . . have for the physiologist. . . . The abnormal reveals and defines the normal" (Howerth 1894, 129). It was a reply that avoided any commitment to reform.

In defining their subject, however, sociologists had to do more than create a field that was logically sensible to themselves as intellectual workers and to other social scientists. They had to accommodate that definition of subject matter to constraints generated by their workplace in the academy. Silva and Slaughter describe some of the limits of that setting:

> University presidents, such as Arthur Twining Hadley of Yale, William Rainey Harper of the University of Chicago, David Starr Jordan of Stanford, Daniel Coit Gilman of Johns Hopkins, and Nicholas Murray Butler of Columbia, saw themselves as directors of brain trusts at the disposal of political and corporate leaders ready to solve contemporary problems. . . . [T]he new social scientists were to accept role limits defined by resource influentials external to the university, not act as independent intellectuals. (1980, 804)

The most dramatic demonstration of this constraint is traced by Furner (1975) through a number of academic freedom cases, primarily involving economists. Sociologists watched as many universities purged or pressured their more radical faculty, including social scientists Henry Carter Adams, Edward W. Bemis, John R. Commons, Richard T. Ely, and E. A. Ross. The Bemis case at Chicago may have particularly impacted sociology. Bemis, an economist on the social science faculty, was first marginalized because of differences in theory with the head of the economics faculty and then asked to resign because of his radical stances—he campaigned for public ownership of municipal utilities (supposedly costing the university its usual reduction in rates) and championed labor in the Pullman strike of 1894. Bemis, turning to Small as a senior colleague, reported that Small counseled caution, saying, "I do not say your conclusions are wrong . . . but in these days a man is not considered scientific, who claims to speak on more than one small corner of a subject. . . . I am now going . . . as far as possible from . . . reform [so as to] establish the scientific nature of my department" (Bemis, as quoted in Furner 1975, 177). Small remained all his life deeply divided on the question of objectivity versus advocacy. A year after the Bemis case, in "Scholarship and Social Agitation," he made a strong case for their combination: "let us go about our business with the understanding that . . . there is first science, and second something better than science. . . . I would have American scholars, especially in the social sciences, . . . repeal the law of custom which bars marriage of thought with action. . . . I would have them advance from knowledge of facts to . . . control of forces in the interest of a more complete social and personal life" (Small 1896, 564).

The pressures were enormous, leading fairly rapidly to an academic culture whose criteria for academic legitimacy were a practice of value-neutral expertise and a rhetoric consistent with academic decorum. Sociology thus emerged as a discipline by locating itself in the process of academic professionalization, and in that context by defining its subject matter as the objective investigation through science of human social relations. Although opportunism and conformity helped produce this outcome, there are other qualities that need to be factored into this story. Furner observes, discussing Cooley, that

> People were often attracted to their inquiries for highly personal reasons, and not . . . primarily as part of a coordinated group effort to construct a discipline. . . . One could almost say that Cooley was attracted to sociology because it allowed him to make a profession of being what he already was. . . . Contemplative and solitary . . . Cooley . . . [b]y rigorous intellectual preparation, . . . hoped to understand the social questions and help to find the bases for a just society. Yet he feared that any involvement in the "active life" of philanthropy or reform would sap the strength . . . for true intellectual achievement. . . . For such a man at such a time the academic life and sociology were natural choices. (1975, 306–7)

In 1905, sociologists formed their own association, the ASS, with no ideological bent to the constitution, and following the procedures pioneered by the APSA, which had organized the year before with a membership that was about 35 percent nonacademic (Haskell 1977/2000, 320). To contemporaries, this moment, which a hundred years later we treat with so much ceremony, was a logical next step in the journey toward professional academic standing and not one of high emotion. According to the *AJS* report "Organization of the American Sociological Society" (1906), the AEA concurred that the time was ripe for such a step. The objective of the association, as stated in article 2, was "the encouragement of sociological research and discussion, and the promotion of intercourse between persons engaged in the scientific study of society." Significantly for our story, the main discussion was about this article 2 and whether it "might not be interpreted to exclude those interested mainly in practical sociological work." Giddings and David Wells (of Dartmouth) assured everyone that the wording was intended to "include everybody. . . . [For] while the society, as a society, is mainly interested in the scientific and critical, rather than the popular or propagandist, aspect of sociology, it does not follow that its members must be exclusively interested in theoretical sociology" (1906, 567). The records of the first ten years of annual meetings show that nonacademics did participate but that academics steadily increased in representation.

By 1905, sociology had a base in the universities, a professional association, a professional journal, a growing body of credentialed practitioners, and some agreement about subject matter. But as Jessie Bernard (1929) notes in a review of the history of the discipline, academic sociology still lacked a method, a distinctive knowledge base, and a communicable technique—the qualities that Flexner had challenged social workers to find. That final achievement for academic sociology would only occur after 1921, as announced in the Park and Burgess text and realized in the "first" Chicago school of sociology. Turner and Turner (1990, 50, 46–47) note that although Chicago may be a special case "not generalizable to the broader discipline," Park succeeded in turning the reform sentiment of students "motivated by a desire to solve social problems into an equally intense commitment to a distinctive kind of sociological curiosity." This change in purpose becomes perhaps one of the professional hallmarks of academic sociology.

By 1921 sociology and social work had assumed separate but distinctly different professional identities. Sociology saw itself as an academic profession, claiming a specialized knowledge based in the value-neutral pursuit of abstract generalizations about human relations. That academic base was overwhelmingly the domain of white privileged-class men. Social work had established itself as a service profession, seeking to counsel the needy and troubled in practical and immediate ways, working primarily in private and public service bureaucracies, and training in clearly demarcated university-based programs. In both the relief agencies and the university training programs, social work professionals were overwhelmingly women—typically white privileged-class women, because the membership rules of the AASW excluded those many nondegreed workers who performed the routine labors of aid administration. For these reasons, the members of the two disciplines felt little attraction to each other's fields, and each field was thus ultimately less effective than it might have been had they been able to find a more mutual basis of thought and practice. We look at those attempts in the following section.

THE CONTINUING RELATION

From approximately 1865 to 1890, sociology and social work had been an intertwined project of the Social Science Movement; from approximately 1890 to 1921 the two carved out separate professional identities. Yet in that period of professionalization and the decade that followed, they continued to be linked in multiple ways.

For one thing, they remained linked in the public mind. Indeed, ironically, since both were distancing from radical reform, Jeffrey Brackett, head of the Boston School for Social Workers, complained in 1909 that the American public could not distinguish among "social work, sociology and social-ism" (as quoted in Shoemaker 1998, 184).

More concretely, sociologists remained in active relationship to social work in various ways. They served as colleagues in the same department with social work practitioners, like Small and Henderson did at Chicago (the latter was the only sociologist to serve as president of the National Con-ference of Social Work). They shared research topics, such as charity, with social work practitioners, as Giddings and Cooley did. They offered courses on social work topics (in 163 of the 185 departments surveyed by Frank Toll-man for a 1902 *AJS* article). And they founded or administered social work programs, as E. Franklin Frazier and F. B. Washington did at the Atlanta School of Social Work, Susan M. Kingsbury at Bryn Mawr, Howard Odum at the University of North Carolina–Chapel Hill, Edith Abbott at the Uni-versity of Chicago, Earle E. Eubank at the University of Cincinnati, J. E. Cutler at Western Reserve University, U. G. Weatherly at Indiana Univer-sity, J. L. Gillin at the University of Wisconsin–Madison, and E. Stuart Chapin at the University of Minnesota (Conrad 1929, 151; Reisch and An-drews 2001, 45). Four of these—Chapin, Frazier, Odum, and Weatherly—served as presidents of the ASS. Odum used *Social Forces,* which he founded at North Carolina in 1922, as a forum for frequent discussions about the re-lationship of sociology and social work (e.g., Brown 1939; Burgess 1923; Jocher 1947; Karpf 1925; Klein 1931).

There was a continuing overlap of program presenters and membership between the ASS and various social work organizations (Klein 1931). In the 1890s Giddings, Cooley, Henderson, Blackmar, H. H. Powers, Charles A. Ellwood, and Frank Fetter all presented at the NCCC, and between 1923 and 1928 "124 persons having affiliations with social work organizations" participated in ASS programs, about equal to one-third of the 371 appear-ances by persons affiliated only with the ASS (Klein 1931). In 1928, by Earl Klein's reckoning, about 14 percent of the members of the ASS also held memberships in social work organizations. In 1927 the ASS formed the sec-tion Sociology and Social Work, which was still functioning effectively at the time of Klein's 1931 study.

Despite these relational ties, the disciplines were divided partly by the internal logic of each and partly by a politics of gender that interpenetrated that logic. Several studies of social workers' attitudes toward sociology showed that the majority of social workers felt they derived no benefit from sociological training (Eliot 1924; Walker 1928). M. J. Karpf, the head of a large Chicago social agency, complained in *Social Forces* that the "sociologist looks down upon the social worker with a goodly measure of contempt . . . as persons who meddle in other people's affairs, and . . . do their work by rule of thumb" (1925, 420). In turn, Karpf writes, "the social worker who reads the sociological literature and who sees great promise and hope for a more scientific type of social work in the sociological point of view, finds himself in the condition of the thirsty wanderer in the desert who sees a mirage and expects to drink his fill only to be bitterly disappointed at the frustration of his hopes" (421). Social workers wanted materials that would lead fairly directly to solutions to the problems their clients confronted; sociology's quest for generalizations seemed a great distance from the immediate reality faced by the social workers.

The tension between practical and theoretical understandings of a problem had institutional impacts. Shoemaker cites as one example the case of Samuel McCune Lindsay, who was hired to run the New York School of Social Work in 1907 and "took [it] on an immediate sociological and policy-oriented turn, teaching courses in social theory and labor legislation" (Shoemaker 1998, 185). The New York School's Education Committee, which included the head of the Russell Sage Foundation, John Glenn, objected that Lindsay's plans were "academic" rather than "technical" (185). Lindsay resigned in 1912 and went on to Columbia University, where he was able to realize his vision of a policy-oriented social work in the Department of Political Science.

The case of the Boston School, as Shoemaker (1998, 187) recounts, illustrates the ways gender scripts overlay debates about education for casework or for public administration. From the beginnings, a gender script had shaped the school; one trustee, Robert Woods, of the South End Settlement, had argued that social work was ideally suited to women as "a reflection and extension of their domesticity . . . [but] that young men were not interested in such work 'which centers in the needy family and individual.'" In 1916, after twelve years of cooperation, Harvard withdrew from the arrangement with Simmons Female College and the Boston Associated Charities for much the same reason: Harvard president Charles Eliot voiced the belief that "many men were not temperamentally well suited to work with the 'defectives' and the 'unattractive mass of human beings'; . . . most men . . . prefer to work with 'the normal human being.'" Woods, Eliot, and Brackett all seemed to agree that working with "defectives" required a certain "missionary spirit," which women had and which made them willing, Brackett posited, to "take what can be paid" (as quoted in Shoemaker 1998, 187).

The same gender script massively affected the organization of academic sociology during this period—as we show in the next section on critical history.

Essentially, sociology and social work faced each other "with affection beaming in one eye and calculation in the other," each wishing for something from the other—social workers wanting some useful theory, and sociologists wanting some base for practical action. There may be a tendency in the social history to exaggerate tensions between the two disciplines because of the troubled relationship between the two at the University of Chicago (see Costin 1983; Muncy 1991), which is so large a player in the history of social science in the United States that its experience frequently is taken for the whole. One insight, to which we return in the conclusion, is Turner and Turner's suggestion that "the fact that sociologists were so heavily involved during the formation of social work as a professional discipline diminished their sense that they should create a separate professional niche for themselves" (1990, 185). Certainly, given the amount of writing about the relationship that occurred between 1900 and 1940, it seems clear that social work occupied a place of possibility in the sociological imagination. But as sociologists turned to disinterested generalization and hypothesis testing (Park and Burgess 1921) and social workers turned to casework, they continually disappointed each other.

The Critical History Narrative

The critical history narrative is a product of the liberationist movements of the last third of the twentieth century—the women's movement, the African American civil rights movement, the antiwar movement, and the antipoverty campaigns. Those movements worked to privilege the views of groups who had been written out of history—a tale proverbially told by the victors. By the 1920s, the victors in both sociology and social work were people who defined professionalism in terms of objectivity. The sociologists were seeking fundamental laws of society, and to do this, it was argued, they could not be advocates of any particular solution. The social workers saw their primary duty as making an objective diagnosis of individuals who were having problems of social adjustment; while their work might suggest some ideas for reform, their job was not to advocate but to counsel. Although not all academic sociologists or professional social workers were satisfied with this arrangement, there was a consensus, even among critics, that social work "could not have survived as the profession for the poor" (Popple and Reid 1999, 27). Similarly, academic sociologists living through the potent academic freedom cases of the 1890s could not have believed that sociology could survive in the academy as the science of agitation. Yet there was another possible location for sociology and social work in the society, a location in which they were not separated. The critical history narrative is the story of that alternative.

The critical narrative both of sociology's past and of its relation to social work has five main themes: (1) that between 1885 and 1920 there existed in the United States a location for both sociology and social work other than the professional bases of the academy and relief agencies—that location was the settlement house; (2) that the project of the settlement movement was to reform society by using knowledge derived from a particular understanding of social science; (3) that that understanding combined sociology and social work into "a science of reform," developing a coherent theory and methodology and a body of social science research that mobilized public opinion to effect legislative change; (4) that the settlement social scientists saw themselves as part of the emerging disciplines of both sociology and social work, but their distinctive and activist stance led to their marginalization or erasure from the histories of both; and (5) that at every stage, including the final act of erasure, settlement sociology turned on a particular politics of gender. Two more points are important to this narrative. First, although the primary location for sociology as a science of reform was in the settlement house, there were also bases in other settlement-inspired projects—organizations for progressive reform such as the Consumers League, the Urban League, the Association of Collegiate Alumnae (forerunner of the AAUW), the National Association for the Advancement of Colored People, and government agencies like the Children's Bureau and Women's Bureau. Our focus is on the settlement house as the associational thread linking these progressive groups. Second, within this narrative, Jane Addams (1860-1935) and the Hull House settlement (established 1889) are major actors, with Addams serving as both prototype and archetype for the emergence of women into public life and for the ways women participated in the founding of American sociology.

The critical history narrative rests on a body of interdisciplinary feminist scholarship by both men and women, beginning about 1980. In sociology, this critical history has been voiced by a generation of feminist scholars (Deegan 1988, 2002; Feagin 2001; Fish 1981, 1985; Hill and Deegan 2004; Lengermann and Niebrugge-Brantley 1998, 2001, 2002; McDonald 1994, 1998; Reinharz 1992; Rynbrandt 1999; Terry 1983); their efforts have been aided and paralleled by work in history and other disciplines (most notably, Fitzpatrick 1990; Flexner 1959; Gordon 1994; Lasch-Quinn 1993; Leach 1980; Muncy 1991; Palmieri 1995; Rosenberg 1982, 1992; Seigfried 1996;

Sklar 1995; Silverberg 1998; Yellin and Van Horne 1994) and studies of their own history by social workers (we rely on Costin 1983; Franklin 1986; Popple and Reid 1999; Reisch and Andrews 2001; Shoemaker 1998; Specht and Courtney 1994). The primary sources for our account here are Deegan's *Jane Addams and the Men of the Chicago School* (1988) and *Race, Hull-House, and the University of Chicago* (2002), Reinharz's *Feminist Methods in Social Research* (1992), and our own work, *The Women Founders: Sociology and Social Theory, 1830–1930* (1998) and "Back to the Future: Settlement Sociology, 1885–1930" (2002).

A POLITICS OF GENDER

In the critical narrative, the relation of sociology and social work is seen as shaped by a politics of gender as women sought a base from which to participate in public life; out of that quest they came to the social settlement, a location from which they could and did become important actors in the making of public policy. The circumstances of these women was captured with extraordinary prescience by Addams in her senior essay at Rockford Female Seminary in 1881, in which she interpreted the story of Cassandra as representing a problem for all women: "to be in the right and always to be disbelieved and rejected." She argues that women must find a way to attain "what the ancients called *auethoritas* [*sic*], right of the speaker to make themselves heard" (Addams 1881, 37). One thesis in the critical narrative is that Addams's life project was to find a way that she as a woman in a patriarchal world could act and speak with *auctoritas*—with "dignity," "influence," "consequence." If for Addams, and other women like her, the quest for *auctoritas* was the problem, then not simply the settlement but settlement sociology, the practice of sociology as the science of reform, was the solution.

The women in the critical narrative are not randomly drawn from all categories of women; they are largely upper-middle-class women—or working-class women who somehow fought their way to a college education. (This focus is true for both white and black women in the settlement movement; the two groups mostly moved in parallel class structures that were unequal in resources. Because of racism and its effects on material and biographical circumstance, for the black women associated with American sociology, most notably Ida B. Wells-Barnett and Anna Julia Cooper, the settlement was a volunteer activity rather than a career. See Deegan [2002].) The white settlement women came from backgrounds similar to that of Addams (see, for instance, Palmieri's 1995 study of Wellesley): the daughter of an affluent household; her father, a business and community leader; a member of the first generation of college-educated women in the United States; a woman shaped by the ethical posture of her middle-class, mid-western, Protestant background—values that were then reinforced at her college, Rockford Female Seminary—which gave her an absolute sense of her duty to act for good in the world. Yet Addams, like other women simi-larly located, found that in that middle-class late nineteenth-century world, her gender severely limited what she could hope for as a life project.

Nearly all the women who shaped settlement sociology were college graduates and shared an anomalous relation to higher education. On the one hand, in the post–Civil War period, the colleges and universities that were being founded and expanded needed students, and women would do. Rosenberg estimates that "in 1870, 1 percent of Americans attended college, of whom 20 percent were women. By 1900 4 percent did so, and 36 percent were women" (1992, 26). On the other hand, no one knew what to do with the women graduates. Fitzpatrick summarizes their plight: "The great con-tradiction of the revolution in women's higher education was that it pre-pared the first college graduates for a world of opportunities that did not really exist. . . . Thus the problem of what to do after graduation was a troubling one for the first generation of college women" (1990, 8).

Addams lived through, reflected on, and tried to find a solution to this crisis in her social theory (1893, 1902, 1910b, 1912); that solution is funda-mental to her analysis of the role of the settlement house, which, if not uni-versally practiced, nevertheless became the theoretical underpinning of the settlement movement in America. Her first presentation of this theory, in 1892 at the School of Applied Ethics in Plymouth, Massachusetts (among other speakers was Franklin Giddings), launched her as a major figure in the world of social reform; in it she distinguishes the settlement from tra-ditional social work, establishing its distinctive character. The settlement was not to be understood as charity but as a life choice in which the settle-ment resident reaches to fulfill the most fundamental desire of the human organism—"'a proper outlet for active faculties' . . . I have seen young girls suffer and grow sensibly lowered in vitality in the first years after they leave school . . . if no work is provided for [them]. . . . The desire for action, the wish to right wrong and alleviate suffering, haunts them daily" (Addams 1893, 12–13). The settlement experience offered residents the opportunity to participate actively in fundamental social issues: "Hull House endeavors to make social intercourse express the growing sense of the economic unity of society. It is an effort to add the social function to democracy. It was opened on the theory that the dependence of social classes on each other is reciprocal; . . . [it is motivated by] the desire to make the entire social organism democratic, to extend democracy beyond its political expression" (1–2).

THE AMERICAN SETTLEMENT MOVEMENT

The settlement idea was taken over from England's Toynbee Hall, an organization that attempted to bridge class differences by having privileged-class young men live among the working poor. In 1886 Stanton Coit, after a brief stay at Toynbee Hall, started the first American settlement on the Lower East Side of Manhattan. In September 1889, unaware of Coit's efforts but also imitating Toynbee Hall, Addams and Ellen Gates Starr opened Hull House, in Chicago's desperately poor nineteenth ward. That same year, in October, Vida Scudder, Jean Fine, and other Smith College graduates opened the College Settlement in New York City. In 1891 Andover House (later South End House) was started in Boston by W. J. Tucker and Robert A. Woods; in 1893, Lillian Wald established the Henry Street Settlement on New York's Lower East Side; in 1894, Graham Taylor started the Chicago Commons on the West Side of Chicago. By 1897 there were 74 American settlements; 103 by 1900; 204 by 1905.[6]

The 1911 *Handbook of Settlements* compiled by Woods and Albert J. Kennedy showed that by 1910 there were 413 U.S. settlement houses in 33 states and Hawaii, with particularly dense concentrations in the major cities— New York, Chicago, Boston, Philadelphia, Los Angeles, San Francisco. The *Handbook* also shows a significant gender pattern: there were 1,077 women residents and 322 men; 5,718 women volunteers and 1,594 men; 216 women as head residents and 85 men.[7]

This gender pattern is crucial to, although not the sole determiner of, the kind of sociology the settlements practiced and the way they came to interpret social work. Certainly part of the appeal of the settlement idea to young college-educated women like Addams was that it gave them an open field in which to begin to try to work their will: the colleges and universities they attended had traditionally been male-dominated and may also have seemed removed from the world of public affairs that they wished to enter; and in the early years of the settlement movement, the traditional social work programs had no role for women of their class save in the capacity of friendly

6. Debates about figures usually involve whether to count organizations with a strong religious affiliation and nonresidential "centers."

7. This count does not include those settlements reported in the *Handbook*, which listed only "volunteers" without any breakout, nor does it include paid employees or students doing settlement work as part of a degree. Including these would, of course, increase the numbers.

visitor, which at that time was an occasional volunteer activity rather than a vocation.

A SCIENCE OF SOCIAL REFORM

The critical narrative argues that settlement sociology was as complete a school as any in the history of the discipline: it had a coherence of theory, method, practice, and purpose; it had a major theorist in Addams; it had an ongoing process of communication through the settlement networks and publications; and it had a research agenda that, consistent with the original purposes of the Social Science Movement, focused on producing major social reforms. Where academia constrained sociology and the bureaucratic caseload controlled social work, the settlement sociologists worked from a base that they had constructed, could adjust, was consistent with their sense of sociology, and had a built-in practice of reflexivity. Typical of this reflexivity is William Horace Noyes's 1899 warning against settlements becoming institutionalized: "Good institutions—i.e., institutions that have proved themselves useful—like good habits lend themselves easily to the conservative forces of society" (1970, 62). Similarly, in 1900 Vida Scudder urged that settlements not lose touch with their original radical ethical impulses: "that the conditions of life forced by our civilization upon vast numbers of the working classes, especially upon the poor in our great cities, are undemocratic, un-Christian, unrighteous; that only the surrender of life itself, probably of many lives of more than one generation can change them; but that in the name of American democracy, changed they must be" (Scudder 1970,72).

THEORY

The critical narrative here is similar to the natural history narrative in that it emphasizes ideas as an independent source of action. It argues that like Durkheim and Weber, the settlement sociologists sought a theoretical understanding that would intellectually order the massive and disruptive social change that surrounded them and be an alternative to Marx. It sees their thinking affected by a number of currents, of which the most important were British Fabian socialism and American pragmatism. (The critical narrative, perhaps wrongly, downplays the role of the Social Gospel movement in the production of settlement's social theory, but it acknowledges that for many settlement leaders—like Mary Simkovitch, Vida Scudder, and Graham Taylor—this activist and liberal-leaning Christianity provided a valuational motive for embarking on settlement work as a way of life.) What the settlement theorists found most fruitful in Fabian socialism was the argument, made most especially by Beatrice and Sidney Webb, that solutions to the chaos produced by capitalist industrialization were emanating naturally from small-scale actions by ordinary people, such as the cooperative movement, and that these actions needed to be studied by social scientists and implemented by government on a broader scale. This thesis appealed in part because it affirmed the importance of local initiatives and offered reform as an alternative to Marxist revolutionary practice. But even more fundamentally, it appealed because it resonated with the basic philosophic stance of American pragmatism as held by many settlement sociologists, notably Addams.

Undergirding settlement sociology's theory was the pragmatist principle that "Truth *happens* to an idea. It *becomes* true, is *made* true by events. Its verity *is* in fact an event, a process: the process namely of its verifying itself, its veri-*fication*. Its validity is the process of its valid-*ation*" (James 1907a/1948, 161). This principle perhaps described the lives they were leading as women on what their colleague Graham Taylor (1930) named "the social frontiers." Applying this principle to sociology itself, settlement sociology was "a theory of social relations" (Brandt 1910, 722) that could only be proved if lived or done. Where Park and Burgess (1921, 44) felt that the collection of information "merely for the purpose of determining what to do in a given case" was a sign that sociology was still struggling toward science, the settlement sociologists saw that process as sociology's fundamental purpose.

Addams's theory opposes the Marxian call for revolution with a call for radical reform in which class conflict is not inevitable, class differences can be bridged by an ongoing communication between classes, and the structural causes of class division can be resolved by bringing the democratic process fully into engagement with a capitalist economy, a process she captured in the phrase "to socialize democracy." From the beginning, she saw the settlement as a social invention in "the becoming true" of this theory:

> The Settlement, then, is an experimental effort to aid in the solution of the social and industrial problems which are engendered by the modern conditions of life in a great city. It insists that these problems are not confined to any one portion of a city. It is an attempt to relieve, at the same time, the over-accumulation at one end of society and the destitution at the other. . . . It should demand from its residents a scientific patience in the accumulation of facts and the steady holding of their sympathies as one of the best instruments for that accumulation. It must be grounded in a philosophy whose foundation is on the solidarity

of the human race, a philosophy which will not waver when the race happens to be represented by a drunken woman or an idiot boy. Its residents must be . . . content to live quietly side by side with their neighbors until they grow into a sense of relationship and mutual interests . . . [,] to see the needs of their neighborhood as a whole, to furnish data for legislation, and use their influence to secure it . . . [,] to regard the entire life of their city as organic, to make an effort to unify it, and to protest against its over-differentiation. (Addams 1893, 21–23)

This working proposition—that the privileged-class settlement residents "grow into a sense of relationship and mutual interests" with their poor and working-class neighbors in the latter's neighborhoods—is based in three theoretical claims: (1) that Marx's concerns could be redressed by fully operationalizing the principle of democracy, (2) that association is the underlying principle of change in the modern world, and (3) that ethics serve as an independent variable in social life, interacting with, affected by, and affecting material production.

Settlement sociology was fully cognizant of socialist theory in both its Marxist and Fabian forms. It was read by Addams and debated and practiced by Hull House clubs—which, for instance, studied Beatrice Potter's *The Co-operative Movement in Great Britain* (1891). The Chicago Woman's Club, whose affluent members helped fund Hull House, studied *Capital* (Scott 1992, 120). Addams's ally Florence Kelley, an active socialist, published the first English translation of Engels' *The Conditions of the Working Class in England in 1844* (Engels 1887) and maintained her relationship with Engels until his death. Settlement sociologists identified economic class as the main variable explaining the human pain they saw around them, saw unrestricted capitalism as the primary cause of that pain, and believed labor organization and legislation were critical to worker emancipation. Kelley attempted to fit Marxist arguments to U.S. social structure by calling consumers into being as a class through the creation of the National Consumers' League in 1899.

Settlement sociologists saw "the power to combine [as] the distinguishing feature of our time" (Addams 1895, 184). They argued that the effective practice of association had made possible capitalism's capacity for industrial and commercial expansion and that its absence among any group would render that group incapable of responding in its own interest to the conditions of the times. In practice, this argument brought them in on the side of labor (at the same moment that Bemis was being dismissed from the University of Chicago for these ideas): "If the settlement, then, is convinced that in industrial affairs lack of organization tends to the helplessness of the isolated worker, and is a menace to the entire community, then, it is bound to pledge itself to industrial organization . . . more technically known as the labor movement" (Addams 1895, 90). The bridge between privileged-class members and working-class members could be built through the ongoing process of relating, and associations like the settlement existed to facilitate that relating.

Class conflict could be transformed in part by organizing the worker into a counterforce to the capitalist corporation. But to make the discourse between those two constituencies constructive rather than conflictive there must be a system of shared values and practices, which Addams called "ethics." In Addams's analysis of society, ethics is a key concept, a dynamic not "outside" of society or of the scope of sociological analysis but a central societal structure. Addams traces the origins of ethics to the human impulses to sociability and kindness—"the evolutionists tell us that the instinct to pity, the impulse to aid his fellows, served man at a very early period, as a rude rule of right and wrong" (1902, 22). That the desire for sociability is transformed into an ethical mandate of responsibility toward the other is a key argument in Addams's theory: individual emotional experience undergirds societal structures, which in turn help pattern the emotional experience of the social actor. What is needed in her own day, she argues, is a *social ethic,* a set of behavioral guidelines for "right relationship" that emphasizes both the actor's responsibility to an enlarged community and the importance of group or democratic processes as the way to fulfill that responsibility. This social ethic, like any ethic, cannot be acquired by study of abstract principles but has to be learned by interactional practice, which is made possible through associations.

Addams was deeply committed to a radical group process within these associations. While admitting the difficulties of learning to relate as equals across lines of difference—"we have all been at times entertained by the futile efforts of half a dozen highly individualized people gathered together as a committee"—she insists that the process is as important as the outcome: that the "associated effort . . . which appears ineffective . . . may represent a finer social quality than the more effective individual action" (1902, 137–38).

METHODOLOGY AND RESEARCH

The critical narrative stresses the extraordinary research productivity of settlement sociology in terms of individual projects, methodological sophistication, and practical social outcomes. It shows how settlement sociology worked to create a science of reform. In this telling, settlement sociology's methodology grew directly out of its social theory and also reflected the women's quest for *auctoritas*. The social theory demanded that ideas be tested and refined through real-life experience; its methodology argued that that real-life experience would come through the "neighborly relation."

Settlement methodology addressed directly the problem of constructing a neighborly relation across enormous divisions of class and culture. In a 1914 *AJS* article, Woods of the South End Settlement analyzes the neighborhood as an associational unit that in its very nature gives rise to a particular relational intimacy:

> One of the most striking facts about the neighborhood is that, though it is not essentially an intimate circle, it is at bottom always a hospitable one, always ready to receive new recruits. The first impact of a new arrival may be chilling, but in due time the newcomer begins almost automatically to go through the degrees of this greatest and freest of human free-masonries. As Mark Twain has suggested, when a man sits down beside you in the railroad car, your first feeling is one of intrusion; but after a little something happens to make your being in the same seat a matter of common interest, and the feeling of recoil dissolves into a continuous friendly glow. It is surely one of the most remarkable of all social facts that . . . the man who establishes his home besides yours, by that very act begins to qualify as an ally of yours and begins to have a claim upon your sense of comradeship. (Woods 1970, 152)

Woods posits that one problem in social science research is that social scientists come from the "unneighborly classes": "Nearly all highly educated persons are snatched out of neighborhood experience at an early age, and few of us ever really have it again. Thus our opportunity for experimental, pragmatic study of typical human relations is lost—lost so far that in most cases we forget that we are suffering loss" (1970, 153). He describes the technique of the neighborly relation as being similar to the way "one friend comes to know about another friend"—bit by bit, learning details as events occur in the friend's life and the friend makes disclosures, being drawn into the emotions as well as the material circumstances of a situation. From this point of view as neighbor, Addams argues, the settlement is naturally drawn into advocacy for: "by virtue of its very locality . . . it has put itself into a position to see, as no one but a neighbor can see, the stress and need of those who bear the brunt of the social injury" (1895, 183).

To be a successful advocate, settlement sociologists needed to build up, out of what they learned as neighbors, information that would be accepted by a wider public as valid. In this quest for accurate and graspable information, the settlement sociologists developed a rich methodology. They used multiple research and data collection strategies, drawing on both qualitative and quantitative techniques. They concretized social problems in terms of empirical experiences of human pain. They analytically demonstrated that that pain occurred not randomly but in a pattern caused by social structure. They presented their information and analysis in an accessible form for a general public. And they concluded their research with proposals for change—actions to be taken and policies to be enacted.

For American sociology they pioneered the use of many strategies now taken for granted by academic sociologists: the survey, the interview, the questionnaire, personal budget keeping, participant-observation, key informants, and secondary data analysis (which included the census, legislation, memoirs and diaries, wage and cost-of-living records, court reports, social worker reports, tax rolls, nursery rhymes, and industrial accident reports). They were equally pioneering in methods of presentation, using photographs, detailed colored maps of neighborhoods, tables, bar charts, graphs, statistical analyses, narrative accounts, and extended quotation from subjects.

The critical narrative stresses that settlement sociological research produced some of the major empirical studies of classical American sociology (see table 3.2). And beyond all these, literally thousands of papers were published by settlements large and small, all across the country, as reports to the public and local governments and as articles in journals and magazines.

The critical narrative locates this methodological and research achievement in part in the quest of the women residents for *auctoritas*. The women recognized that in seeking to gain an entry into public life, they could make knowledge into power. From the very beginnings of the Social Science Movement, leaders had been concerned about the absence of information on social problems. Settlement workers in general and women in particular set out to remedy this absence, both for the purpose of arriving at solutions themselves and for advocating for public policies. Although they recognized the need for both "sympathetic understanding" and "the information of the statistician" (Addams 1910a, 70), they made—perhaps in a determination to reject gender stereotyping—a concerted effort to gather what we today call "hard" data. So successful were they in this that Gordon (1994, 171)—remarking on the irony of the "malleability of gender"—records that for some years in American social science, quantitative techniques were seen as detail or busy work by the male academics in search of larger general principles. The women, Gordon argues, understood quantification as one route to authority and expertise. But settlement sociologists also pioneered participant observation studies that let them bring back firsthand reports

Table 3.2 Examples of settlement sociology research

Year	Author or principal researcher	Title	Settlement
1895	Residents of Hull House, directed by Florence Kelley	*Hull-House Maps and Papers by the Residents of Hull-House*	Hull House, Chicago
1898	Robert Woods	*The City Wilderness: A Settlements Study by Residents and Associates of the South End House Boston*	South End, Boston
1899	W. E. B. DuBois with Isabel Eaton	*The Philadelphia Negro*	College Settlement, Philadelphia
1902	Robert Woods	*Americans in Process: A Settlement Study by Residents and Associates of the South End House— North and West Ends Boston*	South End, Boston
1904	Frances Kellor	*Out of Work: A Study of Unemployment*	Henry Street Settlement, New York City
1905	Lillian Brandt	*Five Hundred and Seventy Four Deserters and Their Families: A Descriptive Study of Their Characteristics and Circumstances*	Greenwich House Settlement, New York City
1909–14	Paul Kellogg	*The Pittsburgh Survey,* 6 vols.	Kingsley House, Pittsburgh; Russell Sage Foundation
1909	Elizabeth Butler	*Women and Trades: Pittsburgh, 1907–1908*	Kingsley House, Pittsburgh; Russell Sage Foundation
1910	Margaret Bynington	*Homestead: The Households of a Milltown*	Kingsley House, Pittsburgh; Russell Sage Foundation
	Crystal Eastman	*Work Accidents and the Law*	Kingsley House, Pittsburgh; Russell Sage Foundation

Table 3.2 continued

	John Andrews Fitch	*The Steelworkers*	Kingsley House, Pittsburgh; Russell Sage Foundation
	Emily Green Balch	*Our Slavic Fellow Citizens*	Denison House, Boston
1911	Mary White Ovington	*Half a Man: The Status of the Negro in New York*	Greenwich House, New York City
1914	Paul Kellogg	*The Pittsburgh District Civic Frontage*	Pittsburgh Survey
		Wage-Earning Pittsburgh	Pittsburgh Survey
1917	Grace Abbott	*The Immigrant and the Community*	Hull House, Chicago
1923	Robert Woods and Albert J. Kennedy	*The Zone of Emergence: Observations of the Lower Middle and Upper Working Class Communities of Boston, 1905–1914*	South End House, Boston
1936	Edith Abbott	*The Tenements of Chicago, 1908–1935*	Hull House, Chicago

Source: Lengermann and Niebrugge-Brantley 2002.

from the social frontiers of unemployment, department store work, and sweatshop labor (e.g., Kellor 1904; MacLean 1899).

ADVOCACY

Some of the most exciting chapters of the critical narrative trace the ways the settlement research was put into the service of reform. From the publication of *Hull-House Maps and Papers* on, settlement sociology argued that "insistent probing into the lives of the poor . . . and the personal impertinence of many of the questions asked, would be unendurable and unpardonable were it not for the conviction that the public conscience when roused must demand better surroundings for the most . . . long-suffering citizens of the commonwealth" (Holbrooke 1895, 13-14). Kelley, in *Ethical Gains through Legislation* (1905), wrote a paradigmatic statement linking research and reform, arguing that an ethically informed public, empowered by social science research, could bring about legal changes designed to re-form structures that hurt the most vulnerable.

Two accounts of victories for research are almost legendary. One is the story of the "Brandeis brief." In 1908 in *Muller v. Oregon*, a case concerning the constitutionality of an Oregon law limiting the maximum hours that women could work, attorney Louis Brandeis, for the first time in legal his-tory, presented an argument that used only a few pages of formal legal rea-soning and citation and rested instead on hundreds of facts supplied by settlement sociologists to argue the case. He had been hired by the National Consumers League headed by Kelley; his strategy of using social science data became known as the "Brandeis brief"—and he won the case. The other story is that of Crystal Eastman's research victories for workmen's compensation during her work for the Pittsburgh Survey, a massive social science survey conducted over six years under the leadership of Paul Kel-logg, originally of the Greenwich House Settlement and editor of *Survey*, the social science journal of the settlements. The story is well told by Rein-harz (1992, 176-77) of how Eastman, finding that neither the employer nor the state kept any records of accidents in the work place, hit on the idea of using coroner's records to get some sense of their occurrence:

> We got permission to use these and made a record of every industrial fatality reported to the coroner during the twelve months from July 1906 to July 1907, taking down on a separate card for each case, the name and address of the man killed, his age, occupation and conjugal condition, the name of his employer, the circumstances of the accident, the names of important witnesses, and the verdict. The plan was to learn from the evidence in the coroner's record, how each accident happened, and to learn from visiting the family what happened after the accident, i.e., how great a financial loss was suffered by the family of the workman killed, how much of this was made up by compensation received from the employer, and how the family was affected in its economic life by the accident. (Eastman 1910, 789)

Eastman's work led her to conclude that in about one-third of the cases, no one was at fault, in about one-third the company was at fault, and in one-third the worker; against these figures, she pointed out the unfairness that "the risks of trade [should be] borne through all these years by the work-men alone" and that it "should in all wisdom and justice be shared by the employer" (Eastman 1910, 789-94). The passage of workmen's compensa-tion legislation was one of the settlement movement's major victories.

More broadly, it was during the years that settlement leaders were presi-dents of the NCCC that that body drafted its landmark position paper

"Social Standards for Industry," which became the basis for much of U.S. welfare policy and quality-of-life guidelines; the paper proposed the ideal of a living wage, the standard of biweekly pay, old-age pensions, unemployment insurance, workmen's compensation, the eight-hour day, and the six-day week.

RELATION TO SOCIOLOGY AND SOCIAL WORK

Settlement social scientists conceived of their project as a seamless combination of theory and practice in the service of social reform. As such, they identified easily both with sociology as a method for thinking about the causes of social problems and with social work as a project for practically addressing those problems. It is an irony of history that eventually they would be relegated to the margins of sociology because they were "too practical" or "applied," and to the margins of social work because they were "too theoretical" or "abstract." They were rejected by both groups for the very combination of traits and accomplishments of which they were justifiably proud. Underlying both acts of rejection, by academic sociology and professional social work, was another charge: that the social settlements engaged in advocacy and as such lacked the objectivity required of a profession.

In the 1890s and 1900s, however, as sociology and social work professionalized, settlement residents moved easily among those who practiced as academic sociologists and those who did the social work of providing public relief. Many residents traced their journey to settlement work through sociology—Graham Taylor, Mary Kingsbury Simkhovitch, Edith Abbott, Sophonisba Breckinridge, Florence Kelley, Vida Scudder, Mary Roberts Smith, and Robert Woods included. Reports from settlements across the country show them self-defining as engaged in sociology. For example, the College Settlement in Manhattan listed first among its activities "Investigations": "The house has for many years carried on a series of sociological studies; largely into aspects of women's and children's life and labor" (Woods and Kennedy 1911, 193-94). Settlement sociologists published in the *American Journal of Sociology* and the *Annals of the American Academy of Political and Social Science* (e.g., Edith Abbott, Grace Abbott, Addams, Kelley, Julia Lathrop, Benjamin C. Marsh, Mary McDowell, Mary White Ovington, Mary Simkhovitch, Taylor, and Woods). Settlement sociologists taught courses for university sociology departments (e.g., E. Abbott and MacLean). And many academic sociologists did research in various ways connected with the settlement and clearly saw the settlement as part of the practice of sociology—for example, Emory Bogardus, W. E. B. DuBois, Franklin Giddings, and Charles R. Henderson.[8]

The settlements' relationship with social work was as close but more complicated. The closeness is illustrated by numerous ties: Addams served as the first woman president of the NCCC; Edith Abbott (Hull House resident during 1908-20) and Sophonisba Breckinridge (Hull House during 1907-20) were cofounders of the School of Social Service Administration at the University of Chicago; Grace Abbott (Hull House resident during 1908-17) was president of the National Conference of Social Workers in 1923-24; Robert Woods (Boston's South End Settlement chief resident) was on the board of the Boston School for Social Workers; and Graham Taylor (of the Chicago Commons settlement) was another past president of the NCCC. Taylor in particular was moved by the long tradition in which he stood. He writes of his experiences: "It was the National Conference of Charities and Corrections which more than any other platform occasion opened to me the fellowship with many of those who became my inspirers . . . in the field of social thought and action. . . .There I met the 'elder statesman' of the social realm. . . . Foremost in this group was Mr. Frank B. Sanborn . . . secretary of the American Social Science Association's Committee which initiated and convened the Conference" (Taylor 1930, 411).

There were, however, deep disagreements with social workers about practice, disagreements rooted in differences of theory and method. The social work case method forced attention to be focused on the individual, and it urged an individual ethic of self-reliance. Yet the most basic position of settlement sociology was that social structure is repeatedly implicated in people's problems and that, especially for Addams, what is needed is not individual morality but social ethics—a willingness to work with the group to arrive at solutions. The settlement sociologists had not necessarily started from this position; it was an idea that had become true based on their personal experience of living in settlement neighborhoods. The social workers urged individual responsibility—or were at least so interpreted by Addams and other settlement workers—whereas the settlement saw social problems in terms of "lack of organization."

This tension is most illustrated by the struggles over social work education, which was really code for the struggle of a sociological versus a psychological understanding of the social worker's role. Edith Abbott and

8. For more details on the relationship between academic and settlement sociologists, see Lengermann and Niebrugge-Brantley (2002).

Breckinridge and the Chicago School of Social Service Administration were the key advocates for a social work oriented toward creating public policies as opposed to the counseling individuals. But they were on the losing side as Abbott's comments in her 1931 *Social Welfare and Professional Education* indicated:

> The academic curriculum of most of the professional schools [of social work] is now poor and slight and covers . . . only the various aspects of a single field. . . . But casework is very far from being the whole story. There are great reaches of territory, some of them yet unexplored and stretching out to a kind of no man's land—the great fields of public charitable organization, of law and government in relation to social work, of social economics, of social insurance, of modern social politics—all of which are required if the social worker is to be an efficient servant of the state. (Quoted in Trattner 1979, 198)

The tension is also reflected in the uneasy relationship between Addams and COS leader Mary Richmond. Whereas Addams thought, wrote, and acted in terms of associational practice, of building solidarity so that in the old labor slogan "the injury to one becomes the injury to all," Richmond thought, wrote, and acted in terms of handling immediate individual need. In her 1899 article "The Settlement and Friendly Visiting," aimed at Addams's criticisms of the charity visitor made at a previous NCCC meeting, Richmond says, "If I could choose a friend for a family fallen into misfortune and asking for relief . . . I would rather choose for them one who had this practical resourcefulness than one who had a perfect equipment of advanced social theories. . . . The former would find the most natural and effective way out . . . the other would say that the whole social order was wrong and must pay a ransom for its wrongness by generous material help to its victims" (as quoted in Franklin 1986, 511).

ERASURE

The processes that marginalized or erased the memory of the settlement sociologists have been analyzed in most of the works listed at the beginning of this section—notably those by Deegan, Reinharz, and ourselves. It can be said that the settlement sociologists constituted what we might call "the radical middle"—radical not so much in their social programs, which were fundamentally reformist, but in the alternative they offered for both sociology and social work. This radical middle practiced sociology, social work, and social science as "the science of reform." Within the critical narrative they are remembered heroically, but within sociology and social work they are relatively forgotten because in the end they were on the losing side with both groups. The sociologists have classified them as social workers who lacked any formal theory and have argued that it is formal theory that gives one a permanent place in sociology (see, e.g., Collins and Makowsky 1998, 227). The social workers considered them too sociological. Both professional groups defined them as too radical or activist.

What finally explains their erasure from the history of sociology is partly a politics of gender, partly a politics of knowledge, and partly a politics of professionalization. We have traced elsewhere in detail the politics of gender (Lengermann and Niebrugge-Brantley 1998), describing its main features in a Schutzian analysis: even when present, the woman-other is not typified as a fully rational, theoretically capable human; when absent, she disappears into the vast category of "other" or "woman." We show this happening particularly in the case of Addams, who despite leaving an impressive and challenging body of theory, has been remembered for good deeds rather than complex thought because that is how the culture best understands women. But there is also a politics of knowledge: the social theory developed out of the settlement was too radical for either sociology or social work. And finally there is a politics of professionalization: the settlement proved in the end a fragile base from which to practice a science of reform. Part of that fragility perhaps came in the demands it made on its practitioners. The settlement sociologists wanted from the social science community a commitment to work for fundamental social change, a willingness to live in a neighborly relation with the most vulnerable, a life not just a career—Franklin (1986) notes that Addams never really reconciled to the idea of social workers who wanted to put in an eight-hour day and go home.

Conclusion: The Present Relation

By the 1930s, sociology and social work had established themselves as separate areas of social science professionalization, the former overwhelmingly male, the latter predominantly female. The social settlements, which had held to the vision that a union of the two fields in "a science of social reform" was possible, were in a period of dramatic decline from which they never recovered. We now look first at what is left of the original union of the two fields and then at what each lost in their separation. We conclude with a brief review of what seems to us the most important aspects of this history of sociology: the ways in which its development continues to this day along the lines of tension and opportunity as suggested by the multiple narratives about sociology's long relation to social work. These lines interweave in complex ways among the century-old issues of public perception of utility, of advocacy versus objectivity, and of gender boundaries.

There are continued linkages between the fields. At present there are somewhere between 37 and 45 joint programs of sociology and social work (the variation in the final number is produced by varying the criteria for inclusion used by different agencies). Moreover, in ASA publications (ASA 2005), in the preprofessional training guidelines typically provided by schools of social work, and on such career Web sites as CollegeBoard.com, a major in sociology is claimed to be as useful a preparation for social work as psychology is. And evidence suggests that a significant number of undergraduate sociology majors have traditionally moved on to employment in social service occupations (Watts and Ellis 1989).

Their separation left both sociology and social work with an absence, an incompleteness. Sociology, unlike social work, still struggles to establish its utility—or at least a sense of utility—in the mind of the public. News features analyzing why students select the majors that they do frequently select sociology as an example of a major that is undertaken for "love" rather than for "money" (e.g., Koeppel 2004). The same could certainly be said of social work, but social work clearly leads to an identifiable job with a salary (even if not a high one). Social work became a field of practical problem-solving, focusing on individuals and small groups experiencing "social maladjustment." Its culminating degree is typically the MSW. Its practitioners, in forfeiting the high-profile academic research track as well as by relinquishing the project of social generalization, lack the authority of the "expert witness," one whose specialized knowledge of society is called on as a guide for public policy. That some discontent exists among social workers over this situation is witnessed in Reisch and Andrews's important revisionist history *The Road Not Taken* (2001), subtitled *A History of Radical Social Work in the United States*.

Sociology has built a public role for itself as the expert witness. But with its separation from social work, sociology lacks a clearly defined sphere of professional practice and employment for its undergraduate majors and master's students. It also may seem to lack a base from which it can directly impact the lives of individuals but must instead work indirectly through its research to try to affect public policy. This absence has many costs for the discipline. For example, the American Sociological Association in 2004 had less than 14,000 members, while the National Association of Social Workers (which has been criticized by its own constituency as unnecessarily *restrictive* in its criteria for membership) had over 150,000. If public assessment of a field's significance can be deduced from the categorizations of the

Bureau of Labor Statistics, it is noteworthy that that agency had identified social workers as a distinct occupational category (as are economists and psychologists), while sociologists are grouped with archaeologists, political scientists, and anthropologists as "other social science." Sociology programs and the ASA itself continue to struggle with the question, "What can you do with a sociology BA?" (Spalter-Roth 2005).

For good or ill, sociology still seems in the public mind to address that century-old yearning for a "science of social reform"—and this seems true whether the public is understood as elites with resources to withhold or confer on the field or as the college student seeking a major. As Michael Burawoy (2004b) has noted, sociology's first public is in its student clientele and in those students who flock to sociology in periods of heightened liberationist activism, like the 1960s and 1970s, but turn away from it when the public mood grows conservative, as in the Reagan era, when professional sociologists were forced by dwindling enrollments to make the case that sociology provides a good foundation for those bent on a business career (Ruggiero and Weston 1986). Further, drawing on personal observation, we suggest that whatever the political climate and overall attitudinal profile of the student body, sociology is constant in its ability to provide a major and a home for the more progressive members of the student body. At the present moment, elite organizations, in their public role, have honored sociologists for research that could certainly be defined as part of a "science of social reform." In 2005, the National Science Foundation's Waterman Award went to Dalton Conley—the first time a sociologist has won this national award for young research scientists across all fields of science—for "empirical research demonstrat[ing] how certain social and economic conditions are the basis of persistent racial differences in key areas of life—from educational success to the likelihood of relying on welfare" (Ebner 2005, 1). And Guggenheims went to Andrew Cherlin, who heads a team investigating the impact on parents and children of 1996 welfare reform legislation, and to Bruce Western, who has looked critically at the effects on U.S. society of the increasing use of imprisonment.

In combination, the narratives of sociology's separation from social work suggest that the earlier period was patterned by a politics of gender and a politics of knowledge. Today, as a result of the second great wave of feminist mobilization that began in the 1960s, the gender politics of sociology has been transformed from one of exclusion to one of negotiation. More than half the ASA membership is female; among its most powerful interest groups are its largest section, Sex and Gender, and the related association Sociologists for Women in Society, both of which are deeply feminist in orientation. Both women and men committed to the value of gender equality are elected year after year to the top executive positions of the association.

Finally, both the social and the critical narratives highlight a politics of knowledge that shaped sociology's struggle for professional standing and revolved significantly around a supposed tension between objectivity and advocacy in the struggle by sociology for professional standing. And both narratives lament the discipline's separation by 1930 from its activist roots in the reform social movements of the nineteenth and early twentieth centuries. Indeed, the triumph of the natural history in the discipline's key teaching texts suggest that the argument for objectivity won the day as well as the power to pattern the field's sense of its own development. But the argument for objectivity over advocacy has never gone unchallenged by those who espouse a more activist stance for the field. And since the 1960s, the politics of that debate, too, have been transformed from one of exclusion to one of negotiation. Indeed, in recent years, especially since 2000, the ASA membership has repeatedly tilted toward the advocacy argument in its selection of presidents. President Michael Burawoy's theme for the 2004 annual meeting—Public Sociologies—voiced the desire of many to see sociologists play a more activist role. As Burawoy wrote:

> As a mirror and conscience of society, sociology defines, promotes and informs public debate about class and racial inequalities, new gender regimes, environmental degradation, multiculturalism, technological revolutions, market fundamentalism, and state and non-state violence. More than ever the world needs public sociologies—sociologies that transcend the academy and engage wider audiences. . . . Academic sociology also needs the world. In stimulating debates about issues of the day, public sociologies inspire and revitalize our own discipline. (Burawoy 2004b)

This call seemed to touch a chord with ASA membership in that the 2004 meeting was the best attended on record (although Burawoy's vision did not go unopposed; see DeFlem 2004a and Godard 2004). In the centenary-year election of 2005, both presidential candidates—Lawrence Bobo and Frances Fox Piven—had built careers on the premise of social science as a tool for social justice. The election of Piven has a particular resonance with the debates of a hundred years earlier. It can be read as representing the change in gender dynamics within the profession, an acceptance of the permeability of conventional academic boundaries, in that she trained as a political scientist; it can also be read as a return to a union with social work in that her role in antipoverty campaigns has made her an important figure in radical revisionist histories of social work (see Reisch and Andrews 2001). Set in the context of sociology's long march toward a usable definition of itself, the internal politics of the profession in the last few years have affirmed, by vote of the membership, the century-old ties of sociology to what the Bernards in 1943 called "a great historic movement, almost heroic in its aspirations.

FOUR

A Life in the First Half-Century
of Sociology: Charles Ellwood
and the Division of Sociology

Stephen Turner

The customary division of the history of American Sociology into the periods before and after 1945 is well grounded. In 1944, Charles Ellwood, one of the first PhD's in sociology and a former American Sociological Society president, published his bitter final message, his "Valedictory" (Ellwood 1944), which testified both to the changes in the discipline and to his loss of hope for it. He began the article by saying that, "as I retire, my critics may well say that I have failed in all my distinctive endeavors." He listed four such efforts: (1) getting sociologists "to recognize that the intangible and imponderable factors in the human mind are the most important factors with which they have to deal"—a recognition that the drift to "natural science methods[,] which take into account only the observable and the measurable," precluded; (2) standing for peace, whereas the drift was "toward the use of force"; (3) standing for humanized religion based on humanized science, whereas the drift was toward "a theological religion which emphasizes supermundane values"; and (4) endeavoring to make the study of human relations central to education, whereas the drift was toward physical science in service to the military (1944, n.p.). He died in 1946 at the age of seventy-three. At the same time, a new generation was taking over American sociology, and taking it over both at an unprecedentedly young age and in what turned out to be almost unprecedented conditions of growth.

Ellwood disappeared from the collective consciousness of sociology very quickly under these circumstances, and the rapidity and completeness of his disappearance is grounds enough for interest. It is a sign of the extent to which the discipline changed and a clue to what changed. But Ellwood is worth thinking about on his own, as a significant figure in the history of the discipline. He was the founder of two graduate departments with PhD programs, at the University of Missouri and Duke University, and midwife to the founding of a third, at UCLA. He was president of the Institute Internationale de Sociologie and leader of the critical 1935 International Congress of Sociology. He was also a public intellectual whose books reached a wide audience and who was much in demand as a public speaker. Moreover, he was the author of one of the most successful textbooks in the history of sociology, *Sociology and Modern Social Problems* (1910),[1] a book that created the field of social problems as a teaching area. To the extent that "influence" on the public comes from the classroom, one would imagine that this book had some influence on the many students who studied it, and indeed, its major thrust, to regard education as the only ultimately effective response to social problems, fits closely with the subsequent biases of the social policy enacted by the generation that was taught social problems with this text. Finally, he was a source, though to what extent is disputed, of symbolic interactionism and the originator of the critique of mainstream American sociological methodology (Ellwood 1933b).

My main concern in this chapter is not with his influence or even with his ideas. Instead, my aim is to recapture, through a consideration of Ellwood's career, something about the world of pre-1945 sociology and the larger world of publics, national and international, that he inhabited. Most of the themes I take up are discussed in a more general way in other chapters of this volume—the relation of sociology to social work and social welfare, the phenomenon of the public intellectual, internationalism, and so forth. Ellwood is particularly revealing with respect to these subjects, not so much because he was typical but because he shows the complexities behind the typifications. Many of the clichés about early sociology apply to him: he grew up on a farm, was a scholarship boy at a state university, was motivated specifically by Christian social concerns and social problems, wrote textbooks, and did much of this in what Robert Friedrichs (1970) has called the prophetic mode, condemning social evils. But in other ways Ellwood belies the typifications, as will become evident. His career also reveals why a history of American sociology focused on Chicago, Columbia, and Harvard, and on the current canon, must be inadequate. The mundane world of academic sociology he inhabited was quite different, and so were the aspirations and opportunities of those who inhabited it. But his career is also important in illuminating one of the critical questions in the history of American sociology: how did the fundamental and persisting conflicts in American sociology originate?

Reformism and the Origins of Academic Sociology

In 1884 the president of Cornell, Andrew White, sought to establish "a course of practical instruction calculated to prepare young men to discuss

---

1. There are many editions of this volume: *Sociology and Modern Social Problems* (1910), new and enlarged edition (1913), new edition (1919), new edition revised (1924), and new edition (1943) titled *Sociology, Principles and Problems*.

intelligently such important social questions as the best methods of dealing practically with pauperism, intemperance, crimes of various degrees and among persons of different ages, insanity, idiocy and the like" (Woodward 1884, 2). In 1886, Frank Sanborn, secretary of the Massachusetts Board of Charities and of the American Social Science Association, was appointed as a special lecturer for this purpose. The arrangement continued through 1889, and the course became the largest taught in the Department of History and Political Science. In 1892, after the course work in social science was rearranged, a full-time resident professor was appointed, Walter F. Willcox, who had just written the first American statistical dissertation on a recognizably sociological topic, divorce, at Columbia under Richmond Mayo-Smith.[2] E. A. Ross, then a new PhD from Johns Hopkins, arrived at the same time, as an economist.

Ellwood arrived at Cornell as a student the same year. The idea of social science was not new to him. He had been exposed to the writings of Richard T. Ely, economist and "Christian sociologist," in high school, through Ely's writings for the Chautauqua movement (Ellwood n.d.b). The atmosphere was heady. Cornell was enlivened by a strong interest in evolution that figured in various ways in the curriculum, and even in the outlook of the philosophy department, which was an American outpost of German neo-Kantianism. Ellwood organized a YMCA program on the family (motivated, it is supposed, by his own troubled family life),[3] to which Samuel Dike (then secretary of the American League for the Protection of the Family) and many of the social science faculty at Cornell contributed. Ross took a personal interest in Ellwood and encouraged him to become a teacher of sociology, a field that barely existed as an academic subject. Ellwood wrote a senior thesis on the topic of sociology as a basis for a science of ethics, under the supervision of political scientist Jeremiah Jenks, and he began to form, through his relations with his teachers, a sense of sociology, and a specific sense of his own tastes in sociology. He disliked Willcox's ideas about a scientific sociology that stressed the interpretation of official statistics, which had been Mayo-Smith's stock in trade, but he seized on a remark that Willcox made to him to the effect that a psychological approach to sociology might be fruitful (Ellwood n.d.b).

Each of these figures, Ely, Ross, and Willcox, was the product of a prominent element in reformism. Ely, a founder of the American Economic Association, had created a circle of "Christian sociologists" that had in-

---

2. For background on Columbia during this era see Turner (1991).
3. This issue is discussed in Whitaker (1972).

cluded Albion Small. The breakup of this group represented one of the first divisions in sociology: between sociology understood as a movement of Christian socialists or as an academic discipline, the understanding subsequently promoted by Small. Ross represented the trickle of "progressive" economists who eventually emigrated into sociology as economics, by shedding its socialists and reformers, became a conventional discipline. Willcox, Mayo-Smith's most successful student, practiced a style of statistics rooted in the aim of the founders of the faculty of Politics and Economics at Columbia—to provide an educated class of civil servants for the United States on the European model, which was taken to require expertise in official statistics.[4] This was part of a movement of governmental reform that had many offshoots and consequences, including the efficiency and municipal research bureau movements of the early decades of the twentieth century (and eventually the professionalization of the field of public administration in the 1930s).

Immediately after graduating from Cornell in 1896, Ellwood went to the University of Chicago for graduate work in sociology, but without a scholarship (although he obtained one once his PhD was in sight). Chicago is often depicted as a machine that transformed eager reformist students interested in such problems as broken marriages and delinquency into scholars who promoted the idea of sociology as a theoretical discipline (e.g., Kaesler 1990, 13-14). Ellwood needed no converting: his thesis on sociology and ethics was already theoretical, and he came with definite, if ill-defined ideas about what sociology should be, ideas that he developed during his career but never abandoned. The Department of Sociology was, of course tiny, consisting of Albion Small, W. I. Thomas,[5] George Vincent, and Charles R. Henderson, and students took courses in related fields. Ellwood was especially impressed, he tells us in the autobiographical statement he wrote for L. L. Bernard, with Dewey and Mead (Ellwood n.d.b).

There was nothing parochial about the education Ellwood received at Chicago nor about Ellwood's tastes. As a student he published an article on LePlay's method in the second volume of the *American Journal of Sociology* (1897), and spent the same year in Berlin, with Georg Simmel, for which he had been given an honorary traveling fellowship. He got little from Simmel,

4. Richmond Mayo-Smith, an exponent of the tabular tradition of nineteenth-century statistics, is discussed in Turner (1996). His papers are at the University of Chicago.

5. Ellwood's relationship with Thomas was in many respects that of a rival: both were social psychologists, though at this point Thomas was known primarily for his study of social origins and his sociobiological speculations; his popularization of the concept of attitude was far in the future.

finding G. Schmoller and F. Paulsen more stimulating and receptive to the idea of social science as a basis of ethics. But his negative reaction to Simmel—whom he dismissed as a metaphysician of the social[6]—was consequential, for it was in a paper he wrote in Germany in response to this experience that he formulated the basis of what was later to become his methodological critique of sociology (cf. Jensen 1946-47). When he returned to Chicago, he published his dissertation on the psychological basis of sociology in sections in the *American Journal of Sociology* (1899a, 1899b, 1899c, 1899d). His PhD committee, which included not only the four sociology faculty members but also Dewey, Mead, and the economist T. Lawrence Laughlin, Veblen's mentor, who brought Veblen to Chicago, passed him magna cum laude in June of 1899. His dissertation was an argument for a social psychological approach to the problem of understanding the foundations of social life, and for the idea of a psychological (or process) approach to the problem of the nature of society, an approach he later contrasted with the social contract and organic theories of society. The dissertation prefigured his life's work as a sociological theorist.[7]

What did this pioneering degree and immaculate pedigree get him in the burgeoning academic market of 1899? Not exactly nothing, but close to nothing. When he first entered the job market, his letter writers, including all the sociologists, Dewey, Mead, and president of the university William Rainey Harper, carefully avoided, with a few ambiguous exceptions, any mention that his degree was in sociology. Dewey suggested that he would be an excellent teacher of philosophy, and others suggested that he could teach in any of the social sciences, in a couple of cases burying the mention of sociology in a long list of other fields (e.g., Dewey, March 25, 1899; Henderson, March 30, 1899; Small, March 30, 1899; all in the Ellwood papers). Small, in a letter of May 15, 1899, to President Lemuel H. Murlin of Baker University, does mention sociology, and the reference is curious: he says that Ellwood "studied sociology from the standpoint of the philosopher rather than the agitator" (Ellwood papers). The language is almost certainly

---

6. At this point in Simmel's career, this appraisal was accurate. Later Ellwood would arrange for the translation of some of Simmel's work by his first PhD student, William Elwang, for the *AJS*.

7. Ellwood is often regarded as a source of symbolic interactionism through his role as the teacher of Blumer. In one crucial respect this characterization is true: Ellwood (along with Charles Cooley) pioneered the argument that "society" is no more than a way of talking about a set of interlinked psychological processes. For the mature Ellwood, most importantly, these were processes of mutual learning and adaptive learning, whose content he identified with culture.

a reference to the Bemis affair of 1895. Bemis, an instructor in the University of Chicago's extension division, who was identified as an economist and sociologist, was fired for a speech in which he criticized the railroads for "their open violations of the inter-state commerce law and their relations to corrupt legislatures and assessors testify to their part in this regard" (Hofstadter and Metzger 1955; Boyer 2002, 3–4). The remarks indicate how serious the consequences were for the fledgling sociology program. These letters were written to no avail. In the end, Ellwood was saved from unemployment only by Henderson, who had heard of a position for a Charity Organization Society (COS) director in Lincoln, Nebraska. With the directorship came the possibility of teaching some courses at the university. The president of the local COS assured him that they could raise funds to pay his salary of $800 for the year, so Ellwood, then twenty-seven, took the position. When he got to Lincoln, he discovered that he has been snookered— the COS was defunct and broke, and he was obliged to spend much of his time raising money to pay his own salary, in addition to coming up with money to support the 350 families in his charge. Moreover, he found that any teaching he did for the university would be for free.

Ellwood nevertheless succeeded brilliantly. He gave public lectures on the topic of modern charity and the need for a scientific approach, which were reprinted in the newspaper, and he raised money so that the COS was left with nearly $500 in the till at the end of the year. He also taught, without pay, two courses that other faculty had already organized, in sociology and social psychology. (The courses were given to him by the creator of the course, Cornell-trained philosopher A. Ross Hill, who had an appointment at Nebraska as professor of psychology and later would be president at the University of Missouri during Ellwood's time there.) He taught two others as well, one in "modern charities" and the other in "criminology." In the end the board of regents of the University of Nebraska made him a regular instructor of sociology with the title Lecturer, with pay. But when, in the spring of 1900, an offer arrived from the University of Missouri for a full professorial appointment at $1,500 a year, he quickly accepted. The position, at least as understood by T. H. Jesse, the president of the university, was continuous with the work he had done at Nebraska. Ellwood taught philanthropy, founded a COS in Columbia, and, as we shall see, did much more to fulfill the expectations that were placed upon him.

Ellwood's experience of the job market tells us something important about the way sociology worked at the time, about the Chicago department, and about the dependence of sociology on the reform movement. Henderson is typically treated in department histories as a joke—pious, ministerial, boring, and a poor substitute for Jane Addams. In fact, as Ellwood's experience shows, he was critical to the success of the department. Ellwood was talented and well trained. He had fulsome letters of recommendation. But these didn't open any doors. A letter from Jane Addams, a controversial figure, might have closed them more tightly. Henderson, however, was another matter. He was a prominent, respected, gutsy, and well-networked member of the philanthropic and reform world on which sociology depended, and his ministerial role and background allowed him to get away with serving as a public conscience. Nor was he a trivial person. In 1899 Henderson was fifty-one, the oldest member of the department, at the peak of his influence. He was serving as president of the National Conference on Charities and Corrections, the major "social work" and social reform organization of the time, and was the author of a string of influential works on charities and reform activities. He was certainly the best known and most published member of the department faculty. When he negotiated his relationship with the department and university, he insisted on taking the job of university chaplain—a position of influence on its own.[8] Moreover, the Christian tradition of witnessing against evil, together with his status as a minister and Christian, gave him a degree of special protection that enabled him to speak out "as a Christian" and say things that otherwise would have been regarded as radical and "agitational."

Chicago sociology, in short, needed Henderson far more than he needed Chicago sociology. And as both an ambassador for and proponent of sociology in the reform world in which he had established his reputation, he promoted the field in a way that was critical to its success simply by vocally endorsing and supporting it. Reformers such as Samuel W. Dike and others had earlier promoted the idea that social science as it applied to social problems should be a university subject, but Henderson went beyond this concept. In the entry on Henderson in Bliss's *Encyclopedia of Social Reform* (1897, 570), the much-reprinted bible of the movement, he is identified with the belief "in sociological science as an instrument of coordination of bodies of knowledge which in isolation would be sterile." This notion is a specific form of the influential idea that inspired the Pittsburgh Survey and the "survey movement"—that serious reform required the sharing of information and effort among the various philanthropies and reform movements in a city (cf. Turner 1996). The reformers around *Survey*, the dominant journal

8. The position was replaced, when Rockefeller Chapel was built, by the dean of the chapel, who held the rank of dean and participated in university decision making at the decanal level.

of reform, and notably its editor Paul Kellogg, believed that this coordinating role belonged to "social workers" (a category quite different and broader than the category it would become in the 1920s), who were supposed to have special expertise relevant to coordination.

The dominant point of view among "social workers," the generic term used to describe reform experts in this period, was that what was needed for successful reform were publicity and power, particularly the power to regulate. But they also believed that social workers had no need of research or principles beyond what was already known. They thought they knew, for example, what sort of food was healthy, and needed only to set and enforce standards. It is of course notorious that Jane Addams took neither notice of nor interest in the opinions of those whom Hull House served. The Pittsburgh Survey researchers were similarly insensitive. They railed against the way immigrant families resisted "Americanization" and sacrificed to provide traditional ethnic clothing for the weddings of their children, for example, never grasping that many of these immigrants intended to back-migrate (and very often did) (Morawska 1996) and that this was simply rational behavior. The mentality of the hectoring nanny here is the same as the mentality that supported Prohibition, a favorite cause of the social workers of the preprofessional period, and one they often regarded as a cure-all.[9]

To justify itself, sociology had to make a claim that ran in a different direction—toward the claim that more knowledge was needed—and Henderson was the most prominent member of the older reform movement who was willing to make this argument. Henderson's idea of the special value of sociology in making sense of the connections between different social problems may seem to be so flimsy as to be undeserving of comment. But the idea is central to, and indeed realized in, Ellwood's social problems textbook, which is discussed in more detail later in the chapter. Ellwood, moreover, treated Henderson with respect and responded to him in the classic fashion of academic clientelism, as someone to whom Ellwood owed something and who provided a relationship that Ellwood needed. When Henderson urgently requested that he write a chapter on the history of English poor relief, Ellwood put aside the theorizing that interested him and produced a substantial piece of scholarship for him (1903). Providing for translations of Simmel for the *AJS*,[10] which he also did, was of course clien-

9. It gets ahead of our story, but it is not irrelevant, that the reformers defended prohibition to the end and that there was an important epistemic or methodological dimension to this defense: they claimed to have a special kind of "social work knowledge" not vouchsafed to mere sociologists. The fallout over Prohibition was one reason for the bitterness of the split with sociology in the 1920s (cf. Turner 1996).

10. The translations were done by Ellwood's student (and a minister) Elwang.

telism of the same sort, in this case fealty to Albion Small. But it was Henderson who exerted the greater pull, asking more and getting more.

The relationship of Chicago sociology to Henderson was a variation on a pattern found throughout sociology, which Ellwood himself would soon reproduce in his own Department of Sociology at Missouri. When Franklin H. Giddings began to travel from Bryn Mawr to Columbia University to teach sociology, it was the beginning of Columbia sociology as distinct from the statistics taught by Richmond Mayo-Smith, a topic that had formed part of the original subject matter of the faculty of political science. But teaching principles of sociology was a minor part of what Columbia's sociology courses originally did. Giddings's students—in a program that was exclusively graduate—were overwhelmingly women who were concerned with social problems, and typically they were destined for careers in charities. Giddings himself was appointed only because of the donations and bargaining of Seth Low, board member and social reformer.

The idea that sociology could have even gained a foothold in universities without the support of reformers, or by the rejection of them, in favor of purity or an ideal of science is illusory. It was only in the 1920s, when the Rockefeller philanthropists, and particularly Beardsley Ruml, grasped that the reformers had overstated their knowledge of social problems and that regulation, and power weren't enough, that sociology received serious financial support. But it did so not as an alternative to reform but as an alternative to the reformers, who were seen to have failed: in addition to the disaster of Prohibition there was the failure of the juvenile courts movement to live up to its promised impact on juvenile crime (cf. Sealander 1997) and the failure of the Pittsburgh Survey to produce any long-lasting effects (the reform mayor that it had brought into office was turned out when he ran for a second term). In the face of these failures, sociology and the social sciences came to be regarded as a necessary intermediate step to successful reform. When the expected reformist results from their huge investment in the social sciences were not forthcoming, the Rockefeller investment was rethought and, in the early 1930s, drastically cut. But by this time sociology was established as an academic discipline.

Reform at Missouri

Ellwood's early career shows how closely the expectations of reformers and the assumption that sociology would serve the cause of reform were bound up with the presence of sociology in the university. By 1900, when Ellwood was called to the University of Missouri at Columbia to establish a program in sociology, there was already a long prehistory of "sociology" at the university, indeed one of the longest in American universities. In 1872, Augustus W. Alexander of the state's Board of Guardians had written a lengthy letter about the need for instruction in sociology, which was motivated in part by concerns over what he called "social pathology" but which also displayed considerable knowledge of Comte and Spencer (University of Missouri Archives, UW:1/4/1, box 2, folder 4A). Spencer's sociology was taught in a course given by the president of the university, Samuel Laws, during the 1886–87 academic year, in the Department of Metaphysics; it covered the social sciences and philosophy. The Cornell philosopher Frank Thilly had taught an ethics course that was largely sociological in the years before Ellwood arrived (Bernard papers [Chicago], box 1, folder 5).

The mix of the reform and the academic was always present. Ellwood knew that the position had been created in part as a result of the support of Mary Perry, a prominent Missouri reformer, and that her support needed to be repaid. This was the university president's understanding as well. Shortly after Ellwood arrived, President Jesse gave him the task of studying the state's poor houses and jails. His letter of December 2, 1902, to Ellwood was straightforward: "I do not mean to divert you at all from other forms of work, but I never would have persuaded the curators to establish this chair except through the prospect of having this work done. Nothing would commend the chair so much to the people of Missouri" (Ellwood papers). Ellwood did the survey and fulfilled a good many other requests of the same kind. The results of the survey proved to be highly controversial and were widely reported in Missouri newspapers and beyond. The study made him, briefly, into a national celebrity in reform circles, and he was invited to give a talk at the national conference of Charities and Corrections as a result.

This sort of undertaking was precisely what was expected of him—outside the university and at the level of the president, at a time when the state university was under the most direct sort of scrutiny by state politicians. Letters from the governor (typically, in Ellwood's case, encouraging and supportive) arrived with some frequency. Yet Ellwood was far from willing to be merely a social welfare researcher, and his academic peers also expected more—indeed his very presence in the job reflected the backstage efforts of Thilly and others on behalf of their very scholarly old Cornell friend. Ellwood's own predilections and circumstance led to a set of compromises. He tried to give intellectual content to the problems that he was expected to deal with. And although he did the practical work of both research and networking that reformism and charity work demanded, he was also eager to delegate it. By the middle of the 1910s, he had made the Columbia COS, for which he was responsible in a "volunteer" capacity, into a project that part-time staff of the department could carry out with the help of university students. In the 1920s he withdrew completely from this work, to devote his effort to research and writing. But he created a department in which others could do the work, and the people he hired, such as Augustus Kuhlman, were very good at what they did and became nationally respected leaders in social welfare work.

This example, in the microcosm of Columbia, Missouri, was a pattern that occurred in more complex and variegated forms in universities in the major cities. The connections in New York between Columbia University sociology and the COS were also intense, and Giddings himself served on the boards of settlement houses and the like. But as with Henderson at Chicago, there was a need for a full-time liaison to this world. Giddings, who had been compelled to do the liaison work himself, got two after a decade at Columbia: first, a social worker, Edward Thomas Devine, and shortly after, Samuel McCune Lindsay. Both were, as Henderson had been, leaders of important reform associations. Devine was general secretary of the Charity Organization Society of New York, and Lindsay, a specialist on social legislation, was secretary of the National Child Labor Committee and for several years was president of the American Academy of Political and Social Science. It took Ellwood only five years to get someone to do this work for him; in 1905-6 he was able to employ the first additional faculty member in sociology, another Chicago product, T. J. Riley, for precisely the same purpose.

Establishing the Discipline in the University

Even though Ellwood found people to take up the burdens of training social workers, he never felt a conflict between sociology and reform. He was a leader in creating the Missouri chapter of the National Conference on Charities and Corrections and a founding figure of a school for training social workers. He also made sociology into a successful academic discipline at the University of Missouri. By the mid-1920s the department was expanding quickly, reporting enrollments of 3,000, and no longer dependent on its claim to serve social welfare.

By this time the field of sociology as a whole was booming. In contrast to the state of affairs in 1899, a strong academic market for sociologists had developed. Ellwood was a significant contributor to this market. The department had a strong record of graduating BAs and MAs who went on to prominent academic careers in sociology. Among them were Irene Tauber and Carle Zimmerman, who spent the bulk of their careers at Princeton and Harvard, respectively, and three others who received BAs or MAs during this era who became presidents of the ASS: L. L. Bernard, Herbert Blumer, and E. B. Reuter.[11] It was department practice, long after Ellwood left, to encourage graduate students to earn a PhD elsewhere. But one of Ellwood's few Missouri PhD students, Carl Taylor, became an ASS president, and the Missouri department was ranked sixth in the first reputational ranking of graduate programs by field in 1925.[12] It was also the highest ranked program within the university. The state of Missouri also ranked second nationally in the number of secondary school students taught sociology, reflecting Ellwood's special interest in high school sociology.

How did Ellwood get the program to this level? Much of it depended on his own talent as a lecturer and his personal qualities. The quality of teaching, something that tends to disappear in histories of sociology, is a theme of many of the biographical statements of the sociologists who came into the discipline during this period. L. L. Bernard, who was a student in 1903-4 and later a member of the department, described his experience in this way: "Ellwood proved not to be a radical and his teaching was clear as crystal. I have always felt he had a wonderful power of clarity. He was also personally charming and sympathetic" (Bernard n.d., 3).[13] Growth depended on good teaching: the highly Germanic manner of Max Meyer, the brilliant but eccentric professor of psychology appointed at the same time as Ellwood, kept psychology enrollments low and kept the psychology department from growing.

The way the curriculum developed was partly a matter of Ellwood's preferences but largely a matter of survival. Ellwood began with a list of courses that reflected both the expectations that he would supply training

11. Undergraduate degrees had a large importance for both Ellwood and his earliest students. Ellwood was helped by his Cornell connections and maintained them all his life. In his first job, at Nebraska, it was a Cornell philosopher and psychologist, A. Ross Hill, who later became president of the University of Missouri and gave him the Social Psychology course. Circumstantial evidence suggests that another Cornell contemporary, Frank Thilly, was a moving force behind the creation of a chair in sociology and behind Ellwood's appointment. Ellwood also took a strong interest in the fate of his students. His relation to Irene Tauber was almost paternal. He encouraged her, recommended her to graduate school, and supported her career. She wrote to him regularly until his death. His relation to L. L. Bernard, which was tempestuous, was the most intense that either had with another sociologist. And he kept in touch with Paul Super, one of the first two students to take his courses, who made a career in the YMCA, ending his career as head of the wartime Polish YMCA.

12. Missouri was ranked after Chicago, Columbia, Wisconsin, Michigan, and Harvard and ahead of Pennsylvania, North Carolina, Yale, Illinois, Ohio State, Cornell, and Bryn Mawr.

13. Ellwood was not alone in this. One is struck, in reading the Bernard autobiographies, how often teaching, and particularly high-quality lecturing, was a consideration in the development of interests in sociology that would lead to academic careers.

in charities' work as well as provide scholarly content. But success in competing for students was certainly an important consideration. The major issue that Ellwood faced in attracting students was finding courses beyond the introductory course that would draw students. The introductory course itself was always critical, and Ellwood kept the task of teaching the introductory course for himself. It proved to be a good method of recruiting. In 1901-2 he was drawing a respectable 62 students. But attracting students to a second course was a problem. The next most popular course that was part of the normal curriculum was the course on ethnology, with 15 students, followed by American Charities, with 14. After his second year with the department Ellwood wrote to the university president expressing his concerns: when he had chosen to restrict the introductory class to second-year students, the class had become even smaller. The president was reassuring. He observed that it was to be expected that disciplines like history and mathematics would have greater demand than sociology. But it was clear that student demand would drive the development of the department and that it was essential to attract students to more than the introductory course, and in a few years Ellwood had the number up to 69, with only 3 freshman. The eventual shape of the curriculum was the result of a series of compromises driven by necessity but also shaped by Ellwood's own ideas about sociology, his interest in theory, and his belief in the importance of anthropology to sociology.

It is something of a puzzle, given the importance of reform motives and the demand for social workers, why the more practically minded sociologists did not simply take over the early discipline of sociology. Ellwood's experience shows why. More emphasis on reform topics was not the solution to the problem of enrollment. The American Charities course, with fourteen students, was not popular enough to serve as a base on which much could be built, much less as the core of an undergraduate major. This meant that figures like Henderson were not in a position to seize control of departments, even if they were so inclined. Yet Ellwood never neglected the philanthropic base he was given to work with. As I have noted, he engaged the sociology students as workers in the Columbia COS, which he ran for many years, and in survey work in Columbia that applied the strategies of the "survey movement" generally (of which Ellwood was a strong supporter) and hired social work–oriented faculty to teach fieldwork and social welfare from 1905 on. This hiring reached a peak toward the end of his time at Missouri, in the late 1920s, after Ellwood himself had chosen, in the early 1920s, to withdraw from this kind of work as much as possible to pursue his own research and writing. His appointments in this area included women and at least two scholars who went on to distinguished careers: A. F. Kuhlman, who had been attracted to sociology through working with the community survey (a common pattern that shows up elsewhere in sociology), and Carl Taylor, who wrote a dissertation under Ellwood that was one of the first books on the survey method and became an important rural sociologist (and one of the very few in that field to become an ASS president).

Ellwood's appeal went beyond being an excellent lecturer and the person responsible for education in philanthropic work. He was also a distinctive campus persona, as a result of two special interests of his that were especially relevant to the intellectual life of students at the time: Christianity and evolution. Ellwood was a staunch evolutionist, both biologically and sociologically, though his use of the notion in sociology was anti–social Darwinist and aligned with L. T. Hobhouse's notion that social evolution needed to be understood as a learning process leading to social betterment through the evolution of a more rational, which meant more cooperative and altruistic, morality.[14] Ellwood's evolutionism was vivid and continuously expressed, leading him to become known on campus as "the monkey man."[15] One suspects that had Ellwood been a philosophical materialist and atheist, his views would not have had the same impact on students. But he was not: he was an outspoken Christian. It is clear that part of the attraction to him and his courses grew out of this fact—as did some of the hostility and ridicule that he generated. The two were sides of the same coin, but it was a coin that was important for many students at the time.

Ellwood's Christianity would be a good focus for a chapter of its own, and indeed one was written in the 1940s (Hughley 1948), at a time of theological upheaval. It is the aspect of Ellwood that is the most difficult, a century on, to reconstruct. Yet it is crucial to the story of Ellwood and to the role he played in developing departments in academic sociology. He was hired at Duke (a university founded with a specific Christian identity) in 1930 precisely for his prominence as a Christian sociologist, and the president, William Preston Few, justifiably regarded Ellwood as one of his best appointments, for he fit the task of representing the university as a safe place

---

14. Social Darwinism itself was largely a retrospective invention of Richard Hofstadter, himself a heavily ideological interpreter of American history in the Parsonian "consensus" mold (cf. Novick 1988).

15. One of his former students, R. L. Myers, who became the superintendent of Dade County (Miami, Florida) schools in the 1920s, wrote to him recalling their conversations on the subject while Myers was a student and ruefully admitting that, resistant as he had been to Ellwood's views at the time, he was now a convert (Myers to Ellwood, November 3, 1923, Bernard Papers, Duke University Archives).

to send students. At Missouri, a state university, matters were different. Teaching Christianity itself was out of the question: that was left to a private school of religion operating across the street from the campus and a Christian junior college operating across town. There was, however, constant suspicion among the faculty that Ellwood was teaching religion under the guise of sociology.[16] This was an issue with a course in sociology of religion that he proposed in 1905.

Ellwood addressed this problem in a variety of ways in his career. In his early years at Missouri he taught a course, for credit, but apparently voluntarily and beyond his ordinary duties, titled the Social Teachings of Jesus. Enrollments were so large, 28 in 1901, that by 1905 Ellwood limited enrollment to 17. What role these courses had in promoting sociology is not clear. Certainly they made Ellwood and therefore sociology more acceptable to Christian parents concerned about the consequences of college education, an issue of importance in this period and also later during Ellwood's time at Duke. There was, however, considerable overlap between religion and reform, and especially in the area of philanthropy. Most of the leading figures in philanthropy were religious in background and motivation, and tracts and disquisitions on the social mission of the church formed a significant part of the literature on reform. The Social Gospel, a heterogeneous and increasingly incoherent movement, was part of the theological background justifying reform, so the elective affinities between these aspects of the circumstances of early sociology would have been important whether Ellwood had been a professing Christian or not.

Nevertheless, the effect of instruction in sociology under Ellwood, and later by other faculty in the expanded department of the 1910s and 1920s, was not to promote religion, or even the antimaterialism (and later antibehaviorism) to which Ellwood was committed. Indeed, in the most prominent cases, Bernard and Taylor, his teaching promoted the exact opposite: both were more behaviorist and more materialist as a result of their education at Missouri. To be sure, there were many other sources of these views in the university, not least in the psychology department, but students seemed more likely to be stimulated to rethink their views by exposure to debate than to indoctrination.

16. In the prehistory of sociology, during the era just before and after the Civil War, college curricula routinely finished with a course on moral philosophy that contained sociological elements. In the early part of the period it typically included Paley's *A View of the Evidences of Christianity* (1803) as a textbook, and the intrusion of theological elements was common. In the history of sociology at Cornell given to Bernard, it is wryly observed that in one precursor course, Philosophy of History, "the Divinity bulked large in influence" among "the agents that control the causes and results of history" (Bernard papers [Chicago], box 1, folder 5).

Sociology in the Departmental Ecology of the University

Some interpreters of the history of American sociology have stressed the role of competition and differentiation in the early years of university sociology and suggested that local circumstances produced different solutions to the problem of finding a place for sociology. Charles Camic (1995), for example, argues against those historians of sociology, such as Dorothy Ross (1991) and Robert Bannister (1987), who have stressed the biographical origins of particular intellectual commitments of the founding generation that were manifested in the forms their "sociology" took, claiming that this focus has led them to overlook the local contexts of the shifting definitions and boundaries of sociology as it developed in different departmental traditions. These local academic relationships are difficult to disentangle,[17] but the point is worth pursuing. What Columbia, Harvard, and Chicago became a century later, and remained, in some discernable degree, is still marked by these original circumstances. Missouri presents the same picture: the local circumstances were different, as were the long-term outcomes.

Ellwood, from his undergraduate days, was committed intellectually to the idea of a psychological conception of society, as we have seen. His dissertation was an application of Dewey's functional psychology to the problem of the nature of society. And his important first theoretical book, *Soci-*

17. Some of Camic's claims are misleading. At Columbia, for example, Giddings was not, as Camic argues, swept up in the craze for statistics as a result of the local circumstance of the power of the "economist" Mayo-Smith, whom he sought to emulate. The statistical tradition Mayo-Smith represented was part of the original design of the Graduate Faculty of Political Science, of "statistics" based on the Prussian state statistics model. Mayo-Smith was much less of an economist than Giddings himself. During his pre-academic career in journalism, Giddings (a former student of civil engineering) had played a prominent role in the Connecticut Valley Economics Association, one of the precursors to the American Economic Association, had published a classic economics article on profit sharing, had been fascinated with index numbers (a fascination that continues in his own extensive writings on measurement and in his student F. S. Chapin's famous living-room scale of social class), and had proposed index numbers for measuring inflation. Moreover, his first scientific publication, which was only partly statistical, was with the Massachusetts Bureau of Labor Statistics. What was more decisive for the development of statistics at Columbia were the exam and the requirements system in this faculty, which required two minors. It was a system that encouraged sociologists to take statistics (indeed made it normal and exposed them to some interesting and cutting-edge thinkers such as H. L. Moore and Franz Boas) and encouraged those in other fields to take sociology. R. E. Merriam, the pivotal figure in Rockefeller philanthropy, took a course from Giddings, for example, and it was possible for Columbia students to have careers like that of Harry Elmer Barnes, who combined history and sociology, or in Ogburn's case, economics and sociology.

ology and Its Psychological Aspects (with Howard Jensen; 1912/1915), was on this theme. In his methodological writings he argued that the way for sociology to become scientific was not, in Chomsky's phrase (1967), by imitating the surface features of the natural sciences but by acquainting itself with biology and psychology and making its theories continuous with them. This position was the opposite from Durkheim's idea of the special and distinct character of sociology as a science with an autonomous subject matter, and he resolutely opposed this conception.

The local psychologist, Max Meyer, however, was not a Deweyan but a protobehaviorist (and much more; cf. Esper 1967). Meyer later commented that "I found it necessary to combat the opinion held by some insiders, that is, faculty members, that 'what Meyer taught was not psychology at all, but some kind of materialism'" (Max Meyer Incident papers). This quote is a reference to Ellwood, but Ellwood's students took Meyer's courses (indeed, because of Meyer's relative unpopularity they were an important source of students for advanced classes in psychology) and were deeply influenced by him. Both Blumer and Bernard, and even Taylor, were converted to his views.[18] Despite Ellwood's hostility to this kind of psychology, there was a modus vivendi, and Missouri sociology students were especially inclined to psychology.

Ellwood's own closest connections, however, were to philosophy, which produced another long-term feature of the department: its commitment to theory. Thilly had been on the committee that had recommended the chair in sociology and an appointment for Meyer (initially in a department of philosophy and psychology, although the departments were soon separated). Ellwood considered his connections with philosophy important as a source of scholarly standards and a model of respectability, as a source of political support in the university, and as an outlet for publication. One of his first papers, still available on the Web, was "Aristotle as a Sociologist" (1902), and Ellwood published many articles in ethics journals presenting the sociological point of view. Ellwood was present, and gave one of the eight papers (on Tarde), at the founding meeting of the Western Philosophical Associa-

---

18. There is a debate in symbolic interactionism about what Blumer got from Ellwood and Meyer. Blumer said that he learned scientific methodology from Meyer, but it is likely he learned much more: one of Meyer's books, with the telltale title *Psychology of the Other-One: An Introductory Text-Book of Psychology* (1921), came out when Blumer was a student (see also *Abnormal Psychology: "When the Other-One Astonishes Us"* [1927]), raising the question of how much of symbolic interactionism he possessed before his encounter with Mead at the end of the 1920s. Moreover, Blumer's conception of society and his later critique of the concept of attitude and of Thomas represent Ellwood's similar, and strongly held, views.

tion, of which Thilly was president. This meeting is considered the originating event of the American Philosophical Association. Thilly soon left Missouri, first for Princeton, then for Cornell (where he became dean and continued to keep a supportive eye on Ellwood, and in the 1920s attempted unsuccessfully to engineer his appointment). Among Ellwood's other colleagues in philosophy in his first decade at Missouri were A. O. Lovejoy, later to create the program History of Ideas at Johns Hopkins, and George Sabine.[19] Sabine was to produce the standard one-volume history of political theory (*A History of Political Theory*, 1937/1973), the dominant text for decades; Thilly did the same in philosophy (*A History of Philosophy*, 1914/1957). The books, which consciously combined context and criticism (Leo Strauss denounced Sabine's book as a history of error), were similar in style and approach to Ellwood's own *A History of Social Philosophy* (1938).[20]

Ellwood's academic life after 1925 raises a new set of issues, which I return to in a later section. Before leaving the period of "establishment," however, a few important topics need to be addressed. One is the problem of "schools of sociology." When Ellwood began studying sociology, and for the period up to 1925, Chicago and Columbia, and of course Yale, were distinct schools that shared the discipline of "sociology" as a kind of friendly condominium, without taking one another's approaches very seriously. Yale continued this approach well into the 1930s. These departments did not hire from one another but hired internally to the extent they hired at all. There were a few exceptions, such as Robert Park, but he was in effect a homegrown product as well. In a sense, a discipline is fundamentally an internal market in PhD's with the same label, and the real test of having achieved a wider market is that major departments respect one another's claims to legitimate representation, which implies the hiring of one another's PhD's (cf. Turner 2000). Sociology did not have such a market, in the top departments, until the late 1920s. Ellwood's tenure at Missouri represented a kind of transition from this "schools" stage to that of a full market. He hired five Chicago PhD's in the time he was at Missouri, and another at Duke (including his best hire, Edgar Thompson, made on the recommen-

19. Lovejoy (later to be a founder of the AAUP) was hired at Missouri after being ousted from Stanford for his religious views. Public universities were then still a refuge from persecution. Sabine had been a Cornell undergraduate (see n. 11).

20. This book ends with the conflict between Ward and Sumner over the efficacy of social intervention and contrasts very strongly with the canon of Marx, Weber, and Durkheim that was established after 1945. Like the Thilly and Sabine texts, it includes many minor figures. Ellwood's favorite is Turgot, who has vanished from the "sociological" canon but for whom Ellwood makes a strong case.

dation of Blumer). In this sense Missouri functioned as a Chicago dependent. But Ellwood was also one of the first heads of a major department to hire a Columbia PhD, Maurice Parmelee, in 1910.

There is another aspect of the "schools" issue. Much has been written by Bernard about Ellwood's lack of tolerance of views that conflicted with his own. This is a complex matter. It is clear that Ellwood's hiring and expectations of loyalty, intellectually and personally, reflected the idea that his appointees ought to teach and follow his way of doing sociology, particularly his psychological approach to society and his antimaterialism, and to some extent his Christian viewpoint. In fact, some did and some did not, and he had stormy relations with those who did not, notably Bernard himself, and also Parmalee, who later blamed Ellwood's influence for his inability to get an appointment in sociology (Parmalee to Bernard, August 10, 1945, Bernard papers [PSU], box 36, folder 11). But Parmalee and Bernard had difficulty getting along with anyone, and in practice Ellwood tolerated those whose views and interests were different from his. He was particularly tolerant of personal criticism. Blumer's MA thesis, written under Ellwood's supervision and approved by him, contains pages of criticism, some of it quite scathing, of Ellwood's own work on revolutions, work of which Ellwood was especially proud (1922, 120-24). Yet Ellwood not only hired Blumer, but he supported him and kept up a relationship with him until his death. Most of his students, such as Zimmerman and Taylor, were drawn to what he would have considered materialism and to an idea of objectivity that excluded the idea of scientific social betterment. But Ellwood, like Giddings and Small, did think of himself as having a distinctive system of ideas that justified his treating his department as a school, and he never quite abandoned this idea, although he moderated it over time. In fact, it did not work: his appointments, like Bernard, and his students, such as Taylor, went their own way. But they were also marked by their experience with Ellwood. Bernard was labeled as a theorist in his appointment at Minnesota, and in the thirties he became a rebel against standard sociology; Blumer became an insider at Chicago, but he also became the most prominent critic of what was to become, in Andrew Abbott's phrase, "variable centered sociology."

Inventing "Social Problems" and Separating from "Social Work"

The literature available to "social workers" at the end of the nineteenth century was extraordinarily extensive. A series of the editions of the one-volume *Encyclopedia of Social Reform* (Bliss 1897) contained articles with extensive biographies on every conceivable social problem as well as on such institutions as workingmen's churches and the views of religious denominations on matters related to reform. The literature was not, however, an academic literature. Much of it consisted of official statistics, studies of social welfare schemes of other countries, and hortatory texts taking a stance against a problem or for a policy. Textbooks, and especially comprehensive, balanced, surveys, were harder to come by. The standard book for courses on philanthropy, under which such topics as pauperism and orphans were treated, was Amos Warner's *American Charities* (1894/1989), and this volume was still in use in Ellwood's department in 1910, when he passed the course off to Parmalee.[21]

Ellwood not only produced the first social problems textbook, he did it very early. The first edition, *Sociology and Modern Social Problems,* appeared in 1910. Eventually this text, which underwent various title changes, was to sell over 300,000 copies, an astonishing number given the relatively small size of the American college student population in the era in which it was a dominant text, and the fact that the standardized textbook market was as yet underdeveloped. A few words about this market and its evolution are necessary for us to contextualize this achievement and understand the most important difference between prewar sociology and the sociology that followed. One striking statistic should make this contrast clear. Before 1950 more than 80 percent of the ASA presidents had themselves written an introductory textbook. Ellwood was among those who had not. Yet Ellwood was apparently the single most successful textbook author of them all. Howard Odum, Ellwood's near neighbor for many years and himself a prolific author as well as an editor of an important series for a textbook publisher, repeated the claim that Ellwood had more than a million books in print worldwide. This was an exaggeration, but it points to the legendary stature of Ellwood's achievements.

The trajectory of Ellwood's social problems texts, however, deserves some special discussion. Warner's *American Charities* (1894/1989) was the only book of its kind. It was not merely a descriptive work. Its aim was to understand and explain the underlying principles under which relief had been given in the past, and was in this sense an analytic text, but what it analyzed were not the problems themselves but the means of dealing with them. Ellwood's text covered some of the same material—the poor, dependent children, the feebleminded, the insane, and so forth. But he did some-

21. As Parmalee later said in an April 17, 1945, letter to Sullenger: "I continued to use Warner's book in spite of the fact that I could hardly stomach its vapid and artificial nature" (Bernard papers [PSU], box 36, folder 11).

thing much more radical, which amounted in its own way to a conceptual revolution in thinking about social problems. The basic idea of his social problem text was that social problems were interrelated, that monocausal explanations of social problems were defective, and that, as a consequence of the interrelations between the various social problems and the impossibility of manipulating the causes of social problems in the simplistic fashion favored by monocausal theorists, the only "solution" to the social problem in its full interrelations was education.

Education is a notion that has many meanings in Ellwood's thought, but it is sufficiently central, and points to such a crucial strand in early American sociology, that it deserves some attention. One of Ellwood's last writings, his *History of Social Philosophy* (1938), concluded with a discussion of Lester F. Ward and William Graham Sumner. Written during the Depression and the Roosevelt administration, the work was an endorsement of the ideas of Ward over Sumner, meaning in particular the idea that intelligent social intervention was possible, contra Sumner. Ellwood took the idea of education to be Ward's central idea and central to his sociology, and remained loyal to this idea, and to Ward, through his whole career. In public addresses about social problems, he returned repeatedly to the theme of education, touting education as the only and necessary approach to the solution of crucial social problems, even predicting that students would at some point be given far more extensive education than that under the current school system.

Later critics, notably C. Wright Mills, whose meretricious "The Professional Ideology of Social Pathologists" (1943) attacked Ellwood and others, saw this sort of reformism as namby-pamby and preferred a kind of Marxism, which he accused the "ideologists of social pathology" of having failed to consider. But Ellwood certainly knew what Marxism was about: he had personally sponsored the socialist club at the University of Missouri, had hired Maurice Parmalee, one of the most Red American sociologists, and, when Parmalee left, had replaced him with Max Handman, a Chicago PhD who had written a dissertation on Marx. Ellwood had himself published a major critique of Marx in the *AJS*, "Marx's Economic Determinism in the Light of Modern Psychology" (1911), and included a lengthy discussion of Marxism, under the title "Economic Interpretations of the Social Problem," in the first edition of *Sociology and Modern Social Problems* (1910). The Marxism discussion (1910, 340–50) takes up nearly the entire chapter.[22] To Ell-

---

22. In his later, shorter, "public sociology" book, *The Social Problem: A Constructive Analysis* (1919), the discussion is only a few pages within a larger chapter titled "Economic Elements."

wood, however, Marxism in the end was a monocausal, economistic explanation of the social problem, and it suffered from the usual defects of monocausal explanations. There was no lack of systemic thinking about social problems in Ellwood. Indeed, this was precisely the revolution that Ellwood's textbook introduced. Social problems in Ellwood's hands were societal problems, mutually reinforcing, insoluble by reformists' nostrums, and approachable only by strategies that reflected their interrelation. Some of the interrelations were obvious, and the thesis lent itself to overstatement. The relationship between broken homes and juvenile delinquency, for example, which was a theme both of the textbook and of Ellwood's public speaking, made his point about mutual reinforcement, but did so in a way that did not challenge the moralism of the reform element, and indeed traded on it.

Even this simple example is a useful indication of the contrast between Ellwood and the reformers. Merely providing playground equipment, or a place for the children of the poor to entertain themselves in settlement houses, or special juvenile courts, all of which were major reform initiatives of the time directed at juveniles, were not effective solutions to the problem of juvenile home life and supervision as created by the fact of divorce. And no significant change in juvenile delinquency could reasonably be expected by any of these reforms. Nor indeed could the problem of divorce itself be made to go away without an assault on these systemic causes. This kind of reasoning about social problems, which appears repeatedly both in Ellwood's social problems texts and his public lectures, returns these problems to their sources in particular aspects of the surrounding social life and society. And this in the end became the message of sociology to the social reform movement itself.

Where did this leave "social work"? Ellwood remained, as I have noted, continually involved in charity work until the 1920s. The Department of Sociology at Missouri did as well: as late as 1940 a specialist on social welfare was appointed to a faculty position, and in the late 1920s, at the end of Ellwood's time there, several were members of the department. But Ellwood's role in this work went far beyond, to the point of being a founding figure of social work in the state of Missouri. His major effort was the creation of a training school for social workers in St. Louis, the Missouri School of Social Economy. The school grew out of a series of lectures on social problems in 1906 "under the auspices of a local committee" (Bernard papers [PSU], box 14, file 7). T. J. Riley, the Chicago PhD who was Ellwood's first hire, was made director of the school, and the Russell Sage Foundation (RSF) provided some start-up funds. Appointments to the school soon followed, and in 1909 the first class graduated. The school grew, and both casework and research were part of the training. In 1912 Riley left to become secretary of the Brooklyn Bureau of Charities, and the school was without a head. At this point the local supporters of the school sought to make a connection with a local university, the private Washington University, which agreed to sponsor it, but only on the condition that it cost the university nothing. When the RSF money eventually dried up in 1916, the board went back to the University of Missouri, which provided a small amount of support from the Extension fund. The school expanded rapidly during the war, providing Red Cross workers. After the war, it was quick to expand its casework teaching, psychiatric and psychological training, and training in public health. In 1923 it came to a bitter end when a legislator's amendment to a crucial bill killed the school. The Brown School of Social Work was started almost immediately by Washington University a year later, eventually becoming one of the top schools nationally.

This success story was for Ellwood a source of pride but also of frustration. The ambitious social work program that he inaugurated, as the name of the school indicated, was not just concerned with casework, the inheritance of the COS, but focused on social legislation and larger issues of policy and on understanding social problems sociologically and through community research. This approach proved not to work well with local charities, and the early graduates had difficulty finding employment in St. Louis, partly because the charities were dominated by local elites who preferred traditional COS-style casework.[23] What makes this failure ironic is that the Brown School of Social Work, which was the successor to this experiment and which succeeded in appealing to the local charities, is, seventy-five years later, focused on the same kinds of matters of policy and research that the original school had concerned itself with.

Money, Factionalism, and Science: Sociology Divides

The issue of money is an intriguing theme within the history of sociology, one not unrelated to some of its antagonisms as well as to the professional behavior of its members. The rise of foundation funding in the 1920s cre-

23. The teachers in the school were almost all unmarried women, and more generally in the charities world much of the power was in the hands of strong-minded older women with money, who were customarily approached with deference and respect. The early records of the Russell Sage Foundation (itself, of course, dominated by Olivia Sage) are full of examples, especially in the memorials, written on the death of board members, that are found in the RSF papers. As the names of Ethel Dummer and Helen Calvert make clear, such women also had a great deal of power over sociologists as well—at least until the Laura Spelman Rockefeller Memorial Foundation became the major funder of sociology in the 1920s.

ated a two-class system in sociology. Professors in the foundation-funded class were able to spend summers writing and, in the case of many of those involved with the Social Science Research Council, to spend them in Vermont or New Hampshire near Dartmouth, where the SSRC supported lengthy summer meetings, a practice that continued for many years. Books that were not textbooks were ordinarily published by subsidy, either indirectly through subventions to the university press or directly by grants to authors. Thorstein Veblen, for example, paid guarantees for all his books— only *The Theory of the Leisure Class* made back the guarantee. Foundation funding allowed for direct subsidies of books, as was the case with Parsons's *The Structure of Social Action,* and also provided university presses with the resources to publish social science by the faculty and PhD's of the favored universities. The classics of academic social science before World War II, including *Middletown* (Lynd 1929), were published on a subsidy basis. Ellwood was never supported by Rockefeller money, and even though he had a letter-writing relationship with Raymond Fosdick, a powerful trustee of Rockefeller philanthropies, he was a critic of the gangland-style coercive tactics of the quantitatively oriented scientizers who dominated the SSRC.[24] The issue of money combined with many other issues, generational and intellectual, produced the beginnings of the bitter hostility that has marked sociology ever since.

These issues came to a head in 1928 over the presidency of the ASS. Professional associations like the ASS rarely had contested elections for officers—the positions involved work but were largely honorific, so the idea of proposing and defeating candidates was inappropriate and considered humiliating. It was not until the Vietnam War that the American Political Science Association had a contested election. Sociology had a similarly high degree of comity until the advent of the SSRC and the scientizers. Ellwood was, for example, on good terms with Giddings, who even wrote endorsements for his religious books, and indeed Ellwood was friendly with many other people he did not particularly agree with.[25] The next generation, including his own student, the chronically querulous L. L. Bernard, and W. F. Ogburn (with whom Ellwood nevertheless had a polite relationship), was a different matter. They were eager to push the older generation out, and there was for the first time a strong incentive for collusion and mutual support: capturing the largesse of the SSRC and the Rockefeller philan-

24. Like others in the universities not favored by the foundations, they found themselves on the outside of a system that provided huge benefits to those on the inside.

25. An exception was W. I. Thomas, a consummate insider, whom Ellwood loathed.

thropies. The conflict came to a head with a floor challenge to the selection of Emory Bogardus for the presidency, in favor of Ogburn. Ogburn was elected, charges of conspiracy were traded, and friendships suffered. Ogburn gave a famously truculent presidential address in which he implicitly attacked the earlier generation in the form of praise for a very explicit and very narrow notion of objectivity. The bitterness was consolidated a few years later with the founding of the invitation-only Sociological Research Association, which still functions as an elite faction.[26] Needless to say, Ellwood, whose collected essays criticizing the scientizers appeared in 1933 (*Methods in Sociology*), was excluded from this group.

Ellwood was, however, an exceptionally successful member of what was to become the hostile underclass of sociology. At the time, summer schools at universities were organized as, in effect, separate businesses, often with their own dean. These summer schools provided opportunities to hire faculty from elsewhere, thus exposing their graduate students to these faculty, but also to generate some profit for the university.[27] Students themselves often used the summer to take courses elsewhere, at attractive summer locations. The University of Colorado Summer School became a successful institution, bringing in major teachers, and other universities were able to build up a substantial summer school program that provided employment for professors from other universities. Ellwood was a major factor in the success of the Colorado Summer School, teaching there in 1911, 1915, 1917, 1921, 1922, and 1924. Virtually every other year he taught summer school as well—at Columbia, Wisconsin, the National Summer School in Utah, Chicago, Colorado Agricultural College, University of Southern California, NYU, Harvard, Northwestern, and in 1939 at UCLA, where he had an important impact on the creation of the department (and where he placed one of his most successful students, Duke graduate Leonard Broom).[28] But this was success only in comparison with that of others who were also teaching and writing academics, not in comparison with beneficiaries of foundations. Professors taught because they needed the money,

26. This pattern of factional, semisecret, invitation-only organizations was not unique to sociology. S. S. Stevens had a similar and in some ways even more militant (though smaller) group in psychology.

27. It is said that the rise of Henry Kissinger began with his role in selecting faculty for the Harvard summer school in the post–World War II period, during which time he had contact with the best faculty of other universities.

28. Originally UCLA sociology was not only allied with but subordinated to anthropology, reflecting Ellwood's views on the importance of anthropology. Broom's dissertation was on the Cherokee, also reflecting Ellwood's views.

and money was an issue for Ellwood much of his career. Salary was a source of friction between him and A. Ross Hill, the president of the University of Missouri,[29] in the 1910s and continued to be an issue for him in the 1920s. At some point in the mid-1920s, Ellwood was eager to leave the university, and when he eventually did, for Duke, he gave salary as the explanation.

The better-paid faculty of the East and those with foundation support (two categories that overlapped), as well as those from the richer state universities, such as Wisconsin, lived very differently. They did not teach in the summer and were often supported. Robert Lynd was one of those who were paid well and able to enjoy the benefits of this system. George Lundberg returned to Vermont every summer (near SSRC-supported summer meetings at Dartmouth) even when he was on the faculty at the University of Washington. This allowed for much hobnobbing with other like-minded sociologists, which was basic to the formation of a sociological elite. The pattern continued to the days of Lazarsfeld, who also enjoyed the benefits of this system. Relieved of the necessity of writing textbooks and able to publish research through subsidies, they occupied a world unlike that experienced by the rest of American sociology.

Writing textbooks, like teaching in summer schools, had its rewards. Those who were successful in the market derived some income from it. Charles Horton Cooley, another nonmember of the scientizing faction, used the money to buy a car. Ellwood, who must have made much more, took up motoring as a hobby, especially late in life, and was able to finance sabbaticals in Europe for himself, which included a substantial amount of travel and personal contact with European sociologists. Nevertheless, until he went to Duke, Ellwood felt pinched. And the demands of survival were a great burden on those who were not in the foundation-supported elite. Even Ellsworth Faris, who had five children, was compelled to teach in the summer school at the University of Chicago, and he attributed his lack of productivity to this fact (Odum 1951, 183). So it is not surprising that great works of sociological thought were not routinely produced outside of the circle of the privileged and that the attitudes of the excluded were flavored with resentment.

The academic book market in the United States during Ellwood's career bears no resemblance to that of today. As noted, research books were almost invariably subsidy published, and only those with foundation support or

29. Hill was a model for the university presidents lampooned by Thorstein Veblen, in *Higher Learning in America* (1918), as captains of erudition — the academic analogue to captains of industry. Veblen, whom Hill saved by appointing him at Missouri, was a Yale PhD in philosophy, who had been at Cornell studying economics.

universities whose presses received subsidies, such as Chicago, benefited. Few authors were able to write for the general book market, and writing for the public had its own constraints.[30] Ellwood was a success within these constraints, however; he published for a general intellectual audience from the time of World War I. His first venture into this market was *The Social Problem: A Constructive Analysis* (1915), which was published by Macmillan in a series edited by Ely, a series following the general strategy of the Chautauqua texts that had introduced Ellwood to social science as a high school student. In 1922 he broke into another "public" market, publishing a book titled *The Reconstruction of Religion,* which sold 7,000 copies in its first year. Ellwood's successes with books other than textbooks, with the exception of his *History of Social Philosophy,*[31] were on religious topics. *The Reconstruction of Religion* was the biggest success, and the same themes figured in his two other "religious" books. Understanding them as books requires an understanding of Ellwood as a religious thinker and figure, which is the topic of the next section. But it should be clear that writing for the public could not have been a living for Ellwood. Among sociologists, making a living as a writer was hardly possible except for those like Harry Elmer Barnes, who produced volume after volume on history, sociology, penology, and public issues, and newspaper column upon column (Goddard 1968).

The publishing categories into which Ellwood's books fell are revealing of the constraints under which nonsubsidy publishing operated. His textbooks reflected both his lectures and the development of his sociological thinking. Keeping them up to date compelled him to keep up with and respond to the current literature, and for someone like Ellwood, who was predominantly a theorist, it was a constant challenge to interpret new work and new developments in sociology in a way that was coherent with his basic outlook. Yet Ellwood was flexible, responded to changes in intellectual climate by modifying his own views, and attempted for the most part to provide an evenhanded statement of the issues. Much of this was forced on him by the demands of the market, but it should not be underestimated how

30. The case of *Middletown* (1929) especially reveals how this system worked. The book was produced as a monograph for the Institute for Social and Religious Research, a personal charity of John D. Rockefeller Jr. and was originally anticipated to be published with a subsidy, within the monograph series of the institute. The directors of the institute disliked the book so much they refused to publish it, and it appeared only through the intervention of friends and another subsidy from another foundation.

31. Even this one sold in part to a religious public and was a recommended book for the "religious" book club, although not the main selection, as well as being "recommended" by the Book of the Month Club itself.

difficult the market was. The use of his social problems text, for example, was opposed by fundamentalist ministers for its partiality to evolution and opposed by the local Association for the Advancement of Colored People in Philadelphia for its depiction of blacks, though, as he observed in a letter to Hart of February 16, 1924, not on the grounds of the falsity of anything said in the book (Ellwood papers). Textbook writing, in short, also involved constraints, and yet, as a means of articulating a comprehensive sociological outlook, it could hardly be bettered.

Ellwood's Christianity

What did it mean for Ellwood to be "Christian"? In a practical sense, it meant that he was acceptable to certain audiences and had special access to others. It also meant that he was in a group of persons who had a common interest in having a "Christian" viewpoint preserved against its contraries, which for Ellwood meant philosophical materialism (or scientific naturalism) and behaviorism (because of its denial of human purposiveness), and more generally, ethical nihilism and rejection of the idea of higher ethical demands. These were important issues in the larger intellectual culture of the time, but also in the social sciences; the resolutely secularizing progressive historian James Harvey Robinson was a case in point. These commitments led Ellwood into various alliances. One was with Pitirim Sorokin, who both theorized the problem of materialism and rejected it. Ellwood's first contact with Sorokin came in 1923, when Sorokin wrote him a fan letter about *The Reconstruction of Religion* in which he explained his situation as an exile and his desire to come to the United States (February 13, 1923, Ellwood papers). The letter began a long relationship. But Christianity, as indicated earlier, played a role in academic politics as well. Ellwood opposed appointments to academic positions, sometimes covertly by putting out the word to sympathetic deans or chairs, against those whose sociological views he regarded as unacceptably materialist or atheistic.

Yet Ellwood was far from being a sectarian or fundamentalist. Indeed, the whole thrust of his religious writing was in the opposite direction, against both denominationalism and a theological approach to Christianity, and in favor of accommodating Christianity to science and social science. Writings of this kind often, in retrospect, are closer to the opposition than they appear at the time, so it is important to see who the opponents were. Ellwood's Christianity was "liberal" and indeed about as extreme in its liberalism, in crucial respects, as could be. The fundamentalists loathed him for his evolutionism. Even his Japanese translator, M. Anesaki, with whom he had a particularly close and long-term relationship, in one letter reproached him for providing an account of Christianity in *The Reconstruction of Religion* that was completely ethical, meaning that the account ignored the whole problem of grace, salvation, the divine, and so forth (September 12, 1922, Ellwood papers).[32] This was an accurate criticism. When Ellwood called for the reconstruction of religion in the light of social science, he meant to strip the Christian message of the whole machinery of Protestant theology, which he criticized as divisive and a distraction from the core Christian message, and offensive to the non-Christians with whom cooperation was necessary (cf. 1922, 159). And what was this core message? As usual, Ellwood is crystal clear:

> The solution which positive Christianity proposes of the religious problem of our time . . . is simple. Let the religious leaders of our day grasp the full social significance of religion, drop their theological disputations, give religion the positive humanitarian trend which civilization demands, recognize that their essential work is the maintenance and propagation of rational social values, and teach clearly, as Jesus did, that the only possible service of God must consist in the service of men regardless of their race, class, or condition. Let also the recognized basis of religious fellowship become full consecration to the service of mankind. (1922, 159)

The echo of Comte is wholly intentional. The lesson of sociology, Comte taught, was the fact of our mutual dependence; for Ellwood, it is, as he titled it in his next religious book, *Man's Social Destiny*, a destiny epitomized in the fact that

> the collective life of men which we call society . . . is carried on by the continual exchange of services between men. It is by mutual service that men live. It is this reciprocity of service that is the basis of all human institutions and all civilization. The more intense the change of services, the more social values are produced and the more social life is built up; and the more equal the exchange is, the more satisfying and harmonious is the social life. (1922, 163)

This was, as Ellwood stressed, a frankly anthropocentric conception of religion, and this is the "social religion" of Jesus himself (1922, 162). His last religious book, *The World's Need of Christ* (1940), was squarely in the religious tradition that stressed the imitation of Christ as a guide to life, and it eliminated the rest of Christian dogma. As he put it in a letter to Motwani of January 5, 1944, "Christians, you know, are of two sorts: those who wor-

---

32. The title of the volume alluded to Dewey's *Reconstruction in Philosophy* (1920), which provided an elaborate explanation of the concept of reconstruction.

ship Jesus and those who follow him. I find in Gandhi a follower of Jesus, and I am more closely in sympathy with Gandhi than I am with some of my so-called fellow Christians" (Ellwood papers).

Earlier I noted that Henderson was empowered by his ministerial status to raise moral concerns that would have seemed political or ideological if raised by others. Ellwood, by not only identifying himself as a Christian but by speaking out against various local evils, had a similar protected status. This came at a price: according to Bernard in his memoir of Elwood (Bannister 1987), many of his colleagues at Missouri thought he was a pious fraud and were irritated by him, and some of the students made fun of him. As Bernard tells it, the citizens of Columbia disliked him as well (in part for his support of the local Presbyterian minister), and Bernard claims Ellwood he was often forced to backtrack on his charges. But Bernard omits critical events that were part of the story in which Ellwood stood out as a courageous and influential leader.

The first and most important of these involved a lynching in 1923 that occurred on the edge of campus, as a result of an assault on the daughter of a faculty member. The event was seared into the consciousness of the local black community and has been an issue in race relations in Columbia ever since. The lynching was presided over by several important community leaders; the victim was pulled from the jail by a crowd recruited in part in an organized manner from the rural area around Columbia (presumably through the active Ku Klux Klan presence). Shortly after the event, "a student followed Ellwood to his office to ask a question: 'Do you mean to say that a community in which a lynching occurs has lower moral ideals than the rest of the country?' Ellwood framed his response carefully, but the short answer was 'yes.' The 'student' as it turned out, was a reporter for the St. Louis *Star*, which splashed the professor's condemnation of Columbia at the top of its front page" (Hunt 2004, 142). A local newspaper publisher, a graduate and enemy of the university, took offense at this remark and turned it into a cause célèbre, attempting to get Ellwood to recant. Ellwood refused and was supported in the pulpit of local churches, and beyond, as the lynching was denounced by the national press. Enlightened opinion supported Ellwood: the governor of Missouri, Arthur M. Hyde, for example, wrote him to say "I am glad you are teaching such sturdy Americanism in your class" (May 7, 1923, Ellwood papers). But many others, especially in town, resented his remarks or were irritated by them, and from this point on Ellwood's relation to the university began to sour.[33]

---

33. A related event, a year later, involved Herbert Blumer, then an instructor in the Department of Sociology. Ellwood told the story from the point of view of the department: In Jan-

For Ellwood, at least, his speaking out was continuous with his duty as a Christian. He left the Presbyterian Church and was never again a particularly active churchman. His religious writings after this event are less optimistic about the Church, as constituted, as an agency of civilization. Indeed, as he said in one of his speeches, reported in the press, the lynch mobs were organized by churchmen (Ellwood scrapbook). Ellwood's reaction to Barth and Niebuhr is understandable in light of his own experiences. Barth's antiliberal "Christology," which swept the mainstream churches, was a flight from Christ as an example; Niebuhr's insistence on the sinful nature of man and his use of this notion to justify, indeed oblige, Christians to act violently against evil would have, for Ellwood, represented the politics of the Grand Inquisitor. Christ, for Ellwood, was found in Dostoyevsky's Alyosha. He was acutely aware that "evil" was a concept that could be just as easily employed by lynch mobs, and his own experience with churches led him to see them as obstacles to Christianity. Yet despite his alienation from churches, at Duke Ellwood continued to witness, movingly, for his kind of Christianity to students, who were in turn impressed by him.

Ellwood's writings for his religious audience in the 1920s were sufficiently well received that he was invited to give many lectures and, at Yale and Vanderbilt, to deliver prominent endowed lecture series, and he was taken seriously enough in this domain to be offered a professorship at the Yale Divinity School. His student, L. L. Bernard, in his acid-drenched memoir of Ellwood (Bernard papers [PSU]), claimed that the dean of the Yale Divinity School had gone to Missouri to personally offer Ellwood the position, but when he was greeted at Ellwood's door with the remark, "The mountain has finally come to Mohammed," he rethought the matter and didn't make the offer. Other versions of this story circulated in Columbia (Nelson 2003). Ellwood's own correspondence indicates that the issue was more mundane—money. Ellwood wanted $6,000 in salary, and the dean, who wanted Ellwood, was unable to get consensus on such an offer (Brown to Ellwood, May 19, 1922, Ellwood papers). Ellwood's Duke appointment in 1930 allowed him the best of both worlds: a Christian setting in which his

---

uary 1925, he gave before a small group an informal talk on the Negro problem, which was reported in the newspapers in a sensational way. A committee, known to be members of a secret organization, attempted to compel the president and the board to force the instructor (Blumer) to resign. The university authorities refused to yield to this request, with both faculty and board courageously supporting him and the department. The attempt recoiled on the organization that instigated it, and since then the department has not been troubled by outside interference (Ellwood n.d.a, 32). As Blumer later told this story, he was accosted by a group of toughs, Klansmen, near campus, whom he was able to threaten in return, with the help of his former football teammates (cf. Nelson 2003).

kind of Christianity was respected, and control of a sociology department in which his form of sociology could be protected.[34]

Yet Ellwood was a loser in the theological struggles of his era, and by the time of his last religious book, *The World's Need of Christ* (1940), he was far from the mainstream. This statement requires some explanation, not least because of the profound effects on American religious culture and politics of the struggle he lost. Protestantism in Ellwood's time was dividing over the question of "fundamentals." If one extended the reasoning of the liberal theologians of the nineteenth century, one would reach a position like Ellwood's, in which Jesus was a historical figure, Darwinism was acceptable, the Bible was not to be taken literally without interpretation, the Christian message evolves into an ethical message in which the example of Jesus was central, and the superstitious elements of Christianity, including the whole list of technical theological doctrines relating to salvation, disappear—such as grace, which Ellwood's translator had found lacking. A long line of European, especially German, theology pointed in this direction. In one sense this movement was away from religious belief and toward a kind of humanism that might as well have been secular. Yet there was nothing halfhearted about the spiritual force behind the idea of living like Jesus. Weber, who becomes relevant to this story, as we shall see shortly, took the followers of Tolstoy to be genuine examples of the ethical transformation that commitment to this ideal required. But Weber thought of these Christians as prime examples of an otherworldly orientation, that is to say, people whose Kingdom was not of this world. Ellwood, however, like the Social Gospel thinkers who preceded him, was a liberal optimist—though with a long view of the problem of human progress—and was entirely this-worldly in his conception of Christianity and the significance of Jesus, whose sacrifice was for this world. It was this optimism that was sorely tested by World War I, and the war produced results, especially in Germany, that led to the discredit of theological liberalism and to a revolution in theology that swept aside the kind of thinking that Ellwood advanced.

34. The circumstances of this move are too complex to discuss here, but they coincided with an event in the Department of Sociology at Missouri, which, although it involved Ellwood only indirectly, had a catastrophic effect on the university as a whole, from which it never recovered. One of Ellwood's Chicago hires, Herman DeGraff, had one of his classes develop and distribute a questionnaire on attitudes about gender relations, which was seized on by the same newspaperman who had opposed Ellwood earlier to create a scandal by labeling it a sex questionnaire. The resulting furor had national coverage and led to the firing of Max Meyer, who had assisted by giving some envelopes, and several other faculty. The chaos created by these actions led in a year to the sacking of the president. But the damage was done, and the Depression prevented the university from recovering. Duke was the beneficiary, as other faculty moved there (Nelson 2003).

German ministers and liberal theologians embraced the war, which they justified by a doctrine of Luther's known as the Two Kingdoms. The idea of the Two Kingdoms reflects a phrase of Jesus that became central to Lutheran theology and the Lutheran worldview, that "the world is given over to the devil." If the world is indeed given over to the devil, the Two Kingdoms argument runs, human conduct in this world must be governed accordingly—by the left hand of God, which permits and indeed requires responding to evil with force. The usual idea of Christian conduct is reserved for relations among Christians, or the private sphere. There was no conflict between the two. Both kingdoms were expressions of God's love. If one felt a conflict between the two, one was simply in error about the boundaries between the application of each. Needless to say this was a doctrine that served German militarism nicely in that it both provided a religious justification for war as the response to evil and confined the imitation of Christ to the private world of believers. As a side note, it should be observed that this Lutheran doctrine was alien to Calvinism, which had a strong sense that the structures, including the political structures of the world, were a reflection of divine will, and thus that political authority itself rested on the intentions of the divinity and that, as a consequence, revolution was justified if the people, motivated by the conscience which was the voice of God, willed the removal of bad authorities in accordance with God's structuring of the world. The problem of the justification of political action was settled directly by appeal to the conscience. This Calvinist sense of the nature of political authority allows for and even encourages the idea of political reform in accordance with God's larger purposes, and Ellwood, raised as a Presbyterian, was carrying out this logic in his own reformist thought.

Then came Karl Barth. Barth was to theology what Einstein was to physics or Heidegger was to philosophy—a profoundly transformative thinker.[35] Ellwood was a student during World War I, when he observed, with disgust, the eagerness with which Barth joined the Social Democratic Party and embarked on a radical rethinking of the issue of God's signifi-

---

35. This is the estimate of professional theologians. One might, however, give a more mundane, Weberian, explanation of the popularity and impact of Barth. In the first place, his theology empowered the professional theologian: for him the "word of God" was the life of Jesus, whose meaning was interpretable only through the machinery of the notions of Grace and so forth. Second, Barth found a way around the doctrine of double predestination, that there were people not only predestined to be saved but to be damned, a doctrine that was central to Calvinism but that made it an uncomfortable and indeed unbearably cruel creed. This made mainstream Christianity more attractive but at the same time demotivated it. Without the fear of arbitrary damnation, one need no longer look for the signs of salvation in one's own conduct and conscience (Webster 2000).

cance for human action, beginning with Paul's Epistle to the Romans, the text that is the fount of the theological complexity that Ellwood so carefully avoided. Barth understood himself as an enemy of nineteenth-century German liberal theology, which he regarded as wrongly accommodating religion to science—Ellwood's central idea, which he wished to extend to social science. The key to Barth's thought was the reestablishment of the distance between humans and God—a Calvinist theme—and the de-anthropomorphization of God. This was an attempt to immunize religious thought from the intrusions of science: God was, for Barth, so "other" that nothing but the word of God counted as evidence about God or as relevant to God. By "the word of God," however, he meant the life of Jesus inter-preted in terms of the doctrines of grace, justification by faith alone, and so forth. This was as radical, or more radical, than "fundamentalism," and less democratic, since the word of God was, for Barth, accessible in practice only to professional theologians. Not surprisingly, his views came to serve as a kind of professional ideology of mainstream Protestant ministers. Ethics, however, now became a problem. If God is radically other in Barth's sense, God is also radically irrelevant to human conduct. This was exactly the kind of theologizing that Ellwood rejected.

Barth was a Lutheran who read Calvin only when appointed to a pro-fessorship that required him to teach the subject. Ellwood's other nemesis was Reinhold Niebuhr. Niebuhr had been raised in a denomination, the Prussian Union, that combined Lutheran and Calvinist teachings, and thus, like Barth, he was well prepared intellectually for the ecumenical moment of Protestantism in the twenties. He was born in the United States, but in a German-speaking community. Religion was, until World War I, still highly denominational, and this was especially true for the Lutheran churches in the United States, whose services were still conducted in German or Scan-dinavian languages and formed separate worlds. Niebuhr was close to the editor of the *Christian Century,* to which he was a prolific contributor, and which had earlier been a promoter of Ellwood, and he was offered, and de-clined, the job at Yale that Ellwood had negotiated over. But Niebuhr was a very different thinker. He was to become famous for his violent attacks on liberal optimism about human nature, his articulation of a theological ar-gument against the kind of Christian pacifism that Ellwood stood for, his liberal optimism about the future of society, and his hostility to the idea that had animated the Social Gospel movement, the idea of the realization of the kingdom of God on earth through human effort, associated especially with Walter Rauschenbusch. Niebuhr's *Moral Man, Immoral Society* (1932) was in many ways the final blow against the Social Gospel tradition and provided its own theologically inflected sociology. The title reflected the basic idea of Two Kingdoms theology, that moral man had no business bringing Christian ideals to bear on society. Niebuhr's version of this argument was that "sin" was a central fact of society that precluded such optimism. As a result of the "immoral" character of society, "the dream of perpetual peace and brotherhood for human society is one that will never be fully realized," he wrote in the first chapter; he went on to say that society is "in a perpetual state of war" (Fox 1985, 140). He ridiculed thinkers like Dewey and decried the idea that "myths were superstitions rendered anachronistic by modern science" (165). These kinds of claims, his capacity for finding biblical backing for them, together with a prodigious talent for speech-making and sermonizing, soon placed Niebuhr in the position of moral authority in politics that was unrivaled in the United States and allowed him not only to voice many concerns that politicians were unable to speak to but to serve as the source of Christian approval of the war against the Nazis and later the cold war. This version of the rejection of "Christian politics" was similar to Weber's own, which accounts for the odd historical fact that Weber's (Jewish) follower Hans J. Morgenthau, the creator of the modern field of international relations, considered Niebuhr to be America's greatest political philosopher and became personally close to Niebuhr at the end of his life.

Was Ellwood's religious thought a dead end? One observation about *The Reconstruction of Religion* should suffice to open some doubts. Ellwood spent a significant amount of the text on Nietzsche, whose protofascist power-worship was the main exemplar of Ellwood's concept of paganism, which he understood to be the main enemy of reconstructed religion (1922, 96–98). Reconstructed religion was, as Ellwood understood it, in the enlightenment tradition. His discussion of reconstructed religion, with it emphasis on discussion rather than coercion and preaching, and its aim of creating a space of enlightened and intelligent international public opinion to resist fundamentalism and paganism, points ahead to Habermas, who had his own theological moment. Ellwood's insistence that there was no theological solution to the moral problems of politics points to Michael Walzer's suggestion that keeping the sense of irreducible moral conflict alive is better than intellectualizing solutions. That the question "What would Jesus do?" later became a slogan of fundamentalists (who, in Ellwood's time, were more inclined to use the Bible to search for interdictions) points to its enduring significance and suggests that the attempts of thinkers like Barth and Niebuhr to bury it under theological arcana were failures. Nor was the attempt of mainstream theology to evade the challenge of science by immunizing it a success.

Ellwood's Last Decades: Public Intellectual and Internationalist

Ellwood's major intellectual turning point came in 1914 when he was on sabbatical in England and became more impressed than ever with the importance of culture. The lynching was his major turning point as a public figure and religious thinker. In 1924, he was American Sociological Society (ASS) president. Increasingly he found himself on the losing side of controversies, first over instinct theory, second over the term *social psychology*, which he had used to describe his work on the psychological foundations of society but which, from about 1925 on, had been invaded by psychologists armed with the notion of attitude as a measurable psychological entity. Ellwood responded to these changes by identifying himself as a theorist, by stressing evolution and culture, and by taking a longer view of the issues that excited his younger contemporaries. He was not alone. Some of the best minds of this generation, such as Alexander Goldenweiser, shared his views, and his alliance with Sorokin and Robert M. MacIver on this and on methodological questions deepened.

Ellwood had been an internationalist from the start. His time in Berlin, his sabbatical in England, and an active correspondence with European scholars (as well as friends) led to his recruitment to the International Institute of Sociology. As the most translated American sociologist of the period before World War II, he was not only well known in Europe and Japan but had close relations with his translators, who were also enthusiasts for his work—though often also acute critics and correspondents. The translator of his books into German, Bela Frank, who lived in Vienna, was a Mason and initiated Ellwood.

The Masonic connection provided a new public, but it also placed Ellwood in a position of intimate knowledge of European affairs from the point of view of the hunted. Because of Ellwood's eminence, he was quickly moved up the ranks of Masonry and became a member of the international Masonic council in Paris in the 1930s, precisely at the time that European Masonry was being threatened by both the Catholic Church and the Nazis, for whom the phrase "Masonic-Jewish conspiracy" was standard invective.[36]

In 1928, Ellwood spent much of his sabbatical in Italy. He became a strong opponent of fascism—long before the so-called premature antifascists, whose prematurity was simply a result of following the party line—and used many occasions to warn of the fascist threat to democracy. He was

---

36. In the late 1930s, after Frank's death, his wife escaped Germany, sending her children to Denmark and then emigrating with them to Colombia with Ellwood's help.

in contact with, and aided, the Italian antifascist opposition in getting their message out in the United States. The audience was uncomprehending and uninterested. But Ellwood was relentless. He was able to use his public speeches and interviews on other topics to deliver his warnings. During Ellwood's time teaching summer school at Northwestern in 1936, a reporter sought him out for a discussion of suburban living: he got an earful on fascism and the European situation instead.

Despite his grasp of the centrality of the conflict between Nietzscheanism and Enlightenment values, which informed his perspective on these issues, Ellwood's analyses of fascism were hardly memorable. He tended to regard the falling away from a religious spirit, Paganism, materialism, and the like as critical, and as one of his religious critics later pointed out, he seemed to lack the imagination to see the world from the point of view of Fascism or Communism and thereby to understand them (Hughley 1948). Nor did he have a solution, as Niebuhr did, in a Christian viewpoint that justified real war against fascism. From 1920, he was an opponent of conscription and viewed large standing armies as a cause of war. He was an increasingly vocal opponent in the 1930s, arguing that the unique geographical situation of the United States allowed it to be defended by a small army. His pacifism, which he hung on to very far into the deterioration of the world situation that led to the U.S. entry into World War II, alienated him from his colleagues at Duke. He continued his opposition to conscription and to the militarization of the universities once the war began.

One can certainly fault Ellwood for the limitations of his outlook. His viewpoint was that of a democrat who believed that Christian idealism was necessary in social life and essential to progress. For him, the loss of the spiritual to materialism was the great and causative tragedy of the twentieth century. But before being too dismissive of these now quaint ideas, one should consider the extent to which they were the glue of the internationalism of the time. The basic point of contact of Americans with the third world, as well as with China, came through missionaries, and the only serious voices for peace in the interwar years, serious in the sense of having a capacity to mobilize people across borders and in significant numbers, came from Christianity. Ellwood's diagnosis of the degenerating world situation was that world Christianity had not been strong enough to hold these forces back—and this was a failure that he did understand, because it was a theme of his discussions with his translators in Japan and Europe. That the Christian consensus proved to be too weak was a world tragedy. But there is also a sense that it was the only significant opportunity for a popular rejection of fascism. Ellwood's contemporaries did not do much better. Before 1940, sociologists did a poor job of analyzing fascism, and the peace-keeping efforts promoted by such admired thinkers as John Dewey and the Outlawry of War movement were even less effective. Several prominent American sociologists, notably George Lundberg, pushed their stance of objectivity in the face of fascism so far that they were regarded widely as fascists themselves. Ellwood was an honorable and vocal, if anguished, exception.

Ellwood became the president of the International Institute of Sociology in 1934, the second American to serve, the third to be elected. He organized the Brussels Congress of 1935. The fate and reputation of this organization requires some explanation. In the first place, one may ask, what sort of sociology did it represent? It had been founded in France by René Worms, for whom the Durkheimians, who were not practitioners of intellectual toleration, had nothing but contempt. Yet it became the only significant international sociological organization and sought to become more— a federation of national sociological associations, as the ISA eventually became. Ellwood did his best to get the ASS to affiliate, as he had when he was ASS president, and tried to get the ASS to affiliate with the American Association for the Advancement of Science (AAAS). Both times he was foiled by Chicago sociology. Albion Small objected to affiliation with the AAAS; the Chicago friends of the Durkheimians, who were hostile to the IIS, prevented the ASS from affiliating with the proposed federation of sociological associations. The collapse of international sociology in the 1930s followed.

Ellwood was himself fully engaged in the business of keeping international sociology going despite the drift into war, and in some ways he was the best representative of international sociology as it then existed. His interest in the problem of morality, for example, was part of the basis of his intense relationship with the long-serving secretary of the international organization, the successor to Worms, Swiss sociologist G. L. Duprat. Together they resisted the takeover of the organization by the well-organized Italians represented by the smart and aggressive Corrado Gini. In the end they failed. The refusal of many prominent Americans and the Durkheimians to participate created an imbalance that, combined with inherent weaknesses of the organization that had been inherited from Worms, plus a constitutional structure that required the rotation of the presidency between countries, meant that the large Italian delegation had a right to be heard. Worms had given away memberships to various notables, and the dues structure of the organization and its finances were a shambles. Gini knew all this and called for reform, an accounting of the finances, and the dismissal of Duprat. When Ellwood placed Sorokin in the presidency, to stave off the Italian takeover, he proposed him as a Russian rather than an American, to avoid the constitutional problem that the current president was not to be succeeded in the presidency by a person from the same country. Gini then forced a compromise that would eventually lead him to power. As a result, after the war, the taint of fascism clung to the organization; it was dominated by Italians for generations and rapidly declined in importance. The International Sociological Association, however, took over Duprat's idea of federating national sociological associations as its own.

Ellwood's Legacy

The elements of Ellwood's conception of sociology fit seamlessly with one another and with his theoretical ideas. For him, sociology was a humanitarian science, working for the rational good (necessarily supplemented by a refined ethical religion). It worked through the diffusion of the results of sociology to the public, through what we would call public sociology, by serving as the intellectual basis of reform, and by the training of social workers. His conceptions of method emphasized the holistic community research approach of the Russell Sage Foundation. The relevant notion of objectivity, for him, was nonpartisanship, both with respect to political views and conceptions of reform. What made sociology scientific for him was substantive, not a matter of a special method: sociology was scientific to the extent that it could be based on, and articulate with, existing science. His theoretical conception of society as a psychological rather than an organic or contractual entity, and his idea that it progresses through a social process in which mutual learning plays a large, and rationalizing, role, supported the idea that education in the broadest sense is the major element of social reform and progress. His argument that religion and ethics required reconstruction in the light of sociology and a basis in sociology supported the idea that it was possible, and necessary, to have a moral basis for reform. On the level of politics and international politics, this conception supported democracy and peace as the rational good. Perhaps Ellwood was the last sociologist for whom these elements fit together successfully. There is a sense in which sociology has ever since attempted without success to put the pieces, or some of the pieces, together again, and failed.

Ellwood was cursed with the ability to see the implications of new developments for his own positions, and for the idea of sociology as a science that informed social reform. He grasped immediately the consequences of behaviorism in psychology for the understanding of society, despite the fact that there were few texts articulating these consequences, and from 1918 he developed a response, articulating for the first time the standard critique of conventional sociological methods. He understood that the attitude psychology of Gordon Allport destroyed the "sociological" social psychological notion of the group, and thus destroyed sociological social psychology, a realization later embodied in Blumer's argument that symbolic interactionism was a field that replaced both psychology and sociology. He understood that the quantitative notions of science and objectivity that were promoted by sociologists like William Ogburn and funded by the SSRC, as he put it in the title of one paper, "Emasculated Sociologies" (1933a), meaning that such notions made sociology incapable of critique. He grasped that the power of foundation money was great and that the older model of sociology was doomed. But his greatest prescience was political. An ardent believer in democracy, he understood that fascism was a challenge to democracy and to the intellectual foundations of hope for democracy.

What became of Ellwood's protests? Was he, as his own final statement (1944) suggests, one of history's losers? Suffice it to say that the scientizers came and went, and came again over and over through the rest of the century, but never fully managed to remold the discipline in their own image. The class system in sociology became more entrenched. In the world of the teachers of sociology, courses in Social Problems remained important, and student interest in sociology continued to be driven by social concerns, with sociology enrollments waxing and waning with these concerns. The large underclass of sociology, intermittently rebellious and sharing little with the elite, persisted, with many continuities in commitments and interests from the time of Ellwood. The discipline's troubled return to the idea of public sociology shows how much was lost and why it will not quickly return. Ellwood's particular version of public sociology, like all public sociologies, depended on a receptive audience. His audience was the intellectually inclined Christian community. It shrank, and shrank nowhere more dramatically than in Europe, where it was swept away by fascism, the war, and the secularization of European society. It is an audience for sociology that has never been replaced. Nor did the problems of sociological practice disappear as a result of the methodological "advances" Elwood rejected. Elwood is still with us.

[FIVE] Knowledge from the Field

Marjorie L. DeVault

Sociologists, as students, are inducted into their discipline by way of stories about its origins. As in any field, we learn a pantheon of "greats" and a canon of great works, and we forge disciplinary identities by cleaving to slogans that we build from these materials. Our practice often fits comfortably with the principles we enunciate, but sometimes it may not; like any practice, it always contains more than we can say. The longer development of a career, I've come to see, is in part a process of learning, in a deeper sense, fuller meanings of disciplinary history and its consequences, and discovering the implications of our practice. In the spirit of that learning process, I provide here a story about fieldwork traditions in sociology and the growth of qualitative methods and methodology in the second half of the twentieth century.

Dilemmas of terminology arise immediately, and they are not only problems of labeling but are related to elaborations of qualitative approaches and their movement in multiple directions. Labels have changed over the years, and so has the thing itself. I locate the roots of these approaches in the "social survey" of the late nineteenth century—what we might now call a community case study—but some point back to the early travel writing of cultural sojourners, colonialists, and missionaries. The early sociologists borrowed and shared ideas with anthropological ethnographers but later formalized their practices of observation, reporting, and analysis under the label "participant observation," as sociology and anthropology separated both intellectually and institutionally. The approach broadened (or, as some see it, narrowed) when studies based solely on open-ended interviewing came to be seen as part of (and some say, to dominate) this family of methods. The category has also come to include a variety of related methods of investigation, such as inductive content analysis, visual and some documentary methods, ethnomethodological approaches (a wary alliance on both sides), and, especially recently, varieties of introspective analysis. Many would include historical approaches in the broad field of qualitative sociology as well, though they lie outside the scope of my discussion. Qualitative methods are often associated with microsociologies and may focus on such limited "fields" as the jazz pianist's hand (Sudnow 1978) or the routines of beginning a conversation (Schegloff 1968). But qualitative sociologies are probably better known through broader ranging and widely influential studies of community, class, and power (e.g., to recall only a few of the most influential, *Middletown, Street Corner Society, Worlds of Pain, Manufacturing Consent, A Place on the Corner,* and *Men and Women of the Corporation*), and new strands of qualitative methodology have taken up analyses of global theoretical questions (Burawoy 2000), multi-sited cultural discourses (Martin 1994), and the translocal coordination of social life (Smith 1987; Griffith and Smith 2005). Although many studies in the fieldwork tradition train their gaze on the less privileged, reporting their experience back to policymakers and middle-class audiences, fieldworkers also study "up," providing close-up inspections of professionals and administrative elites (e.g., Strauss and his colleagues on medicine [Strauss et al. 1964; Glaser and Strauss 1965] and the ethnographies of science that later emerged from this group [Timmermans 1999; Clarke et al. 2003]; Daniels [1988] on affluent women as civic volunteers; Rollins [1985], who included the white employers of African-American domestic workers in her study; and Vaughan [1996] on NASA space flight engineers).

In taking up the editorial committee's invitation to write a history of qualitative methods (a phrase not widely used until later in the century), I've adopted a definition that makes sense to me as a contemporary practitioner and that encompasses the work I've come to understand as ancestry for my practice. I use the phrase *fieldwork tradition* to point toward three strategies for data collection—participant observation (also known as ethnography), open-ended (or semistructured) interviewing, and life history work—and the kinds of analysis associated with those approaches, recognizing that qualitative studies will generally apply some mix of these and/or the related strategies mentioned earlier. Participant observation is typically understood, either explicitly or implicitly, as the "heart" of this family of approaches, and it is central to my story. Although fieldworkers often rely on historical data and build history into their ethnographic studies, I exclude historical sociologies based solely on textual sources. Whichever tools are in play, practitioners (mostly) agree that qualitative research tends to be inductive and committed to on-the-ground, everyday, as-it-happens, "thick" accounting and analysis of people's activities, interactions, and perspectives, and the ways those are coordinated. Taylor and Bogdan capture the spirit of this commitment in their 1984 textbook with a key dictum for qualitative researchers: "Go to the people." Emerson (2004) expresses the other side of the same idea with the phrase "bringing back the news."

I weave my narrative around three methodological essays from the second half of the century: Howard Becker's discussion of inference and proof in participant observation; Jack Katz's essay on a social system of analytic fieldwork, based on a study that included both participant observation and "loosely structured interviews"; and Ruth Behar's commentary on methods in a life history study. I mean to bring forward three ideas:

1. Labels, languages, and emphases may have changed over the course of the century, but one can find a sturdy tradition whose shared strategies and commitments have been passed along, explicitly and implicitly, through generations of practitioners.

2. From its early days in social reform activities, the fieldwork tradition of "close-up" investigation has provided openings for "voices from outside"; yet in every period, researchers have struggled over the relation between science and social action, and the topics and consequences of field studies have been shaped by their social and institutional contexts.

3. Women as well as men have contributed to this tradition, but women have too often been "edged out" (Tuchman 1989) of the discipline or simply overlooked. I do not mean to claim a special affinity of women for fieldwork (feminist histories have taught us that women have contributed to all kinds of sociology: Deegan [1991]; Lengermann and Niebrugge-Brantley [1998]); my goal is simply to tell a story more sensitive to gender than most standard histories do.

Chicago School Beginnings

My story begins in the early years of the twentieth century, an era when both theorists and progressive reformers were observing the growth of cities and commenting on urban life and its contexts. The newly established University of Chicago was one center of such activity. Chicago itself, a relatively new city at the turn of the century, had changed very rapidly as it became a crossroads in the nation's new transportation system, an outpost of cultural life in the Midwest, and a city of primarily European immigrant workers. As in other large cities, civic leaders faced labor and public health issues associated with these changes, and the city was one of the centers of the Progressive settlement movement. When the University of Chicago was founded in 1890, its first president, William Rainey Harper, sought to build a new kind of institution that would emphasize research and graduate training. He had philanthropic support from local elites and, by the teens and twenties, substantial support from the newly established Rockefeller Foundation, and he expected that the university would have a strong presence in the city.

Harper made four appointments to the new department of social science: sociologist Albion Small, anthropologist Frederick Starr, associated with the Chautauqua movement, and reformers Charles Henderson, active in the organization of charity work, and Marion Talbot, who taught home economics (or "sanitary science") in the department until 1904, when she was moved to a separate department of household administration. Faculty in this hybrid department were aligned with the pragmatist social philosophy that was strongly represented among Chicago philosophers, and they worked closely with the Progressive reformers at the Hull House settlement, who were documenting the living conditions of laborers and their families, the growth of neighborhood communities and their problems, and the ways in which diverse populations came together in various urban formations. Indeed, some suggest that Jane Addams should be seen as part of this group; Addams worked closely with the sociologists and wrote as a sociologist, though she declined a faculty position (Deegan 1988).

Most important to my story in that founding moment is a spirit of empirical investigation. Drawing from the British social survey tradition of the late nineteenth century—the work of British reformers Charles Booth and Beatrice and Sidney Webb—sociologists who also saw themselves as social reformers investigated conditions of poverty, close-up, in order to raise public awareness, stimulate moral concern, and ameliorate conditions of poverty. They would find out about people in any way that was useful: census data, maps and documents—both official and personal, surveys, informal interviews, and spending time in some neighborhood or type of place.[1] Such investigations, undertaken primarily by Addams and her colleagues at Hull House, produced the first great Chicago-school empirical exemplar, *Hull-House Maps and Papers,* published in 1895. Addams and her colleagues, including at least some of the male sociologists, saw their work as part of a social survey movement, but in the first decades of the century, Chicago sociology faculty began gradually and unevenly to turn away from the "reformism" of the survey movement, at least in their scholarly rhetoric. Deegan (1988) argues that participation in social reform activities, and connections with Addams and other reformers, continued to be important in shaping the thought of at least some of the Chicago founders and the next generation. Other historians of Chicago sociology (Bulmer 1984a; Chapoulie 2001) also note that the sociologists taught, referred to, and drew from the traditions of social survey investigation.

1. The methodological ecumenism of the Hull House work allows both quantitative and qualitative feminists to claim Addams as a foremother, despite her neglect until recently in many accounts of disciplinary history; see Ferree, Khan, and Morimoto, chap. 13, this volume, and Sprague (2005).

In this earliest period, there was no sharp differentiation between qualitative and quantitative methods; the main distinction was between the community survey approach—based in mapping and ecological interpretation and including both qualitative and quantitative elements—and the newer life history approaches, which drew on personal documents and emphasized people's subjective experiences in their social environments. The latter were developed by W. I. Thomas, who joined the faculty in 1894 and in 1910 received a then quite unusual $50,000 grant from local philanthropist Helen Culver to study Polish communities in Europe and Chicago. He recruited Florian Znianiecki as a collaborator, and the two produced a second key exemplar, the two-volume *Polish Peasant in Europe and America* (1918–20), a work that shared with the earlier social survey tradition an emphasis on the lived experiences of urban dwellers. Before he was forced to leave the university, Thomas recruited Robert Park, who came to sociology with a background in journalism and as an assistant to Booker T. Washington; Park, along with his younger colleague Ernest Burgess, would supervise a burgeoning corpus of urban field studies during the 1920s and 1930s.

In these early years, there were roles for women in Chicago sociology, but those roles began to diminish as the century turned. By Bulmer's account—consistent with standard histories of the discipline—the male sociologists began to move toward more "scientific" conceptions of their activity, looking beyond mere cataloguing and description toward theoretically oriented empirical research as opposed to the "do-goodism" of Progressive reform. Deegan and other feminist historians, on the other hand, argue that women sociologists were systematically segregated, channeled into the neighboring fields of domestic science and social welfare, or relegated to subordinate roles in the men's projects; this is a story consistent with gendered accounts of the professionalization of the sciences and the masculinization that accompanied the process (Rossiter 1982). Barbara Laslett (1998) suggests that the gendering of the social sciences in the early twentieth century—both the participation of women in the early years of the century and their segregation and marginalization in the ensuing decades—can be read as efforts to reconstruct gender relations as the nineteenth-century doctrine of "separate spheres" began to erode (Rosenberg 1982).

The twenties appear to be key for this gendered process of disciplinary formation: this was the decade when social welfare moved definitively out of the sociology department into the separate School of Social Service Administration, and when some Chicago sociologists began to champion the scienticity of more quantitative approaches. Sociological fieldworkers aligned themselves more closely with anthropology—the department then included both disciplines—where governing impulses were more theoretical than reformist. Anthropology, like sociology, was professionalizing during this period, and although early field surveys might have been conducted by untrained observers such as colonialists and missionaries, the ideas of Boas and Malinowski were producing an increasing emphasis on long periods of close-up observation as a skilled, professional practice.

During the "Chicago heyday" (Bulmer 1984a) between 1915 and 1930, Park and Burgess began to teach a graduate seminar in urban field studies, sending students out to investigate a variety of urban locales from the lowly to the lofty. These studies, like the early reformist social surveys, drew on many kinds of data. In addition to making use of observation and interviewing, personal documents, maps and records, students were encouraged to draw on their own backgrounds—to write their own life histories in some cases—and to draw on novels and autobiography as those were relevant. An often-quoted characterization of this period has Park instructing students to "get the seat of your pants dirty in real research" (Bulmer 1984a, 97). Beyond this key instruction, there was relatively little methodological self-consciousness in this period and minimal reporting on methods in research monographs. Platt (1994) has shown that such seat-of-the pants "real research" took a wide variety of forms during this period—some data were drawn relatively unreflectively from published sources, accounts of observers, social workers' case reports, and so on—so that later claims about the importance of "firsthand data" appear to have been read back onto Chicago school practice. But the formation of a cadre of student-researchers brought a greater awareness of methods: Vivien Palmer, who coordinated the students' field projects, produced a handbook titled *Field Studies in Sociology* (1928), which began to codify the methods in use at the time.

Many fieldwork projects of the 1920s were undertaken collaboratively, with institutional and foundation support. Charles Johnson, an African American Chicago PhD who worked closely with Park, produced *The Negro in Chicago* (1922) with support from a city Commission on Race Relations established in the wake of race riots in 1919. In 1923, several University of Chicago departments were funded by the Rockefeller Memorial Foundation to establish a Local Community Research Committee. That funding came as a block grant, and the committee functioned as a loosely organized research group, supporting many sociology students who undertook urban field studies. Sociologists were also central to the work of the Institute for Juvenile Research, where a research fund was created in the midtwenties by a committee of leading reform figures to support a strand of work focused on crime and delinquency; oral histories were central to the work of the institute and were understood by practitioners there as part of a program of community organizing and reform (which survived through the Depression and a world war; see Bennett [1987]). This period produced the classic fieldwork studies associated most strongly with Chicago sociology, including, for example, *The Hobo* (Anderson 1923), *The Gang* (Thrasher 1927), *The Ghetto* (Wirth 1928), *Suicide* (Cavan 1928), *The Saleslady* (Donovan 1929), *The Gold Coast and the Slum* (Zorbaugh 1929), *The Jack-Roller* and *The Natural History of a Delinquent Career* (Shaw 1930, 1931), *The Negro Family in Chicago* (Frazier 1932), and *The Taxi-Dance Hall* (Cressey 1932).

By the 1930s, however, Chicago was beginning to lose its prominence in the discipline, as the field grew and differentiated. Sociology and anthropology had split into separate departments in 1929, and sociology faculty were increasingly pursuing different visions of social science (William Fielding Ogburn moved to the department in 1927, for example, and Laslett [1998] and others note his strong and influential advocacy of quantification and a distanced objectivism through more than two decades at Chicago). Park was frequently away from Chicago and retired in 1934, and Burgess seemed less effective without his colleague. But fieldwork investigations continued, even if they were no longer at the center of departmental activity, and the department was no longer so central to the discipline. William Lloyd Warner joined the sociology and anthropology departments with a joint appointment in 1935, and Everett Hughes, a 1928 PhD, came back to the faculty in 1938. Herbert Blumer (another 1928 PhD) took over Mead's social psychology teaching assignment; over time he became a major interpreter of Mead's work and a foundational figure in what would become symbolic interactionism.

As Chapoulie (1996) points out, the discipline of the 1930s and 1940s was becoming large enough to afford space for multiple approaches. So as a new style of survey research began to develop, Hughes and Warner continued to teach and supervise field-based projects. In this period, the studies moved beyond the city of Chicago, and the production of exemplars expanded beyond Chicago-connected researchers. Warner directed a series of community studies in Massachusetts (*The Yankee City* series, 1941–59), Mississippi (*Deep South,* Davis et al. 1941), and a small Illinois town (*Democracy in Jonesville,* 1949), and Hughes investigated ethnic relations in French Canada, where he taught before returning to the University of Chicago. William F. Whyte, at Harvard, did participant observation in the North End of Boston that resulted in *Street Corner Society* (1943), working with anthropologist Conrad Arensberg, and that book became a model for Chicago fieldwork students. At both Harvard and Chicago, there was increasing interest in studies of industrial work and new financing for research in that area. In the 1940s, war would not only interrupt this work but also change the discipline by intensifying the recruitment of quantitative sociologists into the management of modern mass society and communications. After the war, fieldworkers would systematize their methods within this new disciplinary context.

The 1950s: Postwar Professionalism and Participant Observation

Wars inevitably reshape societies, pulling many people out of customary places and practices, and World War II had these kinds of effects for Americans,[2] including Chicago sociologists. Abbott (1999) notes that key figures in the department were absent for extended periods, as is evident in Helen MacGill Hughes's account of being a "faculty wife employed on campus" and taking on increasing responsibility as editorial assistant at the *AJS*:

> Blumer [the journal's editor at the time] went on leave to Pittsburgh to arbitrate "Big Steel." Of the associate editors, Samuel Stouffer was in Washington finding out for the army what the GIs wanted; Everett Hughes and Lloyd Warner were conducting field studies in Chicago factories of man-, woman-, and Negro-power; Ernest Burgess, Will Ogburn, and Louis Wirth, always concerned citizens, were also caught up in war-connected research. I, meanwhile, kept the editorial office open and busy five forenoons a week, having evolved a conception of my work as getting out on time—a substantial achievement in wartime—a journal more meticulously edited and claiming a minimum of the editors' time and energy. (Hughes 1973a, 768)

After the war, the men came back to the university—as they did elsewhere—and postwar demographics brought big changes in higher education and all of the academic disciplines. The GI bill and the group of returning veterans who enrolled in U.S. colleges meant a massive expansion of undergraduate and also graduate education, ushering in a cohort of scholars who would shape scholarly work through the rest of the century. In sociology, as in most other fields, the order of the day was a return to pre-war gender arrangements.

In the discipline, this was the period when survey research consolidated its modern ascendancy. Chicago faculty had begun the transition toward quantification much earlier, but historians agree that the early 1950s mark a watershed. The department was struggling with its administration, in part

2. See Milkman (1987) on women's employment, Wynn (1976) and Morehouse (2000) on African Americans in the military, and Berube (1990) on changes in the lives of gay men and lesbians.

over the department's "parochialism," and members were struggling with each other over the department's past and future (Abbott and Graziano 1995). By 1960, the major figures associated with fieldwork—Blumer, Strauss, and Hughes—would be gone. But the 1950s brought an extraordinary cohort of Chicago graduate students who began to shape a renewed fieldwork tradition. Those often identified as part of this group (some, but not all, returning veterans) include Howard S. Becker, Erving Goffman, Eliot Freidson, Fred Davis, Tamotsu Shibutani, Murray Wax, Ray Gold, Joseph Gusfield, Melville Dalton, and Donald Roy. They came to be seen by some as constituting a second Chicago school—although (as in the earlier period) the coherence of the group is tenuous enough that Gary Fine's book-length treatment (1995) adds a question mark to the phrase in its title.

Women of this period are not always recognized in accounts of their generation (Deegan 1995), though there were a considerable number, and they were also a quite extraordinary cohort. Some continued to pursue field research and had very successful careers, like Virginia Olesen, Helena Z. Lopata, Paule Verdet, Sally Cassidy, and Joan Moore.[3] Some were wives of male students or faculty (like Rosalie Hankey Wax, whose degree was in anthropology) and worked alongside their husbands, as Helen Hughes had in the earlier generation. There is sharp controversy in the emerging literature on the status of the women scholars in this period. Some would later report experiencing painful discrimination, and it is clear that some careers were restricted, especially by the period's nepotism rules (which prohibited spouses from working in the same institution). Yet women scholars made up a significant part of the postwar cohort, and by their own accounts, some felt well supported by Chicago faculty and well integrated into the student group. Lopata remembered that the women, just like the men, brought strength and a richness of experience from their wartime lives. She quotes Gladys Lang, who describes women of the postwar generation as "veterans in our own way," who were

> quite able to speak up for ourselves and well prepared to look out for our own interests. . . . Lopata had fled Warsaw with her mother; Goldstein [Blumberg] taught at a leading "all Negro college" [Fisk], a hardly usual career choice [she came from a New York Jewish family]; Daisy Lilienthal, a "mischling" rescued after the war by her American father had worked as a laborer in Nazi Germany; Maggie Blough had been a test pilot for Boeing and a union organizer in the

3. My list includes those I believe would be most clearly associated with a fieldwork tradition, but see Deegan and Lopata in Fine (1995) on women scholars of the period doing other kinds of work.

Northwest Canning industry; Paule Verdet and Sally Cassidy . . . lived in France and French Canada and were active in resistance and left-Catholic circles. . . . As for myself, [I] worked in D.C., England (during the buzzbomb days), Italy and China. (Lang to Mary Jo Deegan, July 1991, quoted in Lopata 1995, 374–75)

Despite the gender discrimination of the period, these women persisted and found creative ways to pursue productive sociological careers. Lopata suggests that many of the men felt marginalized as well—because they were Jewish, or refugees, or because of their class mobility—and that men and women students of the early 1950s forged a sense of commonality across varying marginal identities. These observations suggest a complexity underlying portraits of the department that portray it as monolithically white and male; they help to explain, perhaps, both women's diverse views of their status at the time and also the fierce resistance of some male scholars to analyses of sexism in the department (see Deegan and Lopata in Fine 1995). It is striking, however, to observe how the women scholars who were present have been neglected or marginalized in written accounts of the period; the feminist historical research that began in the 1970s is just beginning to bring them back into the record.

Everett Hughes and Herbert Blumer were key figures for this generation of fieldworkers, as teachers at Chicago in the early 1950s and through their continuing work, at Brandeis and Berkeley respectively, in the decades that followed. Some historians of the period point to the ways that Hughes's empirical orientation combined with Blumer's philosophy as the foundation for symbolic interactionist theory (Fine [1995], for example, forms the "second" Chicago school around symbolic interactionism); others see Hughes as more aligned with Warner's anthropological approach and stress his research on work and communities. Early on, Hughes responded to the work demands of this large postwar cohort by taking on the introductory graduate course and crafting it as an introduction to fieldwork (Chapoulie 1996). He also convened a project designed to apply sociological analysis to the conduct of fieldwork (Junker 1960), setting an agenda for a more systematic analysis of ethnographic practice. Blumer was more of a methodological critic than a practitioner, but his increasingly sharp criticisms of variable-based survey research provided conceptual tools for those who would develop new theoretical foundations for fieldwork practice.

The characteristic questions of this era dealt not only with urban communities, but with work and workers, the professions and professional institutions, and middle-class community life. Hughes organized a series of studies of educational institutions during this time, including a study of the education of physicians, undertaken by a team of researchers that included Howard Becker, Blanche Geer (whose training was in education), and Anselm Strauss. This Chicago team of researchers was implicitly (or subjectively) in competition with Merton's group at Columbia, who were at work on survey-based studies of the medical profession (Chapoulie 1996, 18). The Chicago group's work was less respectful of the profession—as reflected in their title, *Boys in White* (Becker et al. 1961)—and illustrated the "debunking" potential of participant observation studies of the powerful. Through their participation in this project, Becker and Geer developed increasingly explicit understandings about the rigor and credibility of what they were now calling participant observation research, and they wrote a series of widely read papers on various aspects of the approach: "First Days in the Field" (Geer 1964), "Participant Observation and Interviewing" on interview and observational data (Becker and Geer 1957), and "Problems of Inference and Proof" (Becker 1958). They wanted in these writings to make explicit the kinds of reasoning underlying their analyses and to resist the notion that insights simply arrive in some mystical way or that fieldwork is such a personal practice that only a talented few can get it right. I suggest as well that these texts are shaped by their moment: the authors responded to questions posed in a language of quantification and relied on that rhetoric in their response.

"Problems of Inference and Proof" begins in Becker's characteristically straightforward way: "The participant observer gathers data by participating in the daily life of the group or organization he studies. He watches the people he is studying. . . . He enters into conversation with some or all the participants" (1958, 652), and so on.[4] He goes on to describe participant observation research as a sequential process of data collection and analysis, in which each phase includes both observation and analysis. Although he describes an inductive process, his account relies on a quantitatively oriented rhetoric. In the first phase, the researcher enters the field and begins to become familiar with its characteristic organization, a process of selecting "problems, concepts and indices" (653). The next step is to check "the frequency and distribution of phenomena" (656). The third stage, constructing a social system model, involves expressing "complicated interrelations among many variables" (657). These interrelations could in theory be expressed statistically, but they are usually too complex for numbers and there-

---

4. It would be churlish to rest for too long on Becker's conventional use of the generic *he*, but it is worth noting briefly as an ironic signal of the gender arrangements of the era, especially given his research partnership with Geer.

fore must be expressed in words. The final stage, the "systematic analysis" that leads to a published report of results, requires "rechecking and rebuilding models as carefully and with as many safeguards as the data will allow" (659).

The heart of this essay is in Becker's discussion of "some commonly used tests" (654) for assessing the adequacy of participant observation data. These tests include examination of the credibility of informants (does the informant have reason to lie or conceal the truth? did she or he actually witness the event? and so forth); consideration of whether statements are volunteered or directed; and judgments about the "observer-informant-group equation" (655), or how the interpersonal context, including the observer's presence, might influence what is seen. With these tests in mind, the researcher goes on to consider the soundness of potential findings and "reaches conclusions that are essentially quantitative" (656). Fleshing out this idea, Becker explains:

> In assessing the evidence . . . the observer takes a cue from his statistical colleagues. Instead of arguing that a conclusion is either totally true or false, he decides, if possible, how *likely* it is that his conclusion about the frequency or distribution of some phenomenon is an accurate quasi-statistic, just as the statistician decides, on the basis of the varying values of a correlation coefficient or a significance figure, that his conclusion is more or less likely to be accurate. (656)

To reach firmly grounded conclusions, the participant observer wants a great deal of evidence to weigh in these ways and, more importantly, many kinds of evidence that can be weighed and considered in relation to one another.

Becker's concluding comments are both defensive and optimistic. First, he wishes "to bring out the fact that the technique [participant observation] consists of something more than merely immersing oneself in data and 'having insights'" (660). For an audience of fellow fieldworkers, he also expresses the hope that qualitative research may become "more a 'scientific' and less an 'artistic' endeavor" (660) (but note the scare quotes for each label). The issue here (and it is a persistent one) is how to deploy fieldwork data as evidence. The data are cumbersome, unlike those of the survey researcher (who can distill thousands of communicative interactions into a single number), and it is clearly impractical to present all of it to readers. Thus Becker acknowledges that it may not be obvious how the observer has reached the conclusions presented and suggests that participant observers should display their reasoning more explicitly.

Becker and his colleagues put these ideas into practice in reporting the results of their collaborative participant observation of medical students in *Boys in White* (1961). Results are presented in quantitative and tabular form as well as through narrative supported with excerpts from field-note data and interviews. The now-peculiar look of the text can be confirmed by a glance at a page or two, but it was less peculiar in its own time, when Donald Roy was presenting tabular data (as in Roy 1952) from his fieldwork studies on the restriction of production (and see Davis et al. 1941). The text can be read, then, as a demonstration more than a presentational strategy that lived on. But it articulates a mode of thought that underpins skillful observation, and those of us teaching fieldwork methods still offer it to students as a useful statement about the logic and rigor of observational practice.

Despite the variable-based rhetoric of "Inference and Proof," what Becker and Geer were counting were medical students' "perspectives"; they were not so much concerned with "getting the facts" (in a positivist sense) as they were with showing others how they came to understand the students' views of medical education. What's important for my historical story is that fieldworkers were developing a sharpened methodological self-consciousness. As quantitative and qualitative sociologies split, those doing qualitative work were pushed to make the foundations of their practice more explicit, and they began to develop a corpus of writing about method. Some texts, such as Whyte's appendix to *Street Corner Society* (1955), are written in a straightforward storytelling style (his goal was to give a "realistic" account, which would be useful in teaching the approach [see Platt 1996, 252]); Buford Junker's volume (1960) reporting on the Hughes study of fieldwork practice is organized more as an "archive" of fieldwork experience and wisdom. One can sometimes read, in the margins of these discussions, the effects of writing within an increasingly quantitative field whose concerns focused on the measurement and testing of relations among variables. It was in this context, for example, that Glaser and Strauss (1967) developed their extended discussion based on the distinction between discovery and verification, arguing that fieldworkers should use their close-up knowledge of social settings to build "grounded" theoretical propositions that might later be tested quantitatively. At the same time, all of these authors share an emphasis on fieldwork as an embodied practice and include stories of that practice in their texts, as in the Becker and Geer essays and the writings of Rosalie Wax (collected in Wax 1971), Ray Gold (1958), Arlene Kaplan Daniels (1967), and others. For these authors, participant observation was a "yardstick" by which one might measure other approaches: it offered distinctive advantages, and while they were careful not to claim that it was superior to other methods, it might serve "to suggest what orders of information escape us when we use other methods" (Becker and Geer 1957, 28).

As academic sociology grew during this period, it began to fragment along multiple fault lines. Along with increasing specialization and a proliferation of subfields that become more distinct, there were political divisions. The expansion of the academic world made room for differentiated spaces, and those spaces made room for sociologists to preserve approaches that might otherwise have clashed with those at the center of the field. The founding of SSSP in the early 1950s, for example, made a home for critics of "grand theory" and "abstracted empiricism," as well as more activist sociologists who questioned the increasing scientism of the field (Abbott 1999, 78–79), and that organization became one of the places where field-based research, especially on urban "social problems," continued to thrive. For proponents, these approaches provided an "antidote to abstraction" and a persuasive rhetoric that linked research—though perhaps tenuously—to community organizing and reform (Bennett 1987, 230).

Key fieldwork figures moved from Chicago to departments that would become new centers of activity: Blumer left in 1952 to head the department at Berkeley; Anselm Strauss left in 1958, moving to the University of California at San Francisco two years later (where he began by teaching methods in a doctoral program in nursing and soon founded a new doctoral program in sociology); and Hughes went to Brandeis University in 1960 to found a new PhD program (Reinharz 1995). Chicago students trained in the early 1950s moved into the proliferating and expanding departments of the 1950s and 1960s, places that afforded time and resources for (and demanded) research and writing. This kind of movement and growth inevitably brought diversification in fieldwork practices and new articulations of the unity of fieldwork practice and its place in the discipline. Becker, Geer, and Hughes completed a study of undergraduate education (*Making the Grade*, 1968), and then planned and received funding for a third joint study of education for the trades (*Learning to Work*, Geer 1972). That research continued as they moved to three different institutions (Hughes was already at Brandeis; Becker went to Northwestern and Geer to Syracuse), where each trained a team of graduate students who worked on specific trades. Strauss's program in San Francisco, where Virginia Olesen also taught, formed the nucleus of a grounded theory group; Blumer and others trained students at Berkeley; and John and Lyn Lofland began to pursue fieldwork studies at the Davis campus in California. At Brandeis, the fieldwork tradition was inflected by the European social theory that was strongly represented there, producing a group of especially reflective fieldworkers on the faculty (e.g., Kurt Wolff, Robert Weiss, and Irv Zola, among other Chicago-influenced and fieldwork-oriented faculty) and a group of students that included Robert Emerson, Gaye Tuchman, Barrie Thorne, and Shulamit Reinharz (who returned to Brandeis as a faculty member in 1982).[5] Emerson would move to UCLA, where fieldworkers built productive collaborations with ethnomethodologists and began training students in yet another distinctive version of Chicago-based ethnographic work.[6]

Researchers in social psychology had begun to develop symbolic interactionism as a theoretical ground for the kind of work going forward as participant observation, drawing on Blumer's interpretations of Mead to build a tradition. Arnold Rose, at work on a symbolic interactionist reader, explained to one potential contributor that it was "what they do at Chicago!"; but many of those who were identified as symbolic interactionists during this time seemed a bit bemused to be categorized (Platt 1996, 120). Becker began to write about marijuana use (or more accurately, about the perspectives of users and others), and the essays collected in *Outsiders* (Becker 1963), alongside other work on deviance, became "labeling theory." Erving Goffman took the ideas of "community study" in unique and fruitful directions, with the study of "everyday life" not only in community (1954) but also in institutions and the public spaces of urban life (1959). Goffman's study *Asylums* (1961), despite a rather distanced tone (Becker 2003), had a powerful impact on the field of psychiatry, becoming a key text in the movement for deinstitutionalization of mental patients. These studies and their reception and influence helped to establish this kind of fieldwork as part of a scientific but also broadly liberatory project, based in investigations and affiliations with the "underdogs" of social organizations (Becker 1967).

The Sixties and Seventies: Asserting Alternative Possibilities

The writings of Whyte, Becker and his colleagues, Murray and Rosalie Wax, and Glaser and Strauss, between the late forties and midsixties, form the scaffolding for conceptions of participant observation that identify it as a distinctive research practice, and that make stronger and more distinctive claims than before about the rigor and credibility of fieldwork methods. As the social sciences grew during the 1960s and 1970s, fieldworkers began to

5. Reinharz's case study of the department provides an analysis of how the fieldwork tradition was *"not* transplanted . . . [but] sustained and transformed"* (1995, 302) in a process of cultural diffusion; it represents the kind of meticulous oral history research we need in order to understand the spread and development of fieldwork approaches in this period.

6. For bits of this history, see Psathas (1995), and Pollner and Emerson (2001).

build their own scholarly networks and outlets. A resurgence of fieldwork in the 1970s and 1980s built in two mutually reinforcing, and also sometimes contradictory, directions. On the one hand, it was a period of institution building that included conferencing, organizational development, and the establishment of new journals devoted to qualitative studies. At the same time, rationales for adopting qualitative methods were strengthened by the identity-based movements and then severely challenged by more sophisticated theorizing of identities and their construction, producing the "crisis of representation" to which fieldworkers are still responding.

Efforts at institution building flourished in a moment of tremendous growth and specialization throughout the academic world. Books on the foundations of qualitative research—Glaser and Strauss's *The Discovery of Grounded Theory* (1967), Denzin's *The Research Act* (1970), Phillips's *Knowledge from What?* (1972)—were accompanied by new textbooks, such as those by Bruyn (1966), McCall and Simmons (1969), Lofland (1971), Bogdan and Taylor (1975), and others. The *Journal of Contemporary Ethnography* was born in 1972, under the auspices of Sage Publications and the title *Urban Life and Culture;*[7] the printed policy in the opening issue calls for studies that "strive to convey the inner life and diverse social enclaves and personal circumstances of urban societies," and editor John Lofland elaborates on that call in an introductory essay. *Symbolic Interaction* appeared in 1977, and *Qualitative Sociology* in 1978. Sage began to publish materials focusing specifically on qualitative methodologies and in 1985 issued the first in its series of "little blue books" (of which there are at least forty-eight at the time of this writing), which treat particular topics in qualitative methodology.

The texts and journals of this period gave practitioners of qualitative methods a foundation for pursuing their work through the "invisible college" of academic discourse rather than only through face-to-face apprenticeship. Clusters of fieldwork practitioners developed on the two coasts, around Brandeis and on the northern California campuses at Berkeley, San Francisco, and Davis, and in institutions such as Syracuse, Northwestern, UCLA, and others. Such departments, housing more than the token fieldworker found in many departments of the era, were key sites that sustained the tradition. They provided the kind of apprenticeship that passes on the "craft knowledge" so necessary for the skillful implementation of any research approach. In the writings of this period, one sees a more confidently

7. The journal's name change in 1975 to *Urban Life* was meant to signal its sociological character. Its 1987 rebirth as *Journal of Contemporary Ethnography* reflected a new epistemological consciousness, which I discuss in the next section, and perhaps also a rapprochement with anthropological fieldworkers.

distinctive rhetoric for qualitative research, though one that is still tied to midcentury standards of the discipline and positivist, or at least naturalist, epistemologies. One can also glean, around the edges of these writings, announcements of the new voices that begin to sound throughout the world and in sociology, and the new challenges they will present for qualitative epistemologies.

As exemplar of a more assertive rhetoric for fieldworkers, I consider an essay that appeared in the first edition of Brandeis PhD Robert Emerson's widely used reader, *Contemporary Field Research* (1983). The reader contains selections by both sociologists and anthropologists, and draws illustrations from research on a broad range of cultures, occupations, and activities; it is organized into sections titled "Understanding Members' Worlds," "Theory and Evidence," "Relational and Personal Processes," and "Ethical and Political Processes." Emerson's introductory material notes an increasing methodological self-consciousness among fieldwork researchers, suggesting that participant observers are engaged in an interpretive process, but one that can be rigorously scientific.

A chapter by Jack Katz, titled "A Theory of Qualitative Methodology: The Social System of Analytic Fieldwork" (adapted from the methodological appendix to Katz's book *Poor People's Lawyers in Transition*, 1982), provides both an outline of analytic induction and a response to critics of qualitative field research.[8] Like Becker's article, it takes on the charge of impressionistic looseness and serves as a manifesto of credibility for fieldwork studies. Katz, however, draws a sharper boundary between qualitative and quantitative approaches.

Katz examines the social system of fieldwork in order to address the questions that critics might ask, labeling these the four Rs: representativeness (can we generalize from the study?), reactivity (does the researcher's presence influence what happens in the field?), reliability (can we trust the data?), and replicability (could others repeat the study?). By framing the issues in this way, he accepts the challenge of a quantitative paradigm. Qualitative studies, he concedes, lack the systematic, planful character of quantitative studies: they are improvisational rather than following a fixed design, and they seek categories of analysis "grounded" in the data rather than in preselected coding schemes. But he refuses the usual answers of the

8. Analytic induction is a mode of analysis that seeks a "perfect relation" between data and the researcher's explanation, and can therefore be more exacting and rigorous than the qualitative researcher's more usual search for themes or patterns in the data. It is also, and significantly in this context, the method used by Alfred Lindesmith in his studies of opiate addiction, which inspired Becker's studies of marijuana users (1963).

time: that qualitative researchers do exploratory research or (the Glaser and Strauss formulation) that fieldworkers discover rather than test theory. Rejecting the idea that the improvisational character of fieldwork stands in the way of meeting the tests of the four Rs, Katz develops a series of claims that position fieldwork, on its own terms, as rigorously scientific.

Katz begins by pointing out, briefly, that the planful character of quantitative research is largely illusory; he draws on the emergent insights of ethnomethodology and foreshadows (though faintly) postmodernism's sharp critiques of positivist science. His argument is that fieldwork practices create a social system—social relationships among researchers, subjects, and readers—that has the capacity to produce knowledge we can trust, and that those social relationships constitute fieldwork as scientifically systematic. The "rules" of those relationships—sometimes formalized as methodology but more often carried in the "routine practices" of fieldwork—constitute a community of interpretation, and the constitution of such a community is what makes a science. To develop this argument, Katz outlines the practice of analytic induction—based on a logic of searching for negative cases—and then takes up each of the four Rs in turn. For each potential criticism of improvisational fieldwork, he develops a counterargument that displays the solidity and rigor of the participant observer's method.

For example, with respect to representativeness, Katz asserts that a fieldworker committed to the analytic style creates relationships in the field that promote the discovery of internal variability. That is, in searching for negative cases, the researcher learns more and more about the range of perspectives and practices characteristic of a particular kind of setting. The quantitative researcher would need to narrow the focus of a study, in order to produce data that could be statistically significant. The qualitative fieldworker, on the other hand, can admit a great deal of qualitative variation, producing a corpus of material that is rich in opportunities for comparative thinking, and such a corpus of data equips the researcher quite well for generalizing.

On the third R, the credibility of fieldwork data, Katz points out: "There is no insurance that analytic researchers will make rigorous interpretations, but readers can easily guard against being misled . . . as a practical matter, the researcher faces strong constraints toward reliability" (1983, 141). The crux of this argument revolves around writing and the relationship of the researcher with audiences for the research report. Writing practices encourage the elimination of bias, for several reasons: (1) in the field, we often don't know whether the data we're recording help or hurt the argument; (2) when we present data in our reports, we present such detailed and specific data that readers learn a great deal about the setting, and they can use all that detail and specificity to argue back; and (3) writing in a qualitative format provides continual testing of faithfulness to our data: "The everyday stuff of writing qualitative analysis consists of an ongoing series of retroductive shifts: trying to convince oneself that a quote or episode can be interpreted to fit the analysis until frustration is sufficient to make stepping back and modifying the analysis seem the easier course" (143). Anticipating objections from readers, the researcher is pushed to improve the fit between data and analysis.

Throughout, Katz's argument is that fieldwork is a distinctive practice with its own logic of accountability. Though it may not look like the (fiction of) positivist science, its own systematicity gives it a rigor and validity that may exceed that of statistical analysis. In a move that foreshadows some of the critical ethnography on the horizon, Katz points to the field researcher's "methodologically sanctioned freedom" to "blur the line between fiction and data" (1983, 146). He notes that field data include not only descriptions of the scene but personal experience; that data may be recorded immediately or much later; and that "phenomenologically, the distinction between 'created' and 'recalled' data becomes ambiguous" (146). But he asserts that this is "a very constraining freedom"; it is constraining because any skeptic need only find a disconfirming case in order to undermine the researcher's argument.

Katz's defense of fieldwork responds to the then-dominant paradigm of sociological knowledge production, but does so on the distinctive terrain of qualitative methodology. I would argue that the chapter bears other traces of its historical context as well. The social movements of the 1960s gave legitimacy to critiques of established authority and infused energy into a range of alternative communities and possibilities. They made visible movements of the poor, of the colonized, and of racial-ethnic minorities. Katz, like many sociology graduate students of the period, found a dissertation topic—activist lawyering—connected to the oppositional movements that engaged a generation. And his assertively oppositional rhetoric echoes that of the period's activists, suggesting both a consciousness of marginalization within the discipline and also the confidence that his alternative community has something better to offer. Still, Katz writes as a social scientist, with a studied neutrality. The first-person *I* is not banished from the main text of his book (Katz 1982), but it is subordinated, coming to the forefront only in the methodological discussion.

The kind of writing that Katz and others were doing in this period gave increasingly personal accounts of fieldwork practice. The new journals provided venues for publishing qualitative studies more easily than in the field's generalist outlets. They also encouraged the publication in article form of the fieldwork "tale," a concrete, personal, instructive narrative; since such stories about quantitative research are relatively rare, these texts likely contributed to an increasing sense of distinctiveness. Developing the kind of storytelling that was so effective in Whyte's methodological appendix, authors of these stories became increasingly interested in the fieldworker as a presence in the research, and the social movements of the period provided impetus and legitimation for a style of writing that was more engaged, personal, and explicitly activist. Women fieldworkers of this period—perhaps because of their still marginal roles in the discipline and in many field settings—seem especially drawn to personal accounts that reveal some of the emotional turmoil of fieldwork. Thus, alongside writings like Katz's, we find fieldwork narratives such as Barrie Thorne's "Political Activist as Participant Observer" (1978)—also reprinted in the Emerson reader—on her work in the draft resistance movement of the 1960s, and Arlene Kaplan Daniels's "Self-Deception and Self-Discovery in Fieldwork" (1983), which applies Daniels's characteristically sharp perceptiveness to her own blinders and biases in several projects. These personal accounts do not yet show the explicit marks of feminism, but they begin to address the self in ways that feminist scholars and postmodern attention to writing would soon give theoretical legitimacy (Krieger 1991; Van Maanen 1988).

Alongside the institutional growth of qualitative sociologies, the great liberation movements of the century—the anticolonial struggles around the globe and antiwar movement in the United States; the civil rights and black power movement; the women's liberation movement of the 1960s and 1970s; Stonewall and the beginnings of gay liberation—were percolating into the academy. These activities outside of sociology were not only bringing historically underrepresented groups into the academy but were also giving them a rationale for speaking and organizing on the basis of marginalized but newly valorized identities. By the late 1960s, ASA meetings became sites for this kind of organizing: the Caucus of Black Sociologists (later the Association of Black Sociologists) was founded in 1968, and a Women's Caucus (precursor to Sociologists for Women in Society) first met in 1969 (Roby 1992). In addition to changing the demographic composition of the academic disciplines, these movements and their academic formations were building new and lively audiences for the kinds of knowledge fieldwork can provide. Each of the academic liberation movements began from a critique of knowledge, and in each case that critique eventually became a critique of the process by which knowledge had been produced. Sociology saw a wave of fieldwork-based social movement studies, new urban ethnographies, and feminist studies that found in qualitative approaches an academic counterpart to consciousness raising as mode of knowledge production (DeVault 1996). These new currents also helped to bring ethnographic approaches to greater prominence in the discipline. As in the earlier period, fieldwork was associated with studies of marginalized peoples, but increasingly in this period representatives of those peoples entered the discipline as professionals themselves, bringing a new, often tense dynamic to the practice and interpretation of fieldwork studies.

As social critiques sharpened, so too did internal critiques of the discipline's "center," and these critiques often drew on fieldwork philosophies, such as the idea that marginalized groups should "speak" through social research. Although the critique within the social sciences began with quantitative methods, its logic brought it to bear on fieldwork as well and raised new questions that would shape the practice and development of fieldwork as the century ended.

The 1980s and Beyond: Twists and Turns of Postmodernism

By the mid-1980s some fieldworkers were continuing to institutionalize the craft, while others were in the midst of a profound crisis of representation. Conferences at the time featured intense, often emotional and fractionalizing discussion. It was a period of heightened interdisciplinarity, as historians and anthropologists took up new theoretical and epistemological perspectives from the humanities. Fieldworkers in sociology—who often locate themselves closer than quantitatively oriented scholars to the discipline's border with the humanities—felt these influences particularly strongly. Anthropologists led the way in raising new questions about language, authority, and knowledge. The "narrative turn" in that field, under way for some years, veered sharply toward an interest in writing and rhetoric in the work of the group of "experimental ethnographers" that formed around James Clifford and George Marcus, and found expression in their influential volume *Writing Culture* (1986). Along with theorists like historian Joan Scott (1991) and feminist epistemologists like Sandra Harding (1986; Harding and Hintikka 1983), Donna Haraway (1988), and sociologist Dorothy Smith (1987, 1990), these scholars began to show how thoroughly language and discourse inevitably shape any human endeavor, and especially the production of scholarly knowledge.

For some sociologists, these new insights made it seem impossible to go on practicing fieldwork, which began to seem only a process of inscribing the researcher's own desires for mastery of an object of study (Clough 1992). Others convinced themselves that this "new stuff" was all a fad and that researchers could simply go on as usual. But a new cohort of researchers and the expanded audiences for fieldwork wanted to continue without ignoring new insights: feminists, "native" anthropologists (and "halfies"),[9] critical race and "women of color" theorists, and sexual "outlaws" saw in the fieldwork and ethnographic traditions rich possibilities for joining political practice and scholarly authority. These groups and other critical ethnographers, keenly aware of the marginalization of their perspectives, rejected the positivist "view from nowhere" and began to develop new modes of practicing and presenting ethnography—approaches that are more highly theorized than before, that have a stronger aesthetic or rhetorical consciousness, and that epistemologists might characterize as "partial," though I think of them more as "raw" and "jagged."

Choosing an exemplary work to discuss here is more difficult than in the previous sections, perhaps in part because these concerns are closer to the present, and therefore it is more difficult to sort out the various strands of work that move in braided paths toward the future. One group of fieldworkers have followed the path of subjectivity, developing an "autoethnography" of emotional experience that is primarily concerned with the researcher's own perspectives (Ellis 1995; Ellis and Bochner 1996). Others have focused on linguistic phenomena, experimenting with writing strategies (Richardson 1994, 1997), or producing readings and analyses of narrative data (Mishler 1986; Riessman 1993), an "interpretive order" (Gubrium and Holstein 1997), or of texts, films, and other discursive products (Denzin 1991). Another recent direction for fieldworkers has taken them toward historicized analyses and/or translocal concerns, as in Dorothy Smith's call for ethnographies of "ruling relations" (1999), Michael Burawoy's "extended case method" of global ethnography (2000), and Mitchell Duneier's proposal for "extended place" ethnography (1999). In addition, the last two decades have seen a resurgence and reinterpretation of life-history methods, across disciplines (Personal Narratives Group 1989) and increasingly within sociology (Long 1999; Plummer 1995; Auyero 2003).[10]

Perhaps the strongest theme—and one that has begun to affect even some quantitative sociologies—is a reflexive sense of the researcher as a person whose life and commitments are relevant to research practice, and

9. Abu-Lughod defines the term *halfies* as follows: "people whose national or cultural identity is mixed by virtue of migration, overseas education, or parentage" (1991, 137).

10. Bennett's discussion of contexts and uses for oral history in criminology (1987) might usefully transfer to its deployment in new areas.

a concomitant concern with representations of "others." In an era of memoir and personal story, fieldwork approaches have made space for researchers to come alive in their texts, not only for purposes of "confession" but to reveal more fully the encounter with others that produces field-based knowledge. Judith Stacey (1988), for example, recounts the anguish of an ethical dilemma in her struggle toward meanings in the field; she not only makes herself visible in the book that reports her research (1990) but gives her informant the last word. Barrie Thorne's book about schoolchildren's experiences of gender (1993) includes historical discussions of "sissy" and "tomboy" discourses, as well as reminiscences of Thorne's own elementary-school yearnings and how they might have steered her toward a focus on the "popular" kids. An increasing awareness of the researcher's situated position has led to a period of innovation in fieldwork practices, especially in reporting the findings of qualitative research.

There are notable sociological experiments with new formats for ethnography: I think of works by Judith Stacey (1990), R. Ruth Linden (1993), Mitchell Duneier (1999), Joseph Schneider and Wang Laihua (2000), and Jackie Orr (1990, 2005). Still, it is more in anthropology that experiments in ethnographic practice and presentation have pushed fieldworkers toward new rhetorics. Therefore, I discuss here a work by anthropologist Ruth Behar, focusing on a section of her life-history book, *Translated Woman* (published in 1993)—the account of "crossing the border with Esperanza's story" contained in part 3 and titled "Literary Wetback." Behar's text draws on the cross-disciplinary scholarship of the time—a moment of "blurred genres" and cross-fertilization of fieldwork and literary traditions. She writes as a feminist and a Cuban-American anthropologist, drawing on the kind of "hybrid" identity that scholars were making more visible. And it seems appropriate to examine a life-history text, given the significance of life history in the Chicago school sociology with which I began.

Behar's discussion of crossing the border is her methodological appendix, in a sense, although it is here presented as part of the main (but multi-formatted) text. The book itself is a mosaic of formats and styles, each section multiply framed and voiced. There is an introduction to Esperanza, the subject of the book—a Mexican street peddler—and also a reasonably straightforward discussion of method, which describes how this research collaboration developed. The next two parts of the book present a relatively conventional life history, told in Esperanza's "own voice." In parts 3 and 4, Behar says, her own voice becomes "more interwoven" with Esperanza's, and the story less predictable, as she reflects on the production of the life history and its positioning in the academic world north of the border; some of that reflection includes Behar's autobiographical writing. Part 3, "Literary Wetback," is about border crossings, about life (and perceptions of lives) on the two sides of the U.S.-Mexican border; about who and what crosses that border and how; and about the meanings of crossing as a researcher and bringing back to the United States (as commodities) the stories of people who can't easily cross as their embodied selves. An epigraph (from Fernando Benitez) provides Behar's response to those who emphasize these power relations of ethnography: "even so, the ethnographer must accept her destiny, overcome her frustration, and go on researching. At the very least she can communicate her shame to others, for shame, as is well known, is a revolutionary sentiment" (1993, 225).

The first appearance of Behar's authorial voice in this section calls attention to her own border crossing and explicitly introduces a comparison with crossers from the other side: "Having made the drive to Mexico so many times, we have our own beliefs and practical knowledge, like Mexican migrant workers coming to this country, about how, when, and from where to make the border crossing to the Mexican side." And then she describes a particular crossing, in the specific detail of the field note: "David has prepared a wad of dollar bills and holds them tightly in his hand. . . . I am sitting in the back seat with Gabriel and start to open the door, but the guard tells me I can stay in the car. This is something to be handled between the men. . . . Why am I afraid? I feel as if anything can happen" (227). The essays that follow report in the same kind of specific (and open or, some might say, inconclusive) detail on the various kinds of conversation and shared experience that were part of her work with Esperanza. "Inevitably," she reports, "these talks forced us to take stock of our different locations on the boundaries of power as a Mexicana and a gringa."

Behar aims to consider how the ethnographic project of "cultural translation" is (she quotes now from Talal Asad in *Writing Culture*) "inevitably enmeshed in conditions of power—professional, national, and international" (1993, 229). The accounts in part 3 of her book address those conditions by providing several windows into the research relationship underlying the project and the ways the project was seen by others, both in Mexico and back at home in the United States. They are reports on Esperanza's view of the project (but always, of course, mediated through Behar's presentation), on Ruth's own complicated emotions, and on the practical, material lives that both women were living.[11] Rather than providing closure and the as-

11. I have focused on Behar's account of her relationship with Esperanza. Some of those who have commented on my essay are much less comfortable with the autobiographical section of her text, which they read as "indulgent" (but see Mykhalovskiy [1996] on this kind of

surance of credibility, they offer a kind of archive of possibly competing views. They provide an example of a writing strategy and postmodern approach to validity that sociologist Laurel Richardson (1994) calls "crystallization" (as opposed to "triangulation"). It is a strategy that provides the loose ends of analysis, still a bit loose, presented artfully rather than tidied into a neat scholarly package. And it produces a text quite unlike the social surveys of the reformers (though perhaps closer to *The Polish Peasant*) or the modern participant observation studies of the 1950s and 1960s.

Behar's reference to "the ethnographer's shame" points to a persistent tension in ethnographic work. On the one hand, our construction of fieldwork as a scientific enterprise gives the fieldworker an authority to speak about the lives of others and the social arrangements that shape those lives. Such projects are often conceived as operating on behalf of those others, but a survey of the century's fieldwork legacy also reveals a practice of power, and contemporary ethnographers seem increasingly conscious of these dual (perhaps indeterminable) possibilities. As I review our history in this moment of global transformation, I am conscious, with Behar, of ethnography as a surveillance of "the other," so well meant and so often morally ambiguous, so confident of its truth while continually opening the possibility of other readings. Qualitative methods have been used, traditionally, for "close-up" studies of marginalized groups—sometimes by outsiders with variously "reformist" intentions and sometimes with more radical, liberatory goals, providing one avenue through which "outsider voices" have appeared in the discipline. Such studies may offer possibilities for effective interventions, but they may also carry the limitations and oppressive possibilities of amelioration, which is typically organized by elites, and often for the purpose of containing resistance. Many contemporary fieldworkers, intensely conscious of this dilemma, are working toward sociologies that operate differently, by experimenting with representation (Schneider and Laihua 2000; Orr 2005), by developing innovative analytic strategies (Smith 1999, 2005), or by making advocacy efforts an integral part of the research (Hondagneu-Sotelo 2001).

In the Centennial Year

In this essay I have followed some characteristic accounts of fieldwork practice from the era of quantification ushered in by World War II up to the

---

labeling). While I would agree that the autobiographical segment fits less smoothly with expectations for an academic text, I see these concerns also as arising from a trained incapacity to interpret such rhetorical moves (see DeVault 1997).

present, considering the ways that fieldworkers have talked to themselves and others about fieldwork and the production of sociological knowledge. Postwar fieldworkers spoke about their embodied, interpretive practice in a language of objective science, but before that move was consolidated, the liberation movements of the century began to challenge the very notion of objectivity. Over the last forty years, such challenges have not only fueled a great resurgence of ethnographic methods but have also led qualitative researchers in multiple, fruitful, sometimes contradictory directions.

As the twentieth century turned, qualitative methods, and especially ethnography (rather suddenly the valorized term, across multiple disciplines),[12] experienced a renewed growth and prominence, signaled by the founding of new journals, often explicitly multidisciplinary (*Qualitative Inquiry* and *Ethnography*, for example) or in the applied fields, such as nursing, education, rhetoric, and communications, where qualitative methods are gaining increased prominence. The two labels point to two apparent directions of the current moment. Qualitative methods have achieved enhanced visibility and credibility within professional sociology; at the same time, however, cross-fertilization with new perspectives from the humanities, cultural studies, and psychoanalysis, along with attention to linguistic/discursive and aesthetic aspects of ethnography, continues to move the critical, experimental wing of the fieldwork tradition toward new strategies of investigation and innovative genres and styles of presentation.

New cohorts of graduate students, many influenced by feminist and other identity-based movements, have been strongly drawn to qualitative approaches and have taken them up even in departments where formal training and mentoring have been quite thin; this student and new faculty presence has pushed departments toward new curricular offerings in qualitative methods and toward hiring to support them. Policy research has come, once again, to include qualitative efforts, especially in particular areas of health care (in studies of groups affected by HIV/AIDs, for example, and how services might be provided for "hard-to-reach" populations) and in recent studies of welfare reform efforts and their consequences. These developments have, arguably, been set in motion by stubborn challenges for quantitative methods of policy analysis, and by the work of qualitative researchers like Edin and Lein (1997), whose studies are not inductive but rather are closely focused on the questions of policy analysts and on producing data their standard methods cannot provide (i.e., in Edin and Lein

12. Indeed, Culyba, Heimer, and Petty (2004) suggest that the recent "ethnographic turn" in sociology is a change of labels more than of practice.

[1977], information about how poor women actually survive on budgets that don't add up).

Both of these trends seem to be leading to a new moment of codification, this time driven at least in part by the relatively recent interest of funding agencies in qualitative research at a time when universities face increasing fiscal pressures and engage in heightened competition for relatively scarce external funding. Qualitative researchers are pushing funders to recognize the distinctive features of their approach, and funders in turn profess a new openness and have instituted efforts to achieve some alignment of qualitative methods with their standards and procedures of evaluation. At the same time, those we might call critical qualitative researchers, for want of a better term, continue to innovate in various ways, extending the logic of critique, pushing the boundaries of sociology and disciplinarity itself, and bursting through standard scholarly formats—and some of these new directions reach back into our history for new accounts of ancestors.[13]

Each of the authors I've highlighted—despite their different rhetorics—aims to show us how a fieldworker makes knowledge. Each carries the history of fieldwork in his or her practice, and each brings forward distinct aspects of the complex business of interpretation and representation. Each author's work has changed over time,[14] but all the ideas I have discussed have a continuing life within the field of qualitative sociology. Postmodern ethnographers are not likely to include statistical tables in their research reports, but in a sense, their interest in displaying the inevitable struggle for meaning is of a piece with Becker's desire to show readers how the text and its ideas came to be. And they rely on the social relations that Katz described to ensure that audiences will read their work with the background understandings that ethnographers share.

One of the notable contributions of qualitative approaches to the current state of the discipline is a strong demonstration of the reflexive character of sociology and a variety of associated experiments with methods and formats meant to address the inevitable locatedness of inquiry. Qualitative approaches foreground the fundamentally interpretive character of sociological investigation and also explore the potential for a rigorous and sys-

13. Dorothy Smith, for example, pulls strands of thought from Schutz, Mead, and literary theorists as well as Marx in the development of her approach to "telling the truth after postmodernism" (1999); Michael Burawoy (2000) points to a Manchester tradition of social anthropology as a source for his multi-sited ethnographic method; and Jackie Orr (1995) has begun to excavate what she calls "anti-traditions of ethnography" in the writings of Zora Neale Hurston and in experimental film and performance that rely on ethnographic sensibilities.

14. See Becker (1982), Katz (1988, 2001), and Behar (1996).

tematic basis for interpretive analysis. How the current varieties of qualitative investigation—some more positivist and others more critical—will intersect and combine, and what place each will find within the discipline and a wider public discourse, remains to be seen. At the end of the century, many sociologists have turned toward the idea of "public sociologies," reflecting renewed interest throughout the academy in roles and possibilities for "public intellectuals" and in how sociological research is disseminated. Fieldwork traditions have historically produced knowledge especially accessible to broad (middle-class) publics, often highly successful books (see Gans 1997) that take publics "inside" other realities, helping "us" to see "others." But the scare quotes point to persistent questions about our research processes and the reception and uses of our work: Where do we locate "the field"? What kinds of knowledge do we seek there? On whose behalf? Answers will of course be shaped by developments in the contemporary academy—now in the throes of change wrought by broad economic restructuring—and crafted in the context of our time, a time of global economic change and new world conflicts. Our history provides an array of resources for such reshaping, waiting for new practitioners to find strands that will be knit together in response to emergent challenges.

Acknowledgments

It's a bit harrowing, I've discovered, to write a history in which one's teachers and friends are central characters. As in any fieldwork, one wants to get it right, yet one also always tells the story from a particular point of view, through a lens that focuses some parts of the story and not others. I am especially grateful to Howard Becker and Jack Katz for useful comments on my reading of their work as well as the overall narrative. I also appreciated comments from the following, who have helped me get closer to "right": Bob Bogdan, Arlene Kaplan Daniels, Barry Glassner, Prema Kurien, Julia Loughlin, Wendy Luttrell, Catherine Kohler Riessman, Joseph Schneider, Diane Vaughan, and Judy Wittner. And I have benefited from the responses of those who attended the 2004 Stony Brook University Graduate Student Fieldwork Conference, where I first presented these ideas, and the editors and authors of this volume, who met and discussed our contributions.

[six] Pragmatism, Phenomenology, and Twentieth-Century American Sociology

Neil Gross

From its earliest days, the disciplinary project of sociology has been marked by the effort to define itself over against philosophy. In sociology's formative, predisciplinary period, Karl Marx inveighed against the enterprise of philosophy, accusing it of getting lost in the ideological world of abstraction and neglecting the realm of materiality, while Auguste Comte relegated it to a historical phase—the metaphysical—that had recently been transcended, displaced by a positive concern with social facticity. Later, Émile Durkheim sought to legitimate sociology in an institutional climate still dominated by philosophy (see the discussion in Brooks 1998). This he did by presenting sociology as, in many respects, an alternative to philosophy, a form of inquiry that would generate scientific answers to questions philosophers had long posed about ethics, epistemology, and metaphysics. Max Weber, for his part, was more concerned with the relationship among sociology, history, and economics but nevertheless defended social science against a growing chorus of conservative critics on the grounds that philosophical investigations into value amount to little unless they are pursued in conjunction with empirical studies that take seriously the mandate of value neutrality.

Although most of these attempts to differentiate sociology from philosophy assumed that on-going contact between the two disciplines was essential to the progress of each—a point made even more explicitly by the two classical founders who were more comfortable straddling the divide between sociology and philosophy than trying to reinforce it, namely, Georg Simmel and George Herbert Mead—the intellectual boundary work (Gieryn 1999) they collectively engaged in proved so successful, alongside the growing division of intellectual labor, that today most sociologists are comfortable knowing next to nothing about philosophy (Bunge 1999). As they see it, philosophy studies the world of the ideal—of idealized knowers and political actors—whereas sociology is the study of the real, of how social structures, forms, processes, and mechanisms shape the human experience, often frustrating our pursuit of the ideal. And philosophy has returned the favor, so much so that major new statements concerning what would seem to be intrinsically sociological questions, such as the nature of social reality, can be asked and answered by philosophers outside of any serious dialogue with contemporary sociology (e.g., Searle 1995). To be sure, there are places on the intellectual landscape where sociology and philosophy regularly cross paths, among them the interdisciplinary fields of social and cultural theory (Turner 2004), the philosophy of the social sciences (Turner and Roth 2003, the Searle example aside), the field of science studies (Hess 1997), and new calls to reinvigorate the project of public sociology by, among other things, putting normative concerns back on the sociological table (Burawoy 2005b). But the majority of sociologists—particularly in the United States—continue to define themselves as empirical researchers for whom philosophical investigations into the nature of mind, the foundations of knowledge, the structure of language, the good and the beautiful, and so forth are simply without scientific relevance.

This chapter does not argue directly that sociologists are wrong to take this stance. That claim has been ably advanced on various grounds by other scholars (e.g., Bellah et al. 1985). Instead, and in keeping with the focus of this book, my interest here is historical. What I wish to show is that despite the prevailing attitude that sociology and philosophy are worlds apart, American sociology in the twentieth century has in fact been shaped in deep and profound ways by movements of thought centered in philosophy. Thus, at the same time that most sociologists have turned their back on the philosophical enterprise, the most creative among them have actively drawn on philosophical ideas, mining them for their epistemological, ontological, normative, and action-theoretical insights and potential. As the postmodern moment draws to a close, what may first come to mind in this regard is the antihumanist philosophy of French thinkers like Michel Foucault, Jacques Derrida, or Gilles Deleuze, which has been much discussed in certain sociological circles (e.g., Seidman 1994). Others may think of the impact of feminist philosophy, or the significance for some areas of sociological research of the notion of "practices," associated above all with the thought of Ludwig Wittgenstein (see Schatzki, Cetina, and Savigny 2001). Historians of sociology may recall the importance of operationalism in the 1940s and 1950s, a notion aligned with the verificationist paradigm of the logical positivists. Marxist sociologists—at least of the nonanalytic variety— might nominate G. W. F. Hegel's dialectical approach as having influenced sociological thinking, while contemporary political sociologists may be inclined to point to the salience of new currents in political theory, such as the interest at present in recognition (see Hobson 2003).

By no means do I intend to suggest that these intellectual importations from philosophy into sociology have been unimportant. But in this chapter I focus on two philosophical movements that had an even deeper and more enduring impact on American sociology: pragmatism and phenomenology. The historical contexts out of which these movements emerged are radically different, as is the nature of the philosophical programs they advanced. But they share an intellectual characteristic that made them particularly susceptible to sociological appropriation at key junctures: a concern to understand the distinctive nature of human subjectivity, and an insistence that this understanding preserve the distinction between humans as subjects and humans as objects, that is, the distinction between an image of the human being as an active creature who responds creatively to her environment using the cognitive tools and habits she is endowed with by her culture, and the image of a mere entity pushed along by larger forces, her every action predetermined. Because pragmatism and phenomenology shared these concerns—but without drawing the conclusion that the nature of subjectivity is such as to make social science impossible—they were intensively drawn on at several points over the course of the twentieth century by sociologists who saw the field as otherwise tending in an objectivist and deterministic direction. There was thus a strong element of dissidence in these appropriations, as pragmatism and phenomenology were used as weapons in intellectual struggles with other research traditions, paradigms, and schools, especially positivism and Parsonian structural functionalism. But all scientific and intellectual movements start out as contentious enterprises that challenge some disciplinary status quo. The fact that this was so for pragmatist and phenomenological sociology does not mean that their impact on the field was destined to be insignificant. While advocates of these approaches would no doubt like to see more sociologists drawn under their theoretical umbrellas—particularly so for phenomenology, whose impact on the discipline peaked in the 1970s—twentieth-century American sociology would have been vastly different, and in my view far more impoverished, had pragmatism and phenomenology never entered into the sociological conversation. I retell the story of these two movements here, drawing on original historical and interpretive research done by others.

A caveat about method before proceeding: The social conditions that give rise to scientific and intellectual movements are complex, as Scott Frickel and I have recently argued (Frickel and Gross 2005). Explaining the emergence, diffusion, institutionalization, and eventual decline of such movements requires an analysis of the diverse grievances that lay behind them, of the opportunity structures within, across, and outside various intellectual fields that enable movement actors to achieve success, of the institutional locations they are able to colonize as sites for knowledge production and recruitment, of the organizational forms they develop for enhancing coordination and communication, and of the framing processes by which they enroll others in their cause. I have not carried out the kind of historical research necessary to explain, in these terms, the full trajectory of pragmatism and phenomenology in twentieth-century American sociology.[1] Nor would such an account of two largely unrelated movements fit within the confines of a single chapter. Unlike some contributors to this volume, therefore, what I offer here is not a sociological explanation for a set of developments in the field but rather a more traditional intellectual-historical narrative that gives a synoptic overview of both movements with the aim of familiarizing sociologists with their scope and significance.

Pragmatism and American Sociology

Any history of the origins of American pragmatism immediately confronts an irony: while the classical pragmatists were, as we shall see, critical of those who sought to professionalize philosophy by constituting it as an autonomous arena of intellectual activity unconnected to real-world problems, pragmatism itself could only arise in the institutional context of the early stages of academic professionalization in the United States. Before the second half of the nineteenth century, the U.S. system of higher education remained poorly developed. A few schools, like Harvard and William and Mary, dated back to the 1600s, while others, like Yale, Columbia, Brown, and Princeton, were of eighteenth-century origin. Many more colleges sprang up in the early 1800s as westward expansion redistributed the population and the growing prosperity of the young nation freed up resources for higher learning. The content of this learning, however, was closely tied to religion. Harvard had been started as a school to train ministers, and throughout the eighteenth and first half of the nineteenth centuries most private colleges maintained a close tie with some Christian denomination. Most professors and college presidents were clergymen, and the collegiate curriculum was geared toward religious and moral instruction.

Philosophy had a special role to play in this regard, as the discipline that put reason to use in the service of establishing religious and moral truths. This is not to say that American academic philosophers retreated into biblical commentary. Most engaged the classic questions of philosophy—about

1. On the multidisciplinary revival of interest in pragmatism that began in the late 1970s, see Gross (2005).

epistemology, logic, morality, and metaphysics—and the way they did so was by appropriating ideas developed by Thomas Reid and his student Dugald Stewart during the eighteenth-century Scottish Enlightenment (Flower and Murphey 1977; Kuklick 1977, 2001). Reid held that an understanding of "common sense" provides the key to solving otherwise intractable philosophical problems. Common sense, for him, referred to the mental faculties with which all people are endowed by God. These faculties permit us direct access to the external objects of our perception, which answers the question, central to both John Locke and David Hume, of how our ideas of objects come to link up with the external world. The "commitments" of those like Reid and Stewart "to humanism, to empiricism in method, and to the urgency of the problems raised by Hume [concerning notions of causality]" (Flower and Murphey 1977, 278), when combined with their professions and defense of religious faith, did much to endear them to American philosophers, many of whom, in the northeast at least, were Unitarians and sought a middle road between empiricism, with its putative openness to science, and religious dogmatism. Scottish commonsense philosophy is not nearly as well known today as are more flashy nineteenth-century American philosophical movements like Transcendentalism, but "until the time of the Civil War, Scottish ideas were undisputed both at Harvard and in the academic world at large" (Kuklick 1977, 19). In the late 1870s, 1880s, and 1890s, however, a new philosophy—pragmatism—appeared on the scene.

Two factors lay in the immediate background. One was the controversy over evolution. Most American scientists quickly signed on to the Darwinian position, but other thinkers—like the academic philosophers—who had sought to reconcile science and religion by understanding the study of nature to be the study of God's design found Darwinism a bitter pill to swallow—not merely its denial of the doctrine of Special Creation or its insistence on the randomness of evolutionary change, but its basic assumption that there is no radical discontinuity between humankind and the rest of nature, an assumption that would deny humans are uniquely made in God's image (Flower and Murphey 1977, 527-58). This position, which seemed to depict the universe as devoid of divine beneficence and to make human will a mere instrument in the playing out of larger evolutionary forces, caused real anguish among American cultural elites. To slip into the theoretical language of Randall Collins (1998), a "slot" in the "intellectual attention space" thus opened up for a philosophy that could retain the best elements of Scottish common sensism and empiricism while combining them with Darwinian themes and a continued sensitivity to religious and spiritual concerns. It would be William James who provided such a synthesis, having been thrown by Darwinism (and the Civil War) into a genuine crisis of philosophical and spiritual identity himself (Cotkin 1990).

The second factor was institutional transformation in American academe, namely, the expansion of American scientific research in the last third of the nineteenth century. Although attributable to a variety of causes, this expansion was a product mostly of the revving up of American industrialism. The sciences grew to provide new technologies that industry could harness and to train technical personnel. As scientific research picked up steam and new, research-oriented universities like Johns Hopkins were founded, academicians, especially at elite institutions, came to define themselves as researchers engaged in the quest for new knowledge, not purveyors of philosophically informed theology. The pragmatists gave expression to the worldview of these research-minded scholars, for they took scientific experimentation to be the model on which all thinking and knowing is based (Mills 1964).

But what exactly was pragmatism? In an essay published in 1908, the philosopher and historian of ideas Arthur Lovejoy (1963) claimed to be able to detect some thirteen different versions of pragmatism. While this may have been an exaggeration, it is not wrong to say that classical American pragmatism was never a unified philosophical doctrine but a family of closely related philosophies. At its core, however, and notwithstanding various family disputes, the approach developed by Charles Peirce (1839-1914), William James (1842-1910), John Dewey (1859-1952), and George Herbert Mead (1863-1931) was an attempt to rethink some of the major problems of modern philosophy through the lens of evolutionism. In the pragmatists' view, the Cartesian separation of mind and body would not do, for, deeply impressed by Darwinism, they understood thought to be a tool that human beings use to cope with and adapt to the various environments they face. Thought is merely a phase of action that the human organism as a whole sets into motion, so the notion that mind and body are different substances is untenable. More generally, the pragmatists subscribed to a model of human action according to which there is a constant alternation between habituality and creativity (Joas 1996). In any given situation, the actor either finds herself in possession of the habits and skills needed to move forward and achieve her aims, or does not. The pragmatists held that the habits needed to cope with situations amount to beliefs, or, to put this another way, that a belief is nothing more than a habit of acting in such and such a way when such and such a problem arises. If actors find themselves in possession of the appropriate habits, they will mobilize them. If not, they will have to behave in an essentially experimental fashion, generating novel hypotheses about how to resolve the problem and testing those hypotheses in experience by putting into practice the actions that comprise their meaning. This capacity for experimentation the pragmatists saw as being to our evolutionary advantage. In adjusting to our changing environments and generating new hypotheses and habits, human beings inject novelty into the world; were we unable to do so, the species would not have thrived.[2]

With this view that beliefs arise from experience, the pragmatists showed their debt to the empiricism of Locke, Hume, and Mill. Where they departed from the empiricists, however, was in their claim that knowledge is given in social rather than individual experience. This was true, according to Charles Peirce, because the nature of all thought is semiotic: it involves the bringing into logical relation of signs that, while pointing outward toward the world, nevertheless acquire their meanings only in communities of sign users. Individual experience is therefore made possible not by a priori synthetic categories of understanding, as in Kant, but by the individual's immersion in a semiotic system that is intrinsically social. This view was a criticism not only of the empiricists (and an attempt on the part of Peirce to move beyond Kant, for whose philosophy he had the greatest respect) but of the entire Cartesian tradition as well, for on Peirce's model it is impossible to bracket off the world of sensory experience and immerse oneself through intuition in the solipsistic world of the ego, as there is neither a self nor any other sign that can become an object of meaningful cognition outside the context of semiosis. Later, George Herbert Mead (1934) would extend this argument in the direction of an ontogenetic account of the origins of the self as a structure of consciousness—an extension that denied the substantialist position that the self is innate. Dewey too sought to move beyond classic empiricism. He regarded habits of action as primarily social in nature, transmitted to the individual by means of social learning and composing a cultural repertoire.

The pragmatists, however, did not think that undermining the Cartesian foundations of modern philosophy led to debilitating skepticism. Viewing thought as something that humans do to help them solve problems in their environments, they saw no reason to secure the *indubitability* of belief. Either our beliefs qua habits are inadequate for allowing us to cope with the situation at hand, in which case we experience genuine doubt as to how to proceed and search out some new belief that will allow us to cope, or we

---

2. See Dewey (1910/1978, 1920/1982, 1922/1983), James (1907b/1975), and Peirce (1992, 1998).

find our beliefs adequate and employ them. We can, of course, be more or less convinced as to the adequacy of our beliefs, but there is no difference in action between a belief that effectively solves some problem and one that is indubitable; and, in any case, since all beliefs ultimately contain reference back to the social communities that inform their premises and provide the habits of thought that make them possible, the whole project of trying to escape from the world of empirical reality in order to provide a foundation for it is ill conceived.

From these premises the pragmatists moved in a number of interesting directions. Peirce worked out a pragmatic theory of meaning: the meaning of an idea, he said, is only its consequence for action, so ideas that have no practical consequences are devoid of meaning. At the same time, the pragmatists developed several distinctive theories of truth. Before them most philosophers had subscribed to a correspondence view of truth: true ideas are those that copy, or correspond with, the nature of the external world. By contrast, Peirce maintained that true ideas are simply those that would ultimately be held by a community of inquirers employing the experimental method. It is not that such inquirers are destined to hit upon the true nature of the world; rather, insofar as the experimental method represents the best way of finding solutions to the problems humans face, truth can be nothing more than the final, ideal solution that would be discovered using this method. James was led in a more relativistic direction, declaring that true ideas are those that allow the individual to solve the problems she or he is facing. Consistency with the nature of reality was, for James, an important factor in determining the adequacy of any such resolution, but he saw consistency with the whole of an individual's experience, including her or his unique aims and values, as no less important. It was on these grounds that James (1897/1979) defended the "will to believe" that higher powers are guiding the universe. James argued that belief of this kind is consequential because faith inclines people away from resignation and spurs them toward meliorism and moral strenuousness. As for Dewey, he staked out a halfway point between Peirce and James, declaring truth to be a matter of "warranted assertibility." Finally, certain of the pragmatists—James and especially Dewey—drew out pragmatism's political implications. Just as the mundane problems individuals confront can only be resolved if they have the capacity to adapt to new situations, so too can a democratic polity respond adequately to new social and political challenges only if its citizens possess a "social intelligence" and are able to see their institutions and public policy choices as provisional and experimental, always subject to whatever modifications the situation might demand (see Dewey 1927/1984).

Although far from dominant in U.S. academic philosophy, where various currents of idealism and realism battled it out in disputes over epistemology through the 1930s, pragmatism was nevertheless one of the most talked about philosophical movements in America in the first third of the twentieth century. The historian Henry Steele Commager was hardly exaggerating when he said that for a time pragmatism had been "almost the official philosophy of America" (1950, 95). Institutionalized in a handful of top American philosophy departments, including those of Chicago, Columbia, and Harvard, pragmatism was a major focus of attention at meetings of the newly formed American Philosophical Association, of which both James and Dewey served as president.[3]

Many academic thinkers outside philosophy also found themselves drawn toward pragmatist ideas:

> Legal theorists such as Oliver Wendell Holmes, Jr. and Louis D. Brandeis, economists such as Richard T. Ely, political theorists such as Herbert Croly, theologians such as Walter Rauschenbush and Reinhold Niebuhr, founders of the National Association for the Advancement of Colored People such as W. E. B. Du Bois and William English Walling, and feminists such as Jane Addams and Jessie Taft all derived from pragmatism a conception of experience and a way of thinking about abstract and concrete problems that oriented them to historical analysis and away from inherited dogmas. (Kloppenberg 1996, 106)

Pragmatism's relationship to American sociology was particularly close at the University of Chicago, which would become a major center for graduate training in the field. Although practitioners of each of the human sciences were, at the time, under considerable pressure to demonstrate that their particular discipline was autonomous from the others and represented a legitimate form of inquiry (Camic 1995), this was not enough to bring cross-disciplinary borrowings to an end. Despite the early ascendance of empirical psychology, philosophy remained a prestigious source of insight

---

3. Outside of academia, pragmatism found even larger constituencies. In addition to giving well-attended public lectures at a number of universities, in the United States and abroad, James regularly spoke to national and community groups about philosophical and religious issues, and his books sold widely. Dewey was even more popular. The philosopher Sydney Hook, who first encountered Dewey at Columbia in the 1920s, recalls in his autobiography that Dewey was, at that time, "already a national institution with an international reputation— indeed the only professional philosopher whose occasional pronouncements on public and political affairs made news" (Hook 1987, 82). While James's popularity was due to his effort to effect a rapprochement between science and religion, Dewey's public acclaim was a function mostly of the affinities between his philosophic outlook and the spirit and cultural temperament of American Progressivism (Kloppenberg 1986).

concerning the question of "human nature," and at the newly founded Hyde Park campus, to which Dewey had moved from Michigan in 1894, bringing Mead with him, pragmatism was the most well-regarded philosophical viewpoint right up through the late 1920s (although Dewey himself departed for Columbia in 1904). This was so for a variety of reasons, but not least because the university, under the leadership of its first president, William Rainey Harper, defined itself as a research institution that would harness the energy of social change in the city of Chicago to inject vitality and dynamism into the knowledge production process, thus serving Progressive Era goals. Pragmatism fit with this institutional identity, for it promised a thoroughgoing rethinking of philosophy in light of contemporary social conditions. It therefore appealed to Chicago thinkers of a variety of disciplinary stripes. James Rowland Angell explored pragmatism's significance for psychology. In economics, Thorstein Veblen, Clarence Edwin Ayres, and Wesley Clair Mitchell all mobilized pragmatist themes in the articulation of the loose framework that would be come to be called institutional economics. And in the departments of political science, theology, and education, pragmatism was much in evidence too, providing a "common frame of reference . . . that made it possible for discoveries in one field to be significant for inquiries in another" (Rucker 1969, 162). It would have been strange had sociology bucked this local pattern.

Ideas are rarely appropriated for reasons of institutional fit alone, however, and sociologists had good intellectual rationales for feeling an affinity with pragmatism. As we have seen, pragmatism postulates the existence an inherently social self. At the same time, pragmatism provided Chicago sociologists with a sense of intellectual and political purpose. While early members of the "Chicago school" were committed to professional social science, they tended to look askance—as did the pragmatists—at the fact/value distinction and linked their intellectual engagements to the Progressive value of "preserving the democratic ideals of the self-government of local communities under the new conditions of a hegemony in American society of the great corporations and the central federal government" (Joas 1993, 28). Their studies of Chicago were intended not as value-free inquiries into the nature of urban life but as inductive efforts to identify social laws governing the modernization process, with the ultimate goal of informing the cause of social reform. Pragmatism, especially that of Dewey, explained the role that the nascent social sciences could play in this regard: in an era of increasingly yellow journalism, social scientists were to provide a counterweight by carefully studying and reporting on the consequence of various social-organizational patterns and institutional configurations, thereby lending insight to the public into aspects of the social universe that might otherwise seem mysterious and not at all subject to intelligent regulation and control. Some Chicago sociologists were more taken by this vision than others—the journalistic Robert Park more so than W. I. Thomas, for example, despite Park's avowed skepticism about the project of social reform. But even those like Thomas who pursued a more nomothetic agenda recognized, "as one of the pragmatists has expressed it, [that while] practical life can and must give credit to science, . . . sooner or later science must pay its debts. . . . A science whose results can be applied proves thereby that it is really based on experience . . .—that it is valid" (Thomas and Znaniecki 1918–20/1958, 16).

Yet beyond its insistence on the inherent sociality of the self and on hitching the social sciences to a political agenda, how exactly did pragmatism inform early Chicago sociology? This question turns out to be complicated not only because there have been sharply divergent historical interpretations of the matter (e.g., Faris 1967; Lewis and Smith 1980) but also because, as Andrew Abbott (1999) has noted, there is some question as to whether the "Chicago school" in its day ever had the unity subsequently attributed to it. Given space constraints I sidestep these complexities here. While the differences among Thomas, Park, Ernest Burgess, and other members of the Chicago sociology faculty during its first great period of intellectual creativity should not be minimized, it is fair to say that Chicago sociologists employed pragmatist ideas in two major ways.

The first concerns the phenomena of meaning and interpretation and their place in social life. The pragmatists held that how people respond to situations is closely bound up with the meanings they interpret them to have. Thinkers working in the tradition of German historicism had advanced the same claim before. But it was the pragmatists' great contribution to link it to an empirically informed philosophical anthropology. Peirce, James, and Dewey all made moves in this direction, but it was Mead who developed the insight most fully. What distinguishes human social interaction from interaction among lower organisms, according to Mead, is that humans, immersed in a world of language and culture, always interpret the behavior of others as comprising "significant symbols" indicative of their social intentions and formulate their responses on the basis of those interpretations. Communication—the grasping of another's intentions through such an interpretive process—requires that we take the role of the other in our imaginations, trying to understand what particular symbols mean to her or him. Intersubjectivity therefore hinges on prior processes of socialization in which actors learn not only role-taking skills, including the capacity to take the role of the other with regard to themselves, but also the common meanings of symbols, so that when I engage in an action, you are familiar enough with it to have some idea as to what I'm up to. For this reason, intersubjectivity is easier to achieve when actors share a culture and harder when they do not.

Thomas and Park fell in line with this point of view. Thomas, among the first students to earn his doctorate at Chicago in sociology, had, under the influence of the folk psychology of Wilhelm Wundt, whose ideas he encountered on a study trip to Germany, committed himself early in his career to exploring various social milieux through ethnographic investigation. In 1908 he was offered a large sum of money by the woman who had bankrolled the Hull House settlement house started by Jane Addams and Ellen Gates Starr—themselves much taken with pragmatism (Deegan 1988)—to study the problem of immigration. The book that was eventually published on the basis of the grant, *The Polish Peasant in Europe and America* (1918-20), written with Polish sociologist and philosopher Florian Znaniecki, became a model for life-history research, tracing the "disorganizing" effects of immigration on Polish American community life through an examination of thousands of letters and other documents that revealed immigrants' characteristic "attitudes," "values," and experiences. In the lengthy methodological note that preceded the substantive analysis, Thomas and Znaniecki, following the pragmatist model in certain respects, insisted that the context for social action is always a situation, and that, while situations do have objective qualities, it is how those qualities are subjectively understood that has the greatest impact on the actor's response. "The definition of the situation," they wrote, "is a necessary preliminary to any act of the will, for in given conditions and with a given set of attitudes an indefinite plurality of actions is possible, and one definite action can appear only if these conditions are selected, interpreted, and combined in a determined way and if a certain systematization of these attitudes is reached, so that one of them becomes predominant and subordinates the others" (Thomas and Znaniecki 1958, 68). Later, in *The Child in America* (1928), written with Dorothy Swaine Thomas, William Thomas—who had by then been forced to leave the university on trumped up morals charges—crystallized this insight into a sociological dictum that would become enshrined as one of the great theoretical contributions of Chicago sociology: "If men define situations as real, they are real in their consequences" (Thomas and Thomas 1928, 572).[4] Joas has argued that Thomas's debt to pragmatism here in-

4. On the "Thomas theorem," see the interesting discussion in Merton (1995).

volved not just "attention . . . paid to the social role of the definer of situations" (Joas 1993, 31) but also his theorization of the process by which definitions of the situation themselves, at either the individual or collective level, arise as creative responses to experienced problems and exigencies.

Although Park, for his part, did not think that definitions of the situation arise *only* in this way, he subscribed to a similar position. A student of William James and a former newspaperman who had briefly worked with John Dewey when the pragmatist had tried to start a "philosophical newspaper" (Ryan 1995, 108) in Ann Arbor, Park worked as a public relations consultant and ghostwriter for Booker T. Washington and the Tuskegee Institute before joining the Chicago sociology department in 1914. Deeply interested in race, immigration, and urban life, Park expounded a social theory that was one part Simmel, one part Spencer, and one part American pragmatism. A passage on assimilation included in the 1921 textbook *Introduction to the Science of Sociology*, written with Ernest Burgess—the so-called green bible from which a generation of sociologists learned the field—maintained that "every single act, and eventually all moral life, is dependent on the definition of the situation. A definition of the situation precedes and limits any possible action, and a redefinition of the situation changes the character of the action" (Park and Burgess 1921/1969, 764). It was for precisely this reason, Park and Burgess held, that the assimilation of immigrants was so important. It is culture that leads people to define situations differently, but in a democracy it is especially important "that the people who compose a community and share in the common life should have a sufficient body of common memories to understand one another" (765). Assimilation occurs, therefore, not as an iron law of social life but as a process of cultural adaptation in which old definitions of the situation are modified so as to make social intercourse between heterogeneous groups less problematic.

Second, and somewhat more speculatively, Chicago sociology may have been shaped by pragmatism's vision of human action more generally—and not just definitions of the situation—as an adaptive response to problematic situations. While most classic Chicago school case studies were largely atheoretical, they shared a characteristic orientation toward their empirical materials. Beyond the interest in good description, typically of some slice of life thought to constitute a social problem in need of solution, beyond their invocation of the opposed themes of "social disorganization" and "social control" (see the discussion in Janowitz 1978), and beyond their use of "a variety of research methods and resources—spot maps, census data, rudimentary statistics, newspaper files, police, court, and social agency records, personal documents," and the like (Colomy and Brown 1995, 27), Chicago studies had in common that they identified the practical problems and mundane exigencies that their informants experienced in the course of their everyday lives, and then interpreted behavior as an attempt to somehow deal with or manage those problems. Rather than proceeding on the basis of some well-elaborated macrotheoretical framework, Chicago sociologists assumed that the quotidian difficulties and dilemmas actors face in particular domains of life are, for all intents and purposes, constitutive of those domains and irreducibly complex. What interested them was not simply the unfolding of collective processes that occur behind people's backs, as in the famous phenomenon of neighborhood succession, but how individual and collective agents, endowed with certain interests, attitudes, and dispositions, actually go about dealing with the problematic situations they confront: the forms of practical reasoning they use; the habits, techniques, and attitudes they develop individually and collectively; and the feedback effects of these on situations. Thus it was that Nels Anderson, in *The Hobo* (1923), followed several chapters on "the hobo problem"—the difficulty hobos have staying healthy in the face of alcohol addiction, their need for intimacy, their constant run-ins with the police, and so forth—with a section titled "How the Hobo Meets His Problem," which interprets attempts at organizing the hobos, the emergence of hobo writers and poets, and the hobos' attitudes toward rescue missions as various ways that hobos cope with the situations life has thrown at them (Anderson 1923/1961). Clifford Shaw's *The Jack-Roller* (1930) pursued a similar strategy. Although its ultimate aim may have been to contribute to an understanding of the etiology of crime, the book presented a detailed life history of one juvenile delinquent, Stanley, out of an interest in grasping "(1) the point of view of the delinquent; (2) the social and cultural situation to which the delinquent is responsive; and (3) the sequence of past experiences and situations in the life of the delinquent" (Shaw 1930/1966, 3). The same interest in situational exigency and response also crops up in the famous community studies carried out by early Chicago sociologists—Harvey Zorbaugh's *Gold Coast and Slum* (1929), for example, or E. Franklin Frazier's *The Negro Family in Chicago* (1932). In both books behavioral patterns—ranging from participation in local politics to illegitimacy—are redescribed as reasonable, if sometimes ill-fated, responses on the part of entire communities to difficult social-ecological conditions and situations. Of course, given the lack of explicit theoretical discussion in many of these texts, it is impossible to know with certainty whether their focus on the problematic situation derives from pragmatism or more generally from Park's social-ecological framework—focused on the inherently "contextual" notion of the "natural area" (see Abbott 1999, 193–222)—which owed any number of intellectual debts. But given pragmatism's general influence at the University of Chicago and on Park himself—and regardless of whether Mead figured centrally in the intellectual lives of most sociology faculty members or graduate students (Lewis and Smith 1980)—it is certainly a reasonable hypothesis that Chicago ethnographies proceeded on the basis of something very much like Dewey's functionalist philosophical psychology, which "abandon[s] the psyche as an object" (Rucker 1969, 31) and focuses instead on the reflective act, seen as arising from problematic situations.

Pragmatism's heyday at Chicago was about to come to a screeching halt, however. The precipitating event was the appointment of Robert M. Hutchins as president of the university in 1929. Hutchins was an advocate of the Great Books approach to education and a fierce critic of the Deweyan idea that pedagogical practices should emphasize the cultivation of an experimental attitude rather than rote memorization. He set out to revamp the philosophy department, orienting it away from its pragmatist heritage and toward the neo-Thomist position to which he had come under the sway of Mortimer Adler, a young Columbia-trained philosopher whom he had brought to the university. Hutchins formulated a plan to hire a number of other philosophers—among them Scott Buchanan and Richard McKeon—whom he saw as sympathetic to Adler's program (though McKeon had studied under Dewey and was in fact reasonably sympathetic to certain aspects of pragmatism). Not surprisingly, the philosophy department resisted the incursion. A battle ensued, and when the dust settled Mead and James Hayden Tufts retired. Mead died shortly thereafter, and pragmatism was forced to retreat from its position of dominance in the university as a whole (Cook 1993).

If anything, however, pragmatism's significance for Chicago sociology only increased after Mead's death. Although the department found itself in something of a doldrums in the 1930s and early 1940s, it was not lacking in intellectual talent. Louis Wirth and Herbert Blumer had joined the faculty in 1931, W. Lloyd Warner in 1935, and Everett C. Hughes in 1938 (Abbott 1999, 221). Of these, Blumer is the most important for the pragmatist story. Blumer had been a graduate student at Chicago, writing a dissertation under Ellsworth Faris, who considered himself a Meadian, and sitting in on several of Mead's courses. When Mead fell ill in 1931, Blumer was asked to take over his Advanced Social Psychology course (Morrione 2004, 3), which

Mead had taught regularly since 1918 (see Lewis and Smith 1980, 262–71).[5]
Blumer continued to teach the class for many years until his departure for
Berkeley in 1952. As he did so, he worked to formalize the program for sociological research he saw as clearly implied by Mead's insights. This was a
period when the identity of Chicago sociology was much in question. Increasingly the major centers of disciplinary activity were those departments
focused on the quantitative analysis of survey data, or, in the rather unique
case of the sociology department at Harvard, where grand theory of a Parsonian order was being developed (Turner and Turner 1990). Blumer's
"symbolic interactionism" was intended as a pragmatist alternative to both
positivism and structural functionalism, which he saw as having neglected
essential aspects of subjectivity in favor of a deterministic view of the human actor (Colomy and Brown 1995). On Blumer's reading, Mead's major
achievement was not simply the development of a theory of the emergence
of self but what that theory implied about the self, and, as a consequence,
about social action. The key to Mead's theory, Blumer said, was the notion
that selfhood involves taking oneself as an object of thought and interpreting social situations in light of their significance for that object. Insofar as
this is so, action has an inherently "reflexive" dimension—it "takes the form
of the person making indications to himself," and this in turn means
"stand[ing] against [the thing so indicated] and . . . put[ting] oneself in the
position of acting toward it instead of automatically responding to it"
(Blumer 1969, 63). Whereas positivists and Parsonians had depicted action
as "merely being released from a pre-existing psychological structure by
factors playing on that structure," the Meadian point of view suggests that
"the human being is . . . an active organism . . . facing, dealing with, and
acting toward the objects he indicates" (64–65). But many of the objects social actors confront are subjects, hence social action is less important than
social *inter*action. Whenever two or more selves come into contact, Blumer
argued, two processes become important: "*interpretation,* or ascertaining
the meaning of the actions or remarks of the other person, and *definition,* or
conveying indications to another person as to how he is to act" (66; emphasis in original). Social life is ultimately made up of individuals who,
through interpretive and definitional processes, "fit" their actions together
to produce more or less coordinated "joint acts," and in so doing help to
constitute collective actors of various kinds ranging from families to organizations to states. To the extent that this is so, the task of sociology is to

5. Mead also taught a wide range of philosophy courses, from those on Kant and Aristotle
to courses on Hegel's *Logic* and nineteenth-century French philosophy.

"catch the process of interpretation through which [actors] . . . construct their actions," not by "turning to conditions which are antecedent to the process," but by the sociologist "tak[ing] the role of the acting unit whose behavior he is studying" (86). Continuing the emphasis on fieldwork that was so important to earlier Chicago sociologists, Blumer encouraged his students to get their hands dirty in empirical research, particularly of an ethnographic variety, where the interpretive processes through which joint actions come about and have their existence over time can be observed in situ. Indeed, another way of interpreting his interest in formalizing the Meadian model is to note that by doing so he was providing a theoretical rationale for the fieldwork his students were already doing under the influence of his colleague Everett C. Hughes, who taught the required fieldwork course and who was less concerned with theoretical or methodological codification than with inculcating in students the practical logic of qualitative research.

Although the Chicago department diversified intellectually during Blumer's tenure, his impact was considerable. He and Hughes trained a number of scholars who went on to eminence in the field,[6] and, as important, the two helped perpetuate a departmental culture—whose foundations had been laid earlier—in which the problems flagged by symbolic interactionism were defined as intellectually important. Howard Becker, for example, most closely aligned with Hughes, was also a student of Blumer and made his first big (solo) splash with *Outsiders,* an ethnographic study of jazz musicians (Becker 1963). His chapter "Becoming a Marijuana User" heeded Blumer's calls to catch the interpretive process in action and generated insight into the role that the labeling of behavior as deviant plays in the unfolding of that behavior. Interpretive processes—this time at a collective level—were also the subject of Becker's chapter "Moral Entrepreneurs," which anticipated at least some of the current focus within the social movements literature on the role of rhetoric and persuasion in collective action. This topic was also pursued by another Chicago PhD, Joseph Gusfield (1963), whose work, along with that of Blumer himself and Chicago graduate John Kituse (and coauthor Malcolm Spector), helped inaugurate an interest, persisting to this day, in the social construction of social problems (see Best 2003). Erving Goffman also trained under Blumer and Hughes, though his take on symbolic interactionism was idiosyncratic and original, tempered by other influences, like Durkheim. Where Blumer emphasized the way that actors themselves understand situations, of particular interest

---

6. In concentrating on Becker and Goffman, I follow Plummer (1996).

to Goffman was how actors strategically—though not necessarily consciously and in fact very often unconsciously—manipulate the impressions they give off to others not simply through what they say but through their physical "movements and adjustments" as well (Burns 1992, 24). Goffman sought, among other things, to identify the rules of the "interaction order" in which such processes of "impression management" play themselves out. And there were many more who learned their Mead from Blumer, among them Tamotsu Shibutani and Ralph Turner, both of whom went on to become major figures in social psychology, as well as a host of more "macro"-oriented scholars like Frances Piven and Arthur Vidich, who remained throughout their careers "largely concerned with meaning and how meaning was developed" (Wacker 1995, 153). Anselm Strauss, a Chicago student who returned to the department as an assistant professor in the 1950s before moving on to the newly established sociology program at the University of California's medical school, was also squarely in the Blumer camp (see the discussion in Baszanger 1998). Beyond his substantive contributions to the sociology of medicine, death, and identity, Strauss coauthored with Barney Glaser an enormously popular text on how to inductively build "grounded theory"—especially of an interactionist variety—on the basis of qualitative research (Glaser and Strauss 1967),[7] only one of a number of interactionist methods texts that sprouted up at the time as qualitative researchers faced criticism from more quantitatively oriented scholars and sought to systematize and legitimate their enterprise (Platt 1996, 62–63).

As Becker, Goffman, Shibutani, Strauss, and other Chicago students got jobs elsewhere and attained professional stature in the 1950s and 1960s, symbolic interactionism grew from what had essentially been a local phenomenon into a nationwide network of like-minded researchers. In the 1950s, Manford Kuhn, a Wisconsin PhD, developed a more positivist version of symbolic interactionism that tried "to establish a theory of self that was both testable and usable" (Katovich, Miller, and Stewart 2003, 120). Kuhn transformed the University of Iowa, where he taught, into a major center for interactionist research. But in fact, "by the 1960s, interactionists were being trained everywhere. . . . Many sociology departments had one or several interactionists on staff, training students; even when no interac-

7. Near the end of the book Glaser and Strauss argue that one of the advantages of grounded theory is that whereas only the sociologist can develop it, it stays close enough to the world of everyday meaning that it can be applied by nonsociologists in the service of bettering the human condition. Pragmatism enters into the book, then, not simply via interactionism but also through the realization that, "as John Dewey has clarified for us, grounded theory is applicable *in* situations as well as *to* them" (Glaser and Strauss 1967, 249; emphasis in original).

tionists were on staff, students read Mead, Blumer, Becker, and Goffman and could decide that this was the perspective they found most appealing" (Fine 1990, 121). In the early 1970s Nicholas and Carolyn Mullins (1973) declared the intellectual project of symbolic interactionism to be winding down, but their assessment proved wrong. With the founding of the Society for the Study of Symbolic Interaction and the emergence of a specialty journal, *Symbolic Interaction,* in 1977, the tradition won a new lease on life, particularly as interactionists forged uneasy alliances with phenomenologists, whose project for sociology was in many respects quite different, and recommitted themselves to the study of organizations and institutions, helping to counter the widespread view that interactionism emphasized the micro to the exclusion of the macro. This lease would be renewed in the 1980s and 1990s as some interactionists embraced the diffuse and sometimes interconnected programs of postmodernism, poststructuralism, and cultural studies (see Denzin 1992).

Not all midcentury paths of influence from pragmatism to American sociology ran through Hyde Park, however. At least one other important but often overlooked route of diffusion merits attention, but it can only be meaningfully discussed after some intellectual-historical and institutional background is filled in.

Within academic philosophy, pragmatism's stature was diminished considerably in the 1940s, 1950s, and 1960s as a result of the rise of what is called analytic philosophy. Analytic philosophy began with the efforts of G. E. Moore and Bertrand Russell in England to vanquish the idealism that had become popular there after years when empiricism dominated (Delacampagne 1999). Russell, influenced by the efforts of Gottlob Frege to develop a formal system by which logical propositions could be represented, took the view that new light could be shed on long-standing philosophical problems if attention were paid to the language in which they are expressed, and to the logical assumptions underlying that language. Russell made crucial contributions to the philosophy of mathematics, in which he tried, like Frege, to reduce mathematics to logic, but he also sought to develop an alternative metaphysics according to which objects in the world are seen as composed of logical atoms to which more complex entities can be reduced. The young Ludwig Wittgenstein studied under Russell and picked up where he and Frege left off, arguing in the *Tractatus Logico-Philosophicus* (1922) that facts, not logical atoms or objects per se, compose the world, and that language—which represents facts—does so by "picturing" them in logically valid propositions. On the basis of this assumption, Wittgenstein claimed that many traditional philosophical problems—particularly those concerning ethics, metaphysics, and aesthetics, which do not meet these criteria for picturing—are nonsensical. The task of the philosopher is to distinguish sensical from nonsensical propositions, and thus to "eliminate misunderstandings, resolve unclarities, and dissolve philosophical problems that arise out of the confusing surface features of natural language" (Hacker 1997, 70). Although Wittgenstein would later move past these claims in his posthumously published *Philosophical Investigations* (1953), his early work, like that of Frege and Russell, proved influential not only for other British philosophers in the 1930s and 1940s like Gilbert Ryle and J. L. Austin, who, also "hostile to metaphysics and certainly to the notion that philosophy was a guide to wisdom . . . rather looked at philosophy as an activity that clarified ordinary talk and the structure of science" (Kuklick 2001, 244), but as well to a group of Austrian and German philosophers known as the logical positivists. Setting themselves in opposition to what they saw as the philosophically meaningless but politically dangerous metaphysics of thinkers like Martin Heidegger, the positivists maintained that the major task of philosophy is to shore up the conceptual underpinnings of science. This was to be accomplished by subjecting philosophical claims to withering logical and conceptual analysis, developing a more penetrating form of empiricism that could reduce all scientific claims to statements about sense experience that would be compatible with modern physics, and showing up the ways in which the different sciences could be unified. All meaningful propositions, the positivists held, are either analytic (true by definition) or synthetic (true because they contain a statement about the world that can be empirically verified). Propositions that do not meet these criteria are simply not the purview of philosophy or science.

Although logical positivism would soon come under attack itself—most famously from Karl Popper, who sought to replace its emphasis on verification with the notion of falsification, and then later from those within the analytic movement like the Harvard philosopher W. V. O. Quine, who attacked the analytic/synthetic distinction—the positivists, along with their counterparts at Oxford and Cambridge, had an enormous impact on U.S. philosophy, giving rise to a new style and tradition of philosophical scholarship. With the rise of Nazism, many of the positivists fled to the United States, where they were offered positions in American universities: Rudolf Carnap at Chicago, Hans Reichenbach at UCLA, Alfred Tarski at Berkeley, Gustav Bergmann at Iowa, Herbert Feigl at Minnesota, Carl Hempel at Princeton, and Ernest Nagel at Columbia. American philosophy in the late 1930s and 1940s presented something of an intellectual vacuum. Dewey was still alive and writing, but his best intellectual days were behind him, and for a time no movement seemed as exciting and sure-footed as pragmatism had once seemed. It was in this context that analytic philosophy—a high prestige European and British import—was able to effect a takeover. It offered U.S. philosophers, who were beginning to turn toward logic and more technically oriented pursuits anyway, a clear sense of mission, linking them to the physical sciences, whose prestige in the American university was rapidly increasing. In the late 1940s and 1950s this appeal would only grow in light of the expansion of Big Science, associated first with the war effort and then with the massive infusion of federal monies into the university sector during the cold war. Philosophy, struggling to secure a disciplinary identity for itself in this time of institutional transformation, came to redefine itself around the "analytic imaginary" (La Caze 2002) and its emphasis on language and formal logic; it would be a field of inquiry as rigorous as any other, demanding its own specialized forms of training, privileging technical competence over insightfulness or literary brilliance, and crucial to the successful pursuit of the other sciences. That analytic philosophy, at least in its early stages, downgraded the status of political philosophy may also have helped protect the field from critical scrutiny during the McCarthy era (McCumber 2001). Within the space of a few years, philosophers who saw themselves as working in the analytic tradition came to dominate nearly all the top-ranked U.S. philosophy graduate programs, analytic work became hegemonic in the major academic journals, and analysts came to assume leadership positions in the American Philosophical Association (Wilshire 2002). Pragmatism was marginalized as a consequence. Russell, for his part, had been sharply critical of Dewey, accusing pragmatism of being a philosophy "in harmony with the age of industrialism and collective enterprise" because it involved a "belief in human power and the unwillingness to admit 'stubborn facts,'" which manifested itself in the view that the truth of a belief is a matter of its effects rather than of its causes (Russell 1945, 827, 826). Some American philosophers, like Chicago's Charles Morris, tried to combine pragmatism and logical positivism, while others, like Quine or his Harvard colleague Morton White, brought pragmatism and linguistic analysis together in other ways. Nevertheless, many who worked in an analytic style came to see pragmatism and analytic philosophy as opposed, and pragmatism's reputation went into decline. As Richard Bernstein puts it,

> [The period following the Second World War] was a time of great confidence among professional philosophers. It was felt by the growing analytic community that "we" philosophers had "finally" discovered the conceptual tools and

techniques to make progress in solving or dissolving philosophical problems. . . . Of course, there were pockets of resistance. . . . There were those who defended and practiced speculative metaphysics . . . ; who saw greater promise in phenomenology and existentialism . . . ; who sought to keep the pragmatic tradition alive. . . . But philosophers who had not taken the analytic "linguistic turn" were clearly on the defensive. (1992, 330–31)

Earlier in the century, however, before the first of the émigré logical positivists arrived in the United States, a number of Dewey and Mead students had managed to secure academic positions for themselves. Throughout the 1930s, 1940s, 1950s, and even into the 1960s they quietly published a steady stream of exegetical books and articles on American pragmatism and generated a surprisingly large student following. Although there was no question but that the center of disciplinary activity lay with analytic philosophy, about 9 percent of the philosophy dissertations written in the United States between 1950 and 1959 dealt in some direct way with the pragmatist tradition,[8] a statistic that forces nuance on the claims of those like literary critic Morris Dickstein who declare that "by the middle of the twentieth century, pragmatism was . . . virtually driven from philosophy departments by the reigning school of analytic philosophy" (Dickstein 1998, 1). Six schools where pragmatism had earlier been institutionalized— Columbia, Chicago, Illinois, Michigan, Texas, and Yale—together accounted for 56 percent of these pragmatist dissertations.

The University of Texas at Austin proved to be a particularly important case for American sociology. Two philosophers there—George Gentry and David Miller—had been students of Mead, receiving their PhD's in 1931 and 1932, respectively, and it was under Gentry and Miller that a soon to be famous American sociologist, Charles Wright Mills, took a bachelors and masters degree in philosophy, graduating in 1939 before moving on to Madison, Wisconsin, to complete doctoral work in sociology. It was pragmatism, not Marxism, that served as the entry point for Mills's intellectual and political engagement, and Irving Horowitz has remarked apropos of Mills's early interest in pragmatism that "a man never really overcomes his first love" (Horowitz 1964a, 11). Horowitz's introduction to *Sociology and Pragmatism*, the book version of Mills's 1942 doctoral dissertation, which was published posthumously, goes to great lengths to demonstrate that

8. To obtain this figure I used John Shook's bibliography of pragmatist dissertations (at www.pragmatism.org), retaining only those written in U.S. philosophy departments, and then compared that figure with those on PhD production in U.S. philosophy departments given in the *Digest of Education Statistics*. The statistic is slightly different from the one I give in "Becoming a Pragmatist Philosopher" (Gross 2002) but is, I think, more accurate.

Mills's interest in pragmatism was deep and abiding. The dissertation itself was a major contribution to the sociology of philosophy. It sought to offer a "sociological account of pragmatism" (Mills 1964, 464), linking the rise of pragmatism's "laboratory style of inquiry" to industrialization and professionalization in the American college and university system. But the dissertation was actually much more than this, for it contained long and insightful discussions of the philosophy of Peirce, James, and Dewey that represented Mills's effort to sort out for himself the core contributions of the pragmatists. Although later in his career Mills would become critical of Dewey for having neglected the insights of Marx and Freud—that is, for having failed to fully attend to the structural and psychological impediments to the developments of a progressive community (see the discussion in Hickman 1990)—Horowitz argues that Mills's basic conception of sociology remained centered on the normative ideal of "a pragmatic life" revolving around the "tough-minded pursuit of democratic life-styles" (Horowitz 1964a, 22).

Beyond this, however, the concept for which Mills has become best known, "the sociological imagination," presents striking affinities with the philosophy of John Dewey. The capacity to "grasp history and biography and the relations between the two within society" (Mills 1959, 6)—the phrase that every first-year student in sociology is now forced to memorize—is, for Mills, conceived of not as a revolutionary ideology or worldview or set of beliefs, but as a habit of thinking, a "quality of mind" (15) that may be more or less present in any particular population. Just as Dewey sought to cultivate experimentalist habits of thinking according to which, among other things, people living in modern democratic societies could learn the consequences of the public policy choices they had made so they could adjust these or abandon them if necessary, so Mills sought to cultivate a sociological imagination by which individuals would learn to link their "private troubles" to "public issues" concerning the organization of society. Through such a procedure, "the indifference of publics is transformed into involvement with public issues" (Mills 1959, 5). And how should this disposition be encouraged? Dewey put great hope in social transformation through education but placed particular stress on the need for the intelligentsia to turn its attention toward the great public issues of the day. If thought arises evolutionarily in the service of action, he reasoned, then the institutionalization of thought in the various academic disciplines is severed from its natural foundations if it ceases to address the pressing problems confronting humankind, retreating into a narrow and self-enclosed professionalism. Intellectual work should ultimately face the test of social consequentiality, and with regard to the social sciences, as we have seen, Dewey believed their most important task was to help people understand the effects of social-organizational and institutional choices that were, with the "collapse" of the public, increasingly being made for them by elites. Mills could not have agreed more. Not only did he endorse Dewey's anti-formalist definition of democracy, according to which it is the active discussion of issues in the public sphere, not formal democratic procedures alone, that is constitutive of the democratic ideal. In addition, Mills maintained that the sociological imagination could only grow and spread and undergird discussion in the public at large if academicians—specifically sociologists—resisted the trend toward specialization, careerism, and professionalization for its own sake and concerned themselves instead with "mak[ing] clear" the "unruly forces of contemporary society itself," including "its pervasive transformations of the very 'nature' of man and the conditions and aims of his life" (Mills 1959, 13). It was this view that lay behind his attacks on "abstracted empiricism" and "grand theory," and led him to urge would-be sociologists to imbue their work with a sense of political and moral purpose, just as Dewey had tried to do for philosophy.

It testifies to the extent of pragmatism's marginalization in the 1950s and 1960s—a function not only of the rise of analytic philosophy but also of a "variety of new influences" in other fields like "existentialism, crisis theology . . . , psychoanalysis, European modernism, and a cultural conservatism bred of growing prosperity and the fear of Communism" (Dickstein 1998, 9)—that the pragmatist roots of Mills's program were left implicit at the time, such that sociologists today who routinely invoke the sociological imagination as a justification for their work typically have no idea of the pragmatist connection. Beginning in the late 1970s and 1980s, however, and stimulated in part by a resurgence of interest in pragmatism among philosophers like Richard Rorty and Hilary Putnam, a host of sociologists began to turn their attention back to pragmatism, doing so not by engaging the themes of the symbolic interactionists but by rereading classical pragmatist texts and seeking to incorporate their insights. By the turn of the twenty-first century, pragmatism would once again find itself poised on the leading edge of sociological thought.

The field of sociological theory was the first affected. One major form this took was the invocation of Dewey's philosophy in the name of communitarianism. In *The Good Society* (1991), for example, Robert Bellah and his coauthors, pushing beyond their discussion in *Habits of the Heart* (1985) of the limitations that American cultural traditions of individualism impose on our capacities to forge commitments to one another, adopt a Deweyan view of institutions. Arguing that institutional arrangements should always be seen as experiments subject to the modifications recommended by experience, they suggest that the havoc caused by a largely unregulated market could be minimized were we willing to take an experimentalist attitude toward our basic economic, educational, and religious arrangements. Bellah's Berkeley colleague Philip Selznick advances a similar claim. Selznick's early work on organizations, which focused on the disjuncture between an organization's initial goals and the emergent goals that develop as it tries to navigate the waters of its external environment, seemed inspired as much by Robert Michels's "iron law of oligarchy" as by Dewey's argument that goals are emergent from situations and should not be seen as always preceding them. But his more recent book, *The Moral Commonwealth* (1992), makes repeated recourse to Deweyan themes. Here Selznick takes the position that a communitarian conception of democracy—which he sees as implied by pragmatism—represents a better normative ideal for society than can be provided by classical liberalism.

For its part, the social-theoretical corpus of Jürgen Habermas—much read and commented on in U.S. sociology—has been intertwined with pragmatism since the days of the English-language publication of *Knowledge and Human Interests* in 1971. Habermas's deepest debts are to the tradition of critical theory, but unlike his Frankfurt school mentors, who heaped derision on pragmatism, he has sought to combine his critical commitments with a broadly pragmatist orientation. In *Knowledge and Human Interests,* Habermas's concern with the pragmatists took the form of an examination of the thought of Peirce—an examination intended to show that Peirce, along with Wilhelm Dilthey and Sigmund Freud, made serious efforts to develop an understanding of science that departed from the core assumptions of positivism, in particular the assumption that "the subjects who put forward and criticize . . . [empirically meaningful] statements . . . have no *epistemological* significance" (McCarthy 1978, 841; emphasis in original). Habermas's intention in the book was to show that knowledge is undergirded by three kinds of human interests: a technical interest in controlling nature, a practical interest in maintaining reliable communication, and a critical interest in overcoming naturalized patterns of life. While crediting Peirce with the insight that "the logical analysis of inquiry . . . is concerned not with the activities of a transcendental consciousness as such but with those of a subject that sustains the process of inquiry as a whole, that is with the community of investigators, who endeavor to perform their common task communicatively" (Habermas 1971, 95), Habermas faulted pragmatism's founder for ultimately succumbing to positivism by conceiving of this communication in an essentially monological way, despite the significance that semiotic considerations play in Peirce's corpus. In *The Theory of Communicative Action* (1984–87), Habermas finds in Mead what, in his view, only remained latent in the writings of Peirce: an understanding of the uniqueness of communicative action as a form of mutual adjustment premised on the possibility of intersubjective understanding.

Influenced by Habermas—his first project (Joas 1985) an attempt in part to respond to what he saw as deficiencies in Habermas's theory—Hans Joas, who even before his half-time appointment at the University of Chicago was a major figure in U.S. discussions, has become perhaps the foremost champion of pragmatism in sociological theory (Joas 1993, 1996). For him, pragmatism's outstanding contribution to the theory of social action lies not in its emphasis on communicative processes but in the centrality it accords to creativity. Attempting to overcome the dichotomy of rational versus normative action that has structured so much of sociological theorization in the wake of Parsons, Joas draws on the pragmatists to argue that action inevitably takes the form of an alternation between the employment of established routines and the creative reconstruction of the actor's lines of action when truly problematic situations arise. Joas's point is not that creativity should be seen as a distinct type of action but that the alternation between habit and creativity undergirds both rational and normative action. In his most recent work he has used this insight to explore the social origins of values (Joas 2000) and the creative destruction that may follow from war (Joas 2003).

Other sociological theorists, too, have utilized pragmatist ideas. Norbert Wiley (1994) draws on Peirce to develop a theory of the "semiotic self," centered on the notion of the "internal conversation," a topic that has been taken up again recently by British theorist Margaret Archer (2003). Eugene Rochberg-Halton (1986) suggests that Peirce's realist semiotics can help us understand culture as a living world of signs—a world whose cultivation it is one of the purposes of human life to further. Robert Antonio (1989) mounts a critique of Habermas in the name of pragmatism. Although Habermas bases his theory of communicative rationality on a reading of Mead, Antonio claims that the pragmatists would have rejected not simply the societal evolutionism that underpins Habermas's theory but the entire effort to discover universally valid foundations on which ethical-political judgments can rest. Likewise, Dmitri Shalin (1992, 238) criticizes Habermas's appropriation of pragmatism for failing to emphasize "the pragmatist sensitivity to indeterminacy, contingency, and chaos." More recently, Nina Eliasoph (1998) has drawn on Dewey's practice-centered, antiformalistic theory of democracy and the public sphere to explore the ways in which the norms of different group settings encourage or discourage public-spirited talk. And Mustafa Emirbayer and Ann Mische (1998) have taken as their point of departure Mead's underappreciated theory of temporality, which they see as holding the key to an understanding of human agency that does not veer too far into either determinism or unrestrained voluntarism.

One arena of empirical research that has proven particularly receptive to pragmatist approaches is cultural sociology. In *Talk of Love*, Ann Swidler (2001) attempts to flesh out the "toolkit" model of culture and action she first articulated in an often-cited 1986 article in *American Sociological Review*. Against a Weberian cum Parsonian view that culture shapes action through the intermediary of values, and against the position, associated with Clifford Geertz, that culture consists of more or less well-bounded webs of meaning in which individuals come to be immersed, Swidler draws on Joas to argue that culture involves ways of thinking and acting, or "repertoires," that agents mobilize to help them deal with problematic situations. What sociologists of culture should study, therefore, is *how* and *when* agents use culture, not the "effect" of culture on action. To this end, Swidler—again following pragmatist insights but this time moving up to the level of collective action—suggests not only that agents are likely to use culture with particular intensity during "unsettled times," when their established habits of action prove ineffective, but also that such cultural coherence as exists in a society is a function mostly of the ways in which institutions build common experiences into the lives of large numbers of individuals. Swidler's use of pragmatism has been criticized for its overinstrumentalism, but there is something deeply pragmatic about her culture-in-action approach. Similarly, in their recent attempt to "rethink" the bases of "comparative cultural sociology," Michèle Lamont and Laurent Thévenot advocate a "pragmatist approach to the public space," arguing that national cultural differences are best thought of in terms of "unevenly present" "repertoires of evaluation" mobilized in different contexts (2000, 7, 6, 5).

In economic sociology, too, pragmatist ideas have resurfaced. Josh Whitford (2002), for example, mobilizes Dewey's stress on the ways in which ends often emerge during the course of action in order to mount a critique of rational choice theory. While his argument is applicable in principle to all the empirical domains where rational choice approaches have been used, Whitford illustrates the significance of his claims by pointing to political scientist Charles Sabel's work on the Japanese economy. If we understand ends to be emergent from interaction rather than antecedent to it, we may be in a better position to grasp how the relatively cooperative "Japanese production model" of interfirm relations can be sustained in light of both the "inherently fragile" nature of cooperation described by game theory and the inadequacies of a culturalist model that would explain cooperation as an inevitable outcome of pregiven norms and values. Likewise, German sociologist Jens Beckert (1996), who has published extensively in the United States, draws on a pragmatist concern with situational uncertainty to suggest that the purview of economic sociology should be not the embeddedness of economic transactions within sustaining social-structural, institutional, and cultural frameworks but rather actors' reliance in situations of uncertainty on social conventions—habits, norms, institutionalized ways of doing things, and the like—that, given the unpredictability of outcomes, offer at least the security of familiarity.

By no means has all this pragmatist-inspired work revolutionized late twentieth- and early twenty-first century American sociology. Although sociologists interested in pragmatism have been at the center of a great many disciplinary discussions, questions remain as to what exactly a pragmatist sociology would entail, whether the tradition's emphasis on creativity and indeterminacy would undermine the explanatory goals of social science, whether its skepticism as to the value of the distinction between normative and empirical inquiry can square with the prevailing assumptions of most social scientists, and how exactly pragmatism's insights into the nature of social action can be linked up with analyses of meso- and macrolevel social processes and mechanisms. These questions will be debated in the years to come. What cannot be denied, however, is that the history of American sociology in the twentieth century has been marked by repeated efforts to use the ideas of the classical pragmatists, bridging the divide between philosophy and sociology.

The Rise and Fall of Phenomenological Sociology

The analytic tradition gave U.S. academic philosophy in the post–World War II era a coherent disciplinary identity. Despite its hegemony, however, institutionalized in the APA, analytic philosophy was never able to completely eradicate the philosophical traditions that were its competitors. Throughout the period, as noted earlier, pragmatism maintained at least a shadow presence in a number of departments, as did various strains of idealism and even a number of schools of metaphysics, the bête noire of logical positivism (Kuklick 2001). At the same time, new philosophical currents emanating from Europe began to lap at American shores. One of these— phenomenology—came to comprise an important part of what would eventually be called the Continental tradition. Like pragmatism, it had a significant impact on American sociological theory and research, though somewhat later in the century and in a less enduring way.

While the term *phenomenology* had been used in the nineteenth century by philosophers as diverse as G. W. F. Hegel, Peirce, and Eduard von Hartmann, a pre-Freudian champion of the notion of the unconscious (Schmitt 1967), it did not receive the formulation for which it would become known until the 1910s and 1920s, when the German philosopher Edmund Husserl (1859-1938) and his followers began to churn out a steady stream of publications. Husserl had taken his doctorate in 1881, studying mathematics and logic. This was an exciting time in the history of logic. Gottlob Frege had turned the field on its head by proposing that the elements of a proposition relate to one other in a manner that is essentially mathematical. Moreover, he sought to understand the logic of mathematics itself. In one of his first publications, Husserl tried, in the context of these developments, to shed new light on numbers by examining the psychology of counting. He was publicly rebuked by Frege for doing so, however, on the grounds that numbers and our psychological conceptions of them are not the same thing. In his subsequent work, Husserl radically changed course. He now understood numbers to be universals and essences (Grossmann 1984), and recognized that most of the time, in what he called the "natural attitude," where we take the mundane world for granted, our conception of an essence is really a conception of a particular instance or type of that essence rather than of the essence itself. He maintained, however, that we *do* have the capacity to gain intuitive access to essences—not just to numbers, but to any kind of essence—and the relations among them. To do so, we have to attend to how those essences and objects more generally present themselves to us in consciousness, and more specifically to the structures of consciousness that make that presentation possible. For Husserl this was not an empirical, psychological concern but a philosophical one best approached through controlled introspection. He held that the key to understanding the structures of consciousness is to effect a phenomenological "reduction," trying as best we can to "bracket" or hold at bay the empirical world, and along with it the natural attitude—not by doubting, in a Cartesian move, that the empirical world actually exists, but by self-consciously refusing to let our belief in its existence keep us from examining the structures of consciousness that allow us to perceive it as such. If we take this step, attending closely to how objects are grasped by or "intended in" our consciousness, and in fact are partially "constituted" in consciousness, we might, he hoped, attain a firmer understanding of everything from logic to reason to science itself. Such an understanding could then serve as a solid philosophical foundation on which all the other sciences could rest (see Husserl 1913/2002).

Husserl's philosophical program was no doubt shaped by a variety of influences and concerns, but as Martin Kusch (1995) and Randall Collins (1998) have persuasively argued, the institutional context out of which it arose was one marked most profoundly by the rise of empirical psychology. In Germany, the founding figures of psychology—men like Wilhelm Wundt, Hermann Ebbinghaus, Carl Stumpf, and Franz Brentano—were initially housed in departments of philosophy. Between 1892 and 1913, empirical psychologists went from holding 7 percent of the country's full professorships in philosophy to holding 22 percent (Kusch 1995, 126). Many tried to legitimate their presence by embracing psychologism, or the view that psychology holds the key to solving long-standing philosophical problems. By contrast, nonpsychologists like Husserl (who had studied under Brentano), Wilhelm Dilthey, and the neo-Kantians Heinrich Rickert and Wilhelm Windelband sought to deny that this was so, embracing antipsychologism as part of an effort to protect the independence of philosophy, not to mention the jobs of their students and associates. Phenomenology, which Husserl developed from his positions at the University of Göttingen and then Freiburg, must be seen as connected to a social strategy of what Kusch (1995, 160) calls "role purification."

In both Europe and America the new science of sociology was being institutionalized around this time, so it is not surprising that Husserl's insights were soon translated into a sociological idiom. This occurred first in Austria and Germany. The philosopher and protosociologist Max Scheler, for example, developed a phenomenological sociology centered on the notion of sympathy that inquired into the conditions of consciousness that make intersubjectivity possible; at the same time he was laying out a rudimentary sociology of knowledge. Karl Mannheim, more widely regarded than Scheler as the founder of the sociology of knowledge, turned to phenomenology early in his career as part of an effort to distance himself from what he perceived as the reductionism of Marxian approaches to culture (Kettler and Meja 1995, 41). And while not a phenomenologist himself, Georg Simmel gave expression to a phenomenological sensibility insofar as he regarded the study of social forms not as an empirical enterprise but as an "eidetic" one in which, following Husserl, "eide, or essences," like social forms, would be understood as "*a priori* principles of things that are apprehended intuitively through a methodology that is based on pure description, i.e., description that is not limited by empirical instantiations" (Backhaus 1998, 260).

As Donald Levine (Levine, Carter, and Gorman 1976a, 1976b) has shown, Simmel received more attention from early twentieth-century American sociologists than did any other European or British sociological theorist with the exception of Herbert Spencer. But Simmel's affinities with phenomenology went largely undetected. Instead, it was through the influence of Alfred Schutz that phenomenology's concerns came to shape American sociological discourse. Schutz was born and educated in Vienna. His first book, *The Phenomenology of the Social World* (1932), published while he was working as an advisor to an Austrian banking concern, was warmly received by Husserl, but Hitler's *Anschluss* soon forced him and his family into exile in New York. In the 1940s he became associated with the "University in Exile" at the New School, eventually assuming a full-time position there as a professor of sociology. Whereas Husserl's phenomenology led in the direction of a "transcendental reduction" in which everything but the ego of the observer is bracketed away, Schutz's phenomenology offered a descriptive analysis of the natural attitude itself, which he saw as intrinsically intersubjective. Drawing on Husserl's insights, Schutz argued that intersubjectivity is always experienced in terms of "typifications"—when we interact with a stranger, for example, we do so on the basis of our categorization of her as a person of a particular type, inferring her motives and interpreting her actions accordingly. Schutz thus suggested that the formation of ideal types in Max Weber's sense of the term is a routine, everyday activity in which actors engage. His claim was that the specific content of typifications, as well as agents' "stocks" of practical knowledge about how to interpret and handle situations, are given to them largely through culture and tradition. Insofar as this is so and agents share a culture, there is an objective dimension to what Husserl called "the life-world," or "the domain of our unreflective, simply taken-for-granted being" (Natanson 1973, 17), the interpretive matrix through which we make mundane sense of the world. Nevertheless, Schutz argued that in any *particular* situation our actions and interpretations only make sense in reference to our biographically defined life "projects." Drawing on William James's theory of selective attention, Schutz claimed that which features of a situation we attend to—and, indeed, where we draw the boundaries of the situation itself—is a function first and foremost of the structures of "relevance" with which we are cognitively endowed at a particular point in time. Whether I view the act of buying a cup of coffee as an economic transaction, a habitual part of my morning, participation in an ongoing tradition, or an occasion for striking up conversation with the person behind the counter depends entirely on my idiosyncratic life experiences and my own understanding of the longer-term life tasks in which I am engaged. Am I, at that moment, concerned about my budget, focused on my work and wanting a jolt of caffeine, waxing nostalgic about the meaning of coffee in my childhood home, or trying to make new friends? Schutz rightly saw that the notion of relevance has serious implications for the methodology of the social sciences: it suggests we can never explain an agent's actions in a given situation without inquiring into what *she* or *he* understood to be her or his defining life project at the time. The situations agents face, in other words, are not objective features of the social world that the sociologist can recover by adopting the neutral stance of the scientific observer—they are *inherently* subjective, which rules out as illegitimate any effort to formulate transcontextual causal laws of human action that do not take subjectivity into account. On these grounds Schutz supported Weber's conception of the social sciences as based on the recovery of the subjective meanings of action, even though he thought that Weber had not been enough concerned with individual biography and variation and hence had "suppressed radical differences in meaning structures" (Barber 1988, 29). Later, Schutz would become a critic of Talcott Parsons, charging his "unit act" framework with having reified and objectified the situation, thus twisting Weber further in a nonsubjectivistic direction (see Schutz, Grathoff, and Parsons 1978).

Schutz's ideas gained prominence in American sociology in the 1960s and early 1970s as a result of a convergence of factors. One was the link between phenomenology and existentialism. Existentialism, whose influence on sociology has been rather limited, given its emphasis on the relative freedom of the individual from social structures (but see Douglas 1977; Hayim 1996; Johnson 1977; Tiryakian 1962), became popular in the United States in the 1950s and 1960s thanks to the concerted efforts of intellectual importers, a media frenzy around Jean-Paul Sartre and Simone de Beauvoir that played heavily on anti-intellectualist themes, and the overlaps between the existentialist movement's interest in alienation and authenticity and the driving concerns of the emerging American youth culture (Cotkin 2003). Many existentialists had begun their philosophical investigations with an immersion in phenomenology, so it was natural that the vogue of existentialism would draw attention to the phenomenological movement. Concurrently—and despite the dominance of analytic philosophy—efforts were under way in U.S. academic philosophy to institutionalize the study of various Continental authors, and there was a spillover effect into sociology. In the early 1960s Northwestern University emerged as the major American center for Continental thought, making a bid to reorient the profession in a more pluralistic direction. Members of its philosophy department played key roles in the founding of the Society for Phenomenology and Existential Philosophy (SPEP), which was intended to serve as a counterweight to the heavily analytic APA. The first edition of a specialty journal, *Philosophy and Phenomenological Research,* had been published in the early 1940s out of the University of Buffalo under the auspices of the International Phenomenological Society (IPS), and by the 1960s it had become a major venue for phenomenological research. Scholars associated with SPEP and the IPS, like Richard Zaner, Maurice Natanson, and Marvin Farber, published important exegeses of Husserl, Schutz, and other phenomenologists and brought out English translations of their work, making phenomenology better known. Zaner and Natanson—both philosophers—had been students of Schutz, but there were sociologists who had studied under him as well, and a third reason for phenomenology's popularity in sociology was that these former students now found themselves established in their careers. The most influential were Thomas Luckmann and Peter Berger, but there were others too, like Helmut Wagner. All had received their PhD's from the New School in the mid-1950s, and in the next decade and a half Luckmann and Berger, at least, would rise to disciplinary prominence, trailing the banner of phenomenology behind them. Finally, mention must be made of the intense sense of dissatisfaction with the disciplinary enterprise of sociology that was felt in the late 1960s and early 1970s, and expressed in books like Alvin Gouldner's *The Coming Crisis of Western Sociology* (1970) and Robert Friedrichs's *A Sociology of Sociology* (1970). In an essay written in 1973, Edward Tiryakian noted that "outside the academic setting, there is a new questioning of the meaning and worth of the industrial-technological order. . . . The object-oriented positivistic methodology which has dominated sociological research is tacitly linked to the industrial-technological order, and the increasing tendency to question the adequacy of the latter carries with it a questioning of the adequacy of the former" (Tiryakian 1973, 189). Though this dissatisfaction was born as much of structural developments in the academic field—the boom of the academic labor market in the 1950s and 1960s followed by the slowdown of the 1970s, which led to frustration and anomie—as it was of wider cultural changes, its significance as a motive for intellectual innovation and change cannot be ignored. This was the context for the emergence of phenomenological sociology, for most of its champions used the ideas of Husserl and Schutz to attack Parsons and the positivists, who were depicted as ideological spokesmen for the conservative status quo. As Tiryakian argued at the time, phenomenology's potential to serve as a weapon in this struggle "increased receptivity" to it, "particularly among younger sociologists" (Tiryakian 1973, 189).

Although now cited mostly as an early critique of essentialism, Berger and Luckmann's *The Social Construction of Reality* (1966) originally had a different intention: to steer sociological theory and research in a nonpositivist, non-Parsonian direction. The authors denied that they had any "polemical interest in writing" the book but admitted that their "enthusiasm for the present state of sociological theory is markedly restrained" (Berger and Luckmann 1966, 170). Their proposal was that the sociology of knowledge recover its phenomenological foundations. Under the influence of Mannheim's later thought and Robert K. Merton's formulation of a synthetic "paradigm" for the sociology of knowledge, the field, in their view, had come to center too much on the sociology of intellectuals and their ideas, and too little on everyday knowledge or the cultural schemata that social actors use to help them get by in the various mundane circumstances they face. But theirs was not a call simply to reorient the sociology of knowledge qua sociology of culture in a more populist direction. Instead, their overriding concern was to replace dominant Parsonian conceptions of culture as consisting of values and beliefs with the Schutzian view that it centers on typifications and pretheoretical "recipe knowledge." They went on to suggest that a major axis of social variation concerns the degree to which typifications and recipe knowledge have been institutionalized, or made to seem a taken-for-granted part of life, and when they called for sociologists to attend to the "social construction of reality," they meant that attention should be paid to this institutionalization process. Normative interests underlay this research agenda, as Luckmann made clear in an essay titled "Philosophy, Science, and Everyday Life." Here he accused positivists and Parsonians of subscribing to a mechanistic worldview that was immoral insofar as it proceeded on the basis of a reductionistic vision of human life, and nonscientific because its core theoretical concepts and guiding metaphors—"instincts or drives, game-strategist, personality subsystem" (Luckmann 1973, 159)—were themselves little more than reifications derived from commonsense understandings. Only by engaging in phenomenological investigations of the social, Berger and Luckmann declared, could these problems be avoided and sociology set on footings that were at once more secure and more humane. Later, Luckmann would do even more to make Schutz's ideas known, editing two volumes of his former teacher's papers on the "structures of the life-world." Berger did his part too. In his widely read book *The Homeless Mind,* he, Brigitte Berger, and Hansfried Kellner (1973) combined Schutzian phenomenology with modernization theory and Weberian themes to argue that one of the distinctive features of "modern consciousness" is a "pluralization of life-worlds," and in later substantive and methodological texts he developed an "interpretive sociology" of modernity whose debts to Schutz were obvious.

The year 1973 may have been the highpoint of American sociological interest in phenomenology properly so-called. In addition to *The Homeless Mind* and a volume edited by Natanson titled *Phenomenology and the Social Sciences*, George Psathas, then at Boston University, came out with an edited volume of essays, *Phenomenological Sociology*, many of which had been given as papers at a special session on phenomenology organized for the 1971 ASA meetings in Denver. In a 1975 qualitative methods textbook, Robert Bogdan and Steven Taylor of Syracuse, defining the phenomenological sociologist as one "concerned with *understanding* human behavior from the actor's own frame of reference" (Bogdan and Taylor 1975, 2; emphasis in original), exhorted would-be scholars of such a persuasion to go out "among the people," and that is what at least some of the contributors to the Psathas volume did. While many remained occupied by theoretical issues, Egon Bittner, then at Brandeis and author of a classic ethnographic study on "policing skid row," used phenomenology to examine fieldwork itself, asking what cognitive techniques are required to generate a fieldwork account that appears to be objective. Roger Jehenson of the University of New Mexico applied Schutzian ideas to understand the patterns of typification at work in a psychiatric hospital. And Peter Manning and Horacio Fabrega of Michigan State analyzed body consciousness among residents of the Mexican city of San Cristobal de las Casas. Other empirical studies published around the same time—Lyn Lofland's *A World of Strangers* (1973), for example, an ethnography that examined the decline of social solidarity in the modern city, or the articles collected in a book edited by Jack Douglas of UC San Diego (Douglas 1970)—seemed to express a Schutzian sensibility of sorts because they "explored the problematic and mundane features of everyday life" (Adler, Adler, and Fontana 1987, 222), even though Lofland's acknowledged debt was to symbolic interactionism. All this activity clearly signaled that "there is increasing interest in something called 'phenomenological sociology'" (Heap and Roth 1973, 354)—a trend that, in the eyes of James Heap and Phillip Roth of the University of British Columbia writing in the *American Sociological Review*, was highly suspect, since exponents of the new approach tended to "use the concepts of phenomenology 'metaphorically'" (Heap and Roth 1973, 355) and greatly misinterpreted Husserl, who, according to them, had no real interest in empirical research. In retrospect, however, it would seem that the very looseness with which some self-proclaimed phenomenological sociologists interpreted and linked themselves to Husserl was a condition for the movement's success, short-lived though it was. In an era when critical sociology, for many, meant demonstrating that the concepts and taken-for-granted assumptions employed by those resistant to changing the American power structure—concepts like deviance and normalcy—were little more than arbitrary constructs, the seeming phenomenological injunction to study "the social construction of reality" must also have sounded like an assertion of humankind's potential to *change* reality, a Europeanized and politicized version of W. I. Thomas's claim that to define situations in particular ways is to fundamentally remake them. And indeed, phenomenology's concerns seemed at the time very much affined with those of symbolic interactionism, which had become focused on the labeling of deviance and the "social construction" of social problems.

It was, however, not simply through studies of everyday knowledge of the kind championed by Berger and Luckmann that Schutzian ideas, and phenomenology more generally, entered American sociology. As Heap and Roth and most other commentators noted at the time, another crucial pathway was the program of ethnomethodology. Harold Garfinkel, ethnomethodology's founder, had studied under Parsons at Harvard, receiving his PhD in 1952. While impressed by Parsons's efforts to locate a distinctive theoretical problematic for the discipline in solving the Hobbesian problem of order, Garfinkel was more taken by the insights of phenomenology, with which he became familiar by reading Schutz and having conversations with Aron Gurwitsch, who was developing a phenomenological psychology centered on a field theory of consciousness. Like Schutz, Garfinkel recognized that cognition of the social world is fundamentally an interpretive endeavor and that this interpretation rests on a bed of pretheoretical assumptions and understandings. Our interactions with others, for example, hinge on our capacity to figure out what actions they are engaging in, and this requires that we ascribe motives to their behavior on the basis of typified understandings that are part of our stock of knowledge. Garfinkel's genius was to recognize that there is a crucial connection between these processes of interpretive cognition and the maintenance of social order. In concrete situations of face-to-face interaction, actors must proceed on the basis of the assumption that they share cognitive-interpretive schemata with their interaction partners. Were this assumption impossible to make—that is, were an actor to confront another who seemed totally alien, whose tacit rules for cognition appeared totally different—interaction would grind to a halt because so much of action is "indexical," gaining its meaning from context and requiring that its sense be filled in by others. But there is no reason why even those actors who share the same culture should *necessarily* make this assumption, for life experiences vary greatly, concrete situations are often so complex that general interpretive rules provide underspecific guidance, and misunderstandings are commonplace. Garfinkel thus saw that a condition for orderly social life is that actors *communicate* to one another that they *are* sharing the same interpretive schemata. Actors do this, he theorized, by employing various "ethnomethods," or techniques through which "the procedural accomplishment of [various] activities as actual, concerted behaviors" (Maynard and Clayman 1991, 387) is achieved. In this way of thinking, social norms, which represented Parsons's answer to the question of how the Hobbesian problem of order could be solved, figure not as internalized constraints on action but as resources that actors can mobilize in their efforts to achieve intersubjective intelligibility. In a famous example, Wieder (1974) argued that in a halfway house, residents do not follow the normative rules of the informal convict code but rather use those rules to demonstrate to one another that they share a lifeworld. Ethnomethodology was conceived as the study of this and other ethnomethods. To bring out their significance, Garfinkel looked for or experimentally created situations in which the assumption of a mutually intelligible lifeworld breaks down. He noted the psychic disturbances these situations generate, as well as the efforts made to quickly restore a sense of intelligibility and order. Against what he saw as the Parsonian position that individuals are essentially "cultural dopes," automatons blindly following internalized norms and scripts, Garfinkel insisted on the reality of knowledgeable practice and agency. Though certainly not a positivist, he also maintained that the study of ethnomethods should be empirical and rigorous (Clayman 2002).

The complexity of Garfinkel's ideas and the tangledness of his prose style combined to generate great misunderstanding about his project in the years following the publication of his landmark volume, *Studies in Ethnomethodology*, in 1967. Ethnomethodology was often confused either with symbolic interactionism or with Erving Goffman's studies of the interaction order. But these confusions were not enough to keep Garfinkel from attracting a scholarly following. While the vast majority of sociologists saw— and continue to see—ethnomethodology as tangential to sociology's true concerns, in part because it is concerned with social structures only insofar as reference to them by actors forms part of their ethnomethodological repertoires (Hilbert 1990), and in part become some ethnomethodologists deny the very viability of the disciplinary project of sociology, researchers who take Garfinkel's work as a point of departure have nevertheless "produced a substantial body of work over the past 25 years" that shows genuine "theoretical, methodological, and empirical diversity" (Maynard and Clayman 1991, 386, 411). Much of this work has centered around the sociology department at UCLA, where Garfinkel taught for many years, although ethnomethodology has since diffused out to other schools as well, where it has sometimes been taught under the rubric of social psychology. Whether ethnomethodology has taken a cognitive direction, as in the many studies inspired by Aaron Cicourel, or focused more on the taken-for-granted frameworks through which conversation is organized, as in inquiries that follow the program laid out by Harvey Sacks and Emanuel Schegloff, or concentrated on examination of the ethnomethods at play in various institutional settings like police work or science, the debt to phenomenology is hard to ignore. And, indeed, given that phenomenological sociology of the Berger and Luckmann variety went into decline in the 1980s and 1990s as those who sought philosophical legitimation for their opposition to positivism turned instead to postmodernism—creating a situation in which the original Schutzian program came to be watered down and recast, weakly, as "everyday life sociology" (Adler, Adler, and Fontana 1987)—one could say that ethnomethodology remains one of the primary vehicles through which Schutzian ideas have continued to inform American sociological practice.

Two other sources of continuing influence must also be mentioned, however. The first is contemporary sociological theory. Though with little fanfare, many of American sociology's favorite European theorists of the last quarter century have crafted their intellectual projects by means of an engagement with phenomenology, if often a critical engagement. For Jürgen Habermas, for example, phenomenological sociology of the kind developed by Schutz and Garfinkel is to be appreciated for its focus on the lifeworld. It is in the realm of the lifeworld, according to Habermas, that meaningful experience becomes possible. But contra the claims of phenomenologists, the implication of this for Habermas is not that social science should restrict itself to understanding how individuals experience this meaning or create orderliness in their mundane interactions. On the one hand, despite Schutz's move away from the Husserlian notion of the transcendental ego, Habermas claims that phenomenology remains wedded to a vision of social interaction that starts from essentially monological premises, so that its particular understanding of the lifeworld cannot accommodate the true dialogical nature of human intersubjectivity. On the other hand, focusing exclusively on the subjective dimensions of the lifeworld gives us no access to the objective social structures that shape it. A critical social theory of modernity, therefore, attentive to real human interests, must somehow bridge the gap between the subjective and the objective, inquiring into the social-structural transformations characteristic of modern society as well the impact of those transformations on everyday experience and meaning (McCarthy 1978, 158–62). And it is precisely such a project that Habermas has pursued by means of a reinterpretation of the Weberian thesis of rationalization as a mostly insidious "colonization" of the life-world—home to the vast potential for communicative rationality—by the imperatives and logic of an increasingly differentiated "social system."

In the social theory of Anthony Giddens, phenomenology plays an even more formative role. Here it is not the lifeworld that looms large but the eth-nomethodological critique of the notion of human beings as followers of normative rules.[9] To be sure, the notion of rules figures centrally in Gid-dens's theory of structuration—but neither in the Durkheimian sense of regulative norms, which exert a constraint over action through the threat of social sanction, nor in the Parsonian sense of norms and values that have become introjected. Instead, Giddens suggests that patterns of interaction come to be reproduced across time and space—and this for him is the meaning of the obdurateness of structure—because agents possess a prac-tical knowledge of how to navigate particular social settings. Practical knowledge of the social world consists of "techniques of generalizable pro-cedures" (Giddens 1984, 21), understandings of what is required to get by in some setting in order to achieve one's aims. Most of these techniques are known only tacitly, at the level of what Giddens calls "practical conscious-ness"—a domain that has been explored in "detailed and subtle" ways "only in phenomenology and ethnomethodology" (1984, 7). However, drawing on Garfinkel, Giddens also asserts that an important element of practical knowledge is that agents must always be prepared to move up to the level of discursivity, giving "accounts" of their actions that are meaningful and plausible given what are taken to be the shared understandings that are constitutive of some setting. Social structures take shape and reproduce themselves, as large numbers of actors partake of the same practical knowl-edge and orient themselves, by means of a reflexive monitoring of their conduct, toward the interpretive frameworks they hold to be shared.

Finally, for Pierre Bourdieu, too, phenomenology is important. Like Giddens, Bourdieu embraces phenomenology's emphasis on agency, knowl-edgeability, and practice. Very much like the rules and resources Giddens holds to be constitutive of practical knowledge, the Bourdieuian habitus, which denotes socially structured habits or dispositions, is theorized to

---

9. The argument of Giddens and other social theorists to this effect is also indebted to Wittgenstein (1953/2001).

have significance for the reproduction of social structures because it endows agents with the practical competency to perform in some domain of social activity, or field. At the same time, Bourdieu draws heavily on the work of the French phenomenologist Maurice Merleau-Ponty, who emphasized that our perceptions of the world are tied to perceptions of our own bodies, to argue that socially structured knowledgeability has its home in the body, where the logic of practical activity becomes constitutive of our processes of perception and cognition. The whole point of Bourdieu's theory of practice, however, is to transcend what he sees as the unhelpful divide between objectivist and subjectivist approaches to social theory, and so, like Habermas, he ultimately rejects the larger theoretical program implied by phenomenology on the grounds that it remains inattentive to reproduction of structures (Wacquant 1992).

Beyond contemporary sociological theory, a second source of phenomenology's continuing influence is the program of neo-institutionalism in sociological analyses of organizations. Attempting in a widely influential edited volume to make explicit the theoretical premises underlying the contributions of such organizational theorists as Lynne Zucker, John Meyer, W. Richard Scott, and Ronald Jepperson, Paul DiMaggio and Walter Powell (1991) sought to distinguish the new institutionalism of recent decades from the old institutionalism of Selznick and others. Selznick would subsequently protest that the distinction had been drawn too sharply (Selznick 1996), but DiMaggio and Powell claimed that while both versions of institutionalism depart from the assumptions of rational choice theory, insisting that organizations be understood in terms of the broader social environments that shape them and the cultural understandings of organizational actors, a major difference between them lies in their conceptions of culture. In this regard they charged that Selznick had followed Parsons, conceiving of the cultural material that composes the important "informal" subculture of organizations as consisting primarily of values and norms, bundled together and introjected by individual actors to form their "character." Neo-institutionalists, by contrast, had been more influenced by phenomenology and ethnomethodology. In place of the Parsonian emphasis on valuation and normativity, neo-institutionalists had taken the cognitive turn, viewing the culture of organizations as made up of typifications and other schemata that recurrently pattern action across settings. Neo-institutionalists drew important lessons from Berger and Luckmann insofar as institutionalization, for them too, had referred to the process by which shared, taken-for-granted schemata become obdurate and invisible, and thus determinative of an agent's behavior. But according to DiMaggio and Powell, neo-institutionalism actually went well beyond Berger and Luckmann, for it tended to follow Garfinkel, as well as theorists like Giddens and Bourdieu, in understanding the structuring power of cultural schemata for organizational life to lie not in the fact that they are shared and internalized and hence determinative of action, but rather in the ongoing efforts of agents at the microlevel to achieve intelligibility through the operation of practical reason (DiMaggio and Powell 1991, esp. 19–27).

Conclusion

As recently as 1999, Raymond Boudon noted that "a history of the connection philosophy-sociology remains to be written" (1999, xi). This chapter surely cannot be seen as such a history, for it tells only a small part of the story and, presuming the reader may have little knowledge of philosophy, has done so in a way that passes over much of the complexity and disagreement that is constitutive of the historically important intellectual activity occurring at the intersection of the two fields. Nevertheless, in recounting the rise of pragmatism and phenomenology in philosophy and their subsequent effect on twentieth-century American sociology, I hope to have illustrated the larger lesson implied by Boudon's call, namely, that one cannot fully comprehend the sociological tradition unless one attends to developments in cognate fields from which sociologists have often taken their insights. Historically, philosophy has been one of these fields. But a more extensive historical analysis would show that it is hardly the only one. Indeed, the history of sociology, in America or any other national context, is as much a history of importation from and dialogue with other disciplines—philosophy, anthropology, economics, psychology, literary studies, statistics, and others—as it is a story of self-contained unfolding. In fact, as Andrew Abbott (2001) has recently pointed out, it is one of the great ironies of disciplinarity that, precisely by constituting different intellectual fields as autonomous and bounded arenas of activity, it is possible for some intellectuals to do what is regarded as groundbreaking work by rethinking their own disciplines through the lens of major approaches in other fields, making contributions by virtue of their capacity to translate ideas across disciplinary and paradigmatic divides, folding them into novel syntheses. To the extent, however, that much intellectual innovation takes this form, histories of the various disciplines will be impoverished unless they attend to developments taking place in neighboring fields.

Attention of this kind has not always characterized histories of sociology, however. As Hans Joas has noted, speaking of both sociology and philosophy, "the different disciplines tend to reconstruct their history as if leading figures had mostly drawn their inspiration from within one or the other" (Joas 2004, xiv). Correcting this tendency is not simply a matter of improved historiographic method. For those of us interested in the history of sociology not just for its own sake or because it represents an important object of study from the standpoint of the sociology of ideas, but also because we are convinced that our own attempts at theorizing the social will be richer the more they are in dialogue with an understanding of the diverse intellectual traditions that inform them, opening ourselves up to the history of other fields and thus eschewing the project of what Donald Black (2000) calls "pure sociology" is nothing less than an honest search for our intellectual heritage, one that cannot help but complexify and deepen our understanding of the human condition. The historical connection between sociology and philosophy is particularly strong, though sociologists have drawn on the ideas of philosophers much more than philosophers have been influenced by sociologists. Perhaps now, after more than a solid century of sociological scholarship in the United States, and at a moment when the enormous wave of theoretical creativity that took place across the social sciences and humanities in the 1960s and 1970s seems to have ebbed (Eagleton 2003), the time may be right to examine this connection even more fully than I have done here.

[SEVEN] On Edge: Sociology during the Great Depression and the New Deal

Charles Camic

The 1930s, an age of harsh material conditions and thwarted expectations for millions of Americans, fell hard on American sociologists as well. Encouraged by the progress of their fledgling field during the 1920s, they watched with increasing awareness and frustration as a national societal drama removed them to the sidelines, revoking their newly won position as authoritative social analysts and conferring public stature instead on rival professionals. Scrambling to overcome this setback, sociologists in the era of the Great Depression and the New Deal responded in ways that helped configure and lock in some of the defining intellectual tendencies of mid-twentieth-century American sociology.

This chapter reports this untold episode in the social and intellectual history of American sociology but is limited in at least two basic ways. First, at the level of historical description, it examines the 1930s exclusively through the lens of the Great Depression and the New Deal and does not purport to provide a more comprehensive account of social and intellectual changes in American sociology during this decade. To approach the thirties from this particular perspective is not to deny, however, that this period constituted an important era in the history of the sociology in multiple ways, many of which have little or nothing to do with either the Depression or the New Deal. On the world scene, for example, the age witnessed (inter alia) the spread of dictatorships in central Europe, the Nazis' ascent to power in Germany, Japan's invasion of Manchuria, Italy's conquest of Ethiopia, the Moscow trials, and Franco's victory in the Spanish Civil War—epochal developments that, although initially ignored by most American sociologists in their writings, would soon command their utmost attention (see Bannister 1992).

As well, the 1930s brought an influx of European ideas through several gates. These included the entry into the United States of refugee German scholars in economics, philosophy, psychology, psychoanalysis, political science, and sociology (see Coser 1984); the rising voice of American sociologists who had studied abroad, such as Talcott Parsons, inspired by German social theory, and Samuel Stouffer, impressed with recent British statistical advances; and the appearance of translations of, and commentaries on, a handful of seminal works by European social thinkers like Émile Durkheim, Max Weber, and Vilfredo Pareto.

Such developments intersected in complex ways with various domestic changes that were simultaneously under way. Among these changes were certain basic transformations in the substance and organization of American culture, due, for example, to new means of mass communication (see Pells 1973; Susman 1984); alterations in the demography, ecology, and economics of American higher education at the undergraduate and graduate levels (see Geiger 1986; Buxton and Turner 1992); and a fundamental reordering of the prestige hierarchy of academic disciplines as a result of trends that predated the Depression (see Cravens 1978). Hand in hand with these broad changes, which to some degree affected most American academics, were developments more specific to sociology, most notably, the field's shifting age structure, plus the purely local fortunes of individual departments—sociology's temporary fall from glory at Columbia University and its belated establishment at Harvard University. All these changes say nothing of the progress during the 1930s of various theoretical, substantive, and methodological debates that were in play before the decade began within the several subfields into which American sociology was already divided. Although the interplay of these various forces would have made the era a dynamic one even apart from the Depression and the New Deal, the focus of this chapter is nonetheless restricted to the effects on sociology of the latter events alone.

The second limitation of the chapter pertains not at the level of historical description but with regard to historical evaluation. My aim in this account is to present a historical narrative, not to pass retrospective judgment on the historical actors involved. Accordingly, when I report that sociologists of the 1930s confronted the Depression and the New Deal at a later date and in a less sustained manner than other social scientists of this period did, my point is not to stand above this period and fault sociologists for the decisions they made. In a few instances, to be sure, my sense has been that readers will better understand the precise nature and historical consequences of these decisions if I somewhat enlarge the historical canvas and call attention to choices that were not made, but this shift in historical perspective implies no verdict as to whether the decisions of the past were wrong or right, reckless or wise, from my own viewpoint as a sociologist writing in the early twenty-first century. Given *their own* aspirations in the 1930s, sociologists sometimes grew frustrated and critical with themselves, and, as part of my narrative, I recount these attitudes and try to make sense of them in terms of their historical context. Again, however, this is not to render my own criticism or to suggest that, except to achieve their purposes, sociologists of the period should have engaged the issues of the Depression and New Deal sooner or differently. To interject a judgment of this sort would require me to take an additional step and defend a more atemporal view of what sociology is and of what its intellectual and political objectives (immediate and long-range) should be and then to ask whether the actions of the men and women of the 1930s advanced the agenda of sociology as defined by this standard. This step falls beyond the bounds of this historical analysis.

The State of the Historiography

The impact of the Great Depression and the New Deal on American sociology is a topic that has previously been largely overlooked in the work of scholars who study the discipline's history.[1] This lacuna partly reflects a larger gap in the historiography on American sociology. As Platt (1996, 4) rightly comments, the entire "interwar period has in general been much neglected in recent writing," save for numerous studies of the rise and fall of the so-called Chicago school of sociology in the 1920s and 1930s (see Abbott 1999 for a review of these studies).

What is more, although Platt's (1996) work, and that of Bannister (1987), Turner and Turner (1990), and Hinkle (1994), takes major steps to remedy this neglect, a strong tendency has emerged in the process to lump the years between 1918 and 1939 together into an essentially homogeneous era in the discipline's development. Turner and Turner's account (1990, 39–84), for example, sets off the interwar years as a single period, marked by institutional and intellectual trends that, although they inevitably fell at different points by 1939 than they had in 1918, by and large remain continuous throughout. Hinkle (1994), likewise, presents "the time between World Wars I and II" as a fundamental temporal division. Bannister (2003), Bulmer (1984a, 1992), Martindale (1976a), and Smith (1994) adopt the same convention.

---

1. In contrast, political sociologists have taken a great interest in the Depression and New Deal, and the era has become the center of a series of important theoretical and empirical debates. (For an authoritative summary of this massive literature, see Manza [2000].) While these debates have given considerable attention to the role of intellectuals and other policy experts during the New Deal, they have not (so far as I am aware) focused specifically on the role of sociologists.

In the literature on the history of American sociology, only an earlier study by Gouldner (1970) cast serious doubt on this convention,[2] rending the interwar period in half at the outset of the Depression, and treating the age of the Great Depression and the New Deal as a historical episode with significant independent consequences for the development of sociological thought. The study's narrow concentration on the ideas of a single figure, Talcott Parsons, and his local milieu (combined with its erroneous claims about both matters), however, limit its value for understanding American sociology more broadly during the period. Nevertheless, Gouldner (1970, 152–53) stands alone in raising the possibly of a close connection between the changing professional situation of sociologists during the 1930s and the substance of sociological work—a question lost in subsequent scholarship as the Depression and New Deal have receded into the presumed temporal unity of the interwar years.

The few existing studies of the interwar period do, to be sure, occasionally offer passing comment on the bearing of the Depression and the New Deal on sociological practice. Almost without exception, the focus of these remarks has been the impact of these events on employment opportunities for sociologists. On this point, the scholarly consensus is that, although the Depression cost sociologists some number of academic jobs, the New Deal quickly offset this loss with expanded opportunities for government employment and public service, thus producing a positive net gain in terms of positions and professional standing—thereby leaving the institutional and intellectual fabric of sociology undisturbed. According to Martindale, for instance, "while American universities went into a holding pattern during the Depression, the 1930s were not hard on sociology" because, among other reasons, "the federal government was making more use of social scientists then ever before" (1976a, 140). Similarly, Bulmer states: "One should not infer too much from th[e] fall in [academic positions] during the 1930s, since other avenues of employment opened up. In the federal government, a group of some fifty to sixty sociologists worked in the Department of Agriculture, [while] the Bureau of the Census [employed] a considerable number of sociologists to do demographic research" (1992, 320).[3]

How broadly this placid assessment of the effect on sociology of the Depression and the New Deal is justified remains unclear, however. To date, claims of the type just quoted rest on a pair of taken-for-granted assump-

2. Rhoades's (1981, 18) thinner account does, however, suggest a similar position. See also Lengermann (1979).

3. See also Bannister (2003, 346), Converse (1987, 12, 38), Fisher (1993, 165), Hinkle (1994, 15), Janowitz (1972, 117), and Lengermann (1979, 192); cf. Turner and Turner (1990, 56).

tions visible in the two statements: (1) that federal jobs for "social scientists" meant positions specifically for sociologists; and/or (2) that the availability of positions for sociologists in a few federal agencies meant a wider opening up of such avenues of employment. Later in the chapter I present evidence to the contrary on both points in an effort to initiate more thorough historical research on the larger topic of the consequences of the Great Depression and the New Deal for American sociology as it was understood and practiced during the 1930s.

Sociology in the 1920s

From its rocky beginnings in the 1880s to the close of World War I, American sociology struggled continually for intellectual legitimacy and institutional position within the nation's universities and colleges, but its prospects improved dramatically amid the (relative) economic prosperity and political calm of the 1920s. Formerly, sociology was a virtual cipher—little more than an umbrella term for the ideas of social reformers, meliorators, and visionaries (inspired by the example of Auguste Comte or Herbert Spencer) and for occasional undergraduate courses that part-time instructors offered on social problems, corrections, charity, and social work. As Abbott has written, in this early period sociologists proper still consisted of no more than a couple hundred people "attempting to precipitate out of [a] diverse interest in social life and problems, a specialized academic discourse" (Abbott 1999, 81).

Yet, by the end of the 1920s, sociology stood as an established component of the liberal arts program in an expanding number of universities and colleges, particularly in the Midwest (progress remained slowest in the older, East Coast institutions). In 1928, for example, there were 99 independent departments of sociology, plus 48 more that combined sociology with another social science (Abbott 1999, 87). The decade brought, as well, increasing undergraduate enrollments (Hinkle 1994, 13) and a steady rise in doctorate degrees in sociology, with 13 new sociology PhD's awarded in 1920, 26 in 1925, and 40 in 1930 (Turner and Turner 1990, 63, fig. 2.2). Simultaneously, membership in the American Sociological Society (hereafter abbreviated, by the organization's future name, as ASA) nearly doubled, jumping from 810 in 1918 to 1,558 in 1930 (figures provided by ASA).

Facilitating these improvements in sociology's academic and professional base were gradual but fundamental changes in the field's intellectual coordinates—a topic that requires a brief caveat. Even a modest-sized modern intellectual field, such as sociology was in the 1920s, generates thousands of records, as hundreds of men and women, year by year, formulate and refashion their ideas about multiple issues in the published and unpublished writings they produce in their capacities as scholars, teachers, and administrators. In the absence of a complete survey or (ideally) a systematic sample of these records, generalizations about the intellectual state of a particular field inevitably rest on more or less impressionistic assessments of its features and trends, assessments that, insofar as they succeed in identifying overall patterns, fail to capture either the range or the distribution of the opinions that field members hold on particular points—a problem that renders such generalizations correct only with many necessarily unstated and often unknown qualifications and exceptions.

This said, careful historical scholarship has observed in the sociological literature of the 1920s several important intellectual shifts that served to bolster the discipline's stature. The first of these was the reshaping of sociology as a science of culture rather than of nature. Late nineteenth- and early twentieth-century American sociologists, operating under the spell of the then-ascendant biological sciences, had, as Cravens (1978) documents, predicated their conceptions of sociology heavily on "natural science determinants, analogies, metaphors, and levels of explanation," only to watch imperialist biological scientists then appropriate this development as a justification for arrogating the study of human beings and social conditions to the natural sciences—and thus dispensing with sociology as an academic field (quoting Cravens 1978, 121). During the 1920s, however, sociologists launched a successful counterattack, abandoning their reliance on biology and mobilizing the concept of culture, as recently reworked by anthropologist Franz Boas and his students, to demarcate an autonomous realm that was irreducible to the biological and, as such, constituted the proper sphere of the social sciences. In this context, sociologists joined anthropologists in conceiving culture, in the broadest possible way, as "man's social heritage," understood as humankind's entire stock of material objects, skills, customs, beliefs, and attitudes, as well as the whole realm of economic, political, legal, religious, and familial institutions (see Camic 1986, 1989, 2005; Cravens 1978; Hinkle 1994).

A second intellectual trend evident in the period involved the growing acceptance of what scholars of the period have called scientism (see Bannister 1987; Platt 1996). For present purposes, scientism may be taken as a combination of two methodological doctrines commonly referred to by other terms: positivism, the belief that the social sciences are modeled after the natural sciences and, as such (i.e., given contemporary understandings of natural science), aim principally to produce general statements of objective fact, as distinguished in particular from normative statements or other value-laden claims; and empiricism, the belief that objective statements of fact derive from systematic observations arrived at through research procedures that are impartial (or ethically neutral) in that they do not vary with the researcher's personal political and moral convictions (for elaboration, see Camic 1987; see also Steinmetz 2005e). As sociologists of the 1920s broke away from the concepts of the natural sciences at the explanatory level, they increasingly embraced the example of the natural sciences at the methodological level, in part as a tactic to differentiate themselves from the social reformers and applied practitioners who had previously dominated their ranks. In the process, some sociologists, particularly those trained at Columbia, became ardent "objectivists" whose empiricism drew them toward data amenable to precise quantitative measurement and, thereby, to statistical analysis (see Bannister 1987; Camic and Xie 1994)—a development that ignited early debates over the merits of quantitative versus qualitative research (see Platt 1996). Yet, while never without critics, the scientistic stance extended more widely, attaining softer but succinct expression in the message that Robert Park instilled in many cohorts of University of Chicago graduate students when he told them that "the world was full of crusaders and that 'their role was to be that of the calm, detached scientist who investigates . . . with the same objectivity and detachment with which the zoologist dissects the potato bug'" (quoted in Bulmer 1984a, 76). At no point, however, was scientism a retreatist movement, counseling the sociologist to turn inward and abandon issues on the public agenda. Disdaining what they perceived as the partisan advocacy of earlier generations, proponents of scientism nevertheless envisioned that sociologists would respond as the public called on them to use their expanding stock of factual knowledge in various service capacities as "advisor[s regarding] means rather than ends . . . the *how* rather than the *why* of public policy" (quoting Bannister 1987, 6; see also Janowitz 1972; Ross 1991; Smith 1994). Commitment to the sociologist's public role, understood in these terms, ran deep through sociology at this time, even as it received comparatively less emphasis and more equivocal formulation amid calls for objective empirical research.

Diffusion of this scientistic outlook was abetted by the growing separation of sociology from social work, the era's quintessential meliorative field.[4] Historians of social work count the 1920s as the central turning point

4. The following is a preliminary effort to pin down a complicated trend that scholars have yet to investigate in sufficient detail. The relation between sociology and social work is a subject that generally hovers at the margins of the exiting secondary literature, where various discrepant views are stated. The contemporary sources cited in this paragraph barely skim the

in the discipline's professionalization, as social work not only acquired its own graduate training programs, journals, and autonomous professional associations but simultaneously forged a new identity for its growing membership by relinquishing its previous emphasis on the social aspects of welfare services in favor of practical interventions predicated on individual casework informed by the teachings of psychiatry (Ehrenreich 1985, 56–81; Gordon 1992; Leiby 1978, 163–216). Where social workers had formerly drawn heavily on sociology and regarded the ASA as a major associational base, their sociological interests waned by the late 1920s, as did the proportion of social workers belonging to the ASA (Deardorff 1932; Karpf 1928; Klein 1931; Mulligan 1954). For their own part, however, sociologists were somewhat slower to sever all ties—though the situation was complex. On the one hand, social work, because of its overwhelmingly female composition and (resulting) low salaries, remained a low-status profession whose direct services to needy recipients were not seen as a suitable occupational task for the scientific sociologist (Gordon 1992; cf. Deegan 1996). On the other hand, sociologists' need to maintain undergraduate enrollments continually encouraged course offerings geared to students on a social work career track (Queen 1934b). Further, social work agencies and, even more, the populations of recipients whose traits social workers recorded offered ready research sites and data sources for empirical sociological research (Bossard 1932). In this context, the domain of social work continued to hold intellectual interest for members of the ASA and to serve as a research focus even for some of sociology's arch objectivists long after their interest in the frontline practice of social work faded (Duncan and Duncan 1933; Karpf 1928; Chapin and Queen 1937).

As this concern with data sources and research sites suggests, the new scientism was more than a hallow rhetorical posture. Not only did sociologists of the twenties espouse an interest in empirical research, in expanding numbers they practiced what they professed, demonstrating in their writings, and in their expectations for doctoral students, "a markedly more empirical orientation" (Bulmer 1992, 318). In this decade, the abstract theoretical debates that occupied sociologists before World War I lost centrality as theory qua theory—and a wide range of continuing theoretical controversies—retreated to the backwaters of introductory textbooks (Hinkle 1994), while monographs and articles based on data gathered by qualitative and quantitative methods of research appeared with growing frequency. To

---

surface of untapped primary materials. For this reason, the picture I present can no more than a sketch what appear to be some of the main lines of development.

be sure, even in the leading journals, nonempirical articles continued to outnumber significantly those based on empirical research, and authors of empirical studies "were often extremely vague about the status and origins of their data" (Platt 1996, 191, 34). Nevertheless, at the University of Chicago and the University of North Carolina, at Columbia University, and at such other institutions as the Universities of Wisconsin, Minnesota, and Michigan—the locations of the era's top-ranked sociology departments—faculty members and graduate students now took for granted that carrying out empirical projects was the hallmark of sociological research. And the ASA was quick to see the effects of this development, as empirically based papers became a more substantial presence at annual meetings and members carved out sections devoted to specialized research interests, establishing eight such divisions by 1930: sections on rural sociology, family, community, religion, education, statistics, social work, and psychiatry (see the ASA Web site, www.asanet.org/governance/sechistory.html).[5] At the time, few sociologists expressed concern about this trend, although it accelerated tendencies in the discipline toward interstitiality—toward constituting fields of empirical research around the assorted leftovers of other social sciences (on this feature of sociology, see Abbott 2001; Calhoun 1992)—and toward fragmentation into discrete topical subfields.[6]

The timing of this turn to empirical research attests in part to a conspicuous change then under way in sociology's standing outside the academic institutions where the field was anchored. Before the 1920s, sociologists aiming to conduct new empirical research were, as Bulmer (1982, 187) has remarked, entirely "dependent upon [local] university budgets or on the work they could fit into their spare time, perhaps with some *ad hoc* outside funding," and these traditional sources of research support were meager at best. The 1920s were marked, however, by the emergence of regular sources of large-scale external funding for research. For rural sociologists, the vehicle of this funding was the Purnell Act of 1925, under whose terms the U.S. Department of Agriculture awarded agricultural colleges and experimental stations ongoing support for the study of the economic and sociological aspects of agriculture, but this remained a singular instance of governmental financing. For other sociologists, fresh avenues of research

5. A ninth section was created that focused not on research but on teaching.

6. To echo the above caveat about description versus evaluation: this and subsequent comments about fragmentation and the like are statements depicting organizational structure—here, the differentiation of the ASA into subunits without the concomitant creation of institutional devices to coordinate these subunits—not a critical judgment. Whether fragmentation in this sense is good or bad obviously depends on one's evaluative yardstick.

support opened up with the intervention of private foundations and the various collateral organizations that these made possible, even as much empirical work continued to rely on more traditional funding mechanisms.[7]

Why large American foundations, such as Rockefeller and Carnegie, gravitated to the funding of social scientific research at this time forms part of the complex history of American philanthropy (Fisher 1993; Geiger 1986; Karl and Katz 1981; Lagemann 1989) and lies beyond this chapter. Of relevance here is the consequence of this development: the sudden infusion of large sums into sociological research, now publicly valorized as a worthy object of private largess. In the celebrated case of Rockefeller support, such resources reached sociology both through direct and through indirect channels. Directly, for example, the Laura Spelman Rockefeller Memorial — after 1929, the Division of Social Sciences within the Rockefeller Foundation — allocated to social research between 1923 and 1928 more than $20 million dollars (roughly $215 million in 2005 dollars), typically funneling these monies through block grants to interdisciplinary research organizations at a small number of target institutions, such as the Local Community Research Committee (LCRC) at the University of Chicago and the Institute for Research in Social Science (IRSS) at the University of North Carolina. By this mechanism, the funds went, at the discretion of the local figures authorized to distribute them, to support faculty release time, graduate traineeships, data collection, clerical staff, and so on, underwriting many of the classic urban community studies of the students of Robert Park and Ernest Burgess and much of the research of Howard Odum and his colleagues and students on the social institutions of the South (see Bulmer 1980, 1982, 1984a; Johnson and Johnson 1980).

Concurrently, Rockefeller trusts supported several intermediary organizations that, in turn, channeled resources for sociological research to academic institutions (often the same ones just named) as well as to individuals. Among these organizations was the New York–based Institute for Social and Religious Research (ISRR), which funded during the period seventy-five separate projects, including Robert Park's West Coast Race Relations Survey and Robert and Helen Lynd's 1929 study *Middletown* (Bulmer 1992, 326; Turner and Turner 1990, 41–45). Still more importantly, Rockefeller grants helped to build and maintain the Social Science Research Council (SSRC). Founded in 1923, SSRC originally took its model from the National Research Council (NRC) and the American Council of Learned Societies

---

7. Platt's sample of empirical articles in the *American Journal of Sociology* and *Social Forces* during the 1920s finds that only 6 percent were externally funded (see Platt 1996, 192).

(ACLS). Much as the NRC served the shared professional interests of those in the natural sciences and ACLS the interests of those in the humanities (although it nominally included the social sciences also), SSCR was designed by prominent economists, political scientists, and sociologists as a federation of the nation's principal social science associations (see Bulmer 1982), although the council immediately became a major presence in its own right, since its financial support derived not from its member associations but from separate sources, chief among them the Rockefeller Foundation. Indeed, throughout the 1920s, SSCR loomed as one of the leading recipients of Rockefeller funds, which it then allocated—on the advice of a governing board and program committees composed of social scientists—to support star-studded research conferences on substantive and methodological topics, pre- and postdoctoral fellowships, and institutional projects grants, including awards to Burgess's Institute for Juvenile Research, another fountain from which several notable Chicago school studies flowed (Fisher 1993, 52–53).

As the examples of the LCRC, IRSS, ISRR, and SSRC all show, sociologists were by no means the sole beneficiaries of the new sources of external funding for empirical social scientific research. Virtually all the great foundations had, as their chartered mission, the task of promoting the "well-being of mankind" (Karl and Katz 1981, 25); although, by the 1920s, leading foundation officials accepted that the road to applied knowledge had first to cross a wide expanse of research on fundamentals, "social welfare," "social technology" "the improvement of the conditions of life" were goals that, however nebulous and fungible, remained squarely in view (quoting Geiger 1986, 149; more generally, see again Fisher 1993; Geiger 1986; Lagemann 1989). Accordingly, while open-minded toward sociological projects, foundations proved even more favorable to the research of economists and political scientists. For example, of the sixteen American universities that Bulmer and Bulmer (1981, 387) count as the largest recipients of funds from the Laura Spelman Rockefeller Memorial, at only two of these, Chicago and North Carolina, did sociologists constitute a major presence (Turner and Turner 1990, 51). Otherwise, resources went elsewhere, including to schools of business and law, with economics and (secondarily) political science strongly favored. So much were these preferences in force that the Rockefeller Foundation—along with the Carnegie Corporation, which had a long-standing interest in bringing economists, in particular, into public policy arenas (Lagemann 1989, 82)—funded several independent research institutes in these fields "as a means for pursuing [foundation] interests in *current social issues*" (Geiger 1986, 148; emphasis added). These initiatives included the high-profile National Bureau of Economic Research (NBER), which began in 1920 with the purpose of carrying out cumulative quantitative studies of national income and business cycles, while also providing statistical analyses of economic data at the request of government agencies (see Alchon 1985), and a trio of entities that would merge in 1927 to form the Brookings Institution: the Institute of Government Research, started in 1916 to improve the efficiency of government administration at the national level; the Institute of Economics, launched in 1922 to study the effects of international economic reconstruction on American agriculture, industry, and commence; and the Brookings Graduate School of Economics and Government, which opened in 1924 as a freestanding postgraduate program to train policymakers (see Critchlow 1985; Lyons 1969). No comparable institute for sociology emerged in this period.

That foundation officials concerned with public welfare and public policy seized particularly on the work of economists and political scientists accurately reflected contemporary thinking about which academic groups possessed the authority, knowledge, and technical skills to play leading roles in discussions of issues on the public agenda. Confronted with the problems of the day, U.S. presidents going back to the start of the century regularly assembled study commissions: Theodore Roosevelt did so 107 times, William Taft 63, Woodrow Wilson 150, Warren Harding 44, and Calvin Coolidge 118; as president, Herbert Hoover repeated this practice 44 times (Karl 1969, 385-86). Although such commissions brought together the usual sorts of prominent figures in finance, industry, labor, agriculture, politics, engineering, medicine, and private and public law, they also included—depending on the topic—natural scientists and social scientists. Significantly, the social scientists were predominately economists, with another large contingent coming from one of the principal fields of political science, public administration. When, for example, Hoover, as secretary of commence, appointed Harding's Conference on Unemployment and Coolidge's Committee on Recent Economic Trends, he gathered advice and then drew committee membership from circles of NBER economists—launching, in the second instance, a project that resulted in *Recent Economic Changes in the United States* (1929), a much-publicized two-volume study that showcased the expertise of some of the country's leading academic economists (Karl 1969). Similarly, when the demands of World War I necessitated that personnel oversee and staff temporary agencies like the War Industries Board, the Food Administration, and the Central Bureau of Planning and Statistics, the Wilson administration called to Washington academics from the fields of government and, more so, economics (Lyons 1969, 26-30; Karl 1969, 350).

This was only part of the picture that took shape by the 1920s. Looking beyond high-level governmental advisory roles and temporary administrative posts, economists also formed, in their capacity as analysts of statistical data, a growing phalanx in the departments of Agriculture, Treasury, Commerce, and Labor, as well as on the Federal Reserve Board and in several other independent federal agencies (Barber 1981, 177; Duncan and Shelton 1978, 12–13). Even so, to focus on select government jobs understates the growing social scientific presence. This is so because economists—and political scientists, to a lesser degree—scarcely needed the federal government (or state and local governments) to thrust them onto the public stage. To judge by their regular letters to newspapers, their frequent journalistic ventures, their unsolicited petitions to elected officials, and their active organizational efforts for and against protective labor legislation, old-age pensions, securities and utility regulation, tariffs, and other policies, these groups by now took for granted that the public stage was theirs to occupy.[8]

While sociologists of the 1920s had little of this storied record of public service behind them, they nonetheless felt hopeful—optimistic that the boom times around them, which were bringing institutional growth inside the academy and generous support from without, were boosting their own stock as publicly esteemed social analysts and promising greater returns just ahead. This confidence, part and parcel of their scientism, their conviction that the more they advanced the frontiers of knowledge the more they would be called on to share that knowledge in applied contexts, seemed to find confirmation in the decision of foundation officials to incorporate sociology in the interdisciplinary mix from which measures to improve human welfare were anticipated, as well as in sociology's inclusion, right alongside economics and political science, in SSCR councils where contemporary problems were translated into research projects. And even more tangible signs appeared. When, after the 1919 Chicago race riot, the Chicago Commission on Race Relations launched a major fact-finding inquiry, the director of research was a sociologist then studying with Robert Park and assisted by other sociologists under Park's guidance (Bulmer 1982, 74–78; Janowitz 1972, 124). Likewise, when the Bureau of Agricultural Economics within the U.S. Department of Agriculture sought ways to improve the condition of American farm families, it created the first sociological research unit inside the federal government, the Division of Farm Population and Rural Life, which employed during the twenties a small group of rural sociologists (see Larson and Zimmerman 2003).

8. See Barber (1985), Dorfman (1959), Farr and Seidelman (1993), Gordon (1992), Hamilton (1991), Manza (1995), Moss (1996), and Rockoff (1997).

Above all, there was the prominent recognition that the president of the United States, Herbert Hoover, accorded sociology as one of the core fields that would lay the foundation of social knowledge necessary to inform the executive decisions and policies of the Great Engineer. This recognition came in one of Hoover's first initiatives after assuming office in March 1929, his establishment of the President's Research Committee on Social Trends. At the apex of this committee, long among Hoover's favorite undertakings, the president installed three academic social scientists from the SSRC-NBER orbit—an economist, a political scientist, and a sociologist; the last, William F. Ogburn, was newly arrived at the University of Chicago from an appointment at Columbia and was sitting president of the ASA (on Ogburn, see Laslett 1990, 1991). Furthermore, although the economist and the political scientist received top billing as committee chairman and vice chairman, Ogburn, as director of research, along with Hoover's choice as assistant research director, incoming ASA president Howard Odum, shouldered the primary task: that of producing what Hoover envisioned as "a complete, impartial examination of the facts" regarding the condition of economic organization, labor, government activity and public administration, legal institutions, rural and urban communities, education, religion, the family, and other core features of American society (Hoover 1932/1933, v). With the help of an army of collaborators and data collectors, flush with foundation support, the result, ready only at the close of Hoover's presidency, was *Recent Social Trends in the United States* (1933), 40 percent of whose chapters were likewise the handiwork of sociologists. While Hoover's successor in the White House would show little interest in this report and critics would fault it for downplaying the momentous intervening event, the Great Depression, these aftereffects were still to come. At the time, at least one sector of the academy was jubilant: "The appointment of the [Recent Social Trends Committee] seemed to place a permanent seal of approval on [the academic disciplines involved]. Never before had social scientists had such status bestowed upon them or been given such an opportunity to influence and formulate national policy" (Fisher 1993, 111, 104; see also Karl 1963, 1969; Lyons 1969; Tobin 1995). What was more, in this big success story of 1929, sociologists were no longer sidelined but at the very center of the action, as Ellsworth Faris (University of Chicago) triumphantly recalled to ASA members several years later: "When the head of the most powerful government in the world [wanted] to make a study of our social trends that [could] be used in the formation of far-reaching public policies," he "appeal[ed] to a former president of this society" (1938, 9–10). As the audience knew too well, however, such appeals had, in the interim, grown few and far between.

Sociology in the 1930s

THE HISTORICAL SETTING

The Depression and the New Deal overtook America in successive waves.[9] The first of these hit unexpectedly on October 29, 1929, with a massive sell-off on the U.S. stock market that soon drained the economy of more than $26 billion, one-third the value of stock assets—albeit with little immediate or direct consequence for the majority of Americans. Irregularly over the course of the next three years, however, economic conditions sharply deteriorated, for reasons that economic historians still debate. By late 1930, with more than 25,000 business failures recorded, housing construction was plummeting, industrial production contracting, and unemployment climbing to an estimated 4 million, while the agricultural sector, stagnant since the early 1920s, atrophied, at which juncture an epidemic of bank closures rippled through the country. Despite efforts by the Hoover administration to stem this fast slide—indeed, more efforts than his administration has generally been credited with—the next year brought still worse by all these measures, transforming what had up to this point looked to most contemporaries like a severe cyclical downturn into the Great Depression by late 1931–early 1932, when the nation's unemployment rate approached 20 percent (50 percent in cities like Chicago and Detroit). A year later, with 13 million workers jobless, the unemployment rate stood at 25 percent, amid a carnage that had by then reduced the value of stocks by 75 percent, shut 5,000 banks, cut the GNP to half its early 1929 level, and cost millions of Americans their savings and their homes, as they endured the brutal daily realities of long breadlines, blighted farms, and widespread human displacement.

In the presidential election of 1932, Franklin D. Roosevelt resoundingly defeated Herbert Hoover and in March 1933 entered office on high promises of recovery and reform that, with starts and fits, unleashed two great swells of legislation, which (for the purposes of the chapter) encapsulate the New Deal. By the middle of 1933, he won from the U.S. Congress measures intended to reequilibrate and rationally order the nation's fractured economy with the assist of newly instituted federal planning agencies: most notably, the National Recovery Administration (NRA), formed to build industrywide compacts, or codes, to control production levels, prices, and wages; and the Agricultural Adjustment Administration (AAA), established to balance farm production and the volume of agricultural consumption. Also significant was the creation of the Tennessee Valley Authority (TVA)—a

---

9. This summary follows the magisterial account of Kennedy (1999).

public corporation charged with revitalizing the Tennessee Valley region though rural electrification, flood control, and the expansion of industry, education, and health care—plus several modest steps aimed at unemployment relief, including the Federal Emergency Relief Administration (FERA), the Civilian Conservation Corps (CCC), and the Public Works Administration (PWA). Then, while public controversy swirled around these initiatives (particularly the NRA and the AAA, which the Supreme Court nullified in 1935), Roosevelt saw through Congress in mid-1935 the Emergency Relief Appropriations Act, which allocated billions for work relief, eventually creating more than 8 million jobs, through the CCC, the PWA, and the new Works Progress Administration (WPA); the Wagner Act, which recognized labor's right to unionize, required employers to bargain with elected union representatives, and set up the National Labor Relations Board (NLRB) to supervise this process; and the Social Security Act, which established, in a fell swoop, contributory old-age pensions for retired workers, state-level unemployment insurance programs, and grants to states to assist the indigent elderly and children in fatherless households (ADC). While economic recovery proved defiantly elusive in the face of this legislative tsunami—and, indeed, would remain elusive until the onset of World War II—the outcome, nevertheless, was an alteration of the scale, scope, and mission of the national state so extensive and ramifying as to constitute what historians describe as "one of only a handful of episodes in American history when . . . the country was, in measurable degree, remade" (Kennedy 1999, 377).

As these changes engulfed the nation, they buffeted American higher education as well, hitting with force with the economic meltdown of 1931–33. Undergraduate and graduate student enrollments (and tuition payments), for example, while still rising during the 1930–31 academic year, thereafter reversed course, entering a precipitous slide by the fall of 1932 (Geiger 1986, 247; see also Hinkle 1994, 13).[10] Concurrently, university budgets dwindled, as Geiger has described:

> The year 1932 was when the ax first fell on [pubic research universities in] California, Michigan, Minnesota, and Wisconsin. . . . For Michigan [in 1933], state appropriation was 44 percent lower than that for 1929; cuts in other states ranged from 30 percent in Wisconsin to 15 percent in California. With numerous companies defaulting on interest and dividend payments, the decline in investment income at the private universities was almost as severe. . . . General

10. This trend reversed direction again in the second half of the decade, as high school and college graduates, unable to find suitable employment, opted to pursue additional degrees, thereby boosting enrollments (Hinkle 1994, 13).

and educational expenditures everywhere were down considerably [by] 1933–34 from the levels two years earlier. (1986, 247–48)

Confronted with this bleak situation, colleges and universities imposed hiring freezes to reduce faculty size, which fell by 7.9 percent at private institutions and 6.9 percent at public institutions between 1930 and 1934, dwindling opportunities for new PhD's (Kuznick 1987, 28). Administrators as well resorted (everywhere but at Harvard, Yale, and Princeton) to salary reductions, sometimes graduated to tax senior faculty most heavily; the University of Washington, for instance, cut professors' salaries by 29 percent, associate professors' by 23 percent, and instructors' by 15 percent (Kuznick 1987, 29). "For American higher education as a whole," reports Geiger (1986, 249), "faculty salary cuts averaged 15 percent (1931–33), and by the end of the decade less than half of that loss had been recouped."

Since this series of reductions blanketed the academy, inevitably it spread to sociology, although historians of the discipline have for the most part neglected the consequences (in particular, the incidence, size, and impact of staff and salary cuts). In terms of graduate education, after peaking at 50 in 1932, the number of new PhD's fell in each of the following three years (down 28 percent by 1935 to 36), before beginning a slow rebound (Turner and Turner 1990, fig. 2.2). Even with the number of doctorates declining, the ASA felt the need in 1933 to establish a special committee "to study the opportunities for trained sociologists in non-teaching fields" (quoted in Rhoades 1981, 19); by 1934, leaders of the profession were in public alarm over whether "graduate departments of sociology [were] overproducing trained personnel," that is, too many PhD's for the small number of academic job openings, given "the present decline in the financial resources of universities, the drop in their enrolment, [and] the closing up of small colleges" (Chapin 1934a, 506–7; see also Faris 1934).[11] While Turner and Turner (1990, 62) doubt that such fears were borne out in retrospect,[12] Lengermann (1979, 193–96) provides evidence of widespread "career anxiety" among sociologists during the mid-1930s.

Looking beyond universities to the condition of the national associa-

11. In this period, the *American Journal of Sociology* instituted a "personnel exchange" service: a listing of ASA members "available for appointment to positions in research, teaching, or administration." As the editors commented: "the present financial situation warrants this effect to serve the interest of our members" ("News and Notes" 1933, 941).

12. Without citing evidence, Turner and Turner (1990, 82) refer to the "unexpected expansion of demand for [sociology] Ph.D. holders in the colleges and the continued expansion of undergraduate teaching," presumably in the second half of the decade. These developments would accord with the growth of college enrollments in the later 1930s (see n. 10).

tion, we find that after 1931, membership in the ASA declined steeply, plunging by more than one-third (from 1,567 to 1,002) by 1936 and hovering around 1,000 for the rest of the decade, eroding all the gains from the 1920s (figures provided by the ASA). Although it is unlikely that this contraction had a single cause, Lengermann (1979) and Pease and Hetrick (1977) plausibly attribute it (in part) to the financial burdens of belonging to the ASA and attending its annual meetings for those in straitened financial circumstances. These scholars have observed as well the rise of lower-cost substitutes with the emergence of regional and quasi-regional societies during this same period: the Pacific Sociological Association (founded ca. 1929-31), the Eastern Sociological Society (1930), the District of Columbia Sociological Association (1933), the Southern Sociological Society (ca. 1935-38), the Midwestern Sociological Society (ca. 1936-37), the North Central Sociological Association (1938), the Rural Sociology Society (1937), and the American Catholic Sociological Association (1938) (Abbott 1999, 105; Turner and Turner 1990, 155; see also the more extensive list in Rhoades 1981, 29). In a related development, as individuals terminated their ASA memberships, they lost their required (half-priced) subscription to its relatively expensive journal—the *American Journal of Sociology* prior to 1936, afterward the *American Sociological Review*. This situation created a market for some of the less costly and evidently more useful specialty journals that proliferated around this time: the *Journal of Educational Sociology* (begun in 1927), the *Journal of Social Psychology* (1930), *Population* (1933), *Rural Sociology* (1936), *Public Opinion Quarterly* (1937), *Sociometry* (1937), and the *Journal of Marriage and the Family* (1939) (this listing draws from Abbott 1999, 105).

For those who remained members of the ASA and continued to attend its annual meetings, this period brought a significantly transformed professional association—in part, again, because of the Depression. Behind this transformation lay long-festering frustrations centering on the Department of Sociology at the University of Chicago: among other reasons, for its commandeering of the lion's share of foundation funding during the 1920s; for monopolizing, under ASA bylaws, the office of secretary-treasurer, which had power over programs at ASA meetings; and for controlling the editorship and the policies of the society's journal, the *American Journal of Sociology*, which the University of Chicago Press owned. As Lengermann has shown, the Depression brought these grievances to a head between 1931 and 1935, for as younger sociologists faced a deteriorating academic job market, "competition became intense for survival in existing jobs [and] for new employment opportunities," ratcheting up the "hostility and resentment [against Chicago for its] inner-circle pattern of job recommendations, its editorial control over what was published in the *AJS,* its influence on what was selected for presentation at . . . annual meetings," and more (1979, 194). In this climate, anti-Chicago camps formed within the ASA, wrested control of several of its key committees, and mobilized sufficient votes from discontented rank-and-file members to remove the secretary-treasurer position from Chicago and permanently to sever the ASA's ties with the University of Chicago Press and, thus, with the *AJS* (among several other new organizational policies) (see Lengermann 1979; Rhoades 1981, 24–32). As part of the break with the *AJS,* ASA moved to expand its existing quarterly periodical, the *Publication of the American Sociological Society,* into a bimonthly journal, now retitled the *American Sociological Review* (*ASR*), and to establish this, under a non-Chicago editorship, as the society's official journal (Abbott 1999, 106–17). Taken together, these changes ended Chicago's decades-old dominance of the discipline (Abbott 1999, 111) and, according to Turner and Turner (1990, 57–65), ruptured the ASA, already splintered by the growth of specialty sections and the rise of regional societies, into antagonistic factions that would bedevil the association long into the future.[13]

The Depression also took a severe toll on the external sources of research support that had flowed into sociology during the 1920s. Here, the downturn occurred with a noticeable lag, since funds allocated in the late 1920s were often committed to institutions and projects for multiyear periods that extended into the 1930s. Between 1934 and 1937, however, social scientists experienced a reduction of over 45 percent in private foundation support, with further cutbacks still to come (Geiger 1986, 253, table 12). Analyzing the reasons for these reductions, Geiger (1986, 160, 255) cites the adverse effect of the Depression both on the assets of existing foundations and on the private fortunes of wealthy Americans who might otherwise have launched new foundations. In sociology the trend toward reduced support was exacerbated by a dual reorientation in the funding policies of the Rockefeller Foundation and its SSRC satellites: first, a move away from institutional block grants and toward specific project awards targeted to the applied problems of the Depression era; and second, the corresponding decision to concentrate on three particular areas of research—business finance and industry, public administration, and international relations[14]—areas that favored economists and political scientists over sociologists

13. Turner and Turner (1990, 61) see the founding at the same time of the invitation-only Sociological Research Association as furthering this process.

14. The last of these areas indicates growing foundation concern with the problems transcending the domestic scene, particularly the growth of Nazi power and Japanese militarism.

(Fisher 1993, 88–89, 116–20, 136, 134, 164). These developments basically terminated support for principal centers of sociological research like the LCRC and the ISRR as early as 1932 (Turner and Turner 1990, 45, 51), while leaving Odum's IRSS barely enough to survive as the Depression forced deep budget cuts at the University of North Carolina (Johnson and Johnson 1980, 108–13). Meanwhile, outside the ambit of sociology, foundation resources actually rose for independent institutes for policy research such as the NBER and the Brookings Institution (see the figures given by Geiger [1986, 254]).

The sole countervailing force in this colder climate for sociological research funding came in a roundabout manner from the New Deal, particularly its work relief programs.[15] The New Deal relief agencies famously set jobless Americans to work building highways, bridges, schools, and hospitals, but they supported as well more than 5,000 projects to create employment for men and women with college educations and more advanced levels of training, who, like millions of the less educated, "would otherwise have been destitute" (WPA 1938–39, 3:iii): projects in chemistry, biology, mathematics, history, philosophy, and education; more than 1,600 projects in economics; and also some 800 projects classified as "social research" (see WPA 1938–39). Many of the latter were projects designed by job-holding academic sociologists, who made use of workers paid with the government funds to collect, tabulate, and analyze their data. Platt describes a colorful instance of this: working on his dissertation, Philip Hauser requested from the WPA "two assistants for a study of differential fertility and mortality in Chicago, and was asked if he could use more people; he ended up with 150 clerks, and so could use data on all births and deaths for 5 years instead of a sample" (1996, 153). While Hauser was already a rising star at the University of Chicago and while work relief programs assisted the research of many leading figures in established sociology departments, the government was by no means so exclusive; its job monies flowed to colleges and universities throughout the country, enabling sociologists who had never received a dime of foundation support to conduct empirical studies on rural life, urban communities, race, crime, social institutions, and other sociological topics of the period (see the item-by-item list in WPA [1938–39]). By this process—a little-known development that actually marked the entry of the federal government into the broad-scale funding of sociological research—

15. A secondary path by which the New Deal impacted sociological research was through the research that those sociologists who held government positions performed while on the job. The next section briefly returns to this point.

"it became possible for the first time for sociologists outside government [and foundation circles] to collect data on a large scale and to learn from experience about the practical and intellectual problems of undertaking such work" (Platt 1996, 153). This unexpected side-benefit of high levels of professional unemployment notwithstanding, government spending on project jobs did not negate the loss to sociology of general-purpose foundation dollars or preserve the hotbeds of collective research that had flourished when support had flowed, less democratically, to a few universities. But these points were moot. Beset by unwanted changes in their student enrollments, their salaries, their national association, and their funding sources, sociologists of the 1930s had come on harder times—and they had still to reckon with other challenges.

PROFESSIONAL EXPERTISE ON THE PUBLIC STAGE

Speaking at the tenth anniversary of the opening of the Social Science Research Building at the University of Chicago just before the crash of 1929, Henry Bruere, a New York business leader and budget reformer, as well as an observer aware of the negative financial impact of the 1930s on higher education, adjudged that "the decade of 1929-1939 [was] the period of greatest opportunity for the social sciences that America had known" (Bruere 1940, 5). By this he referred to the progress social scientists made during these years not inside the academy but outside of it, in the public arena, where consensus had emerged "that trained intelligence, the capacity to analyze, as well as to gather data, and acquaintance with theoretical reasons . . . are indispensable to any serious effort to deal constructively with the problems of society" (6). Bruere illustrated his claim by parading the names of familiar figures who had "supplied very great assistance to the government in recent efforts to deal with its problems," presenting a list consisting entirely of economists, political scientists, and legal academics— the real beneficiaries, by his account, of the "opportunity for the social sciences" that the decade had brought (9-10).

The glaring omission of any sociologist from this roll of esteemed academics who had shaped pubic policy in the decade was an outcome presaged at the start of the New Deal when Roosevelt entered the presidency surrounded by his much-publicized brain trust, a small (and short-lived) circle of advisors at whose core stood three members of the faculty of Columbia University—a professor of economics, a professor of political science, and a professor of law—in conspicuous contrast with the economist, the political scientist, and the sociologist who had been at the center of

Hoover's Recent Social Trends Committee. The brain trust model would re-peat itself on a far larger scale throughout the New Deal as a variety of other professional experts continually dwarfed sociologists in the public arena.

Because sociologists of the time compared their public fortunes mainly with the situation of economists, political scientists, and (to a lesser degree) legal authorities, these three professional groups are the focus of the dis-cussion that follows, although to adopt this focus is not to mistake the standpoint of sociologists for the fuller historical picture. By most histori-cal accountings, the lead professional players during the New Deal were lawyers, economists, and social workers—roughly in that order—with oth-ers, like industrial relations experts, also a visible presence (see Manza 1995).[16] Yet sociologists of the 1930s paid scarcely any heed to industrial relations in its own right (perhaps lumping IR experts with economists, the group to which they usually belonged), and they rarely compared them-selves with social workers. This was so even though some of the principal policymakers and administrators in the New Deal had roots in social work,[17] and government relief efforts created positions for upward of fifty thousand case workers and other welfare workers (Ehrenreich 1985, 104, 108; see also Bremer 1975; Gordon 1992). These developments simply could not eradi-cate sociologists' understanding of social work as a low-status female pro-fession (see Gordon 1992). Accordingly, while sociology departments con-tinued to offer courses for aspiring social workers, and social work agencies and client groups continued to hold empirical interest for sociological re-searchers, professional sociologists further distanced themselves from the occupation of social work (Gordon 1992).[18] Of far greater concern for them

16. Like most other historical writings on the subject, this statement takes the New Deal from the inside. On the circles of radical East Coast intellectuals who viewed it from without and wrote critically about contemporary events in various semipopular publications, see Pells (1973). The relationship, if any, between these leftist circles and the political and other activi-ties of academic sociologists of the 1930s has not yet been studied. Joseph Dorman's 1998 doc-umentary film *Arguing the World* does, however, locate two future sociologists, Daniel Bell and Nathan Glazer, then students, in relation to this milieu (see also Brick 1986). As biographies of figures from this generation appear, they will presumably throw light on these currents of po-litical activism (see also Lipset and Ladd 1972).

17. These include Grace Abbott, Harry Hopkins, Paul Kellog, Eduard Lindemann, Henry Morgenthau Jr., and Frances Perkins.

18. This is not to dispute that, in the nation's depressed job market, social work provided employment opportunities both for those with undergraduate degrees in the field and for those with advanced degrees but no academic prospects. Bucking the national trend, the de-mand for caseworkers—and those in correlative areas like corrections, probation, and parole—skyrocketed during the New Deal, quickly outstripping internal supplies. Ehrenreich writes: "The new social workers were necessarily drawn from outside of the profession, [since] so-cial work schools were turning our fewer than a thousand trained workers a year. . . . The

was the growing centrality of economists, political scientists, and legal scholars and practitioners as the recognized authorities on the central issues of public debate.[19]

For economists, this valued status did not await the coming of the New Deal. From the earliest stages of the Depression, economists commanded the lead, in part through their own initiatives. Within months of the market crash, leading members of the economic profession, consciously seeking to extend "the idea that economists could serve more effectively as advisers on public policy," volunteered to the White House their assessment of impending tariff legislation in a petition that carried a thousand signatures, and they continued to air their policy recommendations in the ensuing years, convening much-publicized conferences on the nation's economic plight and unleashing on the president (who regularly sought economists' counsel on his own accord), and also on Congress, federal agencies, and the press, a torrent of statements on the proper methods for achieving recovery and preventing future depressions (Dorfman 1959, 673–66, quote at 673; see also Barber 1985). When the New Deal arrived, the country's orthodox economists, greatly alarmed about state intervention into the economy, resorted to the same tactics, speaking out publicly against the new administration's programs as well as releasing volumes of learned criticism; Harvard economists issued one such attack in 1934 and another in 1937, while Yale economists offered their own in 1934 (Barber 1996). Meanwhile, economists wrote countless journal articles and monographs analyzing the depression's causes, consequences, and possible remedies (Dorfman 1959). What was more, the public proved receptive to their voices. When in 1931, for example, the newly organized National Advisory Council on Radio undertook programming on subjects of public concern, it began with a six-month series (broadcast nationwide over fifty-five stations) that consisted of thirty addresses on "aspects of the depression," twenty-nine of them by eminent economists[20]—and the council then hurried the popular series into book format, complete with a bibliography of more than thirty books that economists had already published on the subject in 1930 and 1931 alone (see Morley 1932; see also Morley 1933, a subsequent radio series). Intro-

---

new social work recruits were typically young, unemployed graduates" from any and all fields (1985, 108).

19. While sociologists of the period drew in their academic work from psychology and anthropology, psychologists and anthropologists figured little in their thinking about the pubic arena, most likely because the situation in these fields was no better that in sociology (see, e.g., Nicholson 1998, 2003).

20. The thirtieth address was an effort by Jane Addams to cover the "social consequences of business depressions."

ducing the series, Columbia University president Nicholas Murray Butler (a philosopher) explained its rationale: "few things, if any, are more needed by the American people . . . than insight into the fundamental principles of economics" (quoted in Morley 1932, vii). Likewise, in late 1932, when Butler sought publicly to demonstrate the contribution his own university could make to the nation, he assembled a commission of economic authorities to report on the deficiencies of the existing price and credit system (see MacIver 1934a).[21]

The operations of the New Deal catapulted economists into even greater public prominence and repute. William Barber has written that, for heterodox economists, the entire New Deal provided a "laboratory" for policy experimentation in the midst of previously unimagined amounts of "opportunity to make hands-on contact with the world of events" (1996, 2). During Roosevelt's first two terms, economists not only participated in policy deliberations at the highest level about management of the economy as well as about labor, industry, agriculture, economic security, and more, but they helped to design and draft landmark legislation in all these areas, they testified before Congress in support of these measures, they filled the upper echelons of new federal agencies and regulatory commissions, and they occupied positions at all rungs of existing departments, agencies, and commissions (Barber 1996; Lubin 1937; Morgan 2003; Rockoff 1997). Not surprisingly, the slogan in Washington, D.C., by the mid-1930s was that "the Federal Government is the economist's heaven" (quoted in Sims 1938, 30). At times, there seemed scarcely enough economists to go around, as "virtually every university in the country was combed by the various federal agencies for competent economists," causing "leaves of absence [from the academy to become] numerous and widespread" (Lubin 1937, 216). The state's expanding demand for statisticians operated to the same effect, since the planning and execution of New Deal programs generated an immediate need for vast quantities of data and skilled data analysis throughout departments and agencies, and the main qualification for work as a statistician remained training in economics (see Anderson 1990; Duncan and Shelton 1978; see also Rice 1934b).[22] One contemporary study, limited to

21. Robert MacIver, who chaired this commission, was a sociologist, though, perhaps because he was alone in this capacity, the commission report bears no traces of his sociology.

22. Seeking to fill these positions, the Civil Service Commission in 1936 sent 29,000 announcements "to every college and university in the United States, to departments of economics, statistics, and political science, to the American Farm Economic Association, the American Economic Association, the American Statistical Association, and the American Political Science Association" (White 1937, 214). The omission of departments of sociology and of the ASA is, once again, striking.

regular civil service positions (and thus omitting positions in all of the New Deal's special agencies and commissions), found that "583 new positions in economics and 129 new positions in statistics" were created between January 1935 and October 1936 alone (White 1937, 211). Another study, somewhat broader in its coverage, reported that as of December 1938 the federal government employed (exclusive of social workers) 7,075 professionals in "the social science field," of whom 2,025 fell in "miscellaneous categories" and 5,050—an impressive 71 percent—were economists (McDiarmid 1945, 74).[23] These figures do not include the heavy presence of economists on the New Deal's top-level advisory and planning councils (see Barber 1996; Goldberg 1980; Manza 1995).

Although compared with economists, political scientists occupied a considerably smaller public role during the 1930s, they nevertheless probably formed the largest contingent among these "miscellaneous" social scientists in the New Deal. Like economists, political scientists came fast out of the gate at the onset of the Depression, with symposia, radio programs, and writings on the causes and possible legislative solutions for the nation's crisis as well as with empirical analyses of its electoral consequences,[24] and their efforts along these lines continued as the 1930s wore on. No less important were political scientists' quick actions in asserting their indispensability—as "experts in the business of government"—to the future of the nation and in warning that "it would be [a] poor service . . . to the American public to use economists outside their proper sphere," that is, to trust them regarding anything more than the "strictly economic factors in a business depression" (Holcombe 1931, 918; Reed 1932, 138).

That political scientists could plausibly define themselves as experts in the business of government had much to do with the high-profile specialty of public administration, one of the core subfields into which political science had been divided since the late nineteenth century and on the basis of which it had since established outposts both in law schools and in several graduate programs in public administration (see Caiden 1984).[25] Concerned with the principles and practices of successful organizational management (in areas such planning, staffing, reporting, and budgeting), public

23. I thank James Sparrow for directing me to McDiarmid's valuable chapter, as well as to Judd (1938) and Sims (1938), which I draw on in this section.

24. See, e.g., Corwin (1931), Field (1931), Gaus (1931), Gosnell (1933), Holcombe (1931), Jacobson (1932), Myers (1931), and Reed (1933), a radio series.

25. Because their specialty was based in political science, public administrative experts tended to be classed as political scientists even when institutionally located in such outposts rather than in political science departments—or, alternatively, departments of "government" or "politics."

administration experienced "heightened demand" during the 1930s with the proliferation of government agencies at all levels and the felt need for expert guidance in running these effectively (Oren 2003, 82). Accordingly, as Oren has written, "during the depression years, public administration bucked the trend of austerity in the American academy, as its members were able to attract funds and build new institutions," including the Graduate School of Public Administration at Harvard, one of several ventures responsible for the growth in the number of doctoral degrees granted in the field by the decade's end (2003, 86). Likewise, even as the Rockefeller Foundation slashed overall funding for social science research to concentrate on the urgent problems of the 1930s, it increased support for work on public administration, ensuring the incorporation of political scientists on New Deal planning and advisory committees (Fisher 1993, 165). By these and other pathways, "political scientists [came] to have an enormous impact through public positions" during the New Deal (Farr and Seidelman 1993, 109); "Roosevelt liked political scientists and put many of them in prominent places in his administration, [including committees on] national economic and resource planning, the federalization of social welfare and labor policies, civic education, even experiments in ownership like the TVA" (Seidelman 1985, 108). As the growth of the federal bureaucracy during the New Deal revived, by mid-decade, earlier calls for government reorganization, both the president and the Senate (the latter with funds from the Brookings Institution) assembled expert committees and research subcommittees to tackle the issue and to design reorganization plans, bringing to Washington many of the current and future leaders of political science and pressing into service seemingly "everyone of note" in public administration (quoting Caiden 1984, 66; more generally see Karl 1963).

A still more considerable force, both at the helm and down through the inner chambers of the New Deal, added a third element to the professional mix: expertise in law. This came as a result of the influx into the Roosevelt administration of distinguished legal academics and of ordinary practicing lawyers, some of the latter fresh out of Ivy League law schools, where their training had put them in touch with the social sciences (see Auerbach 1976; Irons 1993). To be sure, not only did the public policy involvement of members of the legal profession long predate the New Deal (see Manza 1995), but many elite lawyers of the 1930s actively opposed New Deal reforms and mounted public campaigns against them (see Shamir 1995). Even so, in Auerbach's words, "the New Deal was a lawyer's deal," conferring on those with knowledge of the law "direct access to [the state's] newest and most critical levers of power" (1976, 226). As in the case of economists, this development occurred by multiple means. Legal scholars formed part of Roosevelt's inner clique of advisors (Auerbach 1976); they and scores of government attorneys participated "in drafting, shaping, [and] formulating . . . the avalanche of new statues" that the New Deal called forth (Shamir 1995, 3); lawyers headed up new agencies and commissions and infiltrated deep into established departments, providing (among other things) the frontline team for negotiating and enforcing New Deal regulations (Irons 1993; see also Herring 1938); and, as one new program after another faced judicial challenge, government lawyers devised litigation strategies and waged hundreds of publicized courtroom battles (Irons 1993). The swelling size of the government's legal apparatus indicates the magnitude of these developments: between 1931 and 1937 the number of lawyers in civil service positions (and only those jobs located in Washington) rose by 108 percent to over 3,100 (Judd 1938, 49, table 1), and civil service posts apparently constituted merely a quarter of the government's legal staff (Auerbach 1976, 225). Even by such rough figures, there were more lawyers in the service of the New Deal than there were economists, although which was in greater demand probably passed unnoticed to most contemporaries. More conspicuous was that the events of the Depression and the New Deal had publicly validated both groups (and those in public administration) as authoritative experts on the nation's most pressing issues and offered vastly expanded opportunities for their members to exercise that authority.

Amid these changes, sociologists of the 1930s figured as distant also-rans, and the dramatic professional setback—or so it appeared to them when they compared their situation with that of other social scientists and recalled the progress they felt that they had made in the 1920s—soon registered on them. Scattered exceptions did not obscure for them this reality, though the exceptions may have softened the blow. While Hoover remained in office, the Recent Social Trends Committee and the sociologists it involved proceeded onward with their work, and this remained in the public eye. Further, as the Depression set it, Hoover appointed other advisory committees that included sociologists. Burgess, for instance, chaired one of the task forces of the President's Conference on Child Health and Protection, the Subcommittee on the Function of Home Activities in the Education of the Child, and he enlisted several sociologists in the subcommittee's work (see Stanley and Burgess 1934, xiv); James Ford, a Harvard ethicist whose appointment after 1931 was in the university's new Department of Sociology, supervised the White House Conference on Home Building and Home Ownership and edited its twelve-volume 1933 report (Johnston 1995, 89). Even so, a contemporary anecdote, apparently pertaining to the closing days of the Hoover administration and the period just afterward, ran tellingly as follows: "A prominent American sociologist remarked, as he ate his luncheon in a Washington restaurant, 'I'm almost lonesome here at the capital.' And he elaborated by asking, 'Why it is that in this city, overrun with economists, political scientists, statisticians and even historians, one cannot find a sociologist unless he is here in the guise of one of these others?'" (Willey 1934, 213).

The scene somewhat brightened, to be sure, as the New Deal geared into action. After an early round of staff cutbacks caused by Roosevelt's initial plan to balance the federal budget, the Division of Farm Population and Rural Life within the Department of Agriculture's Bureau of Agricultural Economics (BAE) grew substantially between 1935 and 1941—up from 5 to 57 members, the majority of whom were rural sociologists (half in Washington, half in regional offices)—in response to the need for "sociological knowledge for policy development and programs aimed at improving the well-being of agriculture and rural people" (Larson and Zimmerman 2003, 4–5). Furthermore, while the division remained the government's only sociological unit for the entire New Deal, sociologists made their mark as well in the Census Bureau of the Commerce Department. University of Pennsylvania statistician and sociologist Stuart Rice served as the bureau's assistant director in the mid-1930s, before becoming head of Roosevelt's Central Statistical Board; Rice also chaired the SSRC-sponsored, Commerce-affiliated, Committee on Government Statistics and Information Services. In turn, this committee recruited Samuel Stouffer and Philip Hauser to consider (with the help of personnel supported through work relief agencies) the measurement of unemployment by sampling—a project that eventually revolutionized the design of the 1940 Census, on which Hauser served as assistant chief statistician (Anderson 1990, 173–90; Berland 1962, 232–33).

Outside of established departments, sociologists also occupied positions on New Deal advisory councils and emergency agencies. Ogburn, seemingly omnipresent, served as a member of Roosevelt's National Resources Committee, as a special advisor to the Resettlement Administration, and as director of the NRA's (short-lived) Consumer Advisory Board—the last a committee to which Robert Lynd (Columbia) also belonged. Odum chaired the North Carolina branch of both the Civil Works Administration and the Emergency Relief Administration. His colleague Rupert Vance worked for the Social Security Board and the National Resources Committee. Nels Anderson, George Lundberg, and Thomas McCormick served as Federal Emergency Relief Administration (FERA managers, while McCormick, along with rural sociologists Paul Landis, Dwight Sanderson,

Thomas Woofter, and Carl Zimmerman, held posts in the WPA's Division of Social Research, which produced a large number of monographs and research bulletins during this period (see WPA 1937; see also Converse 1987, 39).[26] A contemporary observer reported that sociologists were active as well in "relief and recovery programs in all parts of the country" (Price 1934, 215), programs presumably based not only in federal but in numerous state and local agencies.

Yet these various instances, rather than the tip of some great iceberg as past scholarship has assumed, probably constituted a good share of the sociological presence in toto. The data set that Abbott and Sparrow have assembled for chapter 8 of this volume identifies a total of 61 instances of service by sociologists or rural sociologists in select government agencies between 1930 and 1939: 17 in the Agriculture Department; 5 in the Labor Department; 7 in the Census Bureau; 4 on the National Resources Planning Board; 5 in the Farm Security Administration; 6 in FERA; and 17 in the WPA—numbers closely in line with the individual cases just cited. What is more, these figures aggregate over the entire decade; as such, they imply considerably smaller numbers during any one portion of this period—the more so in view of the brevity of government service for some sociologists and the possibility that, because some of the same people shuffled across several agencies, certain individuals may be counted more than once. To be sure, the Abbott and Sparrow data include only certain agencies, exclude sociologists born before 1890 and off the ASA membership rolls by the 1940s, and classify as sociologists only holders of PhD's in sociology or rural sociology—thereby omitting those who, in the depressed economy, may have discontinued work toward a degree but obtained civil service employment on the basis of their sociological training. That the ranks of the latter were large, however, is doubtful; a contemporary study of the civil service commented: as for the sociologist, "there are no jobs for him—or rather just a few. The Division of Population of the Bureau of the Census and the Farm Population Division [of the BAE] are the best examples of agencies employing sociologists—at that, only a few. And, of course, these sociologists must be statisticians as well" (Sims 1938, 33). Hinkle (1994, 400) cites an unpublished, "untitled study of about 110 sociologists *and anthropologists* [emphasis added] working for the federal government during the New Deal era," thus hinting at a figure perhaps larger than Abbott and Sparrow's (generated, one presumes, using less precise criteria), but a meager figure

---

26. I draw these examples principally from Odum (1951), supplementing this source with other gleanings from my study of this period.

still. Whatever the precise number, the New Deal was for sociologists hardly the vast public employment agency that it became for lawyers, economists, or even some political scientists.

At first glace, figures of this sort—suggesting upward of five thousand economists in federal employment during the New Deal, perhaps twice that number of lawyers, but fewer than one hundred sociologists—call out for other figures. Were there not, after all, more economists, lawyers, and even political scientists in this period than sociologists? Although full membership counts do not exist for these fields, the size of their respective national professional associations speaks broadly to this question—with the proviso that, in each case, there were professionals who did not belong to the national association, particularly during the 1930s, when membership in all these bodies (except for the American Political Science Association [APSA]) dropped. In 1935, for example, when the membership of the ASA stood at 1,141, the American Economic Association (AEA) had 2,544 members, the APSA 1,854, and the American Bar Association (ABA) 25,000.[27] From this perspective, while economists, lawyers, and political scientists considerably outnumbered sociologists, sociologists were scare in government positions during the New Deal even relative to their small numbers.

This said, we should resist the temptation to concentrate too much on specific numbers. If the figures just cited were comparable, one might compute a ratio for each group by dividing the number of government positions by the number of professional group members. But even taking figures for membership in the national associations as the appropriate denominators here, the numerators would lack comparability—each comes from a different source counting according to different criteria. More seriously, however, even exacter statistics, unless they were known and well publicized in the 1930s, would cloud understanding of the historical situation. No more than the rest of us when we sense that our group has been excluded—as, say, when theorists within the ASA of today feel underrepresented in its journals and governing councils—did sociologists of the 1930s first calculate positions-per-member fractions by group, compare these across groups, and only then form their perceptions. While loosely aware that they were fewer in number than economists, lawyers, and political scientists, what stood out to them were not the statistics (which they did not know) but the looming presence on the public stage of experts from these groups—with

27. I thank the ASA, AEA, APSA, and ABA for providing these data. For comparison, consider the figures at either end of the decade. For 1930: ASA, 1,567; AEA, 2,797; APSA, 1,819; and ABA, 26,773. For 1940: ASA, 1,034; AEA, 3,148; APSA, 2,857; and ABA, 31,626. Of the four associations, only ASA was smaller in 1940 than in 1930.

their frequent writings about events on the national agenda, their opinionated voices on the radio and in the press, their authoritative counsels in demand from elected officials and average citizens alike—in stark contrast to sociologists. This disparity antedated the opening of a single position for economists, lawyers, and men and women in public administration during Roosevelt's presidency, though sociologists recognized that the advent of the New Deal made these professions all the more ubiquitous, a solid mass at every turn. Even had sociology been *overrepresented* for its size, sociologists likely would have found this a galling situation.

How this disparity developed is an important question that historians of sociology have yet to investigate, and the primary research needed for this task exceeds the remit of this chapter. From bits of evidence turned up in the current project, however, I tentatively propose the interplay of two factors as among the reasons that sociologists occupied a lesser role than economists, political scientists, and legal experts on the public stage of the Great Depression and the New Deal. The first of these factors has to do with the self-reinforcing effects of preestablished networks. Compared with sociologists, economists, lawyers, and scholars in public administration entered the 1930s with thicker history of public involvement. Part and parcel of this history were official and unofficial ties to state actors at all levels, connections to the press and other popular media outlets, and so on—linkages that all these parties could activate as the crisis of the 1930s unfolded.

One sees this process vividly during the New Deal as the Roosevelt administration turned immediately to what Abbott and Sparrow describe (in chap. 8 of this volume) as "old-boy methods" of recruitment. The New Deal relied on these methods from its beginnings, building advisory councils, staffing new agencies, and enlarging existing departments by tapping into networks anchored in the top Ivy League schools, the established eastern liberal arts colleges, and the universities in the Washington area, and then, as these sources exhausted themselves, spanning outward via the same networks. This practice comparatively disadvantaged sociology from the start because these were the very institutions that typically lacked sociology departments well into the 1930s (and even afterward); equally important, the discipline had scarcely existed in any form at these institutions back in the schooldays of Roosevelt and his advisors, in striking contrast with the traditional fields of law, economics, and political science. Writing in 1934, Maurice Price (a sociologist later at the University of Illinois) noted the problem: "Important and long-prestiged educational institutions close to Washington have no sociological departments as yet, and leading social science and history men in them are frequently not aware that Yale, Harvard, and Columbia Universities . . . really take any stock of sociology as such" (1934, 218). That the one sociologist on constant display during the New Deal—Ogburn—possessed strong Columbia connections; that the one government department where sociologists (rural sociologists) secured their own base—the Department of Agriculture—was headed by an Iowan (Henry A. Wallace) heavily reliant on his own ties to agricultural colleges of the Midwest, where (rural) sociology was a well-established field (see Gilbert 2000, 2001; Gilbert and Baker 1997)—such instances, too, suggest the role of the network factor.

Second, and operating alongside this factor, were contemporary understandings of the historical period and its problems, that is, the common framing of the national situation. Franklin Roosevelt and his counselors conceived of the New Deal, and liked to describe it publicly, as a move by "government" to assume greater responsibility for the problems of "economic life" (quoted in Barber 1996, 19), and in expressing themselves this way they spoke a language familiar to the times. That the stock market crash, business failures, mortgage foreclosures, and spiraling unemployment were "economic" issues, that "government" should assist, at least by legislating emergency measures for citizens in greatest need: these were views voiced at almost every point along the ideological spectrum—and they were views that seemed to confer a kind of natural monopoly on the accepted experts on "economic life" and "government," that is, economists, political scientists, and lawyers. That these groups constituted the nearly exclusive professional owners of the great issues then on the public agenda generally seemed so self-evident at the time, both inside and outside the administration, as to go without saying. Capturing part of this mentality, sociologist Henry Fairchild (New York University) wrote regretfully in 1937 that the crisis of the age "was commonly regarded by the public, and doubtless by the President himself, as an 'economic' situation and of course economic matters should be dealt with by economists first of all" (1937, 2). Further, insofar as governmental attacks on this situation were at issue, the same attitude extended, just as "naturally," to lawyers and experts in public administration—as well as to social workers to the extent that direct services to the needy were involved. This framing left sociologists out of the picture (see Price 1934, 217-18).

Manza (personal communication) has remarked on the general absence from New Deal policy debates of "social" issues such as race, family organization, and urban problems qua urban problems, and he has plausibly suggested that inclusion of these issues on the national agenda would have opened the way for greater sociological involvement. It is well to recognize further, however, that to declare a subject "economic" or "governmental" by no means necessarily excludes the sociologist—witness European contexts where sociologists, whether from Weberian, Marxist, or other traditions, have been centrally concerned with the economy, the state, and law and regular participants in public discussions of these topics (witness too the many other lines of sociological inquiry that have addressed these issues). This heritage was familiar to American sociologists of the early twentieth century (Hinkle 1994), but into the 1930s they continued—with a few notable exceptions—their practice of constituting sociology otherwise, still mainly around the leftovers of disciplines such as economics and political science. This, at any rate, is a pattern discernable in affiliations to the evolving roster of ASA sections. In 1931, for example, the percentages of ASA members professing interest in the different specialty sections were as follows: Social Psychology, 50 percent; Social Research, 42.4 percent; Family, 41.7 percent; Social Work, 39.8 percent; General and Historical Sociology, 38.3 percent; Community Problems, 34.9 percent; Psychiatry, 30.6 percent; Teaching, 29.9 percent; Religion, 24.1 percent; Education, 23.2 percent; Rural Sociology, 22.2 percent; Statistics, 19.3 percent; and Social Biology, 9.8 percent (Duncan and Duncan 1933, 211, table 2). While "general sociology," "social research," and "community problems" were commodious categories that by no means precluded sociologists' attention to "economic life" and "government," plainly the latter were not topics square at the forefront of professional sociology at the outset of the Depression. As late as 1934, sociologist Malcolm Willey (University of Minnesota) described the Depression era as belonging "naturally [to] economists" because "the immediate issues were economic"—"problems . . . of banking and credit, etc." (1934, 214; see also Ogburn 1934c, 29). From this angle, then, a basic congruence seems to have existed between the way sociologists understood the purview of their discipline and the common consensus about which disciplines could address the contemporary situation.[28]

Yet there was no natural inevitability about this shared framing, as the

28. Given that, in the figures just reported, 40 percent of ASA members express an interest in social work, the question may also arise as to why professional sociologists were largely absent not only from the New Deal's frontline relief effort (this part of the question is probably answered in terms of their growing disinterest in the *practice* of social work) but also from the policy debates and activities that lay behind the passage of the Social Security Act. As Gordon (1992) and Manza (1995) have shown, however, different provisions of this act emerged from different policy circles—a (largely female) social workers' circle in the case of ADC, a (largely male) network of economists and lawyers for social insurance programs—and, significantly, sociologists generally fell outside of both networks.

important counterexample of rural sociology shows. The principal New Deal agency for confronting the crisis of rural America was the Department of Agriculture, and in this instance a mentality differing from the common consensus developed, particularly within the BAE. Here, while agricultural economists were always the dominant force, the assumption prevailed that the research of rural sociologists was naturally integral to understanding rural institutions—whether churches, schools, and communities, or local government, or banks, industries, and marketing organizations—as well as to mounting an effective attack on the massive problems of rural areas (Larson and Zimmerman 2003). In this setting, the expertise of rural sociologists came to be in great demand, and rural sociologists, inside and outside government positions, stepped up and responded not by turning away from the topics of economic life and government, but by incorporating these into wide-ranging studies of rural social conditions (Larson and Zimmerman 2003, esp. 4). One sees clearly here the reciprocal interaction of framing and networks factors: the modest entry of rural sociologists into the BAE (and into agricultural colleges) in the period before the Depression established ties between agricultural economics and rural sociology and led members of the two fields to cooperate in the study of rural life; with this pattern in place, the plight of rural America during the Depression era was framed as the professional province of both groups; given this framing and the existing network ties, the Department of Agriculture called on more rural sociologists to study rural life, thereby confirming their co-ownership of the subject and, in so doing, further increasing demand for their work. Beyond these restricted circles, however, the same reciprocal process seems to have produced the opposite effect: situated outside the networks that wired academics into the public arena, nonrural sociologists fell largely outside frame that brought into focus the expertise needed to address the plight of nonrural America; falling outside this frame, sociologists then remained outside the network structure. Eventually, they grew exasperated.

SOCIOLOGISTS REACT

In a context characterized by the network and framing factors just described, sociologists' intellectual engagement with the events of the Depression era started slowly—in fact, with a delay of roughly four to five years in most corners of the discipline.[29]

29. In the following analysis, my interest is with how sociologists responded to the Depression and the New Deal in their capacity as professional sociologists, rather than in their roles as classroom teachers, voters, members of political parties and churches, citizens of local communities, and so on. When the collective biography of sociologists of this era is written, it

Annual proceedings of the ASA chronicle the field's hesitant start. At the first meeting after the stock market crash, held in the nation's capital in December 1929, Ogburn used the presidential podium to push the objectivist position, which had generally accepted sociology's involvement in the public arena, to what some listeners saw as a hands-off extreme, insisting that "sociology as a science is not interested in making the world a better place to live . . . or in guiding the ship of state, [but] in one thing only, to wit, discovery of new knowledge" (1929, 2). That the person who spoke these words sat, at that moment, on the high advisory council of Hoover's Recent Social Trends Committee speaks tellingly about Ogburn's own thought and character (see Laslett 1990, 1991), but a year later Odum sounded a similarly Olympian note in a presidential address on regionalism which gave no inkling that the country was then in the grips of a deepening depression (see Odum 1930). Apart from Emory Bogardus's (USC) muted references to contemporary conditions in his announcement the next year that sociologists should develop a "social process theory of social problems [to lay the] foundation for the development of programs of social amelioration" (1931, xii)—a stock line out of social problems textbooks of the 1920s—the pattern repeated itself in 1931, 1932 (see Bernard 1932), and 1933. In the latter instance, Ernest Reuter (Iowa) took for his presidential theme the "major universals in the natural story of race and culture contact," and when the ASA met in December of 1933—the darkest hour of the Great Depression—its program featured Ellsworth Faris speaking on "Culture and Personality among the Forest Bantu." Nor, in this respect, were the ASA's presidents out of step with its participating members. Indeed, to judge from the titles of the papers they presented at the annual meetings,[30] before 1934 nothing about the Depression—not its causes, its diverse ramifications, nor any other aspect of it—roused the interest of sociologists as a topic for academic investigation or as an entry point into policy discussions. Members connected to the sections Rural Sociology and Social Work were the only exceptions.[31]

Publications from the period tell the same story. Aside from studies in the area of rural sociology,[32] the early 1930s brought forth from sociology

---

may well show that these men and women were deeply engaged with the events of the 1930s in these other roles, but this is a subject distinct from my concern here.

30. Volumes 24–28 of the *Publication of the American Sociological Society* give the paper titles.

31. Looking backward in 1934, a contemporary observer noted this same silence: "the almost complete disregard of the depression in the programs of important sociological meetings" (Fairchild 1934, 179).

32. The most notable of these was probably Brunner and Kolb (1933). One of several companion volumes to the final report of the Recent Social Trends Committee, the book contained only a short chapter on the period, "1930 and After"; however, because the research for the

(so far as I am aware) only one book focused on the Depression, *Human Aspects of Unemployment and Relief* (1933) by James Mickel Williams, a sociologist (from Hobart and William Smith colleges) situated well outside the professional mainstream and its tributaries. Book production took time, of course, and a few major sociological studies that subsequently appeared were already in progress, notably Robert C. Angell's *The Family Encounters the Depression* (1936), a project started in the spring of 1931—albeit less out of interest in the Depression than in order "to test some notions about the research method in sociology" (Angell 1936, 265). Even so, sociologists in the early 1930s seem to have had limited interest in what other social scientists, who did complete books on the Depression at this time, had to offer on the topic. During these years, the *AJS*—still the ASA's official journal—ran hundreds of book reviews, often of works by economists, political scientists, and others; yet it took little notice of the scores of titles pouring out on the Depression and the New Deal.[33] More striking still, mirroring the pattern of papers presented at the ASA meetings (and excepting, once again, work in rural sociology), *AJS* published during the entire 1930–34 period *only one* sociological research article with a focus on the Depression (Hart 1933), a few deceptive titles notwithstanding.[34]

In addition to regular research articles, *AJS* also devoted one of its six issues each year to the topic of current social trends. These special issues, which began in 1928 with Ogburn's move to the journal's home base at the University of Chicago and onto its editorial board, consisted of invited

---

book served as the second wave of Brunner's earlier survey of 140 agricultural communities, the volume prepared the way for the third wave, which was the basis for Brunner and Lorge's more important *Rural Trends in Depression Years* (1937). In related work on the rural south, staff members at Odum's IRSS conducted during the early 1930s some twenty-four projects, whose results went mostly unpublished, although a few yielded articles in *Social Forces* (Johnson and Johnson 1980, 139). More generally, *Social Forces*, when compared in this period with the *American Journal of Sociology* (as characterized later in the text), and in part due to its linkages with rural sociology, showed itself more attentive to aspects of the Depression and the New Deal, running numerous short entries on unemployment, farm movements, planning, the NRA, and so on (see also Johnson and Johnson 1980, 219, on Odum's various other work at this time). Apparently written in many cases as assignments delegated to Odum's students or to other members of IRSS's multidisciplinary staff, rather than by academic sociologists, these entries provide little insight, however, into the broader state of the profession.

33. This claim and those later in the text about *AJS* are based on my own examination of issues of the journal from the period.

34. Tibbitt's "Majority Votes and the Business Cycle" (1931) actually dealt with the years 1878–88; Hurlburt's "Prosperity, Depression, and the Suicide Rate" (1932) concerned the 1902-25 period; and Schmid's "Suicide in Minneapolis, Minnesota: 1928-32" (1933) scarcely registered the depression then in progress.

summary reports on developments during the previous year in the various domains of American life that interested Ogburn: population, inventions, production, labor, employment, legislation, rural life, family, religion, education, and so on. With this format in place, the Depression could hardly avoid some mention in the journal's pages amid the events of the early 1930s, and mention it did receive, with growing frequency, as these annual reports duly recorded falling levels of production, declining wages, rising unemployment, and so on (see the May issues of *AJS*, 1930–33). Significantly, however, even in this readymade forum for sociological treatment of the causes and consequences of the Depression, sociologists barely connected with the topic. Year after year, in these thematic issues of the journal of their own professional association, sociologists were outnumbered by nonsociologists, as Ogburn assigned the majority of trend reports to academic and government economists, political scientists, and social workers. What was more, even when Ogburn involved sociologists, they mostly confined their reports to official statistics regarding the assigned subject (Groves's article on the family, for example, described the increasing frequency of "family relief on account of the industrial depression" [1931, 993]), with no indication of any sociological research otherwise under way on the questions at stake.

Only in 1933 did a different pattern of response start to emerge. Slow to address the nation's plight, sociologists began shifting their posture when increasingly faced with their own relative deprivation as a professional group. As the New Deal moved into action in mid-1933, valorizing (and increasingly employing) economists, lawyers, and experts in public administration, sociologists recognized their exclusion almost immediately. As they did so, they quickly set about to reverse the perceived setback, blaming themselves for heretofore "following the example of the emperor Nero [and] fiddl[ing] while the world burns down about them" (Brearley 1934, 192).[35] Price (1934, 215) reports that, in December 1933, F. Stuart Chapin (Minnesota) and E. A. Ross (Wisconsin; retired) took to the floor at the ASA meeting to urge sociology to join other social sciences in confronting the

---

35. In this self-critical mood, a number of sociologists attributed their discipline's previously subdued response to the scientistic outlook that had emerged in the 1920s, berating the spokesmen for scientism for detaching sociology from the problems of the 1930s (see, e.g., Brearley 1934, 192; Eliot 1934, 181; Fairchild 1934, 179; Krueger 1934, 193; Todd 1934, 196). Expressions of this critique provide an interesting window onto the mid-1930s but should probably not be mistaken for a fair historical account. As observed earlier, even ardent proponents of scientism generally accepted that sociology would play an important advisory role on issues of public policy.

Depression. By 1934, with New Deal programs mushrooming, sociologists from all tiers of the profession frankly acknowledged their comparative marginalization:[36]

Chapin: "Many statisticians, economists, and political scientists have been drawn into the various Recovery Administration divisions," which neglect "the point of view of the sociologist" (1934b, 473).

Fairchild: "In the imposing array of professors that constitute the 'brain trust' economists outnumber sociologists by an . . . impressive proportion" (1934, 180).

Thomas Eliot (Northwestern): "Sociologists have proved relatively less influential and effective, in the current national crisis, than representatives of other so-called social sciences, [especially] economic and political scientists" (1934, 181).

H. C. Brearley (Clemson): "The present . . . crisis reveals clearly the impotence of sociology . . . [sociologists] are playing far less important roles than the economists" (1934, 192).

W. P. Meroney (Baylor): Amid "present economic, political, and social conditions, . . . college professors calling themselves sociologists [have] little influence and scant recognition" (1934, 198).

Stuart Queen (Washington University): "Judging from events of the recent past sociologists will not be called upon in significant numbers to assume administrative responsibility [or to advise on] problems of agriculture, industry, or relief" (1934a, 207).

Price: "The Planning Board of the P.W.A. and the planning sections of certain other recovery organizations have overlooked [sociologists]—not to mention the permanent government agencies" (1934, 218).

Rice: "There are [in Washington] dozens and dozens of bureaus, divisions, offices, and sections which have in their title the name 'statistics' or 'economics,' but where is sociology found?" (1934a, 220).

Burgess: "No demand has been made of sociology to mobilize and direct upon the consideration of politics and programs of economic and social reconstruction its distinctive point of view and methods of research" (1934, 1).

36. These quotations are ordered earliest to latest, so far as I have been able to determine their chronological sequence.

By no means were these sentiments an exclusively 1934 phenomenon. Three years later, for example, Odum still complained of "the minor role which sociologists have apparently played in the 'New Deal' program at Washington" (1937, 327). Relevant here, however, is the galvanizing effect that such sentiments produced as they spread through sociology in the mid-1930s, for in tandem with sociologists' recognition of their exclusion from the public arena came sudden efforts to secure inclusion. Admittedly, some members of the profession scorned this move, stridently so in the instance of future ASA president (and *ASR* editor) Frank Hankins (Smith College): "The sociologist has no special facilities for devising the ends which society should set up; [and] it is quite certain that if the ends were set up, the sociologist could not tell . . . how to get there. . . . I do not see that he has anything of a clearly scientific nature to contribute to the major problems of a sick capitalist society. He may think he has, but his contribution is almost certain to be tainted with . . . self deceptive wishful thinking" (1934, 202). But few sociologists embraced Hankins's viewpoint. To the contrary, the majority, rankling at the privileged status of economists and others, took active organizational and intellectual steps to thrust sociology forward and to display the contribution the field could make in the age of the Depression and the New Deal.

Broadly, these catch-up efforts fell into three clusters. The first centered on the infrastructure of the ASA. While committees elsewhere in ASA were busy fomenting various anti-Chicago proposals, other committees quickly set to work devising organizational initiatives that might remove sociologists from the national sidelines. These bodies were clear about the problem: in December 1934, the ASA's Research Planning Committee expressed alarm that "certain of the new services of the government have been hampered by the lack of sociological counsel" ("Report of the Research Planning Committee" 1935, 4), while its Committee on Opportunities for Trained Sociologists reported in 1935 that, "although there had been 'a marked increase in the use of social scientists in public service,' sociologists did not benefit from it as much as economists, political scientists, lawyers and social workers" (Rhoades 1981, 19). As remedies, these committees recommended that the ASA adopt measures that included assisting departments in "equipping [graduate] students for technical positions in Federal bureaus," creating a Publicity Committee "to send releases to the press [regarding] developments in sociology," and opening a headquarters for the ASA in Washington, D.C., to "facilitate a working integration of the services of sociologists with governmental departments" ("Official Reports and Proceedings" 1937, 92; "Report of the Research Planning Committee" 1935, 7).

Attesting plainly to sociologists' interest in participating more fully in the New Deal, all these proposals nonetheless foundered at the time for lack of funds.

Simultaneously, however, sociologists proceeded on a second front. Taking cues from the economists and the political scientists, they held conferences and symposia designed to showcase the public importance of their sociology. The three most important of these events occurred on the heels of one another in 1934. In May of that year, Ogburn turned *AJS*'s annual issue on social trends into a special issue on the New Deal. In December, Odum ran a special issue of *Social Forces* devoted to "Questions for Sociology? What is the Role of Sociology in the Current Social Reconstruction? What are the Sociological Implications of the New Deal? What is the Place of Sociology in the Federal Government? What is the Matter with Sociologists?" Finally, also in December, Burgess, then ASA president, convened the association's annual meeting, devoted explicitly to the topic Human Problems of Social Planning, with particular reference to "recent economic, social, and political changes" and "sociological aspects of the New Deal" (Program Announcement 1934). Following the meeting, Burgess rushed what he regarded as the conference's main papers into print in a 1935 book of the same lead title (see Burgess and Blumer 1935).

What effect these various publications had on men and women within the public arena is unknown. Had any nonsociologists come across them, their impressions would most likely have run counter to the vital image that sociologists hoped to propagate about their field. Ogburn's New Deal issue of *AJS* followed the pattern of his earlier special issues. Most articles, including "Economic Recovery," "Unemployment and Relief," "Labor," and "Education," were not even written by sociologists; further, those by sociologists, with the slight exception of MacIver (1934b), left the contribution of sociology implicit at best. Odum's special issue went to the opposite extreme; here sociologists furnished a long list of what sociology could offer the nation, but they seemed only to posture since in no case did they base their claims to expertise on existing sociological research on the topics at stake. Leanest of all was Burgess's volume; bringing together what some of the biggest names in the discipline had to say about the neglected "sociological aspects of the New Deal," it revealed that not one of these luminaries (aside from Burgess himself) had any more than a passing comment to make about any issue then on the national agenda.[37]

37. Ironically, the 1934 meeting included papers actually on point. In contrast to those of previous meetings, this program offered some two dozen empirical papers on different aspects

If contrary in outcome to their intended purposes, however, these symposia and conferences—and others like them[38]—expose an important current in sociological thought during the mid 1930s. Before this period, as observed earlier in the chapter, sociologists generally assumed they had a public role to play; under the influence of various forms of scientism, however, they typically viewed this role as a mandate the public would fashion and then call upon them to undertake—as the Chicago Commission on Race Relations called on the expert advice of Park's students, as Hoover summoned Ogburn and Odum to conduct research on recent social trends. *But what if the pubic went looking elsewhere for expertise, so that the calls to sociologists began to drop off fast?* Here was the conundrum that confronted sociologists of the 1930s as they compared their opportunities with those of economists, lawyers, and political scientists, and it prompted a major rethinking of their public mission. In the course of this rethinking, sociologists not only strongly reasserted their public role but also served notice that they were no longer content to wait upon the public to write and deliver the mandate.

Almost inevitably, this development proceeded along different pathways. For some of the men and women who took part in the rethinking, sociologists properly belonged not only inside the academy but as well in established government positions. Luther Bernard (Washington University), for example, proposed that the president of the United States immediately create by his side a permanent Social Science Commission, with separate subcommissions for sociologists, economists, and political scientists, in order to advise on the "present social situation"; that the sociologically trained serve as "secretaries of War, Labor, and the Interior"; and that "there are hundreds and thousands of other positions, local, state, and national, which could better be filled by sociologists than by others" (1934a, 165–67, 170; see also Brearley 1934). Rice's (1934) somewhat less-sweeping ground plan installed sociologists at the middle and lower rungs of every department of the federal government (including State, Treasury, and Justice) and in all

---

of the Depression and the New Deal (see *Publication of the American Sociological Society* 29[3]: iv–vi), though perhaps because most of these were authored by the society's rank and file, Burgess chose not to publish them.

38. The focus, for example, of several papers at the December 1935 ASA meeting was the theme of Social Theory and Social Action, which Chapin, as president, had decided on because "we are still in the midst of the great depression, and . . . it seems important to consider fundamental principles of sociological theory and research which permit analysis, illustration, and application in terms of the problems of the times" (1935b, i). Similar concerns recurred at the 1936 meeting (see Fairchild 1937).

emergency agencies; Meroney's even more ambitious proposal—declaring that society's "goals and the routes thereto are sociologically derived"—made sociologists the actual "statesmen of the new order," the initiators of the needed "far reaching social reorganization" of American life (1934, 199-200).

The later proposal overlapped with the view of those who believed that sociologists belonged primary within college and universities but should serve as the nation's supreme moral arbiters nonetheless. Representative of this position were James Bossard (University of Pennsylvania), who saw sociology as the vehicle for "the objective determination of social values" (1934, 190); Arthur Todd (Northwestern), who believed that sociology would furnish "a new categorical imperative of social truth which will provide a [firm] basis for social reconstruction" (1934, 197); and Charles Ellwood and Howard Jensen (Duke), who held that, at the feet of sociologists, "the masses must be taught to see that their troubles have come from the wrong traditions, wrong values, and wrong attitudes; and that the remedy for the evils of our social life lies in the right traditions, right beliefs, and right attitudes" (1934, 187; see also Bogardus 1934; Hart 1934; Wood 1934).

To be sure, these ambitious (yet divergent) efforts to redesign the sociologist's public role did not uproot the scientistic belief that the province of the sociologist is to eschew the realm of goals and values and to serve the public only as an academic advisor to policymakers facing the choice of means. Stating that "it is not the function of the sociologist to tell the world what *should* be done, but rather how, what the world wants done or desires to do, *can* be done" (1934, 111), Louis Wirth (Chicago) encapsulated what persisted as a widespread viewpoint.[39] Even so, since partisans of this view knew as well as other sociologists—given their shared experiences during the New Deal—that the "world" might well never seek the sociologist's counsel, even these figures quietly amended their position in significant ways. These amendments included (1) allowing issues currently on the public stage to shift the agenda for sociological research, so that sociologists would set to work on their own on the recognized problems of the age (see, e.g., White 1934); (2) taking active steps to get the word out, that is, disseminating the results of sociological work through teaching, publishing, lecturing, and use of the media (see Queen 1934a); and (3) enjoining sociologists to raise the hard questions that the public evaded, so that sociology would "mak[e] explicit hidden assumptions or neglected aspects in social

---

39. This is not to assert that proponents of this viewpoint lived according to it in practice—only that they continued to espouse the position.

programs and policies" (Wirth 1934, 113; see also MacIver 1934b). Of these options, the last gained a particular following as sociologists, seeking a voice about the New Deal's many planning boards but not invited to opine, revived the ancient idea of the "unanticipated consequences of purposive social action" and, building on this idea, unleashed a torrent of criticism calling into question the very possibility of successful government planning (the phrase comes from Merton [1936], his youthful intervention into a discussion among Chapin [1936], Fairchild [1936], Hankins [1936, 1939], and Sorokin [1936] on the viability of planning).

While the symposia and conferences that brought forth these various plans to reshape the sociologist's public role were still under way, sociologists launched the third (and, in the end, the final) phase of their campaign to assert their expertise regarding the Depression and New Deal. Six years after the stock market crash, they started doing what economists and political scientists had been doing since the outset—they began bringing out substantive work on the subject. Excepting publications in rural sociology once again, the first of these writings (again, so far as I am aware) was Chapin's 1935 *Contemporary American Institutions*. In this text, Chapin sought to sociologize the market crash and its aftermath by viewing these as the result of the earlier growth of "the modern network of communicating systems" that linked previously insular parts of the nation and exposed them all to reverberating shocks, as a stock sell-off in one location rippled though "distant centers in runs on banks, speculative manias, epidemics of business failures . . . and other form of mass behavior" (1935a, 5–6). As well, Chapin outlined "A Sociological Approach to the New Deal" and a "Sociology of Leadership and Planning in the New Deal" (1935a, 281–316).

Hastily produced and speculative, Chapin's treatise was followed by a small flow of actual empirical studies: Angell's (1936) long-gestating analysis of the impact of the Depression on family stability; Sutherland and Locke's *Twenty Thousand Homeless Men: A Study of Unemployed Men in the Chicago Shelters* (1936), a project that started in early 1934; the Lynds' *Middletown in Transition* (1937), a report on Robert Lynd's 1935–36 revisit to the location of his earlier research in order to study the effects of the Depression; and Cavan and Ranck's *The Family and the Depression: A Study of One Hundred Chicago Families* (1938), a study also begun in 1934. Differing among themselves, these volumes sounded one high note in common, namely, that their respective topics defied reduction to the categories of economics and demanded sociological treatment. For Angell, "the effects of the depression upon the interrelationship among family members . . . is a question of social psychology and social organization, not economics," because the question rests on "attitudes and sentiments" (1936, 4, 45); for Sutherland and Locke, living in a homeless shelter is not simply "a matter of destitution, [but] of attitudes, traditions and custom in regard to [accepting] relief" (1936, 19); for the Lynds, Middleton's big story lay beyond "economics statistics" in the "drama of competing values" and the undulations of "culture" and "the think blubber of custom" (1937, 9, 490); while for Cavan and Ranck, "the depression [is] not primarily an economic crises but a crisis in the organization . . . of family life" and in the family's controlling "traditions and ideals" (1938, 2,3). Of these studies, however, only the Lynds' book, which drew praise in the national press, attracted much notice outside of sociology.

By this time, however, sociologists were already pursuing another avenue. Aware that these scattered empirical projects, even combined with a modest number of others then in progress,[40] would never outweigh the vast amount of relevant empirical research by specialists in economics and public administration, Ogburn and a few other notables intervened to prime the sociological research pump. In 1936, they secured from SSRC support for an entire series of commissioned volumes, titled Studies in the *Social Aspects* of the Depression (emphasis added to title; on SSRC's role here, see Fisher [1993, 162–63]), and they lost no time in assigning these volumes to prominent or up-and-coming authors—Chapin, Queen, Sanderson, Stouffer, Paul Lazarsfeld (then at the University of Newark)—and in turning out the finished products. In 1937, all thirteen monographs appeared in print, under SSRC's imprint, with the titles standardized in the form of *Research Memorandum on [X Topic] in the Depression*. The thirteen topics covered were family, religion, education, rural life, internal migration, minority peoples, crime, health, recreation, reading, consumption, social work, and relief policies.[41]

In the foreword to the series, Ogburn and his co-organizers, Malcolm Willey and Shelby Harrison, made their objectives plain, announcing that

40. Of note here, once again, are the work relief funds that federal agencies were channeling in this period to colleges and universities for use (among other things) on "social research" projects. Although the later encompassed a good deal more than projects by sociologists or projects focused on the Depression and New Deal, in many cases they did take this form. Further, while only a subset of this subset of projects resulted in publishable work, this yield formed part of the stream of contemporary empirical sociological work (for a discussion of some of this work, see Johnson and Johnson [1980, 188–89]). In the summer of 1937, however, the Roosevelt administration drastically cut its work relief programs.

41. To the best of my knowledge, this illuminating series is nowhere discussed in the literature of the history of sociology, though James Short's chapter in this volume takes note of the series and gives the thirteen titles in full.

they wanted "no studies of an exclusively economic and political nature" but, instead, "*to stimulate* the study of the depression effects on various social institutions," since these effects "have been only partially recorded" (1937, v; emphasis added)—a quiet admission of the extent to which sociological research still lagged behind work in economics and political science. In monograph after monograph, moreover, authors returned to this theme, asserting the importance of attending to those phenomena that economics (always the larger target than political science) excluded. Young, for example, called for studies not only of the "material differences" between minority groups but also of "less tangible differences in cultural patterns" (1937, 13); Steiner criticized economists for viewing leisure time "in terms of the efficiency of workers and the possible effect of shorter hours upon the cost of production and the reduction of unemployment," while neglecting "the study of the modification in popular attitudes" toward leisure (1937, 23-24); Thompson questioned the "study of the economic aspects of migration" and urged "sociological studies of migration which will yield knowledge of mental attitudes and adjustment" (1937, 85-86); and Vaile observed that, although consumption "might be considered the special province of the economist," the subject really involved a nest of "sociological problems," centering on "changes in social organization and ethical evaluations" (1937, 1).[42]

Aside from this unifying thread, however, the series was too scattershot a production to promote empirical sociological research on the Depression effectively. The thirteen topics the organizers included had little common; for the most part, they simply reproduced the diverse interests in the roll of existing ASA sections, with a few novelties—reading, recreation, and consumption—added according to no obvious selection principle. What was more, while a few authors took pains to present a clear line of sociological argument and supporting empirical evidence (see especially Sanderson 1937; Young 1937), most were satisfied to slice the assigned subject into diverse subtopics, discuss data sources, call for better quantitative and qualitative research in the future,[43] and provide lengthy lists of possible hy-

42. To be sure, not all authors in the series held positions in sociology departments. Kincheloe (author of the volume on religion), for instance, was a professor of the "sociology of religion" in a theological seminary, while Vaile was a professor of marketing. But Ogburn knew whom to tap; regardless of the nature of their own academic appointments, the contributors still harked to the economics versus sociology theme.

43. While Turner and Turner (1990), among others, present this period as one of deep animosity between quantifiers and others, the monographs in the series consistently called for more statistical studies and for more observationally based case studies. Stouffer and

CHARLES CAMIC · 270

potheses and a miscellany of unanswered questions. After some two thousand pages in this vein, there seemed, as of 1937, almost nothing that sociologists did know about the "social aspects" of the depression still gripping the nation. And that conclusion was opposite the message that Ogburn hoped to convey about the utility of sociology, for it could only justify—to anyone from the public actually watching—sociology's position on the sidelines of contemporary policy discussions and initiatives. As if to acknowledge as much, the series foreword tried to divert attention away from the crisis of the 1930s as Ogburn and his collaborators conjured up *a future time* when present-day sociological studies would finally demonstrate their public value "as an especially important preparation for meeting *the shock of the next depression* if and when it comes" (1937, v, emphasis added; see also Chapin and Queen 1937, viii.).

For all this, the series Studies in the Social Aspects of the Depression formed a watershed of an ironic sort. Originally launched "to stimulate" more empirical research by sociologists on the Depression, the series marked the beginning of the end of studies on the Depression and the New Deal by sociologists of the period. Although a number of the relevant projects that were still in progress subsequently reached completion and in some cases publication (on these projects, see Lundberg 1937), the flow of new ones—save, again, in the area of rural sociology—quickly dried up from this point onward, not to resume until later generations of sociologists returned to the period with questions that had never been asked about its women and children; its social movements; the structure and dynamics of its economic, political, and legal institutions; the origins and effects of its policies regarding labor, social security, unemployment insurance; and more. Significantly too, the period from 1937 forward brought fewer calls from sociologists to expand their public role in regard to the Depression and the New Deal. A 1940 study tellingly reported that "no article in either *The American Journal of Sociology* for 1937-38 or in the *American Sociological Review* recommended any specific social action" in any of the policy domains that constituted the New Deal (Davis 1940, 171).

A plausible explanation of this retreat would attribute it to the onrush of history: to the redirection of sociological attention that resulted as international events engulfed the United States and the Roosevelt administration began preparations for World War II. Yet, although this is not incorrect

---

Lazarsfeld, often remembered as two of the staunchest proponents of quantification, repeated throughout their volume the need for both types of research (see Stouffer and Lazarsfeld 1937).

in the long view, in 1937–38 the Depression, as well as the New Deal's initiatives in Social Security, labor relations, government reorganization, and so on, continued to occupy the national center stage. Indeed, although the early months of 1937 brought renewed signs of the country's gradual economic recovery, by August this trend reversed course and by October another recession was well under way, accompanied by falling production, eroding stock values and corporate profits, soaring unemployment (two millions layoffs occurred in winter 1937–38), and swelling relief rolls—a "depression within a depression," as Kennedy has described it (1999, 350). Stunned by this massive setback, the Roosevelt administration turned again to economists inside and outside the government for expert counsel in designing and implementing a new (ultimately more Keynesian) economic strategy (Barber 1996). At the same time, the president vastly expanded the Justice Department's Anti-Trust Division with an infusion of hundreds of additional lawyers (who were already in growing demand as the work of the NLRB skyrocketed), while political scientists hammered out plans for the reorganization of the executive branch. While the consequence of such developments was a set of government policies and programs significantly different from those formulated in the early New Deal (see Brinkley 1995), the experts involved, at levels high and low, hailed from the same professional groups as they had in the past. To the chagrin of sociologists, none of their own efforts in the interim (nor any concurrent changes) had visibly altered the public framing of the nation's crisis—as an "economic" situation that required action by "government"—or the administration's reliance on its established networks to enlist those who remained the taken-for-granted authorities on these subjects—economists, lawyers, and public administration scholars.

Shut out again, and sensing the almost-certain futility of further steps to assert their professional expertise with regard to the Depression and the New Deal, sociologists by late 1937 all but abandoned the pursuit. Ernest Burgess and a coauthor delivered the post mortem the following year. It was severe: "Social scientists . . . missed a unique opportunity during the past ten years for increasing our knowledge of the functioning of social institutions as affected by marked fluctuations of the business cycle"; "the greatest depression in the history of the United States has had no adequate recording by students of society. The social sciences individually and collectively failed, at the appropriate time, to collect the available data necessary for any accurate and systematic analysis of the effects of the depression upon social institutions and upon the human behavior" (Schroeder and Burgess 1938, xii, vii). Burgess chose his words skillfully, allowing sociologists somewhat to conceal themselves in the collective mass of "the social sciences," although—as his audience knew—economists and political scientists were hardly liable on charges of neglecting the effects of the Great Depression.[44] But, stripping away the camouflage, Burgess, as well informed and as generous a partisan as sociology has ever had, here took clear contemporary measure of the field during the 1930s.

In Retrospect

Since, like others, sociologists prefer to recall their accomplishments rather than episodes of self-perceived "failure," it is little wonder that sociology's history during the Depression and the New Deal has previously fallen outside of the discipline's collective memory. Situated between sociology's (relative) boom period in the 1920s and its successful reemergence on the national stage in the 1940s, the 1930s—as seen from the perspective of sociologists who experienced the years between World War I and the end of World War II and recollected them for later generations—formed an interlude that interrupted the triumphal story of the discipline's progressive development and so, in hindsight, scarcely seemed to belong to the story at all.

By one yardstick, history has confirmed this contemporary judgment about the 1930s. Occasional later-day opinion polls on the "great books" in sociology all but completely exclude works of American sociologists from the Depression era (Miller 1986; International Sociological Association 1998).[45] Yet this is not a final verdict. Depending on where any particular sociologist, at a particular subsequent point in time, stands in relation to any of the many trends identifiable in sociology during the 1930s, he or she brings to bear a different standard by which to decide whether the decade was a progressive or regressive one. As I stated at the outset, however, my

44. To be sure, depending on how narrowly Burgess understood "adequate recording," "necessary data," and a "systematic analysis of the effects of the depression on social institutions and upon human behavior," one might interpret his words so that his charge does stick to economists and political scientists. Of most relevance here, however, is not Burgess's view of other disciplines but his assessment of sociology.

45. These polls are not systematic studies. Insofar as they together provide any credible evidence, however, the only works from the 1930s by American sociologists on the all-time hit lists—that is, Miller's Top 55 and the ISA's Top 100—are Parsons's *The Structure of Social Action* (1937), Lundberg's *Foundations of Sociology* (1939b), and Lynd's *Knowledge for What?* (1939). (I exclude 1930s editions of books previously published or of lectures previously given, as well as entries by émigré Pitirim Sorokin). Of these three books, only Parsons's treatise, a work notable for entirely ignoring American sociology in the 1930s (see n. 47), makes both lists, while the other two books squeeze in only in the last year of the decade.

concern in this chapter is not with the multiple trends at work in American sociology during the 1930s, nor with providing an evaluation of the period, but only with examining the immediate and longer-term impact on sociology of the Depression and the New Deal.

Viewed through this lens and in light of the evidence in the previous section about immediate impact, the Depression and the New Deal appear to have affected sociology, its practices and its ideas, in certain more permanent and significant ways. By no means did these historical events revolutionize the field. Few equivalently brief historical episodes have ever produced that result—among other reasons, because of the substantial continuity across adjacent periods of the institutions of sociology and of the men and women who occupy those institutions. Except for eras marked by a large infusion of new intellectual and material resources or a high degree of internal unity among the discipline's practitioners—conditions that did not hold in the 1930s—most decade-long intervals in the modern history of sociology have continued on from where they began, appropriating some of the developments already at work but then pushing these in this direction rather than other possible directions.

The generalization applies to the 1930s, which saw sociologists selectively building on and shaping certain developments present in the 1920s, moving thereby both to lock these tendencies in as characteristics of the field during the mid-twentieth century but also to configure these developments in distinctive ways that in part reflected sociology's situation during the Depression and the New Deal. This is not to say these events were the major causes of the outcome. Because my analysis has approached sociology during the period from a narrow angle, omitting many features of the historical setting both inside and outside of sociology, it supports no claims for the Depression and the New Deal as standalone determining forces. Even so, several developments in sociology, which at the least were closely interwoven with the Depression and the New Deal, stand out.

Most conspicuous among these was the increasing organizational and intellectual splintering of sociology, which already in the 1920s had begun breaking down into specialized areas of empirical research and distinct methodological camps (superadded to older theoretical rifts). Turner and Turner (1990, 57–65) have rightly characterized sociology by the end of the 1930s as a divided discipline, made up of groups that either fought openly or sealed themselves off from one another, and the Depression appears to have abetted this trend. As observed earlier, the divisive battles for organizational control that ripped through the ASA, as well as the sudden proliferation of regional societies and specialty journals, were developments that the Depression fostered by decreasing academic employment opportunities in sociology and sociologists' financial resources. Moreover, in the context of these developments, the discipline fractured still further as sociologists realized, with the coming of the New Deal, their loss of public stature (compared with that of economists, political scientists, and lawyers) and attempted to correct the damage by reshaping their public role and displaying their field's empirical contributions. For, in rethinking sociology's public role, sociologists dissolved into increased discord, advocating proposals that cast sociologists, variously, as top presidential advisors, functionaries in sundry government agencies, architects of society's ends and values, or academically based critics of the means the public uses to accomplish its ends. Likewise, when sociologists sought to elevate their standing by demonstrating the significance of sociological research for understanding the problems of the Depression, they spread out in all directions: they focused on topics as diverse as rural migration, urban homeless shelters, family stability, religion, education, crime, and recreation; and whatever the topic, they pursued to a wide variety of questions and approaches. In other words, as the Depression and the New Deal heightened sociologists' desperation to vindicate their field, they fell all the more into the practice of seizing any interstitial topic and, now too, any imaginable opening in the public sphere as their professional preserve—further fragmenting their public mission and their research agenda in the process.

Yet even as sociologists increasingly diverged among themselves in these areas, consensus began to widen and crystallize regarding three fundamental issues that sociologists' experiences during the Depression and the New Deal help to make salient. The first of these concerned the public role of sociology. During the 1920s, the scientistic outlook that was on the rise in sociology existed in a pliable state. Whether in its harder (objectivist) or softer (Parkian) forms, scientism generally combined the belief that sociological investigators should eschew value-laden statements and other expressions of partisanship with a commitment to sociologists' involvement in public policy discussions, with the balance between these two themes shifting now in one direction, now in the other, depending on the sociologist who was expressing these views and the occasion for which he or she was writing. By the late 1920s and early 1930s, however, the weight seemed subtly to shift in favor of a narrowing of sociology's place in the public arena; both the papers presented and the presidential addresses delivered at ASA meetings during this period, at any rate, suggest that such a shift was under way. Be this as it may, sociologists' jolting recognition during the early New Deal of their comparative exclusion from opportunities in the public sphere stopped cold any tendency to disengagement from the national agenda and pushed them to affirm sociology's public mission strongly and unequivocally. Occasional exceptions like Hankins notwithstanding, this movement occurred en masse, garnering support from those at the major institutional centers and from those in peripheral locations, from senior members of the profession and from figures with little professional standing, and from researchers in all empirical subfields of the discipline.[46] Hereafter, although sociologists could neither agree on the nature of their public role nor hold themselves to research focused on issues on the public agenda, they nevertheless stood convinced that, in principle, sociology belonged square in the public arena and had major public contributions to make. On this article of faith, even the fractious members of the ASA concurred as they set about to use the society to link sociologists to the press, to government policymakers, and so forth.

A second point of convergence was the spreading involvement in empirical sociological research. While the 1920s gave rise to sociology's self-definition as a field predicated primarily on empirical methods of research, the majority of publications from the period remained nonempirical. For example, on the basis of a sample of articles published in *AJS* and *Social Forces*, Platt reports that during the 1920s only 38 percent of articles were empirically based. The 1930s, however, saw a substantial turn in the empirical direction, as evidenced in the rising proportion of empirical articles appearing in these journals (plus *ASR*), a figure that then soared to 64 percent—by far the largest single-decade gain that the discipline would experience (Platt 1996, 191-92). To date, historians of sociology have offered no explanation for this major shift, which occurred in the face of steep Depression-era cuts in external foundation funding for sociological research. Significantly, however, this same period brought two changes that worked in the opposite direction. The first of these was the entry of the state, via federal work relief programs, into the government financing of data collection and analysis, an intervention the made empirical sociological research a reality at many more academic institutions than the foundations had supported. The second was a new impetus to carry out empirical studies: seeking to overcome their disadvantage with regard to economics and political science, sociologists were spurred to demonstrate that sociological research brought to light important phenomena that economists and others had ignored—an objective championed by Angell, Sutherland

---

46. Gouldner (1970) to the contrary, even theorists like Parsons joined the swelling chorus (see Camic 1997a).

and Locke, the Lynds, Cavan and Ranck, and the contributors to the Studies in the Social Aspects of the Depression series. To be sure, these empirical studies, diverse among themselves, still appeared alongside sociological writings lacking in empirical data; as remarked earlier, the 1930s saw the arrival of European theoretical currents that inspired American sociologists to undertake work more expressly concerned with theory.[47] Viewed as a whole, however, American sociology in the course of the 1930s became a discipline tilted predominately toward empirically based research.

A final area of expanding agreement among sociologists of the period concerned their understanding of sociology as a science of culture. In the 1920s, American sociologists reinvented their discipline as a science of culture in order to fend off the enemy forces of the natural sciences by associating their own field with a subject matter that resisted reduction to natural-scientific categories. In that context, sociologists comprehensively defined *culture*, following the work of contemporary anthropologists, as enfolding everything that they could secure from the encroachment of natural scientists: that is, as humankind's entire stock of material objects, techniques, customs, attitudes, and institutions, whether economic, political, legal, religious, or familial. True, sociologists typically adhered to what Fairchild (1937, 4) later described as an "unwritten Gentlemen's Agreement," according to which the detailed study of economic processes fell "naturally" to economists and the organization of the state and law to political scientists and legal scholars. Even so, economic organization and the state formed no less a part of the sociology's working conception of culture than other features of "man's social heritage," and both topics constituted staples in the sociological curriculum (see "Recommendations of the Committee" 1933).

Sociologists of the 1930s, however, significantly revised this view. Because they did so in a thoroughgoing fashion, neither all the various dimensions of this revision nor the complex reasons for it can be adequately treated here. Significant, however, is the connection between certain aspects of this change and sociologists' interest in improving their marginal position relative to the accepted authorities on the economic life and government. Reaffirming their focus on culture, sociologists simultaneously modified their way of conceiving culture as they now redeployed the concept—diverting it from combat with their vanquished former antagonist, the natural sciences, and using culture instead to mark off and over-

47. Parsons provides the most famous instance of this, although during the 1930s, as he wrote *The Structure of Social Action* (1937), he worked as well on an empirical study of the medical profession.

take territory that they felt their rivals on the public stage of the Depression and the New Deal seriously neglected.[48]

Broadly, this revision involved one of two congruent strategies, which spread widely through sociology in the mid-1930s (again, for several reasons). The first of these retained anthropology's all-embracing conception of culture, but resurrected Ogburn's (1922) popular "cultural lag" thesis. According to this formulation, changes in economic and governmental institutions were secondary to changes in a more foundational component of culture, "material culture," or the condition of science and technology. Applied to the 1930s, Ogburn's thesis made the Depression and the New Deal mere expressions of "long-term cultural trends," as the explosion of technological invention in the nineteenth century rippled outward, in succession, to economic, political, community, religious, and familial institutions, causing inevitable short-term dislocations and maladjustments along the way (Ogburn 1934c). From this point of view, economists and political scientists erred in viewing the Depression and the New Deal "as something apart" from the wider "setting [of] the culture of the time"—a cultural setting that belonged intellectually to sociologists, whose special province was the analysis of the driving process of technological transformation and its institutional reverberations (quoting Ogburn 1934a, 729; see also Ogburn 1934b, 1934c). Chapin's writings from the period built on the same ideas: that the economic and political changes associated with the Depression and the New Deal were but "swirling eddies" on the surface of underlying trends in the cultural "whole"; that the "economist and the political scientist" could furnish, therefore, only "a partial view" of the contemporary situation; and that the federal government thus required sociologists to "supplement politico-economic planning" with "differential social planning" (quoting Chapin 1935a, xv; 1934b, 473). MacIver (1934b) and the Lynds (1937), among many others, voiced similar views.

A second (and sometime overlapping) strategy pared down the broad concept of culture in order to rout sociology's professional competitors from

---

48. By no means do I intend by this argument to present this period as sociology's first encounter with these rivals—political scientists and, particularly, economists. In other places (western Europe) and other times (America in the 1890s), economics, for example, was also preeminent among the intellectual and organizational forces that sociology opposed. During the 1920s, however, when American sociologists embraced "culture," their chief threat came from the natural sciences, not from the other social sciences (albeit with notable variations in the pattern across different higher educational institutions). When events of the 1930s returned economists (along with authorities on government) to the forefront, sociologists adjusted their new concept to fit the altered terrain.

another side. Rather than underplay economic and governmental institutions by turning the focus onto material culture, proponents of this variant approach honed in (using vocabularies not yet standardized) on mores, customs, values, ideals, and attitudes, and on the particular institutions that anchored these nonmaterial elements (religion, family, community)—effectively elevating what had been, according to the encompassing anthropological view of culture, only one aspect of culture into culture per se. With this conceptual move, sociologists acquired their own distinctive professional purchase on the Depression and the New Deal, and the move quickly enlisted a wide following.

Examples are plentiful. Burgess's presidential address insisted, for example, that the raison d'être of sociology was "to take account of a . . . group of factors which had been overlooked and neglected by economics and political science," namely "mores" or "culture," and to advance a "theory of cultural determinism," which would supersede economistic perspectives on the contemporary crisis (1934, 1–2). Lamenting that "the sociologist has not been called [upon] by men of practical affairs," Burgess held that the success of New Deal initiatives would actually "turn upon the so-called intangibles" of America's cultural situation because viable policies had to "proceed within the traditional framework of [established] values"; conversely, if, in the design and implementation of programs like the TVA, "the customs, attitudes, and reactions of the people are not as fully studied [as the] economic situation, the Tennessee Valley project is likely to be a partial, if not a complete, failure" (1934, 4, 15, 10).

Variations on these themes became sociologists' stock-in-trade. According to Park, effective social planning demanded an "underground foundation" in "attitudes and sentiments" and recognition of the fact that the "existing moral order . . . cannot be suddenly decreed or legislated out of existence" (1934, 28, 25). According to rural sociologist Arthur Morgan, TVA soil conservation efforts require "changes of mental attitudes" in local communities and, therefore, the guidance of sociologists (1937, 163–64). For Stouffer and Lazarsfeld, writing in the Social Aspects of the Depression series, sociologists needed to study the family as a crucible of "attitudes and habits," because family-based "economic attitudes" played an "important role" in the nation's "recovery from depression" (1937, 4–5, 7–9, 61).

Culture, attitudes, custom, traditions, values, ideals—these concepts emerged as the leitmotiv not only of the entire Social Aspects of the Depression series but also of all the other major empirical studies of the Depression from the mid-1930s, as the previously cited statements by Angell, Sutherland and Locke, the Lynds, and Cavan and Ranck attest. Still further, these concepts occupied the foreground when sociologists issued critiques of New Deal planning efforts for neglecting "unanticipated consequences," for here their recurrent objection was that "the prevalent mores and their associated sentiments set limits to and define the direction" of societal possibilities, regardless of the designs of economic and governmental planners (Hankins 1939, 12–13; see also Chapin 1936; Merton 1936; Sorokin 1936). In related work that also spotlighted the nonmaterial elements of culture, MacIver attributed the New Deal's transformation of the state to the decay of laissez-faire beliefs resulting from the rise of a "new social philosophy" and a "definite shift in attitudes"—phenomena that "provide a new opportunity, a new role, for the sociologist" (1934b, 835–37, 840). As well, in a major amendment to his cultural lag thesis, Ogburn held not only that "ideals and social philosophies" will "determine" the future direction of economic and political trends (1934b, 847) but also that changes in religious "ideas" and "values" sometimes "precede invention," the motor of so-called nonmaterial culture (1934c, 37). Formulated slightly differently, this strong accent on culture appeared even more forcefully in the assertion—by figures as diverse as Burgess (see Schroeder and Burgess 1938), Stouffer and Lazarsfeld (1937), and the young Parsons (see Camic 1997a)—that the prolonged trauma of the Depression was merely an instance of the larger sociological phenomenon of "crisis": a crisis in values, traditions, attitudes, or morals; a crisis whose analysis and solution would demand the expertise of the sociologist, not that of specialists in economics, public administration, or law.

While no two sociologists articulated this argument in an identical manner, a groundswell was nevertheless well under way. For all their internal divisions on other issues, sociologists from all sides concurred. In their view, the intellectual authorities who had been publicly valorized during the Depression and the New Deal overlooked attitudes, values, mores, traditional beliefs, and the like, and so sociology, the period's excluded field, would constitute itself around culture understood in these particular terms. By the same token, sociologists would henceforth either cede the economy, law, and the state outright to the discipline's public rivals or reduce these institutions to side effects of broader cultural forces. These trends marked the end of the alliance sociologists had begun to forge in the 1920s (in arenas like the Committee on Social Trends and the councils of SSRC) with economists and political scientists, and prepared the way for their realignment in the decades ahead, inside and outside the academy, with cultural anthropologists and social psychologists, fellow students of attitudes, beliefs, and cultural values—and professionals also comparatively marginalized during the Depression and the New Deal.

As the 1930s progressed, a few sociologists tried to arrest this development, at least with respect to the study of economic life. Bernard proposed that "more attention should be given in this country to the Sociology of Economic Relations" (Bernard 1934a, 167); Fairchild held that "wages, prices, trade unions, corporations, factories, the standard of living, all [were] fit subjects for sociological treatment"—adding that, were sociology to engage *these* topics and stop treating them as the natural preserve of economists, the discipline could finally help address "the needs of the contemporary world" (Fairchild 1934, 180; 1936, 8). But such voices were more and more in the minority. In the course of the Great Depression and New Deal, economic sociology, the sociology of the state, and the sociology of law were among the intellectual possibilities that sociologists bypassed as they stood before historically unprecedented changes in the American economy, the state, and the state's legal apparatus, seeking territory unclaimed by the political scientists, lawyers, and economists who had emerged as the professional owners of those great changes.

Acknowledgments

I thank Gabi Abend, Howard Becker, Michael Burawoy, Craig Calhoun, Neil Gross, Ira Katznelson, Gail Kligman, Jeff Manza, Jennifer Platt, and an anonymous reviewer for valuable comments on this chapter. I am extremely grateful also to Andy Abbott and James Sparrow for generously sharing with me their data on the careers of midcentury sociologists and for addressing my questions about these data. I thank as well their helpful assistant Geoff Guy.

[EIGHT] Hot War, Cold War: The Structures of Sociological Action, 1940-1955

Andrew Abbott & James T. Sparrow

Despite the immense impact of the Second World War on American society, its effect on American sociology has been little considered. This oversight reflects in part the difficulty of measuring—indeed, even conceptualizing—the war's impact. It is perhaps not surprising that so daunting an intellectual task has not been attempted.

In this chapter, we make a preliminary analysis of American sociology during the war and postwar period. We begin with a brief sketch of the broader social changes attending the wars—two hot and one cold—that defined the period 1940-55. We then look at the discipline in 1940 and in 1955. Having thus set out what might loosely be imagined as our story's beginning and end, we evaluate how the events of the war period changed the demographic, institutional, and intellectual structure of sociology. We aim at the same time to analyze the role of sociology (as of the other social sciences) in shaping the new society that emerged after the war. We close with a discussion of the new stance of sociology during the postwar decade.

Society, War, and Sociology, 1940-55

The years 1940 to 1955 saw the United States emerge from the economic catastrophe of the Great Depression, transforming itself in a few years' time into a high-production, high-employment society of unprecedented affluence and global influence. Driving this transformation was a historically unprecedented centralized state, which even after postwar demobilization dwarfed the New Deal precursor that had seemed so large only half a decade before. It is difficult now to recall the dramatic nature of this change. In 1939, a mere 3.9 million Americans (3 percent of the population and 7 percent of the labor force) paid income tax. In 1955, nearly all working families paid income tax. The 44 million federal taxpayers were 27 percent of the population and 66 percent of the labor force. In 1939, at the high tide of New Deal spending, 9.77 percent of the GNP was government expenditure. In 1955, after the New Deal had been beaten back and a conservative president occupied the White House, federal outlays were 17.2 percent of the GNP. In 1939 a tiny handful of American men served in the military. By 1955, 64 percent of men between ages 16 and 34 had served.

The social landscape also was transformed in the years during and after the war. The number of high school and college graduates more than doubled between 1940 and 1957. The percentage of American families who owned their homes went from 44 percent in 1940 to 55 percent in 1950, and then rose again to 62 percent in 1960. The median family income went from $1,231 in 1939 to $4,594 in 1957, an increase of 65 percent in real terms. The percentage of foreign born dropped from the low teens in the early part of the century to 8.8 percent in 1940, 6.9 percent in 1950, and 5.4 percent in 1960. The percentage of married women in the labor force rose steadily from 15 percent in 1940 to 24 percent in 1950, to 30 percent in 1960.

To be sure, most of these changes had begun before the war. Government expansion had begun in 1930s, as had married women's move into the labor force and the expansion of consumption-based leisure. The rise in mobility and the decline in immigration were also long-standing trends. But all of these were sharply accelerated by the war years. Even nationality, the least affected of the trends, was recast by a historic surge in naturalization driven by memories of the previous war's vigilante-style Americanism and by the desire to avoid the fate of the Japanese interned from the West Coast. More than 1.5 million people received U.S. citizenship between 1941 and 1945—the highest rate of naturalization for any five-year period up to that date (Ueda 1996, 202).

Driving this rapid change were great events. The Second World War was brief but apocalyptic. For the United States, the ordeal lasted only three years and nine months. But its 16.4 million soldiers included fully a third of all men aged 15 to 50 as of 1945. These men served an average of 33 months in the war, with 73 percent of them going overseas for an average of 16.2 months. Over 400,000 died, nearly three-fourths in battle, while more than 670,000 sustained nonfatal wounds or injuries. The war's cost—civilian and military—drove federal government expenditures to an astounding 46.4 percent of GNP in 1945, while federal debt soared to its all-time high of 129 percent of the GNP that year. Roughly half the total labor force worked directly for the military, the government, or war industry.

From the churning upheavals of total war issued ever-expanding ripples of postwar changes. Approximately 25 million Americans moved to another county or state between 1940 and 1947, a proportion of the population (21 percent) considerably larger than the proportion (13 percent) who had moved during the second half of the 1930s, and even greater than the proportion who had moved during the first half of the Depression (Johnson 1993). Even while the housing markets and employers tried to absorb this mobility, war-induced programs produced new problems. The GI bill's housing loans provided critical impetus to suburbanization (and hyperseg-regation; see Jackson 1985, and Cohen 2002), while its educational provi-sions remade post-secondary and vocational campuses nationwide (Frydl 2000). Politically, the tenuous wartime deadlock between liberalism and conservatism broke into open conflict, producing a partisan battle to de-fine the postwar fate of New Deal reform, as well as the mounting security mania that would lead to McCarthyism. The end of the war decade found the new geopolitics of the cold war firmly in place, as the "loss of China" focused American attention on the Far East and remade the Japanese from racialized enemies into respected allies. The Marshall Plan and NATO marked a comparable transformation of the West Germans. By the summer of 1950 the United States was again at war, this time against a proxy adver-sary whose sponsorship by the Soviet Union produced sufficient bipartisan agreement to underwrite the permanent erection of a national security state modeled heavily on its World War II precursor. Such were the trends and events of the years 1940 to 1955. It was a time of almost unimaginable domestic transformation, driven by global upheaval.

What were the equivalent changes in sociology? In 1940, sociology had itself just finished a transformative decade. The 1930s had seen the found-ing of the major regional associations as well as such specialty associations as the Population Association of America and the Rural Sociological Soci-ety. Also founded were a host of specialty journals—from *Public Opinion Quarterly* to *Rural Sociology* and *Journal of Marriage and the Family*. By now about half of the colleges and universities surveyed by the American Coun-cil on Education had freestanding departments of sociology, and nearly all the rest had sociological instruction (Marsh 1940). The Depression and the maturing of social work had driven most of the active reformers out of the American Sociological Society. (We use hereafter the modern name and the abbreviation ASA for this organization.) Coupled with the growth of alternative societies and the Depression itself, this academicization had shrunken ASA membership to 999 in 1940, down from 1,558 in 1930. The discipline had also shed its umbilical connection with the University of Chi-cago, whose personnel (as ASA secretaries and editors), journal (the *Ameri-can Journal of Sociology* [*AJS*]), and money (the ASA subsidies provided by the University of Chicago Press) had translated into what many felt was al-most feudal vassalage. The leaders of this revolt—whose greatest achieve-ment was the transformation of the ASA quarterly *Proceedings* into the bimonthly *American Sociological Review (ASR)* in 1934–35—found their victory somewhat Pyrrhic. This new elite, with its quantitative methods and foundation funding, quickly displaced the Chicago school. It took control of the *ASR* within two or three years of its founding and soon came to control the ASA as well.[1]

Intellectually, the 1930s had seen the waning of the Chicago ecological paradigm. Robert Park retired in 1934. His leadership of community studies was replaced by that of Everett Hughes and Lloyd Warner, who approached community quite differently than had Park, studying midsize towns rather than large cities and following a functionalist framework that came from anthropology (Warner's field of training). The decade also brought sociology new statistical rigor borrowed from agricultural and psychological research; the earlier, descriptive use of correlations and cross-tabulations tightened slowly into a more formal and rigorous methodology (Platt 1996; Turner and Turner 1990). The first election studies and survey-based market research date from the mid-1930s (Converse 1987), and even Chicagoans like Burgess turned to prediction—of parole, marital duration, and occupational success. The late 1930s also brought Parsons's *Structure of Social Action* (1937), with its resounding rejection of American social science in order to answer an English "problem of order" by a curious combination of French social absolutism and German historicism. Given the tendency of American intellectuals and reformers in the late 1930s and 1940s to obscure or ignore the European influences that had recently informed academic and reform circles (Rodgers 1998), Parsons's insistence on the insertion of Weber and Durkheim into the American social scientific canon is striking indeed.

The discipline in 1940 had thus recently weathered significant changes. What did this discipline look like in 1955? The ASA was five times the size it had been in 1940. It now met jointly with a new society founded by people who had rebelled against it, the Society for the Study of Social Problems (SSSP). An enormous generation of war-detained students had pushed through graduate school into a tertiary education sector already expanding to absorb veterans and women, and soon to face the baby boom. Sociology was enthroned in the popular imagination in books like *An American Dilemma* (1944), *The Lonely Crowd* (1950), and *The Organization Man* (1956), which the new multitudes of undergraduate sociology students were read-

1. Basic sources for the history of sociology in this period are Abbott (1999) and Turner and Turner (1990). On the founding of the *ASR* in particular, see also Lengermann (1979). On methods, see Platt (1996).

ing even while they aimed at the careers traditionally identified with sociology—teaching, social work, and ministry (Zetterberg 1956, 10). Sociological market researchers were peddling the concepts of brand image and market segmentation essential to the new consumerism, while pollsters were rapidly becoming electoral fixtures (on soft-core market research, see Karesh 1995 and Levy 2003; see Cohen 2003 on political advertising).

Intellectually, the discipline was now dominated by the odd marriage of survey analysis and Parsonian theory, symbolized by the pairings of Stouffer and Parsons at Harvard and Lazarsfeld and Merton at Columbia. Methodologically this self-proclaimed mainstream had rejected ethnographic and institutional analysis and had embraced big-project sociology (see the essays in Zetterberg [1956], and Lazarsfeld and Rosenberg [1955]), emulating the paradigm-shaping big science that had produced the atomic bomb, radar, and other techno-scientific fixtures of the already-forming World War II mythos. In the SSSP lurked a residue of reformists, ethnographers, radicals, and critics, all of them outside the elite circle of what had become an eastern sociological establishment rooted in Columbia, Harvard, and the New York foundations. Not surprisingly, SSSP-type research and the collections that conveyed it (undergraduate course readers) proved far more accessible and interesting to college students than did the high words and formal science of the elite, producing a structural disparity between undergraduate and graduate sociology that persisted for decades. Most important, by the mid-1950s large portions of sociological writing were not sociological at all in the older sense. They were not studies of social groups, group conflict, or group relations. Rather they were studies of atomized individuals characterized by variable properties and located in a larger and indefinite field—"the collectivity," "the social group," "the society." Given the influence of social psychology as an interdisciplinary platform for wartime social scientific expertise, this shift is perhaps not surprising (see Greenwood [2003] on the earlier decline of the genuinely social dimensions of social psychology), although the degree and timing of social psychology's influence require explanation.

In short, postwar sociology was bigger and more publicly successful than prewar. It was institutionally more solid. It had changed paradigm almost completely, the dominant sociologies of the 1920s having been shoved aside into the SSSP and the undergraduate world. To know how much these changes in sociology owed to the massive social changes and dramatic events of the war years and the early postwar period, we must consider the details of the discipline's wartime experience—its demography, institutions, and intellectual development.

The Demographics of Disciplinary
Experience during and after World War II

The career experience of sociologists in the war comprised two types of service—in war-related research and in the military. These involved, in effect, two different generations. Only a few sociologists combined military service with war-related research; Arnold Rose (a military fieldworker for the War Department's Research Branch) and Morris Janowitz (a soldier attached to OSS in London) were such rare exceptions. In general those working in war-related research were established sociologists who served as civilians, like Samuel Stouffer who ran the Research Branch and Herbert Blumer who worked at the Office of War Information and later the War Labor Board. Only a few were young people who served as civilian researchers in wartime agencies and then entered graduate study in sociology after the war. (For obvious reasons, these were mainly women—e.g., Gladys Lang.) In contrast, the sociologists who were veterans were mostly men of the younger generation, who either left school for the service and returned later to finish or took up sociology from scratch after the war.

Sociological service in war-related government research was relatively concentrated in certain agencies, although many agencies ended up with at least a few sociologists. This pattern probably grew out of the old-boy methods used to staff up agencies in periods that could be as short as one month. The Office of Strategic Services Research and Analysis (OSSR&A) Branch is the most famous case. The OSS founders tapped diplomatic historians James Phinney Baxter III and William Langer to organize and staff the R&A Branch (Katz 1989, 5ff.). Baxter's and Langer's disciplinary connections in turn guaranteed that OSSR&A would be particularly strong in historians and that it would attract historicist émigrés like Franz Neumann (who in turn recommended his colleagues at the Institute for Social Research). OSSR&A also became strong in economists, through Edward Mason, who moved in from the Office of Production Management to start the OSSR&A economics group. The Office of War Information (OWI), by contrast, was full of psychologists and anthropologists. Its Foreign Morale Analysis Division (FMAD), under psychiatrist-anthropologist Alexander Leighton, was typical in containing predominantly members of its director's anthropological specialty: 10 anthropologists to 5 sociologists overall and 8 to 1 in the OWI/FMAD staff proper. (OWI sociologists were mostly Research Branch loaners [Leighton 1949, 223–25].) By contrast, the Department of Agriculture, with long-standing survey and field study branches, had dozens of social psychologists and sociologists (Larson and Zimmerman 2003).

To gain a more detailed picture of wartime service, we have developed a biographical data set of sociologists in the 1940s by combing a wide variety of biographical sources for information. The data set includes 3,385 people, all of whom meet one of two criteria: (*a*) they published an article in the *American Journal of Sociology* before 1965 and were born after 1890; or (*b*) they were members of the ASA in at least two of the years between 1940 and 1949. Since there is no sharp edge to any academic field, our data set of course includes many people identifiably in other fields as well as transient members of the ASA—social reformers, students who didn't finish in sociology, and so on. It includes 1,885 individuals with PhD's whose field is known, of whom 1,314 had PhD's in sociology or rural sociology. This subgroup of 1,314 is what we mean by the word *sociologist* in the paragraphs that follow.[2]

Because of this very broad sampling strategy, the figures we present from this biographical data set are by no means exact. However, the difficulty of assembling data from diverse biographical sources means that the estimates of sociological participation are more likely underestimates than the reverse; false negatives are far more likely than false positives. Also, given our sampling strategy, the probability of our discovering individuals does not vary much from agency to agency, so the *relative* predominance in our data of sociologists in one agency as opposed to another is likely to be a reasonable estimate of the true ratio.[3]

The core of this data set, then, is a group of roughly 1,300 people who ultimately received PhD's in sociology. Of these, 9 percent saw government

2. The other PhD's with known fields are scattered: about 60 each in anthropology, economics, education, and psychology, and about 30 each in history and political science. Another 287 individuals had PhD's but in an unknown field. So far as we know, 1,500 individuals lacked PhD's. Many of these were transient members of the ASA or young reformist writers from *AJS* of the 1920s and 1930s.

3. Searching by agency is extremely difficult, as most agencies employed thousands of individuals and lack separate lists of social scientists or sociologists in their employ. In the few cases where we do have exact listings by agency, it seems that our underestimate within a given agency may be as much as 20 percent. For example, our data set misses about a quarter of the recognizable sociologists in the Research Branch of the War Department, all of whom are listed (along with many others—mostly psychologists and nonprofessional field staff) in the first volume of *The American Soldier*. On closer investigation, however, it turns out that we have data set knowledge of all but one of the "missing" people in government service elsewhere. They participated in the Research Branch as loaners or as military personnel detailed to work on the project as field surveyors. This underscores the fact that many people in government service moved between agencies and even within the military, both formally and informally. Note that by ending the ASA frame in 1949, we may have missed a number of veteran sociologists and younger people who worked in government service during the war.

service at some point in their careers, the vast majority of them during the war years. Another 5 percent saw government *and* military service, and 22 percent saw military service alone. In total, then, over a third of these sociologists did something outside their academic activities in the war, and over a quarter saw military service in particular, a topic to which we return later in the chapter. Here we are concerned with the 14 percent who saw agency service.

By far the most important location for sociologists in government during this entire period was the Department of Agriculture (USDA): 52 PhD's in rural sociology, sociology, or social psychology worked in USDA at some point, at least 42 of them during the war period. Already large in 1940, the USDA sociology program (discussed at length in Larson and Zimmerman 2003) expanded in wartime. Of particular importance for later sociology was the social psychology team under psychologist Rensis Likert, which developed many of the standard forms of survey analysis. The USDA was, however, not the only government location for sociologists before the war. The Census Bureau had employed sociologists for years, and 18 of our sociologists served in the census at some point. (Of the 10 who worked there during the war, several were seconded to other agencies at various times; many individuals served in two, three, or even four agencies during the war, often through informal rather than formal transfers.) The Labor Department also hired a few sociologists, some in the Bureau of Labor Statistics (BLS) and some elsewhere (8 total, mostly in the 1930s). Alongside these longtime employers of sociologists, a number of the new agencies employed sociologists. The Federal Emergency Relief Administration hired a few sociologists (8 in our data), as did the Farm Security Administration (9). However, the most important location for sociologists in the New Deal per se was the Works Progress Administration (WPA), in which 21 sociologists in our data set saw service at one point or another.

Of the war agencies proper, the Research Branch of the War Department hired the most sociologists, hardly surprising given Samuel Stouffer's position as director. Our data set locates 21 sociologists there, including Stouffer, John Clausen, John Dollard, Arnold Rose, Louis Guttman, Robin Williams, Shirley Star, and Leonard Cottrell, to give only the big names. Later in the chapter we consider the branch's great postwar product—the four-volume *American Soldier* (Stouffer et al. 1949–50).[4] Although often seen

4. The studies commonly known as *The American Soldier* were in fact issued by Princeton University Press in four separate volumes whose official series title is Studies in Social Psychology in World War II. Of these four volumes, the first two share the main title *The American*

as sociological, the Research Branch projects were squarely on the boundary between sociology and psychology. The branch contributed almost as many major figures to psychology (e.g., Irving Janis and Carl Hovland) as it did to sociology.

Although the Office of Strategic Services—and in particular its R&A Branch as opposed to its cloak-and-dagger operations—has loomed large in the mythos of sociology, this eminence reflects mainly the accident of Neumann's having brought his soon-to-be famous Frankfurt cohorts Horkheimer, Marcuse, Adorno, and Lowenthal into the Washington office. In fact, the sociological presence in OSS was not very large—only 13 in our data set, although it includes such celebrated names as Morris Janowitz and Edward Shils (both in the London branch, after service with Harold Lasswell in his Library of Congress research operation), as well as Barrington Moore and Alex Inkeles. The Office of War Information actually had more sociologists (18), including Clarence Glick, Warren Dunham, Herbert Blumer, and Hans Speier.

Sociologists were scattered elsewhere in the government. The War Relocation Authority (or WRA, which ran the Japanese internment camps) had six sociologists in our data set, working within a "Bureau of Sociological Research" directed by Alexander Leighton at Poston, Arizona. More an anthropological than a sociological enterprise, this bureau was an extension of the anthropologists' long-standing involvement in the Bureau of Indian Affairs (Hayashi 2004, 24–25). (These researchers are not to be confused with the Nisei "participant observers" who studied the WRA's camps under the leadership of Dorothy Swaine Thomas, whose findings were reported in twin 1946 volumes, *The Salvage* and *The Spoilage*.) The War Production Board hired 4 data set sociologists, the War Labor Board 14, among them Herbert Blumer (who arbitrated a long Pennsylvania strike) and Delbert Miller. The Office of Price Administration hired 11 sociologists, and the National Resources Planning Board 9, among them Louis Wirth and August Hollingshead. Another 5 worked for the Selective Service System, among them William Sewell.

Sociologists also worked in special postwar service. Some served on the

---

Soldier, the first being subtitled *Adjustment during Army Life* and the second *Combat and Its Aftermath*. Historical convention has generalized the main title of these first two volumes to the whole series. Volume 3 is actually titled *Experiments on Mass Communication* and volume 4 *Measurement and Prediction*. Even more confusingly, the four volumes have different author lists, although they involve many of the same people (just in different order). To save the reader confusion, we have cited these works throughout as *The American Soldier* (Stouffer et al. 1949–50), using volume numbers as usual with serial publication.

Strategic Bombing Survey—a multimethod investigation of the "effectiveness" of the saturation bombing that, in addition to its military mission, had incinerated over half a million German and nearly a million Japanese civilians, leaving another million or more injured and homeless. Occupational military government in Germany or Japan involved a much larger number of sociologists—20 in all. Sociologists also filtered into the State Department after the war, some through the temporary transfer of OSS to State Department jurisdiction, others through individual intergovernmental transfers.

Sociologists thus saw a wide variety of service in the government. Given that the ASA had about a thousand members during the war years, the fact that 17 percent of the organization (171 PhD-level sociologists in our data set) saw government service during the war may, however, seem surprisingly modest. But it should be recalled that higher education itself ran on skeleton schedules during the war because of the lack of students. Many of those who remained in college teaching were in fact teaching in ROTC programs and other such schemes for keeping colleges and universities in business during the lean years.[5] And many senior sociologists served as consultants to agencies without formal employment in them.

We shall return later to the institutional and intellectual impact of this wartime agency service and the research that grew out of it. Here, we turn to the other side of sociological participation in the war—military service. The extent of military service in the discipline is hard to capture. Of the sociologists in our biographical data set, more than a quarter served in the military. But veterans who finished degrees during the 1950s may have been missed by our sampling criteria. And there are no master lists of veterans, much less of veterans who were or became sociologists.[6] To provide an estimate, we have established exact figures for veterans in the immediate postwar era at the University of Chicago's sociology department, taking advantage of the requirement that all GI bill transcripts had to be stamped with the statement "Registered under Public Law 346." A total of 204 sociologists took PhD degrees from the department between 1945 and 1960. Of

5. The number of ROTC units jumped to 505 (at 352 schools) in 1952, up from 160 in 1941. In addition to ROTC courses, many schools hosted intensive classes for army ASTP and navy V-5, V-7, and V-12, with roughly half a million men in uniform taking such courses during World War II. Another federal source of military training on campus were the Engineering, Science Management, and War Training programs. See American Council on Education 1952, 6, 69–70.

6. A master list of veterans would be little use in any case, as it would not be electronic yet would contain 16.5 million names. We have looked for, but have not uncovered, evidence for the existence of an informal association or list of veterans who were sociologists.

these, 87 were veterans. Among the others, 26 were male foreigners (nearly half of them Canadians, several of whom had served in British forces), and 33 were women (both foreign and American; none served). Seventeen (15 whites and 2 blacks) of the 59 American male nonservers were too old (36 years old in 1941: in fact, men this old were virtually exempt from the draft) or too young (not 18 years old by August 1945) to serve. Ten American non-servers were known to be either conscientious objectors (COs), vital industry workers, interned, or physically handicapped. There remain, out of the 204 total degrees, 23 white and 8 black males of draftable age who did not serve and for whom we do not know the reason.[7]

Overall then, no less than 45 percent of all Chicago graduate students who finished in this fifteen-year period were veterans, and of those students who were white American males of draftable age, a *minimum* of 80 percent were veterans. Military experience was thus almost a universal for young American male sociologists. Most of these, however, had not seen combat. Given that the armywide percentage of combat service was around 25 percent (Stouffer et al. 1949–50, 1:165; Linderman [2000] suggests that no more than 10 percent of soldiers saw extended combat) and that the World War II military assigned military occupations with considerable attention to education and achievement (more so than the Vietnam military; see Flynn 1993, 234), the proportion of all graduate students who had seen combat was certainly not above 10 percent and was more likely 5 percent or less.[8]

On the basis of this estimate, it is likely that half or more of the sociologists coming out of American graduate schools in the decade immediately after the war were veterans. Did this commonality have intellectual effects?

---

7. The number of blacks is unsurprising, since the segregated military and racist draft boards usually did not want blacks, and many highly educated blacks in particular saw little reason to serve in a military that would constrain them to menial work. The nonserving whites may have had CO or vital industry status, or had physical deferments unknown to us (we know these only on an adventitious basis), and all but 8 of them were old enough to have married and possibly produced children in time to make their draft vulnerability low. Some veterans may not have used GI bill benefits. For example, veteran PhD candidates before service could write their dissertations away from Chicago, which often waived its requirement of registration in the quarter the degree was taken.

8. This measure of sociologists' (more properly protosociologists') service is probably an underestimate for the field as a whole, because of Chicago's relatively large contingent of foreign students, female students, and blacks. An SSRC survey found 72 percent of social science graduate students in 1946–47 drawing on GI bill funds, which provided over 50 percent of per capita monthly receipts across all graduate students (Sibley 1948, 116). However, the SSRC sample was heavily weighted toward the fields of economics and history, where alternative means of support may have been less.

After all, the veterans had shared experiences unlike those of any previous sociological generation: career disruption, heteronomous work for huge and often irrational organizations, erratic mobility in both geographic and social space, and exposure to the peculiar mixture of volunteerism, propaganda, and coercion that undergirded the citizen-soldier concept.

Although this common history may have unified the veterans in some ways, military life was not everywhere the same. The diversity of veteran experience is evident in the March 1946 *AJS* special issue ("Human Behavior in Military Society"), which featured 31 young social scientists whose graduate education was interrupted for war service. The issue combined an anonymous piece about the glories of the combat infantry with discussions of GI language and erotic behavior, examination of fighter squadron social hierarchies, a discussion of army delinquency (including black market trading and looting by U.S. GIs in both friendly and occupied Europe), and a portrayal of an embittered and cynical group of teacher volunteers ground down by army contempt and irrationality. The various papers make it clear that the social scientific impulse survived within the military experience but that the enormous diversity of that experience militated against any single impact.[9]

What about combat? As we noted, relatively few sociologists experienced combat. But combat drove some to sociology. Frank Westie's experience as a bomber pilot over Dresden made him believe "that one could make a greater contribution to world peace through sociological research and teaching than through any other occupation" (Westie 2004). But in the absence of more general data, we can only speculate about the impact of combat on what men later wrote. On the one hand, the bitterness of the combat soldier cries out from the tables of *The American Soldier*. On the other hand, it is common belief, both within the military and outside it, that combat soldiers do not like to talk or think about the experience. So its impact may have gone unrecognized or tacitly overlooked by this generation.

If the military and combat experiences had no clear intellectual impact on the discipline, the demographic cycles induced by the GI bill *did* have a very clear impact. The war in effect stopped graduate education altogether for about four years (Turner and Turner 1990, 87). When graduate school reopened, the GI bill flooded pent-up demand into the system and graduate departments ballooned. As a result, over three-quarters of the ASA mem-

9. During the war the *AJS* featured a number of special issues that provide a window into sociological thinking during the conflict. These issues were as follows: January 1941, "War" (note date); November 1941, "Morale"; May 1942, "Recent Social Change"; November 1942, "Impact of the War on American Life"; and March 1944, "Postwar Preparation."

bership in 1955 came from the post-1945 graduate school cohort; the discipline became extremely young. Moreover, tertiary education's continuing expansion through the 1950s and 1960s meant boundless job prospects not only for this cohort but also for several generations of its students. As a result, whatever was the sociological orthodoxy of the moment during the first postwar generation's training years would be spread without interruption for decades. To the extent that there was such an orthodoxy, it happened to be Parsonianism and survey analysis, and so it is not surprising that these dominated sociology until 1970 and, in the case of survey analysis, even beyond. This demographic account, however, does not address the antecedent question of *why* the dominant themes that the postwar demography so massively diffused should have been what they were. As we shall see, that is a more complicated question.[10]

The War and Sociological Institutions

The war and postwar period had a number of important effects on the institutional structure of sociology. In the first place, the imperative speed of the war mobilization of social scientists confirmed the dominance of sociology's new elite. There was, to be sure, an attempt to mobilize the discipline more generally. The ASA appointed a committee to oversee cooperation with war mobilization in 1940 (Queen 1941). Sociologists also signed up with the National Roster of Scientific and Technical Personnel, a voluntary listing of persons announcing themselves available for service. As of September 1, 1941, a total of 151,726 people had signed up with the National Roster, including 933 sociologists (see National Roster of Scientific and Technical Personnel 1942). The roster was rapidly folded into war mobilization agencies and from there into the civil service. Its records have disappeared, so there is little way of telling whether the 933 sociologists were mostly ASA members (at a time when the organization had only about a thousand members) or mostly laypeople—perhaps reformers and social welfare workers—seeking work at a time when unemployment was still high. (The roster opened for business in July 1940 [National Roster of Scientific and Technical Personnel 1942].) Nor is it evident whether the roster actually served as an important source for recruitment of sociologists into federal agencies. In fact, the lists of those who actually served in agencies

---

10. The splendid job prospects for the postwar generation make clear that the eclipse of the Chicago school of 1920–35 was in part demographic. Its graduates [and, even more, those they trained] faced the worst job market in American history.

make it plain that elite professional networks, and in particular those of the New York foundations and the Social Science Research Council (SSRC), mattered a great deal. Arnold Rose is a good example: he worked under Stouffer on the Carnegie Race Relations study in the early years of the war and then moved into the field staff of the Research Branch (under Stouffer) when he entered military service.

If, however, recruitment tended to privilege elite networks, far more important was the simple existence of a large and uncompetitive market for professional work. Interuniversity competition, geographic dispersion, and increasing specialization had all tended to move the discipline away from elite dominance in the 1930s. But the war changed that. In the first place, competition declined through sheer concentration. Many federal agencies had more PhD sociologists working for them than did the typical major university department. (Chicago, for example, had seven professors at all ranks in its sociology department for most of the 1940s. No more than five were ever in residence at the university at once. As we have seen, several federal agencies had two or three times that number.) Second, geographic dispersion declined. Transportation and time costs concentrated a large portion of wartime social scientists in the northeastern corner of the country, where social science funding had already concentrated. A substantial minority of the work was in Washington alone. Finally, specialization also declined. Agency service and the new large project model brought sociologists into intimate contact across specialties and indeed across disciplines, continuing a process of interdisciplinarity that had its roots in the movement for the SSRC in the 1920s. Indeed, war experience helped make social psychology—a completely interdisciplinary area staffed equally from both disciplines—one of the dominant subfields of sociology.[11]

In summary, the war created a large, publicly funded research sector within which personnel moved with considerable ease and which drew on university-sector consultants without regard for much more than research convenience. Such an environment fostered the coalescence of a new professional elite. Already emerging in the 1930s, this elite was rooted in the New York foundation community and the major East Coast universities, although drawing heavily on the great midwestern departments as well. After the war, it would locate securely on the East Coast, a move symbolized by Stouffer's move from Chicago to Harvard.

11. The term *social psychology*, however, took on hundreds of meanings. In Merton's influential paper "The Social Psychology of Housing" (1948), taking a social psychological approach meant, to all intents and purposes, looking at the housing situation with much greater subtlety, imagination, and rigor. Today we would say "Be more sociological!"

Wartime research also hardened the emerging belief—which came from this foundation-centered elite—that major sociological work should be centrally dominated, multidisciplinary, team-based research employing a deep division of labor. The template for this approach was the Race Relations Project (the *American Dilemma* project), many of whose dozens of subcontracted researchers were working with wartime agencies within a year or so of completing their work for the Carnegie Foundation. Myrdal's study was not, to be sure, the first such massive project. Warner's Yankee City project took this form, although on a smaller scale, and one could argue that the Chicago school's Local Community Research Committee—with its dozens of students making maps and writing vaguely interrelated dissertations—was a more loosely constructed version of the same thing. But during wartime this model became absolutely dominant, in part because the national scope of wartime agencies required research projects of a comparable scale. Likert's ability to marshal his national field staff within a week of Pearl Harbor earned him the immediate patronage of research directors within key civilian war agencies. Stouffer's comparable capacity to implement a "spot" survey using far-flung, theater-based research teams gave the Research Branch's work a timeliness that was absolutely essential for War Department support (Converse 1987; Stouffer et al. 1949-50, 1:31-53).

The new model for research practice had distinct intellectual implications. Theoretical and conceptual unification became extremely difficult. Neither Myrdal nor Stouffer could manage to produce a cohesive theoretical result despite great effort, for the wartime burst of research was not spawned by a clear set of theoretical questions or even hypotheses. Its overriding task was to monitor populations for bureaucratic compliance and tractability, or to check the pulse of the American people. Indeed, the sheer abundance of facts and findings issuing forth from the wartime government may have provided a heuristic advantage to structural-functionalist analysis, promising as it did to provide an operationalizing scythe that could harvest vast fields of data.

The political climate confronting sociologists in the postwar period also served to advance the new research approach at the cost of the old ones. As scientists basked in the glow of the Manhattan Project and other wartime wonders, Congress moved to fund a new National Science Foundation but did not include the social sciences in the new agency. In his 1946 report on the legislative developments that led to this exclusion, Talcott Parsons quickly identified the problem. Beyond the particular dynamics of the Office of Scientific Research and the Defense Department's insider politics, which had heavily shaped the contours of the final bill, there was the added problem that social scientists as a group "have been associated with liberal causes and have absorbed reformist traditions in ways which are more or less closely associated with their professional work. . . . This tendency seems . . . to be associated with broad undercurrents of sentiment which are related to the differences of social status and function of the two groups" (i.e., "hard" and "social" scientists). But if liberalism and the associated failure to develop a "social technology" with promise comparable to that of natural technology hurt sociology's political fortunes in the immediate postwar years, Parsons felt that the "new social sciences" were moving in directions that warranted support. Pointing to "theoretical advances" and to improvements in the "range and accuracy" of new methodologies (e.g., "the analysis of opinions and attitudes"), Parsons underscored the promise of social science—indeed, its urgent necessity in the age of the "atomic bomb." Of particular promise was the advancing use of "statistical information," based on recent advances in sampling, to allow the social sciences to approach "the logical equivalent of the experimental method." "If," he closed, "we are to be moving more and more into a scientific age, and science is to help solve its social problems, it must be social science which does so" (Parsons 1946; see also Klausner and Lidz 1986).

Parsons's line of reasoning failed to persuade Congress. While the discipline as a whole waited for inclusion in the National Science Foundation, many individuals pursued contracts with research departments in the Office of Naval Research, the Defense Department, the State Department, and the organization that came to be known as RAND. These patrons placed the same burdens of pragmatism and scientism on their consultants as had been placed on them in World War II (Lyons 1969). As the mainstream of sociology shifted toward the eastern establishment that had charted this new course of research, a contingent of dissidents countered by forming the Society for the Study of Social Problems (SSSP) in 1951. Led by Alfred McLung Lee, who was outspoken in his criticism of the shift in priorities presided over by Stouffer, Lazarsfeld, and the East Coast fraternity, the SSSP spoke to fears that the discipline had gone from bad to worse, replacing "liberal rationalists of the status quo" with enthusiastic "instruments of those in power" (Lee and Lee 1976). The goal was to launch an alternative movement comparable to the rural sociologists' formation of the Rural Sociological Society in the 1930s (Skura 1976, 23, 24–27). Despite the security that Burgess provided as the first president and the active assistance of the major figures Arnold Rose, Louis Wirth, Reinhard Bendix, and Florian Znaniecki, the SSSP's focus on classic social problems such as juvenile delinquency and racial and ethnic conflict (Henslin and Roesti 1976, 57) could not budge the mainstream literature. The fate of the SSSP showed that the new model of research not only flattened the social topography it studied but also marginalized alternative modes of study by sheer absorption of resources and scholarly attention during the years of its ascendancy.

The Intellectual Effects of the War

Like its effects on the discipline's institutional structure, the war's intellectual effect mainly consisted in hastening developments already under way. This hastening can be seen in each major element of the postwar mainstream: its methodological stance of scientism as articulated through large project surveys; its political stance of detachment; and its model of the social world as a mass of atomic individuals located in a larger "system" or "collectivity." Method, politics, and model all had their roots in the 1930s or even the 1920s. The war established their dominance.

SCIENTISM

Scientism obviously owed much to the war. Although it was the weapons systems that persuaded the public of science's importance, intellectual elites knew that the scientific contribution to military success was much broader— from code breaking to ballistics calculation to operations research. Social scientists were well aware of their own contributions to military performance and production. In sum, among both elites and the public, the prestige of "science" in the immediate postwar period was unparalleled in American history. It is hardly surprising that the new sociology claimed scientific legitimacy.

By this time, however, science had been the banner of sociology for many years. Robert Park had rejected reformism in the name of science in the 1920s. And Talcott Parsons's 1937 *Structure of Social Action* opened with a "scientific" analysis of action that could have come straight from Cohen and Nagel's (1934) enormously influential naturalist philosophy of science.[12] Nor can one ignore the empiricist scientism implicit in the new survey analysis of the 1930s, itself looking to the statistical revolution then being made by Fisher, Yule, Neyman, and Pearson. The 1930s were also the decade of the "social physics" of Lundberg, Dodd, Zipf, and others (Platt

12. Cohen and Nagel's book was the urtext of the positivism it became fashionable to reject in the 1980s. A purely rationalist theory of science, it was uninfluenced by the sociological subtleties of Fleck, the linguistic doubts of Wittgenstein, or the fatal logic of Godel—all of them publicly available, if quite obscure, by the time Parsons wrote.

1996, 212ff.). Science in sociology was thus old news. To be sure wartime sociology certainly played the science card very forcefully, as Stouffer did in showing what sometimes degenerated into contempt for ethnography, general theory, and most of preexisting sociology in the opening chapter of *The American Soldier* (Stouffer et al. 1949–50). But his position was merely an extension of common earlier views.

On a less abstract level, the war had implications for sociological methodology in particular. The most evident effect came through sheer finance: wartime agencies invested enormous amounts of public money in sociology, nearly all of it for various forms of survey analysis—from the more than 176 individual studies done by Stouffer's War Department Research Branch to the endless USDA surveys of farmers and the many OWI studies of morale. Such support whetted sociologists' appetite for survey analysis, even as it created a body of results in which to triumph (see Merton and Lazarsfeld 1950). But the more important methodological implications were negative. Perhaps the most important alternatives to survey analysis were the ethnography, geography, and institutional analysis characteristic of the Chicago school and its era. These all identified their objects of research in a manner incompatible with national security, which in wartime extended not only to military installations but also to the war industries and their communities. Even in postwar publication of surveys, the military sometimes insisted on concealed sample sizes lest the actual figures betray military secrets (e.g., Wachtel and Fay 1946, 396). The ethnographic war industry studies—which made clear the chaos on many shop floors—were not publishable until after 1945. And Tamotsu Shibutani (1978) waited thirty years before publishing his amazing chronicle of the dissolution of a Nisei military unit. Even where secrecy was not an issue, the wartime need for unity and national devotion militated against the kinds of methodologies that would most easily uncover the dynamics of conflict and disorganization. In survey analysis such disunity could be sanitized as "problems of morale." And when studies did investigate such major "disunity" events as breakdown of morale, the race riots in Detroit, or the racial tensions in southern military camps and overseas posts, group conflict disappeared behind clashing white and black "attitudes" that were presumed to be tinder waiting for a spark—any spark—to ignite it.

Yet sociology stopped short of extreme scientism. Among the other results of the intelligentsia's experience in depression and wartime was a serious interest in scientific planning and social engineering. Indeed, the latter was a theme in works as diverse as *An American Dilemma* and Norbert Wiener's *The Human Use of Human Beings* (1950). A number of sociologists flirted with social planning as a model—Louis Wirth, for example (Salerno 1983). Certainly social planning was pervasive in postwar Europe and indeed in the reconstruction of postwar Japan under American rule. But in the United States itself, social planning got a bad name after the war. In part this came from the spate of sociological wartime community studies, nearly all of them studies of the heroic problems in bureaucratically planned communities: the great shipyards in Oakland, California (Archibald 1947) and Seneca, Illinois (Havighurst and Morgan 1951), the 25,000-employee B-24 plant at Willow Run, Michigan (Carr and Stermer 1952), and above all the internment camps for Japanese Americans,[13] which produced a flurry of work from sociologists (e.g., Thomas and Nishimoto 1946), applied anthropologists (Leighton 1945), and political scientists (Grodzins 1949). (The most important planned communities—the many new army bases and such extraordinary places as Oak Ridge—were of course unstudiable for military reasons. But postwar research showed that Oak Ridge, for example, had been hastily erected by the Army Corps of Engineers as a cross between an encampment and a company town, without the advice or guidance of social scientists [Johnson and Jackson 1981, chap. 1].) Selznick's (1949) famous book on the TVA—another wartime study of bureaucracy published after the war's end—would make the same point about the failures of planning and bureaucracy.[14]

An even more important force against postwar planning was the example of Germany and the emerging belief that planning was a step toward totalitarian regimentation. (As the cold war deepened, fear of the USSR with its five-year plans also contributed to the notion that planning was totalitarian.) As Ido Oren (2003) has pointed out, although the Nazi government before 1936 was decried for its racial policies, it was nonetheless admired by some as a model for effective public administration. This respect for fascist "efficiency" dated back to Mussolini's successes in the American press, which came as early as 1925 (Alpers 2002, chap. 2). The postwar recognition that Nazi administrative efficiency had facilitated not only street cleaning but also human extermination created a rejection of public administration

13. We use the term *internment camps* because it was the phrase used at the time. The camps were, however, concentration camps in the literal sense of taking a dispersed population and concentrating it in one place.

14. Thomas and Nishimoto (1946) is the extreme example of this. Johnson and Jackson's 1981 retrospective analysis of Oak Ridge, based on unclassified documents, makes much the same argument, despite its apologetic tone. Given that these bureaucratic studies of failure fit into the growing postwar pessimism about administration, it is curious that they disappeared from the canon of the bureaucracy literature.

that not only destroyed the field in political science but also combined with the right's longtime revolt against interventionist government to produce a complete revulsion against social planning in the late 1940s. Only in some areas of urban studies did the notion of social planning survive the decisive wartime demise of the National Resources Planning Board and most of the New Deal public works projects (Brinkley 1995, 245-58; Porter 1980).

Planning and social engineering did not die away entirely in the postwar years but rather flowed within the narrower and more intensely concentrated channels of the national defense establishment. It is significant that the major experiments in social planning and engineering in this period were all conducted by the military or justified in the name of national defense. Domestically, this happened through the integration of the armed forces, the construction of an interstate highway system, and the bolstering of education through both the GI Bill of Rights (1944) and the National Defense Education Act of 1958. Internationally, it happened through the "reconstruction" of Europe, Japan, and the "third world" by means of foreign aid (the European Recovery Program, or Marshall Plan), the United Nations Educational, Scientific, and Cultural Organization (UNESCO), financial support (the World Bank and the International Monetary Fund), and the export of New Deal–style public works projects.[15]

In summary, the war furthered and perhaps consummated sociology's love affair with science. But it did not originate that affair, nor did it lead sociology to what might seem like the logical outcome—an applied science of openly recognized social planning based on esoteric social knowledge—even though the latter was extensively discussed both during the war and after. As we have seen, fear of just this possibility—because of the inherently political nature of social knowledge—had played a central role in the debate over a National Science Foundation directorate for social sciences.[16]

15. UNESCO exemplifies those sites for sociological activity where American sociologists—including such eminences as Frazier, Angell, and Wirth—would have encountered European social scientists and their ideas. Although the implications of this cross-national contact may have been considerable, the topic lies beyond the scope of our investigation. Similarly important were such international organizations as the ISA, which Wirth helped to found in 1949-50 (Salerno 1987, 29).

16. Even social scientists with strong interests in planning tiptoed around the "problem" that planning might be antidemocratic. Differentiating a possible American or democratic social engineering from totalitarianism was central for works like Mead (1942) and Leighton (1949, 205-18). Even Parsons made some of the same arguments in his (never accepted) SSRC brief for "nationalization" of the social sciences. All the same, social science–based manipulation of the public mind was practiced widely in the United States. And no one seemed to con-

THE SOCIOLOGY OF DETACHMENT AND
THE INDIVIDUAL-COLLECTIVITY MODEL

The downfall of planning left sociology with a de facto ethic of detachment, which in turn implied an acceptance of the social status quo as something that did not need to be explained, at least in any focused way. Such an ethic was, of course, frankly expressed in wartime. Although Stouffer was in the abstract a relativist, in practice he identified with the command and scientific points of view:

> The concept of personal adjustment is here viewed from the point of view of the Army command. One might have looked upon adjustment from other viewpoints. [As examples, he mentions adjustment defined as minimizing individual anxiety, maximizing democratic participation, or conforming to informal rather than formal Army rules.] But it seemed useful, both for the engineering task of serving the Army and for the analytic task of producing these chapters, to view adjustment in terms of adaptation as viewed by the Army command. (Stouffer et al. 1949-50, 1:82)

Indeed, the very subtitle of its most widely read volume tells us that *The American Soldier* is about the "adjustment" of the soldier to army life and to combat. After the war, sociology focused less on adjustment per se, taking a more detached view; in Robert Merton, an individual's problems with social structures became not maladjustment but simply "anomie" (Merton 1949a). Detachment was complete.

As the Merton citation suggests, the political stance of detachment was mixed up with another, more purely intellectual change, the move to what we may call the "individual-collectivity" (IC) model of social life. According to the IC model, social life is best conceived at two abstracted levels: individual and collective. The relation between these two levels was theorized in various ways: as microcosm/macrocosm (the individual contains a picture of the "larger" society or its values); as normative (society provides "rules" that govern or "integrate" individuals); and as purely aggregative (society is merely the appearance of individual attitudes or behaviors taken

---

sider social science-based advertising a form of undemocratic social engineering. The New York, New Haven, and Hartford's legendary "Kid in Upper 4" advertisement was actually part of a precisely engineered campaign to deflect complaints about the railroad's terrible service. The adman who devised it, Nelson Metcalf, proposed to create an ad that would "make everybody who read it feel real ashamed" and thereby defuse civilian discontent. Yet its gently sleeping soldier became one of the icons of war morale (Twitchell 2000, 80-87; Fox 1975, 74-75).

as aggregates). But all three modes shared the concept of sharply separated "levels," related in ways that were abstract and timeless.[17]

The IC model and the concept of adjustment both loomed very large in wartime social science. American propaganda as crafted by the OWI, and the Advertising Council offered an especially individualistic vision of national purpose, consistently portraying the war effort as a natural extension of liberal self-interest rather than relying primarily on the heavy-handed appeals to ideology or jingoism that had discredited the Creel Committee after World War I (Fox 1975; Westbrook 2004; Winkler 1978). Even in the absence of this distinctively liberal conception of war aims, however, full mobilization demanded an unprecedented degree of national unity, at least on the surface of things, if only to advance beyond the politicized stalemates that had deeply divided society during the late New Deal.

Social scientists worked hard at this unification in such organizations as the Committee for National Morale, a private organization founded in June 1940 and dominated by prominent exponents of interventionism, including Margaret Mead, Ruth Benedict, Gregory Bateson, Gordon Allport, Hadley Cantril, Erich Fromm, and Robert Yerkes, all of whom sought an expedited mechanism to ensure that American preparedness was guided by the most advanced social science (Herman 1995, 49–50). In work after work—Gunnar Myrdal's *An American Dilemma* is only the most famous—the "American character" and "American creed" emerged as broad unifying concepts. The unity they portrayed—or wished to summon into existence—was not in any way a reality. We now know that the war years saw new levels of conflict, social dislocation, and disorganization on the "home front," as it was all too tellingly called. There was social chaos within the munitions plants and their communities. Work stoppages reached record numbers, cresting at 4,956 in 1944, only 29 short of the all-time high in 1946. Turnover among manufacturing employees more than doubled, leaping from a monthly rate of 4 percent in 1940 to over 9 percent in 1943. There were race riots in New York, Detroit, and Los Angeles, as well as lesser violent con-

17. For classics statements of the IC view, see Parson's review (1942) of Angell, *The Integration of American Society*, and Shils and Young's famous paper (1956) on the coronation. The IC view can be opposed to the notion (characteristic of the Chicago school both in social psychology and urban ecology) that both individual and collective phenomena emerge and reciprocally define each other in a social process in which overlapping and interconnected groups contact, compete, and accommodate. In such a view, all social phenomena flow in time, and levels are merely analytic appearances. Social problems are solved not by "adjusting" individuals to a procrustean social bed but by modifying the conflicts and interactions of groups so that socially destructive conflict is minimized.

flicts in dozens of other American cities, not to mention in numerous military camps and forts throughout the South and West. The U.S. divorce rate rose dramatically and steadily throughout the war, from 8.8 per thousand married women in 1940 to a peak of 17.9 in 1946, when many hasty wartime unions were reconsidered. It did not settle back down to prewar levels until the second half of the 1950s. In the military, as Stouffer's Research Branch found, there was a very real and thoroughgoing lack of enthusiasm for the dangerous work of combat. In such a political setting, the focus on processes of conflict and accommodation that dominated much earlier sociology—particularly the Chicago school's concept of urban ecology—was simply unacceptable. This was America, and "we" were "all Americans." So wrote the distinguished cultural relativist Margaret Mead in her 1942 book *And Keep Your Powder Dry*, a book whose entire aim was precisely to conjure this "American character" out of the vast, inchoate diversity of the nation.[18]

If the IC model was a logical necessity of the very concept of national morale, it was even less surprising that adjustment was central to the applied social science of wartime. Once the collectivity's interest became the overwhelming one of war, it logically followed that individuals would have to "adjust" to social needs. The proximate groundwork for this approach had already been laid in a 1941 memorandum by Stouffer, Burgess, Cottrell, and other members of the prediction subcommittee of the SSRC's Committee on Social Adjustment. This memorandum framed both the civilian and military aspects of the defense program as a question of "efficient use of human resources," to be mined from the social soil much as other vital resources would be extracted from nature (Burgess et al. 1941).[19] The adjustment model meant that there were no competing groups in the *American Soldier* volumes, none of the particular units, and gangs, and squads, and brothels, and contending branches that would have filled the pages of a Chicago-style study of the army. Nor, indeed, is there any sense of the situatedness of social experience, either in particular social settings or in the particular life

18. Even so consistent a radical as Alfred McClung Lee felt it necessary, in his book on race riots (Lee and Humphrey 1943), to toe the line on the IC image as contained in the concept of Americanism: "Thirty-four Americans died in the Detroit race riots of the week of June 20, 1943. They died while their relatives were fighting in American Uniforms on the battlefields of a war for freedom. It is sincerely hoped that this book points to a few of the lessons we Americans must learn from this hysterical attack upon democracy and American morale" (Lee and Humphrey 1943, ix).

19. Many of the topics considered in this memorandum, such as "personnel placement in the military services," "selection of officers in the armed forces," "selection of aircraft pilots," and "prediction of adjustment to military life," read like a prescient chapter outline for the volumes of *The American Soldier* that would be so influential a decade later.

courses of individual soldiers. The soldiers are no more than sample points—arbitrary "representative" individuals. There is nothing linking those individuals to the collectivity (or to each other) other than their surveyed "attitudes" and, perhaps, the bureaucratic structure of the military.[20]

The practical meaning of the adjustment approach to war becomes clear if we read the two chapters of *American Soldier* on air corps morale (Stouffer et al. 1949-50, vol. 2, chaps. 7, 8) in parallel with the 1995 war novel *Ash Wednesday '45* by Frank Westie, a bomber pilot who became a sociologist studying intergroup conflict. The *American Soldier* chapters speak of high morale, even though a third or more of the flyers said they would not volunteer for combat flight if they had the choice to make over again. The chapters talk of "satisfaction" among flyers. But Westie's novel portrays profound demoralization, a black bitterness that leads his hero to refuse to firebomb Dresden a second time, making the choice Westie himself must have thought about. (He refused all military decorations after his own Dresden flights [Westie 2004].) Only once, at the very end of the *American Soldier* chapters, does Westie's world intrude into the Research Branch view of the world; there we read that the six-month casualty rate for the heavy bomber crews was 71 percent killed or MIA plus 18 percent wounded in action (Stouffer et al. 1949-50, 2:407). In all but name this was a suicide corps.

To such men, at such a time, the Research Branch and its questionnaires must have seemed literally incomprehensible. In reality, the aim of the *American Soldier* air corps morale investigations was to decide how long a tour should be—what number of sorties would get the maximum of skill and performance out of the flyers before they burned out to the point of collapse. *The American Soldier* was specifically *not* a conceptually driven inquiry into the sociology of military life, interesting as that would have been; it was a work of morale engineering and management using sociological methods (and drawing heavily on commercial market research [see Stouffer et al. 1949-50, 1:38]). The sociology was added as an afterthought or sideline (a criticism sometimes also made of Paul Lazarsfeld's later market research work [Converse 1987, 270-72]).

20. The main exception to this statement is the reciprocal anger and distrust between combat and noncombat troops. In *The American Soldier* this conflict is a static attitude conflict between types, even though it is clear that men rotated through both settings in their army careers. The organizational-level dynamics of this conflict, however, are never made clear. (Westie [1995] tells the interesting story of a combat flyer who sends a recalcitrant member of his noncombat ground crew off to France, combat, and probable death.) The *American Soldier* volumes do not consider the various "disorganizations" of army life—personal vendettas, looting, atrocities, goldbricking, subversion, and so on—other than as signs of weak morale. Nor does it consider interunit rivalry and conflict, even though any veteran knows this to be a crucial and often destructive factor in army life.

We see then that the IC model and adjustment were central in wartime social science. But they were not new wartime ideas. They dated from the 1920s. The idea of adjustment had originated in the vast expansion of psychiatry out of the mental hospitals after 1900.[21] As physician promotion slowed and mental illness proved intellectually intractable, psychiatrists flooded into criminology, industrial psychology, pastoral counseling, and dozens of other areas. They achieved institutional success in the juvenile court system and "child guidance" systems, and found public recognition in the shell shock controversy of the First World War and the "mental hygiene" movement. Adjustment was the core concept of all this "social psychiatry," which also developed the life-course concept (the "dynamic psychiatry" of Adolf Meyer) and indeed the very concept of personality.[22] By the late 1920s, the American Psychiatric Association was organizing joint meetings with the SSRC and the Laura Spelman Rockefeller Foundation about the possible contributions of psychiatry to social science. Organized by W. I. Thomas, these meetings brought together the Chicago sociologists, the leaders of American outpatient psychiatry, of child guidance and of delinquency studies, and a variety of luminaries from other social science disciplines.[23]

By the early 1930s, all this ferment about adjustment and personality had coalesced into two major streams. One was the strongly anthropological culture-and-personality movement centered at Yale (later Columbia), of

21. Psychiatry as of 1920 was not the low-status specialty it is today. Practitioners were a small (approximately 1,500) but powerful group deriving cultural authority from its nationwide control of about 250 mental institutions, which contained almost half as many patients as there were undergraduates in all of America's colleges and which cost the states about 10 percent of their total budgets. This discussion of the adjustment literature rests on Abbott (1982, chaps. 7, 11, and 12).

22. The idea of—and certainly the word—*adjustment* was also taken up by psychologists (Napoli 1981). Although in the child guidance clinics, the psychologists were subordinate to psychiatrists, the idea of mental and personality testing—psychology's main stock-in-trade at this point—spread far beyond the military and the guidance clinic, which were its first two areas of application. By the late 1920s, testing was nearly universal in industry, school, court, and society. The psychologists did "preventive" adjustment: they made sure square pegs went into square holes. The psychiatrists did the sanding when the pieces weren't quite square with the holes they happened to be stuck in. Together, these two things constituted a notion of adjustment that was absolutely pervasive in American culture in the 1920s.

23. Astonishingly, the Chicago sociology department's Society for Social Research focused its 1926 summer meeting on the subject of the relation between psychiatry, psychology, and sociology, even though in the standard histories this moment was the supposed apogee of the Chicago school's focus on urban sociology and ecology. Much of this history is based on materials identified and supplied to us by Rainer Egloff of the Collegium Helveticum. We thank Mr. Egloff for his generous sharing of this material, which challenges many presumptions about the history of the social sciences in the 1920s. Another source, excellent in its detail but not always careful about chronology, is Darnell (1990).

which the major figures were anthropologists Edward Sapir, Margaret Mead, Ruth Benedict, political scientist Harold Lasswell, psychiatrists Harry Stack Sullivan and Abram Kardiner, and the heavily psychoanalytic sociologist John Dollard. Out of this school came Benedict's popular success *Patterns of Culture* (1934) and the ensuing national character studies such as Mead's rhapsodic *And Keep Your Powder Dry* and Benedict's OWI-sponsored *The Chrysanthemum and the Sword*. For anthropologists, "culture and personality" had a natural fit, since at this time they were dedicated to studying small groups that were in themselves "whole societies," without clear internal subgroupings and intragroup conflict. The IC model came naturally.

The other stream was what we may call the "adjustment" school. Its clearest exemplar was Ernest Burgess, who spent most of the 1930s on large-scale studies of prediction of individual outcomes like probation violation and divorce. Here too the concept of personal continuity over time—the notion of personality—was central, but the focus was on *personal* adjustment in given social structures like marriage and everyday behavior, not the culture-and-personality school's loose configurational resemblance between the individual personality and the "larger culture." By the late 1930s, Burgess and Samuel Stouffer were running an SSRC subcommittee on prediction of personal adjustment. (Burgess was chairing the parent Committee on Social Adjustment [see Young 1941, 873; Horst 1941].) This work moved toward an IC model of the world, although sometimes retaining Thomas's insistence that "the moral good or evil of a wish depends on the social meaning or value of an activity which results from it" (Thomas 1923, 38).

The IC model was, however, not solely a product of the adjustment and culture/personality schools. The vision of "a national society" is also implicit in the celebrated *Recent Social Trends* volumes of the Hoover commission, which wrote, in 1932, with great prescience:

> In times of war and imminent public calamity it has been possible to achieve a high degree of coordinated action, but in the intervals of which national life is largely made up, coordinated effort relaxes and under the heterogeneous forces of modern life a vast amount of disorganization has been possible in our economic, political and social affairs. It may indeed be said that the primary value of this report is to be found in the effort to interrelate the disjointed factors and elements in the social life of America, in the attempt to view the situation as a whole rather than as a cluster of parts. (President's Research Committee on Social Trends 1933, 1:xii–xiii)

Indeed, much of the politics of the 1930s had searched for just such a national society and, significantly, used the analogy of war (specifically, the precedent of World War I) to tie New Deal reforms to patriotic values, as in Gen. Hugh Johnson's use of the Blue Eagle as a badge of compliance with the NRA (Leuchtenberg 1995, chap. 2). At such a national level, the view of social changes had to be segmentary and topical, rather than interwoven, and so in the Committee on Social Trends' volumes, as indeed in the contemporary community studies of the Lynd–Warner type, social life became a list of functions (education, family, childhood, consumers, and so forth) on the one hand and of problems (welfare activities, crime, health, and the like) on the other, all located within a giant, overarching "society" of which they were simply different aspects.

Thus the wartime focus on adjustment and insistence on a cohesive "American character" and "American culture" were not only necessities of mobilization but also logical developments of long-standing trends in social science more broadly. The major sociological classics throughout the war period and postwar follow the IC model almost without exception. Nothing could make this clearer than Myrdal's *An American Dilemma* (1944), for which the research strategy was designed well before the war. Although he came from a social engineering/social democracy background, Myrdal organized his analysis around a culture-and-personality argument. The roots of the American dilemma lay in the contradiction between the master values of the American creed and the particularities of racial prejudice. Although *An American Dilemma* discussed many of the social structures of racism, Myrdal ultimately viewed those structures as an expression of an attitude of bigotry rather than as the loci of intergroup conflicts in which racism was itself produced. Louis Wirth, by contrast, had objected to this aspect of the design from the beginning. (See his analysis of Myrdal's original project design for Carnegie's Frederick Keppel, in a letter of January 28, 1939.)[24]

As a widely celebrated study, *An American Dilemma* contributed much to the "disappearance of the middle ground" that was characteristic of the IC model of social life. Similar personality arguments became standard in the voluminous postwar literature on the origins of Nazism. The celebrated *Authoritarian Personality* (Adorno et al. 1950) and the enormous literature on prejudice took a personality-based view of prejudice in which actual social

24. Wirth papers, box 55, folder 12. Like other sociologists in the Parkian race relations tradition, Wirth preferred a processual approach to race conflict, in which racism like other social values was produced in the crucible of actual, ongoing interaction between social groups rather than being an ex ante personality or cultural quality. To Myrdal, however, Wirth's view was "pessimism." He did not see the strength of the processes that maintained what would later be called "institutional racism."

conflict and group relations played almost no role. Adorno himself had been highly dissatisfied with the study's failure to place the psychology of prejudice more firmly within a critically articulated social analysis, which suggests the power of the IC model and of survey methodology in that period, even for a veteran of the Frankfurt school's critical approach (Jay 1973). Not until the 1970s would there be serious attempts to seek the social dynamics of Nazism; it is striking in this connection that Neumann's *Behemoth* (1944) did not become one of the great texts of modern social science, while *The Authoritarian Personality* did.

Finally, the dominance of the IC model explains the otherwise enigmatic postwar marriage of the florid abstractions of Talcott Parsons with the dowdy concreteness of survey analysis. *The Structure of Social Action* clearly presupposed two levels of social life: the individual and the collectivity. In principle, the collectivity might be any size or shape of group, but in effect the very abstract framing of the book essentially opposed the individual and the total society, following the Durkheimian logic in which occupations, religious institutions, the family, and so on figure not as actual social groups with real qualities and conflictive existence but simply as conduits for "forces" between the actor and his "collectivity."

To be sure, the IC model had considerable empirical justification. As we noted earlier, American society really was transformed during the war era. Much of that transformation took the form of eradicating or overwhelming what had been stable intermediate structures of interwar society. The vast increases in geographic and occupational mobility, the move of women into the workplace, the dislocations and homogenization of military service, the new possibilities for housing and education, the massification of government, the consolidation of mass culture reinforced by rapid suburbanization and a national consumer market: all these things meant that those who talked of a larger "society" were indeed talking about something that was far more of a reality in 1950 than it had been in 1930. In such a context, the IC model made more sense than before. At the same time, the IC paradigm led mainstream sociology to miss the inevitable emergence of new middle-level structures in the mid- and late 1960s. It also led sociologists to ignore the role of quantitative sociology in *creating,* as much as finding, the new society. But all this was perhaps hard to see in 1955.[25]

25. James Coleman (1978, 1980) argued this position at length, saying that a new society called for a new sociology. Coleman's argument ignored two other things: first, the problem of direction—sociologists played an important role in defining and constituting national society; and second, the extraordinary fecundity of social processes in producing new dimensions and groupings of differences within what appeared to be a highly individualized mass society. It is

Sociology in the Postwar Decade

MCCARTHYISM

Although the wartime and postwar flowering of applied scientistic research grew naturally out of past trends in sociology, the rising climate of anti-communist suspicion ensured that some aspects of the discipline—in particular the "liberal" propensities noted by Parsons in 1946—would be suppressed, if not on grounds of objectivity and scientific detachment then on grounds of loyalty. Yet so many sociologists had been involved in reform or meliorism that it is unclear what principle determined which scholars were singled out for judgment. And if, as seems likely, the process was in fact an arbitrary drive by anti-intellectuals and red baiters uninterested in fine distinctions, and intended simply to squelch all critical thought, then the intellectual impact of the purges remains unclear. (See Schrecker [1986] on the general climate of intellectual self-suppression and Lazarsfeld [1958] on the varied and nuanced responses of social scientists to anticommunist pressure.) Yet we can get a sense of the nature of anticommunism's impact on sociology by looking at the investigation of none other than Samuel Stouffer, a man whose lifelong Republican politics, extensive government service, and distanced methodology should have been above reproach in the new postwar climate.

In 1955, not long after McCarthy had been censured by the Senate, Stouffer had the temerity to publish a definitive national study of public attitudes toward the elephant in the living room. *Communism, Conformity, and Civil Liberties* investigated whether Americans really were anticommunist. Despite the unusually rigorous sampling methodology employed (dual independent national samples, one by Gallup, one by NORC), Stouffer was investigated and subsequently lost his security clearance. Stouffer's scientifically established reputation, his position in the Harvard Department of Social Relations, and the near-universal recognition accorded *The American Soldier* upon its publication in 1949 were not enough to protect him from suspicion. Nor did his avoidance of a "social problems" approach help him. The book overlooked the explosive class conflicts, racial antagonisms, and local power struggles that drove anticommunism: it rose above such lo-

---

the latter process that always defines the limits of survey analysis. The IC view eventually began to recognize the existence of intermediate structures, but these were always concentric: neighborhood, community, state, society. One can follow the methodologists' gradual unpacking of this series in the debate, started by Robinson's celebrated 1950 paper, on the ecological fallacy and the true "level" of variables. For a good contemporary overview, see Lazarsfeld (1993, chap. 8) and Menzel (1961).

cal events as particular unionization drives, or civil rights challenges, to the bloodless abstraction of "conformity." But all this did not suffice. Simply for investigating anticommunism in the context of conformity and civil liberties, one of America's best-positioned conservative sociologists lost for a time his position in the government funding game.[26]

Stouffer's plight suggests that McCarthyism may have operated as a general field effect rather than as a decisive agent favoring one sociologist over another. Yet the proliferation of such safe abstractions as "anomie," "conformity," "adjustment," and "mobility" during this period, tied so often to respectable and "objective" methodology, raises the possibility that fears of conservative pressure may have led many sociologists to take cover in the shade of the IC model.

NEW TOPICS

Postwar sociology turned to a number of new topics (for a general overview, see Kinloch 1988). The first of these was social mobility, which emerged in the 1950s as one of the field's central preoccupations. By 1954, study of mobility was on the cusp of transformation. Earlier mobility work (e.g., the Six Cities study reported in Palmer 1954) had been geographically based. Later work would all be national, partly because of the IC model and because of governmental and commercial efforts to monitor and shape the economic and political choices of the geographically mobile society that had emerged in the war years and after. Once government and industry regularly produced national data sets, which became the standard practice during the war and after, it would be difficult for social scientists to ignore the siren song of national generalizability.[27] The ideology of "national is better" was argued quietly but forcefully in Hebert Parnes's influential review of mobility studies. In Parnes's conceptual chapter (1954, chap. 2) one can see how the embedding of labor in geographical labor markets, in individual life cycles, and, ultimately, within particular employers or even employment sectors had become an inconvenience to the project of generalization, which would by the 1960s consider only the education, age, race, gender,

26. For an extended investigation of FBI surveillance of American sociology, see Keen (1999). Chapter 10 of the Keen volume discusses the case of Samuel Stouffer.

27. Of course national studies and data sets had been produced before, most notably the Census, but also data from the departments of Commerce and Labor in the 1920s, and various New Deal agencies such as the WPA. The shift here is to note that the war permanently increased the need for national data sets corresponding to the policy domains of military and civilian agencies.

and occupation (not employer) of workers. Codable and replicable nationally, these variables not only enabled the study of national level mobility; they also constituted it as a social phenomenon.

The second major new topic of the postwar era was the new mainstream's candidate for an intermediate institution between individual and society, its replacement for the acting groups and conflicting structures of the Chicago school. Not surprisingly, given wartime experience, the new candidate was bureaucracy. In 1944 some 3.3 million civilians worked for the now-enormous federal government, along with 12 million in the armed forces and some 19 million in defense production, the vast majority of it contracted to gigantic firms. In short, about half the total labor experience in wartime America was in large organizations. Moreover, federal bureaucracies had touched Americans in a thousand ways, from rationing to draft registration to the mass income tax.

This postwar importance of bureaucracy was utterly new in sociology. Neither the Chicago school nor its various competitors in the 1930s had taken the problems of bureaucracy seriously.[28] Most work on bureaucratic employees and employment during that period took place in the engineering and business schools, where the descendants and opponents of Taylorism studied the restless entrails of business. Other than psychology, the social sciences proper had little to do with this work.

Parsons, however, featured the Weber analysis of bureaucracy in *The Structure of Social Action* in 1937 and published a translation of the famous Weber essay on bureaucracy in 1947 (Weber 1947). The wartime community studies, as we noted, mostly concerned bureaucracies, as did Selznick's innovative study of the TVA. In 1952, Merton and others published a reader on bureaucracy (Merton et al. 1952) that drew together work from the "engineering" tradition of management (Simon, Veblen), the business studies tradition (Berle and Means, Gordon, Bernard), and historical sociology (Weber, Bendix, Michels). The book even took a crack at what had become the dominant social question of the day—why Nazism?—by including a section from Neumann's *Behemoth* and a commissioned paper giving a Weberian (rather than Neumann's more political and historicist) interpretation of National Socialist bureaucracy.[29]

28. Only seven articles on bureaucracy and bureaucratization appeared in the forty-five volumes of the *AJS* before 1940, while fifteen appeared in the next twenty-five volumes ("Cumulative Index" 1965).

29. Missing from the book, however, is the optimistic analysis of bureaucracy that had been characteristic of the political science subfield of public administration before the war; see Oren (2003).

After the war, community studies would become obsessed with the sub-urbs—Crestwood Heights, Levittown, "exurbia," Park Forest, and so on. But the theme of bureaucratic employment remained central to these studies as well, and a number of their subjects were themselves planned communities posing the same intellectual problem (how do "natural" communities form in bureaucratically structured settings) as had Seneca, Willow Run, and the internment camps during the war. The same bureaucratic theme emerged in such general interpretations as Riesman's *Lonely Crowd* and Whyte's *Organization Man.*

The concept of bureaucracy supplied the IC model of society with an intermediary institution between the individual and the collectivity. Bu-reaucracy—which in the guise of the military had been just such an inter-mediary institution for an entire generation of young American men—thus replaced the Chicago school's ethnicities, churches, voluntary and business associations, gangs, clubs, and so on as the basic "type" of social organiza-tion. Role theories abounded, but built not so much on the dramaturgical roles of Goffman as on the job-description roles of the social psychologists. Even communities, as we have seen, were often interpreted as planned (or at least "functional") structures, in which the "natural histories" of the Chicago school were mere eddies downstream from bureaucratic design. Thus bureaucracy's static, hierarchical systems of roles and rules became the model for social life, replacing the collective behavior, ecological com-petition, and interaction cycles of the Chicago school. Formal organization became the foreground, "informal organization" the background. In the distance lurked the notion of society as efficient, which had in fact been quite explicit in the wartime studies of munitions plants. Indeed, in Par-sons's postwar writing, norms themselves became organized into quasi-military hierarchies of sub- and superordinate.

Weaving all these strands into a global system was modernization the-ory, the great paradigm of postwar social science and the most important bridge between academic work and national policy during the high cold war. With its immediate intellectual roots in Parsonian structural function-alism and the intellectual culture of the Harvard Department of Social Re-lations, modernization theory was quickly developed and applied to a wide range of social science and policy questions by the legions of graduate stu-dents issuing forth from Harvard and Columbia in the 1950s (Gilman 2003). Presenting the abstracted and decontextualized model of "modernity" as the end state of an ahistorical "process" of development, influential schol-ars such as Gabriel Almond, Lucien Pye, and Walt Rostow finally achieved the Washington influence that social scientists had sought since the earliest years of Progressivism. Calling for massive social surveys to enable the technocratic management of personal and social adjustment required by the bureaucratic rationality of modern society, large-scale plans such as Project Camelot aimed to remake the "third world" in the idealized image of the United States, placing it on the fast track to "modernity." Only modern social science could so elegantly reduce the complexities of nonindustrialized societies to a manageable matrix of key factors in need of strategic manipulation before unleashing the full potential of the "free world." In the context of a global struggle against Communist seduction of "undeveloped" nations, such knowledge would be powerful indeed.

At this brink of technological mastery, cold war social science blinked. And in that moment, all its achievements came down like a house of cards, blown to pieces by the controversial winds of the 1960s. But that is another story.

Acknowledgments

The authors thank Geoffrey Guy for his adept assistance in the preparation of the ASA/AJS data set. We also thank those members of the ASA who shared memories of war service, both civilian and military, with us. Although we have not cited any of them directly, their voices have guided us to many important themes.

[NINE] American Sociology before and after World War II: The (Temporary) Settling of a Disciplinary Field

George Steinmetz

The central problem I address in this chapter on American sociology between the early 1930s through the mid-1960s is the shift from an epistemologically splintered discipline before World War II to a more hegemonized situation afterward.[1] I analyze sociology *internally* in terms of its fieldlike qualities (or lack thereof), in Bourdieu's (1985b) sense, asking about the emergence of agreed-upon definitions of unequally distributed social scientific capital. The drawback to a strictly field-level analysis, however, is that it cannot explain why certain definitions of scientific capital—in this case, broadly positivist positions—are ascendant in particular historical periods. Specifically, the Bourdieuian approach cannot explain why methodological positivism was only able to triumph after the war. The actor-network approach pioneered by Bruno Latour is enlightening about the sorts of strategies scientists use in seeking to expand their influence or scientific capital, but it cannot explain why the same techniques succeed in one historical context and fail in another. Both of these compelling approaches to the sociology of science need to be supplemented by attention to the ways in which epochal changes in the organization of society influence the ways scientists think about their objects of inquiry and the nature of scientific activity.[2] The extra-field determinant that is emphasized in most of the existing literature on the sociology of the social sciences is money. The story of social science scientism rightly emphasizes the massive influx of federal funding during and after World War II, which bolstered the impact on sociologists' epistemological orientations of the already significant levels of private funding (Turner and Turner 1990; Kleinman 1995;

1. See Steinmetz (2005a, 2005g) and Steinmetz and Chae (2002) for a more detailed elaboration of this use of the term *epistemological*.

2. This is not to say that Bourdieu entirely ignored the effects of the environing "field of power" on production internal to scientific fields (see, for example, Bourdieu 1991d). My contention is rather than Bourdieu did not adequately theorize the relations between the specific field (e.g., philosophy, sociology) and everything that lay outside the field; see Steinmetz (forthcoming b) for discussion of this point.

Price 2003). But while funding was certainly *part* of the conjuncture that catapulted methodological positivism to its leading position in postwar sociology (and in political science, psychology, and some other social science disciplines), material resources alone do not provide a sufficient explanation. After all, significant research money for "scientific" forms of sociology had been available before World War II, both from private sources like the Laura Spelman Rockefeller Foundation and from the federal government in the New Deal work relief programs (Ross 1991; Camic, chap. 7, this volume). Moreover, the styles of sociology geared toward serving the state and industry and the flood of resources that supported those activities were *both* part of the broader Fordist social formation that emerged after the war.[3] In other words, the causal arrows running between funding and social epistemology are not unidirectional, and these relations were themselves mediated through the larger societal complex of Fordism.

Fordist forms of societal regulation resonated powerfully with social science positivism. The spontaneous social epistemologies that were encouraged by Fordism contributed to the epistemic realignment in sociology by making positivism seem more plausible. American sociologists participated individually in Fordist forms of societalization in their everyday lives, and their personal assumptions about the social came to be more closely aligned with positivism than had been the case before the war. Fordism as a mode of social regulation insisted on the ontological reality of "the social" as an object, and this was the very object over which sociology as a discipline claimed jurisdiction. As a result, sociologists were especially fixated on the predictable, repeated regularities of social existence inside the U.S. metropole. By contrast, disciplines like anthropology and area studies that claimed jurisdiction over the global South were confronting the turbulence of decolonization and revolution rather than a world that resonated with epistemological notions of general laws and "constant conjunctions of events." Analyzing the relations between Fordism and the social sciences undermines the internalist versus externalist division in the study of science insofar as the internal workings of sociology were intrinsically linked to more encompassing patterns of social life.

The burden of my argument in this chapter is to track the postwar narrowing of sociology's intellectual diversity or, more precisely, the shift from a relative equality between nonpositivist and positivist orientations in terms of scientific prestige to a condition in which positivism as defined

---

3. On Fordism in the United States see the foundational text by Aglietta (1987); for a brief overview see Steinmetz (forthcoming a).

here was clearly dominant. Because I have explored the causal linkages between Fordism and postwar positivism elsewhere (Steinmetz 2005a, 2005g, 2005d, forthcoming b) this chapter focuses on establishing in more descriptive detail the epistemological dimensions of the midcentury shift. Specifically, I examine the epistemological characteristics of some of the leading sociology departments and disciplinary publications of the middle third of the century.[4] In the conclusion I summarize my arguments and findings from previous studies concerning the specific ways that postwar Fordism seemed to provide immediate confirming evidence for social science positivism.

Methodological Positivism in American Sociology before World War II

Methodological positivism was already well represented in U.S. sociology before 1945. By *positivism* I am referring neither to pure logical positivism (Ayer 1959) nor to Comte's (1975) classical doctrines but rather to a historically specific set of practices, conventions, and assumptions about social science that emerged between the late nineteenth and mid-twentieth centuries and that continues to evolve and flourish in the social sciences today.[5]

There are three main dimensions of methodological positivism. The first element is an *epistemological* commitment to covering laws, that is, to the identification of Humean "constant conjunctions" of events, or to the

4. Given the ongoing discussions about whether this postwar formation has in fact disappeared, I will not try to establish a specific date for its dissolution. Calhoun (1996) points implicitly to the continuing domination of the discipline by the position I call methodological positivism, and Somers (2005) suggests that a neopositivist formation is currently being consolidated within U.S. sociology. I elaborate two distinct futures for sociological positivism in Steinmetz (2005a, 2005g) without forecasting either of them.

5. This definition is based primarily on discussions in the critical realist philosophy of science, but it is also adjusted to the peculiarities of actual sociological practice. Alternative terms that attempt to capture a similar cluster of scientific tendencies include "instrumental positivism" (Bryant 1985), "objectivism" (Bannister 1987), and "standard" (Mullins and Mullins 1973) or "mainstream" (Calhoun and VanAntwerpen, chap. 10, this volume) sociology. Because these alternative terms neglect to differentiate between empiricist *ontology* and positivist *epistemology*, however, they cannot register more recent changes in sociological positivism, especially the increasingly widespread combination of depth-realist concepts (that is, *nonempiricist* ontology) with a commitment to general laws (*positivist* epistemology); for one defense of this version of positivism see Kiser and Hechter (1991). A comparative overview of the actually existing forms of positivism in the various U.S. social science disciplines during the twentieth century is provided by the essays in Steinmetz (2005e); Abbagnano (1967) compares philosophical definitions of positivism.

probabilistic variants of covering laws that were accepted as legitimate by logical positivist philosophers in the mid-twentieth century. This is the central, defining element.

The second component is an empiricist *ontology*, according to which scientific statements link empirically observable events. The terms *logical positivism* and *logical empiricism* were almost interchangeable during the period discussed in this chapter. By the same token, epistemically positivist sociology was usually empiricist. In more recent decades we have seen the emergence of nonpositivist empiricism and nonempiricist positivism. Postpositivists like Foucault reject "depth hermeneutics" in favor of a kind of neoempiricism, whereas new versions of social science positivism define general laws as linkages between nonempirical depth-realist mechanisms and surface-level events.

A third component or set of assumptions stems from *scientism*, that is, the belief that the social and natural sciences should approach their objects of study in an identical fashion. For the social sciences, this premise means that its objects of study can be treated as brute material facts whose identity is independent of what people think about them. It also means that social facts, like natural ones, are subject to "invariable natural Laws" (Comte) independent of time and place.[6] Scientism's specifically methodological implication has been that the social sciences should strive to become quantitative and experimental like the natural sciences and should eschew normative evaluations.

Several historians have maintained that this broadly "methodological" syndrome was prevalent in U.S. social science during the first half of the twentieth century (Bannister 1987; Bryant 1975, 1985; Ross 1991).[7] Stephen Turner (1994) presents a thesis of strong epistemic continuity that dates from Columbia sociology department founder Franklin Giddings through to the present. This persistence, according to Turner, is maintained by a set of tacit and explicit commitments, passed on from generation to generation, privileging quantitative data (especially surveys) and statistical techniques.

6. Bryant (1975) identified two distinct traditions of positivism: Comte's version and the strand running from Locke and Hume through to Mach and Pearson, twentieth-century logical positivism, and finally to Ernest Nagel (1961/1979). The depth-realist version of positivism was already present in Carnap's later writing (Steinmetz 2005e). With respect to the doctrine of invariable laws (whether social or natural), Comte's position is identical to this more recent one. Note that my use of the term *scientism* here differs from Camic's in chapter 7 of this volume; he connects it to the turn toward more empirical research in 1920s sociology.

7. I am using the adjective *methodological* here in the sense of *méthodos*, which refers in philosophical contexts to the "pursuit of knowledge, investigation," and by extension "a plan or strategy for carrying out an investigation" (Baxter 2002, 42–43).

Other writers emphasize the adherence of many other founders of U.S. sociology to a version of positivism inspired by Karl Pearson, whose own epistemological views were indebted to Ernst Mach.[8] Franklin Giddings trained a large number of sociologists who went on to shape the leading sociology departments in the United States.[9] During the interwar period, numerous American sociologists endorsed what at the time was called the "natural science" perspective, that is, the "naturalist" view that sociology should pattern itself on the biological and/or physical sciences.[10] In his presidential address to the American Sociological Society in 1926, John L. Gillin (PhD, Columbia, 1906) revealed the positivists' disciplinary ambitions, stating bluntly that "the application of scientific method and the increased emphasis upon objective data have been acting as *selective* agents in consigning these *enemies* of sociology"—theorists and social reformers— "to a deserved desuetude."[11] Philosopher Otto Neurath (1931) was already defending a version of social science based on logical positivism before the war. The positivist philosophers' most influential statements came afterward, culminating in Ernst Nagel's widely read *Structure of Science* (1961). Sociologist George Lundberg, who taught at the University of Washington from 1945 until his retirement in 1961, promoted philosophical foundations for the discipline based on the Vienna school of logical positivism (Lundberg 1939a, 1939b, 1964; Platt and Hoch 1996). Lundberg had earned his doctorate with Giddings's student Stuart Chapin (PhD, Columbia, 1911) at Minnesota in 1925. In his 1943 presidential address to the sociological association, Lundberg referred to the distinction between the "vague processes by which [scientists] arrive at hypotheses" and the rigorous "context of verification." This was an allusion to the distinction between the "context of discovery" and the "context of justification" proposed by philosophers Hans Reichenbach (1938) and Karl Popper (1934). Lundberg's Washington colleague Stuart Dodd (1942) was perhaps the most scientistic adherent of methodological positivism in twentieth-century U.S. sociology.[12] And lest we dismiss positivism as restricted in this period to the Columbia depart-

8. See Platt (1996, 71–72, 76); Giddings (1896); Mayo-Smith (1895). The exalted status of Pearson among these founders and their students (and students' students) is suggested by Stouffer's remarks (1958); see also Bulmer (1984a, 176, 179).

9. These included W. F. Ogburn, Frank A. Ross, F. Stuart Chapin, and Stuart A. Rice.

10. For exemplary naturalist statements by sociologists in this period see Bain (1927, 414; 1935, 486), Cobb (1934), and Chapin (1935c).

11. Gillin (1927a), quoted in Oberschall (1972, 242); my emphasis. The adjective "selective" indexes the prestige of social Darwinism in early American sociology.

12. Dodd's influence and reputation within sociology should not be overstated, of course (Platt 1996).

ment and to the sociological provinces, as some have suggested, we should recall that even the ostensibly antipositivist Talcott Parsons insisted in the 1930s that sociology's goal should be the discovery of "analytical laws" that formalize "a uniform mode of relationship between the values of two of more analytical elements."[13] In 1943 C. Wright Mills (1943) assailed American sociology textbooks for their atomism, empiricism, and doctrines of value neutrality. An analysis of sociology textbooks from this period finds widespread agreement on the need to emulate the natural sciences (McCarthy and Das 1985, 27–30).

A closer look at the pre–World War II period reveals, however, that scientistic positivism was far from hegemonic in the discipline or, more importantly, in the leading departments, during the 1930s and the first half of the 1940s.

Epistemological Stalemate in an Unsettled Field: American Sociology, 1930s–45

American sociology was particularly riven during the ideologically turbulent 1930s.[14] There had already been a decline in the use of the Chicago-style case study, leading to a methodological and theoretical interregnum (Lengermann 1979; Kuklick 1973; Wiley 1979). The Chicago approach was not simply replaced by structural functionalism, as has sometimes been suggested; instead, "grand theory" now coexisted with the "ideographic" case study, both of which were coming under attack by the "natural science" approach. Explicit, philosophically sophisticated resistance to scientism emerged in the discipline during this period (Evans 1986–87, 119). The result was an epistemological stalemate or, better, a sort of pluralism. No single epistemological/methodological position was dominant in the leading departments during the 1930s and early 1940s, with the exceptions of Minnesota and UNC–Chapel Hill.

13. Parsons (1937/1949, 622). Despite Parsons's emphasis on values or norms, he fell into an *objectivist* analysis of the subjective, as Camic (1989, 64–69) argues, reducing it to the single category of the means–ends schema (see below).

14. Many writers on this period acknowledge U.S. sociology's epistemic disunity, although often with disapproval; see, for example, Kuklick (1973), who refers to an "identity crisis" in the profession between 1930 and 1945, based partly on "intellectual obsessions." It seems to me sociological, however, to treat disunity per se as identical to crisis, since all social fields (and all semiotic systems) are constructed around differences. What is distinctive about the 1930s is that no single position was dominant in sociology, lending the field a degree of openness that is unsettling to the same people who have been decrying sociology's "crisis" since the 1970s (see Steinmetz and Chae 2002).

Any interpretation of this pre-1945 lack of consensus would certainly need to attend to both external and internal developments. Outside the academy, wrenching social and economic disruptions provided tactile evidence against any project of subsuming social life under repeatable, general laws (Arendt 1994). The decline of external sources of research support undercut the momentum of many big science projects, although New Deal work relief programs partly compensated for the drop-off (Camic, chap. 7, this volume). The influx of intellectuals from fascist Europe brought a greater level of philosophical sophistication to American sociology, including interest in logical positivism as well as its well-informed critics. For example, Herbert Marcuse's first book in English, *Reason and Revolution* (1941), included an extended critique of positivism. The personnel of American sociology departments became more diverse and less rural although still overwhelmingly white and male.[15] The sociological association was riven into different camps fighting against Chicago's domination, leading to the creation of the *American Sociological Review* and various factions, specialty sections, and regional associations (Camic, chap. 7, this volume; Turner and Turner 1990). Critiques of capitalism, although not inherently linked to antipositivism (witness the scientistic formulations of much Marxist analysis in that period), may have introduced some skepticism about foundation funding, which at the time tended to reward positivist approaches (Ross 1991).

My aim in revisiting this period is not to explain its fractured condition, which would require a different and much longer analysis, but simply to establish it in order to set up a contrast with the postwar era. Sociology between the 1930s and 1945, unlike the discipline during the two postwar decades, was not a well-ordered, hegemonized field. After 1945, by contrast, the methodological positivist definition of field-specific capital came to be almost universally *recognized* by all members of the field, regardless of whether they approved of it or adopted it themselves. The difference between the pre- and postwar periods does not have to do with the *availability* of relevant ideas and procedures, all of which were present even in the nineteenth century. What differed was the effectiveness with which adherents of methodological positivism could defend their position as a general measure of scientific capital.

Before trying to establish the distinctiveness of pre-1945 U.S. sociology

15. Whereas a quarter of the authors of *AJS* articles between 1895 and 1900 were members of the National Conference of Charities and Corrections or the American Prison Congress, this percentage decreased to 4 percent in the 1935–40 volumes (Oberschall 1972, 204, citing Sutherland 1945).

it is important to recall that the multivocality of discourse, perception, and practice is a precondition for the functioning of any field in a sociological sense. A discipline can be divided and heterogeneous and still be "structured in dominance." To use a more current sociological language, a discipline that is internally fragmented can still be structured like a field, with widely acknowledged definitions of distinction. Any social field combines *heterogeneous* practices and perceptions with *homogeneous* principles of domination. Indeed, without some internal diversity (for example, disagreements about epistemology within a social science) there would be no raw material that groups seeking domination could wield as weapons of distinction. Scientific domination does not work by means of intellectual *Gleichschaltung* or an all-encompassing paradigm, along the lines proposed by Thomas Kuhn (1962), by Althusser in his theory of ideology (1971), or by Horkheimer and Adorno in their work on mass culture (1944). On the contrary, for a field to be con-figured in Bourdieu's sense, new differences will be invented or discovered even where they had not been previously perceived. The opposite of a well-structured field is an unsettled field, that is, an assemblage of practices in which no single definition of cultural capital holds sway.

The methodological upshot is that a historical sociology of sociology cannot establish the existence of a dominant intellectual structure simply by examining undergraduate textbooks (e.g., Inkeles 1964, 8–9), the topics of master's and doctoral theses (e.g., Bain 1927), the role of influential leaders like Giddings and his students and students' students (e.g., Turner 1994), or citation lists of the most famous sociologists (e.g., Oromaner 1969), although all of these provide important bits of evidence. Conversely, a historical sociology of sociology cannot establish an open, pluralistic, or fragmented condition simply by pointing to the existence of divisions, conflicts, debates, or dissidents. The mere presence of a C. Wright Mills in postwar U.S. sociology, centrally located at Columbia, does not tell us much about scientific power or scientific pluralism. Nor does the fact that there were as many opponents as there were supporters of the "natural science" approach among ASA presidents during the 1945–65 period reveal a lot about the field's power structure, since all members of the ASA could vote in presidential elections, including those located in less influential depart-ments.[16] Book awards are also an ambiguous criterion of status in an article-

16. None of these "opponents" among ASA presidents rejected the methodological posi-tivist formation vigorously, except for Sorokin late in his career (1956/1976; see below). Par-tial opponents of the natural science perspective among ASA presidents included Louis Wirth, E. Franklin Frazier, Robert C. Angell, Florian Znaniecki, Herbert Blumer, Howard P. Becker, Everett C. Hughes, Pitirim Sorokin, Talcott Parsons, and Robert Merton.

driven field such as that of (postwar) American sociology.[17] The ASA's main book award was named after Robert M. MacIver from 1956 to 1968 and after Pitirim Sorokin between 1968 and 1979. Both writers were associated with elite universities and leading departments, and both rejected the positivist trends in the discipline. MacIver was a "decisively antiscientistic" critic of "neopositivist methodology" all along, and Sorokin had turned harshly against the scientistic mainstream in the 1950s. Some responded by calling Sorokin shrill and eccentric, and indeed, his position in *Fads and Foibles in Modern Sociology* (1956) was eccentric in that decade.[18]

It makes more sense to look at the epistemological positions and scientific politics that were associated with the top-ranked departments and leading sociological publications.[19] Both of the leading journals, *American Journal of Sociology* (*AJS*) and *American Sociological Review* (*ASR*), were edited before 1945 by sociologists who were critical of methodological positivism. Opponents of the "natural science" approach in sociology were not only employed by the leading departments but also headed some of them. It is impossible to measure the epistemic disunity of the prewar period or the dominance of the positivist position after the war in quantitative terms, since many texts are internally heterogeneous. Nor can methodological positivism be identified by the use of quantitative methods. Patterns of citations in the *ASR* or *AJS* cannot be used to track dominant epistemologies, since only a handful of books or articles were cited more than once during any given year.[20] It makes sense to examine these journals in more substantive terms, however, and to look more closely at five of the leading departments in this period: Columbia, Chicago, Michigan, Wisconsin, and Harvard. These departments produced the largest number of PhD's among ASA members during the 1950-59 period, which is linked to one of the

17. Thus most research on the diffusion and status rewards of "core publications" in sociology deals exclusively with articles; see, for example, Oromaner (1986).

18. First quote from Hałas (2001, 28); second quote from Coser (1971, 508); see also Sorokin (1956).

19. As identified by peer rankings by all heads of sociology departments and by statistics on the suppliers of PhD's to those departments. See also Camic, chap. 7, this volume, who names the same departments as top ranked in this era.

20. A preliminary analysis of the *ASR* for 1950 found that only a few books or articles were cited twice, and only three were cited more than twice. Each book or article was assigned one point regardless of the number of times it was cited in a given ASR article, two points if it was cited in two different *ASR* articles, and so forth. Self-citations were eliminated. This suggests that epistemological homogeneity is revealed not through the citation of common texts but through similar assumptions. Thanks to Prasanna Baragi for help with this citation analysis.

main correlates of departmental prestige, the exchange of PhD's among departments (Burris 2004). The fact that the top-ranked departments in a given discipline are not necessarily located at the top-ranked universities means that we have more diversity even within this small sample than meets the eye. Two departments that were highly ranked in the interwar period but that are excluded from this analysis are UNC–Chapel Hill and Minnesota.[21] The first of these was described by Turner and Turner (1990, 52) as a "bastion of correlational methods," and Minnesota was given over to "a positivistic orientation" (Martindale 1976b, 77).

The argument for focusing on leading departments rather than, say, a random sample is also directed against the notion (Shils 1972) that peripheries typically share the same values with the center. Although all members of a settled field agree on what counts as symbolic capital, the dominated may still hold proudly to a dissonant set of "values" and even develop a taste for necessity, a taste for their own cultural domination.[22] We should not exaggerate the importance of dissidence or difference, which are as likely to reproduce power hierarchies as they are to disrupt the operations of a field.[23]

The other aspects of this small sample that are worth mentioning are the geographic location of the departments and the distinction between private and public universities. Sociological positivism was not concentrated in public as opposed to private universities, or in the Midwest as opposed to the East Coast during the interwar period (nor is it distributed that way today). Columbia played a central role in the positivist disciplinary formation before the 1930s and after 1945, while Chicago and Michigan were the *least* positivist of the leading departments before 1930. Nor should the impact of postwar Fordism on sociologists—an argument I take up in the conclusion—be understood as being mediated by their physical proximity to the sites of Fordist industrial production, since Fordism at that time was as much about consumption and federal-level policies as it was about the point of production. Fordism is named after a social experiment that started in Highland Park and Dearborn at a time when the Michigan sociology department, under the leadership of Charles Cooley, firmly rejected scientism. For that matter, even the Ford Motor Company's own "sociological depart-

21. Figures on departmental rankings from Riley (1960, 918). Minnesota, which ranked near the top of the prestige rankings in 1934 (Burris 2004, 241), is analyzed by Martindale (1976b).

22. Bourdieu (1984); see Breslau (2005) for an example of this from the economics field.

23. Of course it would still be useful to compare the elite departments with less highly ranked ones, along the lines of Bourdieu's comparative studies of prestigious and dominated groups in fields like art and music.

ment" pursued some remarkably unscientific strategies, like the famous "melting pot" ceremony for Americanizing immigrant workers.[24] Postwar Fordism as a societywide phenomenon was unevenly distributed across geographic space. The U.S. South and rural America in general had less direct contact with Fordism. But as a "cultural dominant" it shaped everyday life in Cambridge and New York, Ann Arbor and Chicago, and all of the other sites of the leading departments.

EPISTEMOLOGY AND THE LEADING U.S. SOCIOLOGY DEPARTMENTS, 1930s–1945

COLUMBIA. As one of the first departments, Columbia occupies a central place in narratives of American sociology. From the beginning Columbia was a center of the "natural science" approach. This is usually attributed to Giddings, Columbia's first sociology professor and a leading figure there for almost forty years. Giddings insisted on empiricism, scientism, and statistical methods (for others, if not always for himself). He called for "men" who were "not afraid to work; who will get busy with the adding machine and the logarithms, and give us *exact studies,* such as we get from the psychological laboratories, not to speak of the biological and physical laboratories. Sociology can be made an exact, quantitative science, if we can get industrious men interested in it" (Bernard 1909, 196, quoting from Gidding's response to a questionnaire). According to Seymour Martin Lipset (1955, 286), another Columbia PhD, "philosophically [Giddings] always remained a positivist" (see also Manicas 1991, 65; and Hinkle 1994, 34–46).

At the same time there was, in contrast to Chicago, "a strong theoretical element in the sociological milieu at Columbia" during the 1920s and 1930s, one that was also promoted by Giddings. Doctoral dissertations were written on "the works of the great European sociologists" by students like Theodore Abel (1929), who was praised by Giddings and appointed at Columbia in 1929 as lecturer and two years later as assistant professor.[25]

24. In 1916, "Ford rented the largest public meeting hall in the city. On the stage stood a replica immigrant ship and in front of it a giant kettle, a 'melting pot' . . . the ceremony literally stripped the worker of his past identity and gave him a new one: 'Down the gangplank came the members of the class dressed in their national garbs . . . [then they descended] into the Ford melting pot and disappeared.' Teachers used long paddles to 'stir' the pot. Before long, 'the pot began to boil over and out came the men dressed in their best American clothes and waving American flags'" (Zieger and Gall 2002).

25. Quote from Hałas (2001, 31); see also Lipset (1955, 294). Platt reports that Abel "went so far as to take the opportunity to criticize his colleagues" for their "undue empiricism" in comments to a member of a congressional committee (1996, 202n).

Robert MacIver, a theorist, ethnographer, and explicit antipositivist, was recruited in 1929. In a paper given to the American Sociological Society meetings in 1931 MacIver attacked the "would-be imitators of the natural sciences," especially the "extreme behaviourists," who "would even jettison their proper subject in order to claim the name of science for a beggarly residue" by imitating "at all costs the mathematicians and the physicists." For MacIver, "imitation, though always bearing the signs of the inferiority complex, may nevertheless succeed when, in following its original, it is applying like tools to like materials. But it is most apt to fail when it applies like tools to unlike materials, and this is just what the social scientist is in danger of doing" (1931, 27–28). MacIver opposed empiricism, arguing that "science is never . . . merely empirical" but is "concerned with phenomena as they reveal an order, a system of relationships." Social relations, unlike natural ones, were inherently both subjective or meaningful and objective. Hence the impossibility of a purely statistical sociology: "we do not comprehend legal codes by measuring them" (MacIver 1931, 33, 28). Three years later MacIver suggested "that social relationships are in such flux that no laws can be formulated" at all. By 1937, as the global social crisis deepened, he held "that the task of sociology is essentially that of interpretation" (Abel 2001, 158, 252).

Other Columbia faculty working in theoretical and qualitative ways in the 1930s included Bernhard Stern and Robert Lynd (C. Wright Mills did not arrive until 1945). Stern was a Marxist in the 1930s who wrote for the journal *New Masses* and founded *Science and Society,* in addition to writing numerous books in the sociology of medicine and other fields. Before moving to Columbia, Stern had been fired in 1930 from the University of Washington for being "too liberal" and was subsequently "harassed by the Catholic Church and academic administrators during his years at the University of Michigan" (Peace 1998, 85). His interest in sociology had been awakened by Charles Cooley at Michigan in 1920. As a student at Columbia, where he was influenced by Franz Boas, who by that time was quite skeptical about "the possibility of establishing significant 'laws' in the cultural realm" (Stocking 2001, 40). Stern rejected the approach of Giddings and the social Darwinists and aligned himself instead with founding sociologists like E. A. Ross and Albion Small.[26] Summarizing his own views in 1949, seven years before his death, Stern wrote that "if the social sciences are denuded

---

26. See Stern (1959a), vii–x; Merton (1957a). Stern had written his dissertation with Ogburn at Columbia, who strongly supported him; see Bloom (1990), who also discusses Stern's appearance before HUAC and the support offered to him by his colleagues at Columbia.

of value judgments they are really naked of value" and condemned to waver "between the discourse of shallow empiricism, which seeks refuge in the assemblage of particulars, and abstract philosophizing" (1959b, 33). His comment on "history and sociology" is startlingly contemporary:

> Sociologists once talked of imbuing historians with correct perspectives. But now the situation is frequently reversed and it is the historian who can serve as an example to sociologists. . . . The frailty of sociologists lies in their tendency to abstract from historical reality 'ideal types' that are applicable everywhere and nowhere, beyond time and space, and hence in a netherworld of unreality. . . . Sociologists do not stress the great importance of the dimension of time. . . . It renders much of attitude testing fatuous. . . . Sociology will remain one-dimensional and hence shallow, and its concepts empty shells . . . unless the examination of historical concepts becomes a meaningful and disciplined task of sociologists. (1959b, 34)

A much more influential figure than Stern at Columbia and in national sociology was Robert Lynd, author with Helen Lynd of *Middletown: A Study in Contemporary American Culture* (1929). Although the Lynds had not felt it necessary to defend their noncomparative, nonquantitative approach in *Middletown,* their follow-up study in 1937, *Middletown Revisited,* insisted that the "big story lay beyond 'economics statistics' in the 'drama of competing values'" (Camic, chap. 7, this volume). Despite his empiricist stance (Abel 2001, 267–68), Robert Lynd's 1939 *Knowledge for What?* rejected the "natural science" paradigm, ontological atomism, and doctrines of value neutrality. Here he described history as "the most venerable of the social sciences" and speculated (like Stern) that sociologists would begin to do their own historical writing. Lynd understood sociology as inherently concerned with cultural meaning; indeed, sociology itself was for him just another "culture-crystallization." Most strikingly, in light of the clamoring of the "natural science" crowd during the 1920s, Lynd suggested that the social sciences should emulate the humanities and seek a closer rapprochement with "novelists, artists, and poets," who provide "insights that go beyond the cautious generalizations of social science" (Lynd 1939, 116, 129, 138, 153–54, 178).

Along with MacIver, Lynd helped Max Horkheimer make the connections that allowed the Frankfurt Institut für Sozialforschung to move to Columbia (Jay 1973, 39; Wiggershaus 1994). Although the Institute jealously guarded its autonomy, it was not isolated from the Columbia sociology department. The Institute's *Zeitschrift für Sozialforschung* (renamed *Studies in Philosophy and Social Science* in 1940) carried articles by members of the Columbia faculty, and Institute members lectured and taught at Columbia after 1936 (Jay 1973, 40, 114–16, 188, 192). One émigré who received support from the Institute in the 1930s was Paul Lazarsfeld, who was recruited by the Columbia sociology department in 1941. Lazarsfeld worked on some Institute projects, including the study of German workers' mentalities that was headed by Erich Fromm, and he collaborated briefly with Adorno in the context of his Princeton Office of Radio Research (forerunner of the Bureau of Applied Social Research at Columbia). Lazarsfeld's Rockefeller Foundation grant allowed Adorno to write the first of his famous essays on jazz music and the "regression of listening" (Adorno 1938; Béthune 2003).[27] This relationship is even more remarkable when we consider that the *Zeitschrift* was publishing critiques of logical positivism by Marcuse. An enthusiastic review of *Knowledge for What?* by Franz Neumann (1939) summarized Lynd's book as "fundamentally a renunciation of positivism and empiricism" and "even more important because it appears at a time when logical empiricism, which in the United States is closely linked to sociology, makes ever growing claims." Lazarsfeld published an article (1941) in the volume of the *Zeitschrift* that carried a review of Marcuse's *Reason and Revolution*. Such close proximity between critical and affirmative sociology (to use Horkheimer's [1937] terms) would no longer be possible even several years later.

CHICAGO. Chicago was the first American sociology department (founded in 1892) and was considered to be the leading department throughout the first three decades of the twentieth century. The founder of the department and the *AJS*, Albion Small, earned his PhD at Johns Hopkins in 1889 with a thesis on the birth of American nationalism and the Continental Congress (Small 1890). Small had been exposed to the German historicist school of political economy during his studies in Berlin and Leipzig (1879–81), and he wrote a detailed studied of the central European cameralist tradition (Small 1909a). Although Small eventually moved toward a version of scientific naturalism, his early predilections for abstract theory and concrete historical studies set the tone in the department and the *AJS* during its early years.[28] The central figure in the department's rise to prominence was

27. After Adorno's falling out with Lazarsfeld, his music project was cut from the renewed grant in the fall of 1939 (Jay 1973, 223).

28. See Vidich (1985, chap. 8); Dibble (1975); and Fuhrman (1978, 98). American sociologists long recognized the relevance of the nineteenth-century German methods debate to their own conflicts (Mills 1943, 168; Hinkle 1994, 48–57). On Small and Giddings see also O'Connor (1942).

Robert E. Park, who taught at Chicago from 1914 until 1933. Park had studied in Germany with Georg Simmel—his only formal sociology training—
and he wrote his PhD thesis in Heidelberg under Wilhelm Windelband
(Coser 1977, 368), according to whom the social sciences belonged to the
Geisteswissenschaften, which investigate unique and subjectively meaningful phenomena. Park's antiscientistic tendencies were even stronger than
Small's, at least initially. Park was openly disdainful of statistical social science (Bulmer 1984a, 153), although he was not averse to importing natural
science models, for instance, in coining the term *human ecology* and in instructing his students to avoid subjective value-judgments (Camic, chap. 7,
this volume). The "Chicago style" case study, associated with Park and
Ernest Burgess, eschewed grand theory and conceptual categories and remained strictly empirical. At the same time its focus on detailed studies of
unique places avoided the positivist covering-law format.[29] Some of the
early Chicago case studies were presented in narrative form, lending themselves to a more historical understanding of the task of sociology. For a variety of reasons (some of them detailed by Abbott 1999), the Chicago sociology department did not move solidly into the scientistic camp until the
second half of the 1950s (Fine 1995). Other faculty who did not fit the positivist mold at Chicago included W. I. Thomas (at Chicago 1895–1918), Florian Znaniecki (1914–20), Louis Wirth (at Chicago through 1951), Everett
Hughes (through 1960), and Herbert Blumer (who was at Chicago until
1952 before moving to Berkeley). Statistical approaches were represented in
the department after the recruitment of William F. Ogburn in 1927, but Ogburn later recalled that he found at Chicago a "much more hostile attitude
to statistics than had existed at Columbia" (Bulmer 1984a, 181). Louis Wirth,
who taught at Chicago starting in 1926, supported Ogburn's appointment
and was seen as part of the empirical wing of the department. But Wirth
expressed dismay in 1947 about sociology's "aura of pseudo-scientific
glamour." As editor of the *AJS,* Wirth criticized the growing enthusiasm for
"complicated scientific gadgets" and "super-refined techniques for ordering and summarizing the . . . accumulation of mountains of authentic but
meaningless facts" (1947, 274).

MICHIGAN. One of the leading proponents of what is nowadays sometimes called "humanistic" sociology was Charles Horton Cooley, a founder
of the American Sociological Association and one of its early presidents

---

29. The positivist antipathy to the case study was already well established in the 1930s and
continues to this day (Steinmetz 2004a).

(1918). Cooley taught the first sociology course at Michigan in 1894 and was a professor there until his death in 1929. Cooley's own master thinkers included William James and Ralph Waldo Emerson, and he had taken courses with John Dewey in the Michigan philosophy department. He was also acquainted with George Herbert Mead, who taught at Michigan while Cooley was in graduate school there (Cooley 1930b, 6; Coser 1977, 343). Cooley's "ideal sociologist" was Goethe, and in his personal journals and "several of [his] books there are more references to Goethe than to any social scientist" (Coser 1971, 319; Cooley 1918, 402).

Cooley's concept of the "looking glass self" (1927, 194) and his recognition of the inherently ideational-meaningful character of social practice and the need to study social life in its total context are often hailed as examples of the alternatives to positivism that were available in early twentieth-century U.S. sociology. One study of early American sociologists concludes that Cooley was the only one who "did not express a belief in the discovery of social laws" (Fuhrman 1978, 100, 96). Hinkle (1994, 61) describes Cooley as being firmly antipositivist. He is perhaps the only American sociologist cited approvingly by Adorno (1991, 121). For U.S. sociologists in the first third of the twentieth century he provided a bridge to the earlier "revolt against positivism" (Hughes 1977, 33) among the generation of the 1890s.

Cooley is best known for his argument that social research had to be grounded in "sympathetic participation" because "the Social Order can be understood only as a complex of ideas." Cooley gave the example of "the Virgin" in 1200 AD, who, though ectoplasmic, "was a most important member of the social order" (Cooley journals, March 16, 1927, vol. 23, 56). As his nephew noted, Cooley "was preaching *verstehende Soziologie* in *Human Nature and the Social Order*" (published 1902) before Weber began publishing on the topic, and many years before Weber became well known in U.S. sociology (Angell n.d., 10a; Platt 1985).[30] For Cooley, the "materials themselves" of social research were "living wholes which can only be apprehended by a trained sympathy in contact with them" (1927, 156). Sociologists who try to "dodge the mental and emotional processes in which society consists," Cooley argued, were engaging in "pseudo-science" (1927, 154). This view distinguishes Cooley from Ward and the other first-generation theorists in Amer-

30. Parsons (1968, 55) believed that the "intellectual traditions which set the stage for Weber were . . . somewhat unfamiliar to Cooley, ignoring the fact that Cooley had ordered Weber's (1905/1958) *Protestant Ethic* for the Michigan library and had taken courses in "foundational problems of ethnics" and "general natural history" in Munich in 1884 (Angell n.d., 9; Cooley papers, Bentley Historical Library, box 2, folder of student notes from 1884).

ican sociology who emphasized "the virtues of working at a remove from" the social object of study (Breslau 1990b, 427). Cooley found statistics deeply misleading in sociology, even though he had received training in statistics as an engineer (Wood 1930, 710; Angell n.d., 10). The "exclusive devotion of one class of students to statistical and descriptive work of narrow scope" was as problematic as the devotion of a second group to "philosophical dissertations on method, general laws, etc" (Cooley journals, vol. 10, 24). Sociologists' belief that "only quantitative methods should be used" was "an idea springing ... from an obsolescent philosophy," one that "physicists themselves are beginning to discard" (1928b, 248, 249n1). Cooley especially recommended Whitehead's *Science and the Modern World*, since the author was "an eminent physicist" who advocated not a "mechanistic and atomistic perspective" but an organic one that also "answers to the evident facts of society" (1928b, 249n1). Cooley recommended "life-like description covering a period of time," which he called the "life-study méthod," a method of "grasping life in its organic reality" (1928b, 248). Such studies could certainly be empirical, as long as they attended to mental states and were conducted in a dialogue with social theory. But statistics could never approach the level of "descriptive precision that may be attained by the skilful use of language, supplemented, perhaps, by photography, phonography and other mechanical devices" (1928b, 249). Other good models for sociology included psychoanalysis, anthropology, photography, and literature (1928b, 250-53; Cooley journals, vol. 22, 51).

Prediction was for Cooley a "false ideal inconsiderately borrowed from the provinces of natural science" (Cooley 1918, 398). This belief stemmed from his view of social reality as a web of conscious (and unconscious) meaning and intention. In social life, "nothing is fixed or independent, everything is plastic" (44). A decade later Cooley responded in more detail to the sociological advocates of prediction:

> Generally speaking the less *life* there is in a phenomenon, the less it is involved in that complex and cumulative interaction that in its culminating human form tends to bring *everything* into play at once, —the more possible is exact understanding and prediction. But, you say, some phenomena of life (of heredity, for example), can be shown to be precise and predictable. This is true but only shows that the life-stream contains, as it were, undissolved mechanical elements which do not change their form. (Cooley journals, vol. 22, 103)

At best, he believed, "one who claims to be a sociologist" might "attempt predictions at least as to the proximate future of the main social currents" (vol. 22, 104).

Cooley was open-minded about the various forms that social knowledge might take. He insisted on a sociology that was both interpretive and causal, and he was therefore skeptical about merely descriptive approaches. Nonetheless, within the dominant split in U.S. sociology in the interwar years, he defended the increasingly embattled case study as against statistical surveys, maintaining that "the phenomena of life are often better distinguished by pattern than by quantity." "What," he asked, "could be more precise, as a record of visible human behavior, than a motion picture? Yet it is not quantitative. Its precision is total, not incremental, a matter of patterns rather than of minute differences in space" (Cooley 1930a, 314). The sociologist's interpretative work could not take a standardized form but needed to be "imaginative" and rooted in a "dramatic vision" (Cooley 1918, 395-97). Indeed, the "'scientific' and the 'literary'" were not "antithetical terms." Sociology was at once a science, a philosophy, and "an art also" (Cooley 1927, 160). As a result, "the method appropriate to sociology must be learned in part from the great men of letters, who alone have dealt strongly with the facts of human life" (Cooley journals, vol. 13, 48). In a prescient warning against what Adorno called the "higher forms of reification" occasioned by mass-produced "teamwork" in social science (Adorno 1972, 498), Cooley noted that all sociological work was "in a certain sense, autobiographic" (Cooley 1930a, 317; 1918, 402, 404). His own writing was personal, conversational, and essayistic.

Cooley was thus the only founder of a leading U.S. sociology department who firmly opposed scientism. But Anthony Oberschall is grievously mistaken in his claim that Cooley prevented *empirical* sociologists from being hired at Michigan—or else he is confusing the adjectives "empirical" and "empiricist" (1972, 223-24). Cooley's hires were sympathetic to his holistic and interpretive approach, but all of them engaged in empirical research.[31] Most consequentially for the future of the department, Cooley hired his nephew, Robert Cooley Angell, as assistant professor in 1924. Angell's first book, *The Campus*, was based on Cooley's method of "sympathetic insight" and defined its object as "a mental unity" (Angell 1928, viii, 1).

The year after Cooley's death in 1929, Michigan hired Roderick McKen-

31. For example, Cooley hired Arthur Evans Wood, a progressive criminologist and penologist, in 1917 as an instructor. Wood stayed at Michigan until his retirement in 1951. Cooley also hired rural sociologist Roy Hinman Holmes as assistant professor in 1922 and Lowell Julliard Carr in 1925. Carr was a former *Detroit Free Press* writer who had studied in London with Hobhouse, Malinowski, and others and who worked in the fields of industrial sociology and delinquency (Cooley 1930b). Information from the University of Michigan, *Proceedings of the Board of Regents,* and *Annual Register,* various years.

zie, who chaired the department until his death a decade later. McKenzie was the creator, along with Robert Park and Ernest Burgess, of "human ecology," and he is credited with writing the first monograph rooted in that perspective (Gaziano 1996; M. Gross 2002, 31). McKenzie aligned Michigan firmly with the Chicago side of the opposition between the case study and statistical surveys—that is, with a position that was perhaps empiricist but not overly scientistic.[32] McKenzie brought in Chicago sociologists Robert Park, Louis Wirth, Herbert Blumer, and Ellsworth Faris as visiting professors. In 1938 two young instructors were added to the teaching staff as instructors, Werner Landecker and Amos Hawley. Landecker taught European social theory in the department for many years and contributed to theories of social class crystallization. He had written a dissertation in Berlin in 1936 on legal sociology that attacked legal positivism (Lüschen 2002).[33]

McKenzie's successor after his death in 1940 was Robert Cooley Angell, who had been promoted to full professor in 1935 and remained chair of the department until 1952. Angell's long tenure thus began during the *Sattelzeit* (saddle period) between the interwar pluralism in U.S. sociology and the postwar hegemony of methodological positivism. As at Chicago, the consolidation of positivist control did not occur overnight or immediately after 1945 but emerged during the 1950s. Angell's initial hiring efforts were marked by his leaning toward Cooley's tradition. In 1940 he wrote to Ernest Burgess at Chicago,

> we are looking for a social psychologist to add to our staff. . . . I am very anxious that we obtain a man who would be sympathetic to the Cooley tradition and at the same time one who would carry forward fruitful research. It seems to be a difficult combination since most able researchers are being developed in statistics and nothing else. I should want our men to be competent in statistics but would also wish him to have conceptual originality. (Angell to Ernest Burgess, November 5, 1940, 1-2, Angell papers)

Angell's first hire, in 1941, was social psychologist Theodor Newcomb, who was about to publish the results of his landmark four-year study of attitudinal change among students at Bennington College. At the time this

32. As Gaziano (1996) notes, little of the work by McKenzie, or by Park and Burgess for that matter, actually refers to evolutionary ideas.

33. Landecker and his family had belonged to the German-Jewish *Kulturbund* in Berlin. Along with five other refugees he was brought to the University of Michigan in 1937 with funds raised by the University of Michigan Hillel Foundation. He became assistant professor in 1942-43, obtained a PhD in sociology in 1947, and retired in 1981. His dissertation was finally published in 1999.

represented an innovative hire, since, as his later colleague Daniel Katz writes, "it was unusual for sociology departments to offer tenure appointments to psychologists, but . . . Angell saw in [Newcomb] a true social psychologist in the tradition of Charles Horton Cooley" (Katz 1986, 295). At the same time, as David Riesman remarked on a "follow-up study in the 1960s of the Bennington alumnae whom Newcomb had studied in the early years," what seems missing in such attitudinal research was "any ethnographic material" that might provide the reader with some idea "what the scholars are really scholarly about" or "how creative and idiosyncratic the Creative Individualists really are" (Riesman 1968, 628). Although Parsons imagined psychoanalysis as part of his postwar interdisciplinary social relations mixture, the version of social psychology represented by Newcomb (quantitative and based on surveys or experiments) pointed in a different direction.

Newcomb was called away almost immediately after arriving in Michigan to work for four years "for the government in the Bureau of Overseas Intelligence in order to decipher foreign broadcasts and gain an understanding of enemy morale" (Johnson and Nichols 1998, 57). Angell later noted that by late 1940 "the likelihood that the country would soon be at war was obvious" and "it was not a time to attempt innovations in academic departments." Angell himself left for service in the army air force in 1942 and remained "absent on leave" through 1945 (Angell 1980, 76).

Angell's own research in the interwar period remained loyal to the basic principles of Cooley's approach. His third book, *The Integration of American Society* (1941), was discursive and theoretical and contained no tables or figures at all. Angell continued in the interwar period to defend Cooley's view that only a "pseudo-science" could deny that "the essential facts of social life are mental" and believed "that the sociologist must deal in large measure with interactive behavior." This entailed "the use of the case method in one of its numerous forms" (1930, 340-41; 1931, 204). According to Angell, "the quarrel which many of us have with the usual use of statistical analysis in sociology is that it deals with small segments abstracted from tremendously complex wholes and does not preserve what seems most important—the pattern or configuration of the parts of the whole" (1933, 85). Like Cooley he held that statistics were often "out of place" and a "source of . . . laborious futility" (1930, 342). Against "the school" of the positivist-oriented sociologist F. Stuart Chapin and Ogburn, which "advocates the quantification of our data," Angell defended the position of "the late Professor Cooley and Professor MacIver," who feel "that measurement is only applicable to external things and that such externals constitute only the shell of social relations, not their essence" (Angell 1932, 208). Statistical research that failed to enquire into what we would nowadays call the causal mechanisms producing the relationship would remain inadequate. Angell recommended instead a research design that would select "fairly homogenous" entities for study and focus on the effects of one "condition" or mechanism (1931, 205).

The study that grew out of this methodological orientation was *The Family Encounters the Depression* (Angell 1936). The book was closer in style to Shaw's *The Jack-Roller* (1930) or to Thomas and Znaniecki's *The Polish Peasant* (1918–20) in that each case was presented in the form of a short (six- to twelve-page) narrative rather than being disaggregated into "variables." Angell made clear that he was interested in causal relations, however, namely, in the impact of a "severe decrease in income from accustomed sources" resulting from the economic depression on family life (1930, 258). He was groping toward means of doing "statistical analysis" in a way that "would preserve the wholeness of the cases instead of mutilating them to the extent most statistical analysis does" (Angell n.d., 25). But the family narratives are the most (indeed the only) interesting aspect of this study from our own contemporary point of view. As with Shaw, Thomas and Znaniecki, McKenzie, and other sociologists teaching or trained at Chicago in the 1920s and 1930s, the key to the continuing readability of works like this is the authors' commitment to a holistic case-study method as against the replacement of the names of people and places by the names of "variables."

Another way of classifying work like Angell's *Family* was as "documentary" research. British filmmaker John Grierson had appropriated the term to describe Robert Flaherty's ethnographic film *Moana* in 1926, and it later was turned into a noun. In the social sciences, *documentary* was used as an adjective to describe qualitative source materials, typically usually sources produced by others (Glaser and Strauss 1967, 161). Because of his well-known belief that sociology had to be based on "sympathetic insight" gained through and perhaps recorded and presented in the form of qualitative documents, Angell was invited in 1940 by Ernest Burgess to contribute the chapter on sociology to a planned SSRC volume titled *The Use of Personal Documents in History,* whose publication was delayed by the war until 1945. In his chapter Angell singled out authors such as Franklin Frazier, Clifford Shaw, Edwin H. Sutherland, Frederic M. Thrasher, and Harvey Zorbaugh as leading examples of the documentary approach in sociology. For Angell, personal documents were one way for sociologists to grasp "the objectives toward which men are striving and how . . . situations are interpreted" (Angell 1945, 178). Angell saw no reason why the term *nomo-*

thetic could not be used also to "cover laws that have been worked out for, and are applicable to, individual cases only" (229). Needless to say, this definition of the words *nomothetic* and *law* departed sharply from positivist understandings. Angell again insisted that sociologists had "no option" other than to engage in "sympathetic understanding," that is, in the "painstaking plodding along the trail which Cooley and Mead long since blazed," even though "many have gone to the extreme" of believing "that facts could speak for themselves" (230–31).

If we follow Cooley's lead and attempt to summarize the interwar field of U.S. sociology in terms of participants' own understandings, it seems that the basic conflict pitted advocates of statistical surveys and experiments against champions of more holistic case studies. The latter were pursued in a more psychological and cultural vein (like Angell) or in a more materialist vein, as in McKenzie (1923). Angell's work after 1930 embodied a middle-ground interpretivist position associated with his illustrious relative and the increasingly prestigious "scientific" approach. Between 1930 and 1945 his research seems to express the balance of epistemological forces in the discipline at large. As we shall see, he tried to continue to reach a kind of compromise in departmental appointments after the war, but forces larger than his own limited power as departmental chair pulled the department in the positivist direction.

WISCONSIN. Edward A. Ross, longtime chairman at Wisconsin and another founder of American sociology, opposed making sociology scientific at the cost of political relevance (M. Gross 2002). Ross was internationally oriented, writing on the Russian Revolution firsthand (Ross 1918, 1921b, 1923) and visiting and reporting on numerous other countries, including China, India, Mexico, Portuguese Africa, and South Africa. This global perspective stood in marked contrast to the U.S. centrism of most interwar and postwar American sociology (Connell 1997; Oberschall 1972, 224–25). Ross criticized the "natural science" crowd for describing society as a "theater of mechanical forces." Unlike positivists nowadays, Ross did not see causal and interpretive knowledge as alternatives but insisted instead on "a causative interpretation of social facts" that "must consider the thoughts and feelings of the units whose behavior is to be explained" (1903, 114). Something of an interpretivist, Ross criticized sociology's fondness for "the objective statement of the behavior of associated men in preference to the subjective interpretation" (1903, 106). Of course his well-known *Social Control*, first published in 1896, was framed broadly in the terms of the social evolutionary views that were widespread in the nineteenth century. Just a few years later, however, he rejected the notion that "culture epochs answer to the gradations in the intellectual life of mankind" and insisted that "it is vain . . . to correlate closely the actual course of evolution of a society with intellectual development, seeing that so many other factors influence it" (1903, 111). Here his words sound quite contemporary—or like a throwback to Herder: "Far from traveling a common highway the peoples have followed routes as various as have been their conditions of life. . . . Vain, likewise, is it to frame a universal law for the succession of political forms" or social ones (1903, 115–16; cf. Gaonkar 2001 and Noyes 2006). Half a century later he argued that the sociologist cannot conduct true experiments but is "really a field observer with a notebook" and insisted that transhistorical generalizations were impossible in sociology since "the behavior of man varies so much from age to age" (1945, 491–92).

Howard P. Becker, who was hired to replace Ross, was a social theorist who had translated Leopold von Wiese's *Systematic Sociology* (1932). Becker attacked scientism in his writings and in clashes at Madison with Ogburn's student, statistician T. C. McCormick (Martindale 1982, 31, 35, 38). In 1934 Becker coauthored *The Fields and Methods of Sociology* with Luther Lee Bernard, a student of Albion Small and president of the American Sociological Society in 1932. Although Bernard had initially defended behaviorism, he was one of several sociologists in the 1930s and 1940s who decried the putative links between positivism and fascism (Bannister 1992).[34] However exaggerated these arguments, the discussion is suggestive of the splintered and nonhegemonized character of U.S. sociology from the 1930s to 1945. Hans Gerth came to Madison in 1940 and, according to C. Wright Mills, was "the only man worth listening to in this department" (quoted in Martindale 1982, 2; see also 27). Gerth had studied with Horkheimer, Adorno, and Fromm in Frankfurt during the early 1930s (Greffrath 1982, 18). He harshly criticized the ahistoricism and antitheoretical bent of U.S. sociology (Gerth 1959). Mills himself was a strong local presence during his two years as a student at Wisconsin (1939–40) and was already publishing prolifically.

HARVARD. Harvard is a special case, and discussed mainly in the next section, because the sociology department was founded only in 1931 when Pitirim Sorokin was hired and then was dissolved into the new interdisciplinary Department of Social Relations in 1946. During the 1930s Sorokin

34. This anticipated the arguments of other sociologists like Frank Hartung (1944, 337), Marcuse (1941) and Horkheimer and Adorno (1944), which linked positivism to Nazism (Bannister 1992, 185). Bernard provocatively characterized sociologists who "aped the physical scientists" as "Fascists at heart" and occasionally in point of fact (Bernard 1940, 344, 342, 340).

was seen as "a leading figure in American sociological positivism." He had received his training at the Psycho-Neurological Institute in St. Petersburg (Nichols 1992, 215; Sorokin 1963, 67–73). Sorokin's defense of a scientific approach to sociology, in contrast to the reformist and religious precedents that had dominated sociological teaching at Harvard before his appointment, gave him the reputation of a positivist, but his writing was more complicated. One of Sorokin's major works, *Social and Cultural Dynamics* (1937–41), rejected empiricist claims to exclusivity, arguing that "Sensate culture" was just one of three different forms of truth. But as Hans Speier pointed out in a review of the book, Sorokin's study was itself "imbued with the spirit of the doctrine that he desires to refute" and was "expressive" or "derivative" of its own civilization rather than being a critique of it. Sorokin "discusses the philosophical problems which he raises . . . with the help of quantitative methods" without ever asking about the adequacy of these methods for this sort of question, that is, "without ever disentangling the ethical problem of what is good from the essentially meaningless one" of trying to *quantify* the good (Speier 1948, 891). Although Sorokin now proposed a thoroughly culturalist interpretation of society that flew in the face of his own earlier behaviorism, he saw societies as progressing through cultural stages in a predictable logic of development, in a sort of idealist mirror image of the orthodox Marxism that he rejected. Sorokin thus exemplifies the widespread phenomenon in this period of epistemically hybrid sociology, while the work of Adorno, on the one hand, and Lundberg, on the other, represent the purified epistemic extremes.

OTHER INDICATORS OF THE EPISTEMOLOGICAL STANDOFF IN THE DISCIPLINE BEFORE 1945

The *ASR* reveals an epistemological and methodological diversity in the decade before 1945 that is striking in comparison with subsequent decades. Theoretical articles only declined gradually in the journal's pages (Wilner 1985, 16, table 10). The first two volumes of the *ASR* ran essays on psychoanalysis by Karen Horney (1936), "Language, Logic, and Culture" by C. Wright Mills (written while he was still an undergraduate at Texas), and on topics like "imagination in social science" (Bowman 1936) and Lenin's theory of revolution (F. Becker 1937). The journal carried a critique of Comtean positivism by the founder of the original version of critical realism, philosopher Roy Wood Sellars (1939). Anthropologists were free to publish discussions of the culture concept in the *ASR* during this period, a topic that would be exiled from sociology after the war when Kroeber and

Parsons (1958) divided up the social-ontological field like the European powers splitting up the colonized world at the Berlin West Africa Conference.

Another sign of the philosophically labile condition of U.S. sociology in the 1930s concerns its relationship to Freud. Psychoanalysis is often difficult to reconcile with empiricism and aculturalist behaviorism, even though it is open to biologizing interpretations (Elliott 2005; Jacoby 1983) and was used by some early sociologists in politically conservative ways (Schwendinger and Schwendinger 1974, 345–80). Cooley (1907, 675) had already argued at the first annual meeting of the American Sociological Society in 1906 that the "social mind" had to be seen as encompassing an *unconscious* dimension. Even the would-be positivist Read Bain was driven into a more epistemically ambiguous position in the mid-1930s, writing in the *ASR* that "sociologists have always known that social and societal phenomena" are "indeterminate, relativistic, [and] non-mechanistic." Sounding more like his former Michigan PhD adviser, Charles Cooley, Bain concluded that "F. S. Chapin's statement about latent culture patterns" should be reinterpreted as a form of "societal unconscious" (Bain 1936, 204). The *AJS* published a special issue on psychoanalysis and sociology in 1939, the year of Freud's death, with essays by A. L. Kroeber, Harold Laswell, Karen Horney, and Kenneth Burke (writing on "Freud and the Analysis of Poetry"), along with articles by medical doctors, psychiatrists, and sociologists. This collection suggests a lower level of anxiety about disciplinary boundaries than in later periods and an openness to the depth-realist categories and concepts of psychoanalysis.[35] One of the contributors to the 1939 *AJS* issue even remarked that "sociology is sufficiently mature to adopt the methods" and categories of psychoanalysis, including "the phenomenon which Freud called the return of the repressed," which was "of particular importance to sociology" (Zilboorg 1939, 341). It goes almost without saying that the concept of the "return of the repressed" has not figured centrally in most postwar American sociological writing.

There are other indicators of the epistemically unsettled nature of U.S. sociology in this period. Individual texts were internally heterogeneous.[36] A volume on the "family in the Depression" by Stouffer and Lazarsfeld (1937), who are "often remembered as two of the staunchest proponents of quantification, repeated throughout their volume the need for both types

35. Each text has to be examined closely to determine *which* Freud is being endorsed — the "radical" version or the repressive, biologistic one.

36. Such epistemic slippage and ambivalence also characterize some would-be sociological positivists today; see Steinmetz (2005a) for a case study of one such text.

of research" (Camic, chap. 7, this volume). It may not tell us much about the field's epistemic power structure to register that the American Sociological Society was divided between "value-neutral" positivists and "humanistic" social activists. It is revealing, however, that the Sociological Research Association was itself divided between the scientistic operationalists like Lundberg, Bain, and Stuart Rice, and more interpretivist "Chicago men" like Herbert Blumer.[37] The SSA was an invitation-only professional group that was formed in 1936 in response to battles within the ASS.

Edward Shils worried in 1948 that the still feeble efforts toward theoretical development in sociology were "in danger of being suffocated in the stampede for concrete results with immediate descriptive or manipulative value," adding that "the post-war financial prosperity of American sociology with the vast sums of money made available by governmental bodies, foundations, and private associations and firms makes this danger a very real one" (Shils 1948, 55). This prophetic phrase (from someone who played both sides of the street, epistemologically speaking) leads us directly to the (re)consolidation of the discipline after 1945.

The Postwar Settlement

By 1950 this balanced or splintered epistemic condition had disappeared, and sociology was becoming a well-structured field. Sociologists had so little in common in substantive terms that their disagreements and settlements necessarily revolved around the politics of method and epistemology. Methodological positivism was becoming orthodox or even *doxic,* that is, its practices and proclamations were increasingly recognized even by its opponents as a form of scientific capital, however much they disliked it.[38] As noted earlier, epistemic unanimity within a field is not a prerequisite for the hegemony of one particular position. A journal like *Qualitative Sociology,* for example, publishes work that is sometimes distinct from the hegemonic model; at the same time, however, its very title seems to acknowledge its own dominated status.[39] But during the 1950s and well into the 1960s

37. Farris (1967); Evans (1986–87, 123); Bannister (1987, 189, 218; 1992).

38. The (Hegelian) category of recognition is at the heart of Bourdieu's analysis of the working of fields (Steinmetz 2005b).

39. *Qualitative Sociology* was founded in the late 1970s, a period that saw a resurgence of positivist hegemony. One reader of this chapter commented that similar claims were made with respect to the Society for the Study of Social Problems (founded at a meeting in Chicago in 1951) and its journal *Social Problems.* The founding statement of the SSSP differed from the scientistic model in ways that were so coded as to be almost unnoticeable. Emphasizing social

(and perhaps beyond), methodological positivism prevailed in the leading sociology journals, in the most widely used textbooks and methods books, in the top departments, and in the tastes of the relevant funding agencies. In addition to the continuing efforts of the prewar camp (Bain, Lundberg, Lazarsfeld, Ogburn, Dodd, and others), there was an influx of entirely new characters. Many of them, like the statistician and survey methodologist Leslie Kish at Michigan, rotated into the discipline from wartime jobs with government agencies.[40] James S. Coleman entered sociology from a job as a chemist at Eastman Kodak with a self-described "positivist orientation . . . carried over from the physical sciences," an orientation he was able to polish in courses he took with Ernest Nagel on the philosophy of science (Coleman 1990, 75, 96, 98). Nagel was probably the most widely read positivist philosopher in sociology during the postwar decades. Although Coleman came from the same evangelical Protestant background as Lynd, he rejected the latter's antiscientist and meliorist orientation in favor of a more "modern" mathematical and utilitarian brand of sociology.

Let us look briefly at the same four departments examined earlier and cast a brief glance at Harvard's postwar Department of Social Relations, which ascended to top ranking in the postwar decades.[41]

---

problems was a mild critique of value-free social science and was linked to a sense of the SSSP as providing a defense of sociologists who were under "attack by representatives of vested interests and of reactionary groups" (Burgess 1953, 3). The emphasis on interdisciplinary collaboration with anthropologists and psychologists rather than economists or natural scientists (Burgess 1953) was also a polite rejection of the scientistic approach.

40. Kish was a political radical who fought in the Spanish Civil War in 1937–39. He helped found Michigan's Institute for Social Research in 1947, before joining the sociology department four years later. Most of the logical positivist philosophers were also on the political left, of course. Epistemology and politics were orthogonal.

41. Most specialists (e.g., Oromaner 1973) locate these departments through the late 1960s among the top five, along with Berkeley, which I leave aside here due to the paucity of secondary literature, the fact that it was not in the top rankings before the war, and the contributions of Burawoy and VanAntwerpen (n.d.) and VanAntwerpen (2005). As VanAntwerpen notes, Berkeley's Department of Social Institutions was founded in 1923 and changed its name to the Department of Sociology and Social Institutions in 1946. Glenn and Villemez's (1970) comparison of departments in the 1965–68 period finds the same six departments in the lead, although UNC sometimes ranks ahead of Harvard on two of their productivity indexes. This suggests to me that we need to know more about departments than productivity rates in order to assess their relative status. For example, Oromaner's data (1969, 333) on the top American sociologists according to graduate student reading lists and *ASR* citations during the late 1950s and early 1960s show three of those sociologists at Harvard (Parsons, Homans, and Sorokin), two at Columbia (Merton and Lazarsfeld), one at Chicago (Shils), and one formerly associated with Michigan (Cooley), but none at UNC or Wisconsin.

EPISTEMOLOGY AND THE LEADING
U.S. SOCIOLOGY DEPARTMENTS, 1945–1965

COLUMBIA. Lazarsfeld's Bureau of Applied Social Research constituted a center of methodological expertise and research in the positivist spirit. Whereas relations between Lazarsfeld and the Institute for Social Research had been on a more equal footing before the war, Lazarsfeld now suggested that the Institute be integrated into his Bureau (Jay 1973, 220). Lazarsfeld's work became "more academic" as he moved "toward academic respectability." At the same time Merton "was becoming more quantitatively empirical" (Coleman 1990, 81). He had written a series of influential historical and theoretical essays on the sociology of science and knowledge during the 1930s and 1940s that had little in common with the quasi-positivist "program for concentration on 'theories of the middle range'" for which he became famous in the postwar period (Parsons 1937/1968, 1:ix; Merton 1968a). Lazarsfeld and Rosenberg's influential *Language of Social Research* (1955), its title redolent of the Vienna Circle with which Lazarsfeld had once maintained contact, contained a section on the "philosophy of the social sciences" that was based entirely on the nomothetic-deductive approach, which was itself a child of logical positivism. This section included a chapter by Nagel, who ran a series of seminars together with Lazarsfeld on mathematical sociology (Coleman 1990, 88). *Language of Social Research* also included an excerpt from Hans Zetterberg's *On Theory and Verification in Sociology* (1954), which argued that axiomatic or deductive theory was "the most satisfactory" type. Zetterberg gave examples of the "if A then B" variety and defended additional positivist postulates such as an a priori preference for "parsimony" in explanation (1954, 534).[42] According to Mullins and Mullins (1973, 218), Zetterberg's book was "the accepted philosophical basis for theory in standard American sociology." Hans Zeisel, Lazarsfeld's lifelong friend and his coauthor (with Marie Jahoda) of the famous Marienthal study (1933), published a popular book on the use of mathematical figures and tables in social science (1947/1957). Zeisel insisted that there was "no logical difference between the study of voting or of buying" and argued for the superiority of social surveys over experiments (xviii, 131–33).[43] A former Columbia student who wrote a dissertation on Durkheim, Harry Alpert,

42. Mullins and Mullins (1973) discuss Zetterberg alongside others in what they call the "positivist style."

43. As Dan Breslau (1998) shows, experimentalists lost struggles with econometricians over control of research on U.S. labor market policy, even though both were broadly positivistic. Zeisel began teaching at the law school at Chicago in 1953 (Sills 1992, 536).

went to the Programs Analysis Office of the newly created National Science Foundation, where he determined the conditions under which sociologists and other social scientists could attain NSF funds. Alpert privileged what he called "the hard-science core of the social sciences" (Cozzens 1996, 3), and in a series of articles he laid out the conditions under which sociologists would be eligible for NSF funding.[44] The first of these was "the *criterion of science,* that is, the identification, within the social disciplines, of those areas characterized by the application of *the* methods and logic of science" (Alpert 1955, 656; my emphasis). This criterion necessitated the "convergence of the natural sciences and the social sciences." Attention to the "national interest" constituted a third prerequisite for funding, suggesting that sociologists would be expected to draw predictive and practical lessons from their research and that value neutrality would have to remain blind in one eye. Alpert concluded one of his articles with a warning: "the social sciences . . . are here to stay, but their future growth and development"— that is, their access to government funding—would "depend largely on their capacity to prove themselves by their deeds" (1955, 660). Alpert's NSF division funded research carried out at Lazarsfeld's Bureau (see Menzel 1959, 199n) and at other centers.

C. Wright Mills was not a bulwark against this positivist tide. James C. Coleman (1990, 77) recollected that when he was a student, Mills "seemed to matter little" in the Columbia "social system of sociology"—or that he "mattered only to those who themselves seemed to matter little." This statement provides a poignant sense of the local and the disciplinary marginalization of one of the most important U.S. sociologists of the twentieth century during this era of cold war and hard science.

CHICAGO, WISCONSIN, AND MICHIGAN. Sociology at the other three universities discussed earlier—the second "Capitoline triad" in postwar U.S. sociology, alongside Parsons, Merton, and Lazarsfeld[45]—was also increasingly dominated by methodological positivism, although the timing

44. As Keat and Urry (1975, 91) point out, Alpert's PhD thesis (1939) was influential in making Durkheim palatable to positivist sociology in the United States by arguing that Durkheim "did not adhere to such a strong interpretation of the social as had often been claimed" and because he inductively built up "general laws of social life through the accumulation of statistical findings." After serving in various other foundation functions, Alpert moved to the University of Oregon in 1957 as dean of the graduate school and served as president of the Pacific Sociological Association in 1963.

45. The Capitoline triad was the union of three Roman deities who shared a temple on Rome's Capitoline Hill. Bourdieu (2001b, 198) discussed the "triade capitoline" of Parsons, Merton, and Lazarsfeld.

and modalities of this shift varied. At Chicago, representatives of the new paradigm did not gain firm control of a highly factionalized department until 1957. Their takeover then was so complete, however, that the editor of a recent volume felt compelled to seek a "valorization, a vindication" of the years 1946–52 as the era of a "second Chicago school" centered around Herbert Blumer, Everett Hughes, and Anselm Strauss (Fine 1995, 1–9). As Fine notes, by 1960 the Chicago department had become more "scientific, modern, [and] positivist" (9). About half of the PhD theses written in Chicago's sociology department between 1946 and 1962 "used entirely quantitative methods"; two-thirds of the journal articles published by Chicago sociology faculty in this period were quantitative (Platt 1996, 266). New quantitative faculty hired in this period included demographers Don Bogue (from 1954), Otis Dudley Duncan (from 1951), and Evelyn Kitagawa (from 1951) and mathematician Leo Goodman (from 1950); Ogburn remained at Chicago even after his retirement in 1952 (Fine 1995, 404–5). And although the qualitative party still had a "coherent focus" (Abbott 1999, 56–58) in 1955 during the chairmanship of Everett Hughes, it had completely dissipated by 1957. David Riesman later recalled that "when the demographers . . . took over, the climate of the Department changed. . . . Students began to worry that unless they had tables in their theses, they wouldn't get their Ph.D.'s" (Bainbridge 2002, 4). A report by chairman Philip Hauser from 1958 spoke tellingly of "the complete disappearance of the earlier bipolar division of departmental interests" (quoted in Abbott 1999, 59).

At Wisconsin, William Sewell Sr. was "instrumental in building [the] powerful and notoriously positivist sociology department and in obtaining a place for sociology at the federal feeding trough, especially at the National Institutes of Mental Health and the National Science Foundation" (Sewell Jr. 2005; see also Sewell Sr. 1988). Together with Michigan and Chicago, Wisconsin pioneered the so-called new causal theory in sociology, using path modeling and related techniques.[46] There were a few exceptions at Wisconsin: Warren Hagstrom, a sociologist of science, who arrived from Berkeley in 1962; Joseph Elder, a comparativist South Asianist and student of Parsons, who arrived in 1963; and Robert Alford and Jay Demerath, who came from Berkeley several years later. But they were located within a large and rapidly expanding department that was dominated by stratification research, demography, and experimental social psychology. Not until the arrival of Maurice Zeitlin in the second half of the 1960s, the visiting profes-

---

46. Faculty in this area at Wisconsin before 1965 included Sewell Sr., Vimal Shah, J. M. Armer, Archibald Haller, and Edgar F. Borgatta.

sorships of Manuel Castells in the mid-1970s, and the recruitment of Erik Olin Wright at the end of the 1970s did the department's monolithic character begin to diversify.

What about Michigan? After the war Robert Angell returned home to chair the sociology department until 1952. He also returned home to an academic field that was expanding rapidly and undergoing turbulent growth. Several developments were especially important as immediate or proximate causes of change at the local level. One was the cycling into sociology departments of researchers from government and wartime agencies (Turner and Turner 1990). Related to this was the expansion of federal funding for social science research from "military, intelligence, and propaganda agencies" such as the U.S. Army and Air Force. These agencies remained the most important sources of funding for social research "until well into the 1960s" and often initiated "social science concepts and projects" (Simpson 1999, xiv). The massive involvement of military funders entailed "a marked preference for quantitative analysis as opposed to historical, qualitative, or other forms of social research that seemed 'soft' by comparison" (Solovey 2001, 177). Another important development that was more internal to the academic and sociological field was the decision at Harvard to allow Talcott Parsons to create an interdisciplinary social relations department. While the shifts related to the war and military policy tipped the hand of those who wanted to channel departments like those at Michigan and Chicago toward the "natural science" approach, Parsons's social relations model resisted the temptations of scientism to some extent by bringing in cultural anthropologists and psychologists who were sometimes willing to engage with psychoanalytic concepts and theories. The postwar Harvard model replaced the interwar Chicago case-study approach as the leading alternative to full-bore scientism in sociology.

Angell's activities after 1945 were closely attuned to these countervailing tendencies. On the one hand, he and Theodor Newcomb founded the Survey Research Center in 1946. This was the precursor of the Institute for Social Research (ISR), which was created in 1949, the same year in which Horkheimer returned to Frankfurt with his identically named Institut für Sozialforschung (Jay 1973, 282; Frantilla 1998, figs. 1-4). Of course, the difference between the two institutes could not have been more profound, and Adorno almost seemed to have the Michigan ISR in mind when he wrote his critique of "teamwork in social research" (1972). Michigan sociology cannot be equated with the ISR, given the institutional separation of the two entities and the fact that many members of the ISR have been nonteaching research scientists or members of psychology and other departments. At the same time, one cannot separate postwar Michigan sociology from the ISR milieu, as Hollinger (1996) has demonstrated and as anyone who has spent time in that department during the past five decades can corroborate. Angell served on the executive committee of the ISR for many years.

On the other hand, Angell described himself as being strongly "attracted by the broad coverage of behavioral science that had been worked out in the Social Relations Department at Harvard," which entailed an integration of cultural anthropology, psychology, and area studies. His first move as department chair in 1946, therefore, was to recruit anthropologist Horace Miner on "the strong recommendation of Robert Redfield to give us a capability in social anthropology" (Angell n.d., 30). Miner had already published an ethnography of St. Denis, a French Canadian parish. He was promoted to associate professor in sociology and anthropology in 1947, but his salary continued to come from the sociology department. Miner served on sociology's executive committee continuously from 1951 to 1979 (Griffin 1995, 291). He wrote books on Timbuktu, Algeria, and Fez, Morocco, carried out research in other parts of Africa, and taught courses on African studies in the sociology department from the 1940s onward. In 1952, the last year of his tenure as department chair, Angell hired a fresh anthropology PhD from Columbia, David F. Aberle, who had published a book the previous year on Hopi culture. Aberle conducted research during the coming years on Navaho and Ute peyotism and taught courses in the sociology department on culture contact.

Angell's commitment to anthropology and international area studies thus expressed itself at the local departmental level, and not just in his better-known activities with UNESCO's social sciences department and as president of the International Sociological Association, or in his often-expressed belief that the national state is an anachronism. Angell was also one of the first to recognize the significance of history for sociology. In his notes for a presentation titled "What Does History Offer Sociology" in 1962 with historian Sylvia Thrupp, Angell wrote, "from about 1918 strong emphasis on improved research techniques, statistical methods, close study of contemporary scene. History and social evolution largely ignored, at least in this country. . . . Sorokin a lonely figure in American Sociology." He then alluded to a "third period" that

> begins with great interest in underdeveloped world with throwing off of colonialism in the 1950s. Sociologists . . . don't deal with the underdeveloped world much. Well trained sociologists found out how to use historical sources—

Marion Levy, Robert Bellah, Ed Swanson. Two at least have focused on particular historical processes—Eisenstadt on the growth of empires, and Barrington Moore on alternative processes of change from agrarian to industrial societies. Excellent studies.[47]

Angell's interdisciplinary, international, anthropological, and historical orientation was almost completely marginalized in the department, however, until the hiring in 1969 of Charles Tilly, a student of the "lonely" Sorokin, as a professor of sociology and history. The only part of the interdisciplinary social relations model that survived after 1952 was the social psychology axis, which was powerfully aligned with positivism. The psychological faculty and graduate students in this program tended to use experiments, while the more sociological members used surveys and organizational analysis. All were imbued with the same strong "scientific" spirit, according to one graduate of the program.[48]

Angell's other appointments between 1945 and 1952 struck a sort of balance between the less positivist approach and the new scientism that was rapidly gaining momentum in the discipline and locally at Michigan. Some of these appointments were more strongly associated with the first side of this division, such as Guy E. Swanson and Gerhard Lenski (both hired in 1949), and Morris Janowitz (hired in 1951). Others were associated with the latter tendency, especially Ronald Freedman (hired 1946) and Rensis Likert, who taught sporadically in the sociology department in this period.[49] But all of the new hires except Miner apparently felt the pressure to become more statistical and "scientific," applying "unsympathetic" methods to phenomena that Cooley would have insisted required "sympathetic understanding." Gerhard Lenski went the farthest in the direction of scientism. During his time at Michigan (1950–63) he was a sociologist of religion, which had traditionally been one of the least scientistic of sociological subfields, concerned as it was with meaning. But Lenski based his 1961 opus *The Religious Factor* on survey research from the 1957–58 Detroit Area Study.

47. Cooley papers, Bentley Historical Library, box 2, Outlines of Talks folder.

48. Personal communications from Mayer Zald (University of Michigan PhD, 1961).

49. Likert had been director of research for the Life Insurance Agency Management Association in Hartford, Connecticut, from 1935 to 1939, when he was appointed director of the Division of Program Surveys in the Bureau of Agricultural Economics of the U.S. Department of Agriculture in Washington, DC. His various activities in World War II are discussed in Johnson and Nichols (1998). Likert was initially hired as director of the Survey Research Center in 1946 and was professor of sociology in 1946–47 without salary (University of Michigan, *Proceedings of the Board of Regents,* October 1946, p. 562), and professor of sociology and psychology from 1956 to 1963.

In subsequent work he expanded on the technologically reductionist evolutionary theory of Michigan anthropologist Leslie White (Lenski 1966) and articulated an explicitly "neopositivistic" epistemology and radically empiricist ontology (Lenski 1988).

Angell's own work became two-pronged. On the one hand he moved closer to what he felt was a more legitimate and scientific perspective, writing that "sociology was proud that it was becoming truly scientific, and I wanted to be an up and coming sociologist" (Angell n.d., 21). His first postwar project on "the moral integration of cities" (1951) departed from the style of his earlier work. Here he examined the effects of ethnic heterogeneity and mobility on low crime rates and high levels of welfare effort ("moral integration") in a sample of cities, using methods that have been recognized as an early example of the use of regression analysis in sociology (Angell 1951). But there was no attention to the actual mentalities or discourse of people living in cities except for a survey using a Likert-style scale of how much people liked living in their hometowns. In his work on transnational movements and international conflict resolution Angell remained primarily theoretical and qualitative. Indeed, he seemed to swing back toward his youthful skepticism toward the natural science perspective as the years went on. He praised a book by a philosophical sociologist who made the relativist argument that "the standards of scientific validity are themselves social products so that no scientist can ever really prove that his theory is correct" (Angell 1956, 235). Three years after his retirement Angell praised the "suggestiveness" of Erving Goffman's (1959) work for "exploring image control by governments" (Angell 1972, 115). This was around the same time that Goffman was being trumpeted by Alvin Gouldner (1970) as the standard-bearer for a long overdue postpositivist revolution in U.S. sociology.

Thus with very few exceptions, the Michigan sociology department was dominated in the postwar period by adherents of methodological positivism. The hegemony of this perspective was expressed in the expansion of the Institute for Social Research (figs. 9.1–9.4), which threatened to extinguish Cooley's legacy of respect for autonomous theory, humanism, interpretivism, and the holistic analysis of specific places and historical processes.[50]

The 1956 Michigan textbook *Principles of Sociology*, edited by Ron Freed-

---

50. The publications from the Michigan department in the 1950s and 1960s are suggestive of this thoroughgoing positivism. An edited volume on Cooley opened with an essay on Cooley as "demographer" (Schnore 1968), indicating the degree to which that particularly positivistic social-science subspecialty had made inroads into sociology (the author was a 1955 Michigan PhD).

Figure 9.1 TOP LEFT: Postwar technoscience at the (Michigan) Institute for Social Research; the ISR building, completed in 1965. Courtesy of ISR.

Figure 9.2 TOP RIGHT: Inside the Institute for Social Research. Courtesy of ISR.

Figure 9.3 BOTTOM LEFT: Rensis Likert, director of the Survey Research Center, 1948–49 and of the Institute for Social Research, 1949–70, with data files. Courtesy of Bentley Historical Library, University of Michigan, Ann Arbor.

Figure 9.4 BOTTOM RIGHT: Charles Cannell, director of field operations at the Survey Research Center, with interviewers. Courtesy of ISR.

man, Amos Hawley, Karl Landecker, Gerhard Lenski, and Horace Miner, replaced the earlier, less positivistic Michigan textbook by Cooley, Angel, and Carr (1933). Although the individual chapters were diverse, the book's introduction defined sociology as a science of "human groups . . . subject to study by the same methods as other natural phenomena"; the discipline's aim was to "discover systematic . . . observable relationships between . . . phenomena" (Freedman et al. 1956, 5). Sociology was both inductive and deductive, and it was "nonethical" since "the scientist has not techniques by which he can determine what the ultimate ends of a society should be," although his knowledge may well be "instrumental" (6, 12). Another key Michigan methods text that was widely read in the joint PhD program in social psychology was Festinger and Katz's *Research Methods in the Behavioral Sciences* (1953), which enshrined the experimental social psychology laboratory framework with its notorious tendency to let college sophomores stand in for "man" in general. Festinger and Katz did not employ a formal philosophical framework (Hollinger 1996). Another relevant Michigan faculty member was philosopher Abraham Kaplan, a student of Bertrand Russell and "by training a positivist," who wrote *The Conduct of Inquiry: Methodology for Behavioral Science* (1964). Unlike the works of Nagel and Lazarsfeld, this text explicitly combined logical positivism with methods for the behavioral sciences.[51] Although it is difficult to know how widely any of these books were read, Robert Friedrichs (1970, 36) mentioned Kaplan's volume as part of a small explosion of new philosophical writing that sociologists were reading during the first half of the 1960s.[52]

The postwar epistemo-methodological realignment in sociology fundamentally transformed the Michigan department. After Angell's term as chair, the department added Hubert Blalock (1954–64), a statistician-cum-sociologist whose positivism inspired refutations by professional philosophers (e.g., Miller 1987, 240–41); Lillian Cohen (1950–57), who wrote an introduction to statistical methods for social scientists (Cohen 1954); demographer Harry P. Sharp (1955–61), a 1955 Michigan PhD; and demographer-statistician Otis Dudley Duncan (1962). Among the rare exceptions in this period were Allan Silver, who had written a Michigan dissertation with Janowitz and Swanson in 1963 and taught in the department during the next decade (1954–64), and East Asian specialist Robert Mortimer Marsh, hired in 1958. The ideological hegemony of methodological positivism was so powerful that when Angell died he was eulogized by a member of the department as a statistician and survey researcher who created a department devoted to quantitative research (Ness 1985, 10). As late as the 1980s the required methods course for all graduate students in sociology at Michigan was the Detroit Area Study, in which they studied survey methods. Only in very recent years has this methodological hegemony started to crumble.

HARVARD. Harvard presents the most complicated departmental story and seems at first glance to be another exception (with Berkeley) to the postwar rule of positivism. Sociology was located between 1946 and 1970

---

51. Abraham Kaplan (1918–1993) taught at Michigan from 1962 to 1972 before moving to the University of Haifa and was named one of the top ten teachers in the United States by *Time* magazine in 1966.

52. According to the OCLC catalogue, 1,417 copies of Kaplan's text are owned in total by U.S. libraries, as opposed to 1,096 copies of the Festiger and Katz volume.

in the Department of Social Relations, which was founded by academics who were fascinated with theory and "what were then considered the 'softer' sides of the social sciences, especially the relations between personality, culture, and society" (Homans 1984, 294). The social relations program nonetheless quickly began attracting hundreds of applicants annually (Nichols 1998, 90). It produced 80 PhD's between 1946 and 1956 (Johnston 1998, 34). Moreover, Harvard was at the very top of the departmental rankings by sociology department chairs in 1957 (Keniston 1959, 146). In 1964 it was second only to Berkeley, which had shot up from seventh place during the intervening years (Burris 2004). These events would seem to indicate that sociological theory was central in U.S. sociology during the 1950s. In his 1950 presidential address to the ASA, Parsons (1950, 5) argued that the "wave of anti-theoretical empiricism has, I think fortunately, greatly subsided." One common view of this situation is that Harvard played the role of theory maker to the more empirical remainder of the discipline. As Kuklick writes (1973, 16, citing Rossi 1956), "after the Second World War the occupational roles of theoretician and bureaucratized research worker became entirely distinct."

If we examine this picture a bit more closely, however, things quickly become more complex. First, the division of labor between theory and *empirie* in sociology, to the extent that it actually existed, was superimposed on deeper agreements about basic principles and goals. The alleged struggle between "operationalism" and "functionalism" did not go to the heart of the consensus on what counted as scientific capital. The 1953 collection *Working Papers in the Theory of Action,* for instance, included an entirely empirical paper by Bales (Parsons, Bales, and Shils 1953). Second, aside from Sorokin (who had been marginalized in the meantime), Parsons was Harvard's only theorist, if we consider theory as more than a restatement of causal relations among variables. Parsons's main coauthor in his theoretical texts written during the 1950s, at the height of his (and Harvard's) power and influence, was not one of his Harvard colleagues but Edward Shils, who taught at Harvard as a visitor. Most of the Harvard sociology PhD's from this period who went on to illustrious careers pursued Mertonian "middle-range" topics and theories.[53] Kingsley Davis (1959, 767), a student of Par-

---

53. Craig Calhoun made this point in earlier comments to the author. One might include in this list of early Department of Social Relations PhD's whose dissertations were in this "middle-range" vein Marion Levy (1948), James A. Davis (1955), Robert N. Bellah (1955), Neil Smelser (1958), and Ezra Vogel (1958). Harold Garfinkel (PhD, 1952) had more microscopic research objects, but his theoretical ambitions were sweeping, while Edward Tiryakian's work after his 1956 dissertation moved in the direction of sociological theory.

sons from the prewar days, insisted that sociology should be concerned with discovering relations among *observable* phenomena (empiricism).

Third, Parsons muted and even recanted some of his prewar antipositivism during the 1950s. Parsons was criticized by Gouldner in 1970 for his alleged positivism, but he had explicitly rejected "the positivistic-utilitarian tradition" in his *Structure of Social Action* (1937). Yet Parsons also argued, both before and after the war, that "the same philosophical principles that guided the natural sciences were at the heart of the social sciences" (Klausner and Lidz 1986, vii). *Working Papers in the Theory of Action* opened with two illuminating chapters by Parsons on the superego and symbolism, but the subsequent chapters, coauthored with Robert F. Bales and Edward Shils, employed a scientistic language derived more from physics and cybernetics and terms from the older lexicons of biology and evolution. The social system was described here as a space-age orrery populated by "particles," "inertia," "flows," "phase movements," "feedback loops," "orbits," and "input–output processes" (quotes from Parsons, Bales, and Shils 1953, 164–68, 210, 212, 214, 217–22). Thus the archpositivist Lundberg (1956, 21) could write convincingly in the mid-1950s that there was now "considerable agreement among the systems" of Parsons-Bales and Stuart Dodd.[54] Finally, the interdisciplinarity of the social relations department bore little resemblance to some current versions of interdisciplinarity as a playground of epistemic diversity and experimentation. Parsons's vision of a convergence of theory in the various social sciences rather recalled the logical positivist dream of the unity of science (Carnap 1934). As Parsons wrote in his preface to the programmatic book *Toward a General Theory of Action*, "these many streams of thought are in the process of flowing together" (1951, viii).

Nor was Parsons the only Harvard sociologist whose own antipositivism was muted or nonexistent. Statistician Samuel Stouffer, who ran the Harvard department's Laboratory of Social Relations, was seen as having "destroyed one of the principal contentions of the case-study side" of the

54. I am skeptical of Platt's (1996, 202–3) claim that Parsons's "lack of methodological commitments" meant that his influence had "no consequences for method." Platt also maintains that Lundberg was *not* taken too seriously (although she herself devotes considerable space to him). But Theodor Abel (2001, 323) criticized "the influences of Parsons and of Lundberg" in one breath in 1950 and discussed Lundberg repeatedly in his diaries between 1931 and 1957; see also Angell (1930, 345; 1945, 229–30). Four years later Hinkle and Hinkle discussed Lundberg as one of five contemporary U.S. sociologists in detail, describing him as "the leading exponent of neo-positivism in contemporary American sociology" and concluding that his "continuing endeavor to develop a sociology modeled upon the physical sciences, especially physics, has had considerable influence among younger sociologists" (1954, 54). Sorokin considered Lundberg important enough to include him as a target of his 1956 antiscientistic tract.

debate over statistics versus the case-study method in his Chicago dissertation (Faris 1970, 114). Alex Inkeles rendered Parsons's *implicit* modernization theory more explicit (Gilman 2003, chap. 3). Modernization theory was
essentially positivist in denying that causal mechanisms and paths of development vary across time and space (Gaonkar 2001; Harootunian 2004;
Steinmetz 1999). Inkeles (1974) combined these ontological assumptions
with survey methods, measuring individuals' levels of modernity in various
countries. The most influential counterweight to Parsons in the sociology
wing of the social relations department in this period was George Homans,
who had replaced Parsons as the most-cited sociologist in the United States
by 1964 (Chriss 1995). Homans disliked "grand theory" and claimed to have
told Parsons in a faculty meeting that "no member shall be put under any
pressure to read" Parsons and Shils's (1951) new treatise (Homans 1984,
303). Homans was explicitly positivistic (1947, 14) and invoked Ernst Mach,
the godfather of post-Comtean social science positivism, insisting that
"science consists of the 'careful and complete description of the mere facts'"
and avoids "why" questions to focus on "how" questions. According to
Dennis Wrong (1971, 251), Homans dismissed "all intellectual traditions in
sociology stemming from nonempiricist philosophies as 'guff.'" Homans
also staked out a methodological individualist ontology, arguing that Durkheim was simply wrong ("that is, untrue") in claiming society to be "an entity *sui generis,* something more than the resultant of individual human beings" (Homans 1984, 297–98).

ALTERNATIVE DIAGNOSES OF
POSTWAR AMERICAN SOCIOLOGY

Several arguments have been mobilized against the thesis of postwar dominance of positivism in U.S. sociology.[55] Some point out that sociologists interact with people from other disciplines, that they read widely, and that
they are not restricted to sociology departments. Sociologists would therefore be exposed to a more varied epistemological menu. But this no more
challenges the fieldlike character of sociology than pointing to individual
dissenters or even entire departments of dissenters: such diversity is one of
the very conditions of existence of a field. A second counterargument can
also be quickly disposed of. This concerns the lack of explicit references to
positivism by those associated with the tendencies I am calling method-

---

55. The first two counterarguments have been made explicitly to me by anonymous reviewers and by discussants of an earlier draft of this chapter.

ological positivism. American sociologists more or less agreed about what positivism was. The widely used 1944 *Dictionary of Sociology* provided a concise definition of the term (Fairchild 1944, 226). Lundberg pounded it into them in article after article and book after book. Students at Columbia and elsewhere read Nagel. By 1983, Raymond Williams could remark that positivism was "a swear-word, by which nobody is swearing" (although he also acknowledged that "the real argument is still there"; 1983, 239). But these overwhelmingly pejorative connotations of positivism date to the 1960s. Moreover, any philosophical realist will admit that unnamed social structures exist and can influence empirical events. Even though the logical positivists and their successors in sociology started to drop the term *positivism* in favor of alternatives like *nomothetic-deductive,* they continued to argue for (1) general and empirical laws (or a "postulate of regularity in the sequence of events"; Shils 1961a, 1419); (2) a view of the social as a closed system (such closure is a precondition for "regularity determinism"; Bhaskar 1975/1978); (3) doctrines of prediction and forecasting (Comte's "savoir pour prévoir et prévoir pour pouvoir"—"from knowledge comes prediction, and from prediction comes power") and (4) falsification (the Popperian reformulation); (5) a spontaneous preference for "parsimonious" explanations (forgetting that the first definition of *parsimonious* is "stingy"); (6) a belief that mathematical and statistical modes of analysis and representation are superior to linguistic forms; and (7) adherence to an idealized view of the natural sciences as a model for the human sciences, that is, to scientism.

According to a third argument, there is a lack of fit between positivist philosophical doctrines and actual sociological research practices. Mullins and Mullins (1973, 218) asserted, for example, that "the simple fact is that almost no theories" of the positivist kind "were ever tried in sociology" (see also Platt 1996 for a similar objection). But this assumes that the only relevant definition of positivism is in terms of some philosophical urtext. Mullins and Mullins (1973, 221) also point to a cluster of "new causal theorists"—a.k.a. positivists—"scattered" across a number of universities. Some writers (Kuklick 1973) argue that twentieth-century positivism was usually deductivist, while mainstream sociological practice has been largely inductivist (throwing data into a computer program and coming up with ad hoc explanations for correlations) and hence not positivist. But as Roy Bhaskar (1975/1978, 1979) argued, the patron saint of the spontaneous positivism of scientists is David Hume, theorist of the inductively discovered "constant conjunctions of events." Moreover, some logical positivists were willing to adjust their theory in the direction of the actual practices of positivist social researchers. In 1951 Hans Reichenbach (1951) proposed a loosening of the Humean "necessity" model of the scientific law to allow for probabilistic "laws" in the social sciences, and this was developed further by Nagel (1961/1979, 503–20).

A final argument insists on the diversity of sociological practices even during the 1950s and 1960s.[56] Berkeley's sociology department, which was at the top of the comparative rankings by 1964, had a number of people like Erving Goffman, Neil Smelser, William Kornhauser, Reinhard Bendix, and Herbert Blumer who pursed nonpositivist styles of research. Like Bendix, a student of Wirth who wrote a Chicago thesis (1943) on German sociology and began teaching at Berkeley in 1947, most of them seem not to have worried publicly about the divergence between their own styles of sociology and the dominant model at the time (Bendix 1990).[57] It is remarkable, however, that muted criticism of positivism came from Herbert Blumer in the pages of the *AJS* against the doctrine of value neutrality in 1940 and again in 1956. Smelser later (1986) published a penetrating critique (in German) of American sociological scientism called "The Persistence of Positivism in American Sociology."[58] Lipset commented frequently on social science positivism. But my argument about the postwar settlement really extends only to the mid-1960s, and public disciplinary recognition of Berkeley seems to come at the very end of this period, despite the fact that many members of this crew had already been there for some time. Did Berkeley change or were the conditions undergirding the postwar settlement beginning to crumble, allowing less positivist forms of sociology to gain recognition?

Even with respect to the 1945–65 period, one might also point out that there was a handful of epistemological dissidents even in the early 1960s, many of them contributors to Irving Louis Horowitz's (1964b) collection in honor of C. Wright Mills, optimistically titled *The New Sociology*. A handful of recognized sociologists continued to criticize methodological positivism directly and publicly during the 1950s. Gerth's epistemological leanings had to be gleaned mainly from his decisions about what to translate (and his teaching), although one published essay attacked sociology for its ahistoricism and antitheoretical bias (1959; see also Gerth and Mills 1964). There was a "humanist" rebuttal at the 1962 meetings to ASA president Paul Lazarsfeld's call for an empiricist sociology, but this came not from a sociologist at all but from historian Arthur Schlesinger Jr. (1962). Alvin Gouldner inched up to his full-blown epistemological critique of U.S. sociological

56. This argument was proposed by the editor of this volume to the author.

57. The same goes for Leo Lowenthal, the only member of the Institute of Social Research who had a career in U.S. sociology.

58. This article has, to my knowledge, never appeared in English.

positivism only gradually. His *Patterns of Industrial Bureaucracy* quoted Homans to the effect that "sociology may miss a great deal if it tries to be too quantitative *too soon*" (Gouldner 1954, 17; my emphasis)—conceding that quantification was the field's ultimate goal. During the early 1960s, as Friedrichs noted (1970), there was a small but noticeable uptick in works arguing that sociology should be seen as part of the humanities, discussing its links to history and philosophy, questioning value neutrality, and proposing a more self-reflexive approach to the discipline, a "sociology of sociology" (see Wolff 1959; Nisbet 1962; Berger 1963; Horowitz 1963; Bierstedt 1960).[59]

A sociology of sociological epistemology would have to determine whether these dissident positions could match the positivist mainstream in terms of their symbolic capital. In fact, many of the critics were not centrally located according to a sociological map of disciplinary ranking. Adorno's writings on sociology from the early 1960s were the most sophisticated critiques of positivism in this period, but they were not translated into English until 1976. Shils (1961a, 1407) could thus assert that "the seed of German sociology ripened only when it was transplanted to America," ignoring (or suppressing) the fact that the editors of the leading pre–Nazi era German sociology journal (*Zeitschrift*) were at the time of his writing already back in Germany and restarting critical sociology in Frankfurt. Marcuse worked as an intelligence analyst for the U.S. army during the war and then headed up the Central European Section of the Office of Intelligence Research. When he finally returned to teaching in 1951 it was in philosophy rather than sociology departments, so it is difficult to count him as an American sociologist.[60] Berkeley may have been a top-ranked department by 1964, but American intellectual life and academic sociology had never been significantly located on the West Coast, and it would take some time to change that.

Finally, some of the earlier critics toned down or subtly adjusted their antipositivism (perhaps not deliberately) in ways that made their work more compatible with the new framework. It is difficult to say whether this was instrumental and intentional or the result of the hegemonic sway of the newly dominant ideas in the discipline—or of the positivist worldview's en-

59. Bierstedt, in his 1959 presidential address to the Eastern Sociological Society, insisted that "great sociologists . . . were humanists first" and reminded his listeners that "Veblen used no questionnaires, Sumner no coefficients of correlation" (1960, 5). I. L. Horowitz's antiscientism in this period is discussed in Steinmetz (2005c).

60. The same can be said of a handful of theorists and "qualitative" sociologists like Daniel Bell (Waters 1996) and Barrington Moore Jr. (D. Smith 1983), who were able to stay aloof from the mainstream, partly because of their idiosyncratic career patterns and self-confidence.

hanced plausibility. After Sorokin was marginalized at Harvard by Parsons, he began to turn sharply against methodological positivism, fulminating against "sham-scientific slang," "sham quantification," "the cult of numerology," "pseudo experimentation" posing as "real experiments," social "atomism," sociological "simulacra" of natural sciences, and empiricist philosophy.[61] But Sorokin still did not break with doctrines of predictability and uniform social laws (1956, chap. 11, 312). Even C. Wright Mills, whose 1959 critique of U.S. sociology is often seen as a heroic cri de coeur from the scientistic wilderness, had drifted toward the mainstream, in contrast to his essays from the 1940s. Mills now cast aspersions not only on "abstracted empiricism" but on "grand theory" as well.

THE FIT BETWEEN POSTWAR SOCIOLOGY AND METHODOLOGICAL POSITIVISM

It may be helpful to back up for a moment and specify the linkages between the main dimensions of methodological positivism and the sociology of the postwar period. The most important component of the former was the belief in general social laws of the "if *a,* then *b*" variety, or the probabilistic variants. The case study was therefore unacceptable since one could not generalize from an "*N* of 1" (Stouffer 1930; Steinmetz 2004a). There was a general movement away from the study of the town, neighborhood, or the single individual and toward the survey, whose unit of analysis was the individual, multiplied (Coleman 1990, 92).[62] Nonsurvey researchers followed suit. Guy Swanson's *Birth of the Gods* (1960) used statistical methods on a sample of fifty "simpler societies" to test a Durkheimian model of religion, gathering information from Swanson's "idiographic" colleagues like Horace Miner, who had written a book on Timbuktu (1960). The existence of Berelson and Steiner's (1964) inventory of 1,045 sociological "findings of proper generality"—some of them couched in multiple ceteris paribus clauses[63]—suggests that assumptions about causal regularity were wide-

61. Several years later Sorokin ended his autobiography with the suggestion that the empiricist "sensate order" was leading to the destruction of mankind and an "abomination of desolation" (1963, 324).

62. As one reviewer of this essay pointed out, many early postwar surveys were actually conducted in a limited geographic area but presented as if they had sampled the entire United States

63. An example, taken almost at random: "Recourse to prayer under combat conditions is common among (American) soldiers, especially for those under great stress and with few personal resources for coping with the situation" (Berelson and Steiner 1964, 447). Needless to say, this was based on Stouffer et al. (1949-50), the template for much of the postwar work in this vein.

spread at the time. Historical sociology was considered out of bounds, except as a means of increasing the number of data points (Sorokin 1956, 50).

Despite this holy grail of the universal law, there is no ontological reason to expect the social world to exhibit such regularities. This failure of the real world to conform to positivist philosophical assumptions meant that empirical social scientists had to loosen the constraint of universalism, emphasizing *probabilistic* laws instead. Hans Reichenbach (1951, 122) argued soothingly in a symposium with the nation's leading social scientists in 1951 that "whoever wants to carry on Humean empiricism in modern times must be willing to accept the frequency interpretation of probability." Social statisticians came up with the idea of "scope conditions," which gestured toward social reality while sticking to the ontological assumption that social causes are *normally* universal, that is, independent of time and space. By the same token, the concept of "path dependency" is epistemically incoherent unless one starts from the positivist assumption that social or historical processes are ideally, essentially, or usually *not* determined by a contingent array of prior conditions and processes. In attempting to force their data into the framework of if–then statements, statistical sociologists also began resorting to interaction terms. But they could not agree to represent history as the result of ever-changing congeries of causal processes or mechanisms, even though this was in fact more adequate to the real qualities of the social world (Bhaskar 1975/1978; Sewell 1996; Steinmetz 1998). Instead, the social was at least implicitly treated as a *closed system*. Parsonian functionalism was famously unable to account for change. Even when Parsons began more explicitly laying the groundwork for a modernization-theoretical account of historical change, history was constrained to follow a path that flattened it out in ways that allowed for an "essential section" of historical time, "a break in the present such that all the elements of the whole revealed by this section are in an immediate relation with one another, a relation that immediately expresses their inner essence" (Althusser 1970, 94). Such closure is not just politically conservative, as was often argued in the 1960s and 1970s; it is also an ontological precondition for the existence of general laws, even if these were laws involving depth-realist concepts as their *explanans*. This is one sense in which structural functionalism, which Mullins and Mullins (1973, 39) called "the faith of our fathers" and Kuklick (1973) analyzed as a triumphant Kuhnian paradigm, corresponded to methodological positivism at the level of its deepest assumptions, even if its depth realism and "hyper-theoreticism" made it a target of dismissal by the more empirically oriented sociologists (who were located on both the left and the right politically).

The second sign of this realignment was the increased emphasis on strictly *empirical* concepts and "theories" (see Willer and Willer 1973). The supposed theoretical dominance of Parsons does not sit well with this claim that empiricism was pervasive. However, Parsons was more often admired than emulated (at least until Niklas Luhmann came along). The officially approved Mertonian formula of "middle range theory" combined with empirical research guided most of Parsons's ostensible followers. Platt (1996, 192) finds a continuous *decrease* in theoretical articles and an *increase* in empirical ones in the three leading sociology journals during the 1920–90 period, with the sharpest decline occurring between the 1950s and 1960s. Depth-realist concepts also dropped out of sociological writing. Operationalist methods were often described as empirical measures that tapped underlying entities (Kaplan 1964, 297), and social statisticians sometimes talked about the murky issue of the *substantive* adequacy of their measures to those deeper objects. But in sociology, at least, "latent" variables were usually construed as also being located on the empirical level, even if they were not directly measured. Lazarsfeld (1951, 156) recommended that the researcher involved in creating concepts should start "with fairly concrete categories." Even after Carnap and other logical positivists began to acknowledge that scientific concepts could *not* be reduced "to the given, i.e. sense-data, or to observable properties of physical things" and to admit the possibility of "theoretical concepts" (Carnap 1956; also 1966, chap. 23), the latter were "regarded as mere devices for deriving the sentences that *really* state the empirical facts, namely the observation sentences" (Putnam 2002, 24).

Empiricism was linked to the doctrine of value neutrality. As Herbert Marcuse pointed out at the debates about Weberian social science at the 1965 German Sociological Congress, "Weber's notion of value freedom simply meant that he refused to subject his own values to any kind of rational criticism" (Zimmerman 2006, 74; Marcuse 1971). And as critics often pointed out during the 1960s, sociology had implicitly allied itself with the reproduction of the current social order by declaring the unobservable or the speculative off limits for scientific discussion.

U.S. sociology also moved away from the interpretivist approaches inspired by Mead, Cooley, Freud, and the various tendencies grouped under phenomenology and symbolic interactionism (despite the just-mentioned short burst of activity in the latter movement during the 1950s). The existence of a "culture concept" in functionalist sociology or an interest in psychology or even psychoanalysis does not really contradict this point. Culture, personality, and subjectivity could all be treated positivistically, as in rational choice theory (Somers 1998). In their analysis of "theory groups" in U.S. sociology, Mullins and Mullins (1973) argued that the "cluster stage"

1945–51 "was notable intellectually for the introduction of Freudian psychology." But the richer and more interpretive Freudian categories such as the unconscious, irrationality, and "the return of the repressed" were largely absent now, and most sociologists seem to have ignored Parsons's own intense interest in at least the superego elements of psychoanalysis. As Kuklick (1973) and Camic (1986) show, postwar sociology's "revolt against behaviorism" also led it to reject what it saw as biological approaches, including the concept of habit. Psychoanalysis was thus rejected both for its antibiologistic and depth-psychoanalytic concepts like the unconscious and for its biologistic tendencies.

The tendency to understand the mechanisms and laws of the social sciences as universal was related to postwar American sociology's geographical and temporal focus, which typically took the United States in the present as its object or, in modernization theory, as the standard for comparison. Categories like "social class" or "social development" were assumed to exist transhistorically and trans-spatially, meaning that it was unproblematic to apply them to earlier historical periods and distant, disparate places. There was a view of historical sociology as "merely the sociology of the past" and as "valuable above all because it increases the number of data points" (Sewell 1996, 246). By the same token, positivist comparativism recommended "replacing proper names of social systems by the relevant variables" (Przeworski and Teune 1970, 30).

The question of sociology's treatment of historical time is complicated by the fact that social evolutionary theory in the eighteenth and nineteenth centuries had already construed colonized parts of the world as earlier stages of the modern West (Fabian 1983). This was reinvigorated in the postwar period under the guise of modernization theory.[64] Connell (1997) sees American sociology's inward turning and its geospatial provincialism as beginning earlier in the twentieth century and continuing after World War II. But this is too general. There were few leading disciplinary figures during the postwar period who were as globally oriented as Edward Ross (1936), but Connell ignores Russian/Soviet specialists like the early Barrington Moore Jr. or Alex Inkeles, Africanists like Immanuel Wallerstein and Horace Miner, as well as comparativists working on "simper societies" like Guy Swanson. The point is not that modernization theory ignored the rest of the world but that it applied the "parochial" concepts of the European-American "ethnosocial sciences" to foreign realities. Such theories do not ig-

---

64. In addition to the references given previously on modernization theory, see also Tripp (1973), Mazrui (1968), and Cooper and Packard (1997).

nore difference so much as they disavow it by subjecting the other to a standardizing logic (Lambek 1991; Clifford and Marcus 1986; Bhabha 1994).

An even simpler approach to global difference was expressed by adherents of the "natural science" approach in postwar sociology. Here the difference between self and other was collapsed altogether, and the life of "non-Western" cultures was equated with the American way of life. The popular postwar sociology textbook by Lundberg, Schrag, and Larsen (1954) pursued such cross-cultural equations relentlessly (see fig. 9.5). S. Dodd's *Project Revere* research for the Korean War effort of the air force examined the effectiveness of air-dropped leaflets in rural towns in Washington State. The explicit assumption here was that rural Washingtonians were identical to Korean peasants rather than being located at a higher stage of a uniform developmental trajectory (DeFleur and Larsen 1958; Robin 2001, 100). Horace Miner mocked such beliefs in his notorious analysis of "Body Ritual among the Nacirema" (1956).

Lest one think that these gestures were found only among the now disparaged acolytes of the "natural science" approach, it is important to recall that the leading voices of postwar sociological theory often claimed to be developing an all-encompassing approach. Edward Shils coauthored with Parsons the chapter in *Toward a General Theory of Action* (1951, chap. 1) that introduced the infamous "pattern variables" that provided modernization

PLATE 11. Similarities in Preliterate and Modern Dress and Adornment. The bustle: Girl at left is the daughter of a Mayogo chief in the Belgian Congo. Her bustle, called a "negbe," is made of dry leaves from a banana tree, trimmed with the red leaves from the banana flower. It is worn fastened at the hips. The round beehive hat is richly decorated with multicolored feathers. Figure at the right illustrates the modern fan bustle, a revival of the Congo style, quite similar to the original in its design.

Figure 9.5 A figure from Lundberg, Schrag, and Larsen (1954), illustrating "similarities in preliterate and modern dress and adornment." Courtesy of Harper & Bros.

theory with some of the categories used to characterize traditional societies (ascription, particularism, and so forth; see Gilman 2003, 86–88). But in the concluding essay of *Theories of Society,* Shils wrote: "Sociological theory as it stands today is . . . [a] sort of short-hand description of the chief features of 'modern society,' with occasional extensions to non-western and nonmodern societies. It is the aim of general theory to become genuinely universal and transhistorical . . . attain[ing] a generality of scope . . . that render[s] it equally applicable to all societies of the past and present" (1961a, 1424). In some respects this approach was even better suited to American imperialism than modernization theory. Since the Suez crisis, the United States had started to support decolonization (Louis and Robinson 1993). The preferred American modus operandi was informal domination that left local sovereignty intact, even insisting on self-rule (Steinmetz 2005f; Liu 1999). Modernization theory infantilized non-Western peoples but at least predicted their eventual convergence with modernity, whereas the colonial rule of difference (Chatterjee 1993) deferred such convergence indefinitely and therefore generated ideologies of the non-Westerner's inherent inferiority.

Here and elsewhere, Shils criticized American sociology's technocratic and manipulative scientism, its empiricism and positivism, its "deficient sense of the past," and even the "disposition to universalize what is, in fact, particular to one society and one epoch." He commented appreciatively, if superficially, on psychoanalysis and on the humanities and the "geisteswissenschaftliche analysis of the realm of symbolic forms," and called for self-reflexivity, the study of history, and attention to the classics. But none of this prevented Shils from insisting that sociology was fundamentally about the search to discover the "variables" underlying "general laws" of action.[65]

Finally, the scientistic program encompassed a new level of enthusiasm for statistical research and for the accoutrements of scientific high modernism (see figs. 3 and 4). As Charles Lindblom (1997, 227) wrote, "in the 1940s and 1950s . . . thanks to new techniques and the computer, the social sciences were perceived as becoming harder, that is, more like the hard sciences" (see also Inkeles 1964, 43). Although we cannot equate quantitative

65. Shils (1961a, 1427, 1433, 1444, 1411, 1417); also Shils (1948). Nor, it might be added, did this prevent Shils from asserting with spectacular arrogance and without referring to a single shred of empirical evidence that contemporary "Western societies" (by which he clearly meant the United States) were "more decently integrated" in the sense that "there is more mutual awareness, more perception of others, more imaginative empathy with the states of mind and motivations of others, more fellow feeling" than in "any societies that have preceded them in world history or are contemporaneous with them in other parts of the world" (1961a, 1429).

or statistical methods with methodological positivism, they clearly certainly had elective affinities. In an analysis of the methods used in the main sociology journals, Platt (1996, 191–93) finds the greatest decadal increase in the use of quantitative methods between the 1940s and 1950s and between the 1950s and the 1960s. By the 1960s a substantial majority of total articles were quantitative.[66]

Conclusion: Fordism and the Awakening of Spontaneous Positivism among the Sociologists

The consolidation of the sociological-scientific field after World War II cannot be explained simply in terms of disciplinary maturation or generational succession. Nor is it satisfying to argue that new sciences tend to emulate the currently most prestigious disciplines.[67] Other newcomer disciplines that emerged at the end of the nineteenth century, most notably anthropology, did not follow the same path as sociology (Keane 2005), and sociology itself did not converge around emulation of any particular "harder" science, whether physics, biology, or economics, during the interwar period. Bourdieu's theoretical framework cannot account for the specific substantive contents of a settled scientific field, that is, it cannot explain why certain epistemologies or theories are felt to be more distinguished than others. There is no universal reason, intrinsic to the study of the social, why methodological positivism came to have more field-specific capital than nonpositivism.

The Holocaust and the cold war made the postwar period inherently different from the prewar period. The impact of the cold war has been rightly emphasized in historical writing about area studies and modernization theory in this period, and the role of emigration from Europe and the Holocaust on American social science has also been explored (e.g., Suedfeld 2001; Srubar 1988). But the impact on sociology of the epochal shifts in the organization of social life in the advanced capitalist world has not been ad-

66. It is also crucial, as R. Miller (1987, 240–41n11) suggests in a discussion of Blalock, to examine statistical as well as broader methodology texts. This is especially true since statistics courses have long been the prime venue for the communication to sociology graduate students of overarching metaphysical and epistemic premises. As Inkeles (1964, 42) pointed out, many sociologists who use statistical methods "would be somewhat surprised if you were to point out that in the mere adoption of a particular statistical technique they are accepting a certain" social ontology, or a model as an "appropriate description of the social world." For one discussion of the ontological implications of different statistical methods, see Abbott (2005).

67. This argument is made by Camic (1995; Camic and Xie 1994), although it is certainly not his entire account.

dressed in any detail. The most significant and all-encompassing new condition after the war was the consolidation of the social forms that retrospectively have come to be known as Atlantic Fordism. By the 1950s and early 1960s, the intellectual, financial, and political forces that had existed before 1945 within sociology combined with the ideological effects of the newly consolidated Fordist mode of regulation to help lift methodological positivism to triumph. On the one hand, the Fordist security state relied to a greater extent than previous regulatory forms on the skills of sociologists, and this entailed a greatly enhanced level of state funding for sociological research. Sociologists' opportunistic efforts to cash in and curry favor with political, military, and business elites played a powerful role in the postwar convergence of the field around positivism. Cold war anticommunism also played a role in convincing some sociologists to embrace the "value-free" ethos and in marginalizing people like C. Wright Mills who retained a political commitment to the "wrong" side. The antiscientific policies and the overall irrationalism of the Nazi and Stalinist regimes played an additional role in convincing some people that politics and science did not belong together, although for the most part the "antitotalitarian" impetus for positivism set in after the 1960s and 1970s with the turning against "political correctness."[68]

The social patterns that regulation theory groups under the heading of Fordism played an equally important role in making methodological positivism seem more plausible to a larger group of sociologists. The Fordist patterning of many aspects of social life in the advanced capitalist world resonated with positivist approaches to social explanation for people who were exposed to those new logics. This is not to say that sociologists actually described the new Fordist conditions. As Camic notes with respect to the Depression, most sociologists display a "head-in-the-sand response to contemporary events," and the postwar period was no different. Sociologists' métier consisted in observing and making sense of the social, but the new social conditions had a powerful impact in ways that did not figure centrally in their writing and that they may not even have perceived consciously.[69] The deeply unstable conditions of the interwar period partly ex-

68. An instructive case in point is Irving Louis Horowitz, who shifted from being an ardent critic of sociological "scientism" and the "suppress[ion] of values at the expense of facts" (in 1964a) to attacking the "bobble heads" who "speak contemptuously of . . . positivism" and "empiricism" (Steinmetz 2005c, 487–89).

69. Other social science disciplines responded to the emerging Fordist formation in ways conditioned by their location in the university field and their particular objects of inquiry. Anthropology, specialized in the cultures of the colonial and postcolonial peripheries, was more

plain why positivism was less compelling at that time as a description of society. After the war, social reality became more orderly and was presented using tropes of stability, repetition, and "the end of history." All of this corresponded more closely to the positivist expectation that social practices can be subsumed under universal covering laws. Social actors now seemed increasingly atomized and interchangeable, losing any distinctive cultural peculiarities, and thus lending themselves to general models of subjectivity (behaviorism, rational choice, and positivist versions of psychoanalysis). Because social practices were more regular and repetitive, it was plausible to forecast and even to control them.[70] For historically contingent reasons, in other words social reality now resonated powerfully with methodological positivism.

Six aspects of postwar Fordism were especially central to this process.[71] (1) The role of science (including social science) in *state policy* was greatly enhanced within the Fordist form of governmentality in comparison to the previous period. The Fordist state relied on a whole panoply of social and fiscal policies to smooth out the bumps in the crisis-ridden process of capitalist accumulation, and it relied on armies of social scientists to design, evaluate, and administer these programs. This integration of sociology into the domestic and foreign policy scientific infrastructure somewhat paradoxically validated the claim that science was "value free," since social scientists could conceive of themselves as a separate and autarkic scientific community only after they had freed themselves from the private corporate organizations that had dominated social research funding during the prewar period (Mirowski 2005). (2) Fordism contributed indirectly to positivism's plausibility by dampening economic crisis through fiscal policies and by lessening some of the economic turbulence in the individual life course via wage and welfare state policies. These developments, which affected unionized industrial workers and the middle wage-earning classes (including many sociologists), made it more plausible that social practices actually repeated themselves in ways that could be represented with gen-

immune to these positivism-enhancing effects, since the global periphery was only marginally brought under the sway of Fordism and was highly unstable in the postwar period. The "behaviorialist revolution" in political science responded to the form and demands of the Fordist state and politics. Keynesian economics, which emerged before Atlantic Fordism, was still highly regarded. Fordism was also connected to various movements in aesthetic modernism (see T. Smith 1993).

70. See the essays in Crawford and Biderman (1969) for confident statements of this forecasting and control perspective.

71. For more detail see Steinmetz (2005a, 2005d, and forthcoming b).

eral covering laws, statistical models, and replicable experiments, thus allowing predictions. Historical analysis became irrelevant for sociology because history had effectively "ended." (3) The increasingly *depthless* and *postideological* culture of Fordism that was replicated serially across regions and social groups and classes enhanced the credibility of models predicated on a picture of universal, interchangeable subjectivity, including behaviorist and rational-choice approaches. Interpretive and semiotic approaches to culture could therefore be abandoned. (4) Fordism's specific *spatial* regime made positivism's denial of the importance of geographic difference seem reasonable. Most social practices, including economic transactions, were not located at multiple and shifting scalar levels and sites but were instead concentrated within the "container" of the nation-state. This encouraged social scientists to take the level of the nation-state for granted as a unit of analysis. Fordism also tended to homogenize this national space internally, even if fewer policies were implemented in the United States than in West Germany or northern Europe to undercut uneven regional development (Brenner 1998). (5) A final aspect of this formation that heightened the credibility of positivism was the emerging foreign policy role of the United States. American imperialism did not begin with Fordism, but the United States now became a global hegemon. As the leading economic power, U.S. hegemony after World War II was oriented toward shaping the world into an open capitalist market via an anticolonial stance (Louis and Robinson 1993; Bergesen and Schoenberg 1980). The United States eschewed direct colonization and was therefore not compelled to enforce a racial "rule of difference" (Chatterjee 1993) in its peripheral dependencies but could promote the convergence of its peripheries with the American way of life. Competition with the USSR for the hearts and minds of the third world also meant that the state encouraged counterinsurgency research like Project Camelot, as long as it promised to yield applicable "lessons for empire" (Steinmetz 2004b). "Ideographic" researchers who learned the languages and histories of specific places tended to be relegated to dominated corners of the discipline, from whence they have only recently been emerging.

In this chapter I have traced the emergence of a hegemonic disciplinary formation and identified some of the ways Fordism resonated with (and directly promoted) sociological positivism after World War II. To claim that sociologists' spontaneous images and theories of the social were influenced by the wider social structures they inhabit does not mean that such images directly *reflect* social reality. Rather, sociologists (like other people) tried to make sense of their own social world, and one of the available models was the positivist one. They were aided in this by the fact that the Fordist mode of regulation was accompanied by a series of self-interpretations. Some of the mainstays of stable Fordism were broadcast constantly to the denizens of the Fordist metropolises as the American Way of Life. These included economic stabilization through demand management, the homogenization of consumer tastes, labor peace, and a steady increase in standards of living, with wages pegged to the cost of living—a system introduced in the General Motors–United Auto Workers contract of 1950 that was termed the Treaty of Detroit by sociologist Daniel Bell in *Fortune* and in the Ford contract of 1955 that gave the UAW a modified version of Walter Reuther's demand for an annual wage (Bell 1950; Lichtenstein 1995, 280–85). When positivists pointed out the connections between existing social patterns and their preferred manner of studying society, reality seemed to ratify their approach.

One result of this conjuncture was the solid implantation of methodological positivism as doxa in the sociological discipline. U.S. sociology's own view of itself followed a narrative of steady progress from social meliorist beginnings toward scientific maturity. In the main historical treatment of the field from the 1950s, Hinkle and Hinkle (1954, 22) described a field becoming ever more focused on "scientific method," which they defined as the quest to discover laws of behavior and a "preference for concrete, empirical work." Despite differences of taste or viewpoint, most of the players in the field recognized common stakes and definitions of field-specific cultural capital. Reputational, social, and economic capital in sociology tended to accrue to more positivist, empiricist, and scientistic positions. Fluency in these idioms began to function as a form of scientific prestige. Even those who disagreed with positivism tended to collude in its dominance. If they refused, they were channeled into less rigidly positivist fields or into poorly regarded sociology departments. Sociology at last became a well-structured field. By returning to this period we may begin to understand some of the ways in which contemporary sociology is still haunted by the specters of this somewhat remote past.

Acknowledgments

Thanks to Craig Calhoun, Christian Topalov, Immanuel Wallerstein, and Jonathan VanAntwerpen for their comments on drafts of this chapter.

[TEN] Orthodoxy, Heterodoxy, and Hierarchy: "Mainstream" Sociology and Its Challengers

Craig Calhoun & Jonathan VanAntwerpen

What is needed is a new and heightened self-awareness among sociologists, which would lead them to ask the same kinds of questions about themselves as they do about taxicab drivers or doctors, and to answer them in the same ways. Above all, this means that we must acquire the ingrained habit of viewing our own beliefs as we would those held by others.

ALVIN GOULDNER, *The Coming Crisis of Western Sociology*

The social sciences deal with pre-named, pre-classified realities which bear proper nouns and common nouns, titles, signs and acronyms. At the risk of unwittingly assuming responsibility for the acts of constitution of whose logic and necessity they are unaware, the social sciences must take as their object of study the social operations of *naming* and the rites of institution through which they are accomplished.

PIERRE BOURDIEU, *Language and Symbolic Power*

Sometime around 1970, sociologists began to refer to an illusive phenomenon called mainstream sociology. Most of those who used the term at first saw this mainstream as a hegemonic force that oppressed them personally and blocked desirable paths for sociology's development. The mainstream was typified by the "ASA leadership," by the *American Sociological Review*, and by a few elite departments like those at Harvard and Columbia. It was more East Coast than West Coast, and indeed some major and influential West Coast sociology departments—like Berkeley's—derived a certain glamour from appearing more insurgent than mainstream. Yet the battle between the alleged mainstream and its critics was also played out within departments, and as much within the Berkeley department as any other. It was a battle of graduate students against faculty, junior against senior, sometimes women and people of color against the evidently white, male mainstream. It was also a battle of theoretical and methodological perspectives, though one has to recover a good bit of context and trajectory to grasp why the alignments took the shape they did.

On the insurgent side, Marxists lined up with ethnomethodologists, symbolic interactionists joined heterodox Weberians, and feminists found common cause with fieldworkers. In the alleged mainstream, survey researchers swam with mathematical modelers, modernization theorists treaded water with organizational theorists, policy researchers probed the same shallow waters as demographers, and functionalists dominated all and claimed to knit everything together in a common theoretical framework. Or so, at least, the mainstream looked to those outside it. But this was only a bit less of an oversimplification than saying that those in the mainstream had grey hair and wore suits.

The sides were drawn in a particular moment, one charged with the energy of large-scale social movements—civil rights, antiwar, women's, environmental—and fueled by the demographic momentum of the baby boom and the expansion of the university system. The sides had a certain elective affinity with long-running distinctions, such as quantitative versus qualitative research, but didn't map neatly onto them. Indeed, such crude distinctions mask internal fissures, such as the extent to which new developments in quantitative methods during the 1960s—path analysis and LISREL, for example—could make scions of the previously dominant Lazarsfeldian version of quantitative sociology feel suddenly outside a new mainstream, where the fastest-flowing channels were carved by analytic statistics rather than data-gathering techniques, and even quantifiers were assigned to the backwaters if they weren't causal modelers or minimally users of multiple regression techniques.[1]

The odd lines of opposition had perhaps their greatest influence not as they were staked out in the late 1960s and early 1970s, but in the decade or two after that. For if "mainstream" had been an epithet tendentiously hurled by radicals in the earlier period, it was a positive virtue claimed no less tendentiously by those who consolidated their influence in the wake of the upheavals. During the difficult decades from the late 1970s through the early 1990s, when jobs were scarce and tenure cases especially likely to be both contentious and terminal for the candidates, being "mainstream" became a mark of merit. It was in fact not under the Old Regime but after the failed Revolution that it mattered most who was judged to be part of the mainstream.[2] This was so, not least, because there were stakes—jobs, and

---

1. On how dramatically quantitative methods changed in the 1960s, see Raftery (2005).

2. It was in the late 1970s and early 1980s, for example, that tenure was famously denied to a number of left-leaning sociologists who had won major prizes for their work—like Jeffrey Paige at Berkeley and Theda Skocpol and Paul Starr at Harvard. The attempt to assert the authority of the mainstream after a hundred flowers bloomed required more repressive measures

NSF grants, and acceptances from the *ASR*—and because those stakes were much more inequitably distributed. In the 1960s, the expansion of the university system ensured an ever-wider availability of jobs. From the mid-1970s, not only were there fewer new jobs but there were more graduate students finishing degrees and there was a growing "backlog" of those who were un- or underemployed. Demands for pre-employment publications shot up, and it became common for those considering tenure cases to insist on achievements far different from those they had earlier been obliged to demonstrate themselves. It was when sociology contracted that it most clearly revealed itself to be a field that differentially distributed rewards and resources in accord with a dominant ideological self-understanding or set of values.

It is not that the discipline did not absorb any of the old radicals; on the contrary, many were tenured, though few in the most elite departments. And the discipline also made room for Marx in the canon of classical theory and for new emphases on race, class, and gender in the curriculum. The new pattern incorporated heterodoxy but further normalized hierarchy. No sociological theory could claim to knit together the concerns of the field as a whole or even to provide a common vocabulary. Subfields proliferated, many founding their own journals and ASA sections. But this is just the point. When sociology contracted, a long-standing differentiation between the undergraduate—and even to a considerable extent the graduate—curriculum and the typical contents of the *ASR* became much more acute. Sociology's majority—employed mostly in teaching positions, sometimes in "applied" research or practice but mainly outside the elite research universities—began to look more and more different from its elite.[3] And the resources and rewards that flowed differentially to the elite began to diverge more sharply from those available to the rest—a trend that continues into the present. Harvard faculty always had higher salaries, more internal research support, more graduate students, and lighter teaching loads than

---

than were in place before—though as sociologists have long observed, resort to actual force often reveals a weakness in authority. It is worth noting that at the time that Paige and Skocpol were denied tenure, they were disciplinary academics—publishing in "mainstream" sociological journals and winning prizes from the ASA—although they challenged dominant approaches. Starr, by contrast, had won the Pulitzer Prize and considerable recognition outside the discipline but was less active within it. There was a different sense in which he deviated from orthodoxy. Obviously other factors were at work in each case, including Skocpol's gender.

3. We refer here to conditions of work and intellectual orientations, but it is also true that as women and people of color entered sociology in greater numbers, they found positions disproportionately outside the elite research departments. See Ferree, Khan, and Morimoto, chap. 13, this volume.

professors at small colleges and nonflagship branch campuses of state universities, not to mention those with less job security than most state university faculty members. The gap simply grew—a lot.

Under these conditions, hierarchy was renewed and intensified, ironically making the concept of the mainstream even more significant but also making clear that it could have at least two meanings (whose distinction was implicit in the original invocations). On the one hand, "mainstream" was the "core," the direction of the future, the heart of the discipline, to which "stars" contributed "cutting-edge" research (to mix a number of metaphors frequently mixed in departmental personnel committees). On the other hand, "mainstream" might have meant the direction in which the majority moved, the source of the waves that occasionally rocked the boat of the *ASR* when insurgents thought it should represent the whole field more. It usually did not. Both the 1960s critics and the 1980s advocates used "mainstream" to describe a particular elite and to give the illusion of its nearly uncontested dominance in the field. A more accurate picture would stress the differentiation between "mass market" sociology, produced especially for and through teaching, though also through a great deal of research and analysis, and a brand-name sociology staking primary claim to the mantle of disciplinary science.

This self-reinforcing stratification system is the sort that Pierre Bourdieu described as typical of developed fields, academic and otherwise. Sociology is a weaker field than some, less able to defend its boundaries, but it is a field well enough organized to distribute its own form of capital, recognizing and rewarding some sorts of performances more than others. In the United States, the postwar period was crucial to the consolidation of sociology as a field, as Bourdieu argued:

> Indeed, it is no exaggeration to say that the universe of sociology, which had begun to function like a *field* in the interwar period—that is, as a space of competition, of struggles, and of genuine debate (there were also the Chicago school, Marxists, and many of the currents that were to emerge later in the so-called period of crisis)—this universe was soon organized into a veritable hierarchical corporate body, a *corporatio* unified around a common vision of science founded upon a few common principles and on a great many exclusions. (Bourdieu 1991a, 378)

Although our analysis is informed by Bourdieu's perspective on fields, he greatly overestimated the extent to which there was a single unified structure organizing the American sociological field in the postwar period. Bourdieu claimed that the elite leaders of American sociology "succeeded in imposing a true intellectual *orthodoxy* by imposing a common corpus of issues, stakes of discussion, and criteria of evaluation." The terms in which Bourdieu evoked the orthodoxy were familiar from C. Wright Mills's famous challenge to it, centered on his telling, but tendentious, suggestion that American sociology was caught between two sources of irrelevance: "abstracted empiricism" and "grand theory" (Mills 1959). In Bourdieu's words, a blend of "functionalist theory" and "positivistic methodology" had come to dominate sociology in the United States. "Establishment sociologists" had put forth a "professional ideology" with global influence. This notion is not altogether false, but it both exaggerates the cohesion and dominance of sociology's postwar elites and neglects the extent to which the "mainstream" only became visible in the 1960s and 1970s clashes over it, and in attempts to impose authority that became more effective in the 1970s and 1980s.

In what follows, we focus first on the retrospective construction and invocation of the category of "mainstream sociology," with special attention to the heroes of the insurgents, Mills and Gouldner. We then turn to the era of postwar expansion most frequently associated with the rise and dominance of the so-called mainstream, discussing the figures Bourdieu referred to as the Capitoline triad—Parsons, Merton, and Lazarsfeld—and continuing with a broader view of the postwar elite, including especially developments at the University of Chicago. We return in conclusion to a critical consideration of the discourse of mainstream sociology. In this chapter we are engaged throughout with the interplay of hierarchy, diversity, orthodoxy, and heterodoxy within postwar American sociology.

A Folk Theory

The mythic image of a postwar "sociological establishment" was embedded in a historical narrative of American sociology that is emblematic of a common set of understandings regarding the trajectory of the discipline in the postwar period. Indeed, we take it to be exemplary of a particularly widespread narrative of the history of postwar sociology, and one that demands further attention and interrogation. In brief, that narrative goes something like this. During the interwar period, American sociology was a pluralistic field full of competing visions and "schools" of sociology. After World War II, the discipline witnessed the installation and imposition of a new orthodoxy, the rise of a "new sociological Establishment," and the formulation of the "professional ideology" of establishment sociologists—what came to be known as "mainstream sociology." "Mainstream sociology" and the establishment sociologists who were its beneficiaries and spokespeople were then subjected to vigorous critique and challenged by disciplinary insurrection. This revolt, carried forward by a "disobedient generation" that came of age in the late 1960s and early 1970s, ultimately led to, and was further propelled by, intellectual fragmentation, increasing diversification, and disciplinary "crisis."[4]

This account of the sociological establishment and its demise typically focuses on "the three great figures" of postwar American sociology: Talcott Parsons, Robert Merton, and Paul Lazarsfeld. As Bourdieu claimed: "Based on their preeminent university positions, the three great figures of the Capitoline triad of the American sociological Pantheon were able to dominate, both in the United States and in other major Western countries, not only teaching institutions but also official publication outlets, professional associations, and even—more or less directly—access to the resources necessary for empirical research" (Bourdieu 1991a, 378). It is a surprisingly individual-centered analysis for a usually relational thinker, but one solidly linked to standard accounts of postwar American sociology.[5] Not entirely without insight, these all-too-familiar accounts can also obscure and mislead. In particular, standard accounts of postwar sociology overestimate the pre-1968 consensus, neglect important older lines of struggle, and exaggerate the extent to which one among many contending claims to the disciplinary mainstream clearly dominated. Yet an emphasis on a few powerful individuals has pervaded numerous critiques of mainstream sociology, both in books and articles and, even more frequently, in ordinary conversations among sociologists. Although the concept of "mainstream sociology" is ambiguous enough to mean many different things, it has been repeatedly tied to a small number of key figures in sociology's dominant postwar elite, especially among those American sociologists who came of age in the 1960s and 1970s,

---

4. For personal accounts of American sociology's "disobedient generation," see Sica and Turner (2005).

5. Of course, neither Harvard nor Columbia was "preeminent" in American sociology before the arrival of Parsons, Merton, and Lazarsfeld; if anything, Chicago was. Harvard and Columbia were extremely valuable institutional bases, but not in themselves determinant. Bourdieu had some experience of U.S. sociology, though not enough to prevent him from thinking Robert Merton an old-line patrician and George Homans a man of the people. (Merton came, in fact, from a family of impoverished Jewish immigrants, while Homans was a Boston Brahmin.) Bourdieu had his longest stay in the United States in 1972–73—when criticism of mainstream sociology was in full flow. He was probably closest to Erving Goffman and more generally derived his understanding of postwar orthodoxy in American sociology—and his image of a sociological establishment that was preceded by pluralism and followed by fragmentation—from rebel sociologists within the U.S. field. Mills and Gouldner were also prominent among these.

during the period when the discourse of mainstream sociology first began to circulate widely.

While it would be difficult to argue that there were no hegemonic projects in postwar sociology, we emphasize the diversity of stances articulated by the actors within the supposedly unified, consensual, and singular projects suggested by the concepts of "mainstream sociology" and the "sociological establishment." Standard accounts of mainstream sociology and the postwar establishment, we think, lack adequate historical reflexivity. There were both attempts to impose orthodoxy and energetic and effective resistance to them.

Common accounts of mainstream sociology not only exaggerate the cohesion and dominance of the postwar establishment but also underestimate the regional and institutional differentiation of the field. Adequately assessing the breadth and depth of success enjoyed by attempts to "impose" a "common corpus of issues, stakes of discussion, and criteria of evaluation," we would argue, requires substantial historical research, including an examination of the field that extends beyond the major PhD-granting departments and the most influential individuals.[6] The present chapter offers only a first step, emphasizing diversity within the disciplinary elite but not analyzing the field as a whole. By interrogating familiar, received understandings regarding these key disciplinary actors, however, we seek to promote a renewed debate about the shape, substance, and stakes of postwar sociology, a debate that might lay the basis for the more detailed research we envision.

Laid down in the struggles of the 1960s and 1970s, and in their aftermath, the conception of a dominant sociological mainstream unrestrained by intellectual opposition has had a powerful effect on the way that American sociologists understand their discipline's history. Once a discursive strategy, a "classificatory epithet," and a weapon of critical sociologists, the notion of the "mainstream" has become an analytic tool for periodizing postwar sociology, even as it also lives on as a label with which to carve up the contemporary field.[7] Yet such accounts of postwar American sociology, drawing at least indirect inspiration from the earlier invocations of the mainstream, frequently beg a significant set of historical questions about one of the most important and dramatic periods in sociology's short history as a discipline. They do so, we suggest, because they rely too heavily and uncritically on the "folk theory" of disciplinary development embedded in the discourse of mainstream sociology.

6. For a similar suggestion, see Bulmer (1994).

7. For the notion of a "classificatory epithet," see Bourdieu (1988).

Take, for example, a *New York Times* op-ed piece, published in May 2002, in which Harvard sociologist Orlando Patterson lamented the passing of David Riesman, author of *The Lonely Crowd,* one of the best-selling books ever written by an American sociologist (Gans 1997). Riesman's work, Patterson claimed, "inevitably raises questions about the claims and limitations of academic sociology today." By Patterson's lights, the discipline of sociology was in decline, hampered by intellectual limitations that were rooted in "the rise in professional sociology of a style of scholarship that mimics the methodology and language of the natural sciences"—a style that ignored or pushed aside many significant social, cultural, and political issues. The problem, Patterson wrote, was "mainstream sociology," a dominant approach to the discipline that had abandoned its "important mission" to engage the American public in an analysis of "how they live." "Mainstream sociology," Patterson charged, "eschews any exploration of human values, meanings and beliefs because ambiguities and judgment are rarely welcomed in the discipline now." By contrast, Riesman, and a group of other publicly oriented sociologists—from Erving Goffman and C. Wright Mills, to Daniel Bell, Nathan Glazer, Peter Berger, and William F. Whyte—had both engaged and influenced public culture in the United States, practicing a form of sociology "different in both style and substance from that of today" (Patterson 2002).

So, what is—or was—mainstream sociology? While at pains to elaborate its particular pathologies, Patterson nonetheless took for granted that his audience would understand what he meant when he used the phrase. To be in the mainstream is to be at the center of a prevailing trend, to belong to an established tradition or field of activity, to be conventional rather than avant-garde, a denizen of the middle and a defender of the golden mean—one who floats comfortably in the wide river, rather than exploring one of its many tributaries. Patterson's readers would likely have understood at least this much of his meaning. In an age when politicians and journalists, musicians and religious leaders are regularly judged to be in or out of the mainstream, why not sociologists as well?

Riesman, Patterson wanted it known, had been anything but a mainstreamer. Rather, he had embraced an independence of mind and possessed "the nerve of failure," defined—and it was with this image that Patterson closed his piece (a sort of obituary both for David Riesman and for a discipline he saw as in deep decline)—by "the courage to face aloneness and the possibility of defeat in one's personal life or one's work without being morally destroyed." Those in the mainstream had given in to the temptation to simply go with the flow. Not so David Riesman. Not so C. Wright Mills.

If we—either as contemporary sociologists or readers of the *New York Times*—could have been expected to understand what Patterson meant by "mainstream sociology," it is curious to note that the same might not have been said of Riesman or Mills, had they been reading this rendering of the discipline in the late 1950s or early 1960s.[8] The notion of "mainstream sociology" is of relatively recent vintage. Indeed, although critics of "mainstream sociology"—and here Patterson is only the most recent in a long line of sociologists who have taken aim at this particular bogeyman—have often invoked figures such as Riesman and Mills, it is not clear that either of these writers actually ever used the phrase.

Where, then, did the concept of "mainstream sociology" come from? Its precise origins are difficult to pinpoint, in part because the phrase has appeared as much, if not more, in ordinary conversations among sociologists as it has in books and articles. Nonetheless, reference to "mainstream sociology" seems to have begun to spread through the field in the late 1960s and early 1970s. These were years of unrest and fragmentation. They were also the years during which opposition to mainstream sociology became much more prominent and pointed—some would say "critical" and "incisive," others "uncivil" and "overwrought."

Some indication of the commonality and significations of the discourse of "mainstream sociology" in the early 1970s can be gathered from a book review written by Lewis Coser (1974) and published in the journal *Social Forces*. Reviewing William J. Goode's *Explorations in Social Theory*, Coser welcomed the collection of essays as a sign of health in sociology, and in particular as a sign of the strength of a unifying "theoretical approach" associated with "functionalist analysis." From Coser's perspective, Goode's functionalism was of the "flexible and pliable" sort, open to grappling with conflict in ways that Coser (1956) considered fundamental to understanding human affairs. The book was also an indication that critics of the sociological "mainstream"—in this case functionalism—had rashly and perhaps ignorantly announced its impotence and demise. Calling Goode's

---

8. Both Riesman and Mills had significant "establishment" sides. Riesman came to sociology from law and sought to engage a broader public than professional sociologists, but he had strong roots in what would later be seen as the disciplinary "mainstream." He taught first at Chicago, then Harvard and was a visiting part of the Lazarsfeld-Merton group at the Bureau of Applied Social Research (see fn. 34 below). Though Mills came from Texas by way of Wisconsin—not an East Coast establishment background—his intellectual roots lay more in pragmatist philosophy and Weber than in Marx. As Becker (1994) notes, he was always determined to maintain his base at Columbia and in New York as a publishing center.

work an "impressive achievement," Coser (1974, 564) wrote in closing: "If those who have recently come to proclaim the 'death of mainstream sociology' from the rooftops were to bring themselves to read it, they might conceivably be led to recognize that their obituaries are decidedly premature."[9]

Who were these naysayers? Why were they prophesying (or perhaps just calling for) the "death of mainstream sociology"? And why did Lewis Coser see the need to chastise them? The critics of mainstream sociology were themselves a motley bunch, including a variety of radical sociologists, Marxists, feminists, phenomenologists, symbolic interactionists, and ethnomethodologists. In the late 1960s and 1970s, these loosely knit "critical" sociologists participated in various forms of disciplinary revolt and intellectual insurrection.[10] In the process, they retrospectively reconstructed the postwar sociological "establishment" to which Bourdieu would later refer, critiquing an elite group of sociologists who purveyed what came to be called "mainstream sociology" and at times making the case for their preferred alternative.

Inventing the "Mainstream"

For many, the watershed year was 1968.[11] As one sociologist told us, it was at the 1968 meetings of the American Sociological Association, held in Boston, that the term *sunshine boys,* a reference to the liberal center of the field in the United States, began to circulate more widely. In an article for *The Activist* written in 1964, Dusky Lee Smith had used the term to describe Seymour Martin Lipset, Nathan Glazer, and Amitai Etzioni (Smith 1964). But already in 1959 Mills had identified "sunshine moralists" as a central tendency in sociology and linked to a broader "liberal practicality" (Mills 1959, 78, 88).

It was also at the 1968 ASA convention that a graduate student from Brandeis University named Martin Nicolaus gave an address titled "Fat-Cat Sociology" in which he repeatedly lambasted the discipline's established elite.[12] "The ruling elite within your profession," he told an audience full of

---

9. The proclamations of the critics notwithstanding, this discourse of death does not seem to have gotten quite as frenzied in the United States as it did in France, where Daniel Cohn-Bendit and his student comrades produced an article titled "Tuer les sociologues" (Kill the sociologists). See Steinmetz and Chae (2002, 112).

10. For more detail, see Fuller (1996), Laslett and Thorne (1997), Levine (2004), McAdam (chap. 11, this volume), Sica and Turner (2005), and VanAntwerpen (2006).

11. See, for instance, Wallerstein, chap. 12, this volume.

12. Nicolaus (1968). Gouldner (1970) famously took Nicolaus's "remarks" as a jumping-off point for discussion on the "coming crisis" of Western sociology.

sociologists, "is in charge of what is called Health, Education, and Welfare." Nicolaus shared the platform with Wilbur Cohen, then secretary of health, education, and welfare. "The department of which the man is head," Nicolaus said, referring to Cohen, "is more accurately described as the agency which watches over the inequitable distribution of preventable disease, over the funding of domestic propaganda and indoctrination, and over the preservation of a cheap and docile reserve labor force to keep everybody else's wages down. He is Secretary of disease, propaganda, and scabbing."

Richard Flacks has called this speech "one of the more electrifying moments in the history of the ASA" and one that "provided an opening for 'radical sociology'" (Flacks 1991, 19). Nicolaus's criticisms of Cohen were outdone only by his criticisms of the sociologists and the "ruling class" they served: "Sociology has risen to its present prosperity and eminence on the blood and bones of the poor and oppressed; it owes its prestige in this society to its putative ability to give information and advice to the ruling class of this society about ways and means to keep the people down. . . . The professional eyes of the sociologist are on the down people, and the professional palm of the sociologist is stretched toward the up people."[13]

While Nicolaus took aim at the entire profession and worried that calls to reform sociology were, in 1968, too little and too late, he reserved particular scorn for the elite leaders of the discipline, those "fat cats" who gave his short talk its title. "The honored sociologist, the big-status sociologist, the jet-set sociologist, the fat-contract sociologist, the book-a-year sociologist, the sociologist who always wears the livery—the suit and tie—of his masters," he told his audience, "this is the type of sociologist who sets the tone and the ethic of the profession, and it is this type of sociologist who is nothing more or less than a house-servant in the corporate establishment." The members of the American sociological "establishment," in short, had become—indeed, had long been—what Bourdieu, more than twenty years later, would call the "organic intellectuals of the dominant class" (1991a, 378).

Two year later, Sociologists for Women in Society (SWS) was formed, yet another sign of discontent and transformations afoot within the discipline.[14] Indeed, many feminist sociologists who entered the discipline in the late 1960s and early 1970s were also Marxists or radicals and thus considered themselves part of a broader "critical sociology movement" that called for attention to issues of race, class, and gender. As both women and people

13. Or even more forcefully: "Sociologists stand guard in the garrison and report to its masters on the movements of the occupied populace" (Nicolaus 1968).

14. See Ferree, Khan, and Morimoto, chap. 13, this volume, for an account a SWS's collective advocacy on behalf of women, and its active protest against the marginality of women within the ASA.

of color entered the discipline in greater numbers, they began to challenge dominant sociological paradigms regarding race and gender, often thereby challenging the "mainstream."[15]

Critiques of "mainstream sociology" were not always at the same time prophesies of its immanent death. They might be, instead, demands for its immediate or future transformation, a transformation that would involve moving underrepresented sociologists or sociological perspectives "from the margin to the mainstream" (see Metz 1994). Thus, Ruth Wallace's edited volume, *Feminism and Sociological Theory* (1989), made the greater inclusion of feminist sociological theory within the "mainstream" one of its explicit aims. Although Wallace's volume came at the end of the 1980s, as feminist theory was consolidating its gains and assessing its continuing challenges, the call for inclusion and the quest for disciplinary transformation were already intertwined in an earlier period, both among feminists and other critical sociologists. As Doris Wilkinson wrote in her review of James E. Blackwell and Morris Janowitz's *Black Sociologists: Historical and Contemporary Perspectives*, "perhaps what is required in the postfunctionalist period, as American sociologists reflect on their heritage, is an ideological metamorphosis and exorcism of racialist elements permeating the sociological consciousness." Wilkinson evinced hope that the volume she was reviewing would push forward the "future incorporation of black sociologists' conceptual paradigms into mainstream sociology."[16]

By the early 1980s, the extent to which the notion of a "mainstream sociology" was familiar in feminist circles was evidenced by the appearance of a telling variant. After Mary O'Brien coined the notion of the "malestream" in her 1981 *The Politics of Reproduction,* feminist sociologists quickly

15. See Laslett and Thorne (1997), Brown (1991), and Collins (chap. 17, this volume). It remains an open question how closely linked the pursuit of more equitable inclusion within sociology's mainstream was to its intellectual transformation and where the balance fell in different projects.

16. Wilkinson (1975, 462). In a similar vein, although from the vantage point of methodology rather than conceptual paradigms, R. Stephen Warner (1976, 68) cited ethnomethodology's "potential contribution to mainstream sociology." See also the introduction to *Radical Sociologists and the Movement,* in which the authors suggest that radical sociology amounts to "a vibrant intellectual countertradition" that "emerged *within* mainstream sociology" (Oppenheimer, Murray, and Levine 1991, 5; our emphasis). Indeed, many radical scholars were attracted to sociology precisely because they saw it as a discipline at least somewhat hospitable to their critical perspectives, concerns about the dominance of the "mainstream" notwithstanding. As Erik Olin Wright puts it, in his contribution to *A Disobedient Generation,* "in sociology, Marxism was treated as a real rival to more mainstream traditions, so even though most sociologists disagreed with me, I felt that my ideas were taken seriously" (2005, 342). It remains an open question how closely linked the pursuit of more equitable inclusion within sociology's mainstream was to its intellectual transformation and where the balance fell in different projects.

took up the term. "What women need to do," O'Brien wrote, "is to be able to demonstrate that male dominant culture and the male-stream thought which buttresses and justifies it are both, in some sense, prejudiced by the very fact that they are masculine."[17] Although *The Politics of Reproduction* was mainly concerned with political theory, the notion of a "male-stream" resonated in sociology as well. If opposition to "mainstream sociology" had connected feminists to others on the discursive and disciplinary margins, opposition to "male-stream" sociology set them apart once again, sharpening a gendered critique of disciplinary hierarchies and inequalities. While feminists were part of a broader "critical sociology movement" then, "mainstream sociology" was not feminism's only target. Feminist sociologists were just as willing to critique Marxists and radicals for their "male-stream" assumptions, just as women of color would critique white feminists for unquestioned assumptions and privilege of their own.

The concept of "mainstream sociology" was invoked as well by Marxists and other critical sociologists, who employed it at times as an alternative to the Marxian notion of "bourgeois sociology," or alongside references to "Establishment Sociologists." And in the late 1970s and early 1980s, just as the feminists had, Marxists and radicals relied on the term to story their own recent past within (and against) the discipline.

In an article published in 1982 in the *American Journal of Sociology*, for instance, Michael Burawoy used the notion of "mainstream sociology" as seeming shorthand for the structural functionalism he took to be dominant in the immediate postwar period. "The two decades after World War Two," Burawoy wrote, "were dominated by Talcott Parsons's grand synthesis of Weber, Durkheim, Pareto, Marshall, and subsequently, Freud. *The Structure of Social Action* (1937) set new parameters and directions in the heyday of an expanding field. It was during this period that Parsons, together with a number of eminent colleagues and students, developed and consolidated the basis of structural functionalism, lending American sociology at least the appearance of an overarching coherence" (Burawoy 1982, S1).

Since "there were few Marxists able to sustain a creative dialogue and critique to counter the euphoria of 1950s sociology," Burawoy suggested, Parsonian structural functionalism had "pursued its totalizing mission unhindered by an intellectual opposition that might have brought its premises into line with the emerging political realities and social movements of the 1960s" (1982, S3). Indeed, in 1965 Parsons had called Marxian theory "ob-

---

17. O'Brien (1981, 5). O'Brien's criticisms of male-stream thought had a clear affinity with prominent criticisms of both male-dominated and "mainstream" sociology. In each case, the emphasis was on the specific social sources from which "mainstream" or "male-stream" sociological theory sprung and on the resulting ideological effects of those sources.

solete." Yet Parsons, Burawoy suggested, was not only oblivious to the Marxist literature after Marx; his theory had also proven to be oblivious to much of the world around it and to "the new historical forces being unleashed on its own doorstep." "Isolated" and "abstract" in character, Parsonian theory was out of step and ill-equipped to deal with the "burgeoning collective disaffection of the 1960s."[18] As a result, "the 1960s involved the rejection of mainstream sociology," a rejection epitomized most forcefully by the work of two frequently cited sociological rebels, C. Wright Mills and Alvin Gouldner. As Burawoy wrote: "Vilified by C. Wright Mills, and later given a more nuanced critique by Alvin Gouldner (who sought to recover the emancipatory potential, the voluntaristic moment of structural functionalism), mainstream sociology came under relentless assault. 'Conflict theory' replaced 'consensus theory'; contradiction replaced equilibrium; critiques of capitalism replaced its celebration" (1982, S4).

Burawoy's account of these changes within the sociological field was intended to fit a specific purpose, introducing an *AJS* issue devoted to "Marxist Inquiries." Thus, in his brief rendering of postwar American sociology, he attempted to situate and contextualize a "resurgence of Marxism in American Sociology," a revival whose impetus had come from "the protests and disillusionments of the 1960s and early 1970s" (Burawoy 1982, S7). Burawoy himself was an important part of that resurgence. When in the mid-1970s, Erik Olin Wright and others succeeded in getting the Department of Sociology at the University of California, Berkeley, to consider Burawoy for a position, letters were solicited from Burawoy's professors at the University of Chicago, where he had received his PhD. In the midst of a long and contradictory letter evaluating Burawoy's sociological work and potential, Edward Shils wrote to Robert Bellah: "It is my impression that Mr. Burawoy is hampered intellectually by excessive and unrealistic preoccupation with what he regards as conflicts between himself and the prevailing trends of sociological analysis in the United States. He seems to think that he must struggle to prevent himself from being overpowered or seduced by 'mainstream sociology.'"[19]

By the mid-1970s, then, the notion of "mainstream sociology" was in

18. Burawoy's rendering appears to have been representative of a widely held view among critical sociologists. To cite another example, more than ten years earlier, Steven Deutsch made a similar point in his review of Alvin Gouldner's *The Coming Crisis of Western Sociology:* "While American cities burn and American military might destroys a people and culture in Southeast Asia, Talcott Parsons and his fellow Establishment Sociologists launch their celebration of American society" (Deutsch 1971, 322).

19. A portion of this letter is reproduced in Burawoy's chapter for *A Disobedient Generation* (Burawoy 2005a).

the disciplinary air, and by the early 1980s, Burawoy could confidently use it to refer to structural functionalist orthodoxies. Yet, as the letter from Shils indicates, at this point the term was being used largely as a means of intervening critically in debates about the discipline. Indeed, Shils's image of Burawoy's "excessive and unrealistic preoccupation" with "mainstream sociology" was no doubt indicative of the self-image of the so-called mainstream. Shils's use of scare quotes is instructive. From Shils's perspective, "mainstream sociology" may as well have amounted to a figment of Burawoy's imagination. It was a fantasy that paid no intellectual dividend, a counterproductive and misguided obsession.

From the perspective of Burawoy and his peers, however, it was precisely the "struggle" (not only individual but collective) between mainstream sociology and its others—whether Marxism, feminism, or some other form of "critical" sociology—that would generate genuine intellectual progress. The invocation of a sociological "mainstream" sharpened the conflict between the previously dominant structural functionalism and its ascendant opponents. Like its feminist variant, "male-stream," the notion of "mainstream sociology" employed a binary logic, differentiating between those individuals or forms of sociology that were in the mainstream and those that were willing to stand—consciously and conspicuously—outside it. This binary gave the notion of "mainstream sociology" some of its power and helps to explain in part why it captured the imagination of a generation of critical sociologists who were opposed to what they saw as dominant trends within the discipline.

Two key touchstones for sociologists of this generation, many of whom mobilized the discourse of mainstream sociology in order to critique the discipline, were Alvin Gouldner and C. Wright Mills. Indeed, E. Digby Baltzell once referred to Mills as "the great disestablishmentarian guru." "In my day at Columbia," Baltzell wrote, "when ambitious graduate students still looked to Brooks Brothers rather than the local Army and Navy Store for their sartorial standards, Professor Mills was a prophet in lifestyles, as well as in sociology, as he roared up to Fayerweather Hall on a motorcycle, clothed more often than not in the style now cultivated as a badge of baptism by the followers of Professor Gouldner."[20]

As Gouldner would later suggest, the sentiments of the New Left and the

20. Baltzell (1972, 215-16). As Howard G. Schneiderman (1991, xv) notes in his introduction to Baltzell's *The Protestant Establishment Revisited*, Baltzell's cool memories of Mills were at least in part related to his claim that Mills had included one of Baltzell's long papers in his book *White Collar*, without attribution. See also Wrong 1999. By the 1990s, Baltzell's own sartorial standards had returned to fashion and were celebrated in a J. Peterman catalogue that hawked an "E. Digby Baltzell Memorial Tweed Suit" in tribute to the past glory of the WASP.

"Psychedelic Culture" of the 1960s were "deeply dissonant with the sentiments and assumptions embedded in the Parsonian synthesis"—so much so, he suggested, that "the mind boggles at the thought of a Parsonian hippie" (Gouldner 1970, 160). Mills, on the other hand, represented a clear alternative. "My first image of sociology," Harvey Molotch (1994, 231) has written, "was through the writing of C. Wright Mills, whom I also imagined as an album cover. He merged with Jack Kerouac, Lenny Bruce, and Henry Miller in my mind; they were all heroes who knew the world through its edges—deviant, strident, and/or dirty-mouthed."

While he has often been celebrated as a sociological rebel, C. Wright Mills was much more than just a maverick on a motorcycle. In fact, this image of Mills-the-rebel, as Daniel Geary has suggested, may be one of the reasons that Mills-the-sociologist has frequently been both mythologized and misunderstood. An unstinting critic of American sociology, Mills was alienated from the professional and academic center of his discipline, including some of his most powerful colleagues in the field. Yet his intellectual approach and sociological interests were importantly connected to powerful currents within the discipline, in no small part due to his place at Columbia University. As Geary puts it, "Mills' approach to social science was distinctive, yet it shared important elements with mainstream work."[21]

A critic of what would come to be called mainstream sociology, Mills seems never to have used the term himself. But is it the sort of term he might have used? Is the understanding of sociology as embedded in the discourse of "mainstream sociology" an understanding Mills would have embraced? In at least one sense, the answer to this question is clearly yes. Those who employed the notion of mainstream sociology often relied on an either-or logic, differentiating those individuals who were in the mainstream from those who were willing to stand outside it. Its use therefore often involved an important element of intellectual self-identification, if only of the negative sort. Mobilizing the discourse was a way to position oneself within the discipline and discourse of sociology, if only by saying what one was not. This is the sort of critical disciplinary position and intellectual identity Mills cultivated, especially as his career developed.

In another sense, however, it is less clear that the discourse of "mainstream sociology"—pro or con—fits with Mills's position and perspective all that well. First, although an intellectual outsider in a variety of ways, Mills spent the greater part of his career in the sociology department at Columbia University, one of the two universities most widely associated with

21. Geary (2004, xi). We draw substantially on Geary's reading of Mills and his milieu.

the postwar hegemony of mainstream sociology, and home to both Merton and Lazarsfeld.[22] From an institutional perspective, at least, Mills was a member of what would later be called the "sociological establishment," even if he would not be counted as an establishment sociologist. Second, and perhaps more importantly, there is a sense in which the notion of mainstream sociology implies the existence of an alternative approach to sociology, and perhaps an alternative sociological tradition. Yet Mills never really elaborated such a tradition.

In *The Sociological Imagination,* for instance, while he referred to the possible continuation of a "grand tradition" of "classical sociology," Mills largely ignored existing alternative trends within the discipline. The much-vaunted notion of the "sociological imagination" did not draw on examples of contemporary works of sociology—those occupying what Mills had earlier called a "third camp"—and thus did not seem to represent a currently viable alternative to the two leading styles of sociological research that were the book's primary targets. It was rather presented as an outsider's vision of what social science might be or might become, if not for the dominance of Parsonsian "grand theory" and Lazarsfeldian "abstracted empiricism."

To a certain extent, Mills's hope that such dominance would give way to a greater flowering of the sociological imagination can be gathered from the title he initially gave to what was to become his most famous book. Prefiguring the discourse that announced the "death of mainstream sociology," *The Sociological Imagination* was originally to be called *Autopsy of Social Science.* In the end, Mills decided that what sociology needed was not an autopsy of its already dead body but a "diagnosis" of its present sickness, and one that might presage a "coming health" (Mills 1959, 132; see Geary 2004, 230–33). Mills's rhetorical style nonetheless left the impression that he saw himself as one of the very few sociologists capable of administering the appropriate shot in the arm. "I must ask that you *not* mention any of this to our friends, especially on Morningside Heights," he wrote to a friend with whom he had discussed the first draft of his book. "I want it to be just one big, dandy surprise: as from a prophet who comes in from the desert" (see

22. Mills's contempt for Columbia's proprieties and authorities is celebrated. It is sometimes suggested that it was either occasioned by or the reason for a refusal to appoint him to the graduate faculty. Mills spent his entire Columbia career affiliated with the undergraduate college and not the graduate school. Irving Louis Horowitz (1983) presents this as evidence of repression by Lazarsfeld and Merton (who recruited him), and there may be truth to this. But it seems as likely to be Mills's way of preserving autonomy from the Merton/Lazarsfeld team—though of course at considerable cost in chance to influence graduate students.

Geary 2004, 232). If Mills was to be remembered as a maverick on a motor-cycle, then, this was at least in part a myth of his own deliberate making. And he would not be critical sociology's last self-proclaimed prophet.

Straddling the boundaries among disciplinary professionals, left critics, and more publicly oriented writers was another self-styled prophet and critic of the postwar mainstream, Alvin Gouldner. Gouldner spent most of his career as an academic sociologist, however pugnacious and "ill-adjusted" he was to that role. He was among Robert Merton's most brilliant students and certainly the one most likely to leave a trail of blood and con-troversy. Earlier in his career he produced sociology in the Columbia mode of problem-oriented, modestly critical, broadly functionalist (but just a little bit Marx-inspired) inquiry. Later he founded *Theory and Society* and pushed for an alternative to "mainstream sociology," among other things seeking to connect Western sociology better to Marxism and all sociology better to classical social theory.

Until the late 1960s, wrote Richard Flacks and Gerald Turkel, radical voices in sociology had been "cries in the wilderness" (1978, 198). Yet little more than a decade after the publication of Mills's *The Sociological Imagina-tion*—and in just the period during which, according to Flacks and Turkel, "the radical polemic began to have a real impact on sociology's character"—came the publication of another book that captured the imagination of a new generation of sociologists critical of their discipline's "mainstream." With *The Coming Crisis of Western Sociology,* Gouldner had an improbable bestseller, yet it was perhaps a sign of the times, and of the centrality of so-ciology to those times, that the *New York Times Book Review* named it one of the Twelve Books of the Year for 1970. *The Coming Crisis,* wrote Steven Deutsch in an *ASR* symposium on the book, was a "monumental work" that went "beyond the writings of C. Wright Mills, whose writings have had great impact on anti-establishment thinking, and whose concerns were with the ideological factors in social theory." Just as Mills's work had chal-lenged the social theorists who dominated the field, and thus drawn their ire, so *The Coming Crisis,* Deutsch predicted, would sit uncomfortably with "Establishment Sociologists in the functionalist tradition."[23] As one sociol-ogist told us, Gouldner's critique of these elite sociologists, and especially Talcott Parsons, may have been "overdone," but it was also "damning," and the book became "a kind of rallying text" for a new generation of politically engaged critical sociologists. As Flacks and Turkel put it (1978, 197): "What

---

23. Deutsch (1971, 322). In the course of his review, Deutsch used "mainstream sociology" as a marker for the work of these "Establishment Sociologists."

had been in the 1950s a rhetorical underground within the discipline, became by the late 1960s a critique in action; for the new-left activists challenged not only national policymakers and the university managers, but also their own professors."

One key feature of Gouldner's work, not infrequently adopted and adapted by his New Left followers and fellow travelers, was a distinction—one of the most memorable of Gouldner's "ubiquitous dichotomies"—between the "Academic Sociology" produced by the "Establishment Sociologists" and the form of sociology Gouldner championed, which he referred to as "Reflexive Sociology."[24] Like Mills's *The Sociological Imagination,* the bulk of Gouldner's *The Coming Crisis* was concerned with a critical consideration of the "sociological establishment," embodied by the figure of Parsons. Yet "Reflexive Sociology," Gouldner's explicitly "radical" alternative, was intended to be not only a "nay-saying or a 'critical sociology,'" but also the basis for articulating a positive vision of sociology and society (Gouldner 1970, 500).[25] While Academic Sociology misrecognized the social world in which it was situated, Reflexive Sociology would be positioned to grapple with that world, and thus to achieve a "distinctive awareness of the ideological implications and political resonance of sociological work" (499). If Parsonian theory was facing an "impending entropy," in good part because it was out of step with the political and social spirit of the times, Reflexive Sociology provided a recipe for a self-critical radical sociology. Since Parsonian sociology was "no longer instrumentally or expressively appropriate to the time," Gouldner wrote, "it withers as an intellectual paradigm."[26] In the face of an emerging "polycentrism" in American sociology, in which Parsons and his followers were being de-centered, an opening appeared for the development of a more reflexive approach.[27]

24. On Gouldner's "ubiquitous dichotomies," see Lemert and Piccone (1982). For more on Gouldner, see Chriss (1999).

25. As other sociologists appropriated and adapted Gouldner's approach, several different and not entirely commensurable dichotomies were put into play: "academic," for instance, was clearly a broader category than "mainstream."

26. On the "impending entropy" of Parsonianism, see Gouldner (1970, 159–62). In contrast with Burawoy's later characterization of Parsonian theory's inability to deal adequately with the "burgeoning collective disaffection of the 1960s," which emphasized the civil rights movement, the antiwar movement, and the student movement (Burawoy 1982, S4), Gouldner (1970, 162) emphasized that Parsonianism was "out of phase" with both a "mature Welfare State" and with an "emerging Psychedelic Culture."

27. On the emerging polycentrism, see Gouldner (1970, 22, 157). At the same time, it should be noted that Gouldner's own book reproduced the overwhelming emphasis on theory—in more or less the Parsonsian sense—as constitutive of sociology.

Behind the Myth of the Mainstream: Harvard and Columbia

Functionalism became a favorite target of the insurgents partly because they were interested in storming the citadel of high theory. They needed to challenge Parsons. But more generally, functionalism had become a general vocabulary for sociology, assumed except where a specific effort was made to supplant it.[28] As Immanuel Wallerstein notes in his contribution to this volume, structural functionalism was the "dominant theoretical label" of this period, and Parsons's 1937 *The Structure of Social Action* was the defining text. Beginning his project of intellectual synthesis and general theory building in the 1930s, Parsons had some very important collaborators, like Edward Shils, and a very advantageous institutional position at Harvard. He quickly moved into the forefront in the postwar period, famously arguing that Weber, Durkheim, Marshall, and Pareto had all converged on a common theory of action (Parsons 1937).

There was, however, another convergence. At the heart of Parsons's "functionalism" was an argument about the essential interconnection of innumerable disparate aspects of social life, issues in social reform, possibilities for social policy. These were all part of a "system." What this meant, to some extent, was that piecemeal projects of empirical research, social reform, and policy intervention were doomed to underperformance if not failure unless they took account of the deep interdependence of parts within the system as a whole. Thus, Parsons reproduced the concern for "interdependence," which Thomas Haskell (1977) has identified as basic to the move away from the old nineteenth-century approach that embedded social science deeply in specific reformist ventures and idealized individual commitments to them. At the end of the nineteenth century, increasing engagement with interdependence doomed the American Social Science Association and helped spur the development of academic social science disciplines, including especially sociology. It was a central theme of the *AJS* in the 1890s. The "general theories" of the day were much looser than those of Parsons (whether Sumner's Spencerian social Darwinism or the integrative approaches of Ross, MacIver, Giddings, and similar earlier generalists). Although Parsons's approach to sociology would thoroughly displace these earlier theories, he was to a large extent taking up an analogous intellectual agenda. And if early on he would famously ask "who now reads Spencer?"

28. One crucial condition of this was that Merton and Lazarsfeld chose to play on the functionalist team. The differences between Columbia and Harvard were kept muted rather than elevated into a clash of paradigms, and the rapprochement helped to sustain the notion that functionalism was a singular "mainstream."

and later reveal that he seemed to read Spencer more than most, it was partly because he was taking over the intellectual space claimed by the American Spencerians, but in a far more professional way.[29]

It hardly needs repeating that Parsons's theoretical writings were influential, though many have pointed out that the actual substantive influence was perhaps less than frequency of citation or borrowing of terminology might suggest. Parsons's earliest students included several of the key figures of postwar sociology.[30] The Department of Social Relations he helped to found played an important role in anthropology and to a lesser extent psychology. Hardly simply conservative, despite its later reputation, it was an expression of the optimism felt by many social scientists that they were finally going to achieve a systematic, integrated, and cumulative approach to knowledge. This was, moreover, a liberal optimism, for the social scientists expected their work to inform government policy. It was in large part as the country as a whole became more conservative, not least in the McCarthy era, that Parsons and many colleagues turned their hopes away from state-led reform, at least within the United States. This is one reason why so many turned their attention to modernization, which was, as Nils Gilman (2003) has suggested, not only a reflection of America's cold war competition with the USSR but an externalization of liberalism from domestic affairs into the "development" of the non-Western world. Probably the most widespread and influential engagement with Parsons's general social theory came through modernization theory and related projects of comparative research (though it should be recalled that Edward Shils also played a leading theoretical role here). Modernization theory was taken up more by political scientists, like Gabriel Almond and others who took up the comparative study of political behavior (partly under the influence of the committee Almond long led at the SSRC), or by anthropologists like Clifford Geertz, who, along with Shils, took up the study of "new nations."[31] But in

29. As Alan Sica (1997) notes, this much-cited question about the reading of Spencer was not Parsons's own invention, but was rather borrowed from his Harvard colleague Crane Brinton. It is also worth noting that sociology has tended to swing back and forth between periods in which theoretical synthesis was dominant and periods in which analysis in various empirical subfields grew with only loose connections to one another, if any. The Spencerians were the most important synthesizers arguing for interdependence before Parsons.

30. Examples included Robert Merton (and some others shared with Sorokin), Kingsley Davis, Wilbert Moore, Herbert Garfinkel, Renee Fox, Robert Bellah, Neil Smelser, Robin Williams, and Marion Levy.

31. Geertz's calls for "local knowledge" would later appeal to a variety of rebels against functionalism; his roots as a student of Parsons and a functionalist analyst are not always recognized.

sociology as well, it was perhaps at the very "macro" level of what societies were supposed to be like and how they could be compared that the Parsonsian system revealed most purchase.[32] And it is therefore no accident that when functionalism went into decline, many of the most ferocious challenges focused on modernization theory (most prominently bringing various versions of Marxist theory into play).

Domestically, Parsons himself wrote on the American university, and others of his students developed aspects of his theory in different empirical domains, from religion to medicine. But as suggested previously, Parsons's theory was most important where concerns were the most general—and accordingly, in the Parsonsian sense, theoretical. Kingsley Davis and Wilbert Moore, for example, famously extended Parsonsian theory directly into empirically informed analyses of domestic social stratification. The Davis-Moore argument as to the functional value of inequality became a shibboleth for insurgents in the 1960s, who sought to show how functionalism legitimated the existing order and neglected the role of power.

In many active lines of empirical research there was only a nod toward Parsonsian functionalism. In quite a few of these lines of research, the project of "functionalism" was more substantially influenced by the work of Robert K. Merton. Merton had studied with Parsons toward the end of his graduate school years at Harvard, though his primary mentors were Pitirim Sorokin and the historian of science George Sarton. He gave Parsons generous credit for showing him a more analytically integrated view of the enterprise of sociological theory, but already in the 1930s he had argued with the budding general theorist, suggesting that his "formulations were remote from providing a problematics and a direction for theory-oriented empirical inquiry into the observable worlds of culture and society." Merton would go on to state his "case for 'theories of the middle range' as mediating between gross empiricism and grand speculative doctrines."[33] In other words, Merton claimed the middle ground between "abstracted empiricism" and "grand theory" even before Mills used the terms as so effective an indictment. But Merton's "middle-range theory" was different from the kinds of analyses Mills produced in *White Collar* or *The Power Elite*. The latter were works aimed not only at professional sociologists but at a broader

32. Parsonsian comparative sociologists like Marion Levy have been nearly completely forgotten but were very influential for decades. Some others like Robert Bellah remained prominent as they shifted topics from comparative research to communitarian inquiry into American society. And indeed, as Gilman has noted, modernization theorists not drawn to neoconservatism were apt to become communitarians.

33. This is Merton's recollection in "A Life of Learning" (Merton 1994).

public. Though their analyses and (more or less implicit) theoretical frameworks were different, Mills's writings were in crucial ways more akin to David Riesman's *The Lonely Crowd* than to the works of either Merton or Parsons.[34]

Merton's idea of middle-range theory focused on transposable explanatory constructs—what in contemporary literature are often evoked by the "mechanisms" at their core. These had both a manifest and a latent function. The former was to focus sociologists' attention on explanatory problems that could be tackled effectively and be the basis for what Lakatos would later dub a progressive research program (Lakatos and Musgrave 1970). The latent function was to secure some autonomy from Parsons without direct confrontation. Together, both manifest and latent functions contributed to the success Merton enjoyed in creating an approach to sociological explanation that offered sociologists not merely a vocabulary, a theoretical framework, or a belief system but a craft skill. Merton had been hired at Columbia as part of a compromise—MacIver would get a theorist and Lynd an empiricist.[35] In fact, both MacIver and Lynd were supplanted by the new guys, who quickly formed a strong team. The empiricist was Paul F. Lazarsfeld, though it needs to be emphasized again that although styled the "theorist" in this relationship, Merton was in fact consistently engaged in empirical research (and even innovated technique, as, for example, by developing the "focused group interview" or "focus group"). The idea that theory and empirical research should be combined was already prominent at Columbia; Giddings had stressed as much in the early twentieth century. But Merton and Lazarsfeld gave this new substance and form.

34. Riesman's differentiation from the Columbia sociologists should not be exaggerated. Merton's account of "social structure and anomie" shaped the concepts of anomie, adjustment, and autonomy pivotal to *The Lonely Crowd*. With Nathan Glazer, Riesman tried out the conceptual framework by reanalyzing the interviews Mills's students had conducted for *White Collar*. And he contributed a warm memoir to the festschrift for Paul Lazarsfeld, crediting the latter with influencing his decision to leave law for sociology. As he wrote, "It is hard to give a sociology student today a sense of the excitement that surrounded the Bureau of Applied Social Research in the decade 1948–58—an atmosphere from which I learned and drew colleagueship and friendship. It was a shop where all kinds of studies were underway and in which substantive explorations of then relatively new areas . . . were proceeding simultaneously with methodological inquiries . . . ideas were freely shared, hunches tried out, languages of social research elaborated" (Riesman 1979, 212).

35. In fact, the story of their hiring and eventual partnership is more complicated and interesting. At first, indeed, they barely spoke and showed little interest in each other—until Lazarsfeld decided he simply ought to be gracious and acknowledge his opposite number by going around to say hello. The rest is history, though not adequately written history. See Hunt (1961), Lazarsfeld (1975), and Merton (1994).

They pioneered what became a widespread and normatively approved approach to formulating research projects and journal articles.[36] If Parsons's early students were central to modernization theory and the most general arguments about social structure and inequality, Merton's and Lazarsfeld's students became leaders in a wide range of specific research programs.[37]

Parsons looms larger in histories of sociology than his actual influence warrants, not only because he has been a regular target of critics (a fact that has tended to retrospectively inflate his disciplinary centrality), but also because histories by sociologists tend to focus disproportionately on theory. Parsons's theory is treated as an icon representing the whole postwar era. But this is partly because it can be deployed as an exemplar of a general theory and set alongside other putatively analogous theories in a classical canon. This is the approach of textbooks, but equally of much serious theoretical reading and writing (for example, Jürgen Habermas's *Theory of Communicative Action*). It was exemplified in Parsons's own *The Structure of Social Action*. And the form or genre itself is in important ways one of Parsons's influences. Drawing on his German education and European reading, he helped to establish the sociological canon.[38] There had long been histories of social thought—by Howard P. Becker and Harry Elmer Barnes, for example, and many of the other great figures of early twentieth-century sociology (see Sica, chap. 21, this volume). But most of these ranged over all manner of social thought from ancient Greece to medieval scholastics, early modern moral philosophers, and political economists. Parsons cre-

36. Before he ever got to Columbia, Merton had published articles in three of the five first volumes of the *ASR*, as well as the *AJS* and *Social Forces*. He was among the first sociologists whose reputation would rest more on articles than books. Merton and Lazarsfeld published relatively little jointly, considering how much each influenced the other. Only a single co-authored article (Merton and Lazarsfeld 1943) marks the extent to which their separately published wartime inquiries into communications and mass persuasion were in fact mutually informing. Their important edited collection, *Continuities in Social Research* (Merton and Lazarsfeld 1950), served as something of an advertisement for their shared perspective. In it they both paid tribute to Stouffer's *American Soldier* studies and showcased their own different styles of analysis—notably in Merton and Alice Rossi's chapter on reference groups.

37. The students included Peter Blau, James Coleman, Lewis Coser, Rose Coser, Alvin Gouldner, Seymour Martin Lipset, Alice Rossi, Peter Rossi, and Philip Selznick.

38. What Parsons thought belonged in this canon is suggested by the anthology he edited with Edward Shils, Kaspar D. Naegle, and Jesse R. Pitts, *Theories of Society* (Parsons et al. 1961). Parsons was also active in translation and in advising the Free Press on its selection of canonical works to publish in English. The Free Press publications of the 1950s and 1960s were themselves a considerable influence on American sociology and especially the understanding of sociological theory within it.

ated a new genre of specifically sociological theory—as distinct from social thought more generally (albeit with a tenuous argument as to the convergences that defined the canon). This was part of what Robert Merton (1994) recalled of Parsons's teaching at Harvard—"the corpus of social thought which Sorokin summarized," Merton claimed, "Parsons anatomized and synthesized"—and it amounted to a crucial act of field formation, in Bourdieu's sense, as much because of its exclusions as its inclusions. Parsons's critics have emphasized his failure to give Marx much prominence in his identification of the crucial resources he presented to the sociological "mainstream." Certainly his canon, like any, was skewed. And later readings of Parsons suggest he learned rather more from Marx than he was inclined to emphasize in the 1950s.[39]

Parsons's act of canon formation has, however, been both influential and misleading in quite another way as well. It established each of those authors included as a producer of general theory in the same sense as Parsons himself sought to produce it. But neither Weber nor Durkheim—to take the two most central examples—was so purely an abstract systematizer as was Parsons. To render each a "theorist" required placing emphasis on one dimension of their intellectual production and specifically underemphasizing the extent to which each was—and more or less inseparably—a pioneering empirical researcher. Merton did not produce much abstract general theory in this sense—what Mills labeled "grand theory." He did seek generality through middle-range theories, each of which would transcend particular contexts of explanation. One might thus use the theory of deviance or reference groups or role sets in explaining patterns of crime or science or educational attainment. Merton was in the business of giving working sociologists tools with which to produce publishable research and to evaluate publications and see what should be retained as part of cumulative scientific knowledge.[40]

The same pragmatic orientation that helps explain why Merton figures

39. See, for example, Jeffrey Alexander's own effort to read theory in the Parsonian mode, *Theoretical Logic in Sociology* (1982). Also on Parsons, see Robertson and Turner (1991), Camic (1987, 1989), and Howard Brick's useful efforts to trace Parsons's movement from a state-centered vision of social engineering in the 1930s to a more conservative and impressively apolitical social theory in the 1950s (Brick 1993, 2000).

40. Merton's somewhat unsatisfactory distinction of the history of theory from its systematics attempted both to express this approach to scientific knowledge and to claim something of the ground of general theory that Parsons dominated. It was a distinction at once informed by and in tension with much of his own empirical research on science. See Merton (1968b).

less than he should in disciplinary histories helps also to explain why Lazarsfeld is much more widely and centrally remembered than Samuel Stouffer—in a sense Lazarsfeld's Harvard counterpart. Lazarsfeld himself regarded Stouffer as a titan and a major influence on his own work. But Stouffer has faded from memory—and indeed in his lifetime his influence faded, despite his major work in sociological statistics and the prominence he received from the *American Soldier* studies (see Abbott and Sparrow, chap. 8, this volume). Lazarsfeld's greater fame no doubt reflects in part his influence on the substantive field of communications research. It is also the product of his institutional activism. He founded not only Columbia's highly productive Bureau of Applied Social Research but the Center for Advanced Study in the Behavioral Sciences as well. If Merton was the key leader in the sociology department, Lazarsfeld was in each of these other institutions.[41] Surely Lazarsfeld's influence stemmed importantly from his partnership with Merton (and vice versa). And the lack of corresponding teamwork between Parsons—with his more self-sufficient version of theory—and Stouffer helps to explain why Stouffer is less well known today.[42] But equally important is the specific approach that Merton and Lazarsfeld took up together. This approach focused on identifying problems—often practical as well as intellectual, which was a crucial reason for Lazarsfeld's capacity to keep the Bureau and their larger project funded—and seeking to resolve these in a way that would contribute to cumulative scientific knowledge without depending on prior theoretical synthesis.

Whatever its implications for their retrospective fame, the "craft" orientation Merton and Lazarsfeld developed equipped their students (and many others) with a set of skills oriented toward pragmatic problem solving and intellectual production. Their influence came through the students and the approach as much as their own specific publications. Even many of the concepts Merton originated may be thought of in this way. "Unintended consequences" was an idea running through the whole of functionalist analysis. What Merton did in his 1936 article on the topic was to frame it in a way that made it a workable tool for sociologists. Likewise, "role model," "Matthew effect," "self-fulfilling prophecy," and other Mertonian coinages passed not only into the general vocabulary but into the sociologist's tool

41. The founding of the center was the occasion for a rare falling out between Merton and Lazarsfeld, when the former broke ranks with the latter's plan for a more hierarchically structured organization centered on the training of junior members by senior.

42. At the Lazarsfeld centenary conference, September 29, 2001, Merton suggested that at the time Stouffer was recruited to Harvard there was a conscious intention to create such a partnership, but that this never took off.

kit. They were not so much theories to be tested as equipment for constructing explanations.[43]

The point is of more general relevance, however. Merton and Lazarsfeld contributed at least as much to the mainstream of American sociology as Parsons did—if by this we mean the process of continually producing more sociology. Mills skewered Lazarsfeld—a bit unfairly—with his invocation of "abstracted empiricism" as one of the sources of sociological irrelevance. But as we have discussed, Merton was not in the grand theory business. Both Merton and Lazarsfeld—and their numerous students—were already engaged in a project that escaped the dualism. But their project did not escape the authority or normalization structures of American sociology. Indeed Merton and Lazarsfeld were extremely influential gatekeepers. Most centrally, though, if Parsonsian theory gave postwar sociology its preeminent ideology of unity and generality, Merton and Lazarsfeld provided the most influential exemplification of how theory and research fit together, and with their students they produced the canonical model for expressing this combination in journal articles and monographs.

Merton himself reflected on their relationship as having given sociology its "original odd couple": "Paul was and remained the matter-of-fact but methodologically demanding positivist; I was something of a doubting Thomas about positivism who, in my very first published paper, had dared to satirize, rather than adopt, the 'enlightened Boojum of Positivism'" (Merton 1994, 170). It is crucial to grasp that the Boojum is a snark, from Louis Carroll's poem "The Hunting of the Snark," and although it is the most dangerous of snarks, it is nonetheless an imaginary creature. This characterization did not stop positivism from becoming an important target for the critics of mainstream sociology in the 1960s and 1970s. "Positivism" encompassed at once Mills's "abstracted empiricism," philosophical positions more directly indebted to either Comte or the Vienna positivists, and more generally the production of false certainties about social life. Merton's early satire did not immunize the Columbia team against the criticism. Neither did the fact that he introduced some Marxian influences into the functionalist corpus (a point Alvin Gouldner acknowledged in *The Coming Crisis*).

Merton was more liberal than Parsons—or perhaps better said, more to the left, since in many ways Parsons was also a liberal (if a rather conserva-

---

43. Stephen Cole (2004) has pointed to Merton's disinterest in testing the theories that stood behind concepts like "Matthew effect." Cole may be right that Merton simply thought this a lesser task better delegated to lesser mortals. But it is also important to see Merton's engagement in providing usable tools—*bonnes à penser*, in Lévi-Strauss's sense, concepts good to think with—rather than only tested propositions for more or less positivist accumulation.

tive one). And while Lazarsfeld was in important senses an empiricist-positivist, he confounded the stereotype that this was an antipolitical position. He remained oriented by his youthful socialist convictions and more general notions of the practical usefulness of social science even as he insisted that researchers must avoid a short-circuiting of the connection between science and politics. More importantly, though, neither man addressed questions of fundamental social change. Even when taking up concerns for social structure, they did not address its largest parameters: capitalism, nationalism, global power structures. As meliorist liberals, they sought improvements in society within a perspective not dissimilar to Merton's notion of middle-range theory—making progress on one problem at a time.

Lazarsfeld was more drawn to the idea of social scientists as "experts" shaping policy—an ideal he shared with his student James Coleman. Coleman would go on to establish a remarkably productive team at Johns Hopkins in the 1960s. With Peter Rossi and Arthur Stinchcombe as other leading lights, the Hopkins group pursued something close to the Columbia agenda—with perhaps a stronger emphasis on policy relevance and methodological sophistication.[44] Merton was both less confident about this and more drawn to the purely intellectual dimensions of social science. Nonetheless, he was proud that his study of an integrated community informed Kenneth Clark's testimony in the landmark desegregation case of *Brown v. the Board of Education*. But with the signal exception of Merton's early work on science, neither Merton nor Lazarsfeld engaged the question of whether society could in basic ways be different. "Macro" questions about society as a whole were left largely to Parsons, within an intrafunctionalist division of labor. Merton and Lazarsfeld showed little interest in modernization theory, though some of their Columbia students and colleagues did—notably Seymour Martin Lipset and Immanuel Wallerstein.

The suggestion that the empirically measurable conditions of actually

44. Coleman's mobilization of his research to inform court decisions about school integration produced perhaps the single most famous impact of high quality sociological research on policy (made all the more interesting by Coleman's later research on white flight and private schools, and his concern that the policy his earlier research and testimony had informed was counterproductive). In addition, he pioneered mathematical modeling as a sociological research technique. Rossi pioneered risk assessment, the study of disasters, and scientific approaches to program evaluation (as well as conducting a "community study" with an accent on the question of policy and choice—focused on the politics of race and class in a nearby Maryland planned community). Stinchcombe made pivotal contributions to organizational research and the development of economic sociology, and also wrote an influential manual for the construction of middle range (or even slightly more specific) sociological theories.

existing social life did not exhaust the possibilities for social organization was central to critical theory, and more generally to critical alternatives to positivism and sociology's mainstream. Indeed, positivism became an omnibus term of accusation (and sometimes embrace) partly because of the influence of Lazarsfeld's sometime colleague Theodore Adorno and other Frankfurt school critical theorists. These figures had spent the war years in the United States, the early part of them in New York, with hospitality from the Bureau of Applied Social Research. Lazarsfeld involved Adorno in some of his research on radio communications and propaganda. The relationship was one of respect, although they eventually fell out. The issue was not so much theoretical differences as Lazarsfeld's conclusion that Adorno simply could not be practical in relation to empirical research. Lazarsfeld saw the researcher as an expert informing policy, while Adorno maintained a central European conception of the researcher as philosopher-intellectual. Adorno got huffy about Lazarsfeld's déclassé turn to "administrative research." He found Lazarsfeld's integration into American culture and styles of work troubling, a threat to his very self-conception as intellectual. Lazarsfeld got tired of Adorno's unwillingness to get on with new work in the United States (rather than returning to recycled German work). He later wondered, though, whether he had failed as a manager, since Adorno played a more productive role in the studies that would become *The Authoritarian Personality,* with its famous f-scale and deployments of survey research. Adorno's brief transit through Columbia was not without influence. When he returned to Germany after the war, he actually tried to teach survey techniques (more cynically, he found that claiming to be an expert on empirical research methods was a valuable source of distinction). Indeed, the project of joining empirical social science to theory was basic to the Frankfurt Institute of Social Research, both before and after the war, even if perhaps more fully achieved in the Lazarsfeld-Merton years at Columbia.[45]

Back in Germany, Adorno helped launch a "positivist dispute" in German sociology. This was a curious debate, because no important figure argued the case for positivism—certainly not Karl Popper, who was invited to speak to the German Sociological Association in 1961, explicitly refusing the label "positivist" and attacking inductivist and naturalist conceptions of science. Popper's position somewhat disarmed Adorno, who was to speak next, but he and his colleagues still challenged the logical positivists of early twentieth-century Vienna. They saw these as intellectually serious but mis-

---

45. On the Frankfurt school, see Wiggershaus (1994).

taken on two key issues. One was their faith in the unity of science—the Comtean project by which distinctions between the human and natural sciences would vanish as humans came to be understood entirely objectively. Building on Dilthey and Weber, the Frankfurt theorists insisted that such understanding of human actors could never be complete. Moreover, they argued that if pursued without a critical complement that gave greater respect to the distinctiveness of human beings and the importance of action, such positivism would inevitably do violence to humanity. Second, they objected to the positivists' notion of science as outside of history and free from social influence. This allowed the illusion of perfect scientific certainty, but that could only be ideological and potentially condone disastrous overconfidence (generally on the lines of being certain enough of ends to claim justification for troubling means, as in various twentieth-century projects of social engineering).

It was largely in the terms of this debate—though refracted through many circuits of reception—that "positivism" became the omnibus label for reductionist empiricism and a scientism that denied both social influences and social responsibilities.[46] Although both Lazarsfeld's students and his opponents were happy to see him exemplifying the positivist pole of this formative dualism, it partially distorts his work—mainly because the argument implied in the positivist/critical split is so poorly joined (witness Popper's resistance to it). It does so also because the later deployment of the opposition mapped it onto one between "apolitical" research and political engagement, obscuring the more precise distinction between the public role that Lazarsfeld sought for sociologists—as experts with objective knowledge—and the more directly political roles advocated by his critics, who would have had sociologists more often addressing the general public, and not only policymakers.

Statistical Innovation, Symbolic Interactionism, and Fieldwork at Chicago

Lazarsfeld was a major influence on quantitative methods in sociology through the 1950s, but by the 1960s, other individuals and groups had taken the lead. The most prominent of these was probably Otis Dudley

46. This—and more generally engagement with the critical theory of the Frankfurt school—is also the source of reliance on the term *critical* to describe a range of perspectives challenging positivism and "establishment sociology" in the 1960s and 1970s. Much critical sociology was not specifically critical theory in the narrower Frankfurt sense. Marxism itself became important in a variety of different forms, and more "homegrown" radicalism and the

Duncan, though Hubert Blalock, Leo Goodman, Leo Srole, and many others were also important. Although Lazarsfeld had trained in mathematics as well as psychology and made important innovations in statistical analysis, his actual practice centered far more on data gathering. His approach was to find the best facts he could, innovating in ways of collecting them where necessary, and presenting them in a systematic fashion. Eventually the actual conduct of surveys would move out of sociology departments into the hands of specialists. And despite persistent worries over the quality of data and the influence of technical features of survey design, analytic statistics would become the primary focus of graduate methods courses.[47]

For Lazarsfeld and others in the mid-twentieth century, analytic statistics meant starting with cross-tabulations and then developing ways of studying patterns of variation in distributions. Lazarsfeld's latent structure analysis (now more familiar as latent class models) improved, for example, on the sort of work earlier sociologists like Giddings (which tended mainly to consist of deriving average values for characteristics of whole social categories). The next generation of leaders in sociological statistics showed still more interest in analytical statistics—and benefited both from the spread of computer technology and the availability of new and better data sets. Some took up econometric techniques. More sophisticated use of probability estimates transformed thinking about causal attribution in sociology.[48] By the 1970s, hazard models would extend this work dramatically, making possible new kinds of dynamic analyses. Blalock, Duncan, Goodman, and others pioneered linear regression and its extension into path models, structural equation models, and event history models. While the general ideas of regression and path analysis had older histories and were used in other fields, Duncan both brought them into sociology in connection with well-recognized analytic problems—like measuring social mobility—and brought them to bear on newly available unit-level survey data.

---

social problems movement also informed both the critical turn in sociology and the U.S. New Left generally.

47. On the persistent questions about survey design, see Schuman and Presser (1981).

48. In many ways, the statistical innovations of the 1960s and 1970s centered on causal analysis; Blalock's *Causal Inferences in Nonexperimental Research* (1961) helped to pave the way. Blalock spent most of his career at the universities of Michigan, North Carolina (where he had earlier done his PhD), and Washington. Though he spent three years at Yale, the series of major state universities at which he taught is indicative of where much of the action was in the development of quantitative sociology. Odum had helped to pioneer this topic at North Carolina (as Ogburn had at Chicago). Wisconsin was not intensively quantitative until the 1960s, when William Sewell Sr. led the remaking of a department that previously had been headed by Howard Becker and Hans Gerth.

This made possible the extraordinarily influential study *The American Occupational Structure,* which both launched status attainment research and called attention to the power of the new statistical techniques.[49] Its appearance was followed quickly by the founding of *Sociological Methodology* in 1969 and *Sociological Methods and Research* in 1972 (with Edgar Borgatta of the University of Washington playing the leading role in establishing each).

It is instructive to recall how recently these major innovations in statistical analysis came to sociology and that they were more or less simultaneous with the "crisis" of mainstream sociology in the 1960s. Positivism (if that is the right word) was gathering steam even while it was under attack, and it arguably survived the attack better than the attackers did.

Duncan's primary methodological innovations came while he was on the University of Chicago faculty. Just how many Chicago schools there have been depends on the interests and perspective of the enumerator—urbanists may count differently from other sociologists.[50] But in general terms, the first Chicago school was that associated with the discipline's founding and the leadership of Albion Small, and continued into the heyday of Park, Burgess, and W. I. Thomas. The second was centered on the mid-twentieth-century years when Everett Hughes and Herbert Blumer taught at Chicago and W. Lloyd Warner held a joint appointment in anthropology and sociology. This appointment solidified a common engagement with ethnography for both sociologists and anthropologists at Chicago, at a time when the disciplines were pulling farther apart in the rest of the United States. Generations of field researchers were trained in the department, from Howard S. Becker and others who studied with Hughes and Blumer to those trained later by Morris Janowitz and Gerald Suttles (both Chicago products themselves). The fieldwork approach was also integrated—at least loosely—with the symbolic interactionist theoretical framework Blumer and others synthesized, drawing on the work of George Herbert Mead. At the same time, while "Chicago school" usually referred to the fieldwork tradition, Chicago was home to William Fielding Ogburn, Philip Hauser, and Leo Goodman (as well as Duncan) and a center for innovation in quantitative sociology, including especially demography and human ecology. Park's human ecology tradition was systematized and renewed at Chicago by Duncan (and at Michigan by Amos Hawley). The post-

49. Blau and Duncan (1967). This built on earlier work in which Duncan developed the multiple indicator socioeconomic index (as a replacement for mere prestige ratings) as well as on his elaboration of path analysis. See Duncan (1961, 1966).

50. On Chicago, see Bulmer (1984a), Fine (1995), Abbott (1999), and the introduction to this volume.

war Chicago department was more heterogeneous than the common link of "Chicago" to urban ethnography would suggest, as important as that was.

Here, in short, was a distinctive competitor for the mantle of "mainstream." Of course, Chicago was a collaborator as well as a competitor. Among its most distinguished faculty members was Edward Shils—who had helped invent both the Committee on Social Thought and the Committee on the Study of New Nations. Shils was central to the birth of modernization theory and had a hand in many of the other distinctive intellectual projects of the postwar era. And he was Parsons's collaborator, not least on the influential *Working Papers in the Theory of Action*.[51] Still, Chicago represented the old guard from which the founders of the *ASR* had sought to break away. It remained among the most prestigious and influential of departments. And as a major producer of PhD's, Chicago was peopling other programs: notably Northwestern and Berkeley, and more generally a range of universities in the Midwest and West.

On the one hand, the Chicago fieldwork tradition carried forward a tradition of inquiry focused especially on the marginalized, disadvantaged, and rebellious. Even when studying elites, the Chicago fieldworkers were irreverent—especially compared to the more affirmative studies from the Columbia and Harvard functionalists. The contrast is evident in nearly simultaneous studies: *The Student-Physician* (Merton, Reader, and Kendall 1957) and *Boys in White* (Becker et al. 1961). This difference in style helped foster a greater tendency to write for the broader public and for undergraduate students, compared to the East Coast functionalists. The issue is not just prose clarity, for while it is easy to mock Parsons on that score (and masterful mockery helped Mills's critique greatly), Merton's prose was as limpid as any sociologist's. The issue has more to do with descriptive detail, perhaps, and with interest in individuals as well as social patterns, but most of all with the intention to inform a general understanding of social life rather than either policy decisions or the accumulation of tested propositions in a positivist model. Many of the fieldworkers resisted professionalization or identified themselves as teachers and writers as well as sociologists. They

51. Parsons, Bales, and Shils (1953). Shils did do empirical work, perhaps most notably *The Intellectual between Tradition and Modernity: The Indian Situation* (1961), but he is best known as a theorist. In a sense, this makes him anomalous for a Chicago department that viewed "pure theory" with suspicion (and to be sure, Shils was a man of Chicago's interdisciplinary committees, not primarily the Department of Sociology). Donald Levine, for example, was told as a student in the 1950s that one couldn't make it at Chicago as a theorist and so had better do empirical work. Whatever the other merits of this advice (which he seems to have resented), it led to major studies of Ethiopia—including the classic *Wax and Gold* (Levine 1965).

sought to be not the government's "experts" but the voice of those they studied. They were seldom recipients of NSF support.

The fieldwork tradition was commonly linked to symbolic interactionism, which provided a loose interpretative framework. Few of the studies were theory driven, though, and to a considerable extent the fieldwork tradition was hostile to theory—especially grand theory of the Parsonsian variety, but even middle-range theory as well. There were efforts to develop symbolic interactionism as a theory, notably by Blumer. And interactionism came to be presented in textbooks as a theoretical alternative to functionalism—alongside "conflict theory," which was itself a loose euphemism for Marxist, Weberian, and other perspectives that challenged the consensus orientation of functionalism but did not necessarily have much else in common. It is possible that neither symbolic interactionism nor conflict theory would have figured as "theories" were it not for the establishment by Parsons and other functionalists of a specific idea of what a theory was and how it worked in securing the scientific status of sociology. What many fieldworkers drew from symbolic interactionism was less a theory than an injunction to pay attention to actual patterns of interaction among real people. "Respect the nature of the empirical world," Herbert Blumer repeatedly implored his readers. The way to respect that world, Blumer (1969, 32) maintained, was to go out into it and, through a "direct examination" and a "diligent effort," to put one's ideas to the test of its complicated reality. In this sense, interactionist research had an inevitably anthropological dimension. Doing sociology meant going out into public.

Blumer's "theorizing" notwithstanding, symbolic interactionism often came to mean "micro-sociology" as much as it meant a specific theoretical orientation. Indeed, there were arguments against theory and in favor of approaching fieldwork with as few preconceptions as possible. In this tradition, learning was often organized as much through the reading of previous case studies as through mastery of a theoretical apparatus. Likewise, it was not until later that there was a significant movement to formalize qualitative methods, including fieldwork, and this came under pressure to match the formalization of quantitative methods (see DeVault, chap. 5, this volume).

On the other hand, Chicago's newer quantitative wing helped to bring demography firmly into sociology. Demography developed in close relationship to quantitative methods, including not only survey research methods but also new analytic statistics. When the Rockefeller Foundation made funds available in the 1960s to establish population research programs, almost all the universities with major PhD programs in sociology were recipients. At Harvard and Columbia, however, sociology stayed mostly aloof from research programs that developed more in public health. Demography did not develop into a major part of graduate studies or research in sociology, as it did at Chicago, Michigan, Wisconsin, North Carolina, and Berkeley, where there were closer ties between population research centers and sociology departments. Yet clearly, both demography and quantitative methods were emerging into the sociological "mainstream" in important ways.

The expansion was not primarily theory driven but rather supported by methodological advances, new large-scale data sources, and of course external funding. Internally, the field of population studies was rent by some of the same division between problem-oriented, often applied research and more abstract "pure science" orientations that divided sociologists generally. Funds from Rockefeller and Ford were made available mainly on the basis of the sense that "population problems" were of immediate importance—both because of a broad worry about overpopulation and, in more focused ways, because of the perception that population expansion stood in the way of economic development, poverty reduction, and environmental protection.[52] There was, however, a conceptual framework that offered a notion of sociology in which population was central. This was human ecology, which was developed in this period especially by Otis Dudley Duncan (Hauser and Duncan 1959) and Amos Hawley (1950). Duncan provided the acronym POET to articulate the basic premise that human social life was based on the intersection of population, organization, ecology, and technology. Although this was not presented mainly as a challenge to functionalism (in the way that would be typical of the revival of Marxism in sociology a generation later), it did suggest an alternative approach to what Parsons was calling the "functional requisites" of society (Parsons, Bales, and Shils 1953). It also gave more emphasis to material conditions (though not in anything like the Marxist approach). And if Parsons's account of the social system had the advantage of articulating a specifically sociological level of analysis within which individual researchers could feel their particular studies gained general significance, the POET paradigm had the advantage of suggesting both closer links to other fields of science and greater practical relevance.

The fieldwork and human ecology dimensions of Chicago sociology converged in urban and community studies. These had been central since the earliest days of Chicago sociology. Community studies research was also

---

52. The Rockefeller Foundation came to its postwar concern with population issues in a trajectory shaped by its earlier engagements with eugenics as well as by neo-Malthusian fears and optimism about technological responses like the "green revolution."

important to sociology more generally, and there were other important traditions. Hans Gerth nurtured a Wisconsin school of community studies, the most prominent exemplar of which is probably *Small Town in Mass Society* by Arthur Vidich and Joseph Bensman. Robert and Helen Lynd's *Middletown* remains one of the most influential of all community studies. Community had also been a primary interest of Robert Lynd's Columbia colleague MacIver; Herbert Gans continued this tradition there. "Community" was an intermediate construct between individuals and small groups and society at large. So too were various specific sorts of "acting groups": for example, unions, newspaper writers, musicians, and gangs.[53] And so of course were more abstract constructs like formal organizations of bureaucracy, which grew in importance in the 1940s and 1950s.

While the precise place of Chicago sociology within the discipline's postwar elite would be a matter of continued debate among historians of sociology, its disciplinary importance clearly endured in various ways. The department remained highly ranked. It continued to produce larger numbers of PhD's than any other American sociology department, and only in the late 1970s and early 1980s was it equaled or surpassed by Michigan, Wisconsin, and Berkeley.

"Mainstream Sociology" Revisited

In 1978, Richard Flacks, who had his own contentious personal history with the Chicago department, coauthored an article with Gerald Turkel on the emergence of neo-Marxian perspectives in American sociology. In that

53. See Lipset, Trow, and Coleman (1956), Janowitz (1952), and Becker (1963). All of these were conceptualized more or less concretely, as specific kinds of groups. This contrasted with a growing emphasis in the postwar years on more abstractly conceptualized kinds of social phenomena—e.g., bureaucracy—rather than concrete groups. This was part of an effort to create a more scientific sociology, pursuing generalization by abstracting from particulars of cases. As dramatically different was the replacement of all specific attention to intermediate associations of various sorts—a core theme since De Tocqueville and throughout sociology's history—with the dichotomy "individual/collective." Parsons's approach to the social system certainly allowed for the existence of a variety of groups, and Parsons even implied this was a good thing. But his theory saw systematicity—and thus science—at the levels of personality, culture, and social system. These were alternatives to economic conceptions of abstract market systems (always the "other" against which Parsons constructed his approach). The various specific groups were only particulars to be understood by the general theory: community was a social system and thus an instance of the collective. The general process needed to be understood, and the shift from community to association reconceptualized in terms of pattern variables and modernization. But specific communities were mere particulars if they were of sociological interest at all.

article, Flacks and Turkel claimed that it was "no longer possible to speak of a mainstream in sociology or to argue that a monolithic consensus surrounds any perspective or paradigm." There had been, they suggested, an "unraveling of the postwar consensus in the discipline," an unraveling to which radical sociologists and other critics of the mainstream had contributed. The "crisis" that academic sociology faced in the 1960s had brought about a "climate of shattered confidence and consensus," and by the end of the 1960s those who dominated sociology in the immediate postwar period had been put "on the defensive" (Flacks and Turkel 1978, 198). By implication, of course, it had once been possible to speak of a coherent "mainstream" in sociology and to argue that there was a "monolithic consensus." To speak of something shattered is to imply that it was once whole. Yet in an important sense the "mainstream" was an invention of the very New Left that Flacks and Turkel sought to story, as was the wider use of the notion of "Establishment Sociology." Sociologists would continue to refer to the "mainstream," critically and otherwise—and not just retrospectively. At the same time, "Establishment Sociologists" would maintain their "confidence," although the shape of the sociological establishment, as Flacks and Turkel noted, was changing by the late 1960s and would continue to change in the decades that followed.

By the late 1970s, the field of American sociology had grown enormously. Throughout the postwar era, public universities played an increasingly important role within the discipline, with major departments at Michigan, Wisconsin, Berkeley, and Chapel Hill producing hundreds of PhD's throughout the 1970s alone. Both Michigan and Wisconsin had become exemplars of yet another version of the sociological mainstream, albeit one with close affinities with and connections to the quantitative wing at Chicago (see Steinmetz, chap. 9, this volume). In self-conscious contrast to—but certainly not in disconnection from—the professionalizing projects pursued here and elsewhere, the rising department at Berkeley sought a different strategy. As Berkeley sociologist Philip Selznick recalled, the "implicit mission" at Berkeley during the postwar years was "to turn marginal fields into mainstream fields" (Burawoy and VanAntwerpen n.d.). Under the leadership of Blumer and others, Berkeley engaged in what Seymour Martin Lipset would later dub a "catholic sociology," cultivating a plurality of sociological approaches and intellectual agendas. And by Lipset's lights, this emphasis on diversity had "created a time bomb that finally exploded," as the Berkeley department was beset in the late 1960s by internal struggles and political controversies, caught up in the crisis of a "self-destructive discipline" (Lipset 2001, 266).

Such narratives of disciplinary crisis and self-destruction, at times accompanied by an explicit yearning for a supposedly lost age of unity and consensus, bear striking resemblance to critical accounts of the postwar mainstream and its demise. Yet, as we have argued, critical discourses regarding "mainstream sociology" have tended to overestimate the degree of unification among the postwar "establishment" and thus have risked exaggerating the degree of disciplinary rupture wrought by the 1960s and 1970s. Was a "monolithic" postwar "consensus" really "shattered" by the sixties, or is the story of postwar sociology somewhat more complicated than that? Although we have not attended in detail here to the disciplinary effects wrought by the struggles of 1960s and 1970s, we have suggested that the postwar sociological elite was not the narrowly defined monolith it was sometimes imagined to be. Likewise, failure to establish deeper roots in earlier dissident sociological traditions may have undermined the rebels of the 1960s and 1970s, obscuring the more complicated realities of their disciplinary situation.[54]

Writing in 1991, Richard Flacks reconsidered the assumptions the rebels had once made about their discipline:

> We were, it turns out, wrong to believe that there was a self-conscious and powerful "establishment" in sociology that could or would mobilize real power against us. We were, in fact, wrong to think that sociology had become a crucial vehicle for maintaining social control. Indeed, we shared with analysts like Daniel Bell and other theorists of the post-industrial society an exaggerated belief in the strategic centrality of the university for shaping the society's future—a belief that led us to think that our challenge to the discipline and to the university was more weighty than it turned out to be.[55]

54. See Flacks and Turkel (1978, 195): "The polemic against Establishment Sociology in the US has a long history. It became a significant underground force after World War II as sociology became a consolidated academic discipline, and as sociological research became an institutionalized adjunct of policy and management." Like others, Flacks and Turkel seemed to use the terms "Establishment Sociology" and "mainstream sociology" almost interchangeably. Mills, as we have suggested, chose to present himself as bringing a completely new critical vision to sociology, making less of his previous engagements with pragmatism than he might have (perhaps maintaining distance from the Chicago school) and also linking his project to Weber and Marx (thus appealing, like Parsons, for European prestige). He also chose to work at Columbia and in New York in order to be at what he took to be the "center" of American intellectual and public life. For more on Mills, see Becker (1994).

55. Flacks (1991, 25). A page later, however, Flacks writes: "If there was an establishment sociology twenty years ago, we helped do it in; and so, for good or ill, and despite rearguard resistance in some departments, the field is to some extent ours."

By the early 1990s, Flacks realized that it was somewhat anachronistic to speak of a sociological "establishment." But what of the sociological "mainstream"? While the discourse of "mainstream sociology" still resonates widely today, it remains difficult to call up the most appropriate label for its opposites or "others." Are they tributaries? Eddies? Cataracts? Narrows? However suggestive, none of these metaphors seems likely to capture the imaginations of graduate students or critical sociologists wondering about how to figure their place within the discipline. References to "Establishment Sociology," especially common in the wake of Gouldner's *The Coming Crisis,* dwindled in the 1980s and have now more or less disappeared. Yet in the same period the discourse of "mainstream sociology" has proliferated and continues to be common throughout the discipline, even as its users and referents have become more diverse.

The discourse of the "mainstream" has shifted along with the discipline itself. As the theoretical, methodological, ideological, and even regional and institutional shape of the sociological "establishment" has, in many ways, been transformed, so has the ever elusive (if not illusive) "mainstream." What is mainstream sociology today? Is it in public or private universities, mass or elite sociology? It is often difficult to say. Yet the word is still bandied about throughout the discipline, both as both a positive and negative classification. As one sociologist told us: "When you are trying to make a new senior hire and a dean needs to see a grant record, you use the word 'mainstream' to indicate admirable strength of character and likely productivity; when you want to hire somebody who is creative and unorthodox, you say that they 'challenge the mainstream in a responsible manner' or some such nonsense. It's mostly ideological claptrap."

No doubt the tendency of "mainstream sociology" to function as a floating signifier served to promote its diffusion, especially in the 1960s and 1970s. If there was ever a time when "mainstream sociology" had a fairly stable primary meaning, it was between Mill's 1959 critique of the twin evils of "grand theory" and "abstracted empiricism" and Gouldner's 1970 declaration that the rebels were winning. The key targets of critics of the "mainstream" were frequently the same "three great figures of the Capitoline triad" that later figured prominently in Bourdieu's retelling of the rise of the new sociological establishment. As one veteran of the earlier struggles put it: "I doubt there is a mainstream anymore, ever since Parsons died. Surely Merton, Lazarsfeld, Parsons, Shils, and their followers in the '50s and '60s embodied the mainstream, even if they themselves argued against such a notion. That kind of hegemony isn't available anymore, so far as I can see."

Yet the desire to claim and to contest the alleged mainstream remains strong. Indeed, something like the notion of "mainstream sociology" is perhaps built into the very disciplinary project that establishes a struggle over authoritative knowledge, legitimate intellectual perspectives, and the conditions and rewards of sociological work.

Although the recurrent preoccupation with "mainstream sociology" may thus be seen as a product of endemic struggle over the state and structure of American sociology, it is a preoccupation that remains liable to obscure as much as it reveals, thereby contributing to oversimplified understandings of both the discipline's postwar history and its present condition. The application of the "mainstream" label, we have argued, was rooted in a specific discursive formation within the field of American sociology. It functioned as a sort of classificatory epithet, lumping together a range of otherwise disparate dominant sociologists and sociologies under one undifferentiated, and usually derisive, category.[56] "Mainstream sociology" was simultaneously a category of historical analysis and a discursive strategy mobilized largely by a new generation of opponents and critics of the discipline's postwar establishment.[57] But it was also readily appropriable after the rebel ascendancy by those who sought to resume a more "professional" disciplinary project. In the midst of such disciplinary developments and transformations, discourses of mainstream sociology became a pervasive and widely circulating piece of disciplinary "common sense," a key component of a "folk theory" of American sociology's postwar development, subsequent crisis, and ensuing attempts at disciplinary reconstruction.

In seeking to historically situate and critically assess the emergence and circulation of such discourses, our aim has not been to suggest that they are

56. As Murray Hausknecht (1972) pointed out in his review of J. David Colfax and Jack L. Roach's *Radical Sociology,* applying the label "mainstream sociology" had at times the effect of suggesting that a supposedly radical work of sociology was in fact not radical enough, particularly if it did not break sufficiently with mainstream methodologies. It was thus a classificatory epithet aimed not simply at the key figures of the sociological establishment but sometimes at critical sociologists who would otherwise have in various ways represented alternatives to that establishment.

57. Thus, at least at the beginning, to refer to the "mainstream" or "establishment" sociologist was generally not to engage in a discourse of self-identification, although it may be argued that the use of such terms often involved the staking of a specific sociological identity. Just as Gouldner's mind boggled at the thought of a Parsonian hippie, so too would it be baffling to imagine Smelser or Lipset identifying with a project called "Establishment Sociology." Indeed, from the perspective of many so-called mainstream sociologists, the sociology they practiced required no modifier. As Kingsley Davis (1959, 771) put it in his ASA presidential address, "structural-functional analysis *is* sociological analysis."

entirely or essentially without merit. While some invocations of the sociological "mainstream" may indeed amount to little more than "ideological
claptrap," it is also clear that discourses of mainstream sociology can sometimes serve an effective and productive purpose, not least in the hands of
those seeking further disciplinary transformation, efforts that frequently
revolve around the critical appraisal of sociology's recent past and present
possibilities. From the point of view of sociologists writing and rewriting
the history of their discipline, however, the relevant issue is what sort of
critical purchase or epistemic gain might be afforded by an analysis that
employed a suitably reflexive conception of the disciplinary mainstream.
The challenge for historians of sociology engaged in such analysis would be
to craft a conception of mainstream sociology that succeeded in breaking
with the potentially misleading commonsense understandings associated
with the term, while not being so discontinuous with these understandings
as to be unrecognizable. With this challenge in view, we close with a brief
consideration of one significant effort to make critical use of the concept of
mainstream sociology in the writing of American sociology's history.

In one of the few book-length treatments of the history of American sociology, Stephen Turner and Jonathan Turner have offered an account of
the "postwar synthesis" not altogether different from the one we have proposed here. In the closing chapter of *The Impossible Science,* Turner and
Turner argued that while Parsons, Merton, and others made an ambitious
attempt to unify the discipline of sociology in the years after World War II,
"there was never a single, clear, consensual model of the new sociology." Indeed, they suggested, what consensus there was in this period was "both extremely limited and extremely tenuous." The Turners nonetheless viewed
such synthesizing attempts as forwarding a "highly persuasive general image of the scientific future of the discipline," an image that they associated
with a new "mainstream" of American sociology, a mainstream linked to
developments in both "theory" and "quantitative methods" (Turner and
Turner 1990, 188–92).

In a subsequent article, which was in part a response to critics of the
book, Stephen Turner elaborated substantially on this conception of the
"mainstream," writing that "the basic *historical* story line of *The Impossible
Science,* however concealed," was a narrative of "the rise and triumph of
mainstream sociology" (Turner 1994, 46). Emphasizing the methodological
side of the story and referring to "mainstream sociology" as a "methodology tradition" whose "hidden source" was Franklin H. Giddings, "a figure
neglected, abused, or ignored by virtually the whole historical literature
produced by sociologists on American sociology," Turner referred to other

major and much-discussed developments in postwar American sociology—including both "Parsonsianism" and "the Lazarsfeld-Merton BASR survey model"—as "sideshows" that had been of "little long term significance" (48, 43, 46). By contrast, "the long quest to create a quantitative science" of sociology, while largely an intellectual failure, had been a huge political success for a privileged and dominant network of elite sociologists—though this success would be repeatedly and hotly contested by the discipline's recalcitrant "underclass" (55). Thus, if there was a "core" to mainstream sociology, it was to be found in a quantitative tradition that was linked together historically by tacit knowledge passed down from well-positioned and influential teachers to doctoral students, through "the Apostolic succession of apprenticeship" (50).

Although the details of Turner's provocative and fiercely argued thesis cannot be neatly summarized or adequately reproduced here, his narrative regarding the "origins" and "success" of mainstream sociology both intersects with and disconnects from the folk theory we have described, in interesting and potentially instructive ways. First, on Turner's account, mainstream sociology has been from its very beginnings the project of a disciplinary elite. Like the critical sociologists of the 1960s and 1970s, Turner represented the "mainstream" of sociology not as a majoritarian enterprise but rather as a minority movement that attempted to impose its scientific vision of sociology from the top down. Aided by its access to substantial resources and its establishment in major journals and powerful graduate departments, this movement nonetheless faced stiff resistance from those in sociology whom it sought either to reform or to exclude. "The rest of the discipline," Turner writes, "did not go along gently," providing one explanation for "the distinctive awfulness of sociology's internecine squabbling" (1994, 46, 55).

While one might expect the presuppositions and sociological practices of the "mainstream" to be defined as those that were most widely accepted throughout the discipline, in fact the term has been used repeatedly to refer to the prerogatives and attempted dominance of a narrowly defined disciplinary elite. This was true even of those critics of mainstream sociology who self-conceived as critically avant-garde or cutting edge, situating themselves outside the mass of the sociological mainstream, and thereby conflating an opposition to the top of the disciplinary hierarchy with an opposition the middle or center of the disciplinary majority.

Although Turner made no such claims to cutting-edge status, his association of mainstream sociology with a disciplinary elite did not stray far from the commonsense understandings embedded in the discourse of mainstream sociology. A second element of his argument represented a more distinct departure, however. Clearly delimiting what he meant by "mainstream sociology," Turner implicitly set his conception of the mainstream apart from the numerous understandings that had placed Bourdieu's "Capitoline triad"—and particularly Parsons—at the center (although his article dealt in detail with the case of Parsons, as did *The Impossible Science*). This displacement of the supposedly hegemonic postwar theorists had the virtue of giving Turner's rendering of mainstream sociology greater analytic clarity. But it also risked disconnecting that rendering from some of the most prevalent understandings of what—and who—the "mainstream" was. In and of itself, this need not be seen as problematic. Indeed, much of Turner's argument might be read as a sustained interrogation of the received understandings of mainstream sociology we have critically examined here. Yet because he never explicitly acknowledged it as such—because, in other words, he did not seek to account not simply for the rise of something he called mainstream sociology but also for the historical emergence and circulation of the "mainstream" label itself—the effects of his interrogation were muted. When, a decade after his article was published, renewed discussion of "mainstream sociology" surfaced in the midst of debates over the promotion of "public sociology," the terms of those debates were still largely defined by conceptions of mainstream sociology inherited from the critical discourses of the 1960s and 1970s. This was in part the result, to be sure, of the fact that many contemporary sociologists in the United States do not read widely in the history of American sociology. But it might also be seen as a product of a general failure on the part of historians of sociology to adequately historicize the master concepts around which they have built their historical narratives and explanations. Historicizing such concepts—especially when those concepts have wide purchase throughout the discipline—would be one way to engage less historically inclined sociologists in direct dialogue. This project of historicizing sociology should also be a central element of any attempt to critically examine the history of the discipline.

American sociologists in recent years have shown an increasing interest in the history of their own discipline. As American sociology's past, present, and future—public, professional, and otherwise—continue to be debated, historians of sociology can and should seek to historicize and critically inform the stakes of those debates. A central claim of this chapter has been that debates regarding the postwar sociological establishment and its challengers would benefit from a more historicized and more reflexive conception of mainstream sociology. Engaged in struggles over the future of their discipline which were at least in part "struggles over classification," the insurgent sociologists of the 1960s and 1970s projected the politicized categories of their present onto the past, retelling the history of postwar sociology in the process.[58] For them, the notion of "mainstream sociology" was as much a discursive strategy as it was an objective historical category. It was a resonant rhetorical tool, a critical classification, constituted and mobilized by the critics, and employed at various points in battles over the present meaning and future shape of the discipline. The pasts it projected in the midst of such struggles should be seen in this light.

Acknowledgments

Thanks to a variety of interlocutors for sharing their reflections on "mainstream sociology," including Gabi Abend, Howard S. Becker, Michael Burawoy, Randall Collins, Arlene Kaplan Daniels, Kai Erikson, Daniel Geary, Todd Gitlin, Charles Lemert, Harvey Molotch, David Nasatir, Tom Scheff, Alan Sica, Dorothy Smith, Judith Stacey, Barrie Thorne, Stephen Turner, Immanuel Wallerstein, Erik Olin Wright, Mayer Zald, Harriet Zuckerman, and participants in the NYU workshop on the history of sociology.

58. For commentary on the danger of this approach in the history of sociology, see Camic (1994). For "struggles over classification," see Bourdieu (1991b).

[ELEVEN] From Relevance to Irrelevance:
The Curious Impact of the Sixties
on Public Sociology

Doug McAdam

During his term as ASA president, Michael Burawoy (2005b) called for much more attention to, and debate about, the role of "public sociology" in the discipline. While *any* attention to this issue is welcome in my view, there is no shortage of ironies associated with the contemporary conversation about the matter. As we internally debate the merits of different versions of public sociology, the external—or public—disregard for sociology is palpable. One fears that even if we were to embrace a credible version of public sociology, we would struggle mightily to get a host of important real-world constituencies to care very much.

It was not always this way. Without overstating the case, I think it fair to say that in the quarter century following World War II, sociology enjoyed a public presence and policy resonance that far exceeds its influence today. And yet, or perhaps because of this, there was little self-conscious conversation within the discipline about the nature of, or call to, public sociology. Already broadly committed to various forms of public sociology, sociologists apparently felt little need to discuss or debate the matter.

The question is, how did we get from the engaged, successfully public sociology of the immediate postwar period to the current desultory state of affairs? A full answer to this question is beyond the scope of this chapter. Instead, I confine myself to just one strand of the story—the ironic impact that the baby boom cohorts had on the tradition of engaged, public sociology that so thrived in the post–World War II period.

The chapter, then, takes up one aspect of a very complicated legacy, that is, the impact of the 1960s on contemporary sociology. I begin with two clarifying comments and a caution. The first clarifying comment concerns the decidedly nonchronological definition of the sixties that I adopt in the chapter. The sixties that I refer to here is not the ten-year period, 1960-69, but that distinctive bundle of political, social, and cultural trends that we popularly—if erroneously—associate with the decade. In this more amorphous cultural sense, the sixties is very much a moving target, an evolving sensibility that took hold at very different times in very different places and institutional settings within the United States.[1] And so while it may very well be that the peak of the sixties in San Francisco came with the Summer of Love in 1967, most of the sixties trends within sociology that I discuss in this chapter were played out in the 1970s (and even the early 1980s) rather than the 1960s.

The second clarifying remark is analytic but follows directly from the definition of the sixties offered here. In seeking to assess "the impact of the sixties on contemporary sociology," it is not the events of the period that are presumed to have exerted a direct effect on sociology. Rather it is the generational dynamics associated with the period that I see centrally implicated in the disciplinary changes on offer here. This then is principally an impressionistic assessment of life-course effects—a story of how a particular academic (qua political) generation, powerfully influenced by its times and interacting with its disciplinary elders, reshaped American sociology in complicated and unintended ways. In this sense, the story is similar to one I told some years back about the volunteers who went to Mississippi in the summer of 1964 to take part in what came to be known as the Freedom Summer project (McAdam 1988). The volunteers were very much the products of the unique confluence of history, biography, and social structure that Mills (1959) so powerfully invokes in *The Sociological Imagination.* They then experienced the shared crucible of Mississippi in that not so distant and violent summer. Needless to say, they were changed by the experience, but in acting on those changes they became an active force in history themselves.

Though the baby boomers who committed to careers in academic sociology are a far larger and more amorphous group than the Freedom Summer volunteers, I conceive of them in a broadly similar fashion. They too were products of particular combinations of history, biography, and social structure. Indeed, the modal "package" of social influences they brought to sociology closely resembled the background of the Freedom Summer volunteers. Overwhelmingly both groups were liberal idealists who had grown up in relatively privileged circumstances, bringing their concern for social

---

1. Nor is this more amorphous version of the sixties a U.S. phenomenon only. The "new social movements" that developed in most western European countries in the 1970s reminds us that there too a "sixties sensibility" took hold and exerted a powerful political and cultural influence. Then too, when the Berlin Wall came down in 1989, a good many East Germans claimed that the revolution was their "sixties." For all the narrowly chronological histories of the 1960s, it has always seemed to me that this necessarily subjective definition of the sixties is far and away the more interesting phenomenon to study. And it is this sixties—sociology's sixties—that is the subject matter of this chapter.

issues and a strong sense of generational identification to Mississippi and sociology respectively.

The biographies of our budding academics were powerfully shaped by their socialization into sociology. But, like the Freedom Summer volunteers, they were agents of change no less than the passive products of social influence. In interaction with themselves and their generational elders, the baby boomers reshaped the substantive and institutional contours of sociology. The nature of these contours is the subject of this chapter.

Now for the caution. This chapter is decidedly *not* a piece of systematic empirical scholarship. Though I deploy bits and pieces of data throughout, mine is, at best, an informed but still largely personal, impressionistic, and *polemical* account of the how the sixties generation reshaped certain aspects of sociology. Specifically, I seek to highlight and tease out the links between several sixties trends that over the years have, in my view, served, ironically, to transform the discipline from one known for its "relevance" to a field largely hostile to "applied" work and increasingly irrelevant to a set of real-world constituents about whom we profess to care deeply.

One final note. I am very much a member of the generation about which I am writing. My own intellectual sensibilities—the topics I have chosen to study, the methods I use to do so, the scholars I most admire—were shaped by coming of age during the 1960s and being trained in that extended "sixties" that was graduate school (at least in sociology) in the 1970s. I mention this only to say that I enthusiastically embrace much of the sixties legacy in contemporary sociology. Despite that, it has long seemed to me that the era's impact on the discipline can, from at least one perspective, be seen as one of those classic cases of "unintended consequences" we sociologists are so fond of documenting. Attracted by its "relevance" and progressive sensibilities, record numbers of baby boomers (and pre-boomers) streamed into sociology between 1965 and 1975. Motivated by generally left-of-center political views, we had strong real-world commitments and hoped that sociology would be an effective vehicle for acting on those commitments. But if our presence served to politicize the discipline, it did so in a peculiar way, with ultimately ironic consequences. While stridently political in much of its rhetoric and consciousness, contemporary American sociology is generally a nonfactor in policy debates and irrelevant to the lives of a host of real-world groups about whom we purport to care deeply (e.g., the poor).

How did this happen? How did the rapid recruitment of so many politically attuned and motivated scholars in the 1960s and 1970s result ultimately in the politically marginal position the discipline finds itself in today? The chapter is an attempt to answer that question and to encourage a broader discussion of the role of sociology in contemporary political life. I begin with a discussion of trends.

Sociology and the Sixties: Five Trends

THE RAPID EXPANSION OF THE FIELD

Extraordinary growth took place in the field during the sixties, as can be seen clearly in figure 11.1, which shows the trends in ASA membership from 1910 to 2000.

The story is a simple one. Membership in the association remained low and remarkably constant until the end of the Second World War. Then, reflecting the postwar faith in science and an exponential growth in higher education, ASA membership grew steadily through the late 1940s and 1950s. But even this growth was just a prelude to what was to come in the sixties. ASA membership totaled only slightly more than 6,000 in 1959. Ten years later the figure stood at more than double that number (13,485). As more and more baby boomers poured into graduate school in the late sixties and early seventies, the total kept rising, finally peaking at 14,934 in 1972. In a scant thirteen years, membership in the association had risen by nearly 150 percent.

The figure has dropped some since but still stands at roughly the same level as the end of the 1960s. So the current size of the ASA—and presumably the broader institution of American sociology—very much bears the imprint of the 1960s. I discuss what I see as the significance of the size of the discipline later in the chapter. For now, it is simply worth noting that nowhere else in the world is the discipline of sociology anywhere near as

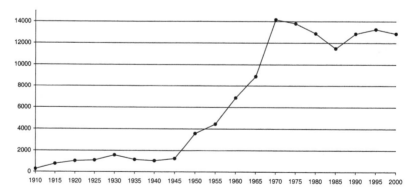

Figure 11.1 ASA membership, 1910-2000.

large as it is in the United States. By comparison, the national sociological association of Germany has under 1,400 members, one-tenth the total of the ASA.

SIGN OF THE TIMES: THE LEFTWARD DRIFT OF AMERICAN SOCIOLOGY

I have heard sociologists—generally, older sociologists—complain that the sixties "politicized" the discipline. But this suggests that American sociology was apolitical or ideologically neutral before the sixties. This, of course, is nonsense. Without denying variation in individual political views, I think it is clear that the discipline as a whole was broadly liberal in its politics before and throughout the sixties. This is not to suggest, however, that there were no political divisions within the field before the "invasion" of the baby boomers. On the contrary, the chronological sixties had already served to sharpen tensions between two large groupings within the discipline. Insofar as Calhoun and VanAntwerpen's chapter 10 in this volume takes this division as its principal focus, I am spared the need to describe it in great detail. For my purposes, a stylized description of the two groups suffices.

There were those who were committed to, and identified with, a broadly mainstream effort to "professionalize" sociology, through the spread of sophisticated empirical methods and the embrace of "value-neutral" scientific practices. The other group, much inspired by the events of the chronological 1960s, were those who favored a more engaged, problem-oriented approach to sociological practice. We should not, however, reify this division overmuch. Some of the seminal figures associated with the "professional project" (e.g., Merton, Lazarsfeld) were very much attuned to real-world issues in their work. And most of the "social problems" practitioners were committed to the same "scientific" vision of the discipline favored by the "professional project" types. There was, however, a discernible rift here, one that was to grow wider during the late 1960s and early 1970s.

The baby boomers who began pouring into the discipline in the late 1960s and 1970s owed allegiance to neither of these older camps. Indeed, to the extent they were aware of the division at all, they tended to view it with much the same mix of disinterest and lack of comprehension as the New Left regarded the partisan splits within the Old Left. The generation gap had come to sociology.

Besides the gap itself, the most salient distinction for the baby boomers concerned the political views of their age peers. The generational flood that washed over the field brought two very different political groupings into the discipline. The smaller of the two groups constituted what I will call a "hard left," with Marxists the numerically and intellectually dominant segment of this formation. The second and far larger group represented what I will call sociology's "soft left." These were baby boomers with liberal/leftist sensibilities who, early on, came to identify with the fragmented multicultural politics that are still very much with us today. (This second group has always lacked the ideological/intellectual coherence of the hard left. Indeed, in fairness, it is something of a "residual" grouping, defined more by a rejection of hard left views as by the force of any single soft left alternative.)

So the generational clash within sociology involved more than a simple confrontation between young and old. Much of the characteristic dynamism of the period involved simultaneous interactions within and between generations, as was true in American society more generally. Though opaque at the time, from the vantage point of thirty to thirty-five years the broad outcomes of these complicated dynamics seem clear enough now. Highly visible in the late 1960s, the hard left grew in influence throughout the 1970s, only to fade in the early 1980s. (It is tempting to believe that "external" events—principally Ronald Reagan's election in 1980 and the return of the cold war—had something to do with this.) In contrast, the soft left (and their socialized heirs in the next generation) grew steadily over time and is now numerically dominant in the discipline. The fate of these two lefts can be seen in the ebb and flow of members in the Marxist Sociology and the Sex and Gender sections of ASA.[2] Figure 11.2 reports the annual membership totals for these two sections from 1976 to 2001.

As the older of the two sections, Sex and Gender was briefly the larger of the two sections, but Marxist Sociology, reflecting the ascendance of the hard left, edged past its soft left counterpart in 1978 and retained its membership edge until 1983. After that, the fortunes of the two sections reversed. Sex and Gender grew rapidly though the 1980s, topping 1,000 members in 1991. In the very next year it became the largest section in ASA, a distinc-

2. I use these two sections as crude proxies to illustrate my equally crude distinction between the "hard" and "soft" left within sociology. The key word here is *crude*. I am well aware that throughout their histories, a good many members of these sections have fit comfortably into neither the "hard" nor "soft" left, while others have blended aspects of both lefts. Marxist feminists, for example, are very likely to have belonged for some time to *both* sections. Still, I think it fair to surmise that, throughout its history, the overwhelming majority of members of Marxist Sociology have been hard leftists. The percentage of Sex and Gender members who fit neatly under the soft left umbrella has, no doubt, been smaller (and more variable) over time, but I would bet they have always comprised a majority of the section.

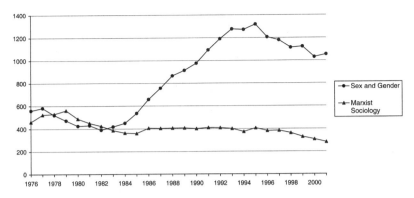

Figure 11.2 Membership in the Sex and Gender and Marxist Sociology sections of ASA, 1976–2001.

tion it retains today. In contrast, Marxist Sociology slowly declined through the 1980s and 1990s, bottoming out at 280 members in 2001.

And what of the two groups in evidence before the baby boom invasion? Both suffered at the hands of the "invaders," but the longer-term fate of the two intellectual traditions has been very different. The "professional project" of those interested in a higher-status, more "scientific" sociology suffered as both "lefts" criticized the "value-neutral" stance of the "professionals" as undesirable and unattainable. The "naïve positivism" of the "professionals" also came in for attack, weakening the normal science consensus that had characterized the discipline in the post–World War II period. In the end, though, this segment of the discipline survived, and indeed, continues very much in evidence today. Though still roundly criticized in many quarters, "mainstream sociology" continues to prize the same general elements—technical innovation, normal science, basic research—as were associated with the older "professional project."

The fate of the "social problem" tradition has been quite different. Initially, many in the soft left identified with and embraced the "relevance" of the "social problem" approach, granting it a certain intellectual/moral cachet vis-à-vis the "professional project." But this privileged position did not last long. Both lefts, but especially the Marxists, excoriated the "problems" orientation as blind to broader structural inequities and inherently compromised by its "applied" ties to mainstream institutions and the American state. And although under attack themselves, the "professionals" continued to draw an invidious distinction between their commitment to "basic research" and the social problem community's embrace of "applied" work. The ironic effect of these multiple critiques was to substantially weaken the tradition of "engaged" sociology, even as ASA absorbed thousands of new members attracted by the discipline's "relevance." This devaluation of "applied" work is clearly mirrored in a third trend evident during this period.

THE GROWTH AND CHANGING
NATURE OF ASA SECTIONS

As the 1970s dawned, the ASA had only eight official sections. These eight (with their founding dates in parentheses) were Methodology (1961), Social Psychology (1961), Medical Sociology (1962), Crime, Law, and Deviance (1966), Sociology of Education (1967), Family (1967), Theory (1968), and Organizations, Occupations, and Work (1970). What do these sections have in common? Aside from the generic sections on theory and methods, all of the others (save Social Psychology) are oriented to mainstream social institutions. As such, they capture the comfortable fit between sociology and the central institutions of postwar American life. They also speak to the dominant vision of sociology as an "engaged," policy-oriented social science. Reflecting the influence of the "social problems" tradition, much of the work in these fields was motivated by a desire to engage in progressive "social engineering" designed to redress social problems and improve the overall "functional" fit between this or that institution and society as a whole.

The sections organized in the 1970s and early 1980s could not have been more different. The next eleven sections approved by the association were Sex and Gender (1973), Community and Urban (1973), Environment and Technology (1977), Marxist Sociology (1977), Peace and War (1978), Population (1978), Sociological Practice (1979), Aging and the Life Course (1980), Political Economy of the World System (1981), Collective Behavior and Social Movements (1981), and Racial and Ethnic Minorities (1981). The new additions clearly expressed the topical interests and value commitments of those within both lefts who were then streaming into the discipline. As such, these new additions also read like a litany of progressive causes: women, environment, peace, race, global economy, and the like.

These newer sections also speak to a more general change in the relationship of American sociology to American life. Although there is no definitive data on the subject, I think we can confidently offer the following portrait of the modal sociologist, circa 1965. This portrait applies equally to those identified with both of the established orientations—"professional" and "problem"—described earlier. Demographically, we are talking about a middle-age, middle-class male, married with children; in brief, someone living a broadly normative, mainstream life. More importantly, in life-course terms, this is someone whose value commitments were almost certainly shaped by New Deal politics and the Second World War. For the most part these were liberal Democrats who embraced the idea of social science as a vehicle for achieving more enlightened and effective social policy. More to the point, these are sociologists who accept—indeed, typically *embrace*—the links between sociology and state actors and other mainstream policymakers. Even those sociologists associated with the "professional project" were comfortable with these links. Indeed, they advocated for a more prominent public role for an increasingly high-status professional sociology.

The modal sociologist in, say, 1977 presents a stark contrast to the above portrait. Demographically, *he* is almost as likely to be a *she,* to be young and unmarried. The number of racial minorities in sociology remains small but significantly exceeds the comparable figure for 1965. The ideational and life-course contrasts are just as striking. Having come of age during the 1960s, the typical baby boomer sociologist combines (some flavor of) leftist views with an active distrust of state actors and a disdain for "applied" work. The practical effect of this combination is to politicize the discipline while largely "privatizing" the expression of those politics. That is, *in their formal academic roles,* the value commitments of the new generation of sociologists come to be expressed primarily in their teaching and campus politics rather than through an active scholarly engagement with policymakers or other public actors. "Private" commitments (to alternative institutions, social movement groups, and the like) aside, the ironic impact of both lefts has been to undermine and impoverish a certain version of "public" sociology that was clearly ascendant in the post World War II period.

EMERGENCE/TRANSFORMATION
OF SPECIFIC SUBFIELDS

The general intellectual transformation of sociology just described expressed itself in countless substantive changes in the structure and content of disciplinary subfields. In many cases, the changes consisted of the establishment of whole new fields of inquiry within sociology. The founding of a good many of the sections mentioned merely formalized the emergence of these new subfields. Such fields as feminist sociology, environmental sociology, Marxist sociology, and world system research have their roots in the period. In other cases, the subfields were not so much new as thoroughly transformed by the influence of variants of leftist thought and/or value commitments. Two specific cases serve to illustrate the more general intellectual impact that was everywhere evident during this period.

COLLECTIVE BEHAVIOR TO SOCIAL MOVEMENTS. I begin with a case I know well: the rise of social movement studies at the expense of the older field of "collective behavior." The list of ASA sections shows that one titled Collective Behavior and Social Movements was established in 1981. The name suggests a harmonious blend of the old and the new. But at the time the section was established, the reality was very different. The early business meetings featured heated exchanges and simmering hostility between the adherents of the older collective behavior tradition and the upstart social movement scholars. What were the animating logics of these two perspectives and how do they express the more general tensions characteristic of sociology during the 1970s and early 1980s?

As a field of study, collective behavior had long focused on what might be thought of as the "error term" of social life. These are forms of action that appear to represent departures from normative routines and which, in that sense, are fairly rare and typically short-lived. A list of the forms traditionally grouped under this heading reflect the "error term" view. These forms include fads, crazes, panics, disasters, crowds, and social movements.

Like so much else in American sociology, the collective behavior perspective has its roots in the Chicago school. Robert Park (Park 1967; Park and Burgess 1921) was probably the most influential progenitor of the approach. Park himself was heavily influenced by the French analyst of crowds, Gustave Le Bon (1960), who in turn owed a heavy intellectual debt to Durkheim. However, it remained for one of Park's students, Herbert Blumer (1946, 1955) to systematize the perspective in a series of reviews that elaborated its substantive and empirical elements. With a heavy emphasis on the emergent character of collective behavior and social movements, the approach was in turn further refined by a still later generation of theorists, including Turner and Killian (1957) and Lang and Lang (1961). Though ostensibly in the same tradition, Neil Smelser's important book (1962) moved the field away from its earlier emphasis on process and toward a social structural conception of collective behavior as a response to strain.

In this sense, Smelser's work marked both a return to the field's Durkheimian roots and an embrace of 1950s-style structural functionalism. Like these twin influences, Smelser's work assumed a normative order, interrupted only occasionally by these exceptional (read: aberrant?) forms of behavior. And lest we be tempted to assign positive functions to these forms of behavior, we are told explicitly that they have none, save perhaps as an "early warning" to rational policymakers that there exists some underlying "strain" that must be addressed to restore normative order.

Opposition to the dominant collective behavior paradigm began to develop among a group of sociologists in the early 1970s. This opposition reflected both intellectual influences (e.g., revitalized Marxism, power elite theory, new social history) and the disconnect, in many cases, between the lived experience of movement politics and the fundamental understanding of social movements reflected in the collective behavior perspective. I, for one, first encountered the collective behavior framework as a college sophomore in 1971. Fresh off a year in Washington, D.C., working for a coalition of peace churches on draft-related issues, I was keen to learn as much as I could about the formal scholarship done on social movements. Toward that end I took two political science courses that sounded promising, only to be disappointed by the absence of material on the topic of movements. As disappointed as I was by the silence in these classes, I was equally surprised— and dismayed—when I finally stumbled upon work on the topic in a course on *abnormal psychology!* Imagine my surprise to learn that I—and most of my friends—were psychologically different from the well-adjusted populace at large and engaged in an activity that had little or nothing to do with substantive political ends.

Born of such experiences, a group of sociologists began to formulate alternatives to the collective behavior framework. The resulting critique of collective behavior focused on two principal elements of the perspective.

- A reappraisal of the "normative order." Amid the turbulence of the 1960s and early 1970s it became harder and harder to believe in the kind of normative order envisioned by structural functionalists and implied by the collective behavior perspective. This was not simply a disagreement about the "normal" state of social life but also a challenge to the seeming unquestioning acceptance of the normative order by established sociologists. Even if there was substantial order in American life, perhaps it reflected enduring power differences and enforced patterns of exclusion (e.g., of minorities, of women, and the like) rather than some overarching functional social system. When viewed in this way, some of the infrequent episodes of collective behavior began to look more like legitimate efforts to challenge a closed and coercive system rather than dysfunctional departures from an overarching salutary normative order.
- Social movements as legitimate objects of study. Influenced by this view, a small group of sociologists seized on the study of social movements as a legitimate field in its own right. Differentiating between social movements and the other traditional forms of "collective behavior," these sociologists argued for the normalcy of collective action and its inextricable links to the broader study of power and politics. In this spirit, McCarthy and Zald (1973, 1977), sought to reframe the study of social

movements as but a part of organizational sociology. For their part, Gamson (1975), Tilly (1978; Tilly, Tilly, and Tilly 1975), and others sought to reclaim the study of social movements and revolutions as a central aspect of a more conflict-oriented political sociology.

By the time CBSM was formally recognized as a section in 1981, the influx of (mostly) soft left types into the field had decisively altered the balance of power between the adherents of the older collective behavior tradition and the newer self-defined social movement scholars. The skirmishes so common during those years reflected the increasing dominance of the latter at the expense of the former.

FROM STRATIFICATION TO SOCIAL INEQUALITY. The second case presents an interesting contrast to the first. Although "collective behavior" was hardly a major subfield within sociology in the 1960s, "stratification" clearly was. Indeed, for many it was the proud embodiment of "mainstream sociology." But here too the substantive imprint of the sixties would seem to be evident in the evolution of the field since the 1960s.[3]

The hallmark of traditional stratification research is, of course, Blau and Duncan's *The American Occupational Structure*. Originally published in 1967, the book was not only a groundbreaking piece of scholarship but, with its (for the time) technical sophistication and emphasis on basic research, it was the very embodiment of the "professional project" I've touched on. To say the book had a big impact on the field is severe understatement. More accurately, it set the agenda for stratification research for years to come.

As the influence of both lefts came to be felt more intensively in sociology, however, the work inspired by *The American Occupational Structure* grew increasingly critical in tone. The fundamental complaint by both the hard and soft left was that the status attainment model reflected a structurally impoverished conception of occupational attainment. For Marxists, the exclusive focus on families and family members—to the neglect of formal class relations and the structural properties of the economy—not only truncated the analysis but served to mask gross inequities and confer a certain individualist legitimacy on a system they viewed as fundamentally corrupt. Among other Marxist-inspired lines of work, dual labor market theory rose to prominence in the late 1970s/early 1980s as an alternative perspective on occupational attainment and inequality in general (Beck,

3. My "outsider's" knowledge of the field was greatly enhanced by talking with and reading the work of one of the foremost scholars of inequality, Paula England, in the United States.

Horan, and Tolbert 1980; Tolbert 1983; Hodson and Kaufman 1981, 1982; Horan 1978; Wright and Martin 1987).

For its part, the soft left objected primarily to the implicit "one model fits all" claims of the adherents of the status attainment approach. Although not discounting the processes stressed earlier by Marxists, these "other" leftists came in the 1980s and early 1990s with their singular contribution—an emphasis on the ways in which "race, class, and gender" interact to shape the life chances and material circumstances of individuals (Bielby and Baron 1986; Coverdill 1988; England 1979; Neckerman and Kirschenman 1991; Reskin 1984; Tolbert 1983). Long gone was the concern with universal mobility processes, which was replaced by a sharp focus on division, inequality, and segregation in occupational dynamics. For all this discontinuity, however, one reassuring constant could be seen in the field over time. Regardless of perspective, work in the field retained its high status within the discipline.

DEVALUATION OF "APPLIED" WORK

The spread of a diffuse leftist sensibility within the discipline did more than simply motivate the creation or reconstitution of a host of more explicitly "political" subfields. It also served to discredit and undermine the "problem"-oriented public sociology that had flourished in the postwar period. So thoroughgoing was the Left's critique of American society and American politics that almost all "applied work" came to be seen as suspect by virtue of its connection to "the state." If the modal sociologist of the 1950s and early 1960s was a progressive social engineer seeking solutions to society's problems, his counterpart, circa 1980, was an "outsider" far removed from the mainstream institutions and practical policy questions that had been the focus of so much scholarship in the postwar period. The decline in "applied" work can be clearly seen in the trend in section memberships since 1970.

Figure 11.3 shows variations in the percentage of memberships in ASA sections with a strong applied orientation.[4] In 1971, before the real influx of the baby boom cohorts, a majority of section memberships were in these "applied" sections. By 1982, less than a third of the memberships were of

4. For the purposes of this analysis, I defined the following sections as those characterized by a strong applied emphasis: Medical Sociology; Crime, Law, and Deviance; Sociology of Education; Family; Population; Aging and the Life Course; Mental Health; Alcohol, Drugs, and Tobacco; Sociology of Children and Youth; and International Migration. All others are treated as "non-applied" sections.

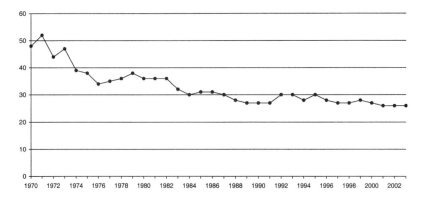

Figure 11.3 Percentage of membership in applied sections, 1970–2003.

the applied variety. Today barely a fourth of all memberships are in sections with an applied orientation.

Nor is it simply the balance between more and less applied work that has changed over the past three decades. I think it fair to say that the *status* and *visibility* of applied work has declined sharply over the same period of time. This may be changing, but it is still the case that the most applied subfields are virtually absent from the highest-ranked sociology departments in the country. Consider the case of medical sociology. This subfield is currently the second largest section in ASA. (The fact that this statement tends to be greeted with incredulity by colleagues in top departments helps to make my point.) Yet as of 2003 none of the top ten–ranked U.S. sociology departments included a medical sociologist among the tenure track faculty. The other major applied subfields find themselves similarly underrepresented in the higher-status departments.

In short, the balance between more or less applied work has shifted dramatically over the past three to four decades in the direction of the latter. And with it, the overall stature and visibility of an "engaged," policy-oriented sociology has declined as well. Ironically, the critical shift in this regard came with the infusion of the baby boom cohorts, attracted by the real-world "relevance" of sociology.

From Relevance to Irrelevance: Whither Sociology?

The sixties have powerfully shaped contemporary sociology. Much of the effect has, in my view, been positive. For instance, I think our understanding of a host of traditional disciplinary topics has been greatly advanced by the distinctive life experiences of sociologists born immediately before and during the baby boom. Social movements, inequality, and race/ethnicity are only a few of the topics that have benefited from a thoroughgoing conceptual makeover at the hands of the baby boom cohorts. More importantly, sociology now boasts a richer, more vibrant mix of subfields than it did in the 1950s and 1960s. Critical dimensions of the human experience—sexuality, emotions, and gender, to name just a few—that were essentially missing from the discipline in these earlier years have been given powerful voice by sociologists whose scholarly sensibilities were shaped by the political and cultural ferment of the 1960s and 1970s.

These gains, however, must be tallied against a marked drop in the visibility, stature, and relevance of contemporary sociology among a host of important external publics. The various trends reviewed here have helped cause this decline. As I have argued, these trends have

- Weakened the tradition of "engaged" scholarship that we rightly associate with sociology in the United States, from its celebrated beginnings in the Chicago school to the great postwar exemplars of the tradition (e.g., Merton, Lazarsfeld, Mills). There is, as I have noted, great irony in this, since the baby boom cohorts who flooded the discipline in the 1960s and 1970s did so out of a desire for "relevance" and "to make a difference."
- Marginalized various subfields within sociology that have not simply been the locus of narrowly applied work but central to the development of general social theory. Criminology is perhaps the best example of this, with the work of Sutherland, Cressey, Merton, and others concerned as much with foundational social processes as real-world implications. As a result of this marginalization, many of the practitioners in these areas feel estranged from sociology and identify almost exclusively with their subfields (e.g., as criminologists, demographers), thereby further divorcing high-quality engaged sociology from the discipline as a whole.

These effects have convinced most external audiences of the irrelevance of sociology. And here I am not simply talking about the Right's distrust of "liberal" social science. Far more damning and worrisome is the entirely understandable skepticism of liberal policymakers, sympathetic foundations, crusading journalists, and progressive advocacy organizations. My duties as director of the Center for Advanced Study in the Behavioral Sciences and as a board member for the Social Science Research Council have obliged me to make the case for the relevance of social science (and sociology in particular) with various real-world constituencies. Nothing in these roles has been more disheartening than the generalized skepticism and disdain that typically greets my efforts to make a case for the continuing relevance and vitality of American social science (and sociology in particular).

Yet the sheer size of the discipline—itself a product of the sixties—has allowed sociologists to largely insulate themselves from the disdain and skepticism of these real-world critics. Sociology is now largely organized as a set of insular, self-referential, communities of scholars who, through regular conferences, specialty journals, and tight network connections (aided by e-mail and the Web), reinforce the importance—indeed the *political* significance—of their narrow subfield-based work, even as that work grows ever more disconnected from the concerns of a host of important real-world constituencies. It is not clear how long sociology can sustain this stance without measurably impacting the long-term institutional and intellectual health of the discipline.

Acknowledgments

My thanks to Michael Murphy and Janet Astner at the American Sociological Association for furnishing much of the data used in this chapter. I am also indebted to Craig Calhoun and an anonymous reviewer for their extremely useful feedback on a draft of the chapter.

[TWELVE] The Culture of Sociology in Disarray: The Impact of 1968 on U.S. Sociologists

Immanuel Wallerstein

In two previous papers, I argued that scholarly disciplines should be seen as a combination of three phenomena: an intellectual construct creating boundaries of a field of study, an institutional structure that defines the rules of participation, and a cultural community that imposes norms of appropriate modes of performance.[1] Here I attempt an interpretation of the consequences for the culture of sociology of the events of 1968 in the United States and elsewhere in the world.

Most discussions of disciplines concentrate on the other two phenomena: the evolving nature of the intellectual construct and/or the parameters of the institutional structure. It is obvious that, as an intellectual construct, sociology (as well as every other scholarly subject matter defined as a discipline) is very complicated. The more one looks at it in detail, the more subtle complexity one finds. One can conclude such a close view with a very idiographic description of the reality one has perceived. Or one can stand back and try to outline the construct in relatively broad brush strokes, thereby risking the accusation that one has ignored important variations and deviation from the mode. The choice is more or less analogous if one analyzes sociology as an institutional structure.

When, however, one analyzes sociology as a culture, particularly as a "national" culture, one needs to worry less about variation and deviation. For we can take it as a given that the norms of group cultures (at all levels) are never fully observed by all members of the group. The important thing, therefore, is not to describe the fact that some, even many, members do not observe the norms but rather to discover what is in fact normative, that is, what is the behavior for which members tend to be rewarded and punished by the community. That said, it is not easy to give firm evidence for what one

1. See my more elaborate discussion of this distinction in my address in 1998 as president of the International Sociological Association (Wallerstein 1999) and in the Ninth Sidney W. Mintz Lecture in Anthropology, Johns Hopkins University, in 2004 (Wallerstein 2004).

defines as the culture of a group, certainly not a group as physically dispersed and as intellectually contentious as U.S. sociologists. In addition, of course, cultures vary over time as well as place.

Still, we can draw some very large canvases at a succession of levels: (1) the world of knowledge over the history of the modern world-system; (2) the location of sociology as a culture in that world of knowledge; (3) the particular features of the culture of sociology within the United States; (4) the historical evolution of this culture in the United States; and (5) the impact of the politico-cultural world revolution of 1968 on the practice of sociology in the United States since then. I describe the first four canvases rapidly in order to concentrate on the impact of the world revolution of 1968.

The most striking thing about the world of knowledge over the history of the modern world-system is the very unusual form it has taken, compared to worlds of knowledge in all previously existing (and studied) world-systems. In the modern world-system, the world of knowledge, which in all earlier systems had been dominated by a single epistemology, suffered the so-called divorce between philosophy and science, referred to summarily as the emergence of the "two cultures." There are a few things to be noted about this divorce. First, it took shape intellectually only in the second half of the eighteenth century and was institutionalized only in the mid-nineteenth century. It could be said to have reached the apogee of clearly etched division only in the period 1945–68, which is indeed rather recent.

Second, once launched, the epistemological battle between the sciences and the humanities became ever sharper over time. The extreme cultural position on each side was to deny intellectual validity to the alternative epistemology. The moderate position was to accept a tacit truce and division of the intellectual domain (and therefore of the institutional turf). Basically, the epistemological debate involved a separation of the long-standing human search for the true, the good, and the beautiful—once thought inseparable—by assigning to the sciences exclusive jurisdiction over the search for the true and to the humanities exclusive jurisdiction over the search for the good and the beautiful.[2]

Third, the social sciences emerged as a superdomain (alongside the natural sciences and the humanities) only in the mid- to late nineteenth century. From the outset, this third domain had difficulty situating itself vis-à-vis the epistemological divide that had taken shape and was dominating the

2. The term *two cultures* was invented by C. P. Snow (1965) in his Cambridge lectures in 1959, in which he expounded the differences and the conflicts between them. For an analysis of the historical development of this struggle, see Lee and Wallerstein (2004, esp. pt. 1).

world of knowledge. While individuals took different sides, the multiple institutional collectivities (that is, social science disciplines) tended to attach themselves to one side or the other of this so-called *Methodenstreit*. Sociology, on the whole and more and more over time, defined itself as a nomothetic (scientistic) discipline rather than an idiographic (humanistic) one.[3]

Fourth, in the cultural battle between science and humanities for social recognition (and hence institutional and financial advantage), science steadily got the upper hand in the eyes of governments, foundations, universities, and the general public. This preference became virtually unquestioned in the period 1945–68 in the wake of extensive practical achievements by the scientists plus the needs of the military and industry in a cold war world.

The prevailing culture of U.S. sociology in the post-1945 period was shaped by two main happenings: the publication in 1937 of Talcott Parsons's *Structure of Social Action*, which invented the "canon" of sociological theorizing,[4] and the institutional preeminence of two departments—Harvard and Columbia. Both departments emphasized the necessity to combine theory and empirical research, and each was led by a team representing this combination—Parsons and Stouffer, Merton and Lazarsfeld. Columbia was probably more important for three fundamental reasons: it was larger and produced many more graduates; it undertook deliberate international outreach (the particular contribution of Lazarsfeld); and its version of theorizing—middle range as opposed to "grand"—was more usable by workaday sociologists (the particular contribution of Merton).

The two happenings—the publications of Parsons's book(s) and the dominance of Harvard and Columbia—are of course linked. Before 1945, Parsons was not widely read, and neither Harvard nor Columbia was a dom-

3. See Lepenies (1988). Lepenies's original title in German was *Drei Kulturen*, which was not translated directly and used as the English title, unfortunately. See also Wallerstein et al. (1996).

4. For Parsons, the canon was Durkheim, Weber, and Pareto. In fact, U.S. sociology adopted Durkheim and Weber but not Pareto. Furthermore, they added Marx, whom Parsons clearly wanted to exclude. What it was about Durkheim, Marx, and Weber that seemed so attractive is something I discussed in my presidential address to the 1998 International Sociological Association (Wallerstein 1999).

Pareto seems to me have fallen flat as a member of the canon for a number of reasons. He was not needed in terms of the basic themes that I suggest account for the combination of Durkheim, Marx, and Weber. He didn't have a strong support group in the way that French sociology supported Durkheim, German post-1945 sociology supported Weber, and the world Left supported Marx. And finally, Pareto was tainted by his association with Italian Fascism, which mattered in the post-1945 years.

inant department in U.S. sociology, but rather Chicago and to a lesser extent Washington. The question of how Parsons and the two departments came to define the culture of U.S. sociology is not an easy one to answer. One element is that the prevailing triumph of scientism in U.S. culture made Chicago ethnography seem too "soft," while the simple positivism espoused by Washington and many other departments seemed unable to deal with the larger sociopolitical questions that loomed so large in the post-1945 U.S. worldview. A second factor, linked to the first, was that Columbia especially was able to exert significant influence on funding agencies such as the Ford Foundation, Guggenheim, and the National Science Foundation, and also of course on the Center for Advanced Study in the Behavioral Sciences, in whose creation both Merton and Lazarsfeld played a major role.

The dominant theoretical label of the time, espoused notably by Columbia, was structural functionalism. On the whole, U.S. sociologists defined themselves in relation to what was seen at its premises—most accepting them, a few defying them. The gatekeepers—the American Sociological Association in its multiple activities and elections; the main sociology journals; the foundations; the Center for Advanced Study in the Behavioral Sciences; and not least, the university committees deciding who should be appointed, promoted, and given tenure—tended to use adherence to this theoretical framework as a prerequisite for reward. The doctrine spread to the hinterland and spread internationally.

We know its main cultural features—methodological positivism; the validation of the scientific method; the centrality of survey analysis and the fourfold table; and adherence to value neutrality (while at the same time engaging in applied sociology, which was problem solving).[5] There were of course many variants on this theme, but essentially, no important department of sociology and no major gatekeeper failed to insist on some version of this set of cultural norms as a basis for supporting the work of the individual sociologist. No doubt there were surviving dissenters, but for the graduate student, the norms that were most helpful to career advancement were clear.

It has been regularly noticed that U.S. sociology in this period was overwhelmingly the study of what was going on in the United States. This is not hard to explain. First of all, the United States was the world's hegemonic power and therefore de facto, in the eyes of most sociologists, a model society. Second, there was next to nothing in the training of graduate students

5. Many other articles in this collection describe this combination of norms, in particular that of George Steinmetz.

that oriented them to acquiring the knowledge skills (including the lin-guistic skills) that would enable them to do research outside the United States. No one seemed to think this important. Third, it was easier to do work nearby. Fourth, U.S. sociology seemed to dominate world sociology, and sociologists from other countries seemed to want to learn about U.S. so-ciology. There seemed little incentive to reverse the orientation. But most of all, the methodological positivism that dominated the scene was universal-istic in tone. It followed that whatever one discovered about behavior in Iowa should in principle be true of behavior anywhere (and any time)—so why not go to the sites of the most reliable data? Notice that these are for the most part cultural, not intellectual, assumptions. To be sure, in most countries, there was a particular emphasis by social scientists on studying itself (and its empire). But at least, in other countries, everyone read the lit-erature written by U.S. sociologists about the United States. This pattern was not at all reciprocated on the whole by U.S. sociologists.

In the 1960s, these cultural assumptions began to erode slowly. I re-member, as a young assistant professor at Columbia, that new cohorts of entering graduate students from 1963 on included a significant number of persons who had served in the Peace Corps. These persons had a far less U.S.-centric view of the world, and many of them wished to use their new empirical knowledge about another part of the world—indeed usually of what was then called the third world—as the basis of their doctoral re-search. These students had usually acquired the practical linguistic skills necessary to do this. They demanded new courses in the curriculum. The area studies programs that had been created in the 1950s but even more in the 1960s offered them encouragement (Wallerstein 1997).

The political atmosphere in the United States was beginning to change. The 1960s saw the rise of an antiwar movement, with particular reference to Vietnam, starting with the teach-ins at the University of Michigan in 1965. It also saw the emergence of a new militant civil rights movement—Congress of Racial Equality, Student Nonviolent Coordinating Committee, Martin Luther King, Malcolm X, Black Power. And Berkeley in 1964 be-came the site of a Free Speech Movement, initially organized around the rights of students to conduct overt political activity. The Free Speech Move-ment received national press coverage.

By the time the first uprising occurred on a university campus in 1968—at Columbia in April—all these issues had been fused. The students who oc-cupied the buildings were protesting Columbia's involvement with the In-stitute for Defense Analysis (which did research supporting the United States' role in the Vietnam War) and Columbia's proposal to build a gymnasium on public property in Morningside Park (seen by Black students as an incursion on the social space and rights of the Harlem community). At Columbia, as on many other campuses, the department with the highest percentage of graduate students directly involved in the actions was that of sociology. In the Ad Hoc Faculty Group, created to mediate the crisis at Columbia, four of the fifteen or so members of its executive committee were from the sociology department.

The uprisings on university campuses in the United States continued for three years, only dissipating in the fall of 1970. This period was traumatic for the universities and for the departments of sociology. What happened as a result?

There was some institutional reform—more participation by students and junior faculty in decision-making bodies. And there was considerable reduction of formality in the university and extensive loosening of the restrictions on students' nonacademic behavior. The concept of the university in loco parentis crashed. Indeed, the parents themselves were cut out of the equation entirely in the name of the privacy rights of the students. But all this was relatively minor in terms of its impact on the intellectual climate of the universities.

The real change was the demise of the canon. It is not that those who accepted the cultural premises that pervaded U.S. sociology from at least 1945 to 1968 all of a sudden ceased to believe in the canon. Far from it. But this set of cultural premises moved from the status of being virtually self-evident to that of being one possible set of premises. And the hypothetical percentage of believers declined as the decades went by, especially among the younger recruits to the discipline. Over the next thirty years, there came to be less and less of a coherent culture of sociology—or one could say that the culture was in disarray.

The first major incursion into older premises was constituted by the claims of the "neglected" peoples and zones. Politically, the 1960s and 1970s were times of great turbulence. Those who were once denoted and conceptualized as minorities began to insist on being called and conceptualized as peoples or as identities. They demanded not only political, economic, and social rights but what might be called intellectual rights. They argued about the names used to designate their group—in the popular press and in academic discourse. Negroes became first Blacks and then African Americans, and the discussion is still continuing. The term Hispanics arose, to be replaced by Latinos, and then by Latin@s. American Indians became Native Americans. And so forth (Wallerstein 2005). Names turned out to be very important but so were concepts. "Race relations" was replaced by "racial/

ethnic conflict" and "prejudice" by "racism." The foundational assumptions of the new terms were quite different from the old.

The same thing happened with women. Classically, the category "women" was biological, and women were studied primarily by sociologists of the family. But politically, the 1960s and 1970s saw the flourishing of the second wave of feminism and the demands by women for multiple, new kinds of rights—rights over their bodies, rights in the workplace, rights to parity in the political arena. "Sex" as a category was replaced by "gender," a term that was designed to emphasize the constructed nature of the concept. Names were important here too, and again so were concepts. What happened with "minorities" and "women" was repeated for other groups— homosexuals became ultimately gay, lesbian, bisexual, and transsexual (GLBT) persons; the disabled became other-abled; the deaf became the hearing-impaired; and on and on.

In each of these cases, there were common elements, or perhaps a common sequence. There was the emergence in the larger political world of a movement that became strong. There was the discovery that, in the academic world, these peoples had been neglected. There was the rise of specialized studies (programs of study and research, scholarly journals, and new scholarly associations) to remedy the neglect. And, within U.S. sociology, there were the new fundamental categories of race and gender, which were now considered to be basic elements in every sociological analysis.

The second thing that happened was the rediscovery and reinterpretation of class as a sociological category. Class had been part of the armory of concepts throughout the history of sociology in the United States (and elsewhere). Chicago sociology was essentially a mode of research about the urban working classes. The urban workers were to some extent treated ethnographically and to some extent as a "problem" in "deviant" or "violent" behavior that had to be addressed. But class was never out of the picture. It is not that most U.S. sociologists were Marxists; they were not. But if one didn't want to call it class, one called it, more aseptically, "strata." Stratification was a major subdiscipline within U.S. (and world) sociology.

Politically, the movements of racial/ethnic identity and the feminists felt they had to battle assumptions on the political left that issues of race and gender were secondary to issues of class. In a sense, their advocates spent much energy combating the primacy, and even the significance, of class. But as the racial/ethnic and women's movements became more important and successful, they began to have internal battles that seemed to reflect to some extent issues of class. And to the degree that these movements were worldwide, they began to feel that sometimes race and gender were in fact, at least in part, surrogates for class. So the concern with race and gender of the 1970s became by the 1990s a concern with race-class-gender. In the process, the term *stratification* practically disappeared from the standard vocabulary.

The third thing that happened is that U.S.-centrism began to seem outmoded, or dubious, or even patently nefarious. The so-called third world within called attention to the third world without. Indeed, such academic categories as Afro-American studies often became studies of the Black world. And the area studies programs, which had cut up the world into geographical spheres, began to feel pressure to see various regions as part of the South or as the "periphery" of a world-system. Added to this thrust, which reflected leftist critiques of the existing social structures, came the eminently mainstream emphasis on globalization as a new framework within which to analyze the contemporary world. It was no longer thought that studying Iowa would give us the needed tools to study all the rest of the world. This trend was reinforced by the sudden large increase in non-U.S. students in graduate departments.

The world revolution of 1968 was not merely a rejection of the dominant geoculture, of centrist liberalism as the only possible legitimate ideology, and therefore of what had passed as mainstream sociology as the only possible legitimate mode of sociological analysis. The Old Left in its multiple forms (Communism, Social Democracy, and national liberation movements) came under similarly withering criticism from those who participated in the various student uprisings. The Old Left was seen as collusive with the Establishment, as failures historically in transforming the world, as "part of the problem and not part of the solution."

The political consequences of this volcanic upsurge of political sentiment were enormous. But equally enormous were the consequences for the cultures of the university. The critics of mainstream sociology had long emphasized the economic underpinnings of social processes and their political consequences. Their emphasis was on what is sometimes called political economy. These critics, like their counterparts in the Old Left movements, had regarded, or at the very least seemed to regard, the negatives of race and ethnicity, the imbalances of gender, as derivative of allegedly more fundamental factors in the social structure. They thus believed that these "problems" would be resolved eventually when (and only when) the "fundamental" imbalances were corrected. This assumption of so-called critical sociologists was not so different in practice from the Whiggish assumption of mainstream sociologists that the negatives would be erased as the system inevitably developed over time.

Those who called for a new emphasis on race/ethnicity and gender found these assumptions intolerable. Since a good deal of the new theorizing centered around the revalidation of identities, it was quite regularly expressed in terms of the centrality of culture—now not a prerequisite for social integration and development, as in the post-1945 Weberianism so prevalent in U.S. sociology, but as a justification for a radical reanalysis of social processes and at the same time of university curricula. This group joined a transdisciplinary movement called cultural studies, with its emphasis on the "hermeneutic turn" and discourse analysis.

The consequence of these new emphases was an effort to upend the cultural prejudices of U.S. sociologists. The years 1945–68 had seen the final triumph of quantitative methods as the only truly legitimate mode of doing research. The post-1968 counterreaction was to revalidate qualitative analyses, whether in the form of cultural analyses or in the form of historical sociology. It is not that no one did quantitative work any more. It is simply that there came to be a greater balance between quantitative and qualitative work in the community. By the late 1990s, the *American Sociological Review,* while still largely quantitative, would publish some qualitative work, and departments openly advertised for persons doing qualitative work.

A more contentious but probably more important cultural challenge to what had been mainstream sociology was the challenge to "value neutrality" as the indispensable cloak of scholarly work. To the argument, which had been dominant in the 1945–68 period, that scholars could and should segregate radically their scholarly judgments and their moral/political preferences, a new generation of scholars opposed the view that it was not really possible, and not necessarily desirable at all, that sociologists make the attempt.

This argument was not a plea for subordination of scholarship to political tactics of the moment but a rereading of Weber's careful and somewhat ambiguous discussions of "substantive" (or material) rationality as opposed to formal rationality. Weber, who had been the icon in the 1945–68 period of value neutrality, seemed, on closer look, not to follow the views his acolytes alleged were his. In any case, what had been an unquestioned norm now became a matter of scholarly debate, as can be seen in the discussions that revolved around the theme of public sociology at the 2004 meetings of the ASA.[6]

One of the intellectual consequences of the upheavals of 1968 was the opening (or reopening) of the questions about the intellectual boundaries

6. See the articles on "public sociologies" in the various 2004 issues of *Footnotes,* in particular the letter-debate between Mathieu DeFlem and Michael Burawoy in the July/August 2004 issue (pp. 9–10), about the ASA Council's resolution on a proposed amendment to the U.S. Constitution.

of sociology. Such figures as Durkheim and Weber wrote widely about themes that seemed to cross what some later thought were strict disciplinary boundaries. Was Durkheim's *The Elementary Forms of Religious Life* a work of sociology or of anthropology, or indeed of religious studies? Was Weber's *General Economic History* anything other than economic history? Weber did not identify himself as a sociologist until late in life, and even then he considered himself also an economic historian. And Durkheim said there was no difference between sociology and history.[7]

By the time I became a graduate student, such a lax view of the relation of the separate disciplines was considered to be heresy, and many continue to think it so. In the period 1945–68, and largely due to Talcott Parsons's *The Structure of Social Action,* Durkheim and Weber were reinterpreted, and the boundary lines of sociology (as distinct from economics, political science, and history) raised high. The field of sociology now included neither the state nor the market. To be sure, almost as soon as this was decreed as official doctrine, it began to break down. One of the reasons was the expansion of the university system, hence the expansion of the number of PhD's, and therefore the necessity in all the disciplines to find niches of originality for them. Already in sociology in the1950s, the new fields of political sociology and economic sociology began to emerge. And their practitioners worked hard to show that somehow they were different from political scientists and economists. By the 1960s, the field of historical sociology announced itself. Confusion about boundaries was growing.

The upheavals consequent upon 1968 pushed the matter much further. On the one hand, many sociologists (and university administrators) began to praise the virtue of multidisciplinary studies. The defining feature of such studies was either a research team made up of people with PhD's in two or more disciplines or, more rarely, an avowal by an individual scholar that he/she was reading in and drawing from work identified with two or more disciplines. Intellectually, this often resulted in mishmash and seemed largely a ploy to attract fund-givers. In particular some of the scholars identified with the new "identity" fields or with gender analysis began to feel that the intellectual boundaries of the traditional social science disciplines were not merely fluid but even useless or at least served to constrain serious analysis. Some began to demand intellectual revision of disciplinary boundaries, which certainly went against the culture of sociology that prevailed in the 1945–68 period.

The furthest revision was the one called for by those who questioned the

7. See Durkheim (1898a). I discuss Durkheim's arguments in Wallerstein (1998).

legitimacy of the concept of the two cultures—the total distinctiveness between science (theoretically driven empirical research) and the humanities (the attempt to understand hermeneutically the intellectual production of others). This distinction had been validated within the social sciences by the so-called *Methodenstreit* between nomothetic and idiographic epistemologies. As late as the eighteenth century, this distinction had had little or no purchase among serious intellectuals. However, beginning in the nineteenth century, and especially during 1945–68, it became doxa. But in the late twentieth century, the question has been reopened.

Many will argue that all these post-1968 questions have always been on the table. And no doubt, they have been. What one can say, however, is that the period 1945–68 saw a particular crystallization of the culture of sociology, what we now retrospectively call mainstream sociology (in the United States, in particular). This culture legitimated a particular intellectual definition of the field and was normatively enforced by the organizational apparatus of U.S. sociology. The upheavals of 1968 in the external political arena of U.S. sociology broke the crust of the culture by redefining what had seemed self-evident consensus as merely a particular viewpoint—perhaps one that still enjoyed majority support, but not one that was the unique legitimate definition of the field.

The culture of sociology is today in limbo. It would be a brave professor who would propose to incoming graduate students a set of premises and norms that command overwhelming support among the practitioners of sociology today. Perhaps this is not at all unhealthy. Students have before them many uncertainties and, if they are serious, will have to struggle with the rest of us in seeking more stable ground for future creative work.

[THIRTEEN] Assessing the Feminist Revolution: The Presence and Absence of Gender in Theory and Practice

Myra Marx Ferree, Shamus Rahman Khan
& Shauna A. Morimoto

In the first decade of the twenty-first century, sociology offers a wide range of theoretical tools for understanding the development and effects of gender relations. Empirical studies of gender expectations and power relations range from the micro- to the macrolevel. At least to some degree, gender has become a concept theoretically understood to refer to "social relations based on perceived differences between the sexes and . . . a primary means of symbolizing power" (Scott 1986, 1067). Gender has become recognized as a major social force, perhaps best described as a core institution of all societies (Martin 2004), and the location of significant structural inequality. Gender inequality is a focus of attention in many institutional settings, and how gender shapes the way that people relate to each other and to broader social structures is widely recognized as an important question. This was not always so.

The extent of change in how gender relations are understood sociologically is perhaps best illustrated by comparing this approach to the functionalist understanding of "sex roles" that dominated American sociology in the early 1960s. This view drew on Talcott Parsons's perception of natural differences between sexes as legitimating a general binary division of expressive and instrumental functions for men and women, demanding a division of family life into separate "roles" of domesticity and paid labor, and seeing "the adult female anchored primarily in the internal affairs of the family, as wife, mother, and manager of the household" (Parsons and Bales 1955, 355). In this approach, the equation of women with the family was nearly absolute, since women's "domestic role" meant that both women's exclusion from public life and men's "private" violence against women went unremarked. The invisibility of women went still further, since race and class—both recognized as important—were seen as social processes primarily having to do with men. This was apparent in functionalist stratification studies based on male workers and "heads of households" no less than in "conflict sociology," where research on power structures recognized only the presence and interests of men in social movements, unions, and corporations, yet assumed these to be "ungendered." Moreover, studies conducted from men's point of view defined deviations from these familial and interpersonal norms as "social problems." Women were therefore rarely of interest to sociologists, unless as deviants ("nuts and sluts") or as wives and mothers (family sociology being understood largely by studying women, and only women). Women's subordinate status was not even recognized, much less defined as a social problem.

The feminist mobilization that began in the 1960s changed all this, but not immediately, nor even yet completely. Feminism itself, connecting the recognition of social inequality in the relations between women and men to a commitment to empower women and reduce men's domination, stirred on the streets after a long period of quiescence (Taylor 1989; Freeman 1975). In the 1970s, American feminist mobilization inside institutions spread from the small groups of activists "in the woodwork" of political parties, unions, and state offices to encompass new forms of activism in churches, schools, and workplaces (Ferree and Hess 2000). Academic feminist activism, including the new arena of women's studies, encompassed challenges both to university structures and disciplinary biases that reproduced gender inequality. Sociologists were among those who mobilized to change gender relations in and outside academia, and sociology was one of the many social institutions that they changed.

In this chapter, we trace the process of these transformations in the United States. We argue that the dramatic increase in the number of women in sociology since the early 1970s has produced a still-ongoing process of remaking sociological theory, methods, and organizational practice by drawing attention to two previously ignored phenomena: the social structures that produce gender and the gender relations that shape all social structures. Central to this project is the overthrow of the sex roles model of the 1950s. Feminist sociologists went beyond their initial critique of its normative prescription of a specific form of family relations to reject its underlying assumption of binary social roles. As a result, a new, structural understanding of gender has emerged that draws from and contributes to the sociological analysis of inequality in general.

We argue that women's own struggle to enter and change sociology has been the engine driving this theoretical transformation from the end of the 1960s through the present. Although this has been an international process, our focus here is on the dynamics of American sociology in particular. Over this period, we demonstrate a marked increase in the originally male-defined discipline's willingness to consider both women scholars and gender issues as important. Indeed, to the extent that women have brought feminism into sociology and have forced the abandonment of the sex roles model, sociology's approach to gender has become more genuinely sociological: focused on relations among individuals and groups, social practices and social structures. But we also suggest that this transformation is still incomplete. Even though American sociology has increasingly included women in its departments, journals, and organizations, and has developed flourishing fields of feminist theory and empirical scholarship on gender, it has not brought the insights of these fields into the everyday practice of "doing sociology."

We begin by examining how women entered the discipline and changed the demographics and organizational practices of American sociology between 1960 and 2004. Gaining such standing was a difficult and controversial process, provoked by deliberate feminist action, as women organized to overcome long-established barriers. We then demonstrate just how striking the change in the presence of women, whether feminist or not, has been for sociological research. Once sociology's subjects no longer could be simply assumed to be men, basic ideas and approaches came into question. Filling in the gaps made it obvious that these exclusions were built into the substance of theories and not superficial shortcomings. Made aware of the significance of gender by feminism, both male and female researchers looked for sociological ways to understand the subordination of women. Drawing from and contributing to women's and gender studies, they provided a different and initially controversial perspective on once seemingly settled issues of inequality. Bringing women into the picture changed the framing of such sociological concepts as stratification, work, and violence. Relating gender to such core sociological concerns as power, inequality, and social change undermined the basis for understanding it as binary "sex roles" and as only relevant for studying women.

After considering how the increased presence of women as objects of sociological study forced a revision of the inherently but invisibly male-centered approaches of the discipline, we look at the deeper transformation of sociological theory that feminist research initiated. This structural understanding of gender, not simply of women, now challenges ideas of inequality and interaction embedded in sociological theory as a whole. We examine how the new view of gender and the older sex roles models are expressed in the way that research is done, published, and taught. Because this theoretical conflict is ongoing, we look at some recent challenges to methods and theory that exemplify the current tension between these paradigms. Finally, we suggest some issues for the future prospects of resolving this conflict.

Sociology as Gendered Work

The process of professionalization that created sociology as a discipline was gendered, with men actively excluding women from the departments and associational roles that established the field (Magdalenić 2004). At the beginning of the twentieth century, Julia Lathrop, Grace Abbot, and Ethel Dummer were members of the ASA executive, and in 1906 there were fifteen women members of the ASA, including Jane Addams and Charlotte Perkins Gilman. By 1926, however, women's exclusion from sociology departments was reflected in the association. Women scholars formed alternative networks, such as the one around Hull House in Chicago, not typically defined as sociological (Deegan 1990). Women's participation in ASA became limited to support roles like administrative officer or managing editor. Although to most men the ASA and the discipline of sociology appeared to be gender neutral, the domination of men and the marginalization of women were not so invisible to the women who felt the brunt of them (Bernard 1973; Hughes 1973a, 1973b; Riley 1988). This gendered exclusion only began to be made visible as feminism created opportunities to discuss and challenge it.[1]

CREATING AN ORGANIZATIONAL PRESENCE

When the American Sociological Association held its 1969 annual meeting in San Francisco, Alice Rossi, then a professor at Goucher College, confronted the organization's leadership (which included ASA secretary Peter Rossi) at the business meeting. On behalf of the newly formed Women's Caucus, Alice Rossi offered nine resolutions on topics such as hiring and promotion practices, child care at the annual meeting, the inclusion of women in research designs, and the development of course material on women. Council supported these resolutions, but the ad hoc women's caucus formed that summer decided to meet again that winter in order to sustain its momentum. Sociologists for Women in Society (SWS), a feminist organization of both women and men, was formed at that 1970 winter meeting.

As a collective advocate for women, SWS first became highly visible in 1972 at the ASA meeting in New Orleans (Roby 1992). In this era, the sit-ins

1. Today's readers would find the blatant consignment of women and gender relations to social irrelevance, common in the 1960s, to be astonishing. For example, Glenn and Weiner (1969) "decided to exclude" all women from their study of changing social origins of sociologists, while deploring the declining number of (male) sociologists from rural backgrounds as a loss of "a perspective that probably has considerable value to the discipline."

to desegregate lunch counters in the South were spilling over into comparable sit-ins, by newly forming feminist groups, at restaurants, bars, and clubs across the country with male-only policies. A number of sociologists (among them Jessie Bernard, Arlene Kaplan Daniels, Nona Glazer, Beth Hess, Alice Rossi, and Erving Goffman) decided to sit-in at the Monteleone Hotel's all-male lunchroom. The protesters made clear that they saw exclusion from the bar and grill in the meeting hotel as a symbol of the overall marginality of women in ASA's program and activities.

SWS, as an organization autonomous from ASA, offered its own alternative program to give women and feminism a space to be heard; it also brought direct pressure to bear on ASA. From the start, SWS melded the collectivist feminist style of organizing projects for direct service (in this case, offering substantive paper sessions and career support) and the bureaucratic feminist style of lobbying and lawsuits (endorsing candidates for ASA elections, bringing member resolutions, sending observers to ASA Council meetings, and funding sociologists' sex discrimination cases). The ASA Council, partly in response to this mobilization, established an office for women and minority affairs in 1972, with Doris Wilkinson, a SWS member, as the first program officer. This office began to systematically collect data on women and nonwhites in sociology.

The picture they found was bleak. In 1966 there were no women serving as elected decision makers in ASA (on the Council, the publications committee, or in any section), and women made up only 10 percent of all ASA journal editorial board members (Roby 1992). By 1971, initial pressure had jumped women's representation to 19 percent of elected committee members and 8 percent of elected section officers. These numbers began to change even more as SWS mobilized its members to vote in ASA elections. The fact that SWS members voted at a significantly higher rate than did ASA members overall made the SWS an effective lobby and helped move women into ASA office in numbers higher proportionally than the number of women holding nonstudent memberships (D'Antonio and Tuch 1991; Rosenfeld, Cunningham, and Schmidt 1997). Although in 1973 the ASA elected Mirra Komarovsky as only its second woman president (the first being Dorothy Swaine Thomas in 1952), in the ensuing twenty elections between 1974 and 1994 just three women were elected president. In 1994, controversy arose, generating protest write-in candidates, when the official ASA nominating process produced an all-woman set of candidates, most of whom were also SWS members, for its three top offices (president, vice president, and secretary).

The representation of women in ASA office has since then become non-controversial. In 2004, unlike 1994, the election of feminist women sociologists as president and vice president in that year's election did not create a backlash. Since 1983 the ASA Council has generally been composed of at least 50 percent women (Rosenfeld, Cunningham, and Schmidt 1997). However, the proportion of women nominated and the odds of a nominated woman being elected have both declined since 1994. Women are no longer overrepresented in leadership roles relative to their percentage of faculty appointments (Committee on the Status of Women in Sociology [CSW] 2004).

Since the 1970s, ASA meetings have changed in substance as well as in their representation of women. ASA introduced child care at meetings, began to import SWS-originated programming ideas (e.g., mentoring workshops on how to publish and network), and established the section Sex Roles. Renamed Sex and Gender in 1976, the section has been the largest single one in ASA since 1988. Women's share of presentations on the ASA program also began to rise in the 1970s, and with it attention to gender inequality as a sociological issue. By the 1980s, research on gender issues was a vital force at ASA meetings. Analyses of program participation by the ASA's Committee on the Status of Women in 1995 and 2004 show no differences by gender in amount or types of participation (CSW 2004). Although certainly not all women sociologists do research on gender, nor are all those who study gender women, the more extensive incorporation of women researchers clearly directed greater attention to gender as an object of study. By the mid-1990s, SWS felt it was no longer necessary to offer substantive program sessions on women's status and gender research, since its members and concerns were now well incorporated in the overall ASA program. Changing ASA as an organization, however, was easier than transforming the discipline as a whole.

CHANGES IN THE COMPOSITION OF THE DISCIPLINE

Some of the rapid rise in women's organizational standing in the discipline reflected an overall increase in women researchers. As table 13.1 indicates, this growth represented less of a change in women undergraduates' interest in sociology than in women's access to advanced study. In the 1960s, graduate work was still defined as male. Arlene Kaplan Daniels recounts, "we were all boys together; there was no other choice. The notion that women might have different agendas or interests or problems was unheard of . . . so in the end, I was the only woman in my cohort who completed the Ph.D. program" (1994, 32). Even though women were already a majority among sociology undergraduates in the 1960s, the overall share of ad-

Table 13.1 Percentage of degrees in sociology conferred on women, 1966–2001

Year	Bachelor's (%)	Master's (%)	PhD (%)
1966	60	31	15
1971	59	37	20
1976	59	42	30
1981	70	52	40
1986	69	55	44
1991	69	60	50
1996	68	65	52
2001	70 (2000)	66 (2000)	58

Note: The percentage of bachelor's and master's degrees conferred during 2001 were unavailable, so those of 2000 are substituted.

vanced degrees going to women was much lower (30 percent of master's degrees and only 15 percent of PhD's in 1966). As feminist protests began, this proportion began to rise significantly, and once begun, the shift at the PhD level accelerated substantially, with the percentage of women receiving PhD's going up to 20 percent in 1971 and jumping to 40 percent only ten years later. By 1980, sociology departments were granting a majority of their master's degrees to women, and by 1988 gave a majority of their PhD's to women as well.

The impact of opening doors to women for advanced study was felt across the social sciences. The share of psychology doctorates going to women rose from 22 percent in 1965–69 to 66 percent in 1995–99, and in political science from 9 percent to 33 percent, while in sociology women's share rose from 19 percent to 55 percent (CSW 2004). Sociology was unusual, however, in that the field experienced a huge increase in the number of men doing graduate work during this period, with men receiving just over 200 PhD's in 1966 compared to 500 PhD's in 1972. Women did not initially match this rate of increase (see fig. 13.1). The exceptionally large babyboom cohorts of men (450–500 per year) earning degrees in the 1970s are still moving slowly through the "python" of the academic system. By contrast, women earned fewer than 50 PhD's in 1966, and this number rose steadily to about 220 in 1977. The late 1970s saw a drop in numbers as the

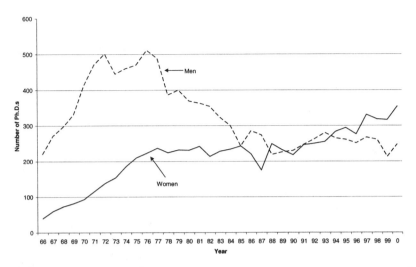

Figure 13.1 Number of sociology PhD's awarded to men and women, 1966-2000.
Source: CSW 2004.

labor market contracted (Roos and Jones 1993), but from the mid-1980s on, the number of men receiving PhD's appears to have stabilized at around 250 per year, while the number of women began again to rise—from about 220 per year throughout the 1980s to 325-50 per year in the late 1990s and early 2000s. Thus, although a first wave of women broke into sociology with energy in the 1970s, their institutional presence was initially muted by the large "boom cohort" of men who were a source of both solidarity in pursuit of social change and competition for increasingly scarce jobs.

How well women made it into the academic mainstream was affected by this historical transformation. Men of the boom generation moved up in rank before the new wave of younger women entered in the late 1980s, making men as a group both older and more likely to be full professors in 1999 (see table 13.2). That women faced obstacles in an increasingly tight academic labor market was evident in January 1984, when ASA Council approved "departmental hiring goals" that asserted that "the proportion of women holding tenured positions in academic departments of sociology in 1990 should be equivalent to the proportion receiving Ph.D.s between 1950 and 1980. The appropriate figure is 27 percent or approximately one in four." That figure was not actually reached until 1997.

Using a similar standard for 2000 (i.e., the proportion of women among 1960-90 PhD's) indicates that departments have caught up (women comprised 28 percent of the graduates during this period and 32 percent of the

Table 13.2 Age and rank structure of academic sociologists by gender, 1969 and 1999

	Year			
	1969		1999	
	Women	Men	Women	Men
% over 40 years old	70	55	74	84
% full professors	27	40	28	52

Source: 1969 Carnegie Survey of Higher Education, as cited in *CSW* 2004.

tenured faculty). However, other factors suggest less optimism. Although the share of assistant professorships held by women closely matched the share of PhD's awarded in 1975 (approximately 30 percent) and 1984 (approximately 42 percent), by 1999 women were earning 60 percent of the PhD's but receiving only 50 percent of the assistant professor positions, and the gap between the percentage of tenured women and the percentage of women who had earned a PhD ten years earlier again seemed to be widening (fig. 13.2). The proportion of women among full professors (10 percent) barely increased at all before 1984 and was still only 20 percent in 1991, suggesting that many women faced considerable delay in getting this promotion. And while the large male boom cohorts will be retiring in this decade, sociology departments now are shrinking and the odds of being promoted to full professor falling, making it less likely that women in the cohorts to follow will benefit from these openings at the top (CSW 2004).

It is also important to acknowledge how institutionalized forms of discrimination (e.g., the continuing stereotyping of women researchers as less qualified, the shunting of women into teaching-intensive jobs, resistance to accepting women in positions of authority over men) kept the older cohorts of women sociologists on the margins. As Matilda White Riley notes, "in my early years, sex discrimination was taken for granted" (1988, 28), and Helen McGill Hughes, with PhD in hand, was relegated to the role of editorial assistant for *AJS*, "a job that would never have been offered to a male Ph.D. or even to a male doctoral student" (1973a, 772). Although the Civil Rights Act of 1963 and the Education Amendments of 1972 clearly defined discrimination against women faculty as illegal, it took lawsuits by courageous women (such as sociologists Margaret Cussler, Nancy Stoller Shaw, and Natalie Allon, whose own careers typically were destroyed in the lengthy process) to hold universities accountable for changing their hiring, promotion,

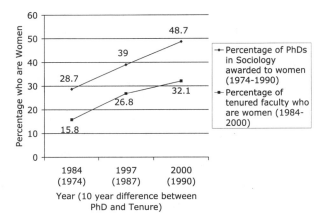

Figure 13.2 Proportion of PhDs in sociology awarded to women (1974–1990) compared with the proportion of tenured women faculty (1984–2000).

and pay practices. Thus, as table 13.2 also indicates, the rank held by the relatively few women in the academy in 1969 did not reflect their seniority. The boom generation made faculty men younger as a group than faculty women in 1969 (45 percent of the men were forty or younger, compared to only 30 percent of the women), yet 40 percent of all men in sociology were already full professors at that point, compared to only 27 percent of the women.

RESEARCH STATUS AND AUTHORITY

Indeed, the presence of important women sociologists such as Jessie Bernard, Helen McGill Hughes, and Matilda White Riley in the discipline in the 1960s and 1970s did not mean that they enjoyed the same prestige or institutional resources granted the typical male academic researcher. From 1948 to 1970, for example, not one woman was hired in a tenure-track position at Berkeley (Delamont 2003, 40). For several pioneering women, partnership with men sociologists relegated them (via institutional nepotism rules) to non-tenure-track positions or jobs in nearby teaching-intensive liberal arts colleges (for example, consider Alice Rossi at Goucher College when Peter was at Johns Hopkins, Rose Coser at Wellesley when Lewis was at Brandeis). In the 1970s, some schools began to open up the possibility of dual-career hiring (the University of Massachusetts at Amherst hired the Rossis and SUNY Stony Brook hired the Cosers as couples). But elite schools remained less interested in even top women scholars. Only in the 1980s did this resistance began to crack. When the Harvard sociology department denied tenure to Theda Skocpol in 1980, she received offers to teach at other leading departments and sued the university. Unlike those whose careers were destroyed by the arduous process of bringing a discrimination case, Skocpol taught for several years at Chicago before being invited back to Harvard (Skocpol 1988).

Still, leading gender scholars had limited access to departments most engaged in training the next generation. Neither the University of Massachusetts nor Stony Brook was a top-ten department when each made its pathbreaking appointment of a couple, and although both departments rose in status as a result, graduate students studying gender either had to go to such a lower-ranked schools or do innovative work in a higher-ranked department on their own. Through the mid-1980s, leading scholars, who in the 1990s would be recognized by being recruited at major schools and winning top prizes for their work, were often denied tenure (e.g., Evelyn Nakano Glenn at Boston University). Others remained in departments with limited graduate programs (e.g., Barrie Thorne at Michigan State) or were positioned on the margins of sociology (e.g., Joyce Ladner and Patricia Yancey Martin in social work).[2] Stephen Kulis analyzed the top twenty-seven ranked departments in 1984 and found women comprised 19 percent of these faculty compared to 24 percent of others, but also that among the top-ranked faculties almost three of five men were full professors but only one in three women were (1988, 206, 209). Looking just at the top twenty sociology departments (ranked by the National Research Council) in 1984 and 2000, we find that the percentage of tenured faculty members who were women at these elite schools lagged behind the field as a whole, as did the proportion of women among all faculty members (see fig. 13.3). Although the data show that women have now made inroads into the leading departments, their progress is remarkably recent, coming only in the 1990s. Even today, SWS's ranking of graduate departments in terms of support for gender scholarship and proportion of women faculty shows that "the higher one moves up the ladder of institutional prestige, the fewer women one will find, the less diversity overall, and the less concern with gender and inequality scholarship" and argues that the trade-off remains between "seeking work and education in the most prestigious departments or choosing to surround themselves with women faculty and scholars interested in gen-

2. In the nonrandom sample of eminent women sociologists whose autobiographical essays are collected in three volumes (Goetting and Fenstermaker 1995; Laslett and Thorne 1997; Meadow Orlans and Wallace 1994), no less than ten of the forty-two report denial of tenure (Delamont 2003, 29).

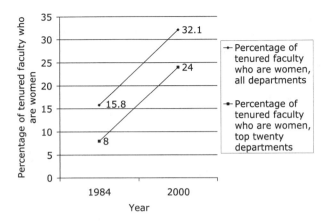

Figure 13.3 Percentage of tenured faculty who are women, in the top twenty departments versus all departments, 1984–2000.

der" (Hays and Risman 2004). Overall, women are slower to acquire tenure and promotion and less well represented in the most advantaged research settings.

FEMINIST RESEARCH AND GATEKEEPING

The marginal position of women in the academy in the 1960s and 1970s meant that feminist research began outside the mainstream and first became visible at the intersection of scholarship and social protest. In the early 1970s, women's studies programs emerged as a space where an interdisciplinary and activist challenge to the "male-stream" could be posed. Initially engaged in what would be called an "add women and stir" approach (McIntosh 1983) to the exclusion of knowledge about women, women's studies quickly found that even such a small stirring in could cause explosive reactions, both of creative discovery and hostile rejection.[3] Working in dual mode to transform the conventional disciplines as well as establish a secure extradepartmental basis for research that placed women at the center of the discovery process, women's studies drew feminist sociologists into interdisciplinary research and curriculum transformation projects (e.g., Andersen 1987).

3. Imber (1999) offers a good example of the continuing backlash against feminist gains. He attacks both ASA and sociology departments for their attention to gender and race, he attacks the substance of the field as a whole but does not cite specific feminist work, and he couches political vituperation as a defense against politicization.

Sociologists both provided theoretical tools for activists and were guided to new research questions by the challenges to institutional structures posed by women's movement groups. Barbara Katz Rothman's work on the practices of childbirth informed and inspired feminist nurses and mid-wives while also feeding their experiences and insights into her critique of institutional medicine. Jessie Bernard, Pauline Bart, and Nancy Chodorow figured prominently in such classic early mass-market feminist readers as Gornick and Moran's *Woman in Sexist Society* (1971), which focused on rela-tionships and structures in gender inequality. Hannah Papanek, Joan Huber, Barrie Thorne, Elise Boulding, Lise Vogel, Jean Lipman-Blumen, and Joan Acker were featured in the first volume of *Signs: A Journal of Women in Cul-ture and Society* (1975), the new and soon to be leading journal in women's studies. Sociology's own journals initially showed interest in this research as well, but after first opening their doors, they failed to institutionalize ap-propriate ways of evaluating feminist studies.

Already in the 1970s, some women began to gain access to gatekeeping roles, including in the leading journals. In 1971, the *Journal of Marriage and the Family* published a special issue on women and feminism (edited by Pauline Bart) that drew attention to issues previously invisible to family so-ciologists, including violence against women. This topic does not show up in the big three sociology journals until 1984, with an *AJS* article "Toward a Phenomenology of Domestic Violence" by Norman Denzin; the article does not particularly offer a feminist perspective on the issue, but at least it notices the topic's significance. The 1973 special issue on gender that *AJS*, quite unusually, commissioned Joan Huber to edit marked another critical step toward recognition that this new topic was indeed of sociological in-terest.[4]

This first taste of feminist research was not followed by a feast of new ideas in mainstream journals, however. Although it became increasingly possible to publish research focused on women, the failure of sociology journals to publish much feminist research done on its own terms, rather than compensatory research done within the still male-defined terms of the discipline, created a powerful desire among sex and gender researchers for a journal of their own.

In 1985, at the Washington, D.C., annual meeting, the Sex and Gender section of ASA made application to Council, formally requesting permis-sion to launch a new journal in this area. Council rejected this request both

4. Delamont (2003, 23) says that Andrew Abbott describes this as an "exciting time" in the history of *AJS*, "when the managing editor, Florence Levinsohn, tried to make the journal more controversial and exciting. The special issue was 'immensely successful' but Levinsohn was sacked in 1974" and the strategy was not repeated.

on the official grounds that sections were not allowed to publish journals (a rule ASA later changed) and on the unofficial but openly stated rationale that this would "divert good papers from *ASR*." Since feminist scholars had good reason to believe that *ASR* reviewers were disinclined to accept their work, SWS took advantage of its autonomy from ASA to set up *Gender and Society* on its own. Under the skilled leadership of its first editor, Judith Lorber, *G&S* published pathbreaking papers of gender scholarship such as West and Zimmerman's "Doing Gender," which had already collected a pile of rejection letters from the mainstream journals. In 2005, its nineteenth year of publication, *G&S* has become the most frequently cited social science journal in women's studies. Rather than "diverting" feminist scholarship from *ASR*, *G&S* probably encouraged *ASR* to compete more effectively to publish such work.

Rita Simon, a criminologist, was appointed the first woman editor of *ASR* in 1978, but under her tenure feminist issues such as violence against women still failed to find a home in this journal. By the time Paula England, noted for her feminist research on sex stratification, became editor of *ASR* in 1994 (having started her career, like so many other gender scholars, at a teaching-intensive school, the University of Texas at Dallas), her appointment was seen as a recognition of her individual contributions to the field, as an opportunity for the journal to encourage more submissions from feminist scholars, and as a means of drawing in a more diverse pool of reviewers. Although succeeding in expanding and diversifying the editorial board in other ways, England kept the gender composition relatively stable (at 33–37 percent, as it had been under both previous editors). The proportion of women rose to 50 percent under editors Charles Camic and Franklin Wilson (2000–2003). Despite these gains, women remain less likely to edit the set of ASA journals than they are to be among the elected chairs of sections (CSW 2004). Thus, although there have been major transformations in the status of women in the profession, gender remains an institutional obstacle, particularly at the highest levels.[5]

Recognition of women as scholars also lags. Women's scholarship in general (including but not limited to gender subjects) remains less likely to be singled out for special recognition, even when it proves over time to be an important contribution. Thus, although books by women authors were cited in retrospect among the pool of "most influential" of the past twenty-

---

5. Individual university studies (Rutgers, Duke, MIT) indicate that the glass ceiling effect can pose a problem for women professors who are among the luminaries in their field or subfield. Looking at the scholarly honors conferred by ASA committees, such as a Distinguished Scholarly Publication award or an editorship, suggests this glass ceiling may be true of the ASA as well.

five years ("Ten Most Influential Books" 1996) at or above the proportion that one might expect based on women's representation in the discipline (31 percent), the Distinguished Scholarly Publication Award given by ASA went much less often to women (10 percent of awards between 1970 and 2002; CSW 2004).

CONNECTING WOMEN RESEARCHERS AND GENDER SCHOLARSHIP

Issues pertaining to women and gender would never have been raised if women had not brought their concerns about women's subordination into the discipline, yet the connections between the presence of women and gender scholarship reflect a dynamic social process, not a one-to-one identification between them. Women graduate students often organized and pressed their home departments for courses on gender as well as for women on the faculty. Much of the new faculty hiring of women was intended to bring "someone" studying women into the department, all too often in a single token position. The context of feminist activism that opened doors in the 1980s blurred the lines between being a woman, studying women, and being a feminist sociologist. Feminist researchers who studied other subjects, including those women of color who worked to bring awareness of gender into research on race (see, for example, pioneering studies by Evelyn Nakano Glenn, Bonnie Dill, Doris Wilkenson, Esther Chow, Judith Rollins, and Cheryl Gilkes), sometimes had difficulty being recognized by their male colleagues or their feminist peers. The Sex and Gender section of ASA (which is oriented toward advancing research on women and gender issues) and SWS (which is directed toward feminist activism and advancing the status of women in the profession) still have heavily overlapping memberships and often are not perceived as representing distinct interests.

While the degree of overlap is exaggerated and can be misleading, the link itself is no accident. On the one hand, because active political mobilization made it possible for sociologists to claim a legitimate expertise in studying women's lives and status, feminists pressured sociology to recognize and incorporate this expertise within the discipline. On the other hand, the recognition of women and gender as fields of study created a niche for women scholars as well as an attractive opportunity for personally meaningful research. However, the equation of women with gender tends to define all research on gender issues as relevant only to or for women sociologists, and women sociologists as good only at studying women. Although a few American men (among them, Steve Buechler, Gary LaFree,

Bill Bielby, Michael Kimmel, Steve Kulis, James Baron, and Jerry Jacobs) ventured early on into the study of gender, most male sociologists saw the appropriate division of labor as one in which men studied ostensibly ungendered "general" issues while women should study the "particular" case of women. It remains all too true that, as Jessie Bernard noted thirty years ago, "a great deal of research focuses on men with no reference to women [but] . . . research on women in their own right, without reference to a male standard, is not viewed as worthy of male attention" (1973, 787).

Segregation within the discipline has been interpreted as methodological, with women being identified with qualitative and men with quantitative methods. Although this stereotype is an exaggeration (and inverts the early history of the discipline, when the men of the Chicago school were known for their ethnographies and the women around the Hull House group for their quantitative social budgets), there are real developments behind it. Mainstream sociology's ever sharper turn toward quantitative research in the 1980s, as massive expansion of computing capacity made large-sample studies ever easier and more revealing, ran counter to the feminist emphases on interdisciplinary legibility, sensitivity to including the actual voices of women, and reflexivity and awareness of power dynamics in the research process, all of which tended to privilege qualitative styles of work (Grant, Ward, and Rong 1987). For the most part, computer-intensive, grant-funded quantitative research was harder to do in smaller, teaching-oriented colleges, where women faculty remain overrepresented. The desire to theorize from a grounded basis in experience rather than to fit women into existing categories also pushed many feminist researchers away from the hypothetico-deductive approaches typified by quantitative studies. While many gender scholars questioned the exclusions and inappropriateness of existing models for understanding women's experience, Dorothy Smith was one of the strongest voices calling for "institutional ethnographies" that would expose the interests involved in defining women as problems to be managed, reveal the interconnections between ostensibly separate "private" and "public" matters, and allow the development of new theory that rested on women's own perspectives and on their "everyday/everynight" lives (Smith 1987).

Despite these real connections between gender and method, the stereotype equating women and qualitative research obscures other, more complex processes at work, including vigorous feminist calls for more use of quantitative methods (Jayaratne 1983). The study of occupational segregation and wage discrimination, the focus on women's exclusion from textbooks and media, and the challenge to the unequal division of labor in the home and women's marginalization in the academy demanded quantitative data and increasingly sophisticated statistical analysis to rebut the continued charge that women "chose" a separate and unequal status. Feminist sociologists such as Paula England, Jerry Jacobs, Barbara Reskin, Bill Bielby, Leslie McCall, and Patricia Roos were and remain crucial contributors to this essential, interdisciplinary project.[6] The greater prestige given today to quantitative methods (unlike the stature that qualitative work held for the early twentieth-century Chicago school) also tends to be interpreted as consistent with men's higher status (variously understood as cause or result). In fact, articles about gender in mainstream sociology journals, whether written by women or men, are more likely than other articles to use quantitative methods (Mackie 1985; Grant, Ward, and Rong 1987; Swygart-Hobaugh 2004).

The gendering of authorship is reinforced through citation practices: highly cited authors in books and journals tend to form "two distinct populations" centered around qualitative and quantitative research, respectively (Clemens et al. 1995; Cronin, Snyder, and Atkins 1997); women are less well represented as authors in the most quantitative, highest-status journals (Karides et al. 2001); women are more likely to cite women's work and gender-focused articles than men are (Ward, Gast, and Grant 1992); and relative to the population of articles and researchers in an area, men undercite women's work (Davenport and Snyder 1995; Delamont 1989; Ferber 1988). Sociology's pattern of undercitation of women by men is echoed in neighboring disciplines of economics (Ferber 1986), psychology (Fine 1999), and anthropology (Lutz 1990), despite their different methodological styles. The combined result of status effects by both gender and method on citation practices is that the actual diversity and theoretical contributions of the work of feminist scholars fail to be recognized within sociology, and the contributions that women scholars make, across methods and topics, are still underacknowledged by their male colleagues.[7]

6. Yet the opposite misperception, that sociologists bring data rather than theory to women's studies, is belied by the interdisciplinary significance of theorists such as Dorothy Smith, Judith Lorber, and Patricia Hill Collins and theory-generating qualitative researchers such as Arlie Hochschild, Evelyn Nakano Glenn, Barrie Thorne, Barbara Katz Rothman, Judith Stacey, Elizabeth Higginbotham, and Joan Acker.

7. The cascading consequences for women's status that derives from men's failure to acknowledge women's contributions has been dubbed the "Matilda effect" in honor of suffragist author Matilda Joslyn Gage, who both described and endured this denial of credit. The Matilda effect is a counterpoint to the Matthew effect, which was ascribed to Robert Merton but (as he himself later acknowledged) actually was described by Harriet Zuckerman and him together (Rossiter 1993).

Although men still dominate the ASA sections that are defined as most "abstract" (in 2004, men accounted for more than 60 percent of the members of the Theory, Methods, Economic Sociology, and Rational Choice sections), the greatly increased organizational presence of women in sociology responded to and reinforced wider changes in the definition of sociology's core concerns. Theory remains an area where women sociologists and gender perspectives are strongly marginalized, but their exclusion followed different lines in neighboring disciplines. In political science, for example, the field of theory is richly populated by women and feminist questions. Scholars such as Seyla Benhabib, Wendy Brown, Nancy Fraser, Carole Pateman, Hanna Pitkin, and Iris Marion Young are widely cited, and their analyses are part of the core of this area. Although there is nothing inherent to either gender or theory that would make these interests incompatible, the position of women in this area of sociology, as in quantitative methods, remains precarious and subject to stereotypes.

Nonetheless, the ability to study women and gender issues and to have this scholarship lead to a job, tenure, recognition, and tangible rewards in sociology increased substantially from the mid-1970s to the present. It is clear that the increased presence and organizational influence of women changed sociology's gatekeeping norms. Institutionalized practices from hiring to reviewing to publishing and promoting came under pressure and over time became more open to women. As Sandra Harding (1991) argues with regard to "strong objectivity" as a standard of science, the inclusion of researchers from a greater variety of social locations allows greater recognition of the biases and exclusions in theory. The invisible dominance of male experiences and perspectives in defining the "general" began to be challenged as women became a self-conscious group and made their presence known.

Already in 1973, Jessie Bernard optimistically suggested that "so far as the activist phase in the profession is concerned, it has been remarkably successful. . . . Now the question is, 'will the harder phase—that of reorienting the paradigms to take account of women—be equally successful?'" (Bernard 1973, 788). We turn now to consider the continuing struggle for the conceptual remaking of the field.

Challenging the Definition of Core Concerns

The exclusion of women from sociology is a double-sided process with a long history. On the one hand, what women social scientists before the 1960s did was not considered sociology. Although the label "sociology" was not clearly defined during this period, the discipline was eager to embrace men who did social analyses that it saw as valuable, regardless of what these men called themselves. However, the women who developed theory and methods for studying society—such as Harriet Martineau, Beatrice Webb, or Jane Addams—were denied recognition as part of the discipline (Deegan 1990; Magdalenić 2004). Later, Jessie Bernard, Alice Cook, and Matilda White Riley were excluded from tenure-track positions in mainstream departments as a result of explicit discrimination against them as women (Hughes 1973b). Such ongoing marginality made women's work harder and less likely to be recognized as sociologically significant, although it may have placed women in a good position to contribute significantly to professional schools and applied disciplines where they were more welcome.[8] Women of color continue to find that the interdisciplinary resonance of their work is perversely used to signal that they are less authentically or exclusively sociologists. Their marginality is manifest in that they are invidiously compared among themselves, remain isolated as single hires, and are recruited more often for positions newly created for them rather than for a position constructed around a department's needs (Glenn 1997; Misra, Kennelly, and Karides 1999).

On the other hand, theorizing women's social position was also not considered part of sociology's historical tradition and was distinctly unwelcome in contemporary departments. In the early twentieth century, when women's education and suffrage were active policy questions, male and female social theorists such as Gilman, Simmel, Weber, and Bebel energetically debated the status of women. The centrality of gender in these theorists' work was erased from memory when sociology's "canon" was constructed in midcentury (Connell 1997; Adams 1998; Gerhard 2001; Sprague 1997). The relationships among patriarchy, industrialization, democracy, and modern family structures either devolved into Marxist ideological certainties or disappeared from consideration. Connections between the status of women and the structure of society, a lively topic for debate in the 1910s

8. Researching the relation between sociology and such applied areas of study as public opinion, business management, and social work would be another paper, but it should be noted that the American Association of Public Opinion Research, which includes both applied and academic practitioners, had gender-balanced membership and women in leadership positions long before ASA did. A leading sociologist of organizations, Rosabeth Moss Kanter, was recruited by the Harvard Business School while failing to win any sociological prize for her work. Social work has long offered a home to those women scholars whose research interests include organizations, communities, and politics, while these subfields remained defined as male domains within sociology itself.

and 1920s, vanished from sociology's research agenda in the years after World War II. The integration of personal experience, political sensibility, and sociological imagination sometimes attributed to the sixties generation (Lemert 1988) did not come easily to feminist scholars in sociology or elsewhere in the academy, where their concerns were trivialized, obscured, or excluded by dominant definitions of who and what mattered.[9]

Indeed, examining the dissertation topics of women sociologists who were pioneers of the field of sex and gender makes clear how few were able to study women in the 1950s and 1960s: Helen Hacker's (1951) dissertation, "A Functional Approach to the Gainful Employment of Married Women," and Pauline Bart's (1967), "Depression in Middle-Aged Women," are atypical in explicitly focusing on women but otherwise characteristic of the discipline's functionalist paradigm in which women's employment and aging were social problems, and family and social psychology were the areas in which women could be seen at all. Mirra Komarovsky's (1941) dissertation, "The Unemployed Man and His Family," expresses in its title the way women were folded invisibly into the concept of family and men link the family to the wider world.[10] Other scholars who, like Komarovsky, later offered pioneering work on gender issues once feminism revived this concern wrote their dissertations on families and communities without naming women as being of particular interest (e.g., Helena Lopata's dissertation, in 1956, "The Functions of an Ethnic Community, 'Polonia'"; and Francesca Cancian's, in 1963, "Family Interaction in Zincantan").

As feminist consciousness-raising began to spread, dissertations that engaged directly with women's status began to reemerge in sociology. One of the earliest was Valerie Kincade Oppenheimer's "The Female Labor Force in the United States: Demographic and Economic Factors Governing Its Growth and Changing Composition" (1966). A turning point appears to have come around 1968–69, as concern with women begins to be evidenced

9. In fact, as Lemert argues, "many feminists in institutionally marginal programs, often in other than first-rank universities, subjected to well-known secret doubts about the 'objectivity' of their knowledge, have been forced to develop a theory and practice of knowledge consistent with the social experience of exclusion. Hence the critical difference of feminist theory" (1988, 801).

10. Melvin Kohn's classic study *Class and Conformity* (1969) well illustrates both theoretically and empirically the pervasiveness of this model. The book connects a father's blue- or white-collar job to the way a family's children were raised, but without considering whether a father actively participated in childrearing or whether a mother's own education or work experience might affect her behavior with and aspirations for her children. For the most part, mothers were simply invisible links in a chain of transmission from fathers to the next generation.

in what would become a new tide of dissertations; Cynthia Fuchs Epstein (1968) on women lawyers, Arlie Hochschild (1968) on "a community of grandmothers," and Elise Boulding (1969) on the effects of industrialization on women's participation in society were among them. What is notable is the shift in focus: these new studies address women's work as an issue of power and inequality rather than as a disruption of the functional order of sex roles.[11]

By 1975, forty-five women and five men listed in the ASA directory the topic "women and gender issues" as their focus of interest (Roby 1992). This group included those who earlier had written dissertations on nongender topics (such as Jessie Bernard and Alice Rossi) and later published path-breaking work in the area (such as Rossi's 1964 article in *Daedalus*, "Equality between the Sexes: An Immodest Proposal," and Bernard's classic 1971 study of men's and women's different perceptions of marriage). These "fore-mothers" as well as the "breakthrough generation"—the new cohort of sociologists inspired by feminism to break the taboo on studying women in their dissertations—together established "women and gender" as a field of legitimate sociological concern.

Still, studying women as such was deemed not very important to the overall sociological enterprise, since biology and psychology could better address the "underlying differences" among individuals, which were presumed to generate "sex roles." The dynamics of the overall social order were located elsewhere, in a supposedly "ungendered" political economy or modernization/development process. The debate (in textbooks and graduate schools) of the 1970s was often framed as one between functionalists' endorsement of the contemporary social order (as anchored in mainstream departments and in the ASA) and "critical" or "conflict" approaches to sociology (as anchored in SSSP and encompassing everything from Marx to Goffman).

The "critical sociology" of the period, however, was initially no more inclusive of women than its functionalist alternative. Leftist thinking often relied on the socialist orthodoxy that working-class women were best served by raising men's wages to a "family wage" so that wives could "stay home" and "not work" (see the debate between Wright [1978] and Ferree [1976, 1984]). Gender issues were addressed by explaining class; the status

11. Although many of these were studies of work (e.g., dissertations by Reskin [1973] and Bose [1973]), radical feminist questions of power and embodiment also shaped thinking about what counted as work and how it was done. For example, Pamela Roby's 1971 dissertation addressed the politics of prostitution.

of women was seen as a "residual category" that would be resolved with the alleviation of class domination. To seriously bring women into sociology meant recognizing women as workers with interests of their own, with problems that went beyond their class position, and seeing where and how they fit or didn't fit "the male model" (e.g., see Feldberg and Glenn [1979] on jobs and Acker [1973] on the concept of the head of household). Thus one of the most fruitful early feminist challenges to the sociological status quo involved trying to bring women into the various male-dominant approaches to class, stratification, mobility, and economic disadvantage.

Reworking the Paradigm of Work

Since neither the view of stratification as a hierarchy of rewards nor the view of class as relations of production took women's work into account, trying to fit women's experiences into prevailing models began to expose fundamental flaws in the models' conceptualization. Along with a set of "relations of production" in which women participated, there were "relations of reproduction" that were socially significant but sociologically invisible. Although initially generating a "dual systems theory" that kept patriarchy and capitalism in their separate spheres, the struggle to encompass women's lives in a coherent, macrosociological understanding of gender began here (Hartmann 1979; Sargent 1981; Sokoloff 1980).

Rosabeth Moss Kanter's *Men and Women of the Corporation* (1977) set an agenda for a new, more social structural analysis of work and workplaces. First, it defined tokenism and blocked mobility as practices that produced apparent gender differences via structural rather than sociobiological mechanisms. This opened a space for seeing gender as a social process in an organization rather than an individual trait and was enormously influential in launching studies of gender as a mesolevel organizational characteristic (e.g., sex ratio). Second, it retold the history of the corporation in a way that made the emergence of managers and secretaries an explicitly gendered process. This resonated with the macrolevel interests of social historians in understanding the emergence of the category "work" as peculiarly male and "housework" and "dependence" as female (Fraser and Gordon 1994).

Mainstream models in the 1970s did not frame stratification as including gender relations, though in an unmarked way they did so: by defining the object of stratification as the head of household, by basing social mobility studies on fathers and sons, and by defining a family's social class as a function of men's education and employment alone. The process of confronting these male-centered assumptions produced a wave of empirical research. Feminist sociologists tried to bring women into men's models by assessing how mothers' and fathers' attributes contributed to social mobility (Rosenfeld 1978) and how both women's and men's characteristics mattered to household social stratification (Goldthorpe 1983; Crompton 1996). Measures on which men's sociology had relied, such as occupational prestige (based on rating jobs with male incumbents) and labor force participation (based on instructions to Census interviewers that undercounted women's work), were exposed as biased (Bose 1985; Deacon 1989). The finding that women's and men's prestige scores were approximately equal when their wages and access to authority on the job were grossly unequal undermined the overall meaningfulness of prestige scores as characteristics of occupations (Roos 1981; England 1979).

In the 1950s and 1960s, differences in women's and men's incomes were still invisible to sociology. It was remarkable for a social scientist even to take note of the fact of persistent wage differences (Gross 1968), since economic theory held that discrimination against women would simply disappear as a market inefficiency. This idée fixe among economists (and some sociologists, as Jackson [1998] shows) has itself proved resistant to disappearing in the face of a vast literature attesting to the resiliency of the wage gap (Powell 1999). New debates emerged between those who attributed earnings differences to natural efficiencies in the specialization of women and men for different roles (Becker 1981) and those who saw discrimination institutionalized in labor market structures, routine hiring practices, and the different evaluations of women's and men's abilities (Reskin and Roos 1990; England 1992a). Practical policy questions of addressing occupational segregation and job evaluation highlighted the political construction of labor markets in gendered terms (Steinberg 1987; Acker 1989; England 1992a).

Stratification had to be fundamentally reconceptualized once gender was really brought into the picture. Recognition of the degree of occupational sex segregation in labor markets widened the conceptualization of mobility to include moves across gender lines (Jacobs 1989), directed more attention to hiring and other intraorganizational processes (Bielby and Bielby 1996; Rosenfeld 1992), and encouraged new research on the historical transformations of occupations and firms (Crompton 1984). Both within and between occupations, taking account of the presence of women changed sociology's understanding of paid work, one of its most central concepts. In addition, bringing women in conceptually to the study of work meant acknowledging the invisible and unpaid labor done outside of the formal, waged economy of modern industrial societies.

DISCOVERING HOUSEWORK AS WORK

Sociology's sharp division between work and family, public and private, men and women, erased housework from view. Like those other aspects of life left out of the standard account of what "really mattered" because they were associated with women—emotions, community life, culture, informal organizations, children—housework did not seem in the 1950s or 1960s to have any broad sociological significance. Indeed, housework was unable to be seen as work at all, not only because, being in the home, it was privatized and personalized but also because it was defined as a nonproductive, non-instrumental, expressive activity.

Feminist research took a different approach to the sociology of the family, one that highlighted the connections between politics and families, work and families, and schools and families. This approach brought the family out of its segregated and isolated ghetto into a dynamic relationship with other core institutions (see, e.g., Stack 1974; Smith 1987; Luker 1984). In this new model, housework played a critical role in establishing women's subordination, as it did in the feminist theories being developed within the consciousness-raising groups of the women's movement itself (see Mainardi's classic "The Politics of Housework" [1968]). Dorothy Smith especially challenged the public/private "sphere" model that placed family relations outside of the organizing work of society, while Ann Oakley, a British sociologist, opened a new empirical field for research on the household division of labor as an arena of politics. In addition to the rich studies of paid domestic labor done of and by women of color (e.g., Glenn 1986, 1992; Rollins 1985; Romero 1992), which exploded the idea that "the home" was not a workplace, and the studies by social historians on the changing nature of the hidden work women performed under the label "housework" (e.g., Luxton 1980; Strasser 1982; Cowan 1983), multiple studies addressed the division of labor between women and men and the resistance by men to performing this unpaid work (e.g., Coverman 1983; Pleck and Pleck 1980). The discovery that the time women spent doing housework had not declined since the 1920s (Vanek 1974) overturned the functionalist view that women were only going out to work because they had nothing left to do at home.

Over the next decade, as feminist researchers studying housework documented the range of attitudes toward the division of labor, the time budgets of families, and the actual share of tasks that husbands performed (compared to that of wives and unmarried men), the centrality of housework as work became clearer and the separation of "spheres" by gender became untenable (see Ferree 1990). New questions arose about how doing more or less of this work affected the pay gap between women and men (England 1992a) as well as how unpaid work hidden behind the label of housework was essential to the functioning of other institutions such as hospitals (Glazer 1993) and schools (Smith 2000). The "expressive" aspect of labor, once seen as merely part of women's "domestic role," became recognized as "emotion work" in paid jobs as well (Hochschild 1983) and as a crucial— and teachable—part of the modern service economy, whether in the United States (Leidner 1993) or China (Otis 2002).

Studies of the household division of labor, however, often remained embedded in conceptualizations based on "roles" in which the issue of women's employment was taken as a matter of overcoming "old-fashioned" attitudes and adopting more "modern" views consistent with the economy's demand for women workers. As it emerged that popular beliefs could more readily change to include women in "men's sphere" of paid employment than to challenge domestic arrangements (Mason, Czajka, and Arber 1976), the issue of men's interests and rational, political resistance to change became clearer (see also the issue of resistance at the workplace raised by Reskin [1988] and Cockburn [1991]). The discovery that even married women who were successful in "leaving the home" to pursue careers remained responsible for the household chores was christened "the second shift" (Hochschild 1989).

The conceptualization of paid work and housework as opposite, gender-typed "roles" thus collided with recognition of the reality of women's labor in both paid and unpaid forms. Feminist scholars' discovery of housework as work challenged sociology's conception of the household as unpolitical, women's labor force participation as progress and development, and traditional attitudes as the fundamental obstacle to women's emancipation. These findings reopened the question—ignored in the sociological canon since the early twentieth century—about the relationship between gender and modernity as a whole. Scholars debated whether the emergence of postmodern theories was a useful complement to feminist rethinking of the categories of modern life such as "work" or a way of devaluing subjectivity, citizenship, and formal equality just as these benefits of modern life seemed within women's grasp (Delamont 2003). But the practical need to understand gender relations as political struggle came to be widely accepted among feminist scholars. Contemporary mobilizations against gender equality, whether found in antimodern fundamentalisms or family values rhetoric, potentially make the connection between modernity and gender more salient, but gender theories remain surprisingly segregated and marginalized in the sociological agenda (see discussion, led by section chair Michèle Lamont, in the Theory section's newsletter [Gross 2004]).

Who or What Is the Problem?

Interdisciplinary women's studies and feminist theorizing outside the boundaries of the academy provided a crucial impetus for rethinking sociology. *Another Voice*, a 1975 feminist anthology of efforts to reimagine social science approaches to topics such as medicine, law, deviance, and sexuality, led the way in defining a new research agenda in each of the substantive fields it covered. This volume showed that the social sciences had typically defined women as being "social problems" both within and for institutions, and inverted the argument to show how institutions posed problems for women. Centered on inequality and power, *Another Voice* laid the groundwork for the incorporation of men into a sociological theory of gender.

From women's perspective, a key social problem was male violence in a variety of forms: rape, battering, incest, sexual harassment. Violence against women was discovered primarily by feminists working outside of sociological paradigms (especially helped by Susan Brownmiller's *Against Our Will* in 1975) but was taken up as a political issue in need of research by sociologists such as Pauline Bart, who questioned the common wisdom that women's resistance to male violence was futile or dangerous (Bart 1981). Lynda Lytle Holmstrom and Ann Wolbert Burgess (1978) explored the options for battered women's shelters or other ways of socially responding to protect women. Gary LaFree, one of the earliest men working in this area, raised questions about institutional recognition and responses to rape (LaFree 1980). Controversially, Straus, Gelles, and Steinmetz developed a "conflict tactics scale" that both obscured the gender dimensions of institutionalized violence in the family and directed attention toward measuring the prevalence of the problem in women's lives (Straus, Gelles, and Steinmetz 1980; see critique by Brush 1990).

Eventually, the ability to focus on national, institutional, and situational variation in men's violence (see Sanday 1990; Martin and Hummer 1989) and to relate it to variation in men's attitudes (Scully 1990) began to deconstruct the supposedly natural connection between men and violence. This opened up new questions about masculinities (Messerschmidt 1993) and the institutionalized forms in which "masculine" aggression is expressed, such as pornography (Dworkin 1981) and militarism (Enloe 1989). The commercial exploitation of women's bodies and the institutionalized violence of the traffic in women were aspects of the economy and polity that had not been even noticed in male-defined sociology.

Political strategies adopted by feminists, such as pay equity (also called comparable worth [Acker 1989; England 1992a]), affirmative action (Reskin 1998), and antirape organizing on campus (Martin and Hummer 1989) drew on sociological analyses. No sharp line was drawn between data, theory, and activism as feminist sociologists sought to transform not only their discipline but their society. These new kinds of studies demanded a better analysis of the social processes of gender subordination than conventional sociological studies of sex role attitudes could provide. As Carole Turbin (1998) shows, E. P. Thomson's *Making of the English Working Class* was the model on which some feminist scholars drew as they began to unpack Simone de Beauvoir's claim that that women are "made not born." Women began to be seen as a group whose meaning was constructed by changing macrosocial relations, not only as individual selves with identities and attitudes generated in microsocial socialization processes. Rather than biology and psychology alone, history and politics were now seen as vital for understanding gender.[12]

Breaking with the sex roles notion of women as a static and unitary biological category, feminist research in sociology began to see women as a social group with internal diversity as well as commonalities created by the processes of categorization and sociopolitical subordination. Dissertations by African American feminist sociologists such as Joyce Ladner (1968), Rose Brewer (1977), Cheryl Townsend Gilkes (1979), and Bonnie Thornton Dill (1979) made it obvious that not all the women were white, nor were all the blacks men (Hull, Scott, and Smith 1982). Their work also undermined the separate spheres model by showing the distinctive ways in which African American women connected family with politics (Brewer, on political socialization among black adolescents), education and work (Dill, on black mothers as domestic workers and childrearers), and civic life (Gilkes, on religion and black women community workers). Seeing differences among women as not merely historical but entwined in ongoing processes of racial/ethnic subordination, Judith Rollins (1983) focused attention on how relationships of domination between women of different races (white employers and black domestics) were distorted by merely thinking of them

12. This was in tune with the spirit of the times. Postsixties sociology was "returning to the primordial ground out of which sociology, the discipline, arose and in which it was still certifiably a social theory. A new political economy, strong ties between sociology and history, a sociological philosophy (or philosophical sociology)" was emerging (Lemert 1988, 798). This was nowhere more evident than in the study of the status of women.

as differences. These intersectional studies raised the question of how gender constituted relationships among women (and so also among men), not
merely between women and men. Insofar as contemporary research claims
to be concerned with the intersections among race, class, and gender but remains focused on difference rather than domination, it still fails to incorporate the challenge to sociological concepts of stratification posed by this
early and ongoing work by women of color.

When it brought both historical transformation and intragender power
relations to the fore, feminist research launched the more fundamental critique of the sex roles model that the next section explores. But even the
most simple feminist questioning of the "natural" invisibility and incon-
sequentiality of women had an effect on the journals. The extent to which
the major sociological journals cover topics about women steadily grew
(Karides et al. 2001). As figure 13.4 shows, in the 1950s the number of abstracts in *ASR*, *AJS*, or *Social Forces* that mentioned the word *women* is virtually zero. Helen Hacker's classic article "Women as a Minority Group"
(1951) stands out in this wasteland. Even in the 1960s, when some notice is
paid to women, it is still couched largely in conventional theoretical terms.
By the 1970s, there is intensified interest in attitudes toward women and
changes in women's roles, and by the 1980s, the debates over core theoretical terms—their applicability to women specifically and their general
usefulness if they cannot incorporate women—have become very visible.
Overall, on the basis of just this examination of abstracts, the rise in sociological attention to "women" as a topic is steady and considerable throughout the entire second half of the twentieth century.

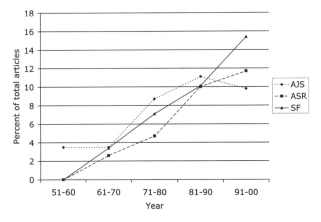

Figure 13.4 Percentage of articles in *AJS*, *ASR*, and *Social Forces* with
the word *women* in the abstract.

The bulk of feminist research in the 1970s and early 1980s—both within and outside of sociology—still drew for the most part on the classic concept of sex roles. Sociologists Helena Lopata and Barrie Thorne played a critical role in challenging this framework with their classic 1978 article in *Signs,* "On the Term *Sex Roles,*" in which they pointed out the functionalist basis of this term and the glaring inconsistency between the way that sociology generally conceptualized a role and the status and power dimensions that the term *sex role* was being used to describe. They noted that there were good reasons why sociologists did not usually speak of "race roles" but of "race relations."[13] As Lopata and Thorne (1978) pointed out, the key issue was to identify and critique the structural and power dimensions of a supraindividual process. The eventual shift to a structural theory of gender relations produced a wide-ranging reframing of when, where, and how gender was sociologically relevant.

From Sex Roles to Gender Relations

Beginning in the 1980s, and becoming established in the 1990s, a new paradigm for research on what could now be called gender relations emerged (see review in Hall 2000). It was partly initiated by programmatic articles such as Stacey and Thorne's "Missing Feminist Revolution" (1985), West and Zimmerman's "Doing Gender" (1987), Joan Scott's "Gender as a Useful Category for Historical Analysis" (1986), and Joan Acker's "Gendered Organizations" (1990). It also arose organically from the accumulating body of feminist work that struggled with and against the conventional terms of sociological research to reformulate questions about women as questions about society as a whole. The differences between structural gender models and sex roles models are truly profound enough to warrant the term *paradigm change.*[14]

13. In psychology, the concept of sex role was also under attack, but with the critical difference that the problematic aspect of the term was *sex* rather than *role*. Since feminist psychologists emphasized the distinction between *sex* as a bio-physiological fact and *gender* as a social-cultural acquisition, the notion of "sex role" was seen as theoretically inconsistent and "gender role" was deemed more logical.

14. There is also some debate as to whether this new paradigm should be called a gender relations model, a structural understanding of gender, or gender as a social institution. Within the paradigm, the term *gender* alone is typically used to convey this understanding, but all three of the mentioned labels are compatible with the overall theory and are used interchangeably in this essay. As we show later in the chapter, the concept of intersectionality (in which race, gender, and class are understood as mutually constitutive) is an aspect of this paradigm, but we do not consider this a label for the paradigm itself.

"Sex roles" taught that people belonged to one or the other dichotomous group and practiced a role with more or less fidelity to a traditional dualist stereotype across situations and over the life course. In contrast, the gender model did not define women and men as intrinsically opposite but saw change and contradiction in how traits, behaviors, feelings, and statuses were assigned to each group and looked for the interests at work when individuals resisted, accommodated, or enforced such rules for themselves and others. The new theory problematized in several revolutionary ways the division of people into two and only two oppositional sex role categories.

THE CONTOURS OF GENDER THEORY

First, "sex roles" were understood now more as "the organic ideology of modern society" (Connell 1987) than a theory capturing reality. The mythic representation of women and men as binary, homogeneous groups could be used to *justify* a division of labor that disadvantaged women across the board but did not *explain* social practices that worked with diverse and historically changing idealized types of femininity and masculinity to make social role assignments. If social organization in practice generated and used multiple masculinities and femininities that changed over time, how could a single dichotomous role acquired largely in childhood help to explain what these masculinities and femininities were and how they changed (Connell 1987; Scott 1986)? One needed instead to move to the system level and analyze culture itself. Functionalism obscured empirical understanding of both social conflict and historical change by positing as traditional a particular dualist past that, if it existed at all, was only brief and local (Stacey and Thorne 1985).

Second, sex roles were viewed as overindividualized and unsociological concepts (Lopata and Thorne 1978; Connell 1987). Recognition of the diversity and inconsistency in gendered behavior across situations and over the life course was combined with the acknowledged diversity in statuses of race, class, sexuality, and age to emphasize gender as a structural rather than individual characteristic (Kanter 1977; Lorber 1994; Epstein 1993). The macrolevel arrangement of rewards and costs by politics and social policy (cf. Skocpol 1992; O'Connor, Orloff, and Shaver 1999) and the meso-structural properties of organizations and groups (e.g., routines of work and evaluation; Acker 1990) were understood as part of the gender system. Even in social psychology, gender began to look microstructural: more like an aspect of social status and location that would contribute to shaping behavior from the outside via perceptions and expectations than a personal trait or individual role generating a certain pattern of action (Deaux 1976; Ridgeway and Correll 2000; Risman 1998). The internalized aspects of gender, now considered part of a complex and nondichotomous gender identity rather than a singular role, would shape or be shaped by extraindividual demands, and individuals had to negotiate the conflicts between them (Kennelly 2002).

Interaction particularly emerged as the site at which gender was "done" (West and Zimmerman 1987). Such doing was increasingly viewed in "intersectional" terms in which gender combined with race, class, sexualities, and age (Espiritu 1997; Calasanti 2001; see also Collins, chap. 17, this volume). Explanations of social facts based only on individual features of the actor, whether emergent from biological predisposition or social upbringing, were viewed as inherently inadequate (Lorber 1994; Risman 1998). The sociological focus on "doing" gender, and its methods for studying this interaction, complemented and contributed to the social philosophy of gender as "performative" (Butler 1990). Features of the settings in which gender is done are especially likely to be brought to the fore by sociologists. Studies by Ferguson (2000) on black boys doing gender in school and Salzinger (2003) on Mexican women and men performing gender in diverse maquiladoras demonstrate the social construction of supposed traits of aggression and docility respectively.

Third, the gender relations model included the experiences of women as embodied actors. Because sex role theory set up nature and nurture as competing explanations for behavior, it engaged in continual debates between biology and socialization as explanations of individual-level traits, typically positioning feminist social scientists as defending the idea that there were no meaningful differences between men and women. Such theories implicitly deny the social significance of experiences of pregnancy, birth, menstruation, and all other ways that women experience their female bodies as such. The gender relations model, by contrast, had little difficulty acknowledging that women and men have different bodies as well as different social locations, since the question was not where individual differences (of all sorts) come from but what society makes of them.

As embodied individuals, women and men are also—and variably—tall and short, fat and skinny, old and young, healthy and ill, and their bodies are shaped by their gendered (and race- and class-specific) experiences to develop calluses, high blood pressure, or well-defined muscles (Connell 1995). To deny biology any role in making gender would demand abstracting away from actual people in their material circumstances, expressed in social relations of reproduction and production, and insist on women as pseudo-men. But gender theory also argued that to grant biology a causal priority would be to de-historicize how biology works—in social relations that raise and lower life expectancies, hormone levels, age at menstruation, and even bone densities (Brumberg 1997; Bourdieu 2001a; Fausto-Sterling 2004). Biology was redefined as offering a different level of explanation (like chemistry or physics) of bodies rather than a competing explanation of social structural facts about how bodies are used.

Recognizing embodiment as socially significant but not determinative means that transsexuals and intersexuals provide interesting cases for understanding the work being done at the boundaries between the supposedly dichotomous categories of gender. Rather than a test case for nature-versus-nurture arguments, as in the sex role approach, for those working in the gender model the fact that some individuals successfully "pass" across these borders is an opportunity to see the interactions that routinely display and recognize gender (like using gender-segregated public restrooms) when they are being done most self-consciously. All types of gender ambiguity entail more awareness of the boundaries and more social risk in gender performance (Lucal 1999; West and Zimmerman 1987) and offer opportunities for protesting the generally perceived naturalness of the gender dichotomy (Rupp and Taylor 2003). The structures of gender that individuals navigate and the border work they do are the source of sociological interest for a gender relations model. For example, that healthy babies with ambiguous genitalia are surgically forced into one gender category or the other leads gender theorists to ask questions about the way medicine is practiced, not about whether the babies "really were" boys or girls (Fausto-Sterling 2000). In the gender paradigm, this latter question is viewed as uninteresting because the categories themselves first have to be socially constructed in order to answer it.

Finally, and most critically, the structural gender model puts issues of power in central position in the model, at all levels from macro to micro. While the sex role approach reduced domination to diversity and made passively existing "differences" between men and women its focus, the gender approach highlights not only face-to-face interaction but also structured relations of inequality that are part of the social order of countries no less than of corporations. All social institutions, regardless of their gender composition, are affected by gender ideology, engage in gendered practices, and experience gendered interaction. When the sex role model studied both women and men, it made "difference" its primary concern, and treated men and predominantly male institutions as the unmarked case that provided the norm against which women "differed." But for the gender relations model, both men and women are caught up in gendered social relations. The operation of gender within all-male institutions, be it football or fraternities, is no less interesting than the interactions of women and men across this gendered boundary. Gender as a source of hierarchy, exclusion, and violence is far more sociologically interesting than "difference" alone could be.

In sum, the paradigm change from sex roles to gender relations that characterized feminist research in sociology in the 1980s and 1990s altered the kinds of questions that can be asked and the kinds of data that are relevant for answering them in profound ways. The resultant interest in gender as ideology and culture made social and intellectual history more important, and promoted connections between current feminist theory and the early twentieth-century work of Charlotte Perkins Gilman, Marianne Weber, Thorstein Veblen, and others who considered modernization itself a gendered process. This encourages theorists to address patriarchy as a social relation of the early modern world (e.g., Pateman 1988; Adams 1998). The definition of gender as structure has moved the social psychology of gender away from studies of traits and attitudes, and toward interactions and perceptions in a framework of status and institutions. The relation of sociology to biology has changed from a competition for causal priority to examination of how science, law, and other social institutions make biology matter, and for what purposes. The dynamic model of gender as power relations also moved feminist research toward understanding domination and resistance, accommodation and change in gender structures, as they affect both women and men.

The Still-Missing Feminist Revolution in Sociology

In 1975 Arlene Kaplan Daniels wrote optimistically on the coming feminist revolution within sociology, suggesting that the discipline of sociology was ideally structured to incorporate feminist insights. Ten years later Stacey and Thorne reflected back on Daniels and asked why sociology had been so little transformed by feminist rethinking. Their answer was that the discipline as a whole was too functionalist to take change and conflict seriously, that it defined gender as only having to do with women and relegated women to the family arena alone, and that it allowed its commitment to the sex role paradigm to block out the relevance of gender relations for power and inequality, its own core concerns. Ten years after Stacey and Thorne, Joan Alway (1995) reflected again on this lack of transformation. She argued that the blame could no longer be laid on functionalism; the discipline as a whole had moved away from such theorizing. Instead, she proposed that feminists "displace the problematic of modernity with the problematic of gender" (220). However, the relation of gender and modernity was fundamental to many of the classic writers (e.g., Marx and Simmel) and only disappeared again in the mid-twentieth century (Delamont 2003). Ten years after Alway, sociology's failure to make feminist theory a core aspect of its work on modernization, globalization, and social change remains puzzling (Gross 2004).

Despite women's gains in access to sociology as a discipline, contemporary feminist scholarship is still struggling to be recognized and incorporated within the research and teaching of the rest of the discipline. There is still a pervasive failure by scholars who do not do gender research, whether or not they consider themselves to be politically feminist, to consider these models in their own work, even where they would be most relevant. The gatekeepers of the discipline have not marked such a failure as a deficiency.

In research articles, the widespread acceptance of the term *gender* rather than *sex* provides evidence of a superficial level of change. As figure 13.5 shows, in the three major journals, *Social Forces, ASR,* and *AJS,* there was a shift in the mid- to late 1980s away from use of the word *sex* and toward that of *gender* (at least in the articles' abstracts) as well as an overall increase from the year 1960 to 2000 in the number of articles dealing with sex/gender taken together. The separation of "biological" sex from the social category "gender" in this terminological fashion, however, does not get at the paradigm shift that reconceptualizes gender as a social relation or structure rather than a "role." The frontier science of gender has moved on, but the discipline as a whole has not moved with it.

The version of gender that migrates from the cutting edge of research

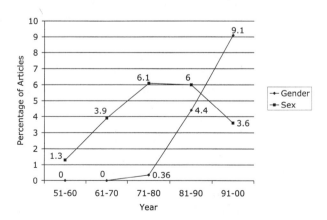

Figure 13.5 Percentage of articles in *AJS, ASR,* and *Social Forces* the words *sex* and *gender* in the abstract.

Table 13.3 Percentage of articles with race, class, and/or gender in the abstract, in four sociology journals, 1991–2000

	ASR	*AJS*	*Social Forces*	*G&S*
Gender	9.5	5.72	11	53.9
	(55/579)	(21/367)	(59/534)	(171/317)
Class	8.46	7.90	7.68	19.6
	(49/579)	(29/367)	(41/534)	(62/317)
Race	5.70	1.91	8.05	13.90
	(33/579)	(7/367)	(43/534)	(44/317)
Race and class	1.55	0	0.936	9.46
	(9/579)	(0/367)	(5/534)	(30/317)
Race and gender	1.21	0.27	1.69	10.7
	(7/579)	(1/367)	(9/534)	(34/317)
Class and gender	1.04	0.27	0.562	13.2
	(6/579)	(1/367)	(3/534)	(42/317)
Race, class, and gender	0.69	0	0.375	8.20
	(4/579)	(0/367)	(2/534)	(26/317)

and into textbooks also lags. The examination of introductory sociology textbooks from the 1980s (Ferree and Hall 1996) suggests that the explanations of stratification offered there place gender as a microlevel issue of socialization and attitudes, race as a mesolevel problem of intergroup relations, and only class as a macrolevel structure relevant for organizing a whole society. The continued separation of gender from race and class in the abstracts of articles published in mainstream journals (although notably not in *Gender and Society*) indicates that the segregation of concerns by level of analysis is still widespread. As table 13.3 shows, only 1.4 percent of the total articles in *ASR, AJS,* and *Social Forces* between the years 1991 and 2000 used at least two of the concepts of race, gender, and class in their abstracts. Closer analysis reveals that of the 21 articles (out of 1,480), only a handful use these terms in a way that went beyond simple variable analysis. The segregation of these three forms of stratification into three different conceptual levels, not only in teaching but in the way many sociologists define their research problems, makes them difficult to combine (but see McCall 2001; Cotter, Hermsen, and Vanneman 1999). Although, as figures

13.4 and 13.5 indicated, the quantity of work on gender in leading socio-logical journals has increased, the critical turn for the discipline, one in which a structurally oriented gender perspective would inform sociology as a whole, has yet to happen.

CONTESTED EXCLUSIONS IN THEORY AND METHODS

As one initial indication of how gender enters the mainstream, we looked at the citations in *ASR* and *Sociological Theory* for the years 1990 and 2003. Al-though the number of articles pertaining to gender rose, and these articles, of course, cite works by gender scholars, in 1990 the 61 articles not explic-itly related to gender cited barely any gender scholarship (we found a total of 31 citations to scholarship pertaining to gender). In 2003, in the 53 arti-cles not directly about gender, there were 134 citations of scholarship about gender. Although this clearly indicates an increase in the extent to which a study of gender is seen as having some general relevance, it also indicates how marginal these concerns remain. Feminist theory is positioned as an outsider critique of grand theory rather than incorporated as an aspect of contemporary sociological theorizing. As Delamont summarizes her own extensive review, "histories and overviews of the grand narrative of sociol-ogy ignored women and feminism 30 years ago, *and still do*" (2003, 98).

These exclusions do not go uncontested. For example, a 1994 list of twenty-one "neglected theorists," drawn up in a call for papers for a special issue of *Sociological Theory,* was composed entirely of men, leading feminist scholars to protest; *Sociological Theory* responded by publishing special arti-cles on women theorists. The failure to notice contemporary scholarship done by feminists about classic theorists, and thus redoubling their neglect in the canon, is also exemplified by Bermingham's (2003) commentary and translation of Marianne Weber's "Authority and Autonomy in Marriage" in *Sociological Theory.* In introducing the article, Bermingham discussed the "urgent need" to study Marianne Weber's work as that of both a feminist and an undiscovered sociological scholar. Feminist scholars Lengermann and Niebrugge-Brantley (2003) replied, arguing that Bermingham misled readers into thinking that no work has been done on Weber when there is a sizable feminist literature on Weber's works and noting Bermingham's failure to cite this work. One assumes that the gatekeepers for this journal were equally ignorant of contemporary feminist scholarship on Weber or they would have demanded that the author take account of it.

Ignorance of contemporary feminist scholarship is still viewed as ac-ceptable in the realm of empirical methodology as well. A good example is the publication in *ASR* of an article that revived the old nature/nurture debate (Udry 2000). The methodological approach that Udry took to his data assumed that the properties of femininity could be measured as universal traits fixed within individual women's personalities either by their socialization via their mothers or by their hormones. Feminist scholars were incensed that a major journal would overlook what a structural gender model would define as fundamental flaws in measurement, such as treating historically variable social norms like wearing lipstick or jewelry to be traitlike expressions of levels of femininity in an individual (see replies by Kennelly, Merz, and Lorber 2001; Risman 2001). Gender scholars were also offended by the apparent lack of any reviewers drawn from the gender area who could have pointed out the inadequacy of the outdated sex role literature that Udry cited for his characterizations of feminist research. Udry's assertion that dueling biological and sociological models were only now to be reconciled, to the advantage of biology, was not only notable for its explicitly antifeminist polemic but for the unsociological understanding of gender that a major sociological journal allowed to pass with impunity through the review process. The controversy as a whole underlined the way in which the paradigm of gender relations research can still be treated as unimportant and unnecessary for serious scholarship (and negative reviews by gender scholars disregarded; Firebaugh 2001, 620).

In the realms of both theory and methods, then, the feminist reframing of gender has not had enough impact to make major journals question the misleading assertions of scholars who do not know or use the tools of contemporary sociological work in this area. Those in gatekeeper roles remain sufficiently ignorant of the paradigm change that has occurred such that egregious exclusion and misrepresentation can pass by without their awareness or critique. But the prominence of the Bermingham and Udry debates also highlights the active work feminist scholars are doing in challenging these exclusions and the increased willingness of journal editors to respond to them as legitimate critics. The accountability for change continues to come from protest, particularly from feminist women scholars working on gender analysis.

Conclusions: Standing and Framing in Sociology

If *standing* is defined as the right to a legitimate voice in a discussion and *framing* as the nature of the perspective and ideas expressed (Ferree et al. 2002), it is clear that women have gained markedly in both dimensions since the 1960s. Women organized, struggled, and eventually won a place

in the ongoing scholarly discussion that constitutes the discipline of sociology. Beginning in the 1970s, women's standing rose dramatically in graduate schools, on university faculties, in organizational offices, and in gatekeeper roles in the major journals, and it seems still to be increasing. In
struggling to gain a voice in the discipline, women also used their social locations as a source of critical insight not only to reframe women as inherently interesting objects of study but also to challenge the dominant framing of sociology. The conceptual division between public and private that
marginalized women and rendered invisible the significant relationship
between families and other social institutions was undermined. The definition of work and stratification that only worked for men was expanded and
redrawn so that familiar terms such as *prestige, social mobility,* and *class* acquired different meanings. The division of labor in the home, the gender
segregation of occupations, the persistent inequality of women's and men's
wages, and the social impact of violence against women were discoveries
brought into sociology by feminist research that are now taken for granted.
Sociology's overall conception of modern society and the nature of what it
means to be a modern individual have changed, sometimes subtly and
sometimes dramatically, by noticing gender in social organization. Although it is self-evident now, as it was not in the 1960s, that women are citizens and workers, not merely wives and mothers, the issue of gender
conflict that is part and parcel of this transformation remains underrecog-
nized, even as women scholars and the knowledge they have created remain undercited and underrewarded.

These very real gains in standing and framing have to be balanced by a
sober consideration of the ways in which feminist research is still positioned as an outsider to the main business of sociology, which remains
defined as the research that men do. Women sociologists' identification
with feminism and with gender research has tended to conflate the two
concepts, leaving the sociological awareness of gender to those who are presumed to have a stake in changing it. Women who do not study gender are
therefore (falsely) assumed not to be feminist or interested in the status of
women, and those who study gender are assumed to be women. Yet to study
gender means studying a set of relations in which *all* actors participate and
which intersects all other social institutions at multiple levels. Resistance
and denial are part of these relations, as evidenced by how minimal men's
awareness of gender as an aspect of their own lives remains. Delamont's
analysis of the life histories written by "silverback" American men in sociology notes that "not one single man mentioned that his formative environment was a male one, or that he experienced it as all male, or that he

remembered it as all male. Not one single man mentioned that male undergraduates, or graduates, or young faculties in the 1990s would have a different experience because they have women teachers and might even experience their discipline as a co-educational or feminised one" (2003, 122). We think that the expansion of gender studies among more recent cohorts of male sociology students shows that this institutional change does make a difference. Feminist teaching about the pervasive institutional force of gender is bearing fruit, at least among those exposed to the new paradigm, but here the highest-status institutions continue to lag behind.

Our examination of the journals in recent years suggests that the failure of men sociologists to take account of feminist work in the relevant area remains a problem. *Gender and Society,* for example, has a strong impact in the social sciences as a whole (it ranks 16 in total citations), but its impact is low in sociology itself in that it ranks 43 out of 93 journals in the Institute for Scientific Information (ISI) database for sociology. Recent studies continue to document patterns of undercitation of women's research by men scholars (Swygart-Hobaugh 2004). This type of exclusion is being actively challenged today, as the two recent debates we cited in *ASR* and *Sociological Theory* show. The continued willingness of feminist scholars to raise the issue of exclusion, as Michèle Lamont did in constructing this as a topic for the Theory section's newsletter, also bodes well for the increase in women's standing to contribute to the reframing of gender and feminist research as core to the discipline.

We suggest that the underlying problem lies in the ignorance that many men trained in sociology before the 1980s still have about the new gender paradigm. Even for those with feminist sympathies, the conceptual revolution came after they were trained. They persist in believing that gender is not relevant in their particular area of study, reject feminist scholarship on the basis of their own outdated stereotypes about sex roles research, and fail to read contemporary research done by gender scholars in their area. They not only have allowed the discipline to move on in significant ways without them, but they are not sanctioned by the gatekeepers of the discipline for the resultant lacunae in their knowledge. Although there has been a significant growth in the presence of women in the discipline and of scholars, both men and women, working on gender from a structural perspective in its gatekeeping roles, this influence has not been effectively incorporated into studies that are not directly about gender.

We suggest that the transformatory potential of gender relations theory for a more thorough feminist revolution in sociology is limited by two profoundly political processes. First, the association of women with gender and men with the "rest" of sociology (especially its most abstract core) as an un-marked and invisibly gendered domain produces the *gender identification* of fields of study in sociology. The new field of gender, no less than the old ar-eas of family and social psychology, is identified as "women's," just as core areas, especially theory and methods, are identified as "men's." Gender ide-ology is even mobilized at times to suggest that certain methods also are gender identified, arguing falsely that quantitative methods are not "wom-en's" or feminist, which would surely come as a surprise to many of the feminist pioneers discussed earlier (Oakley 2000). As gender theory sug-gests, we should look at this gender identification as a social and political process that depends on organizational and institutional practices in grad-uate school, departments, funding agencies, and other actors, not merely on the internal preferences of individual sociologists, whether men or women. How differences in styles of research are constructed, taught, published, cited, and rewarded should be of interest as a sociological question about gender, since the differential status given to the areas identified with men and women are not "natural facts" about sociology but politically con-testable outcomes of organizational practices. Men's sociological education, no less than women's, can and should change as women's standing in the dis-cipline makes it more feasible to challenge these institutional rules. The re-framing of both theory and methods is crucial to this reconstruction.

The gender identification of what is framed as theory as being an espe-cially male domain continues to keep gender theory positioned as an out-sider critique rather than as a core aspect of the development of sociologi-cal thinking, a position not found in political science. Pierre Bourdieu presents this marginalization process as a social one, in which men's "at-tention and discussion focus on a few female theorists, capable of excelling in what one of their critics called 'the race for theory,' rather than on magnificent studies . . . which are infinitely richer and more fertile, even from a theoretical point of view, but are less in conformity with the—typi-cally masculine—idea of 'grand theory'" (2001a, 98). This focus on a few se-lect, highly sought-after "grand" women as representing feminist theory then leads to exclusions in which, for example, no one identified as a femi-nist theorist can be found who has not "already committed her work else-where" to represent feminist theory in a collection on the sixties generation (Lemert 1988). The most elite universities are excused for their underrep-resentation of women in tenured positions by the patterns of exclusion of scholarship by gender and method from top journals and by women's undercitation by men. Gender scholarship remains defined as a typically lower-status niche for women.

Thus the gender identification of subfields and methods seems in this case to have led to *gender polarization* of sociology as a discipline. Women and men sociologists are assumed to be different in regard to their interest in and appreciation of gender research, and men are excused from the intellectual responsibility to know when and how it is relevant to their work, or to identify more than a few "canonized" (and tokenized) feminist authors and theorists. With differential status still attached to maleness and femaleness as principles, it is not surprising that men can still publish work that recapitulates or draws invisibly on earlier feminist work in the field and by doing so convert a "women's" issue into one that is now "general." Thus, for example, decades of feminist research on women's community organizations and activism are now seen as merely precursors to the real (men's) discovery of civil society. Similarly, men who go into the lower-status "women's" field of studying gender may profit from the "glass escalator effect" (Williams 1995) or have their heterosexuality challenged (Kimmel 2001), both forms of gender dynamics that need more scrutiny in sociology as well as in other disciplines, such as biology, that have experienced substantial changes in gender composition in the past decades.

Given the gender identification and gender polarization that characterize sociology and that militate against an incorporation of the feminist revolution in the entire discipline, it is realistic to expect continued struggle in future years. What might the discipline look like if such struggles were to bear full, ripe fruit? Since fields of study would be free of gender identification and gender polarization, gender theory would be integrated into relevant sociological models at all levels. This is more than the "and gender" approach of today, where gender is added as a variable or placed as an afterthought or caveat to the analysis. It means recognizing how gender (like race and class) is part of the "big stuff" of social relations and noticing all the "daily 'hard work' conducted at micro- and macro-level by individuals and collectivities that goes into reproducing gender as a fundamental feature of social life, indeed a more ubiquitous feature than social class" (Chafetz 1997, 116). It implies integrating the insights of gender theory from the start of any sociological project.

Yet we are reflexive enough to know that the process we are up against is gender itself, that gender as an institution is itself the primary problem. In some ways the struggle is to "unmake" gender in sociology no less than in the rest of the social order. This project is not necessarily to make individual gender irrelevant in all regards but continually to work against the ways in which gender structures produce and reproduce power and inequality. That struggle will continue to include ensuring that women can acquire academic jobs and are as likely as men to get tenure once they have such jobs, to be in leadership and graduate training roles within the top departments, to receive rewards and recognition for their work, and to be gatekeepers and decision makers for the discipline as a whole. Although feminist sociologists have gained a large and influential room of their own within the discipline, transforming "the master's house" with the tools sociology provides remains their unfulfilled aspiration.

Acknowledgments

We offer our heartfelt thanks for the thought-proving input and useful comments provided by Chris Bose, Craig Calhoun, Paula England, Lowell Hargens, Jerry Jacobs, Michèle Lamont, Judith Lorber, Patricia Yancey Martin, Joya Misra, Cameron Macdonald, Patricia Roos, and Sylvia Walby.

[FOURTEEN] Feminist Sociology in the Twentieth-Century United States: Life Stories in Historical Context

Barbara Laslett

Feminist sociology in the United States, originally associated with the second-wave women's movement of the late 1960s and 1970s, led to a major innovation in sociological thought. Although not the first or only group to do so, feminist sociologists have raised questions about the social bases of sexual inequality, about patriarchy, in both its legal and cultural forms, and about power and sexuality, that have been a concern of few sociologists in the past. We have also raised new questions about the gendered division of labor in the family and in the society as a whole. We have examined changes in women's participation in the paid labor force, in social and political movements, and in public life more generally. We have also asked questions about masculinity and men's participation in domestic and public life. We have asked about race, class, and historical differences in gender relations in employment, politics, and culture. Recently, new attention has been paid to immigration and globalization. And we have acted on our belief in the importance of these questions and of gaining professional recognition and legitimacy for them. There have been institutional innovations as well as intellectual ones associated with the development of feminist sociology. We have built scholarly organizations, held conferences, founded journals, established new academic programs, and have advocated for positions in feminist scholarship. We have promoted the hiring of feminist scholars that have affected those who get these positions and the students who study with them. Women and gender studies programs have been founded, and changes have been made in the criteria for academic appointments and tenure decisions.[1] As a consequence, a context in which feminists and feminist scholarship have a substantial presence in academia has developed.

How can we understand these developments? In *Feminist Sociology*, Bar-

---

1. Although varying by institution and time period, I have in mind here the willingness to consider articles published in interdisciplinary and feminist academic journals such as *Signs* when writing faculty reviews and making tenure decisions and to consider partner, spousal, and family relations when making academic appointments. Needless to say, controversy has not been absent as these practices have emerged.

rie Thorne and I (Laslett and Thorne 1997), looking back over the past thirty-five years, have tried to provide some answers to that question. But feminist sociology, and feminist scholarship in the social sciences more generally, extends back in time much further than its most recent appearance. Using primarily three volumes of life stories—the commanding biography of Elsie Clews Parsons (Deacon 1997b), the sociologist turned anthropologist who received her PhD from Columbia University in 1899; the biography of Jessie Bernard (Bannister 1991), whose life and sociological work spanned most of the twentieth century; and a volume of primarily autobiographical essays collected from women involved in building contemporary feminist sociology (Laslett and Thorne 1997)—I explore this part of twentiety-century U.S. history. My analysis suggests how and why this intellectual innovation emerged as it did at two points in U.S. history, during the end of the nineteenth and beginning of the twentieth centuries, and why it was silent from then until the 1970s.

But why have I chosen a life story methodology for this purpose? Life stories, by which I mean accounts of all or some period of a person's life, such as biographies, autobiographies, and life history interviews, especially those of single individuals, are an unusual basis for sociological research in the United States.[2] And why am I looking at the development of feminist scholarship as opposed to any other intellectual innovation in twentieth-century sociology. The answer is partly autobiographical. At the University of Minnesota, between 1990 and 1995, Ruth-Ellen Joeres and I were editors of *Signs: A Journal of Women in Society and Culture*,[3] the interdisciplinary journal of feminist scholarship published by the University of Chicago Press. From this editorial seat, as a sociologist active in teaching, research, and writing, and as a feminist, I was able to observe processes by which knowledge is constructed, evaluated, and disseminated.[4] Being a partici-

2. Barrie's and my attention to life stories (as in Laslett and Thorne 1997) is by no means original. See, for instance, Dollard (1935) and Allport (1965), although their purposes were quite different than my own. See also Thomas and Znaniecki (1927). But as the discipline became more scientistic after World War I and gained further importance after World War II, the use of life stories in sociology did not develop. Greater attention was given to technical questions about sampling, representativeness and generalization, reliability and validity, and statistics and quantitative analysis, as criteria for defining scientific knowledge. Although other methodological practices have existed simultaneously (see DeVault, chap. 5, this volume), quantitative approaches have come to dominate the discipline. Indeed, they have become central to the idea of the discipline itself.

3. Ruth-Ellen Joeres is a highly regarded scholar of German literature, particularly on women's contributions to it, in the nineteenth and twentieth centuries.

4. *Signs* was not my first editorial assignment. I was also the editor of *Contemporary Sociology*, the book review journal of the American Sociological Association, during 1983-86.

pant observer of the development and growth of feminist scholarship, in sociology and in other academic disciplines over the past thirty to thirty-five years, made me both an insider and an outsider of these innovations.

For sociologists to use life stories for research is to examine individual lives in context. It is to examine how historically specific conditions, relationships, institutions, cultures, and psychologies can shape individual behavior. But individuals within the same contexts and sociological categories do not necessarily behave in the same ways. Individuals, in my view, need to be seen as social beings whose life experiences and social locations shape their feelings, actions, and beliefs. Indeed, that is the major assumption of contemporary sociological work in general. At the same time, however, individuals are not determined by the contexts in which they live their lives. Individuals interpret their experiences, construct meanings, and act on them in ways that are also shaped by individual emotions, fantasies, and experiences.[5]

In addition, life stories provide opportunities to examine motivations in more nuanced ways than is the current fashion in much contemporary social theory in the United States. They allow us to observe whole persons, and the actual and constructed connections they make between various aspects of their lives, within, for instance, personal, political and historical contexts, family, work, religious and cultural institutions, within social relationships, and under particular material conditions, and how these may (or may not) change over lifetimes. Life stories can suggest how individuals give meanings to events and, very important in my view, how emotions shape these meanings, relate to ideas, and are catalysts for action (and inaction). Finally, although this list is certainly not exhaustive, life stories can show whether, how, and what individuals learn from experience over the life course.[6]

Women's capacity for collective self-organization is also a concept central to the analysis being presented here. This capacity has existed in vari-

5. It also needs to be noted that the narrative character of life stories, and the sociohistorical and literary contexts in which they are produced, is relevant to their analysis. This point is discussed at length in Maynes and Pierce (2005). See also, among others, Somers and Gibson (1994) and Halbwachs (1992).

6. This "list" of relevant advantages does not attend to the methodological complexities of using life stories in sociological research. Among other things, these complexities include asking how age, memory, and emotions may affect the stories that are told; how particular sources—archival, textual, and interview—were generated; how historical and social conditions, personal meanings, and literary forms affect narratives about life events and experiences; and many other such issues. It is not clear to me, however, that the use of life stories, with these complexities, poses more daunting methodological barriers to disciplined research than the use of other source materials. In addition, feminist scholarship has developed the con-

ous forms; it can be seen in early twentieth-century Barcelona, the United States, and South Africa (Kaplan 1982, 1997); in women's support of striking coal miners in mid-twentieth-century Lancashire (Beckwith 1996); in women's unique participation in independence struggles in mid-twentieth-century Tanzania (Geiger 1997); and in many other instances. Women's collective self-organization also reflects the gendered division of labor in the family and in the society as a whole. Thus, another key concept in this analysis is social reproduction, which refers to the socially necessary caring labor required to maintain life over the life course and intergenerally. (For extended discussions of this concept, see Brenner and Laslett [1986, 1991] and Laslett and Brenner [1989].) Although varying by class, race, and historical context, social reproduction involves physical, social, and emotional work, work that has usually been assigned to women.

Two of the contexts I examine in this chapter fostered academic feminism and feminist scholarship in the United States; the other did not. The first case can be found in the work of late nineteenth- and early twentieth-century social science. This reflected in part the political self-organization of reform women (and men), who hoped to ameliorate social and political problems in the expanding cities. The settlement house movement, for instance, fostered educational opportunities and practical support for the poor in contrast to the policy of providing charity that had preceded it historically. In relation to the rise of feminist sociology, women's self-organization included *intellectual* as well as political activities. These activities brought women together as actors in the public realms of politics, policy, and practices. Elsie Clews Parsons began her intellectual and public life in the context of the settlement house and reform movements in New York City.

The second period that has been more favorable to the inclusion of feminist insights into American academic thought grew out of the social movements, the women's movement in particular, of the late 1960s and 1970s, and can be dated by the founding of two scholarly journals, *Feminist Studies* and *Signs: Journal of Women and Culture in Society,* in 1972 and 1975, respectively. Building on the experience of other social movements, such as the civil rights and antiwar movements that preceded it, the women's movement, as it developed an academic presence, again brought women together in institutions, such as colleges and universities, and affected most of the

---

cept of reflexivity, an important addition to our methodological tool bag, which refers to a self-analytic consideration of how our individual characteristics and experiences may influence both our empirical observations and interpretations.

women whose life stories are told in *Feminist Sociology*. Women's collective self-organization was once again facilitated institutionally and by a political ideology of liberation. Derived in part from contemporaneous domestic and international political movements, this ideology provided a powerful ground for the emotional and intellectual commitments that supported the development of a new academic subject called feminist sociology. Among the issues that came to define feminist scholarship, in sociology and in other disciplines, were critiques of existing definitions of objectivity, quantification as the primary basis for scientific knowledge, and personal distance of the researcher from his or her research subject(s). In sociology, at the time, these were primary criteria for constructing such knowledge.

Intellectual discourses and professional practices—those that advocated logical positivism, behaviorism, and quantification—shaped the beginning of Jessie Bernard's professional life. Scientism in twentieth-century American sociology was less favorable to feminism or feminists, as it was to all intellectual perspectives that were thought to value commitments, personal or political, over objectivity and detachment. Recent feminist historians and philosophers of science, as well as sociologists, have questioned these tenets of objectivism, recognizing the relationship of investigators' social interests and ideologies, as well as their psychological propensities, to the generation of new knowledge. This critique also examined mostly men's feelings about masculinity in modernism.[7]

Perhaps the most important intellectual innovation in feminist scholarship has been the development of a broad concept of gender relations, by which I mean social, sexual, emotional, and power relations between women and men, between women, and between men as gendered actors, that is, as persons for whom being a woman or a man is central to understanding who they are and what they are doing. The concept of "gender relations" is thus considerably broader than the concepts of "sex differences" and "sex roles" and can be used to examine politics, economics, and the production of knowledge as well as personal and family life. As I show, historical changes in gender relations outside and within the academy are important dimensions of the contexts that both fostered and inhibited the development of feminist scholarship. They allow us to see why women organized, with what goals in mind, and within what range of alternatives. Personal, political, emotional, as well as intellectual grounds for critique all contributed to the development of feminism and feminist sociology in late

7. See, for instance, Harding (1986), Harding and Hintikka (1983), Keller (1985), Longino (1990), and Stacey and Thorne (1985).

twentieth-century United States. They can be seen in the life stories at the center of my analysis, of Elsie Clews Parsons, of Jessie Bernard, and of the autobiographers in *Feminist Sociology*.

Elsie Clews Parsons

Elsie Clews Parsons was born in 1874 into a wealthy, socially prominent family that moved between the elite circles of New York and Newport, Rhode Island, where the roles for women, young and old, were constricted by narrow and limiting social conventions.[8] Tensions within her immediate family, between Elsie's mother and father, were a recurring aspect of the context in which she lived. Until she was about ten years old, Elsie was educated at home by governesses and thereafter at a small private school with high academic standards. During these years, Elsie became an avid reader, having learned that one escape from family tensions was through books.

In the social circle in which Elsie was brought up, there was opposition to young women going to college, especially if it involved them leaving home. Elsie, headstrong and rebellious, was spared having to battle for a college education by the founding of Barnard College in 1889, an institution of higher education affiliated with Columbia University in New York City. There she could pursue her studies while living at home and continuing, at least in form, to participate in social obligations as defined by her set in general and her mother in particular. Elsie entered Barnard in the fall of 1892 and in 1894 was introduced to sociology by Franklin Henry Giddings, who inspired many soon-to-be prominent social scientists of that generation.[9]

As a result of her studies in sociology, Elsie became involved in the world of social settlements as well as with several groups of New York intellectuals, where she met women who provided support for the unconventional path she was pursuing. In 1897, Elsie embarked on a doctoral program at Columbia University. Having an intellectual calling, however, did not relieve Elsie of the social obligations that fell on the shoulders of single women from her social set. Yet despite a suitor whom she loved and with whom she shared many of her values for social service, Elsie was wary of

8. Most of the life story of Elsie Clews Parsons that follows is taken from Deacon (1997b). For a less laudatory view of Parsons, see Banner (2003). See also Deacon (1997a), Deegan (1991), and Rosenberg (1982).

9. Elsie wrote a master's thesis on poor-relief in New York City, under Franklin Giddings's supervision. Although her master's degree was in sociology, her further graduate education, for a PhD, was in anthropology. For a description of the process that changed Parsons's intellectual interests and professional activities, see Deacon (1997b, esp. chap. 8).

marriage, partly as a consequence of observing the unhappiness of her parent's relationship and partly because of a conviction that marriage was incompatible with women's development. Nevertheless, in September 1900, Elsie Clews married Herbert Parsons, a lawyer from her family's social set who, between 1904 and 1910, was also a member of the U.S. Congress.

During the years when Elsie was considering marriage to Herbert, changes in gender relations, in attitudes toward marriage, in women's capabilities, and in women's sexuality were taking place. Elsie's wish to have children, as well as her belief in these changes, was among the reasons that she consented to marry Herbert. But she saw her marriage as an experiment, as an opportunity to create a new form of intimacy among women and men, one that widened women's capacities rather than narrowed them. Within six weeks of the wedding, Elsie became pregnant and was glad to have the opportunity to put her theories about marriage, parenthood, and a woman's pursuit of an active work life outside the family to the test.[10]

Among the activities in which Elsie was immersed professionally was writing a college textbook on family life based on a course she taught at Barnard from 1902 to 1905. From 1905 onward, Elsie focused on the conventions surrounding sex relations, particularly among white middle-class women and men, as the crucial arena in which the battle for equality had to be fought. Her text, *The Family,* published in 1906, demonstrated her knowledge of the comparative ethnographic and psychological literatures on family organization and sexuality that were becoming available. She eagerly embraced this new scholarship, seeing in the message of cultural relativity a scientific basis for her own rebellion against conventional ideas about the family. In *The Family* Elsie recommended, among other things, early trial marriage, divorce without public condemnation, and economic independence for women. Immediately upon its publication, *The Family* was greeted with substantial hostility and condemnation from many quarters (see Deacon 1997b, 68–69).

Although never holding a regular academic appointment, Elsie was active as a member of the group of young anthropologists surrounding Franz Boas who were creating a revolution in cultural anthropology. This revolution emphasized ethnography and fieldwork.[11] Boaz and his students were "busily reconstructing the discipline . . . [developing] a distinctive

10. In total, Elsie and Herbert had six children, two of whom died in infancy.

11. Elsie became a prodigious fieldworker for both intellectual and personal reasons. Not only was fieldwork a research activity but, as she had found with books earlier in her life, it was an escape from some of the tensions in her immediate family life. It also enabled her to travel with lovers.

approach to the studies of cultural diffusion that now replaced evolution as anthropology's central concern" (Deacon 1997b, 149). Elsie's conversion to anthropology was also based on positivism as a philosophy of science, not positivism as viewed by interwar, objectivist sociologists (see Bannister 1987) but rather a critical positivism as presented by Ernst Mach, an Austrian physicist and historian of science born in 1838. Mach believed that all scientific systems of thought had to be continually challenged and historicized; his ideas were very attractive "to innovative intellectuals, and to the women and men who were beginning to call themselves 'feminist'" (Deacon 1997a, 177–79). Learning about Mach's ideas through her colleagues in anthropology provided Elsie the intellectual and social support she needed to continue her critique of the rigid concepts and social life she had fought against in her writings on the family. She found, in these ideas and in their discussion, the reinforcement she needed to continue her challenge of orthodoxy and habit, despite the reception of *The Family*.

Having reconstructed herself as an anthropologist, Elsie participated fully in the intellectual and professional developments in cultural anthropology, through her own research and by providing financial support for both projects and persons.[12] She was a prodigious fieldworker and is particularly well known for her work as an ethnographer of the Southwest, the Bahamas, Haiti, Mexico, Ecuador, and African American communities of the Atlantic Coast. She was also active as a public intellectual and supported women in anthropology and women's causes more generally. She died unexpectedly in 1941, a few days before she was scheduled to deliver her presidential address to the American Anthropological Association.

What, then, led Elsie to become a feminist and a scholar? The foregoing analysis suggests several elements of her life story that are important. Becoming a scholar in the context in which she lived made it possible for her to construct a life for herself that was very different from her mother's and that was free of the constraints that the elite set in which she had grown up imposed on women. Having early been involved in the settlement house movement, she found encouragement there and among the avant-garde modernists whom she was meeting. The intellectual world that she found at Barnard College and Columbia University also provided supportive colleagues, as did the major changes taking place in cultural anthropology. Through them, she was able to learn about bodies of thought, such as

---

12. See, for instance, Banner (2003, 151), in relation to Ruth Benedict, even though Benedict and Parsons did not get along, either intellectually or personally. Deacon (1997b) provides many examples of Parsons's financial support for the new anthropology and its practitioners.

Mach's, that were supportive of what she was trying to do intellectually and how she was trying to live her life, as wife, mother, and anthropologist, although it was not without difficulties. The actual work of being an anthropologist, particularly fieldwork, provided her with opportunities to satisfy both intellectual interests and personal needs. Her wealth undoubtedly shielded her from much of the labor associated with social reproduction and made both motherhood and her excursions into the field possible. And social changes in gender relations made it easier for women and men to have collegial relations, whatever else these relations may also have been.

Elsie Clews Parsons called herself a feminist from very early on in her adulthood, but feminism, at least feminism of the settlement house variety, could not hold her commitment for long. It was the new anthropology, and finding colleagues who supported her interests and efforts, that captured her. She participated in and supported financially the collective enterprises taking place in her chosen discipline. The social organization of social reproduction and changing gender relations, then, were central to Elsie's life, as was her personal wealth. But the new anthropology also captured her attention and loyalty for personal reasons, for the ways it provided outlets and made possible some ways of dealing with her wishes, fantasies, and desires.

Jessie Bernard

Jessie Ravitch was born June 8, 1903, into a Jewish family in Minneapolis, Minnesota, the daughter of immigrant parents who had attained a comfortable middle-class lifestyle.[13] The family had membership in a conservative synagogue, and Jewishness was an important presence in Jessie's home, as was anti-Semitism in the city in which she grew up. Nevertheless, Jessie believed that she was an American first and only incidentally Jewish (Bannister 1991, 27).

Jessie entered the University of Minnesota in 1920, during the heyday of the post–World War I vitality, which brought with it changes in both personal and intellectual life. Fashion, bobbed hair, and bras were only a few manifestations of the new culture for white, middle-class women in the United States. Although originally planning to major in English, Jessie found that the department that won her heart was sociology. "The outcome," Bannister writes (1991, 36), "was an exhilarating blend of new ideas, new experiences, and apparent liberation from the cloistered world of [her family].

13. Most of the materials for this section come from Bannister (1991). See also Deegan (1991) and Bernard (1973).

For four years, without her parents' knowledge, she carried on a clandestine affair with her professor, Luther Lee Bernard, while embracing the teachings of modern sociology with the passion of the convert." When they first met in 1921, Luther was forty-seven, and Jessie Ravitch was seventeen.

Luther's background was nothing like that of Herbert Parsons, Elsie's husband. He had grown up in a poor family in Texas, and eventually received a BS degree from a Baptist college in southwest Missouri and a BA from the state university; his doctorate was from the University of Chicago in 1910. By 1924, Luther had a reputation as a leading proponent of sociological behaviorism. He had decidedly negative ideas about women and about Jews and was also a womanizer on a grand scale, as recorded in detail in papers currently housed in the Pennsylvania State University archives. A scandal that followed a romantic relationship with another young student in 1924 forced Luther to leave the University of Minnesota in 1925. Jessie and Luther were married that same year, a move that shattered Jessie's relationship with her family and with the community and associations she had known throughout her youth.

Jessie's willingness to put up with Luther's opinions and actions are hard to fathom; certainly it provides no inkling of the importance that feminism would have for her later in life (Bernard 1973). It may, of course, have contributed to that importance. Like Elsie Clews Parsons, Jessie had dreams and desires that were shaped in part by the newly relaxing constraints on gender and sexual relations that affected the lives of white middle-class as well as upper-class women in the early part of the twentieth century.

After a temporary appointment at Cornell University followed by a fellowship year (for Luther) in Argentina (1926), the Bernards moved to Tulane University (1927–28), to the University of North Carolina (1928–29), and finally to Washington University in St. Louis, where Luther remained from 1929 until his retirement in 1945. Jessie, however, did not remain in St. Louis throughout all these years. While acting as Luther's unpaid research assistant for most of the first ten years of their marriage, Jessie also pursued her own sociological education. In Chicago, where Luther taught summer sessions, Jessie studied with some of the luminaries in that sociology department. At Tulane she completed most of the course work for her doctorate, and in St. Louis she was writing and publishing in sociology. Jessie received her PhD from Washington University in 1935, her dissertation a statistical study of patterns of settlement within neighborhoods.

Jessie's professional debut was at the American Sociological Society meetings in 1924 in a session chaired by William F. Ogburn, soon to be one of the leading proponents of objectivist sociology in the discipline (Bannister 1987; Laslett 1990). In this way, and in many of the years that followed, Jessie participated in what she called the first of her four revolutions (Bernard 1973). The idea of empirical research, in contrast to "the high level papers the giants addressed to one another," caught on in the ASS/ASA (Bernard 1973). By 1932, with a presentation at that meeting and another a year later, Jessie found her career was on its way.

The tumultuous nature of her marriage, however, had not abated, and two of the issues that had shaped her early relationship with Luther remained constant sources of contention: Luther's views about women and his anti-Semitism. In April 1936, after discovering Luther in another affair, Jessie filed for divorce and, doctorate in hand, moved to Washington, D.C. There she worked at a series of jobs funded by the federal government, jobs that made it possible for her to pursue her passion for measurement and quantification and provided her with financial independence. She remained in Washington for the next four years, refusing a series of pleas from Luther that she return home. The price for calling off the divorce was Luther's agreement that they would have children. In 1940, Jessie obtained a position at Lindenwood College, outside of St. Louis; then their first child was born in 1941, and her first book, *American Family Behavior*, was published in 1942.[14] Although it was soon to be questioned, her faith in science and her devotion to statistics continued. But as with many social scientists, belief in science began to falter in the context of World War II and the rise of fascism in Europe, especially Nazism in Germany.[15] Central to Jessie in these debates was her increasing skepticism that science was inherently good and her rejection of the idea that science was or should be value free.

Jessie taught at Lindenwood for seven years, when both she and Luther received appointments at Pennsylvania State University—Jessie as an assistant professor and the newly retired Luther as a lecturer. Jessie's intellectual eclecticism took many forms in the years to follow: interest in conflict sociology, in game theory, and continuously, in family sociology. Perhaps her most long-lasting contribution to family sociology and feminist thinking was her development of ideas about two marriages, his and hers, (Bernard 1972), and the differential subjective realities of wives and husbands that could explain it—no mean acknowledgment from a once confirmed behaviorist. She continued to add other related topics, particularly women and

14. Their second child was born in 1945 and the third in 1950. Perhaps not surprising given the organization of social reproduction, both Jessie Bernard's and Elsie Clews Parsons's first books were on the family, although their perspectives were very different.

15. This was also the case for Elsie Clews Parsons and many of her colleagues in anthropology, although in Elsie's case it was also a reaction to racism in sociology (Deacon 1997b, 152–53).

sexism, to her long list of sociological interests, and the vitality of her thinking and writing continued well into her retirement years.

Luther died in 1951, and Jessie faced difficult years as a single parent. Great as the responsibilities of parenting three children were, one born just a few months before his father's death, it was not the problems of parenting alone that she confronted. For the first time in her life, Jessie became solely responsible for domestic chores such as food shopping, cooking, and seeing to the upkeep of their large home. The full complement of work associated with social reproduction was upon her. Although Jessie was by no means in the same category of affluence as Elsie Clews Parsons, finances were no longer as much of a worry to her as they had been earlier in her marriage. As Bannister puts it: "Bernard's single parenthood was thus partly a story of the things money makes possible: an endless succession of baby sitters, a live-in housekeeper, summer camps, and private schools. . . . Despite her resources and her toughmindedness, a chief hazard for Bernard herself was a guilt that was palpable not only in retrospect, but throughout her years as a single parent" (1991, 171, 172). Dealing with children's psychological problems, along with her own guilt, was part of the emotional work of social reproduction for Jessie Bernard.

During these same years, Jessie was tremendously prolific professionally, producing four books and several dozen articles (Bannister 1991). In the last three of these books, according to Bannister, it is possible to trace the development of Jessie's thought, leading to an increasingly open and explicit incorporation of feminist thinking into her work. After taking early retirement in 1964, Jessie moved back to Washington, where she researched and wrote *Academic Women,* published the same year. With this book, Jessie began the transition to her fourth revolution, the feminist revolution, in which she became an éminence grise through her writings and her personal support and friendships with women, especially younger women sociologists.

In the late 1960s, in the context of the women's movement, existing gender relations were coming under attack. Jessie attended her first feminist meeting in 1968, and thereafter her relations with women became more important to her. Women were a resource that she had not appreciated earlier in her life, when she had been oriented toward men. This was a social as well as an individual phenomenon. Johanna Brenner and I (1991) argue that marriage and gender relations changed between the Progressive Era at the end of the nineteenth and beginning of the twentieth century and the post–World War II period. White middle-class women's more female-centered social relations in the former and their more heterosexual orientations in the latter affected their capacity for collective self-organization, with consequences for both feminism as a social movement and the development of feminist thought. It was only when women's relations with other women became important again, from the late 1960s onward, that this change in gender relations could be seen.

Bannister concludes his study of Bernard's life and work by saying that "she may be better remembered as a mentor and role model than as feminist theorist" (1991, 221). This implies, in my view, an unfortunate assumption that mentorship and support are less significant contributions to the construction of knowledge than theory and perhaps an insufficient appreciation of the social processes by which such knowledge is generated (see Longino 1990). Jessie died in 1996 at the age of ninety-three. A memorial session for her was held at the 1997 meetings of the American Sociological Association. It attests to the intellectual and social impact of her sociology and her presence on younger sociologists, particularly those working on family and feminist subjects. It also was a testimony to the love and respect in which she was held as sociologist, role model, and friend.[16]

Later Twentieth-Century Feminist Sociology

If summarizing in a few pages the full and rich lives of Elsie Clews Parsons and Jessie Bernard was difficult, I found it even more so to quickly describe the twelve women and one man whose life stories appear in *Feminist Sociology:* Joan Acker, R. W. Connell, Desley Deacon, Marjorie DeVault, Bonnie Thornton Dill, Sarah Fenstermaker, Evelyn Nakano Glenn, Elizabeth Higginbotham, Susan Krieger, Judith Stacey, Barrie Thorne, Lynn Weber, and myself.[17] These authors write from different positions of race, class, religion, sexual orientation, and national origin and, with one exception, have spent most of their academic careers within the United States. Their careers span the years from the 1940s to the present.[18] Political commitments and

16. A similar session was held at the 1973 meetings of the ASA for Mirra Komarovsky, the second woman president of the ASA. The first was Dorothy Thomas, in 1952, but she was seen as a stand-in for her husband, W. I. Thomas, who was then under a cloud of professional disapproval.

17. Thorne's and my choice of autobiographers was by no means random: intellectual, political, and personal connections shaped who we invited to prepare these essays. Not all whom we invited to write for *Feminist Sociology* accepted our invitation to do so. For autobiographical essays by Arlene K. Daniels and Dorothy E. Smith, see Meadow Orlans and Wallace (1994). See also Goetting and Fenstermaker (1995).

18. R. W. Connell has spent part of his academic career in the United States, but he has pursued it primarily in Australia. Desley Deacon, a professor of American studies at the University of Texas, Austin, was born, raised, and received her university degrees in Australia.

activism during the 1940s and 1950s, and the growth of the civil rights, antiwar, and women's movements during the 1960s and 1970s, also enter into these life stories. Childhood fears and adventures, lovers, marriages, motherhood, divorces, experiences of racism, sexism, homophobia, and elitism, struggles to establish careers often in the face of considerable obstacles, professional successes, disappointments, recognitions, and slights are all part of these autobiographies, as are the ideas, emotions, and psychological responses that these experiences engendered. But we have all lived our lives as sociologists while there was a women's movement, although the timing of our engagement with it differed. In each instance, this movement made possible a consciousness, both intellectual and personal, that would otherwise have been more inchoate.

Barrie Thorne and I begin the introduction to *Feminist Sociology* with three quotations from the autobiographers that provide a flavor of the life stories the volume contains. Joan Acker, professor emerita at the University of Oregon, wrote: "Feminism helped me to begin to make some order in my theoretical thinking and to understand why sociology has been alienating and confusing to me" (Acker 1997, 35). We faced, however, more than intellectual problems. Evelyn Nakano Glenn, a professor of ethnic studies and women's studies but not sociology, at the University of California, Berkeley, put it this way: "But, I confess, there is anger. . . . My anger may be somewhat inexplicable to the colleagues who, despite the best intentions, have difficulty understanding at a gut level the injuries inflicted through large and small acts of arrogance by white men as they go about their business" (Glenn 1997, 95). And Susan Krieger, who has published award-winning, innovative work in feminist scholarship but has never had a regular academic job, writes: "Homophobia has a hidden nature because it is a fear. Acts that stimulate that fear are interrelated. They are also, I think, disabling. I have found the repeated job rejections I have experienced to be disabling, not only externally, but internally, in terms of my self-confidence and ability to do my work" (Krieger 1997, 204; see also Krieger 1996, esp. pt. 2).

The life stories in *Feminist Sociology* reflect on personal experience—families, childhoods, growing up, friendships, and intimate relations—as well as schooling, waged work, politics, and intellectual life; they illuminate two decades of convergence between a political movement and an academic discipline. We have all been part of that movement, and the careers we have fashioned have been strongly affected by it. For those of us—Joan Acker, Evelyn Nakano Glenn, and myself—whose graduate education took place at times and in institutions where feminist insights and organizations did not yet exist (the University of Oregon, Harvard University, and the

University of Chicago, respectively), feminism provided a place for personal and intellectual growth. Evi Glenn speaks of the importance to her of the Women and Work group of which she was a part, funded by a small grant from the American Sociological Association, where she was able to develop ideas about women's paid and unpaid labor. Lynn Weber, Elizabeth Higginbotham, and Barrie Thornton Dill tell of the intersection of their individual lives and the founding of the Center for Research on Women at the University of Memphis, which provided an important staging ground for raising class and race issues in feminist discourses in sociology. The center, through its workshops and conferences, created opportunities for women of color in academia to meet each other, exchange ideas, and learn about each other's work. Barrie Thorne describes the institutional conditions and culture of her graduate training at Brandeis University that also fostered the growth of feminist thought. The faculty at Brandeis, many of whom were refugees from Nazism in Europe, was not enthralled by the scientism that was hegemonic throughout most of the discipline. The newness of the program and the faculty's positive sense of collective marginality created the conditions in which women graduate students could organize themselves to explore feminist questions; a remarkable list of feminist scholars came out of this program. And although arriving there later than the period Barrie describes, both Judy Stacey and Elizabeth Higginbotham also attended Brandeis as graduate students.

Sarah Fenstermaker received her graduate training at Northwestern University, where, until the very end of her graduate student days, there was one woman only on the faculty: Janet Abu-Lughod, a prolific and award-winning scholar. But, as Sarah describes it, there was an open and self-designated creative identity among the faculty that supported innovation. Women graduate students relied on each other to explore questions about their own positions in personal and professional life and developed a remarkably long-lasting sense of sisterhood in the process. The visit of Dorothy Smith to the University of California, Santa Barbara, where Sarah was a young faculty member, created the conditions for developing a feminist lens through which to interpret her research on housework. Marj DeVault, the youngest of the autobiographers in *Feminist Sociology*, also did her graduate training at Northwestern, although somewhat later than Sarah. By the time Marj got there, Arlene Daniels, who became her dissertation advisor, was on the faculty, and Dorothy Smith was a visiting scholar for a term. Marj was therefore able to benefit from the increasing presence of feminist women faculty in the department and the feminist thinking they brought with them. But Marj also witnessed two young feminist scholars being denied tenure and in the process noticed that the women scholars, however powerful and productive as sociologists, were also distant from the graduate curriculum and departmental decision making.

Although certainly not alone in doing so, we participated in building feminist institutions within the discipline: Sociologists for Women in Society (SWS) and local study groups, such as Red Wednesday in Los Angeles, of which I was a member, and the mothers and daughters group at Brandeis in which Barrie participated. We also provided peer reviews of the emerging corpus of feminist writings for journals such as *Feminist Studies* and *Signs* and served as editors of some mainstream sociology journals, where it was possible to expand the attention given to feminist scholarship. We participated in building women's studies programs, and many of us were nourished by the scholars from other disciplines with whom we came into contact in the process. SWS created safe spaces at often unwelcoming professional meetings and organized sessions of special interest to feminist scholars. We became members of antidiscrimination committees in our professional associations, which were responding to feminist demands for greater gender equity. Through all of these activities, we faced reactions from most of our male colleagues that ranged from amusement and incomprehension to refusals of positions and promotions. We also made invaluable friendships (and some enmities, too, it must be said), exchanged syllabi for the new courses feminists were fashioning, read papers for each other, organized sessions on feminist subjects at regional and national meetings, and provided conversations and consultations on the numerous issues, personal and professional, that made up our lives. Women's collective self-organization was alive and well.

The intellectual outcomes of this work have been impressive. Joan Acker's theoretical and empirical work on women in organizations; Evi Glenn's research on Japanese families and her historical studies of the race, class, and gender dimensions of domestic labor; Barrie Thorne's prolific writing on families and her wonderful book on children in schools; Judy Stacey's theoretical work on women and families in socialist China and in the United States and now her engagement, as a public as well as an academic intellectual, with current political debates about family values; Sarah Fenstermaker's original research on housework; Marj DeVault's wonderful book, *Feeding the Family,* which documents the physical and emotional labor it entails; Susan Krieger's study of lesbian lives and her innovative and award-winning methods; Lynn Weber, Elizabeth Higginbotham, and Bonnie Thornton Dill's research and writings on race and class in the lives of women domestic workers and working-class women's lives more generally.

And, of course, there is Desley Deacon's biography of Elsie Clews Parsons as well as my own work on the history of the family and of sociology, on how gender relations and emotions have affected the discipline, and more recently, on the contributions of life stories to sociological research. One way or another, the gendered structure of social reproduction and changes in gender relations—particularly ideas about sisterhood, whether actual or rhetorical, and some men's increasing capacities to tolerate and even support our careers—affected the questions that we asked and the ways we pursued them.

This picture of solidarity, creativity, and innovation, however, is only part of the story. Friendships, marriage, and jobs have been lost as well as gained, and personal as well as professional lives have been transformed. There have been many defeats as well as successes, especially in the face of defensive reactions within the discipline and the often angry, and legitimate, responses of women of color, in this country and abroad, to the sense of exclusion from the developing feminist discourses in the United States and the inattention to those developing elsewhere. And there have been changes in feminist scholarship itself, with important contributions from feminist colleagues in other disciplines, especially in historical, literary, and cultural studies. Yet some of us have survived, and many of us have been brave in the face of sometimes malicious opponents. We have also prospered, and the alienation and confusion that Joan Acker expressed is less now than would have been the case without a women's movement and without the growth of feminism in the academy.

Discussion

Nested intersections of historical context, class and race relations, personal life, gender relations, and social reproduction are keys to answering questions about the rise and institutionalization of feminist sociology. I have not given attention to many details of historical periods or to race and class relations during them, but not because I consider such relations unimportant either empirically or theoretically. The importance of race relations (including the privileges of whiteness) and of class (including the privileges of wealth, economic autonomy, and security) can be seen clearly in the individual life stories. I have not, however, elaborated on them in more macrohistorical or institutional terms. To do so would have taken me too far beyond the focus of this paper on the growth of feminist sociology during the twentieth century in the United States and the importance of life stories for understanding that growth.

Elsie Clews Parsons's fortune and her white upper-class status affected the ways in which she was able to live and to think about her work. Jessie Bernard's less cosmopolitan background than that of Parsons, her less elite education, her lack of economic independence, and her Jewishness affected the choices she made earlier in her life and had consequences for her adulthood and her sociology. Elizabeth Higginbotham grew up in a black, working-class family in New York City and went to public schools for her primary and secondary education; most of her undergraduate work was done at City College of New York. Bonnie Thornton Dill grew up on the South Side of Chicago in the 1950s and learned about race and class as a child. Both of her parents were professionals, and she attended the University of Chicago Laboratory School from nursery school through twelfth grade. Lynn Weber's father was a steam fitter and her mother was a secretary. Both of her parents worked hard to provide their children with the possibility of a college education, but ultimately it was sports (tennis) that gave her a ticket to college and the middle class.[19]

To me, this variability in race, class, and educational experiences make clear their importance to any full-scale analysis of innovations in sociological life and ideas in the United States during the twentieth century. The analysis I have presented here, however, also suggests the power of social reproduction, gender relations, and sexuality as theoretical concepts for addressing the same question, as does women's capacity for collective political self-organization. These concepts have, however, been largely excluded from sociological understandings of intellectual and scientific innovations. In what follows, I focus on these concepts in relation to the development of feminist sociology in the twentieth-century United States.

One aspect of gender relations that is key to understanding feminism and the development of feminist sociology is women's capacity for political self-organization under different historical conditions. Both Elsie Clews Parsons and contemporary feminist sociologists were part of collectivities, women who met in the settlement house movement and intellectual groups that were exploring new ideas. Of the women discussed here, it was only Jessie Bernard who spent the early decades of her long career isolated in the world of mostly male sociologists. She belonged to no collectivity of feminists with whom to struggle for the intellectual insights she was ultimately able to articulate, especially in studies of marriage and family life. It was then, when feminists and feminist thinking began to have a presence in so-

19. See Laslett and Thorne (1997) for more about these lives and those of the other autobiographers in the volume.

ciology and in society as a whole, that she began to develop ideas about differences between "his" and "her" marriage (Bernard 1972). Attention to power relations and economic independence within an institution normatively considered primarily "companionate," or as specializing in "socio-emotional" and "expressive" functions, and perhaps attention to her own experiences of marriage and family life, may well have contributed to those insights. It was only when she became part of the feminist revolution in sociology that her ideas could be developed further. Having experienced support from a collectivity with a feminist consciousness, she was, through her mentorship, able to provide the same to a new generation of women in the discipline.

Closer to our own times, women scholars in the feminist movement have found relationships with each other and with women in their discipline to be significant personal, political, and intellectual resources. We have worked collectively to demand day care at professional meetings, exchanged views on personal as well as intellectual concerns, shared gossip and food as routine parts of informal seminars, and viewed our graduate school and early career experiences through a newly emerging feminist lens. We also challenged the existing norm, and theory, that separated professional and private lives for both men and women. The increasing visibility and presence of feminists in sociology, however, as Marj DeVault observed while a graduate student, did not immediately result in increasing professional power. This was to come later, when women sociologists, both feminists and nonfeminists, were asked to evaluate grant proposals, review manuscripts for professional journals, and review the work of feminist colleagues for tenure and promotion.

Jessie Bernard's career had a different trajectory. Her intellectual focus was shaped by the behaviorism that her husband and other, younger, men of the discipline strongly espoused. (See, for instance, Bannister [1991], on Jessie's relationship with George Lundberg, an anti-Semite and prominent behaviorist like Luther.) Her focus helped her career in some ways but also hindered it, and perhaps made more protracted her struggle to find new ways of thinking as a sociologist.

Shifting sexual conventions and desires are also important to the intellectual innovations discussed in this chapter. Elsie Clews Parsons pursued sexual freedoms in her own personal and professional life and wrote about their importance in her work on marriage and the family. Jessie Bernard's Jewishness and her childhood in a practicing, Jewish-identified family are important for understanding her actions, even if she did not publicly acknowledge the salience of her heritage (Bannister 1991). For Jessie, increasing sexual freedoms seem to have had a more immediate impact than did anti-Semitism.

Recognition and discussion of women's sexual desire were, as Elsie Clews Parsons believed more than a decade earlier, part of a modernism that both women sought. The family, class, and community context in which Jessie grew up certainly differed from Elsie's. Although as a young girl Elsie felt constrained by her class and social standing, as an adult her position and personal fortune made certain freedoms more available to her than they were to Jessie Ravitch. The social and psychological differences between the men they married had considerable impact on their lives as well. It was when Jessie entered university that her personal rebelliousness exploded. The possibility of such freedoms and the mixture of rationality, emancipation, and assimilation that Jessie became aware of in the Minneapolis Reform Jewish community suggest that desire was only one part of her attraction to Luther. It is likely that, for Jessie, this attraction reflected a wish for emancipation from her family as well as sexual desire.

It is more difficult to understand the place of sexuality and issues of femininity in contemporary feminist life stories because they are, as would be expected, diverse. They are also less likely to be disclosed for an audience of sociologists than are intellectual or political commitments. Yet lesbianism has been central to the contemporary women's movement, to feminist scholarship, and certainly to the individual life story of Susan Krieger (1997; also 1996, esp. pt. 2), as has the continuing debate over heterosexual women's desire and pleasure. If more muted in the other life stories of contemporary feminist sociologists, issues of sexuality are, nevertheless, present and perhaps hold the same meanings they held for Jessie Bernard: sexuality as pleasure, sexuality as emancipation, and sexuality as rebellion, but it is now not only within heterosexual relations. Contemporary feminists, with the support of other women in the academy, women with gendered consciousnesses, were able to rebel in intellectual as well as personal ways by questioning many of the disciplinary and professional ideas and practices that had been the basis of their sociological training.

Each of the feminists whose life stories I have discussed here was involved in an intellectual revolution. Elsie Clews Parsons participated in the revolution in cultural anthropology, which for her stimulated ideas about cultural relativism and culture contacts through extensive and innovative fieldwork. Jessie Bernard was also part of an intellectual revolution; she called it her second revolution (Bernard 1973)—one that fostered and institutionalized empiricism and quantification in sociology. These innovations opened up minds to new intellectual possibilities, but not in ways that were equally attractive to women and men. The scientism that developed in American sociology after World War I called for a personal distance from one's subjects of study and distrust of emotions and advocacy (Laslett 1990). This more "robust" type of sociology helped to define a newly emerging culture of masculinity among intellectual men who either were professionals or wished to become so. Reform had engaged many of the first generation of men as well as women sociologists, but its momentum began to dissipate after World War I. This newly emerging culture of masculinity was also likely to have affected women's involvement in the discipline. Social problems and social work, which had been part of sociology, and economics, especially home economics, which had been part of political economy, became professions for women. Toward the end of her career, Jessie called the scientism of the sociology she had practiced "masculine." I would agree, but not because empiricism or quantitative methods in science are intrinsically so; rather, these methods engendered a more "masculine" professional culture in sociology.

I would argue that just as greater sexual freedom was part of the modernizing project for twentieth-century American women, the culture of scientism in academic sociology was an attempt to modernize white, middle-class masculinity. The problems of masculinity for white men in academia had been building since the end of the nineteenth century; they found a temporary solution in scientism. Under changing economic conditions, the status of religion, the background of many of the earliest sociologists in the United States, and small proprietorship were declining in status. Scientism raised the social standing of the white, male professoriate. The association of sociology with science, especially the stereotypical idea of the "hard" sciences, was used to attract funding for academic research from outside the university, such as from the newly developing foundations. Second-wave feminists began to critique the claims made under the banner of science with their own epistemological claims about the importance of emotions and reflexivity, not "unfeeling knowledge" or personal distance. Recognition and appreciation of this work also made it possible for feminists to establish academic careers as well as provide a focus for their intellectual interests and individual preferences.

To summarize: innovations in intellectual life, at least in the case of feminist sociology, involved women's collective self-organization for action in the professional world of scholarship and a willingness to confront intellectually some of the social forces that inhibited such ideas. To do this, it has been necessary to challenge male dominant gender relations in the profession and within marriage, the family, and sexual life. Yet many feminist women did not give up their loyalty to aspects of older definitions of femininity and feminism. It is not by chance, or by natural inclination, that so many of the women whose lives have been discussed here are scholars of the family, nor that for Elsie Clews Parsons and Jessie Bernard, as well as for women of the more contemporary period, having children was of great importance. Raising these questions, however, and finding feminist answers are not due to personal feelings alone. The contexts also have fostered or repressed the questions and the answers; these include progressive social movements, international wars and liberation movements, an increasingly centralized economy, and most recently, globalization. As can be seen in the life story of Jessie Bernard, male dominance in the profession and a sociological culture particularly unfriendly to women go a long way toward dampening feminist inquiry, although not forever.

The intellectual project with which modern feminist scholarship has been centrally concerned—understanding sexuality and gender relations—has posed new questions. It is here, therefore, that we can see intellectual innovation in its clearest form, growing, as it did, not solely out of earlier sociological discourses but also out of political movements that spoke to the experiences of women in their daily lives (see, for instance, Smith 1987). And the institutionalization of feminist scholarship has been possible because of the feelings, commitments, and advocacy of feminists as intellectuals and as social actors. For others to understand this innovation, life stories in context make an invaluable contribution.

The picture I have presented here is complex, if still incomplete. I have been attentive, although to different extents, to multiple levels of analysis: personal, professional, political, and historical. My analysis, particularly of gender relations and social reproduction, would not have been possible, however, without the life stories on which I have reported. Life stories in context provide important evidence for sociologists. Considering some of the individual lives that have contributed to feminist sociology in the United States has led us well beyond them—to vibrant and diverse social and political movements, to macrohistorical transitions, and to emotionally significant identities and relationships both within and outside of the academy. Life stories have also contributed to recognition of the importance of context and culture, of material resources and power, of relations of race, class, gender, sexuality, and social reproduction to intellectual innovation. Analyzing individual lives in context can be a powerful tool for sociological analysis of intellectual innovations and social action.

The theoretical concepts I identified at the beginning of my analysis—women's capacities for self-organization, social reproduction as socially

organized labor, and the broadened definition of gender and sexual relations—are important to understand the emergence, decline, and reemergence of feminist scholarship in the United States during the twentieth
century. Each of the historical periods presented women with different
resources and limits to their sociological and personal understanding of
what they were doing intellectually and to their capacity to pursue their self
and collective interests together. The result has been important intellectual
innovations in sociological theory and practices.

Acknowledgments

An early version of this chapter was presented at Pennsylvania State University in 1998 to mark the transfer of the American Sociological Association archives and the Jessie Bernard papers to their library.

[FIFTEEN] Sociology of Race and W. E. B. DuBois: The Path Not Taken

Aldon D. Morris

American sociology has devoted serious attention to the study of race. Indeed, from the outset, sociology and the social sciences could not ignore race, given its explosive nature, uncertainty, and prominence in all aspects of American life. Thus, for over a hundred years extensive sociological scholarship has attempted to unravel the mysteries that have plagued the relationships between Black and white Americans. The study of race, no matter the intentions of the scholar, has never been neutral because it concerns power, inequality, oppression, and the moral fiber of the nation. It probes who Americans are and raises fundamental questions about social justice in the context of a society that prides itself as the world's preeminent democracy.

American sociologists have produced a vast literature that has probed race from a variety of theoretical, empirical, and methodological standpoints. This field can be assessed in terms of the value and quality of its scholarship. Its sociological conceptualizations, findings, and theories can be interrogated to determine their analytic power and whether they square with reality.

Failed Perspective

Sociologist James McKee has conducted a masterful interrogation of sociology's literature on race, beginning with work undertaken at the turn of the twentieth century through the 1970s. His book *Sociology and the Race Problem: The Failure of a Perspective* (1993) reaches a definitive conclusion: American sociology of race prior to the civil rights movement failed because its perspective generated a body of theories and empirical findings that did not match the racial realities actually occurring in the society. He asked why no American sociologist of race anticipated the American civil rights movement and the urban rebellions of the late 1960s. In search of an answer, McKee conducted a thorough investigation of seven decades of scholarship on race to discover its limitations and blind spots, as well as the reasons it failed to grasp the actual race relations occurring on the ground.

McKee argued that the sociological perspective on race failed because its theorizing and assumptions led to the manufacturing of a Black people who did not exist. American race relations could not be examined accurately when one of the major groups in the equation was so caricatured that its members imitated myth rather than reality. This perspective was not capable of anticipating the civil rights movement or understanding real racial dynamics. The source of that failure, according to McKee, was rooted in the racial assumptions of white sociologists, which they shared with the majority of white Americans. The guiding assumption—belief in Blacks' inferiority—was shared by white sociologists of race during the closing years of the nineteenth century and throughout three-quarters of the twentieth century. It was responsible for producing a sociology of race that was marred from the start.

Could it have been otherwise? In this chapter I argue that a superior sociology of race relations containing a great deal more analytic accuracy and predictive power could have been developed if DuBois's conceptualizations of race had guided the field. DuBois completely and unequivocally rejected the thesis of Blacks' inferiority. In all of his work he attacked the accepted sociological wisdom by hammering against the presumption that Blacks were subhuman, existing outside the human fold. By assuming that Black people were full members of the human family shaped by history, culture, and social structure, DuBois constructed a realistic sociological picture of Black people.

Because he saw Black people as a distinctive and creative group, he also rejected the widely held view of white sociologists that Blacks' only salvation was assimilation. As a result of rejecting both the inferiority and assimilation theses, he produced unique cultural and structural analyses of Black people, their institutions, movements, culture, leaders, shortcomings, and capabilities.

In fact, DuBois attributed agency to Black people and conducted painstaking pathbreaking research to illustrate it. In the process, DuBois also created a different view of white people and racial interactions than those painted by white sociologists. One cannot caricature Blacks without also doing the same for whites. The portrayals of whites were mythic too because their agency was greatly exaggerated and the nature of their racial interactions was obscured. Worse still, this flawed scholarship was incapable of accurately informing Americans about the racial scene or about the actions needed to change a system of racial oppression deeply rooted in the foundations of a society lurching slowly toward democracy.

The belief that sociology could and should be used for the initiation of change was another pivotal feature of DuBois's scholarship. This aspect set his work apart from that of the Chicago school, which preached scientific objectivity and detachment despite the fact that its work on race was based on the prescientific assumptions of the inferiority of Blacks and the saving graces of assimilation. By linking scholarship and activism, DuBois was at the center of historic efforts for social change; in the process he became a major public intellectual and the pioneer of public sociology.

At the center of my argument is the view that the dual theses of racial inferiority and assimilation produced a sociology of race that was incapable of enlightening Americans about the state of their race relations. If DuBoisian ideas had guided the field, there would have been no need for the discipline to lose a century before catching up to his insights. However, white sociologists ignored DuBois's scholarship on race and thus missed the opportunity to develop a framework that would have been superior in explaining actual race relations in America and the world and the direction in which they were headed. From the vantage point of the twenty-first century, we can see that it is DuBois's work that prefigured the best contemporary scholarship on race. Moreover, if DuBois's public sociology had been embraced, perhaps we would live in a less oppressive world today and sociology's relevance to that world would be undeniable. I argue here that DuBois's rejection of the theses of Blacks' inferiority and assimilation, coupled with his development of public sociology, enabled him to construct a novel approach to race and inequality that prefigured the seminal ideas of the current field.

DuBois's path was not taken, however. Indeed, white sociologists continued to view Black people as either biologically or culturally inferior or both. During the first two decades of the twentieth century, both the natural and social sciences made explicit claims backed by "scientific proof" that Black people were biologically inferior. The founders of American sociology, including luminaries such as Frank Giddings, E. A. Ross, Herbert Spencer, and William Graham Sumner, accepted the view that Blacks represented a lower species clearly inferior to whites. Even progressive sociologists who rejected the thesis of the biological inferiority of Blacks, as did W. I. Thomas and Robert Park, clung to notions that Blacks were endowed with mental qualities that differed from those of whites.

By the 1920s a cadre of anthropologists, aided by a few sociologists, had marshaled sufficient evidence that refuted the claims that races and racial differences were determined by biology. To remain creditable, social scientists were forced to abandon the biological thesis of racial inferiority. As a result, culture became the new analytic framework through which racial dynamics were to be grasped. This paradigm shift appeared to be good news for African Americans, for it contained the possibility that they could break free of the claims that God had made them inferior.

For Blacks, however, the good news was fleeting. American white sociologists, many of whom had not completely abandoned the biological inferiority thesis, were incapable of shedding their deep-seated assumption of Blacks' inferiority. They were to trap Blacks within another analytical box of inferiority by viewing them as culturally inferior. McKee (1993, 79) captured the change that emerged in the 1920s: "What was only dimly evident here, but would soon be more evident in the work of other sociologists less inclined to hold fast notions of innate inferiority, was the beginnings of a new tendency: to abandon the idea of inherent inferiority and replace it with the idea of cultural inferiority. Even as black people were about to be freed from the bondage of biological inferiority, they were soon to be confined by that of cultural inferiority." This assumption of cultural inferiority determined the questions asked, the concepts developed, and the body of knowledge assembled by generations of race relations sociologists. Thus, the analytic perspective laboriously constructed across three-quarters of a century rested on the bedrock assumption that African Americans were an inferior people.

This approach, by denying the agency of Blacks, produced a fundamental flaw in race scholarship. Thus African Americans, their culture, institutions, and leadership were viewed as primitive and in need of white guidance and civilization. The baseline premise maintained that the slave experience had destroyed the African cultural traditions of the bondsmen, rendering them a cultureless people. Their only choice was to adapt white culture, but this task was daunting because they lacked the capabilities to fully grasp the sophisticated ways of white folks.

Black institutions—family, schools, associations, and the church—were conceptualized as inferior and lacking stability because they were rooted in social disorganization and unbridled emotions. For example, the church was viewed as highly emotional and incapable of providing moral direction for a backward people. Edward Reuter, a major contributor to the race literature, summed up the position on Black institutions: "The institutions developed by the Negroes are more or less faithful copies of corresponding white institutions but, in the nature of the social process, they will be inferior to the originals ... separate institutions are inferior institutions" (Reuter 1927, 412). Thus Black institutions were substandard vehicles incapable of elevating the masses to a modern state of civilization.

Blacks were viewed as incapable of producing either competent or great leaders. The prominent leaders of Black Americans during the twentieth century were unquestionably Black pastors. To be sure, there were intellectual and business leaders, but Black pastors were dominant in sheer numbers and power, and they too were viewed as inferior. Again, Reuter expressed the consensus when he argued that the Black clergy were "men of mediocre ability and a limited education" and that they usually possessed low moral standards (Reuter 1927, 326, 327). Howard Odum, another major architect of this literature, concurred, arguing that Black pastors were untruthful, did not understand the needs of their people, and were highly ignorant (Odum 1910, 86–88). In short, like all other Black institutions, the Church was inferior, and it was out of step with the requirements of a modern religious institution. The leadership of an inferior clergy exacerbated these institutional defects.

From this perspective, the notion of white superiority was a taken-for-granted reality. It argued that Black people needed to master white culture and demonstrate that they could measure up to the standards of European civilization (McKee 1993, 118). Yet white superiority served as a default category because no systematic comparative analyses were conducted to demonstrate that white culture, institutions, and leadership were in fact superior. It was merely assumed that white immigrants were superior because they had arrived as ethnics with an intact foreign culture that prepared them to assimilate rapidly into the American melting pot.

Most assuredly, this mode of analysis assumed that Black people did not possess agency. Because agency in this literature was assigned to whites, the race problem was viewed as the white man's burden, and it was up to him to decide whether changes in the status quo were conceivable. Because white agency was theorized as front and center, the literature developed elaborate formulations and measurements of white attitudes, the intensity of white prejudice, and the degree of social distance with which whites were comfortable.

Much of the race relations literature accepted Park's race relations cycle. That argument maintained that as different groups came into contact, they passed through phases of competition, conflict, and accommodation, which ultimately ended in assimilation (Park 1935). Indeed, the melting pot itself was a consortium of assimilated groups who underwent a cultural and physical merging that made them indistinguishable. This cycle specified the ways social change occurred and the process by which variegated groups became full-fledged Americans.

For the American Negro, however, the cycle was especially problematic. In particular, how could a culturally inferior and backward people with unique physical characteristics assimilate into American society? McKee concluded that most white sociologists postulated that in some vague undetermined future Blacks would be able to assimilate. However, given the persistent and deep-seated prejudices of whites, coupled with the cultural inferiority of Blacks, the assimilation of Blacks had to proceed gradually, methodically, and free of conflict and violent struggle. The pace and extent of Blacks' assimilation could only be determined by the dominant white society.

In this view, Blacks had little say regarding the prospect of racial change. Indeed, they did not have the capacity to make change given their inferior culture, institutions, and leaders. Thus Myrdal, in his monumental *An American Dilemma* (1944), reached this conclusion even though he found that Blacks were deeply involved in organizational activity because they joined organizations at a significantly higher rate than whites did. Rather than considering this organizational involvement as strategic capacity, Myrdal argued that Blacks were merely imitating whites in a pathological manner and thus behaving as exaggerated Americans. Like the white sociologists before him, Myrdal robbed Blacks of agency by fully embracing, through his analysis, the cultural inferiority thesis: "In practically all the divergences, American Negro culture is not something independent of general American culture. It is a distorted development, or a pathological condition of the general American culture" (Myrdal 1944, 928). Myrdal went on to admonish Blacks that they needed to become assimilated into American culture and "to acquire the traits held in esteem by the dominant white Americans" (929).

Myrdal's statement on America's race problem was probing, and he developed richer accounts of Black culture than had previously existed in the race relations literature. Yet Myrdal's embrace of the cultural inferiority thesis reveals the power this frame exercised over the imagination of white analysts. Myrdal displayed his progressive leanings when he urged whites to take action to decrease the gap between their racial practice and the American creed. But because he assigned all agency to whites, Myrdal never envisioned Blacks as having the capacity to transform American race relations. David Levering Lewis captured the spell that the thesis of Blacks' inferiority cast on Myrdal's thinking: "The Negro was deprived of agency and rendered a problem that the white man was challenged to solved in *his* country for the sake of *his* shining values, lest the pathologies of oppressed, degraded, though still salvageable people of color pollute the wellspring of civic virtue" (Lewis 2000, 452).

After McKee meticulously deconstructed the race relations literature, laying bare the determinative racial assumptions on which it rested, he provided a convincing explanation of why no sociological scholar anticipated the civil rights and Black power movements. Secondarily, he argued that "most sociologists were ideologically uneasy with an image of collective action and group conflict as a way of altering the segregated patterns of race relations" (McKee 1993, 146). But the crux of the failure stemmed from the image these sociologists held of African Americans: "a people so culturally inferior would lack the capability to advance their own interests by rational action. Viewed as lacking a trained and experienced leadership, as still ignorant and mostly uneducated, and as incapable of participating in the political process, blacks were portrayed as a people unable on their own to effect changes in race relations and thus dependent on white leadership; race was still the 'white man's burden'" (McKee 1993, 8). Only the political explosions of the 1950s and 1960s were capable of chipping away at this racially denigrating image that served as the foundational assumption of white sociologists.

McKee's groundbreaking analysis of the race relations perspective clearly demonstrates that white sociologists accepted and reinforced the view that whites and their culture were superior. This perspective assigned agency for potential changes to whites, for their attitudes and actions were decisive. The ultimate goal for Blacks, they thought, was to assimilate into whiteness through a gradual nonconflictive process. Such assimilation would take decades and perhaps centuries to materialize. This perspective had no chance of anticipating the agency-driven Black rebellions of the 1950s and 1960s.

Enter W. E. B. DuBois

Although W. E. B. DuBois offered sociology another path through which to understand race, it was not taken. In 1899 DuBois published *The Philadelphia Negro,* which was the first major sociological study of race in America. This classic work predates Robert Park's Chicago school by a quarter century. Other works on race by DuBois, including his Atlanta studies published between 1897 and 1914, and the classic *Souls of Black Folk* (1903), preceded the Chicago school's race studies by decades. Yet Park and the Chicago school are credited with founding the field, and for the balance of the twentieth century this tradition provided the theoretical framework for research on race (Wright 2002a). In other words, DuBois produced major studies on race that preceded much of the work that did in fact found the "mainstream" American sociological approach to race, yet his work did not found that tradition (Wright 2002b, 336). Although DuBois wrote early and important sociological works on race, other early American sociologists did not follow his lead as they might have, and so he was not the pivotal founder of the tradition that he might have been, and the tradition was the worse for it. As a result, DuBois had to be—and still has to be—rediscovered and reappreciated.

Indeed, as late as the 1980s DuBois's work was rarely read in American graduate departments of sociology. Graduate students as well as seasoned scholars interested in alternative accounts of race found no easy path to DuBois. Black social scientists often knew of DuBois's work because of its centrality in Black intellectual thought (Dennis 1996). Yet even Black sociologists tended not to incorporate DuBois's work in a substantive manner. To be sure, a DuBoisian mode of analysis was not the currency that launched or sustained academic careers, no matter the race of the scholar. To this day, DuBois's work is rarely at the center of sociological discourse on race. Thus, McKee's incisive analysis of race relations scholarship shares a prominent feature of the failed perspective; it largely ignores the scholarship of DuBois. McKee references DuBois's work and hints that it probably differed from the accepted paradigm and that he received "little recognition from white sociologists" (1993, 31). McKee, sensing DuBois's importance, wrote that "hovering around the margins of the discipline in this first decade was W. E. B. DuBois, committed to empirical research as a source of knowledge to replace ignorance about race, and firmly believing that such knowledge was the basis for movement toward social equality" (31). Yet McKee leaves DuBois "hovering" by failing to interrogate his scholarship. This is a curious oversight because DuBois's scholarly output on race was prodigious given that he authored 20 books, 33 pamphlets, 19 edited volumes, 58 edited studies, and 2,000 articles for periodicals and newspapers (Johnson 2003). It is from this corpus of scholarship that I selectively draw to construct the DuBoisian perspective on race relations. Other scholars (Blackwell and Janowitz 1974; Broderick 1974; Rudwick 1974; Green and Driver 1978; Marable 1986; Anderson 1996) have produced important works on DuBois's life and scholarship, but my goal here is to construct his sociological framework and the assumptions on which it rests.

Social Science, Black Inferiority, Assimilation, and Race

For DuBois, the goal of science was the search for truth by using the best scientific methods available. In particular, he argued that sociological generalizations and interpretations needed to be based on carefully collected empirical data and measurement. Thus, "we must more and more school ourselves to the minute study of limited fields of human action, where observation and accurate measurement are possible and where real illuminating knowledge can be had" (DuBois 1904, 85). DuBois argued that vast generalizations and biological analogies, such as those associated with Herbert Spencer, were not useful in sociology because they imply knowledge but do not supply it, and they suggest but do not furnish lines of investigation (DuBois 2000, 40). DuBois maintained that the mission of sociology was to produce social scientific truths irrespective of their moral and political implications. Regarding his studies he declared: "We never consciously conceal an unpleasant truth that militates against our assumptions, nor do we allow ourselves to be swept by the prevailing dislike of the race into conclusions unwarranted by the facts or beyond the evidence. We are seeking the truth and seeking it despite the urging of friends and clamor of enemies; and in this seeking we demand and think we deserve the sympathy and aid of scientific men" (DuBois 1904, 88). At the dawn of the twentieth century, DuBois set out to discover the unbiased truths of Black people and of race relations through the science of sociology.

In a striking departure from the mainstream social science of his day, DuBois rejected the assumption of Blacks' inferiority and he also rejected the view that the ultimate goal of Blacks was to assimilate into America's melting pot. Neither his temperament nor his scholarly reasoning resonated with claims of Blacks' inferiority. Upon discerning a racial insult during grammar school, DuBois made a personal pledge to outperform whites, stating that his sky was bluest "when I could beat my mates at examination-time, or beat them at a foot-race, or even beat their stringy heads" (DuBois 1903, 2). At twenty-five he wondered whether it was the "silent call of the world spirit that makes me feel that I am royal and that beneath my scepter a world of Kings shall bow . . . I am either a genius or a fool" (quoted in Lewis 1993, 134).

In his scholarly work, DuBois frequently made his position on Blacks' inferiority abundantly clear. It must be remembered that at the turn of the twentieth century, claims for the inferiority of Blacks were rampant in the social sciences and in other writings. Thus, in Carroll's book *The Negro A Beast* (Carroll 1900), it was argued on the basis of science and the Bible that Black people were part of the animal world and that unlike whites they could never be human. In the midst of these insulting proclamations, DuBois always insisted that Black people were full members of the human family and refers to them repeatedly as one of the great races of that family. DuBois was well aware that some basic assumptions had to serve as a foundation on which to study Blacks and racial dynamics. He maintained that "some assumptions of this kind are necessary. They must be held tentatively ever subject to change and revision; and yet the scientific investigation must start with them." Nevertheless, he maintained that "the study of men however, is peculiar in being especially liable to the influence of prejudice which makes the inevitable scientific assumption with which all investigators must start difficult to agree upon" (DuBois 1904, 87). DuBois stated his position on the assumption of Blacks' inferiority clearly and unequivocally:

> Now we at Atlanta University in making some small beginning toward the scientific study of the American Negro have made certain tentative assumptions. We have assumed that the Negro is a Constituent member of the great human family, that he is capable of advancement and development, that mulattoes are not necessarily degenerates and that it is perfectly possible for the Negro people to become a great and civilized group. In making these assumptions we have kept before us the facts that every student knows, namely: That there is no adequate historical warrant for pronouncing the Negro race inferior to other races of the world in a sense of unalterable destiny. To be sure we do not dogmatically assert what place the Negro really occupies in the human scale. We merely assume that clear evidence to the contrary being absolutely wanting, it is fair to place a great race of men who have for centuries come in contact with the world's greatest civilizations as a part and parcel of that world of men. We assume further the Negro's capability of advancement, not so much because of the progress he has already made, as because of the repeated failure of those theories that have placed metes and bounds to his development. (1904, 87)

Thus DuBois rejected the inferiority thesis that served as a foundational principle of the white perspective. For him, social groups and their culture were historical phenomena that evolved through time and were shaped by the social environment. He argued that to understand the Negro and his culture one must pay special attention to the far mightier social environment (DuBois 1899/1973, 5).

Although DuBois profoundly understood how the inferiority thesis justified Black oppression, his strongest rebuke was leveled at social scientists:

> Finally, the American Negro deserves study for the great end of advancing the cause of science in general. No such opportunity to watch and measure the history and development of a great race of men ever presented itself to the scholars of a modern nation. If they miss this opportunity—if they do the work in a slip-shod, unsystematic manner—if they dally with the truth to humor the whims of the day, they do far more than hurt the good name of the American people; they hurt the cause of scientific truth the world over, they voluntarily decrease human knowledge. (DuBois 1898a, 10–11)

DuBois rejected assimilation as the ultimate solution to America's race problem. In his view, all great races had particular gifts and messages that could enrich human civilization. Early on, he advanced the claim that Black people, because of their unique historical experiences, possessed special gifts that would enhance humanity and that these gifts would be stunted or even destroyed if Blacks assimilated. Writing in 1897 DuBois staked out his position:

> Manifestly some of the great races of today—particularly the Negro race—have not as yet given to civilization the full spiritual message which they are capable of giving. . . . For this reason, the advance guard of the Negro people—the 8,000,000 people of Negro blood in the United States of America—must soon come to realize that if they are to take their place in the van of Pan-Negroism, then their destiny is *not* absorption by the white Americans. (DuBois 1986, 4)

He went on to argue that American culture could be revitalized by the cultural gifts of Black folk if there was a realization that Blacks

> are a nation stored with wonderful possibilities of culture, then their destiny is not a servile imitation of Anglo-Saxon culture, but a stalwart originality which shall unswervingly follow Negro ideals. (DuBois 1986, 4)

He then addressed his message to the Black race:

> As such, it is our duty to conserve our physical powers, our intellectual endowments, our spiritual ideals; as a race we must strive by race organization, by race solidarity, by race unity to the realization of that broader humanity which freely recognizes differences in men, but sternly deprecates inequality in their opportunities of development. . . . Have we in America a distinct mission as a race—a distinct sphere of action and an opportunity for race development, or is self-obliteration the highest end to which Negro blood dare aspire? (DuBois 1986, 5)

DuBois also rejected assimilation in personal terms, declaring that "there was not the slightest idea of the permanent subordination and inequality of my world. Nor again was there any idea of racial amalgamation. I resented the assumption that we desired it" (DuBois 1940, 101). Having laid out his position on assimilation in 1897, DuBois remarked a quarter century later that he was still in great agreement with himself regarding assimilation. Thus, DuBois firmly rejected the Black assimilation thesis that served as a key pillar of the white perspective. Indeed, contemporary scholars (Takaki 1979; Rumbaut 2005) have followed DuBois's lead by showing that the assimilation thesis was flawed because of its inability to describe the experiences of people of color and even of some whites like the Irish who could assimilate only if they bleached themselves into whiteness.

By the turn of the twentieth century, DuBois had begun to embrace and develop a social constructionist view of race. He was thoroughly versed in the work of anthropologists like Frank Boas, who argued that races were cultural creations rather than biological categories. In 1897 DuBois defined race as a "vast family of human beings, generally of common blood and language, always of common history, traditions and impulses, who are both voluntarily and involuntarily striving together for the accomplishment of certain more or less vividly concerned ideals of life" (DuBois 1986, 2). Although he failed to completely sever the biology/race nexus, DuBois was clear about what he considered to be the most important determinants of race. He argued that while race identity and common blood mattered, what was more important was "a common history, common laws and religion, similar habits of thought and a conscious striving together for certain ideals of life" (1986, 2). By 1911 DuBois agreed with Boad and Seal that races were not unchangeable accomplished facts but growing developing entities such that the old idea of the absolute stability of racial types must be given up (Zuckerman 2004, 27). For DuBois, a dynamic social process produced races, and these races were always undergoing social development, and at bottom racial content reflected a social heritage. Thus as early as the 1920s, DuBois argued that whiteness was a social construction used as the new religion to exploit nonwhite peoples (Zuckerman 2004, 32–37).

Again DuBois rejects a key element of the white perspective. While white sociologists conceptualized races as pure, unchangeable categories, DuBois argued that there were no hard and fast racial types among men. Rather for him "race is a dynamic and not a static conception, and the typical races are continually changing and developing, amalgamating and differentiating" (Zuckerman 2004, 32). The DuBoisian scholar Phil Zuckerman was correct to point out that DuBois was the first sociologist to argue explicitly that race is ultimately a social construction.

DuBois's sociology of race, therefore, broke radically from the white perspective. His conceptual framework was driven in a novel direction because of its insistence from the beginning that sociological interpretations should rest on empirical data rather than grand theorizing; it rejected the thesis of Blacks' inferiority and its associated claims of Blacks' assimilation as foundational principles; and it conceptualized races as social constructions rather than immutable categories.

THE WORK

A DuBoisian perspective on race can be constructed from the vast scholarship DuBois produced stretching across seven decades. Although elements within the perspective change through time, they are always nestled within a definite conceptual framework. That framework contained a causal analysis of racial oppression and a detailed account and analysis of a distinctive Black agency. It also specified the social location of the agency required to change the rigid system of racial oppression that prevailed prior to the modern civil rights movement. I construct this DuBoisian perspective, paying particular attention to how its analytical complexity increased through time.

In DuBois's earliest work, white discrimination and prejudice were conceptualized as the fundamental causes of racial inequality. These factors were argued to be the root causes of two and a half centuries of slavery and decades of Jim Crow rule. In 1898 DuBois wrote that aside from the relative importance of the many problems experienced by Blacks, "we must realize definitely that not only is he affected by all the varying forces that act on any nation at his stage of advancement, but that in addition to these there is reacting upon him the mighty power of a peculiar and unusual social environment which affects to some extent every other social force" (Green and Driver 1978, 75). At the center of this environment rested the powerful feeling of white prejudice. Thus for DuBois, "this feeling, widespread and deepseated, is in America, the vastest of the Negro problem" (DuBois 1899/1973, 387). White prejudice was the motivation that led whites to exploit Blacks economically, disenfranchise them politically, and oppress them socially. So powerful was this prejudice that it even caused whites to act counter to their own economic interests if those actions prevented them from having close associations with the Negro (DuBois 1899/1973, 146).

Prejudice and discrimination created the hostile and peculiar social environment that caused racial inequality. Although such causal analyses are not novel today, this was far from the case at the turn of the twentieth century, when sociologists routinely blamed racial inequality on cultural inferiority and the inability of Blacks to measure up to white standards. In contrast to DuBois, white sociologists reversed the causal chain so that Blacks' inferiority caused white prejudice and discrimination because the dominant majority feared that racial assimilation and equality would drag white America into mediocrity and decay.

DuBois's scholarship did not evade the illiteracy, high crime and death rates, poverty, and moral shortcomings of Blacks highlighted in the causal schemes of white sociologists. DuBois fully acknowledged these challenges and preached to Blacks to overcome them despite their causes. He even engaged in moralizing sermons about how Blacks needed to clean themselves up and abandon bad habits. But when engaging in causal analysis, DuBois argued that these "defects" were triggered by the social environment, and he used comparative analyses of white Europeans to demonstrate that they too were victims of such "defects" when similar social conditions existed (DuBois 1899). DuBois insisted that once historical and evolutionary conditions were factored into the analysis, the cultural, economic, and political progress of Blacks was unparalleled. Hence the role of the social environment was central in DuBois's analysis of racial inequality, and this set him apart from his white contemporaries, who clung to Blacks' inferiority as the explanatory factor.

In DuBois's framework, severe racial oppression did not destroy the ability of the oppressed to develop a creative community, agency-laden social institutions, and a complex inner life. DuBois was an empirical sociologist who eschewed theories of human behavior manufactured in the cloistered confines of the ivory tower. DuBois actually observed and conducted research on Black communities in both the urban North and rural South. He was intimately familiar with Black slums, the tavern, lynchings, the family, the church, and their work environment. It was these settings that afforded DuBois the opportunities to collect data and formulate causal explanations. In short, DuBois knew the Black community and the souls of Black folks firsthand. His writings escort the reader inside the world of Black people, revealing their cultural formations, their organizational and institutional dynamics, and their tears, triumphs, and inner conflicts. DuBois opened the door on the real Black world, but white sociologists could not really see it because their sociological imagination was trapped in racial caricatures.

Analyses of the social differentiation and complexity of the Black community were a hallmark of the DuBoisian approach. He critiqued the dominant tendency of white sociologists to categorize Black people as a homogeneous mass. He pointed out that the inferiority thesis rested on this flimsy lumping, wherein the entire community was judged by the behavior and standards of its lowest classes. He pleaded for a sociology that would capture all facets of the Black community.

Throughout DuBois's work he analyzed how the national Black community was stratified into distinct social classes with a small upper class, a vast working class, and an ultrapoor submerged class (DuBois 1899/1973, 309–21). These classes afforded their members different life chances and experiences, but all classes were severely limited by the hostile white social environment. DuBois also analyzed regional differences in the Black community, revealing that Blacks had greater economic and political freedoms in large northern cities but that the effects of racism and discrimination were prevalent throughout the land. DuBois developed finely tuned gender analyses of the Black community, demonstrating how gender mattered in this context. He examined the limited variety of occupations available to the sexes, and, clearly anticipating Wilson's (1987) analysis of female-headed households, he established the presence of an unbalanced women-to-men sex ratio that negatively impacted the marriage pool for women (DuBois 1899/1973, 97–146). DuBois probed the gendered nature of work available to Blacks and the different social consequences that flowed from occupationally based gender segregation. He revealed the dangerous working conditions faced by the vast majority of women engaged in domestic work in white homes. While adult women were vulnerable to sexual abuse on the job, the same held true for their young daughters left unprotected and unsupervised at home. DuBois also conducted detailed studies of educational differences among the various strata of the Black community and the ways that life chances varied according to educational opportunities. Through these analyses of the concrete types of differentiation within the Black community, DuBois shed light on the complexities of Black folk that completely escaped the purview of the white perspective on race.

DuBois developed groundbreaking analyses of Black social institutions and community organizations. He conducted studies of the Black family, the church, business organizations, secret societies, and voluntary associations (see the Atlanta University Studies 1898–1914). Unlike Myrdal and the other white sociologists who viewed such institutions and organizations as crude and inferior, DuBois analyzed their social functions and the vital roles they played in serving the needs of an oppressed community. For example, he provided accounts of the secret and beneficial organizations located in communities throughout the Black world. In his study of a rural farming community, DuBois wrote, "next to the churches in importance come the secret and beneficial organizations, which are of considerable influence. Their real function is to provide a fund for relief in cases of sickness and for funeral expenses" (DuBois 1898b, 35). Culturally speaking, these organizations served as mechanisms of solidarity because their business functions were made attractive by a "ritual, ceremonies, officers, often a regalia, and various social features" (36). Unlike the white perspective, these detailed and nuanced analyses of the organized life of African Americans painted realistic portraits of a complex Black community.

DuBois's classic analysis of the Black church has stood the test of time, and no serious study of the Black community can afford to ignore the monumental role of the church (Frazier 1964; Lincoln and Mamiya 1990; Billingsley 1999; Gilkes 2001). DuBois's view of this institution stands in sharp contrast to those of the white sociologists, who argued that the Black church was culturally inferior and incapable of directing the spiritual life of the

Black masses given the inferior qualities of its clergy. In contrast, DuBois argued that the Black church was the most unique and important Black institution because it served immense familial, political, economic, educational, and spiritual functions. Analyzing the church in the small community of Farmville, Virginia, in 1898, DuBois wrote:

> The most highly developed and characteristic expression of Negro group life in this town, as throughout the Union, is the Negro Church. . . . Various organizations meet here, entertainments and lectures take place here, the church collects and distributes considerable sums of money, and the whole social life of the town centers here. The unifying and directing force is, however, religious exercise of some sort . . . however one must not hastily form the conclusion that the religion of such churches is hollow or their spiritual influence bad. While under present circumstances the Negro church can not be simply a spiritual agency, but must also be a social, intellectual, and economic center, it never the less is a spiritual center of wide influence. (DuBois 1898a, 34)

Thus in DuBois's sociology, the church was the institutional backbone of the entire Black community.

The white perspective portrayed the Black pastor as an inferior moral and social leader. DuBois directly challenged this view by developing an ideal typical analysis of the Black pastor. Writing in *The Philadelphia Negro* he maintained that "the preacher is sure to be a man of executive ability, a leader of men, a shrewd and affable president of a large and intricate corporation. In addition to this he may be, and usually is, a striking elocutionist; he may also be a man of integrity, learning, and deep spiritual earnestness" (DuBois 1899/1973, 206). DuBois found this ideal type of pastor in both rural and urban America. Thus, in Farmville, Virginia, in 1898 he provides a snapshot of the two leading pastors: "Both are graduates of theological seminaries and represent the younger and more progressive element. They use good English and no scandal attaches to their private life, so far as the investigator could learn. Their influence is, on the whole, good, although they are not particularly spiritual guides, being rather social leaders or agents. Such men are slowly but surely crowding out the ignorant but picturesque and, in many particulars, impressive preacher of slavery days" (DuBois 1898a, 16). This is the mode of analysis that anticipates the rise of great clerical leaders like Adam Clayton Powell Jr., Malcolm X, and Martin King Jr. DuBois unraveled the political nature of this institution by conceptualizing Black churches as governments of men. Moreover, those pastors at the top of the church were portrayed as having a genius for leadership—else they would not have been bishops (DuBois 1899/1973, 248). Indeed, "the bishops who preside over these organizations throughout the land are among the most powerful Negro rulers in the world" (DuBois 1900, 617). Here then is an analysis that suggests that a Black movement for change would center in the church because of it potent agency (Morris 1984). Engaging in prediction, DuBois declared in 1899 that "all movements for social betterment are apt to centre in the churches. The race problem in all its phases is continually being discussed, and, indeed, from this forum many a youth goes forth inspired to work" (DuBois 1899/1973, 207).

DuBois also dissected the rich inner life rooted deeply in the souls of Black people. His famous insights into what he called the inner ethical life of Black people maintained that they possessed a conflictual double consciousness that was always seeking a creative synthesis (Dennis 2003). This double consciousness led Blacks to ask a piercing question, "What, after all, am I? Am I an American or am I a Negro? Can I be both?" (DuBois 1986, 5). This psychic-based dialectical conflict hounded the inner life of Black folk, for "one ever feels his two-ness—an American, a Negro; two souls, two thoughts, two unreconciled strivings, two warring ideals in one dark body, whose dogged strength alone keeps it from being torn asunder" (DuBois 1903, 3). For DuBois this complex subjectivity pivoted on this pendulum of double consciousness, which was always conditioned by the system of white oppression. Thus during the heyday of bondage, slaves adopted the doctrines of passive submission offered up by Christianity, but during the abolition period they were seized by the ideals of attaining freedom. During each period, Black music, art, and literature reflected the corresponding tendency of their social predicament.

The inner life of Black people during the Jim Crow era was shaped by the profound questions pertaining to their civil, political, and economic status. DuBois spoke directly to the issue:

> They must perpetually discuss the "Negro Problem"—live, move, and have their being in it, and interpret all else in its light or darkness. With this come, too, peculiar problems of their inner life,—of the status of women, the maintenance of Home, the training of children, the accumulation of wealth and the prevention of crime. All this must mean a time of intense ethical ferment, of religious heart-searching and intellectual unrest. (DuBois 1900, 622)

DuBois maintained that during this period the pendulum of Black inner life swung between conservatism and radicalism. However, he thought that the clashing of these psychic tensions would eventually resolve themselves in a

Hegelian-like fashion, flowering into a higher synthesis of mental creativity. Indulging in prophecy fully a half century before the civil rights movement, DuBois declared:

> But, back of this, still brood silently the deep religious feeling of the real Negro heart, the stirring, unguided might of powerful human souls who have lost the guiding star of the past and are seeking in the great night a new religious ideal. Some day the Awakening will come, when the pent-up vigor of ten million souls shall sweep irresistibly toward the Goal, out of the Valley of the Shadow of Death, where all that makes life worth living—Liberty, Justice and Right—is marked "For White People Only." (DuBois 1900, 624–25)

This portrait of Black inner life diverged sharply from the white perspective, which depicted the subjective world of Black people as simple and only capable of crudely imitating white cultural patterns. Where they saw mental simplicity, DuBois saw complexity. Where they saw a crippling Black mental world locked in a Sisyphus-like eternal futility, DuBois described one capable of supporting creativity and agency.

Breaking new intellectual ground, DuBois established early in the twentieth century that Black people had developed a distinct community teeming with its own culture, institutions, and organizations and a rich complex inner life. Despite the mighty weight of white oppression, DuBois explained, "under these circumstances there has grown up a Negro world in America which has its own economic and social life, its churches, schools, and newspapers; its literature, public opinion, and ideals. This life is largely unnoticed and unknown even in America, and travelers miss it almost entirely" (Green and Driver 1978, 107). The dual assumptions of Blacks' inferiority and their eventual assimilation blinded DuBois's white contemporaries, causing them to miss this prominent sociological reality. But there can be no mistake that DuBois was the first to plow these intellectual grounds, thus setting the stage for the next generation of Black sociologists to fully reap the bountiful harvest.

Expanding and Deepening the Framework: Gender, Class, and Global Racism

DuBois explored the link between race and gender oppression in America. He argued that women were similarly oppressed economically and politically as Blacks and that similar ideological justifications were used to maintain gender domination. DuBois debunked the particular inferiority thesis used to subjugate women, declaring in 1915 that "the statement that woman is weaker than man is sheer rot: It is the same sort of thing that we hear about 'darker races' and 'lower classes.' Difference, either physical or spiritual, does not argue weakness or inferiority" (DuBois 1915, 29). Critiquing gender inequality in the family, DuBois argued that women "existed not for themselves, but for men. They were named after the men to whom they were related and not after the fashion of their own souls" (DuBois 1920, 163). He made it clear that women needed the vote because they were central to economic production across the world, given that "the actual work of the world today depends more largely upon women than upon men" (DuBois 1915, 29). Thus, women needed a voice in the direction of work.

DuBois clearly revealed the link between racial and gender inequality when he examined the plight of the Black female worker. He first observed that more Black women worked to support their families out of necessity, given the low pay Black men received due to racial discrimination. DuBois observed that there were "in 1910 two and a half million Negro homes in the United States. Out of these homes walked daily to work two million women and girls over ten years of age,—one half of the colored female population as against a fifth in the case of white women" (DuBois 1970, 141). He added that Black women were not the recipients of the usual sentimental arguments that they were to be spared from the workplace to protect their womanhood. Nevertheless, for DuBois all women needed independence and political rights because they were going to become far more important as workers in the future, and he deemed Black women to have prefigured this development and to have "had a direct influence upon it" (DuBois 1970, 142). Gender and race inequalities were so closely linked for DuBois that he called for a shared solution for dismantling them: "What is today the message of these black women to America and to the world? The uplift of women is, next to the problem of the color line and the peace movement, our greatest modern cause. When, now, two of these movements— woman and color—combine in one, the combination has deep meaning" (DuBois 1920, 181). Here we see DuBois rejecting the inferiority thesis across the board, arguing that a potentially transformative agency existed in all subordinate groups.

In DuBois's framework, race and class inequality came to be closely linked as well. As pointed out earlier, DuBois initially identified the peculiar social environment as the central cause of Black inequality. White prejudice was the key mechanism in that environment in that it was responsible for Blacks' economic exploitation, political disenfranchisement, and racial segregation. Yet DuBois was acutely aware that economic factors played a crucial role in Black poverty and restricted life chances. He routinely delved into the occupational structure to reveal the depths of economic exploitation and discrimination that Blacks encountered. Nevertheless, in DuBois's early analyses, prejudice, not economics was the root cause of race inequality.

A new causal ordering entered DuBois's conceptual framework in the late 1920s and remained there throughout his scholarly career. With this analytic shift, economics replaced prejudice as the driving force of social and racial inequality. DuBois came to accept a Marxian analysis, which emphasized that worldwide class exploitation of workers by capitalists was the fundamental cause of working-class poverty and suffering. Moreover, because the overwhelming majority of American Blacks were workers, DuBois came to see Negro workers as Black proletarians. His economic analysis stressed the worldwide capitalist organization of industry as the force that enabled capitalists to realize private profits through the exploitation of workers. This exploitation produced both class and race inequality. In critiquing his previous causal logic, DuBois highlighted the relation between race and wealth and came to the "realization that the income-bearing value of race prejudice was the cause and not the result of theories of race inferiority" (DuBois 1940, 129). He concluded that white supremacists had either a conscious or unconscious determination to increase their incomes by taking full advantage of the ideology of white prejudice. In reversing the causal order between prejudice and capitalist exploitation, DuBois boldly declared that it was Marx's analysis of the class struggle that changed his thinking and that "we see in Karl Marx a colossal genius of infinite sacrifice and monumental industry, and with a mind of extraordinary logical keenness and grasp" (DuBois 1933, 103). The 1917 Russian Revolution and DuBois's visits to the Soviet Union in 1926 and 1936 helped to solidify his adoption of the basic elements of the Marxian framework (Baldwin 2002).

Yet DuBois's racial experiences and his analytic grasp of American racism prevented him from elevating the economic factor to the status of sole determinant of racial inequality. His analysis stressed the effects of the potent interaction between race and class. He argued that even though formally the vast majority of Negroes belonged to the proletariat, white racism and exploitation prevented them from becoming a part of the white proletariat. Thus Black workers endured a special brand of exploitation not experienced by white workers because the "Negro is exploited to a degree that means poverty, crime, delinquency and indigence. And that exploitation comes not from a Black capitalistic class but from the white capitalists and equally from the white proletariat" (DuBois 1933, 103). Moreover, this race/class dynamic allowed white capitalists to use Black workers as scabs and replacement workers to drive down the wages of the entire working class. Here DuBois clearly prefigured the split labor market analysis of racial inequality developed by Bonacich (1972) that would hold sway in the late twentieth century.

This interactive effect had profound political implications. It meant that for Blacks to be emancipated from racial and class domination they needed to develop their own independent struggle, because white workers and their labor unions would not find it in their racial interest to lead or support Black liberation. Because of the unique circumstances of the Black proletariat, DuBois exclaimed that the "man that has a grievance is supposed to speak for himself. No one can speak for him—no one knows the thing as well as he does" (DuBois 1907, 110). Thus, DuBois was clear that for the class struggle to succeed, a specific Black agency needed to be exercised. This brand of class analysis sets DuBois apart from those neo-Marxists who neglected the racial dimension of class dynamics. Similarly, DuBois's approach also differed from that of the Black Marxist Oliver Cox (1948), who denied the importance of Black agency by arguing that Blacks would be led to the promised land only by white proletarian revolutionaries.

This marriage between class and racial analysis further sets DuBois apart from his white contemporaries. White sociologists of the period were too American and conservative to embrace Marx in the land where capitalistic logic, coupled with the belief in Blacks' inferiority, still propelled conceptual frames for understanding the Negro problem. Nevertheless, this conceptual marriage represented a new theoretical departure because DuBois's work sought to unravel the linkages of worldwide poverty, racism, and gender and class domination.

In this comprehensive approach DuBois came to view the race problem as a global phenomenon whose various manifestations could be explained by a common set of causal factors. An international perspective is apparent even in DuBois's earliest scholarship. His first scholarly publication, *The Suppression of the African Slave Trade to the United States of America, 1638–1870* (1896), explored the role of international exploitation. In that work he examined the interconnected roles of Europe, Africa, and the Americas in the trading of human beings and the rise of modern capitalism. Early on he saw the need for Africans throughout the world to organize collectively in a common struggle to overthrow racism. In 1919, 1921, 1924, and 1927 he organized historic Pan-African Congresses, which brought together Africans throughout the world to analyze racial domination and develop common strategies for its overthrow.

The first pillar of DuBois's global analysis was the proposition that the African slave trade and Black slavery gave rise to the industrial revolution and modern capitalism. He followed Marx's argument that "slavery is an economic category just as any other," and he embraced Marx's view that "direct slavery is the pivot of bourgeois industry, just as are machinery and credit, etc. Without slavery there is no cotton; without cotton, there is no modern industry. It is slavery that has given value to universal commerce, and it is world trade which is the condition of large scale industry. Thus, slavery is an economic category of the first importance" (Marx, as quoted in DuBois 1975, 138). Following this logic, DuBois documented the locations to which slaves had been shipped, including America, South America, and the Caribbean. He examined their perilous journey across the seas, their labor as slaves, and the raw materials upon which they worked. He riveted his analysis on the role played by European nations, including Portugal, France, Belgium, and especially England, in directing and benefiting from the slave trade and from slavery for over four hundred years. From their colonial outposts, Europe built capitalist empires off the backs of millions of slaves, who produced the textiles, gold, coffee, ivory, cotton, and raw materials that gave rise to large fortunes and were "transferred to the mother country and invested" (DuBois 1975, 139). DuBois emphasized that these slaves were colored people and that the crux of it all could be explained by understanding "the relation between European capital and colored labor involving high profit, low wages and cheap raw material" (Zuckerman 2004, 87). Thus, DuBois concluded, "the basis of the English trade, on which capitalism was erected, was Negro labor" (DuBois 1975, 138), and the driving force behind this racial domination was the pursuit of profit.

For systems of economic domination to flourish, however, they required a legitimating ideology. For DuBois, the same white prejudice prevalent in the cotton fields of Mississippi provided the ideological substance that justified the exploitation of Black slavery flourishing in various locations across the globe. Thus, "the theory of the innate and eternal inferiority of black folk was invented and diffused" (DuBois 1975, 128). DuBois concluded that this ideology "is simply passionate, deep-seated heritage, and as such can be moved by neither argument nor fact" (DuBois 1920, 73). He argued that it was the capitalist motive of private profit coupled with the ideology of white supremacy that fueled racial domination worldwide.

With the overthrow of formal slavery, a crack appeared in the armor of slave regimes. The white capitalist empires faced a real threat because their survival depended on Black slave labor. In DuBois's view, European capitalists hit upon the solution: "If the slave cannot be taken from Africa, slavery can be taken to Africa" (DuBois 1920, 64). This solution gave rise to African colonies and semicolonies around the globe. DuBois defined the phenomenon in this way: "a colony, strictly speaking, is a country which belongs to another country, forms a part of the mother country's industrial organization, and exercises such powers of government, and such civic and cultural freedom, as the dominant country allows" (Zuckerman 2004, 89). The African colonies established by various European conquests "become . . . a vast business organization to reap profits for European investors out of the invested capital and forced labor of Africa" (91). DuBois agreed with Marx that these "colonies provided a market for the rising manufactures and the monopoly of this market intensified accumulation" (Marx, as quoted in DuBois 1975, 141). Because these colonies were economic units for European capitalists, their only political interests stemmed from the need to control a conquered indigenous labor force. That control was furnished by local elites installed by capitalist interests. In this scheme, the mission of the local people was to provide cheap, heavily exploited labor. As a result, the indigenous Africans "are a mass, poverty-stricken, with the lowest standard of living; they are for the most part illiterate and unacquainted with the systematized knowledge of modern science; and they have little or no voice in their own government, with a consequent lack of freedom of development" (Zuckerman 2004, 89). Given similar racial conditions, the plight of the colonized African was strikingly similar to that of the American Negro.

DuBois argued, through his concept of the semi- or quasi-colony, that the vast majority of colored people around the world were coming to share a similar fate because of European capitalist domination of the world. He maintained that semicolonies existed because there were "manifestly groups of people, countries and nations, which while not colonies in the strict sense of the word, yet so approach the colonial status as to merit the designation semicolonial" (Zuckerman 2004, 89).

Semicolonies have their own cultural heritages and a recognized political independence, yet structurally they behave like colonies because each of them is dependent on "European and North American industrial organization, in commerce, in sale of raw materials and especially in obtaining the use of capital in the shape of machinery and manufactured materials" (Zuckerman 2004, 92). This dependence is the linchpin linking colonies and semicolonies in that both are "dependent on financial interests and cultural ideas quite outside the land itself" (92). This dependence ensures that the exploitation and human degradation of the masses in semicolonies are not qualitatively different from those in formal colonies. DuBois argued that semicolonies engulfed almost the entire colored world, including peoples and countries in Asia and South America, the Indians of the Americas, and the Negroes in the United States. Indeed, "for the most part, . . . the colonial people are colored of skin" (DuBois 1945, 18). This was no accident, for there existed a robust correlation between race and the economic dynamics of capitalism.

Not surprisingly, the same ideology declaring colored people inferior and subhuman was used to exploit people trapped in colonies across the world. In DuBois's terms it was the same: "more or less conscious feeling, wide-spread among the white peoples of the world, that other folk exist not for themselves, but for their uses to Europe; that white Europe and America have the right to invade the territory of colored peoples, to force them to work and to interfere at will with their cultural patterns, while demanding for whites themselves a preferred status" (Zuckerman 2004, 87). Thus, for DuBois, the cause of global racism was the European pursuit of capitalist interests, which were legitimized by an ideology that denigrated people of color throughout the world.

Before any other American sociologist, DuBois developed a sophisticated and comprehensive framework that explained how the linkages between race, gender, class, and worldwide capitalism combined to produce social inequality. But DuBois's mission was not merely to produce illuminating scholarship. For him, the ultimate purpose of sociological knowledge was its value as an intellectual weapon to guide liberation struggles.

DUBOIS: THE PREEMINENT PUBLIC SOCIOLOGIST

Before the turn of the twentieth century DuBois was well on his way to becoming a public intellectual and using sociology to emancipate the oppressed (Morris and Ghaziani 2005). In so doing, DuBois broke radically from the Chicago school, whose practitioners followed Park's advice that "their role instead was to be that of the calm, detached scientist who investigates race relations with the same objectivity and detachment with which the zoologist dissects the potato bug" (Coser 1977, 372). But DuBois lived in a completely different world from that of most Chicago school sociologists; he was often the victim of racism, and he abhorred the pain it inflicted on both himself and his race. Speaking of a particularly gut-wrenching lynching, after which he saw the victim's knuckles on display in the window of a local grocer, DuBois wrote: "One could not be a calm, cool, and detached scientist while Negroes were lynched, murdered and starved" (DuBois 1968, 222). This stance led him to pioneer American public sociology and to become the discipline's first preeminent public sociologist long before it was lucrative and celebratory to be a public intellectual.

Today a cadre of sociologists wants to push sociology out of its academic confines and into the public arena. These scholars worry that academic sociology has become too insular, and they believe the task of developing core principles, bodies of knowledge, methodologies, and empirical findings of professional sociology should be paired with expressing to the world those important things sociology has to say that could help humanity face its problems and move toward solutions (Burawoy 2004a; Burawoy et al. 2004). Moreover, they argue that public sociology should not only engage publics beyond the academy in dialogue about matters of political and moral concern, but it should create publics and forge identities for movements of social change.

Unbeknown to most of them, these sociologists are attempting to reclaim a heritage fathered by DuBois over a century ago. Indeed, DuBois decided to develop his sociology as a weapon of liberation by using scientific knowledge to change white minds, awaken Blacks to the power of education, and reshape how they saw themselves. In 1895 he explained, "I returned ready and eager to begin a life-work, leading to the emancipation of the American Negro. History and the other social sciences were to be my weapons, to be sharpened and applied by research and writing" (DuBois 1968, 192).

As a public sociologist, DuBois organized and founded historic publics and social movements, including the National Negro Academy, the Niagara Movement, the National Association for the Advancement of Colored People, and four Pan-African Congresses held in Europe and America during the 1920s. These publics and movements initiated major efforts to overthrow racism nationally and internationally, and they were always driven by sociological scholarship. DuBois disseminated this knowledge through the innumerable lectures he gave and the thousands of articles he wrote for newspapers and periodicals. His major mode of public sociology was expressed through the magazine genre, where he was one of the first to convey sociology through literature.

DuBois, a founder of the NAACP, became director of its Department of Research and Publicity in 1910. In this capacity he founded the *Crisis Magazine* and edited it for a quarter century. The *Crisis* became DuBois's major vehicle for merging sociological scholarship and activism. Through this magazine he used his scholarship, as well as that of others, to educate the world about the devastating effects of racism and inequality. Here DuBois presented his theories of race, class, and gender inequality. He expounded on how ruling classes divided Black and white labor so that both groups could be exploited. He explained how women's disenfranchisement was a tool promoting racism, sexism, and capitalist domination. He ceaselessly uncovered the role ignorance played in oppressing people and sought to develop the knowledge needed for their liberation. He sought to disentangle those social factors that produced wars from those that promoted peace. He analyzed protest and movements nationally and internationally, always interested in the lessons of social change they provided.

The analyses disseminated through the *Crisis* intended to spur social action and social movements that could build a more just and equal world. The *Crisis* counseled the oppressed to engage in unceasing protest and agitation. It published literature and scholarship aimed at building and promoting race, feminist, and class consciousness. It opened its pages to scholars and writers whose ideas promoted progressive thinking. Many of the writers who birthed the Harlem Renaissance were first published in the *Crisis*. Not only did the *Crisis* openly support activists and movements for change, but it repeatedly called for action to attack inequality.

DuBois's public sociology was intelligent and did not condescend to the masses. Yet he made sure that it was presented clearly and provocatively so it could reach large audiences. He employed different genres to attract attention, including poems, novels, interviews, plays, and literary works. As a result, the *Crisis* was an instant success. By the 1920s it had over a million subscribers, many of whom were African Americans. One subscriber stated, "I know in my family the *Crisis* was the magazine to read and take leadership from." Another exclaimed, "I don't know where the Bible was in the house but I knew where the *Crisis* was" (Johnson 2003, 140). Never before or since has there been such an effective organ that disseminated a sociological perspective to millions. DuBois's achievements in organizing and sustaining publics and social movements have been influential in American and world politics. His work demonstrates that sociology can marry science and activism to build a better world. In so doing, DuBois enhanced sociological scholarship and demonstrated that the discipline is capable of diffusing its important messages to the world through public sociology.

The Meaning of All This

DuBois's prolific scholarship focuses attention on a number of issues. Foremost among them is the enormous impact that prescientific assumptions can have in shaping the content and theoretical guideposts of scholarship. Indeed, the dominant white perspective developed particular explanations of American race relations and produced certain kinds of confirming evidence that were congruent with the assumption of Blacks' inferiority and the ideal of assimilation. These assumptions led white sociologists to develop a perspective that produced very different portraits of Black and white Americans. They led white sociologists to formulate two contrasting sociological populations: whites were civilized, endowed with agency, and superior; Blacks were subhuman, bereft of agency, and inferior. For DuBois, on the other hand, whites and Blacks were members of the same human family, both equally capable of exercising agency and both equally endowed intellectually. Oppression, history, and discrimination produced observed racial differences, not inferiority of any sort. Inescapably, different theoretical formulations and predictions followed from these diametrically opposed assumptions. Clearly, political and moral values held by scholars can shape the intellectual landscape of their scholarship.

These opposing assumptions led DuBois and the white scholars to very different conceptualizations regarding the agency capable of producing racial change. The white sociologists believed change could only occur if whites engaged in action to produce that change because they alone possessed a superior power anchored in a superior culture and institutional vehicles. DuBois, on the other hand, believed agency existed in the oppressed Black community, and he analyzed its culture, institutions, and subjective world to reveal that agency and its potential. Sociology was not alone regarding the lack of Black agency, for the view was common throughout the social sciences. Thus historians of the Reconstruction era (Dunning 1965; Burgess 1902) attributed no agency to Blacks in the overthrow of slavery, the defeat of the South in the Civil War, and the construction of progressive state governments during Reconstruction. In his classic work *Black Reconstruction*, first published in 1935, DuBois demonstrated empirically that Black action was crucial to the overthrow of slavery, that military action of Black soldiers was crucial to the Union's defeat of the Confederacy, and that Black elected officials provided creative leadership in developing progressive state governments during Reconstruction. As a result of DuBois's novel interpretation, the historiography of Reconstruction had to change radically to accommodate the decisive role of Black agency. Similarly, DuBois attributed major agency to worldwide Black labor in the formation of industrialization and modern capitalism. It was DuBois's scholarship that conducted war on the dominant view that whites, because of their superiority, determined the fate of the people of color the world over.

McKee's key question was why, given a thoroughly developed sociological perspective, no sociological scholars anticipated the Black-led civil rights movement and the urban rebellions? White sociologists did not predict this development because they assumed all such efforts would have to be led by whites and that at best Blacks were capable of a minor supporting role. To the contrary, DuBois insisted such an effort could only be launched by Blacks because they alone had the interest and the cultural and institutional resources to overthrow Jim Crow. Making bold predictions about such a struggle, DuBois thundered in 1913 that

> When the American people in their carelessness and impudence have finally succeeded in welding 10,000,000 American Negroes into one great self-conscious and self-acting mass, they will realize their mistake . . . in another generation . . . we will have in this country a mass of people of colored blood acting together like one great fist for their own ends, with secret understanding, with pitiless efficiency, and with resources for defense which will make their freedom incapable of attack from without. (Arndt 1970, 103)

Again, in 1934, DuBois anticipates the coming Black struggles:

> It is the race-conscious black man cooperating together in his own institutions and movements who will eventually emancipate the colored race, and the great step ahead today is for the American Negro to accomplish his economic emancipation through voluntary determined cooperative effort. (DuBois 1934, 20)

Moreover, as Arndt (1970, 145) has demonstrated, DuBois also comprehended the relevance of Gandhi's movement in India for the coming Black American struggle because

> He saw in Gandhi the new kind of savior, a leader of dark people who got power without bloodshed and who used power without selfishness or rancor. He saw in the tactics evolved by Gandhi new weapons for the struggle of the black man in the United States and colored fold throughout the world. Boycott, noncooperation, conquest through peace, agitation—all became watchwords of the evolving DuBois position. (Arndt 1970, 145)

Indeed, DuBois confidently predicted a major Black struggle, exclaiming that "the great day is coming" (Arndt 1970, 60). To be sure, DuBois anticipated what the white perspective on race precluded—a Black movement successfully led by Black folks to overthrow Jim Crow.

Generations of Black sociologists who came to maturity after DuBois's groundbreaking scholarship journeyed in his footsteps by conducting research showing that Black people had developed their own unique community, race consciousness, institutions, and discontentment with racial oppression and that they did not wish to be fully assimilated into white culture (see Frazier 1939, 1949; Johnson 1934; Drake and Cayton 1945). There are contemporary scholars, including some who are white (e.g., Aptheker

1961; Myrdal 1944; Foner and Mahoney 1995; Winant 2001), whose scholarship has been influenced by DuBoisian thought. Indeed, the most famous and influential study on race, *An American Dilemma,* was deeply influenced by DuBois's scholarship. In that work DuBois was cited eighty-three times, in contrast to nine citations of Park. Myrdal made his debt clear when he wrote, "We cannot close this description of what a study of a Negro community should be without calling attention to the study which best meets our requirements, a study which is now all but forgotten. We refer to W. E. B. DuBois, *The Philadelphia Negro,* published in 1899" (Myrdal 1944, 1132). Yet it was the Black sociologists immediately following DuBois who were the original heirs of DuBois's intellectual work. These Black scholars embraced and further developed the DuBoisian message, but, as McKee explained, the white sociologists refused the message: "Though they were widely read and cited often and appreciatively by their white sociological colleagues, they nonetheless put forth some assessments of race relations that violated the assumptions of the perspective. When that happened, their deviant views were effectively ignored by those same white colleagues" (McKee 1993, 4).

McKee was correct in this assessment, but he represents the DuBoisian message as coming solely from Black sociologists rather than giving DuBois credit for having plowed these intellectual grounds and making it possible for the next generation of Black scholars to further develop the perspective. The neglect of DuBoisian thought by white sociologists suggests that Kuhn's argument (1962) was right—that intellectual politics can limit the receptivity of radical ideas that challenge dominant paradigms. In this instance, these politics marginalized the pioneering scholarship of DuBois, and even today the struggle continues to move it from the periphery to the center of mainstream sociological discourse. Black sociologists also played a role in DuBois's marginalization because even though they cited him in streams of footnotes, they seldom brought the messenger and his message front and center. Thus Frazier, in his 1948 presidential address (Frazier 1949), lays out an essentially DuBoisian agenda for scholarship on race but fails to mention or even cite DuBois. DuBoisian thought was not the route to professional achievement and recognition.

It is clear that DuBois's work, by pointing out the powerful links among race, gender, and class inequalities, anticipated the important and current scholarship investigating the interlocking and reinforcing nature of race, gender, and class inequalities (see Collins 1990; Dill 1983; King 1988; Morris 1992). DuBois's work on race and class also prefigured Bonacich's work (1972) on a split labor theory of racial antagonism. Indeed, a lasting contribution of DuBois's work is its theoretical recognition that systems of domination often interlock.

Centering racial oppression in an international framework was a key DuBoisian innovation; it allowed him to demonstrate that Black Americans and Africans were linked because they shared those cultural elements that survived slavery. For DuBois such cultural analyses were deeply intertwined with structural and cultural analyses. By dissecting the slave trade, slave regimes, and the ruthless creation of colonies around the globe, DuBois formulated theories of the rise of modern capitalism and global racism. He delineated the structural kinship among oppressed people of color around the globe by demonstrating how the European capitalist nations fashioned colonial arrangements that linked the subordinated fates of colored people worldwide. Here we see the seeds of Diaspora studies that are currently seizing the imagination of scholars around the world (Drake 1987, 1990). This work also prefigured that of Fanon (1976) and Blauner (1972), who have analyzed the nature of internal racial colonies. It has also inspired the work of Winant (2001), who has explicitly used DuBois's theories of racism and capitalism to explain worldwide capitalism.

Conclusions

A fair assessment must conclude that DuBois produced pathbreaking scholarship on race and social inequality. Yet it has taken sociology one hundred years to catch up and begin to incorporate his insights into the core of the discipline. Though one can only speculate, it seems self-evident that the current field of race and inequality would be extraordinarily farther down the road if DuBois's work had been at the center over the last century.

DuBois's groundbreaking scholarship was largely ignored by mainstream sociology. Indeed, it has received scant attention in the *American Journal of Sociology*, the *American Sociological Review*, *Social Forces*, and the general literature. Without a major academic post, access to ably prepared students, and the sponsorship of white colleagues and philanthropy, DuBois was isolated institutionally and intellectually: "So far as the American world of science and letters was concerned, we never 'belonged'; we remained unrecognized in learned societies and academic groups. We rated merely as Negroes studying Negroes, and after all, what had Negroes to do with America or science?" (1968, 228).

Moreover, his scholarly work suffered perennially from lack of adequate funding, causing DuBois to constantly beg white philanthropists for research support. He reported that each year while conducting the first empirical studies on the Black community at Atlanta University between 1900 and 1910, he was on a budget of $5,000, which included his salary, costs of publication, investigations, and annual meetings. This treatment stood in sharp contrast to the hundreds of thousands of research dollars funneled to the white sociologists of the Chicago school (Coser 1977, 533; Stanfield 1985). Indeed, white scholars, including Park at Chicago and Odum at the University of North Carolina, were deeply ensconced in national philanthropic networks, making it possible for their own and their students' research to be funded handsomely and continuously (Fisher 1993; Yu 2001). Similarly, Myrdal received $300,000 in the 1940s for the research and writing of an *American Dilemma,* while at the same time DuBois was refused funding for a major research project (Lewis 2000, 450). White philanthropists, supported by the powerful Black leader Booker T. Washington, largely closed the research coffers to DuBois.

Additionally, because of DuBois's academic marginalization, he was never in a position to mentor students who could have assisted him in developing a DuBoisian school of race on a par with the Chicago school. Yet DuBois's work profoundly affected intellectually, if not institutionally, the generations of Black sociologists who would follow. Even Black sociologists often failed to give DuBois the credit he deserved for creating a counter-perspective on race, probably because he did not have the resources to affect their careers or determine their placement in the academy. This academic marginalization is beginning to recede because of the sheer impact of DuBois's scholarship, yet DuBois still does not receive the honor and distinction appropriate for one of the discipline's pivotal thinkers. Even the century-old American Sociological Association obscures DuBois's intellectual originality and status as a founder of American sociology by indiscriminately lumping his contributions with that of other important Black sociologists as reflected in the association's DuBois/Johnson/Frazier Award. There is a difference between the founder and master of an intellectual framework and those who creatively pick its fruits.

But hope does spring eternally. Indeed, after a hundred years, sociology is finally embracing the pathbreaking sociology of W. E. B. DuBois. Yet it behooves contemporary scholars of social inequality to examine the deep-seated assumptions they bring to their scholarship and fathom the ways their perspectives are shaped by them. Thus, could it be that a hundreds years in the future, sociologists of science will discover that similar assumptions prevalent during DuBois's time actually guided the contemporary thesis that race is no longer a dominant factor in American racial inequality (Mills 1997; Holt 2000; Brown et al. 2003). Because of the intellectual gems still buried in DuBois's work and the promise it holds for building a better world, may we hasten to beat a path to DuBoisian sociology so as to claim and build upon a rich professional and public heritage.

Acknowledgments

I thank Walter Allen, Craig Calhoun, Charles Camic, William Gamson, Amin Ghaziani, Marie Jones, David Levering Lewis, Kim Morris, Michael Schwartz, and Phil Zuckerman for their useful comments on drafts of this chapter. I thank Michael Flug and Bob Miller of the Vivian G. Harsh Research Collection and Kathleen Bethel of the African American collection at Northwestern University for all of their assistance. I dedicate this chapter to Michael Schwartz—a mentor, friend, and admirer of DuBois's scholarship.

[SIXTEEN] The Dark Side of the Force: One Hundred Years of the Sociology of Race

Howard Winant

What was the racial scene at the time of the American Sociological Society's founding in 1905? How race conscious and racially organized was the world the founding "fathers" saw at that moment? How racialized were U.S. social ties and identities, and those of the 1905 intellectual world, broadly conceived? On a general level these questions answer themselves. Of course race was present, as present (at least) as it is today in the everyday life and social structure of the United States. Race has always been present, indeed foundational, since the earliest moments of modernity.

But what race *meant* in 1905 is less certain. How has that meaning changed, how has it developed, and how has it been challenged as it came down to the present day? To what extent has sociology influenced general conceptions of race, and to what extent has the field itself been shaped by racial meanings and racial conflicts? These questions require our consideration; they are the subject of this chapter.

As a sociohistorical concept race connects to numerous familiar themes: the body and its social meaning, territoriality, (in)equality, identity/difference, collectivity, and politicization. But this has not always been the case. One hundred years ago the physiognomic, corporeal dimension of race was the dominant theme in nascent sociological thought. Although an alternative view was beginning to take shape—one that conceived of racial difference as largely sociocultural—the idea of race as a political phenomenon, a matter of movement activity and policy formation, went virtually unheard in 1905. Race was not viewed as a political issue except by opponents of the disciplinary consensus, such as W. E. B. DuBois.[1]

---

1. While I do not concentrate on these problems here, it is important to note that at its founding the American Sociological Society was composed almost exclusively of white men, that the participation of sociologists of color in the society or in its successor organization (the ASA) was limited until the rise of the racial movements of the 1960s, and that even today the field lacks a truly representational racial profile.

Background

At the turn of the twentieth century, biologistic views of race were in command. Evolutionism had taken over. "Race war" was a source of anxiety to early sociologists. Race was about migration and fertility, "breeding," and human genetics as it was then understood. It was also about development, though this too was conceived in a biological way. Empire and colonialism were comprehended and justified (in Europe most centrally, but elsewhere as well) as the logical outcomes of racial differences among the world's peoples. Non-Europeans, seen as backward and uncivilized, were thought to need and benefit from the uplifting forces of colonial rule.

In the United States it was seen as "natural" that the black South and Native American peoples would be subdued by the "more advanced" white races. The U.S. Supreme Court had recently (in 1896) handed down the *Plessy* decision. What we would now call "ethnic cleansing" of indigenous people (seen most centrally in the 1887 Dawes Act) had been completed; it was widely supported as "civilizing" these supposedly backward and savage nations (or tribes). Tensions on the Mexican border were merely "normal" in 1905 but would soon intensify with the Mexican Revolution's onset in 1910; the border states and the Southwest were rife with anti-Mexican racism (Almaguer 1994). The restriction of Asian immigration (the Chinese Exclusion Act was reenacted in 1904; the "Gentleman's Agreement" with Japan would be concluded in 1907) was considered natural as well, for in America Asians were viewed as unassimilable aliens: their presence en masse was perceived as so threatening (especially to labor) that their widespread influx could not be tolerated.

On the other hand a new imperial age was dawning: the "little brown people," as McKinley called them (Rusling 1987, 22–23), of the Philippines, Puerto Rico, and Cuba, were now ripe for U.S. colonization. This too was "natural," a patent continuation of the expansionism of the nineteenth century. Not only would the United States prosper from heightened control of the Caribbean, the isthmus of Panama, and the Pacific Rim, but the areas thus subjected would gain as well: they would be civilized and Christianized by imperial activity.[2]

In 1905 race was as much a global issue as it was a U.S. one. Colonial

2. The Philippines, though majority Catholic as a result of centuries of Spanish rule, also contained a substantial minority of Muslims. Religious conflict between invading Christians and colonized Muslims, a theme redolent both of pre-modern Europe and of our own time, has received relatively little attention in respect to the U.S. conquest of the Philippines. For an exception, see Kramer (2006).

resources and labor fed, clothed, and housed the imperial countries that exploited their riches. In the Congo King Leopold's massacres continued unimpeded, a fact reported in detail by Robert E. Park (not yet installed at the University of Chicago) and by George Washington Williams, another pioneering journalist/sociologist of race (Hochschild 1998). "Semper novi quid ex Africa!" DuBois repeated in his analysis "The African Roots of the War" (1915/1995). Imperial rivalries shaped international relations, an arena in which the United States was a newcomer, albeit a formidable one. On the Russian front, the Japanese defeated the czar in the Pacific in 1905, and the first Russian Revolution erupted that same year; it featured strikes, mutinies (on the *Potemkin* and elsewhere), and government troops shooting down unarmed demonstrators in the streets of St. Petersburg.[3] These events all had racial dimensions.

These were but some of the main events that shaped the sociopolitical context in which the founding sociologists were working. Although they were necessarily subject to the "common sense" prevailing at the field's founding moments, they were far from wholly subservient to it. To some of the field's founding fathers such as Sumner and Giddings, race was a matter of human biological nature, instinctual, "hardwired." It was an intractable matter, a question of evolution, not sociality. But other leading sociologists—such as Lester Frank Ward, the American Sociological Society's first president, and Albion Small, founding editor of the *American Journal of Sociology*—had been publishing critical appraisals of what we would now call racism since before the American Sociological Society's founding in 1905. In his 1980 assessment of the twentieth-century sociology of race, Thomas Pettigrew noted that "critical work is in the minority throughout" the whole arc of mainstream sociological writing on the subject (Pettigrew 1980, xxv). But challenges to the received wisdom were still present from the first in such publications as the *AJS*. These critical reappraisals of the received racial wisdom included contributions by such vital figures as W. I. Thomas, Charlotte Perkins Gilman, W. E. B. DuBois, Monroe Work, and various writers associated with Jane Addams and Chicago's Hull House

3. Theodore Roosevelt negotiated the end of the Russo-Japanese War, for which he would receive the Nobel Peace Prize in 1906. Roosevelt's imperial orientation and support for eugenics coincided with a racial position that was relatively more tolerant, toward black people at least. He was more aware than his predecessors had been (and than many of his successors would be) of the ongoing U.S. obligation to secure citizenship rights for blacks. But Roosevelt's attitudes toward "other others"—Asians, Native Americans, and Latin Americans—was less free of the racism of his time. For a generally laudatory assessment of Roosevelt's orientation toward race matters, see Gerstle (2002).

(Deegan 2002).[4] Still, in 1905 and for a long time thereafter, the sociology of race took shape almost exclusively as a conversation among whites, even though this required the marginalization of W. E. B. DuBois, who was not only the founder of the field in its modern, empirical, and theoretically sophisticated form but also arguably the founder of modern American sociology tout court.[5]

The origins of American sociology considerably predate the founding of the American Sociological Society in 1905. Just as in Europe the field developed to interpret onrushing social change, so too in the United States sociology developed in response to pressing demands for new social knowledge. In France sociology was invented during the era of Comte and de Tocqueville as a "positive science of society," a tool to explain industrialization, the downfall of absolutism, and colonial war.[6] In the United States sociology arose in response to racial upheaval and the crisis of the slave system. The onset and intensification of U.S. convulsions over racial slavery roughly paralleled the European transition from absolutism to democratic rule, as well as the trajectory of industrialization. The Civil War was among other things a semirevolutionary battle to overthrow absolutism in its American incarnation, as DuBois argued (see below). So it should come as no surprise that in the United States the nascent field found in the racial problematic some of its earliest and most foundational explanatory tasks.[7]

In 1873 Herbert Spencer's *The Study of Sociology* crossed the Atlantic to

4. Addams was the only sociologist to win a Nobel Prize (1931).

5. Also largely ignored were such other black figures as Kelly Miller, professor at Howard University; Monroe Work, head of the Division of Records and Work at Tuskegee, who was the first black sociologist published in the *AJS* (in 1901); and William T. B. Williams and Thomas Jesse Jones at Hampton, who were instrumental in organizing and establishing the *Southern Workman*. This list could be expanded considerably.

6. The term did not attain currency even in France until much later, however. Durkheim founded *L'Année Sociologique* only in 1898, more or less at the same time that the *AJS* was being launched.

7. The fall of the Confederacy—the end of slavocracy and the death of the "noble cause"— is of course the fundamental text of the American right. See Genovese (1998). DuBois addressed this issue in *Black Reconstruction* as follows: "The chief obstacle in this rich realm of the United States, endowed with every natural resource and with the abilities of a hundred different peoples—the chief and only obstacle to the coming of that kingdom of economic equality which is the only logical end of work is the determination of the white world to keep the black world poor and themselves rich. A clear vision of a world without inordinate individual wealth, of capital without profit and of income based on work alone, is the path out,— not only for America but for all men. Across this path stands the [American] South with a flaming sword" (DuBois 1935/1977, 706–7).

the United States. Spencer, a contemporary of Darwin,[8] asserted that a racial instinct was crucial to human evolution and thus joined a long list of taxonomists whose preoccupation was the racial ranking of human groups. Spencer's influence was crucial in launching U.S. academic sociology; the title of Spencer's first book (*Social Statics*), was a phrase he had borrowed from Comte.

Spencer's was not the first sociological voice to make itself heard, however. In the United States the sociology of race had predated the arrival of Spencer's ideas. Societal transformations that commenced with the rise of abolitionism, continued through the Civil War and its horrors, and were perpetuated by the partial emancipation and then virtual reenslavement of southern blacks, provided the earliest demand in the United States for something called "sociology." The first avowed U.S. sociologists anteceded the American Sociological Society's debut by more than half a century. Some were defenders or apologists for slavery—intellectuals like Henry Hughes (Hughes 1854; see also Lyman 1985; Fredrickson 1971) and George Fitzhugh; others were critics of the institution, like Hinton Rowan Helper (Wish 1960). Hughes's 1854 tract—proslavery, agrarian, anti-industrialist, and at its core romantic—was the first to use the term *sociology* in the United States. When DuBois in 1935 interpreted the Civil War as the second stage of the American Revolution, the completion of the transition from absolutism to democracy in the United States, he was linking the political sociology of slavery and abolition to that of European empire and the industrial revolution.[9]

So there were direct lines connecting early U.S. sociology to racial matters. The ranks of both advocates and critics of racial slavery included self-described sociologists, because—as in Europe—the process of socioeconomic development and the ferocious conflicts it generated demanded explanation, both at the elite and mass levels. Racial conflict played a parallel role—that of generating a "great transformation" (pace Polanyi) in the

8. Although the subject is too extensive to be covered in this chapter, Darwin's involvement with race issues at least merits a note. In *The Descent of Man*, the volume that succeeded *The Origin of Species* (1871), Darwin attempted what might be called a "racialist" account of human evolution. In *The Origin of Species* Darwin also evinces some of the racialism of his time; note the full title, for example: *On the Origin of Species by Means of Natural Selection, or the Preservation of Favored Races in the Struggle for Life*. Darwin's cousin Francis Galton was the founder of the eugenics movement and the great man's most assiduous popularizer, at least where "the descent of man" was concerned. For more extensive comment, see Gould (1981).

9. Barrington Moore (1966/1993) made similar arguments, unfortunately failing to note DuBois's pioneering work of thirty years earlier.

United States—to the one played by the downfall of absolutism and the on-set of capitalism in Europe. Racial slavery and native conquest and slaughter displayed an absolutism all their own, of course. But beyond that the rise of capitalism also followed an expropriative policy toward lives and labor and land—some of Polanyi's "fictitious commodities" (1944/2001)—in the United States. DuBois saw a resemblance here to Marx's "primitive accumulation," and indeed so did Marx.[10] In the United States this process was greatly shaped by race, since substantial conflict and confusion surrounded the race/class distinction there. For example, building on DuBois, Roediger examines the paradoxical identities of white workers in the antebellum United States: were they "freemen" or "servants"? Since the category of "servant" described enslaved blacks, white men resisted it. Especially in the Jeffersonian, southern tradition, where whiteness conferred the status of "master"—that is, a self-possessing, "yeoman," property-owning, citizen—no honorable white male could have a master over him; no white could be a servant. Yet propertyless whites could not avoid a sort of U.S. "enclosure" in the developing capitalist system: this was the making of the American working class, so to speak. Only by reinforcing racial distinctions—through which becoming a worker meant joining the class of masters, the white men—could the opprobrium of enslavement be avoided (Roediger 1991).[11]

Approaching Race

So what constitutes the sociology of race anyway? No positivisms of any type allow us to answer this question, any more than old accounts by travelers or travestied applications of Darwinian concepts would.[12] To grasp the

10. "The discovery of gold and silver in America, the extirpation, enslavement, and entombment in mines of the aboriginal population, the beginning of the conquest and looting of the East Indies, the turning of Africa into a warren for the commercial hunting of blackskins, signalized the rosy dawn of the era of capitalist production. These idyllic proceedings are the chief momenta of primitive accumulation. On their heels treads the commercial war of the European nations with the globe for a theater. It begins with the revolt of the Netherlands from Spain, assumes giant dimensions in England's AntiJacobin War, and is still going on in the opium wars with China, etc." (Marx 1967, 351).

11. These ideas have enormous implications and evoke literatures far exceeding this chapter's scope. On the sociology of slavery, see Patterson (1982); on antebellum white working-class formation, see Lott (1995) and Foner (1995). For a comparative Caribbean-focused account, see Stinchcombe (1997). Note also, finally, how early U.S. tensions over the race/class dimensions in capitalist development also involved crucial gender-based elements: for example, Foner's "free *men*," or the Jeffersonian yeo*man* farmer or artisan.

12. Or shall I say "Galtonian" concepts? See Zuberi (2001).

sociologies of race (and "racial studies" more broadly understood as well) proposed over the last century and down to the present is to understand the field *genealogically*. Here I survey the trajectory of the sociology of race over the last hundred years by means of a discussion of the rise and fall of four racial paradigms within the field: the *biologistic* paradigm, the *pragmatist* paradigm, the *structural-functionalist/civil rights* paradigm, and the *social-movement-versus-neoconservative* paradigm.

These four "moments" or episodes in the recent history of the field were deeply linked to broader sociopolitical trends. In this account the developing sociology of race is seen as a series of competing and episodic efforts both to contain political conflict over race and to foment it.

Politically the field may be divided, like Gaul, into three parts: mainstream, insurgent, and reactionary. Broadly speaking, *mainstream* sociological approaches to race have sought to explain and help contain upsurges in the ongoing racial conflicts that characterize U.S. society; *insurgent* approaches have endeavored to explain those challenges in order to advance them; and *reactionary* sociologies of race have tried to explain these challenges in order to reverse them. When threats and disruptions affecting societywide—and disciplinary—understandings of the meaning of race have grown too formidable, too dangerous to ignore, the field of sociology has been forced to respond. When race riots, racially based mass mobilizations, and race-related opposition to established political leaderships have confronted the U.S. status quo too fiercely, sociological research on the subject of race has ramped up. Continuing racial inequalities have been noted, explanatory accounts developed, and policy reforms advocated. That has been, mutatis mutandis, the mainstream sociological approach to race.

Insurgent sociologies of race arise from time to time in alliance with these same challenges: radical, nationalist, and egalitarian voices have repeatedly made themselves heard, most notably in the post–World War II period. The field's allegiances and commitments are typically called into question by insurgent positions within it. Racial challenges are often linked to global tensions, to parallel political issues like class and gender conflict, and to crises of American identity and purpose. In the post–World War II era, for example, racial crisis intersected with cold war issues, anticolonial and antiwar movements, the rise of the second wave of feminism, and an intense period of soul-searching over national identity and public morality.

Reactionary approaches to race are also common responses to racial conflict. Intellectual tendencies considered dead and buried have a habit of resurfacing in respect to race. For example, biologistic accounts and religious explanations of racial difference and inequality, as well as appeals to racial nationalism and nativism, have frequently reemerged at times of heightened racial conflict. These positions also exhibit global linkages and affinities with parallel political universes: in the heyday of eugenics, biologistic racism spanned the globe; the rise of fascism and its easy articulation with traditional U.S. white supremacy is another familiar example; racial reaction, homophobia, antifeminism, and anticommunism go together nicely as well. In the sociology of race, these positions typically take the form of condemnation of government interventionism and celebration of racial laissez-faire (benign neglect and the like), calls for more vigorous law enforcement, and victim blaming.

Race has always been a deeply political subject, whether or not it was recognized as such in sociology. Hence mainstream writers, radical egalitarians, and reactionaries have time and again deployed all the theoretical and empirical resources they could muster in their efforts to reformulate the enigma of race in U.S. society. But for all the significance of racial politics, sociological approaches to race have been driven by other influences as well: our own rationalistic impulses, our hunger for scientific status, and our sense of political and moral obligation have forced us continually to reinvent the sociology of race, in the process recurring to ideas that had been thought discredited and refighting old battles. As much as the movements, identities, and social relationships studied within the field of sociology, the discipline itself has periodically been a zone of contention.

So the field of sociology is necessarily part of the problem it is trying to explain. The sociology of race has been severely criticized for its "failure of perspective," as two well-known books on the subject were subtitled (Lyman 1972; McKee 1993). The field has also been seen as progressing, however unevenly, away from its own racism and toward a more scientific as well as tendentially more egalitarian perspective (Pettigrew 1980).[13] Spokespersons for the organized discipline of sociology have frequently sought to foster racial reformism in U.S. society at large; just consider the names of various post–World War II sociological schools of thought about race— assimilationism, pluralism, race relations, multiculturalism. Yet reformism is better understood as incorporation and absorption of conflict than as conflict resolution. That is the meaning of Gramsci's term *hegemony*.

From the vantage point of a century's intellectual experience, we can see that each of these three politically oriented "perspectives"—the main-

13. In my judgment the first view (Lyman and McKee's "failure of a perspective") is too harsh and the second (Pettigrew's evolving "race relations") is too incrementalist as well as overly optimistic.

stream, insurgent, and reactionary approaches—has proved inadequate in the face of a set of racial conditions (not problems but fundamental structures) endemic not only to the United States but to the "modern world-system" as a whole.

In the roughly diachronic account that follows, I address the conditions in which studies have been carried out and theories elaborated in the sociology of race. No attempt is made to consider the literature systematically; that would be impossible anyway in this space. Rather I provide a sort of periodized conceptual history, a *genealogy,* of the sociology of race. Basing my approach on the claim that social thought is "demand driven," I begin by discussing the *biologistic paradigm:* the theoretical formulations and research frameworks on view in the early sociology of race. From that point forward, I make bold to say, the field has gone through a series of crackups, a sequence of periodic reformulations and re-searches, reiteratively trying to make sense of race. At each crisis point the contradiction between the dominant sociological paradigm of race and the larger explanatory "work" that paradigm was required to perform became too great, too explosive. Under these conditions the field retreated into a confused interregnum of sorts while a new paradigm was framed, usually on the basis of the radical criticisms that had subsisted at the margins of the discipline before the paradigmatic crisis struck with full force. Sometimes too, reactionary critics have been able to intervene in the field, forcing a sociological "retreat from race" when the going got too rough.

Between crisis points, critical standpoints have developed in semi-independence. This claim is particularly true of insurgent approaches but applies as well to reactionary views. Under "normal" conditions in the discipline, the mainstream paradigm rules; although contending views may be marginalized, they are not entirely in abeyance. Critics are concerned with sociopolitical anomalies beneath the racial radar of the sociological biens-pensants of the day. When crises occur and a moment of paradigm shift approaches—which is often not a moment at all but a more gradual breakdown in established sociological "ways of seeing" race—these alternative viewpoints are in position to exercise their greatest influence.[14]

What forces shape the sociology of race? What impels crisis, insurgency, reform, and consolidation? I have already noted a rough correspondence between conflict over race and the field of sociology's attempts to address the broad societal demand for explanations. But clearly something more

14. As will be obvious, I am borrowing here from Thomas Kuhn (1962/1970), although adding a rather stronger political flavoring.

problematic has been at stake in the United States where race was concerned, for over the entire course of the past century the field has moved only gradually and incrementally toward a recognition of the breadth and depth of the U.S. (not to mention the global) racial problematic. Deep social crises and traumatic societal upheavals have been required to demonstrate that sociological attitudes toward race could be altered even incrementally. Not unlike U.S. society as a whole, the field has maintained a default position of benignity vis-à-vis race, operating in what may be characterized as the "as if" mode:

- *as if* American democracy were not sharply called into question by U.S. racial conditions;
- *as if* the U.S. rise to global power did not have significant racial dimensions;
- *as if* the founding scenarios of U.S. society—conquest, settlement, slavery, and immigration—were not fundamental racial traumas;
- *as if* those themes were somehow relegated to the past, not constitutive of periodic social upheavals, both in a larger political sense and in terms of the field's attempts to explain them.

By recognizing the presence of this "default" mode, we can better understand the seemingly small shifts the sociology of race has undergone, even as previous conceptions have been cast aside. These revisions have by and large been brought about by the actions of the racial "others" themselves and helped along by their representatives and allies within the field itself. It is this combination—periodic rejection of the dominant sociological paradigm by those whom it purportedly describes, and the efforts of sociologists themselves to make sense of the new situation, to craft a new and more effective account of race—that I describe as "the dark side of the force."

The Biologistic Paradigm

As the field was organizationally consolidated (roughly from the turn of the twentieth century until the 1920s) it was dominated by the *biologistic paradigm*, whose affinities were social Darwinist and eugenicist. The initial preeminence of the biological account of race was largely residual. A long meditation on the meaning of racial identity and difference had accompanied and indeed shaped modern intellectual life from the Enlightenment to the dawning twentieth century. This body of thought was preoccupied with the "nature" of race: corporeal form, intellectual capacity, and physical beauty were among its key themes; these were all characteristics deemed to be intrinsic and intractable. German idealists, English empiricists, French philosophes, and U.S. founding fathers such as Jefferson and Franklin all expatiated on these matters. As the human sciences developed in the nineteenth century, race was investigated (after a fashion) through such methods as cranial capacity measurement and phrenology (Gould 1981; Gilman 1985; Mosse 1978). European authorities like Lapouge and Broca continued to exercise influence over early twentieth-century sociologists of race. Indeed, Lapouge's "Old and New Aspects of the Aryan Question" appeared in the *AJS* in 1899, in some respects channeling Gobineau into American sociology at the fin de siècle and foreshadowing the linkages between eugenics and fascism.[15]

James McKee writes that "throughout the first decade of the [twentieth] century, race still fell within evolutionary theory and the vocabulary of race reflected that: [*American*] *Journal* [*of Sociology*] articles spoke of civilization and savagery, of advanced and backward races. 'Civilization' defined the highest stage within social evolution; the lesser stages of development were 'barbarian' and 'savage,' and people of African origin were declared to have come from a savage culture" (McKee 1993, 29). This was "commonsense" evolutionism, but it intersected well with the social Darwinism and eugenicism that constituted racial science in this epoch. At the turn of the century eugenics was nearing the height of its influence.[16] Although biologistic theories about race long predated nineteenth-century science, they acquired new credibility with the ascent of evolutionary theory after Darwin. The term *eugenics* was coined by Darwin's cousin Francis Galton with his 1869 book *Hereditary Genius*. The evolutionist approach to race was also supercharged by the claims of Spencer regarding the social significance of racial instinct, and the social Darwinism of Sumner among others. Further influences proceeded from the everyday debates of the times.[17]

15. On these connections see Chase (1977).

16. Its fall would not come until the 1940s, when its association with Nazism became unavoidable. See Barkan (1992).

17. At the turn of the century anxieties abounded regarding the continuing tidal waves of European and Asian immigration, and uncertainties abided about the status of blacks, particularly in the South but also in the North. Many sociologists identified with the progressivism of Theodore Roosevelt (and later of Woodrow Wilson), a racially ambiguous brew at best. Progressivism's uncertainties were theirs as well: uncertainties about urbanism, industrialism, and the din and tumult of cities teeming with garlic-eating European immigrants, "inscrutable" Asians, and menacing Negroes, all of them impoverished and eager for any job, no matter how low-waged. Eugenics was embraced. White working-class nativism played a role in shaping this climate as well (Higham 1955/1994).

Eugenics offered a seemingly far more objective, quantitatively sophisticated methodology for the study of racial matters than had previously been available in the social sciences. Indeed it is to eugenics that we owe the introduction into sociology of inferential statistics, calculus, and the concept of regression to the mean (Marks 1995; Zuberi 2001; Kevles 1985). Eugenics deeply influenced all the social sciences; it was embraced not only by mainstream psychologists, historians, anthropologists, and other academics but also by many feminists and socialists, who saw in it a rationality and commitment to science that contrasted with the residual superstition of older ways of thinking about population, sex, and such social problems as education, public health, housing, and especially crime and deviance (Rafter 1997).

In the United States eugenicist thought was most centrally applied to issues of immigration, but it also operated in debates about poverty and race. How was the United States to deal with the hordes of immigrants arriving around the century's turn from racially "other" areas of the world—Jews, Greeks, Italians, and Slavs, not to mention Asians—in effect, all the world's "others," its non-English-speaking, non-Protestant, huddled masses?[18] How were blacks, now emancipated and citizens (at least in theory), to be regarded? There were strong affinities between eugenics-based viewpoints and American nativism, as there were between eugenics and antiblack views.[19] The 1916 publication and wide circulation of Madison Grant's *The Passing of the Great Race* signified a general trend toward immigrant exclusion on the grounds of "natural" racial hierarchy.[20] William Graham Sumner's social Darwinism probably best exemplified this trend (Sumner 1963). Edward A. Ross's work (1914; 1920, 59–70), though more nativist than social Darwinist, also reflected some of these biologistic presumptions.[21] A

18. It goes without saying that the raciality of these peoples was unevenly theorized, to put the matter kindly. The present chapter does not afford the requisite space to discuss processes of racialization or the social construction of racial categories. I have addressed these problems at length in other work, however. See Omi and Winant (1994) and Winant (2001).

19. U.S. eugenics also included a strong anti-"white trash" component that condemned and sought to sterilize those it called feebleminded. This form of racism had complex roots: in the plantation agricultural system, in the striving antiprovincialism of urban elites, and in Malthus and early capitalist political economy. See Chase's discussion (1977) of the Jukes and Kallikaks.

20. Although not a sociologist, Grant wielded influence as a principal of the American Museum of Natural History and friend of Theodore Roosevelt. His book was probably the key intellectual force behind the restrictive immigration policy of 1924.

21. A committed progressive of the Wisconsin school and former student of Richard Ely, Ross combined biologistic racism with populist and socialist sympathies, an admixture that

host of early sociological writings and debates treated race as a "natural" phenomenon.

Biologistic understandings of the sociology of race were competing with cultural ones by the 1910s. In part this was an outcome of the insurgent sociology being produced by black writers and researchers at this time. DuBois's voice reached social scientific readers (albeit only sporadically) through publication in both the *AJS* and the *Annals of the American Academy of Social and Political Science.* His volume *The Philadelphia Negro,* published in 1899, was an entirely pathbreaking work that combined urban and labor sociology, studies of what we would now call social stratification, criminology, the sociology of religion, and historical and political sociology as well. The book's formidable empirical commitments far outstripped anything else written during that epoch and anticipated Chicago urban studies by two decades or more. But it received little attention.[22] *The Souls of Black Folk* (1903) did better, selling particularly to black readers; some sections of the book had appeared previously as articles in the *Atlantic* and elsewhere.

An early pragmatist as well as racial radical, DuBois had become a sociology professor at Atlanta University in 1897, while still working on *The Philadelphia Negro.* He remained at Atlanta until 1910, producing with the help of students and associates a steady stream of empirical studies on black institutions (religious, educational, economic, among them), on the social conditions of black folk, particularly in the South, and on U.S. racial dynamics. Although not without flaws and constantly limited by inadequate resources, the Atlanta studies remained the most empirically detailed and sophisticated sociological analyses of racial conditions available in the United States until the arrival in the South of Park's black Chicago graduates (notably Charles S. Johnson)[23] in the late 1920s and 1930s.

During this period as well there was significant growth in sociological activity at black colleges and universities. For example, at the Hampton In-

---

was common enough in the early twentieth century. See Ross (1901a, 1921a). In his autobiography, published in the 1930s, Ross (1936) repudiated his earlier racism. See also Frazier (1980, 153n).

22. See Elijah Anderson's enlightening introduction to the centennial edition of the book (Anderson 1996); see also David Levering Lewis's comments on the book's production and reception (Lewis 1993, 201-10).

23. Johnson received his PhD at Chicago in 1917. After studying the 1919 Chicago race riot (an assault on black neighborhoods by white mobs that paralleled dozens of others in cities around the country that year) and publishing *The Negro in Chicago* (1921), Johnson became research director for the National Urban League in New York. He arrived at Fisk University to become professor of social research in 1927, and became the first black president of Fisk in 1946.

stitute the Negro Conference was created under the leadership of Thomas Jesse Jones, where it continued for two decades. Hampton was also the institutional base for the research journal *Southern Workman*, which from 1903 to 1935 published empirical research that paralleled DuBois's Atlanta University studies. At Howard University the mathematician Kelly Miller established the sociology department in 1895 and taught there for forty years; the Howard department came to include such crucial black sociologists as E. Franklin Frazier and Alain Leroy Locke.[24]

Racial biologism was confronted during and after World War I by a range of phenomena it could not readily explain: most centrally the newly apparent agency of racially defined minorities, whose widespread urbanization, incorporation into the industrial working class, and incipient political mobilization clearly exceeded the logic of the old paradigm. This was the era of the Harlem Renaissance, the Garvey movement, and the *Crisis*. As a result a "cultural turn" began to take hold in the sociology of race. The culturalist trend appealed to many mainstream sociologists disaffected with social Darwinist and Spencerian evolutionism, and dismayed by the intractability the biologistic paradigm assigned to race. So racial themes and race itself now began to be recognized as "social problems." Initial challenges to biologism were timid, merely replacing its overtly "natural" framework with one based on concepts of cultural backwardness and disadvantage. These were handicaps, matters that could be transformed, but only gradually, over many generations.

Early tendencies in this direction were evinced in the work of Franklin Giddings and Howard Odum. Giddings had been active in shifting the biologistic racial paradigm toward issues of instinct, proposing a racial theory based on the concept of "consciousness of kind." A quantitatively oriented, positivistically inclined thinker and committed evolutionist, Giddings became the first professor of sociology at Columbia (in 1894). He grounded his sociology of race in a four-stage philosophical anthropology, of which only the final stage (the "demogenic") was seen as fully civilized. Many human "types" had not yet attained this stage; indeed Giddings saw evolu-

---

24. Kelly Miller, professor of mathematics at Howard, founded the sociology department there in 1895 and taught at Howard until 1935, when he retired as dean of Arts and Sciences. A prolific author, Miller, in his book *Race Adjustment* (1908), sought to reframe the dispute between Booker T. Washington and W. E. B. DuBois. In a 1897 review of economist Frederick L. Hoffman's *Race Traits and Tendencies of the American Negro,* one of the leading eugenics-based works to argue for the innate inferiority of African Americans, Miller used census data to argue that Hoffman's claims were statistically flawed. See Miller (1897), and Stepan and Gilman (1993).

tionary differences as besetting society even in its most modern configurations and necessarily generating inequalities of various types. Giddings's notions of instinct had a strong commonsensical quality; they may still be observed today in popular explanations about such matters as racial segregation ("like cleaves to like," and so forth) and in laments about the so-called self-segregation phenomenon among racially defined minorities.[25]

The shift from accounts based in supposedly inherent biological characteristics to theories grounded in concepts of instinct was not only symptomatic of a declining biologism but also signified the expanding explanatory ambition of the field. Here was an early appearance of a social concept of race, though obviously the sociality that an instinct-based theory could recognize was still limited. Instinct remained a nearly natural concept; it still signified something intrinsic and largely unalterable. But there was a shift here too: that something could be explained by social patterns and structures that gave rise to it over time—"folkways," for example.

This early recognition of the sociality of race is visible in the work of Howard Odum, who suggested that black isolation from the dominant (that is, white) culture was profound enough both to forestall "civilizing" influences and to preserve uniquely black (but also implicitly backward) cultural characteristics. Odum's *Social and Mental Traits of the Negro* (1910) was originally a dissertation completed under Giddings. His later work on southern black music and folk tales simultaneously chronicled the complexities of African American life in the "black belt" and documented its isolation. A committed social reformer and sometimes embattled white racial "moderate" in the segregationist South, Odum looked at black culture with real attention and respect. Yet his preoccupation with folk traditions tended to reify the racial separatism linked to Jim Crow and to minimize the extent to which an oppositional black modernity was emerging in the United States—and in the South—in the early decades of the twentieth century. Thus we find in Odum's work foreshadowings and hints both of the "separate development" arguments of black nationalism and of the "culture of poverty" arguments that would stress black "disadvantage" as an explanation for inequality in the 1960s. His cultural sociology of race was able to retain a good deal of the old framework of racial hierarchy that had earlier been a mainstay of the biologistic paradigm, while dispensing with some of the overt racism inherent there.

In fact Giddings, Odum, and colleagues were by no means devoid of a

25. See Tatum (2003) for a present-day social-psychological critique of this school of thought.

paternalistic racism of their own. The very designation of African American relationships and institutions as "folkways"—implicitly premodern and sociohistorically retarded—depreciated and dismissed the black (and indigenous, and colonized, and immigrant) presence in the modern world. These leading (and most other following) scholars remained blithely ignorant of black political activity as well as black sociological research and analysis. Nor did they generally understand "other others"—Asians, Latin Americans, indigenous people, Arabs, and so on—as capable of self-activity, collective or organized, in civil society. Needless to say, conflict over inequality, political and civil rights, and the meaning of race did not preoccupy this viewpoint.

During the 1910s and 1920s debates over race and culture expanded significantly throughout the social sciences; these debates deeply affected sociological thought on race. Three crucial developments must be noted, necessarily far too briefly, in this chapter: the advent of Boasian cultural anthropology as a challenge to the physical anthropology that then dominated the field; the development of IQ testing in psychology under Lewis Terman, a process that was first linked closely with eugenicism and the "feeble-minded," and then later adopted its own version of culturalism in the quest for an "objective" measure of intelligence; and the seemingly definitive vindication of slavery in American academic history with the publication of Ulrich Phillips's *American Negro Slavery* in 1918.

Franz Boas's work was devoted above all to the claim that cultural variation among distinct peoples could not be ranked hierarchically or classified along a scale that ran from civilization to savagery. Boas sought both to counter nativist and eugenicist positions in the public sphere and to rethink cultural anthropology so as to surpass such positions. He bequeathed a remarkable antiracist, though of course somewhat uneven, legacy. His contributions were based on decades of work at Columbia and through the American Museum of Natural History, where he had to coexist (and contend) with various eugenicist stalwarts, politicians, and trustees. In the antiracist annals of American social science, Boas's contribution is exceeded only by that of DuBois. He trained dozens of influential anthropologists (among them Hurston, Freyre, Benedict, and Herskovitz) and deeply reoriented the field in the United States.[26]

26. In the process he reoriented the field at the American Museum of Natural History, where Boas had to combat the eugenicism of Madison Grant and the elite racism of Henry Fairfield Osborn, the paleontologist who became the Museum's president and chief primatologist. See Harraway (1990).

Intelligence testing, first developed by Binet in France during the 1890s, was employed by psychologist Lewis Terman to sort military recruits during World War I. Terman, along with such other early influential psychologists as Robert Yerkes and Carl Brigham, linked racial difference (by which they meant southern and eastern European migrants as well as U.S. blacks) to differences in "IQ," thus reinforcing Galtonian arguments. Justice Oliver Wendell Holmes Jr. invoked this racial "science" as late as 1927 in *Buck v. Bell*, to justify an order of coercive sterilization of a "feeble-minded" white girl from the rural South. Later, in the face of concerted arguments from such prestigious figures as Walter Lippman, Terman collaborated with anthropologist Alfred Kroeber to design IQ tests that were supposedly culturally neutral. Debates over "hereditary genius" (that is, intelligence) resurface steadily, most recently in the controversies sparked by Herrnstein and Murray's *The Bell Curve* (1994), a book that focused on putative differences in intelligence and their supposed correlation to race.[27]

Phillips's account of slavery as a benevolent institution caring for uncivilized and culturally backward blacks, and of the South as falling prey to merciless and money-grubbing northern capitalists and carpetbaggers who invaded under the cover of Reconstruction, summarized and justified the cause of southern irredentism on a national scale. The romance of the noble "lost cause" achieved a degree of acceptance (among whites at least) that has still not been entirely reversed, despite DuBois's masterpiece of refutation, *Black Reconstruction in America* (1935), and a flood of revisionist historical studies of slavery that were produced during and after the 1960s. The "invaders" were shown by DuBois to have included numerous black and white schoolteachers (many of them Quaker and Methodist women), thousands of northern blacks who saw themselves as returning from exile to minister to a homeland devastated by war and suffering, many Radical Republicans intent on fostering land reform and political democracy, and not incidentally a great many ex-slaves who had *emancipated themselves* through resistance (unarmed and armed) during the course of the Civil War. This alternative viewpoint on Reconstruction remained unnoticed, despite the efforts of DuBois and colleagues, until the 1960s; it was swept away by *Birth of a Nation* and the thousand other irredentist accounts, both academic and popular, that flooded the popular imagination and the academic marketplace, especially after Phillips's book (Blight 2002).

27. For more extensive discussion of this set of issues, see Chase (1977), Gould (1981), Fischer et al. (1996), and Fraser (1995).

The Pragmatist Paradigm

The wide-ranging debates about race in the first few decades of the century focused their attention—despite great variation in their political orientations and commitments to racial (in)equality—on the issue of cultural variation across racial categories. All displayed a diminishing commitment to the biologistic model of racial difference. This culturalist approach to race acquired ever-greater weight in sociology during the 1920s, notably in the work of Edward Reuter. An early population specialist and lifelong race theorist, Reuter developed positions that overlapped to a considerable extent with the emerging perspective of Robert Ezra Park and his group of students and associates at the University of Chicago. Reuter emphasized "culture contact" and race mixing as dynamic processes that shifted the social dimensions of "the American race problem" over time. He situated U.S. racial patterns in a global context, influencing Park. (Reuter's *The Mulatto in the United States* [1918] was written initially as his dissertation, directed by Park.)[28]

Park's importance in developing the sociology of race can scarcely be exaggerated; he is eclipsed by few figures besides DuBois. Notably, he only slowly detached his position from a belief in "racial types" (a quintessentially culturalist viewpoint) and from the highly deterministic "race-relations cycle" he had charted while supervising a field research project in Hawaii.[29] Still Park's humanistic and personal antiracism contrasted sharply with the views of most of his contemporaries. His early journalistic work had put him directly in touch with southern black poverty and the horrors of imperial rule in Africa. At Chicago his group consolidated their

28. Reuter's *The American Race Problem* first appeared in 1927 and was revised in 1938, reflecting the author's developing racial liberalism. The trajectory of his writings from his (1918) *The Mulatto in the United States* to the revised edition of *The American Race Problem* is quite striking. In the former book he argues in traditional fashion that the "white element" in mixed-race persons' identity provides them with their highest and most civilized features, while the "black element" embodies primitive and even animalistic characteristics; in the latter he stresses the American principle of "fair play" for the Negro, in some ways anticipating Myrdal. Reuter's final academic position was in the Department of Sociology at Fisk University.

29. Park's four-stage "cycle," which began with "contact" and ended with "assimilation," tended to neglect variability and agency, key points in any pragmatist approach to race. Although he recognized the importance of conflict and incorporated a global perspective, his model also tended to conflate racial groups with the national ones whose struggles for independence he had observed during his doctoral study years in Germany. In his later work Park repudiated the "cycle."

pragmatist approach over the course of the 1920s and 1930s, first by rejecting biologism for a more sociocultural approach and then by developing
their views on the agency and capabilities for collective action inherent in
racially (and ethnically) defined minority communities.[30] Park resolutely
insisted on placing U.S. racial dynamics within a global and historical context, at first emphasizing "culture contact" as Reuter had done but later situating that theme in the context of empire building and colonialism, as well
as linking racial conflict to nationalism (Park 1950).

Park initiated various aspects of his work—on race, the city, empirical
methods, and cultural contacts—at roughly the same moment. His students
became accustomed to treating the city as a vast sociological laboratory.
Chicago was also the first top-ranked sociology department to admit significant numbers of racially defined minority graduate students. Early
black graduate students included Ira De A. Reid and Charles S. Johnson,
who would become leaders in the field; they were followed later in the department by E. Franklin Frazier and Oliver C. Cox, among other notables.
In some ways reinventing the pragmatist sociological wheel that DuBois
had constructed in Philadelphia and Atlanta,[31] the Chicago department
modernized and democratized the sociology of race, albeit in uneven ways.
Chicago became identified not only with a new racial sociology but with
an approach that addressed such matters as urbanism, immigration, and
imperialism (the "racial frontier") with far greater effectiveness than its
predecessors did. The resurgent racial reaction and nativism of the 1920s—
visible in widespread antiblack rioting, anti-immigrant legislation, depor-

30. The distinction between race and ethnicity is a complex matter, requiring more space
than I can devote to it here. Let it suffice for the present to associate racial difference with the
corporeal or "phenotypical" attributability, the "color coding" and ascriptive assignment of
racial identity that operates on the commonsense level in everyday life; and let us identify ethnicity with the cultural distinctions that attend group differences in respect to language, religion, national origin, and tradition. There is substantial overlap between these two sets of attributes in practice, owing to the flexibility of both categories. Ethnically defined groups are
often racialized, as has occurred among the former Yugoslavs, in Britain and Ireland, in Nazi
Germany, in Rwanda and Burundi, and in many other instances. Racially defined groups can
be ethnicized (or de-racialized), as has occurred in the United States with many European immigrants who were formerly classified as racially "other" but who are now firmly defined as
"white." See Omi and Winant (1994).

31. Both Park and DuBois were deeply influenced by pragmatist philosophy, and indeed
were both students of William James at Harvard. DuBois's pragmatist orientation, as well as
that of other black contemporaries such as Alain Locke, has received attention only recently.
See West (1989) and Fraser (1998).

tation of thousands of immigrants in consequence of the Palmer raids, and the disgraceful demonstration of hundreds of thousands of KKK members at the Capitol in Washington, D.C., also disturbed the discipline's progressives, for whom Chicago was headquarters.

A renovative approach to immigration also characterized the pragmatist sociology practiced in Chicago during these years. Over three years (1918–20) Chicago sociologists W. I. Thomas and Florian Znaniecki published their five-volume study *The Polish Peasant in Europe and America,* which significantly reconceptualized the sociology of migration.[32] This enormous project combined a great deal of primary data with an unprecedentedly humanistic account of migration. Although Thomas and Znaniecki weren't primarily concerned with race, their work still broke new ground by dispensing with the racism common in contemporary work on immigration. They theorized their subjects as world-aware agents who comparatively assessed their situations in central Europe and Chicago by using political, economic, and cultural criteria. This was a quite different perspective on the "huddled masses"; Thomas and Znaniecki should be seen as the founders of today's sophisticated sociology of migration.

In rethinking race via the pragmatist tradition, the Chicago "school" was returning this uniquely American philosophical complex to its roots, which lay in abolitionism and the reactions of Oliver Wendell Holmes Jr. (he of *Buck v. Bell*), and Charles S. Peirce to the Civil War and its aftermath. Pragmatism also shaped William James's attention to problems of agency in social psychology and John Dewey's concern with the practical problems of fostering and maintaining a democratic public (Menand 2001; Joas 1993; West 1989; Bulmer 1984a; Abbott 1999; Feffer 1993). The work at Chicago, linked on the one hand to this primary U.S. philosophical tradition and on the other to American Progressivism, represented a tremendous infusion of realism and attentiveness into the field of sociology.

The Chicago approach to race also remained limited, however. Park's aversion to political sociology and insistence on value-free methodology, always a chimera in social scientific research, inhibited the effectiveness of Chicago sociology as racial critique. Racial inequality and injustice were not seen as outcomes or objects of state policy but as phenomena of civil society. Lacking a focus on the racial state, Park (and to varied extents the

32. During that same year, Thomas was dismissed from the university under a morals charge that was never proven and that his supporters claimed was retribution for his pacifism and support for the feminist movement. Despite his difficult exit from Hyde Park, Thomas was elected president of the American Sociological Society in 1926.

Chicago researchers he mentored) argued that racial conflict itself would generate egalitarian and inclusive pressures; this was the essence of the "race relations cycle" (Lyman 1972, 27–51). Political alliances with progressive whites, feminists, the labor movement, or even among racially defined minorities themselves were not considered viable; this view may have descended from Park's association with Booker T. Washington. Park's sociology of race also tended to analogize U.S. racial struggles with the European national conflicts he had observed during his graduate school days in Heidelberg. In his view the European model of "ethnocracy" (Persons 1987, 79–83) paralleled U.S. racial stratification, explaining both prejudice and discrimination (whites' defense of their privileged status) and the ineluctable pressures of assimilation (blacks and other minorities overcoming the cultural disadvantages imposed by slavery and exclusion).

Still, Park and his students managed to validate racial conflict as an engine of social change and an essential component of American democracy. They recognized the agency of the racially subordinated and oppressed, and indeed understood it as a species of nationalism. Their departure from the generally static and structurally determined sociology of race that Chicago had inherited constituted a dramatic innovation, an important reform in the field. The combination of all the developments I have just enumerated (and many more factors I cannot examine here, such as the centrality of microlevel work at Chicago as developed by Mead and extended and modified by Blumer)—revitalized the sociology of race in numerous ways. In particular the Chicago school's emphasis on an empirically driven approach to race brought new attention to issues of variability, agency, and conflict among racially defined groups. Work at Chicago at long last incorporated at least some of the insurgent insights pioneered by DuBois—long relegated to sociology's margins because of his radicalism as well as his race—into the disciplinary mainstream.

Despite numerous limitations, Chicago sociology attended to race in a far more nuanced, respectful, and democratic way than had its mainstream predecessors. Chicago scholars talked to blacks and Asians, trained black researchers, and paid attention to the complex sociohistorical environment in which race operated. However unevenly and tendentially, Park, Thomas, Wirth, Blumer, and colleagues broke with the biologism and the unquestioning white supremacism that had characterized the field before their arrival.

By the 1930s the pragmatist sociology of race was losing authority. Numerous factors were responsible for the changes under way. A major social-psychological turn in the 1930s, the rise of quantitatively oriented survey research,[33] and most centrally the onset of the Depression reoriented the field's mainstream, rendering less attractive Chicago's preoccupations with cities, immigration, and group conflict/accommodation. On the margins of the field, Marxist currents gained influence: here interest in race continued and even grew, but these approaches centered on labor, inequality, and class in general, thus narrowing the scope of racial studies.[34] To be sure, the influence of the Chicago school remained, helping to shape at least one more epochal study of the Chicago urban landscape, St. Clair Drake and Horace Cayton's *Black Metropolis: A Study of Negro Life in a Northern City*. This mammoth community study, which appeared in 1945, remained very much in the pragmatist tradition, devoting extensive attention to the self-organization of the community named Bronzeville. With its emphasis on economic life, family structure and ties to the South, education, housing, and so forth, *Black Metropolis* evoked the tradition not only of Park and Wirth's Chicago sociology but also of DuBois's *The Philadelphia Negro*, the founding work in American pragmatist sociology.[35] *Black Metropolis* was in many respects the last hurrah of the Chicago sociology of race.

Chicago sociology had provided a comprehensive account of race, however imperfect and uneven, especially as concerned the United States. This approach was at once interactional, local/urban/national, and situated in a global field of population movement, culture contact, and empire.[36] But at the same time, in good pragmatist fashion, it was decentered and subject to the interests, identities, and interventions of the conscious actors it studied. Chicago sociology was relatively nontheoretical, with the exception of those theories we would now consider "middle range": such was Park's "cycle" or Blumer's symbolic interaction. Chicago's incipient holism, its lack of a fun-

33. The growth in survey research occurred especially after the establishment, at Columbia University (in 1940), of the Bureau of Applied Social Research under Paul Lazarsfeld.

34. A renewed interest in Marxism led black sociologists—often Chicago trained (Frazier, Johnson, Cox)—to "bring class back in." Other black academics—Howard University political scientist Ralph Bunche, for example—also flirted seriously with Marxism. DuBois's *Black Reconstruction*, certainly his most Marx-oriented work, appeared in 1935.

35. St. Clair Drake, one of the book's coauthors, was the pioneering black urban anthropologist. Horace Cayton, the other coauthor, was a protean figure who went from employment as deputy sheriff in Seattle (where his father—an ex-slave—was a leading black Republican newspaperman), to an appointment in the Chicago sociology department under Wirth and Park, to a position as special assistant to Secretary of the Interior Harold Ickes, to director of a WPA research program (he was recommended for that post by W. Lloyd Warner), to writing *Black Metropolis* in the early 1940s. See Hobbs (2002).

36. "Interactional" refers to the whole Cooley/Mead/Blumer tradition, itself fraught with debate and dispute.

damental, unifying conceptual frame,[37] and its openness to conflict prepared the way for the structural-functionalist account in the United States, at least as much as did any importation by Parsons, Shils, and others, of Weber and Durkheim (the usual reason given for structural functionalism's rise).

The Structural-Functionalist Paradigm and the Civil Rights Movement

The field's center of gravity, meanwhile, moved east from Chicago to Columbia and Harvard, where during the 1940s and 1950s the structural-functionalist paradigm would attain the dominant position in sociology. Not only was the pragmatist stress on conflict and agency—especially as seen in its Chicago version—incompatible with the political and cultural unity demanded by wartime conditions, but sociology was proving itself useful to the powers, corporate and state-based,[38] that wielded most of the resources the field needed to operate, first in depression, then in wartime, and then in the "twilight struggle" of the cold war. The New Deal–sponsored work on labor conditions and cultural matters that had shaped sociology in the 1930s gave way to wartime government research, which was oriented to planning, military recruitment, and shifting demographics and opinions in the United States.

Structural functionalism's rise with the onset of World War II also seemed to surpass Chicago's pragmatist approach to race. Whereas U.S. sociology (including the then leading Chicago department) had been roiled in conflict over the United States' entry into World War I in 1917, no such discontent or criticism in the field had been precipitated by World War II. Like every other profession, the field of sociology harnessed itself to the war effort, an enterprise that (after Pearl Harbor, anyway) encompassed left and right, rich and poor, white and black. With their focus on social integration, structural functionalism's chief architects aspired to a disciplinary consensus never before achieved.[39] They tended to ignore or dismiss radical ten-

37. A good example would be the AGIL (Adaptation, Goal Attainment, Integration, Latency) framework Parsons would provide, or the classical theories' central themes: class struggle/forces versus relations of production in Marx; rationalization in Weber, and so on.

38. Lazarsfeld's work on public opinion helped reshape the marketing strategies of modern media (ratings) and politics (polling). His partnership with Frank Stanton of CBS typified postwar collaboration between sociology and business.

39. To refer in this blanket way to "structural functionalism" is to agglomerate a wide variety of perspectives rather harshly. Parsonian sociology with its regulatory cultural norms and emphasis on systematicity is only poorly equated with vast range of inquiry pursued by

dencies (Marxism most notably) and assiduously sought to incorporate a wide range of social conflicts in their effort at systematization.

Race relations (no longer understood as racial "conflict") was no exception. The structural-functionalist approach was notable for its racial liberalism and integrationism. The Chicago sociology of race had viewed integration (or more properly, assimilation) as the end-stage of a prolonged process of conflict and accommodation whose realization in the United States remained a long way off. Chicago's successors in Cambridge and Morningside Heights were considerably more sanguine about racial progress. This change may be explained not only by the appearance of highly influential new work (notably the Myrdal study; see below) but also by the shifting experience of race relations, especially in the 1940s. An increase in racial solidarity (in the Durkheimian sense) accompanied the war and achieved some theoretical function, so to speak, at least in early structural-functionalist thought. Well into the 1960s, that approach seemed to inform and support the post–World War II civil rights movement; indeed structural functionalism may be characterized as the *paradigmatic expression of the civil rights movement in the sociology of race*. The chief spokespersons for structural functionalism—Parsons, Merton,[40] and Robin Williams, among others—wrote extensively and effectively about race, analyzing prejudice and discrimination.

Racially, the war mobilized every sector of society, finally bringing an end to the Depression. The war provided racially defined minorities with industrial employment, entry into the armed services, and a degree of social inclusion they had previously lacked. It fomented black, Mexican, and Puerto Rican migration from the sharecropping plantations of Dixie (and Texas, Arizona, and Ponce) to the industrial North, the Midwest, and the developing West. It diminished the poverty and suffering of the Depression years and tendentially narrowed the gaps and tensions that had previously divided racially defined groups. Not that the war signified an all-out effort for racial inclusion and equality; in practice it was a more contradictory

---

Merton, who gives far more latitude than Parsons did to conflict and uneven social integration. The functionalism espoused by Kingsley Davis hardly comported with Merton's or Parsons's work either. Without the latitude here to explore adequately these variegated currents, I still argue that they shared a view—descended more centrally from Durkheim than from Weber—that emphasized the self-regulatory and integrative features of modern social structures and that consequently minimized the continuity and fundamentality of key social cleavages in U.S. society. Race was certainly such a cleavage.

40. See Merton (1949b) for an early effort to develop Myrdal's insights within a broadly structural-functionalist framework sympathetic to civil rights.

affair, racially speaking, for the United States. The Atlantic war was democratic, tolerant, and inclusive; the Pacific war was rife with racism toward the "Japs." This racism was imported into the domestic milieu by a ferocious bigotry, which culminated in the notorious 1942 Executive Order 9066 and its internment of Japanese Americans.[41] No comparable outrage was committed against German or Italian Americans, although there were some detentions in those communities as well.

The structural-functionalist framework generally stressed the unifying role of culture, and particularly American values, in regulating and resolving conflicts. This approach was notably in evidence with respect to the sociology of race and converged with the argument of the Myrdal study, *An American Dilemma* (1944). I use the verb *converged* because it is difficult to say that the work of Myrdal, a Swedish parliamentarian and social democrat as well as a social scientist, was greatly influenced by that of Parsons et al. More likely the reverse—Parsons was a racial liberal and Merton had been involved in civil rights activity in his undergraduate days[42]—but in any case the consensual political climate of the war years provided an appropriate moment for calls for racial reform. Myrdal made this position clear in his book's concluding pages, pointing out the inconsistencies and contradictions inherent in a racially exclusionary and discriminatory society leading a war for democracy.

Myrdal's book was perhaps the single most influential work ever published on the sociology of race. His central thesis about the discrepancy between racial injustice and "the American creed" was deeply linked to mainstream liberalism, racial gradualism, and the ideal of racial assimilation. The product of an enormous group effort in which a great many sociologists were involved,[43] *An American Dilemma* also reflected its author's extensive

41. The "relocation" received relatively little sociological attention during the war. For some distinguished exceptions, see Thomas and Nishimoto (1946) and Thomas, Kikuchi, and Sakoda (1952). See also Broom (1943).

42. Robert Merton, personal communication.

43. Myrdal's secondary authors were Arnold Rose, an American sociologist, and Richard Sterner, also a Swedish economist. Political scientist Ralph Bunche was Myrdal's guide and "native informant," so to speak, in two sometimes perilous research voyages through the wartime South. Among the project's other collaborators were sociologists E. Franklin Frazier, William F. Ogburn, Samuel A. Stouffer, Edward Shils, and Dorothy Swaine Thomas. Leading black intellectuals Sterling Brown, Doxey Wilkerson, Alain Locke, and Kenneth Clark were consultants as well. W. E. B. DuBois was kept at a discrete distance from the effort at the insistence of Frederick Kappel, the Carnegie Commission organizer of the project, whose racial politics were hardly progressive. Myrdal's involvement was sought to provide some degree of hoped-for social science objectivity. See Southern (1987), Jackson (1990), and Stanfield (1985).

observations and inquiries in African American social settings, much of which was undertaken with the aid and guidance of political scientist and neo-Marxist (as well as future diplomat and Nobel laureate) Ralph Bunche. Myrdal's sympathy with American blacks and his vast documentation of the injustices visited upon them did not result, however, in a denunciation of U.S. racism, perhaps because he resolutely sought to address the American "mainstream," perhaps because he undertook his project in the shadow of World War II, which despite all its limits and illusions he still properly understood as a struggle for democracy, and perhaps because his patrons at the Carnegie Foundation and elsewhere would not have accepted so radical a critique, especially in wartime (Jackson 1990; Southern 1987; Stanfield 1985). So, rather than presenting his "dilemma" as something endemic and foundational in U.S. society and culture, he framed racism (a word he did not use) as an aberration, a retardation and obstacle besetting the higher virtues of U.S. democracy. He combined this account with a Fabian faith in progress over the historical medium to long term: the theory of "cumulative and cyclical development" that he was later to apply to the global problem of economic development (Myrdal 1963). He also presented assimilation as an unproblematic objective of racial reform, a position that surely differed from the views of many of his black informants.[44] In short, Myrdal's devotion to the cause of racial reform—the product of many determinations and influences—drove his project at its most fundamental level. This treatment resonated deeply with the structural-functionalist perspective.

Another major sociological study that tackled race issues at this time was Stouffer et al.'s *The American Soldier.* Research for this project was initiated in 1941 with War Department/Department of Defense support; it was published in 1949–50 (Stouffer et al. 1949–50; see also Merton and Lazarsfeld 1950). Stouffer and colleagues devoted significant attention to racial attitudes in the wartime military and to the experiences of the more than one million black members of the U.S. armed forces. In its explicit examination of the tensions of racial segregation and the aspirations for racial progress

---

44. Black reaction to the Myrdal volume varied significantly. E. Franklin Frazier heaped praise on the work. Myrdal, he wrote, "revealed a remarkable facility for getting the feel of the racial situation in the United States. His objectivity was apparent from the very beginning in his relations with Negroes. They were simply people to him" (Frazier 1945, 557). Ralph Ellison, however, criticized Myrdal for his assimilationism: "aside from implying that Negro culture is not also American, [he] assumes the Negroes should desire nothing better than what whites consider highest. . . . It does not occur to Myrdal that many of the Negro cultural manifestations which he considers merely reflective might also embody a *rejection* of what he considers 'higher values.' There is a delusion at work here" (Ellison 1964, 301; emphasis in original).

that characterized the wartime armed forces, *The American Soldier* strongly paralleled the Myrdal study, which had preceded it by some five years. In Stouffer et al.'s interviews, white soldiers continued to express their Negrophobia, while blacks articulated their expectations—as they had in World War I—that their sacrifices in wartime would be recognized and rewarded later. Stouffer et al. suggested that the war reduced the degree of white racism. Although this claim was not vacuous, the extent of this meliorism has since been called into question. To be sure, the armed forces remained segregated, various race riots (and even gun battles) took place on U.S. bases, and U.S. servicemen of color were often discriminated against and assaulted, sometimes even while in uniform.[45]

Although Myrdal's was the predominant voice in the 1940s' sociology of race, Stouffer et al.'s influence was also significant, especially since the latter's work appeared at roughly the same moment that the U.S. military was finally desegregating. Both studies departed from the conflict-oriented approach that had largely informed the sociology of race into the 1930s. Viewed in conjunction with other mainstream sociological work of the period (notably MacIver 1949), these works must be seen as definitively introducing an integration-oriented perspective on U.S. race relations into mainstream sociology.

While recognizing the gravity of segregation and racial prejudice, the structural-functionalist view of race consistently stressed the integrative qualities of U.S. society; thus the overlap of the two uses of the term *integration*—one that summarized the key civil rights demands of the era, and one that framed sociological explanations in terms of social unity and commonality—is more than a casual synecdoche. Deep-seated conflicts were not amenable to the structural-functionalist account; at most they could appear as "social problems" or be understood as having "latent" functions (Coser 1956) of an integrative sort. An understanding of race and racial injustice as foundational elements in U.S. society and culture (not to mention as world-historically significant issues) was not possible within this viewpoint, which thus tended to marginalize radical accounts such as those deriving from the DuBoisian tradition, anticolonialist and Pan-African thought, or Marxism.

Once properly reconceptualized as symptoms of the tensions inherent in societal self-regulation, however, racial matters could be understood as amenable to reform. Racial conflict received little attention in Talcott Par-

---

45. For additional commentary see Kryder (2000); for a valuable fictionalized account, see Killens (1963).

sons's early work, but after the appearance of *An American Dilemma* he began writing more about race. In the late 1940s, drawing on Allport and focusing largely upon microsociological phenomena, Parsons began thinking about prejudice as a problem of values (that is, white values). The edited work *Toward a General Theory of Action* (Parsons and Shils 1951) contains a substantial essay by Allport in which he takes this approach.[46] Parsons begins the essay "Full Citizenship for the Negro American? A Sociological Problem," written for *The Negro American* (Parsons and Clark 1967) at the height of the civil rights struggle, by arguing social-psychologically. He recognizes the values conflict that exclusion and the experience of white prejudice engender in blacks, echoing Myrdal's diagnosis of the "dilemma." A reform-oriented transition is under way, he suggests, in which inclusion is first advanced by legal action, then by politics, and finally by state-based guarantees of social citizenship and even redistribution of resources (Parsons and Clark 1967, 718). The informed reader must have struggled with this hypothesis even in 1967, notably with its underestimation of white resistance—from overt "backlash" politics on down to limited reform—that such a program would face, and indeed was already confronting "up North" as well as "down South."

Looking back on Parsons's account of race, what is most striking is his ungainly combination of sympathy ("moderate," to be sure) with the civil rights movement and his striking unfamiliarity with the nonwhite world. He manages some criticism of white prejudice and discrimination, but he depicts U.S. "race relations" as undergoing a steady progress toward inclusion of blacks, a condition he seemed to think was on the verge of accomplishment in 1966. A deeper interest in black life and thought, however, eludes him.[47]

Parsons's co-editor was the eminent black psychologist Kenneth B. Clark, whose work in *The Negro American* took a much less rosy view of U.S. racial politics of the mid-1960s.[48] That edited collection appeared roughly simultaneously with Clark's book *Dark Ghetto* (1965), in which he

46. This essay, "Prejudice: A Problem in Psychological and Social Causation," is an early version of Allport's *The Nature of Prejudice* (1954), a work that was to have a significant impact in social psychology.

47. This tendency contrasts sharply with that of Parsons's co-editor, Kenneth Clark, and the other black voices in the book (among them John Hope Franklin, Markin Kilson, St. Clair Drake, and even Whitney Young, director of the National Urban League).

48. See Clark's introduction to the volume, titled "The Dilemma of Power"; see also John Hope Franklin's chapter in the volume, titled "The Two Worlds of Race" (1967).

began to reassess what had been a lifelong commitment to integration.[49] Clark's analysis of black exclusion and white racism invoked the "internal colonialism" framework; his influential book anticipated Blauner's important radical analyses (1969, 1972) that extended and popularized the concept several years later. Clark had been the first tenured black professor at City College of New York, where he began teaching in 1942. He is perhaps best known for the influence his early work on internalized prejudice (the famous "doll experiments," carried out in collaboration with his wife, Mamie Phipps Clark) had on the Supreme Court's 1954 *Brown* decision. But his social psychological approach to racism and black identity, both collective and individual, has shaped thinking about racial "identity politics" more generally, right down to the present day. In rough parallel to DuBois's trajectory, Clark's early work envisioned racial progress as occurring through integration and the adoption of rational and democratic racial norms on the part of U.S. whites; with this lens we can see his affinities with the Myrdal model, as well as with Parsons's attempted systematization. But his doubts were already visible in the mid-1960s and became more pronounced throughout his vast later oeuvre. These led him to more radical— and in some respects more "nationalist"—positions as similar tendencies gained increasing traction in the black community.

At its apogee the structural-functionalist approach to race sought to meld (or incorporate) sociological thought into a different kind of nationalism—the mainstream, U.S. kind (Bell 1964; Gouldner 1970). Not long after sociology's embrace of civil rights came a new round of racial anomalies: above all, the Black Power revolt and its cousins, brown power, yellow power, and red power. In addition, race began to appear as a global issue, not just a U.S. domestic problem. Earlier sociological paradigms had recognized this better than the post–World War II approaches did: for all their limits, the biologistic approach had located race in the sphere of "development," and the Chicago pragmatists had seen its intimate connections with imperialism.

During the later 1960s, structural-functionalist sociology's heavy hitters encountered the limits of their double-edged integrationism. The larger panoply of post–World War II racial issues—the crisis of the old European empires, and the suppression during the 1940s and 1950s of radical (black and racially mixed) organizations opposing continuing colonialism in Africa,

---

49. *The Negro American* was initially a two-issue collection published in the journal *Daedalus*. It later went through several book-length editions.

the Caribbean, and Asia—exceeded racial moderates' framework: the paradigm could not grasp these conflicts for the deeply racialized issues that they were on their native soils in Africa, Asia, and Latin America but also as they were mirrored in movement activity at home.

Sociology's leading lights were cold warriors; they had taken up the civil rights banner at a time when segregation, lynching, and discrimination against racially defined minorities had become deep embarrassments for the United States. Did Parsons read Fanon or even DuBois? Did Merton consider the sociology of African development proposed by his onetime junior colleague Immanuel Wallerstein? Did Kingsley Davis—who wrote on population in South Asia, comparative urbanization, and the sociology of the family and reproduction in global perspective—ever address anticolonialism? According to Lipset at least (1994), these leading figures, and many others as well, came to sociology after youthful involvement with socialism and communism. No doubt they were nervous in the late 1940s and 1950s; this was quite logical: many of them were being watched.[50]

From the vantage point of the present, racial dynamics can be seen as deeply structuring all these issues. But during the 1950s and 1960s, racial issues appeared largely to be U.S. domestic problems. They were not to be confused with the battle against communism. Racial integration was supported, while the purges and witch-hunting that stigmatized and disemployed some of the field's most active advocates for racial justice were condoned, at least in part.[51] The major figures associated with the structural-

50. The scandalous McCarthyite harassment (and at one point, indictment) of the octogenarian DuBois in the 1950s occurred without notable protest from within the field. FBI surveillance extended to such mainstream figures as Samuel Stouffer, Herbert Blumer, Robert Bellah, Robert and Helen Lynd, E. Franklin Frazier, Alfred McClung Lee, and of course C. Wright Mills. Some leading sociologists, we know, cooperated with witch-hunters, most notably Pitirim Sorokin, but most remained cautious, at least through the late 1940s and 1950s (Keen 1999; Lipset 1994). Mass dismissals did occur on occasion, and surveillance was widespread (Slaughter 1980). Particular attention was paid to area studies, notably Russian and Chinese, but also to those of the insurgent "third world" (Simpson 1999; for parallels in anthropology, see Price 2004). A striking aspect of a great deal of this late 1940s–1950s academic repression and red-baiting was how much of it related to race. A major signal to the FBI, HUAC, and other similar agencies that a given scholar or teacher was ripe for purging, or at least needed watching, was that he or she participated in antiracist activities or attended mixed-race events. A certain cold war orthodoxy was mandatory; this in itself resulted in a muting of sociological criticism of U.S. racism. For larger treatments of the links between the cold war and the civil rights movement, see Dudziak (2000), Borstelmann (2003), and Kelley (1999).

51. The battles of the McCarthy period of course engulfed the black movement as well, as DuBois, Robeson, and others were reframed as pariah figures and racial "moderates" strove to distance themselves from them.

functionalist paradigm of race did not oppose the Vietnam War or consider its racial implications. King's 1967 denunciation of the war from the pulpit of New York's Riverside Church was condemned by such "moderate" sociologists of race as Daniel Moynihan, as it was by such "moderate" civil rights leaders as Roy Wilkins and Whitney Young. In the 1960s such figures as Milton Gordon and Nathan Glazer combined support for the "moderate" tendencies in the civil rights movement and rejection of "negative" discrimination (the exclusionary kind) with denunciation of "positive" discrimination (a.k.a. affirmative action).[52] Thus they prefigured or perhaps launched the neoconservative racial reaction and the "color-blind" resurgence of the post–civil rights era (Steinberg 1995).

Sure enough, racial radicalism did dismiss the significance of integration, both the movement kind and the functionalist kind. To the consternation of the racial "moderates" and structural functionalists, that radicalism, redolent of the 1930s, reappeared in the later 1960s. It posed a discomfiting question: how much integration—in both the sociological sense and the racial sense—was American society willing to deliver?

The elective affinity between movement-oriented racial reformism and the sociological critique of racial prejudice and discrimination was real but not permanent. Reformism made sense in the period before *Brown* and continued to represent a vital political current until the mid-1960s or so. The assimilationism advocated so unequivocally by Myrdal and the integrationism put forward by Parsons and Clark, however, were soon exceeded by the vast agenda that meaningful racial reform entailed. This point was made forcefully by the new wave of race riots beginning in Harlem in 1964, by the assassinations of Malcolm and Martin, by the resurgence of black nationalism and the Black Power revolt, and by the doomed U.S. defense of neocolonialism in Asia. Although Parsons, Merton, and other moderates tried valiantly to advocate an incrementalist and integrationist view of race and civil rights, by the later 1960s the reassertion of a conflict-oriented sociology of race (Ladner 1973) and the emergence of identity politics were the key problems confronting the sociology of race. Structural functionalism was ill equipped to face this challenge, though many of its key approaches would resurface again in the 1970s under the banner of neoconservatism.

52. In a later edited work, Glazer and Moynihan (1975) did try to address the comparative sociology of race (in their framework, "ethnicity"). By this time structural functionalism was effectively dead, though. Neoconservatism was emerging as its successor.

The Social Movement Paradigm
versus the Neoconservative Paradigm

By the later 1960s the civil rights paradigm had been ruptured in sociology, as it had in American politics. Views of race were divided between a *social movement paradigm* that criticized the civil rights reforms of the 1960s as inadequate and tokenistic, and a *neoconservative paradigm* that called for "color blindness" despite comprehensive and continuing racial stratification in U.S. society. All the standard sociological subjects were in play, and debated, between the two antagonistic positions, which we may once again label, in good sociologese, the "integrationist" versus "conflict-based" views. On the one hand, urban riots, radical antiracist movements, significant waves of state-sponsored racial repression, neocolonial foreign policy, and military intervention in the "third world," and deepening ghettoization and inequality at home, all seemed to negate the civil rights movement's accomplishments. On the other hand, overt racial prejudice seemed to be declining, U.S. imperial projects were losing ground both in the jungles of Southeast Asia and in the face of popular protest at home, and middle-class racially defined minorities, at least, were experiencing heightened mobility. By the 1970s, in a virtually unprecedented development, civil rights laws and practices were coming under fire from the political right as "reverse discrimination," and forceful claims were being made that the United States was entering a "postracial" era of "color blindness" and meritocracy.[53]

These contradictions were effectively captured in what was probably the most thorough survey of racial beliefs ever undertaken in U.S. sociology, Schuman et al.'s *Racial Attitudes in America* (1985/1997). This book remains notable for its recursive commitments: the authors relate their findings to historical trends informed by political conflict, cultural developments, and shifting concepts of identity; they also seek to distinguish between respondents' professed attitudes and their applied beliefs, their "attitudes in practice." This refinement of Merton's (1949b) distinction between prejudice and behavior expresses more than the frequently noted disconnect between

---

53. "My proposal for dealing with the racial issue in social welfare is to repeal every bit of legislation and reverse every court decision that in any way requires, recommends, or awards differential treatment according to race, and thereby put us back onto the track that we left in 1965. We may argue about the appropriate limits of government intervention in trying to enforce the ideal, but at least it should be possible to identify the ideal: Race is not a morally admissible reason for treating one person differently from another. Period" (Murray 1984, 223). See also Gilder (1981) and Sowell (1983).

expressed racial attitudes and underlying practice; pondering the effective socialization of their respondents to racial attitude research (in which research subjects conform to post–civil rights norms of tolerance), Schuman et al. question the methodological effectiveness and accuracy of racial attitude research itself.[54]

As organized American sociology ended its first century, a prolonged period of irresolution and paradigm conflict continued in the sociology of race. To grasp the unresolved state of the sociology of race at the turn of the twenty-first century is to consider race from a political sociological point of view. What has been the outcome of the racial reforms extracted by social movements from various regimes—both in the United States and globally—over the tumultuous post–World War II decades? In part as a consequence of the civil rights and antiapartheid campaigns, as well as anticolonialist and indigenous rights struggles, the sociology of race underwent a shift toward a new *social movements paradigm.*[55] This approach drew on neo-Marxist political economy, organization theory (resource mobilization and the like), and cultural studies to propose a political process approach to the sociology of race (McAdam 1982; Morris 1984; McAdam et al. 1996). Invoking postmodern concepts such as "contested racial meanings" and returning to pragmatist sociological ideas of "role taking," stigma, and DuBoisian "double consciousness" (Omi and Winant 1994; Winant 2001; Kelley 2003; Balibar and Wallerstein 1991; Hall 1980; Dawson 2001), the "new social movement" approach sought to understand the radicalization of the racial justice movements of the post–civil rights, postcolonial, and even post-apartheid (after 1994) period.

The movement influence (and movement critique) in these works was palpable. Notably, significant attention was devoted to intersectionality—the complex linkages among racial, gender-based, and class-oriented forms of domination and exploitation. Some examples: the prevalence and attitudes toward miscegenation and mixed-race identities were analyzed as indices of racial rule and resistance to racism, as well as instances of divergence and conflict among feminist, antiracist, and working-class movements

---

54. See Andrew Hacker's review (1988). The difficulties noted by Schuman et al. have led more recent researchers to develop methods for testing the depth and sincerity of professed racial attitudes. For example, Sniderman and Piazza (1993) directed their interviewers to argue with respondents about affirmative action so as to determine the degree of their commitment to their own beliefs.

55. Such allied movements as feminism, human rights, environmentalism, and gay liberation contributed to the shift as well.

(P. H. Collins 2004; Higginbotham 2001; Romero and Stewart 1999). Race and gender were studied as key determinations of labor regimes and citizenship structures in the United States (Glenn 2002).

At the same time, however, the partial but important effects of civil rights reform in palliating racial injustice, permitting some desegregation and upward mobility, and limiting if not eliminating racial discrimination in employment, education, immigration, and cultural production (and other areas as well) had tangible consequences for the sociology of race. Advancing arguments for a *neoconservative paradigm*, this current—also quite vast—analyzed U.S. racial dynamics in a manner that often seemed to suggest a structural-functionalist approach. Beginning with a largely policy-oriented body of work critiquing affirmative action and welfare policy (Glazer 1975; Murray 1984; Sleeper 1997; Patterson 1997; Thernstrom and Thernstrom 1997), neoconservatism developed, from about 1970, into a center-right political project with a growing mass base. Its centerpiece was the claim that, confronted by protest and by the civil rights movement's insistent reminders of American values—"I Have a Dream," for example— U.S. society had moved decisively though imperfectly toward racial integration and toward a mainstream, postracial ideology based on the idea of color blindness. Movement orientations were now anachronistic or worse: they advocated "reverse discrimination" and practiced victimology (McWhorter 2000). Drawing on long-standing black conservative traditions (some of them "nationalist" in their own right), on free market economics (of another "Chicago school," that of Friedman, Hayek, Becker, et al.), and claiming a post–civil rights orientation of their own, neoconservative writers made significant headway in the sociology of race.[56] By the later 1990s, neoconservatism had graduated from postracialism to postimperialism: its chief interests were the consolidation of a "new American empire."

Everything seemed uncertain in this emerging post–civil rights political and intellectual climate. Old problems once stressed by the pragmatists resurfaced: Park's linkage of race and empire, and Blumer's connection between prejudice and racial hierarchy, to pick just two. DuBois's Pan-Africanism reappeared as third worldism; Garveyism reappeared as Afrocentrism. Even debates on biologistic views of race returned: the neoconservative bible *The Bell Curve* (1994) received intense criticism from sociologists (Hauser 1995; Fischer et al. 1996; Fraser 1995) and in critical racially oriented sociologies of science, genomics, and health (Duster 1990,

---

56. For criticism of these positions in sociology, see Brown et al. (2003), Winant (1998), and Steinberg (1995).

2001; Nelkin and Tancredi 1989). Neoconservative assaults on affirmative action contended with spirited defenses and attempted reframings of such policies (Thernstrom and Thernstrom 1997; Massey et al. 2002; Kahlenberg 1996). Such leading figures in the field as William J. Wilson argued that race was "declining in significance" (Wilson 1978) and proposed a class-based (or class-reductionist) view of race. Wilson's attempt to reconcile the social movement paradigm (with its redistributionist core) and the neoconservative paradigm (with its blame-the-victim framework) necessarily cracked under the pressure. His position was grounded not in an argument that racial inequality was disappearing but in a strategic orientation he described as social democratic (Wilson 1999).[57] This view made too many concessions to the developing neoconservative consensus of official "color blindness." It tended to minimize the ongoing, and in some ways deepening (see Massey and Denton 1993), racial inequality that accompanied (and indeed was reinforced by) the neoconservative "color-blind" position.

So we are in a quandary, we sociologists of race: as the twenty-first century begins, we lack a dominant theoretical paradigm of race. Although this situation has all the characteristics of an interregnum, it is far from a peaceful one. If the neoconservative viewpoint continues to gain ground in the field, that can only be as a result of larger political developments: the evisceration of the welfare state with its attendant contempt for the poor and commitment to incarceration as a social policy, the reversion to empire now being urged vis-à-vis Islam and the Middle East,[58] or the rise in Latino population and influence, which stokes nativist impulses (Huntington 2004; Brimelow 1995) not unknown in sociology.

Speaking intuitively, however, and recalling the experience of attending recent annual meetings of the American Sociological Association, I find the prospect of a recrudescence of the racial right in the discipline of sociology unlikely. No matter how beset by uncertainties, the sociology of race remains movement oriented. This can be attributed to the deep influence of the postwar black movement. I have argued elsewhere that the racial upsurge in the United States was but one manifestation (albeit a very impor-

---

57. Wilson's views on this matter overlapped (somewhat ironically) with those of legal scholar Derrick Bell, a founder of the "critical race theory" school that greatly influenced (and was influenced by) radical sociologists of race. Bell's "convergence hypothesis" suggested that progress toward racial equality for blacks only occurred in U.S. society when the state policies designed to achieve it also and immediately benefited whites. See Bell (1992).

58. On the new imperialism see Gardner and Young (2002) and Kagan and Kristol (2000). For an overview of neocon positions, see Kristol (1999) and Gerson and Wilson (1996). On the racialization of Islam see Halliday (1999), Aidi (2003), and Lamont (2000).

tant one) of a global convergence of egalitarian and democratic currents in the sphere of race, a political rupture or break that was only contained with great difficulty over the latter decades of the twentieth century (Winant 2001). By no means has the influence of this break yet disappeared from the field of sociology.

But that racial upsurge was certainly contained, both as a global and domestic political force. It was incorporated in the United States and elsewhere in a range of "postracial" political hegemonies, of which U.S. "color blindness" is but one variant.[59] It has undoubtedly made some gains in sociology as well: not only on the right, where a "color-blind" view is upheld by more scholars than the Thernstroms, but also on the left, where an antiracist humanism that dismisses the utility of the race concept altogether is acquiring influence (Gilroy 2000). If a reversion to the sociological integrationism of Parsons et al. is not in the cards (under neoconservative auspices or any others), neither is a resurgence of the social movement–oriented racial radicalism of the Black Power (and brown power, yellow power, and red power) era.

Neoconservative claims that we have entered a postracial era are vitiated by the omnipresence of race consciousness and the continuities of structural racism: by almost every conceivable indicator researchers can bring forward, the same racial inequalities that existed in the past persist today, modified here and there perhaps but hardly eliminated and not even much reduced in scope, especially in terms of black–white disparities. This is not the place to inventory the data, but whether we look at wealth/income (in)equality, health, access to/returns to education, segregation by residence or occupation, rates of surveillance, punishment by the criminal "justice" system, or the many other indicators that compare racial "life chances," we find patterns strikingly similar to those of the past. The sorts of inclusionist reforms sought by Myrdal and the civil rights moderates who became neocons have simply not materialized.

Meanwhile the radical demands of the great antiracist movements of past decades have also been damaged by the cunning of history. Largely nationalist and class based, these positions come up short in an age of globalization and diaspora, when racially defined "peoplehood" is spread across the planet and hard to express (not to mention to organize) in traditional

---

59. Other examples are European "racial differentialism" (Taguieff 1988/2001), the postapartheid adaptation in South Africa of the African National Congress's "nonracialism" (Barnard and Farred 2004), and the reworking of Brazilian "racial democracy" to include limited commitments to "group rights" and affirmative action policies (Telles 2004).

nationalist terms. The decline of socialism, however prone to criticism the "actually existing socialist regimes" may have been, has hardly helped political programs calling for racial redistribution.[60]

So a full century after the American Sociological Society was founded, the quandary of race, the theme that claimed so much attention so long ago, stubbornly refuses to disappear. No new sociological paradigm of race has appeared in quite some time, as the field struggles—and the nation and the world struggle—with the ongoing racial crisis of the post–civil rights, post-apartheid, postcolonial era. The old has died, but the new cannot be born.

60. Affirmative action lives on in various settings: in India, South Africa, and Brazil, for example, as well as the United States, where it has suffered significant setbacks. It remains a small gesture in the direction of redistribution, however. Reparations demands are also still extant, sparking community meetings in U.S. ghettos and conferences on campus. They have also generated some high-profile lawsuits against major U.S. corporations charged with having profited from slavery. Reparations as a global issue was a much-discussed topic at the UN World Conference on Racism that took place in Durban, South Africa, in August 2001.

[SEVENTEEN] Pushing the Boundaries or Business as Usual? Race, Class, and Gender Studies and Sociological Inquiry

Patricia Hill Collins

At the 2003 annual meetings of American Sociological Association (ASA), I attended a session on future directions in race, gender, and class studies. I enjoyed the panel, yet I found it unnerving to hear once again the familiar clarion call to sociologists to "do" race, class, and gender studies. Unlike the 1980s, when scholars who wished to synthesize the separate fields of race, class, and gender searched for one another inside and outside sociology, or the 1990s, when academics across many disciplines claimed variations of the phrase "race, class, and gender" as a new hot topic, by 2003 sociologists were already "doing" race, class, and gender studies. During its first two decades, the field of race, class, and gender studies had carved out an established niche within sociology, and by the 2003 ASA meeting the field seemed to be doing fine.

The speed with which the phrase has caught on appears unprecedented. For example, in 2004, a search of scholarly journals and popular press turned up hundreds of hits where authors had invoked variations of the phrase "race, class, and gender" in their titles, abstracts, and texts. The diversity of venues that are publishing scholarship on the topic of race, class, and gender is truly staggering. Between 2002 and 2004, journals as diverse as the *American Journal of Public Health,* the *Columbia Journal of Gender and the Law,* the *Journal of Social History, Latino Studies,* the *Journal of American History,* the *British Journal of Social Work,* and the *American Bankruptcy Law Journal* all included articles that invoked this phrase.

Similar enthusiasm seemingly permeates American sociology. There too, journals such as the *Sociology of Religion,* the *Social Science Quarterly,* and the *American Sociological Review* have all published articles with race, class, and gender in their titles. Undergraduate college courses in this area have grown rapidly (Weber 1998, 14). For example, so many colleges have continued to adopt *Race, Class, and Gender: An Anthology* after its initial publication in 1992 that a sixth edition is scheduled for 2006 (Andersen and Collins 2004). Other signs of rapid institutionalization have occurred within sociology. By 1996, adherents of race, class, and gender studies within the ASA had garnered the two hundred dues-paying members needed to launch a Race, Class, and Gender section.[1] The subdiscipline's institutional visibility within graduate education in sociology has also increased. For example, a survey of 211 graduate sociology programs listed in the 2003 ASA *Guide to Graduate Programs* found that 54 programs classified themselves as specializing in race, class, and gender, 30 programs classified themselves as offering a specialization in stratification, and 8 programs self-reported that they specialized in both areas.[2]

When a new, interdisciplinary area grows this rapidly across fields as diverse as history, literature, cultural studies, psychology, and sociology, it spills out in many directions at once, attracting converts and opportunists alike.[3] Within American sociology, for example, despite graduate program reports of specialties in race, class, and gender studies, far fewer programs had faculty members who listed race, class, and gender as an area of specialization in their own research. The phrase "race, class, and gender" may appear as a marketing tool for graduate programs in sociology, yet few programs that claim this specialty offer graduate courses with this title. Programs may offer courses on race *or* class *or* gender and leave the impression that adding these separate components together, or incorporating them within prevailing understandings of social stratification, yields a race, class, and gender framework.

Because the broader, interdisciplinary field of race, class, and gender studies is so new and has grown so rapidly, it encompasses many constituencies and agendas. At this point, it may be prudent for sociologists to stop and ask some tough questions. Within sociology, a discipline whose

1. The Race, Class, and Gender section also launched a journal and sponsored several national conferences. As the main professional association of American sociology, ASA embodies the institutionalized image of the discipline. Mapping the ebb and flow of subspecialties within ASA constitutes one way of mapping intellectual trends within sociology. For a discussion of this process within ASA, see Daipha (2001).

2. I am indebted to Tamika Odum for research on this topic.

3. This essay uses a taxonomy of subdisciplinary specialties, interdisciplinary fields, transdisciplinary fields, and supradisciplinary syntheses to map race, class, and gender studies (Levine 1995, 292). Within this framework, I distinguish between the more narrow sociological specialization of race, class, and gender studies (as evidenced by the formation of a section) and the broader interdisciplinary/transdisciplinary area of race, class, and gender studies that encompasses many different academic disciplines. Moreover, while related, interdisciplinarity and transdisciplinarity are not interchangeable. Interdisciplinarity typically encompasses strategies of border crossing and cross-disciplinary collaboration. In contrast, transdisciplinarity implies some core principles that characterize a new field, within Levine's schema, the presence of supradisciplinary syntheses. For a discussion of transdisciplinarity, see Horlick-Jones and Sime (2004).

practitioners have been in the forefront of race, class, and gender scholarship, the issue may be less one of convincing sociologists to do race, class, and gender studies than of specifying what constitutes race, class, and gender studies within the historical, intellectual, and professional context of American sociology. Since its inception, the broader field of race, class, and gender studies has challenged its practitioners to push the boundaries of established knowledge and to eschew doing business as usual. Yet the initial stance of critique that generated such apparent scholarly enthusiasm now confronts the issue of what constitutes business as usual *within* this interdisciplinary field. The concern is especially important for sociology, a discipline with a recognized specialization in race, class, and gender studies. In what ways, if any, is the sociological subdiscipline of race, class, and gender studies developing the analytical strategies, interpretive paradigms, and core principles that advance the larger endeavor of race, class, and gender studies? Does this specialization push the boundaries of sociological inquiry or is it simply stratification in drag?

The theme of boundary making constitutes an important challenge both for the sociological specialization of race, class, and gender studies as well as for the broader interdisciplinary field in which it also participates. Boundary making is an important component of the power relations that catalyze academic disciplines, including sociology, as well as sociological knowledge itself. A fluid process of boundary making in social and symbolic space shapes the contours of race, class, and gender studies both within and outside sociology.[4] Negotiating boundaries constitutes a major challenge for the field of race, class, and gender studies—not to seal the borders from interlopers but rather to ensure safe passage across them. In

4. Lamont and Molnár distinguish between social and symbolic boundaries. They define social boundaries as "objectified forms of social differences manifested in unequal access to and unequal distribution of resources (material and nonmaterial) and social opportunities" (Lamont and Molnár 2002, 168). Within this definition, race, class, and gender as social categories produce social groups with histories of unequal access to resources and opportunities, including the ability to become the professional sociologists who legitimate the very categories of race, class, and gender. In contrast, symbolic boundaries are "conceptual distinctions made by social actors to categorize objects, people, practices, and even time and space. They are tools by which individuals and groups struggle over and come to agree upon definitions of reality" (Lamont and Molnár 2002, 168). Lamont and Molnár present symbolic and social boundaries as recursive and interactive rather than categorical and static. They note that "only when symbolic boundaries are widely agreed upon can they take on a constraining character and pattern social interaction in important ways . . . only then can they become social boundaries" (168–69). In the argument presented here, I explore how the sociological subdiscipline of race, class, and gender studies unfolds in both social and symbolic space and how the process of boundary construction and boundary contestation is central to this process.

essence, how can race, class, and gender studies define its own boundaries in a meaningful fashion when a large part of its very reason for being *is* to challenge the whole notion of existing boundaries?

American sociology provides a useful social location for exploring some major challenges that frame boundary making for race, class, and gender studies. First, sociology, itself a border discipline, has long contained dual aspirations of being both a positivistic and an interpretive social science. One sees constant renegotiation within the discipline between its positivistic and interpretive tendencies, often in response to social issues that lie outside its boundaries. Second, sociology encompasses and influences its own object of study. Because social relations of race, class, and gender within American society shape and are shaped by sociological practices, more so than in other disciplines, sociology must come to terms with its own recursive relationship with the dynamics of race, class, and gender within American society. Third, American sociology has identifiable subdisciplines of class and race, and has implicitly contained an analysis of gender within the subdiscipline of family studies. Because the broader interdisciplinary field of race, class, and gender studies implies new social and symbolic relationships among academic disciplines, sociology's efforts to synthesize its own subspecialties of race, class, and gender constitutes a microcosm of this larger, interdisciplinary project. Finally, sociology's long-standing efforts to negotiate the relationships among its own micro-, meso-, and macrotraditions may shed light on the type of interdisciplinary work required across levels of social analysis within race, class, and gender studies.[5]

The Logic of Segregation and the Sociological Study of Class, Race, and Gender

During its hundred-year history, in response to social conditions within American society, American sociology has studied race, class, and gender differently. In particular, sociological practices during its formative years in the early twentieth century, the installation of functionalism in the 1940s and 1950s, the disruption of sociological business as usual in the 1960s and 1970s, as well as the subsequent emergence of a sociological specialization

---

5. Within sociology, one can find micro-, meso-, and macrolevels of analysis that roughly parallel corresponding disciplines of psychology, literature, and history (micro); anthropology, social psychology, racial/ethnic studies, and some versions of cultural studies (meso); and political science, economics, and law (macro). Here I make broad comparisons. Whereas all the disciplines may have all three levels of analysis within them, each typically emphasizes one more so than the others. For example, law relies on narrative testimony, the microlevel, yet its primary focus lies on macrolevel processes of the legal system itself.

in race, class, and gender studies from the 1980s to the present all constitute key moments in how race, class, and gender were conceptualized and studied. During all of these periods, different versions of a logic of segregation shaped all aspects of American society, including American sociology. Reviewing how the logic of segregation affected early modern sociological practices as well as tracing how American sociology of the 1940s and 1950s studied class, race, and gender as separate (segregated) areas provides a context for understanding the emergence of contemporary race, class, and gender studies as a critique of these earlier practices.

By the time of ASA's founding in 1905, it was apparent that the United States was undergoing a period of unprecedented change that involved the marking of multiple social and symbolic boundaries. Installing and then following a pervasive logic of segregation, the makers of social policies set out to classify, rank, and foster differential treatment of places and peoples, specifically, neighborhoods, colonies, and nations as well as social groups formed using criteria of nation, class, race, gender, and sexuality. Taking a lead from European colonial powers, the United States entered an imperialistic period, supporting policies that continued the process of divvying up the globe into nation-states and colonies and its own population into groups of first- and second-class citizens. The expansion of big business and industrialization fostered massive immigration and the growth of a ghettoized ethnic, working-class, urban population. In 1896 the Supreme Court handed down *Plessy v. Ferguson*, the landmark decision that codified the separate but equal doctrine as the linchpin of racial segregation and crystallized a racial formation that led William E. B. DuBois to claim that the "problem of the twentieth century would be the color line." Within the broader relations of class and race, women were further segregated by gender: they were confined to the private sphere of home and family, where supposedly they were protected by a "man of the house," who earned a "family wage." The same logic of segregation supported binary categories that increasingly defined so-called normal sexuality and marked the emergence of homosexuality as a new and stigmatized identity. Despite the massive changes at the turn of the century, or perhaps because of them, the logic of segregation framed social relations of nation, class, race, gender, and sexuality, which in turn helped foster a sense of order within these rapidly changing social relations.[6]

6. This highly abbreviated history links a vast literature on nation, class, race, gender, and sexuality, respectively. For a theoretical analysis on intersections among these concepts, see P. Collins (2001). For scholarship on this period that engages in the intersectional analysis suggested here, see McClintock (1995), Somerville (2000), and Bederman (1995). None of these au-

Expressing a dual impetus to study modernity via interpretive and positivistic means, American sociologists participated in, reproduced, and challenged this overarching logic of segregation. As a concept that shapes not only social boundaries of class, race, and gender within American society and American sociology, but also the symbolic boundaries of knowledge about these concepts, this core logic of segregation has several distinguishing features.[7] First, within the logic of segregation, everything has *one* place, places have meaning only in relation to one another, and every place has its rank. Thus, the logic of segregation is essential in constructing social hierarchies of class, race, and gender. Second, social practices involuntarily assign individuals to segregated spaces. Working-class men, women, and African Americans may appear to go willingly to their assigned places, especially when hegemonic ideologies naturalize these identities. On a societal level, however, individuals inherit specific social positions and must grapple with the positive and/or negative attributes associated with their assigned places. Third, the logic of segregation relies on essentialism, a set of ideas that assumes that people who share assigned social classifications also share some basic attributes. For those in privileged spaces, essentialist thinking fosters and rewards homogeneity. On the basis of the belief that equates elitism and exclusivity with excellence, people who seemingly pollute the sameness of privileged spaces are routinely barred from the "best neighborhoods," the "best schools," the "best jobs," and the "best sociology programs." Finally, maintaining segregated spaces requires boundary maintenance. To distribute social goods, one needs to know who truly belongs to the category at hand and who is an interloper. Thus, relations of inclusion and exclusion become vital to defining the segregated spaces.

On one level, at its inception American sociology was uniquely positioned to grapple with the forms that the logic of segregation took because its very reason for being was to uncover and study the rules of social structure that were invisible in everyday social interaction. The logic of segregation that framed class and race and gender relations was one such rule. Within a society that was preoccupied with the class conflict and urbaniza-

---

thors is a sociologist, a fact that supports a claim that historians, literary critics, and scholars in the humanities often find it easier to develop intersectional analyses.

7. Here I rely heavily on Michel Foucault's discussion of the panoptical discipline to develop this argument concerning segregated space (Foucault 1979). For the links between segregated space and segregated knowledge, I draw from Foucault's seminal work on knowledge/power relations (Foucault 1980). The concept of essentialism also encapsulates this process of assigning one meaning to people, ideas, and social space that is categorized in this fashion (Fuss 1989).

tion of industrial capitalism, social structures of race that grappled with the legacy of American chattel slavery, and the problem of unmarried working women, sociologists could observe how the logic of segregation organized American social structures of class, race, and gender. On another level, because these very same relations of race, gender, and class segregation created and institutionalized sociology, it simultaneously incorporated these very same assumptions concerning the logic of segregation into its characteristic modes of sociological practice and producing knowledge.[8]

Take, for example, how the distinguishing features of this logic of segregation affected the symbolic organization of American sociology itself. First, within the logic of segregation, the impetus is to classify ideas in *one* predetermined category (usually a theory). Ideas thus have meaning only in relation to a ranked symbolic order (demography gains stature in relation to the populist sensibilities of the sociology of education). Moreover, some ideas garner social rewards, whereas others are stigmatized (demographic research garners a higher salary than teaching sociology of education at a community college). Within this logic, entire specializations can gain stature or fall from grace, depending on their classification within symbolic hierarchies of knowledge. Second, involuntarily classifying holistic ideas to segregated spaces can compromise their worth because the classification process itself requires reducing ideas to their seemingly essential attributes. Third, the logic of segregation that fosters and rewards homogeneity within privileged space makes it difficult to conceptualize excellence in terms other than elitist. Using a reputational method of citation, sociologists are encouraged to cite the classics in a field and thus uncritically perpetuate the guiding assumptions of an area. The more elite the area, the more homogeneous it becomes, and the more difficult it becomes to introduce ideas that lie outside its borders. Finally, segregated spaces require maintaining social and symbolic boundaries. Under the logic of segregation, admissions committees, editorial review boards, tenure requirements, letters of recommendation, and similar gatekeeping mechanisms maintain social boundaries that exclude people and ideas that seem to fall too far outside sociological norms. As a result, the ideas that are included reflect a homogeneity that remains hegemonic if unchallenged by sociological insiders. Overall, in its quest to establish the social and symbolic boundaries as a bona fide science

8. Scholars of science point out how the logic of science, namely, a belief in classification, objectivity, and empiricism, resembled these social relations of this logic of segregation. In essence, the norms of the logic of segregation are remarkably similar to the norms of normal science. See, for example, Sandra Harding's analysis of scientific norms as well as my own discussion of these issues (Harding 1986; P. Collins 1998, 95–123).

of society, American sociology's adherence to norms of classification, separation, and ranking may have limited its ability to see how the logic of segregation influenced its own professional identity.

The Separate Study of Race, Class, and Gender: The Logic of Segregation and Sociological Subdisciplines of the 1940s and 1950s

Throughout most of American sociology's history, exclusionary practices associated with the logic of segregation ensured that African Americans, working-class and/or poor people, and women were largely excluded from the profession of sociology (Blackwell and Janowitz 1974; Deegan 1991; P. Collins 1998, 95–123). Denied opportunities as professional sociologists, individuals from these groups did not participate in any significant fashion in shaping what would count as sociological knowledge. Each group seemingly belonged to one ranked place, and for the most part that place was not in American sociology.

These exclusionary practices associated with the logic of segregation meant that a homogeneous group of individuals shaped all sociological knowledge, including each distinctive sociological specialization of class *or* race *or* gender under consideration here. These subdisciplines developed as discreet areas that typically paid scant attention to one another. As a result, this logic of segregation simultaneously specified the social and symbolic boundaries of the separate sociological subdisciplines of class or race or gender but also limited their ability to grapple with questions that might concern them all. If the study of marriage and the family was "covering" women, why should the subfield of race and ethnicity concern itself with gender? If race and ethnic studies specialized in African Americans, why include race in either functionalist studies of labor markets or Marxist critiques of them? If class analysis focused on jobs and labor markets, why would the study of marriage and the family concern itself with topics so far outside its symbolic borders?

Briefly summarizing American sociology's approach to the study of class or race or gender in the 1940s and 1950s not only illuminates how the logic of segregation operated; it also illuminates some catalysts for the emergence of race, class, and gender studies in the 1980s and 1990s. Each sociological subdiscipline of class, race, and family (gender) had a distinctive yet similar history. Social class claimed the lion's share of attention. Given the prominence of class stratification within American sociology, the trajectories that the two main macrosociological perspectives on class have taken remain vitally important to contemporary sociology. Despite a plethora of terms applied to the two main perspectives, functionalist (consensus) and Marxist (conflict) approaches to social class influence how contemporary sociologists conceptualize not just social stratification but social structure itself.

When Talcott Parsons published his classic piece in 1940 on the theory of social stratification, he advanced a functional theory that not only sought rules for social phenomena; it also represented how the logic of segregation affected mainstream sociology (Parsons 1940). For a scholar of Parsons's background and from his social location at Harvard University, a science of society meant developing a science of segregation. Within this logic of segregated space, Parsons presents two spheres of class analysis, one of achievement and the other of kinship. Foreshadowing the gendered public and private spheres of social organization (and civic and ethnic nationalism for that matter), Parsons confines his analysis to the realm of individual achievement. He then identifies the main sphere of class analysis:

> In our own society, apart from hereditary groups at the top in certain sections of the country, the main criteria of class status are to be found in the occupational achievements of men, the normal case being the married man with immature children. Authority is significant partly as a necessary means of carrying on occupational functions, but in turn the authority exercised is one of the main criteria of the prestige of occupational status. Authority, especially that of office, is again important as a reward for past achievements. (Parsons 1940, 856)

Parsons was not using the word *men* metaphorically—he meant actual men. Here women lacked individuality—"family" as a concept excises women from the basic sociological vocabulary of authority, occupations, status, and achievement. Naturalized by assumptions concerning their biology, women stood outside society, happy to care for home and hearth. Parsons also eliminates another unstated "hereditary group" from this model of social stratification. Blacks become by default a racialized hereditary group whose experiences remained as much outside class analysis as did those of the hereditary group of elite white males who did not follow society's rules but rather established them. With women, African Americans, and elite families outside the symbolic boundaries of class analysis, those white men who remained not only inherited by default the individuality that enabled them to enter the public sphere as citizens but they became the archetypal subjects of sociological analysis. Within functionalist logic, social class became the purview of white men, with occupational achievement elevated as one core dimension of social structure. Moreover, defining social class in this fashion as seminal for social stratification simultaneously elevated class to the level of macrosociological analysis and rendered race, gender, ethnicity, sexuality, age, ability, and similar forms of structural inequality as derivative of this most fundamental system.

Functionalist analyses interpreted racial segregation not as a social problem but rather as part of the normal workings of societies. By specifying the implied connections among individual achievement, white men as the basic unit of social class analysis, and social stratification itself, sociologists Kingsley Davis and Wilbert Moore (1944) took this assumption one step further. Not only was this version of social class the way society worked, but this particular organization was *functional* to the smooth workings of society. In a section titled "The Functional Necessity of Stratification," they argue that "as a functioning mechanism a society must somehow distribute its members in social positions and induce them to perform the duties of these positions. It must thus concern itself with motivation at two different levels: to instill in the proper individuals the desire to fill certain positions, and, once in these positions, the desire to perform the duties attached to them" (Davis and Moore 1944, 242). Keep in mind that denying individuality to women and African Americans excluded them from this achievement process. The very wealthy also fell outside of functionalist analysis—apparently they could remain unmotivated to fill positions and escape duties altogether. In a tautological tour de force, Davis and Moore also defend the necessity of social inequality for the smooth functioning of society: "If the rights and perquisites of different positions in a society must be unequal, then the society must be stratified, because that is precisely what stratification means. Social inequality is thus an unconsciously evolved device by which societies insure that the most important positions are conscientiously filled by the most qualified persons" (243). When combined, the functionalist theories of Parson, Davis and Moore, and others legitimated the existing social inequalities of class, race, and gender within American society, which granted them careers as professional sociologists. Moreover, drawing symbolic boundaries around class analysis in this fashion left the social mobility of white men as the focus of social stratification research.

Marxist social theory, a second macrosociological theory of class, challenged the individualistic assumptions of functionalism as well as its seemingly uncritical endorsement of capitalism. In contrast to the functionalist achievement model, Marxist social theory argued that wealth and power created social groups that were locked in antagonistic relationships with one another. The working class and the capitalist class had opposing interests. Yet by focusing on the site of production as the penultimate place of class analysis, Marxist sociology also excluded the concerns of women and African Americans from analysis and/or treated their concerns as derivative of much larger issues. Although an improvement on functionalism, Marxist social theory still relegated race and gender to a secondary and often derivative status in relation to class. Moreover, like its functionalist counterpart, it failed to challenge the macrosociological assumptions shared by both that installed white men at the center of sociological inquiry. Unlike functionalism, Marxist sociology faced an inhospitable political context. In the social context of the 1950s, fears of communism that reflected the constraints of cold war politics limited the ability of Marxist sociology to challenge functionalist stratification models. Mainstream American sociology effectively distanced itself from Marxist social class analysis.[9]

The subdiscipline of race (and ethnic) studies within American sociology reflected this same logic of segregation, yet with emphasis on studying race on the mesolevel of group culture. Drawing on Robert Park's race relations paradigm of competition, conflict, accommodation, and assimilation, sociological studies of race and ethnicity typically assumed that white ethnic groups could assimilate and wondered whether African Americans ever could. By defining African Americans as a biologically distinct hereditary group, sociologists seemed to be saying that their study required distinctive rules.

E. Franklin Frazier, Oliver Cromwell Cox, and other African American scholars who worked as professional sociologists in the 1940s and 1950s challenged prevailing functionalist paradigms regarding race. They identified institutionalized racism as a core yet neglected principle of sociological analysis. Such scholars saw class, race, and culture as tightly bundled entities, but not in the ways advanced by either functionalist or Marxist class analyses. Instead, they argued for more attention to issues of political economy, specifically, how racial discrimination shaped the social class outcomes and subsequent behavior (culture) within African American society. Cox in particular echoed William E. B. DuBois's earlier global frameworks and, by linking race, class, and caste in a global context, advanced a structural analysis of racism (Hunter and Abraham 1987). In essence, by pointing to structural barriers as a compelling explanation for racial disadvantage and conflict theory as useful in explaining how changes were actually

9. In this climate, African American sociologist Oliver Cromwell Cox's work on race and world systems theory constitutes an especially important achievement (Hunter and Abraham 1987).

occurring, they drew on macrosociological theories of class to criticize the limitations of mesosociological perspectives on race. Yet because common-sense assumptions about the alleged deviancy of African American culture remained so deeply entrenched within American society, African American sociologists of this period focused on mesolevel questions of African American culture (see, e.g., Frazier 1948). Moreover, because African American men constituted the vast majority of such scholars, they failed to challenge the sexist assumptions in their own scholarship, for example, the wide-spread tendency to associate the status of people of African descent as a group with the welfare of African American men.

When compared to race, the sociological study of gender had a similar yet distinctive history. For one, like race, gender lacked the status of an ex-planatory category of macrosociological analysis and was even more likely than race to be defined as an essentialist, natural, biological attribute. Treat-ing gender, and by implication, sexuality, as a case of biological difference confined the study of gender and sexuality to the level of microsociological analysis. It also gave plausibility to the notion of sex roles, Talcott Parsons's perceptions of the allegedly natural differences between the sexes. These differences suggested that society consisted of instrumental and expressive functions for men and women that were foundational to the division of so-ciety into roles of paid labor for men in occupations and unpaid domestic-ity for women within the family. Within this deployment of the logic of segregation, the experiences of adult women were best analyzed primarily within the internal affairs of the family—as wives, mothers, and managers of the household (Ferree, Khan, and Morimoto, chap. 13, this volume). This naturalization of gender had grave consequences for women because com-partmentalizing gender into two mutually exclusive categories and relegat-ing women to the inferior sphere made it virtually impossible to raise is-sues of women's oppression or even to look at gender itself as socially constructed. Within sociology, it was widely accepted that African Ameri-cans as a group occupied an inferior position in American society. De-bates around race pivoted on the causes of and potential remedies for this accepted social fact. In contrast, few sociologists thought to challenge the gender hierarchy that relegated women to family and treated women's in-terests as coterminous with policies that strengthened families. Women re-mained an unaffiliated constellation of individuals and certainly not a so-cial group with shared interests in a system of gender inequality.

This brief genealogy of the study of class, race, and gender as separate subdisciplines within American sociology in the 1940s and 1950s suggests that because the practitioners associated with stratification/class or race or gender routinely worked within social conditions of segregation, their scholarship reflected this logic of segregation. Moreover, this same logic further compartmentalized these subdisciplines so that they focused on macro-, meso-, and microlevels of analysis respectively. Thus, stratification/class became the purview of white men, and its main emphasis on macrosociological processes as well as on categories of work and occupations reflects the widespread tendency to equate white male experiences with society overall. As for race and ethnicity, because so few African American female sociologists entered the field, dialogues about race fell mainly to a short list of African American men, who debated their white male counterparts. Preoccupied with mesolevel questions of culture, this group stressed concepts of assimilation drawn from the experiences of white ethnic groups. As for gender, white women found themselves either contained within the so-called helping profession of social work and/or relegated to their so-called natural sphere—the subdiscipline of family studies. Preoccupied with the microlevel of interpersonal family dynamics and fraught with essentialist ideas about women's nature, gender analysis remained contained by the language of social psychology and individual social interaction. Overall, the effect of the logic of segregation on each subdiscipline lay in its emphasis on different levels of social structure as well as its inability to consider the ways in which other subdisciplines might be germane to its own functioning.

The Transitional Period: The 1960s and 1970s

In the 1960s and 1970s, social movements by African Americans, Latinos, women, and lesbian, gay, bisexual, and transgendered (LGBT) people catalyzed important changes in the legal climate in the United States. In a span of less than twenty-five years, legal reforms set the stage for the erosion of a wide array of mechanisms that buttressed a segregated American society. After the 1954 *Brown v. Board of Education* Supreme Court decision that banned racially segregated public schools, a series of laws in the decades that followed dismantled the legal edifice of segregation. For example, the Civil Rights Act of 1964 prohibited discrimination based on race, color, religion, sex, age, ethnicity, or national origin, and the Fair Housing Law of 1968 prohibited discrimination against people seeking housing. The Voting Rights Act of 1965 outlawed local discriminatory practices against African American voters and was amended in 1975 and 1982 to include linguistic minorities. The Immigration Act of 1965 removed barriers to immigration for people from primarily nonwhite nations. The 1967 *Loving v. Virginia* Supreme Court decision removed all legal barriers to interracial marriage.

In 2003, in *Lawrence and Garner v. Texas*, the Supreme Court struck down an antisodomy law that made it illegal to impose different standards of sexual conduct on same-sex partners as opposed to different-sex partners, in effect ruling that privacy laws applied to the sexual practices of LGBT people. Collectively, this new legal infrastructure provided a legal context for challenging a deep-seated logic of segregation that shaped virtually every American social institution. Rigid boundaries that had historically confined African Americans, women, Latinos, poor people, and native peoples to specific jobs, schools, and neighborhoods gave way to new rules governing social interaction. Ideally, a new logic of desegregation that would dismantle segregated schools, jobs, neighborhoods, and other social institutions would eliminate the deep-seated logic of segregation.

The social movements of the 1950s and the 1960s not only challenged the logic of segregation within American social institutions but also revealed how this same logic compromised sociological knowledge. For example, American sociology's insularity apparently blinded it to the rumblings of African American unrest that exploded into sit-ins, marches, protest rallies, and urban upheavals. When, in the 1950s, African Americans turned their backs on accommodation and engaged in widespread social protest, sociologists were caught off guard. Even Marxist social theory, which understood how social conflict catalyzed social change, failed to see how African Americans might use social institutions such as families, churches, neighborhoods, and community organization not as conduits of biological and cultural debasement but rather as sites of political organization. Moreover, the absence of a gendered analysis in both Marxist social theory and the sociological subdiscipline that studied race rendered African American women's political activism especially invisible. By the 1960s, it was apparent that sociologists of race relations had misunderstood their own object of study. As James McKee points out, "the sociologists of race relations had not simply failed to predict a specific event; rather, they had grievously misread a significant historical development. The race relations that appeared in their writings were incongruent with the race relations to be found in the society around them" (McKee 1993, 2). The limitations of the study of race in explaining African American and Latino activism, the persistence of disparate racial effects that could not be explained by attitudes, and the shift from a melting pot theory of society toward cultural pluralism and multiculturalism all raised doubts about the ability of traditional approaches to race in explaining contemporary social phenomena.

The women's movement of the 1960s and 1970s pointed out major problems in the sociological study of gender. Large numbers of obviously dissatisfied middle-class white wives and daughters refused to accept their secondary status. Instead, they argued that the types of structural forces that oppressed African Americans as a hereditary group oppressed women in a similar fashion. For example, within the women's movement, middle-class white women, African American women, and Chicanas advanced distinctive arguments that collectively challenged basic assumptions about the family (Roth 2004). In this case, neither social stratification/class analysis nor sociological approaches to race and ethnicity could explain women's anger and activism. Within the logic of segregation, defining *public* sphere activities as being both more important for society and thus the privileged site of macrosociological analysis ranked private sphere family activities as a secondary concern. This emphasis left no space for critical studies of women's labor force participation, domestic violence, sexual harassment, reproductive rights concerns, inequitable social welfare policies, discriminatory treatment in science classrooms, and other contemporary women's issues.

The increasing percentages of women in American sociology in the 1960s and 1970s challenged historical patterns of exclusion within the field, opening the door to an upsurge in gender scholarship. Women's increasing participation in sociology raised a simple yet profoundly complex question—how could sociological knowledge have much validity if it omitted the experiences of half of the human population? This question catalyzed a rethinking of sociological concepts, paradigms, and theories as well as sociological practices as a science of society. For example, the limitations of the functionalist construct of sex roles developed under the logic of segregation became readily apparent. Redefining gender as a category of analysis with explanatory power created visibility for a new subdiscipline within sociology. Unlike class and race, the study of gender had to struggle for the right to be a valid area of sociological inquiry.

By the 1960s and 1970s, it became increasingly apparent that the sociological subdisciplines of class or race or gender of the 1940s and 1950s could not explain the social conditions that surrounded them. The core assumptions of each specialization as well as their essentialized perceptions of African Americans and other people of color, of women, and of poor people limited their capacity to understand the social movement politics of these groups. In particular, reflecting the essentialist logic of segregation, African American men became symbolic representatives of race whereas white women became symbolic representatives of gender. Black women had both race and gender but rarely at the same time. In contrast, white men avoided this race and gender essentialism—they ostensibly had neither race nor gender all of the time.

These assumptions had a deep-seated effect on the sociological study of class, race, or gender not only in the 1940s and 1950s but also throughout the transitional period of the 1960s and 1970s. For example, when they appeared at all, the subdisciplines of race and gender often depicted African American women as extreme examples of how a given trend affected the allegedly normative group. Within gender studies, functionalist sociologists could use African American women's problem-ridden experiences as single mothers to highlight white women's positive family experiences. Feminist critics of mainstream family values could invoke the same family research to illustrate how bad things really were for women; for example, things were bad for white women, but they were especially odious for African American single mothers. Within studies of race, sociologists could claim that racism may have harmed African American men. Ironically, the special burdens that racism imposed on African American women due to gender could then be reinserted into existing racial paradigms, for example, the well-known matriarchy thesis, to focus on how African American women's work and family experiences created their own special burden for African American men. This moving target of race and gender that was applied to African American women often erased alternative explanations of their ideas and experiences. Yet, at the same time, discounting the workings of race and gender in the lives of white men enabled mainstream sociologists to emphasize the significance of social class. By default, social class became the purview of white men, with questions of social class stasis and conflict, upward social class mobility, and the rationality of market relations deemed to be far more important issues within sociological analysis that the seeming special interests of less important groups.

Despite challenges to the logic of segregation in the 1960s and 1970s, the beliefs and social practices that accompanied it did not disappear overnight. Upending Jim Crow laws and the legal infrastructures of other forms segregation did not mean that social inequalities of race, class, and gender disappeared. By the 1980s, four new trends became increasingly evident. First, segregation persisted in many areas of American society. Racial segregation of African Americans in neighborhoods and jobs, the persisting gap between the numbers of men and women choosing careers in math and science, and the increased difficulties faced by poor and working-class youth in attaining college educations all pointed to the persistence of various forms of segregation in housing, jobs, and schooling. Second, social hierarchies based on exclusions and rankings became supplemented by a parallel set of mechanisms for reproducing social inequalities within ostensibly integrated spaces. Inequalities of race, class, and gender were increasingly maintained *both* by exclusionary practices of segregation *and* by a panoply of seemingly benign practices that included historically oppressed groups in schools and the workplace yet marginalized them.[10] Third, because the old markers of race and gender no longer gave clear signals as to who belonged, strategies of boundary maintenance grew in significance. One could no longer assume that one's doctor would be a white man and one's cleaning lady would be a woman of color. With race and gender no longer so tightly mapped onto social class relations, broader and fuzzier border zones replaced the either/or dichotomies that upheld the segregated practices of the past. Finally and most strikingly, new laws and customs discredited the logic of segregation, with desegregated, multicultural spaces installed as the new model for American social organization. An ethos of color blindness and gender neutrality, and the resurrection of old ideas about the American meritocracy, made room for those handpicked individuals whose seeming success masked the persisting disadvantage of the many (Guinier and Torres 2002).

Dismantling the Logic of Segregation: Race, Class, and Gender Studies within Contemporary American Sociology

The emergence of race, class, and gender studies in the 1980s and 1990s not only challenged prevailing practices within sociological subdisciplines of stratification/class, race, and gender; it also assailed the logic of segregation that shaped Western scholarship itself. Not sociology, psychology, economics, or any other single academic discipline could adequately address the initial questions that preoccupied race, class, and gender scholars. In the context of new social movements that attacked segregation in American society and that dismantled colonialism in the global context, as well as a changing intellectual environment that advanced poststructuralist and postcolonial social theories, a growing number of American scholars began to engage in so-called border work. This new form of transdisciplinary activity entailed making links between scholarship and practice as well as across disciplinary boundaries (Horlick-Jones and Sime 2004). Describing the greatly

---

10. Étienne Balibar and Immanuel Wallerstein's analysis of internal and external racisms examines the inclusionary (desegregation) and exclusionary practices (segregation) described here (Balibar and Wallerstein 1991). They suggest that these two forms of racism may be analytically distinct but that they work together. The legal distinction between formal and substantive citizenship rights, where a group may possess the formal rights of membership but be denied the full benefits of it, also refers to this distinction. For analysis of this relationship, see my essay on how racisms of exclusion and inclusion have framed American national identity (P. Collins 2001).

changed context that catalyzed these processes of boundary contestation and construction, Donald Levine observes, "the most interesting work now takes place within other kinds of boundaries: in subdisciplinary specialties, transdisciplinary forays, and supradisciplinary syntheses" (Levine 1995, 292). Levine's complex analysis is commonly collapsed into the term *interdisciplinary*, a term that references the constellation of social practices and knowledges that result from dismantling the logic of segregation. This term typically flattens the kind of complexity that is actually at play, yet it constitutes a recurring theme within race, class, and gender studies. In essence, the broader field aimed to synthesize subdisciplinary and disciplinary knowledges into new interdisciplinary areas that in turn might continue on the path toward transdisciplinary.[11]

Two key moments facilitated the emergence of race, class, and gender as a field of study within sociology. First, in the 1980s, under the leadership of Bonnie Thornton Dill, Lynn Weber, and Elizabeth Higginbotham, the Center for Research on Women at Memphis State University (now the University of Memphis) sponsored curriculum workshops and research institutes in race, class, and gender studies for scholars across a range of academic disciplines as well as independent scholars and community activists. These workshops and research institutes not only fostered increased understanding of race, class, and gender studies; they simultaneously organized a national network of academic and public intellectuals. Second, in September 1992, under the editorship of Margaret Andersen, *Gender and Society* published a special issue on race, class, and gender studies. The volume of high-quality papers submitted for this special issue enabled the journal to publish a second special issue in June 1993. In her introductions to these

11. Transdisciplinary forays by a range of scholars catalyzed entirely new overlapping and cross-fertilizing fields of study. New interdisciplinary fields were highly significant in breaking the social boundaries among academic disciplines as well as the symbolic boundaries that encased disciplinary knowledge. For example, women's studies enabled gender scholars who were spread across various disciplines to gather, compare, and contrast the study of women within their distinctive disciplines, then migrate back into those very same disciplines with this new knowledge. Lynn Weber, an early leader in race, class, and gender studies, suggests that "it is in Women's Studies—not in racial or ethnic studies, not in social stratification (class) studies in sociology, not in psychology or in other traditional disciplines—that race, class, gender, and sexuality studies first emerged" (Weber 1998, 14). In essence, women's studies practitioners participated in a form of border crossing and boundary breaking that has by now come to be not only accepted but lauded as the new frontier for research itself. Given the size and breath of the community of women's studies practitioners, the growth of race, class, and gender studies within women's studies also explains the rapid spread of race, class, and gender studies across fields that were ostensibly very different from one another.

special issues, Andersen discusses some of the parameters of the then emerging field of race, class, and gender studies: "The central question that has guided new studies of race, class, and gender is, How are race, class, and gender interrelated and how do they appear in the experiences of women and men in different social locations at different points in time?" (Andersen 1993, 158). After these initial issues, *Gender and Society* served as an important outlet for sociological scholarship in race, class, and gender studies thereafter.

Within American sociology, the emergence of the subdisciplinary specialization of race, class, and gender studies was buoyed by these new social networks of scholars as well as by a publishing venue that was sympathetic to this new scholarship. The subdiscipline's emergence, however, required crossing at least two sets of borders. One consisted of the external borders that linked sociology with women's studies, Africana and Latino studies, cultural studies, critical race studies, postcolonial studies, and similar interdisciplinary areas. The other comprised the internal borders among sociological subdisciplines that had developed under the logic of segregation. In this context, established sociological subdisciplines could not claim ownership over the topics of class, race, and gender as they had when the logic of segregation held sway (Tucker 1994, 103). Instead, both inside and outside sociology, many sociologists who were engaged in border work within race, class, and gender studies came to recognize the benefits of transdisciplinary forays and the new insights that they often engendered. For example, sociologist Evelyn Nakano Glenn, a prominent scholar in the field of race, class, and gender studies, describes how transdisciplinarity shapes her scholarship:

> As I struggle to formulate an integrated analysis of gender, race, and class, I have relied on a historical comparative approach that incorporates political economy while taking advantage of the critical insights made possible by poststructuralism. I use a social constructionist framework, which considers how race, gender, and class are simultaneously constituted in specific locations and historical periods through "racialized" and "genderized" social structure and discourse. I try to inhabit that middle ground between essentialism and antiessentialism by looking at the ways in which race, gender, and class are constituted relationally. (Glenn 1998, 32)

The synthesis both of fields of study and of levels of analysis in Glenn's description exemplifies the kinds of transdisciplinary forays that permeate the interdisciplinary field of race, class, and gender studies.

Glenn's description of working within these parameters shows the benefits of the creativity catalyzed by transdisciplinarity, yet it also identifies the difficulties associated with delineating the field's symbolic boundaries. On the one hand, transdisciplinarity should produce new supradisciplinary features that come to characterize the core of the field. In essence, transdisciplinarity should catalyze new centers for fields such as race, class, and gender studies. Without such centers, what the field is *not* continues to define it, and patrolling the boundaries of the field to exclude interlopers takes on added importance. On the other hand, sealing the symbolic boundaries of the field may suppress the dynamic border work that created the field itself. Permeable boundaries, the ostensible solution to this challenge, however, suggest two potential outcomes. For one, maintaining the fluidity of field may foster supradisciplinary syntheses that reflect the broad, democratic processes that brought very different types of scholars together to work on common interests. For another, fluid boundaries also create space for the types of opportunistic, mechanistic "race, class, and gender" studies described at the beginning of this essay.

These tensions raise one fundamental question, namely, what is the status of race, class, and gender studies both in specifying the supradisciplinary syntheses that might lie at its core and in supervising its border work? One way of cutting into such a large question lies in examining how practitioners in the field of race, class, and gender studies describe its distinguishing features (e.g., its nascent supradisciplinary syntheses that in turn define its symbolic boundaries). In 2001, sociologist Bonnie Thornton Dill surveyed seventy faculty members from seventeen colleges and universities in the United States, many of whom had helped launch the field itself, on their perceptions of the core features and status of race, class, and gender studies. Dill's study provides an important starting point for tracing theoretical, epistemological, and political developments within the broader, interdisciplinary/transdisciplinary area of race, class, and gender studies. It also provides a useful framework for exploring how the subdiscipline of race, class, and gender studies has fared within American sociology.

Dill identifies three interdependent, distinguishing features of work in this field: (1) researchers analyze social relations by use of a dynamic centering on ideas and experiences of multiple social groups; (2) they use intersectional paradigms to study the relationships among race, class, and gender as mutually constructing structures of power; and (3) they view the ultimate goal of race, class, and gender scholarship as fostering a more just society.[12]

---

12. Dill does not explicitly identify these three areas, but they are implicit in her more holistic analysis. As Dill points out, "what I take from these interviews is that work 'at the inter-

How has each of these three distinguishing features of the symbolic boundaries of race, class, and gender studies fared within contemporary sociology? Moreover, just how does each feature engage the initial questions of this essay, namely, how might each both push the boundaries of sociological inquiry and constitute business as usual?

A New Analytical Strategy?
Dynamic Centering on Multiple Social Groups

Black women, other women of color, and working-class white women were early advocates for race, class, and gender studies,[13] primarily because traditional disciplines had excluded or marginalized them. Beginning in the 1960s and gaining momentum in the 1970s and 1980s, increasing numbers of African Americans and women entered American sociology. Because these groups often brought social movement sensibilities with them, they raised new kinds of questions *within* sociology. One feature became immediately clear—no one sociological subdiscipline could adequately address the types of issues raised by these new border crossers. Because sociology as well as the segregated subdisciplines within it had historically excluded African American women, many challenged the applicability of class-only, or race-only, or gender-only theories to the social problems that they faced.

Take, for example, Joyce Ladner's 1968 groundbreaking dissertation on African American adolescent girls, which is an early work within sociology that explicitly set out to examine African American women's experiences through the lens of race, class, and gender. Published in 1972 as *Tomorrow's Tomorrow*, Ladner's scholarship marks a fundamental shift toward what is now called intersectional scholarship (Ladner 1972). Like Ladner, African American women saw their lives as influenced by the intersections of race, class, and/or gender, and they questioned the prevailing pressure that they

---

sections' is an analytical strategy, an approach to understanding human life and behavior rooted in the experiences and struggles of marginalized people. It is also an important tool linking theory with practice that can aid in the empowerment of communities and individuals. Finally it is a theoretical perspective that insists on examining the multi-dimensionality of human experience" (Dill 2002, 6).

13. In the following sections, I place these guiding principles of race, class, and gender studies in dialogue with well-known concerns within sociological research. This is a huge theme, and I can only sketch out a preliminary argument here. I condense Denzin and Lincoln's schema of the research process into three areas, namely, theoretical perspectives and paradigms, research strategies, and interpretation and presentation. These three areas roughly correspond to the three distinguishing features identified by Dill's subjects (Denzin and Lincoln 1994, 12).

choose one as more important and let the others go as secondary (P. Collins 1998, 111–14).[14]

Within American sociology, this initial analytical strategy of centering on the ideas and experiences of African American women and other historically oppressed groups stimulated an outpouring of new empirical work on them. More importantly, practitioners redefined centering as a way of working that required the ongoing study of numerous social groups, with practitioners typically trying to understand a group's angles of vision on the world.[15] The goal of centering was not to install a new normative center— for example, to replace the implicit white male center within sociology with a female one—but rather to develop a more inclusive sociology that continually constructed and evaluated its own social and symbolic boundaries.

This dynamic centering as a way of working catalyzed at least three potential contributions to American sociology. First, it revealed how permanently installing an imagined white male subject at the center of sociological analysis distorted understanding of core sociological concepts. Take, for example, the meaning of the term *work*. African American women's reproductive labor under slavery and their unpaid family labor, low-paid domestic work, and service work within the segmented labor markets of advanced capitalism do not fit many taken-for-granted concepts within the sociological subdisciplines of class, race, and gender, respectively. Each subdiscipline examines some aspect of work, yet individually and collectively none adequately explains African American women's work histories. Because both stratification and class analyses treated race and gender as residual problems that would subside as a result of advanced industrialization or class struggle, both gave scant attention to African American women's work.

14. I provide a comprehensive discussion of this theme of African American women's engagement in *Fighting Words* (P. Collins 1998, 95–123). I use examples from African American women's scholarship and experiences, primarily because this group has been at the forefront of developing this area and because African American women's experiences provide important illustrations of more general processes. Yet the basic principles were neither peculiar to African American women nor applicable only to this group.

15. Sociology has long studied the experiences of historically oppressed groups, but largely through paradigms framed within the logic of segregation. In contrast, this new emphasis on centering suggested that the analyses that social groups brought to bear on their own lived experiences constituted important knowledge that might not only challenge existing fields, in this case the findings of the separate subdisciplines, but also that might generate new questions, paradigms, or supradisciplinary syntheses. Because standpoint theory encapsulates this process of centering as well as a valorization of the agency of oppressed groups, it has come under sharp criticism. For a discussion of standpoint theory and the form of intersectionality suggested by race, class, and gender studies, see P. Collins (1998, 201–28).

The race relations framework focused on racially segmented labor markets yet typically simply ignored women altogether, believing that gender-segmented labor markets were natural whereas racially segmented labor markets constituted discrimination. Within family studies, scholars typically did not see women's reproductive labor as work because was it unpaid. Centering on African American women's work thus served as a corrective to multiple yet partial meanings of the very term *work*. Using dynamic centering for multiple social groups with diverse configurations of race, ethnicity, sexuality, class, age, gender, ability, and citizenship status should expand sociological knowledge even further. Continuing this ongoing process of dynamic centering should, over time, yield a more complex and robust understanding of the concept of work.[16]

Second, a dynamic centering on multiple social groups potentially stimulates new interpretations of prevailing sociological theories. Recall how Marxist sociology's historical trajectory of centering on white men limited its understandings of social class. Here, a dynamic centering on other groups might generate new directions for materialist analyses. For example, French sociological theorist Colette Guillaumin's materialist analysis focuses both on the economy (the exploitative dimension of appropriation for various social systems such as slavery and social institutions such as marriage) and on questions of power and domination. However, Guillaumin presents these arguments outside of traditional functionalist and Marxist analyses of stratification/class (Guillaumin 1995). In contrast to traditional social class analyses that begin their analysis with the *sale* of labor power within capitalist relations, Guillaumin's materialist framework originates in the appropriation of the body that contains the labor power itself. Because no form of measuring the value of labor in isolation from the body itself exists, Guillaumin contends that racism and sexism both draw on this physical appropriation of bodies. Guillaumin identifies slavery as the fundamental historical relationship that fostered modern understandings of ideologies of race. Enslaving African bodies constituted the original theft—the stealing of labor came later. Racial ideologies explaining this process emerged after slavery was in effect. By identifying the seizure of time, the products of the body such as children and sexual services, and the physical care of children, the elderly, the sick, as well as healthy men as tangible expressions of the appropriation of women, Guillaumin's theory of the sexual oppression of women (her analysis of *sexage*) follows a similar logic.

16. Work occupies a central place in race, class, and gender scholarship within sociology. For a solid review of this research, see Browne and Misra (2003).

Guillaumin points out that people only take publicly that which they feel already belongs to them, and she identifies the public harassment of women on the street, in the workplace, and elsewhere as expressions of men who, as a class, feel that they can appropriate the bodies of women as a class.

A third and related contribution of dynamic centering on multiple groups concerns how this analytical strategy fosters a more robust understanding of social structure. For example, African American women routinely point out that their race or gender is not the problem. Instead, they identity the social meanings attached to these categories by racism and sexism as the real culprit. This shift moves race and gender from the realm of descriptive, individual identity categories with little power to explain American social institutions, and installs racism and sexism as causal and intersecting systems of oppression that define social structure. Focusing sociological attention on questions of power, the term *matrix of domination* describes this overall social structure within which such oppressions originate, develop, and are contained. Just as intersecting oppressions take on historically specific forms that change in response to human actions, so the shape of domination itself changes. As the form assumed by intersecting oppressions in one social location, any matrix of domination can be seen as a historically specific organization of power in which social groups are embedded and which they aim to influence (P. Collins 2000, 227–29, 274–76). Claims that race, class, and gender constitute mutually constructing features of social structure foster a basic rethinking of social institutions. In this fashion, dynamic centering on multiple groups without privileging any one group's experiences can prove to be especially important for rethinking not just race and gender but also the social structural matrix of domination of American society.

Beyond these potentially important contributions, this analytic strategy of dynamic centering on multiple groups faces one significant challenge. Ideas about hierarchy may be so deeply embedded in the cognitive structures of Western science that they can be uncritically imported into the centering process itself. In other words, sociologists who participate in actual social relations of intersecting oppressions of race, class, and gender may have difficulty divesting themselves of the benefits they gain within power relations in order to pursue this dynamic centering agenda. For example, because this strategy of centering emerged from the experiences of historically oppressed people, centering remains closely associated with oppressed groups. Yet in the eyes of many, understanding race, class, and gender studies primarily as the study of African American women and other less important people, an association that is heightened within assumptions of centering, diminishes race, class, and gender studies because its subjects of study remain devalued in actual social relations. Moreover, this association between dynamic centering and oppressed groups also facilitates a facile shift to an "adding different voices" model whereby the formerly excluded are included, but their presence does little to disrupt business as usual. One can center on African American women for a moment and then return to business as usual, now holding the moral capital of having modeled inclusivity. Thus, dynamic centering's efficacy to challenge sociological business as usual can become lost in cosmetic efforts to include the excluded in order to avoid accusations of impropriety.

A related issue concerns what happens when the experiences of the privileged become the center of analysis. The danger here also lies in conducting business as usual. Take, for example, the case of using race as an analytical category to examine whiteness. Amanda Lewis identifies several theoretical and methodological challenges that frame whiteness studies. One concerns how the context of color-blind racism enables some whites to claim that they do not experience whiteness at all. Lewis also points out that scholars do not conduct studies of whiteness in a vacuum, namely, that the material realities that create whiteness also influence racial discourse (Lewis 2004). If whiteness scholars become unduly preoccupied with studying whiteness, especially if their studies suggest puzzles such as that identified by Lewis, then such scholars may inadvertently reinstall white privilege as a the center of attention once again. Whiteness studies raise some important issues about the limits of dynamic centering in a social context that remains organized around principles of racial hierarchy.

Using Intersectional Paradigms

Practitioners within the field of race, class, and gender studies also advance a second important knowledge-claim, namely, the importance of conceptualizing race, class, and gender as mutually constructing constructs that in turn describe interconnected structures of hierarchical power relations. Gender, race, or class, each as a separate entity, constitutes a distinctive *structure* of hierarchal power relations that have patterned organizational outcomes on the micro-, meso-, and macrolevels of analysis as well as discourses that frame these social relations. However, although race, class, and gender constitute distinctive structures of power, they also only make sense in relation to one another, often through commonsense analogies (Stepan 1990). Intersectionality is the concept most often used to name these interconnections among race, class, and gender (Crenshaw 1991; P. Collins 1998, 201-28; Browne and Misra 2003, 489-94).

Within American sociology, this notion of intersecting, mutually constructing social structures emerged in the context of desegregating the social structures of American society as well as desegregating knowledges, in this case, the sociological subdisciplines of stratification/class, race, and gender. Central to intersectionality is the tenet that racism and sexism operate as mutually reinforcing systems of inequality (P. Collins 2001). Within sociological traditions, intersectional theory views race, gender, and class as neither fixed and discrete categories nor properties of individuals but rather as social constructs that both reflect and reinforce unequal relationships among classes, racial groups, and genders. Within American sociology, this focus on structural analyses is a hallmark of race, class, and gender studies. For example, using a simple analogy, Lynn Weber describes the essence of intersectionality: "People's real life experiences have never fit neatly into the boundaries created by academic disciplines: Lives are much more complex and far reaching. Just as the social, political, economic, and psychological dimensions of everyday life are intertwined and mutually dependent, so too are the systems of inequality—race, class, gender, and sexuality—that limit and restrict some people while privileging others" (Weber 1998, 13).

Currently, intersectionality may be described as an emerging paradigm that is in the process of analyzing and replacing prevailing paradigms (e.g., segregated sociological subdisciplines of class, race, and gender). Following Thomas Kuhn's definition, paradigms consist of shared assumptions within a field that define certain problems as significant, identify relevant evidence, and produce agreed-upon social facts (solutions) as well as troubling anomalies (Kuhn 1970). To acquire the status of a new scientific paradigm, a scientific achievement must (1) convincingly resolve a sufficient number of previously recognized problems; (2) attract enough specialists to form the core of a new agreed-upon paradigm; and (3) have enough unresolved problems to provide the puzzles for subsequent research practice.

The concept of intersectionality seemingly meets these criteria.[17] For one, it addresses gaps in existing knowledges produced under the logic of segregation by pointing out that interdisciplinary and transdisciplinary for-

---

17. In its everyday usage, a paradigm consists of a typical example or model to be replicated or followed. When used to guide political behavior, a paradigm would contain a list of orienting strategies for coping with concrete situations. Paradigms enable individuals to copy the behavior of others whom they want to emulate. The actions and beliefs of exemplars of the paradigm provide sets of rules that one can follow. Although they may contain visionary content, paradigms typically do not aim to predict or develop causal relationships about reality. Instead, political paradigms represent guidelines to follow and shortcuts to assist people in everyday life.

ays outside of sociology can yield better results (for example, the case of work). For another, as illustrated by the wide range of scholars who invoke the phrase "race, class, and gender" in their scholarship, intersectionality broadly understood has accumulated a broad base of new practitioners. The rapid growth of sociologists who formed new alliances across subdisciplinary boundaries shows the general success of race, class, and gender studies and intersectionality as the subdiscipline's guiding paradigm. Finally, as the breadth of journals and graduate program activities cited in the beginning of this essay suggests, studying the dynamics and institutional outcomes of structural intersections of race, class, and gender seemingly provide endless puzzles.

In a sense, because intersectional paradigms focus on the relationships among ostensibly discrete entities, they reverse the process of abstraction (also predicated on the logic of segregation) that has been central to constructing both social relations of intersecting oppressions as well as Western science itself. As Canadian sociologist Himani Bannerji notes, "an abstraction is created when the different social moments which constitute the 'concrete' being of any social organization and existence are pulled apart, and each part assumed to have a substantive, self-regulating structure. This becomes apparent when we see gender, race and class each considered as a separate issue—as ground for separate oppressions" (Bannerji 1995, 49). Thus, one can only analyze systems of oppression as separate systems by violating the concrete—"pulling apart" material reality and assigning essential qualities to each part. Intersectional paradigms that start with the concrete as the point of origin (Guillamin's theory of bodily appropriation or African American women's work experiences) aim to build abstractions not by pulling apart but by examining connections. In this sense, intersectional paradigms may be especially well suited to explaining contemporary social relations of desegregation in the United States and postcolonialism and transnationalism in a global context.

Intersectionality may signal the emergence of a new paradigm, yet how does one go about using it? Here British feminist sociologist Floya Anthias provides a helpful approach. Anthias suggests that intersectionality is best defined as a *heuristic device* or orienting framework that potentially generates new questions, avenues of investigation, and interpretations of existing and new knowledge. In this sense, intersectionality is not a theoretical perspective in the same way that functionalism, feminism, Marxism, Pan-Africanism, and world systems theory are because these theories all strive to *explain* the world. As a heuristic device, intersectional paradigms suggest certain core questions that should shape the sociological research process as well as propose frameworks for interpreting findings. Using intersectional paradigms as a heuristic device can mean analyzing one specific social location, social practice, group history, or commonsense hegemonic representation. This typically means choosing a particular topic that is already the subject of investigation and trying to find the workings of race, class, gender, sexuality, and nation where only one or two constructs ostensibly were operating. This approach has enriched sociological research on topics as diverse as how white supremacist literature may mirror mainstream American attitudes on race, class, gender, and sexuality (Ferber 1998), how race and gender affect upward social class mobility (Higginbotham 2001), and how labor markets are structured (Browne and Misra 2003).

By now, several defining texts in the field of race, class, and gender studies expand on these ideas or use intersectional paradigms as heuristic devices. Some are in sociology, but most are not.[18] Such texts use intersectional paradigms to identify what types of questions and concepts are important, what to look for in conducting research, and how intersectional analyses might help explain their research findings. British sociologists Floya Anthias and Nira Yuval-Davis's 1992 volume *Racialized Boundaries: Race, Nation, Gender, Colour and Class in Anti-Racist Struggle* represents an important text that deploys and advances a paradigm of intersectionality (Anthias and Yuval-Davis 1992). Broadly defined, postcolonial theory has housed the lion's share of theoretical work in race, class, and gender studies, with its major texts traveling into many traditional disciplines (Stoler 1995; Young 1995; McClintock 1995; Gilman 1985; Alexander and Mohanty 1997).

The theme of using intersectional paradigms constitutes a significant challenge for sociology generally and sociological research in particular. Because sociology occupies a distinctive position as a border discipline that encapsulates *both* an interpretive, humanistic tradition *and* a positivistic social science (as evidenced by the current shorthand qualitative versus quantitative methods), scholars of race, class, and gender studies are still experimenting with how to use intersectional paradigms. It is not so much the method per se that guides whether an analysis can be accomplished in intersectional terms so much as the frame of reference that the researcher brings to the initial research question, the research design, and/or his or her interpretation of findings. Stated differently, the methodological issues that

18. American political economists Teresa Amott and Julie Matthaei's 1991 volume on women's work broke new ground in drawing conceptual links in class, race, and gender studies (Amott and Matthaei 1991). Recent sociological work builds on this tradition (Browne and Misra 2003; McCall 2001). I would also categorize both editions of my own work *Black Feminist Thought* in a similar fashion (P. Collins 2000).

accompany the use of intersectionality for empirical research may differ, depending on the type of empirical research conducted—for example, demographic, ethnographic, comparative historical, life histories, or narrative—yet no one methodology is more inherently suited to intersectional research than another. At the same time, the history of empirical research within the new subdiscipline of race, class, and gender studies suggests that researchers have been much more likely to use qualitative methodologies over others. This may stem from the newness of the field rather than from an inherent advantage or disadvantage in the methodology itself.

Dividing sociological research into the familiar yet overly generalized categories of qualitative and quantitative research methods provides one way of highlighting some of the issues that accompany the use of intersectional paradigms within sociology.[19] Qualitative methods have been especially attractive to sociologists concerned with persisting inequalities of race, class, and gender. The fieldwork tradition is one location where so-called outsider voices appear and narrative methods generally allow the voices of the marginalized to be showcased. Moreover, the energy and ideas of liberation movements have been important for the development and current resurgence of ethnographic methods. Because such methods traditionally have been used for close-up studies of marginalized groups, qualitative methods also posses the potential for helping those who are harmed by racism, sexism, and/or class exploitation.[20]

When it comes to using intersectional paradigms for sociological research, quantitative strategies may face distinctive challenges.[21] One lies in

19. Qualitative strategies have a range of study designs that guide methods of data collection and analysis that seem especially amenable to intersectional paradigms. The use of case studies, ethnographies, strategies of participant observation, as well as ethnomethodology; grounded theory, biographical method, historical method, action and applied research; and clinical research all take on new directions if intersectional paradigms are used. At the same time, none of these methods inherently contains an intersectional framework. Primarily because qualitative strategies are more closely aligned with the narrative and historical approaches of the humanities, researchers who use them have led the way in using intersectional paradigms. For example, ethnography and participant observation lend themselves to intersectional paradigms simply because good ethnographies do not ignore the workings of race, class, and gender in their research settings. Similarly, case studies and biographical method are close cousins to the narrative traditions of history and the humanities and thus benefit from greater ease of synthesis within telling a good story.

20. I thank Marjorie DeVault for this observation.

21. Quantitative strategies also have standard study designs that guide methods of data collection and analysis: survey research, demographic methods, simple statistical analysis (e.g., descriptive, correlations, ordinary least squares, regression), and more complex statistical analysis are typical.

basic definitions of race, class, and/or gender within quantitative studies. Defining race and gender as transparent, descriptive variables coupled with the lack of definitive definitions of class limits the type of intersectional research that views race, class, and gender as explanatory constructs and/or as subjects of analysis. Another barrier lies in how researchers conceptualize the relationship among race, class, and gender within the research design. Including race *and* gender *and* class in the same study is not new for quantitative research. Rather, how the study manipulates the relationship among these three concepts matters. Within traditional sociological research, when both race and gender appear in any given study, the purpose often is to study *either* race *or* gender and control for the other statistically through regression. For example, when studying race within the assumptions of positivist social science, one controls for gender or class to make sure that the research design is not affected by these other variables. Yet the purpose of controlling for either race or gender neglects how they intersect and, in effect, can ensure that they do *not* intersect.[22]

Despite these difficulties, some quantitative researchers who strive both to make race, class, and gender the focus of study versus descriptive variables and to treat these constructs as intersecting entities produce important and complex work. For example, in their sociological scholarship both Leslie McCall (2001) and Chris Bose (2001) use an intersectional paradigm as well as quantitative methods to study women's work. Both of these scholars not only use race/gender intersectional frameworks but they also recognize how American sociology's treatment of social class affects all quantitative research on social stratification. If social stratification remains defined solely as individualized mobility within a static social system, then it is difficult to see that race and gender are more than additional individual attributes that help or hinder the mobility of the individual. In contrast, because both authors treat social class as a changing structure of economic power, they gain a better view of how race and gender articulate with labor market changes.[23]

At the same time, because quantitative strategies have the capacity to

22. Part of the problem with quantitative approaches when dealing with race, class, and gender simultaneously is that one of the three categories gets held constant due to the complexity of examining all three as part of the interlocking nature/process of inequality (as opposed to being just as a variable). Quantitative methodologies might be more successful if distinct composite variables were constructed to identify how the race, class, and gender categories work in combination to form a different category of experience from that of any of the categories originally combined.

23. I am indebted to Myra Marx Ferree for this insight.

measure and describe large-scale social processes, they are ideal for the study of social structure on the macrolevel. One goal of race, class, and gender studies is to expand the study of social structure in the direction of highlighting the distinctive elements of race and class and gender as mutually constructing yet distinctive systems of power. It is unlikely that sociologists will understand a theoretical question with this level of complexity without sophisticated quantitative strategies. The need for macrolevel, structural analyses that use large-scale data sets is evident. The task is to examine how sociologists might better use existing quantitative tools in order to better understand intersections of race, class, and gender for macrolevel social structures.

Fostering a More Just Society

Dynamic centering on multiple groups and the use of intersectional paradigms certainly constitute a fruitful starting point for exploring the question of the ways in which race, class, and gender studies may push the boundaries of sociological inquiry. Yet fostering more just societies, the third distinguishing feature identified by race, class, and gender practitioners, may not be so easily resolved. Research in race, class, and gender studies need not deliberately set out to better society, yet the types of questions that preoccupy race, class, and gender scholars often go beyond describing race, class, and gender as intersecting systems of power or developing innovative ways to deploy intersectional paradigms within traditional social science research. Just as sociologists who work from positions of privilege generally defend sociological business as usual, the historical exclusion and/or marginalization of sociological newcomers often catalyzes a heightened sense of social justice. The African Americans, Latinos, women, immigrant populations, and working-class whites whose social locations provided them with opportunities to develop a distinctive and often critical standpoint on sociological business as usual often were first to point out the harm done to sociology by multiple forms of segregation.

Dynamic centering has reinvigorated existing sociological categories and intersectional paradigms that show great promise in sparking new directions for sociological research. Yet how will supporters of this third theme of fostering a more just society negotiate important changes in the political climate of postsegregation American society? Doug McAdam contends that contemporary sociology bears a contradictory imprint from the upheavals of 1960s, the same social rupture that catalyzed race, class, and gender studies (McAdam, chap. 11, this volume). McAdam suggests that several trends over the years have transformed sociology as a discipline known for its engagement in social problems to a field that remains cool to applied work as well as ineffective in speaking with and for the constituents of race, class, and gender studies, in particular, the poor. As McAdam points out, "while stridently political in much of its rhetoric and consciousness, contemporary American sociology is generally a nonfactor in policy debates and irrelevant to the lives of a host of real world groups about whom we purport to care deeply."

Sociologists Joe Feagin and Hernán Vera (2001) agree. They contend that, "oddly enough, in U.S. colleges and universities, we have numerous courses on social *problems* but very few on social *solutions*. To map and analyze the dimensions of social problems—crime, inequities, racism, corporate control, and environmental hazards—is seen as scientific research. To discuss and describe alternative practices and develop solutions is seen as moving toward politics and advocacy—areas that are perceived as a threat to the objectivity of research" (Feagin and Vera 2001, 193). The founding of organizations such as the Society for the Study of Social Problems in 1951, the Association of Black Sociologists in 1970, Sociologists for Women in Society in 1971, and the Association for Humanist Sociology in 1976 suggest that many sociologists support this impetus to highlight and solve social problems.

Despite these initiatives, if McAdam is correct, one might ask if an established discipline such as sociology with a century-long history of engagement in social problems finds itself increasingly irrelevant within contemporary society, then how might the less-legitimated, more amorphous, shape-shifting, transdisciplinary area such as race, class, and gender studies foster a more just society? Here Feagin and Vera provide a partial answer when they argue that social justice traditions have a long and distinguished history within both American sociology and other national sociologies. Race, class, and gender scholars who wish to place sociology in service to social justice by pursuing social solutions might revitalize sociological dialogues from earlier periods of sociology's history.[24] Michael Burawoy's

---

24. In developing a more robust reading of the sociological record, Feagin and Vera revisit some familiar names through the lens of liberation sociology. They reassess selected classical sociological theorists, giving a new reading of the works of Auguste Comte, Harriet Martineau, Max Weber, Émile Durkheim, Karl Marx, and Herbert Mead. They argue that the earliest sociologists in Europe and in the United States viewed sociology as generating new knowledge and as being directly applicable to building a better society. Feagin and Vera also recover the work of lesser-known U.S. sociologists whose contributions have been ignored, such as Jane Adams, urban sociologist Saul Alinsky, and William E. B. DuBois (Feagin and Vera 2001).

provocative analysis of public sociology also provides potentially important new directions for framing social justice agendas within American sociology (Burawoy 2005b).

The desire that race, class, and gender scholarship serves the cause of social justice constitutes a noble objective for individual scholars, but this theme of knowledge in service to social justice constitutes a direct challenge to prevailing norms of scientific objectivity that view advocacy as antithetical to science. This tension between an ethically informed and interpretive sociology and a seemingly value-neutral sociology has framed the discipline since its inception. Contemporary sociologists are not likely to solve this puzzle, nor should they. Instead, continuing to negotiate this basic tension that lies at the heart of sociology may comprise one of its greatest strengths.

In this regard, the theme of fostering a more just society as a new center both for the broader transdisciplinary field of race, class, and gender studies and for its new subdiscipline within the discipline of sociology returns us to the basic theme of what holds fields together. Border work, the crossing of boundaries, hybridity, and other states of liminality constitute one part of the puzzle. Can there be a field with permeable boundaries yet no center? What criteria may ultimately bind scholars and practitioners who claim the field of race, class, and gender studies? The strategies of centering on multiple groups and on using intersectional paradigms may define the boundaries of the field. In contrast, social justice concerns may lie at the core.

The fundamental challenge to race, class, and gender studies lies in continuing to clarify its own boundaries while simultaneously maintaining the creative tension that destabilizes them, all the while remaining open to ethical concerns that motivated the practitioners in Dill's study. They remind us that the field of race, class, and gender studies never aspired to be a destination, a closed system. Rather, in the spirit of true scholarship, it remains an unending aspiration to ask better questions and to figure out how best to answer them.

[EIGHTEEN] Criminology, Criminologists, and the Sociological Enterprise

James F. Short Jr. with Lorine A. Hughes

Historical Background

By the time the American Sociological Society (ASA) was founded, social science perspectives on crime and deviance were an integral part of sociology as it had developed in Europe. They were integral as well to the early history of sociology in the United States.[1] Sociology continues to be central to criminology, but relations between the discipline and the field are no longer as close as they once were. My task is to trace and, if possible, account for the intellectual, professional, organizational, and institutional developments related to this change.[2]

Increased specialization and professionalization of fields *within* areas of deviance, especially criminology, and the inherently interdisciplinary character of these fields are major processes *internal* to criminology and other areas of deviance. As these same centrifugal processes threaten sociology, the discipline has sought to define its distinctiveness and to establish status criteria that are sui generis (Bourdieu 1991c; Burris 2004). Together, these push and pull processes account for the changed (and changing) relationships between sociology and these areas of study.

The constitutive forms of criminology and studies of deviance attracted the attention of governments, reformist movements, and organizations long before the notion of deviance entered the sociological lexicon in the 1950s (Lemert 1983; see also Lengermann and Niebrugge, chap. 3, this volume; Rothman 1971). Conceptual and definitional issues plague both areas of study. Deviance has been conceptualized in terms that are absolutist, statistical, legalistic, reactive, and a function of group evaluations (Tittle 2002). Definitions of crimes and criminals are equally diverse except for

---

1. "Positivist" approaches to the study of crime emerged from preoccupations with codes of law and philosophical debates about the nature of man and the state's responsibilities for crime control only in the nineteenth century. The earliest of these sought to identify characteristics of individuals and social conditions associated with crime (and thought to be their causes). See Bernard (2002), Drapkin (1983), and Vold (1958/1979).

2. See also, in this volume, Lengermann and Niebrugge, chap. 3; Gross, chap. 6; Camic, chap. 7; Abbott and Sparrow, chap. 8; McAdam, chap. 11; and Walters, chap. 19.

their dependence on the criminal law—and that too is controversial (see Short 1985, 2002a). In the broadest sense, criminology is a special area within studies of deviance (Uggen 2003).

Although historically the linkage of criminology and studies of deviance is long standing politically and in reformist movements (as well as in undergraduate and graduate sociology curricula and training), the main focus of this chapter is on criminology, and within that broad field primarily on research and theory devoted to explaining criminal behavior. Studies of trends and processes of law making, criminal punishment, incarceration rates, and capital punishment are here given scant attention, as are policing, prosecution, sentencing, and prisons. Each of these topics has a large literature of its own, much to the benefit of sociological scholarship in social change and social control, social organization, professionalization, and the varied societal reactions to crime and deviance. In later sections I briefly discuss efforts to integrate and formalize these and other literatures and an ambitious project to make control the central idea of sociology.

Although these fields remain intertwined, they have become separate areas of specialization; within both, special interests divide scholars and professions organized around them. Studies of suicide (venerable though they are in the history of sociology), mental health, drug abuse, and alcoholism, for example, are increasingly interdisciplinary and separate from one another and from criminology and sociology. Specialization notwithstanding, however, these areas continue to draw upon one another in many ways, theoretically and methodologically. They should, and they do, enrich each other.

PRE- AND EARLY ACADEMIC CONCERNS
WITH CRIME AND DEVIANCE

Early European scholars, journalists, and reformers were the first in the Western world to engage the areas of crime and deviance.[3] Statisticians studied the distribution of crimes and other social conditions, for example, leading Adolphe Quetelet (1796–1874) to observe that "society prepares the crime and the guilty is only the instrument by which it is accomplished" (Vold 1979, 168). Nineteenth-century journalistic accounts such as May-

3. One of these reformers was Henry Fielding, best known as the author of *Tom Jones*, who became magistrate at the Bow Street Court in London. A severe critic of the criminal justice system, Fielding proposed a number of changes—"experiments," in the view of Lawrence Sherman, who regards Fielding as the "first social scientist of crime to publish in the English language" (Sherman 2005, 120).

hew's 1849–50 *London Labor and the London Poor* (1968) and Charles Boothe's monumental survey, *Life and Labor of the People of London* (1902–3), begun in 1886, brought to the attention of broader publics stories about crime and criminals, deviance and deviants, and documented social conditions associated with them. Boothe's "commonsense" and pragmatic focus presaged the Chicago school's philosophical underpinnings (Gross, chap. 6, this volume) and the empirical sociology of the city that was its hallmark, as well as later studies of community social stratification and organization (Pfautz 1967, 6).

The most influential of the nineteenth-century scholars of criminology clearly was Émile Durkheim, whose doctoral dissertation, published as *The Division of Labor in Society* (1893/1947), forecast both the sociology of law and theoretical concerns with social solidarity. *The Rules of Sociological Method* (1895/1964) raised the level of theoretical debate concerning social science methodology as no previous work had done, and *Suicide* (1897/1951) served as a model for typologies of crime and deviance that were to come. Durkheim's comparison of the social distribution of suicide rates and those of other forms of deviance, especially homicide, resonate with scholars to this day.[4]

A wide range of public and institutional concerns accompanied, and in some cases preceded, the academy's involvement with matters related to crime and deviance. Social movements and movement organizations influenced institutions of law, courts, and procedures for the disposition of those caught in the toils of the law, with important consequences for scholarly work. Establishment of the Metropolitan Police of London in 1829 (imported to the United States soon thereafter), for example, both broadened the scope of public responsibility for wrongdoing and made that responsibility problematic. A century later, concern that police training and performance were inadequate led police leaders to involve the academy in efforts to professionalize the police (Fosdick 1920). The organization spawned by these efforts later became the American Society of Criminology (Morris 1975).

"Child saving" (the major precursor to the idea of juvenile delinquency) was part of a social movement that promoted "asylums" as a solution to a host of social problems. These institutions included "penitentiaries for the

---

4. Studies of suicide have since taken many forms, the most formal and structural of which is Gibbs and Martin (1964). Theories that posit suicide and homicide as self versus other objects of aggression or violence include Henry and Short (1954) and Unnithan et al. (1995); see also Maris (1981). Suicidology has become a special area of study with its own professional association (the American Association of Suicidology) and official journal, *Suicide and Life Threatening Behavior,* and a strong clinical and applied emphasis.

criminal, asylums for the insane, almshouses for the poor, orphan asylums for homeless children," and, late in the nineteenth century, the juvenile court (Rothman 1971, xii; see also Platt 1969). Scholarly participation in these developments took the form of the nineteenth-century Social Science Movement and the organization it spawned, the American Social Science Association (ASSA), both of which were important to the social history of American sociology (Lengermann and Niebrugge, chap. 3, this volume). Patterned after the National Association for the Promotion of Social Science in Britain (established in 1856), the ASSA was comprised of individuals and organizations brought together (and stimulated) by the perceived need to employ scientific means for solutions to social problems generated by industrialization. The objects of the ASSA, as set forth in its constitution, included inter alia guidance of the "public mind to the best practical means of promoting . . . the Prevention and Repression of Crime, the Reformation of Criminals, and the Progress of Public Morality" (Lengermann and Niebrugge, chap. 3, this volume, quoting Haskell 1977/2000, 100-101). Among the "hivings off" of the ASSA was the American Sociological Society (ASA).

ENTER THE AMERICAN JOURNAL OF SOCIOLOGY AND THE AMERICAN SOCIOLOGICAL ASSOCIATION

"Social problems" and what would now be called "criminology" articles appeared in the *American Journal of Sociology* (*AJS*) even before it became the first flagship journal of the ASA. The articles were primarily descriptive and evaluative of ameliorative programs: C. D. Randall's "The Michigan System of Child Saving" (1:710-24), Clare DeGraffenried's "Some Social Economic Problems" (2:190-201), and Hastings Hart's "Immigration and Crime" (2:369-77). Although these early articles had the ring of social commentary rather than theory or research, by the second decade of the twentieth century more systematic studies began to appear in the sociological literature.

In 1912, Sophonisba P. Breckinridge and Edith Abbott published a study of the geographical distribution of cases of juvenile delinquency brought to the juvenile court of Cook County (Illinois) for the years 1890-1909. The study documented higher numbers of delinquents in community areas characterized by high population density, steel mills and stockyards, "segregated vice," and racial and ethnic minorities (Breckinridge and Abbott 1912, 153). Three years later Ernest W. Burgess, surveying social conditions in Lawrence, Kansas, documented lower rates of delinquency in wards of that city that were removed from "the industrial and business part of the community," where rates were much higher (Blackmar and Burgess 1917, 72). These and other early studies culminated in Clifford R. Shaw and

Henry D. McKay's *Juvenile Delinquency and Urban Areas* (1942), which effectively launched the human ecology tradition of crime, delinquency, and other social ills.[5]

Scholarly concerns with crime and criminals, delinquency and delinquents, deviance and deviants thus reflected the general movement away from informed commentary, philosophical debate, and reform and toward more rigorous study (Abbott 1999). They also signaled a shift toward the location of both sociology and criminology in the academy. A distinctly American criminology developed slowly, as empirical research accumulated and courses on the topic were added to college curricula. Early texts by Maurice Parmelee (1918), Edwin Sutherland (1924), and John Gillin (1926) followed, marking the beginning of criminology as an autonomous field.[6]

Among early American sociologists, it was Sutherland who set the tone for the sociological criminology that came to dominate the field. Sutherland defined criminology as the body of knowledge that regarded crime as a social phenomenon, including "the processes of making laws, of breaking laws, and of reacting toward the breaking of laws" (Sutherland 1924, 3). This formulation set the parameters for the sociology of law and of justice systems—criminal, juvenile, civil, and regulatory—as well as for study of crime and delinquency, of criminals and delinquents, and of white-collar violators of both criminal and noncriminal statutes.[7]

Sutherland later studied professional crime, and his student, Donald Cressey (1969), became the foremost scholar of organized crime. It was to Sutherland that William F. Ogburn, director of research for the President's Research Committee on Social Trends, turned for the chapter "Crime and Punishment" in the massive *Recent Social Trends in the United States* commissioned by President Herbert Hoover in 1929 (President's Research Committee on Social Trends 1934; Sutherland and Gehlke 1934).[8]

---

5. Shaw and McKay (1942, 12–13) provide a "partial list" of early studies.

6. These texts were preceded by other works, notably Charles R. Henderson's *Introduction to the Study of the Dependent, Defective, and Delinquent Classes,* first published in 1893 (Henderson 1901), and *The Cause and Cure of Crime* (1914); and Philip A. Parsons's *Responsibility for Crime* (1909). See Gaylord and Galliher (1988).

7. Regarded by many as "the most influential criminologist in the twentieth century" (Laub 1983, 17; see also Gibbons 1979), Sutherland became the twenty-ninth ASA president. Elizabeth Briant Lee and Alfred McClung Lee suggest that ASA "gatekeepers" were "alarmed by the attention given" Sutherland's 1939 ASA presidential address, "White-Collar Criminality" (Lee and Lee 1976, 4).

8. The President's Committee was chaired by economist Wesley Mitchell. William F. Ogburn was a member of the committee as well as director of research. The volume consists of twenty-nine chapters and more than 1,600 pages. Ten research monographs were also prepared under the direction of the committee.

RESEARCH METHODS AND EMPIRICAL RESEARCH

The research momentum that was achieved during the early decades of the twentieth century prompted methodological concerns among adherents of all the social sciences. In 1926 the Social Science Research Council (SSRC) Committee on Scientific Method began deliberations that would result in a large-scale survey of the varied methods employed by the social sciences in the conduct of research (see Rice 1931, Appendix A).[9] The committee's report, *Methods in Social Science: A Case Book,* eventually comprised critiques of some fifty-two cases selected from recommendations made by advisory committees representing seven professional associations, among them ASA.[10] The "list of books and articles of importance in sociological method and standpoint," as submitted by the ASA advisory committee, revealed the breadth of the sociologists' interests. Twenty-two items, including works by anthropologists and psychologists, were recommended, ranging broadly over topics such as "Systematic Treatises," "History of Social Institutions," "Case-Study Methods: Ecological and Survey Types," and "Statistical or Quantitative Methods." Nine of these had foundational significance for criminology.[11]

Parallel with the methodological concerns of social scientists, govern-

9. In 1926 SSRC president Charles E. Merriam suggested that "the chief work of the Council" should encompass review "of the special research projects under way, approval of significant plans, bringing together of unrelated works, stimulation of research where now neglected, emphasis on the vital importance of more severely scientific methods, the inadequacy of methods often employed, and the neglect of many important fields altogether" (Rice 1931, 732). The phasing "more severely scientific methods" is especially interesting in view of disagreements between Merriam and Ogburn concerning science and methods (Bulmer 1984a, 182–83).

10. The ASA advisory committee consisted of Kimball Young (University of Wisconsin) and Robert E. Park and Ogburn (University of Chicago). The six other professional associations were the American Anthropological Association, the American Economic Association, the American Historical Association, the American Political Science Association, the American Psychological Association, and the American Statistical Association. The first case analysis, one of six under "Section I: The Delimitation of Fields of Inquiry," was "The Method of Auguste Comte: Subordination of Imagination to Observation in the Social Sciences," by McQuilkin DeGrange of Dartmouth College.

11. Durkheim, *De la division due travail social;* Sumner, *Folkways;* Burgess, *The Growth of the City;* Healy and Bronner, Judge Baker Foundation Case Studies, nos. 1–20; Shaw, *The Jack-Roller;* Thomas and Znaniecki, *The Polish Peasant in Europe and America;* Goring, *The English Convict;* Slawson, *The Delinquent Boy;* and Dorothy Thomas, *The Social Aspects of the Business Cycle.* Burgess's pioneering work on parole violations was also included in the total of fifty-two case studies, paired with studies by Ogburn in "Section VII: Attempts to Determine Relations among Measured but Experimentally Uncontrolled Factors."

ments at all levels were beginning to play a more active role in addressing crime problems. Importantly, the 1920s witnessed the first large-scale federal involvement in such efforts. The nation's first major crime commission, the National Commission on Law Observance and Law Enforcement, was appointed by President Herbert Hoover shortly after his inauguration.[12] The Wickersham commission,[13] as it came to be called, brought the sociological analysis of crime to public attention on a scale previously unknown. Especially important in the history of studies of juvenile crime and delinquency was Clifford R. Shaw and Henry D. McKay's *A Study of the Community, the Family, and the Gang in Relation to Delinquent Behavior* (Shaw and McKay 1931), published as volume 2 of the commission's report. Coincident with *Methods in Social Science* and the crime commission reports, a survey with even greater institutional significance for both sociology and criminology was under way.

Recent Social Trends in the United States

On the cusp of the Great Depression, in September of the fateful fall of 1929, President Herbert Hoover "asked a group of eminent scientists to examine into the feasibility of a national survey of social trends in the United States" (President's Research Committee on Social Trends 1934, v). In December he commissioned the President's Research Committee on Social Trends (v).[14] The committee's report was released on October 11, 1932, at the depth of the Depression, just before Mr. Hoover was voted out of office.

The committee's "summons"—"to examine and to report upon recent social trends in the United States with a view to providing such a review as might supply a basis for the formulation of large national policies looking to the next phase in the nation's development" (President's Research Committee on Social Trends 1934, xi)—was a unique challenge. Although the emphasis throughout the committee's report was largely on description— of the state of the natural and the built environments, of people and insti-

---

12. A 1925 commission appointed by President Calvin Coolidge with the charge of investigating steps to reduce crime apparently "met with little success and much opposition and jealousy from state counterparts" (Cronin, Cronin, and Milakovich 1981, 28).

13. Former U.S. attorney general George W. Wickersham chaired the commission.

14. Charles E. Merriam and William F. Ogburn were also members of the President's Research Committee, and Ogburn was its director of research. More than a third of the chapters were authored or coauthored by persons with Chicago connections (including Sutherland), three times the number of any other institution. The choice of chapter topics and the tone of the committee report clearly reflected Ogburn's interest in and theory of social change.

tutions and their relationships with one another, and above all on social change and adaptation—identification of social problems and policy approaches to them were common themes. Sutherland's chapter in *Recent Social Trends* dealt primarily with trends in "criminal law, the amount and kinds of crime, the police, the criminal courts and the treatment of convicted persons," giving little attention to the causes of crime or to "analysis of the present situation," which was being "ably carried out" by the Wickersham commission (Sutherland and Gehlke 1934, 1115).

Recent Social Trends in the United States marked a new public role for social science, a role that developed out of active collaboration among foundations such as Rockefeller and Russell Sage, academic social scientists, and SSRC.[15] The Great Depression, just under way as the *Recent Social Trends* social scientists began their work, reached its depth as they completed their tasks. The decade that followed greatly expanded the role of disciplinary expertise in advising social policymakers, particularly at the federal level (see Camic, chap. 7, this volume). World War II expanded and consolidated that role (Abbott and Sparrow, chap. 8, this volume). Still, as we shall see, sociologists—certainly including criminologists—continued to agonize and debate the proper role of sociology and sociologists in social policy (see Demerath, Larsen, and Schuessler 1975). But that is another story, to be discussed later in the chapter.

Together, *Methods in Social Science* and *Recent Social Trends* were the culmination of efforts of a distinguished group of social scientists assembled to bridge disciplinary boundaries in the service of knowledge acquired by scientific means. In contrast, as a harbinger of things to come, the Wickersham commission served to further differentiate criminology from its principal disciplinary parentage.

"The last five years of the 1920s," writes Donald Fisher, "was truly a gilded age for the social sciences in the United States" (Fisher 1993, 111). For the first time, the struggles of social scientists to establish their legitimacy in the larger society received substantial philanthropic support. Much of the "gild" of this period was in the form of grants by the Laura Spelman Rockefeller Memorial and the Rockefeller Foundation, which provided

15. Rockefeller Foundation's priorities changed markedly during the 1920s; for example, they stopped promoting policies such as eugenics and began creating and supporting institutions, including support of the SSRC. The chapter titled "Privately Supported Social Work" in *Recent Social Trends*, written by Rockefeller Foundation's Sydnor H. Walker, concludes, however, with the statement that "public health, mental hygiene, eugenics and birth control activities have potentialities for reducing dependency due to physical and mental disorder" (Walker 1934, 1223).

funding at previously unheard of levels for the encouragement of centers of excellence in addition to their support of SSRC.[16] Martin and Joan Bulmer (1981, 357) attribute private foundation support for social science to "beliefs about the conditions under which these disciplines could develop and the benefits that development would bring about."

> The need to be objective implied that the support for theoretical propositions advanced should rest on reliable and if possible quantitative data, collected by methodical, first-hand observation. . . . Effective practical use of the results of social science would be hindered by the partisanship of the investigator. Rather, it depended on first developing disciplined, theoretical and empirical understanding of how the contemporary world works. . . . Everything had to be done methodically; casual observation was to be avoided. (Bulmer and Bulmer 1981, 337–38)[17]

Fisher, who writes appreciatively of both *Methods in Social Science* and *Recent Social Trends* as triumphs of social science, casts a skeptical eye, viewing the relationship between Rockefeller philanthropy and the social sciences as a lost opportunity (Fisher 1993, also 1983), charging that fundamental development of the social sciences was diverted to the cause of empiricism and that policy concerns won out over science. Instead of forging lasting bridges between social science disciplines, he argues, SSRC efforts resulted in retrenchment and overidentification of the social sciences with the state. The driving force was the Rockefellers' class-related interests in practical affairs devoted to increasing human welfare and preserving liberal democratic capitalism (see also Brown 1979).[18]

Both the Rockefeller Foundation and SSRC were acknowledged in the President's Research Committee's report, the former for providing funds for the work, the latter "for various services and personnel" (1934, lxxvii). The committee's summary of findings noted that SSRC "may prove an instrumentality of great value in the broader view of the complex social problems, in the integration of social knowledge, in the initiative toward social

---

16. The history of SSRC is a virtual cataloguing of the most prominent social and behavioral scientists of the era. It is also controversial.

17. Chicagoans, who were never of one mind methodologically, were nevertheless at the forefront of such "practical" research enterprises as parole prediction and marriage adjustment. Although the Chicago school is often identified with qualitative fieldwork, many of the monographs with which the tradition is identified also used statistical measures. Shaw, McKay, and others exemplified this melding of empirical approaches (see Fine 1995).

18. Fisher's interpretations were vigorously challenged by Martin Bulmer and equally vigorously defended by Fisher (Bulmer 1984a, 1984b; Fisher 1984). Interdisciplinarity soon proved to be a "mirage" in any case (Abbott 2001, 132 passim).

planning on a high level" (lxxiii). SSRC also published thirteen research memoranda on social aspects of the Depression; they focused on institutional and demographic problems and crime.[19]

Encouraged by SSRC, the Rockefellers, and self-interests, social scientists participated in guiding the collection of data by governmental agencies as new federal data systems—including the Federal Bureau of Investigation's Uniform Crime Report system—were put in place. Research conducted under government auspices increased vastly during the Depression, World War II, and afterward (Abbott and Sparrow, chap. 8, this volume; Bulmer 1987; Camic, chap. 7, this volume). Funding and motivation for support of the social sciences notwithstanding, the vision that animated sociologists at Chicago and other universities clearly had more to do with the excitement of advancing disciplinary and interdisciplinary (Bulmer 1984a), ameliorative, and scientific interests than did either ideology or class interests. The outpouring from Chicago in particular was the product of a remarkable faculty who inspired students to view the city as a laboratory for research (Faris 1967).

Although sociological study of crime and deviant behavior became staples of teaching and research in most colleges and universities throughout the country, Chicago's influence waned somewhat as the theoretical center of the discipline shifted eastward to Harvard and Columbia, to structural functionalism and survey research methodology (Abbott 1999; Camic 1995; Abbott and Sparrow, chap. 8, this volume). Despite this shift, Chicago-style research and theorizing dominated criminology throughout most of the twentieth century.

Sociological Theory and Criminology

Sociology's hegemony owed much to theories associated with the Chicago school of urban sociology as well as its methodological and empirical work

19. The thirteen are as follows: Thorsten Sellin, *Research Memorandum on Crime in the Depression;* Educational Policies Commission, *Research Memorandum on Education in the Depression;* Samuel Stouffer, Paul Lazarsfeld, and A. J. Jaffe, *Research Memorandum on the Family in the Depression;* Warren Thompson, *Research Memorandum on Internal Migration in the Depression;* Donald Young, *Research Memorandum on Minority Peoples in the Depression;* Jesse Steiner, *Research Memorandum on Recreation in the Depression;* Samuel Kincheloe, *Research Memorandum on Religion in the Depression;* Dwight Sanderson, *Research Memorandum on Rural Life in the Depression;* Roland Vaile, *Research Memorandum on Social Aspects of Consumption in the Depression;* Selwyn Collins, Clark Tibbitts, Arch Clark, and Eleanor Richie, *Research Memorandum on Social Aspects of Health in the Depression;* Douglas Waples, *Research Memorandum on Social Aspects of Reading in the Depression;* Clyde White, *Research Memorandum on Social Aspects of Relief Policies in the Depression;* and Stuart Chapin, *Research Memorandum on Social Work in the Depression.*

(Short 2002a). Early criminology texts, including Sutherland's, espoused a "multifactor" approach that attributed the causes of crime and deviance to a combination of "factors," a popular view that had the virtue of bringing together perspectives from a variety of disciplines and fields of practice (see also Glueck and Glueck 1930, 1934; Healy 1915). Sutherland was never satisfied with this approach, however, and after a decade and a half of research, correspondence, and discussion of his misgivings with friends and students, he revised his thinking in the form of the principle of "differential association" to account for the cause of delinquent behavior (see Gaylord and Galliher 1988). First explicitly stated in the third edition of his text (1939), differential association was a bold affirmation of the importance of culture (and culture conflict) and the learned nature of behavior at a time when such ideas were not generally accepted (Cohen, Lindesmith, and Schuessler 1956). That "a person becomes delinquent because of an excess of definitions favorable to violation of law over definitions unfavorable to violation of law" now seems arcane in view of more sophisticated psychological theories of operant conditioning and social learning, but empirical studies have been strongly supportive (see, e.g., Kaplan 1980; Matsueda and Heimer 1987), and its theoretical impact has been enhanced by linking it with those psychological theories (Burgess and Akers 1968; Jackson, Tittle, and Burke 1986).

To account for variations in crime rates, Sutherland invoked a related principle, differential group (or social) organization (Cohen, Lindesmith, and Schuessler 1956). In doing so he drew on a large body of research and theory concerning cultural and normative conflict, social disorganization, socialization, and social control. Although these literatures recognized the importance of structural position for human experience, they lacked systematic attention to social structure. It was here that the influence of sociology's shift from Chicago's natural history approach to the abstractions of structural functionalism had its greatest impact. Robert K. Merton's "Social Structure and Anomie" (1938) filled an important theoretical void. Described as "the most influential single formulation in the sociology of deviance" (Clinard 1964, 10), the paradigm has proven to be more important to criminology than to the study of forms of deviance such as mental illness and retardation, sexual deviance, drug use, and "good people" doing "dirty work" (Hughes 1964).[20]

Merton's focus on deviant adaptations to structural limitations on goal

---

20. Everett Hughes's article "Good People and Dirty Work" is among those treating a variety of forms of deviance in Becker (1964). See also selections in Clinard (1964) for discussion of the influence of Merton's work on research and theory in several areas of deviance.

achievement was, as both men acknowledged, complementary to Sutherland's delineation of the mechanisms of cultural transmission in the theory of differential association (Merton 1997, 519; see Cohen 1983). Much of the theoretical flowering in criminology during the mid-twentieth century essentially assumed Sutherland's position and extended or elaborated Merton's, or contested both with social constructivist perspectives called variously "labeling" (Becker 1973) or societal reaction theories (see Goffman 1963; Erikson 1966; Lemert 1967; Cicourel 1968; Spector and Kitsuse 1977/1987).[21]

Beyond such pivotal influences, the inherently interdisciplinary nature of criminology and the failure to reach agreement on competing perspectives render organization or summary of criminological theory extraordinarily difficult. Theories ranging from the most positivistic and formal (Gibbs 1989, 1994) to the most stridently ideological and philosophical (Henry and Einstadter 1998; Milovanovic 1997) have been advanced and are as controversial among criminologists as they are among sociologists in general (Laub 2004; Sampson 2002; Sampson and Laub 2003; Short 1998b; Vold 1958; Vold, Bernard, and Snipes 2002). Relatively few criminologists embrace either of the extremes. Increasingly, however, theorists—and most researchers—attempt to express their ideas in testable terms and eschew overt ideological positions (see selections in Meier 1985). None is as insistently formal as Jack P. Gibbs (1972).

Gibbs's challenge is that the failure of sociologists to agree on a central notion is debilitating to sociology, retarding its theoretical power and contributing to fragmentation and the lack of cumulative knowledge. Drawn initially to the topic of control by his research on deterrence (Gibbs 1975), Gibbs later advanced the notion as a candidate for sociology's core (Gibbs 1989). Two macrolevel theories about control followed: the first is a formal statement, "A Theory about Disputes and the Efficacy of Control" (Stafford and Gibbs 1993); the second a more elaborate theory concerning the efficacy of control attempts, together with research using nations as units of analysis and applications to specific topics of sociological concern, for example, stratification, environmental problems, as well as deterrence (Gibbs 1994).

Criminology's other theoretical pole makes no pretense of restricting the field to lawbreaking behavior or to science. Stuart Henry and Werner Einstadter "encourage criminologists among others to cease investing in constructing the existing structures of power and oppression and to begin

---

21. The rise and decline of constructivist positions (Abbott 2001) does not negate the substantial contribution to sociological theory of symbolic interactionist analyses of the social construction of organizations and institutions, for example, Aaron Cicourel's *The Social Organization of Juvenile Justice* (1968).

investing through replacement discourse in new, less harmful structures" (1998, 418). Dragan Milovanovic accuses criminologists of "worshipping the very alienating, hierarchical creations that are our own" and urges abandonment of "the futile search for causes of crime because that simply elaborates the distinctions that maintain crime as a separate reality" (Milovanovic 1997, 90).

These theoretical poles reflect, and parallel, developments in sociological theory and beyond, toward formalism on the one hand and critical assessments identified with other disciplines and fields on the other.[22] Within each there are variations directed toward different substantive questions as well as questions of method and analysis. Tracing the history of such extreme diversity is daunting to say the least. John Laub's "Life Course of Criminology in the United States" (2004) is useful in this regard. Building on Glen Elder's (1998) life-course principles in the study of lives, Laub identifies three life-course eras in criminology: 1900-1930, the "Golden Age of Research"; 1930-60, the "Golden Age of Theory"; and 1960-2000, which he characterizes as the most confusing because it is the most diverse and contradictory of the periods (2004, 6). Laub further identifies five turning points that in his view shifted the intellectual trajectory of criminology. Historically, Shaw and McKay's work was especially important because it addressed the problem of crime from multiple levels of analysis.[23] The second, the Sutherland-Glueck debate, references Sutherland's critique of Sheldon and Eleanor Glueck's longitudinal studies of male offenders in the Massachusetts State Reformatory (Glueck and Glueck 1930, 1937). Ironically, Sutherland's attack on multiple factor theory discouraged multidisciplinary research and set the course for the use of theory and theory evaluation "for much of the latter half of the twentieth century" (Laub 2004, 11).[24]

22. Critiques of criminology abound from within as well as outside the field (see, e.g., Williams 1984). Crime has become a central theme of many fields and disciplines outside of criminology: "Feminism, cultural studies, economics, town planning, architectural design, film, political science, risk analysis, social theory in its various forms" (Garland and Sparks 2000, 201).

23. Shaw and McKay's work was the only one of Laub's turning points to address multiple levels of analysis explicitly and with data. The others are concerned primarily with the individual level of explanation, although inferences can be made to other levels from them.

24. Laub is not critical of the substantive points made by Sutherland, namely, that the Gluecks' data and analyses were inadequate to support their conclusions regarding changes in delinquent careers and psychological factors that were invoked to explain such changes. Sutherland's critique, written in 1937, was extended and later published in *The Sutherland Papers* (Cohen, Lindesmith, and Schuessler 1956). The critique was directed toward the first two of the Gluecks' several studies over a period of nearly forty years (Glueck and Glueck 1930, 1934, 1937, 1950, 1968).

With Robert Sampson, Laub had earlier argued that Sutherland's critique was motivated by personal ambition, a commitment to the method of analytic induction, and his wish to establish sociology as the proper home for criminology.[25] Turning point number three, Travis Hirschi's *Causes of Delinquency* (1969), was important both as theory (social control in the form of social bonding) and as an approach to theory testing. Measuring delinquent behavior and theory testing by means of self-reports had become common by the late 1960s, but Hirschi's work set a standard of theory development and testing that continues to be emulated. Number four, the Philadelphia birth cohort study by Marvin Wolfgang, Robert M. Figlio, and Thorstein Sellin (1972), was a massive data collection effort, using police data, that resonated widely beyond the academy, bringing renewed attention to longitudinal studies of crime and focusing attention on the small percentage of juvenile offenders (about 6 percent) who were responsible for approximately half of the crimes committed by members of the cohort. The latter finding, since extended and replicated on another cohort in Philadelphia and in similar studies elsewhere (Shannon et al. 1988; Wolfgang, Thornberry, and Figlio 1987), set off a flurry of research attempts to identify early in their lives individuals who are most at risk of becoming involved in crime. Policy implications of such research, although seemingly clear, remain elusive despite major support from foundations, the National Research Council, and agencies of the federal government (see, e.g., Blumstein et al. 1986; Tonry, Ohlin, and Farrington 1991). Number five, political scientist James Q. Wilson's *Thinking about Crime* (1975), "literally changed thinking about crime by focusing on the role of the criminal justice system, not as criminogenic as claimed by popular theories such as labeling theory during the 1960s, but as a tool to influence the individual decisionmaking of offenders" (Laub 2004, 13). The argument, and Wilson's prominence, discouraged pursuit of "root causes" of crime and lent support to research that could mechanistically identify risk factors virtually devoid of context, the antithesis of much sociological research and theory.[26]

Although different scholars doubtless would choose different turning points, few would disagree with Laub's assessment of the historical importance of these works. Developments in criminology over the most recent of

25. Although Sutherland was successful in his ambitions for sociology and himself, with notable exceptions analytic induction never became the preferred method of doing research and theorizing among criminologists. For an insightful and appreciative depiction of Sutherland's life and work, see Gaylord and Galliher (1988) and Schuessler (1973).

26. Wilson's argument is vigorously challenged on many grounds, by Laub and others (Hirschi 1979).

his "eras" are complex, involving as they do multiple theoretical perspectives and increased emphasis on theory testing. A useful summary is Charles Tittle's review of the state of criminological theory and research at the turn of the century. Tittle classifies criminological theories in terms of four explicanda: "differences in criminal behavior among individuals," "differences in crime at different times in the lifecycle," "differences in crime rates among societies, cities, communities, neighborhoods, or other sociopolitical units," and "differences among social situations in criminal outcomes" (Tittle 2000, 52).

A variety of themes within each of these categories reflect and build upon theories that were developed in psychology, biology, economics, and political science, as well as sociology.[27] Theories at the individual level vary in the extent to which they attribute differences in criminal behavior to personal defects, learning, strain/deprivation, identity, rational choice, and control/integration. Tittle's review quickly leads to the conclusion that, although each is important, none is sufficient to account for individual offending, and that in many ways they are mutually reinforcing rather than mutually exclusive. Moreover, the effects of each are dependent in some measure on factors, contingencies, and processes occurring at other levels of explanation.

The most macrolevel of the several suggested elaborations of the Merton paradigm is *Crime and the American Dream* (1994), in which Steven Messner and Richard Rosenfeld present the thesis that Merton failed to appreciate fully the role of institutions in the production of crime. Pressures generated by the American Dream—"a strong achievement orientation, a commitment to competitive individualism, universalism, and most important, the glorification of material success" (Messner and Rosenfeld 1994, 75)—result in domination of the entire institutional structure by economic institutions and the consequent inability of other institutions to regulate and control those pressures.

Conversely, "general strain theory" strays considerably from macrolevel concerns. Robert Agnew, the theory's most persistent advocate, seeks explicitly to explain both crime rates and individual offending, arguing that a broad range of personal strains provoke criminal behavior by individuals

27. Editions of the *Encyclopedia of Crime and Justice* (1985, 2002) follow identical patterns, with entries introducing the field of crime causation followed by entries devoted to biological, economic, political, psychological, and sociological theories. Each of the entries is written by a different author or set of authors, and all emphasize the interrelationships among theories based on these disciplines. Entries in the second edition place greater emphasis on integration of such theories.

(Agnew 1992) and that unequal distribution of such strains among individuals accounts for variations in crime rates (Agnew 1999; Broidy 2001).

Though not generally phrased specifically in strain terms, recent attempts to account for the extreme variability in the effects of sanctions on offenders, their families, and communities follow this tradition. Theorizing about mechanisms of social control and their effectiveness, John Braithwaite (1989) draws on a broad range of theory and research to develop the thesis that formal and informal controls are interdependent, and that shaming of offenders can—and should—be integral to both. Theoretically, bringing offenders and victims together and shaming offenders, provided it does not stigmatize (a very important proviso), can effectively deter offenders from future offending and promote community integration—hence the terms *reintegrative shaming* and *restorative justice* (Braithwaite 1998).

More recently, Braithwaite (2005) builds on analysis of the South African Truth and Reconciliation Commission, the experience of the Aboriginal Corrections Policy Unit in Canada, and the results of "restorative antibullying programs in schools" (in several countries) to develop the counterintuitive argument that confrontation combined with mercy for offenders is more effective in arriving at the truth (compared to a criminal trial) and as a means of achieving reconciliation of offenders and victims. Conventional deterrence theory is challenged as well:

> A systematic presumption in favour of mercy delivers more effective deterrence than proportional punishment. The fear of conventional deterrence theorists is not just that mercy erodes deterrence; it is also that a presumption in favour of trying mercy first (with court enforcement of punishment as a backstop) will cause the rational calculator to behave badly for as long as mercy is on offer, and then switch to responsible behavior only when there is a switch to punishment. It is a "free hit" incentive structure. (Braithwaite 2005, 297)

Braithwaite denies this interpretation. "What it does is shift the focus from punishing the commission of crime to punishing the failure to engage with the prevention of crime" (297).[28]

28. Braithwaite's argument is similar to that advanced by "high reliability organization" theorists that an organizational culture of learning and prevention is an important factor in preventing accidents in complex, tightly coupled, high hazard organizations that nevertheless are relatively accident free (Laporte and Consolini 1991; cf. Perrow 1984/1999; Vaughan 1996; see also Clarke and Short 1993). Both HRO theorists and Braithwaite invoke the air traffic safety system (ATSS) to make the point. The ATSS rewards airline pilots for reporting "near misses" of accidents but punishes them if they fail "to engage energetically with high integrity truth seeking, active responsibility and prevention" (Braithwaite 2005, 297).

Similarly, Lawrence Sherman (1993, 2003) argues that, absent respect for the dignity and the bonding of offenders to their communities so that they are motivated to become reintegrated with them, sanctioning processes produce defiance rather than a desire to desist from further offending. A growing literature addresses these issues, based in large part on symbolic interactionism's stress on the importance of individuals' sense of self and the influence of others and of situational elements in behavior (Birkbeck and LaFree 1993; Stryker 1980; see also Felson 1993; Luckenbill 1977). Self-concept studies have produced impressive support for this theoretical tradition (Kaplan 1980, 1995; Matsueda 1992). Systematic study of situational influences, however, remains relatively undeveloped.

Clifford Shaw and his associates and Frank Tannenbaum (1938) had noted that official responses to delinquent behavior often were defining events in the lives of delinquents and for other community residents as they related to delinquents, implying important situational elements in the production and control of delinquency and crime. Others noted that criminal behavior was influenced by the nature of relationships between criminals and their victims (von Hentig 1948). Despite these early insights, and the ready availability of rich contexts for empirical study, research concerning such influences has been slow to develop.

Marvin Wolfgang's careful study identified 26 percent of homicides in Philadelphia as "victim-precipitated," in the sense that the victims were "the first to commence the interplay or resort to physical violence" (Wolfgang 1967, 75). A study of Chicago street gangs found that gang leaders often responded to situational status threats by inciting violence and that episodes of group violence involved similar threats to the collectivity (Short and Strodtbeck 1965).[29] Responses to specific situations also varied a great deal among gang members, casting doubt on theories that attributed gang behavior to gang norms. More recently, however, gang norms are reported to play an important role in gang homicides (Papachristos 2004). Mixed empirical findings such as these create problems and paradoxes that remain to be deciphered.

Other recent work in criminology has enriched still other general sociological perspectives. Life-course research and theory has been enriched by the work of John Laub and Robert Sampson (Laub and Sampson 2003;

---

29. Further analysis of disputes involving these same gang members found that the manner in which disputes were resolved (violently or without violence) was influenced by rational considerations and situational factors such as the nature of dispute pretexts, the role of third parties, alcohol and other drugs, firearms and their use, and the presence of authority figures (Hughes 2005; Hughes and Short 2005; also Cooney 1998; Luckenbill 1977).

Sampson and Laub 1993), who challenge developmental and typological theories associated with both sociology and psychology (Farrington 2003; Gibbons 1985; Moffitt 1993).[30] Community theory and the study of neighborhoods and communities also have experienced a resurgence of empirical research, methodological innovation, and theoretical advance as a result of the work by criminologists.[31]

Arguably, Tittle writes, "within a probabilistic framework" theorists in criminology "are now able to broadly outline the causes of criminalization, criminal behavior, and variations in rates of crime among situations, communities, societies, and other social entities, as well as across the life course" (2000, 84). He acknowledges, however—and few criminologists would disagree—that theories generally are weak in explanatory and predictive power and that they apply mainly to aggregate populations rather than to individual behaviors.

Tittle is a primary advocate for a general theory of deviance, arguing that simple theories all fail one or more of the criteria of breadth, comprehensiveness, precision, and depth. His candidate is *Control Balance* (Tittle 1995), which seeks to understand both conforming and deviant behavior by the "balance" between controlling and controlled forces in individuals' lives.[32] Less sweeping general theories of criminal behavior have been proposed that stress social control (Gottfredson and Hirschi 1990), social learning theory (Akers 1998), and integration of developmental, interactional, and social structural perspectives (e.g., Thornberry 1987). All such theories receive a measure of empirical support in the research literature, but there is no consensus and the search for closure goes on.[33]

Organizational Change and Context

From its beginning, ASA counted criminologists and students of deviance among its most active members. Four sociologists whose work is identified primarily with criminology and studies of deviance have served as ASA

---

30. The development of the life-course perspective owes much to criminology, as reflected in biographies and autobiographies such as the life histories gathered by Shaw and his colleagues, and in Sutherland's *Professional Thief* (1937).

31. See, e.g., Bursik (1999), Bursik and Grasmick (1993), Hagan and McCarthy (1997), Sampson, Raudenbush, and Earls (1997), and Sampson, Morenoff, and Gannon-Rowley (2002).

32. See Tittle (2004); see also Tittle and Paternoster (2002) for citations of related empirical research and refinement of the theory.

33. See, e.g., Janet Lauritsen's (2005) critique of interaction theory. Criminology evidences all of the features of Abbott's "fractal" vision of the social sciences and the "self-similar" theories that emerge from research and theoretical ferment, much to the consternation—indeed, disgust—of some and the delight of others (Abbott 2001).

presidents and virtually all of the others have influenced scholarly development in these fields.[34] Criminologists have served as editors and members of editorial boards of the *ASR* and other official ASA publications, as well as *AJS, Social Forces, Annual Review of Sociology*, regional society journals and many specialty publications.

The first issue of *ASR*, which became the association's official journal in 1936, contained exchanges between several mainline sociologists focused on the relationship between scholarly work and social action, a persistent and continuing problem with special relevance for criminology due to the political nature of laws and their enforcement. Several of the early *ASR* articles were remarkably value laden. "Social Theory and Social Action" by Stuart Chapin (1–11), was followed by Pitirim Sorokin's "Is Accurate Social Planning Possible?" (12–28), and "Discussion" by Henry Pratt Fairchild (25–28).[35] The third in the series, E. A. Ross's "Some Contributions of Sociology to the Guidance of Society" (29–32), was discussed by F. H. Hankins.

ASR's first volume included stock-taking articles by criminologists: Nathaniel Cantor's "Recent Tendencies in Criminological Research in Germany" and Elio Monachesi's "Trends in Criminological Research in Italy," Pauline Young's "Social Problems in the Education of the Immigrant Child," Marie Kopp's "Legal and Medical Aspects of Hygienic Sterilization in Germany,"[36] Donald Taft's "Nationality and Crime," and Ferris Laune's "The Application of Attitude Tests in the Field of Parole Prediction." The last issue of that first *ASR* volume returned to the theme of the first, with Merton's "The Unanticipated Consequences of Purposive Social Action," which to this day bears rereading.[37]

Sociologists have also been active participants in other emerging professional associations devoted to criminology and special areas within de-

34. In addition to Sutherland, John Gillin, Kai Erikson, and James Short, Jack Gibbs and Albert Reiss were nominated but not elected. Elijah Anderson served as ASA vice president, and John Hagan was nominated for that office.

35. Fairchild's final sentence is worth repeating, if for no other reason than as a warning against impressionistic judgments: "With reference to the Soviet Union . . . After having spent the entire summer there . . . far from sharing Professor Sorokin's view that it is a lamentable failure and a proof of the futility of social planning, I regard it as an amazing and impressive body of evidence that a determined rational, and intelligent societal plan may work out in very nearly the manner that was intended" (Fairchild 1936, 28).

36. Kopp quoted approvingly "the guiding spirit of a truly constructive social policy for any country," citing Justice Holmes's comment that "three generations of imbeciles are enough" (Kopp 1936, 770).

37. One of the major questions in Gibbs's delineation of types of control is "What are the consequences of control attempts and why are some of the unanticipated and/or unrecognized?" (Gibbs 1989, 71).

viance. The presence of Merton among the founders of the Society for the Study of Social Problems (SSSP, in 1951) notwithstanding, the organization came into being as a result of the disaffection of sociologists who felt that social problems were being given inadequate attention by the new ASA elite and the shift from Chicago-style inquiry to the abstractions of structural functionalism (Skura 1976; Abbott 1999; Abbott and Sparrow, chap. 8, this volume). Virtually all of the SSSP founders, officers, committee chairs, and the first editor and advisory editors were sociologists, and most SSSP presidents have been sociologists.

An officially commissioned history of the American Society of Criminology (ASC), however, reveals a very different picture, demonstrating both continuity and change in institutional, organizational, and disciplinary/ field relationships (Morris 1975). In the early 1930s August Vollmer, a former chief of police in Berkeley, California, and a pioneer in university-based police training, began discussions with his students and others about the educational and training needs related to professionalization of the police. Formally organized (in late 1941) as the National Association of College Police Training Officials, the organization grew slowly, renaming itself the Society for the Advancement of Criminology in 1946, at which time there were "over 40 dues-paying members" (Morris 1975, 129).[38] The name was again changed (to its present form) in 1957. At this time the organization had achieved a measure of institutional stability, becoming an affiliate of the American Association for the Advancement of Science in 1950, with formal representation at International Congresses in Europe, and "mutually supportive relations with the International Association of Chiefs of Police, the American Academy of Forensic Sciences, the American Correctional Association, and the National Probation and Parole Association (now the National Council on Crime and Delinquency" (131). It remained small and primarily law-enforcement and education oriented, however, with only sixty-four members.[39] Although Vollmer believed that professionalization of police forces "required that police—and especially police administra-

---

38. The 1946 SAC constitution defined criminology as "the study of the causes, treatment and prevention of crime, including, but not restricted to: a) Scientific crime detection, investigation and identification; b) Crime prevention, public safety and security; c) Law enforcement administration; d) Administration of criminal justice; e) Traffic administration; f) probation; g) juvenile delinquency control; h) related aspects of penology" (Morris 1975, 128).

39. All were male, and most were either engaged in police administration or teaching in college police and law enforcement programs; 11 were teaching college courses in criminology, 2 were professors of law, 4 were in correctional work, 8 in related areas, "e.g., clinician, fiscal investigator, textbook publisher . . . and the occupations of 3 were unknown" (Morris 1975, 134).

tors—become broadly informed in the entire area of criminology and in the principles of such related areas as public administration, political science, psychology and sociology" (127), it was not until 1964 that a sociologist (Walter Reckless) became the first non–police professional to serve as ASC president. Thereafter, however, with few exceptions, the primary disciplinary identification of ASC presidents has been sociology.

This is not the case for the Academy of Criminal Justice Science (ACJS), which remains more oriented toward law enforcement and corrections than is ASC. Membership in the two organizations overlap, but ACJS (founded in 1963) is also more representative of the view of criminology as an independent discipline than is ASC. That view remains controversial within both organizations and troubling to many. A 1983 encyclopedia article characterized efforts of social and behavioral scientists to resist the development of criminology (including criminal justice studies) as an independent discipline as "empire building" (Lejins 1983, 689). Others similarly argue that criminology's grounding in criminal law and its multidisciplinary, multimethod approach constitute a sufficient disciplinary "intellectual core" (see, e.g., Wolfgang and Ferracuti 1967).

Conversely, a special journal issue devoted to "mutual engagement of criminology and sociology" advances the view that criminology lacks an intellectual core and is necessarily multidisciplinary, with special grounding in sociology (Savelsberg and Sampson 2002).[40] Criminology's pulling away from sociology, it is argued, comes at great cost, putting at risk the academic integrity of the field because of its vulnerability "to extra-scholarly influences, especially those of the state" (Savelsberg and Sampson 2002, 99).

Papers following Savelsberg and Sampson's introductory essay illustrate the mutual engagement of sociology and criminology in a variety of ways. Susan Silbey discusses the Durkheimian conundrum that crime is viewed both as "episodic ruptures of the social fabric and as a normal feature of healthy societies," noting that these "contradictory cultural representations and experiences help sustain a hegemonic reality in which crime is both a usual feature of ordinary social life to be understood and managed like any other mundane matter, and an episodic event that need not challenge confidence in what is in effect a reified conception of society" (Silbey 2002, 163; see also Black 1976). She concludes that "the segregation of criminology from mainstream sociology reduces the probability of being a science with a firm systematic theoretical foundation. . . . Outside of sociol-

40. This issue of *Crime, Law, and Social Change* was edited by Savelsberg and Sampson. The published papers were prepared originally for a 1999 ASA session.

ogy, and removed from the sociology of law, criminology is more likely to see crime as a rupture than as a normal and constituent part of the law" (Silbey 2002, 173).

Diane Vaughan, in "Criminology and the Sociology of Organizations," compares "family violence and corporate crime as examples of organizational misconduct, foregrounding the organizational setting in order to examine links between . . . levels of analysis" (Vaughan 2002, 117).[41] Vaughan's scholarly work demonstrates the value of crossing boundaries between and within disciplines in the pursuit of both criminological and sociological theory (e.g., Vaughan 1996). John Hagan brings social stratification into the picture by examining the experience of U.S. citizens who resisted the draft and military service in Vietnam by "dodging" and "deserting" military service and migrating to Canada. In addition to demonstrating the highly contingent relationship between class and crime, the case illustrates the principle that "class circumstances follow from as well as causally precede crime" (Hagan 2002, 137).

Sociology and sociologists are mutually engaged with still other fields with special relevance to criminology. In the 1960s the Law and Society Association (LSA) brought together scholars in legal and all social science communities. LSA soon became the leading professional organization for this purpose, serving an international constituency and becoming more autonomous as a special field. More recently (2005) Annual Reviews announced that volume 1 of the *Annual Review of Law and Social Science* would appear in December of that year, with sociologists John Hagan and Kim Lane Scheppele as editor and associate editor, respectively (political scientist Tom R. Tyler is also an associate editor), further evidence of the institutionalization of law and society as an autonomous field.

While sociologists have served—and continue to serve—in a variety of capacities with other criminological associations that focus on various forms of deviance, linkages *between* these organizations, and among sociologists with widely varying interests, have not always been smooth.

Institutional and Intellectual Change

Because criminology was aligned with the SSSP discontents, the most important effect as sociology moved away from Chicago-style work was

41. The levels-of-analysis (or explanation) problem has been addressed by many social scientists, several of whom have cited research in criminology in the search for solutions (see, e.g., Inkeles 1959; Reiss and Roth 1993; Short 1998a).

methodological rather than theoretical, namely, the increasing use of survey research methods. Encouraged by the success of *The American Soldier* research and vastly improved survey methods, many criminologists selected surveys as their method of choice. The advent of self-reported delinquency surveys had a major impact on criminology (see, e.g., Elliott et al. 1983), as did initiation of the National Crime Victims Survey (NCVS); both elicit responses from individuals concerning their own delinquent behavior or, in the case of the NCVS, household members' victimization. Survey research informed the demographics of crime and delinquency, but its focus on individuals often left out considerations of group, community, and cultural influences.[42] Rapprochement with sociology's shifting theoretical posture came with publication of two volumes: Albert Cohen's *Delinquent Boys: The Culture of the Gang* (1955), a blending of structural functionalism and Chicago-style sociology through Cohen's association with both Harvard and Sutherland;[43] and Richard Cloward and Lloyd Ohlin's *Delinquency and Opportunity* (1960), the result of Cloward's mentoring by Merton and Ohlin's Chicago upbringing.

Sociology's postwar mainstream focus on bureaucracy found expression in studies of white-collar, organizational, and organized crime. Although the modernization synthesis sought in some circles had less initial impact, international research in crime and delinquency, and scholarly attention and collaboration have grown rapidly. An even greater effect can be expected from the burgeoning literature on globalization, spurred by the events and the aftermath of 9/11, and increasingly problematic aspects of the phenomenon, such as displaced populations, international migration related to criminal enterprise, exploitation of women and children, and growing informal and often illegal markets (see Hagedorn 2006).[44]

Although such studies have brought criminology closer to the mainstream, other centrifugal forces eroded the once close ties between crimi-

42. The NCVS employs a household-based sample. Self-reports, ironically, were given impetus by Clifford Shaw's suggestion that the field needed a "Kinsey-type" study of delinquent behavior—which, he was confident, would reveal a good deal more delinquent behavior among middle-class boys and girls than was to be found in official reports of such behavior—a prediction that was confirmed by many such studies (see, e.g., Elliott and Ageton 1980; Nagin, Farrington, and Moffitt 1995).

43. Before publication of Cohen's book, portions of the dissertation on which it was based were circulated in some criminology circles. It first came to my attention through contacts with Henry McKay and Solomon Kobrin at the Illinois Institute for Juvenile Research.

44. In December 2004, the SSRC convened, in South Africa, a workshop on youth in organized violence. The phenomenon a child soldiers is part of the much larger problem of the global exploitation of child labor.

nology and sociology. Increasing specialization is perhaps the most obvious of these, as evidenced by the emergence of professional associations organized around many different areas such as those noted earlier.[45] Sociological specialization is most obvious in the number and variety of sections within ASA, virtually all of which have interdisciplinary ties. These forces exacerbate the "structural weakness" of sociology (Halliday and Janowitz 1992), that is, the relatively low level of interdependence *among sociologists* (but see Moody 2004).

The impact of both specialization and interdisciplinarity on criminology has been marked by large-scale institutional changes, as well. These include, especially, the rapid growth of academic programs in criminology and criminal justice (many in large state institutions), the increase in the professionalization of law enforcement, and the growth of political policies that are captured in the "war on crime" metaphor—that is, emphasis on punishment of criminals rather than rehabilitation, and incarceration rather than community-based alternatives. These policies, it should be noted, are in direct opposition to the theory and the experimental—and quasi-experimental—work of Braithwaite and others discussed earlier. The impact of these changes is especially great because, among sociological specializations, criminology is perhaps the most highly professionalized; it is also the most identified with government and therefore (some argue) subject to political influence (see Bourdieu 1991c; Savelsberg, Cleveland, and King 2004).

Changes in the academic organization of criminology mirror these trends. Whereas courses in criminology once were taught exclusively in departments of sociology, the advent of criminal justice as an academic field has brought about departments of criminal justice, as well as departments of sociology and criminal justice, of sociology, anthropology and criminal justice, and of criminology and criminal justice. Colleges and schools of criminal justice, with *criminology* sometimes preceding and sometimes following *criminal justice* in the title, are now common. Arizona State University has a School of Justice and Social Inquiry. A few departments continue to include *social work* in their titles. Sociologists tend to be leading lights in

---

45. Correctional reform organizations in this country antedate the republic. Many of their successors, for example, the National Council on Crime and Delinquency (formerly the National Probation and Parole Association) have existed for many years. At the other end of the historical scale, the Justice Studies Association met for only the sixth time in 2004. Many of these have publication programs. ASC, for example, publishes a newsletter (*Criminologist*) and two journals, *Criminology* and *Criminology and Public Policy*, the latter in its fourth volume in 2005.

all of these academic units, and the teaching of criminology continues to have a strong sociological slant, but such changes inevitably weaken the criminology/sociology nexus.[46]

These changes have left in their wake varied assessments, with some criminologists viewing the glass as "half empty" because the field has strayed from its parent disciplines and become more insular. For others the glass remains at least "half full" *because* explanations of crime and deviance seem clearly to require input from many disciplines.

Soul Searching among Criminologists

Criminologists are ambivalent regarding these changes. Sociologist Gilbert Geis writes (with Mary Dodge) that "criminology and criminal justice split off from sociology, where they were regarded—along with marriage and the family—as waifs, tolerated because they kept enrollments high. Their later structural independence demonstrated clearly enough that the problems they addressed often were considerably more significant than the more esoteric menus offered by their parent discipline. Indeed, as sociology has tended to wane, criminology and criminal justice studies have flourished" (Geis and Dodge 2002, xlii; see also Abbott and Sparrow, chap. 8, this volume). Low regard for criminology is evident in some circles. In his 2003 ASC presidential address, John Laub expressed his surprise at "the disdain that prominent academics, policymakers, and politicians have" for criminology. Laub quotes a state governor, who responded to research showing that "boot camps" are ineffective in reducing crime by stating: "Nobody can tell me from some ivory tower that you take a kid you kick him in the rear end, and it doesn't do any good"; a police officer and a big city mayor, both of whom denigrated criminologists and research evidence; and political scientist John DiIulio, who told the *Washington Post* that he "would most definitely rather be governed on crime policy by the first 100 names in the local phone book than by the first 100 names on the membership roll of the American Society of Criminology" (Laub 2004, 16).

Such appraisals sting, and many criminologists bristle in response.

---

46. Criminologists in a few departments of sociology outnumber and/or outproduce noncriminologists. Sociologists in the Department of Criminology and Criminal Justice in one large state institution considerably outnumber those in the Department of Sociology and are far more distinguished. I was recently invited to visit this university as an outside consultant in an effort to rebuild the Department of Sociology. Although the obvious solution was closer cooperation between the two departments, it is not clear that departmental and university politics will make this possible.

Statements by respected mainline sociologists especially rankle. Geis earlier had remarked that "scholars at so prestigious an institution as Columbia University barely deign to work in the field of crime" (1974, 287), noting that Merton once wrote in self-criticism of his "slum-encouraged provincialism of thinking that the primary subject-matter of sociology was centered on such peripheral problems of social life as divorce and juvenile delinquency" (Merton 1957b, 17).

Merton, however, later wrote warmly of his respect for Edwin Sutherland and of his "long standing appreciation of Sutherland's foundational work in criminology." When, in 1996, he received the Edwin H. Sutherland Award, ASC's highest scholarly award, Merton responded graciously that he regarded "Sutherland's specialized theorizing in criminology as having "contributed to general theorizing in sociology," just as his (Merton's) "general theorizing in sociology may have contributed to specialized theorizing in criminology" (Merton 1997, 518). His extended remarks credited Sutherland's work on white-collar crime with "conceptual clarification" of the meaning of crime data. He noted that much of the theoretical ferment of the 1950s and 1960s in criminology involved the fusion of the ideas to be found in Sutherland's theory of differential association and his own theory of differential opportunity and anomie (519–20). He concluded with the observation that he, the pluralist, was like the fox, who "knows many things," while Sutherland, the monist, was like the hedgehog "knowing one big thing"—a personalized version of Isaiah Berlin's (1953) famous essay.[47]

Autobiographical statements by prominent criminologists often reveal ambivalence about their involvement in the field and the role of chance in guiding their intellectual interests and career choices. John Laub's oral history, *Criminology in the Making* (Laub 1983), notes that the criminologists he interviewed "took jobs on a chance basis and 'rolled with the punches' rather than planning their professional careers in advance."[48]

47. On this same occasion Merton, after tracing the evolution of anomie theory in his own thinking and in work of his students and others over a period of more than fifty years, noted that in an unpublished paper Sutherland once acknowledged that "opportunity" was a factor in criminal behavior that was "at least partially extraneous to differential association" (Cohen, Lindesmith, and Schuessler 1956, 31). Toward the end of his talk Merton quoted a note he once received from Sutherland, to wit, "I marvel at your ability to write so much on such varied topics," perhaps a not-so-subtle judgment that he (Merton) was the more important scholar.

48. Laub's primary interviewees were Hans Mattick, Leslie Wilkins, Solomon Kobrin, Daniel Glaser, Edwin Lemert, Donald Cressey, Thorsten Sellin, Albert Cohen, and Lloyd Ohlin; all except Willkins were sociologists. Also interviewed were three associates of Shaw at the Illinois Institute for Juvenile Research and the Chicago Area Projects: Anthony Sorrentino, Joseph Puntil, and Yale Levin.

"I came into criminology quite by accident" wrote William Chambliss (1987, 1).[49] Charles Tittle reflects that "happenstance led me to investigate certain sociological problems that resulted in my being labeled a criminologist" (2002, 23; see also Tittle 1991). Francis Cullen (2002, 2) notes that his intellectual development and career was "a mixture of an idiosyncratic biography situated in a particular historical era." Robert Bursik (1988, 7) writes that his substantive interests turned to deviance as a result of summer employment with a circus. I titled one of my own forays in this genre "Aleatory Elements in a Criminologist's Career" (Short 1988).[50]

Lessons of Criminology (Geis and Dodge 2002), a volume of autobiographical essays by prominent criminologists, includes chapter titles such as Jackson Toby's "Ignoring Warnings, I Became a Criminologist" and Tittle's "Reflections of a Reluctant but Committed Criminologist." Malcolm Klein, a social psychologist by training, reports that he simply "followed the money" in his choice of graduate school and later "quite accidentally . . . became a sociologist" (Klein 2002, 49). Still, the field has proven to be seductive to its adherents. Klein, a foremost student of street gangs, introduced his book, *Street Gangs and Street Workers* 1971, 1), with the comment, "I've had it with gangs"; yet he returned to study them and to head up an ambitious cross-national study of gangs (see Klein et al. 2001).[51]

Linking Sociology and Its Specialties

Among criminologists, as was true of the early American sociologists, boundaries between and linkages among disciplines have occasioned a

49. Chambliss also reflected that he became disillusioned with "traditional" criminology and that the more he wanted to understand crime, "the farther away from criminology" he had to go. Where he went was to the "study of political and economic structures," to Marx, history, and the study of crime and corruption in other societies (Chambliss 1987, 7).

50. I studied with Clifford Shaw and greatly admired him. Perhaps for this reason I have never been ambivalent about being a sociologist/criminologist. The "aleatory" elements in my career were less intellectual than experiential, especially during military service (see Short 1988; also 2002c).

51. I did much the same, after a hiatus of several years (Short 1998a; Hughes and Short 2005). Albert Reiss told me many years ago that he had "virtually left" criminology, yet he went on to become one of the world's most prominent criminologists. Conversations with a few much younger sociological criminologists suggest that while they are not ambivalent about being criminologists, they feel that their criminal justice counterparts often are not well schooled in sociological theories and methods. One colleague expressed that in one sociology department with which she is familiar, criminology was the "900-pound gorilla" and the object of envy, and in some cases resentment.

good deal of thought and no little concern. Ronald Akers, when he was president of the Southern Sociological Society, set the theme for the annual meeting of that society with the paper "Will the Center Hold? Linking Sociology to Its Specialties and Other Disciplines" (Akers 1992).

It is not simply that criminology has pulled away from sociology, of course. With notable exceptions, sociology has also pulled away from criminology, particularly as taught and studied at elite institutions.[52] Michael Allen reports that when he looked at the frequency with which five criminology journals were cited in three "core journals" (*ASR, AJS,* and *Social Forces*), all five lost ground relative to other journals between 1988 and 2001 (Allen 2003).[53] Although *Criminology* fell from a rank of 13 in 1988 to 21 in 2001, its "core influence score" increased from .88 to .99 over this period, the only criminology journal to do so. Allen's work has been criticized both for his designation of "core journals" and his measure of influence (Koffler 2004; Marsh 2004). Aside from such criticisms (and Allen's response), several developments relevant to this chapter may have affected the measures and their interpretation.

Criminology, the official journal of the American Society of Criminology, hugely improved in quality during the last quarter of the twentieth century. Before then, many sociologist/criminologists rarely read it. Many new criminology journals entered the field during the period studied by Allen, and core journal editors may not be as accepting of criminological research as they once were.[54] The *Journal of Quantitative Criminology* (*JQC*), which is in Allen's study, publishes many articles of general interest to sociologists. If *JQC*'s 2001 core influence score is added to that of *Criminology,* the latter's

52. Among elite institutions, the centrality of criminology depends heavily on the presence of particular sociologists, for example, Wolfgang, and now Sherman, at Penn; Ohlin and Sampson at Harvard (previously at Chicago); Melvin Tumin at Princeton; and Reiss and Stanton Wheeler at Yale. Ohlin and Wheeler held appointments in the law schools of Harvard and Yale, respectively.

53. "The core influence of a journal is defined as the number of times that articles published in that journal have been cited by the three core journals in sociology in a given year divided by the number of articles published by that journal in that same year" (Allen 2003, 7).

54. A fall 2004 survey inquiring as to the quality of journals in criminology listed an astounding sixty-nine journals. While revising this essay, an e-mail from a distinguished criminologist (well published in the core journals) informed me that the editor of *Social Forces* recently refused to send out for review an article he had written with a colleague on the grounds that "it was merely about cities and crime, not something sociological." *Social Forces* editor Judith Blau explains her policy of "diverting . . . to specialty journals" some papers, mentioning specifically "criminology, public health, and urban planning" (Blau 2004, 460); for a response by one criminologist, see DeFlem (2005). Ironically, Blau is the senior author of a major article on cities and crime (Blau and Blau 1982).

score would increase substantially in both rank and core influence. Among journals in which criminologists publish, some are well established, whereas others are relatively new.

Membership in the American Society of Criminology grew rapidly during the period studied by Allen. Criminologists who once submitted their work first to *ASR*, *AJS*, or *Social Forces* now may be more likely to submit first to *Criminology*. Most importantly, scholars who read only the "core" journals miss out on a good deal of research of general interest that appears in more specialized journals.[55]

Aside from such controversies, specialization and interdisciplinarity clearly pose serious problems—and opportunities. Although both may contribute to the pulling away of special subfields from sociology, neither is a sufficient explanation of problems besetting criminology. Sociology as a discipline has become more specialized and interdisciplinary, and being a sociological generalist, as many of us aspire to be, has become virtually impossible. The interpenetration of sociology, psychology, economics, anthropology, political science, and biology (increasingly, as a result of human problems associated with advances in molecular biology, biotechnology, and evolutionary theory; see Heuveline 2004)—affects us all.[56]

Applied Research and Public Sociology

Ironically, another reason for sociology's "pulling away" from its subfields may be the association of the latter with applied social research, which has been a growth industry and a primary means of professional employment and achievement, if not always of professional recognition (Rossi 1980). The irony is amplified by the recent resurgence of interest in the public roles played by sociologists (Burawoy 2005b), as well as by the undeniable mutual enrichment of applied social research and sociology from the beginning—enrichment in methods, data sets, and opportunities for data generation and theoretical development.

Rossi notes that applied research often requires more technical prepa-

55. In defense of his measures Allen remarks—incorrectly—that "researchers who publish in the core journals ignore much of the work published in these specialty journals" (Allen 2004, 11). Although reading all specialty journals would not be possible, scholars who publish in core journals find it essential to pay careful attention to specialty journals that publish articles of general interest and relevance.

56. We have come a long way from my recollection of Louis Wirth's casual dismissal of the influence of biological factors on human behavior, to the effect that a person's "belly ache" might affect one's behavior!

ration than many sociologists possess, with the result that much applied research is poorly conceptualized and executed. Moreover, universities—unless they include research centers or institutes that are prepared to respond quickly to "requests for proposals" (and timely execution)—tend to be ill prepared to respond to the demands of such research.[57] More than timing and the technical research demands of applied work are involved, however. Some applied research is simply pedestrian, lacking in conceptualization or theoretical significance. Devaluation of much applied research also occurs as a result of social constructionist arguments that weaken support for positivist perspectives on social conditions and their amelioration. Conflict arguments that threaten the status quo weaken support from both public and private sectors (see Turk 1982). Among sociologists, surveys that focus attention on individual variation rather than social organization and institutions often seem to miss the sociological point. Moreover, objectified policy-related variables—those regarding which change is most feasible—typically are found to relate only weakly to desired outcomes.

The challenge to objectification of social conditions by social constructionism, conflict and critical theory, and postmodernist thought has special salience for criminology because public policy so often seems to require objectification in order to provide leverage for amelioration. Arguments that lack objectification seem also—falsely—to "explain away" social problems and thus to discourage control efforts. Perversely, both constructionist and realist theories often study "root causes" of phenomena such as crime, which, as noted earlier, some argue are not amenable to change. Although they enriched theoretical dialogue and controversy, constructionist perspectives were less adaptable to the applied researchers' armamentaria and tended to discourage policymakers from supporting social science research.

Applied social research embraced sample survey methods because of their power, ease of administration and analysis. Sociologically, however, the choice was unfortunate. The focus on individual variation deflected attention from social processes and change, on organizations, institutions, social movements, and groups—the heart and soul of the early works that were most attractive to sociology and to many policymakers. Poorly designed and cross-sectional sample surveys neglected the interaction of individuals within intimate and other relationships, failing to capture the effects of change and the dynamic character of social life. All of the social and behavioral sciences suffer the consequences of poorly designed and ex-

---

57. For discussion of this problem with regard to service on national commissions see Komarovsky (1975).

ecuted research, of course, but criminology is especially vulnerable because so many of the issues studied have policy implications and are emotionally charged and politically sensitive.

Although much applied research finds its way into the public domain, public sociology should not be conflated with applied sociology. Public sociology existed long before its current renaissance, especially in criminology. The Wickersham commission was only the first presidential commission to have sociologists among its chief contributors. Other commissions include the President's Commission on Law Enforcement and Administration of Justice (appointed in 1965), the United States National Advisory Commission on Civil Disorders (the Kerner commission, in 1967), the National Commission on the Causes and Prevention of Violence (1968), and the U.S. Commission on Obscenity and Pornography (1968).[58] The political nature of national commissions is amply illustrated by commissions that were appointed (with little or no participation of social scientists) at least in part to counter conclusions and recommendations of earlier such efforts (e.g., the Attorney General's Commission on Pornography, in 1986, and the Attorney General's Task Force on Violent Crime, in 1981, whose report contained sixty-four recommendations, many of which "were off-the-shelf conservative bromides; others were hastily conceived in an atmosphere of high enthusiasm and substantial misinformation" (Zimring and Hawkins 1983, 355).

The Sociology of Criminology

For many of us the state of criminology is both good and bad news. The institutional forces that created opportunities for growth and funding for research and positions (academic and applied) contributed as well to the erosion of close ties with sociology. Although relationships among disciplines are a source of constant debate (see, e.g., McCarthy 2002), ties of criminology with other fields and disciplines—notably legal scholarship, psychology, economics, political science, and anthropology—have been strengthened. Inevitably this has weakened sociology's hegemony and contributed to the loss of the high status that criminology once enjoyed in sociology (and vice versa).

Histories of sociology and criminology include periods of sometimes

58. Komarovsky (1975) presents case histories of three of these commissions, plus that of the Commission on Population Growth and the American Future, and discussion of sociologists' roles in them.

problematic association with other institutions, for example, with religion and religiously inspired scholars (e.g., the Social Gospel sociologists), with social work, and for criminologists, with law enforcement. Some such problems have been countered by increasingly rigorous efforts to study phenomena associated with crime, by use of both dispassionate observation and abstract theoretical development, though these are not unmixed blessings. Relationships with the broader public and the state raise issues for all disciplines. In the early years such relationships may have been a minor concern for sociology, but as sociologists began to contribute to data collection systems and to participate in governmental programs, identification with the state became more problematic, as it has always been for criminology by virtue of its dependence on the criminal law and the state's vital interests in crime.

Efforts to legitimate the social and behavioral sciences customarily stress their institution-serving functions, often to the neglect of their critical role vis-à-vis those institutions. Sociology has been more successful than criminology in maintaining that delicate balance. As noted at the beginning of this chapter, the maturity of sociology has been marked by the development of status criteria that are sui generis (Bourdieu 1991c; Burris 2004). Similar efforts by criminology have been less successful in establishing an identity apart from law enforcement and the interests of the state.

Neoinstitutional Perspectives

A series of papers by Joachim Savelsberg and his colleagues suggests that the changing institutional environment of criminology and sociology's pulling away from criminology are causally and reflexively related to one another (Savelsberg and Flood 2005; Savelsberg, Cleveland, and King 2002, 2004; see also Dowdy 1994). Analyses of articles published in sociology, criminology, and criminal justice journals focus on "historical periods" between 1951 and 1993, funding sources, and substantive, theoretical, and methodological orientations to make the case.[59]

Criminal justice policy became more punitive late in the twentieth century as crime rates rose dramatically and penal policies changed. By the late 1960s governmental funding for criminological research had shifted from

59. The journals, with the number of articles included in each in parentheses, were *ASR* (132), *AJS* (78), *Social Forces* (85), *Social Problems* (75), *Criminology* (579), *Journal of Criminal Justice* (116), *Journal of Criminal Law and Criminology* (55), *Journal of Research in Crime and Delinquency* (336), and *Law and Society Review* (156).

agencies such as urban development, housing, and health to the U.S. Department of Justice and constituent agencies such as the Law Enforcement Assistance Agency, the National Institute of Justice, and the Office for Juvenile Justice and Delinquency Prevention. Over time, research funding from these agencies increasingly emphasized "strategic funding of agency-defined research projects" and appealed to the scholarly community to produce "relevant" research (Savelsberg, Cleveland, and King 2004, 1278).[60] More and more universities, often with government encouragement, initiated programs designed to professionalize law enforcement. Both cohort and period effects on criminology research were related to these changes (Savelsberg and Flood 2004).

Findings from this research program support hypotheses derived from neoinstitutional theory (DiMaggio and Powell 1983; Powell and DiMaggio 1991). For example, as a result of political funding, the field has seen increased research on such political priorities as drugs, multiple offending, incapacitation of offenders, and recidivism, as well as increased research based on control theories. Sociology journals were more likely to publish articles emphasizing social conditions and criminal behavior; criminology journals and research based on politically funded research published more articles on control institutions (Savelsberg, Cleveland, and King 2004, 1287). For the most part, however, independent variables such as period effects, political funding, and justice funding were not related to theory confirmation variables.[61] Thus, "while the questions asked are influenced by funding and organization, empirical conclusions are independent" of such considerations (1294).

Criminologists do not need to be reminded that governmental priorities heavily influence the availability and direction of research funding. The fact that they do so, however, is the subject of much controversy, and a sober reminder that the academy exists at the sufferance of broad and sometimes conflicting constituencies (Heydebrand 1990). For sociologists it demonstrates as well the interdependence of the law and its enforcement, and what is defined as crime and who is defined as criminal.

---

60. Policymakers in both executive and legislative branches also direct initiatives to non-justice organizations such as the National Science Foundation (NSF) and the National Academy of Sciences, as well as to more applied-mission funding agencies.

61. Political funding included non-justice-policy-related agencies such as the National Institutes of Mental Health and NSF.

Conclusion

Criminology and criminologists share with others in the social and behavioral sciences the many challenges of ever-changing societies. Observers of global change theorize forces that, it is argued, alter fundamental social bonds and institutions. Scholars from a variety of disciplines suggest that at the turn of the millennium, risk rather than crime "has become the central cultural register of social interaction" (Lianos and Douglas 2000, 261). The "globalizing logic of risk management" may make criminology's traditional concerns decreasingly "relevant to the new harms, risks, and mechanisms of control that are emerging today" (Braithwaite 2000, 222; see also other chapters in Garland and Sparks 2000). Such challenges and possibilities lie beyond the topic of this chapter. Necessarily and inevitably, however, they are of concern both to criminology as a special field and to sociology as a discipline.

Like problems associated with the increasing politicization of governmental research funding,[62] institutional environments of all disciplines and fields are influenced by social change. Criminology may be especially vulnerable, but we are all in some measure "in the same boat." The slings and arrows of critics notwithstanding, criminologists continue to contribute to sociology and to profit from our continued association. Surely, we can do better than "just be friends" (Heuveline 2004).[63]

Acknowledgments

The research and writing of multiple drafts of this chapter have been greatly facilitated by constructive comments from Bob Bursik, Gilbert Geis, Jack Gibbs, John Laub, Bob Meier, Charles Tittle, Javier Trevino, and especially Craig Calhoun.

62. Problems of political influences on research funding are noted frequently in editorials and articles in the journal of the American Association for the Advancement of Science (*Science*) and elsewhere.

63. On an autobiographical note, my choice of risk analysis as the topic for my ASA presidential address (Short 1984) was viewed by some, incorrectly, as an indication that I was either embarrassed or disillusioned with criminology. At the time, I felt that risk analysis had too long been neglected by sociologists and was in need of sociological thinking. Moreover, I felt that I had said all that I had to say about youth gangs and violence. Subsequent developments have proven the latter judgment incorrect, as new gang studies and research opportunities have rekindled my interest in both youth gangs and violence (Hughes and Short 2005; Short and Hughes forthcoming).

NINETEEN

Betwixt and Between
Discipline and Profession: A History of
Sociology of Education

Pamela Barnhouse Walters

The study of education has occupied the attention of sociologists from the very birth of the discipline. Indeed, the man often credited with founding sociology, Émile Durkheim, was interested throughout his career in the theory, history, and practice of education. Since the time of Durkheim, the centrality of education and schooling to the discipline of sociology has waxed and waned, but it has never entirely disappeared from the field. Further, sociology of education (or educational sociology, as it was first called) emerged as an important specialty shortly after the founding of American sociology, but its location with respect to its parent fields—sociology and education—and its prominence within sociology exhibit a series of interesting continuities and discontinuities. In this chapter I situate the development of the subfield in the context of intellectual and organizational developments in the discipline of sociology more generally, the development of professional schools of education within the American university, shifts in prevailing understandings of the problems that beset education, and methodological developments within sociology. Throughout, I argue that the ways in which scholars have managed the fundamental tension between two approaches to the sociological analysis of education—scholarship that uses the case of education to advance sociological theory versus scholarship oriented to the improvement of educational policy and practice—has shaped and constrained the development from its inception of what came to be known as the sociology of education.

The Founding Fathers, European and American

That said, let us return to Durkheim. Although he is not best remembered as a sociologist of education (except, perhaps, among sociologists of education), education was among his earliest interests, and it remained an abiding one.[1] For Durkheim, education was "a privileged applied field where so-

---

1. Durkheim's most important books on education are *Education and Sociology, Moral Education,* and *Evolution of Educational Thought.*

ciology could make its most important contribution to that regeneration of society for which he aimed so passionately" (Coser 1977, 146). His first academic appointment, at the University of Bordeaux, was in sociology and pedagogy. He moved to the Sorbonne in 1902; shortly thereafter he was named professor of the science of education and then, in 1913, professor of the science of education and sociology. Consistent with his overall views on society and social change, Durkheim was interested in education as a social system and in the relationship of education to the larger political and economic structure. His two most abiding contributions to the sociological study of education were to establish the interdependency of education and other social institutions and to show that education is closely related to societal values and beliefs (Filloux 1993; Karabel and Halsey 1977). Durkheim set an agenda for the study of the functions of education for societal stability and the role of education in social change, but his framework does not direct attention to issues of destabilization, conflict, or social inequality—all of which came to the fore in the hands of later generations of scholars.

Durkheim's career, and his body of scholarly work, cannot be understood apart from developments in French education. He was influenced by, and in turn contributed to, a secularization movement in late nineteenth-century France to loosen the Church's hold on education. Indeed, in the 1880s Durkheim was developing into the world's first "educational sociologist" just as Jules Ferry, the French minister of public instruction, "was laying the foundations of a secular, compulsory and egalitarian school system" (Filloux 1993, 306). It is probably not an accident that Durkheim was weighing questions about the relationship of education to the larger society at the same time that France was establishing a new system of public education to better serve the needs of the French nation. As we shall see, the intellectual twists and turns within the sociology of education throughout the twentieth century similarly cannot be understood apart from changes in the ways in which universities provided teacher training, nor apart from the social problems or needs the schools were expected to address.

During the same time that Durkheim was helping to found sociology and to establish education as an important field of study within it, American sociology was also getting its start.[2] Although the founders of American sociology similarly considered education to be central to the enterprise, one cannot find the fingerprints of Durkheim on the first generation of Ameri-

2. Between 1889 and the early 1890s, the first independent departments of sociology in American universities were established at Kansas, Harvard, Columbia, and Chicago. The American Sociological Association was founded in 1895, and the first issue of the *American Journal of Sociology* was published in 1905 at the University of Chicago.

can sociologists. The intellectual origins of American sociological interest in education lay elsewhere, in the service of late nineteenth-century social reform, and were intertwined with the development of the American social sciences more generally. For example, the university leaders who founded the American Social Science Association (ASSA) in 1865 promoted empirical study as a tool of social reform and considered educational reform to be a high priority (Haskell 1977).

Whereas the beginnings of sociological research on education in France coincided with the development of universal public education, in the United States mass education (the common school movement) preceded the start of sociological research on education by several decades. By the time sociology was emerging as a discipline, the educational issue on the public agenda was not the purpose of a system of free, public education in society; rather, it was how to solve what were seen as a series of vexing problems with the operation of the system.[3] Education, many agreed, was in serious need of reform.

Among sociologists and other social scientists, this reformist impulse led to an emphasis on school improvement as a means of advancing society; the importance of schools lay in their potential to develop students' mental abilities, which in turn was seen as an important engine of social progress. The leading psychologists of the day were at the forefront: John Dewey focused his attention on a child-centered curriculum;[4] G. Stanley Hall and James Cattell collected data on children's cognitive and emotional development in an effort to create a developmentally appropriate pedagogy; and based on his research showing that intelligence was largely inherited, Edward Thorndike promoted a differentiated curriculum (Reuben 2003). Lester Ward and Albion Small, who each played significant roles in establishing American sociology,[5] were similarly interested in educational improvement

---

3. In the United States, the common school movement successfully created a system of free, universal public education outside the South in the first third of the nineteenth century (Kaestle 1983). By the turn of the century, education was seen as a key means of dealing with the enormous social problems and dislocations brought about by rapid industrialization and urbanization and the rapid influx of "new" immigrants (Tyack 1974).

4. In addition to his academic work at the University of Chicago, Dewey was also active in a wide range of Progressive Era reform movements.

5. Lester Ward had an appointment in the sociology department at Brown. He was the first president of the American Sociological Association (then known as the American Sociological Society), serving from 1905 to 1907. Albion Small established the first department of sociology in the United States at the University of Chicago in 1892 and chaired it for over thirty years. In 1895 he established the *American Journal of Sociology*. He too served as a president of the American Sociological Association, from 1912 to 1913.

as a means of promoting greater individual development, albeit in different ways than the psychologists: Ward argued that social progress depended on achievement fostered through education (Dealey 1926; Kulp 1929), and Small thought the curriculum should be reformulated to fit the individual's experience in society (Reuben 2003). Both treated education as a way of incorporating individuals into the broader society (Dreeben 1994).

The attention Durkheim paid to the relationship between schools and the larger society was by no means completely absent, but the emphasis was different. For the American sociologists, the schools were linked to the larger society through the potential that lay in them for perfecting humanity and society (Parelius and Parelius 1987). Whereas Durkheim saw education as an institution that responds to social change, the American progressives saw education as the key means to alleviate social problems. Thus American educational sociology (as it was then called) had its origins in the Progressive impulse to reform society and to ameliorate social problems and dislocations. Importantly, schools' contribution to societal reform was fixing or improving *individuals*. As we shall see later, a similar mission restored education to prominence among sociologists in the 1960s after a long absence, although in service of the solution of different kinds of social problems.

The educational sociology of the early twentieth century was a cooperative endeavor between sociologists and educators, brought together by their shared commitment to improve society. They shared a pragmatic focus on school and classroom organization, administrative problems, and means of managing conflict between schools and other institutions (Parelius and Parelius 1987). This cooperative endeavor preceded the era of specialization in sociology (and was likely made possible by the absence of internal divisions within the discipline) and took place at a time when the study of what would now be considered relatively applied questions had great currency in the social sciences; as Bulmer puts it, the early American sociologists had "an enduring commitment to the production and application of socially useful knowledge" (1992, 317). This allowed those sociologically minded scholars who studied educational problems—whether formally located in sociology or education—to be central figures in their respective fields and to be remembered today as founders of sociology or education rather than as pioneers in "educational sociology." The tension that would emerge shortly thereafter between scholarship in the service of advancing sociological theory and scholarship in the service of solving educational problems was not yet apparent; at the time, sociological scholarship could be both.

By the 1920s, the Progressive Era commitment to scholarly inquiry in the service of societal improvement waned, taking with it the common ground on which sociologists and education scholars had together stood. Scholarly and organizational developments within the discipline of sociology and the field of education furthered the split. During the first two decades of the twentieth century, American sociology endeavored to establish its scientific legitimacy, and the research tradition took stronger hold in the American university system more generally, both of which called into question within sociology the practical, pragmatic, and applied nature of educational sociology as it had previously been practiced. At the same time, because educational sociology was not able to deliver on its original promise of solving educational problems, much less perfecting society, many educators became disillusioned with the enterprise.

Further, the increasing institutionalization of the American research university in the first decades of the twentieth century made it increasingly difficult to maintain a joint intellectual enterprise between leading sociologists and educators. As academic sociology departments and professional schools of education developed stronger (and more distinct) identities, the centers of gravity in education and sociology moved farther apart and the boundary between them became more firmly established. Thus the deepening organizational boundary between sociology and education made it increasingly difficult for the leading scholars in each area of study to maintain an identity that crossed the divide, although it did not remove education as a significant area of study for leading sociologists. That is, the question of whether sociologists continued to contribute in significant ways to the study of education—including those who were not identified as "sociologists of education"—is different from questions about the development of a distinct subfield known as educational sociology or sociology of education.

Education Inside Sociology: The 1920s to the 1940s

We have seen that education was a core concern of many of the leading American sociologists of the first generation and that around the turn of the century the boundary between sociology and education was relatively fluid.[6] By the 1920s, however, work that crossed that boundary was considerably rarer, and leading American sociologists partly turned away from the study of education. The turning away was not, however, thoroughgoing.

---

6. Their interests in education were more applied than theoretical, however. That is, they placed more emphasis on school improvement than on developing a theoretical understanding of how schools work. (I am indebted to Aaron Pallas for this point.) Note that this orientation put them in the mainstream of sociology of the time. It was consistent, for example, with the dominant approach of the Chicago school: social reform, broadly defined.

The second generation of American sociologists included several leading figures who devoted considerable attention to education (although they are not generally identified as specialists in education), and as the Progressive Era drew to a close, the organizational foundation for an academic specialty area in educational sociology was laid (although its members were generally not among the leading sociologists of the day).

Nonetheless, the prevailing approach to the study of education within sociology shifted between the first and second generation of scholars. The progressive sociologists and education scholars had studied education in the service of solving educational and societal problems. From the 1920s, this approach continued to be apparent (indeed, was heightened) in scholarship produced in schools of education but not by and large in that produced by sociology departments. By the 1920s, schools of education gained a much stronger institutional base in American universities and, in the process, moved away from the disciplines, especially philosophy, history, and sociology (Katz 1966); ties with psychology were maintained and perhaps even strengthened. In seeking an autonomous professional status akin to law or medicine, schools of education moved toward an applied empirical investigation of the child and the school (Katz 1966, 328). In Katz's view, then, education defected from sociology (329); this defection included eschewing theory for empiricism (332). The tradition in sociology, on the other hand, shifted to the application of sociological theory to the study of education and to the use of research on education and educational processes to advance sociological theorizing.

Between the Progressive Era and the 1950s and 1960s, three major themes characterized research on education by leading American sociologists: Research on social mobility, as exemplified by the work of Pitirim Sorokin; research on education and community, especially the work of Lloyd Warner and August Hollingshead; and research on school organization and social control, embodied in the work of Willard Waller. As I discuss later, with the partial exception of Waller these scholars worked outside of the subfield that came to be called educational sociology, yet they made a far greater contribution to research in sociology of education after midcentury than did any of the educational sociologists of the same era.

THE MOBILITY TRADITION

Sorokin, a Russian émigré, came to the United States in 1923. From 1924 to 1930, he had an appointment in sociology at the University of Minnesota; in 1930 he accepted an appointment as the first chair of sociology at Harvard University, which he held until his retirement in 1955 (Coser 1977). He was thus a key figure in the institutionalization and maturation of the discipline, at least through the middle years of his career at Harvard; his later work on altruism and love, however, moved him away from the intellectual center.[7] He is best known for his theory of mobility—as expressed especially in his 1927 book *Social Mobility*—and it is in this context that he made a long-lasting contribution to a sociological understanding of education.

Unlike later mobility scholars, Sorokin was not primarily interested in the determinants of *individuals'* prospects for mobility (Dreeben 1994; Bidwell 1999). Rather, he understood mobility as a process of exchange among groups. He identified education as the most significant channel of vertical mobility in most societies—a significant mechanism of social selection and distribution of individuals to distinct, hierarchically ordered social strata. Its significance to modern society, then, was its role in the social selection and distribution of the members of society to social strata (Coser 1977). His concern with the efficient allocation of talent foreshadowed the emergence some years later of functionalism within American sociology (Bidwell 1999), although his understanding that the social exchange made possible by education could have negative as well as positive consequences for society sets him apart from mainstream functionalist theorizing (including the work of his younger Harvard colleague who came into great prominence later, Talcott Parsons).

Sorokin's influence, albeit an indirect one, can be seen in the pioneering research of Blau and Duncan some decades later (Dreeben 1994). All in all, though, Sorokin's influence on subsequent attention to education within sociology was not as significant as the work of the education and community and school organization scholars to whom I turn later in the chapter. By the time the role of the school in social mobility was again at the center of the sociological research agenda, in the 1960s and 1970s, the question had been transformed. The later generations of sociologists investigated the individual-level determinants of "status attainment," abandoning Sorokin's conception of social positions located within classes or status groups in favor of a model of attainment as a continuum of status scores (Bidwell 1999).

EDUCATION AND COMMUNITY

Education was not at the center of the rich sociological community-study tradition of the 1920s to the 1940s, but that research tradition nonetheless

---

7. It was not until well after his retirement, in 1965, that Sorokin's lasting contributions to the discipline were recognized through his election to the presidency of the American Sociological Association.

led to attention to the school as a community—and a community of adolescents at that. By the 1930s, the transformation of the high school from an elite to a mass institution and the establishment of the practice of social promotion created a new kind of social environment of age-peers in most American high schools, not all of whom were serious or well-prepared students. Sociologists who pioneered the community-study tradition made important contributions to our understanding of the social dynamics of educational communities and social cleavages within them. Robert and Helen Lynd's studies in the 1920s and 1930s of "Middletown" found that a distinct minority of students were enrolled in academic tracks;[8] further, few students worked hard or even reported learning as their aim in attending high school. The Lynds established a new tradition of stratification research in American sociology and, in part through their close analysis of education, showed that equality of opportunity was more elusive than real.

Through his cultural anthropological studies of community, sociologist Lloyd Warner introduced to the field the concept that American society consisted of three main strata: the upper, middle, and lower classes.[9] He concluded that the school reflects the local status order in everything it does. Status, for example, shapes how students got sorted and selected in the schools (Dreeben 1994). One of Warner's enduring contributions was his introduction of the concept of "equality of educational opportunity" to American sociology. Similarly, August Hollingshead's study of "Elmtown" showed that student status was correlated with track placement, IQ, aspirations, and the like.[10] Both Warner and Hollingshead "demonstrated the manner in which schools tend to favor and select out children of the middle classes" (Becker 1952b, 452);[11] this agenda continues to be vigorously examined today by a range of contemporary sociologists of education.

In many respects, the Lynds, Warner, and Hollingshead set an agenda for sociological research on education that has been continuously examined from the time of their research to the present. The continuity between their work and James Coleman's 1961 *Adolescent Society*, for example, is obvious: Coleman examined how the school as a social system functioned and how individuals' actions are shaped within it (Schneider 2003). All were

8. Their classic books are *Middletown* (1929) and *Middletown in Transition* (1937).

9. Warner's publications most explicitly concerned with education are his 1944 book (with Havinghurst and Loeb) *Who Shall Be Educated? The Challenge of Unequal Opportunities* and two articles he published in the *Journal of Educational Sociology* in 1936 and 1943.

10. Hollingshead's *Elmtown's Youth* was published in 1949.

11. Warner's contribution here was mainly through his 1944 book with Havinghurst and Loeb, *Who Shall Be Educated?*

considered to be among the leading sociologists of their day and held positions at universities that were among the most prestigious in the country (Columbia, Chicago, and Yale, respectively), but none was identified as a scholar of education.[12]

SCHOOL ORGANIZATION AND SOCIAL CONTROL

Whereas Sorokin, like Durkheim, was interested in the relationship between education and the larger society, another line of research and theorizing within American sociology between the 1920s and the 1940s examined the relationship between the social structure of the school and the individuals within it. These studies move inside the school but not necessarily inside individual classrooms. The key figure here is Willard Waller; his classic 1932 book, *The Sociology of Teaching,* made significant contributions to the sociological understanding of school organization, social control, and the exercise of authority (Dreeben 1994) by providing "the first rounded account of the nature of schools as organizations to be encountered in either the sociological or the educational literature" (Bidwell 1999, 89).[13] Waller addressed key questions about the functioning of schools, such as how do teachers organize their classes for instruction, how do teachers provide learning opportunities for students, and how do students respond to teachers and to school authority more generally (Schneider 2003)?

The *Sociology of Teaching* is widely recognized as a classic in sociology of education, and Waller is seen today as a founding father of the subdiscipline (e.g., two decades ago the Sociology of Education section of the ASA named its annual prize after him). Nonetheless, Waller was not identified by his contemporaries as a scholar interested primarily in education; his main focus was on interaction, and classrooms were but one of the many sites where he studied it.[14] Further, Waller's research agenda about school organization was not taken up again by sociologists for more than three decades. Charles Bidwell's now classic 1965 article, "The School as a Formal

12. Robert Lynd was a sociology professor at Columbia from 1931 to 1961. Helen Lynd did not have a PhD or a faculty appointment at the time of either Middletown study. She received a PhD in the history of ideas from Columbia in 1944 and subsequently taught at Sarah Lawrence. Warner taught in the sociology department at Chicago from 1935 to 1959 and published a number of important books on American communities and stratification in the 1940s and 1950s. Hollingshead was a longtime member of the sociology faculty at Yale.

13. Waller's other main interests were in the sociology of the family and the sociology of war.

14. See, for example, Willard Wallers's obituary written by Kingsley Davis that appeared in the *American Sociological Review* in October 1945.

Organization," put this line of research back on the sociological agenda; it was furthered by the publication in 1970 of Robert Dreeben's *The Nature of Teaching* and in 1975 of Dan Lortie's *School-Teacher: A Sociological Study.*

Some of the themes Waller addressed about the social structure of the schools and interactions within it reappear in a variety of ways in the work of a handful of prominent sociologists in the 1950s and 1960s, such as Howard Becker's studies of Chicago teachers (Becker 1952a, 1952b, 1953); Neal Gross, Ward Mason, and Alexander McEachern's (1958) research on the role of school superintendents; and, most importantly, Talcott Parsons's classic article "The School Class as a Social System" (1959). These studies do not, however, act as a foundation for a later line of scholarship in the sociology of education, perhaps because they do not cohere into a research tradition, and attention to social processes in education did not prove to be among the lasting interests of the individual scholars.

In any case, the line of research that originated with Waller has a greater affinity with the concerns of educators than does Sorokin's work on social mobility or with the Lynds', Havinghurst's, and Hollingshead's work on community and stratification. It addresses issues of classroom organization and management that educators must confront in their professional routines. I find it significant, then, that Waller was not nearly as well placed or (at least eventually) as highly regarded within the discipline of sociology as was Sorokin, Havinghurst, Hollingshead, or Robert Lynd. Waller was educated at Chicago, but at the time of the publication of *The Sociology of Teaching* he was in sociology at the University of Nebraska; he later moved to the sociology department at Barnard.

Thus Waller's work, alone among the sociological research of the 1920s to the 1940s that I consider here, straddled the fields of sociology and education and spoke to issues of interest to education scholars and educators. But it was much less visible and highly regarded within sociology than were the other two lines of research, perhaps because by the time Waller was writing, the coin of the realm in sociology had shifted from social problems to theoretical advancements. When Waller's research agenda was revived, three to four decades after the publication of *The Sociology of Teaching,* the scholars who did so similarly straddled education and sociology. Indeed, all three were either partly or fully in the Department of Education at Chicago, which had an unusually close relationship with the Department of Sociology.[15] Charles Bidwell started his career with an appointment in the De-

---

15. Alone among the elite programs in education in American universities (what David Labaree [1998] calls "schools of education studies," to distinguish them from the "schools of

partment of Education at Chicago; he served as chair of the Department of Education and later, after moving to sociology, as chair of Sociology. Robert Dreeben spent his career in the Department of Education at Chicago, serving for a period as chair, and he had close ties with Sociology. Similarly, Dan Lortie was a professor in the Department of Education at Chicago, where he moved after an initial period at Harvard.

Reuben (2003) argues that social scientists' (including sociologists') interest in education waned between the Progressive Era and the 1960s. This brief review suggests a different interpretation. Throughout the 1920s to the 1940s, some of the most eminent sociologists of the day devoted considerable attention to educational processes, even though their work was not generally considered to be in the field of educational sociology and did not address questions of concern to educators or education scholars. The double exception among those discussed is Willard Waller. His work spoke to matters of social control and authority in the classroom—matters of vital interest to educators and education scholars—and he was a mainstream sociologist. Yet perhaps the price he paid is that he received only a partial embrace from each group of scholars. He was not seen at the time as an "educational sociologist,"[16] nor is he remembered today as one of the leading sociologists of his era.

The Subfield: Educational Sociology in the 1920s to the 1940s

Ironically, the formal creation of the subfield of educational sociology, straddling the discipline of sociology and the professional field of education, coincided with the breaking down of the loose cooperative endeavor among social scientists and education scholars in the service of education reform at the end of the Progressive Era. There are several markers of the institutionalization of educational sociology as a subfield located partly, but not fully, within the discipline of sociology. First there must be courses devoted to it: the first known class in educational sociology was taught in

---

education" whose primary mission is teacher training), education at Chicago was in a department located in the Division of the Social Sciences. The other elite "schools of education studies" (e.g., Harvard and Stanford) were separate schools, standing apart from the social sciences, and were much more closely associated with professional education than was the Department of Education at Chicago (although less closely associated with teaching training than most schools of education).

16. Waller published but one article in the official journal of the subfield, the *Journal of Educational Sociology* (see Waller 1936); more significantly, even though *The Sociology of Teaching* is now revered as a classic in sociology of education, it was never reviewed in the journal.

1907–8 at Teachers College of Columbia University by Henry Suzzallo, and by the mid-1920s nearly one-third of sociology departments offered an educational sociology class (Szreter 1980). Another indicator of institutionalization is an organizational basis: the National Society for Study of Educational Sociology (NSSES) was established in 1927 in the School of Education at New York University. A third marker is a specialty journal, whose establishment is a sign of strength and legitimacy of a new branch of knowledge: the NSSES started a new journal, the *Journal of Educational Sociology*, at the time of its founding in 1927, located in the School of Education. In 1932, however, the journal was taken over by the sociology department at NYU, thus establishing it as an "academic" journal for an academic audience (Szreter 1980). This move signaled the intent of the newly formally organized subfield to focus on the theoretical concerns of sociology rather than on the applied and practical concerns of educators and education scholars.

It is clear that the founders of the NSSES and the *Journal of Educational Sociology* intended the subfield to be primarily sociological. The inaugural issue of the journal, for example, included an article by Charles A. Ellwood (sociology department, University of Missouri) called "What Is Educational Sociology?"[17] He identified the subfield of educational sociology as "the very heart, so to speak, of general sociology" (Ellwood 1927, 25). And he emphasized its great potential by, in part, clearly differentiating it from education: "It should be primarily sociology, not education" (25). He also emphasized the essentially social nature of the sociological study of education by differentiating educational sociology from educational psychology and by claiming (in opposition to educational psychology) that the field would "speedily put an end to the individualistic view of education and all the evils that have followed in the train of that view" (28). Nonetheless, education scholars were welcome (albeit apparently on the terms of sociology): he

17. Ellwood's numerous books and prolific publications in sociology journals show that the center of gravity of his research was not in education. He published on a wide range of topics in the *American Journal of Sociology* (a total of twenty-two articles between the 1890s and the 1930s) and the *Journal of Social Forces* (eight articles during his career). In contrast, he published only twice in the *Journal of Educational Sociology*. Of his dozen major books, none focused on education (Odum 1951). Some years after his article in the inaugural issue of *JES*, he moved to the sociology department at Duke University. His prominence in the discipline of sociology is suggested by, among other things, his membership on the Committee of Ten that reported to the American Sociological Society in 1912 on subject matter for a fundamental course in sociology (Cooley et al. 1912) and his term as president of the American Sociological Society in 1924. Nonetheless, he was not as central to the discipline as was Sorokin, the Lynds, Warner, Hollingshead, or even Waller.

called for "educationists" to "make their work scientific" by devoting themselves enthusiastically "to the development of educational sociology."

The members of this new circle of officially organized educational sociologists, however, seem to have been concerned primarily with relatively applied questions and affiliated primarily with schools/departments of education. The second issue of the journal included an overview article titled "Research in Educational Sociology" by Harvey Zorbaugh (1927) of the School of Education at NYU,[18] in which he outlined a research agenda for the field. The field should apply "sociological technique to human nature problems arising in education" (Zorbaugh 1927, 19) rather than focus on some of the (apparently too abstract and esoteric) questions that preoccupy many sociologists. Zorbaugh warned the educational sociologist not to dally "on the banks of the Nile, trading stones with naked savages" or to dream "in his study of why the mills of the Gods grind slowly and fine" (19). The same issue included an article by Ross L. Finney (1927),[19] the first president of the National Society, reporting on replies to a letter he'd sent to members asking for their definitions of the field of educational sociology. Most of those who replied were affiliated with schools of education rather than sociology departments.

Because of its overwhelming focus on producing knowledge that would be useful to educators and educational policymakers, the new field of educational sociology "connected only slightly to mainstream sociological teaching and research in departments of sociology" (Bulmer 1992, 324). Even though, shortly after the founding of the NSSES and the journal, Daniel H. Kulp II (1929) argued that educational sociologists could choose between two possible approaches—to orient their work to "pertinent prac-

18. Zorbaugh published twenty-two articles in the *Journal of Educational Sociology* between 1927 and 1958, and no other publications in major sociology journals. He also did not have a record of publishing in any of the other major education journals. He moved to NYU shortly before publishing his first piece in the *JES*, after a period as a faculty member in sociology at Chicago where, as part of the Chicago school, he did the research for his classic 1929 book, *The Gold Coast and the Slum* (which was his only book). After his move to NYU he became, unlike Ellwood, fully "located" in the new subdiscipline.

19. Finney's appointment at Minnesota was as an assistant professor of educational sociology. Before that, he had been affiliated with the State Normal School in Valley City, North Dakota. Despite publishing a few articles in sociology journals (*Journal of Social Forces* and the *American Journal of Sociology*), he seems to have had an orientation closer to the field of education than the discipline of sociology. In *A Sociological Philosophy of Education*, published in 1929, for example, he expressed the view that the purpose of educational sociology was societal improvement (social evolution) through school improvement. Of the seven books he published, three were sociology texts to be used in the schools and three were analyses of education.

tical applications in education" or to study educational problems "to discover sociological findings and methods" (311)—it is clear that in practice the former largely eclipsed the latter among those who identified themselves and were identified by others as educational sociologists. In the trade-off between speaking to the educator versus speaking to the sociologist, the new field chose the educator, with the result that, from the perspective of sociology, the subfield became an "intellectual ghetto" (Bulmer 1992, 325).

Systematic analyses of the content and authorship of articles in the *Journal of Educational Sociology* similarly indicate that in the early years it was more oriented toward the interests of "educationists" than "sociologists," the original definition offered by Ellwood notwithstanding. Clearly, educationists and sociologists disagreed about what the objectives of the field should be (Jacobson 1962). During the first five years, the articles were primarily descriptive of current educational practices rather than analytical; there was little evidence of the application of sociological theories and concepts (Szreter 1980). The institutional affiliation of the authors reflected this as well. In the early years those with appointments in schools of education outnumbered those with appointments in sociology departments by a ratio of about 7 to 1 (Szreter 1980), although the proportion of articles contributed by sociologists increased between the 1920s and the 1950s (Jacobson 1962). Reflecting the dominance of educationists in the early years, most of the early articles were "practical-minded" pieces (e.g., on the curriculum, on civic education, on questions of student adjustment to school). Most adopted a normative approach (common to the field of education) and were concerned primarily with the solution of educational problems (Szreter 1980).

Those who published in the *Journal of Educational Sociology* in the early years were also anxious to establish the scientific legitimacy of the subfield and felt that its scientific advancement compared unfavorably with educational psychology. The inaugural editor, E. George Payne of the School of Education of New York University, argued in 1928 in his first editorial that educational psychology (unlike educational sociology) had attained the status of a science. Educational sociology's ability to realize its potential for promoting social progress, he continued, depends on "the extent to which sociologists are interested in the development of a scientific basis of educational procedure, as the psychologists have done" (Payne 1928, 242). Early on, it seems, the chief competitor of educational sociology for a social scientific analysis of education was educational psychology. In hindsight, given the social geography of schools of education in recent decades, this is significant.

We see, then, that although the subfield of educational sociology gained a firm organizational basis in the 1920s, in the early decades it straddled discipline and profession and was less sociological than "educationist." It gradually became more sociological, however, through the 1950s (Jacobson 1962). As we saw earlier, a number of the leading American sociologists devoted considerable attention to educational questions in the first half of the twentieth century; they were not, however, closely associated with the formally organized subfield. Most never published in the *Journal of Educational Sociology* (e.g., Sorokin, Hollingshead, and the Lynds). Although Waller is in hindsight most closely identified as an educational sociologist than any of the others commonly considered to be the fathers of sociology of education, recall that he published only one article in the journal and that *The Sociology of Teaching* was never reviewed in the journal. Of those seen today as the fathers of the subdiscipline, Warner published the most in the *Journal of Educational Sociology:* two articles.

To what prominent figures in sociology did the subfield of educational sociology turn? As discussions of the intellectual continuities in the field have suggested (Dreeben 1994; Bidwell 1999; Schneider 2003), here we see the influence of Sorokin, Warner, and the Lynds. The *Journal of Educational Sociology* published reviews of four of Sorokin's books, two of Warner's, and a review of the Lynds' *Middletown in Transition* (but not the original *Middletown,* published in 1929). Again, this suggests that the subfield did draw inspiration from some of the leading sociologists of the time, but the connection between the discipline and the subfield seems to have primarily operated in one direction. This pattern is consistent with Szreter's (1980, 180) argument that the founding of the journal "led to the expansion" of the subfield as well as "the potential isolation of the study of education as sociology's major specialism." Because of the journal's (and subfield's) pragmatic concerns with social problems in education, "its epistemological contribution to the laying of the foundations for sociology of education as we know it today, was limited," and "the kind of sociological perspective it stood for did not endure" (180).

Our sense of the prominence and standing of educational sociology in the period from the 1920s to the 1940s depends, then, on whether we look at the period from the point of view of an intellectual history or an organizational history. One can trace a near-continuous interest in education on the part of a number of leading sociologists from the time of the founding of the discipline, both in Europe and the United States, to the 1950s, even if for the most part these leading scholars were not primarily identified as educational sociologists. One can also consider the establishment of a formal organization and a specialty journal devoted to educational sociology as evidence of the increasing legitimacy of the subfield, although we have seen that it was generally isolated from the intellectual interests of the most prominent scholars in the discipline, that its center of gravity was more in schools of education than in sociology departments, that the subfield's key figures were not key figures in sociology in general, and that the work of the educational sociologists of the period has had little lasting impact on the present subdiscipline of sociology of education.

From Educational Sociology to the
Sociology of Education: The 1950s to 1970s

Between the 1950s and the mid-1960s, the subfield underwent a significant transformation, owing to organizational developments and to changes in the intellectual currents in sociology more generally. Essentially, I argue that the subfield became a subdiscipline, in the process moving closer to the center of the discipline of sociology.[20] At the same time, sociologists at the center of the discipline were increasingly turning their attention to educational processes.

Let us first consider the organizational transformation from subfield to subdiscipline. Between 1950 and 1965, educational sociology gradually developed into a scholarly specialty more closely associated with sociology than education; in the process, it came to be called the "sociology of education" (Dreeben 1994).[21] Two main developments mark this transition. In 1960, the Sociology of Education section of the American Sociological Association (ASA) was established, and in 1963 the ASA took over the *Journal of Educational Sociology* and renamed it *Sociology of Education*. The change in sponsorship and title of the journal was far more than symbolic. There was

20. I use the phrase "center of the discipline" cautiously. One of the critiques of sociology is that there is no center—instead of having a singular theoretical approach or set of important problems/questions to address, we have what might best be described as competing centers. I remain agnostic about whether this is good or bad for scholarship in sociology, but it is clear that scholars whose work is of interest to (and admired by) a broad range of sociologists are more likely to attain a position of prominence within the discipline and influence the direction of the discipline. It is with these understandings that I argue that sociology of education as a subfield (or subdiscipline, for that matter) has greater legitimacy *within sociology* when it is closer to the "center of the discipline."

21. Note, however, that as recently as 1961 the main issue concerning the status of the field of educational sociology with which its members were preoccupied was the proper subject matter for courses, not research—most of which were taught to prospective teachers in schools or departments of education (see Hoyme 1961; Quintana and Sexton 1961).

a dramatic shift in content. From 1961 to the final issue of the *Journal of Educational Sociology* in July 1963, the main topics investigated pertained to matters close to the instructional core of education: teaching, curriculum, school management, school transitions, testing, and—the farthest removed from the instructional core—racial segregation. In the first two and a half years of *Sociology of Education,* in contrast, little attention was paid to matters of instruction, classroom management, or other problems commonly faced by educators. The focus was far more on the relationship between school and society, and the topics covered included stratification and mobility, student culture, segregation, and educational attainment. Further, a number of articles on education in other countries appeared. The main common ground between educational sociology and sociology of education, it seems, was an interest in racial segregation and the problems associated with it.[22]

It is not entirely clear what occasioned the transition from educational sociology to sociology of education, but it was likely aided by the 1954 Supreme Court decision in *Brown v. Board of Education,* which brought questions of social inequality in general, and racial inequality in education in particular, to the forefront in the social sciences (Reuben 2003; Schneider 2003). The common thread of an interest in racial segregation both before and after the change in journal sponsorship and title is consistent with this argument. The discipline's and subdiscipline's interest in questions of social and educational inequality was furthered by other national developments throughout the 1960s, including the War on Poverty, the Elementary and Secondary Education Act (ESEA) of 1965 (which for the first time provided significant amounts of federal funding for disadvantaged students to state and local school systems), and the Civil Rights Act of 1964. Schneider (2003, 210), for example, identifies the *Brown* decision and the ESEA legislation as federal policy changes that "demonstrated a historical shift whereby education became publicly identified as a central mechanism for both social mobility and equal access to and participation in society." Questions of mobility and equality began to dominate sociology; as a result of the centrality of education to these processes, sociologists who studied education had ample opportunity to speak to the center of the discipline.

These same factors led to a revival of interest in education within other social sciences, although the revival was most dramatic in sociology (Reuben

22. In the period I examined (1961–65), the departmental affiliations of authors were not provided in the journal. Nonetheless, I recognized far more names of sociologists among the authors after the renaming of the journal in 1963 than before.

2003). Among the other social sciences, the growth of interest in education was especially noteworthy in economics. Radical economists Samuel Bowles and Herbert Gintis's (1976) *Schooling in Capitalist America* was highly influential throughout the social sciences and among education scholars, along with the work of revisionist historians such as Michael B. Katz (1968, 1971). This vibrant interdisciplinary line of research signaled a shift to a critical theory of education to which a number of sociologists of education (many located in schools of education) contributed.[23] Despite the contributions of a few leading sociologists to this tradition (see, e.g., R. Collins 1971, 1979), however, the center of gravity of the critical tradition in education was not in sociology, nor did it substantially affect sociology as a discipline.[24]

Two burgeoning areas of interest constituted an important bridge between sociology of education as a subdiscipline and the center of sociology during the 1960s: research on educational equality, as most visibly represented in the work of James Coleman and his colleagues, and the status attainment tradition associated with William H. Sewell and his colleagues.[25]

23. The growth of schools of education during this period, and the need to offer training in "social foundations" of education to prospective teachers, opened up job opportunities for sociologists in schools of education. Further, the establishment or strengthening of programs in the social sciences at most elite schools of education also provided opportunities for sociologists within schools of education (Lagemann 1996). In the past couple of decades, however, the presence of sociologists of education in schools of education has diminished. At present, educational psychology is the highest-status field within education, and educational psychologists far outnumber sociologists of education on the faculties of schools of education.

24. For a careful review, see Davies (1995). It is telling that the three main reviews of the intellectual history of the sociology of education as a subdiscipline (Dreeben 1994; Bidwell 1999; Schneider 2003) do not consider the critical tradition, nor do they trace any influence of Marx or Marxist thought on sociology of education. Perhaps it is because it was not a tradition centrally located in sociology, or even sociology of education; it spanned sociology, education, economics, and anthropology. Nonetheless, it was highly influential among scholars of education.

25. A significant body of research on higher education was produced during this period by a number of highly regarded sociologists. As Aaron Pallas reminded me, this includes Theodore Caplow and Reece McGee's 1958 *The Academic Marketplace*, Daniel Bell's 1965 *The Reforming of General Education*, Peter Blau's 1973 *The Organization of Academic Work*, and Christopher Jencks and David Riesman's 1968 *The Academic Revolution*, to name just a few. For reasons I do not fully understand, neither this body of research on higher education nor, with the partial exception of Jencks, the researchers who produced it were thought of as located within the subdiscipline of sociology of education. Conversely, until very recently, scholars identified as "sociologists of education" have paid little attention to higher education, focusing the vast majority of their attention on K-12 education and leaving the topic of higher education primarily to scholars in departments of higher education or educational administration in schools of education. I suspect part of the reason for American sociologists' recent overwhelming attention

Both lines of research were associated with sociologists at the center of the discipline, and each influenced research in sociology of education for years to come. I consider each in turn.

EQUALITY OF EDUCATIONAL OPPORTUNITY

The most obvious impact on sociology as a result of politicians' "discovery" of poverty in the early 1960s and the public's new attention to problems of social inequality was James Coleman's and his colleagues' landmark 1966 report *Equality of Educational Opportunity*.[26] The report was ordered by the U.S. commissioner for education in response to a mandate in the Civil Rights Act of 1964 to conduct a survey of the availability of equal educational opportunities in the United States (Karabel and Halsey 1977, 20). Contrary to the expectation that the well-known disparities in educational achievement between white and black students could be explained by racial inequality in school resources and facilities, the study found that school resources had little effect on student achievement, over and above family background. In other words, families are implicated in the creation of inequality in educational outcomes, but schools are not. Despite widespread debate over the measures and methods used in the study, the findings of the Coleman Report and another highly influential study published in 1972, Christopher Jencks and his colleagues' *Inequality: A Reassessment of the Effect of Family and Schooling in America,* which similarly showed that measures of school resources poorly predicted students' academic performance, were widely interpreted to mean that "schools don't matter." This interpretation begs the question of why poor and minority students tend to get clustered together in school and tend to go to schools with fewer resources (Walters 2001), but this alternate line of questioning went largely unexplored.

The Coleman Report was enormously influential in a number of ways. It directed sociologists' attention to the processes that affect individual students' academic achievement (Bidwell 1999; Dreeben 1994), thus laying the foundation for the full development of the status attainment tradition. It brought leading sociologists' attention to questions of educational inequal-

---

to K-12 education at the expense of higher education has to do with the field's individualist turn (see my later discussion of the status attainment tradition) and the ease of conducting individual-level analyses on K-12 students (due to the availability of a number of public-use data sets), whereas comparable individual-level public-use data on college students are not available.

26. Recall that Warner first introduced this concept in the 1940s.

ity.[27] Conversely, the widespread acceptance of the schools-don't-matter finding had two types of influences. It effectively directed social scientists' attention away from questions about the distribution of educational opportunities for most of the last four-plus decades (Walters 2001), but it also initiated a line of research on school effects and effectiveness as scholars attempted to identify what about schools *does* make a difference.

STATUS ATTAINMENT

By the 1950s, sociology as a discipline had taken an "individualist turn" (Bidwell 1999). One important realization of this turn was the development of what has come to be called the Wisconsin social-psychological model of status attainment by William H. Sewell and his colleagues in the 1960s. Based (eventually) on several waves of longitudinal data collected on Wisconsin youth, this research tradition examined the connections among individuals' family background, educational and occupational aspirations, and both educational and occupational attainment. A series of important articles by Sewell and his colleagues in the late 1960s, based on the first two waves of data (e.g., Sewell and Shah 1967, 1968; Sewell, Haller, and Portes 1969) laid out the longitudinal model and was largely responsible for putting status attainment research at the center of both the discipline of sociology and the subdiscipline of what had by then come to be known as the sociology of education.[28] Sewell and Hauser's 1975 book, *Education, Occu-*

27. Coleman was in the sociology department at the Johns Hopkins University at the time he conducted the study; in 1973 he moved to the sociology department at the University of Chicago, where he remained until his death in 1995. Coleman was one of the most influential sociologists of the second half of the twentieth century. He was honored by, among other things, election to the National Academy of Sciences in 1972 and the presidency of the ASA in 1992. Jencks was a sociologist at the Graduate School of Education at Harvard at the time that *Inequality* was written. He later moved to the sociology department at Northwestern; recently he moved back to Harvard in the Kennedy School of Government. He was elected to the National Academy of Sciences in 1997. Jencks and Coleman are both recipients of the ASA Sociology of Education section's award for a distinguished career of scholarship.

28. Blau and Duncan's now-classic book *The American Occupational Structure,* published in 1967, laid out a model of the role of education in social mobility and the intergenerational transmission of inequality that showed that achievement outweighs ascription in these processes. The Blau and Duncan volume provided the basic framework on which Sewell and his colleagues elaborated (Kerckhoff 1976), and the book was enormously influential in the discipline (e.g., the retrospective on *The American Occupational Structure* published in *Contemporary Sociology* in 1992 establishes that a large number of major lines of research in sociology can be traced to the volume). The impact of their joint work is also evident by the honors they received. Duncan was elected to the National Academy of Sciences in 1973. Blau served as ASA

pation, and Earnings, constitutes the most complete presentation of the Wisconsin status attainment findings.[29]

The status attainment tradition shifted the prevailing view of the relationship between education and larger social processes in important ways. Educational outcomes were explained in terms of individual attributes, and the models neither incorporate the social organizational and cultural processes identified by earlier generations as important determinants of social outcomes (Bidwell 1999) nor account for the effects of allocation—the way in which schools select, process, classify, and assign students—on educational attainment (Kerckhoff 1976). As such this line of research is not an intellectual descendant of Warner's, Sorokin's, or others' earlier sociological work on mobility (Dreeben 1994). Nonetheless, it is fair to say that the reinvigoration of sociology of education in the 1960s and 1970s, following the organizational shifts described previously, was built on the back of status attainment research (Dreeben 1994)—it was that dominant both within the discipline at large and within the subdiscipline.[30]

The kind of research embodied in the status attainment tradition would not have been possible were it not for the development of high-speed computers and multiple regression techniques (Dreeben 1994). The diffusion of the methodological and theoretical approach exemplified by the status attainment tradition was also made possible by the collection of a number of large-scale data sets by the federal government that were then made available to researchers for secondary analysis (e.g., High School and Beyond, the National Longitudinal Study of the High School Class of 1972, the National Longitudinal Survey of Youth). We see, then, that the questions sociologists address are shaped by the limits and possibilities represented by the availability of data and methodological advances as much as by shifting theoretical perspectives in and of themselves. As a result of these methodological advances and the "opportunities" represented by the new data sets, research on mechanisms whereby schools shape student outcomes, on the

president in 1974 and was elected to the National Academy of Sciences in 1980. Nonetheless, Sewell, through his status attainment work, had a far greater impact on the *subdiscipline* of sociology of education than did Blau or Duncan.

29. Sewell was a longtime faculty member in the sociology department at the University of Wisconsin. He served as president of the ASA in 1971 and was elected to the National Academy of Sciences in 1976. Robert Hauser, also a longtime member of the sociology department at Wisconsin, was elected to the National Academy of Sciences in 1984.

30. By the mid- to late-1970s, after status attainment research came to full fruition and the tradition was adopted by many other scholars (made possible, in part, by the availability of a number of large-scale, longitudinal data sets), there was some concern in the subdiscipline that *Sociology of Education* was seen as a de facto journal of status attainment.

role of social and cultural factors in educational processes, and on macro-level educational change (through historical and/or comparative analysis) went into retreat (Bidwell 1999). This retreat was aided and abetted by the new availability of federal funding for research on education to address policymakers' concerns, especially questions of (individual-level) opportunity and achievement.

By the 1970s, then, the individualist turn in the sociology of education was complete. Although status attainment research no longer dominates the subdiscipline as it did throughout the 1970s and 1980s, research at least loosely in this tradition—using large-scale secondary data sets to examine the individual-level determinants of student achievement—is still the bread and butter of sociology of education. It also remains well represented in the flagship journals of the discipline. In that respect, it represents an important bridge between sociology of education and the center of the discipline.

Research in the status attainment tradition, and the Coleman Report and research on school effects that followed from it, has found a wide audience within the sociology and education communities. That is, these research traditions simultaneously address issues central to the discipline as well as concerns central to policymaking in education (if not classroom practice). In this respect, they are a relatively rare exception to the commonly experienced trade-off between the goals of using education as a case to advance sociological theorizing versus generating knowledge of practical use to educators. That exceptionality may explain their wide influence. Interestingly, they follow (probably unwittingly) the direction Brookover laid out in 1949 for sociology of education (as distinct from educational sociology): "the analysis of the educational system as a pattern of social interaction and its relation to other social systems" (1949, 411) rather than the problems of the technical core of instruction that dominated educational sociology.

The 1980s and Beyond

The publication in 1983 of *A Nation at Risk,* which warned of the rising tide of mediocrity in America's schools, changed the public and political agenda concerning education from that of equality to one of excellence and shifted the kind of educational research projects federal and foundation funders were willing to support; that shift in emphasis moved education out of the center of interests of social scientists. This especially affected sociologists: research on educational equality and stratification could be placed at the very center of the discipline, but the questions that follow from the new ex-

cellence agenda—primarily about learning and academic achievement—
are not central to sociology. If sociology of education had adopted this
agenda, it would have returned to the issues that occupied the attention of
the preceding generations of educational sociologists that were connected
only tenuously to the mainstream of sociology. For better or for worse.

Since the 1980s, sociology of education has continued to be an active
and energetic field, but it is not as close to the center of sociology as it was
in the early decades of the twentieth century or in the 1960s and 1970s,
when a reform/equality agenda dominated sociology (and much of the social sciences). The increasing specialization of sociology has made its mark
on sociology of education as well. One can identify any number of strands
of research on schools and schooling on the part of sociologists in the past
few decades, and one can trace the lineage from some lines of research that
dominated in earlier decades to the present. But at present there is nothing
comparable to the agenda-defining work of Coleman or Sewell and his colleagues from the 1960s and 1970s.

To be sure, there have been important new developments in sociology
of education that have made their mark in sociology in general, of which the
theory of social capital is the prime example. The French sociologist Pierre
Bourdieu introduced the concept of social capital to English-speaking sociologists in a text on the sociology of education in 1985. He argued that the
social networks and groups in which an individual participates give the individual resources that can be converted to personal benefits. In a careful
study of the ways in which social capital furthers the individual's pursuit
of educational credentials, American sociologist James Coleman (1988)
focused attention on "the role of social capital in the creation of human
capital" (Portes 1998, 5) and brought the concept to greater prominence
in American sociology. In the numerous empirical studies of the consequences of social capital for individual advancement that followed, the
differences between Bourdieu's and Coleman's definitions are blurred, and
"social capital stands for the ability of actors to secure benefits by virtue of
membership in social networks or other social structures" (Portes 1998, 6).

Research on social capital is related to sociology of education in two important ways. First, the case with which both Bourdieu and Coleman
worked out their theoretical accounts of social capital was education, and
from its development with respect to education the concept has come to be
enormously influential throughout the discipline. Second, social-capital
models of educational achievement and attainment have become increasingly dominant in the subdiscipline. Despite the attention drawn in theoretical models of social capital to links between individuals and social groups,

most of the empirical research in sociology of education that deploys the concept explores individual-level processes of achievement and attainment. As such, most research on education in the social capital tradition is of a piece with the individualist orientation that predominated in the 1960s and 1970s and, conversely, only loosely derived from the mobility studies of early twentieth-century sociologists such as Sorokin, who focused their attention on the locations of social groups rather than the attainment of individuals.

Other more fully macro approaches, however, have come into their own; further, to some degree these research agendas have been taken up outside of sociology of education. I am thinking here especially of the "neo-institutional" tradition most closely associated with John Meyer and his colleagues (e.g., Meyer and Hannan 1979; Meyer, Ramirez, and Soysal 1992) that locates the development of national systems of schooling in the context of the development of the nation-state and a world culture of modern individual rights and citizenship (see discussion in Bidwell 1999; Schneider 2003). This work has close connections with broader sociological interests in institutions and organizations. Also important is the work discussed earlier of Dreeben, Bidwell, and Lortie (all in education or education and sociology at the University of Chicago) on the organization of the school, especially the way in which school bureaucracy affects the work of teachers and the school's ability to fulfill its mission. One can place in this same general line of research Karl Weick's (1976) theory of "loose coupling" between the school organization's productive activities and its administrative cadre; similar themes were also taken up by John Meyer. Much of this work connects with research on formal organizations outside of sociology of education. It derives partly from the research tradition established by Willard Waller but is more closely connected to the main currents of sociology as a discipline than was Waller's work. Tellingly, the main figures in these lines of research each have a foot in sociology of education and a foot in another subdiscipline that, at the time, was closer to the core of sociology than was sociology of education.[31]

There is little in current research in sociology of education that draws directly from the rich community-study tradition of the 1920s to the 1940s, exemplified by the Lynds, Warner, and Hollingshead. Based as it was on field research and the methods of cultural anthropology,[32] this kind of research has been harder to sustain in the climate of recent decades that places a high

31. These figures reinforce Pallas's (1998) advice to budding sociologists of education to develop dual subspecialties.

32. As Craig Calhoun reminded me, Warner's influence on contemporary anthropology is evident.

premium on what is seen as legitimate science and the drive to establish generalizable patterns among large populations and cases (Bidwell 1999). Recent ethnographic work on schools and families (e.g., Lareau 2003) and on adolescent peer culture within schools (e.g., Eder, Evans, and Parker 1995) can, however, be seen as an indirect descendent of the community-study tradition.[33]

The roads not taken in sociology of education and the bodies of work not claimed as part of the subdiscipline are as telling as the areas of proliferating research. For example, the rich functionalist theories of the early twentieth century and midcentury work in the functionalist tradition (consider, e.g., the substantial and varied work on education of Parsons [1959a], Parsons and Platt [1973], and Inkeles and Smith [1974]) do not appear to be carried forward in contemporary research in the sociology of education. This is of a piece with the more general pattern in sociology of a turning away from functionalism, at least until recently. From the point of view of intellectual contributions alone, it is hard to understand why Willard Waller is considered to be among the leading figures in sociology of education of an earlier generation but other scholars who worked in a similar vein, such as Howard Becker, are not. Perhaps it is that Waller, who died in 1945, was available to be claimed as an ancestor in the 1960s, when the subfield of educational sociology was being actively reconstituted as the subdiscipline of sociology of education, a process that could be aided by laying claim to a recognized sociological ancestor whose body of work was complete.

Perhaps most importantly, however, contemporary sociologists of education pay little attention to the questions of school improvement that preoccupied American educational sociologists and established a common ground for sociologists interested in education and education scholars during the Progressive Era. Sociologists who today turn their attention to education generally prefer to study how schools work than to try to figure out how to make schools better. Notably absent from the intellectual agenda of sociologists of education today are questions about learning, curriculum, and instructional practices (see Hout and Walters 2000). Importantly, this means that at present sociology of education is much closer to sociology than to education, whereas at the time of the organizational founding of the subfield it clearly had a closer affinity to schools of education than to departments of sociology.

33. Further, much current work in the community-studies tradition speaks to questions about education indirectly if not directly, even though most is not explicitly focused on education.

Perhaps in recent decades sociologists of education turned more fully to sociology than to education because of perceptions that education is a low-status field (Pallas 1998; Schneider 2003; also see Labaree 2004). But scholars of education have also increasingly turned away from sociology since the 1970s—indeed, from the social sciences in general (except psychology, which is seen as making valuable contributions to the science of learning; Reuben 2003). The increased orientation of education research to applied problems facing educators was furthered by the passage of No Child Left Behind and the creation of the Institute of Education Sciences in the federal Department of Education (e.g., see the research agenda outlined in Whitehurst [2003]). As a result of these trends, sociologists of education are far more marginalized within schools of education at present than they were a decade or two ago, and their numbers are much reduced. Importantly, unlike the situation during the Progressive Era, in which a loose interdisciplinary group of social scientists interested in education drew heavily on sociology and psychology, there is little evidence of a link between sociologists interested in education and educational psychologists at present. Although the increasing isolation of sociology of education from the mainstream of scholarship in schools of education and from the concerns of educators may be a boon to the scholarly status of the subdiscipline within the field of sociology in that it puts a greater distance between the subdiscipline and a lower-status professional field of study, it removes from the subdiscipline a potentially valuable source of intellectual vitality.

There is a further intellectual and organizational divide within the subdiscipline of sociology of education at present that works at cross-purposes to subfield coherence. Some of the roads not taken in the sociologically rooted wing of American sociology of education were taken by the education school–rooted wing. The "new sociology of education" that was interpretive rather than quantitative and that emerged primarily in England in the 1960s and 1970s never gained a widespread following among American sociologists who study education (Karabel and Halsey 1977), although it did attract the attention of a number of education scholars in American schools of education (see Davies 1995). It was decidedly antipositivist at the time that status attainment research and other quantitative traditions seemed to hold the promise of making sociology more scientific.

In important respects, then, sociology of education in the American academy is today a bifurcated field, with one base in sociology that is generally focused on studying educational processes in the service of theory development and the other base in schools of education that is primarily devoted to improving education. This intellectual divide within the subfield parallels the organizational divide between sociology and the professional field of education. More importantly, it is problematic for the intellectual endeavor. Whereas sociology of education was at the time of the founding of the American Sociological Association a shared endeavor between sociologists and educationists, at present sociology of education is internally divided. In other words, there is at present no "invisible college" that brings together the leading scholars within the field.[34] It might be more accurate to talk about the two sociologies of education.

Acknowledgments

I am indebted to Jenny Stuber for her research assistance; to Elizabeth Armstrong, Mitchell Stevens, Craig Calhoun, Aaron Pallas and his seminar students, and two anonymous reviewers for their generous and helpful comments on a draft of this chapter; and to Brian Steensland and Tom Gieryn for answering questions for me at important junctures.

34. The term is Crane's (1972). Those who study the development of scientific fields show that in coherent scientific communities, elites are closely bound by a wide variety of shared communication ties and shared scientific understandings (Crane 1972; R. Collins 1989; Friedkin 1998). These conditions that make possible a field are lacking at present in sociology of education.

[TWENTY] Internationalism and Global Transformations in American Sociology

Michael D. Kennedy & Miguel A. Centeno

How has the world beyond the United States of America shaped the development of American sociology over this last century? To what extent has American sociology treated empirical reality outside of the United States as part of its professional "sample"? Should American sociology cultivate more international perspectives?

We begin this chapter by clarifying the range of things to which sociologists might refer when they use the word *international* to mark sociology in America. We use that provisional clarification to guide a historical review of American sociological internationalism over the past century. We focus on the last fifty and especially the most recent twenty-five years of our disciplinary practice, simultaneously a time of globalization and a new "golden age" of comparative and historical sociology (R. Collins 1999b). We also draw on surveys of published materials and correspondence with more than seventy American sociology department members evidently international in their scholarly commitments. We learned from them about the most important contributions to scholarship in their field and received additional valuable commentary on the status of the international in American sociology.

On the basis of these sources, the discipline looks more ethnocentric than one might expect, even as it is more global. American sociology faces a double bind—obliged by its location to engage the world, but blinded by its location to recognize the full scope of American power. That double bind is even apparent in the definition of *international*.

What Is International?

To specify "international" one must be able to recognize "American" sociology. Some might wonder if there is any part of the discipline that may not be described as international. Are there any circumstances in which we can find that native-born American citizen employed in an American sociology department filled with similar sorts, reading only about America by American authors, using American data to teach American citizens and to publish in American journals? This is atypical, if it exists at all.

Of course the best place to recognize what is American sociology may be to focus on the organization devoted to its promotion; as the sponsor of this very volume, and therefore indirectly of American sociological internationalism's very recognition, we could consider how ASA practices denote the international. We therefore use the ASA, and its principal constituency, as our background for this analysis.

Alternatively, we could have looked at American participation in organizations devoted to international sociology, for example, the International Institute of Sociology, founded in Paris in 1893, or the International Sociological Association, an organization formed by UNESCO with the express purpose of supporting sociology across the world.[1] The latter's research committees and conferences are often cited by American sociologists as critical interventions in extending their American sociology, and its publications might be a good source for identifying the ways in which American sociologists engage the world.

We don't, however, pursue a formal organizational or institutional analysis of American sociological internationalism but instead address the question more in cultural and historical terms. In particular, we seek to clarify the contentions around American sociological internationalism's meanings, and the variety of those contentions across the discipline and over time and space in the world. After all, every American sociologist is no doubt an advocate of extending the global foundations of the American sociological imagination. At the very least, most would agree that the wider the scatter of data points in search of general theory, the better.[2]

One obstacle to differentiating a national from an international perspective rests in the apparent failure of many American sociologists to recognize the national accent in their work. While the limits of covering laws or general explanations might be specified, these constraints are posed typically without marking national references, or without explicitly theorizing the context of the enabling social relations or social theory.[3] Consider those

1. In regard to the International Institute of Sociology, see http://www.tau.ac.il/~iisoc/about.html; in regard to the International Sociological Association, see http://www.ucm.es/info/isa.

2. For example, "Internationalization means that knowledge is broadly applicable without reference to national and other boundaries" (Smelser 2003, 645). See also Kohn (1987).

3. Even our discipline's histories rarely problematize our national location. Abbott's (2001) institutional analysis, for example, emphasizes the peculiarity of American higher ed-

methodological and theoretical treatises that have no particular place in mind, or those discussions of society that might apply to any nation, or at least to any industrial or postindustrial place. Aspirations to develop general sociology or universal laws may even find the identification of national particularities a hindrance, rather than a help, in their work. From this perspective, sociology, like physics, should know no empirical borders. We might improvise on the Thomas theorem to offer our caution: to define things as absent does not mean they are absent in their effects.

American sociology has focused substantially, if not exclusively, on American society and its intellectual products. It has developed practices that elevate and evaluate with American references and, secondarily, those of nations that most resemble it. This American privilege varies considerably by specialization, but even those specializations committed to understanding the world beyond the United States face pressures that reproduce the discipline's national presumption in its international work. This happens typically without acknowledgment because it is so apparently natural, so commonsensical. But national boundaries can be quite powerful when they work implicitly. For a global sociology to reduce those constraints, we need first to recognize them, and this requires some consideration of why national constraints are hard to see, especially in the United States.

Given the power and privilege of American sociology in the world, it is easy to imagine the world in American terms. When the influence of American power in that world's definition combines with the capacities of American sociology to recruit scholars and students from around the world to its institutions and into collaboration with American research projects, American terms may not look ethnocentric. As the American part of the global story becomes increasingly prominent, the American perspective on the world seems to be even more justifiable. Too, given the diversity of standpoints *within* the United States, and their influence on our discipline, it is common to slide directly from American multiculturalism right into internationalism when we speak of our nation's sociology of the world. Given

---

ucation with its disciplinary formation and professional organization, in this sense provincializing American institutional structure much as Chakrabarty has provincialized that of Europe (Chakrabarty 2000). But unlike the latter, with his regional cultural focus, Abbott still treats sociology's cultural formation in a comparatively generic fashion, noting its extreme interstitiality and fractal qualities in knowledge cultures and career making, but without noting the discipline's American accent. Nationality appears only implicitly when a work, with author or substance from elsewhere, finds a place in the list of the exemplary, whether in reference to the migration of Polish peasants or the making of the English working class. Thanks to Mel Kohn for this very helpful way of framing the problem.

the diversity of American sociology's engagements with that world, it is also difficult to recognize a single national paradigm at work.

How, then, can we speak of American presumption? We acknowledge this variety, but consider it central to an explanation of how ethnocentrism functions in the constitution of the "sociological imaginary" of American sociological internationalism.[4]

At one level, some colleagues consider using data sets from other countries to be evidence of internationalism at work. With the wider distribution of data points for American theory, the discipline can become simultaneously more global and more American at the same time, to the extent Americans set the terms of the data collection, interpretation, and argument, and conduct the collaboration in English.

Other scholars find a more robust internationalism to exist when American scholars use other nations' cultures and historiographies to shape not only those data's interpretations but also the questions used to gather the material. These collaborations are also more likely to move beyond American cultural terms and language, but they may remain focused on nations and scholarships that are more similar to the national and professional imaginaries of American sociology.[5]

Still others find internationalism's challenge more fully embraced when the cultural logics of distant civilizations shape the ways in which we recognize similarities and differences, and even envision space and time in social analysis (Wallerstein 1999). Here, we might raise the epistemological issue of the extent to which local context can ever be properly understood by any external observer. From one postmodern extreme, American sociology can never be anything but American and attempts at internationalism merely mask that particular.

Anthropology has faced many of these challenges and questions and has arguably become much more "global" in its perspective than American sociology. American anthropologists have historically focused on cultures beyond the United States, or if within its national boundaries, on societies

---

4. We build on work around the "social imaginary" here. Although he has not been its original or exclusive theorist, Charles Taylor (2004, 23) offers one of the most concise and useful presentations of the "social imaginary"—"how people imagine their social existence, how they fit together with others, how things go on between them and their fellows, the expectations that are normally met, and the deeper normative notions and images that underlie these expectations."

5. For example, Poland became a major case for comparative studies of socialist and capitalist societies because its intellectual infrastructure and geopolitical orientation were closer to those of America (Kennedy 2004b).

perceived as alien if not also in danger of disappearance. With this effort, the distinction of and problem for American identity has been central in the analysis of these explicitly "other" societies. As well, the problem of the "native anthropologist" moving into the American discipline, and into the field that was once home, has been extensively discussed.[6] America's relative marginality from anthropology's disciplinary focus has thus contributed significantly to the problem of Americans knowing others. American sociology has not had similar focus.

Political science and history, at least in organizational terms, are also better off than sociology. They have worked much more than sociology at defining this American peculiarity. Both are more explicit about the place of the international in their disciplinary makeup in part because American studies has a much stronger, and more distinctive, place in each of them (although this may be changing, especially in political science).

American sociology is different because of American studies' *implicit* centrality. This area study is powerfully important within sociology, as it is in history and political science, but this regional focus is not so easily distinguished as a field given the heterogeneity of interests, from conversation analysis to wayward Puritans, that might go into American sociology's dominant area study. Most importantly, it is not clear where the line dividing American studies within sociology from sociology in general lies. General sociology masks American sociology's dominant focus, and when it focuses on the "other," its dominant others have been within the nation. American sociology has wrestled mightily with the challenge of difference within America, most especially around race, migrant status, class, gender, and sexuality, but has not devoted similar effort to those others beyond the nation.

It is clear, given this variety within the discipline, and the distinction of the discipline from other approaches, that although "international" is part of our discipline's imaginary, it is not as theoretically rigorous or organizationally distinct as it might be. We therefore cannot treat the international as a simple categorical distinction from American sociology, or within American sociology. It rather functions in association with the discipline's debates about method, theory, and above all standpoint. Indeed, we argue that this standpoint is especially difficult to recognize given that American national identity and identification provide such a powerful lens through which to present a global view and a world sociology.[7]

---

6. This might be exemplified at the end of the nineteenth century by Cushing (1979) and by scholars like Nazif Shahrani in the end of the century (1994).

7. Consider, for example, how American identity infiltrates general visions of society when no place is identified explicitly but American society obviously is in the author's mind.

Part of our challenge, then, is not only to offer an account of internationalism's history in American sociology but to consider how various qualities of internationalism are embedded in, and distant from, American sociology's historical practice. This is made more difficult with the generally complicated relationship between theory and history (Somers 1998), especially between theory and histories beyond sociology's typical ancestry, beyond its Anglo-American heritage, and beyond central and western Europe too.

Given the relative difficulty of articulating theories developed in one context with alien historical contexts, many sociologists who work with these more distant histories develop their arguments in what some might call atheoretical, or even antitheoretical, terms. By epistemologically privileging the particular context of a region, such colleagues eschew universalistic claims in their own work and sometimes even challenge others' attempts to establish these general theories. In part, this defense of the particular against the universal stems from the professional experiences of regional experts.

Colleagues who work outside of the United States frequently complain about journal editors who ask them to justify the significance of a set of findings since they only apply to country A or region Y beyond the United States, or who recommend that the article be placed in an area studies journal rather than in a journal dedicated to general sociology. This alienation grows when these colleagues observe similar work based only on the United States finding a place in a publication dedicated to general sociology. Thus, for many regional experts, "theory" or "generalizability" has become nothing more than a cover for American centrism. Moreover, social theory *is* frequently grounded in a Western if not predominantly American condition (Centeno and Lopez 2001).

By making "international" a more robust theoretical category, we can help to extend the discipline's global reach by issuing a more explicit challenge to American sociology's theoretical range, and not only its empirical scope. By making the limitations of national presumption explicit in theory, we might increase the discipline's reflexivity about the national conditions of its own production and invite further work to reduce the ethnocentrism

---

It is also apparent when American sociologists analyze other societies within a framework more closely associated with an American disposition than are the studied society's civilizational concerns or contentions. It might be apparent when scholarship about a world region refers only to American scholarship about that region, and nothing from that region, even in translation, appears in the bibliography. That American lens may even be more apparent in a region's absence, where certain parts of the world not implicated already in an American story fail to become part of American sociology.

of American sociology. Such work might not only reduce ethnocentrism but also help to constitute more sober ambitions in the realization of global sociology, recognizing the possibilities, and limits, of utopian visions that purport to transcend locales of various sorts in sociology's making. But we don't see this only as a matter of theory.

Global transformations, social organization, and personnel matter. To the extent, for example, that comparative and historical sociology is more prominent in a site than is experimental social psychology, we should expect the international to be more apparent.[8] To the extent that our discipline is populated by people from other world regions, those regions should become more prominent in the discipline's explicit and implicit practice. Of course, too, global transformations also influence the importance of any subject—revolutions and wars involving America make regions important in ways that impoverishment and health crises do not. And of course places without crisis appear hardly relevant to a sociology assuming the universality of its culture (Kennedy 2004b).

We do not only seek to understand variations, however. There are important continuities within American sociology's engagement of the world beyond its borders. It has been profoundly western and central European in focus for most of this century. Prominent arguments about social structures and dynamics in other world regions become visible typically when global transformations or American intellectual debates direct the national gaze toward that region. These general observations are made better, however, with reference to the historical transformations of our discipline in its engagement of the world, helping us to appreciate the enduring engagements, and problems, of American sociological internationalism.

Historical Patterns in American Sociological Internationalism

The discipline's founding in the midst of substantial immigration, European intellectual engagement, and the explosion of imperialism, revolution, and war presumed quite broad international reference in American sociology. Too, sociology was more closely tied to anthropology in its first half century, enabling world regions subsequently removed from the discipline's primary focus to have a relatively substantial presence in the early

---

8. Although even here the burgeoning interest in culture and cognition, in psychology at least, suggests great promise for globalizing studies of the self. One of the major contributions in this regard is from Markus and Kitayama (1991). Sociologists, especially ethnographers, are also working to extend studies of the self (e.g., Glaeser 2000).

years (Steinmetz, chap. 9, this volume). However, given his subsequent dominance at Harvard, in the discipline, and in the definition of that quintessential social scientific internationalism, modernization theory (Gilman 2003), one typically references Parsons's (1937) attempt to codify that international influence in *The Structure of Social Action*. But that would overlook a much broader European, and even global, engagement.

For example, Harry Elmer Barnes (1948b) suggested the world vision of American sociology with his edited volume. Chapters were written by very distinguished American sociologists, attending initially to the "pioneers of sociology"—the Frenchman Comte, the Englishman Spencer, the Austrian Gumplowicz,[9] and the Americans Morgan, Sumner, and Ward. It's especially useful to note Sumner's influence here, for his founding of the "Yale school" of sociology not only had that typically Christian reformist bent (Vidich and Lyman 1985) but also an international reference. Often identified as America's Spencer (Breslau, chap. 2, this volume), Sumner was also a vigorous opponent of American militaristic imperialism and its advocates in sociology, including Giddings. Sumner argued that "imperialism, like paternalistic legislation, imposes upon the population burdens which quite outweigh the benefits which are forthcoming. The increased expenses of government are thrown upon the middle class, and imperialistic administration necessitates a curtailment of liberty and the adoption of militaristic measures which seriously threaten the existence of free republican government and industrial democracy. . . . It invariably creates an attitude of political arrogance and chauvinism" (Sumner 1913, as quoted in Barnes 1948c, 168). Keller and Murdock, the latter the founder of the Human Relations Area Files project, succeeded Sumner at Yale. Their comparative reach led much of Yale sociology to become part of anthropology, although its influence remained apparent in the work of Parsons, Lenski, and others.[10]

It is also worth noting that, in contrast to the myth about focusing on modernity's making within the metropole, and the singular focus on the canonical trinity of Marx, Weber, and Durkheim typically invoked by histories of classical sociological theory, these American sociologists read very broadly and did not consider contemporary industrial society as their only object of study (Connell 1997).

American sociologists offered chapters on their peers from Germanic countries (Wundt, Toennies, Simmel, von Wiese, Max Weber, Troestsch,

9. Or is he better understood as "doubly without a country—as a Jew and a Pole" (Gella 1964, 227)?

10. We are indebted to Gil Merkx for this recollection. See also Bannister (1991).

Sombart, Oppenheimer, Alfred Weber, Freyer, Ratzenhofer, Spann, and Stein), France (Fouillée, Tarde, Le Bon, Durkheim, and de Greef), and England (Kidd, Hobhouse, Westermarck, Briffault, Geddes, Branford, Wallas, and Toynbee). They attended to sociologists of a few other nationalities—two Russians (Novicow and Kovalevsky), a chapter on Italians (Pareto, Loria, Vaccaro, Gini, and Sighele), and a chapter on the "Lester Ward" of Spanish sociology, Adolfo Posada. Too, in the volume's concluding section on American sociology one finds more than a European reading list.

This familiar roster of early American sociologists—Small, Giddings, Cooley, Ross, Hayes, Thomas and Ellwood, as well as a couple less familiar, including J. H. W. Stuckenberg—enjoyed extensive European travel and research. W. I. Thomas was most vigorous in that ambition. His volumes, authored with Florian Znaniecki, became a signpost for theoretically and empirically ambitious scholarship (Thomas and Znaniecki 1918–21). It also exemplified transnational intellectual engagement around a manifestly global process, even if its practical and empirical concerns were grounded in America. Thomas even took it upon himself to learn Polish and spent more than two-thirds of his time between 1908 and 1913 in Polish lands in order to understand the communities from which his Chicago residents came (Burawoy 2000).[11] But Thomas was by no means alone among European travelers.

Stuckenberg moved to and from Germany during the latter part of the nineteenth century, advancing both Christian ministry and sociology. Another Christian author, Ellwood, was also a major activist in promoting world peace in Europe, through whose ties he ultimately became president of the International Institute of Sociology between 1935 and 1936 (Barnes 1948a, 857). Ross was the first American sociologist to be seriously engaged in the Russian Revolution, investigating it "on the spot"; he also wrote a book on the Mexican Revolution shortly thereafter and studied social change in China and India (Kolb 1948, 822–23)

No American sociologist was more influenced by the Russian Revolution (Sorokin 1925, 1950), however, than was the Barnes volume's contemporary "systematizer"—the Russian émigré Pitirim Alexandrovitch Sorokin. His prominence in American sociology at that time is too easily overlooked today, perhaps partially attributable to what the chapter's author characterized as his experience during the Russian Revolution: "His [Sorokin's] hatred of communism, many of his anti-progressive and reactionary political

---

11. Znaniecki was not, apparently, so much a coauthor as a translator, but he contributed "the 'values' concept for which Thomas has given him full credit" (Barnes 1948d, 797–98).

opinions, and his rejection of the ideals of modern, Western civilization as a whole may be traced to this period of his life" (Spier 1948, 884). American sociology does not have such an easy antimodernist guise, but Sorokin's own troubled relationship with many colleagues, including Talcott Parsons, cannot be overlooked either (Johnston 1995).

Sorokin is not the only distinguished international sociologist to disappear from the American sociological imagination, of course. Florian Znaniecki is another prominent sociologist of American sociology's middle age who had profound international interests (see, e.g., Znaniecki 1954). His contributions to global and cultural sociology are also largely overlooked in contemporary American sociology (Halas 2005). We might simply attribute this ignorance to American sociology's amnesia regarding disciplinary history (Turner, chap. 4, this volume), but that would miss the unevenness of this forgetfulness. Both Znaniecki and Sorokin helped develop important collaborative ties for their national compatriots to American sociology, with relatively enduring appreciation in those networks for the consequent benefits provided (Johnston 1995; Halas 2005).

Of course, while much of American sociology's internationalism took place during study of and collaboration with its European counterparts, it was not just about Europe. European engagement shaped an outlook on the rest of the world, a quality evident even in the final contribution in the Barnes collection in which the systematic sociology of the Latin American sociologist Mariano H. Cornejo was addressed in a larger context of the history of Latin American sociology. The article, while summarizing a great deal of work, nonetheless identifies the "generally backward character of Latin-American sociology," even as it notes the region's original contributions in interpreting the "impact of the native culture and the frontier upon the European culture and the struggle between the antagonistic types of civilization arising there from" (Bernard 1948, 909–10). Even here we find powerful European reference and grounding.

One cannot typify American sociology at this time very easily, whether in degrees of or attitudes toward internationalism. Although one might read the Sumner/Giddings debate about imperialism to reflect European concerns even in disagreement, W. E. B. DuBois clearly signaled a tendency in American sociology to challenge not only white but also Western presumption. He was not included in the Barnes collection, however.

DuBois studied first at Fisk University and then at Harvard in 1888–90. From William James and Albert Bushnell Hart he took interest in the social sciences and began his study of the slave trade in America. After writing his thesis, he studied at the University of Berlin for two years and traveled throughout the Continent, where his outlook on life was "modified profoundly" (DuBois 1968, 156). He enjoyed his stay, but returned to days of disillusion on his arrival in "'nigger'-hating America" (183). He returned occasionally to Europe, but between 1918 and 1928 he made four trips that gave him "a depth of knowledge and breadth of view which was of incalculable value for realizing and judging modern conditions and above all the problem of race in America" (270). World War I's putative fight against militarism and for democracy failed to yield the emancipation for which he had he hoped (274), but it set in motion his commitment to Pan-Africanism and communism that influenced his subsequent assessment of and intervention in world history.

His story continues well beyond this era, beyond the discipline's first half century, and thus is something to which we shall return. However, even his story captures the main point of this first stage of American sociology's internationalism: this discipline was worldlier than one might expect, if still Eurocentric in its extra-American interest (Wallerstein 1999). But what European vision meant changed radically in the middle of the 1930s.

DESTRUCTIONS, EMIGRATIONS, AND AMERICAN EXTENSIONS

Nazism and Fascism changed the meaning of sociology in the world. Their destruction of human lives and social institutions, and the war mobilized to stop it, ended an alternative center of world sociology and social science in central Europe. Although the imperial cores may have continued to shape the sociological imaginations of their past and present colonial nations, with the murder and emigration of central European intellectuals and the subsequent repression of others in the heyday of Stalinism,[12] America became much more vital to the definition of a world sociology. And sociology became closely tied to state interests.

Ruth Benedict's (1946) characterization of Japanese character and Adorno and colleagues' (1950) account of the authoritarian personality symbolized that alliance between military/state and academy,[13] but in fact this engagement was much broader and was concentrated especially in the U.S. Department of Agriculture. For those focused more on the war per se,

12. We are grateful to Georgi Derluguian for this observation.

13. Benedict's is not the only "national character" study of this era to be sure; sociologists also contributed to this effort, complete with accomplishments and pitfalls. For both general comment and a particularly interesting discussion of how an American text comes to inform the interrogated nation's sensibility, see Lie (2001).

Samuel Stouffer recruited many into the Research Branch of the War Department (Abbott and Sparrow, chap. 8, this volume). More notable were those who worked in the Office of Strategic Services Research and Analysis, who produced a number of studies directly related to psychological warfare, like the one Edward Shils and Morris Janowitz (1948) undertook in their studies of German POWs (Robin 2001, 96–100). This World War II exercise cannot be reduced to a tale of service to the state, however, given the ways in which intellectual exiles from fascism, who were disproportionately Jewish, used their antifascist political and moral commitments to shape their own commitment to American social science.

Lewis A. Coser was only one among a number of refugee scholars in America, but he assessed their impact and experiences in general and in sociology in particular, with noted attention to the import of Critical Theory and the New School for Social Research, in addition to other distinguished scholars noted for their contributions to methodology (Lazarsfeld), phenomenology (Schutz), and studies of Asian societies (Wittfogel).[14] Borrowing from H. Stuart Hughes, Coser offered his summary assessment in terms of the "deprovincialization of the American mind," made possible by the exiles' marginal status as "strangers" (1984, 10, 14). They brought European thought to America, once again, but also they brought recognition for how bad things could be. Most of all, they reminded American sociologists that a focus on difference within the nation was hardly a worldly sociology.

Two streams of scholarship from this emigration remain vitally important, if easily overlooked in our traditions. Lazarsfeld, of course, helped to establish the rigorous quantitative sociology to emerge in opposition to the influence of the ethnographic styles of the Chicago school. His Austrian origins were not so evident in this development, although those ties figured in his work to extend collaborations during the cold war with Polish and other national sociologies from central Europe.

The Frankfurt school's importance was apparent in sociology's 1960s critical turn. Including Theodor Adorno, Max Horkheimer, Herbert Marcuse, and Friederich Pollock, this group became central to the theories and formation of the New Left, especially with regard to the combination of psychoanalysis and cultural sociology, studies of authority, Nazism, mass cul-

---

14. Coser (1984, 86–87) also mentions Hans Gerth, Kurt H. Wolff, and several other central European sociologists who relocated to America, but he does not elaborate on their contributions, although there are many. Wolff is especially notable for his promotion of Simmel's work, and Gerth not only for his work on Weber but for his mentorship of many other native-born American sociologists, including C. Wright Mills, whose sociological imaginings remain among the most widely read texts in American sociology.

ture and aesthetic theory, and the philosophy of history (Jay 1973). Horkheimer, Adorno, and Pollock returned to Germany in 1950, but Marcuse
stayed to influence substantially a subsequent generation of critical theorists and activists in American sociology, less so for his critique of Soviet
Marxism (Marcuse 1958) than for his search for a revolutionary subject
(Marcuse 1951).

Despite these European influences, some sociologists actively worried
whether our discipline was "ethnocentric" (Hughes 1961). Subsequent writers even identify this period as one of retreat from the earlier world sociological focus on difference between metropole and colonized (Connell
1997). In these accounts, the American sociological problematic shifted its
focus to industrial societies, leaving anthropology to study the premodern
or less developed and historians to study noncontemporary conditions. But
this critique overlooks important work that moves beyond not only the
United States but also advanced industrial societies. During the cold war,
American social science, including sociology, embarked on one of the most
remarkably internationalist projects ever through its development of the
modernization problematic.

It is difficult to date this project's start, although Nils Gilman (2003, 1–2)
argues for one founding moment in 1959, when Edward Shils addressed a
group of modernization theorists and turned the development question
into one of modernization, where new postcolonial states would become
democratic, egalitarian, scientific, economically advanced, and sovereign,
something like America itself (Gilman 2003, 19).

The American state directly supported this academic work. The govern-
ment/academic affinity was already apparent during the Korean War, when
some sociologists helped understand the North Korean mind by interviewing prisoners on Koje Do (Robin 2001). Sociologists were not the lead actors
here or in subsequent efforts to apply rational choice theory to repressive
counterinsurgency models for containing the communist threat.[15] They
were part of that debate (e.g., Short 1971), but they were much more prominent around Project Camelot (Horowitz 1967).

Because sociology was perceived as useful in predicting political turbulence and influencing its course, senior social scientists, and in particular
one sociologist, Jesse Bernard, led in this application of social science to

15. Leites and Wolf (1966) offered the most ambitious statement in this regard. Princeton's
then director of the Center of International Studies, Klaus Knorr, challenged them and argued
that the military should focus more on civic action (Robin 2001, 188).

confront violence (Robin 2001, 206–25). While known for her work on gender, Romania-born Bernard coauthored a major volume in 1934, *Sociology and the Study of International Relations*. She was herself committed to the search for nonviolent solutions to conflict and was among Project Camelot's most thoughtful critics after the fact. She reflected at substantial length on the challenges of cross-cultural research and ideological conviction, whether in favor of insurgents' historical role or system stability (Bernard 1967). Other sociologists, including Neil Smelser, served as consultants on the project, and the volume that reported the project included several prominent sociologists of the day.[16]

This major collaboration between the academy and the military came to a diplomatic crash, however, when one of its anthropology participants misrepresented the sponsor of his research to Chilean colleagues in 1965. The Chilean government protested, and a scandal emerged over the autonomy of social science. The publicity led to the project's cancellation and the reassignment of foreign area research oversight from the military to the State Department (Robin 2001, 206–25). It also led a generation or more of sociologists to cease working for, or at least doubt the intellectual integrity of working for, the U.S. government on questions of national security.

Of course sociologists were also working well beyond government contract; modernization and its variants provided a very powerful lens for internationalizing American sociology. On the one hand, this approach helped to locate one recently defeated and one newly threatening totalitarianism on its scale. Fascism could be understood as modernity denied, with premodern populism gaining power, and communism as a kind of pathological modernity (Gilman 2003). This approach led to investigations of Japan, among other societies, and how they developed functional substitutes for the Protestant ethic (Bellah 1957). Such a concern for modernity became especially developed in the study of the Soviet Union and other communist-led societies, with scholars interested to know whether capitalism and socialism were on paths of convergence, leading away from the extreme economic inequities of the former and the totalitarian tendencies of the latter (Jones 1976; Lenski 1978).

Within and against this framework, extensive collaborations with social scientists from the Soviet Union and especially Eastern Europe developed. Gerhard Lenski (1966) became quite influential on the macrosociological

16. Klausner (1967) presented the papers from the conference, with many sociologists, including Edward Tiryakian, Amitai Etzioni, Fredric Du Bow, and Ithiel De Sola Pool.

side, and Mel Kohn's (1969) work was broadly embraced more on the microsociological.[17] The debates about convergence also spawned their own literature well beyond the modernization domain, partially because these societies were "closed" to normal social scientific research and their sociologists were obliged to incorporate Marxist inspiration in their own social research through the mid-1970s. Modernization had much greater influence in, and engagement with, developing societies, therefore.

The exemplar, published many years after the completion of data collection, was *Becoming Modern* (Inkeles and Smith 1974), in which the authors, using survey research, explained how individuals came to embrace increasingly modern views on social life in six developing nations—Argentina, Chile, India, Israel, Nigeria, and Bangladesh. This work is in many ways emblematic of some of the difficulties facing "international" perspectives, and it exemplifies some of the problems of modernization theory. It obviously expanded the relevant sample used for formulating sociological theories, but the basic assumptions underlying these theories were so much based on American experiences and perspectives as to make the exercise less obviously international than the range of comparison suggests.

Modernization's greatest impact came, however, through one of its principal expressions—demography.[18] While usefully considered as its own subdiscipline, demography might also be considered one of the principal vehicles through which American sociology engaged the "third world." Dennis Hodgson (2001) offers a remarkably concise history accounting for the rise of demography within American sociology in precisely these terms. The Ford and Rockefeller foundations helped to set up a "neo-Malthusian" movement to lessen population growth throughout the third world; the movement considered academic research as a first step to convince political leaders of the need to reduce fertility in order to realize development. Fellowships were established to bring students from the third world to study demography at American universities. With this support, demography developed into one of the most coherent, and internationally focused, aspects

17. One of the fruits of this collaboration was Kohn and Slomczynski (1990), which represents Polish sociologists' long-standing engagement with Kohn's work. Wlodzimierz Wesolowski, to whom the volume was dedicated, viewed Kohn's 1969 *Class and Conformity* as "providing a vehicle for the comparative analysis of the social psychology of stratification in capitalist and socialist society" (Kohn and Slomczynski 1990, xi). This in turn led to extensive collaboration among many U.S. and Polish sociologists, and Japanese sociologists as well.

18. Recent scholars have sought to challenge this presumption, even while identifying how the presumptions embedded in this historiography have also shaped family formation in non-Western societies. For a discussion of this trajectory, see Thornton (2004).

of American sociology. With declines in extramural funding, however, it has also become less focused on international fertility. The influence of American philanthropic and political interests is not limited to demography, of course, nor could it be considered only a matter of money and power.

Modernization theory was an exceptionally American enterprise. Not only did America represent the pinnacle of modernism, but its proponents even revised European thinkers to minimize their pessimism and accentuate the positive (Gilman 2003, 55). While this was about explaining how other societies might change, it was also about America itself and its view of the good society. But concerns about its own society also fed into the modernization paradigm's anxieties, in the wake of the crisis of liberalism in a United States racked by civil rights protest, antiwar activism, and a Vietnam War that denied modernization theory's sensibilities (Gilman 2003, 205–14). As such, modernization theory and its problems reflected American intellectual politics.

COMPARATIVE, HISTORICAL, AND CRITICAL WORLD SOCIOLOGY

An evaluation of Talcott Parsons's contribution to American sociological internationalism suggests the broader challenge. On the one hand, Parsons was the leading, and perhaps prototypical, American sociologist of his generation, whose extended stays in Europe shaped his work and vision. He led the effort to bring Max Weber's work to an American audience, even as he Americanized that scholarship. He benefited in his struggles for recognition at Harvard from his obviously American style, in contrast to Sorokin's enduringly foreign manner (Johnston 1995). He also was at the center of this simultaneously ethnocentric and globally ambitious modernization movement. Combined with his own efforts to reconstruct social science at Harvard, and his alliance with Shils and other social scientists from Chicago, Parsons developed an enormously coherent project for research, enabling area studies of particular world regions to find a common theoretical language in which to conduct their research and their debates. Much of modernization theory's protest also focused on Parsons.

In powerful contrast, W. E. B. DuBois was closely tied to communist groups and quite distant from any hint of collaboration with American intellectual or political powers. His lifetime travels coincided with movement away from his identification as sociologist, becoming much more the intellectual advocate for communism and Pan-Africanism. His admiration for the Soviet Union (DuBois 1968, 29–43) hardly fit with the tenor of America's cold war times, nor does it ring very appealing today. His and other re-actions by "political pilgrims" certainly suggested the power of communist propaganda (Hollander 1982) made all the more compelling by an American racism hardly fitting with claims to be the pinnacle of a modernity defined by meritocracy and universalistic values. This dilemma is what Gunnar Myrdal (1944), a Swede, did so much to bring into broader American academic and public focus. But it was the comparisons to other societies that made much more of this American peculiarity.

The most important series of comparisons seemed to develop among the most retrograde (South African apartheid) and progressive (Brazilian), with American society somewhere in the middle (Lieberson 1961; Van den Berghe 1970; Telles 1992) and always at risk of being associated with the former (Denton and Massey 1993). Some also invoked India's caste system to recognize the American peculiarity, as in Cox's (1948) *Caste, Class, and Race*, but the comparisons were mainly formulated with the American racial imaginary of black and white in mind. Although there were occasional efforts to understand other regions' racial divisions with this American prob-lematic (Hertz 1988),[19] this view on race was not so easily transported, and other regions' perspectives on race and identity were not so easily adapted to the American environment. While obviously an anomaly for modernization theory, studies of American racism did not function principally as a chal-lenge for American ethnocentrism. Modernization theory's academic de-mise came more from a contest on its own grounds (Gilman 2003, 218–25).

Joseph Gusfield (1967) argued that tradition and modernity cannot be so easily distinguished, given the results of his study of India. Dean Tipps (1973), in a celebrated essay in *Comparative Studies in Society and History*, found modernization theory hopelessly muddled. Finally, comparative and historical sociology and their allied historians took up the simple schemes that modernization offered and contended that things weren't so directed, or simple. Reinhard Bendix (1967) offered a more modest modernization program, one that Charles Tilly (1975) and Raymond Grew (1978) helped to complicate even further. The debate carried on beyond the specificities of modernization theory per se; the debate between Robert Nisbet (1969) and Gerhard Lenski (1975) demonstrated that this contest was not just a matter of data but a dispute over epistemology and the philosophy of history (Kennedy 2004a).

---

19. Not only did émigré Poles such as Hertz explore the similarities between Polish Jews and African Americans, but so did DuBois himself, who during one of his travels to Poland, in 1893, was identified as a Jew in Poland and housed accordingly (DuBois 1968, 175).

Modernization theory suffered an even greater international challenge from the Latin American "dependency" school. This outlook, most commonly associated with Fernando Henrique Cardoso and Enzo Faletto's *Dependency and Development in Latin America* (originally published in Spanish in 1970, translated into English in 1979), is arguably Latin America's major contribution to American social science. Originating in the work of the CEPAL economists of the 1950s and borrowing from work in Africa as well, this perspective challenged the "convergence" assumptions of modernization. It theorized that, given the radically different history of the global South, this region could never expect to reproduce the development of the North. In fact the development of the global haves and have-nots was intrinsically linked and could not be understood in isolation. This particular kind of critique was also important because it was a theoretical perspective grounded in the intellectual culture of another world region.[20] Alongside this Latin American accent came a North African one as well, with Samir Amin's (1974) work finding powerful resonance within the discipline among those who sought to explain development in neocolonial terms.

Dependency theory's development was powerfully extended into world systems theory. Although African studies was Immanuel Wallerstein's original focus, he reshaped a substantial part of American, and international, sociology by arguing that we should not only locate change in macrostructures but that it was the world system, not individual societies per se, that should organize our research (Wallerstein 1976). This scholarship, with its associated section of the American Sociological Association, has done much to internationalize the discipline even as it provided an important vehicle for scholars from other parts of the world to enter the American disciplinary discussion. Although substantial debate has ranged about the adequacy of this perspective, whether class relations or state power were properly theorized for instance, it is one of the most consequential international interventions in American sociology. It also reflected its historical environment with its implicit critique of capitalism and question about the conditions for its own demise (Wallerstein 1974).

More than system collapse, however, the cold war clearly articulated the sociology of revolution. One might even argue that American sociology's comparative historical renaissance began with the sociology of revolution. Barrington Moore's influential *Social Origins of Dictatorship and Democracy* (1966) is central to this tradition, with its argument that the character of

20. This influence was augmented by important works in the United States (e.g., Evans 1979).

class conflict and qualities of revolution shape the conditions for modernity's political expression. This volume was followed in the 1970s by works such as Jeff Paige's *Agrarian Revolution* (1975) and Theda Skocpol's *States and Social Revolutions* (1979) and was even extended to other periods, notably with Jack Goldstone's (1990) work. These works developed new and important analytical perspectives in their own stream as well as in combination with the new systematic comparative work, notably associated with Charles Tilly (2003a, 2003b), on contentious politics. When these streams in contention are considered alongside the world system approach, one can easily see why Collins (1999b) has recognized this as "the golden age of comparative historical sociology," with its return to the classical questions that began the European tradition of the discipline.

Much of that golden age's comparative and historical sociology of state formation and social transformations endures in importance and finds important refinement in subsequent scholarly work. The class, culture, community, and gender associated with capitalist class relations and state formation (e.g., Calhoun 1982; Markoff 1996; Somers 1995; Rose 1993; Steinmetz 1999; Lachman 2002; Tilly 1990; Centeno 2002; Adams, Clemens, and Orloff 2005) have been among the most obviously important intellectual transformations to emerge from that period. As important if not equally consequential has been the wider historical and geographical range of this scholarship, from pristine state formation to empire's transformation in relation to western Europe and beyond it (Mann 1986, 1993; Gocek 1995; Lo 2002; Zeitlin 1998).

Given this range, it is difficult to identify the consequence of this work in simple terms. Much of it is apparent, for example, in the distinguished publication awards of the American Sociological Association, of which, since 1974, about half have been awarded for work comparative or international in reference. One might also appreciate this influence in terms of public impact on the societies about which they are written. This is especially evident in terms of the analysis of genocide.

William Gamson (1995) delivered his 1994 ASA presidential address on the subject, and Helen Fein (1979) won recognition in 1979 from the American Sociological Association for her book on the topic (see also Fein 1993), but sometimes the public impact is greater than the academic recognition. Jan Gross (2001), for example, initiated with his publication a substantial reconsideration in the Polish public about Poles' roles in the Holocaust.[21]

---

21. Here the symposium and associated articles in *Polish Sociological Review* 137(3) from 2002 was quite important, as well as Borkowicz et al. (2001). Another Polish émigré has writ-

Taner Akcam (2004) has also inspired substantial conversation in Turkey over the definition and causes of systematic exodus and deaths of Armenians in 1915. Suny and sociologist Muge Gocek (2002) have woven this discussion into their work on the Ottoman Empire. George Steinmetz (2006) has made the 1904 destruction of the Herero nation in former German Southwest Africa (Namibia) central to his argument about the pre-1914 German overseas empire, and with colleagues he initiated an appeal to the German government to support the call by Herero and other Namibians for reparations for the 1904 genocide and for the use of slave labor from the POW ("concentration") camps between 1904 and 1908 for government projects and countless private ones, including the building of railways. When we think about American sociological internationalism, therefore, we should not overlook how that sociology affects publics abroad. But we should also note how the discipline recognizes that work, for although each of the scholars just listed has been trained as a sociologist, much of this discussion takes place beyond the discipline.

More scholars working on genocide identify with political science and history than with sociology,[22] as is evident in the employment of sociologists Gross and Akcam in those departments, respectively. Although one might argue that genocide should not be central to the American sociological imagination, it is hard to appreciate why the study of this most basic kind of inequality is not at the center of a discipline focused on power, privilege, and destitution. It might have something to do with the extranational focus of this work, but even the study of genocide against Native Americans within the New World is not central to disciplinary practice.[23] It may be because genocide does not fit with the dominant macrosociological debates in American sociology, organized as they are around the effects of slavery on contemporary American society (e.g., Patterson 1985) and around the dynamics of a generic capitalism with its socialist counterculture (Bauman 1976). Ironically, revolutions, long an interest of the latter, would shift that macrosociological sense, beginning with 1979.

The Nicaraguan Revolution drew great interest and attention from American sociology, in part because of its proximity, its implication in American power, and its fit with the discipline's own imaginary of history (Paige 1997). But it was the Iranian Revolution that offered the greatest challenge

---

ten powerfully on the implications of the Holocaust for our understanding of modernity, but because of his British location he is officially beyond this review (Bauman 1991).

22. Consider the absence of sociologists in Gellately and Kiernan (2003).

23. See, e.g., Stannard (1993). Some sociologists have written in this vein, however; see, e.g., Thornton (1990).

and piqued more interest for it. On the one hand, a substantial number of efforts went toward interpreting the revolution in both structural and mobilization terms (Arjomand 2001; Parsa 1989; Skocpol 1982) but with relatively limited challenge to the larger imaginary within which it was constructed (Kurzman 2004). It could still be understood as a challenge to imperialism, even if its socialist accent was lost to religious expression. We return to this challenging revolution later, but it is worth noting that this revolution did not shake the larger cold war sociological imaginary like communism's collapse did.

Although antisystemic conditions and movements were noted and theorized under communism, it was not so simple to interpret these tendencies within the cold war framework still operative in sociology in the 1970s and 1980s (Kennedy 1991). There was considerable interest in dissident texts and studies, but their implication in sociology was itself complicated by their articulation with a critical perspective on American power and the capitalism it represented. Sociologists like Alvin Gouldner (1979) undertook substantial efforts to identify the third way in this critical sociology, explaining why Marxist critical sociologies of communism were so important, from Djilas (1957) to Konrad and Szelenyi (1979).[24] With their continuing focus on class and inequality, relatively few in sociology anticipated civil society's centrality in 1989's revolution against the revolutionary tradition, even if there are some partial exceptions (Arato 1994; R. Collins 1999a).

This revolution offered not only a radical but also a nonviolent embrace of "normality," of markets, pluralism, and publicity instead of a vision of radical if necessarily violent change in the name of greater equality and substantive justice (Eglitis 2002). It reinforced the broader and growing literature on democratization that, while predominantly a political science discourse, had important sociologist contributors (Stephens, Rueschemeyer, and Stephens 1992). Although some authors doubted the range of civil society's articulation with other continents' political imaginations (Comaroff and Comaroff 1999), "transition culture" within the postcommunist world helped to establish the centrality of globalization as the broad metanarrative in which sociology's internationalism might be practiced (Kennedy 2002).

With Soviet-inspired alternatives gone, Eastern European leaderships seeking accession to transnational bodies from NATO to the European Union, and Chinese and Indian openings to global markets inspiring alter-

24. For commentary on the abiding significance of this volume, see the symposium in *Theory and Society* (Verdery et al. 2005) recognizing the twenty-fifth anniversary of this volume's translation into English.

native visions of development, a new generation of sociology began to consider the study of capitalism's genesis and variety to be the key question of sociology's formation. The study of economic change in the postcommunist world did not emphasize globalization as much as it did internal factors driving change, but it fit with the new metanarrative associated with globalization. Rather than a history of radical alternatives, this was a world with important variations on the capitalist theme available to it, to which countries and individuals had to adapt (Burawoy 2001; Eyal, Szelenyi, and Townsley 2001; Stark and Bruszt 2001; Kennedy 2001; Borocz 2001).

This emphasis on adaptation, however, did not resonate simply with the traditional centrality of the nation-state in the world's organization. Especially for communist states whose sovereignty was restricted by obeisance to Moscow, communism's collapse alongside globalization's constraints inspired a new wave of nationalism and renewed scholarly interest in the subject. Although historians and political scientists dominated the field, and European sociologists were more prominent than their American colleagues (e.g., Smith 1986), sociologists became newly evident in nationalism's study (Calhoun 1997), whether in more historically nuanced and theoretically sophisticated versions of older national character studies (Greenfeld 1992; Brubaker 1992) or in studies that embedded the nation in historical explanations of social dynamics (Brubaker 1996; Eglitis 2002; Lo 2002; Kennedy 2002). At the same time, comparative cultural sociology was resuscitated, with regional emphases shaping their formulation of the national question.[25]

GLOBALIZATION, TERROR, AND EMPIRE

Like nationalism's study, that of globalization has not been mainly an American sociologist's game; those who might consider it part of their purview have tended to address similar issues in world system terms that concentrate on the enduring, rather than novel, quality of this globalization focused on capital (e.g., Arrighi and Silver 1999). Given the debate about the significance of currencies, and trade and capital flows in the new global economy, economists have typically had a prominent position in its definition (Stiglitz 2002; Bhagwati 2004). Political scientists, given the importance of global governance in globalization's discussion, have also been par-

---

25. Contrast, for example, how Suny and Kennedy (1999), with their East European perspective, focused on historical trajectories, whereas a Euro-Atlantic emphasis enables more enduring patterns of national identity to be highlighted (Lamont and Thevénot 2000).

ticularly prominent (e.g., Roseneau 1992). Geographers treated it, famously, as a question of time/space compression and therefore have an important position to stake out (Harvey 1989). Anthropologists have used it to liberate themselves from bounded studies of community (Appadurai 1996). European sociologists, more accustomed to studies of empire, on the one hand, and of European Union expansion, on the other, appear to be more influential than their American colleagues (Beck 2000; Hirst and Thompson 1996; Featherstone 1995; Tomlinson 1998). Even one of the leading American theorists of globalization, long at the University of Pittsburgh, returned to Europe in his relocation to the University of Aberdeen (Robertson 1992; Robertson and Inglis 2005). There are, of course, important exceptions to this extra-American sociological rule.

Saskia Sassen (1998, 2001), initially with her work on the global city but later with her work on globalization per se, is among the leading theorists of this transformation. Manuel Castells (1996), with his focus on the network society, flows along with globalization to emphasize the importance of the information and communication technology revolution for redefining social inquiry. John L. Campbell (2004) develops an institutional perspective to bear on the phenomenon. Edna Bonacich and Richard Appelbaum (2000) have brought a more familiar sociological approach to globalization with their emphasis on the race to the bottom in sweatshop labor. Indeed, more consistent with this latter orientation, *Social Problems* devoted their fall 2001 issue to the question, focusing on what globalization makes worse more than what it might improve.

Globalization has also influenced other fields, including social movements (Smith, Chatfield, and Pagnucco 1997; McAdam, McCarthy, and Zald 1996; DellaPorta and Kriesi 1999; Guidry, Kennedy, and Zald 2000) and economic sociology (Evans 1995; Fligstein 2001), but more typically through the critique of globalization's dominant conceptions than in their extension. Debate about the name under which the compression of time and space is considered also became important—was this world society, globalization, glocalization, grobalization, or McDonaldization (Meyer et al. 1997; Ritzer 2003, 2004)?[26] Each choice has implications for the methods and sense for addressing global transformations. Perhaps even more important, some scholars question whether this new global integration is more appropriately considered as empire. Here again, however, most of the

---

26. Ritzer's *The McDonaldization of Society* (1993) itself represents among the most globalized scholarly products, with translations into German, Czech, Polish, Japanese, Spanish, Danish, Italian, French, Turkish, Korean, Chinese, Romanian, Hungarian, Portuguese, and Greek.

leading interventions take place either beyond the discipline or the nation (Hardt and Negri 2000), although some sociologists employed at U.S. universities have made important interventions in this discussion (Mann 2003).

Ironically, perhaps, both imperialism and globalization allow for America's restoration to the center of an international sociology. Because America figures so prominently in the definition of either, it also offers an opportunity to move beyond America while not entirely moving beyond America. One can find (and one often does find) studies of globalization within the United States itself (e.g., Burawoy et al. 2000). Studying empire requires too a critical sense of American strategy, interests, and benefits from its global reach. The American lens can shape American sociology in the reflection of American power, whether military or economic.

While perhaps not appropriately called imperialist, the globalization of American sociology can accompany either aspect of world reach. These questions might be formed with American political concerns in mind, whether in support or in opposition. They also might have more academic overtones, shaped by the search for new environments in which to ask enduring academic questions, testing out whether other places and nations responded differently or similarly to processes discovered in America. Much like modernization theory, therefore, all of these starting points tend to be framed with American concerns, rather than with other world regions and their intellectual cultures, as starting points. After the attacks of September 11, 2001, the limitations of this presumption become evident.

Most American sociological studies of global change framed their problem and conducted their research within American, or Western, tradition. Among other distinctions, Randall Collins's (1998) work on a global theory of intellectual change was an important exception for its engagement with extra-European intellectual communities and religious influences in particular. Otherwise, little sociological attention was given to those dynamics deemed beyond the pale of McWorld, although the political scientist Benjamin Barber's (1995) jihad in some ways anticipated the next global transformation that would shake the international imaginary guiding our discipline. Culture becomes newly prominent in this post 9/11 sociology of globalization, moving beyond its technologically or economically derivative status to ask whether a view of the world, from globalization or imperialism's standpoint, misses something important. Shouldn't we learn more than what Americanization or Westernization allows us to consider (Tomlinson 1998), the cross-cultural theorists ask. Religion may be an especially good place to start.

The secularization thesis, while contested in America, led much of

American social science to look at the rest of the world as if religion did not matter. There were of course important exceptions—from Berger's (1967, 1999) work on the sacred canopy to Murray's book on Indian culture (1994) and Casanova's book on public religions (1994). However, religion was not so prominent in the definition of international sociology as it might have been, and it remained much more a focus among sociologists of religion than a central part of social theory and comparative and historical sociology (Calhoun 1999).[27] Globalization did not help either, given its emphasis on flows and the disappearance of national distinction. Such "traditional" concerns as religion appeared anachronistic. Juergensmeyer's (2000) work on violence and religion was, one might argue, the most prescient and underappreciated for the world that would emerge after September 11, 2001.

Many rushed to figure the meaning of this horrific event (e.g., Calhoun, Price, and Timmer 2002). The temptation was to ask how it changed American society most of all, or how it changed America's view of the world. It was more difficult to figure out how it changed the rest of the world, or how it might have led Americans to ask questions that other parts of the world have considered more salient to their own mission (Hershberg and Moore 2002). Although there have been new and concentrated efforts,[28] this focus could issue major challenges for the conventional frames of the discipline. Of course it might be understood as a variation on the conventional study of contentious politics (Tilly 2004) or of criminology (LaFree 2004), but it also might require new conceptualizations (DeFlem 2004b). This might involve, for example, new comparisons and microsociologies (R. Collins 2004). It might require thinking beyond the factors that shape biography and history in the United States, as well as consideration of new combinations of world systems theory and biographical analysis in order to imagine someone whom Russians might call a Chechen terrorist and Georgi Derluguian (2005) could name a student of Pierre Bourdieu.

Despite this new energy, the relative novelty of this focus on religious terrorism and Islam's relationship to violence, development, and democracy is striking, with American sociology looked remarkably ill prepared. This focus is all the more remarkable given the discipline's interest in the Iranian Islamic Revolution of 1979.

Most of the interest in that revolution was devoted to understanding it in conventional social scientific terms, around political opportunity, mobi-

27. Philip Gorski (2003) represents the return to religion in social theory and historical change for a classic theme in historical sociology. Zubrzycki (forthcoming) takes that theme to more contemporary discussions of cultural politics.

28. See, e.g., *Sociological Theory*'s special symposium, published in 2004, on terrorism.

lization of resources, cultural dispositions, economic cycles, or military capacities. None of this scholarship really attended to what was so remarkable about the event. From the point of view of participants and analysts alike, this was an "unthinkable" revolution and an invitation to rethink our presumptions about modernity, Islam, and the organization of cooperation and contest in the world system (Kurzman 2004).

That failure to consider Iran as a harbinger of more than revolution, and as an invitation to move beyond our lenses, suggests just how disinterested American sociologists were in questions beyond their national imagination. Nevertheless, after 9/11, the interest in Islam and its world has grown, signified by the 2004 Distinguished Scholarly Publication Award and the growth of interest in the comparative sociology of religion and its application to understanding apparently nonreligious issues such as globalization (Juergensmeyer 2003).[29] American sociology may be on the verge of important change in both regional and thematic interest. American sociology had, however, already been changing in another way. China has been growing steadily more central in American sociology for at least three different reasons.

First, with China's abiding importance in the definition of American security and the relatively great attention it won from American private foundations, a significant number of several generations of American students have been supported to undertake Chinese studies in a number of fields, including sociology.[30] Second, this interest in China does not only depend on Americans acquiring Chinese expertise, given the large number of students from China in American graduate programs and their relative success in the job market. While these scholars are not always defining their research agendas with regard to changes in Chinese society, their language and cultural facility enable China to figure prominently in research agendas ranging from demography to stratification, much as other immigrant intellectuals shaped American agendas with their own cultural capacities. Finally, given China's size and economic dynamism, it is increasingly important as a reflection of globalization itself and sociology's abiding interest in the study of capitalism. In many ways, the study of Chinese capitalism appears to be increasingly a field of its own making.

Of course not one of these features by itself explains China's growing

29. The 2004 Distinguished Scholarly Publication Award was given to Charrad (2004).

30. The Tiananmen Square rebellion of 1989 also sparked substantial interest both within the area studies community and beyond, but this interest has not been sustained as much as one would think, perhaps because the protest seems to have had no systemic effect. For two important sociologies of this movement, see Calhoun (1994) and Zhao (2004).

importance in American sociology. For example, given its importance in the world economy, one would expect Japan to be more central than it is in American sociological discussions, but for reasons associated with historically incommensurate knowledge cultures and greater opportunities within Japanese academia, Japan has not realized the influence that China recently has realized within American sociology (Lie 1996). Nevertheless, Japan is more prominent in sociology than Africa, the Middle East (at least before 9/11), South Asia, and Southeast Asia. None of these areas has produced a major stream of graduate students—a large problem that articulates with American national security—nor a problematic that resonates powerfully with American sociological concerns. Individual sociologists produce individually important works, but they have not yet been as effective in capturing the discipline's imagination at large.

In some cases, of course, this problem is not peculiar to sociology. Southeast Asian studies, with Benedict Anderson and James Scott (both political scientists) as the notable exceptions, has not been prominent in any discipline. In other cases, this appears to be more of a disciplinary peculiarity. For example, the number of exceptionally influential scholars in South Asian studies is greater in both anthropology and political science and even economics than in sociology, despite the importance of sociology in India itself.[31] Nevertheless, this is changing with generations and new thematic and theoretical developments in international sociology.

In particular, there is a relatively young stream of scholars globalizing gender studies that promises to transform not only American sociology's approach to gender but also that of their respective regional studies in the American academy. Although some of the most notable work in comparative gender studies engages Europe (Ferree et al. 2002), with some of the most destabilizing work for critical sociology being undertaken in postcommunist central Europe (Gal and Kligman 2000; Weiner 2005), South Asia and the Middle East also show promise as challenging and innovative sites for developing feminist theory (Lal 1999; Ray 1999). The motors behind these transformations are different, however.

On the Indian side, the growth of transnational ties and careers between South Asia and the United States has contributed significantly to the growth of that conjunction between South Asian and gender studies. The Middle East's engagement, while also dependent on globalization, finds

31. Veena Das, for example, one of the most prominent anthropologists in the United States who has focused on this region, studied sociology in India as an undergraduate before coming to the United States for graduate work in anthropology.

additional inspiration in the complicated relationship between war and women's rights.

Other world regions without the advantage of theoretical familiarity, globalizing networks, or public centrality face additional challenges. Consider, for example, the award-winning book by Oyeronke Oyewumi (1997) on Nigerian gender relations. It was not reviewed extensively in sociology or gender studies journals, perhaps because few gender experts knew enough about Africa, and few Africanists were sufficiently sophisticated in feminist theory to assess it critically. More generally, however, as one scholar has told us, unless "foreign" scholars know the right literature, meant to be American literature, they will not likely succeed in refereed American publications.

Beyond these gross continental or subcontinental comparisons, there are also important regional variations. For example, South African apartheid and its end have produced relatively great interest in racial/ethnic studies and studies of memory and justice (e.g., Comaroff and Comaroff 1991, 1999), exceeding substantially the number of sociological studies devoted to other parts of sub-Saharan Africa (Seidman 1999).[32] Similar points could and should be made for other world regions, whether in identifying Hungary's relatively great influence in an American sociology focused on postcommunist Europe, the relative invisibility of China's western regions in the American sociology of China, or Pakistan's limited reflection in either the American sociology of the Islamic world or of South Asia.

The intensity of American sociological internationalism, therefore, varies substantially over time, across regions, and amid sociology's substantive foci and perspectives. We have concentrated on some of the most prominent international work in sociology and have worked to identify some of the factors that have shaped that prominence. Before we turn to the present, therefore, it is worth considering the main features of this historical trajectory.

ASSESSING HISTORICAL TRAJECTORIES

Globalization has made the extension of the American sociological imagination simpler. International collaboration has been facilitated by the compression of time and space, enabling all parts of the discipline to find part-

32. Indeed, at the 2003 American Sociological Association meetings focused on public sociology, the only session devoted to African public intellectuals addressed South Africa sociology, leaving the rest of the continent's issues and intellectuals both distant and implicated. Beyond Oyewumi's work, see also Griswold (2000) and Aminzade (2003) for recent work concerning the west and east of sub-Saharan Africa.

ners and data abroad more readily. Suitably resourced, and with English-language work increasingly dominant, American paradigms travel more easily, with the challenge of difference receding before the opportunities for the extension of American sociological perspectives. But not all regions, and not all substantive areas, are so readily embraced.

Some parts of the discipline emphasize the value of extra-American data or perspectives, while others treat those as additional data points only. If the latter, challenging differences, whether in language, lack of systematic data, or other incommensurabilities, can deter engagement. Even for those parts of the discipline that are explicitly international, resonance with American sensibilities remains a powerful quality for assuring sociological recognition. This familiarity and proximity of a world region and its issues are central to explaining the trajectory of American sociological internationalism.

One should expect that studies of contemporary globalization and empire, as disproportionately American projects, would be among the most prominent avenues for American sociological internationalism. The immigration of scholars (notably European in the first half century and increasingly Chinese in the last decade) can shape this place too, as is evident in the prominence of European theory and Chinese society in our discipline's histories. Too, a region's implication in American power and/or imagination (whether Latin American or, more recently, eastern European) might do it, whether for our discipline's fascination for Latin American dependency and revolution in the 1960s and 1970s, or for Eastern European transition in the 1990s. Translation is also critical, however, to allow a region's interests to be recognizable and suitable for publication and elevation in sociology outlets. Here, the Muslim world represents the challenge. On the one hand, this region and culture should become more prominent, given the currents of war, but that is made more difficult by the paucity of American sociologists expert in the region's history and culture.[33] This, we expect, should produce a major change in American sociology if sociology is responsive to a world transformed. It is not clear, however, how it will change.

Given the differentiation of the discipline, other world regions and global issues can find particular niches, but for them to realize prominence in the discipline more broadly, whether in terms of appointments for their scholars or prominent publication outlets, they must challenge, and transform, an American sociology still ethnocentric by reflex.

---

33. Consider, for example, that in 2003 the Middle Eastern Studies Association had 407 political scientists and 655 historians but only 80 sociologists as members (Arjomand 2004).

Is American Sociology Still Ethnocentric?

To offer broad brush portraits of the international state of our discipline, we must use some relatively simple operationalizations of this sociological imaginary and others' interpretations of our discipline's "required reading" (Clawson 1998). And depending on our measures, we can look either quite ethnocentric or pretty international. Indeed, some of the chapters in this volume focus almost exclusively on studies of American society; they are reflecting, but also helping to construct, a tale of American sociology as an American area studies specialty. But it depends on how you look at what we do.

For instance, if one were to take the American book market as an indicator of our discipline's important works, one would find a remarkably Americo-centric discipline, at least by the end of the 1990s. Nearly all of the top twenty-five books that Herb Gans (1998) indicated as best sellers (that is, selling more than 50,000 copies) were focused on America, with the only (and sometimes only partial) exceptions being Lipset's *Political Man*, Bell's *Coming of Post-Industrial Society*, and Horowitz's *Wargames*. By contrast, our discipline's taste for excellence is decidedly more international. Since 1956 the American Sociological Association has awarded a prize for outstanding scholarly publication—first the MacIver Award (1956–68), then the Sorokin Award (1968–79), and finally the Distinguished Scholarly Publication Award. Approximately half of these award-winning volumes were focused entirely or substantially on societies beyond the United States. Although there are striking gaps in recognition for international works (notably between 1969 and 1973, and 1980 and 1986), it is also striking just how international this field is. Indeed, even some of those who wrote award-winning books about America had substantial investments in learning beyond the nation, as Bellah in Japan (1957).

Nevertheless, it is useful to look at the list more closely to recognize the ways in which the international shapes American sociology's self-understanding. Most works focused on the United States don't bother to mention that national focus in their title, because their audience recognizes the reference and assumes its national location.[34] Second, although about

---

34. Here we need only note the civil rights movement or the wayward Puritans. Of these U.S.-focused works, only six award winners out of twenty-two marked their sociology's national (or more local) substantive focus. Interestingly, both volumes on gender inequality marked their American place, as did the works on religion and occupational structure. Strikingly, of these American books, a plurality of volumes focus on race and ethnicity, but only one of these explicitly notes a regional concentration in its title. By contrast, none of the books with an international focus has race or ethnicity as its principal substantive concern.

half of the internationally oriented volumes have substantial or exclusive western European focus, other parts of the world still find a place, with India, China, and the developing world more broadly finding recognition in these awards. However, most of these international volumes are macrosociological. Their association with the tradition of comparative and historical political, economic, or cultural sociology is apparent, as is the international field's relative emphasis on book, rather than article, publication in its own career tracks.

The discipline's leading journal of book reviews challenges even more strongly the case for a simple American sociological ethnocentrism. *Contemporary Sociology*'s mid-1990s list of the ten most influential books over the preceding quarter century contained seven that looked beyond America, of which several were written by authors who had spent most or substantial parts of their lives outside the United States.[35] *Contemporary Sociology* took that effort one step further to consider different national and regional sociologies, from the Arab world, East Asia, eastern central, Nordic, and southern Europe, Latin America, the Portuguese-speaking world, southern Africa, and South Asia, in addition to considering how gender and formal organization influence that sociology.[36] This collection, with reviewers coming from regions in which the reviewed works had been produced (in English), suggested several thematics particular to those regions, such as transition in eastern central Europe, financial crisis of East Asia, and various forms of dependency in other world regions.

Once we move beyond the book world and toward our discipline's article culture, however, we see a more ethnocentric American sociology (Clawson 1998, 7–9). Miguel Centeno and his colleagues used country and region names, as well as a string of three terms relevant to international subject matter (i.e., "foreign," "international," and "global"), to identify what was international, and what was not, within leading journals associated with our discipline. They reviewed *American Journal of Sociology, Amer-*

35. The controversy over such a list, and over alternative ways to interpret it, is collected in Clawson (1988). For example, in that volume Gerald Marwell suggested that one use the Social Science Citation Index. He found, for 1995, Coleman's *Foundations of Social Theory*, Duncan's *Introduction to Structural Equation Models*, Giddens's *The Constitution of Society*, Goffman's *Frame Analysis*, Jencks et al.'s *Inequality*, Kohn's *Class and Conformity*, and Lieberson's *A Piece of the Pie* deserving of top-ten status; not one of them is explicitly international in reference. One parenthetical—he uses the phrase "journals produced in America," which he says, with tongue in cheek, is "ethnocentric, but easier" (1998, 192).

36. Nevertheless, there are important efforts to reflect on this worldly association. Consider, for example, *Contemporary Sociology*'s reviews of its national accents—in its July 1998 issue, "Symposia; Spanning the Globe: Flavors of Sociology."

ican Sociological Review, Social Forces, Theory and Society, and *Sociological Forum* in selected years between 1990 and 2002 and found 126 international articles from a total sample of 821 articles, or just over 15 percent of all those retrieved for the target dates.[37] Looking at the percentage of international articles in each journal over all five years reveals a striking similarity among *AJS, ASR,* and *Social Forces,* all of which devote approximately 17 percent of their articles to non-U.S. and/or comparative research topics. *Theory and Society* comes next, with 11.83 percent, followed by *Sociological Forum* with 9.09 percent. This distribution looks even worse, however, if we view these articles with not only subject matter but also epistemology or ontology, or even bibliography, in mind.[38]

Turning to expressed research interests by those in leading sociology departments of the United States,[39] Centeno and his colleagues found only

37. They used ISI Web of Science (WOS) online citation databases to search for articles devoted to non-U.S. and comparative research topics (i.e., international articles) in five sociology journals: *American Journal of Sociology, American Sociological Review, Social Forces, Sociological Forum,* and *Theory and Society.* We searched for articles published in the years 1990, 1993, 1996, 1999, and 2002. Searches were conducted using two strings of more than fifty country and region names as well as a string of three terms relevant to international subject matter (i.e., "foreign," "international," and "global"). All searches were conducted in the title, abstract, and keyword fields of the WOS citation databases, and a limit was applied such that only documents classified as articles were returned. Because WOS lacks abstract information for articles published before 1991, supplemental searches using identical search strings were conducted in JSTOR's online database for 1990. These results were added to the total articles discovered in the WOS searches. To determine the baseline number of articles per journal for a given year, we conducted searches as indicated but with one exception: the search strings were not used. In other words, the only search criteria were the journal's name, document type, and publication year. All articles published in a particular journal during a given year were returned in the searches and tallied. Several notes on article classification and region/country counting need to be made. First, articles matching a country or region name were generally included as international articles; rare exceptions were those that focused exclusively on an immigrant population within the United States. Second, articles matching the third search string had to be screened manually because of the varied uses of each term. Articles addressing one or more non-U.S. country or an explicitly cross-border phenomenon such as third world debt were accepted as "international articles." Third, cross-national quantitative studies examining ten or more countries met the criteria for international articles but were not included when counting region and country frequencies. A large cross-national study that can just as easily include or exclude data from a particular country is qualitatively different from an in-depth case study addressing just a few countries and therefore irrelevant to establishing country and region representation.

38. Thanks in particular to Muge Gocek for this very helpful distinction.

39. Following the Gourman Report Rankings of 1997, we examined the amount of self-professed international research being done by professors and graduate students in the top thirty-two sociology departments in the country during the years 1990, 1993, 1996, 1999, and

a slightly greater portion of faculty than articles with expressed international commitments. During the years analyzed, a mean of 21 percent of primary sociology professors reported having an international research interest. This was true both across the discipline and in general within individual departments. (Adjuncts and associated faculty were less likely to be doing international work. They had a mean of 13 percent both per department and for the top thirty-two departments.) PhD students were the most likely to conduct international research. During our time period a mean of 28 percent per department and 30 percent overall wrote internationally oriented dissertations. These percentages have remained remarkably stable over the years, but within departments there has been much greater variation over the past decade.

The distribution of regional interests among those doing international work will not surprise even causal observers of the American academy. Western Europe and Asia predominate, with Latin America a close third. The lack of attention given to Africa and the Middle East is particularly disappointing in light of recent developments. The overall decline in the numbers associating their work with any specific region may be the result of changes in the manner in which the ASA obtained the information, or it could reflect an increasing reluctance to be seen as a "regionalist" and a preference for more generic terms such as "comparative work" or "globalization." Within the regions, the distribution of countries again was not

---

2003. Using the division the departments themselves reported, we classified the sociologists in these departments into three categories: primary, secondary, and graduating PhD students. Primary professors were full-time professors within the sociology department. They could be full, associate, or assistant professors. Secondary professors consisted of professors jointly affiliated with other departments. They too could be at various levels of tenure, but unlike primary professors, the secondary professor category also included emeritus professors. This division seemed appropriate because it hinted at the amount of time being devoted to sociological research and toward sociology graduate students. For the graduating PhD student category, we also used what ASA provides: a list of those who graduated from the department during the previous year. Primary and secondary professors were considered to be doing international sociology if they listed one of the following words or their derivatives as an area of interest: international, global, development, comparative, immigration, world, cross-cultural, transnational, cross-national, and modernization. Professors who mentioned focusing on a specific world region, foreign country, or foreign community were also included as doing international research. Once a professor listed one of these keywords, he or she was counted as doing international work; no single professor was double counted even if they reported two international keywords. ASA only includes PhD students' dissertation titles, and thus PhD students were deemed to do international work if the title of their dissertation employed one of our selected terms.

surprising, with American sociology paying relatively high attention to Japan and China but largely ignoring other major countries.

Centeno and colleagues augmented the data with information from the individual departments.[40] Asked if American sociology is too focused on American society and does not pay enough attention to international topics, most chairs said that U.S. sociology is "parochial" or "provincial," but some felt that the situation is improving. Chairs did recognize the critical importance of doing comparative or international work: "Both theoretically and practically, social problems at the national level can be fully understood only by situating them in the international context and by analyzing them comparatively." Another faculty added: "Clearly, we live in a shrinking world. For quite a while now, social structures and processes have a global effect. Ignoring the cross-national connections of social life provides a most limited view of the kinds of things that are of interest to sociology." Finally one noted that "it is important that Americans understand the rest of the world better than they currently do."

Most respondents, however, agreed that "mainstream U.S. sociology remains something of a national sport." One chair noted that "in general, U.S. sociology is a bit too parochial, both in its focus on American society and its distance from sociological research outside the U.S." Another recognized that "U.S. sociology does enough international work. In graduate school, the pressure to finish in a 'timely fashion' and the lack of adequate funding discourages students from learning languages and from traveling abroad to do research." There was some hope, however, and one chair noted that "in recent years, American sociologists have begun to pay more attention to international topics and contexts, and this has enhanced their research."

In trying to determine how this situation can be resolved, most chairs agreed that a record of international/comparative research was a significant consideration in the hiring of new faculty for a department. But even here there were some divisions in that only half of the sample agreed with

40. We e-mailed the survey to the chairs of 32 top sociology departments, as ranked by Gourman. We got 13 responses, that is, the response rate is 41 percent. In order to contact the approximately three hundred individuals who earned their PhD's from the thirty-two highest-ranked graduate programs in sociology during 2001 and 2002, we used networks, Internet searches, and contact with the faculty and staff of the PhD-granting universities. We were able to locate nearly 85 percent of the individuals who received their doctorates during this two-year period. Rather than conducting in-person interviews or telephone interviews, we decided to reap information from this cohort through the use of an e-mail questionnaire. This questionnaire has provided us with a large enough number of respondents ($N = 74$) to notice trends in our sample.

this statement unequivocally. Only two of the thirteen universities from which we received responses included on their list of universitywide priorities an increase in the number of faculty concerned with international/ global topics. In most cases international focus was a priority when faculty were hired for their particular specializations (comparative, development, global studies, and demography). One chair noted that international focus has been a significant consideration, "although pressures to increase enrollments in other areas also lead us to hire in other more traditional specialties." The general feeling is that "international" topics are seen as merely a subfield within the discipline and that in other substantive fields, an emphasis on the United States is expected and perhaps even desirable.

All thirteen chairs said that their departments offered international courses for graduate and undergraduate students. Only one chair, however, said that the department actively encouraged undergraduate research in international themes. Even this was worded cautiously: "We certainly invite students to consider international topics, though we don't pressure them to do so." Another said, "we encourage them to investigate the issues that interest them most, and we find that most of them work on American topics of various kinds." A typical comment noted that it's "too hard for undergrads to do high-quality original research on these topics." In contrast, seven chairs said that their departments did encourage international dissertations. This encouragement, however, was largely passive in that it took the form of employing faculty who were working on international topics— and therefore graduate students had the option available to them. Two persons mentioned university fellowships meant to support international research as an incentive for graduate students.

Everyone agreed that international students are the ones most likely to pick international topics. As for American students, several respondents linked their interest in international issues to a broader conception of the discipline and structure/macrosociological interests. Several also identified a relationship between a subfield and a focus on international research; that is, those working in comparative or development areas will gravitate toward international topics, while those working in stratification will focus on the United States.

Only half of the respondents said that they perceived increasing interest in international affairs. One noted that

> Globalization has heightened some awareness of international issues but in general; I still have the sense of American sociology being decidedly American in tone and content. To me, much international work is (by many) thought of as

akin to "regional studies" and to some degree ghettoized there by virtue of where it's published. This can, of course, also come into play when people are being promoted. When asked "how well known" is someone? the unstated part of the question is "in American sociology." Ironically, one could be more well known outside of the U.S. than inside it and subsequently have their "value" to a doctoral program diminished!

Required International Reading

Despite this ambiguous embrace of international sociology, leading departments of sociology have an array of faculty explicitly identified with international sociology. Inspired by *Contemporary Sociology*'s example, we wrote to those sociology department members explicitly associated with "international sociology" at several departments known for their position in the field or for their international commitments, as well as to other selected sociologists especially known for their international commitments.[41] Although we wrote to a few retired sociologists, nearly all of our respondents were regularly employed as assistant, associate, or full professors. In total, we

---

41. Literally, Kennedy wrote the following between June 10 and June 19, 2004:

Together with Miguel Centeno, I am writing a chapter for the ASA Centennial history of sociology in America on international dimensions of American sociology. You can imagine the challenge, and therefore we seek your help, given your prominence in defining American sociology's extra-US scholarship. Improvising on *Contemporary Sociology*'s question nearly a decade ago, we are asking you and several others the following question: "Beyond your own contributions, which five books or articles, published in the last fifty years by those working in American sociology, are the most important contributions to scholarship in your field?"

Of course we recognize that you might define your field in several different ways thematically and regionally, but we also hope you might humor us, and suggest the best work in American sociology whose data and/or perspective are grounded outside the US, whose scholarship has been important in its own field, and whose value might be recognized even more broadly.

For your reply to be most useful, we would appreciate receiving it by July 6. We're not yet sure how these replies will inform our essay, but we will be pleased, if you are interested, to send an early draft of this essay to you for your comments. Because this work reflects a longer standing interest on our parts, your replies will certainly be guiding our subsequent work in this area too. Thanks very much.

We identified authors explicitly associated with "international sociology" by their publications or their homepage representation. The departments we wrote to included those at Berkeley, Chicago, Harvard, Wisconsin-Madison, Michigan, Yale, Duke, North Carolina, UCLA, UC Davis, UC San Diego, Northwestern, University of Pennsylvania, New York University, Columbia University, and University of Washington.

wrote to 176 respondents, of which 80 replied. Five scholars replied to decline an answer, for personal or intellectual reasons. Some in that number expressed their discomfort with the question and declined to answer; more expressed their discomfort but answered anyway.

We asked them to tell us, beyond their own publications, which five books or articles, published in the last fifty years by those working in American sociology, were the most important contributions to scholarship in their field.[42] Table 20.1 summarizes those authors most often mentioned.

As one can see, international sociology is not so homogeneous as the adjective would suggest. In general we found that the results of our survey indicated the existence of two "internationalist" groups. On the one hand, there is a very cohesive "comparative and historical" set who tend to share the same bibliographic preferences. On the other, there is a residual group with a broad array of interests and beliefs in "which books matter."

Its sense, if pedigree matters, varies importantly with specialty and regional reference. For those who identify as "comparative and historical," perhaps the dominant sense of the international field, recent times have been characterized as "the golden age," with relative consensus about the most influential books. Demographers, another relatively international section of the America Sociological Association, are unlikely to identify *The Modern World System* or *Social Origins of Dictatorship and Democracy* as central to their genealogy, but they were also less likely to respond to the question than were comparative and historical sociologists. Region also matters. Those who focus on Europe are more likely to identify with the field in general and identify books that transcend region. Those who specialize in China are much more likely to identify other works that have focused on their own region than are those who focus on other world regions. Scholars expert in this region are also quite prominent in our list of respondents, given the growing number of scholars interested in China in leading sociology departments. There are also clear institutional legacies, with graduates from departments citing the works of the leading people with whom they studied.

This list is also unrepresentative of the profession's demographic struc-

42. If they replied with a list of only American sociologists, we then wrote to ask them the following: "Would your answers change if we had not asked you to identify which five books or articles, published in the last fifty years by those working in American Sociology, are the most important contributions to scholarship in your field? In other words, with this condition relaxed, would you have named any sociologists principally employed and engaged outside the USA, or scholars in other disciplines within the USA or beyond, in this list?"

Table 20.1 Authors who have made the most important contributions to scholarship in American sociology in the last fifty years

Authors	Total mentions	Authors	Total mentions
Barrington Moore	20	James Coleman	4
Immanuel Wallerstein	20	Andy Walder	4
Charles Tilly	19	Ernest Gellner	4
Theda Skocpol	13	Gosta Esping-Anderson	4
Pierre Bourdieu	9	Reinhard Bendix	4
Peter Evans	7	Berger-Luckman	3
Ivan Szelenyi	7	Michael Mann	3
Jeff Paige	6	Talcott Parsons	3
Blau/Duncan	6	Georg Homans	3
S. M. Lipset	6	Michael Burawoy	3
Michel Foucault	6	S. M. Eisenstadt	3
Erving Goffman	5	Adam Przeworski	3
Perry Anderson	5	Doug Massey	3
Robert Bellah	4	Victor Nee	3
Robert Merton	4	38 others	2
Manuel Castells	4	107 others	1

Note: Although in most cases a single work was cited (e.g., Barrington Moore), in others (e.g., Tilly), several individual works were mentioned. The number of respondents to the survey was 63.

ture today. Theda Skocpol is the only woman mentioned in this list of twenty-nine top authors, and Victor Nee is the only person without predominantly European origins. American sociological internationalism, at least with its most revered scholars in place, remains more like American sociology in the 1950s than what our profession looks like today.

Although some of our respondents replied only with a list, quite a few wrote back with extensive comments. It's worth considering a few of those themes here, for they shape what is, in the end, the key questions shaping our discipline's internationalism.

IS AMERICAN SOCIOLOGY
SUFFICIENTLY INTERNATIONAL?

There is little consensus on how international American sociology is. One scholar celebrated American sociology's internationalism, at least in contrast to the 1950s and 1960s, when it was a "parochial American-centered discipline." Another scholar found even more reason to question our project, given internationalism's dominance:

> In political sociology, which has arguably been more open to international comparisons than many other fields within sociology, it seems to me that almost all of the great books are internationally oriented. I'm trying to think of an area in political sociology that has not been primarily internationally oriented, and what I come up with are voter studies (until relatively recently) and social movement studies (again, until recently—I'm thinking of this field as a subset of political sociology these days). It occurs to me that one could well invert the premise of your chapter and ask: which fields in American sociology have tended to downplay international dimensions, and why!

There were others, however, who saw it quite differently. One scholar wrote, "I think American sociology is terribly American-centric most of the time, with most of its generically presented ideas about how 'modern society works' in fact a reflection of only how American society works—with little or no comparative control, or awareness that American modernity differs from other versions of modernity." Another said, "Unfortunately, I also feel that sociology has turned its back on important non-American issues. . . . I find fewer and fewer students interested in the world outside our borders, except for some of our demographers."

This answer is certainly localized, based on experience in one's immediate surroundings. It would be useful, sometime, to consider how departmental qualities vary with internationalism. One scholar, for example, suggested that

> American sociology is terrifically parochial and will remain focused on American social problems, particularly race. This is a result of who is in the field, when they were trained, and the way universities see the service function of the field. It is not an accident that the best sociology departments hire mostly without regard to field precisely because they are committed to a broader vision of the

field. As a result: the major people working on international stuff are in the major departments as a result. So, the core of the field is more eclectic and knowledgeable than the periphery on this issue.

While the sufficiency of the international in our discipline might be contestable, and variable across departments, certain world regions are definitely not on the front pages of our journals. One scholar was particularly informative on this point:

> I consider Middle East/Islamic studies to have been marginal in sociology and the social sciences in general, even in fields of study that emphasize global protest, such as world systems theory and globalization studies, not to mention the study of revolutions and social movements—in spite of the fact that Islamist radicalism has been one of the world's largest protest movements, if not the single largest movement, for the past generation. Latin American studies gave us dependency theory in the 1960s and 1970s, East Asian studies helped build the field of economic development in the 1980s, East European studies revitalized theories of civil society in the 1980s and 1990s, and Western Europe has always been central to social science—so what does that leave? African studies and Middle Eastern studies—and African studies at least has Robert Bates to link regional stories with high-profile theoretical debates in political science. Middle East studies has not had such a high-status spokesperson since Said (who did not himself study the Middle East) or modernization theorists such as Daniel Lerner and Leonard Binder. This is notwithstanding the fact that three of the most influential social scientists of the late 20th century—Pierre Bourdieu, Clifford Geertz, and Ernest Gellner—started their careers with studies of Muslim societies. But they have had no discernable effect on the attention paid to these societies in their home disciplines, much less in U.S. sociology.

Not only might we say that some world regions are quite underrepresented in our discipline, but we might say even more emphatically that our discipline tends not to find much inspiration in other regions' scholarship.

BEYOND ATTENTION TO WORLD REGIONS, DOES OUR DISCIPLINE FIND INSPIRATION IN SCHOLARSHIP BEYOND AMERICAN PARAMETERS?

Analyzing various world regions beyond America is one step in internationalism's development, but it is not the only quality of internationalism. One might argue that a discipline, or study, is more international if scholarly works that are informed by other nations' historiographies and cultures shape that research. It might be even more international if that research draws on, and especially if it is inspired by, works produced in other world regions. We designed our method to draw out this distinction.

We designed our question for scholars whose principal research lay outside this country. We subsequently decided to include sociologists who rely on comparisons with America for their work. To our surprise, for those scholars with America as a major case study, our question looked as if it sought two different kinds of answers, marking influential works in their field, and influential works in the sociology of international arenas.

One might argue that for those who focus, at least part of the time, on the "American case," the most important work is often done with America in mind. That may be one sign of American nationalism at work in comparative sociology, even among the internationalists. However, even for those who focus on societies beyond the United States, important works are often those written without place in mind, and rather a theoretical point on edge. Chinese studies is the only field, apparently, where Chinese research is abidingly important; for most other American sociologists with international interests, a theoretical argument is more important than a substantive finding.

We asked those who listed exclusively American sociologists whether their answers would change if we had relaxed the conditions about the important works' national location and discipline. Only a few either declined reply or replied that it would not change; in this sense, most of our international sociologists found inspiration in interdisciplinarity and scholarship from elsewhere. However, in nearly every circumstance, that extranational inspiration came from those providing perspective or theory, not substantive argument. As well, nearly all were European.[43] The only exceptions included Fernando Henrique Cardoso and Enzo Faletto, Oliver Cromwell Cox, Shmuel Eisenstadt, Samir Amin, Frantz Fanon, Aimé Cesaire, and Fei Xiaotong. Several scholars were mentioned, for example, Mahmood Mamdani and Hiroshi Ishida, who were located beyond Europe at one time but who are now affiliated with American universities. One scholar embraced this sociological internationalism more fully than any other when she identified two out of four sociologists important in comparative racial studies, as currently located in Brazil (if American trained), including Carlos Hasenbalg and Nelson do Valle Silva.

One might differentiate among Europeans on this list, given that part of the Continent was relatively inaccessible for much of this last half century,

43. That most were Europeans is evident too in this volume's location of extra-U.S. theoretical innovation. See Gross, chap. 6, this volume.

and was not similarly implicated in the imperial project that shaped so much of American sociology's view of the world. If we focused on those from regions once governed by communists, the number of those beyond the western European/American axis would grow substantially, including Stanislaw Ossowski, Roy Medvedev, Michael Voslensky, Pavel Machonin, Milovan Djilas, J. Obradovic, Wlodzimierz Wesolowski, Jadwiga Stansizkis, Zsuzsa Ferge, Laszlo Bruszt, and of course Ivan Szelenyi, who with Gyorgy Konrad wrote the most frequently mentioned book composed abroad, *The Intellectuals on the Road to Class Power* (Konrad and Szelenyi 1979). Here, however, the Polish and Hungarian dominance is obvious too.

American sociology may be more international in its interests, but its scholarly inspiration remains mainly American (even if imported!). When moving beyond America, Americans look to Europe, but mostly for European epistemology and theory, and less for their research or findings. One of our colleagues reflected on the way he teaches sociology:

> When I do a lecture for my intro classes on the history of American sociology, the story I tell basically involves the separate, parallel development of sociology in the US (social reformers, ethnographers, and Progressive empiricists) and in Europe (social theorists and philosophers). . . . Then, I argue, the influx of refugees in and around WWII brings European sociologists to the US, where, almost (but of course not quite) for the first time they mingle with American sociologists. The productive clash between these two very different ideas of sociology produces what Americans and Europeans generally think of as sociology now. That story is perhaps overly simplified, but may explain some of the complexity.

A European-born sociologist emphasized the importance of European thought for theory.

> France has produced major theorists in the postwar period. . . . I am currently putting together my syllabi for classical and contemporary theory next year. They are both dominated by the Germans and the French! And I don't think these are only my own biases . . . the likes of Bourdieu, Foucault, or Norbert Elias are unsurpassed (again, only, perhaps, by Goffman). If you add to this list the more specialized science studies scholarship (Bloor, Latour, MacKenzie, Shapin, Schaffer), which in my line of research is another huge intellectual development, that is a lot coming from outside the US (even though some of these people have been absorbed by American academia).

Another sociologist born in Europe suggests a similar point, but with American scholarship offering something complementary, and important:

I also continue to be strongly influenced by intellectual traditions which are marked as 'continental' or even 'German' such as phenomenology and hermeneutics, traditions I got into through studying philosophy in Germany. And yet, I very much consider myself an American social scientist. . . . I have a strong empirical and ethnographic/historical bent that I would have never acquired in Germany; but I have a drive towards systematic theoretization which I would not have gotten by just studying sociology here.

We identify these distinctions not to indicate pluralism's intrinsic value but only to note its existence. Some scholars with training in other world regions fully embrace the American tradition for their own scholarship. As one "comparative sociologist," trained in Europe, observed: "As a comparative sociologist, I have gained much of my theoretical insights from American scholarship (Moore, Skocpol, Lipset, Abbott, Dobbin, Biernacki). . . . the French tend to be universalistic in their approach and I did not find much there that was useful to my comparative purpose." Americans don't own comparative sociology, however, at least in some fields. One expert in stratification, after identifying American sociological exemplars, replied to our follow-up with praise for the field's genuine internationalization:

> Comparative stratification research is definitely a field where Americans and America-based researchers do not dominate, even though they are strong. My sense (biased no doubt) is that comparative is one of the most dynamic areas in stratification research right now (the others being the intersections of stratification with health, the family, politics, and migration). The ISA's "research committee" on social stratification (RC28) has played a big role in bringing together an international group of scholars to share data, approaches, and results, and to provide a ready-made network for collaborations. Comparative stratification appears to be the exception, again, that might prove the rule. But here too, it is mainly a European exception, with an occasional Japanese or Israeli scholar, that complicates the mix.

Comparative perspectives do not always inspire our colleagues with international interests, however, given the privilege such comparisons typically assign American viewpoints. One of our colleagues wrote,

> I often employ sociologists who do comparative international work in order to learn how not to do research. I therefore use Barrington Moore, Theda Skocpol, Jack Goldstone, for instance, in order to be aware that (*a*) structural analyses are generally reductionist because they treat historical facts as things, and (*b*) these sociologists inherently compare the rest with the West. The ones I do respect, like Ivan Evans, Bill Sewell, Stuart Hall, . . . [a]re those who study one society in depth, the interpretivists, whose insights I could employ much more suc-

cessfully cross-culturally. . . . The other thing which does travel well across so-cieties is of course interdisciplinary analysis, so I always like Dorothy Smith, Omi and Winant, bell hooks, David Halperin because race, gender and sexuality travel extremely well and provide excellent insights.

In this case, standpoint, not comparison, becomes the principal lens with which international scholarship is reviewed. Interdisciplinary can, however, fit just as well with the comparative as with the standpoint position. One of our more senior, and most comparative, scholars was also among the most moved by interdisciplinary and extra-U.S. scholarship. He wrote,

> I should add that most of the books that have had the greatest impact on my own thinking and development have been by non-sociologists (e.g., V. Gordon Childe, the archaeologist, or Walter Goldschmidt, the anthropologist) or by long-dead scholars, such as Millar, Ferguson, Michels, Marx, Weber, Pareto, etc.) or more recent non-Americans, such as Dahrendorf, Ossowski, Machonin, Wesolowski, Shlapentokh, Duverger, etc.).

This scholar, in fact, notes the divide between the discipline and his own scholarship, for the discipline is inspired first and foremost by its own nationally produced sociology. He found his inspiration elsewhere, as many of our other senior distinguished scholars did.

It may be, however, that with the globalization of American sociology, within America one need no longer find inspiration beyond the discipline or the nation. It may be that as scholars offer collaboration from without to produce for American journals, or as scholars from across the world come to America for employment, that international sociology could become synonymous with what is produced within America, for American sociological audiences. Like globalization itself, one might find the world as much within one's home as in another place. Or it might also be the same illusion.

Conclusions

What can we say about American sociology's internationalism? To be sure, it would be difficult to write in 2004 that American sociology is as ethnocentric as Everett Hughes worried over forty years ago. At the same time, it is difficult to deny that this internationalism is more Eurocentric than it is fully internationalist. To be sure, the discipline has moved well beyond researching only the West. One of the field's great transformations is in the number of scholars studying China in particular, but as well Eastern Europe and other postcommunist sites. Transition certainly became as mainstream a concern as globalization. Terrorism, however, is quite new and hardly grounded in the historical sociology of the region over which American authorities are most concerned. Here, we can say without doubt that our internationalism is uneven in research attention and absolutely uneven in terms of intellectual inspiration.

The story is, of course, complicated. The globalization of knowledge production means that there are many scholars, within American sociology departments, that bring other regional contentions and concerns into our disciplinary discussion. In this sense, American sociology is becoming increasingly less ethnocentric as it brings people, data, and ideas from other world regions into its generalizing ambitions.

It is however absolutely clear, at the same time, that these discussions must be articulated within the frames of reference that guide American sociological discussions, which themselves have been grounded in reference at least to the West or Western power, and often with regard to American society itself. Even those scholars from beyond Europe and America became appealing because they were arguing *against* imperialist or colonial powers, resonating with America's own debate about itself and its role in the world.

This is a tale familiar to many internationally oriented sociologists. Articles and arguments must be justified in terms that sociologists expert on America can recognize. Indeed, very often such scholars must justify not only the question but the place for its address. American sociologists focusing on America do not have such problems.

We would be remiss, however, if we did not acknowledge that there are important conceptual shifts at work in the development of a global sociology with a less exclusively American accent. Latin American scholarship was critical to modernization theory's eclipse as the dominant interpretation of global transformations. East European scholarship is frequently cited in sociologies of transition and postcommunist transformation; civil society is a critical concept in American sociology due, in no small part, to its revival within Eastern European critical theory. Guanxi is known well beyond Chinese-language speakers, finding that network ties are at least as important to understand as father's occupation and educational attainment in explaining socioeconomic status. These innovations, however, are relatively compatible with American sociology's globalization. When boundaries were crossed, and communication and cooperation dominant, the introduction of "foreign" conceptions into a world sociology was politically unproblematic and conceptually advantageous.

In a world at war, however, it is much more difficult to conceive how foreign concepts, especially those that challenge American powers or presumptions, might be entered. In this, the challenge of internationalizing sociology grows, especially if this sociology's cosmopolitanism is not to be an extension of its World War II and early cold war sensibilities. Perhaps we could learn from our discipline's beginning debates about imperialism, but given the Christian, racist, patriarchal, and Western roots of many of those discussions, our history looks particularly inadequate. In many ways, American sociology faces an international challenge greater than ever before. But it is also prepared, if the responses of our colleagues are indicative of the discipline's disposition, to engage the most challenging questions if suitably supported by the broader discipline and larger institutional infrastructure and culture. Will our intellectual infrastructure support a deeper globalization of scholarship, one that goes beyond American presumption in defining the world?

Not only must American sociology consider the sensibilities of those its government defines as enemies and consider their formation's implication in American power, it also must engage a sense of religions distant from the secular presumptions of American sociology. To update Barnes's (1948b) collection today, we would have to go well beyond Christian reformism and European scholarship. We may even have to go beyond globalization's parameters, for its cosmopolitanism is certainly not sufficient for a sociology of a world transformed by global terrorism and American empire. American sociology's double bind may have just become tighter. At least it is also more apparent.

Acknowledgments

We received an enormous amount of good advice on this chapter from those who replied to our query and from those who commented on our work. Thanks go to the essay's anonymous reviewers as well as to Craig Calhoun, Jonathan VanAntwerpen, Charlie Kurzman, Andrew Schrank, Muge Gocek, John Lie, Gerhard Lenski, Georgi Derluguian, Wlodzimierz Wesolowski, Mel Kohn, Gil Merkx, John Comaroff, Chris Smith, Jeff Paige, Genevieve Zubrzycki, Andreas Glaeser, Jozsef Borocz, Arne Kalleberg, Marion Fourcade-Gourinchas, Andrew Perrin, Bill Lacy, Barbara Heyns, Saskia Sassen, Martha Lampland, Adrian Favell, Michael Mann, Min Zhou, Neil Brenner, Nan Lin, Bruce Carrothers, William Brustein, Tukufu Zuberi, Abigail Saguy, Edward Telles, Erik Olin Wright, Ron Aminzade, Doug Guthrie, Don Treiman, Ted Gerber, Julian Dierkes, Duane Champagne, Ming-cheng Lo, Ted Gerber, Rebecca Emigh, David Wiley, Lynne Haney, Gershon Shafir, Immanuel Wallerstein, Ron Rindfuss, Dingxin Zhao, John Hall, Arland Thornton, Eileen Otis, Said Arjomand, Cindy Buckley, Peter Bearman, Tom Gold, France Winddance Twine, Burkhart Holzner, Jeff Goodwin, George Steinmetz, Alberto Palloni, Andy Abbott, Hyun Ok Park, Mark Juergensmeyer, Charlie Hirschman, Gary Gereffi, Phil Gorski, Larry King, Dan Chirot, Neil Fligstein, Carlos Waisman, Oyeronke Oyewumi, Tom DiPrete, Michèle Lamont, Loïc Wacquant, Maciek Slomczynski, Marty Whyte, Deborah Davis, and Elzbieta Halas.

[TWENTY-ONE] Defining Disciplinary Identity: The Historiography of U.S. Sociology

Alan Sica

The Problem of Sociology's Historiography in the United States

There are no definitive, comprehensive histories of sociology as practiced in the United States (or elsewhere) which can be compared favorably with the leading extant accounts of biology, chemistry, economics, philosophy, or psychology. For physics the best histories are not written by practicing physicists but by historians of science who know enough physics to explain how the field developed but who would never compete with laboratory researchers in trying to discover new techniques or ideas. Early historians of sociology wrote foundational chronicles in their "spare time" while giving most of their attention to formulating theories and methods of social research proper. By contrast, historians of science are trained to evaluate archival evidence, imitating their guiding light, George Sarton, who single-handedly invented the modern history of natural science around 1915 (Garfield 1985). Sociology has not thus far been blessed with its own Sarton to show the way toward constructing a reliable, robust, and comprehensive historical record, though several notable attempts were indeed made early on.

Physicists might be the first to point out that their field began three thousand years ago, while the very word *sociology* only appeared on April 27, 1839, in one of Auguste Comte's notebooks (Pickering 1993, 615). So perhaps historians of sociology have simply not found enough archival material to justify their labors. Yet famous histories of economics by Eric Roll, Joseph Schumpeter, and Mark Blaug, among others, demonstrate that solid accounts of an allied field not much older than sociology can indeed be produced given the right author and an attentive audience. However, even in the absence of an agreed-upon historical methodology, or a defining work that sets the pace for subsequent scholars (in the way that Sarton's five-volume *Introduction to the History of Science* so masterfully did), there does exist a neglected corpus of work which can yield revealing insight into sociology's past. Not surprisingly, the earliest of such works were produced by a handful of pioneers ("participant observers") whose historical writings conveyed great enthusiasm for their new professional identity, if occasionally at the expense of factual accuracy in favor of rhetorical zeal. A cursory evaluation of these works occupies this chapter, plus glancing reference to subsequent historiography that has treated sociology's U.S. beginnings.

The earliest American sociologists were as much at home writing rigorously historical studies of sociocultural topics as their descendants today are not. Many were formally trained in the *Geisteswissenschaften* by masters in Germany, which meant that at the time no stark divisions obtained between nascent sociology and its more firmly established sister disciplines. For instance, when Frank Wilson Blackmar (ninth ASA president, in 1919) began his long, steady career of writing scholarly books, it was with works heavily embroiled in matters of historiography: *The Study of History and Sociology* (1890b), a didactic pamphlet written to enlighten recalcitrant Kansas legislators; *Spanish Institutions in the Southwest* (1891), a substantial, award-winning monograph that still remains a fundamental scholarly source; and its briefer companion volume, *Spanish Colonization in the Southwest* (1890a). Coming full circle, and after writing many sociological studies and textbooks, his final book was *History of Human Society* (1926). Similarly, Robert Park's published dissertation on the role of crowds in historical change (*Masse und Publikum*, 1904) was directed by the noted historian of philosophy Wilhelm Windelband and as such kept Park firmly tied to a historical sense of social reality. It is hardly surprising then to learn that Albion Small, also German trained (the indispensable founder of what much later came to be called the Chicago school [see Abbott 1999; Kurtz 1984]), would produce dozens of articles and several books defining sociology as a distinctly historical achievement not only in the United States but also among its forebears in Europe.

Yet despite these auspicious beginnings in favor of paying serious attention to the discipline's past, not until 1978 was there a scholarly journal dedicated solely to the history of the field, even though many articles and the occasional book on the topic had regularly appeared earlier in the twentieth century. Partly this was due to a scientistic attitude common to post–World War II practitioners that demeaned the significance of the "merely historical" in favor of "doing real sociology" (a phenomenon well documented by Jones and Kronus [1976]). The *Journal of the History of Sociology* (1978–87), which I edited and published for a time, quickly lost its frail financial footing. Similarly, the ASA History of Sociology section is still in its infancy relative to other research groups (such as Cheiron) that sponsor study of social science history. These facts might lead one to believe that until recently, the discipline's past has been of only minor interest to the rank and file, or that formally trained historians of the social sciences have not discovered within sociology that same rich vein of archival materials that they have long mined while excavating the origins of related disciplines, particularly anthropology, economics, and psychology. (One might also wonder why, until recently, all graduate students in psychology were required to take a course in the history of the discipline, for which ample textbooks exist, while the same requirement has never obtained within sociology.)

Such a viewpoint apparently contradicts that of a noted historian of the social sciences, as expressed in a synoptic article that bears directly on the topic:

> And from the pattern of professional conduct I have identified we may be able to deduce the reason that the journal devoted to and entitled *History of Sociology* had only a short-lived existence in the early [to mid-] 1980s: while both the International Sociological Association and the American Sociological Association have proven hospitable to organized interest groups devoted to the history of sociology, it may be that there is no market for a specialized journal because research in the history of the field is a routine feature of disciplinary practice, of putative interest to the readers of mainstream journals, no different from, say, work on social stratification. (Kuklick 1999, 234)

Although it is true that a few well-known sociologists have been able to publish strictly historical articles in the main journals, little space in these principal venues is normally "donated" to histories of the field, since "doing sociology" has always been given precedence over "reviewing the past," especially during the two or three decades following World War II. (As editor of *History of Sociology* for several years, I found no lack of credible submissions; the journal's crisis came rather from too few institutional subscribers and the lack of an endowment.) The fact that a few younger social historians—most of whom are *not* formally trained sociologists, since no major American sociology doctoral program offers a specialization in the history of sociology—have over the last two decades or so boldly pursued American sociology's origins and development does not contradict my argument contra Kuklick (who is a historian proper): today's sociologists are in general ignorant about their field's past and have not been persuaded to become otherwise during their graduate educations. They are not encouraged to pursue research along these lines simply because publication opportunities in the principal journals are very slim for that category known as "the history of the discipline."

Despite the odds against such publication, though, a number of solid works assaying the history of U.S. sociology have indeed appeared during the last thirty years (which perhaps inspired Kuklick to express her sanguine view), and which, if taken as a whole, go some considerable way toward illuminating sociology's origins. The fact that they are not routinely assigned for graduate student indoctrination is hardly the fault of their authors but merely reflects what has long been a strong disciplinary norm.[1] Most of these works are neither grand in scope nor strongly polemical by intent (exceptions include Schwendinger and Schwendinger [1974], Deegan [1988], and Turner and Turner [1990]). But they do evidence a sustained attempt by scholars from a number of disciplines to narrate sociology's story in a way that is consistent with contemporary scholarly norms, and, despite the marginality, such works endure among historians proper as well as among everyday sociologists.

These newer works are very far removed in tone, technique, and substance from the earliest historiographical forays, produced between about 1895 and 1940. Taken together, however, the earliest writers provide a fascinating, full-blooded portrait of sociology's institutional and intellectual history during its most self-confident and combative period. Ever since Albion Small's vigorous, sustained ventures in telling sociology's story between 1895 and 1924, a set of scholarly materials has come into existence, often written by prominent members of the guild, which surveyed its historical record. More often than not these took a celebratory form, in order to legitimate a newcomer that scholars from other competing fields disparaged from its very beginnings (at Hopkins in the late 1880s).

As the first ASS (i.e., ASA) president, Lester Ward, put it in his presidential address in December 1906, "a retiring dean . . . in a public address . . . said, among other things, that 'Sociology, far from being a science, was little more than empty verbiage'" (Ward 1907, 582). Similarly, Edward Cummings revealed to Small that prior to 1891–92, when he taught "the first sociology course offered at Harvard . . . no one had given me the slightest encouragement to believe there was any 'academic future' for 'sociological'

1. A sample of these groundbreaking studies (by decade) could include the following: I: Bannister (1979), Fine (1979), Furner (1975), Hardin (1977), Haskell (1977), Matthews (1977), Oberschall (1972), Schwendingers (1974); II: Bannister (1987), Bernert (1983), Bulmer (1984b), Converse (1987), Deegan (1988), Fuhrman (1980), Hinkle (1980), Jones (1983), Kloppenberg (1986), Kuklick (1980), Lewis and Smith (1980), Miller (1986), Phelan (1989), Rhoades (1981), Schwartz (1987), Sica (1983, 1986), Vidich and Lyman (1985), Wallace (1989), Wolff (1985); III: Bannister (1991, 2003), Camic (1995), Camic and Xie (1994), Connell (1997), Deegan (1991), Fine (1995), Finlay (1999), Henking (1992), Herzberg (2001), Hinkle (1994), Käsler (1998), Keen (1999), King (1990), Kivisto (2004), Kuklick (1999), Laslett (1990, 1991), Levine (1995), Platt (1996), Porter and Ross (2003), Rafferty (2003), Romano (2002), Ross (1991, 1993, 1994), Schorske (1997), Sica (1990, 1997, 1998), Sklansky (1999), Smith (1994), Tobin (1995), Turner and Turner (1990), Wald (2002).

work" (Small 1916, 761-62). Aspersions of this type could be multiplied by the hundred. It quickly became a platitude in the academy that those adventurers who embraced sociology as a profession were setting out to sea in a fragile craft, without maps, and with no discernible destination. That "sociology" and "socialism" were chronically conflated in the popular mind did not help the discipline's advancement either (see, inter alia, Gillin 1927a, 24).

In this chapter I survey the key works of sociology's early historiography with an eye toward delineating the principal scholarly and ideological shifts that inhabit this special realm of sociological inquiry. The changes that have engulfed this scholarly subfield—beginning with the earliest formulations from the 1890s and culminating in the latest entry in the genre, the pertinent chapter of the *Cambridge History of Science: The Modern Social Sciences* (Bannister 2003)—are hard to miss. Somewhat surprisingly given the robust rhetoric of sociology's first fifty years or so, the peculiar "reflexivity" that Alvin Gouldner during the 1960s urged his colleagues to adopt so that their self-perceptions might be sharpened has now swamped more traditional motives of historical writing and has itself become orthodoxy. The ultimate meaning and consequences of this epistemological shift toward relentless self-critique are not entirely clear as we head into a new century of sociology's existence—one which in many ways seems eons removed from the giddy founding days of Ward, Giddings, Sumner, and Small, when the value of sociology seemed to them self-evident and indisputably grand.

"Small's Journal" in Its Early Days

Before commenting, even briefly, on the handful of histories that U.S. sociology has inspired, it is necessary to contextualize the discipline's earliest moments during its fierce struggle to legitimate itself as a respectable, widely institutionalized field. The most efficient way of doing this is to consider selected documents published during the first years of the *American Journal of Sociology* (from July 1895), plus the series *Papers and Proceedings* of the ASS, beginning in 1906, also published for some time in the *AJS*. As one would expect, these essays, articles, and other documents evidence a fair amount of undiluted ideological statement and restatement, particularly when transmitted through the practiced and committed offices of Albion Small and his coterie. Yet the level of purely intellectual give-and-take among a number of early guild members concerning the new discipline's most desirable future, and the serene seriousness with which many of these writers delivered their messages to one another as well as to what they hoped would become a wider public, remains bracing, even inspiring. This is especially so when viewed against the backdrop of today's comparatively tepid arguments for sociology's "relevance" to the growth of academic knowledge, as well as its hopeful applicability to various policy spheres.

One way, then, of coming to grips with the discipline's earliest days, as well as with those narratives composed at the time which tried to capture the development of the field during its infancy, is to study the first issues of "Small's *Journal*," as the *AJS* was known privately to Lester Ward, Franklin Giddings, and others less fortunate in their publishing outlets than was their genial competitor in the Midwest (e.g., Giddings's letter to Ward, March 5, 1896 [in Stern 1932, 309]). It is not too much to say that Small's vision of what sorts of material should fill the journal, and thereby define the discipline's initial public identity, became for many years the single most important factor in U.S. sociology's evolution. According to Small, it was William Rainey Harper's surprising challenge to him "late in the spring of 1895" to use money previously and fruitlessly allocated to Harper's favored publication, *University Extension World*—by asking simply, "Are you willing to be responsible for a journal of sociology?"—that spurred Small into the business of running the first such periodical in the United States (Small 1916, 786n1). Needless to say, it was Harper's lavish funding of the department and its new chairman—whose salary was on the order of $7,000 in 1892, an outlandish sum when compared with even the most famous professors' salaries, which rarely exceeded $1,500 per annum—that nudged eastern universities into beginning their own sociology programs, even if with markedly less enthusiasm and institutional support than was the case at Mr. Rockefeller's university.

Small had very strong epistemological ideas, many of them reflecting his postgraduate work in Germany (detailed in his *Origins of Sociology*), about what ought to be recognized as sociology proper and what should be left aside. Despite his own theological background and his passionate belief that sociology should ultimately serve some meliorative societal purpose, he was married to the idea of "objectivity" as the distinguishing trait of "true" sociological research. And even though he is no longer remembered as such, he thought of his own achievement as principally one of championing rigorous "methodology": "The American sociological movement . . . takes on significance, not only for itself but as a phenomenon of social science in general, when it appears as an inevitable phase of that expansion of DEMAND FOR OBJECTIVITY in social science which found voice in Adam Smith, and which became the beginning of a program in the methodology projected by Eichhorn, and Savigny, and Niebuhr, and Ranke" (Small 1916, 748, emphases in original; cf. Small 1910, 681). Though entirely laudable in their own ways, social work, religiously based moral uplift practices, social problems studies of narrow gauge, and any other mode of inquiry that could not be comfortably situated beneath the umbrella of "science" had no place, so Small thought, within sociology's fight to establish itself among its older, jealous sister disciplines. The protosociological fields suffered from a methodological footing too subjectivistic and unstandardized to suit Small's taste, and their ultimate goal—to improve living conditions for contemporary U.S. citizens—clashed with Small's insistence that sociology take the high road to "pure knowledge" as defined by Newtonian science. (This may account in part for the alleged animosity that obtained between Jane Addams and her high-minded colleagues in Hyde Park, as portrayed by Deegan [1988].)

Yet despite all these a priori limitations, the range of articles, book reviews, bibliographies, letters, professional announcements, and comments that Small actually published in his journal cannot fail to amaze the unsuspecting reader. As the self-appointed international ambassador for American sociology, Small never tired of pontificating about the form and substance that sociology ought to assume to reach its potential. His own prescriptions for sociology's future included articles such as "The Organic Concept of Society" (1895), "The Era of Sociology" (1895), "The Sociologist's Point of View" (1897), "The Scope of Sociology" (in seven parts, 1900–1902), "What Is a Sociologist?" (1903), "The Subject Matter of Sociology" (1904), "A Decade of Sociology" (1905), "The Relation between Sociology and the Other Sciences" (1906), "The Meaning of Sociology" (1908), "The Vindication of Sociology" (1909), "The Sociological Stage in the Evolution of the Social Sciences" (1910), and others, up to "The Future of Sociology" (1921), oddly culminating in "Sociology and Plato's *Republic*" (1925), an unsung precursor to Alvin Gouldner's *Enter Plato*. (For a useful if incomplete list of Small's publications, including these dozen or more that defined and redefined the discipline, see House [1926].) And yet either owing to Small's natural catholicity of judgments and professional contacts, or because he was sheerly under pressure to fill vacant pages, the material he allowed to be called "sociology" by showing up in *AJS* proved to be remarkably unfettered.

With the short, pungent clarion call, "The Era of Sociology," Small officially welcomed his new journal into the world of learning and gave notice that the *science* of sociology had taken up permanent residence at the University of Chicago. Witness his opening lines: "Sociology has a foremost place in the thought of modern men. Approve or deplore the fact at pleasure, we cannot escape it" (Small 1895a, 1). His italicized subheads clearly indicate how strongly he felt about the field's prospects, while also shouting a strident rhetorical program that must have irritated other academics who were more accustomed to restrained self-praise: "In our age the fact of human association is more obtrusive and relatively more influential than in any previous epoch" (1895a, 1); "The distinguishing mental trait of our age is undisciplined social self-consciousness" (2); "This inevitable contact of man with men has produced confident popular philosophies of human association" (2); "Popular social philosophy has its counterpart today in a social gravitation or 'movement'" (3); "The facts thus sketched constitute a strenuous demand for authentic social philosophy" (6); "Many capable scholars are beginning to recognize in these conditions a summons to unique forms of service" (7).

After curt forays into the works of Spencer, the detested Benjamin Kidd, and Dr. Edward Aveling (who "has not greatly overrated Marx's true position in placing him alone alongside of Darwin in influencing the thought of the nineteenth century" [Small 1895a, 11]), Small concludes with specific observations about his new journal:

> *The American Journal of Sociology* will be a medium for exchange of thought between scholars upon the work of developing an orderly view of associated human activities as a whole. In this *Journal* a large number of American scholars, with many representative European sociologists will also try to express their best thoughts upon discoverable principles of societary relationship, in such a way that they might assist all intelligent men in taking the largest possible view of their rights and duties as citizens. (13)

Although today's *AJS* does not publicly subscribe to Small's forthright connection between scholarship and improved citizenship, the subtext remains in place within the unspoken creed of sociologists everywhere. We are more publicly modest in our claims but no less committed, I would argue, to Small's vision of the sociological enterprise with regard to its most basic motivations. The 2004 (San Francisco) meeting of the ASA, during which the former presidents of Ireland and Brazil spoke eloquently about the practical role sociologists play in large-scale policy decisions, is one of many possible cases in point.

Wisely, Small invited the "American Aristotle," Lester Ward (see Chugerman 1939), to write the follow-up article in the inaugural issue of *AJS*, titled "The Place of Sociology among the Sciences." Ward's career as a paleobiologist for the U.S. government, plus his polymathic scholarly interests, gave him a reputation qua scientist that neither Giddings nor Small could claim, so they both humbled themselves before the older man while fighting between themselves. Ward cites them both in footnotes 1 and 2 of the article, while determining the etymological origin of the term *sociology*. In characteristically thorough fashion, Ward recounts the history of the modern sciences, taking the lead of Spencer, Comte, and J. S. Mill while trying to position sociology correctly. After some pages, he reaches a Comtean conclusion: "We come then to the last and highest of the sciences, viz., sociology. . . sociology is an advanced study, the last and latest in the entire curriculum. . . . it involves high powers of generalization, and what is more, it absolutely requires a broad basis of induction" (Ward 1895a, 22, 25). Ward thought sociology ought to be exclusively reserved for postgraduates, probably because without a deep and broad background in various traditions of learning (notably from history, political economics, and related fields) on which to practice "induction," the field would not prosper or prove convincing to its legion of detractors.

The balance of the first issue of *AJS* included articles that were probably cobbled together at the last moment, inasmuch as the money for the journal was first proffered to Small in "late spring of 1895," and the first issue appeared in July. Harry Pratt Judson asked "Is Our Republic a Failure?" (which shows the perennial pertinence of certain topics), followed by George Fellows's "The Relation of Anthropology to the Study of History," Paul Monroe's "English and American Christian Socialism: An Estimate," and the first of a nine-article series by Shailer Mathews called "Christian Sociology." Small himself contributed "The Civic Federation of Sociology: A Study in Social Dynamics," and the journal's 112 pages concluded with "Seminar Notes." All of these spontaneous ventures into "official" sociology still make interesting reading, as much for their heartfelt seriousness as for their hopefulness regarding the discipline's future. Ward claimed that most sociologists were being recruited from the ranks of political economy, but it seems, based on the heavy moralizing that saturated many of the journal's earliest contributions, that Christian theology played a central role, if not through formal doctrine then in reflecting the theme of "thy brother's keeper."[2]

Though impossible on this occasion to review many of the articles that Small accepted for *AJS* in its first decade or so, a few deserve comment because they gave shape to an overtly self-conscious effort on his part as well as that of his confederates (W. I. Thomas, George Vincent, C. R. Henderson, and the redoubtable Ward) to enunciate a history of sociology before there

2. See Vidich and Lyman (1985) for the fullest expression of this viewpoint and my review essay (Sica 1986) for a critical response.

was time for a true history to have evolved, while at the same time defining the new discipline's borders. Ward began a long series called "Contributions to Social Philosophy" in the second issue of the journal, Rene Worms contributed "Sociology and Political Economy," Jeremiah Jenks wrote, long before NORC was even dreamt of, "The Guidance of Public Opinion," and Small laid the foundation of his own theoretical work with "Static and Dynamic Sociology" (in addition to providing reviews of three books plus a conference in Paris). Clearly, Small was "setting the sociological agenda" for the succeeding generation; perhaps in part he had to use whatever articles came to hand, but he was also canny in his selection of authors and topics. The third issue of *AJS* led with a long article by Carroll Wright, "Contributions of the United States Government to Social Science," Small indulged in some light muckraking with "Private Business as a Public Trust," while other articles included "Politics and Crime" and "Mr. Kidd's 'Social Evolution,'" about a British competitor who wrote the article on "sociology" for the ninth edition of the *Britannica* which so infuriated Small. C. R. Henderson's first *AJS* piece examined "The Place and Functions of Voluntary Associations," others pursued "Sociology in Italy" and "The Relation of Sociology and Pedagogy," while "Minor Editorials" became a regular feature of the journal, where letters were printed from interested readers (one from Durkheim himself in May 1898), conferences announced, and other professional business outlined. The fourth issue began with another Henderson piece, "Business Men and Social Theorists," coupled with J. D. Forrest's "Anti-Monopoly Legislation in the United States," both of which would seem to be as "relevant" today as they were then, since the Gay Nineties shared many of the political-economic tendencies of our own recent past. (One wonders what Rockefeller would have made of Forrest's comments.)

Small's skillful orchestration of articles that would provide a pedigree for his nascent field continued in the fourth issue (January 1896) with George Vincent's "The Province of Sociology" and James H. Tufts's "Recent Sociological Tendencies in France." The famously independent Jane Addams published her first article in the March 1896 issue (vol. 1, no. 5), as did E. A. Ross, with "Social Control." Another member of his circle, C. R. Henderson, wrote the first of several articles with the intriguing title "Rise of the German Inner Mission," which, when compared with Weber's use of *Innerlichkeit* in his sociology of religion, also seems prescient. Meanwhile, Ward continued his series on "social philosophy," and Shailer Mathews soldiered on with his "Christian Sociology."

In its second year the *AJS* offered articles on the peace movement in Europe, more social control from Ross (which after thirteen installments became an important book), immigration and crime, a useful bibliography by C. H. Hastings (a University of Chicago librarian) that became a regular feature, Simmel's first article (vol. 2, no. 2), a discussion of "distributive justice," many more book reviews (including Small on Giddings's *Principles*), conference reports, and many others which bear a striking familiarity with the tone and substance of sociological work these 108 years later. Small encouraged Ward to produce "The Purpose of Sociology" (1896e) as part of his long series on fundamentals but also included Frank Blackmar's "Smoky Pilgrims" (1897), a quaint yet shocking urban ethnography in Lawrence, Kansas, carried out among the chronically poor by a future president of the ASS. Small's promise to make the journal cosmopolitan, with strong European connections, was exemplified by O. Thon's series "The Present Status of Sociology in Germany," joined by E. Muensterberg's series "Principles of Public Charity and Private Philanthropy in Germany." Hull House was given a lead article, followed by "Socialistic Thought in England" and an instructional piece concerning "the Le Play Method of Monographs on Families." I. W. Howerth began a didactic series, much in keeping with the general spirit of the journal, called "A Programme for Social Study." And the tireless Small reviewed the third volume of Spencer's *Principles*. Thus, the first two years (twelve issues) of the journal had been filled with promise and energetic writing, indicating that Harper had been right in his hunch: the U.S. academic world was ready to write suitable material for a journal of sociological work.

> Thus we see that it was Small's unembarrassed, ingenuous grandiloquence that set the tone for sociology's earliest historiography, e.g., . . . our sense of the present condition is not a sense at all, it is a numbness without this historical approach. We do not fully take in the problems as problems, unless to a certain extent we have put ourselves back into the state of mind of people before our time who were pioneering through blind trails that opened at last upon the problems of our own time, and were experimenting with devices for dealing with pioneering difficulties. (Small 1924, 325)

That the early founders were learned in the demanding Victorian sense—including easy familiarity with multiple languages, history, political economics, and literature, plus standardized graduate study in Europe—is sometimes too easily forgotten, since today's definition of a sociologist does not necessarily include any of these attributes. The quality of their formal writings, discussions (as stenographically preserved), and letters is often very high, driven as much by elevated moral purpose as by scientific and historical literacy.[3] For example, in the foundational work by Small, "Fifty Years of Sociology in the United States (1865–1915)," he offers the entire course guide to the "plan of instruction in the Columbia School of Political Science, as it was projected in 1892." This he viewed as "certainly the best considered, most comprehensive, and most coherent attempt up to that time in the United States to organize team-work in the social sciences so as to cover all the ground which needs to be surveyed in that field" (Small 1916, 737–38). The program "stimulated the inevitable demand for general sociology," which is why Small valued it. It was designed to be Germanic in its thoroughness and difficulty, clearly imitating the universities where Columbia's professors had studied abroad: "The student is supposed to be familiar with the outlines of European history, ancient and modern. . . . It is presumed that students possess a knowledge of the general principles of political economy as laid down in the ordinary manuals by Walker or Mill" (Small 1916, 739, 743); reading lists were in English, German, and French.

A sense of what was expected from students around this time can be gleaned from the 1906 volume assembled by Giddings ("Professor of Sociology and the History of Civilization in Columbia University"), titled *Readings in Descriptive and Historical Sociology*. Its 550 pages began thus: "The chief purpose held in view in preparing this volume has been to offer to the beginner in sociological studies significant examples of the great facts of social evolution, and of their interpretation; and to present them so that collectively, and in connection with a mere outline of theory, they should constitute a fairly complete scheme." To this end Giddings excerpted material from works such as *History of the People of the United States, Some Facts about Alsace and Lorraine, Journal of André Micheaux, China and the Chinese, Irish Life in Irish Fiction, Hull House Maps and Papers,* Taine's *French Revolution,* Morgan's *Ancient Society,* and Josiah Royce's unusual study, *California,* not to mention works of Plutarch, Lecky, and a study of Zwingli. Leaving aside Giddings's organizing theory, students could still learn quite a lot about comparative civilizations from this book, filled as it is with information that is no longer available in introductory sociology textbooks (where graphics have supplanted text).

During its first year, seventy-six students enrolled in the Columbia program that Small admired and were surely thereby among a tiny intellectual elite, conforming to what must now seem to be prohibitive requirements for

3. See especially the Small-Ross-Ward collections edited by Bernard Stern (1932, 1933, 1935, 1936, 1937, 1938, 1946a, 1946b, 1947, 1948, 1949).

admission but which at the time were simply the modus operandi of advanced study. And if one reads the letters, speeches, and formal writings of these early social scientists, it is easy to see how well they were served by their rigorous education, which in its catholicity was far broader than that of their successors. Speaking of the sister organization at the twenty-fifth anniversary of the American Historical Society in 1909, J. Franklin Jameson wrote: "Organization, numbers, and quantities are not all. The graduate student of that time, it is agreed on all sides, was superior to the graduate student of today. . . . The professors were few but they included—to mention only the *stelligeri* in the catalogue—such teachers as Torrey and Gurney, Moses Coit Tyler and W. F. Allen, Herbert B. Adams and Charles Kendall Adams" (Small 1916, 777). These scholars' strong rhetoric and argumentation make it apparent that debating the likely or desirable future of sociology was not for most of their interlocutors an idle hobby but came close to defining their very beings. They staked out this intellectual and political terrain in vigorous opposition not only to other academics but also to a public that remained ambivalent about the connative and denotative meanings of the term *social science* in general and *sociology* in particular.

In tune with its founders' tempered optimism, the American Sociological Association celebrates its centennial as a professional organization in 2005, an achievement that would have seemed improbable and unnecessary to most other members of the academy when it was first organized. It began humbly enough:

> During the summer of 1905, Professor C. W. A. Veditz, of the George Washington University, wrote to a number of the well-known sociologists of the United States with a view to securing an expression of opinion with regard to the desirability and feasibility of forming some sort of an organization of sociologists. This correspondence indicated, among those who participated in it, a unanimous desire for such an organization. Dr. Lester F. Ward, of Washington, believed that there is certainly need for a national sociological association. ("Organization of the ASS" [probably Albion Small] 1906, 555)

The possible need for such a group, one that distinguished itself from psychology, political economics, or history, was thoroughly discussed soon thereafter:

> In accordance with this invitation, the first meeting of those interested was held in McCoy Hall, at the Johns Hopkins University, Wednesday afternoon, December 27, at 3:30 p.m. The meeting was attended by some fifty persons, among whom were a number particularly interested in the practical aspects of sociology. (557)

These "specialists in sociology"—whose professional commitments had originally been to social work, social philosophy, practical theology, journalism, economics, and so on—met in person but were also informed by forty public letters sent to Professor Veditz from other interested parties unable to attend (Rhoades 1981, 1). Many of the actual and virtual participants soon became iconic figures in sociology's history, and much of their early discussion turned into spirited yet optimistic arguments over the direction the discipline and the proposed organization should take. "Professor Giddings, of Columbia University, pointed out that probably in no country in the world is there so much interest in the problems of sociology, whether theoretical or practical, as in the United States. Many, if not most, of our colleges and universities offer courses in sociology" ("Organization of the ASS" 1906, 561).

After two days of talks, Ward was elected president, William Graham Sumner the first vice president, Giddings as second vice president, with E. A. Ross, Albion Small, and others on the executive committee ("Organization of the ASS" 1906, 568). It was agreed to hold the first annual meeting of what was then called the American Sociological Society in December 1906 in Providence, Rhode Island, where 115 members attended, each of whom had paid $3 a year in membership dues (as compared with well over $200 a year in 2005). (The organization's name remained American Sociological Society until 1959, when its acronym was suddenly noted as troubling, so it was changed from Society to Association.) Within several years of that modest beginning, Theodore Roosevelt addressed the society when it met in Washington, apparently the only time a U.S. president has spoken to the ASA's annual meeting. From this humble origin the society steadily grew, with membership rising to 1,021 by 1920, 1,530 in 1930 (when the society's entire annual budget came to $9,160), and 3,241 by 1950. In sharp contrast, the 2004 annual meeting held in San Francisco involved over 5,000 participants from around the globe, which represents only about 40 percent of the association's total membership.

Early Efforts at Historiography

Despite a history reaching at least back to 1840 and the French social philosopher and mathematical prodigy Auguste Comte, sociology has not been especially well served by historians. As already mentioned, the history of sociology remains largely terra incognita, especially when one compares it with large-scale historical accounts of other fields, even those accounts that restrict themselves to the last two centuries. Until quite recently, the number of monographic histories that explore sociology's development as an intellectual venture and an academic specialty (particularly in the United States) was very small when compared with those treating sister disciplines. Preceding this small group of books and partly dependent on them was a 129-page series of four seminal articles organized by Frank Tolman in four consecutive issues of *AJS*. Surely inspired by Small, "The Study of Sociology in Institutions of Learning in the United States" assembled systematic data on sociology courses and professors (carried out by "the Graduate Sociological League at the University of Chicago") that has provided raw material for every subsequent study in the field. This data source was by intention light on interpretation, providing instead unvarnished reports from around the country regarding exact course titles and the names of professors who taught them. Key textual sources were assumed to be few and emphasized Spencer and Lester Ward.

Following Tolman's lead, the ever-enterprising Franklin Giddings was first out of the blocks (in terms of book-length studies) with *Readings in Descriptive and Historical Sociology* (1906), a 550-page textbook designed to introduce students to the field. It incidentally also supplied contextual material that colorfully portrayed sociology's roots, especially in comparative perspective. But Giddings's competitor and nemesis, Small, was hard at work along similar lines and with more attention to detail. In May 1916 he published one of the most important documents in the historiography of early sociology, "Fifty Years of Sociology in the United States (1865–1915)"— so important that its 143 pages were entirely reprinted in the *AJS* in 1947. The data and interpretation reported in this piece set the baseline for subsequent studies and were quoted without critical evaluation for years to come. Some of this dependence reflected admiration for Small's rhetorical gifts, as, for example: "It is no wonder then that the sociologists had to pay the penalty of their interloping crudity when they tried to get room in the sun upon territory already occupied by vested crudity" (Small 1916, 822). Shades of Veblen, Small's sometime colleague at Chicago.

Enlarging his scope considerably, and returning to his German education, Small published the first monograph, *Origins of Sociology* (1924), which attempted to outline the specific beginnings of the field. (For the prickly fraternalism of the Giddings-Ward-Small relationship, with Ward serving as the good-natured, avuncular go-between, see Stern [1932].) After pointing out that the book had appeared as articles in *AJS* during the preceding two years, Small described his contribution:

It does not deal with the maturest, but only with the most elementary, manifestations of the sociological tendency. It is an attempt to show the falsity of the general impression that sociology is like the popular notion of a comet—a monster with an orbit from nowhere to nowhere. The book sustains the main thesis that during the nineteenth century the social sciences were half-consciously engaged in a drive from relatively irresponsible discursiveness toward "positivity" or "objectivity"; and that, at its time, the initiation of the American Sociological Movement was as truly a lineal continuance from the previous tradition of social interpretation as was any other of the tendencies which varied the technique of historiography, or economics, or political science. (Small 1924, v)

In truth the book is a protracted account of nineteenth-century German historiography, with chapter-length treatments of Ranke, Eichhorn, Niebuhr, Schmoller, Treitschke, and others, finally concluding with a single chapter called "The Emergence of Sociology in the United States" (324-51). After 323 pages of historical reconstruction, Small summarizes the meaning of his exploration for sociology in the United States as he had witnessed its rise:

All that has been said in this survey thus far might be compressed into the single sentence which has been repeated in various versions, viz. *Sociology has a venerable genealogy.* Sociology was not like Topsy, not even like Minerva, born in complete maturity from a single creative brain. Sociology is a branch of the great trunk of social science. Social science itself has been developing into increasingly definite self-consciousness, and consequently into increasingly adequate self-expression. . . . Why is it worth while to dig up the record of all these people who are no more to us than we to them? This is the answer: Whatever we may construct as a logical statement of what ought to be true, it is true that *we cannot be as intelligent as we might be about the present problems or the present processes of any science, unless, among other things, we have joined company with the people who have at length differentiated the processes; in other words, unless we have acquired our sense of the present condition of that branch of knowledge in part by the historical approach.* (324-25; emphases in original)

This is vintage Small, of course, toward the end of an illustrious self-imposed career as an institutional founder of the field and its chief propagandist.

Alongside Small's monumental contribution to sociology's founding, other scholars and teachers worked hard to advance the cause, meanwhile finding time to write their own historical accounts. Quickly following Small's 1924 book, Howard Odum and nine colleagues produced *American Masters of Social Science* (1927), a study of as many famous scholars, only three of them (Ward, Small, and Giddings) sociologists. James Quayle

Dealey's chapter concerned Ward and began in a tone of cheering admiration that would seem impossible to take seriously only two decades hence:

> Lester F. Ward in the field of social science is to the United States what Auguste Comte is to France or Herbert Spencer to England. Great pioneer in the development of sociology on this side of the Atlantic, he was often referred to in his later years as the Nestor of American sociologists. At the same time his comprehensive knowledge and his scientific method make him, even yet, an admirable approach to the study of the social sciences. (Odum 1927, 61)

Syntactical awkwardness aside, Dealey's heartfelt encomium exhibits precisely the rhetorical excess one expects regarding a new discipline's recently departed founders. The chapter ends by reprinting flattering "appreciations" from *AJS* (1913) at Ward's death by Ross, Giddings, Ulysses Weatherly, Charles Ellwood, Blackmar, and Small himself. The other two chapters are similarly constructed, connecting biographies of the "great men" with their intellectual and sociopolitical environments, their function being as much to serve as venerational monuments as to give novices an accurate view of sociology's beginnings in the United States. What is missing, of course, is the larger institutional context of the kind so skillfully outlined in Veysey's standard work on American universities (Veysey 1965). And critique of the sort that Marx perfected as a young man is almost nonexistent.

Soon after Odum's book, a still more valuable collection edited by George Lundberg (1929) appeared, dedicated to Cooley, W. I. Thomas, and Luther Bernard. *Trends in American Sociology* is where serious historiography of the field begins. Interestingly enough, the long, detailed opening chapter, "The History and Prospects of Sociology in the United States," was written by Jessie Bernard, her first major work and one for which she should be properly venerated (along with Luther Bernard, whom she quotes and acknowledges throughout). Bernard's 70-page chapter serves as a handy summary of every notable historical account of U.S. sociology that had preceded hers. Though more sober than some of the cheerleading that came earlier, her commentary is nevertheless essentially upbeat and promises a bright future for her field. Unlike Tolman, she lists important sociological books as they appeared and also considers problems that faced the discipline when pivotal changes occurred, for example: "Recently, however, sociology has suffered a serious setback in the decline of the department at Columbia University. This leaves Chicago as the foremost single department in the country. This department has always tended to dominate American sociology, but with a strong department at Columbia this was never possible" (in Lundberg 1929, 50).

The Lundberg collection also featured solid analyses of American sociological theory (Read Bain), social psychology (John Markey), rural sociology (Carl Zimmerman, Pitirim Sorokin's coauthor of a textbook on this topic), urban sociology (Nels Anderson), and methodology (Lundberg), among others. One could argue that with this particular compendium—interestingly enough, published by a commercial house—sociology's history and future prospects came clearly into focus.

By the time Floyd House produced *The Development of Sociology* in 1936 as a McGraw-Hill textbook, a nascent self-consciousness about historiographical possibilities, far removed from Small's mindset, had become evident: "The account of the history of sociology offered in the following pages is intended to be comprehensive but not exhaustive. It is inevitable that, in the preparation of such an account, considerable reliance will be placed upon secondary sources; although sociology is, relatively, a 'new science,' it is old enough to have a literature too extensive for any one person to have first-hand acquaintance with all of it" (House 1936, v). He then credits Dunning's *Political Theories*, Lichtenberger's *Development of Social Theory*, and Sorokin's *Contemporary Sociological Theories*, plus the estimable *Encyclopaedia of the Social Sciences*, with "lightening the task" he tried to accomplish. As intelligent and useful as House's volume was and is, it is not a work of historiography but rather a literature survey, beginning (improbably) around 300 BCE, and rapidly moving toward his own day. He claims to have been inspired by the *Wissens-soziologie* [sic] approach just minted by Max Scheler and Karl Mannheim, plus Alfred Weber's *Kultursoziologie*. His intellectual history is admirable, to be sure, but his attention to historiography proper relied for the most part on Small's *Origins* and allied works.

The first truly indispensable work of history proper, remaining seminal even today, was Luther L. Bernard and Jessie Bernard's *Origins of American Sociology* (1943), published shortly before the Bernards joined the Penn State faculty. This 900-page study was the culmination of Luther Bernard's career and the fruit of many years' joint work, bearing the revealing subtitle *The Social Science Movement in the United States*. The Bernards' work was based on extensive use of secondary sources and extended the range of important surveys that Luther Bernard had carried out among practicing sociologists many years before (Bernard 1909, 1918). But unlike his apprentice survey work, *Origins* is heavily textual and unnecessarily modest in its claims: "Thus the present work is not a history of the whole field of social thought, but only of the significant phase of writing in this field lying chiefly between the years 1840 and 1890 which called itself Social Science or in some way recognized its close kinship with the movement" (Bernard and Bernard 1943, 7). The most important material for a history of sociology narrowly defined arrives after 655 pages of preliminary work, beginning with the subhead, "When Does Social Science Become Sociology?" (657-69). The real utility of this extraordinary work lies in its demonstration of how valuable a detailed recounting of protosociology could be when conceptualizing what the history of the discipline itself should take in.

The Bernards' book was soon followed by a few others that purported to render sociology's history, but in each case they were limited by design or lack of data commensurate with that of the Bernards. Barnes's edited work, *An Introduction to the History of Sociology* (1948), covered global sociology and therefore had little space in which to say much that was original about the U.S. case. Odum's *American Sociology: The Story of Sociology in the United States through 1950* (1950), though valuable then and now, focuses mainly on the biographies of those men who were the first presidents of the ASA. Naturally, this left out most of the practitioners and inadvertently became a study of an intellectual elite, something Luther Bernard had carefully avoided doing in his book. Nearly thirty years later, Bottomore and Nisbet published *A History of Sociological Analysis* (1978), but the emphases fell on schools of thought and methods rather than on the history of the discipline as it was experienced by its teachers and researchers. Like most books of this type, it is intellectual history, but it is not "sociological history" and, more importantly, not a history of sociology.

The last major attempt to give a historical account of American sociology came in 1985 with Vidich and Lyman's *American Sociology: Worldly Rejections of Religion and Their Directions*. When I reviewed this book for *Science* (Sica 1986), I pointed out that it insists on a strongly monochromatic view of the field, sociology as essentially the product of Protestant ministers. No knowledgeable reviewer of the book accepted its general argument, even though it was ingeniously constructed. And with these relatively few volumes, we are well into the second century of academic sociology in the United States—recalling that it was taught as such by Sumner at Yale in the 1870s using Spencer's works as textbooks—and to date still do not have a "definitive" history. But the materials have begun to be collected systematically (e.g., at the new ASA Archive housed at Penn State), and more younger historians within sociology and without are beginning to specialize in chronicling sociology's past. As the globalized social world becomes ever more treacherous, sociology's pertinence becomes too obvious even for its most obdurate opponents to deny. Thus its history, like its future prospects, takes on new and urgent meaning.

[APPENDIX] Histories of American Sociology: Readings and Resources

Alton Phillips & Jonathan VanAntwerpen

From Park and Burgess (1921), Sorokin (1928), and Parsons (1937) to Nisbet (1966) and Gouldner (1970), twentieth-century American sociologists sought to story their discipline's past with a view to existing academic concerns. Recent writings in the history of American sociology have continued to mirror the impulse of these "archetypal narratives" (Levine 1995). Whether attempting to reclaim the classics (Camic 1997b), arguing that canonical commitments must be reconfigured (Connell 1997), or pursuing a new disciplinary vision for the twenty-first century (Burawoy 2005b), American sociologists have continued to look to their discipline's past in order to reexamine its present and revise its future, turning to the history of sociology in an attempt to build or dismantle, construct or deconstruct, one sociological tradition or another. This essay provides a brief overview of the major works in this field over the course of the last three decades, during which time histories of sociology have in various ways become more critical, more reflexive, and more informed by the norms of historical research and scholarship. Although individual works have not always been affected in equal measure by these shifts, increasing interdisciplinary attention to the history of sociology in the United States has given rise nonetheless to a sustained and promising series of scholarly efforts to narrate the discipline's varied histories.

The academic fields most conspicuously involved in these efforts have been history and sociology. While American sociologists have long been interested in the history of their discipline (Sica, chap. 21, this volume), works by historians on the history of American sociology were relatively rare until the 1970s, when a handful of important books were published. Matthews (1977) wrote about Robert Park and the Chicago school, while other historians tackled the early history of American social science more broadly (Furner 1975; Haskell 1977). These books laid the foundation for a number of key contemporary works, including Bannister's (1987) treatment of scientism and the "quest for objectivity" in American sociology, which considered key sociologists of the interwar period, such as Bernard, Ogburn, and Chapin; Ross's (1991) major work on the "origins" of American social science, which stretched from economics and sociology to political science, and emphasized the importance of "American exceptionalism" in the development of the social sciences (see also Ross 1994); and Smith's (1994) attempt to assess the objectivity debates of the 1920s and 1930s through an examination of the careers of five male social scientists, including sociologist Robert Lynd. More recently, historians have moved to consider earlier struggles over "public sociology" (Haney 1998), the rise of modernization theory in the postwar period (Latham 2000; Gilman 2003), and the production and public reception of survey research (Igo 2006).

These historians and others have been joined by historically oriented sociologists, themselves propelled, at least in part, by renewed attention to the practices of historical writing and the project of historical sociology (Abbott 1991; Calhoun 1996; Adams, Clemens, and Orloff 2005; Steinmetz 2005a). Turner and Turner's *The Impossible Science* (1990), an institutional analysis that emphasized the importance of funding and resources in the development of American sociology, continues to be the most ambitious attempt to chart the entire discipline's growth and transformation (see also Bulmer et al. 1994). More recently, Abbott (2001) has analyzed cycles of conflict and disagreement in American sociology in the course of elaborating a "fractal" theory of intellectual continuity and change. Other works have focused in greater detail on specific departments, individuals, historical periods, or events.

A significant volume of literature tells and retells the story of sociology at Chicago. Bulmer's (1984a) book on the Chicago school was a part of the important Heritage of Sociology series, founded by Morris Janowitz. Deegan (1988, 2002) emphasized the overlooked significance of Jane Addams and Hull House, while Fine (1995) collected essays on the question of a second Chicago school. Abbott (1999) assessed the Chicago department's relationship to the *American Journal of Sociology*, along the way providing a detailed treatment of the department's rivalries and politics, and an excellent overview of historical work on sociology at Chicago, while Lengermann (1979) considered the founding of the *American Sociological Review* as part of a "rebellion" against the early disciplinary dominance of Chicago. In a broader view, Camic (1995) compared the early development of sociology departments at Chicago, Columbia, and Harvard, calling for greater attention to local conditions and interdisciplinary interaction. Along with historian Howard Brick (1993, 2000), Camic (1987) has also investigated the early intellectual trajectory of Talcott Parsons, whose work not only became the basis for the rising importance of the Harvard department, the widespread influence of structural functionalism, and the formation of a postwar "canon" of sociological theory but also served as a foil for much of the writing on the discipline's history in the decades that followed.

Although *The Structure of Social Action,* Parsons's "towering first book" (Camic 1989), was published in 1937, its influence on the discipline was felt most widely in the years after World War II, a period frequently associated with a rise of a "new sociological Establishment" (Bourdieu 1991a) and with the dominance of what Mills (1959) called "grand theory" and "abstracted empiricism." Wallerstein (chap. 12, this volume) has suggested that the "prevailing culture" of postwar sociology was shaped in the main both by the publication of *Structure* and by the preeminence of the Harvard and Columbia departments. In an account the postwar establishment of a "new epistemological orthodoxy" that focuses less on Parsons—who explicitly critiqued "the positivistic-utilitarian tradition"—Steinmetz (2005e) has argued that the discipline took "a dramatic turn toward methodological positivism" during these years. Arguing that claims to sociological "science" were structured around a loose understanding of the term, Platt (1996) presented a history of methodological thought that ran from the interwar period through to 1960, and explored the significant slippage between ardent methodological expositions and actual sociological research practices.

The postwar years were a period of rapid expansion and transformation within American sociology, as the number of professional sociologists grew dramatically, new departments were established, new journals founded, and new subfields formed (Turner and Turner 1990; McAdam, chap. 11, this volume). Thus, even as this period's precise shape and significance continue to be debated by historians of sociology, it is one particularly ripe for further research, especially on departments and figures beyond a narrowly defined elite. In that vein, a number of authors have focused on sociology at colleges and universities outside the small handful of usual suspects, including Nebraska (Deegan 1979), Minnesota (Martindale 1980), Kansas (Sica 1983), Wellesley (Deegan 1983), and Indiana (Miller 1986). MacLean and Williams (2005) have considered the development of sociology at black and women's colleges, and Hill (2005) has detailed a number of departmental histories, surveying both unpublished and published work.

Sociology continued to grow throughout the 1960s and early 1970s, and with greater disciplinary inclusion and changing political circumstances came revisionist critiques of the postwar "mainstream," many of them associated with critical sociology and the "sociology of sociology" (Friedrichs 1970; Schwendinger and Schwendinger 1974). Chief among these was Gouldner's *The Coming Crisis of Western Sociology* (1970), which took aim primarily at Parsons, called for greater sociological "reflexivity," and inspired a new generation of disciplinary insurgents. As feminism became more influential, and Marx—previously excluded from the canon—was more widely read, there was an increasing attention to questions of gender and class (and, to a certain extent, race). While the degree to which these changes effectively transformed the discipline continues to be debated, they have had a marked effect on attempts to grasp and assess sociology's past, as new perspectives and purposes have been brought to bear on the writing of disciplinary history. In particular, the turn toward reflexivity and critical histories has contributed to two trends in histories of sociology: the construction and collection of autobiographical reflections, and increasing attention to "marginal" or underrepresented figures within sociology.

Emerging especially in the 1990s, sometimes under the influence of feminism or other forms of critical sociology, collections of autobiographical reflections became a popular form of biographical history (Berger 1990; Goetting and Fenstermaker 1995; Laslett and Thorne 1997; Riley 1988; Sica and Turner 2005). In response, Wacquant (2000) provided a critical perspective on the supposed "reflexivity" of various forms of autobiographical reflection. These autobiographic works join a significant volume of literature that traces the discipline's history through biographies and reconsiderations of key figures, including works on Jane Addams (Deegan 1988, 2002), Daniel Bell (Waters 1995; Brick 1986), Jessie Bernard (Bannister 1991), Anna Julia Cooper (Hutchinson 1982; Gabel 1982), Oliver C. Cox (McAuley 2004), Caroline Bartlett Crane (Rickard 1994; Rynbrandt 1999), W. E. B. DuBois (Lewis 1993; Wortham 2005), E. Franklin Frazier (Platt 1991), Erving Goffman (Burns 1992; Trevino 2003), Alvin Gouldner (Chriss 1999), Charles S. Johnson (Robbins 1996), Alfred and Elizabeth Lee (Galliher 1995), George Herbert Mead (Cook 1993), Robert Merton (Sztompka 1986; Crothers 1987), C. Wright Mills (Horowitz 1983; Geary 2004), William Ogburn (Laslett 1991), Robert Park (Matthews 1977; Lal 1990), Talcott Parsons (Hamilton 1983; Camic 1987, 1989), Albion Small (Dibble 1975; Christakes 1978), and Pitirim Sorokin (Johnston 1995; Ford, Richard, and Talbutt 1996).

As Laslett (chap. 14, this volume) has emphasized, life histories have provided an important source for feminists investigating the history of women in sociology. In particular, investigations of the lives and works of women in sociology and related fields who were active during sociology's formative years have aided the recuperation of women's contributions to the discipline. Substantial books have been written on particular individuals, such as Jane Addams (Deegan 1988) and Jessie Bernard (Bannister 1991), and numerous life histories have been produced. Deegan (1991) has chronicled the life histories of over fifty women making contributions to sociology between the 1840s and the 1990s, in an effort to dispel the myth that women only joined the field after 1930. Similarly, Lengermann and Niebrugge-Brantley (1998) presented the lives and works of fifteen women sociologists of the nineteenth and early twentieth centuries, including Charlotte Perkins Gilman, Harriet Martineau, Beatrice Potter Webb, and Marianne Weber; Broschart (2005) explored the neglected contributions of women sociologists in the American South, such as Anna Julia Cooper and Ida B. Wells-Barnett; and Meadow Orlans and Wallace (1994) collected the autobiographical reflections of women sociologists at Berkeley, including those of Arlene Kaplan Daniels, Arlie Russell Hochschild, and Dorothy Smith. Other works have taken a more broadly institutional focus, including Wilkinson's (1979) report for the ASA on the status of women in the discipline from 1934 to 1977, and Roby's (1992) examination of women's struggles for representation and transformation within the ASA in the late 1960s and early 1970s. Finally, Reinharz (1989) has emphasized the importance of recognizing the sociological contributions of women in the teaching of sociology.

Another product of disciplinary rebellion in the late 1960s and early 1970s, Ladner's *The Death of White Sociology* (1973), explored the reproduction of racism in the discipline's theories, methods, and organizations and set the terms for future considerations of race and the history of American sociology, just as Collins (1990) laid the groundwork for interrogations of race, class, and gender as "interlocking systems of oppression." More recently, Winant (chap. 16, this volume) has assessed the reciprocal effects of race and sociology on one another over the course of the last century; Dickerson (2005) has investigated the roots of the Association of Black Sociologists; and Deegan (2005) has considered the situation of African Americans within the ASA. There have also been a number of biographically focused works attempting to reclaim otherwise unrecognized figures, including those referenced above on Anna Julia Cooper, Oliver C. Cox, Caroline Bartlett Crane, W. E. B. DuBois, E. Franklin Frazier, and Charles S. Johnson. These works join others that have sought to "rediscover" the lives and works of "lost sociologists" (Romano 2002).

If greater attention has recently been given to issues of gender and race within the history of the discipline, the same cannot be said of sexuality. Although a number of life histories engage with issues of sexuality—including Krieger's (1997) contribution to Laslett and Thorne's *Feminist Sociology*—there has yet to be a sustained interrogation of the role of sexuality, desire, and heterosexism in the history of the discipline itself, an analysis that might build on the work of Seidman (1996) and others. Further, a conceptualization of the production of "difference" that stretches beyond the traditional sociological taxonomies of gender, race, class, sexuality, and their intersections remains an underdeveloped endeavor in the history of sociology, as in sociology more generally. Sociologists continue to face the daunting challenge of turning their own modes of analysis back upon themselves.

While the ability to engage in such analysis might be rendered as a potential source of insight for sociologists writing their discipline's history, it has also been regularly conceived as the basis of a certain sort of historical blindness. Indeed, historian Laurence Veysey (1978) once claimed that the sociologist writing a history of sociology was "an amateur, no different in principle from an untrained Mormon writing the history of Mormonism." We disagree. Although sociologists writing histories of their own discipline may still be tempted by the "narcissistic vineyards" of which Veysey warned, they are also well positioned not only to critique the prejudice on the surface of his claim but to prove it wrong in substance. Although much of the scholarship surveyed here appears not to be widely read by practicing sociologists, graduate seminars on the history of sociology remain relatively rare, and no work has yet done for sociology what Novick's magisterial *That Noble Dream* did for the discipline of history, critical attention to the history of American sociology appears to be on the rise. Burawoy (2005b) made a critical history of the discipline an integral part of his call to "public sociology," and his successor as ASA president, Troy Duster, put the wide historical sweep of sociology center stage for the association's 2005 meetings (Calhoun and Duster 2005). In addition to those who contributed chapters to the present volume, contributors to Blasi's edited volume (2005) explore "diverse histories of American sociology," focusing on minority groups and important intellectual movements that did not merge into the "mainstream." Further, the ASA commissioned an update and companion to Rhoades's (1981) brief history of the association (Rosich 2005), while Hill (2005) coordinated a major bibliographic effort on behalf of the ASA's History of Sociology section, a project likely to become a key resource in the future.

REFERENCES

ABBAGNANO, NICOLA. 1967. "Positivism." In *The Encyclopedia of Philosophy*, ed. Paul Edwards, 5:414–19. New York: Macmillan.

ABBOTT, ANDREW. 1982. "The Emergence of American Psychiatry." PhD diss., University of Chicago.

———. 1988. *The System of Professions: An Essay on the Division of Expert Labor.* Chicago: University of Chicago Press.

———. 1991. "History and Sociology: The Lost Synthesis." *Social Science History* 15: 201-38.

———. 1999. *Department and Discipline: Chicago Sociology at One Hundred.* Chicago: University of Chicago Press.

———. 2001. *Chaos of Disciplines.* Chicago: University of Chicago Press.

———. 2005. "The Idea of Outcome in American Sociology." In *The Politics of Method in the Human Sciences: Positivism and Its Epistemological Others,* ed. George Steinmetz. Durham, NC: Duke University Press.

ABBOTT, ANDREW, and EMANUEL GRAZIANO. 1995. "Transition and Tradition: Departmental Faculty in the Era of the Second Chicago School." In *A Second Chicago School? The Development of a Postwar American Sociology,* ed. Gary Alan Fine, 221-72. Chicago: University of Chicago Press.

ABEL, THEODORE FRED. 1929. *Systematic Sociology in Germany.* New York: Columbia University Press.

———. 2001. *The Columbia Circle of Scholars: Selections from the Journal (1930-1957).* Ed. Elżbieta Hałas. Frankfurt: Peter Lang.

ABU-LUGHOD, LILA. 1991. "Writing against Culture." In *Recapturing Anthropology,* ed. Richard G. Fox, 137-162. Santa Fe: School of American Research Press.

ACKER, JOAN. 1973. "Women and Social Stratification: A Case of Intellectual Sexism," *American Journal of Sociology* 78: 936-45.

———. 1989. *Doing Comparable Worth: Gender, Class, and Pay Equity.* Philadelphia: Temple University Press.

———. 1990. "Hierarchies, Jobs, Bodies: A Theory of Gendered Organizations." *Gender and Society* 4:139-58.

———. 1997. "My Life as a Feminist Sociologist; or, Getting the Man out of My Head." In *Feminist Sociology: Life Histories of a Movement,* ed. Barbara Laslett and Barrie Thorne, 28-47. New Brunswick, NJ: Rutgers University Press.

ADAMS, JULIA. 1998. "Feminist Theory as Fifth Columnist or Discursive Vanguard?" *Social Politics* 5:1-16.

ADAMS, JULIA, ELIZABETH CLEMENS, and ANN ORLOFF, eds. 2005. *Remaking Modernity: Politics, History, and Sociology.* Durham, NC: Duke University Press.

ADDAMS, JANE. 1881. "Cassandra." In *Essays of Class of 1881, Rockford Seminary,* 36-39. DeKalb, IL: "News" Steam Press.

———. 1893. "The Subjective Necessity for Social Settlements." In *Philanthropy and Social Progress,* ed. Henry C. Adams, 1-26. New York: Thomas Y. Cromwell.

———. 1895. "The Settlement as a Factor in the Labor Movement." In *Hull-House Maps and Papers by the Residents of Hull-House, A Social Settlement,* 183-204. New York: Crowell.

———. 1896. "A Belated Industry." *American Journal of Sociology* 1: 536-50.

———. 1902/1907. *Democracy and Social Ethics.* New York: Macmillan.

———. 1907. *Newer Ideals of Peace.* New York: Macmillan.

——. 1909. *The Spirit of Youth and the City Streets.* New York: Macmillan.

——. 1910a. "Charity and Social Justice." *North American Review* 192:68–81.

——. 1910b. *Twenty Years at Hull-House.* New York: Macmillan.

——. 1912. "A Modern Lear." *Survey* (November 2): 131–35.

ADLER, PATRICIA A., PETER ADLER, and ANDREA FONTANA. 1987. "Everyday Life Sociology." *Annual Review of Sociology* 13:217–35.

ADORNO, THEODOR W. 1938/1982. "On the Fetish Character of Music and the Regression of Listening." In *The Essential Frankfurt School Reader,* ed. Andrew Arato and Eike Gebhardt, 270–99. New York: Continuum.

——. 1958/1991. "Reading Balzac." In *Notes to Literature* by Theodor W. Adorno, ed. Rolf Tiedemann, trans. Shierry Weber Nicholsen, 121–36. New York: Columbia University Press.

——. 1972. "Teamwork in der Sozialforschung." In *Soziologische Schriften* I by Theodor W. Adorno, ed. Rolf Tiedemann, 493–99. Frankfurt: Suhrkamp.

ADORNO, T. W., E. FRENKEL-BRUNSWIK, D. J. LEVINSON, and R. N. SANFORD. 1950. *The Authoritarian Personality.* New York: Harper and Row.

AGLIETTA, MICHEL. 1987. *A Theory of Capitalist Regulation.* London: Verso.

AGNEW, ROBERT. 1992. "Foundation for a General Strain Theory of Crime and Delinquency." *Journal of Research in Crime and Delinquency* 38: 319–61.

——. 1999. "A General Strain Theory of Community Differences in Crime Rates." *Journal of Research in Crime and Delinquency* 36(2): 123–55.

AIDI, HISHAM. 2003. "Let Us Be Moors: Islam, Race and 'Connected Histories.'" *Middle East Report* 229.

AKCAM, TANER. 2004. *From Empire to Republic: Turkish Nationalism and the Armenian Genocide.* London: Zed Books.

AKERS, RONALD L. 1992. "Linking Sociology and Its Specialties." *Social Forces* 71(1): 1–16.

——. 1998. *Social Learning and Social Structure.* Boston: Northeastern University Press.

ALCHON, GUY. 1985. *The Invisible Hand of Planning.* Princeton: Princeton University Press.

ALEXANDER, JEFFREY. 1982. *Theoretical Logic in Sociology.* 4 vols. Berkeley: University of California Press.

ALEXANDER, M. J., and CHANDRA T. MOHANTY. 1997. "Introduction: Genealogies, Legacies, Movements." In *Feminist Genealogies, Colonial Legacies, Democratic Futures,* ed. M. J. Alexander and Chandra T. Mohanty, xiii–xlii. New York: Routledge.

ALLEN, MICHAEL P. 2003. "The 'Core Influence' of Journals in Sociology Revisited." *Footnotes* 31(9): 7–10.

——. 2004. Reply to Marsh, Koffler. *Footnotes* 32(3): 10–11.

ALLPORT, GORDON W. 1954. *The Nature of Prejudice.* Cambridge, MA: Addison-Wesley.

——, ed. 1965. *Letters from Jenny.* New York: Harcourt, Brace and World.

ALMAGUER, TOMÁS. 1994. *Racial Faultlines: The Historical Origins of White Supremacy in California.* Berkeley: University of California Press.

ALPERS, B. L. 2002. *Dictators, Democracy, and American Public Culture: Envisioning the Totalitarian Enemy, 1920s–1950s.* Chapel Hill: University of North Carolina Press.

ALPERT, HARRY. 1939. "Émile Durkheim and His Sociology." PhD diss., Columbia University.

———. 1955. "The Social Sciences and the National Science Foundation." *Proceedings of the American Philosophical Society* 99 (October 15): 332–33.

ALTHUSSER, LOUIS. 1970. "The Object of *Capital.*" In *Reading Capital,* ed. Louis Althusser and Étienne Balibar, 71–198. London: NLB.

———. 1971. "Ideology and Ideological State Apparatuses." In *Lenin and Philosophy,* by Louis Althusser, 121–72. London: NLB.

ALWAY, JOAN. 1995. "The Trouble with Gender: Tales of the Still-Missing Feminist Revolution in Sociological Theory." *Sociological Theory* 13:209–28.

AMERICAN COUNCIL ON EDUCATION. 1952. *American Universities and Colleges.* 6th ed. Ed. Mary Irwin. Washington, DC: American Council on Education.

AMERICAN SOCIAL SCIENCE ASSOCIATION (ASSA). 1866. *Constitution, Address, and List of Members of the American Association for the Promotion of Social Science.* Boston: Wright and Potter.

AMERICAN SOCIOLOGICAL ASSOCIATION (ASA). 2004a. "A Brief Centennial Bibliography of Resources on the History of the American Sociological Society/Association." Typescript. History of Sociology Section of the ASA. Washington, DC.

———. 2004b. "Trend Data on the Profession." http://www.asanet.org/research/faqintro2002.html.

———. 2005. "Sociology: A World of Opportunity." asanet.org/student/career/world.html.

AMERICAN SOCIOLOGICAL SOCIETY (ASS). 1907a. Announcement of the formation of the American Sociological Society in December 1905. *American Journal of Sociology* 12(5): 579–80.

———. 1907b. Constitution of the American Sociological Society. *American Journal of Sociology* 12(5): 735–36.

———. 1907c. List of members. *American Journal of Sociology* 12(5): 736–38.

AMIN, SAMIR. 1974. *Accumulation on a World Scale: A Critique of the Theory of Underdevelopment.* Sussex: Harvester.

AMINZADE, RONALD. 2003. "From Race to Citizenship: The Indigenization Debate in Post-Socialist Tanzania." *Comparative Studies in International Development* 38: 43–63.

AMOTT, TERESA L., and JULIE MATTHAEI. 1991. *Race, Gender, and Work: A Multicultural Economic History of Women in the United States.* Boston: South End Press.

ANDERSEN, MARGARET L. 1987. "Changing the Curriculum in Higher Education." *Signs* 12(2): 222–54.

———. 1993. "From the Editor." *Gender and Society* 7(2): 157–61.

ANDERSEN, MARGARET L., and PATRICIA HILL COLLINS. 2004. *Race, Class, and Gender: An Anthology*. Belmont, CA: Wadsworth.

ANDERSON, ELIJAH. 1978. *A Place on the Corner*. Chicago: University of Chicago Press.

———. 1996. Introduction to *The Philadelphia Negro: A Social Study*, by W. E. B. DuBois. Centennial ed. Philadelphia: University of Pennsylvania Press.

ANDERSON, MARGO J. 1990. *The American Census: A Social History*. New Haven, CT: Yale University Press.

ANDERSON, NELS. 1923/1961. *The Hobo: The Sociology of the Homeless Man*. Chicago: University of Chicago Press.

ANGELL, ROBERT COOLEY. 1928. *The Campus: A Study of Contemporary Undergraduate Life in the American University*. New York: D. Appleton.

———. 1930. "Cooley's Heritage to Social Research." *Social Forces* 8(3): 340–47.

———. 1931. "Memorandum Concerning a Proposed Research Technique." *Social Forces* 10(2): 204–8.

———. 1932. "The Experimental Approach II: The Difficulties of Experimental Sociology." *Social Forces* 11(2): 207–10.

———. 1933. "The Influence of Severe and Apparently Lasting Decrease in Income upon Family Life." In *Racial Contacts and Social Research: Papers Presented at the Twenty-Eighth Annual Meeting of the American Sociological Society*, 85–89. Chicago: University of Chicago Press.

———. 1936. *The Family Encounters the Depression*. New York: Scribner's.

———. 1941. *The Integration of American Society. A Study of Groups and Institutions*. New York: McGraw-Hill.

———. 1945. "A Critical Review of the Development of the Personal Document Method in Sociology, 1920–1940." In *The Use of Personal Documents in History, Anthropology, and Sociology* by Louis Gottschalk, Clyde Kluckhohn, and Robert Angell, 177–232. New York: Social Science Research Council.

———. 1951. *The Moral Integration of American Cities*. Chicago: University of Chicago Press.

———. 1956. Review of *Science and Social Action* by W. J. H. Sprott. *American Sociological Review* 21(2): 235.

———. 1972. Review of *The Logic of Images in International Relations* by Robert Jervis. *Social Forces* 51(1): 115–16.

———. Ca. 1980. "The Sociology Department, 1940–1975." Manuscript. Archives of the Sociology Department, University of Michigan.

———. 1980. "The Joys of Modest Success." *Society* 18: 72–81.

———. N.d. "Science and Values in a Sociologist's Career." Manuscript. Bentley Historical Library, University of Michigan.

———. Papers and letters. Bentley Historical Library, University of Michigan.

ANTHIAS, FLOYA, and NIRA YUVAL-DAVIS. 1992. *Racialized Boundaries: Race, Nation, Gender, Colour and Class and the Anti-Racist Struggle*. New York: Routledge.

ANTONIO, ROBERT J. 1989. "The Normative Foundations of Emancipatory Theory: Evolutionary versus Pragmatic Perspectives." *American Journal of Sociology* 94:721-48.

APPARDURAI, ARJUN. 1996. *Modernity at Large: Cultural Dimensions of Globalization.* Minneapolis: University of Minnesota Press.

APTHEKER, HERBERT. 1961. *The American Civil War.* New York: International Publishers.

ARATO, ANDREW. 1994. "Revolution, Restoration, and Legitimization: Ideological Problems of the Transition from State Socialism." In *Envisioning Eastern Europe: Postcommunist Cultural Studies,* ed. Michael D. Kennedy, 180-246. Ann Arbor: University of Michigan Press.

ARCHER, MARGARET S. 2003. *Structure, Agency and the Internal Conversation.* Cambridge: Cambridge University Press.

ARCHIBALD, K. 1947. *Wartime Shipyard.* Berkeley: University of California Press.

ARENDT, HANNAH. 1951. *The Origins of Totalitarianism.* New York: Harcourt, Brace.

——. 1994. "Understanding and Politics" (1953). In *Essays in Understanding, 1930-1954,* 307-27. New York: Harcourt, Brace.

ARJOMAND, SAID. 2001. *The Turban for the Crown: The Islamic Revolution in Iran.* Bridgewater, NJ: Replica Books.

——. 2004. "America in the New Age of Global Conflict." Paper presented at the annual meeting of the American Sociological Association.

ARNDT, MURRAY DENNIS. 1970. "The *Crisis* Years of W. E. B. DuBois: 1910-1934." PhD diss., Department of English, Duke University.

ARRIGHI GIOVANNI, and BEVERLY J. SILVER. 1999. *Chaos and Governance in the Modern World System.* Minneapolis: University of Minnesota Press.

ATLANTA UNIVERSITY STUDIES OF THE NEGRO PROBLEM. 1897-1914. Ed. W. E. B. DuBois. Annual conferences. Atlanta: Atlanta University Press.

AUERBACH, JEROLD S. 1976. *Unequal Justice: Lawyers and Social Change in Modern America.* New York: Oxford University Press.

AUYERO, JAVIER. 2003. *Contentious Lives: Two Argentine Women, Two Protests, and the Quest for Recognition.* Durham, NC: Duke University Press.

AYER, A. J. 1959. *Logical Positivism.* New York: Free Press.

BACKHAUS, GARY. 1998. "Georg Simmel as an Eidetic Social Scientist." *Sociological Theory* 16:260-81.

BAGWHATI, JAGDISH. 2004. *In Defense of Globalization.* New York: Oxford University Press.

BAIN, READ. 1927. "Trends in American Sociology." *Social Forces* 5(3): 413-22.

——. 1936. "Sociology and Psychoanalysis." *American Sociological Review* 1(2): 203-16.

——. 1947. "Sociology as a Natural Science." *American Journal of Sociology* 53(1): 9-16.

BAINBRIDGE, WILLIAM SIMS. 2002. "An Interview with Professor Emeritus David Riesman" (1987). *Sociology Lives* (Harvard University, Department of Sociology) 17(1): 3-10.

BALDWIN, KATE A. 2002. "Beyond the Color Line and the Iron Curtain: Reading Encounters between Black and Red, 1922-1963." Durham, NC, and London: Duke University Press.

BALIBAR, ÉTIENNE, and IMMANUEL WALLERSTEIN. 1991. *Race, Nation, Class: Ambiguous Identities.* New York: Verso.

BALTZELL, E. DIGBY. 1972. "Epilogue: To Be a Phoenix—Reflections on Two Noisy Ages of Prose." *American Journal of Sociology* 78:202-20.

BANNER, LOIS W. 2003. *Intertwined Lives: Margaret Mead, Ruth Benedict, and Their Circle.* Knopf.

BANNERJI, HIMANI. 1995. *Thinking Through: Essays on Feminism, Marxism, and Anti-Racism.* Toronto: Women's Press.

BANNISTER, ROBERT C. 1979. *Social Darwinism.* Philadelphia: Temple University Press.

———. 1987. *Sociology and Scientism: The American Quest for Objectivity, 1880-1940.* Chapel Hill: University of North Carolina Press.

———. 1991. *Jessie Bernard: The Making of a Feminist.* New Brunswick, NJ: Rutgers University Press.

———. 1992. "Principle, Politics, and Profession." In *Sociology Responds to Fascism,* ed. Stephen P. Turner and Dirk Kasler, 172-213. London: Routledge.

———. 2003. "Sociology." In *The Modern Social Sciences,* 329-53, vol. 7 of *The Cambridge History of Science,* ed. Theodore Porter and Dorothy Ross. Cambridge: Cambridge University Press.

BARBER, BENJAMIN. 1995. *Jihad vs. McWorld.* New York: Bantam.

BARBER, MICHAEL D. 1988. *Social Typifications and the Elusive Other: The Place of Sociology of Knowledge in Alfred Schutz's Phenomenology.* Lewisburg, PA: Bucknell University Press.

BARBER, WILLIAM J. 1981. "The United States: Economists in a Pluralistic Polity." In *Economists and Government,* ed. A. W. Coats, 175-205. Durham, NC: Duke University Press.

———. 1985. *From New Era to New Deal: Herbert Hoover, the Economists, and American Economic Policy, 1921-1933.* Cambridge: Cambridge University Press.

———. 1996. *Designs within Disorder: Franklin D. Roosevelt, the Economists, and the Shaping of American Economic Policy, 1933-1945.* Cambridge: Cambridge University Press.

BARKAN, ELAZAR. 1992. *The Retreat of Scientific Racism: Changing Concepts of Race in Britain and the United States between the World Wars.* Cambridge: Cambridge University Press.

BARNARD, RITA, and GRANT FARRED, eds. 2004. *After the Thrill Is Gone: A Decade of Post-Apartheid South Africa.* Special issue. *South Atlantic Quarterly* (Fall).

BARNES, HARRY ELMER. 1948a. "Charles Abram Ellwood: Founder of Scientific Psychological Sociology." In *An Introduction to the History of Sociology,* ed. H. E. Barnes, 853-68. Chicago: University of Chicago Press.

———, ed. 1948b. *An Introduction to the History of Sociology.* Chicago: University of Chicago Press.

———. 1948c. "William Graham Sumner: Spencerianism in American Dress. In *An Introduction to the History of Sociology,* ed. Harry Elmer Barnes,155-90. Chicago: University of Chicago Press.

———. 1948d. "William Isaac Thomas: The Fusion of Psychological and Cultural Sociology." In *An Introduction to the History of Sociology,* ed. H. E. Barnes, 793-804. Chicago: University of Chicago Press.

BART, PAULINE B. 1981. "A Study of Women Who Both Were Raped and Avoided Rape." *Journal of Social Issues* 37:123-37.

BASTIDE, ROGER. 1972. *The Sociology of Mental Disorder.* London, Routledge and Kegan Paul.

BASZANGER, ISABELLE. 1998. "The Work Sites of an American Interactionist: Anselm L. Strauss, 1917-1996." *Symbolic Interaction* 21:353-78.

BATES, R. C. 1898. "Character Building at Elmira." *American Journal of Sociology* 3:577-600.

BAUMAN, ZYGMUNT. 1976. *Socialism: The Active Utopia.* London: Allen and Unwin.

———. 1991. *Modernity and the Holocaust.* Ithaca, NY: Cornell University Press.

BAXTER, WILLIAM H. 2002. "Where Does the 'Comparative Method' Come From?" In *The Linguist's Linguist,* ed. Fabrice Cavoto, 1:33-52. Munich: LINCOM.

BEAL, OWEN F. 1944. "The Development of Sociology in the United States with Special Reference to American Pioneers in Sociology." Typescript. Ann Arbor, MI: Edwards Brothers.

BECK, E. M., PATRICK H. HORAN, and CHARLES M. TOLBERT II. 1980. "Industrial Segmentation and Labor Market Discrimination." *Social Problems* 28:113-30.

BECK, ULRICH. 2000. *What Is Globalization?* Cambridge, MA: Polity Press.

BECKER, FRANCES BENNETT. 1937. "Lenin's Application of Marx's Theory of Revolutionary Tactics." *American Sociological Review* 2(3): 353-64.

BECKER, GARY A. 1981. *Treatise on the Family.* Cambridge: Harvard University Press.

BECKER, HOWARD S. 1952a. "The Career of the Chicago Public Schoolteacher." *American Journal of Sociology* 57:470-77.

———. 1952b. "Social-Class Variations in the Teacher-Pupil Relationship." *Journal of Educational Sociology* 25:451-65.

———. 1953. "The Teacher in the Authority System of the Public School." *Journal of Educational Sociology* 27:128-41.

———. 1958. "Problems of Inference and Proof in Participant Observation." *American Sociological Review* 23:652-60. Reprinted in *Sociological Work* by H. Becker. Chicago: Aldine, 1970.

———. 1963/1973. *Outsiders: Studies in the Sociology of Deviance.* New York: Free Press.

———, ed. 1964. *The Other Side: Perspectives on Deviance.* Glencoe, IL: Free Press.

———. 1967. "Whose Side Are We On?" *Social Problems* 14:239-47.

———. 1982. *Art Worlds.* Berkeley: University of California Press.

———. 1994. "Professional Sociology: The Case of C. Wright Mills." In *The Democratic Imagination: Dialogues on the Work of Irving Louis Horowitz,* ed. Ray Rist, 175–87. New Brunswick, NJ: Transaction Books.

———. 2003. "The Politics of Presentation: Goffman and Total Institutions." *Symbolic Interaction* 26:659–69.

BECKER, HOWARD S., and BLANCHE GEER. 1957. "Participant Observation and Interviewing: A Comparison." *Human Organization* 16:28–32.

BECKER, HOWARD S., BLANCHE GEER, and EVERETT C. HUGHES. 1968. *Making the Grade: The Academic Side of College Life.* New York: Wiley.

BECKER, HOWARD S., BLANCHE GEER, EVERETT C. HUGHES, and ANSELM L. STRAUSS. 1961. *Boys in White: Student Culture in Medical School.* Chicago: University of Chicago Press.

BECKERT, JENS. 1996. "What Is Sociological about Economic Sociology? Uncertainty and the Embeddedness of Economic Action." *Theory and Society* 25:803–40.

BECKWITH, KAREN. 1996. "Lancashire Women against Pit Closures: Women's Standing in a Men's Movement." *Signs* 21:1034–68.

BEDERMAN, GAIL. 1995. *Manliness and Civilization: A Cultural History of Gender and Race in the United States, 1890–1917.* Chicago: University of Chicago Press.

BEHAR, RUTH. 1993. *Translated Woman: Crossing the Border with Esperanza's Story.* Boston: Beacon Press.

———. 1996. *The Vulnerable Observer: Anthropology That Breaks Your Heart.* Boston: Beacon Press.

BELL, DANIEL. 1950. "The Treaty of Detroit." *Fortune* 42(1): 53–55.

———. 1964. *The End of Ideology: On the Exhaustion of Political Ideas in the Fifties.* New York: Free Press.

———. 1965. *The Reforming of General Education.* New York: Columbia University Press.

BELL, DERRICK. 1992. *Faces at the Bottom of the Well: The Permanence of Racism.* New York: Basic.

BELLAH, ROBERT. 1957. *Tokugawa Religion: The Cultural Roots of Modern Japan.* New York: Free Press.

———. 2003. *Imagining Japan: The Japanese Tradition and Its Modern Interpretation.* Berkeley: University of California Press.

BELLAH, ROBERT, RICHARD MADSEN, WILLIAM M. SULLIVAN, ANN SWIDLER, and STEVEN M. TIPTON. 1985. *Habits of the Heart: Individualism and Commitment in American Life.* New York: Harper and Row.

BENDER, THOMAS, and CARL E. SCHORSKE, eds. 1997. *American Academic Culture in Transformation: Fifty Years, Four Disciplines.* Princeton: Princeton University Press.

BENDIX, REINHARD. 1943. "The Rise and Acceptance of German Sociology." PhD diss., University of Chicago.

———. 1967. "Tradition and Modernity Reconsidered." *Comparative Studies in Society and History* 9:3.

————. 1990. "How I Became an American Sociologist." In *Authors of Their Own Lives: Intellectual Autobiographies by Twenty American Sociologists*, ed. Bennett M. Berger, 452–75. Berkeley: University of California Press.

BENEDICT, RUTH. 1934. *Patterns of Culture*. Boston: Houghton Mifflin.

————. 1946. *The Chrysanthemum and the Sword*. Boston: Houghton Mifflin.

BENNETT, JAMES. 1987. *Oral History and Delinquency: The Rhetoric of Criminology*. Chicago: University of Chicago Press.

BERELSON, BERNARD, and GARY STEINER. 1964. *Human Behavior: An Inventory of Scientific Findings*. New York, Harcourt, Brace and World.

BERGER, BENNETT M., ed. 1990. *Authors of Their Own Lives: Intellectual Autobiographies*. Berkeley: University of California Press.

BERGER, PETER L. 1963. *Invitation to Sociology: A Humanistic Perspective*. Garden City, NY: Doubleday

————. 1967. *The Sacred Canopy: Elements of a Sociological Theory of Religion*. New York: Random House.

————, ed. 1999. *Desecularization: Resurgent Religion and World Politics*. Washington, DC: Ethics and Policy Center.

BERGER, PETER, BRIGITTE BERGER, and HANSFRIED KELLNER. 1973. *The Homeless Mind: Modernization and Consciousness*. New York: Vintage.

BERGER, PETER L., and THOMAS LUCKMANN. 1966. *The Social Construction of Reality: A Treatise in the Sociology of Knowledge*. Garden City, NJ: Doubleday.

BERGESEN, ALBERT, and RONALD SCHOENBERG. 1980. "Long Waves of Colonial Expansion and Contraction." In *Studies of the Modern World-System*, ed. Albert Bergesen, 231–77. New York: Academic Press.

BERLAND, THEODORE. 1962. *The Scientific Life*. New York: Coward-McCann.

BERLIN, ISAIAH. 1953. *The Hedgehog and the Fox*. New York: Simon and Schuster.

BERMINGHAM, CRAIG R. 2003. "'Authority and Autonomy in Marriage': Translation Bernard, Jessie. 1929. "The History and Prospects of Sociology in the United States." In *Trends in American Sociology*, ed. George Lundberg, Read Bain, and Nels Anderson, 1–71. New York: Harper.

————. 1967. "Conflict as Research and Research as Conflict" In *The Rise and Fall of Project Camelot: Studies in the Relationship between Social Science and Practical Politics*, ed. Irving Louis Horowitz, 128–52. Cambridge, MA: Transaction.

————. 1971. "The Paradox of the Happy Marriage." In *Women in Sexist Society*, ed. Vivian Gornick and Barbara Moran. New York: Basic Books.

————. 1972. *The Future of Marriage*. New York: McGraw-Hill.

————. 1973. "My Four Revolutions: An Autobiographic History of the ASA." *American Journal of Sociology* 78:773–91.

————. 1981. *The Female World*. New York: Free Press.

BERNARD, LUTHER L. 1909/1945. "The Teaching of Sociology in the United States." *American Journal of Sociology* 50(6): 534–48.

————. 1918. "The Teaching of Sociology in Southern Colleges and Universities." *American Journal of Sociology* 23(4): 491–515.

——. 1932/1933. "Sociological Research and the Exceptional Man." *Publication of the American Sociological Society* 27:3-19.

——. 1934a. Contribution to "Questions for Sociology: An Informal Round Table Symposium." *Social Forces* 13:165-70.

——, ed. 1934b. *The Fields and Methods of Sociology.* New York: R. Long and R. R. Smith, Inc.

——. 1936. "Henry Hughes, First American Sociologist." *Social Forces* 15(2): 154-74.

——. 1940. "The Method of Generalization for Social Control." *American Sociological Review* 5(3): 340-50.

——. 1948. "The Systematic Sociology of Mariano H. Cornejo." In *An Introduction to the History of Sociology,* ed. Harry Elmer Barnes, 902-30. Chicago: University of Chicago Press.

——. N.d. "Sociological Life History of L. L. Bernard." Bernard Papers, box 15, file 8. Pennsylvania State University Archives.

——. Papers. Pennsylvania State University [PSU] Archives.

——. Papers. University of Chicago Library Special Collections.

BERNARD, LUTHER L., and HOWARD PAUL BECKER. 1934. *The Fields and Methods of Sociology.* New York: R. Long and R. R. Smith.

BERNARD, LUTHER, and JESSIE BERNARD. 1943. *The Origins of American Sociology: The Social Science Movement in the United States.* New York: Thomas Y. Crowell Co.

BERNARD, THOMAS J. 2002. "Criminology: Intellectual History." In *Encyclopedia of Crime and Justice,* 457-64. 2nd ed. New York: Macmillan.

BERNERT, CHRISTOPHER. 1983. "The Career of Causal Analysis in American Sociology." *British Journal of Sociology* 34(2): 230-54.

BERNSTEIN, RICHARD J. 1992. *The New Constellation: The Ethical-Political Horizons of Modernity/Postmodernity.* Cambridge: MIT Press.

BERUBE, ALLAN. 1990. *Coming Out under Fire: The History of Gay Men and Women in World War Two.* New York: Free Press.

BEST, JOEL. 2003. "Social Problems." In *Handbook of Symbolic Interactionism,* ed. L. T. Reynolds and N. J. Herman-Kinney, 981-96. Walnut Creek, CA: AltaMira Press.

BÉTHUNE, CHRISTIAN. 2003. *Adorno et le jazz: Analyse d'un déni esthétique.* Paris: Klincksieck.

BHABHA, HOMI K. 1994. "Of Mimicry and Man: The Ambivalence of Colonial Discourse." In *The Location of Culture,* 85-92. New York: Routledge.

BHASKAR, ROY. 1975/1978. *A Realist Theory of Science.* Hemel Hempstead: Harvester Press.

——. 1979. *The Possibility of Naturalism: A Philosophical Critique of the Contemporary Human Sciences.* Atlantic Highlands, NJ: Humanities Press.

BIDWELL, CHARLES E. 1965. "The School as a Formal Organization." In *Handbook of Organizations,* ed. James G. March, 972-1022. Chicago: Rand McNally.

——. 1999. "Sociology and the Study of Education: Continuity, Discontinuity, and the Individualist Turn." In *Issues in Education Research: Problems and Possibilities,* ed. Ellen Condliffe Lagemann and Lee S. Shulman, 85–104. San Francisco, CA: Jossey-Bass.

BIELBY, DENISE D., and WILLIAM T. BIELBY. 1996. "Women and Men in Film: Gender Inequality among Writers in a Culture Industry." *Gender and Society* 10:248–70.

BIELBY, WILLIAM T., and JAMES N. BARON. 1986. "Men and Women at Work: Sex Segregation and Statistical Discrimination." *American Journal of Sociology* 91:759–99.

BIERSTEDT, ROBERT. 1960. "Sociology and Humane Learning." *American Sociological Review* 25(1): 3–9.

———. 1981. *American Sociological Theory: A Critical History.* New York: Academic Press.

———. 1988. Review of *One Hundred Years: The History of Sociology at Indiana University, 1885–1985,* by Delbert C. Miller. Bloomington: Indiana University Department of Sociology.

BILLINGSLEY, ANDREW. 1999. *Mighty Like a River: The Black Church and Social Reform.* New York: Oxford University Press.

BIRKBECK, CHRISTOPHER, and GARY LAFREE. 1993. "The Situational Analysis of Crime and Deviance." *Annual Review of Sociology* 19:113–37.

BLACK, DONALD. 1976. *The Behavior of Law.* New York: Academic Press.

———. 2000. "Dreams of Pure Sociology." *Sociological Theory* 18:343–67.

BLACKMAR, FRANK W. 1890a. *Spanish Colonization in the Southwest.* Baltimore: Johns Hopkins Press.

———. 1890b. *The Study of History and Sociology.* Topeka, KS: Kansas Publishing House.

———. 1891. *Spanish Institutions in the Southwest.* Baltimore: Johns Hopkins Press.

———. 1897. "The Smoky Pilgrims." *American Journal of Sociology* 2(4): 485–500.

BLACKMAR, FRANK W., and ERNEST W. BURGESS. 1917. *Lawrence Social Survey.* Lawrence: University of Kansas Press.

BLACKWELL, JAMES, and MORRIS JANOWITZ. 1974. *Black Sociologists: Historical and Contemporary Perspectives.* Chicago: University of Chicago Press.

BLALOCK, HUBERT M. 1961. *Causal Inferences in Nonexperimental Research.* Chapel Hill: University of North Carolina Press.

BLASI, ANTHONY, ed. 2005. *Diverse Histories of American Sociology.* Leiden, Netherlands: Brill.

BLAU, JUDITH. 2004. "Editor's Note." *Social Forces* 83(2): 459–60.

BLAU, JUDITH R., and PETER M. BLAU. 1982. "The Cost of Inequality: Metropolitan Structure and Violent Crime." *American Sociological Review* 47(1): 114–29.

BLAU, PETER M. 1973. *The Organization of Academic Work.* New York: Wiley.

BLAU, PETER, and OTIS DUDLEY DUNCAN. 1967. *The American Occupational Structure.* New York: Wiley.

BLAUNER, ROBERT. 1969. "Internal Colonialism and Ghetto Revolt." *Social Problems* 16(4): 393–408.

———. 1972. *Racial Oppression in America.* New York: Harper and Row.

BLEDSTEIN, BURTON J. 1974. "Noah Porter versus William Graham Sumner." *Church History* 43:340–49.

———. 1976. *The Culture of Professionalism: The Middle Class and the Development of Higher Education in America.* New York: Norton.

BLIGHT, DAVID W. 2002. *Race and Reunion: The Civil War in American Memory.* Cambridge: Harvard University Press.

BLISS, WILLIAM D. P., ed. 1897/1908. *The Encyclopedia of Social Reform; including Political Economy, Political Science, Sociology and Statistics.* New York and London: Funk and Wagnall's.

BLOOM, SAMUEL. 1990. "The Intellectual in a Time of Crisis: The Case of Bernhard J. Stern, 1894–1956. *Journal of the History of the Behavioral Sciences* 26:17–37.

BLUMER, HERBERT. 1922. "Theory of Social Revolutions." MA thesis, University of Missouri.

———. 1946. "Collective Behavior." In *A New Outline of the Principles of Sociology,* ed. A. M. Lee, 167–219. New York: Barnes and Noble.

———. 1955. "Social Movements." In *Principles of Sociology,* ed. A. M. Lee, 99–220. New York: Barnes and Noble.

———. 1969. *Symbolic Interactionism: Perspective and Method.* Englewood Cliffs, NJ: Prentice Hall.

BLUMSTEIN, ALFRED, JACQUELINE COHEN, JEFFREY A. ROTH, and CHRISTY A. VISHER, eds. 1986. *Criminal Careers and "Career Criminals."* Washington, DC: National Academy Press.

BOGARDUS, EMORY S. 1931/1932. Introduction to *Social Problems and Social Processes,* ed. Emory S. Bogardus, ix–xii. New York: Freeport.

———. 1934. Contribution to "Questions for Sociology: An Informal Round Table Symposium." *Social Forces* 13:212.

BOGDAN, ROBERT, and STEVEN J. TAYLOR. 1975. *Introduction to Qualitative Research Methods: A Phenomenological Approach to the Social Sciences.* New York: Wiley. (2nd and 3rd eds. are listed as Taylor and Bogdan 1984, 1998.)

BONACICH, EDNA. 1972. "A Theory of Ethnic Antagonism: The Split Labor Market." *American Sociological Review* 37 (October): 547–59.

BONACICH, EDNA, and RICHARD APPELBAUM. 2000. *Behind the Label: Inequality in the Los Angeles Apparel Industry.* Berkeley: University of California Press.

BOOTHE, CHARLES. 1902–3. *Life and Labour of the People in London.* 17 vols. London: Macmillan.

BORKOWICZ, JACEK, et al. 2001. *Thou Shalt Not Kill: Poles on Jedwabne.* Warsaw: Wiez.

BOROCZ, JOZSEF. 2001. "Change Rules." *American Journal of Sociology* 106:1152–68.

BORSTELMANN, THOMAS. 2003. *The Cold War and the Color Line: American Race Relations in the Global Arena.* Cambridge: Harvard University Press.

BOSE, CHRISTINE E. 1985. *Jobs and Gender: A Study of Occupational Prestige.* New York: Praeger.

———. 2001. *Women in 1900: Gateway to the Political Economy of the 20th Century.* Philadelphia: Temple University Press.

BOSSARD, JAMES H. S. 1932. "Applied Sociology and Major Social Problems." *Social Forces* 11:188–90.

———. 1934. Contribution to "Questions for Sociology: An Informal Round Table Symposium." *Social Forces* 13:189–91.

BOTTOMORE, TOM, and ROBERT NISBET, eds. 1978. *A History of Sociological Analysis.* New York: Basic Books.

BOUDON, RAYMOND. 1999. Foreword to *The Sociology-Philosophy Connection,* by Mario Bunge, xi–xv. New Brunswick, NJ: Transaction.

BOURDIEU, PIERRE. 1979/1984. *Distinction: A Social Critique of the Judgement of Taste.* Cambridge: Harvard University Press.

———. 1985a. "The Forms of Capital." In *Handbook of Theory and Research for the Sociology of Education,* ed. J. G. Richardson, 241–58. New York: Greenwood Press.

———. 1985b. "The Genesis of the Concepts of *Habitus* and Field." *Sociocriticism* 2(2): 11–24.

———. 1988. *Homo Academicus.* Cambridge, MA: Polity Press.

———. 1991a. "Epilogue: On the Possibility of a Field of World Sociology." In *Social Theory for a Changing Society,* ed. Pierre Bourdieu and James S. Coleman, trans. L. Wacquant, 373–87. Boulder, CO: Westview Press.

———. 1991b. *Language and Symbolic Power.* Cambridge: Harvard University Press.

———. 1991c. "The Peculiar History of Scientific Reason." *Sociological Forum* 6(1): 3–26.

———. 1991d. *The Political Ontology of Martin Heidegger.* Oxford: Polity Press.

———. 2000. *Pascalian Meditations.* Trans. R. Nice. Stanford: Stanford University Press.

———. 2001a. *Masculine Domination.* Trans. Richard Nice. Cambridge, MA: Polity Press.

———. 2001b. *Science de la science et réflexivité.* Paris: Éditions Raisons d'Agir.

BOWLES, SAMUEL, and HERBERT GINTIS. 1976. *Schooling in Capitalist America: Educational Reform and the Contradictions of Economic Life.* New York: Basic Books.

BOWMAN, CLAUDE C. 1936. "Imagination in Social Science." *American Sociological Review* 1(4): 632–40.

BOYER, JOHN W. 2002. "Annual Report to the Faculty of the College." *University of Chicago Record* 37(3): 2–15.

BRAITHWAITE, JOHN. 1989. *Crime, Shame, and Reintegration.* New York: Cambridge University Press.

———. 1998. "Restorative Justice." In *Handbook of Crime and Justice,* ed. Michael Tonry, 323–44. New York: Oxford.

———. 2000. "The New Regulatory State and the Transformation of Criminology." *British Journal of Criminology* 40:222–28.

———. 2005. "Between Proportionality and Impunity: Confrontation-Truth-Prevention: The American Society of Criminology 2004 Sutherland Address." *Criminology* 43(1): 283–305.

BRAMSON, LEON. 1961. *The Political Context of Sociology*. Princeton: Princeton University Press.

BRANDT, LILLIAN. 1910. "Review of *Medical Sociology* by J. P. Warbasse. *Survey*, February.

BRANFORD, VICTOR V. 1903. "On the Origin and Use of the Word 'Sociology.'" *American Journal of Sociology* 9(2): 145–62.

———. 1904. "The Founders of Sociology." *American Journal of Sociology* 10(1): 94–120; discussion, 120–26.

BREARLEY, H. C. 1934. Contribution to "Questions for Sociology: An Informal Round Table Symposium." *Social Forces* 13:191–93.

BRECKINRIDGE, SOPHONISBA P., and EDITH ABBOTT. 1912. *The Delinquent Child and the Home*. New York: Russell Sage Foundation.

BREMER, WILLIAM W. 1975. "Along the 'American Way': The New Deal's Work Relief Programs for the Unemployed." *Journal of American History* 62:636–52.

BRENNER, JOHANNA, and BARBARA LASLETT. 1986. "Social Reproduction and the Family." In *The Social Reproduction of Organization and Culture*, vol. 2 of *Sociology from Crisis to Science?* ed. Ulf Himmelstrand. London: Sage.

———. 1991. "Gender, Social Reproduction and Women's Self-Organization: Considering the U.S. Welfare State." *Gender and Society* 5:311–33.

BRENNER, NEIL. 1998. "Between Fixity and Motion: Accumulation, Territorial Organization and the Historical Geography of Spatial Scales." *Environment and Planning D: Society and Space* 16:459–81.

BRESLAU, DANIEL. 1990a. "La science, le sexisme et l'Ecole de Chicago." *Actes de la Recherche en Sciences Sociales* 85:94–95.

———. 1990b. "The Scientific Appropriation of Social Research: Robert Park's *Human Ecology and American Sociology*." *Theory and Society* 19:417–46.

———. 1998. *In Search of the Unequivocal: The Political Economy of Measurement in U.S. Labor Market Policy*. Westport, CT: Praeger.

———. 2003. "Economics Invents the Economy: Mathematics, Statistics, and Models in the Work of Irving Fisher and Wesley Mitchell." *Theory and Society* 32:379–411.

———. 2005. "The Real and the Imaginary in Economic Methodology." In *The Politics of Method in the Human Sciences: Positivism and Its Epistemological Others*, ed. George Steinmetz, 451–69. Durham, NC: Duke University Press.

BRICK, HOWARD. 1986. *Daniel Bell and the Decline of Intellectual Radicalism*. Madison: University of Wisconsin Press.

———. 1993. "The Reformist Dimension of Talcott Parsons' Early Social Theory." In *The Culture of the Market: Historical Essays*, ed. Thomas L. Haskell and Richard F. Teichgraeber III, 357–96. Cambridge: Cambridge University Press.

———. 2000. "Talcott Parsons's 'Shift Away from Economics,' 1937–1946." *Journal of American History* 87:490–514.

BRIMELOW, PETER. 1995. *Alien Nation: Common Sense about America's Immigration Disaster*. New York: Random House.

BRINKLEY, ALAN. 1995. *The End of Reform: New Deal Liberalism in Recession and War.* New York: Knopf.

BRODERICK, FRANCIS L. 1974. "W. E. B. DuBois: History of an Intellectual." In *Black Sociologists: Historical and Contemporary Perspectives,* ed. James E. Blackwell and Morris Janowitz, 3–24. Chicago: University of Chicago Press.

BROIDY, LISA M. 2001. "A Test of General Strain Theory." *Criminology* 39(1): 9–35.

BROOKOVER, W. B. 1949. "Sociology of Education: A Definition." *American Sociological Review* 14:407–15.

BROOKS, JOHN I. 1998. *The Eclectic Legacy: Academic Philosophy and the Human Sciences in Nineteenth-Century France.* Newark: University of Delaware Press.

BROOM, LEONARD. 1943. "Familial Adjustments of Japanese-Americans to Relocation: First Phase." *American Sociological Review* 8:551–60.

BROSCHART, KAY RICHARDS. 2005. "The Neglected Contributions of Female Sociologists in the American South." In *Diverse Histories of American Sociology,* ed. Anthony Blasi. Leiden, Netherlands: Brill.

BROWN, CAROL A. 1991. "The Early Years of the Sociology Liberation Movement," In *Radical Sociologists and the Movement, Experiences, Lessons, and Legacies,* ed. Martin Oppenheimer, Martin J. Murray, and Rhonda F. Levine, 43–53. Philadelphia: Temple University Press.

BROWN, E. R. 1979. *Rockefeller Medicine Men: Medicine and Capitalism in America.* Berkeley: University of California Press.

BROWN, MICHAEL K., MARTIN CARNOY, ELLIOTT CURRIE, TROY DUSTER, DAVID B. OPPENHEIMER, MARJORIE M. SHULTZ, and DAVID WELLMAN. 2003. *Whitewashing Race: The Myth of a Color-Blind Society.* Berkeley: University of California Press.

BROWN, ROY M. 1939. "Education for Social Work: II. From the Point of View of the State University." *Social Forces* 18(1): 65–70.

BROWNE, IRENE, and JOYA MISRA. 2003. "The Intersection of Gender and Race in the Labor Market." *Annual Review of Sociology* 29:487–513.

BROWNMILLER, SUSAN. 1975. *Against Our Will.* New York: Simon and Schuster.

BRUBAKER, ROGERS. 1992. *Citizenship and Nationhood in France and Germany.* Cambridge: Harvard University Press.

———. 1996. *Nationalism Reframed: Nationhood and the National Question and the New Europe.* Cambridge: Cambridge: Cambridge University Press.

BRUERE, HENRY. 1940. "The Social Sciences in the Service of Society." In *Eleven Twenty-Six: A Decade of Social Science Research,* ed. Louis Wirth, 5–22. Chicago: University of Chicago Press.

BRUMBERG, JOAN JACOBS. 1997. *The Body Project.* New York: Random House.

BRUNNER, EDMUND DES., and J. H. KOLB. 1933. *Rural Social Trends.* New York: McGraw-Hill.

BRUNNER, EDMUND DES., and IRVING LORGE. 1937. *Rural Trends in Depression Years.* New York: Columbia University Press.

BRUNO, FRANK. 1957. *Trends in Social Work, 1874-1956.* New York: Columbia University Press.

BRUSH, LISA. 1990. "Violent Acts and Injurious Outcomes in Married Couples: Methodological Issues in the National Study of Families and Households." *Gender and Society* 4(1): 156-67.

BRUYN, SEVERYN T. 1966. *The Human Perspective in Sociology: The Methodology of Participant Observation.* Englewood Cliffs, NJ: Prentice Hall.

BRYANT, CHRISTOPHER. 1975. "Positivism Reconsidered." *Sociological Review* 23 (May): 397-412.

———. 1985. *Positivism in Social Theory and Research.* New York: Macmillan.

The Builder. 1930. Review of *Man's Social Destiny in the Light of Science,* by Charles Ellwood. May, 157.

BULMER, MARTIN. 1980. "The Early Institutional Establishment of Social Science Research: The Local Community Research Committee at the University of Chicago, 1923-30." *Minerva* 18:51-110.

———. 1982. "Support for Sociology in the 1920s." *American Sociologist* 17:185-92.

———. 1984a. *The Chicago School of Sociology: Institutionalization, Diversity, and the Rise of Sociological Research.* Chicago: University of Chicago Press.

———. 1984b. "Philanthropic Foundations and the Development of the Social Sciences in the Early Twentieth Century: A Reply to Donald Fisher." *Sociology* 18(4): 572-79.

———, ed. 1987. *Social Science Research and Government: Comparative Essays on Britain and the United States.* Cambridge: Cambridge University Press.

———. 1992. "The Growth of Applied Sociology after 1945: The Prewar Establishment of Postwar Infrastructure." In *Sociology and Its Publics: The Forms and Fates of Disciplinary Organization,* ed. Terrance C. Halliday and Morris Janowitz, 317-45. Chicago: University of Chicago Press.

———. 1994. "The Institutionalization of an Academic Discipline." *Social Epistemology* 8:3-8.

BULMER, MARTIN, KEVIN BALES, and KATHRYN KISH SKLAR, eds. 1991. *The Social Survey in Historical Perspective, 1880-1940.* Cambridge: Cambridge University Press.

BULMER, MARTIN, and JOAN BULMER. 1981. "Philanthropy and Social Science in the 1920s: Beardsley Ruml and the Laura Spelman Rockefeller Memorial, 1922-29." *Minerva* 19(3): 347-507.

BULMER, MARTIN, CHARLES CAMIC, JAY DEMERATH, HOWARD SCHUMAN, JONATHAN TURNER, and STEPHEN TURNER. 1994. "Symposium on the History of American Sociology Portrayed in *The Impossible Science* by Stephen Turner and Jonathan Turner." *Social Epistemology* 8(1): 3-67.

BUNGE, MARIO A. 1999. *The Sociology-Philosophy Connection.* New Brunswick, NJ: Transaction.

BURAWOY, MICHAEL. 1979. *Manufacturing Consent: Changes in the Labor Process under Monopoly Capitalism.* Chicago: University of Chicago Press.

———. 1982. "Introduction: The Resurgence of Marxism in American Sociology." *American Journal of Sociology* 88:S1–S30.

———. 2000. "Introduction: Reaching for the Global." In *Global Ethnography: Forces, Connections, and Imaginations in a Postmodern World,* by Michael Burawoy et al. Berkeley: University of California Press.

———. 2001. "Neoclassical Sociology: From the End of Communism to the End of Classes," *American Journal of Sociology* 106(4): 1099–1120.

———. 2004a. "Public Sociologies: Contradictions, Dilemmas, and Possibilities." *Social Forces* 82(4): 1–16.

———. 2004b. "Public Sociologies: Theme Statement, Annual Meeting 2004." <asanet.org/convention/2004/theme1.html>.

———. 2005a. "Antinomian Marxist." In *A Disobedient Generation: Social Theorists in the Sixties,* ed. Alan Sica and Stephen Turner, 48–71. Chicago: University of Chicago Press.

———. 2005b. "Presidential Address: For Public Sociology." *American Sociological Review* 70(1): 4–28.

———. 2005c. "Provincializing the Social Sciences." In *The Politics of Method in the Human Sciences: Positivism and Its Epistemological Others,* ed. George Steinmetz, 508–25. Durham, NC: Duke University Press.

BURAWOY, MICHAEL, JOSEPH A. BLUM, SHEBA GEORGE, ZSUZSA GILLE, TERESA GOWAN, LYNNE HANEY, MAREN KLAWITER, STEVE H. LOPEZ, SEÁN Ó RIAIN, and MILLIE THAYER. 2000. *Global Ethnography: Forces, Connections, and Imaginations in a Postmodern World.* Berkeley: University of California Press.

BURAWOY, MICHAEL, WILLIAM GAMSON, CHARLOTTE RYAN, STEPHEN PFOHL, DIANE VAUGHAN, CHARLES DERBER, and JULIET SCHOR. 2004. "Public Sociologies: A Symposium from Boston College." *Social Problems* 51(1): 103–30.

BURAWOY, MICHAEL, and JONATHAN VANANTWERPEN. n.d. "Public Sociology at Berkeley: Past, Present, and Future." Manuscript. Department of Sociology, University of California, Berkeley.

BURGESS, ERNEST W. 1923. "The Interdependence of Sociology and Social Work." *Journal of Social Forces.* 1(4): 366–70.

———. 1934/1935. "Social Planning and the Mores." In *The Human Side of Social Planning,* ed. E. W. Burgess and Herbert Blumer, 1–18. Chicago: American Sociological Society.

———. 1939. "The Influence of Sigmund Freud upon Sociology in the United States." *American Journal of Sociology* 45(3): 356–74.

———. 1953. "The Aims of the Society for the Study of Social Problems." *Social Problems* 1(1): 203.

BURGESS, E. W. and HERBERT BLUMER. 1935. *The Human Side of Social Planning.* Chicago: American Sociological Society.

BURGESS, E. W., L. S. COTTRELL, P. HORST, E. L. KELLY, M. W. RICHARDSON, and S. A. STOUFFER. 1941. "Memorandum on Prediction and National Defense." In *The Prediction of Personal Adjustment*, ed. Paul Horst, 157–78. Bulletin No. 48. New York: Social Science Research Council.

BURGESS, JOHN WILLIAM. 1902. *Reconstruction and the Constitution, 1866–1876*. New York: C. Scribner's Sons.

BURGESS, ROBERT L., and RONALD L. AKERS. 1968. "A Differential Association: Reinforcement Theory of Criminal Behavior." *Social Problems* 14(2): 459–69.

BURNS, TOM. 1992. *Erving Goffman*. New York: Routledge.

BURRIS, VAL. 2004. "The Academic Caste System: Prestige Hierarchies in PhD Exchange Networks." *American Sociological Review* 69(2): 239–64.

BURSIK, ROBERT J. 1988. "A Premature Encapsulation." *Criminologist* 13(5): 1, 6–8, 10, 17.

———. 1999. "The Informal Control of Crime through Neighborhood Networks." *Sociological Focus* 32:85–97.

BURSIK, ROBERT J., and HAROLD G. GRASMICK. 1993. *Neighborhoods and Crime: The Dimensions of Effective Community Control*. New York: Lexington Books.

BUTLER, JUDITH. 1990. *Gender Trouble: Feminism and the Subversion of Identity*. New York: Routledge.

BUXTON, WILLIAM, and STEPHEN P. TURNER. 1992. "From Education to Expertise: Sociology as a 'Profession.'" In *Sociology and Its Publics: The Forms and Fates of Disciplinary Organization*, ed. Terrance C. Halliday and Morris Janowitz, 373–407. Chicago: University of Chicago Press.

CAIDEN, GERALD E. 1984. "In Search of an Apolitical Science of American Public Administration." In *Politics and Administration: Woodrow Wilson and American Public Administration*, ed. Jack Rabin and James S. Bowman, 51–76. New York: Dekker.

CALASANTI, TONI M. 2001. *Gender, Social Inequalities, and Aging*. Walnut Creek: Alta Mira Press.

CALHOUN, CRAIG. 1982. *The Question of Class Struggle*. Chicago: University of Chicago.

———. 1992. "Sociology, Other Disciplines, and the Project of a General Understanding of Social Life." In *Sociology and Its Publics*, ed. Terence C. Halliday and Morris Janowitz, 137–95. Chicago: University of Chicago Press.

———. 1994. *Neither Gods nor Emperors: Students and the Struggle for Democracy in China*. Berkeley: University of California Press.

———. 1996. "The Rise and Domestication of Historical Sociology." In *The Historic Turn in the Human Sciences*, ed. T. J. McDonald, 305–38. Ann Arbor: University of Michigan Press.

———. 1997. *Nationalism*. Minneapolis: University of Minnesota Press.

———. 1999. "Introduction." *Sociological Theory* 17(3): 237–39.

CALHOUN, CRAIG, and TROY DUSTER. 2005. "The Visions and Divisions of Sociology." *Chronicle of Higher Education* 51(49): B7.

CALHOUN, CRAIG, PAUL PRICE, and ASHLEY TIMMER, eds. 2002. *Understanding September 11*. New York: New Press.

CALVERTON, V. F. 1929. "The Sociological Aesthetics of the Bolsheviki." *American Journal of Sociology* 35(3): 383-92.

CAMIC, CHARLES. 1986. "The Matter of Habit." *American Journal of Sociology* 91:1039-87.

———. 1987. "The Making of a Method: A Historical Reinterpretation of the Early Parsons." *American Sociological Review* 52:421-39.

———. 1989. "*Structure* after 50 Years: The Anatomy of a Charter." *American Journal of Sociology* 95 (July): 38-107.

———. 1994. "Reshaping the History of American Sociology." *Social Epistemology* 8:9-18.

———. 1995. "Three Departments in Search of a Discipline: Localism and Interdisciplinary Interaction in American Sociology, 1890-1940." *Source Social Research* 62:1003-33.

———. 1997a. "Parsons and the Crisis of the 1930s." Paper presented at the Heidelberg Conference on the 60th Anniversary of *The Structure of Social Action*.

———, ed. 1997b. *Reclaiming the Sociological Classics: The State of the Scholarship.* Oxford: Blackwell.

———. 2005. "From Amherst to Heidelberg: On the Origins of the Parsonsian Conception of Culture." In *After Parsons: A Theory of Social Action for the Twenty-First Century,* ed. Harold Bershady, Renee Fox, and Victor Lidz. New York: Russell Sage.

CAMIC, CHARLES, and YU XIE. 1994. "The Statistical Turn in American Social Science: Columbia University, 1890 to 1915." *American Sociological Review* 59 (October): 773-805.

CAMPBELL, JOHN L. 2004. *Institutional Change and Globalization.* Princeton: Princeton University Press.

CAPLOW, THEODORE, and REECE J. MCGEE. 1958. *The Academic Marketplace.* New York: Basic.

CARNAP, RUDOLF. 1934. *The Unity of Science.* London: Kegan Paul.

———. 1956. *Meaning and Necessity; A Study in Semantics and Modal Logic.* 2nd ed. Chicago, University of Chicago Press.

CARNEIRO, ROBERT L. 1974. "Herbert Spencer's *The Study of Sociology* and the Rise of Social Science in America." *Proceedings of the American Philosophical Society* 118:540-54.

CARR, L. J., and J. E. STERMER. 1952. *Willow Run.* New York: Harper.

CARRITHERS, DAVID. 1995. "The Enlightenment Science of Society." In *Inventing Human Science: Eighteenth-Century Domains,* ed. Christopher Fox, Roy Porter, and Robert Wokler, 232-70. Berkeley: University of California Press.

CARROLL, CHARLES. 1900. *The Negro A Beast.* Miami: Mnemosyne Publishing.

CARTWRIGHT, D. 1954. "Some Principles of Mass Persuasion: Selected Findings of Research on the Sale of United States War Bonds." In *Public Opinion and Propaganda,* ed. Daniel Katz, Dorwin Cartwright, Samuel Eldersveld, and Alred McLung Lee. New York: Holt, Reinhart.

CARVER, T. N., JOHN B. CLARK, DAVID KINLEY, E. A. ROSS, LESTER F. WARD, HUTTON WEBSTER, and ALBION W. SMALL. 1907. "The Relations of the Social Sciences: A Symposium." *American Journal of Sociology* 13(3): 392–401.

CASANOVA, JOSE. 1994. *Public Religions in the Modern World.* Chicago: University of Chicago Press.

CASTELLS, MANUEL. 1996. *The Rise of the Network Society.* Oxford: Blackwell.

CAVAN, RUTH SHONLE. 1928. *Suicide.* Chicago: University of Chicago Press.

CAVAN, RUTH SHONLE, and KATHERINE HOWLAND RANCK. 1938. *The Family and the Depression: A Study of One Hundred Chicago Families.* Chicago: University of Chicago Press.

CENTENO, MIGUEL ANGEL. 2002. *Blood and Debt: War and the Nation-State in Latin America.* University Park: Pennsylvania State University Press.

CENTENO, MIGUEL ANGEL, and FERNANDO LÓPEZ-ALVES. 2001. *The Other Mirror: Grand Theory through the Lens of Latin America.* Princeton: Princeton University Press.

CHAFETZ, JANET SALZMAN. 1997. "Feminist Theory and Sociology: Underutilized Contributions for Mainstream Theory." *Annual Review of Sociology* 23:97–120.

CHAKRABARTY, DIPESH. 2000. *Provincializing Europe: Postcolonial Thought and Historical Difference.* Princeton: Princeton University Press.

CHAMBLISS, WILLIAM J. 1987. "I Wish I Didn't Know Now What I Didn't Know Then." *Criminologist* 12(6): 1–9.

CHAPIN, F. STUART. 1934a. "The Present State of the Profession." *American Journal of Sociology* 39: 506–8.

——. 1934b. "What Has Sociology to Contribute to Plans for Recovery from the Depression?" *Social Forces* 12:473–75.

——. 1935a. *Contemporary American Institutions: A Sociological Analysis.* New York: Harper.

——. 1935b. "Letter from the President of the American Sociological Society." *Publication of the American Sociological Society* 29(1): 1–2.

——. 1935c. "Measurement in Sociology." *American Journal of Sociology* 40(4): 476–80.

——. 1936. "Social Theory and Social Action." *American Sociological Review* 1:1–11.

CHAPIN, F. STUART, and STUART A. QUEEN. 1937. *Research Memorandum on Social Work in the Depression.* New York: Social Science Research Council.

CHAPOULIE, JEAN-MICHEL. 1996. "Everett Hughes and the Chicago Tradition." *Sociological Theory* 14(1): 3–29.

——. 2001. *La tradition sociologique de Chicago, 1892–1961.* Paris: Seuil.

CHARMAZ, KATHY. 1983. "The Grounded Theory Method: An Explication and Interpretation." In *Contemporary Field Research*, ed. Robert Emerson, 109–26. Prospect Heights, IL: Waveland Press.

CHARRAD, MOUNIRA MAYA. 2004. *States and Women's Rights: The Making of Postcolonial Tunisia, Algeria and Morocco.* Berkeley: University of California Press.

CHASE, ALLAN. 1977. *The Legacy of Malthus: The Social Costs of the New Scientific Racism.* New York: Knopf.

CHATTERJEE, PARTHA. 1993. *The Nation and Its Fragments.* Princeton: Princeton University Press.

CHOMSKY, NOAM. 1967. "The Responsibility of Intellectuals." *New York Review of Books* 8(3). http://www.nybooks.com/articles/12172 (accessed 6/20/05).

CHRISS, JAMES J. 1995. "Testing Gouldner's Coming Crisis Thesis: On the Waxing and Waning of Intellectual Influence." *Current Perspectives in Social Theory* 15:3–61.

———. 1999. *Alvin W. Gouldner: Sociologist and Outlaw Marxist.* London: Ashgate.

CHRISTAKES, GEORGE. 1978. *Albion W. Small.* Boston: Twayne Publishers.

CHUGERMAN, SAMUEL. 1939. *Lester F. Ward: The American Aristotle: A Summary and Interpretation of His Sociology.* Durham, NC: Duke University Press.

CICOUREL, AARON V. 1968. *The Social Organization of Juvenile Justice.* New York: Wiley.

CLARK, JOHN BATES. 1899. *The Distribution of Wealth.* New York: Macmillan.

CLARK, KENNETH. 1965. *Dark Ghetto: Dilemmas of Social Power.* Foreword by Gunnar Myrdal. New York: Harper and Row.

CLARKE, ADELE E., JANET K. SHIM, LAURA MAMO, JENNIFER RUTH FOSKET, and JENNIFER R. FISHMAN. 2003. "Biomedicalization: Technoscientific Transformations of Health, Illness, and U.S. Biomedicine." *American Sociological Review* 68:161–94.

CLARKE, LEE, and JAMES F. SHORT JR. 1993. "Social Organization and Risk: Some Current Controversies." *Annual Review of Sociology* 19:375–99.

CLAWSON, DAN, ed. 1998. *Required Reading: Sociology's Most Influential Books.* Amherst: University of Massachusetts Press.

CLAYMAN, STEVEN E. 2002. "Ethnomethodology." In *The International Encyclopedia of the Social and Behavioral Sciences,* ed. N. Smelser and P. Baltes. Oxford: Elsevier Science.

CLEMENS, ELISABETH, W. POWELL, K. MCILWAINE, and D. OKOMOTO. 1995. "Careers in Print: Books, Journals and Scholarly Reputation." *American Journal of Sociology* 101(2): 433–94.

CLIFFORD, JAMES, and GEORGE MARCUS. 1986. *Writing Culture: The Poetics and Politics of Ethnography: A School of American Research Advanced Seminar.* Berkeley: University of California Press.

CLINARD, MARSHALL B., ed. 1964. *Anomie and Deviant Behavior: A Discussion and Critique.* Glencoe, IL: Free Press.

CLOUGH, PATRICIA. 1992. *The End(s) of Ethnography: From Realism to Social Criticism.* Newbury Park, CA: Sage.

CLOWARD, RICHARD, and LLOYD E. OHLIN. 1960. *Delinquency and Opportunity.* New York: Free Press.

COBB, JOHN CHANDLER. 1934. *The Application of Scientific Methods to Sociology.* Boston: Chapman and Grimes.

COCKBURN, CYNTHIA. 1991. *In the Way of Women: Men's Resistance to Sex Equality in Organizations.* Ithaca, NY: ILR Press.

COHEN, ALBERT K. 1955. *Delinquent Boys: The Culture of the Gang*. New York: Free Press.

———. 1983. "Interview." In *Criminology in the Making: An Oral History*, ed. John H. Laub, 182–203. Boston: Northeastern University Press.

COHEN, ALBERT K., ALFRED LINDESMITH, and KARL SCHUESSLER, eds. 1956. *The Sutherland Papers*. Bloomington: Indiana University Press.

COHEN, LILLIAN. 1954. *Statistical Methods for Social Scientists: An Introduction*. New York: Prentice Hall.

COHEN, LIZABETH. 2003. *Consumer's Republic*. New York: Knopf.

COHEN, M. R., and E. NAGEL. 1934. *An Introduction to Logic and Scientific Method*. New York: Harcourt, Brace.

COLE, STEPHEN. 2004. "Merton's Contribution to the Sociology of Science." *Social Studies of Science* 34:829–44.

COLEMAN, JAMES S. 1961. *The Adolescent Society: The Social Life of the Teenager and Its Impact on Education*. New York: Free Press of Glencoe.

———. 1978. "Sociological Analysis and Social Policy." In *A History of Sociological Analysis*, ed. T. Bottomore and R. Nisbet, 677–703. New York: Basic Books.

———. 1980. "The Structure of Society and the Nature of Social Research." *Knowledge* 1:333–50.

———. 1988. "Social Capital in the Creation of Human Capital." *American Journal of Sociology* 94:S95–121.

———. 1990. "Columbia in the 1950s." In *Authors of Their Own Lives: Intellectual Autobiographies by Twenty American Sociologists*, ed. Bennett M. Berger, 75–103. Berkeley: University of California Press.

COLEMAN, JAMES S., et al. 1966. *Equality of Educational Opportunity*. Washington, DC: Government Printing Office.

COLLINS, PATRICIA HILL. 1990/2000. *Black Feminist Thought: Knowledge, Consciousness, and the Politics of Empowerment*. Boston: Unwin Hyman; New York: Routledge.

———. 1998. *Fighting Words: Black Women and the Search for Justice*. Minneapolis: University of Minnesota Press.

———. 2001. "Like One of the Family: Race, Ethnicity, and the Paradox of U.S. National Identity." *Ethnic and Racial Studies* 24(1): 3–28.

———. 2004. *Black Sexual Politics: African Americans, Gender, and the New Racism*. New York: Routledge.

COLLINS, RANDALL. 1971. "Functional and Conflict Theories of Educational Stratification." *American Sociological Review* 36:1002–19.

———. 1979. *The Credential Society*. New York: Academic Press.

———. 1989. "Toward a Theory of Intellectual Change: The Social Causes of Philosophies." *Science, Technology, and Human Values* 14:107–40.

———. 1998. *The Sociology of Philosophies: A Global Theory of Intellectual Change*. Cambridge: Harvard University Press.

———. 1999a. "The Geopolitical Basis of Revolution: The Prediction of Soviet Collapse." In *Macrohistory: Essays in Sociology of the Long Run* by Randall Collins, 37–69. Stanford: Stanford University Press.

——. 1999b. "Introduction: The Golden Age of Macrohistorical Sociology." In *Macrohistory: Essays in Sociology of the Long Run* by Randall Collins, 37–69. Stanford: Stanford University Press.

——. 2004. "The Micro and Macro Foundations of Terrorism." Paper presented at the annual meeting of the American Sociological Association, San Francisco.

COLLINS, RANDALL, and MICHAEL MAKOWSKY. 1998. *The Discovery of Society.* 6th ed. New York: McGraw-Hill.

COLOMY, PAUL, and J. DAVID BROWN. 1995. "Elaboration, Revision, Polemic, and Progress in the Second Chicago School." In *A Second Chicago School? The Development of a Postwar American Sociology,* ed. G. A. Fine, 17–81. Chicago: University of Chicago Press.

COMAROFF, JOHN L., and JEAN COMAROFF, eds. 1991. *Of Revelation and Revolution: Christianity, Colonialism and Consciousness in South Africa* Chicago: University of Chicago Press.

——. 1999. *Civil Society and Political Imagination in Africa.* Chicago: University of Chicago Press.

COMMAGER, HENRY STEELE. 1950. *The American Mind: An Interpretation of American Thought and Character since the 1880s.* New Haven: Yale University Press.

COMMITTEE ON THE STATUS OF WOMEN IN SOCIOLOGY. 2004. "2004 Report of the ASA Committee on the Status of Women in Sociology." Report presented to the Council of the American Sociological Association, Washington, DC. August.

COMMONS, JOHN R. 1899. "A Sociological View of Sovereignty. I." *American Journal of Sociology* 5(1): 1–15.

COMTE, AUGUSTE. 1975. *Auguste Comte and Positivism: The Essential Writings.* Ed. Gertrud Lenzer. New York: Harper and Row.

COMTE, AUGUSTE, and STANISLAV ANDRESKI. 1974. *The Essential Comte: Selected from "Cours de philosophie positive."* London: Croom Helm.

CONNELL, R. W. 1987. *Gender and Power.* Stanford: Stanford University Press.

——. 1995. *Masculinities.* Berkeley: University of California Press.

——. 1997. "Why Is Classical Theory Classical?" *American Journal of Sociology* 102(6): 1511–57.

CONRAD, IRENE. 1929. "Education for Social Work." In *Social Work Year Book,* 148–54. New York: Russell Sage Foundation.

CONVERSE, JEAN M. 1987. *Survey Research in the United States: Roots and Emergence, 1890–1960.* Berkeley: University of California Press.

COOK, GARY A. 1993. *George Herbert Mead: The Making of a Social Pragmatist.* Urbana: University of Illinois Press.

COOLEY, CHARLES H. 1902/1983. *Human Nature and the Social Order.* New Brunswick, NJ: Transaction Books.

——. 1907. "Social Consciousness" [proceedings of the first ASS meeting]. *American Journal of Sociology* 12(5): 675–87; comments by Edwin Earp, Alvan Tenney,

Charlotte Perkins Gilman, C. W. A. Veditz, James Minnick, and E. A. Ross, 687–94. Also published in *Papers and Proceedings; First Annual Meeting of the American Sociological Society*, 1:97–109. Chicago: University of Chicago Press.

———. 1918. *Social Process*. New York: C. Scribner's Sons.

———. 1920. "Reflections upon the Sociology of Herbert Spencer." *American Journal of Sociology* 26(2): 129–45.

———. 1927. *Life and the Student: Roadside Notes on Human Nature, Society and Letters*. New York: Knopf.

———. 1928a. "Case Study of Small Institutions as a Method of Research." *Publications of the American Sociological Society* 22: 124–25.

———. 1928b. "The Life-Study Method as Applied to Rural Social Research." In *Papers and Proceedings: Twenty-Third Annual Meeting of the American Sociological Society*, 248–54. Chicago: University of Chicago Press.

———. 1930a. "Case Study of Small Institutions as a Method of Research." In *Sociological Theory and Social Research: Being Selected Papers of Charles Horton Cooley*, 313–22. New York: H. Holt.

———. 1930b. "The Development of Sociology at Michigan." In *Sociological Theory and Social Research: Being Selected Papers of Charles Horton Cooley*, 3–14. New York: H. Holt.

———. Journals. Bentley Historical Library, University of Michigan.

COOLEY, CHARLES HORTON, ROBERT COOLEY ANGELL, and LOWELL JUILLIARD CARR. 1933. *Introductory Sociology*. New York: C. Scribner's Sons.

COOLEY, CHARLES H., JAMES Q. DEALEY, CHARLES A. ELLWOOD, H. P. FAIRCHILD, FRANKLIN H. GIDDINGS, EDWARD C. HAYES, EDWARD A. ROSS, ALBION W. SMALL, ULYSSES G. WEATHERLY, and JEROME DOWD. 1912. "Report of the Committee of Ten." *American Journal of Sociology* 17:620–36.

COONEY, MARK. 1998. *Warriors and Peacemakers: How Third Parties Shape Violence*. New York: New York University Press.

COOPER, FREDERICK, and RANDALL PACKARD. 1997. *International Development and the Social Sciences: Essays on the History and Politics of Knowledge*. Berkeley: University of California Press.

CORWIN, EDWARD S. 1931. "Social Planning under the Constitution." *American Political Science Review* 26:1–27.

COSER, LEWIS A. 1956. *The Functions of Social Conflict*. Glencoe, IL: Free Press.

———. 1971/1977. *Masters of Sociological Thought: Ideas in Historical and Social Context*. New York: Free Press; New York: Harcourt Brace Jovanovich.

———. 1974. "Review of *Explorations in Social Theory*." *Social Forces* 52:563–64.

———. 1984. *Refugee Scholars in America: Their Impact and Experiences*. New Haven: Yale University Press.

COSTIN, LELA. 1983. *Two Sisters for Social Justice: A Biography of Edith and Grace Abbott*. Urbana: University of Illinois.

COTKIN, GEORGE. 1990. *William James, Public Philosopher*. Baltimore: Johns Hopkins University Press.

———. 2003. *Existential America*. Baltimore: Johns Hopkins University Press.

COTTER, DAVID A., JOAN M. HERMSEN, and REEVE VANNEMAN. 1999. "Systems of Gender, Race, and Class Inequality." *Social Forces*, 78:433–60.

COVERDILL, JAMES E. 1988. "The Dual Economy and Sex Differences in Earnings." *Social Forces* 66:970–93.

COVERMAN, SHELLEY. 1983. "Gender Domestic Labor Time, and Wage Inequality." *American Sociological Review* 48:623–37.

COWAN, RUTH SCHWARTZ. 1983. *More Work for Mother*. New York: Basic Books.

COX, OLIVER C. 1948. *Caste, Class, and Race*. New York: Doubleday.

COZZENS, SUSAN. 1996. "Social Sciences: Shunned at the Frontier." In *Science the Endless Frontier, 1945–1995: Learning from the Past, Designing for the Future*. Tempe, AZ: Consortium for Science, Policy and Outcomes at Arizona State University.

CRANE, DIANA. 1972. *Invisible Colleges: Diffusion of Knowledge in Scientific Communities*. Chicago: University of Chicago Press.

CRAVENS, HAMILTON. 1971. "The Abandonment of Evolutionary Social Theory in America: The Impact of Academic Professionalization upon American Sociological Theory, 1890–1920." *American Studies* 12:5–20.

———. 1978. *The Triumph of Evolution*. Philadelphia: University of Pennsylvania Press.

CRAWFORD, ELISABETH T., and ALBERT D. BIDERMAN, eds. 1969. *Social Scientists and International Affair: A Case for a Sociology of Social Science*. New York: Wiley.

CRENSHAW, KIMBERLÉ W. 1991. "Mapping the Margins: Intersectionality, Identity Politics, and Violence against Women of Color." *Stanford Law Review* 43(6): 1241–99.

CRESSEY, DONALD R. 1969. *Theft of the Nation*. New York: Harper and Row.

CRESSEY, PAUL G. 1932. *The Taxi-Dance Hall: A Sociological Study in Commercialized Recreation and City Life*. Chicago: University of Chicago Press.

CRITCHLOW, DONALD T. 1985. *The Brookings Institution, 1916–1952*. De Kalb, IL: Northern Illinois University Press.

CROMPTON, ROSEMARY. 1984. *White-Collar Proletariat: Deskilling and Gender in Clerical Work*. London: Macmillan.

———. 1996. "The Fragmentation of Class Analysis." *British Journal of Sociology* 47:56–67.

CRONIN, B., H. SNYDER, and H. ATKINS. 1997. "Comparative Citation Rankings of Authors in Monographic and Journal Literature: a Study of Sociology." *Journal of Documentation* 53(3): 263–73.

CRONIN, THOMAS E., TANIA CRONIN, and MICHAEL E. MILAKOVICH. 1981. *Crime in the Streets*. Bloomington: Indiana University Press.

CROTHERS, CHARLES. 1987. *Robert K. Merton*. New York: Tavistock Publications.

CULLEN, FRANCIS T. 2002. "It's a Wonderful Life: Reflections on a Career in Progress." In *Lessons of Criminology*, ed. Gilbert Geis and Mary Dodge, 1–22. Cincinnati: Anderson Publishing.

CULYBA, REBECCA J., CAROL A. HEIMER, and JULEIGH COLEMAN PETTY. 2004.

"The Ethnographic Turn: Fact, Fashion, or Fiction?" *Qualitative Sociology* 27:365-89.

"Cumulative Index to *The American Journal of Sociology:* Volumes 1-70, 1895-1965." 1965. *American Journal of Sociology.*

CUSHING, FRANK HAMILTON. 1979. *Zuni: Selected Writings of Frank Hamilton Cushing.* Lincoln: University of Nebraska Press.

DAIPHA, PHAEDRA. 2001. "The Intellectual and Social Organization of ASA, 1990-1997: Exploring the Interface between the Discipline of Sociology and Its Practitioners." *American Sociologist* 32(3): 73-90.

DANIELS, ARLENE K. 1967. "The Low-Caste Stranger in Social Research." In *Ethics, Politics, and Social Research,* ed. Gideon Sjoberg, 267-96. Cambridge, MA: Schenkman.

———. 1975. "Feminist Perspectives in Sociological Research." *Sociological Inquiry* 45:340-80.

———. 1983. "Self-Deception and Self-Discovery in Fieldwork." *Qualitative Sociology* 6 (Fall): 195-214.

———. 1988. *Invisible Careers: Women Civic Leaders from the Volunteer World.* Chicago: University of Chicago Press.

———. 1994. "When We Were All Boys Together: Graduate School in the Fifties and Beyond." In *Gender and the Academic Experience,* ed. Kathryn P. Meadow Orlans and Ruth A. Wallace. Lincoln: University of Nebraska Press.

D'ANTONIO, WILLIAM V., and STEVE A TUCH. 1991. "Voting in Professional Associations: The Case of the American Sociological Association." *American Sociologist* 22:37-48.

DARNELL, R. 1990. *Edward Sapir.* Berkeley: University of California Press.

DAVENPORT, E., and H. SNYDER. 1995. "Who Cites Women? Who Do Women Cite? An Exploration of Gender and Scholarly Citation in Sociology." *Journal of Documentation* 51(4): 404-10.

DAVIES, SCOTT. 1995. "Leaps of Faith: Shifting Currents in Critical Sociology of Education." *American Journal of Sociology* 100:1448-78.

DAVIS, ALLISON, BURLEIGH B. GARDNER, and MARY R. GARDNER, directed by W. LLOYD WARNER. 1941. *Deep South: A Social Anthropological Study of Caste and Class.* Chicago: University of Chicago Press.

DAVIS, JEROME. 1940. "The Sociologist and Social Action." *American Sociological Review* 5:171-76.

DAVIS, KINGSLEY. 1945. "Willard Walter Waller." *American Sociological Review* 10:697-98.

———. 1959. "The Myth of Functional Analysis as a Special Method in Sociology and Anthropology." *American Sociological Review* 24:757-72.

———. 1960. "The Myth of Functional Analysis as a Special Method in Sociology and Anthropology." *American Sociological Review* 36:321-26.

DAVIS, KINGSLEY, and WILBERT E. MOORE. 1944. "Some Principles of Stratification." *American Sociological Review* 10(2): 242-49.

DAWSON, MICHAEL C. 2001. *Black Visions: The Roots of Contemporary African-American Political Ideologies.* Chicago: University of Chicago Press.

DEACON, DESLEY. 1989. *Managing Gender: The State, the New Middle Class, and Women Workers, 1830–193.* New York: Oxford University Press.

———. 1997a. "Brave New Sociology? Elsie Clews Parsons and Me." In *Feminist Sociology: Life Histories of a Movement,* ed. Barbara Laslett and Barrie Thorne, 165–93. New Brunswick, NJ: Rutgers University Press.

———. 1997b. *Elsie Clews Parsons: Inventing the Modern.* Chicago: University of Chicago Press.

DEALEY, JAMES QUAYLE. 1910. "The Teaching of Sociology." *American Journal of Sociology* 15(5): 657–71.

———. 1926. "Lester Frank Ward." In *American Masters of Social Science,* ed. Howard W. Odum, 61–98. New York: Henry Holt.

DEARDORFF, NEVA R. 1932. "The Relation of Applied Sociology to Social Work." *Social Forces* 11:190–93.

DEAUX, KAY. 1976. *The Behavior of Women and Men.* Monterey, CA: Brooks/Cole Publishing.

DEEGAN, MARY JO. 1979. "Sociology at Nebraska: 1884–1929." *Journal of the History of Sociology* 1(2): 40–41.

———. 1983. "Sociology at Wellesley College: 1900–1919." *Journal of the History of Sociology* 5(1): 91.

———. 1988/1990. *Jane Addams and the Men of the Chicago School, 1892–1913.* New Brunswick, NJ.: Transaction Books.

———. 1991. *Women in Sociology: A Bio-Bibliographical Sourcebook.* New York: Greenwood Press.

———. 1995. "The Second Sex and the Second Chicago School: Women's Accounts, Knowledge, and Work, 1945–1960." In *A Second Chicago School? The Development of a Postwar American Sociology,* ed. Gary Alan Fine, 322–64. Chicago: University of Chicago Press.

———. 1996. "'Dear Love, Dear Love': Feminist Pragmatism and the Chicago Female World of Love and Ritual." *Gender and Society* 10:590–607.

———. 2002. *Race, Hull-House, and the University of Chicago: A New Conscience against Ancient Evils.* Westport, CT: Praeger.

———. 2005. "Women, African Americans, and the ASA, 1905–2005." In *Diverse Histories of American Sociology* ed. Anthony Blasi. Leiden, Netherlands: Brill.

DEFLEM, MATHIEU, ed. 2004a. "The Proper Role of Sociology in the World at Large—Letter." *Chronicle of Higher Education* (October 1): 17.

———. 2004b. *Terrorism and Counter-Terrorism: Criminological Perspectives.* Oxford: Elsevier Science

———. 2005. "Crime and Deviance at Social Forces." Crime and Juvenile Delinquency Division News. *SSSP Newsletter* (Winter): 2.

DEFLEUR, MELVIN L., and OTTO N. LARSEN. 1958. *The Flow of Information: An Experiment in Mass Communication.* New York: Harper.

DELACAMPAGNE, CHRISTIAN. 1999. *A History of Philosophy in the Twentieth Century.* Trans. M. E. DeBevoise. Baltimore: Johns Hopkins University Press.

DELAMONT, SARA. 1989. "Citation and Social Mobility Research." *Sociological Review* 37(2): 332-37.

———. 2003. *Feminist Sociology.* Thousand Oaks, CA: Sage.

DELLA PORTA, DONATELLA, and HANSPETER KRIESI, eds. 1999. *Social Movements in a Globalising World.* New York: St. Martins.

DEMERATH III, N. J. OTTO N. LARSEN, and KARL F. SCHUESSLER, eds. 1975. *Social Policy and Sociology.* New York: Academic Press.

DENNIS, RUTLEDGE M. 1996. "Continuities and Discontinuities in the Social and Political Thought of W. E. B. DuBois." *Research in Race and Ethnic Relations* 9:3-23.

———. 2003. "W. E. B. DuBois's Concept of Double Consciousness." In *Race and Ethnicity: Comparative and Theoretical Approaches,* ed. John Stone and Rutledge Dennis. Cambridge, MA: Blackwell Publishing.

DENTON, NANCY A., and DOUGLAS S. MASSEY. 1993. *American Apartheid.* Cambridge: Harvard University Press.

DENZIN, NORMAN K. 1970. *The Research Act: A Theoretical Introduction to Sociological Methods.* Chicago: Aldine Publishing.

———. 1991. *Hollywood Shot by Shot: Alcoholism in American Cinema.* New York: Aldine de Gruyter.

———. 1992. *Symbolic Interactionism and Cultural Studies: The Politics of Interpretation.* Oxford: Blackwell.

DENZIN, NORMAN K., and YVONNA S. LINCOLN. 1994. "Introduction: Entering the Field of Qualitative Research." In *Handbook of Qualitative Research,* ed. Norman K. Denzin and Yvonna S. Lincoln, 1-17. London: Sage.

DERLUGUIAN, GEORGI. 2005. *Bourdieu's Secret Admirer in the Caucasus.* Chicago: University of Chicago Press.

DEUTSCH, STEVEN E. 1971. Review of *The Coming Crisis of Western Sociology* by Alvin Gouldner. *American Sociological Review* 36:321-26.

DEVAULT, MARJORIE L. 1996. "Talking Back to Sociology: Distinctive Contributions of Feminist Methodology." *Annual Review of Sociology* 22:29-50.

———. 1997. "Personal Writing in Social Research: Issues of Production and Interpretation." In *Reflexivity and Voice,* ed. Rosanna Hertz, 216-28. Thousand Oaks, CA: Sage.

DEWEY, JOHN. 1910/1978. *How We Think.* In *The Middle Works of John Dewey, 1899-1924,* vol. 6. Carbondale: Southern Illinois University Press.

———. 1920/1982. *Reconstruction in Philosophy.* New York: Henry Holt. Also published in *The Middle Works of John Dewey, 1899-1924,* vol. 12. Carbondale, IL: Southern Illinois University Press.

———. 1922/1983. *Human Nature and Conduct.* In *The Middle Works of John Dewey, 1899-1924,* vol. 14. Carbondale: Southern Illinois University Press.

———. 1927/1984. *The Public and Its Problems.* In *The Later Works of John Dewey, 1925-1953,* vol. 2. Carbondale: Southern Illinois University Press.

DIBBLE, VERNON K. 1975. *The Legacy of Albion Small*. Chicago: University of Chicago Press

DICKERSON, BETTE. 2005. "Blooming in the Noise of the Whirlwind." In *Diverse Histories of American Sociology* ed. Anthony Blasi. Leiden, Netherlands: Brill.

DICKSTEIN, MORRIS. 1998. "Introduction: Pragmatism Then and Now." In *The Revival of Pragmatism: New Essays on Social Thought, Law, and Culture*, ed. M. Dickstein, 1–18. Durham, NC: Duke University Press.

DILL, BONNIE THORNTON. 1983. "Race, Class and Gender: Prospects for an All-Inclusive Sisterhood." *Feminist Studies* 9(1): 131–50.

———. 2002. "Work at the Intersections of Race, Gender, Ethnicity, and Other Dimensions of Difference in Higher Education." *Connections: Newsletter of the Consortium on Race, Gender, and Ethnicity* (University of Maryland) (Fall): 5–7.

DIMAGGIO, PAUL J., and WALTER W. POWELL. 1983. "The Iron Cage Revisited: Institutional Isomorphism and Collective Rationality in Organizational Fields." *American Sociological Review* 48(2): 147–60.

———. 1991. Introduction to *The New Institutionalism in Organizational Analysis*, ed. W. Powell and P. DiMaggio, 1–38. Chicago: University of Chicago Press.

DJILAS, MILOVAN. 1957. *The New Class*. New York: Praeger.

DODD, STUART CARTER. 1942. *Dimensions of Society: A Quantitative Systematics for the Social Sciences*. New York: Macmillan.

DOLLARD, JOHN. 1935. *Criteria for the Life History, with Analyses of Six Notable Documents*. New Haven: Yale University Press.

DONOVAN, FRANCES R. 1929. *The Saleslady*. Chicago: University of Chicago Press.

DORFMAN, JOSEPH. 1959. *The Economic Mind in American Civilization*, vol. 5: 1918–1933. New York: Viking.

DOSKOW, MINNA. 1999. Introduction to *Charlotte Perkins Gilman's Utopian Novels: "Moving the Mountain," "Herland," and "With Her in Ourland."* Madison, NJ: Fairleigh Dickinson University Press.

DOUGLAS, JACK D., ed. 1970. *Understanding Everyday Life: Toward the Reconstruction of Sociological Knowledge*. Chicago: Aldine.

———. 1977. "Existential Sociology." In *Existential Sociology*, ed. J. D. Douglas and J. M. Johnson, 3–73. Cambridge: Cambridge University Press.

DOWDY, ERIC. 1994. "Federal Funding and Its Effect on Criminological Research: Emphasizing Individualistic Explanations for Criminal Behavior." *American Sociologist* 25:77–89.

DRAKE, ST. CLAIR. 1987–90. *Black Folk Here and There*. 2 vols. Los Angeles: Center for Afro-American Studies, University of California.

DRAKE, ST. CLAIR, and HORACE R. CAYTON. 1945. *Black Metropolis: A Study of Negro Life in a Northern City*. New York: Harcourt, Brace and World.

DRAPKIN, ISRAEL. 1983. "Criminology: Intellectual History." In *Encyclopedia of Crime and Justice*, ed. Sanford H. Kadish, 547–56. New York: Free Press.

DREEBEN, ROBERT. 1970. *The Nature of Teaching: Schools and the Work of Teachers*. Glenview, IL: Scott, Foresman.

———. 1994. "The Sociology of Education: Its Development in the United States." *Research in Sociology of Education and Socialization* 10:7-52.

DUBOIS, W. E. B. 1896. *The Suppression of the African Slave-Trade to the United States of America, 1638-1870.* New York: Longmans, Green.

———. 1898a. "The Negroes of Farmville, Virginia: A Social Study." *Bulletin of the Department of Labor* (14): 1-38. Available through the Electronic Text Center, University of Virginia Library, Washington, DC.

———. 1898b. "The Study of the Negro Problems." In *Annals of the American Academy of Political and Social Science*, vol. 11. New York: Kraus Reprint.

———. 1899/1967/1973/1996 [centennial ed.]. *The Philadelphia Negro: A Social Study/ Together with a Special Report on Domestic Service by Isabel Eaton.* Philadelphia: Published for the University; New York: Schocken; Millwood, NY: Kraus-Thomson Organization; Philadelphia: University of Pennsylvania Press.

———. 1900. *The New World.* Vol. 9. Boston: Houghton, Mifflin.

———. 1903. *The Souls of Black Folk.* Chicago: A. C. McClurg and Co.

———. 1904. "The Atlanta Conferences." In *The Voice of the Negro*, 1:85-90. New York: Negro Universities Press.

———. 1907. "The Value of Agitation." In *The Voice of the Negro*, 4:109-10. New York: Negro Universities Press.

———. 1915. "Woman Suffrage." *Crisis* 11(1): 29-30. Reprint. New York: Arno Press.

———. 1920. "The Hands of Ethiopia." In *Darkwater*, 56-74. New York: Schocken Books.

———. 1933. "Marxism and the Negro Problem." *Crisis.* 40(3): 101-16. Reprint. New York: Arno Press.

———. 1934. "Segregation." *Crisis* (January): 20.

———. 1935/1939/1977. *Black Reconstruction in America, 1860-1880: An Essay toward a History of the Part which Black Folk Played in the Attempt to Reconstruct Democracy in America, 1860-1880.* New York: Henry Holt; New York: Athenaeum.

———. 1940. *Dusk of Dawn: An Essay toward an Autobiography of a Race Concept.* New York: Harcourt, Brace.

———. 1945. *Color and Democracy.* New York: Harcourt, Brace.

———. 1968. *The Autobiography of W. E. B. DuBois: A Soliloquy on Viewing My Life from the Last Decade of Its First Century.* New York: International Publishers.

———. 1970. *The Gift of Black Folk.* New York: Washington Square Press.

———. 1975. *Black Folk: Then and Now.* Millwood, NY: Kraus-Thomson Organization.

———. 1986. "Conservation of Races." In *Pamphlets and Leaflets*, compiled and ed. Herbert Aptheker. White Plains, NY: Kraus-Thomson Organization Limited.

———. 1995. "The African Roots of the War" (1915). In *W. E. B. Du Bois: A Reader*, ed. David Levering Lewis. New York: Henry Holt.

———. 2000. "Sociology Hesitant: Thinking with W. E. B. DuBois." Special issue, ed. Ronald A. T. Judy. *Boundary 2* 27(3): 37-44.

DUDZIAK, MARY L. 2000. *Cold War Civil Rights: Race and the Image of American Democracy.* Princeton: Princeton University Press.

DUNCAN, H. G., and WINNIE LEACH DUNCAN. 1933. "Shifts in Interests of American Sociologists." *Social Forces* 12:209-12.

DUNCAN, JOSEPH W., and WILLIAM C. SHELTON. 1978. *Revolution in United States Government Statistics, 1926-1976.* Washington, DC: Department of Commerce.

DUNCAN, OTIS DUDLEY. 1961. "A Socioeconomic Index for All Occupations." In *Occupations and Social Status,* ed. A. J. Reiss, 109-38. New York: Free Press.

———. 1966. "Path Analysis: Sociological Examples." *American Journal of Sociology* 72:1-16.

DUNEIER, MITCHELL. 1999. *Sidewalk.* New York: Farrar, Straus and Giroux.

DUNNING, WILLIAM ARCHIBALD. 1965. *Essays on the Civil War and Reconstruction.* New York: Harper and Row.

DURKHEIM, ÉMILE. 1893/1947. *The Division of Labor in Society.* Trans. George Simpson. Glencoe, IL: Free Press.

———. 1895/1964. *The Rules of Sociological Method.* 8th ed. Ed. George E. E. Catlin. Trans. Sarah A. Solovay and John H. Mueller. New York: Free Press.

———. 1897/1951. *Suicide: A Study in Sociology.* Ed. George Simpson. Trans. John A. Spaulding and George Simpson. Glencoe, IL: Free Press.

———. 1898a. *L'Année sociologique* (1896-97). Vol. 1. Paris: Félix Alcan.

———. 1898b. "Minor Editorials" [a letter in French]. *American Journal of Sociology* 3(6): 848-49.

———. 1956. *Education and Sociology.* Trans. Sherwood D. Fox. Glencoe, IL: Free Press.

———. 1961. *Moral Education: A Study in the Theory and Application of the Sociology of Education.* Trans. Everett K. Wilson and Herman Schnurer. New York: Free Press.

———. 1977. *Evolution of Educational Thought: Lectures on the Formation and Development of Secondary Education in France.* English translation. London: Routledge and Kegan Paul.

DUSTER, TROY. 1990. *Backdoor to Eugenics.* New York: Routledge.

———. 2001. "The Sociology of Science and the Revolution in Molecular Biology." In *The Blackwell Companion to Sociology,* ed. J. R. Blau. London: Blackwell.

DWORKIN, ANDREA. 1981. *Pornography: Men Possessing Women.* New York: Perigee Books.

EAGLETON, TERRY. 2003. *After Theory.* New York: Basic Books.

EASTMAN, CRYSTAL. 1910. "Work-Accidents and Employers' Liability." *Survey* (September 3): 788-94.

EBNER, JOHANNA. 2005. "Dalton Conley Becomes First Sociologist to Receive the National Science Board's Prestigious Alan T. Waterman Award." *Footnotes* 33(5): 1.

EDER, DONNA, CATHERINE COLLEEN EVANS, and STEPHEN PARKER. 1995. *School Talk: Gender and Adolescent Culture.* New Brunswick, NJ: Rutgers University Press.

EDIN, KATHRYN, and LAURA LEIN. 1997. *Making Ends Meet: How Single Mothers Survive Welfare and Low-Wage Work.* New York: Russell Sage Foundation.

EGLITIS, DAINA STUKULS. 2002. *Imagining the Nation: History, Modernity, and Revolution in Latvia.* State College: Pennsylvania State University Press.

EHRENREICH, JOHN H. 1985. *The Altruistic Imagination: A History of Social Work and Social Policy in the United States.* Ithaca, NY: Cornell University Press.

EISENSTADT, S. N. (with M. CURELARU). 1976. *The Form of Sociology: Paradigms and Crises.* New York: Wiley.

ELDER, GLEN H., JR. 1998. "The Life Course as Developmental Theory." *Child Development* 69(1): 1–12.

ELIASOPH, NINA. 1998. *Avoiding Politics: How Americans Produce Apathy in Everyday Life.* Cambridge: Cambridge University Press.

ELIOT, THOMAS D. 1924. "Sociology as a Prevocational Subject: The Verdict of Sixty Social Workers." *American Journal of Sociology* 29:726–46.

———. 1934. Contribution to "Questions for Sociology: An Informal Round Table Symposium." *Social Forces* 13:181–82.

ELLIOTT, ANTHONY. 2005. "Psychoanalysis and the Theory of the Subject." In *The Politics of Method in the Human Sciences: Positivism and Its Epistemological Others,* ed. George Steinmetz, 427–51. Durham, NC: Duke University Press.

ELLIOTT, DELBERT S. 1989. *Multiple Problem Youth: Delinquency, Substance Use, and Mental Health Problems.* New York: Springer-Verlag.

ELLIOTT, DELBERT S., and SUZANNE S. AGETON. 1980. "Reconciling Differences in Estimates of Delinquency." *American Sociological Review* 45(1): 95–110.

ELLIOTT, DELBERT S., SUZANNE S. AGETON, DAVID HUIZINGA, BRIAN A. KNOWLES, and RACHELLE J. CANTER. 1983. *The Prevalence and Incidence of Delinquent Behavior: 1976–1980.* Boulder, CO: Behavioral Research Institute.

ELLIS, CAROLYN. 1995. *Final Negotiations: A Story of Love, Loss, and Chronic Illness.* Philadelphia: Temple University Press.

ELLIS, CAROLYN, and ARTHUR P. BOCHNER, eds. 1996. *Composing Ethnography: Alternative Forms of Qualitative Writing.* Walnut Creek, CA: AltaMira.

ELLISON, RALPH. 1964. *Shadow and Act.* New York: Signet.

ELLWOOD, CHARLES A. 1897. "The LePlay Method of Social Observation." *American Journal of Sociology* 2 (March): 662–79.

———. 1899a. "Prolegomena to Social Psychology I: The Need of the Study of Social Psychology." *American Journal of Sociology* 4(5): 656–65.

———. 1899b. "Prolegomena to Social Psychology II: The Fundamental Fact in Social Psychology." *American Journal of Sociology* 5(1): 807–822.

———. 1899c. "Prolegomena to Social Psychology III: The Nature and Task of Social Psychology." *American Journal of Sociology* 5(2): 98–109.

———. 1899d. "Prolegomena to Social Psychology IV: The Concept of the Social Mind." *American Journal of Sociology* 5(2): 220–27.

———. 1902. "Aristotle as a Sociologist." *Annals of the American Academy of Political Science* 19. http://socserv2.socsci.mcmaster.ca/~econ/ugcm/3ll3/aristotle/ellwood .html (accessed 09/20/04).

———. 1903. "Public Relief and Private Charity in England." *University of Missouri Studies* 2(2). Reprinted in *Modern Methods of Charity: An Account of the Systems of Relief, Public and Private, in the Principle Countries Having Modern Methods,* ed. Charles Henderson. New York: Macmillan, 1904.

———. 1904a. *A Bulletin on the Condition of the County Almshouses of Missouri*. Columbia: University of Missouri Department of Sociology. http://mulibraries.missouri.edu/specialcollections/specmu.htm (accessed 09/20/04).

———. 1904b. *A Bulletin on the Condition of the County Jails of Missouri*. Columbia: University of Missouri Department of Sociology. http://mulibraries.missouri.edu/specialcollections/specmu.htm (accessed 09/20/04).

———. 1907a. "How Should Sociology Be Taught as a College or University Subject?" [proceedings of the first ASS meeting]. *American Journal of Sociology* 12(5): 588–96; discussion by William Graham Sumner, 596–99; Morgan Davenport, 600–602; Jeffrey Brackett, 602–3; Robert Chapin, 603–4; and Elbert Cutler, 604–6.

———. 1907b. "Sociology: Its Problems and Its Relations" ["This paper constitutes the first four chapters of a text in sociology which Professor Ellwood has in preparation"]. *American Journal of Sociology* 13(3): 300–348.

———. 1908. Review of *The Negro Races: A Sociological Study*, vol. 1, by Jerome Dowd. *American Journal of Sociology* 13(6): 855–58.

———. 1909. "The Science of Sociology: A Reply [to Henry Jones Ford]." *American Journal of Sociology* 15(1): 105–10.

———. 1910. *Sociology and Modern Social Problems*. New York and Cincinnati: American Book Company. http://www.gutenberg.net/etext/6568 (accessed 09/20/04).

———. 1911. "Marx's Economic Determinism in the Light of Modern Psychology." *American Journal of Sociology* 17:35–46.

———. 1915. *The Social Problem: A Constructive Analysis*. New York: Macmillan.

———. 1917. "The Present Condition of the Social Sciences." *Science* 46 (November 16): 469–73.

———. 1919/1922. *The Social Problem: A Reconstructive Analysis*. Rev. ed. New York: Macmillan.

———. 1922. *The Reconstruction of Religion: A Sociological View*. New York: Macmillan.

———. 1925. *The Psychology of Human Society: An Introduction to Sociological Theory*. New York: D. Appleton.

———. 1927. "What Is Educational Sociology?" *Journal of Educational Sociology* 1:25–30.

———. 1929. *Man's Social Destiny in the Light of Science*. Nashville: Cokesbury Press.

———. 1933a. "Emasculated Sociologies." *Sociology and Social Research* 17:219–29.

———. 1933b. *Methods in Sociology: A Critical Study*. Durham, NC: Duke University Press.

———. 1934. Contribution to "Questions for Sociology: An Informal Round Table Symposium." *Social Forces* 13:187–88.

———. 1938. *A History of Social Philosophy*. New York: Prentice Hall.

———. 1940. *The World's Need of Christ*. New York: Abingdon-Cokesbury Press.

———. 1943. *Sociology, Principles and Problems*. New York: American Book Company.

———. 1944. "Valedictory." *American Sociologist* 6(3): n.p.

———. N.d.a. "A History of the Department of Sociology in the University of Missouri." L. L. Bernard Papers, box 1, folder 10. University of Chicago Library Special Collections.

———. N.d.b. "Sociological Life History of Charles Ellwood." L. L. Bernard Papers, box 2, folder 2. University of Chicago Library Special Collections.

———. Papers. Duke University Archives.

———. Scrapbook. Duke University Archives.

ELLWOOD, CHARLES A., and HOWARD E. JENSEN. 1912/1915. *Sociology and Its Psychological Aspects*. Rev. ed. New York: D. Appleton.

———. 1934. Contribution to "Questions for Sociology: An Informal Round Table Symposium." *Social Forces* 13:187–88.

ELSHTAIN, JEAN BETHKE. 2002. *Jane Addams and the Dream of American Democracy*. New York: Basic Books.

ELWANG, WILLIAM WILSON. 1904. *The Negroes of Columbia, Missouri: A Concrete Study of the Race Problem*. Columbia: Department of Sociology, University of Missouri.

EMERSON, ROBERT M., ed. 1983/2001. *Contemporary Field Research: A Collection of Readings*. Prospect Heights, IL: Waveland.

———. 2004. Introduction to "Being Here and Being There: Fieldwork Encounters and Ethnographic Discoveries." *Annals of the American Academy of Political and Social Science* 595:8–13.

EMERSON, ROBERT M., RACHEL I. FRETZ, and LINDA SHAW. 1995. *Writing Ethnographic Fieldnotes*. Chicago: University of Chicago Press.

EMIRBAYER, MUSTAFA, and ANN MISCHE. 1998. "What Is Agency?" *American Journal of Sociology* 103:962–1023.

ENGELS, FREDRICH. 1887. *The Conditions of the Working Class in England in 1844*. Trans. Florence Kelley. New York: L. Weiss. Originally published in German in 1846.

ENGLAND, PAULA. 1979. "Women and Occupational Prestige: A Case of Vacuous Sex Equality." *Signs* 5:252–65.

———. 1992a. *Comparable Worth: Theories and Evidence*. New York: Aldine de Gruyter.

———. 1992b. "From Status Attainment to Segregation and Devaluation." *Contemporary Sociology* 21:643–47.

ENLOE, CYNTHIA H. 1989. *Bananas, Beaches, and Bases*. London: Pandora.

EPSTEIN, CYNTHIA FUCHS. 1993. *Women in Law*. Urbana: University of Illinois Press.

ERIKSON, KAI T. 1966. *Wayward Puritans: A Study in the Sociology of Deviance*. New York: Wiley.

ESPER, ERWIN. 1967. "Max Meyer in America." *Journal of the History of the Behavioral Sciences* 3(2): 107–31.

ESPIRITU, Y. L. 1997. *Asian American Women and Men*. Thousand Oaks, CA: Sage.

EVANS, PETER. 1979. *Dependent Development: The Alliance of Multinational State and Local Capital in Brazil*. Princeton: Princeton University Press.

———. 1995. *Embedded Autonomy: States and Industrial Transformation*. Princeton: Princeton University Press.

EVANS, RICHARD. 1986–87. "Sociological Journals and the 'Decline' of Chicago Sociology: 1929–1945." *History of Sociology* 6(2), 7(1), and 7(2) [combined issue]: 109–30.

EYAL, GIL, IVAN SZELENYI, and ELEANOR TOWNSLEY. 2001. "The Utopia of Post-socialist Theory and the Ironic View of History in Neoclassical Sociology." *American Journal of Sociology* 106:1121–28.

FABIAN, JOHANNES. 1983. *Time and the Other: How Anthropology Makes Its Object.* New York: Columbia University Press.

FAIRCHILD, HENRY PRATT. 1934. Contribution to "Questions for Sociology: An Informal Round Table Symposium." *Social Forces* 13:179–81.

———. 1936. "Is Accurate Social Planning Possible: Discussion." *American Sociological Review* 1:25–28.

———. 1937. "Business as an Institution." *American Sociological Review* 2:1–8.

FANON, FRANZ. 1976. *The Wretched of the Earth.* London: Penguin.

FARIS, ELLSWORTH. 1934. "Too Many PhDs?" *American Journal of Sociology* 39:509–12.

———. 1938. "The Promise of Sociology." *American Sociological Review* 3:1–12.

FARIS, ROBERT E. LEE. 1967/1970. *Chicago Sociology, 1920–1932.* San Francisco: Chandler; Chicago: University of Chicago Press.

FARR, JAMES, and RAYMOND SEIDELMAN. 1993. Introduction to *Discipline and History: Political Science in the United States,* ed. James Farr and Raymond Seidelman, 107–12. Ann Arbor: University of Michigan Press.

FARRINGTON, DAVID P. 2003. "Developmental and Life-Course Criminology: Key Theoretical and Empirical Issues—The 2002 Sutherland Award Address." *Criminology* 41(2): 221–55.

FAUSTO-STERLING, ANNE. 2000. *Sexing the Body: Gender Politics and the Construction of Sexuality.* New York: Basic Books.

———. 2004. "Bare Bones of Sex." Lecture given at the University of Wisconsin, Madison. February 23.

FEAGIN, JOE R. 2001. "Social Justice and Sociology: Agendas for the Twenty-First Century: Presidential Address." *American Sociological Review* 66(1): 1–20.

FEAGIN, JOE R., and HERNÁN VERA. 2001. *Liberation Sociology.* Boulder, CO: Westview Press.

FEATHERSTONE, MIKE. 1995. *Undoing Culture: Globalization, Postmodernism and Identity.* London: Sage.

FEFFER, ANDREW. 1993. *The Chicago Pragmatists and American Progressivism.* Ithaca, NY: Cornell University Press.

FEIN, HELEN. 1979. *Accounting for Genocide: National Responses and Jewish Victimization during the Holocaust.* New York: Free Press.

———. 1993. *Genocide: A Sociological Perspective.* London: Sage.

FELDBERG, R. L., and E. N. GLENN. 1979. "Male and Female: Job versus Gender Models in the Sociology of Work." *Social Problem* 26:525–36.

FELSON, RICHARD B. 1993. "Predatory and Dispute-Related Violence: A Social Interactionist Approach." In *Routine Activity and Rational Choice: Advances in Criminological Theory,* ed. Ronald V. Clarke and Marcus Felson, 103–25. New Brunswick, NJ: Transaction.

FERBER, ABBY L. 1998. *White Man Falling: Race, Gender, and White Supremacy.* Lanham, MD: Rowman and Littlefield.

FERBER, MARIANNE. 1986. "Citations: Are They an Objective Measure of Scholarly Merit?" *Signs* 11(2): 381–89.

———. 1988. "Citations and Networking." *Gender and Society* 2(1): 82–89.

FERGUSON, ANN. 2000. *Bad Boys: Public Schools in the Making of Black Masculinity.* Ann Arbor: University of Michigan Press.

FERREE, MYRA MARX. 1976. "Working Class Jobs: Paid Work and Housework as Sources of Satisfaction." *Social Problems,* 23:431–41.

———. 1983. "Housework: Rethinking the Costs and Benefits." In *Families, Politics, and Public Policy,* ed. Irene Diamond. New York: Longman.

———. 1984. "Class, Housework, and Happiness." *Sex Roles* 11:1057–74.

———. 1990. "Beyond Separate Spheres: Feminism and Family Research." *Journal of Marriage and the Family* 52:866–84.

FERREE, MYRA MARX, WILLIAM A. GAMSON, JURGEN GERHARDS, and DIETER RUCHT. 2002. *Shaping Abortion Discourse.* New York: Cambridge University Press.

FERREE, MYRA MARX, and ELAINE J. HALL. 1996. "Rethinking Stratification from a Feminist Perspective: Gender, Race, and Class in Mainstream Textbooks." *American Sociological Review* 61:929–50.

FERREE, MYRA MARX, and BETH HESS. 2000. *Controversy and Coalition: The New Feminist Movement across Three Decades of Change.* New York: Routledge.

FIAMINGO, G. 1895. "Sociology in Italy: The Sociological Tendency of Today." *American Journal of Sociology* 1(3): 334–52.

FIELD, OLIVER P. 1931. "State Constitutional Law in 1930–31." *American Political Science Review* 25: 650–70.

FILLOUX, JEAN-CLAUDE. 1993. "Emile Durkheim." *PROSPECTS: The Quarterly Review of Comparative Education* 23:303–20.

FINE, GARY ALAN. 1990. "Symbolic Interactionism in the Post-Blumerian Age." In *Frontiers of Social Theory: The New Syntheses,* ed. G. Ritzer, 117–57. New York: Columbia University Press.

———. 1995. *A Second Chicago School? The Development of a Postwar American Sociology.* Chicago: University of Chicago Press.

FINE, MICHELLE. 1999. *Disruptive Voices.* Ann Arbor: University of Michigan Press.

FINE, WILLIAM F. 1979. *Progressive Evolutionism and American Sociology, 1890–1920.* Ann Arbor, MI: UMI Research Press.

FINK, ARTHUR E. 1941. "Social Problems of Social Work Education from the Point of View of the State University." *Social Forces* 20:54–64.

FINLAY, BARBARA. 1999. "Lester Frank Ward as a Sociologist of Gender: A New Look at His Sociological Work." *Gender and Society* 13:251–65.

FINNEY, ROSS L. 1927. "Divergent Views of Educational Sociology." *Journal of Educational Sociology* 1:100–104.

FIREBAUGH, GLENN. 2001. "The *ASR* Review Process: Reply to Risman and Udry." *American Sociological Review* 66(4): 619–21.

FISCHER, CLAUDE S., MICHAEL HOUT, MARTÍN SÁNCHEZ JANKOWSKI, SAMUEL R. LUCAS, ANN SWIDLER, and KIM VOS. 1996. *Inequality by Design: Cracking the Bell Curve Myth.* Princeton: Princeton University Press.

FISH, VIRGINIA KEMP. 1981. "Annie Marion MacLean: A Neglected Part of the Chicago School." *Journal of the History of Sociology* 3: 43–62.

———. 1985. "Hull House: Pioneer in Urban Research during Its Creative Years." *Journal of the History of Sociology* 6(1): 33–54.

FISHER, DONALD. 1983. "The Role of Philanthropic Foundations in the Reproduction and Production of Hegemony: Rockefeller Foundations and the Social Sciences." *Sociology* 17(2): 206–33.

———. 1984. "Philanthropic Foundations and the Social Sciences: A Response to Martin Bulmer." *Sociology* 18(4): 580–87.

———. 1993. *Fundamental Development of the Social Sciences: Rockefeller Philanthropy and the United States Social Science Research Council.* Ann Arbor: University of Michigan Press.

FITZHUGH, GEORGE. 1854. *Sociology for the South, or, the Failure of Free Society.* Richmond: A. Morris.

FITZPATRICK, ELLEN. 1990. *Endless Crusade: Women Social Scientists and Progressive Reform.* New York: Oxford University Press.

FLACKS, DICK. 1991. "The Sociology Liberation Movement: Some Legacies and Lessons." In *Radical Sociologists and the Movement: Experiences, Lessons, and Legacies,* ed. Martin Oppenheimer, Martin J. Murray, and Rhonda F. Levine, 17–27. Philadelphia: Temple University Press.

FLACKS, RICHARD, and GERALD TURKEL. 1978. "Radical Sociology: The Emergence of Neo-Marxian Perspectives in U.S. Sociology." *Annual Review of Sociology* 4:193–238.

FLEXNER, ELEANOR. 1959. *Century of Struggle.* Cambridge: Harvard University Press.

FLIGSTEIN, NEIL. 2001. *The Architecture of Markets: An Economic Sociology of Capitalist Societies.* Princeton: Princeton University Press.

FLOWER, ELIZABETH, and MURRAY G. MURPHEY. 1977. *A History of Philosophy in America.* Vol. 1. New York: Capricorn.

FLYNN, G. Q. 1993. *The Draft, 1940–1973.* Lawrence: University Press of Kansas.

FONER, ERIC. 1995. *Free Soil, Free Labor, Free Men: The Ideology of the Republican Party before the Civil War.* Rev. ed. New York: Oxford University Press.

FONER, ERIC, and OLIVIA MAHONEY. 1995. *America's Reconstruction: People and Politics after Civil War.* New York: Harper Perennial.

FORD, HENRY JONES. 1909a. "The Claims of Sociology Examined." *American Journal of Sociology* 15(2): 244–59.

———. 1909b. "The Pretensions of Sociology." *American Journal of Sociology* 15(1): 96–104. (Response by Charles Ellwood in the pages that follow.)

FORD, JOSEPH B., MICHAEL P. RICHARD, and PALMER C. TALBUTT, eds. 1996. *Sorokin and Civilization: A Centennial Assessment.* New Brunswick, NJ: Transaction Publishers.

FOSDICK, RAYMOND. 1920. *American Police Systems.* New York: Century.

FOUCAULT, MICHEL. 1979. *Discipline and Punish: The Birth of the Prison.* New York: Schocken.

———. 1980. *Power/Knowledge: Selected Interviews and Other Writings, 1972–1977.* Ed. Colin Gordon. New York: Pantheon.

FOX, CHRISTOPHER, ROY PORTER, and ROBERT WOKLER, eds. 1995. *Inventing Human Science: Eighteenth-Century Domains.* Berkeley: University of California Press.

FOX, DANIEL M. 1967. *The Discovery of Abundance: Simon N. Patten and the Transformation of Social Theory.* Ithaca, NY: Cornell University Press for the American Historical Association.

FOX, F. 1975. *Madison Avenue Goes to War: The Strange Military Career of American Advertising, 1941–45.* Provo, UT: Brigham Young University.

FOX, RICHARD W. 1985. *Reinhold Niebuhr: A Biography.* New York: Pantheon Books.

FRANKLIN, DONNA. 1986. "Mary Richmond and Jane Addams: From Moral Certainty to Rational Inquiry in Social Work Practice." *Social Service Review* (December): 504–25.

FRANTILLA, ANNE. 1998. *Social Science in the Public Interest: A Fiftieth-Year History of the Institute for Social Research.* Bulletin 45 (September). Ann Arbor, MI: Bentley Historical Library.

FRASER, NANCY. 1998. "Another Pragmatism: Alain Locke, Critical 'Race' Theory, and the Politics of Culture." In *The Revival of Pragmatism: New Essays on Social Thought, Law, and Culture,* ed. Morris Dickstein. Durham, NC: Duke University Press

FRASER, NANCY, and LINDA GORDON. 1994. "A Genealogy of Dependency: Tracing a Keyword of the U.S. Welfare State." *Signs* 19(2): 309–36.

FRASER, STEVEN, ed. 1995. *The Bell Curve Wars: Race, Intelligence, and the Future of America.* New York: Basic.

FRAZIER, E. FRANKLIN. 1932. *The Negro Family in Chicago.* Chicago: University of Chicago Press.

———. 1939/1948. *The Negro Family in the United States.* Chicago: University of Chicago Press; New York: Dryden.

———. 1945. Review of *An American Dilemma* by Gunnar Myrdal. *American Journal of Sociology* 50.

———. 1949a. *The Negro in the United States.* New York: Macmillan.

———. 1949b. "Race Contacts and the Social Structure." *American Sociological Review* 14(1): 1–11.

———. 1964. *The Negro Church in America.* New York: Schocken.

———. 1980. "Sociological Theory and Race Relations" (1947). In *The Sociology of Race Relations: Reflection and Reform,* ed. Thomas Pettigrew, 151–58. New York: Free Press.

FREDRICKSON, GEORGE M. 1971. *The Black Image in the White Mind: The Debate on Afro-American Character and Destiny, 1817–1914.* New York: Harper and Row.

FREEDMAN, RONALD, AMOS H. HAWLEY, WERNER S. LANDECKER, and HORACE M. MINER. 1956. *Principles of Sociology.* Rev. ed. New York: Holt.

FREEMAN, JO. 1975. *The Politics of Women's Liberation.* New York: David McKay.

FRICKEL, SCOTT, and NEIL GROSS. 2005. "A General Theory of Scientific/Intellectual Movements." *American Sociological Review* 70:204–32.

FRIEDKIN, NOAH E. 1998. *A Structural Theory of Social Influence.* Cambridge: Cambridge University Press.

FRIEDRICHS, ROBERT WINSLOW. 1970. *A Sociology of Sociology.* New York: Free Press.

FROMM, E. 1941/1965. *Escape from Freedom.* New York: Avon.

FRYDL, K. J. 2000. "The GI Bill." PhD diss., University of Chicago.

FUHRMAN, ELLESWORTH R. 1978. "Images of the Discipline in Early American Sociology." *Journal of the History of Sociology* 1(1): 91–116.

———. 1980. *The Sociology of Knowledge in America, 1883–1915.* Charlottesville: University Press of Virginia.

FULLER, ABIGAIL A. 1996. "Producing Radical Scholarship: The Radical Sociology Movement, 1967–1975." *Sociological Imagination* 33.

FURNER, MARY O. 1975. *Advocacy and Objectivity: A Crisis in the Professionalization of American Social Science, 1865–1905.* Lexington: University Press of Kentucky.

FUSS, DIANA. 1989. "Essentially Speaking: Feminism, Nature and Difference." New York: Routledge, Chapman and Hall.

GABEL, LEONA C. 1982. *From Slavery to the Sorbonne and Beyond: The Life and Writings of Anna J. Cooper.* Northampton, MA: Smith College Library.

GAL, SUSAN, and GAIL KLIGMAN. 2000. *The Politics of Gender after Socialism.* Princeton: Princeton University Press.

GALLIHER, JOHN F. 1995. *Marginality and Dissent in Twentieth-Century American Sociology: The Case of Elizabeth Briant Lee and Alfred McClung Lee.* Albany: State University of New York Press.

GALTON, FRANCIS. 1904. "Eugenics: Its Definition, Scope and Aims." *American Journal of Sociology* 10(1): 1–6; discussion with Karl Pearson, H. G. Wells, Benjamin Kidd, Lady Welby, Mr. Hobhouse, G. Bernard Shaw, W. Bateson, et al., 7–25.

GAMSON, WILLIAM A. 1975. *The Strategy of Social Protest.* Homewood, IL: Dorsey Press.

———. 1995. "Hiroshima, the Holocaust, and the Politics of Exclusion." *American Sociological Review* 60:1–20.

GANS, HERBERT J. 1997. "Best-Sellers by Sociologists." *Contemporary Sociology* 26:131–35, 790–91.

———. 1998. "Best-Sellers by American Sociologists." in *Required Reading: Sociology's Most Influential Books,* ed. Dan Clawson, 19–27. Amherst: University of Massachusetts Press.

GAONKAR, DILIP PARAMESHWAR, ed. 2001. *Alternative Modernities.* Durham, NC: Duke University Press.

GARDNER, LLOYD, and MARILYN B. YOUNG, eds. 2002. *The New American Empire: A 21st-Century Teach-in on U.S. Foreign Policy.* New York: New Press.

GARFIELD, EUGENE. 1985. "The Life and Career of George Sarton: The Father of the History of Science." *Journal of the History of the Behavioral Sciences* 21 (April): 107–17.

GARLAND, DAVID. 1985. "The Criminal and His Science." *British Journal of Criminology* 25(2): 109–37.

GARLAND, DAVID, and RICHARD SPARKS, eds. 2000. *Criminology and Social Theory.* Oxford: Oxford University Press.

GAUS, JOHN M. 1931. "Notes on Administration." *American Political Science Review* 25:120-34.

GAYLORD, MARK S., and JOHN F. GALLIHER 1988. *The Criminology of Edwin Sutherland.* New Brunswick, NJ: Transaction Books.

GAZIANO, EMANUEL. 1996. "Ecological Metaphors as Scientific Boundary Work: Innovation and Authority in Interwar Sociology and Biology." *American Journal of Sociology* 101(4): 874-907.

GEARY, DANIEL. 2004. "The Power and the Intellect: C. Wright Mills, the Left, and American Social Science." PhD diss., Department of History, University of California, Berkeley.

GEER, BLANCHE. 1964. "First Days in the Field." In *Sociologists at Work,* ed. Phillip E. Hammond, 322-44. New York: Basic Books.

—— 1972. *Learning to Work.* Beverly Hills, CA: Sage. Originally special issue of *American Behavioral Scientist* 16(1).

GEIGER, ROGER L. 1986. *To Advance Knowledge: The Growth of American Research Universities, 1900-1940.* New York: Oxford University Press.

GEIGER, SUSAN. 1997. *TANU Women: Gender and Culture in the Making of Tanganyikan Nationalism, 1955-1965.* London: Heinemann.

GEIS, GILBERT. 1974. "Avocational Crime." In *Handbook of Criminology,* ed. Daniel Glaser, 273-98. Chicago: Rand McNally.

GEIS, GILBERT, and MARY DODGE, eds. 2002. *Lessons of Criminology.* Cincinnati: Anderson Publishing.

GELLA, ALEKSANDER. 1964. Reply. *American Journal of Sociology* 70 (2): 225-27.

GELLATELY, ROBERT, and BEN KIERNAN. 2003. *The Specter of Genocide: Mass Murder in Historical Perspective.* Cambridge: Cambridge University Press.

GENOV, NIKOLAI, ed. 1989. *National Traditions in Sociology.* London: Sage.

GENOVESE, EUGENE D. 1998. *A Consuming Fire: The Fall of the Confederacy in the Mind of the White Christian South.* Athens: University of Georgia Press.

GERHARD, UTE. 2001. "Illegitimate Daughters: The Complicated Relationship between Feminism and Sociology." Paper presented at the Center for German and European Studies, University of Wisconsin,.

GERSON, MARK, and JAMES Q. WILSON, eds. 1996. *The Essential Neoconservative Reader.* New York: Perseus.

GERSTLE, GARY. 2002. *American Crucible: Race and Nation in the Twentieth Century.* Princeton: Princeton University Press.

GERTH, HANS. 1959. "The Relevance of History to the Sociological Ethos." *Studies on the Left* 1:7-14.

GERTH, HANS HEINRICH, and C. WRIGHT MILLS. 1964. *Character and Social Structure: The Psychology of Social Institutions.* New York: Harcourt, Brace and World.

GIBBONS, DONALD C. 1979. *The Criminological Enterprise: Theories and Perspectives.* Englewood Cliffs, NJ: Prentice Hall.

———. 1985. "The Assumption of the Efficacy of Middle-Range Explanation: Typologies." In *Theoretical Methods in Criminology*, ed. Robert F. Meier, 151–74. Beverly Hills, CA: Sage.

GIBBS, JACK P. 1972. *Sociological Theory Construction*. Hinsdale, IL: Dryden.

———. 1975. *Crime, Punishment, and Deterrence*. New York: Elsevier.

———. 1989. *Control: Sociology's Central Notion*. Urbana: University of Illinois Press.

———. 1994. *A Theory about Control*. Boulder, CO: Westview Press.

GIBBS, JACK P., and WALTER T. MARTIN. 1964. *Status Integration and Suicide*. Eugene: University of Oregon Press.

GIDDENS, ANTHONY. 1984. *The Constitution of Society: Outline of the Theory of Structuration*. Berkeley: University of California Press.

GIDDINGS, FRANKLIN HENRY. 1896. *The Principles of Sociology: An Analysis of the Phenomena of Association and of Social Organization*. New York: Macmillan.

———. 1898. *The Elements of Sociology: A Text-Book for Colleges and Schools*. New York: Macmillan.

———. 1900. *Democracy and Empire, with Studies of Their Psychological, Economic, and Moral Foundations*. New York: Macmillan.

———. 1901. *Inductive Sociology: A Syllabus of Methods, Analyses and Classifications, and Provisionally Formulated Laws*. New York: Macmillan.

———, ed. 1906/1923. *Readings in Descriptive and Historical Sociology*. New York: Macmillan.

———. 1912. "The Quality of Civilization" [ASS presidential address]. *American Journal of Sociology* 17(5): 581–89.

———. 1922. *Studies in the Theory of Human Society*. New York: Macmillan.

GIERYN, THOMAS F. 1999. *Cultural Boundaries of Science: Credibility on the Line*. Chicago: University of Chicago Press.

GILBERT, JESS. 2000. "Eastern Urban Liberals and Midwestern Agrarian Intellectuals." *Agricultural History* 74:162–80.

———. 2001. "Agrarian Intellectuals in a Democratizing State." In *The Countryside in the Age of the Modern State*, ed. Catherine McNicol Stock and Robert D. Johnston, 213–39. Ithaca, NY: Cornell University Press.

GILBERT, JESS, and ELLEN BAKER. 1997. "Wisconsin Economists and New Deal Agricultural Policy." *Wisconsin Magazine of History* (Summer): 280–312.

GILDER, GEORGE. 1981. *Wealth and Poverty*. New York: Basic Books.

GILKES, CHERYL TOWNSEND. 2001. *If It Wasn't for the Women: Black Women's Experience and Womanist Culture in Church and Community*. Maryknoll, NY: Orbis Books.

GILLIN, JOHN L. 1926. *Criminology and Penology*. 3rd ed. New York: Appleton-Century.

———. 1927a. "The Development of Sociology in the United States." *Publications of the American Sociological Society* 21:1–25.

———. 1927b. "Franklin Henry Giddings." In *American Masters of Social Science*, ed. H. W. Odum, 191–230. New York: Henry Holt.

GILMAN, CHARLOTTE PERKINS. 1998. *Women and Economics: A Study of the Eco-*

nomic Relation between Men and Women as a Factor in Social Evolution. Berkeley: University of California Press.

GILMAN, NILS. 2003. *Mandarins of the Future: Modernization Theory in Cold War America.* Baltimore: Johns Hopkins University Press.

GILMAN, SANDER L. 1985. *Difference and Pathology: Stereotypes of Sexuality, Race, and Madness.* Ithaca, NY: Cornell University Press.

GILPIN, PATRICK J., and MARYBETH GASMAN. 2003. *Charles S. Johnson: Leadership beyond the Veil in the Age of Jim Crow.* Albany: State University of New York Press.

GILROY, PAUL. 2000. *Against Race: Imagining Political Culture beyond the Color Line.* Cambridge: Harvard University Press.

GLAESER, ANDREAS. 2000. *Divided in Unity: Identity, Germany, and the Berlin Police.* Chicago: University of Chicago Press.

GLASER, BARNEY G., AND ANSELM L. STRAUSS. 1965. *Awareness of Dying.* Chicago: Aldine.

———. 1967. *The Discovery of Grounded Theory: Strategies for Qualitative Research.* Hawthorne, NY: Aldine de Gruyter.

GLAZER, NATHAN. 1975. *Affirmative Discrimination: Ethnic Inequality and Public Policy.* New York: Basic Books.

GLAZER, NATHAN, AND DANIEL P. MOYNIHAN, eds. 1975. *Ethnicity: Theory and Experience.* Cambridge: Harvard University Press.

GLAZER, NONA Y. 1993. *Women's Paid and Unpaid Labor.* Philadelphia: Temple University Press.

GLENN, EVELYN N. 1986. *Issei, Nisei, War Bride: Three Generations of Japanese American Women in Domestic Service.* Philadelphia: Temple University Press.

———. 1992. "From Servitude to Service Work: Historical Continuities in the Racial Division of Paid Reproductive Labor." *Signs* 18:1–43.

———. 1997. "Looking Back in Anger? Re-remembering My Sociological Career." In *Feminist Sociology: Life Histories of a Movement,* ed. Barbara Laslett and Barrie Thorne, 103–25. New Brunswick, NJ: Rutgers University Press.

———. 1998. "Gender, Race, and Class: Bridging the Language-Structure Divide." *Social Science History* 22(1): 29–38.

———. 2002. *Unequal Freedom: How Race and Gender Shaped American Citizenship and Labor.* Cambridge: Harvard University Press.

GLENN, NORVAL, and WAYNE VILLEMEZ. 1970. "The Productivity of Sociologists at 45 American Universities." *American Sociologist* 5(3): 244–52.

GLENN, NORVAL, and D. WEINER. 1969. "Some Trends in the Social Origins of American Sociologists." *American Sociologist* 5 (November): 291–302.

GLUECK, SHELDON, and ELEANOR T. GLUECK. 1930. *500 Criminal Careers.* New York: Knopf.

———. 1934. *One Thousand Juvenile Delinquents.* Cambridge: Harvard University Press.

———. 1937. *Later Criminal Careers.* New York: Commonwealth Fund.

———. 1950. *Unraveling Juvenile Delinquency.* Cambridge: Harvard University Press.

———. 1968. *Delinquents and Nondelinquents in Perspective.* Cambridge: Harvard University Press.

GOCEK, FATMA MUGE. 1995. *Rise of the Bourgeoisie and Demise of Empire: Ottoman Westernization and Social Change.* New York: Oxford University Press.

GODARD, ELLIS. 2004. "The Proper Role of Sociology in the World at Large" [letter]. *Chronicle of Higher Education* (October 1): 17.

GODDARD, ARTHUR, ed. 1968. *Harry Elmer Barnes Learned Crusader: The New History in Action.* Colorado Springs, CO: Ralph Myles.

GOETTING, ANN, and SARAH FENSTERMAKER, eds. 1995. *Individual Choices, Collective Visions: Fifty Years of Women in Sociology.* Philadelphia: Temple University Press.

GOFFMAN, ERVING. 1954. "Communication Conduct in an Island Community." PhD diss., University of Chicago.

———. 1959. *The Presentation of Self in Everyday Life.* Garden City, NY: Doubleday.

———. 1961. *Asylums: Essays on the Social Situation of Mental Patients and Other Inmates.* Chicago: Aldine.

———. 1963. *Stigma: Notes on the Management of Spoiled Identity.* Englewood Cliffs, NJ: Prentice Hall.

GOLD, RAYMOND L. 1958. "Roles in Sociological Field Observation." *Social Forces* 36:217-33.

GOLDBERG, JOSEPH. 1980. "Francis Perkins, Isador Lubin, and the Bureau of Labor Statistics." *Monthly Labor Review* 103(4): 22-30.

GOLDMAN, LAWRENCE. 1987. "A Peculiarity of the English? The Social Science Association and the Absence of Sociology in Nineteenth-Century Britain." *Past and Present*, no. 114 (February): 133-71.

GOLDSTONE, JACK. 1990. *Revolution and Rebellion in the Early Modern World.* Berkeley: University of California Press.

GOLDTHORPE, JOHN. 1983. "Women and Class Analysis: In Defense of the Conventional View." *Sociology* 17:465-88.

GOODE, WILLIAM J. 1960. "Encroachment, Charlatanism, and the Emerging Profession: Psychology, Sociology, and Medicine." *American Sociological Review* 25(6): 902-65.

GORDON, LINDA. 1992. "Social Insurance and Public Assistance: The Influence of Gender in Welfare Thought in the United States, 1890-1935." *American Historical Review* 97:19-54.

———. 1994. *Pitied but Not Entitled: Single Mothers and the History of Welfare.* Cambridge: Harvard University Press.

GORDON, MILTON. 1973. "The Social Survey Movement." *Social Problems* 21:284-98.

GORSKI, PHILIP. 2003. *The Disciplinary Revolution: Capitalism and the Rise of the State in Early Modern Europe.* Chicago: University of Chicago Press.

GOSNELL, HAROLD F. 1933. "Statisticians and Political Scientists." *American Political Science Review* 27:392-403.

GOTTFREDSON, MICHAEL R., and TRAVIS HIRSCHI 1990. *A General Theory of Crime.* Stanford, CA: Stanford University Press.

GOULD, STEPHEN JAY. 1981. *The Mismeasure of Man.* New York: Norton.

GOULDNER, ALVIN W. 1954. *Patterns of Industrial Bureaucracy.* Glencoe, IL: Free Press.

———. 1965. *Enter Plato: Classical Greece and the Origins of Social Theory.* New York: Basic Books.

———. 1970. *The Coming Crisis of Western Sociology.* New York: Basic Books; London: Heinemann.

———. 1979. *The Future of Intellectuals and the Rise of the New Class.* New York: Seabury.

GRAFF, HARVEY J. 2001. "The Shock of the 'New' (Histories): Social Science Histories and Historical Literacies." *Social Science History* 25(4): 483-533.

GRANT, LINDA, KATHERINE WARD, and XUE LAN RONG. 1987. "Is There an Association between Gender and Methods in Sociological Research?" *American Sociological Review* 52(6): 856-62.

GREEN, DAN S., and EDWIN D. DRIVER, eds. 1978. *W. E. B. DuBois: On Sociology and the Black Community.* Chicago: University of Chicago Press.

GREENFELD, LIAH. 1992. *Nationalism: Five Roads to Modernity.* Cambridge: Harvard University Press.

GREENWOOD, J. 2003. *The Decline of the Social in Social Psychology.* New York: Cambridge University Press.

GREFFRATH, MATTHIAS. 1979/1982. "'As in the Book of Fairy Tales: All Alone . . .' A Conversation with Hans Gerth." Trans. Jeffrey Herf. In *Politics, Character, and Culture: Perspectives from Hans Gerth,* ed. Joseph Bensman, Arthur J. Vidich, and Nobuko Gerth, 14-47. Westport, CT: Greenwood Press.

GREFFRATH, MATHIAS, and GÜNTHER ANDERS. 1979. *Die Zerstörung einer Zukunft: Gespräche mit emigrierten Sozialwissenschaftlern.* Hamburg: Rowohlt Verlag.

GREW, RAYMOND, ed. 1978. *Crises of Political Development in Europe and the United States.* Princeton: Princeton University Press.

GRIFFIN, JAMES B. 1995. "Horace Mitchell Miner (26 May 1912-26 November 1993)." *Proceedings of the American Philosophical Society* 139(3): 288-92.

GRIFFITH, ALISON I., and DOROTHY E. SMITH. 2005. *Mothering for Schooling.* New York: RoutledgeFalmer.

GRISWOLD, WENDY. 1981. "American Character and the American Novel." *American Journal of Sociology* 86:740-65.

———. 2000. *Bearing Witness: Readers, Writers and the Novel in Nigeria.* Princeton: Princeton University Press.

GRODZINS, M. 1949. *Americans Betrayed.* Chicago: University of Chicago Press.

GROSS, EDWARD. 1968. "Plus Ça Change . . . ? The Sexual Structure of Occupations over Time." *Social Problems* 16:198-208.

GROSS, JAN. 2001. *Neighbors: The Destruction of the Jewish Community in Jedwabne, Poland.* Princeton: Princeton University Press.

GROSS, MATTHIAS. 2002. "When Ecology and Sociology Meet: The Contributions of Edward A. Ross." *Journal of the History of the Behavioral Sciences* 38(1): 27-42.

GROSS, NEIL. 2002. "Becoming a Pragmatist Philosopher." *American Sociological Review* 67:52-76.

———, ed. 2004. *Perspectives: Newsletter of the ASA Theory Section* 27(3): 1-20.

———. 2005. "Richard Rorty's Pragmatism." Book manuscript.

GROSS, NEAL C., WARD S. MASON, and ALEXANDER W. MCEACHERN. 1958. *Explorations in Role Analysis: Studies of the School Superintendency Role*. New York: Wiley.

GROSSMANN, REINHARDT. 1984. *Phenomenology and Existentialism: An Introduction*. London: Routledge and Kegan Paul.

GROVES, ERNEST R. 1931. "The Family." *American Journal of Sociology* 36:993-1001.

GUBRIUM, JABER F., and JAMES A. HOLSTEIN. 1997. *The New Language of Qualitative Method*. New York: Oxford University Press.

GUIDRY, JOHN, MICHAEL D. KENNEDY, and MAYER ZALD, eds. 2000. *Globalizations and Social Movements: Culture, Power, and the Transnational Public Sphere*. Ann Arbor: University of Michigan Press.

GUILLAUMIN, COLETTE. 1995. *Racism, Sexism, Power and Ideology*. New York: Routledge.

GUINIER, LANI, and GERALD TORRES. 2002. *The Miner's Canary: Enlisting Race, Resisting Power, Transforming Democracy*. Cambridge: Harvard University Press.

GUSFIELD, JOSEPH R. 1963. *Symbolic Crusade: Status Politics and the American Temperance Movement*. Urbana: University of Illinois Press.

———. 1967. "Tradition and Modernity: Misplaced Polarities in the Study of Social Change." *American Journal of Sociology* 72(4): 351-62.

———. 1981. *The Culture of Public Problems: Drinking-Driving and the Social Order*. Chicago: University of Chicago Press.

GUTMAN, ROBERT. 1958. "Cooley: A Perspective." *American Sociological Review* 23(3): 251-56.

HABERMAS, JÜRGEN. 1971. *Knowledge and Human Interests*. Trans. J. Shapiro. Boston: Beacon Press.

HACKER, ANDREW. 1988. "Black Crime, White Racism." *New York Review of Books* 35(3): 36-41.

HACKER, HELEN. 1951. "Women as a Minority Group." *Social Forces* 30:60-69.

HACKER, P. M. S. 1997. "The Rise of Twentieth Century Analytic Philosophy." In *The Rise of Analytic Philosophy*, ed. H. J. Glock, 51-56. Oxford: Blackwell.

HAGAN, JOHN. 2002. "Lessons of the American Vietnam War Resistance in Canada." *Crime, Law and Social Change* 37(2): 137-62.

HAGAN, JOHN, and BILL MCCARTHY. 1997. *Mean Streets: Youth Crime and Homelessness*. Cambridge: Cambridge University Press.

HAGEDORN, JOHN M., ed. 2006. *Gangs in the Global City*. Urbana: University of Illinois Press.

HAŁAS, ELŻBIETA. 2001. "How Robert MacIver Was Forgotten: Columbia and American Sociology in a New Light, 1929-1950." *Journal of the History of the Behavioral Sciences* 37(1): 27-43.

———. 2005. "New Reading of Florian Znaniecki's Contribution to Classical Cultural Sociology." *Studia Socjologiczne* (Sociological Studies) 3(178): 5-34.

HALBWACHS, MAURICE. 1992. *On Collective Memory*. Trans. and ed. Lewis A. Coser. Chicago: University of Chicago Press.

HALL, ELAINE J. 2000. "Developing the Gender Relations Perspective: The Emergence of a New Conceptualization of Gender in the 1990s." *Current Perspectives in Social Theory* 20:91-123.

HALL, STUART. 1980. "Race, Articulation, and Societies Structured in Dominance." In *Sociological Theories: Race and Colonialism,* ed. Marion O'Callaghan. Paris: UNESCO.

HALLIDAY, FRED. 1999. "Islamophobia Reconsidered." *Ethnic and Racial Studies* 22(5): 892-902.

HALLIDAY, TERENCE C. 1992. "Introduction: Sociology's Fragile Professionalism." In *Sociology and Its Publics,* ed. T. Halliday and M. Janowitz, 3-41. Chicago: University of Chicago Press.

HALLIDAY, TERENCE C., and MORRIS JANOWITZ, eds. 1992. *Sociology and Its Publics: The Forms and Fates of Disciplinary Organization.* Chicago: University of Chicago Press.

HAMILTON, DAVID E. 1991. *From New Day to New Deal: American Farm Policy from Hoover to Roosevelt, 1928-1933.* Chapel Hill: University of North Carolina Press.

HAMILTON, PETER. 1983. *Talcott Parsons.* New York: Tavistock Publications.

HANEY, DAVID PAUL. 1998. "Democratic Ideals, Scientific Identities, and the Struggle for a Public Sociology in the United States, 1945-1962." PhD diss., Department of History, University of Texas, Austin.

HANKINS, FRANK H. 1931. "Franklin Henry Giddings, 1855-1931: Some Aspects of His Sociological Theory." *American Journal of Sociology* 37(3): 349-67.

———. 1934. Contribution to "Questions for Sociology: An Informal Round Table Symposium." *Social Forces* 13:202-3.

———. 1936. "Sociology and Social Guidance: Discussion." *American Sociological Review* 1:33-37.

———. 1939. "Social Science and Social Action." *American Sociological Review* 4:1-16.

HARAWAY, DONNA. 1988. "Situated Knowledges: The Science Question in Feminism and the Privilege of Partial Perspective." *Feminist Studies* 14:575-99.

———. 1990. *Primate Visions: Gender, Race and Nature in the World of Modern Science.* New York: Routledge.

HARDIN, BERT. 1977. *The Professionalization of Sociology—A Comparative Study: Germany-USA.* Frankfurt and New York: Campus Verlag.

HARDING, SANDRA G. 1986. *The Science Question in Feminism.* Ithaca, NY: Cornell University Press.

———. 1991. *Whose Science? Whose Knowledge? Thinking from Women's Lives.* Ithaca, NY: Cornell University Press.

———. 2005. "Negotiating with the Positivist Legacy: New Social Justice Movements and a Standpoint Politics of Method." In *The Politics of Method in the Human Sciences: Positivism and Its Epistemological Others,* ed. George Steinmetz, 346-65. Durham, NC: Duke University Press.

HARDING, SANDRA G., and MERRILL B. HINTIKKA, eds. 1983. *Discovering Reality: Feminist Perspectives on Epistemology, Metaphysics, Methodology, and Philosophy of Science.* Dordrecht, Holland: D. Reidel.

HARDT, MICHAEL, and ANTONI NEGRI. 2000. *Empire.* Cambridge: Harvard University Press.

HAROOTUNIAN, HARRY D. 2004. *The Empire's New Clothes: Paradigm Lost, and Regained.* Chicago: Prickly Paradigm.

HART, HORNELL. 1933. "Changing Opinions about Business Prosperity." *American Journal of Sociology* 38:665–87.

———. 1934. Contribution to "Questions for Sociology: An Informal Round Table Symposium." *Social Forces* 13:209–10.

HARTMANN, HEIDI. 1979. "The Unhappy Marriage of Marxism and Feminism: Towards a More Progressive Union." *Capital and Class* 8:1–33.

HARTUNG, FRANK E. 1944. "The Sociology of Positivism." *Science and Society* 8: 328–41.

HARVEY, DAVID. 1989. *The Condition of Postmodernity.* Cambridge, MA: Blackwell.

HASKELL, THOMAS L. 1977/2000. *The Emergence of Professional Social Science: The American Social Science Association and the Nineteenth-Century Crisis of Authority.* Urbana: University of Illinois Press; Baltimore: Johns Hopkins University Press.

———. 1996. "Justifying the Rights of Academic Freedom in the Era of 'Power/Knowledge.'" In *The Future of Academic Freedom,* ed. Louis Menand, 43–90. Chicago: University of Chicago Press.

HASTINGS, C. H., comp. 1897. Bibliography. *American Journal of Sociology* 2(5): 752–69.

———. 1899a. Bibliography. *American Journal of Sociology* 4(6): 854–64.

———. 1899b. Bibliography. *American Journal of Sociology* 5(3): 420–32.

HAUSER, PHILIP M., and OTIS DUDLEY DUNCAN, eds. 1959. *The Study of Population: An Inventory and Appraisal.* Chicago: University of Chicago Press.

HAUSER, ROBERT M. 1995. Review of *The Bell Curve* by Richard J. Herrnstein and Charles Murray. *Contemporary Sociology* 24(2): 149–53.

HAUSKNECHT, MURRAY. 1972. Review of *Radical Sociology. Contemporary Sociology* 1:102–5.

HAVIGHURST, R. J., and H. G. MORGAN. 1951. *The Social History of a War-Boom Community.* New York: Longmans

HAWLEY, AMOS HENRY. 1950. *Human Ecology: A Theory of Community Structure.* New York: Ronald Press.

HAYASHI, G. 2004. *Democratizing the Enemy.* Princeton: Princeton University Press.

HAYES, EDWARD CARY, et al. 1921. "The Work of the American Sociological Society: A Symposium." *Papers and Proceedings of the American Sociological Society* 16:257–63.

HAYIM, GILA J. 1996. *Existentialism and Sociology: The Contribution of Jean-Paul Sartre.* New Brunswick, NJ: Transaction.

HAYS, SHARON, and BARBARA RISMAN. 2004. "SWS Report Card on Gender- and Women-Friendly Sociology Departments among PhD-Granting Institutions." *SWS Report* (August).

HEALY, WILLIAM. 1915. *The Individual Delinquent.* Boston: Little, Brown.

HEAP, JAMES L., and PHILLIP A. ROTH. 1973. "On Phenomenological Sociology." *American Sociological Review* 38:354–67.

HELMES-HAYES, RICHARD. 2000. "The Concept of Social Class: The Contribution of Everett Hughes." *Journal of the History of the Behavioral Sciences* 36(2): 127–47.

HEMPEL, CARL GUSTAV. 1965. "The Function of General Laws in History." In *Aspects of Scientific Explanation and Other Essays in the Philosophy of Science*, 231–43. New York: Free Press.

HENDERSON, C. R. 1896a. "Business Men and Social Theorists." *American Journal of Sociology* 1(4): 385–97.

——. 1896b. "The German Inner Mission. II. The Experimental Stage." *American Journal of Sociology* 1(6): 674–84.

——. 1896c. "Rise of the German Inner Mission." *American Journal of Sociology* 1(5): 583–95.

——. 1901. *Introduction to the Study of the Dependent, Defective, and Delinquent Classes.* 2nd ed. Boston: D. C. Heath

——. 1914. *The Cause and Cure of Crime.* Chicago: A. C. McClurg.

HENKING, SUSAN E. 1992. "Protestant Religious Experience and the Rise of American Sociology: Evidence from the Bernard Papers." *Journal of the History of the Behavioral Sciences* 28 (October): 325–39.

HENRY, ANDREW F., and JAMES F. SHORT JR. 1954. *Suicide and Homicide: Some Economic, Sociological, and Psychological Aspects of Aggression.* Glencoe, IL: Free Press.

HENRY, STUART, and WERNER EINSTADTER, eds. 1998. *The Criminology Theory Reader.* New York: New York University Press.

HENSLIN, J. M., and P. M. ROESTI. 1976. "Trends and Topics in *Social Problems,* 1953-1975: A Content Analysis and Critique." *Social Problems* 24:54–68.

HERMAN, E. 1995. *The Romance of American Psychology: Political Culture in the Age of Experts.* Berkeley: University of California Press.

HERRING, E. PENDLETON. 1938. "The Experts on Five Federal Commissions." *American Political Science Review* 32:86–93.

HERRNSTEIN, RICHARD J., and CHARLES MURRAY. 1994. *The Bell Curve: Intelligence and Class Structure in American Life.* New York: Free Press.

HERSHBERG, ERIC, and KEVIN MOORE. 2002. *Critical Views of September 11: Analyses from Around the World.* New York: New Press.

HERTZ, ALEXANDER. 1988. *The Jews in Polish Culture.* Evanston, IL: Northwestern University Press.

HERZBERG, DAVID L. 2001. "Thinking through War: The Social Thought of Richard T. Ely, John R. Commons, and Edward A. Ross during the First World War." *Journal of the History of the Behavioral Sciences* 37(2): 123–41.

HESS, DAVID J. 1997. *Science Studies: An Advanced Introduction.* New York: New York University Press.

HEUVELINE, PATRICK. 2004. "Sociology and Biology: Can't We Just Be Friends?" *American Journal of Sociology* 109(6): 1500–1506.

HEYDEBRAND, WOLF. 1990. "The Technocratic Organization of Academic Work."

In *Structures of Power and Constraint: Papers in Honor of Peter M. Blau,* ed. Craig Calhoun, Marshall W. Meyer, and W. Richard Scott, 323–57. Cambridge: Cambridge University Press.

HICKMAN, LARRY. 1990. *John Dewey's Pragmatic Technology.* Bloomington: Indiana University Press.

HIGGINBOTHAM, ELIZABETH. 2001. *Too Much to Ask: Black Women in the Era of Integration.* Chapel Hill: University of North Carolina Press.

HIGHAM, JOHN. 1955/1994. *Strangers in the Land: Patterns of American Nativism, 1860–1925.* New Brunswick, NJ: Rutgers University Press.

HILBERT, RICHARD A. 1990. "Ethnomethodology and the Micro-Macro Order." *American Sociological Review* 55:794–808.

HILL, MICHAEL R. 2005. *Centennial Bibliography on the History of American Sociology.* Washington, DC: American Sociological Association.

HILL, MICHAEL R., and MARY JO DEEGAN, eds. 2004. *Social Ethics: Sociology and the Future of Society.* Westport, CT: Praeger.

HINKLE, ROSCOE C. 1980. *Founding Theory of American Sociology, 1881–1915.* Boston: Routledge and Kegan Paul.

———. 1994. *Developments in American Sociological Theory, 1915–1950.* Albany: State University of New York Press.

HINKLE, ROSCOE C., and GISELA J. HINCKLE. 1954. *The Development of Modern Sociology, Its Nature and Growth in the United States.* New York: Random House.

HIRSCHI, TRAVIS. 1969. *Causes of Delinquency.* Berkeley: University of California Press.

HIRST, PAUL, and GRAEME THOMPSON. 1996. *Globalization in Question.* Cambridge: Cambridge University Press.

HOBBS, RICHARD S. 2002. *The Cayton Legacy: An African American Family.* Pullman: Washington State University Press.

HOBSON, BARBARA, ed. 2003. *Recognition Struggles and Social Movements: Contested Identities, Agency and Power.* Cambridge: Cambridge University Press.

HOCHSCHILD, ADAM. 1998. *King Leopold's Ghost: A Story of Greed, Terror, and Heroism in Colonial Africa.* Boston: Houghton Mifflin.

HOCHSCHILD, ARLIE RUSSELL. 1983. *The Managed Heart: Commercialization of Human Feeling.* Berkeley: University of California Press.

———. 1989. *The Second Shift.* New York: Avon Books.

HODGSON, DENNIS. 2001. "Demography: 20th Century History of the Discipline." *International Encyclopedia of the Social and Behavioral Sciences.* Amsterdam: Pergamon.

HODSON, RANDY, and ROBERT L. KAUFMAN. 1981. "Circularity in the Dual Economy." *American Journal of Sociology* 86:881–87.

———. 1982. "Economic Dualism." *American Sociological Review* 47:727–39.

HOFSTADTER, RICHARD. 1944/1955/1959. *Social Darwinism in American Thought.* Rev. ed. Boston: Beacon Press; New York: G. Braziller.

HOFSTADTER, RICHARD, and WALTER P. METZGER. 1955. *The Development of Academic Freedom in the United States.* New York: Columbia University Press.

HOLBROOKE, AGNES SINCLAIR. 1895. "Map Notes and Comments." In *Hull-House Maps and Papers, by Residents of Hull-House*, 3–23. Boston: Cromwell.

HOLCOMBE, ARTHUR N. 1931. "Trench Warfare." *American Political Science Review* 25:914–25.

HOLLANDER, PAUL. 1982. *Political Pilgrims: Western Intellectuals in Search of the Good Society.* New Brunswick, NJ: Transaction.

HOLLINGER, DAVID A. 1996. *Science, Jews, and Secular Culture: Studies in Mid-Twentieth-Century American Intellectual History.* Princeton: Princeton University Press.

HOLLINGSHEAD, AUGUST. 1949. *Elmstown's Youth: The Impact of Social Classes on Adolescents.* New York: Science Editions.

HOLMSTROM, LYNDA LYTLE, and ANN WOLBERT BURGESS. 1978. *The Victim of Rape: Institutional Reactions.* New York: Wiley.

HOLT, THOMAS C. 2000. *The Problem of Race in the Twenty-first Century.* Cambridge: Harvard University Press.

HOMANS, GEORGE C. 1947. "A Conceptual Scheme for the Study of Social Organization." *American Sociological Review* 12(1): 13–26.

———. 1984. *Coming to My Senses : The Autobiography of a Sociologist.* New Brunswick, NJ: Transaction Books.

HONDAGNEU-SOTELO, PIERETTE. 2001. *Doméstica: Immigrant Workers Cleaning and Caring in the Shadows of Affluence.* Berkeley: University of California Press.

HOOK, SIDNEY. 1987. *Out of Step: An Unquiet Life in the 20th Century.* New York: Harper and Row.

HOOVER, HERBERT. 1932/1933. Foreword to *Recent Social Trends in the United States*, 1:v. New York: McGraw-Hill.

HORAN, PATRICK M. 1978. "Is Status Attainment Research Atheoretical?" *American Sociological Review* 43:534–41.

HORKHEIMER, MAX. 1937/1982. "Traditional and Critical Theory." In *Critical Theory: Selected Essays*, by M. Horkheimer, trans. Matthew J. O'Connell, 188–243. New York: Continuum.

HORKHEIMER, MAX, and THEODOR ADORNO. 1944/1986. *The Dialectic of the Enlightenment.* New York: Continuum.

HORLICK-JONES, TOM, and JONATHAN SIME. 2004. "Living on the Border: Knowledge, Risk and Transdisciplinarity." *Futures* 36:441–56.

HORNEY, KAREN. 1936. "Culture and Neurosis." *American Sociological Review* 1(32): 221–30.

HOROWITZ, IRVING LOUIS. 1963. *Professing Sociology: Studies in the Life Cycle of Social Science.* Chicago: Aldine.

———. 1964a. "The Intellectual Genesis of C. Wright Mills." In *Sociology and Pragmatism: The Higher Learning in America*, by C. Wright Mills, ed. I. L. Horowitz, 11–31. New York: Paine-Whitman Publishers.

———, ed. 1964b. *The New Sociology.* New York: Oxford University Press.

———, ed. 1967. *The Rise and Fall of Project Camelot: Studies in the Relationship between Social Science and Practical Politics.* Cambridge: MIT Press.

———. 1983. *C. Wright Mills: An American Utopian.* New York: Free Press.

HORST, P., ed. 1941. *The Prediction of Personal Adjustment.* Bulletin No. 48. New York: Social Science Research Council.

HOUSE, FLOYD. 1926. "A List of the More Important Published Writings of Albion Woodberry Small." *American Journal of Sociology* 32(1): 49–58.

———. 1936. *The Development of Sociology.* New York: McGraw-Hill.

HOUT, MICHAEL, and PAMELA BARNHOUSE WALTERS. 2000. *Report on the Conference on Sociology and Education.* Chicago: Spencer Foundation. Available at http://www.spencer.org/publications/index.htm.

HOWARD, GEORGE ELLIOTT. 1908. "Is the Freer Granting of Divorce an Evil?" *Papers and Proceedings of the American Sociological Society* 3 (December): 150–60, and discussion.

HOWERTH, IRA. 1894. "Present Condition of Sociology in the United States." *Annals of the American Academy of Political and Social Science* 5:260–69.

HOXIE, R. GORDON. 1955. *A History of the Faculty of Political Science, Columbia University.* New York: Columbia University Press.

HOYME, RICHARD G. 1961. "The Current Status of Educational Sociology." *Journal of Educational Sociology* 35:128–33.

HUGHES, EVERETT C. 1961. "Ethnocentric Sociology." *Social Forces* 40:1–4.

———. 1964. "Good People and Dirty Work." In *The Other Side: Perspectives on Deviance,* ed. Howard S. Becker, 23–36. Glencoe, IL: Free Press.

HUGHES, H. STUART. 1977. *Consciousness and Society: The Reorientation of European Social Thought, 1890–1930.* Rev. ed. New York: Vintage.

HUGHES, HELEN MACGILL. 1973a. "Maid of All Work or Departmental Sister-in-Law? The Faculty Wife Employed on Campus." *American Journal of Sociology* 78:767–72.

———, ed. 1973b. *The Status of Women in Sociology, 1968–1972.* Washington, DC: American Sociological Association.

HUGHES, HENRY. 1854/1968. *Treatise on Sociology, Theoretical and Practical.* Reprint. New York: Negro Universities Press.

HUGHES, LORINE A. 2005. *Violent and Non-Violent Disputes Involving Gang Youth.* New York: LFB Scholarly.

HUGHES, LORINE A., and JAMES F. SHORT JR. 2005. "Disputes Involving Youth Street Gang Members: Micro-Social Contexts." *Criminology* 43(1): 43–76.

HUGHLEY, J. NEAL. 1948. "Christian Sociology: Charles A. Ellwood." In *Trends in Protestant Social Idealism.* Morningside Heights, NY: King's Crown Press.

HULL, GLORIA T., PATRICIA BELL SCOTT, and BARBARA SMITH, eds. 1982. *All the Women Are White, All the Blacks Are Men, but Some of Us Are Brave: Black Women's Studies.* Old Westbury, NY: Feminist Press.

Hull-House Maps and Papers, by Residents of Hull House. ca. 1895/1970. New York: Arno Press.

"Human Behavior in Military Society." 1946. Special issue. *American Journal of Sociology* (March).

HUNT, DOUG. 2004. "A Course in Applied Lynching." *Missouri Review* 27(2): 122–70.

HUNT, MORTON. 1961. "A Biographical Profile of Robert K. Merton." *New Yorker* 28:39–63.

HUNTER, HERBERT M., and SAMEER Y. ABRAHAM. 1987. *Race, Class, and the World System: The Sociology of Oliver C. Cox.* New York: Monthly Review Press.

HUNTINGTON, SAMUEL P. 2004. *Who Are We? The Challenges to America's Identity.* New York: Simon and Schuster.

HURLBURT, WALTER C. 1932. "Prosperity, Depression, and the Suicide Rate." *American Journal of Sociology* 37:714–19.

HUSSERL, EDMUND. 1913/2002. *Ideas Pertaining to a Pure Phenomenology and to a Phenomenological Philosophy.* Vol. 1. Trans. R. Rojcewicz and A. Schuwer. New York: Springer.

HUTCHINSON, LOUISE DANIEL. 1982. *Anna J. Cooper: A Voice from the South.* Washington, DC: Smithsonian Books.

IGO, SARAH E. 2006. *America Surveyed: The Making of a Mass Public.* Cambridge: Harvard University Press.

IMBER, JONATHAN. 1999. "Values, Politics and Science." *Contemporary Sociology* 28(3): 255–59.

INKELES, ALEX. 1959. "Personality and Social Structure." In *Sociology Today,* ed. Robert K. Merton, L. Broom, and L. Cottrell Jr., 249–76. New York: Basic Books.

———. 1964. *What Is Sociology? An Introduction to the Discipline and Profession.* Englewood Cliffs, NJ: Prentice Hall.

INKELES, ALEX, and DAVID H. SMITH. 1974. *Becoming Modern: Individual Change in Six Developing Countries.* Cambridge: Harvard University Press.

INTERNATIONAL SOCIOLOGICAL ASSOCIATION (ISA). 1998. "Books of the Century." http://www.ucm.es/info/isa.

IRONS, PETER H. 1993. *The New Deal Lawyers.* Princeton: Princeton University Press.

JACKSON, ELTON F., CHARLES R. TITTLE, and MARY J. BURKE. 1986. "Offense-Specific Models of the Differential Association Process." *Social Problems* 33(4): 335–56.

JACKSON, K. T. 1985. *Crabgrass Frontier.* New York: Oxford.

JACKSON, ROBERT MAX. 1998. *Destined for Equality: The Inevitable Rise of Women's Status.* Cambridge: Harvard University Press.

JACKSON, WALTER. 1990. *Gunnar Myrdal and America's Conscience.* Chapel Hill: University of North Carolina Press.

JACOBS, JERRY. 1989. "Long-Term Trends in Occupational Segregation by Sex." *American Journal of Sociology* 95:160–73.

JACOBSON, HARVEY K. 1962. "The Sources and Subject Matter of Papers in the *Journal of Educational Sociology.*" *Journal of Educational Sociology* 36:98–107.

JACOBSON, J. MARK. 1932. "The Wisconsin Unemployment Compensation Law of 1932." *American Political Science Review* 256:300–311.

JACOBY, RUSSELL. 1983. *The Repression of Psychoanalysis: Otto Fenichel and the Political Freudians.* New York: Basic Books.

——. 1987. *The Last Intellectuals: American Culture in the Age of Academe.* New York: Basic Books.

JAMES, EDWARD R., JANET WILSON JAMES, and PAUL BOYERS, eds. 1971. *Notable American Women, 1607-1950: A Biographical Dictionary.* Vol. 3. Cambridge: Harvard University Press.

JAMES, WILLIAM. 1897/1979. *The Will to Believe, and Other Essays in Popular Philosophy.* Cambridge: Harvard University Press.

——. 1907a/1948. *Essays in Pragmatism.* New York: Hafner Publishing.

——. 1907b/1975. *Pragmatism: A New Name for Some Old Ways of Thinking.* Cambridge: Harvard University Press.

JANOWITZ, MORRIS. 1952. *The Community Press in an Urban Setting.* Glencoe, IL: Free Press.

——. 1972. "Professionalization of Sociology." *American Journal of Sociology* 78: 105-35.

——. 1978. *The Last Half-Century: Societal Change and Politics in America.* Chicago: University of Chicago Press.

JAY, MARTIN. 1973. *The Dialectical Imagination: A History of the Frankfurt School and Institute of Social Research, 1923-1950.* Boston: Little, Brown.

JAYARATNE, TOBY. 1983. "The Value of Quantitative Methodology for Feminist Research." In *Theories of Women's Studies,* ed. Gloria Bowles and Renate Duelli-Klein, 140-61. Boston: Routledge and Kegan Paul.

JENCKS, CHRISTOPHER, and DAVID RIESMAN. 1968. *The Academic Revolution.* Garden City, NY: Doubleday.

JENSEN, HOWARD E. 1946-47. "The Development of the Social Thought of Charles Abram Ellwood." *Sociology and Social Research* 31:341-51.

JOAS, HANS. 1985. *G. H. Mead: A Contemporary Re-examination of His Thought.* Trans. Raymond Meyer. Cambridge: MIT Press.

——. 1993. *Pragmatism and Social Theory.* Trans. Jeremy Gaines, Raymond Meyer, and Steven Minner. Chicago: University of Chicago Press.

——. 1996. *The Creativity of Action.* Trans. Jeremy Gaines and Paul Keast. Chicago: University of Chicago Press.

——. 2000. *The Genesis of Values.* Trans. Gregory Moore. Chicago: University of Chicago Press.

——. 2003. *War and Modernity.* Trans. Rodney Livingstone. Cambridge, MA: Polity Press.

——. 2004. Foreword to *Durkheim's Philosophy Lectures: Notes from the Lycée de Sens Course, 1883-4,* ed. N. Gross and R. A. Jones, xi-xiv. Cambridge: Cambridge University Press.

JOCHER, KATHARINE. 1947. "The Place of Sociology in Education for Social Work." *Social Forces* 25(4): 419-26.

JOHNSON, BLAIR T., and DIANA R. NICHOLS. 1998. "Social Psychologists' Expertise in the Public Interest: Civilian Morale Research during World War II." *Journal of Social Issues* 54(1): 53-77.

JOHNSON, BRIAN LAMONT. 2003. "William Edward Burghardt DuBois (1883–1934): Authorship, Reform Writing and Periodical-Based Leadership." Doctoral diss., Department of English, University of South Carolina.

JOHNSON, CHARLES SPURGEON. 1934. *Shadow of the Plantation.* Chicago: University of Chicago Press.

———. 1937. "Negro Racial Movements and Leadership in the United States." *American Journal of Sociology* 43(1): 5–71.

JOHNSON, CHARLES S./CHICAGO COMMISSION ON RACE RELATIONS. 1922. *The Negro in Chicago: A Study of Race Relations and a Race Riot.* Chicago: University of Chicago Press.

JOHNSON, CHARLES W., and C. O. JACKSON. 1981. *City behind a Fence.* Knoxville: University of Tennessee Press.

JOHNSON, GUY BENTON, and GURON GRIFFS JOHNSON. 1980. *Research in Service to Society: The First Fifty Years of the Institute for Research in Social Science at the University of North Carolina.* Chapel Hill: University of North Carolina Press.

JOHNSON, JOHN M. 1977. "Ethnomethodology and Existential Sociology." In *Existential Sociology,* ed. J. D. Douglas and J. M. Johnson, 153–73. Cambridge: Cambridge University Press.

JOHNSON, M. S. 1993. *The Second Gold Rush: Oakland and the East Bay in World War II.* Berkeley: University of California Press.

JOHNSTON, BARRY V. 1995. *Pitirim A. Sorokin: An Intellectual Biography.* Lawrence: University of Kansas Press.

———. 1998. "The Contemporary Crisis and the Social Relations Department at Harvard: A Case Study in Hegemony and Disintegration." *American Sociologist* 29(3): 1–23.

JONES, ROBERT ALUN. 1983. "The New History of Sociology." *Annual Review of Sociology* 9:447–69.

JONES, ROBERT ALUN, and SIDNEY KRONUS. 1976. "Professional Sociologists and the History of Sociology: A Survey of Recent Opinion." *Journal of the History of the Behavioral Sciences* 12:3–13.

JONES, T. ANTHONY. 1976. "Modernization Theory and Socialist Development." In *The Social Consequences of Modernization in Communist Countries,* ed. M. G. Field, 19–49. Baltimore: Johns Hopkins University Press.

JUDD, CHARLES H. 1938. "Summary of Memoranda on the Research of the Federal Government in the Social Sciences." In *Relation of the Federal Government to Research,* 49–57, vol. 1 of *Research—A National Resource.* Report of the Science Committee to the National Resources Committee. Washington, DC: Government Printing Office.

JUDSON, HARRY PRATT. 1895. "Is Our Republic a Failure?" *American Journal of Sociology* 1(1): 28–40.

JUERGENSMEYER, MARK. 2000. *Terror in the Mind of God: The Global Rise of Religious Violence.* Berkeley: University of California Press.

———. 2003. *Global Religions: An Introduction.* Oxford: Oxford University Press.

JUNKER, BUFORD. 1960. *Fieldwork: An Introduction to the Social Sciences.* Chicago: University of Chicago Press.

KAESLER [KÄSLER], DIRK. 1990. *Sociological Adventures: Earle Edward Eubank's Visits with European Sociologists.* New Brunswick, NJ: Transaction Books.

———. 1998. "Sociology in Search of the Booster: Review Essay" [review of *Visions of the Sociological Tradition* by Donald Levine]. *Journal of the History of the Behavioral Sciences* 34(3): 271–77.

KAESTLE, CARL F. 1983. *Pillars of the Republic: Common Schools and American Society, 1780–1860.* New York: Hill and Wang.

KAGAN, ROBERT, and WILLIAM KRISTOL. 2000. *Present Dangers: Crisis and Opportunity in American Foreign and Defense Policy.* New York: Encounter.

KAHLENBERG, RICHARD D. 1996. *The Remedy: Class, Race, and Affirmative Action.* New York: Basic.

KANTER, ROSABETH. 1977. *Men and Women of the Corporation.* New York: Basic Books.

KAPLAN, ABRAHAM. 1964. *The Conduct of Inquiry: Methodology for Behavioral Science.* San Francisco: Chandler Publishing.

KAPLAN, HOWARD B. 1980. *Deviant Behavior in Defense of Self.* New York: Academic Press.

———. 1995. "Drugs, Crime, and Other Deviant Adaptation." In *Drugs, Crime, and Other Deviant Acts: Longitudinal Studies,* ed. Howard B. Kaplan, 3–46. New York: Plenum.

KAPLAN, TEMMA. 1982. "Female Consciousness and Collective Action: The Case of Barcelona, 1910–1919." *Signs* 7:545–66.

———. 1997. *Crazy for Democracy: Women in Grassroots Movements.* New York: Routledge.

KARABEL, JEROME, and A. H. HALSEY. 1977. "Educational Research: A Review and an Interpretation." In *Power and Ideology in Education,* ed. Jerome Karabel and A. H. Halsey, 1–86. New York: Oxford University Press.

KARESH, M. 1995. "The Interstitial Origins of Symbolic Consumer Research." Master's thesis, University of Chicago.

KARIDES, MARINA, JOYA MISRA, IVY KENNELLY, and STEPHANIE MOELLER. 2001. "Representing the Discipline: Social Problems Compared to ASR and AJS." *Social Problems* 48(1): 111–28.

KARL, BARRY D. 1963. *Executive Reorganization and Reform in the New Deal.* Cambridge: Harvard University Press.

———. 1969. "Presidential Planning and Social Science Research: Mr. Hoover's Experts." *Perspectives in American History* 3:347–409.

KARL, BARRY D, and STANLEY N. KATZ. 1981. "The American Private Philanthropic Foundation and the Public Sphere, 1890–1930." *Minerva* 19:236–70.

KARPF, MAURICE J. 1925. "The Relation between Sociology and Social Work." *Journal of Social Forces* 3(3): 419–27.

———. 1928. "Sociology and Social Work: A Retrospect." *Social Forces* 6:511–19.

KATOVICH, MICHAEL A., DAN E. MILLER, and ROBERT L. STEWART. 2003. "The

Iowa School." In *Handbook of Symbolic Interactionism*, ed. L. T. Reynolds and N. J. Herman-Kinney, 119–39. Walnut Creek, CA: AltaMira Press.

KATZ, B. M. 1989. *Foreign Intelligence*. Cambridge: Harvard University Press.

KATZ, DANIEL. 1986. "Theodore M. Newcomb: 1903–1984." *American Journal of Psychology* 99(2): 293–98.

KATZ, JACK. 1982. *Poor People's Lawyers in Transition*. New Brunswick, NJ: Rutgers University Press.

———. 1983. "A Theory of Qualitative Methodology: The Social System of Analytic Fieldwork." In *Contemporary Field Research*, ed. Robert Emerson, 127–48. Prospect Heights, IL: Waveland Press.

———. 1988. *Seductions of Crime: Moral and Sensual Attractions in Doing Evil*. New York: Basic Books.

———. 2001. *How Emotions Work*. Chicago: University of Chicago Press.

KATZ, MICHAEL B. 1966. "From Theory to Survey in Graduate Schools of Education." *Journal of Higher Education* 37:325–34.

———. 1968. *The Irony of Early School Reform*. Cambridge: Harvard University Press.

———. 1971. *Class, Bureaucracy, and Schools*. New York: Praeger.

KATZ, MICHAEL B., and THOMAS J. SUGRUE. 1998. *W. E. B. DuBois, Race, and the City: The Philadelphia Negro and the City*. Philadelphia: University of Pennsylvania Press.

KEANE, WEBB. 2005. "Estrangement, Intimacy, and the Objects of Anthropology." In *The Politics of Method in the Human Sciences: Positivism and Its Epistemological Others*, ed. George Steinmetz, 59–88. Durham, NC: Duke University Press.

KEAT, RUSSELL, and JOHN URRY. 1975. *Social Theory as Science*. London: Routledge and Kegan Paul.

KEEN, MIKE FORREST. 1999. *Stalking the Sociological Imagination: J. Edgar Hoover's FBI Surveillance of American Sociology*. Westport, CT: Greenwood Press.

KELLER, ALBERT G. 1903. "Sociology and Homer." *American Journal of Sociology* 9(1): 37–45.

KELLER, EVELYN FOX. 1985. *Reflections on Gender and Science*. New Haven: Yale University Press.

KELLEY, FLORENCE. 1905. *Some Ethical Gains through Legislation*. New York: Macmillan.

KELLEY, ROBIN D. G. 1999. "But a Local Phase of a World Problem: Black History's Global Vision, 1883–1950." *Journal of American History* 86(3):1045–77.

———. 2003. *Freedom Dreams: The Black Radical Imagination*. Boston: Beacon.

KELLOR, FRANCES. 1904. *Out of Work*. New York: G. P. Putnam.

KENISTON, HAYWARD. 1959. *Graduate Study and Research in the Arts and Sciences at the University of Pennsylvania*. Philadelphia: University of Pennsylvania Press.

KENNEDY, DAVID M. 1999. *Freedom from Fear: The American People in Depression and War, 1929–1945*. New York: Oxford University Press.

KENNEDY, MICHAEL D. 1991. *Professionals, Power and Solidarity in Poland: A Critical Sociology of Soviet-Type Society*. Cambridge: Cambridge University Press.

———. 2001. "Postcommunist Capitalism, Culture and History." *American Journal of Sociology* 106(4): 1138–51.

———. 2002. *Cultural Formations of Postcommunism: Emancipation, Transition, Nation, and War.* Minneapolis: University of Minnesota Press.

———. 2004a. "Evolution and Event in History and Social Change: Gerhard Lenski's Critical Theory." *Sociological Theory* 22(2): 315–27.

———. 2004b. "Poland in the American Sociological Imagination." *Polish Sociological Review* 4(148): 361–83.

KENNELLY, IVY. 2002. "'I Would Never Be a Secretary': Reinforcing Gender in Segregated and Integrated Occupations." *Gender and Society* 16:603–24.

KENNELLY, IVY, SABINE MERZ, and JUDITH LORBER. 2001. "What Is Gender?" *American Sociological Review* 66(4): 598–605.

KERCKHOFF, ALAN C. 1976. "The Status Attainment Process: Socialization or Allocation?" *Social Forces* 55:368–81.

KETTLER, DAVID, and VOLKER MEJA. 1995. *Karl Mannheim and the Crisis of Liberalism: The Secret of These New Times.* New Brunswick, NJ: Transaction.

KEVLES, DANIEL J. 1985. *In the Name of Eugenics: Genetics and the Uses of Human Heredity.* New York: Knopf.

KILLENS, JOHN OLIVER. 1963. *And Then We Heard the Thunder.* New York: Knopf.

KIMMEL, MICHAEL. 2001. "Masculinity as Homophobia." In *The Masculinities Reader,* ed. Stephen M. Whitehead and Frank J. Barrett, 266–87. Cambridge, MA: Polity Press.

KING, DEBORAH. 1988. "Multiple Jeopardy, Multiple Consciousness: The Context of a Black Feminist Ideology." *Signs* 14(1): 42–72.

KING, ERIKA G. 1990. "Reconciling Democracy and the Crowd in Turn-of-the-Century American Social-Psychological Thought." *Journal of the History of the Behavioral Sciences* 26 (October): 334–44.

KINLOCH, G. C. 1988. "American Sociology's Changing Interests as Reflected in Two Leading Journals." *American Sociologist* 19:181–94.

KISER, EDGAR, and MICHAEL HECHTER. 1991. "The Role of General Theory in Comparative-Historical Sociology." *American Journal of Sociology* 97:1–30.

KIVISTO, PETER. 2004. "What Is the Canonical Theory of Assimilation? Robert Park and His Predecessors." *Journal of the History of the Behavioral Sciences* 40(2): 149–63.

KLAUSA, EKKEHARD. 1983. Review of *Geschichte der Soziologie: Studien zur kognitiven, sozialen, und historischen Identität einer Disziplin,* 4 vols., ed. Wolf Lepenies. *Journal of the History of the Behavioral Sciences* 19(4): 414–18.

KLAUSNER, SAMUEL Z., and VICTOR D. LIDZ, eds. 1986. *The Nationalization of the Social Sciences.* Philadelphia: University of Pennsylvania Press.

KLEIN, EARL E. 1931. "The Relation of Sociology to Social Work-Historically Considered." *Social Forces* 9:500–507.

KLEIN, MALCOLM W. 1971. *Street Gangs and Street Workers.* Englewood Cliffs, NJ: Prentice Hall.

———. 2002. "Surrounded by Crime: Lessons from One Academic Career." In *Lessons of Criminology,* ed. Gilbert Geis and Mary Dodge, 47–63. Cincinnati: Anderson Publishing.

KLEIN, MALCOLM W., HANS-JUERGEN KERNER, CHERYL L. MAXSON, and ELMAR G. M. WEITEKAMP, eds. 2001. *The Eurogang Paradox: Street Gangs and Youth Groups in the U.S. and Europe.* Amsterdam: Kluwer Academic Publishers.

KLEIN, PHILIP. 1968. *From Philanthropy to Social Welfare.* San Francisco: Jossey-Bass.

KLEINMAN, DANIEL LEE. 1995. *Politics on the Endless Frontier: Postwar Research Policy in the United States.* Durham, NC: Duke University Press.

KLOPPENBERG, JAMES T. 1986. *Uncertain Victory: Social Democracy and Progressivism in European and American Thought, 1870–1920.* New York: Oxford University Press.

———. 1996. "Pragmatism: An Old Name for Some New Ways of Thinking?" *Journal of American History* 83:100–138.

KOEPPEL, DAVID. 2004. "Choosing a College Major: For Love for the Money?" *New York Times,* December 5, p. 1.

KOFFLER, RICHARD. 2004. "Mere Degrees of Reflected Lunar Light?" *Footnotes* 32(3): 10.

KOHN, MELVIN. 1969/1989. *Class and Conformity: A Study in Values.* Homewood, IL: Dorsey Press; Chicago: University of Chicago Press.

———. 1987. "Cross-National Research as an Analytic Strategy." *American Sociological Review* 52:713–31.

KOHN, MELVIN, and KAZIMIERZ M. SLOMCZYNSKI. 1990. *Social Structure and Self-Direction: A Comparative Analysis of the United States and Poland.* Oxford: Blackwell.

KOLB, WILLIAM L. 1948. "The Sociological Theories of Edward Alsworth Ross." In *An Introduction to the History of Sociology,* ed. Harry Elmer Barnes, 819–32. Chicago: University of Chicago Press.

KOMAROVSKY, MIRRA, ed. 1975. *Sociology and Public Policy: The Case of Presidential Commissions.* New York: Elsevier.

KONRAD, GEORGE, and IVAN SZELENYI. 1979. *The Intellectuals on the Road to Class Power.* New York: Harcourt Brace Jovanovich.

KOPP, MARIE. 1936. "Legal and Medical Aspects of Hygienic Sterilization in Germany." *American Sociological Review* 1.

KRAMER, PAUL A. 2006. *The Blood of Government: Race, Empire, the United States, and the Philippines.* Chapel Hill: University of North Carolina Press.

KRIEGER, SUSAN. 1991. *Social Science and the Self: Personal Essays on an Art Form.* New Brunswick, NJ: Rutgers University Press.

———. 1996. *The Family Silver: Essays on Relationships among Women.* Berkeley: University of California Press.

———. 1997. "Lesbian in Academe." In *Feminist Sociology: Life Histories of a Movement,* ed. Barbara Laslett and Barrie Thorne, 194–208. New Brunswick, NJ: Rutgers University Press.

KRISTOL, IRVING. 1999. *Neo-Conservatism: The Autobiography of an Idea.* New York: Ivan R. Dee.

KROEBER, A. L., and TALCOTT PARSONS. 1958. "The Concept of Culture and of Social System." *American Sociological Review* 23(5): 582–83.

KROPOTKIN, PETR ALEKSEEVICH. 1908. *Modern Science and Anarchism.* Trans. D. A. Modell. New York: Mother Earth Publishing Association.

KRUEGER, E. T. 1934. Contribution to "Questions for Sociology: An Informal Round Table Symposium." *Social Forces* 13:193–95.

KRYDER, DANIEL. 2000. *Divided Arsenal: Race and the American State during World War II.* New York: Cambridge University Press.

KUHN, THOMAS S. 1962/1970. *The Structure of Scientific Revolutions.* Chicago: University of Chicago Press.

KUKLICK, BRUCE. 1977. *The Rise of American Philosophy: Cambridge, Massachusetts 1860-1930.* New Haven: Yale University Press.

——. 2001. *A History of Philosophy in America, 1720-2000.* Oxford: Oxford University Press.

KUKLICK, HENRIKA. 1973. "A 'Scientific Revolution': Sociological Theory in the United States, 1930-1945." *Sociological Inquiry* 8(1): 3–22.

——. 1980. "Boundary Maintenance in American Sociology; Limitations to Academic 'Professionalization.'" *Journal of the History of the Behavioral Sciences* 16:201–19.

——. 1999. "Assessing Research in the History of Sociology and Anthropology." *Journal of the History of the Behavioral Sciences* 35(3): 227–37.

KULIS, STEPHEN. 1988. "The Representation of Women in Top Ranked Sociology Departments." *American Sociologist* 19:203–17.

KULP II, DANIEL H. 1929. "Educational Sociology." In *Trends in American Sociology,* ed. George A. Lundberg, Read Bain, and Nels Anderson, 297-313. New York: Harper and Brothers.

KURTZ, LESTER R. 1984. *Evaluating Chicago Sociology: A Guide to the Literature, with an Annotated Bibliography.* Chicago: University of Chicago Press.

KURZMAN, CHARLES. 2004. *The Unthinkable Revolution in Iran.* Cambridge: Harvard University Press.

KUSCH, MARTIN. 1995. *Psychologism: A Case Study in the Sociology of Philosophical Knowledge.* London: Routledge.

KUZNICK, PETER J. 1987. *Beyond the Laboratory: Scientists as Political Activists in 1930s America.* Chicago: University of Chicago Press.

LABAREE, DAVID. 1998. "Educational Researchers: Living with a Lesser Form of Knowledge?" *Educational Researcher* 27:4–12.

——. 2004. "Teacher Ed in the Past: The Roots of Its Lowly Status." Chap. 2 in *The Trouble with Ed Schools.* New Haven: Yale University Press.

LA CAZE, MARGUERITE. 2002. *The Analytic Imaginary.* Ithaca, NY: Cornell University Press.

LACHMAN, RICHARD. 2002. *Capitalists in Spite of Themselves: Elite Conflict and European Transitions in Early Modern Europe.* Oxford: Oxford University Press.

LADNER, JOYCE. 1972. *Tomorrow's Tomorrow.* Garden City, NY: Doubleday.

——, ed. 1973. *The Death of White Sociology.* New York: Random House.

LAFREE, GARY. 1980. "Variables Affecting Guilty Please and Convictions in Rape Cases: Toward a Social Theory of Rape Processing." *Social Forces,* 58:833-50.

——. 2004. "Political and Social Correlates of Global Terrorism." Paper presented at the annual meeting of the American Sociological Association, San Francisco. August 17.

LAGEMANN, ELLEN CONDLIFFE. 1989. *The Politics of Knowledge: The Carnegie Corporation, Philanthropy, and Public Policy.* Middletown, CT: Wesleyan University Press.

——. 1996. *Contested Terrain: A History of Education Research in the United States, 1890-1990.* Chicago: Spencer Foundation.

LAKATOS, IMRE, and ALAN MUSGRAVE, eds. 1970. *Criticism and the Growth of Knowledge.* Cambridge: Cambridge University Press.

LAL, BARBARA BALLIS. 1990. *The Romance of Culture in an Urban Civilization: Robert E. Park on Race and Ethnic Relations in Cities.* London: Routledge.

LAL, JAYATI. 1996. "Situating Locations: The Politics of Self, Identity and 'Other' in Living and Writing the Text." In *Feminist Dilemmas in Fieldwork,* ed. Diane Wolf, 185-214. Boulder, CO: Westview.

——. 1999. "Situating Locations: The Politics of Self, Identity and 'Other' in Living and Writing the Text." In *Feminist Approaches to Theory and Methodology,* ed. Sharlene Hesse-Biber, Christina Gilmartin, and Robin Lydenberg. New York: Oxford University Press.

LAMBEK, MICHAEL. 1991. "Tryin' to Make It Real, but Compared to What?" *Culture* 11:43-51.

LAMONT, MICHÈLE. 2000. *The Dignity of Working Men: Morality and the Boundaries of Race, Class, and Immigration.* Cambridge: Harvard University Press.

LAMONT, MICHÈLE, and VIRAG MOLNÁR. 2002. "The Study of Boundaries in the Social Sciences." *Annual Review of Sociology* 28:167-95.

LAMONT, MICHÈLE, and LAURENT THEVÉNOT, eds. 2000. *Rethinking Comparative Cultural Sociology: Repertoires of Evaluation in France and the United States.* Cambridge: Cambridge University Press.

LANE, ANN. 1990. *To "Herland" and Beyond: The Life and Work of Charlotte Perkins Gilman.* New York: Pantheon.

LANG, KURT, and GLADYS LANG. 1961. *Collective Dynamics.* New York: Crowell.

LAPIERE, RICHARD T., and CHENG WANG. 1931. "The Incidence and Sequence of Social Change." *American Journal of Sociology* 37(3): 399-409.

LAPORTE, TODD R., and PAULA M. CONSOLINI. 1991. "Working in Practice but Not in Theory: Theoretical Challenges of High-Reliability Organizations." *Journal of Public Administration Research and Theory* 1(1): 19-47.

LAREAU, ANNETTE. 2003. *Unequal Childhoods: Class, Race, and Family Life.* Berkeley: University of California Press.

LARSON, OLAF F., and JULIE N. ZIMMERMAN. 2003. *Sociology in Government:*

The Galpin-Taylor Years in the U.S. Department of Agriculture, 1919–1953. University Park: Pennsylvania State University Press.

LASCH, CHRISTOPHER. 1991. *The True and Only Heaven.* New York: Norton.

LASCH-QUINN, ELIZABETH. 1993. *Black Neighbors: Race and the Limits of Reform in the American Settlement House Movement.* Chapel Hill: University of North Carolina Press.

LASLETT, BARBARA. 1990. "Unfeeling Knowledge: Emotion and Objectivity in the History of Sociology." *Sociological Forum* 5(3): 413–33.

———. 1991. "Biography as Historical Sociology: The Case of William Fielding Ogburn." *Theory and Society* 20(4): 511–38.

———. 1998. "Gender and the Rhetoric of Social Science: William Fielding Ogburn and Early Twentieth-Century Sociology in the United States." In *Contesting the Master Narrative*, ed. Jeffrey Cox and Shelton Stromquist, 19–49. Iowa City: University of Iowa Press.

LASLETT, BARBARA, and JOHANNA BRENNER. 1989. "Gender and Social Reproduction: Historical Perspectives." *Annual Review of Sociology* 15:381–404.

LASLETT, BARBARA, and BARRIE THORNE, eds. 1997. *Feminist Sociology: Life Histories of a Movement.* New Brunswick, NJ: Rutgers University Press.

LATHAM, MICHAEL E. 2000. *Modernization as Ideology: American Social Science and "Nation Building" in the Kennedy Era.* Chapel Hill: University of North Carolina Press.

LAUB, JOHN H. 1983. *Criminology in the Making: An Oral History.* Boston: Northeastern University Press.

———. 2004. "The Life Course of Criminology in the United States—The American Society of Criminology 2003 Presidential Address." *Criminology* 42(1): 1–26.

LAUB, JOHN H., and ROBERT J. SAMPSON. 2003. *Shared Beginnings, Divergent Lives: Delinquent Boys to Age 70.* Cambridge: Harvard University Press.

LAURITSEN, JANET L. 2005. "Explaining Patterns of Offending across the Life Course: Comments on Interactional Theory and Recent Tests Based on the RYDS-RIS Data." Prepared for a conference on theoretical integration in criminology, School of Criminology, Albany, NY.

LAZARSFELD, PAUL FELIX. 1951. "Qualitative Measurement in the Social Sciences: Classification, Typologies, and Indices." In *The Policy Sciences: Recent Developments in Scope and Method*, ed. Daniel Lerner, 155–92. Stanford, CA: Stanford University Press.

———. 1958. *The Academic Mind: Social Scientists in a Time of Crisis.* Glencoe, IL: Free Press.

———. 1975. "Working with Merton," In *The Idea of Social Structure: Papers in Honor of Robert K. Merton*, ed. Lewis A. Coser, 35–66. New York: Harcourt Brace Jovanovich.

———. 1993. *On Social Research and Its Language.* Ed. Raymond Boudon. Chicago: University of Chicago Press.

LAZARSFELD, PAUL FELIX, and MORRIS ROSENBERG. 1955. *The Language of Social Research: A Reader in the Methodology of Social Research.* Glencoe, IL: Free Press.

LEACH, WILLIAM. 1980. *True Love and Perfect Union: The Feminist Reform of Sex and Society.* New York: Basic Books.

LE BON, GUSTAVE. 1960. *The Crowd: A Study of the Popular Mind.* New York: Viking Press.

LEE, A. M., and N. D. HUMPHREY. 1943. *Race Riot.* New York: Dryden.

LEE, ALFRED M., and ELIZABETH B. LEE. 1976. "The Society for the Study of Social Problems: Parental Recollections and Hopes." *Social Problems* 24(1): 4-14.

LEE, RICHARD E., and IMMANUEL WALLERSTEIN, COORDINATORS. 2004. *Overcoming the Two Cultures: Science versus the Humanities in the Modern World-System.* Boulder, CO: Paradigm Press.

LEIBY, JAMES. 1978. *A History of Social Welfare and Social Work in the United States.* New York: Columbia University Press.

LEIDNER, ROBIN. 1993. *Fast Food, Fast Talk: Service Work and the Routinization of Everyday Life.* Berkeley: University of California Press.

LEIGHNINGER, LESLIE. 1987. *Social Work: Search for Identity.* Westport, CT: Greenwood Press.

LEIGHTON, A. H. 1945. *The Governing of Men.* Princeton: Princeton University Press.

———. 1949. *Human Relations in a Changing World: Observations on the Use of the Social Sciences.* New York: E. P. Dutton.

LEITES, NATHAN, and CHARLES WOLF JR. 1966. *Rebellion and Authority: Myths and Realities Reconsidered.* Santa Monica, CA: Rand Corporation.

LEJINS, PETER P. 1983. "Educational Programs in Criminal Justice." In *Encyclopedia of Crime and Justice,* ed. Sanford H. Kadish, 688-92. New York: Free Press.

LEMERT, CHARLES. 1988. "Future of the Sixties Generation and Social Theory." *Theory and Society* 17:789-807.

LEMERT, CHARLES, and PAUL PICCONE. 1982. "Gouldner's Theoretical Method and Reflexive Sociology." *Theory and Society* 11:733-57.

LEMERT, EDWIN M. 1967. *Human Deviance, Social Problems, and Social Control.* Englewood Cliffs, NJ: Prentice Hall.

———. 1983. "Deviance." In *Encyclopedia of Crime and Justice,* ed. Sanford H. Kadish, 601-12. New York: Free Press.

LENGERMANN, PATRICIA MADOO. 1979. "The Founding of the *American Sociological Review:* The Anatomy of a Rebellion." *American Sociological Review* 44: 185-98.

LENGERMANN, PATRICIA, and JILL NIEBRUGGE-BRANTLEY, eds. 1998. *The Women Founders: Sociology and Social Theory, 1830-1930.* Boston: McGraw-Hill.

———. 2001. "Classical Feminist Social Theory." In *Handbook of Social Theory,* ed. George Ritzer and Barry Smart, 125-38. Thousand Oaks, CA: Sage.

———. 2002. "Back to the Future: Settlement Sociology, 1885-1930." *American Sociologist* 33:5-15.

———. 2003. "Commentary on Craig R. Bermingham's 'Translation with Introduction and Commentary' of Marianne Weber's 'Authority and Autonomy in Marriage.'" *Sociological Theory* 21:424.

LENSKI, GERHARD E. 1961. *The Religious Factor: A Sociological Study of Religion's Impact on Politics, Economics, and Family Life.* Garden City, NY: Doubleday.

———. 1966. *Power and Privilege: A Theory of Social Stratification.* New York: McGraw-Hill.

———. 1975. "History and Social Change." *American Journal of Sociology* 82:548–63.

———. 1978. "Marxist Experiments in Destratification: An Appraisal." *Social Forces* 57:364–83.

———. 1988. "Rethinking Macrosociological Theory." *American Sociological Review* 53 (April): 163–71.

LEPENIES, WOLF. 1988. *Between Literature and Science: The Rise of Sociology.* Cambridge: Cambridge University Press.

LEUCHTENBURG, W. 1995. "The New Deal and the Analog of War." In *The FDR Years: On Roosevelt and His Legacy.* New York: Columbia University Press.

LEVINE, DONALD N. 1965. *Wax and Gold.* Chicago: University of Chicago Press.

———. 1995. *Visions of the Sociological Tradition.* Chicago: University of Chicago Press.

LEVINE, DONALD N., ELLWOOD B. CARTER, and ELEANOR MILLER GORMAN. 1976a. "Simmel's Influence on American Sociology. I." *American Journal of Sociology* 81:813–45.

———. 1976b. "Simmel's Influence on American Sociology. II." *American Journal of Sociology* 81:1112–32.

LEVINE, RHONDA F., ed. 2004. *Enriching the Sociological Imagination: How Radical Sociology Changed the Discipline.* Leiden: Brill.

LEVY, S. 2003. "Roots of Marketing and Consumer Research at the University of Chicago." In *Consumption, Markets and Culture* 6(2): 99–110.

LEWIS, AMANDA E. 2004. "'What Group?' Studying Whites and Whiteness in the Era of 'Color-Blindness.'" *Sociological Theory* 22(4): 623–46.

LEWIS, DAVID LEVERING. 1993. *W. E. B. DuBois: Biography of a Race, 1868–1919.* New York: Henry Holt.

———. 2000. *W. E. B. DuBois: The Fight for Equality and the American Century, 1919–1963.* New York: Henry Holt.

LEWIS, J. DAVID, and RICHARD L. SMITH. 1980. *American Sociology and Pragmatism: Mead, Chicago Sociology, and Symbolic Interaction.* Chicago: University of Chicago Press.

LIANOS, MICHAELIS, with MARY DOUGLAS. 2000. "Dangerization and the End of Deviance: The Institutional Environment." *British Journal of Criminology* 40: 261–78.

LICHTENSTEIN, NELSON. 1995. *The Most Dangerous Man in Detroit: Walter Reuther and the Fate of American Labor.* New York: Basic Books.

LIE, JOHN. 1996. "Sociology of Contemporary Japan." *Current Sociology* 44(1): 1–95.

———. 2001. "Ruth Benedict's Legacy of Shame: Orientalism and Occidentalism in the Study of Japan" *Asian Journal of Social Science* 29:249–61.

LIEBERSON, STANLEY. 1961. "A Societal Theory of Race and Ethnic Relations." *American Sociological Review* 26:902–10.

LINCOLN, C. ERIC, and LAWRENCE H. MAMIYA. 1990. *The Black Church in the African American Experience.* Durham, NC: Duke University Press.

LINDBLOM, CHARLES. 1997. "Political Science in the 1940 and 1950s." *Daedalus* 126(1): 225–52.

LINDEN, R. RUTH. 1993. *Making Stories, Making Selves: Feminist Reflections on the Holocaust.* Columbus: Ohio State University Press.

LINDERMAN, G. F. 1997. *The World within the War.* Cambridge: Harvard University Press.

LIPSET, SEYMOUR MARTIN. 1955. "The Department of Sociology." In *A History of the Faculty of Political Science at Columbia University,* ed. R. Gordon Hoxie, 284–303. New York: Columbia University Press.

——. 1994. "What's Wrong with Sociology?" *Social Problems* 9(2).

——. 2001. "The State of American Sociology." In *What's Wrong with Sociology?* ed. Stephen Cole, 247–70. New Brunswick, NJ: Transaction Publishers.

LIPSET, SEYMOUR MARTIN, and EVERETT CARLL LADD JR. 1972. "The Politics of American Sociologists." *American Journal of Sociology* 78:67–104.

LIPSET, SEYMOUR MARTIN, MARTIN TROW, and JAMES COLEMAN. 1956. *Union Democracy: The Internal Politics of the International Typographical Union.* Glencoe, IL: Free Press.

LIU, LYDIA. 1999. "The Desire for the Sovereign and the Logic of Reciprocity in the Family of Nations." *Diacritics* 29(4): 150–77.

——. 2001. "The State of American Sociology." In *What's Wrong with Sociology?* ed. Stephen Cole, 247–70. New Brunswick, NJ: Transaction Publishers.

LO, MING-CHENG. 2002. *Doctors within Borders: Profession, Ethnicity, and Modernity in Colonial Taiwan.* Berkeley: University of California Press.

LOFLAND, JOHN. 1971. *Analyzing Social Settings: A Guide to Qualitative Observation and Analysis.* Belmont, CA: Wadsworth Publishing.

LONG, JUDY. 1999. *Telling Women's Lives: Subject/Narrator/Reader/Text.* New York: New York University Press.

LONGINO, HELEN. 1990. *Science as Social Knowledge: Values and Objectivity in Scientific Inquiry.* Princeton: Princeton University Press.

LOPATA, HELENA. 1995. "Postscript." In *A Second Chicago School? The Development of a Postwar American Sociology,* ed. Gary Alan Fine, 365–86. Chicago: University of Chicago Press.

LOPATA, HELENA Z., and BARRIE THORNE. 1978. "On the Term 'Sex Roles.'" *Signs* 3:718–21.

LORBER, JUDITH. 1994. *Paradoxes of Gender.* New Haven: Yale University Press.

LORTIE, DAN C. 1975. *School-Teacher: A Sociological Study.* Chicago: University of Chicago Press.

LOTT, ERIC. 1995. *Love and Theft: Blackface Minstrelsy and the American Working Class.* New York: Oxford University Press.

LOUIS, WILLIAM ROGER, and RONALD ROBINSON. 1993. "The Imperialism of De-colonization." *Journal of Imperial and Commonwealth History* 22(3): 462–511.

LOVEJOY, ARTHUR O. 1963. *The Thirteen Pragmatisms, and Other Essays*. Baltimore: Johns Hopkins University Press.

LUBIN, ISADOR. 1937. "Government Employment as a Professional Career in Eco-nomics." *American Economic Review* 27 (suppl.): 216–24.

LUBOVE, ROY. 1965. *The Professional Altruist : The Emergence of Social Work as a Ca-reer, 1880–1930*. Cambridge: Harvard University Press.

LUCAL, BETSY. 1999. "What It Means to Be Gendered Me: Life on the Boundaries of a Dichotomous Gender System." *Gender and Society* 13:781–97.

LUCKENBILL, DAVID F. 1977. "Criminal Homicide as a Situation Transaction." *So-cial Problems* 25(2): 176–86.

LUCKMANN, THOMAS. 1973. "Philosophy, Science, and Everyday Life." In *Phenom-enology and the Social Sciences*, ed. M. Natanson, 1:143–85. Evanston, IL: North-western University Press.

LUKER, KRISTIN. 1984. *Abortion and the Politics of Motherhood*. Berkeley: University of California Press.

LUNDBERG, GEORGE. 1931. "The Interests of Members of the American Sociologi-cal Society, 1930." *American Journal of Sociology* 37(3): 458–60.

—— 1937. "Report of Research Census of 1937." *American Sociological Review* 2: 518–30.

——. 1939a. "Contemporary Positivism in Sociology." *American Sociological Review* 4 (1): 42–55.

——. 1939b. *Foundations of Sociology*. New York: Macmillan.

——. 1945. "The Growth of Scientific Method." *American Journal of Sociology* 50(6): 502–13.

——. 1955. "The Natural Science Trend in Sociology." *American Journal of Sociology* 61(3): 191–202.

——. 1956. "Some Convergences in Sociological Theory." *American Journal of Soci-ology* 62(1): 21–27.

——. 1964. *Foundations of Sociology*. New York: Macmillan.

LUNDBERG, GEORGE, READ BAIN, and NELS ANDERSON, eds. 1929. *Trends in American Sociology*. New York: Harper and Brothers.

LUNDBERG, GEORGE A., CLARENCE C. SCHRAG, and OTTO N. LARSEN. 1954. *So-ciology*. New York: Harper and Brothers.

LÜSCHEN, GÜNTHER. 2002. "In memoriam Werner S. Landecker 30.04.1911–19.05.2002." *Kölner Zeitschrift für Soziologie und Sozialpsychologie* 54: 617–18.

LUTZ, CATHERINE. 1990. "The Erasure of Women's Writing in Socio-Cultural An-thropology." *American Ethnologist* 17(4): 611–27.

LUXTON, MEG. 1980. *More Than a Labour of Love: Three Generations of Women's Work in the Home*. Toronto: Women's Press.

LYMAN, STANFORD M. 1972. *The Black American in Sociological Thought: A Failure of Perspective*. New York: Putnam.

———. 1985. Introduction to *Selected Writings of Henry Hughes, Antebellum Southerner, Slavocrat, Sociologist*, ed. S. Lyman. Jackson: University Press of Mississippi.

LYND, ROBERT STAUGHTON. 1939. *Knowledge for What? The Place of Social Science in American Culture*. Princeton: Princeton University Press.

LYND, ROBERT S., and HELEN M. LYND. 1929. *Middletown: A Study in Contemporary American Culture*. New York: Harcourt, Brace.

———. 1937. *Middletown in Transition: A Study of Cultural Conflict*. New York: Harcourt, Brace.

LYONS, GENE M. 1969. *The Uneasy Partnership: Social Science and the Federal Government in the Twentieth Century*. New York: Russell Sage.

MACIVER, ROBERT M. 1931. "Is Sociology a Natural Science?" *Publications of the American Sociological Society* 25: 25–35.

———. 1934a. *Economic Reconstruction*. Report of the Columbia University Commission. New York: Columbia University Press.

———. 1934b. "Social Philosophy." *American Journal of Sociology* 39:835–41.

———, ed. 1949. *Discrimination and the National Welfare*. New York: Harper and Brothers.

MACKIE, MARLENE. 1985. "Female Sociologists' Productivity through Journal Publications." *Sociology and Social Research* 69:189–209.

MACLEAN, ANNIE MARION. 1899. "Two Weeks in Department Stores." *American Journal of Sociology* 4:721–41.

MACLEAN, VICKY M., and JOYCE E. WILLIAMS. 2005. "Sociology at Women's and Black Colleges, 1880s–1940s." In *Diverse Histories of American Sociology*, ed. Anthony Blasi. Leiden, Netherlands: Brill.

MAGDALENIĆ, SANJA. 2004. "Gendering the Sociology Profession: Sweden, Britain, and the U.S." PhD diss., Department of Sociology, Stockholm University.

MAINARDI, PAT. 1968. "The Politics of Housework." Somerville, MA: New England Free Press.

MANICAS, PETER T. 1991. "Social Science Disciplines: The American Model." In *Discourses on Society: Shaping the Social Science Disciplines*, ed. Peter Wagner, Björn Wittrock, and Richard Whitley, 45–71. Dordrecht and Boston: Kluwer Academic Publishers.

MANN, MICHAEL. 1986. *The Sources of Social Power: A History of Power from the Beginning to AD 1760*. Cambridge: Cambridge University Press.

———. 1993. *The Sources of Social Power: The Rise of Classes and Nation States, 1760–1914*. Cambridge: Cambridge University Press.

———. 2003. *Incoherent Empire*. London: Verso.

MANZA, JEFFREY L. 1995. "Policy Experts and Political Change during the New Deal." PhD diss., University of California, Berkeley. Ann Arbor: UMI Dissertation Services.

———. 2000. "Political Sociological Models of the U.S. New Deal." *Annual Review of Sociology* 26:297–322.

MARABLE, MANNING. 1986. *W. E. B. DuBois: Black Radical Democrat*. Boston: Twayne.

MARCUSE, HERBERT. 1941. *Reason and Revolution: Hegel and the Rise of Social Theory.* New York: Oxford University Press.

———. 1951. *One-Dimensional Man.* Boston: Beacon Press.

———. 1958. *Soviet Marxism: A Critical Analysis.* New York: Columbia University Press.

———. 1965/1971. "Industrialization and Capitalism." In *Max Weber and Sociology Today: Transactions of the Fifteenth German Sociological Congress,* ed. Otto Stammer, trans. Kathleen Morris, 133-51. Oxford: Blackwell.

MARIS, RONALD W. 1981. *Pathways to Suicide: A Survey of Self-Destructive Behaviors.* Baltimore: Johns Hopkins University Press.

MARKOFF, JOHN. 1996. *Abolition of Feudalism: Peasants, Lords, and Legislators in the French Revolution.* State College: Pennsylvania State University Press.

MARKS, JONATHAN. 1995. *Human Biodiversity: Genes, Race, and History.* New York: Aldine de Gruyter.

MARKUS, HAZEL, and SHINOBU KITAYAMA. 1991. "Culture and the Self: Implications for Cognition, Emotion, and Motivation." *Psychological Review* 98:224-53.

MARSDEN, GEORGE. 1994. "God and Man at Yale (1880)." *First Things* 42 (April): 39-42.

———. 1996. *The Soul of the American University.* New York: Oxford University Press.

MARSH, C. S. 1940. *American Universities and Colleges.* Washington, DC: American Council on Education.

MARSH, ROBERT M. 2004. "Is *Social Forces* Still a 'Core Journal'?" *Footnotes* 32(3): 10.

MARTIN, EMILY. 1994. *Flexible Bodies: Tracking Immunity in American Culture from the Days of Polio to the Age of AIDS.* Boston: Beacon Press.

MARTIN, PATRICIA YANCEY. 2004. "Gender as a Social Institution." *Social Forces* 82:1249-74.

MARTIN, PATRICIA YANCEY, and ROBERT A. HUMMER. 1989. "Fraternities and Rape on Campus." *Gender and Society* 3:457-73.

MARTINDALE, DON ALBERT. 1976a. "American Sociology before World War II." *Annual Review of Sociology* 2:121-43.

———. 1976b. *The Romance of a Profession: A Case History in the Sociology of Sociology.* St. Paul, MN: Windflower Publishing.

———. 1980. "The Golden Age of Minnesota Sociology, 1921-1930." *Journal of the History of Sociology* 2:35-60.

———. 1982. *The Monologue: Hans Gerth (1908-1978), a Memoir.* Ghaziabad, India: Intercontinental Press.

MARWELL, GERALD. 1998. "Sociological Politics and Contemporary Sociology's Ten Most Influential Books." In *Required Reading: Sociology's Most Influential Books,* ed. Dan Clawson, 189-95. Amherst: University of Massachusetts Press.

MARX, KARL. 1967. *Capital.* Vol. 1. New York: International Publishers.

MASON, KAREN OPPENHEIM, JOHN L. CZAJKA, and SARA ARBER. 1976. "Change in U.S. Women's Sex-Role Attitudes, 1964-1974." *American Sociological Review* 40:123-47.

MASSEY, DOUGLAS S., ET AL. 2002. *The Source of the River: The Social Origins of*

Freshmen at America's Selective Colleges and Universities. Princeton: Princeton University Press.

MASSEY, DOUGLAS, and NANCY DENTON. 1993. *American Apartheid.* Cambridge: Harvard University Press.

MATHEWS, SHAILER. 1895a. "Christian Sociology: Introduction. *American Journal of Sociology* 1(1): 69–78.

———. 1895b. "Christian Sociology. I. Man." *American Journal of Sociology* 1(2): 182–94.

———. 1895c. "Christian Sociology. II. Society." *American Journal of Sociology* 1(3): 359–80.

———. 1896a. "Christian Sociology. III. The Family." *American Journal of Sociology* 1(4): 457–72.

———. 1896b. "Christian Sociology. IV. The State." *American Journal of Sociology* 1(5): 604–17.

———. 1896c. "Christian Sociology. V. Wealth." *American Journal of Sociology* 1(6): 771–84.

MATSUEDA, ROSS L. 1992. "Reflected Appraisals, Parental Labeling, and Delinquency: Specifying a Symbolic Interactionist Theory." *American Journal of Sociology* 97(6): 1577–1611.

MATSUEDA, ROSS L., and KAREN HEIMER. 1987. "Race, Family Structure and Delinquency: A Test of Differential Association and Social Control Theories." *American Sociological Review* 52(6): 826–40.

MATTHEWS, FRED H. 1977. *Quest for an American Sociology: Robert E. Park and the Chicago School.* Montreal: McGill-Queen's University Press.

MAYHEW, HENRY. 1968. *London Labor and the London Poor: Those That Will Not Work, Comprising Prostitutes, Thieves, Swindlers and Beggars.* New York: Dover.

MAYNARD, DOUGLAS W., and STEVEN E. CLAYMAN. 1991. "The Diversity of Ethnomethodology." *Annual Review of Sociology* 17:385–418.

MAYNES, MARY JO. 1992. "Autobiography and Class Formation in Nineteenth-Century Europe." *Social Science History* 16:517–37.

MAYNES, MARY JO, and JENNIFER PIERCE. 2005. "Telling Stories: Life Histories in the Social Sciences and History." Manuscript.

MAYO-SMITH, RICHMOND. 1895–99. *Science of Statistics.* 2 vols. New York: Macmillan.

MAZRUI, ALI A. 1968. "From Social Darwinism to Current Theories of Modernization: A Tradition of Analysis." *World Politics* 21 (October): 69–83.

MCADAM, DOUG. 1982. *Political Process and the Development of Black Insurgency, 1930–1970.* Chicago: University of Chicago Press.

———. 1988. *Freedom Summer.* New York: Oxford University Press.

MCADAM, DOUGLAS, JOHN MCCARTHY, and MAYER ZALD. 1996. *Comparative Perspectives on Social Movements.* New York: Cambridge University Press.

MCAULEY, CHRISTOPHER. 2004. *The Mind of Oliver C. Cox.* Notre Dame: Notre Dame University Press.

MCCALL, GEORGE J., and J. L. SIMMONS. 1969. *Issues in Participant Observation: A Text and Reader.* Reading, MA: Addison-Wesley.

MCCALL, LESLIE. 2001. *Complex Inequality: Gender, Class and Race in the New Economy.* New York: Routledge.

MCCARTHY, BILL. 2002. "New Economics of Sociological Criminology." *Annual Review of Sociology* 28:417–42.

MCCARTHY, E. DOYLE, and ROBIN DAS. 1985. "American Sociology's Idea of Itself: A Review of the Textbook Literature from the Turn of the Century to the Present." *History of Sociology* 5(2): 21–43.

MCCARTHY, JOHN D., and MAYER ZALD. 1973. *The Trend of Social Movements in America: Professionalization and Resource Mobilization.* Morristown, NJ: General Learning Press.

———. 1977. "Resource Mobilization and Social Movements: A Partial Theory." *American Journal of Sociology* 82:1212–41.

MCCARTHY, THOMAS. 1978. *The Critical Theory of Jürgen Habermas.* Cambridge: MIT Press.

MCCLINTOCK, ANNE. 1995. *Imperial Leather: Race, Gender, and Sexuality in the Colonial Contest.* New York: Routledge.

MCCOBB, HELEN IRENE. 1932. "A Definition of Sociology Derived from Titles of Courses." *Social Forces* 10(3): 355–57.

MCCUMBER, JOHN. 2001. *Time in the Ditch: American Philosophy and the McCarthy Era.* Evanston, IL: Northwestern University Press.

MCDIARMID, JOHN. 1945. "The Mobilization of Social Scientists." In *Civil Service in Wartime,* ed. Leonard D. White, 73–96. Chicago: University of Chicago Press.

MCDONALD, LYNN. 1994. *The Women Founders of the Social Sciences.* Ottawa, Canada: Carleton University Press.

———, ed. 1998. *Women Theorists on Society and Politics.* Waterloo, Ontario: Wilfred Laurier University Press.

MCINTOSH, PEGGY. 1983. "Interactive Phases of Curricular Revision: A Feminist Perspective." Working Papers, series 124. Wellesley College Center for Research on Women.

MCKEE, JAMES B. 1993. *Sociology and the Race Problem: The Failure of a Perspective.* Urbana: University of Illinois Press.

MCKENZIE, RODERICK. 1923. *The Neighborhood: A Study of Local Life in the City of Columbus, Ohio.* Chicago: University of Chicago Press.

MCWHORTER, JOHN H. 2000. *Losing the Race: Self-Sabotage in Black America.* New York: Free Press.

MEAD, GEORGE HERBERT. 1934. *Mind, Self, and Society from the Standpoint of a Social Behaviorist.* Chicago: University of Chicago Press.

MEAD, M. 1942. *And Keep Your Powder Dry: An Anthropologist Looks at America.* New York: William Morrow.

MEADOW ORLANS, KATHRYN P., and RUTH A. WALLACE. 1994. *Gender and the Academic Experience: Berkeley Women Sociologists.* Lincoln: University of Nebraska Press.

MEIER, ROBERT F., ed. 1985. *Theories of Criminology.* Beverly Hills: Sage.

MENAND, LOUIS. 2001. *The Metaphysical Club.* New York: Farrar, Straus and Giroux.

MENZEL, HERBERT. 1959. "Planned and Unplanned Scientific Communication."

In *International Conference on Scientific Information (1958)*, 1:199–243. Washington, DC: National Academy of Sciences–National Research Council.

———. 1961. "On the Relation between Individual and Collective Properties." In *Complex Organizations*, ed. A. Etzioni, 422–40. New York: Holt Rinehart.

MERONEY, W. P. 1931. "The Membership and Program of Twenty-Five Years of the American Sociological Society." *Publications of the American Sociological Society* 25:55–67.

———. 1934. Contribution to "Questions for Sociology: An Informal Round Table Symposium." *Social Forces* 13:198–200.

MERTON, ROBERT K. 1936. "The Unanticipated Consequences of Purposive Social Action." *American Sociological Review* 1:894–904.

———. 1938. "Social Structure and Anomie." *American Sociological Review* 3(4): 672–82.

———. 1948. "The Social Psychology of Housing." In *Current Trends in Social Psychology*, ed. W. Dennis, 163–217. Pittsburgh: University of Pittsburgh Press.

———. 1949a. "Anomie and Social Structure." In *Social Theory and Social Structure*. 1st ed. Glencoe, IL: Free Press.

———. 1949b. "Discrimination and the American Creed." In *Discrimination and the National Welfare*, ed. Robert W. MacIver. New York: Harper and Brothers.

———. 1957a. "In Memory of Bernhard J. Stern." *Science and Society* 21(1): 7–9.

———. 1957b. *Social Theory and Social Structure*. 2nd ed. Glencoe, IL: Free Press.

———. 1968a. "Puritanism, Pietism, and Science" (1936). In *Social Theory and Social Structure*, 628–60. New York: Free Press.

———. 1968b. *Social Theory and Social Structure*. 3rd ed. New York: Free Press.

———. 1973. "The Normative Structure of Science." In *The Sociology of Science*, ed. N. W. Storer, 267–78. Chicago: University of Chicago Press. Essay originally pub. 1942.

———. 1983. "Florian Znaniecki: A Short Reminiscence." *Journal of the History of the Behavioral Sciences* 19 (April): 123–26.

———. 1994. "A Life of Learning." Occasional Paper No. 25. New York: American Council of Learned Societies.

———. 1995. "The Thomas Theorem and the Matthew Effect." *Social Forces* 74:379–424.

———. 1997. "On the Evolving Synthesis of Differential Association and Anomie Theory: A Perspective from the Sociology of Science." *Criminology* 35(3): 517–25.

MERTON, ROBERT K., ALISA P. GRAY, BARBARA HOCKEY, and HANAN C. SELVIN, eds. 1952. *Reader in Bureaucracy*. Glencoe, IL: Free Press.

MERTON, ROBERT K., and PAUL F. LAZARSFELD. 1943. "Studies in Radio and Film Propaganda." *Transactions of New York Academy of Sciences* 6:58–79.

———. 1950. *Continuities in Social Research: Studies in the Scope and Method of "The American Soldier."* Glencoe, IL: Free Press.

MERTON, ROBERT K., GEORGE G. READER, and PATRICIA L. KENDALL, eds. 1957. *The Student-Physician: Introductory Studies in the Sociology of Medical Education.* Cambridge: Harvard University Press.

MERTON, ROBERT K., and MATILDA WHITE RILEY, eds. 1980. *Sociological Traditions from Generation to Generation: Glimpses of the American Experience.* Norwood, NJ: Ablex Publishing Co.

MESSERSCHMIDT, JAMES W. 1993. *Masculinities and Crime.* Lanham: Rowman and Littlefield.

MESSNER, STEVEN F., and R. ROSENFELD. 1994. *Crime and the American Dream.* Belmont, CA: Wadsworth.

METZ, MARY HAYWOOD. 1994. "Running between the Raindrops: From the Margin to the Mainstream." In *Gender and the Academic Experience: Berkeley Women Sociologists,* ed. Kathryn P. Meadow Orlans and Ruth A. Wallace, 219–27. Lincoln: University of Nebraska Press.

METZGER, WALTER. 1961. *Academic Freedom in the Age of the University.* New York: Columbia University Press.

MEYER, JOHN, JOHN BOLI, GEORGE M. THOMAS, and FRANCISCO O. RAMIREZ. 1997. "World Society and the Nation State." *American Journal of Sociology* 103(1): 144–81.

MEYER, JOHN W., and MICHAEL T. HANNAN, eds. 1979. *National Development and the World System: Educational, Economic, and Political Change, 1950–1970.* Chicago: University of Chicago Press.

MEYER, JOHN W., FRANCISCO O. RAMIREZ, and YASEMIN NUHOGLU SOYSAL. 1992. "World Expansion of Mass Education, 1870–1980." *Sociology of Education* 65:128–49.

MEYER, MAX. 1921. *Psychology of the Other-One: An Introductory Text-Book of Psychology.* Columbia, MO: Missouri Book Company.

———. 1927. *Abnormal Psychology: "When the Other-One Astonishes Us."* Columbia, MO: Lucas Brothers.

———. Max Meyer Incident Papers. Western Historical Manuscript Collection, 1929–30, 1/0/1 box 4. University of Missouri, Columbia.

MILKMAN, RUTH. 1987. *Gender at Work: The Dynamics of Job Segregation by Sex during World War II.* Urbana: University of Illinois Press.

MILLER, DELBERT C. 1986. *One Hundred Years: The History of Sociology at Indiana University, 1885–1985.* Bloomington: Department of Sociology, Indiana University.

———. 1989. "The Greatest Books of Sociology." *Footnotes* (December): 13.

MILLER, KELLY. 1897. "A Review of Hoffman's *Race Traits and Tendencies of the American Negro.*" Washington, DC: American Negro Academy.

MILLER, RICHARD W. 1987. *Fact and Method: Explanation, Confirmation and Reality in the Natural and Social Sciences.* Princeton: Princeton University Press.

MILLIS, H. A. 1898. "The Law Relating to the Relief and Care of Dependents, II." *American Journal of Sociology* 3:479–89.

MILLMAN, MARCIA, and ROSABETH MOSS KANTOR, eds. 1975. *Another Voice.* Garden City, NJ: Doubleday.

MILLS, C. WRIGHT. 1943. "The Professional Ideology of Social Pathologists." *American Journal of Sociology* 49(2): 165–80.

———. 1948. "International Relations and Sociology: Discussion." *American Sociological Review* 13(3): 271-73.

———. 1956. *The Power Elite.* New York: Oxford University Press.

———. 1959. *The Sociological Imagination.* Oxford: Oxford University Press.

———. 1964. *Sociology and Pragmatism: The Higher Learning in America.* New York: Paine-Whitman Publishers.

MILLS, CHARLES W. 1997. *The Racial Contract.* Ithaca, NY: Cornell University Press.

MILNER, MURRAY, JR. 1994. *Status and Sacredness: A General Theory of Status Relations and an Analysis of Indian Culture.* New York: Oxford University Press.

MILOVANOVIC, DRAGAN. 1997. *Postmodern Criminology.* New York: Garland.

MINER, HORACE. 1956. "Body Ritual among the Nacirema." *American Anthropologist,* n.s., 58(3): 503-7.

MIROWSKI, PHILIP. 1989. *More Heat Than Light: Economics as Social Physics, Physics as Nature's Economics.* Cambridge: Cambridge University Press.

———. 2005. "How Positivism Made Pact with the Postwar Social Sciences in America." In *The Politics of Method in the Human Sciences: Positivism and Its Epistemological Others,* ed. George Steinmetz, 142-72. Durham, NC: Duke University Press.

MISHLER, ELLIOT GEORGE. 1986. *Research Interviewing: Context and Narrative.* Cambridge: Harvard University Press.

MISRA, JOYCE, IVY KENNELLY, and MARINA KARIDES. 1999. "Employment Chances in the Academic Job Market in Sociology: Do Race and Gender Matter?" *Sociological Perspectives* 42(2): 215-47.

MITCHELL, G. DUNCAN. 1968. *A Hundred Years of Sociology.* Chicago: Aldine.

MOFFITT, TERRIE E. 1993. "Adolescent-Limited and Life-Course Persistent Antisocial Behavior: A Developmental Taxonomy." *Psychological Review* 100(4): 674-701.

MOLOTCH, HARVEY. 1994. "Going Out." *Sociological Forum* 9:221-39.

MOODY, JAMES. 2004. "The Structure of a Social Science Collaboration Network: Disciplinary Cohesion from 1963 to 1999." *American Sociological Review* 69(2): 213-38.

MOORE, BARRINGTON. 1966/1993. *Social Origins of Dictatorship and Democracy: Lord and Peasant in the Making of the Modern World.* Boston: Beacon Press.

MOORE, WILBERT E. 1980. *American Negro Slavery and Abolition: A Sociological Study.* New York: Arno Press.

MORAWSKA, EWA. 1996. "The Immigrants Pictured and Unpictured in the Pittsburgh Survey." In *Pittsburgh Surveyed,* ed. Maurine Greenwald and Margo Anderson, 221-41. Pittsburgh: University of Pittsburgh Press.

MOREHOUSE, MAGGI. 2000. *Fighting in the Jim Crow Army: Black Men and Women Remember World War II.* Lanham, MD: Rowman and Littlefield.

MORGAN, ARTHUR E. 1937. "Sociology in the TVA." *American Sociological Review* 2:157-65.

MORGAN, MARY S. 2003. "Economics." In *The Modern Social Sciences,* 275-305, vol. 7 of *The Cambridge History of Science,* ed. Theodore M. Porter and Dorothy Ross. Cambridge: Cambridge University Press.

MORLEY, FELIX, ed. 1932. *Aspects of the Depression.* Chicago: University of Chicago Press.

———, ed. 1933. *The Economic World Today.* Chicago: University of Chicago Press.

MORRIONE, THOMAS J. 2004. "Editor's Introduction." In *George Herbert Mead and Human Conduct,* by Herbert Blumer, ed. T. J. Morrione. Walnut Creek, CA: AltaMira.

MORRIS, ALBERT. 1975. "The American Society of Criminology: A History, 1941–1974." *Criminology* 13(2): 123–67.

MORRIS, ALDON D. 1984. *Origins of the Civil Rights Movement: Black Communities Organizing for Change.* New York: Free Press.

———. 1992. "Political Consciousness and Collective Action." In *Frontiers in Social Movement Theory,* ed. Aldon D. Morris and Carol McClurg Mueller, 351–73. New Haven: Yale University Press.

MORRIS, ALDON, and AMIN GHAZIANI. 2005. "Du Boisian Sociology: A Watershed of Professional and Public Sociology." In *Souls.* Philadelphia: Taylor and Francis.

MOSS, DAVID A. 1996. *Socializing Security: Progressive-Era Economists and the Origins of American Social Policy.* Cambridge: Harvard University Press.

MOSSE, GEORGE L. 1978. *Toward the Final Solution: A History of European Racism.* New York: Howard Fertig.

MUENSTERBERG, E. 1897. "Principles of Public Charity and Private Philanthropy in Germany." *American Journal of Sociology* 2(4): 589–605; 2(5): 680–98.

MULLIGAN, RAYMOND A. 1954. "Sociology and Education for Social Work." *Journal of Educational Sociology* 27:196–204.

MULLINS, NICHOLAS C., and CAROLYN J. MULLINS. 1973. *Theories and Theory Groups in Contemporary American Sociology.* New York: Harper and Row.

MUNCY, ROBYN. 1991. *Creating a Female Dominion of Reform.* New York: Oxford University Press.

MURRAY, CHARLES A. 1984. *Losing Ground: American Social Policy, 1950–1980.* New York: Basic Books.

MURRAY, STEPHEN. 1980. "Resistance to Sociology at Berkeley." *Journal of the History of Sociology* 2:61–84.

MYERS, WILLIAM STARR. 1931. "Looking Toward 1932." *American Political Science Review* 25:925–31.

MYKHALOVSKIY, ERIC. 1996. "Reconsidering Table Talk: Critical Thoughts on the Relationship between Sociology, Autobiography and Self-Indulgence." *Qualitative Sociology* 19:131–51.

MYRDAL, GUNNAR. 1944. *An American Dilemma: The Negro Problem and Modern Democracy.* With the assistance of Richard Sterner and Arnold Rose. New York: Harper and Brothers.

———. 1963. *Economic Theory and Underdeveloped Regions.* London: Methuen.

NAGEL, ERNEST. 1961/1979. *The Structure of Science: Problems in the Logic of Scientific Explanation.* New York: Harcourt, Brace and World.

NAGIN, DANIEL S., DAVID P. FARRINGTON, and TERRIE E. MOFFITT. 1995. "Life-Course Trajectories of Different Types of Offenders." *Criminology* 33(1): 111–39.

NAPOLI, D. S. 1981. *Architects of Adjustment*. Port Washington, NY: Kennikat Press.

NATANSON, MAURICE. 1973. *Edmund Husserl: Philosopher of Infinite Tasks*. Evanston, IL: Northwestern University Press.

NATIONAL COMMISSION ON EXCELLENCE IN EDUCATION. 1983. *A Nation at Risk: The Imperative for Educational Reform*. Washington, DC: Government Printing Office.

NATIONAL ROSTER OF SCIENTIFIC AND TECHNICAL PERSONNEL. 1942. *Report of the National Roster of Scientific and Technical Personnel to the National Resources Planning Board*. Washington, DC: Government Printing Office.

NECKERMAN, KATHRYN M., and JOLEEN KIRSCHENMAN. 1991. "Hiring Strategies, Racial Bias, and Inner-City Workers." *Social Problems* 38:433-47.

NELKIN, DOROTHY, and LAURENCE TANCREDI. 1989. *Dangerous Diagnostics: The Social Power of Biological Information*. New York: Basic Books.

NELSON, LAWRENCE J. 2003. *The Rumors of Indiscretion: University of Missouri "Sex Questionnaire" Scandal in the Jazz Age*. Columbia: University of Missouri Press.

NESS, GAYLE D. 1985. "Obituaries: Robert Cooley Angell (1899-1984)." *ASA Footnotes*, May, 10.

NEUMANN, FRANZ. 1939. Review of *Knowledge for What?* by Robert Lynd. *Zeitschrift für Sozialforschung* 8 (1-2): 228-32, 469.

———. 1944. *Behemoth*. New York: Oxford University Press.

NEURATH, OTTO. 1973. "Empirical Sociology" (1931). In *Empiricism and Sociology*, ed. Marie Neurath and Robert S. Cohen, 319-421. Dordrecht: D. Reidel.

"News and Notes." 1933. *American Journal of Sociology* 38:941-53.

NICHOLS, LAWRENCE T. 1992. "The Establishment of Sociology at Harvard: A Case of Organizational Ambivalence and Scientific Vulnerability." In *Science at Harvard University: Historical Perspectives*, ed. Clark A. Elliott and Margaret W. Rossiter, 191-222. Bethlehem, PA: Lehigh University Press.

———. 1998. "Social Relations Undone: Disciplinary Divergence at Harvard, 1946-1970." *American Sociologist* 29(2): 83-107.

NICHOLSON, IAN A. M. 1998. "'The Approved Bureaucratic Torpor': Goodwin Watson, Critical Psychology, and the Dilemmas of Expertise, 1930-1950." *Journal of Social Issues* 54:53-78.

———. 2003. *Inventing Personality: Gordon Allport and the Science of Selfhood*. Washington, DC: American Psychological Association.

NICOLAUS, MARTIN. 1968. "Fat-Cat Sociology: Remarks at the American Sociological Association." *American Sociologist* 4:154-56.

NIEBUHR, REINHOLD. 1932. *Moral Man and Immoral Society*. New York: Scribner's.

NISBET, ROBERT A. 1962. "Sociology as an Art Form." *Pacific Sociological Review* 5(2): 67-74.

———. 1966. *The Sociological Tradition*. New York: Basic Books.

———. 1969. *Social Change and History*. New York: Oxford University Press.

NORMANO, J. F. 1931. A Neglected Utopian: Cyrano de Bergerac, 1619-55. *American Journal of Sociology* 37:3 (November): 454-57.

NORTHCOTT, CLARENCE H. 1948. "The Sociological Theories of Franklin Henry Giddings: Consciousness of Kind, Pluralistic Behavior, and Statistical Method." In *An Introduction to the History of Sociology,* ed. Harry Elmer Barnes, 744–65. Chicago: University of Chicago Press.

NOVICK, PETER. 1988. *That Noble Dream: The "Objectivity Question" and the American Historical Profession.* Cambridge: Cambridge University Press.

NOYES, JOHN. 2006. "Commerce, Colonialism, and the Globalization of Action in Late Enlightenment Germany." *Postcolonial Studies* 9(1): 81–98.

NOYES, WILLIAM HORACE. 1950/1970. "Institutional Peril of the Settlements" (1899). In *The Development of Settlement Work,* ed. Lorena M. Pacey, 60–68. Freeport, NY: Books for Libraries Press.

OAKLEY, ANN. 2000. *Experiments in Knowing: Gender and Method in the Social Sciences.* Cambridge, MA: Polity Press.

OBERSCHALL, ANTHONY. 1986. "The Two Empirical Roots of Social Theory." *Knowledge and Society* 6:67–97.

———, ed. 1972. *The Establishment of Empirical Sociology: Studies in Continuity, Discontinuity, and Institutionalization.* New York: Harper and Row.

O'BRIEN K. P., AND L. H. PARSONS, eds. 1995. *The Home-Front War: World War II and American Society.* Westport, CT: Greenwood Press.

O'BRIEN, MARY. 1981. *The Politics of Reproduction.* London: Routledge and Kegan Paul.

O'CONNOR, JULIA, ANN SHOLA ORLOFF, and SHEILA SHAVER. 1999. *States, Markets, Families.* New York: Cambridge University Press.

O'CONNOR, WILLIAM THOMAS. 1942. *Naturalism and the Pioneers of American Sociology.* Washington, DC: Catholic University of America Press.

ODENWALD-UNGER, MRS. J. 1907. "The Fine Arts as a Dynamic Factor in Society" [proceedings of the first ASS meeting]. *American Journal of Sociology* 12(5): 656–65; comments by George Cooke, Lester Ward, Franklin Sargent, and Charles Moore, 665–74.

ODUM, HOWARD W. 1910. *Social and Mental Traits of the Negro: Research into the Conditions of the Negro Race in Southern Towns, A Study in Race Traits, Tendencies and Prospects.* New York: Columbia University Press.

———, ed. 1927. *American Masters of Social Science: An Approach to the Study of the Social Sciences through a Neglected Field of Biography.* New York: Henry Holt.

———. 1930/1931. "Folk and Regional Conflict as a Field of Sociological Study." *Publication of the American Sociological Society* 25:1–17.

———. 1937. "The Errors of Sociology." *Social Forces* 15:327–42.

———. 1951/1969. *American Sociology: The Story of Sociology in the United States through 1950.* New York: Longmans, Green; New York: Greenwood Press.

"Official Reports and Proceedings" [of the American Sociological Society, 1935–36]. 1937. *American Sociological Review* 2:73–97.

OGBURN, WILLIAM F. 1922. *Social Change, with Respect to Culture and Original Nature.* New York: Huebsch.

———. 1929/1930. "The Folkways of a Scientific Sociology." *Publication of the American Sociological Society* 24:1–11.

———. 1934a. "The Background of the New Deal." *American Journal of Sociology* 39:729–37.

———. 1934b. "The Future of the New Deal." *American Journal of Sociology* 39:842–48.

———. 1934c/1935. "Man and His Institutions." In *The Human Side of Social Planning*, ed. E. W. Burgess and Herbert Blumer, 29–40. Chicago: American Sociological Society.

OGBURN, WILLIAM F., SHELBY M. HARRISON, and MALCOLM M. WILLEY. 1937. Foreword to the series Studies in the Social Aspects of the Depression, v–vi in all 13 vols. New York: Social Science Research Council.

OMI, MICHAEL, and HOWARD WINANT. 1994. *Racial Formation in the United States: From the 1960s to the 1990s.* Rev. ed. New York: Routledge.

OPPENHEIMER, MARTIN, MARTIN J. MURRAY, and RHONDA F. LEVINE, eds. 1991. *Radical Sociologists and the Movement: Experiences, Lessons, and Legacies.* Philadelphia: Temple University Press.

OREN, IDO. 2003. *Our Enemies and US: America's Rivalries and the Making of Political Science.* Ithaca, NY: Cornell University Press.

"Organization of the American Sociological Society." 1906. *American Journal of Sociology* 11(4): 555–69.

OROMANER, MARK. 1969. "The Audience as a Determinant of the Most Important Sociologists." *American Sociologist* 4(4): 332–35.

———. 1973. "Productivity and Recognition of Sociology Departments." *Sociological Focus* 6(1): 83–89.

———. 1986. "The Diffusion of Core Publications in American Sociology: A Replication." *International Journal of Information Management* 6:29–35.

ORR, JACKIE. 1990. "Theory on the Market: Panic, Incorporating." *Social Problems* 37:460–84.

———. 1995. "Re/Sounding Race, Re/Signifying Ethnography: Sampling Oaktown Rap." In *Prosthetic Territories: Politics and Hyper Technologies,* ed. Gabriel Brahm Jr. and Mark Driscoll. Boulder, CO: Westview Press.

———. 2005. *Panic Diaries: A Genealogy of Panic Disorder.* Durham, NC: Duke University Press.

OTIS, EILEEN M. 2002. "The Construction of Gender in Service Work: China's Hotel Industry." Paper presented at the American Sociological Association.

OYEWUMI, OYERONKE. 1997. *Invention of Women: Making an African Sense of Western Gender Discourses.* Minneapolis: University of Minnesota Press.

PAGE, CHARLES H. 1940/1969. *Class and American Sociology: From Ward to Ross.* New York: Schocken Books.

———. 1986. "Young Turks in Sociology: Yesterday and Today." *Sociological Forum* 1(1): 158–68.

PAIGE, JEFFERY. 1975. *Agrarian Revolution: Social Movements and Export Agriculture in the Underdeveloped World* New York: Free Press.

———. 1997. *Coffee and Power: Revolution and the Rise of Democracy in Central America.* Cambridge: Harvard University Press.

PALEY, WILLIAM. 1803. *A View of the Evidences of Christianity.* Boston: I. Thomas and E. T. Andrews.

PALLAS, AARON. 1998. "Scholarly Lives on the Boundary: Markets, Demand, and the Erosion of Identity." Paper presented at the annual meeting of the American Educational Research Association, San Diego, CA.

PALMER, G. L. 1954. *Labor Mobility in Six Cities.* New York: Social Science Research Council.

PALMIERI, PATRICIA ANN. 1995. *An Adamless Eden: The Community of Women Faculty at Wellesley.* New Haven: Yale University Press.

PAPACHRISTOS, ANDREW V. 2004. "Murder as Interaction: The Social Structure of Gang Homicide in Chicago." Manuscript. Department of Sociology, University of Chicago.

PARELIUS, ROBERT J., and ANN P. PARELIUS. 1987. *The Sociology of Education.* Englewood Cliffs, NJ: Prentice Hall.

PARK, ROBERT E. 1915. "The City: Suggestions for the Investigation of Human Behavior in the City Environment." *American Journal of Sociology* 20:577–612.

———. 1934/1935. "Social Planning and Human Nature." In *The Human Side of Social Planning,* ed. E. W. Burgess and Herbert Blumer, 19–28. Chicago: American Sociological Society.

———. 1950. "Our Racial Frontier on the Pacific." In *Race and Culture,* by R. Parker. New York: Free Press.

———. 1952. *Human Communities.* New York: Free Press.

———. 1967. *On Social Control and Collective Behavior.* Ed. Ralph H. Turner. Chicago: University of Chicago Press.

———. 1972. *The Crowd and the Public and Other Essays.* Ed. and with intro by Harry Elsner Jr. Chicago: University of Chicago Press. Published in 1904 as *Masse und Publikum.*

PARK, ROBERT E., and ERNEST BURGESS. 1921/1969. *Introduction to the Science of Sociology.* Chicago: University of Chicago Press; New York: Greenwood Press.

PARMELEE, MAURICE. 1918. *Criminology.* New York: Macmillan.

PARNES, H. S. 1954. *Research on Labor Mobility.* Social Science Research Council Bulletin 65. New York: Social Science Research Council.

PARSA, MISAGH, 1989. *The Social Origins of the Iranian Revolution.* New Brunswick, NJ: Rutgers University Press.

PARSONS, PHILIP A. 1909. *Responsibility for Crime.* New York: Columbia University Press.

PARSONS, TALCOTT. 1937/1949/1968. *The Structure of Social Action: A Study in Social Theory with Special Reference to a Group of Recent European Writers.* New York: McGraw-Hill; Glencoe, IL: Free Press; New York: Free Press.

———. 1940. "An Analytical Approach to the Theory of Social Stratification." *American Journal of Sociology* 45(6): 841–62.

————. 1942. "The Integration of Society." *American Journal of Sociology* 48:251-54.

————. 1946. "The Science Legislation and the Role of the Social Sciences." *American Sociological Review* 11 (December): 653-66.

————. 1950. "The Prospects of Sociological Theory." *American Sociological Review* 15(1): 3-16.

————. 1959a. "The School Class as a Social Structure: Some of Its Functions in American Society." *Harvard Educational Review* 29:297-318.

————. 1959b. "Some Problems Confronting Sociology as a Profession." *American Sociological Review* 24(4): 547-69.

————. 1968. "Cooley and the Problem of Internalization." In *Cooley and Sociological Analysis,* ed. Albert J. Reiss, 48-67. Ann Arbor: University of Michigan Press.

————. 1993. *Talcott Parsons on National Socialism.* Ed. Ute Gerhardt. New York: de Gruyter.

PARSONS, TALCOTT, and ROBERT F. BALES. 1955. *Family, Socialization, and Interaction Process.* Glencoe, IL: Free Press.

PARSONS, TALCOTT, ROBERT F. BALES, and EDWARD A. SHILS. 1953. *Working Papers in the Theory of Action.* Glencoe, IL,: Free Press.

PARSONS, TALCOTT, and KENNETH B. CLARK, eds. 1967. *The Negro American.* Boston: Houghton Mifflin.

PARSONS, TALCOTT, and GERALD M. PLATT. 1973. *The American University.* Cambridge: Harvard University Press.

PARSONS, TALCOTT, and EDWARD A. SHILS, eds. 1951. *Toward a General Theory of Action.* Cambridge: Harvard University Press

PARSONS, TALCOTT, EDWARD SHILS, KASPAR D. NAEGLE, and JESSE R. PITTS, eds. 1961. *Theories of Society: Foundations of Modern Sociological Theory.* Glencoe, IL: Free Press.

PARSONS, TALCOTT, and NEIL SMELSER. 1956. *Economy and Society.* New York: Free Press.

PASSERINI, LUISA. 1992. "A Memory for Women's History: Problems of Method and Interpretation." *Social Science History* 16(4): 669-92.

PATEMAN, CAROL. 1988. *The Sexual Contract.* Palo Alto, CA: Stanford University Press.

PATTERSON, ORLANDO. 1982. *Slavery and Social Death: A Comparative Study.* Cambridge: Harvard University Press.

————. 1997. *The Ordeal of Integration: Progress and Resentment in America's "Racial" Crisis.* New York: Perseus Books.

————. 2002. "The Last Sociologist." *New York Times,* Op-ed, May 19.

PAYNE, E. GEORGE. 1928. Editorial. *Journal of Educational Sociology* 1:241-43.

PEACE, WILLIAM J. 1998. "Bernhard Stern, Leslie A. White, and *An Anthropological Appraisal of the Russian Revolution.*" *American Anthropologist* 100(1): 84-93.

PEASE, JOHN, and BARBARA HETRICK. 1977. "Association for Whom: The Regionals and the American Sociological Association." *American Sociologist* 12: 42-47.

PEIRCE, CHARLES S. 1992. *The Essential Peirce.* Vol. 1 (1867-93). Ed. Nathan Houser and Christian Kloesel. Peirce Edition Project. Bloomington: Indiana University Press.

———. 1998. *The Essential Peirce.* Vol. 2 (1893-1913). Ed. Nathan Houser and Christian Kloesel. Peirce Edition Project. Bloomington: Indiana University Press.

PELLS, RICHARD H. 1973. *Radical Visions and American Dreams: Culture and Social Thought in the Depression Years.* Middletown, CT: Wesleyan University Press.

PERROW, CHARLES. 1984/1999. *Normal Accidents: Living with High-Risk Technologies.* New York: Basic Books.

PERSONAL NARRATIVES GROUP. 1989. *Interpreting Women's Lives: Feminist Theory and Personal Narratives.* Bloomington: Indiana University Press.

PERSONS, STOW. 1987. *Ethnic Studies at Chicago, 1905-45.* Urbana: University of Illinois Press.

PETTIGREW, THOMAS F., ed. 1980. *The Sociology of Race Relations: Reflection and Reform.* New York: Free Press.

PFAUTZ, HAROLD W., ed. 1967. *Charles Booth on the City: Physical Pattern and Social Structure.* Chicago: University of Chicago Press.

PHELAN, THOMAS JAMES. 1989. "From the Attic of the American Journal of Sociology: Unusual Contributions to American Sociology, 1895-1935." *Sociological Forum* 4:71-86.

PHILLIPS, DEREK L. 1972. *Knowledge from What? Theories and Methods in Social Research.* Chicago: Rand-McNally.

PHILLIPS, ULRICH BONNELL. 1918/1940. *American Negro Slavery: A Survey of the Supply, Employment and Control of Negro Labor as Determined by the Plantation Regime.* New York: Appleton-Century.

PICKERING, MARY. 1993. *Auguste Comte: An Intellectual Biography.* Vol. 1. Cambridge: Cambridge University Press.

PLATT, ANTHONY M. 1969. *Child Savers: The Invention of Delinquency.* Chicago: University of Chicago Press.

———. 1991. *E. Franklin Frazier Reconsidered.* New Brunswick, NJ: Rutgers University Press.

PLATT, JENNIFER. 1985. "Weber's *Verstehen* and the History of Qualitative Research: The Missing Link." *British Journal of Sociology* 36(3): 448-66.

———. 1994. "The Chicago School and Firsthand Data." *History of the Human Sciences* 7:57-80.

———. 1996. *A History of Sociological Research Methods in America, 1920-1960.* New York: Cambridge University Press.

———. 2003. *The British Sociological Association: A Sociological History.* Durham, UK: Sociologypress (supported by the British Sociological Association).

PLATT, JENNIFER and PAUL HOCH. 1996. "The Vienna Circle in the United States and Empirical Research Methods in Sociology." In *Forced Migration and Scientific Change: Émigré German-Speaking Scientists and Scholars after 1933,* ed. Michell G. Ash and Alfons Söllner, 224-45. Cambridge: Cambridge University Press.

PLECK, ELIZABETH H., and JOSEPH H. PLECK. 1980. *The American Man.* Englewood Cliffs, NJ: Prentice Hall.

PLUMMER, KENNETH. 1995. *Telling Sexual Stories: Power, Change, and Social Worlds.* London: Routledge.

———. 1996. "Symbolic Interactionism in the Twentieth Century: The Rise of Empirical Social Theory." In *The Blackwell Companion to Social Theory*, ed. B. S. Turner, 223–51. Oxford: Blackwell.

POLANYI, KARL. 1944/2001. *The Great Transformation: The Political and Economic Origins of Our Time.* Boston: Beacon Press.

POLLNER, MELVIN, and ROBERT M. EMERSON. 2001. "Ethnomethodology and Ethnography." In *Handbook of Ethnography*, ed. Paul Atkinson, Amanda Coffey, Sara Delamont, John Lofland, and Lyn Lofland, 118–35. London: Sage.

POPPER, KARL R. 1934/1992. *The Logic of Scientific Discovery.* London: Routledge.

POPPLE, PHILIP, and P. NELSON REID. 1999. "A Profession for the Poor? A History of Social Work in the United States." In *The Professionalization of Poverty*, ed. Gary R. Lowe and P. Nelson Reid, 9–28. New York: Aldine de Gruyter.

PORTER, D. 1980. *Congress and the Waning of the New Deal.* Port Washington, NY: Kennikat Press.

PORTER, THEODORE M. 1986. *The Rise of Statistical Thinking, 1820–1900.* Princeton: Princeton University Press.

PORTER, THEODORE, and DOROTHY ROSS, eds. 2003. *The Modern Social Sciences.* Vol. 7 of *The Cambridge History of Science.* Cambridge: Cambridge University Press.

PORTES, ALEJANDRO. 1998. "Social Capital: Its Origins and Applications in Modern Sociology." *Annual Review of Sociology* 24:1–24.

POWELL, GARY, ED., 1999. *Handbook of Gender and Work.* Thousand Oaks, CA: Sage.

POWELL, WALTER W., and PAUL J. DIMAGGIO. 1991. *The New Institutionalism in Organizational Analysis.* Chicago: University of Chicago Press.

PRESIDENT'S RESEARCH COMMITTEE ON SOCIAL TRENDS. 1933. *Recent Social Trends in the United States.* Ed. William F. Ogburn and Howard W. Odum. New York: McGraw-Hill.

———. 1934. *Recent Social Trends in the United States.* One-vol. ed. New York: McGraw-Hill.

PRICE, DAVID H. 2003. "Subtle Means and Enticing Carrots: The Impact of Funding on American Cold War Anthropology." *Critique of Anthropology* 23(4): 373–401.

———. 2004. *Threatening Anthropology: McCarthyism and the FBI's Surveillance of Activist Anthropologists.* Durham, NC: Duke University Press.

PRICE, MAURICE T. 1934. Contribution to "Questions for Sociology: An Informal Round Table Symposium." *Social Forces* 13:215–19.

PRITCHETT, HENRY. 1914. "Reasonable Restrictions upon the Scholar's Freedom." *Papers and Proceedings of the American Sociological Society* 9:150–59.

Program Announcement for the 1934 Meeting of the American Sociological Society. 1934. *Social Forces* 13:223.

PRZEWORSKI, ADAM, and HENRY TEUNE. 1970. *The Logic of Comparative Social Inquiry.* New York: Wiley-Interscience.

PSATHAS, GEORGE. 1995. *Conversation Analysis: The Study of Talk-in-Interaction.* Thousand Oaks, CA: Sage.

PUTNAM, HILARY. 2002. *The Collapse of the Fact/Value Dichotomy and Other Essays.* Cambridge: Harvard University Press.

QUEEN, STUART A. 1941. "Sociologists in the Present Crisis." *Social Forces* 20:1–7.

———1934a. Contribution to "Questions for Sociology: An Informal Round Table Symposium." *Social Forces* 13:207–8.

———. 1934b. "What the Pre-Social Work Student Can Get from Sociology." *Social Forces* 12:475–77.

QUINTANA, BERTHA, and PATRICIA SEXTON. 1961. "Sociology, Anthropology, and Schools of Education: A Progress Report." *Journal of Educational Sociology* 35:97–103.

RAFFERTY, EDWARD C. 2003. *Apostle of Human Progress: Lester Frank Ward and American Political Thought, 1841–1913.* Lanham, MD: Rowman and Littlefield.

RAFTER, NICOLE HAHN. 1997. *Creating Born Criminals.* Urbana: University of Illinois Press.

RAFTERY, ADRIAN. 2005. "Quantitative Research Methods." In *International Handbook of Sociology,* ed. C. Calhoun, C. Rojek, and B. Turner, 15–39. London: Sage.

RAY, RAKA, 1999. *Fields of Protest: Women's Movements in India.* Minneapolis: University of Minnesota Press.

Recent Economic Changes in the United States. 1929. Report of the Committee on Recent Economic Changes of the President's Conference on Unemployment. 2 vols. New York: McGraw-Hill.

Recent Social Trends in the United States. 1933. Report of the President's Research Committee on Social Trends. 2 vols. New York: McGraw-Hill.

"Recommendations of the Committee [of the American Sociological Society]." 1933. *Journal of Educational Sociology* 7:78–82.

REED, THOMAS H. 1932. "Report of the General Chairman of the Committee on Policy for the Year 1931." *American Political Science Review* 26:136–49.

———, ed. 1933. *Government in a Depression: Constructive Economy in State and Local Government.* Chicago: University of Chicago Press.

REICHENBACH, HANS. 1938. *Experience and Prediction.* Chicago: University of Chicago Press.

———. 1951. "Probability Models in Social Science." In *The Policy Sciences: Recent Developments in Scope and Method,* ed. Daniel Lerner, 121–26. Stanford: Stanford University Press.

REINHARZ, SHULAMIT. 1979. *On Becoming a Social Scientist: From Survey Research and Participant Observation to Experiential Analysis.* New Brunswick, NJ: Transaction Books.

———. 1989. "Teaching the History of Women in Sociology: Or Dorothy Swaine Thomas, Wasn't She the Woman Married to William I.?" *American Sociologist* 20(1): 87.

———. 1992. *Feminist Methods in Social Research.* New York: Oxford University Press.

———. 1995. "The Chicago School of Sociology and the Founding of the Graduate

Program in Sociology at Brandeis University: A Case Study in Cultural Diffu-sion." In *A Second Chicago School? The Development of a Postwar American Sociology*, ed. Gary Alan Fine, 273–321. Chicago: University of Chicago Press.

REISCH, MICHAEL, and JANICE ANDREWS. 2001. *The Road Not Taken: A History of Radical Social Work in the United States*. Ann Arbor, MI: Brunner Routledge.

REISS, ALBERT J., ed. 1968. *Cooley and Sociological Analysis*. Ann Arbor: University of Michigan Press.

REISS, ALBERT J., JR., and JEFFREY A. ROTH, eds. 1993. *Understanding and Pre-venting Violence*. Panel on the Understanding and Control of Violent Behavior, Committee on Law and Justice. Washington, DC: National Academy Press.

"Report of the Research Planning Committee [of the American Sociological Soci-ety, 1934]." 1935. *Publication of the American Sociological Society* 29(1): 2–8.

RESKIN, BARBARA F. 1984. *Sex Segregation in the Workplace: Trends, Explanations, Remedies*. Washington, DC: National Academy Press.

———. 1988. "Bringing the Men Back In: Sex Differentiation and the Devaluation of Women's Work." *Gender and Society* 2:58–81.

———. 1998. *The Realities of Affirmative Action*. Washington, DC: American Sociolog-ical Association.

RESKIN, BARBARA, and PATRICIA A. ROOS. 1990. *Job Queues, Gender Queues: Ex-plaining Women's Inroads into Male Occupations*. Philadelphia: Temple University Press.

REUBEN, JULIE A. 1995. *The Shaping of the Modern University*. Chicago: University of Chicago Press.

———. 2003. "Education and the History of the Social Sciences." In *Modern Social and Behavioral Sciences*, 622–34, vol. 7 of *Cambridge History of Science*, ed. Dorothy Ross and Theodore Porter. Cambridge: Cambridge University Press.

REUTER, EDWARD B. 1918/1969. *The Mulatto in the United States, including a Study of the Role of Mixed-Blood Races throughout the World*. New York: Negro Universi-ties Press.

———. 1927/1938. *The American Race Problem: A Study of the Negro*. New York: Thomas Y. Crowell.

RHOADES, LAWRENCE J. 1981. *A History of the American Sociological Association, 1905–1980*. Washington, DC: American Sociological Association.

RICE, STUART A., ed. 1931. *Methods in Social Science: A Case Book*. Compiled under the direction of the Committee on Scientific Method in the Social Sciences of the Social Science Research Council. Chicago: University of Chicago Press.

———. 1934a. Contribution to "Questions for Sociology: An Informal Round Table Symposium." *Social Forces* 13:220–23.

———. 1934b. "Statistical Opportunities and Responsibilities." *Journal of the Ameri-can Statistical Association* 29:1–10.

RICHARDSON, LAUREL. 1994. "Writing: A Method of Inquiry." In *Handbook of Qual-itative Research*, ed. Norman K. Denzin and Yvonna S. Lincoln, 516–29. Thousand Oaks, CA: Sage.

——. 1997. *Fields of Play: Constructing an Academic Life*. New Brunswick, NJ: Rutgers University Press.

RICHMOND, MARY. 1917. *Social Diagnosis*. New York: Russell Sage.

RICKARD, O'RYAN. 1994. *A Just Verdict: The Life of Caroline Bartlett Crane*. Kalamazoo, MI: New Issues Press.

RIDGEWAY, CECILIA L., and SHELLEY CORRELL. 2000. "Limiting Inequality through Interaction: The End(s) of Gender." *Contemporary Sociology* 29:110-20.

RIESMAN, DAVID. 1950. *The Lonely Crowd*. New Haven: Yale University Press.

——. 1968. "Persistence and Change: Bennington College and Its Students after Twenty-Five Years." *American Journal of Sociology* 73(5): 628-30.

——. 1979. "Ethical and Practical Dilemmas of Fieldwork in Academic Settings: A Personal Memoir." In *Qualitative and Quantitative Social Research: Papers in Honor of Paul F. Lazarsfeld*, ed. R. K. Merton, J. S. Coleman, and P. H. Rossi, 210-31. New York: Free Press.

RIESSMAN, CATHERINE KOHLER. 1993. *Narrative Analysis*. Newbury Park, CA: Sage.

RILEY, MATHILDA WHITE. 1960. "Membership of the American Sociological Association." *American Sociological Review* 25:914-26.

——, ed. 1988. *Sociological Lives*. American Sociological Association Presidential Series. Newbury Park, CA: Sage.

RISMAN, BARBARA. 1998. *Gender Vertigo: American Families in Transition*. New Haven: Yale University Press.

——. 2001. "Calling the Bluff of Value-Free Science." *American Sociological Review* 66(4): 605-11.

RITZER, GEORGE. 1993. *The McDonaldization of Society*. Thousand Oaks, CA: Pine Forge Press.

——. 2003. "Rethinking Globalization: Glocalization/Grobalization and Something/Nothing." *Sociological Theory* 21(3): 193-209.

——. 2004. *The Globalization of Nothing*. Thousand Oaks, CA: Sage.

RITZER, GEORGE, and DOUGLAS GOODMAN. 2004. *Sociological Theory*. New York: McGraw-Hill.

ROBBINS, RICHARD. 1996. *Sidelines Activist: Charles S. Johnson and the Struggle for Civil Rights*. Jackson: University Press of Mississippi.

ROBERSTON, ROLAND. 1992. *Globalization: Social Theory and Global Culture*. London: Sage.

ROBERSTON, ROLAND, and DAVID INGLIS. 2005. *Globalization and Social Theory: Redefining Social Science*. London: Open University Press.

ROBERTSON, ROLAND, and BRYAN TURNER, eds. 1991. *Talcott Parsons*. London: Sage.

ROBIN, RON. 2001. *The Making of the Cold War Enemy: Culture and Politics in the Military Intellectual Complex*. Princeton: Princeton University Press.

ROBINSON, JAMES HARVEY. 1921. *The Mind in the Making: The Relation of Intelligence to Social Reform*. New York: Harper and Brothers.

ROBY, PAMELA. 1992. "Women and the ASA: Degendering Organizational Structures and Processes, 1964–74." *American Sociologist* 23(1): 18–48.

ROCHBERG-HALTON, EUGENE. 1986. *Meaning and Modernity: Social Theory in the Pragmatic Attitude.* Chicago: University of Chicago Press.

ROCKOFF, HUGH. 1997. "By Way of Analogy: The Expansion of the Federal Government in the 1930s." In *The Defining Moment: The Great Depression and the American Economy in the Twentieth Century,* ed. Michael D. Bordo, Claudia Goldin, and Eugene N. White, 125–54. Chicago: University of Chicago Press.

RODGERS, D. 1998. *Atlantic Crossings.* Cambridge: Harvard University Press.

ROEDIGER, DAVID R. 1991. *The Wages of Whiteness: Race and the Making of the American Working Class.* New York: Verso.

ROETHLISBERGER, F. J., and W. J. DICKSON. 1939. *Management and the Worker.* Cambridge: Harvard University Press.

ROLLINS, JUDITH. 1985. *Between Women: Domestics and Their Employers.* Philadelphia: Temple University Press.

ROMERO, MARY A. 1992. *Maid in the U.S.A.* New York: Routledge.

———. 2002. *Lost Sociologists Rediscovered: Jane Addams, Walter Benjamin, W. E. B. Du Bois, Harriet Martineau, Pitirim A. Sorokin, Flora Tristan, George E. Vincent, and Beatrice Webb.* Lewiston, NY: Edwin Mellen Press.

ROMERO, MARY, and ABIGAIL J. STEWART, eds. 1999. *Women's Untold Stories: Breaking Silence, Talking Back, Voicing Complexity.* New York: Routledge.

ROOS, PATRICIA A. 1981. "Sex Stratification in the Workplace: Male-Female Differences in Economic Returns to Occupation." *Social Science Research* 10:195–224.

ROOS, PATRICIA, and KATHERINE W. JONES. 1993. "Shifting Gender Boundaries: Women's Inroads into Academic Sociology." *Work and Occupations* 20(4): 395–428.

ROSE, SONYA. 1993. *Limited Livelihoods: Gender and Class in Nineteenth-Century England.* Berkeley: University of California Press.

ROSENBERG, ROSALIND. 1982. *Beyond Separate Spheres: Intellectual Roots of Modern Feminism.* New Haven: Yale University Press.

———. 1992. *Divided Lives: American Women in the Twentieth Century.* New York: Hill and Wang.

ROSENEAU, JAMES. 1992. "Governance, Order and Change in World Politics." In *Governance without Government,* ed. J. Rosenau and E. O. Czempiel. Cambridge: Cambridge University Press.

ROSENFELD, RACHEL A. 1978. "Women's Intergenerational Occupational Mobility." *American Sociology Review* 43:36–46.

———. 1992. "Job Mobility and Career Processes." *Annual Review of Sociology* 18: 39–61.

ROSENFELD, RACHEL A., DAVID CUNNINGHAM, and KATHRYN SCHMIDT. 1997. "American Sociological Association Elections, 1975–1996: Exploring Explanations for 'Feminization.'" *American Sociological Review* 62:746–59.

ROSICH, KATHERINE J. 2005. *A History of the American Sociological Association, 1981–2004.* Washington, DC: American Sociological Association.

ROSS, DOROTHY. 1991. *The Origins of American Social Science.* Cambridge: Cambridge University Press.

———. 1993. "An Historian's View of American Social Science." *Journal of the History of the Behavioral Sciences* 29 (April): 99-112.

———, ed. 1994. *Modernist Impulses in the Human Sciences, 1870-1930.* Baltimore: Johns Hopkins University Press.

ROSS, EDWARD A. 1896. "Social Control." *American Journal of Sociology* 1(5): 513-35.

———. 1898. "Social Control, XI." *American Journal of Sociology* 3:502-19.

———. 1901a. "The Causes of Race Superiority." *Annals of the American Academy of Political and Social Science* 18.

———. 1901b/1969. *Social Control: A Survey of the Foundations of Order.* Cleveland: Press of Case Western Reserve University.

———. 1903. "Moot Points in Sociology. II. Social Laws." *American Journal of Sociology* 9(1): 105-23.

———. 1914. *The Old World in the New: The Significance of Past and Present Immigration to the American People.* New York: Century.

———. 1918. *Russia in Upheaval.* New York: Century.

———. 1920. *The Principles of Sociology.* New York: Century.

———. 1921a. "The Menace of Migrating Peoples." *Century Magazine* 102 (May).

———. 1921b. *The Russian Bolshevik Revolution.* New York: Century.

———. 1923. *Russian Soviet Republic.* New York: Century.

———. 1936. *Seventy Years of It: An Autobiography.* New York: Appleton-Century.

———. 1945. "Fifty Years of Sociology in the United States." *American Journal of Sociology* 50:489-92.

ROSSI, ALICE S. 1964. "Equality between the Sexes: An Immodest Proposal." *Daedalus* 93:607-52.

ROSSI, PETER H. 1980. "The Presidential Address: The Challenge and Opportunities of Applied Social Research." *American Sociological Review* 45(6): 889-904.

ROSSITER, MARGARET W. 1982. *Women Scientists in America: Struggles and Strategies to 1940.* Baltimore: Johns Hopkins University Press.

———. 1993. "The Matthew/Matilda Effect in Science." *Social Studies of Science* 23(2): 325-41.

ROTH, BENITA. 2004. *Separate Roads to Feminism: Black, Chicana, and White Feminist Movements in America's Second Wave.* New York: Cambridge University Press.

ROTHMAN, DAVID. 1971. *The Discovery of the Asylum.* Boston: Little, Brown.

ROY, DONALD. 1952. "Quota Restriction and Goldbricking in a Machine Shop." *American Journal of Sociology* 57:425-42.

RUBIN, LILLIAN. 1976. *Worlds of Pain: A Life in the Working Class Family.* New York: Basic Books.

RUCKER, DARNELL. 1969. *The Chicago Pragmatists.* Minneapolis: University of Minnesota Press.

RUDWICK, ELLIOT. 1974. "W. E. B. as Sociologist." In *Black Sociologists: Historical and Contemporary Perspectives,* ed. James E. Blackwell and Morris Janowitz, 25-55. Chicago: University of Chicago Press.

RUGGIERO, JOSEPHINE, and LOUISE C. WESTON. 1986. "Marketing the B.A. Sociologists: Implications from Research on Graduates, Employers, and Sociology Departments." *Teaching Sociology* 14:224-33.

RUMBAUT, RUBEN G. 2000. "The Melting and the Pot: Assimilation and Variety in American Life." In *Incorporating Diversity: Rethinking Assimilation in a Multicultural Era,* ed. Peter Kivisto. Boulder, CO: Paradigm.

RUPP, LEILA J., and VERTA TAYLOR. 2003. *Drag Queens at the 801 Cabaret.* Chicago: University of Chicago Press.

RUSLING, GENERAL JAMES. 1987. "Interview with President William McKinley." In *The Philippines Reader,* ed. Daniel Schirmer and Stephen Rosskamm Shalom. Boston: South End Press.

RUSSELL, BERTRAND. 1939. "The Role of the Intellectual in the Modern World" [an address to the Sociology Club at the University of Chicago]. *American Journal of Sociology* 44(4): 491-98.

———. 1945. *A History of Western Philosophy.* New York: Simon and Schuster.

RYAN, ALAN. 1995. *John Dewey and the High Tide of American Liberalism.* New York: Norton.

RYNBRANDT, LINDA. 1999. *Caroline Bartlett Crane and Progressive Era Reform: Social Housekeeping in Sociology.* New York: Garland.

SABINE, GEORGE. 1937/1973. *A History of Political Theory.* 4th ed. rev. Hinsdale, IL: Dryden Press.

SALERNO, R. A. 1983. "Louis Wirth: Urbanism as a Liberal Perspective." PhD diss., New York University.

———. 1987. *Louis Wirth.* New York: Greenwood Press.

SALMON, LUCY M. 1912. "Democracy in the Household." *American Journal of Sociology* 17(4): 437-57.

SALZINGER, LESLIE. 2003. *Genders in Production: Making Workers in Mexico's Global Factories.* Berkeley: University of California Press.

SAMPSON, ROBERT J. 2002. "Transcending Tradition: New Directions in Community Research, Chicago Style—The American Society of Criminology 2001 Sutherland Address." *Criminology* 40(2): 213-30.

SAMPSON, ROBERT J., and JOHN H. LAUB. 1993. *Crime in the Making: Pathways and Turning Points through Life.* Cambridge: Harvard University Press.

———. 2003. "Life-Course Desisters? Trajectories of Crime among Delinquent Boys Followed to Age 70." *Criminology* 41(3): 555-92.

SAMPSON, ROBERT J., JEFFREY D. MORENOFF, and THOMAS P. GANNON-ROWLEY. 2002. "Assessing 'Neighborhood Effects': Social Processes and New Directions in Research." *Annual Review of Sociology* 28(3): 443-78.

SAMPSON, ROBERT J., STEPHEN W. RAUDENBUSH, and FELTON EARLS. 1997. "Neighborhoods and Violent Crime: A Multilevel Study of Collective Efficacy" *Science* 277(5328): 918-24.

SANDAY, PEGGY REEVES. 1990. *Fraternity Gang Rape.* New York: New York University Press.

SANDERSON, DWIGHT. 1937. *Research Memorandum on Rural Life in the Depression.* New York: Social Science Research Council.

SARGENT, LYDIA, ed. 1981. *Women and Revolution: A Discussion of the Unhappy Marriage of Marxism and Feminism.* Boston: South End Press.

SASSEN, SASKIA. 1998. *Globalization and Its Discontents.* New York: New Press.

———. 2001. *The Global City: New York, London, Tokyo.* Princeton: Princeton University Press.

SAVELSBERG, JOACHIM J., LARA L. CLEVELAND, and RYAN D. KING. 2002. "Politicized Scholarship? Science on Crime and the State." *Social Problems* 49:327-48.

———. 2004. "Institutional Environments and Scholarly Work: American Criminology, 1951-1993." *Social Forces* 82(4): 1275-1302.

SAVELSBERG, JOACHIM J., and SARAH M. FLOOD. 2004. "Criminological Knowledge: Period and Cohort Effects in Scholarship." *Criminology* 42:1009-41.

SAVELSBERG, JOACHIM J., and ROBERT J. SAMPSON, eds. 2002. "Mutual Engagement: Criminology and Sociology?" *Crime, Law and Social Change* 37(3): 99-105.

SCHATZKI, THEODORE, KARIN KNORR CETINA, and EIKE VON SAVIGNY, eds. 2001. *The Practice Turn in Contemporary Theory.* London: Routledge.

SCHEGLOFF, EMANUEL A. 1968. "Sequencing in Conversational Openings." *American Anthropologist* 70:1075-95.

SCHLESINGER, ARTHUR, JR. 1962. "The Humanist Looks at Empirical Social Research." *American Sociological Review* 27(6): 768-71.

SCHMID, CALVIN F. 1933. "Suicide in Minneapolis, Minnesota: 1928-32." *American Journal of Sociology* 39:30-48.

SCHMITT, RICHARD. 1967. "Phenomenology." In *The Encyclopedia of Philosophy,* ed. P. Edwards, 135-51. New York: Macmillan.

SCHNEIDER, BARBARA. 2003. "Sociology of Education: An Overview of the Field at the Turn of the Twenty-First Century." In *Stability and Change in American Education: Structure, Process, and Outcomes,* ed. Maureen Hallinan, Adam Gamoran, Warren Kubitschek, and Tom Loveless, 193-225. Clinton Corners, NY: E. Werner Publications.

SCHNEIDER, JOSEPH, and WANG LAIHUA. 2000. *Giving Care, Writing Self: A "New" Ethnography.* New York: Peter Lang.

SCHNEIDERMAN, HOWARD G. 1991. Introduction to *The Protestant Establishment Revisited,* by E. Digby Baltzell. New Brunswick, NJ: Transaction Publishers.

SCHNORE, LEO F. 1968. "Cooley as Territorial Demographer." In *Cooley and Sociological Analysis,* ed. Albert J. Reiss, 13-31. Ann Arbor: University of Michigan Press.

SCHORSKE, CARL 1997. "The New Rigorism in the Human Sciences, 1940-1960." In *American Academic Culture in Transformation,* ed. T. Bender and C. Schorske, 309-29. Princeton: Princeton University Press.

SCHRECKER, E. 1986. *No Ivory Tower.* Oxford: Oxford University Press.

———. 1998. *Many Are the Crimes.* Princeton: Princeton University Press.

SCHROEDER, PAUL L., and ERNEST W. BURGESS. 1938. Introduction to *The Family and the Depression: A Study of One Hundred Chicago Families,* by Ruth Shonle Cavan and Katherine Howland Ranck, vii–xii. Chicago: University of Chicago Press.

SCHUESSLER, KARL, ed. 1973. *Edwin H. Sutherland on Analyzing Crime.* Chicago: University of Chicago Press.

SCHUMAN, HOWARD, and STANLEY PRESSER. 1981. *Questions and Answers in Attitudes Surveys: Experiments in Question Form, Wording and Context.* San Diego, CA: Academic Press.

SCHUMAN, HOWARD, CHARLOTTE STEEH, LAWRENCE BOBO, and MARIA KRYSAN. 1985/1997. *Racial Attitudes in America: Trends and Interpretations.* Cambridge: Harvard University Press.

SCHUTZ, ALFRED, RICHARD GRATHOFF, and TALCOTT PARSONS. 1978. *The Theory of Social Action: The Correspondence of Alfred Schutz and Talcott Parsons.* Bloomington: Indiana University Press.

SCHWARTZ, MILDRED A. 1987. "Historical Sociology in the History of *American Sociology.*" *Social Science History* 11(1): 1–16.

SCHWENDINGER, HERMAN, and JULIA R. SCHWENDINGER. 1974. *The Sociologists of the Chair: A Radical Analysis of the Formative Years of North American Sociology (1883–1922).* New York: Basic Books.

SCOTT, CLIFFORD H. 1976. *Lester Frank Ward.* Boston: Twayne.

SCOTT, JOAN FIROR. 1992. *Natural Allies: Women's Associations in American History.* Urbana: University of Illinois Press

SCOTT, JOAN W. 1986. "Gender: A Useful Category for Historical Analysis." *American Historical Review* 91:1053–75.

———. 1991. "The Evidence of Experience." *Critical Inquiry* 17 (Summer): 773–97.

SCUDDER, VIDA. 1950/1970. "Settlement Past and Future" (1900). In *The Development of Settlement Work,* ed. Lorena M. Pacey, 69–73. Freeport, NY: Books for Libraries Press.

SCULLY, DIANA. 1990. *Understanding Sexual Violence.* Boston: Unwin Hyman.

SEALANDER, JUDITH. 1997. *Private Wealth and Public Life: Foundation Philanthropy and the Reshaping of American Social Policy from the Progressive Era to the New Deal.* Baltimore: Johns Hopkins University Press.

SEARLE, JOHN R. 1995. *The Construction of Social Reality.* New York: Free Press.

SEIDELMAN, RAYMOND. 1985. *Disenchanted Realists: Political Science and the American Crisis, 1884–1984.* Albany: State University of New York Press.

SEIDMAN, GAY. 1999. "Is South Africa Different? South Africa in Comparative Perspective." *Annual Review of Sociology* (1999): 219–40.

SEIDMAN, STEVEN, ed. 1994. *The Postmodern Turn: New Perspectives on Social Theory.* Cambridge: Cambridge University Press.

———. 1996. *Queer Theory/Sociology.* Cambridge, MA: Blackwell.

SEIGFRIED, CHARLENE HADDOCK. 1996. *Pragmatism and Feminism.* Chicago: University of Chicago Press.

SEITLER, DANA. 2003. "Unnatural Selection: Mothers, Eugenic Feminism, and

Charlotte Perkins Gilman's Regeneration Narratives." *American Quarterly* 55(1): 61–88.

SELLARS, ROY WOOD. 1939. "Positivism in Contemporary Philosophic Thought." *American Sociological Review* 4 (February): 26–42.

SELZNICK, PHILIP. 1949. *TVA and the Grass Roots: A Study in the Sociology of Formal Organization.* Berkeley: University of California Press.

———. 1996. "Institutionalism 'Old' and 'New.'" *Administrative Science Quarterly* 41:270–77.

SEWELL, WILLIAM H. 1988. "The Changing Institutional Structure of Sociology and My Career." In *Sociological Lives: Social Change and the Life Course,* vol. 2, ed. Matilda W. Riley. Newbury Park, CA: Sage.

SEWELL, WILLIAM H., ARCHIBALD O. HALLER, and ALEJANDRO PORTES. 1969. "The Educational and Early Occupational Attainment Process." *American Sociological Review* 34:82–92.

SEWELL, WILLIAM H., ARCHIBALD O. HALLER, and MURRAY J. STRAUS. 1957. "Social Status and Educational and Occupational Aspiration." *American Sociological Review* 22:67–73.

SEWELL, WILLIAM H., and ROBERT M. HAUSER. 1975. *Education, Occupation, and Earnings: Achievement in the Early Career.* New York: Academic Press.

SEWELL, WILLIAM H. and VIMAL P. SHAH. 1967. "Socioeconomic Status, Intelligence, and the Attainment of Higher Education." *Sociology of Education* 40:1–23.

———. 1968. "Social Class, Parental Encouragement, and Educational Aspirations." *American Journal of Sociology* 73:559–72.

SEWELL, WILLIAM, JR. 1996. "Three Temporalities: Toward an Eventful Sociology." In *The Historic Turn in the Human Sciences,* ed. Terrence J. McDonald, 245–80. Ann Arbor: University of Michigan Press.

———. 2005. "The Political Unconscious of Social and Cultural History, or, Confessions of a Former Quantitative Historian." In *The Politics of Method in the Human Sciences: Positivism and Its Epistemological Others,* ed. George Steinmetz, 173–206. Durham, NC: Duke University Press.

SHAHRANI, NAZIF. 1994. "Honored Guest and Marginal Man: Long Term Field Research and Predicaments of a Native Anthropologist." In *Others Knowing Others: Perspectives on Ethnographic Careers,* ed. Don D. Fowler and Donald V. Hardesty, 15–67. Washington, DC: Smithsonian Press.

SHALIN, DMITRI N. 1992. "Critical Theory and the Pragmatist Challenge." *American Journal of Sociology* 98:237–79.

SHAMIR, RONEN. 1995. *Managing Legal Uncertainty: Elite Lawyers in the New Deal.* Durham, NC: Duke University Press.

SHANAS, ETHEL. 1945. "The *American Journal of Sociology* through Fifty Years." *American Journal of Sociology* 50(6): 522–33.

SHANNON, LYLE W., JUDITH L. MCKIM, JAMES P. CURRY, and LAWRENCE J. HAFFNER. 1988. *Criminal Career Continuity: Its Social Context.* New York: Human Sciences Press.

SHAW, CLIFFORD R. 1930/1966. *The Jack-Roller: A Delinquent Boy's Own Story*. Chicago: University of Chicago Press.

——. 1931. *The Natural History of a Delinquent Career*. Chicago: University of Chicago Press.

SHAW, CLIFFORD R., and HENRY D. MCKAY. 1931. *Report on the Causes of Crime, Volume II: Social Factors in Juvenile Delinquency: A Study of the Community, the Family, and the Gang in Relation to Delinquent Behavior*. Washington, DC: National Commission on Law Observance and Enforcement.

——. 1942. *Juvenile Delinquency and Urban Areas: A Study of Rates of Delinquency in Relation to Differential Characteristics of Local Communities in American Cities*. Chicago: University of Chicago Press.

SHERMAN, LAWRENCE W. 1993. "Defiance, Deterrence, and Irrelevance: A Theory of the Criminal Sanction." *Journal of Research in Crime and Delinquency* 30(4): 445–73.

——. 2005. "The Use and Usefulness of Criminology, 1751 to 2005: Enlightened Justice and Its Failures." *Annals of the American Academy of Political and Social Science* 600(1): 115–35.

SHIBUTANI, T. 1978. *The Derelicts of Company K*. Berkeley: University of California Press.

SHILS, EDWARD A. 1948. *The Present State of American Sociology*. Glencoe, IL: Free Press.

——. 1956. *The Torment of Secrecy*. Glencoe, IL: Free Press.

——. 1961a. "The Calling of Sociology." In *Theories of Society*, ed. Talcott Parsons et al., 1405–48. New York: Free Press.

——. 1961b. *The Intellectual between Tradition and Modernity: The Indian Situation*. The Hague: Mouton.

——. 1972. "Center and Periphery." In *The Constitution of Society*, 93–109. Chicago: University of Chicago Press.

SHILS, EDWARD A., and MORRIS JANOWITZ. 1948. "Cohesion and Disintegration in the Wehrmacht in World War II." *Public Opinion Quarterly* 12:280–315.

SHILS, EDWARD A., and M. YOUNG. 1956. "The Meaning of the Coronation." *Sociological Review* 1(2): 63–82.

SHOEMAKER, LINDA M. 1998. "Early Conflicts in Social Work Education." *Social Service Review* (June): 182–91.

SHORT, JAMES F., JR. 1969. Introduction to *Juvenile Delinquency and Urban Areas*, by Clifford R. Shaw and Henry D. McKay. Rev. ed. Chicago: University of Chicago Press.

——. 1971. "Review of *Rebellion and Authority: Myths and Realities Reconsidered*, by Nathan Leites and Charles Wolf Jr. *American Journal of Sociology* 76:768.

——. 1984. "The Social Fabric at Risk: Toward a Social Transformation of Risk Analysis." *American Sociological Review* 49:711–25.

——. 1985. "Criminology: Modern Controversies." In *Encyclopedia of Crime and Justice*, ed. Sanford H. Kadish, 464–73. New York: Free Press.

———. 1988. "Aleatory Elements in a Criminologist's Career." *Criminologist* 13(3): 1, 3, 6–7.

———. 1998a. "The Level of Explanation Problem Revisited-The American Society of Criminology 1997 Presidential Address." *Criminology* 36(1): 3–36.

———. 1998b. "Review Essay: Criminology through the Lens of Theory, Ideology, and Research." *Sociological Inquiry* 69(4): 659–64.

———. 2002a. "Criminology: Modern Controversies," In *Encyclopedia of Crime and Justice*, ed. Joshua Dressler, 556–66. New York: Macmillan.

———. 2002b. "Criminology, the Chicago School, and Sociological Theory." *Crime, Law and Social Change* 37(2): 107–15.

———. 2002c. "Unwinding: Reflections on a Career." In *Lessons of Criminology*, ed. Gilbert Geis and Mary Dodge, 219–38. Cincinnati: Anderson Publishing.

SHORT, JAMES F., JR., and LORINE A. HUGHES, eds. forthcoming. *Studying Youth Gangs*. Walnut Creek, CA: Altamira Press.

SHORT, JAMES F., JR., and FRED L. STRODTBECK. 1965. *Group Process and Gang Delinquency*. Chicago: University of Chicago Press.

SHUMAN, HOWARD, CHARLOTTE STEEH, LAWRENCE D. BOBO, and MARIA KRYSAN. 1997. *Racial Attitudes in America: Trends and Interpretations*. Rev. ed. Cambridge: Harvard University Press.

SIBLEY, E. 1948. *The Recruitment, Selection, and Training of Social Scientists*. Bulletin 58. New York: Social Science Research Council.

SICA, ALAN. 1979. "Received Wisdom versus Historical Fact." *Journal of the History of Sociology* 1(2): 17–34.

———. 1983. "Sociology at the University of Kansas, 1889–1993." *Sociological Quarterly* 24(4): 605–23.

———. 1986. "Impulses in Sociological Thought" [review essay on Arthur Vidich and Stanford Lyman, *American Sociology*]. *Science* 229 (4719): 1255–257.

———. 1990. "A Question of Priority: Small at Chicago or Blackmar at Kansas?" *Social Thought and Research*, 14(1/2): 1–12.

———. 1995. "A Sociology Archive and the Discipline's Future." *American Sociologist* 26(2): 70–77.

———. 1997. "Acclaiming the Reclaimers: The Trials of Writing Sociology's History." In *Reclaiming the Sociological Classics: The State of Scholarship*, ed. Charles Camic, 282–98. Oxford: Blackwell.

———. 1998. "The Dire Need for History: Amnesia and Sociology in the U.S." *Swiss Journal of Sociology/Schweizerische Zeitschrift für Soziologie* 24(2): 191–98.

SICA, ALAN, and STEPHEN TURNER, eds. 2005. *A Disobedient Generation: Social Theorists in the Sixties*. Chicago: University of Chicago Press.

SILBEY, SUSAN S. 2002. "Criminology and the Sociology of Law." *Crime, Law and Social Change* 37:163–75.

SILLS, DAVID L. 1992. "In Memoriam: Hans Zeisel, 1905–1992. *Public Opinion Quarterly* 56(4): 536–37.

SILVA, EDWARD T., and SHEILA SLAUGHTER. 1980. "Prometheus Bound: The

Limits of Social Science Professionalization in the Progressive Period." *Theory and Society* 9:781-819.

SILVERBERG, HELENE, ed. 1998. *Gender and American Social Science.* Princeton: Princeton University Press.

SIMPSON, CHRISTOPHER, ed. 1999. *Universities and Empire: Money and Politics in the Social Sciences during the Cold War.* New York: New Press.

SIMS, LEWIS B. 1938. *Recruiting Social Scientists for the Federal Civil Service.* Cambridge [?], MA.

SKLANSKY, JEFF. 1999. "Pauperism and Poverty: Henry George, William Graham Sumner, and the Ideological Origins of Modern American Social Science." *Journal of the History of the Behavioral Sciences* 35(2): 111-38.

SKLAR, KATHRYN KISH. 1995. *Florence Kelley and the Nation's Work, 1830-1900.* New Haven: Yale University Press.

SKOCPOL, THEDA. 1979. *States and Social Revolutions: A Comparative Analysis of France, Russia, and China.* Cambridge: Cambridge University Press.

———. 1982. "Rentier State and Shi'a Islam in the Iranian Revolution." *Theory and Society* 11:265-83.

———. 1988. "An 'Uppity Generation' and the Revitalization of Macroscopic Sociology: Reflections at Mid-Career by a Woman from the Sixties." *Theory and Society* 17:627-43.

———. 1992. *Protecting Soldiers and Mothers: The Political Origins of Social Policy in the United States.* Cambridge: Harvard University Press.

SKURA, BARRY. 1976. "Constraints on a Reform Movement: Relationships between SSSP and ASA, 1951-1970." *Social Problems* 24(1): 15-36.

SLAUGHTER, SHEILA. 1980. "The Danger Zone: Academic Freedom and Civil Liberties." *Annals of the American Academy of Political and Social Science* 448 (March).

SLEEPER, JIM. 1997. *Liberal Racism.* New York: Viking.

SMALL, ALBION. 1890. *The Beginnings of American Nationality.* Baltimore: Johns Hopkins Press.

———. 1895a. "The Era of Sociology." *American Journal of Sociology* 1(1): 1-15.

———. 1895b. "Static and Dynamic Sociology." *American Journal of Sociology* 1(2): 195-209.

———. 1896. "Scholarship and Agitation." *American Journal of Sociology* 5:564-82.

———. 1897a. Review of *The Principles of Sociology,* vol. 3, by Herbert Spencer. *American Journal of Sociology* 2(5): 741-42.

———. 1897b. Review of *The Story of Human Progress,* by Frank Wilson Blackmar. *American Journal of Sociology* 2(5): 745-46.

———. 1897c. "Some Demands of Sociology upon Pedagogy." *American Journal of Sociology* 2(6): 839-51.

———. 1900. "The Scope of Sociology. I. The Development of Sociological Method." *American Journal of Sociology* 5(4): 506-26.

———. 1903. "What Is a Sociologist?" *American Journal of Sociology* 8(4): 468-77.

———. 1905a. "A Decade of Sociology." *American Journal of Sociology* 11(1): 1-10.

——. 1905b. *General Sociology: An Exposition of the Main Development in Sociological Theory from Spencer to Ratzenhofer.* Chicago: University of Chicago Press.

——. 1907. "Points of Agreement among Sociologists" [proceedings of the first ASS meeting]. *American Journal of Sociology* 12(5): 633–49; comments by James Hagerty, J. Q. Dealey, and E. C. Hayes, 649–55.

——. 1908. "The Meaning of Sociology." *American Journal of Sociology* 14(1): 1–14.

——. 1909a. *The Cameralists: The Pioneers of German Social Polity.* Chicago: University of Chicago Press.

——. 1909b. "The Vindication of Sociology." *American Journal of Sociology* 15(1): 1–15.

——. 1910. "The Sociological Stage in the Evolution of the Social Sciences." *American Journal of Sociology* 15(5): 681–97.

——. 1913. "The Present Outlook of Social Science" [presidential address to the ASS]. *American Journal of Sociology* 18(4): 433–69.

——. 1916. "Fifty Years of Sociology in the United States (1865–1915)." *American Journal of Sociology* 21(6): 721–864. Reprinted with the *AJS* index to vols. 1–51 (1947): 177–281.

——. 1921. "Evolution of Sociological Consciousness in the United States." *American Journal of Sociology* 27(2): 226–31.

——. 1924. *Origins of Sociology.* Chicago: University of Chicago Press.

SMALL, ALBION WOODBURY, and GEORGE E. VINCENT. 1894. *An Introduction to the Study of Society.* New York: American Book Co.

SMALL, ALBION, and LESTER F. WARD. 1933–35. "The Letters of Albion W. Small to Lester F. Ward" [ed. Bernhard J. Stern]. *Social Forces* 12(2): 163–73; 13(3): 323–40.

SMELSER, NEIL J. 1986. "Die Beharrlichkeit des Positivismus in der amerikanischen Soziologie." *Kölner Zeitschrift für Soziologie und Sozialpsychologie* 38 (March): 133–50.

——. 1962. *Theory of Collective Behavior.* New York: Free Press.

——. 2003. "On Comparative Analysis, Interdisciplinarity and Internationalization in Sociology." *International Sociology* 18:643–57.

SMITH, ANTHONY. 1986. *The Ethnic Origins of Nations.* Oxford: Basil Blackwell.

SMITH, CHRISTIAN. 2003. "Secularizing American Higher Education: The Case of Early American Sociology." In *The Secular Revolution: Power, Interests, and Conflict in the Secularization of American Public Life,* ed. C. Smith. Berkeley: University of California Press.

SMITH, DENNIS. 1983. *Barrington Moore, Jr., a Critical Appraisal.* Armonk, NY: M. E. Sharpe.

SMITH, DOROTHY. 1987. *The Everyday World as Problematic: A Feminist Sociology.* Boston: Northeastern University Press.

——. 1990. *The Conceptual Practices of Power: A Feminist Sociology of Knowledge.* Boston: Northeastern University Press.

——. 1999. *Writing the Social: Critique, Theory, and Investigations.* Toronto: University of Toronto Press.

——. 2000. "Schooling for Inequality." *Signs* 25:1147–51.

——. 2005. *Institutional Ethnography: A Sociology for People*. Lanham, MD: AltaMira.

SMITH, DUSKY LEE. 1964. "The Sunshine Boys: Toward a Sociology of Happiness." *Activist* 4:166–77. Reprinted in *The Sociology of Sociology*, ed. Larry T. Reynolds and Janice M. Reynolds, 371–87. New York: David McKay, 1970.

SMITH, JACKIE, C. CHATFIELD, and R. PAGNUCCO, eds. 1997. *Transnational Social Movements and Global Politics: Solidarity beyond the State*. Syracuse: Syracuse University Press.

SMITH, MARK C. 1994. *Social Science in the Crucible: The American Debate over Objectivity and Purpose, 1918–1941*. Durham, NC: Duke University Press.

SMITH, T. V. 1931. "The Social Philosophy of George Herbert Mead." *American Journal of Sociology* 37(3): 368–85.

SMITH, TERRY E. 1993. *Making the Modern: Industry, Art, and Design in America*. Chicago: University of Chicago Press.

SNEEDEN, DAVID. 1917. "The Waning Powers of Art." *American Journal of Sociology* 22(6): 801–21.

SNIDERMAN, PAUL M., and THOMAS L. PIAZZA. 1993. *The Scar of Race*. Cambridge: Harvard University Press.

SNOW, C. P. 1959/1965. *The Two Cultures, and a Second Look*. 2nd ed. Cambridge: Cambridge University Press.

"Sociological Miscellany." 1895. *American Journal of Sociology* 1(2): 231–36.

SOKOLOFF, NATALIE. 1980. *Between Money and Love*. New York: Praeger.

SOLOVEY, MARK. 2001. "Project Camelot and the 1960s Epistemological Revolution: Rethinking the Politics-Patronage-Social Science Nexus." *Social Studies of Science* 31(2): 171–206.

SOMERS, MARGARET R. 1995. "The Misteries of Property: Relationality, Families, and Community in Chartist Narratives of Political Rights." In *Early Modern Conceptions of Property*, ed. John Brewer and Susan Staves. London: Routledge.

——. 1998. "'We're No Angels': Realism, Rational Choice, and Relationality in Social Science." *American Journal of Sociology* 104:722–84.

——. 2005. "Beware Trojan Horses bearing Social Capital: How Ideational Power Turned Gdansk into a Bowling Alley." In *The Politics of Method in the Human Sciences: Positivism and Its Epistemological Others*, ed. George Steinmetz, 233–74. Durham, NC: Duke University Press.

SOMERS, MARGARET R., and GLORIA D. GIBSON. 1994. "Reclaiming the Epistemological 'Other': Narrative and the Social Constitution of Identity." In *Social Theory and the Politics of Identity*, ed. Craig Calhoun. Oxford: Basil Blackwell.

SOMERVILLE, SIOBHAN B. 2000. *Queering the Color Line: Race and the Invention of Homosexuality in American Culture*. Durham, NC: Duke University Press.

SOROKIN, PITIRIM. 1925. *The Sociology of Revolution*. Philadelphia: Lippincott.

——. 1927. *Social Mobility*. New York: Harper.

——. 1928. *Contemporary Sociological Theories*. New York: Harper.

——. 1936. "Is Accurate Social Planning Possible?" *American Sociological Review* 1:12–25.

——. 1937-41/1957. *Social and Cultural Dynamics.* 4 vols. Boston: Porter Sargent.

——. 1950. *Leaves from a Russian Diary and Thirty Years After.* Boston: Beacon Press.

——. 1956/1976. *Fads and Foibles in Modern Sociology and Related Sciences.* Westport, CT: Greenwood Press.

——. 1963. *A Long Journey; The Autobiography of Pitirim A. Sorokin.* New Haven, CT: College and University Press.

SOUTHERN, DAVID W. 1987. *Gunnar Myrdal and Black-White Relations: The Use and Abuse of an American Dilemma.* Baton Rouge: Louisiana State University Press.

SOWELL, THOMAS. 1983. *The Economics and Politics of Race: An International Perspective.* New York: Quill.

SPALTER-ROTH, ROBERTA. 2005. "What Can You Do with a Sociology BA?" http://www2.asanet.org/footnotes/jan05/fn4.html.

SPECHT, HARRY, and MARK COURTNEY. 1994. *Unfaithful Angels: How Social Work Abandoned Its Mission.* New York: Free Press.

SPECTOR, MALCOLM, and JOHN I. KITSUSE. 1977/1987. *Constructing Social Problems.* Menlo Park, CA: Cummings.

SPEIER, HANS. 1948. "The Sociological Ideas of Pitirim Alexandrovitch Sorokin: 'Integralist' Sociology." In *An Introduction to the History of Sociology,* ed. Harry Elmer Barnes, 884-901. Chicago: University of Chicago Press.

SPENCER, HERBERT. 1892. *Social Statics.* Abridged and rev., together with *The Man versus the State.* New York: Appleton.

——. 1896. *The Principles of Psychology.* New York: D. Appleton.

——. 1929. *The Study of Sociology.* New York: Appleton.

——. 1975. *The Principles of Sociology.* Westport, CT: Greenwood Press.

SPENCER, HERBERT, DAVID DUNCAN, RICHARD SCHEPPIG, JAMES COLLIER, and EMIL TORDAY. 1873. *Descriptive Sociology; or, Groups of Sociological Facts.* New York: D. Appleton.

SPRAGUE, JOEY. 1997. "Holy Men and Big Guns: The Can(n)on in Social Theory." *Gender and Society* 11:88-107.

——. 2005. *Feminist Methodologies for Critical Researchers: Bridging Differences.* Walnut Creek, CA: AltaMira.

SRUBAR, ILJA, ed. 1988. *Exil, Wissenschaft, Identität: Die Emigration deutscher Sozialwissenschaftler, 1933-1945.* Frankfurt: Suhrkamp.

STACEY, JUDITH, and BARRIE THORNE. 1985. "The Missing Feminist Revolution in Sociology." *Social Problems* 32:301-16.

——. 1988. "Can There Be a Feminist Ethnography?" *Women's Studies International Forum* 11:21-27.

——. 1990. *Brave New Families: Stories of Domestic Upheaval in Late Twentieth Century America.* New York: Basic Books.

STACK, CAROL. 1974. *All Our Kin: Strategies for Survival in a Black Community.* New York: Harper and Row.

STAFFORD, MARK C., and JACK P. GIBBS. 1993. "A Theory about Disputes and the Efficacy of Control." In *Aggression and Violence: Social Interactionist Perspectives,* ed. Richard B. Felson and James T. Tedeschi, 69-96. Washington, DC: American Psychological Association.

STANFIELD, JOHN H. 1985. *Philanthropy and Jim Crow in American Social Science.* Westport, CT: Greenwood Press.

———. 1995. "Historical Considerations-Setting the Stage: The Myth of Race and the Human Sciences." *Journal of Negro Education* 64(3): 218-31.

STANLEY, LOUISE, and E. W. BURGESS. 1934. Foreword to *The Adolescent in the Family*, xiii-xiv. Report of the Subcommittee on the Function of Home Activities in the Education of the Child. New York: Appleton.

STANNARD, DAVID E. 1993. *American Holocaust: The Conquest of the New World.* New York: Oxford University Press.

STARK, DAVID, and LASZLO BRUSZT. 2001. "One Way or Multiple Paths: For a Comparative Sociology of East European Capitalism." *American Journal of Sociology* 106:1129-37.

STEINBERG, RONNIE. 1987. "Radical Changes in a Liberal World: The Mixed Success of Comparable Worth." *Gender and Society* 1:466-75.

STEINBERG, STEPHEN. 1995. *Turning Back: The Retreat from Racial Justice in American Thought and Policy.* Boston: Beacon Press.

STEINER, JESSE F. 1937. *Research Memorandum on Recreation in the Depression.* New York: Social Science Research Council.

STEINMETZ, GEORGE. 1998. "Critical Realism and Historical Sociology." *Comparative Studies in Society and History* 39 (4): 170-86

———, ed. 1999. *State/Culture: State Formation after the Cultural Turn.* Ithaca, NY: Cornell University Press.

———. 2004a. "Odious Comparisons: Incommensurability, the Case Study, and 'Small N's.'" *Sociological Theory* 22(3): 371-400.

———. 2004b. "The Uncontrollable Afterlives of Ethnography: Lessons from German 'Salvage Colonialism' for a New Age of Empire." *Ethnography* 5(3): 251-88.

———. 2005a. "American Sociology's Epistemological Unconscious and the Transition to Post-Fordism: The Case of Historical Sociology." In *Remaking Modernity: Politics, Processes and History in Sociology,* ed. Julia Adams, Elisabeth Clemens, and Ann Orloff, 109-57. Durham, NC: Duke University Press.

———. 2005b. "Bourdieu and the Psychoanalytic Theory of the Subject." Paper prepared for the conference Bourdieuian Theory and Historical Analysis, Yale University. April 29-May 1. This paper is forthcoming in the journal *Constellations* as "Bourdieu's Disavowal of Lacan: Psychoanalytic Theory and the Concepts of 'Habitus' and 'Symbolic Capital.'"

———. 2005c. "The Cultural Contradictions of Irving Louis Horowitz." *Michigan Quarterly Review* 44(3): 496-505.

———. 2005d. "The Genealogy of a Positivist Haunting: Comparing Prewar and Postwar U.S. Sociology." *Boundary 2* 32(2): 107-33.

———, ed. 2005e. *The Politics of Method in the Human Sciences: Positivism and Its Epistemological Others.* Durham, NC: Duke University Press.

———. 2005f. "Return to Empire: The New U.S. Imperialism in Comparative-Historical Perspective." *Sociological Theory* 23:4.

———. 2005g. "Scientific Authority and the Transition to Post-Fordism: The Plausibility of Positivism in U.S. Sociology since 1945." In *The Politics of Method in the Human Sciences: Positivism and Its Epistemological Others,* ed. George Steinmetz, 275–323. Durham, NC: Duke University Press.

———. 2006. *The Devil's Handwriting: Precoloniality and the German Colonial State in Qingdao, Samoa, and Southwest Africa.* Chicago: University of Chicago Press.

———. Forthcoming a. "Fordism." In *Encyclopedia of Europe: 1914–2004,* ed. John Merriman and Jay Winter. New York: Charles Scribner's Sons.

———. Forthcoming b. "Fordism and the Positivist Revenant: Response to Fourcade-Gourinchas, Riley, and Burris." *Social Science History.*

STEINMETZ, GEORGE, and OU-BYUNG CHAE. 2002. "Sociology in an Era of Fragmentation: From the Sociology of Knowledge to the Philosophy of Science, and Back Again." *Sociological Quarterly* 43:111–37.

STEPAN, NANCY. 1990. "Race and Gender: The Role of Analogy in Science." In *Anatomy of Racism,* ed. David Goldberg, 38–57. Minneapolis: University of Minnesota Press.

STEPAN, NANCY LEYS, and SANDER L. GILMAN. 1993. "Appropriating the Idioms of Science: The Rejection of Scientific Racism." In *The "Racial" Economy of Science: Toward a Democratic Future,* ed. Sandra Harding. Bloomington: Indiana University Press.

STEPHENS, JOHN, DIETRICH RUESCHEMEYER, and EVELYNE HUBER STEPHENS. 1992. *Capitalist Development and Democracy.* London: Polity Press.

STERN, BERNHARD J. 1932. "Giddings, Ward, and Small: An Interchange of Letters." Social Forces 10:305–18.

———. 1933. "The Letters of Albion W. Small to Lester F. Ward: I." *Social Forces* 12(2): 163–73.

———. 1935. "The Letters of Albion W. Small to Lester F. Ward: II." *Social Forces* 13(3): 323–40.

———. 1936. "The Letters of Albion W. Small to Lester F. Ward: III." *Social Forces* 15(2): 174–86.

———. 1937. "The Letters of Albion W. Small to Lester F. Ward: IV." *Social Forces* 15(3): 305–27.

———. 1938. "The Ward-Ross Correspondence, 1891–1896." *American Journal of Sociology* 3(3): 362–401.

———. 1946a. "The Ward-Ross Correspondence II, 1897–1901." *American Journal of Sociology* 11(5): 593–605.

———. 1946b. "The Ward-Ross Correspondence II, 1897–1901." *American Journal of Sociology* 11(6): 734–48.

———. 1947. "The Ward-Ross Correspondence III, 1902–1903." *American Journal of Sociology* 12(6): 703–20.

———. 1948. "The Ward-Ross Correspondence III, 1904–1905." *American Journal of Sociology* 13(1): 82–94.

———. 1949. "The Ward-Ross Correspondence IV, 1906-1912." *American Journal of Sociology* 14(1): 88-119.

———. 1959a. *Historical Sociology: The Selected Papers of Bernhard J. Stern.* New York: Citadel Press.

———. 1959b. "History and Sociology: A Comment." In *Historical Sociology,* 33-35. New York: Citadel Press.

STEWART, THEOPHILUS BOLDEN. 1903. Review of *Souls of Black Folk,* by W. E. B. DuBois. *American Journal of Sociology* 9(1): 136-37.

STIGLITZ, JOSEPH. 2002. *Globalization and Its Discontents.* New York: Norton.

STINCHCOMBE, ARTHUR L. 1995. *Sugar Island Slavery in the Age of Enlightenment: The Political Economy of the Caribbean World.* Princeton: Princeton University Press.

STOCKING, GEORGE W., JR. 1962. "Lamarckianism in American Social Science: 1890-1915." *Journal of the History of Ideas* 23:239-56.

———. 2001. *Delimiting Anthropology.* Madison: University of Wisconsin Press.

STOLER, ANN L. 1995. *Race and the Education of Desire: Foucault's History of Sexuality and the Colonial Order of Things.* Durham, NC: Duke University Press.

STOUFFER, SAMUEL A. 1930. "Experimental Comparison of Statistical and Case History Methods of Attitude Research." PhD diss., University of Chicago. http://spartan.ac.brocku.ca/~lward/Stouffer/1930/Stouffer_1930_5.html (accessed 7/29/05).

———. 1955. *Communism, Conformity, and Civil Liberties.* Garden City, NJ: Doubleday.

———. 1958. "Karl Pearson—An Appreciation on the 100th Anniversary of His Birth." *Journal of the American Statistical Association* 53(281): 23-27.

STOUFFER, SAMUEL A., and PAUL F. LAZARSFELD. 1937. *Research Memorandum on the Family in the Depression.* New York: Social Science Research Council.

STOUFFER, SAMUEL A., et al. 1949-50. *The American Soldier.* 4 vols. Princeton: Princeton University Press.

STRASSER, SUSAN. 1982. *Never Done: A History of American Housework.* New York: Pantheon Books.

STRAUSS, ANSELM L. 1987. *Qualitative Analysis for Social Scientists.* New York: Cambridge University Press.

STRAUSS, ANSELM L., LEONARD SCHATZMAN, RUE BUCHER, DANUTA EHRLICH, and MELVIN SABSHIN. 1964. *Psychiatric Ideologies and Institutions.* Glencoe, IL: Free Press.

STRAUSS, MURRAY A., RICHARD J. GELLES, and SUZANNE K. STEINMETZ. 1980. *Behind Closed Doors: Violence in the American Family.* Garden City, NJ: Anchor Press.

STRICKER, FRANK. 1988. "American Professors in the Progressive Era: Incomes, Aspirations, and Professionalization." *Journal of Interdisciplinary History* 19(2): 231-57.

STRYKER, SHELDON. 1980. *Symbolic Interactionism.* Menlo Park, CA: Benjamin/ Cummins.

SUDNOW, DAVID. 1978. *Ways of the Hand: The Organization of Improvised Conduct.* Cambridge: Harvard University Press.

SUEDFELD, PETER, ed. 2001. *Light from the Ashes: Social Science Careers of Young Holocaust Refugees and Survivors*. Ann Arbor: University of Michigan Press.

SUMNER, WILLIAM GRAHAM. 1909. "The Family and Social Change." *American Journal of Sociology* 14(5): 577–91.

——. 1913/1919. *War and Other Essays*. Ed. A. G. Keller. New Haven: Yale University Press.

——. 1940. *Folkways: A Study of the Sociological Importance of Usages, Manners, Customs, Mores, and Morals*. Boston: Ginn.

——. 1963. *Social Darwinism: Selected Essays*. Ed. Stow Persons. Englewood Cliffs, NJ: Prentice Hall.

SUMNER, WILLIAM GRAHAM, and ALBERT G. KELLER. 1927. *The Science of Society*. New Haven: Yale University Press.

SUNY, RONALD GRIGOR, and FATMA MUGE GOCEK. 2002. "Discussing Genocide: Contextualizing the Armenian Experience in the Ottoman Empire." *Journal of the International Institute* 10(3). http://www.umich.edu/7Eiinet/journal/vol9no3/suny.htm.

SUNY, RONALD GRIGOR, and MICHAEL D. KENNEDY, eds. 1999. *Intellectuals and the Articulation of the Nation*. Ann Arbor: University of Michigan Press.

SUSMAN, WARREN I. 1984. *Culture as History: The Transformation of American Society in the Twentieth Century*. New York: Pantheon.

SUTHERLAND, EDWIN H. 1924. *Criminology*. Philadelphia: Lippincott.

——. 1937. *The Professional Thief*. Chicago: University of Chicago Press.

——. 1939. *Principles of Criminology*. 3rd ed. Philadelphia: Lippincott.

SUTHERLAND, EDWIN H., and C. E. GEHLKE. 1934. "Crime and Punishment." In *Recent Social Trends in the United States*, by the President's Research Committee on Social Trends. New York: McGraw-Hill.

SUTHERLAND, EDWIN H., and HARVEY J. LOCKE. 1936. *Twenty Thousand Homeless Men: A Study of Unemployed Men in the Chicago Shelters*. Chicago: Lippincott.

SWIDLER, ANN. 2001. *Talk of Love: How Culture Matters*. Chicago: University of Chicago Press.

SWYGART-HOBAUGH, AMANDA J. 2004. "A Citation Analysis of the Qualitative/Quantitative Methods Debate's Reflection in Sociology Research: Implications for Library Collection Development." *Library Collections, Acquisitions and Technical Services* 28: 180–95.

SZRETER, R. 1980. "Institutionalising a New Specialism: The Early Years of the *Journal of Educational Sociology*." *British Journal of Sociology of Education* 1:173–82.

SZTOMPKA, PI. 1986. *Robert K. Merton: An Intellectual Profile*. New York: St. Martin's Press.

TAGUIEFF, PIERRE-ANDRÉ. 1988/2001. *The Force of Prejudice: On Racism and Its Doubles*. Trans. Hassan Melehy. Minneapolis: University of Minnesota Press.

TAKAKI, RONALD T. 1979. *Iron Cages: Race and Culture in Nineteenth-Century America*. New York: Knopf.

TANNENBAUM, FRANK. 1938. *Crime and the Community*. Boston: Ginn.

TATUM, BEVERLY DANIEL. 2003. *Why Are All the Black Kids Sitting Together in the Cafeteria?* New York: Basic Books.

TAYLOR, CHARLES, 2004. *Modern Social Imaginaries.* Durham, NC: Duke University Press.

TAYLOR, GRAHAM. 1930. *Pioneering on Social Frontiers.* Chicago: University of Chicago Press.

TAYLOR, STEVEN J., and ROBERT BOGDAN. 1984/1998. *Introduction to Qualitative Research Methods: The Search for Meanings.* 2nd and 3rd eds. New York: Wiley.

TAYLOR, VERTA. 1989. "Social Movement Continuity: The Women's Movement in Abeyance." *American Sociological Review* 54:761–75.

TEELE, JAMES E. 2002. *E. Franklin Frazier and "Black Bourgeoisie."* Columbia: University of Missouri Press.

TELLES, EDWARD E. 1992. "Residential Segregation in Brazil." *American Sociological Review* 57:186–97.

———. 2004. *Race in Another America: The Significance of Skin Color in Brazil.* Princeton: Princeton University Press.

"Ten Most Influential Books of the Past 25 Years." 1996. *Contemporary Sociology* 25 (3).

TERRY, JAMES L. 1983. "Bringing Women . . . In: A Modest Proposal." *Teaching Sociology* 10(2): 251–61.

THERBORN, GORAN. 1976. *Science, Class, and Society: On the Formation of Sociology and Historical Materialism.* London: New Left Books.

THERNSTROM, STEPHAN, and ABIGAIL THERNSTROM. 1997. *America in Black and White: One Nation, Indivisible.* New York: Simon and Schuster.

THILLY, FRANK 1914/1957. *A History of Philosophy.* 3rd ed. rev. New York: Henry Holt.

THOMAS, DOROTHY SWAINE. 1946. *The Salvage.* Berkeley: University of California Press.

THOMAS, DOROTHY SWAINE, with CHARLES KIKUCHI and JAMES SAKODA. 1952. *The Salvage.* Berkeley: University of California Press.

THOMAS, DOROTHY SWAINE, and RICHARD S. NISHIMOTO. 1946. *The Spoilage.* Berkeley: University of California Press.

THOMAS, WILLIAM I. 1907. "The Significance of the Orient for the Occident." *Publications of the American Sociological Society* 2:111–24; discussion, 125–37.

———. 1923. *The Unadjusted Girl.* Boston: Little, Brown.

THOMAS, WILLIAM I., and DOROTHY SWAINE THOMAS. 1928. *The Child in America: Behavior Problems and Programs.* New York: Knopf.

THOMAS, WILLIAM I., and FLORIAN ZNANIECKI. 1918–20. *The Polish Peasant in Europe and America: Monograph of an Immigrant Group.* 5 vols. Chicago: University of Chicago Press.

———. 1927/1958. *Polish Peasant in Europe and America.* Abridged 2-vol. ed. New York: Knopf; New York: Dover.

———. 1996. *The Polish Peasant in Europe and America: A Classic Work in Immigration History.* Ed. Eli Zaretsky. Urbana: University of Illinois Press.

THOMPSON, WARREN S. 1937. *Research Memorandum on Internal Migration in the Depression.* New York: Social Science Research Council.

THON, O. 1897a. "The Present Status of Sociology in Germany." Trans. Albion Small. *American Journal of Sociology* 2(4): 567–88.

——. 1897b. "The Present Status of Sociology in Germany, II." Trans. Albion Small. *American Journal of Sociology* 2(5): 718–36.

——. 1897c. "The Present Status of Sociology in Germany, III." Trans. Albion Small. *American Journal of Sociology* 2(6): 792–800.

THORNBERRY, TERENCE P. 1987. "Toward An Interactional Theory of Delinquency." *Criminology* 25(4): 863–91.

THORNE, BARRIE. 1978. "Political Activist as Participant Observer: Conflicts of Commitment in a Study of the Draft Resistance Movement of the 1960s." *Symbolic Interaction* 2:73–88. Reprinted, with a postscript, in *Contemporary Field Research*, ed. Robert Emerson, 216–34. Prospect Heights, IL: Waveland Press, 1983.

——. 1993. *Gender Play: Girls and Boys in School.* New Brunswick, NJ: Rutgers University Press.

THORNTON, ARLAND. 2004. *Reading History Sideways: The Fallacy and Enduring Impact of the Developmental Paradigm.* Chicago: University of Chicago Press.

THORNTON, RUSSELL. 1990. *American Indian Holocaust and Survival: A Population History since 1492.* Norman: University of Oklahoma Press.

THRASHER, FREDERIC M. 1927. *The Gang: A Study of 1,313 Gangs in Chicago.* Chicago: University of Chicago Press.

TIBBITS, CLARK. 1931. "Majority Votes and the Business Cycle." *American Journal of Sociology* 36:596–606.

TILLY, CHARLES, ed. 1975. *The Formation of National States in Western Europe.* Princeton: Princeton University Press.

——. 1978. *From Mobilization to Revolution.* Reading, MA: Addison-Wesley.

——. 1990. *Coercion, Capital, and European States: AD 990–1992.* London: Blackwell.

——. 2003a. *Contention and Democracy in Europe: 1650–2000.* Cambridge: Cambridge University Press.

——. 2003b. *The Politics of Collective Violence.* Cambridge: Cambridge University Press.

——, ed. 2004. "Terror, Terrorists, Terrorism" *Sociological Theory* 22(1): 5–13.

TILLY, CHARLES, LOUISE TILLY, and RICHARD TILLY. 1975. *The Rebellious Century, 1830–1930.* Cambridge: Harvard University Press.

TIMMERMANS, STEFAN. 1999. *Sudden Death and the Myth of CPR.* Philadelphia: Temple University Press.

TIPPS, DEAN. 1973. "Modernization Theory and the Comparative Study of Societies: A Critical Perspective." *Comparative Studies in Society and History* 15:199–226.

TIRYAKIAN, EDWARD A. 1962. *Sociologism and Existentialism: Two Perspectives on the Individual and Society.* Englewood Cliffs, NJ: Prentice Hall.

——. 1973. "Sociology and Existential Phenomenology." In *Phenomenology and the Social Sciences*, ed. M. Natanson, 1:187–222. Evanston, IL: Northwestern University Press.

TITTLE, CHARLES R. 1991. "On Being Labeled a Criminologist." In *Lessons of Criminology*, ed. Gilbert Geis and Mary Dodge. Cincinnati: Anderson Publishing.

——. 1995. *Control Balance: Toward a General Theory of Deviance.* Boulder, CO: Westview Press.

——. 2000. "Theoretical Developments in Criminology." In *The Nature of Crime: Continuity and Change,* 51-101, vol. 1 of *Criminal Justice 2000,* ed. Gary LaFree, Robert J. Bursik, Sr., James Short, and Ralph B. Taylor. Washington, DC: Office of Justice Programs.

——. 2002. "Reflections of a Reluctant but Committed Criminologist." In *Lessons of Criminology,* ed. Gilbert Geis and Mary Dodge, 23-45. Cincinnati: Anderson Publishing.

——. 2004. "Refining Control Balance Theory." *Theoretical Criminology* 8(4): 395-428.

TITTLE, CHARLES R., and RAYMOND PATERNOSTER. 2000. *Social Deviance and Crime: An Organizational and Theoretical Approach.* Los Angeles: Roxbury.

TOBIN, WILLIAM A. 1995. "Studying Society: The Making of *Recent Social Trends in the United States, 1929-1933.*" *Theory and Society* 24:537-65.

TOBY, JACKSON. 2002. "Ignoring Warnings, I Became a Criminologist." In *Lessons of Criminology,* ed. Gilbert Geis and Mary Dodge, 137-48. Cincinnati: Anderson Publishing.

TODD, ARTHUR S. 1934. Contribution to "Questions for Sociology: An Informal Round Table Symposium." *Social Forces* 13:196-97.

TOLBERT II, CHARLES M. 1983. "Industrial Segmentation and Men's Career Mobility." *American Sociological Review* 47:457-77.

TOLMAN, FRANK L. 1902a. "The Study of Sociology in Institutions of Higher Learning in the United States: A Report of an Investigation Undertaken by the Graduate Sociological League of the University of Chicago." *American Journal of Sociology* 7(6): 797-838.

——. 1902b. "The Study of Sociology in Institutions of Higher Learning in the United States, II." *American Journal of Sociology* 8(1): 85-121.

——. 1902c. "The Study of Sociology in Institutions of Higher Learning in the United States, III." *American Journal of Sociology* 8(2): 251-72.

——. 1903. "The Study of Sociology in Institutions of Higher Learning in the United States, IV." *American Journal of Sociology* 8(4): 531-58.

TOMLINSON, JOHN. 1998. *Globalization and Culture.* Chicago: University of Chicago Press.

TONRY, MICHAEL, LLOYD E. OHLIN, and DAVID P. FARRINGTON. 1991. *Human Development and Criminal Behavior: New Ways of Advancing Knowledge.* New York: Springer-Verlag.

TORRES, CARLOS ALBERTO, and THEODORE R. MITCHELL. 1998. *Sociology of Education: Emerging Perspectives.* Albany: State University of New York Press.

TRATTNER, WALTER L. 1979. *From Poor Law to Welfare State.* New York: Free Press.

TREVINO, A. JAVIER, ed. 2003. *Goffman's Legacy.* Lanham, MD: Rowman and Littlefield.

TRIPP, DEAN C. 1973. "Modernization Theory and the Comparative Study of Societies: A Critical Perspective." *Comparative Studies in Society and History* 15 (March): 199-226.

TUCHMAN, GAYE. 1989. *Edging Women Out: Victorian Novelists, Publishers, and Social Change*. New Haven: Yale University Press.

TUCKER, WILLIAM H. 1994. *The Science and Politics of Racial Research*. Urbana: University of Illinois.

TUFTS, JAMES H. 1896. "Recent Sociological Trends in France." *American Journal of Sociology* 1(4): 446–56.

TURBIN, CAROLE. 1998. "Introduction to Roundtable-What Social History Can Learn from Postmodernism, and Vice Versa? Or, Social Science Historians and Postmodernists Can Be Friends." *Social Science History* 22(1): 1–6.

TURK, AUSTIN T. 1982. "Social Control and Social Conflict." In *Social Control: Views from the Social Sciences*, ed. Jack P. Gibbs, 249–64. Beverly Hills, CA: Sage.

TURNER, JONATHAN H. 1985. *Herbert Spencer: A Renewed Appreciation*. Beverly Hills, CA: Sage.

———. 1989. *Sociology in the United States: Its Growth and Contemporary Profile*. In *National Traditions in Sociology*, ed. Nikolai Genov, 220–42. London: Sage.

TURNER, JONATHAN, LEONARD BEEGHLEY, and CHARLES H. POWERS. 2002. *The Emergence of Sociological Theory*. 5th ed. Belmont, CA: Wadsworth.

TURNER, RALPH, and LEWIS KILLIAN. 1957. *Collective Behavior*. Englewood Cliffs, NJ: Prentice Hall.

TURNER, STEPHEN. 1991. "The World of the Academic Quantifiers: The Columbia University Family and Its Connections." In *The Social Survey in Historical Perspective: 1880–1940*, ed. Martin Bulmer, Kevin Bales, and Kathryn Kish Sklar, 269–90. Cambridge: Cambridge University Press. Reprinted in *The Classical Tradition in Sociology: The American Tradition*, ed. Jeffrey Alexander, Raymond Boudon, and Mohamed Cherkaoui, 1:142–61. Twelve Oaks, CA: Sage, 1997.

———. 1994. "The Origins of 'Mainstream Sociology' and Other Issues in the History of American Sociology." *Social Epistemology* 8(1): 41–67.

———. 1996. "The Pittsburgh Survey and the Survey Movement: An Episode in the History of Expertise." In *Pittsburgh Surveyed: Social Science and Social Reform in the Early Twentieth Century*, ed. Maurine W. Greenwald and Margo Anderson, 35–49. Pittsburgh: University of Pittsburgh Press.

———. 2000. "Disciplinarity and Its Other." In *Practising Interdisciplinarity*, ed. Peter Weingart and Nico Stehr, 46–65. Toronto: University of Toronto Press.

———. 2004. "Social Theory as a Mature Discipline." In *The Dialogical Turn: New Roles for Sociology in a Postdisciplinary Age*, ed. C. Camic and H. Joas, 141–70. Lanham, MD: Rowman and Littlefield.

TURNER, STEPHEN, and PAUL ROTH, eds. 2003. *Blackwell Guide to the Philosophy of the Social Sciences*. Oxford: Blackwell.

TURNER, STEPHEN P., and JONATHAN H. TURNER. 1990. *The Impossible Science: An Institutional Analysis of American Sociology*. Newbury Park, CA: Sage.

TWITCHELL, J. B. 2000. *Twenty Ads That Shook the World*. New York: Three Rivers Press.

TYACK, DAVID. 1974. *The One Best System: A History of American Urban Education*. Cambridge: Harvard University Press.

UDRY, BRIAN. 2000. "Biological Limits of Gender Construction." *American Sociological Review* 65:443–57.

UEDA, R. 1996. "The Changing Path to Citizenship: Ethnicity and Naturalization during World War II." In *The War in American Culture: Society and Consciousness during World War II*, ed. L. Erenberg and S. Hirsch. Chicago: University of Chicago Press.

UGGEN, CHRISTOPHER. 2003. "Criminology and the Sociology of Deviance." *Criminologist* 28(3): 1, 3–5.

UNNITHAN, N. P., LIN HUFF-CORZINE, JAY CORZINE, and HUGH P. WHITT. 1995. *Currents of Lethal Violence: An Integrated Model of Homicide and Suicide*. Albany: SUNY Press.

VAILE, ROLAND S. 1937. *Research Memorandum on Social Aspects of Consumption in the Depression*. New York: Social Science Research Council.

VANANTWERPEN, JONATHAN. 2005. "Resisting Sociology's Seductive Name: Frederick J. Teggart and Sociology at Berkeley." In *Diverse Histories of American Sociology*, ed. Anthony J. Blasi, 141–77. Leiden: Brill.

———. 2006. "Critical Sociology and the Interdisciplinary Imagination." *Thesis Eleven* 84:60–72.

VAN DEN BERGHE, PIERRE L. 1970. *Race and Ethnicity: Essays in Comparative Sociology*. New York: Basic Books.

VANEK, JOANNE. 1974. "Time Spent in Housework." *Scientific American* 231:116–20.

VAN MAANEN, JOHN. 1988. *Tales of the Field: On Writing Ethnography*. Chicago: University of Chicago Press.

VAUGHAN, DIANE. 1996. *The Challenger Launch Decision: Risky Technology, Culture, and Deviance at NASA*. Chicago: University of Chicago Press.

———. 2002. "Criminology and the Sociology of Organizations: Analogy, Comparative Social Organization, and General Theory." *Crime, Law and Social Change* 37(2): 117–36.

VEBLEN, THORSTEIN. 1918. *The Higher Learning in America: A Memorandum on the Conduct of Universities by Business Men*. New York: B. W. Huebsch.

VEDITZ, C. W. A. 1906. "The American Sociological Society" [announcement of organizational meeting, December 1905, Baltimore]. *American Journal of Sociology* 11(1): 681–82.

VERDERY, KATHERINE, MICHAEL BERNHARD, JEFFREY KOPSTEIN, GALE STOKES, and MICHAEL D. KENNEDY. 2005. "Rereading *The Intellectuals on the Road to Class Power*." *Theory and Society* 34:1–36.

VEYSEY, LAURENCE R. 1965. *The Emergence of the American University*. Chicago: University of Chicago Press.

———. 1978. "Reappraising the Chicago School of Sociology." *Reviews in American History* 6:114–19.

VIDICH, ARTHUR J., and STANFORD M. LYMAN. 1985. *American Sociology: World Rejections of Religion and Their Directions*. New Haven: Yale University Press.

VINCENT, GEORGE E. 1896. "The Province of Sociology. Syllabus of a Course Occupying Four Hours per Week during Twelve Weeks: Given by the Author at the University of Chicago in the Autumn Quarter, 1895." *American Journal of Sociology* 1(4): 473–91.

——. 1904. "The Development of Sociology." *American Journal of Sociology* 10(2): 145–60.

VOLD, GEORGE B. 1958/1979. *Theoretical Criminology*. New York: Oxford University Press.

VOLD, GEORGE B., THOMAS J. BERNARD, AND JEFFREY B. SNIPES. 2002. *Theoretical Criminology*. 5th ed. New York: Oxford University Press.

VON HENTIG, HANS. 1948. *The Criminal and His Victim*. New Haven: Yale University Press.

WACHTEL, S. B., and L. C. FAY. 1946. "Allocation of Grades in the Army Air Forces." *American Journal of Sociology* 51:395–403.

WACKER, R. FRED. 1995. "The Sociology of Race and Ethnicity in the Second Chicago School." In *A Second Chicago School? The Development of a Postwar American Sociology*, ed. G. A. Fine, 136–63. Chicago: University of Chicago Press.

WACQUANT, LOÏC J. D. 1992. "Toward a Social Praxeology: The Structure and Logic of Bourdieu's Sociology." In *An Invitation to Reflexive Sociology*, ed. P. Bourdieu and L. J. D. Wacquant, 1–59. Chicago: University of Chicago Press.

——. 2000. "Academic Portraits: Autobiography and Scientific Censorship in American Sociology." In *Ideology and the Social Sciences*, ed. G. C. Kinloch and R. P. Mohan, 147–58. Westport, CT: Greenwood Press.

WALD, PRISCILLA. 2002. "Communicable Americanism: Contagion, Geographic Fictions, and the Sociological Legacy of Robert E. Park." *American Literary History* 14(4): 653–85.

WALKER, SYDNOR H. 1928. *Social Work and Social Workers*. Chapel Hill: University of North Carolina Press.

——. 1934. "Privately Supported Social Work." In *Recent Social Trends in the United States*, by the President's Research Committee on Social Trends. New York: McGraw-Hill.

WALLACE, ROBERT W. 1989. *The Institutionalization of a New Discipline: The Case of Sociology at Columbia University, 1891–1931*. Ann Arbor, MI: University Microfilms International.

WALLACE, RUTH A., ed. 1989. *Feminism and Sociological Theory*. Newbury Park, CA: Sage.

WALLER, WILLARD. 1932. *The Sociology of Teaching*. New York: Wiley.

——. 1936. "Personality Changes in Practice Teachers." *Journal of Educational Sociology* 9:556–64.

WALLERSTEIN, IMMANUEL. 1974. "The Rise and Future Demise of the World Capitalist System: Concepts for Comparative Analysis." *Comparative Studies in Society and History* 16:387–415.

——. 1976. *The Modern World-System: Capitalist Agriculture and the Origins of the European World-Economy in the Sixteenth Century*. New York: Academic Press.

———. 1997. "The Unanticipated Consequences of Cold War Area Studies." In *The Cold War and the University: Toward an Intellectual History of the Postwar Years,* by N. Chomsky et al., 195–231. New York: New Press.

———. 1998. "Letter from the President, No. 2, 'Sociology and History.'" In *Letters from the President, 1994–1998,* printed for and distributed at the 14th World Congress of Sociology, Montreal. July 26–August 1.

———. 1999. "The Heritage of Sociology: The Promise of Social Science." In *The End of the World as We Know It: Social Science for the Twenty-First Century,* by Immanuel Wallerstein, 220–51. Minneapolis: University of Minnesota Press.

———. 2004. "Anthropology, Sociology, and Other Dubious Disciplines." In *The Uncertainties of Knowledge,* by Immanuel Wallerstein, 166–90. Philadelphia: Temple University Press.

———. 2005. "Latin@s: What's In a Name?" In *Latin@s in the World System: Decolonization Struggles in the 21st Century U.S. Empire,* ed. Ramón Grosfoguel, Nelson Maldonado-Torres, and José David Saldívar. Boulder, CO: Paradigm Press.

WALLERSTEIN, IMMANUEL, ET AL. 1996. *Open the Social Sciences: Report of the Gulbenkian Commission on the Restructuring of the Social Sciences.* Stanford, CA: Stanford University Press.

WALLIS, LOUIS. 1908a. "Biblical Sociology, I." *American Journal of Sociology* 14(2): 145–70.

———. 1908b. "Biblical Sociology, II." *American Journal of Sociology* 14(3): 306–28.

———. 1909a. "Biblical Sociology, III." *American Journal of Sociology* 14(4): 497–533.

———. 1909b. "Biblical Sociology, IV." *American Journal of Sociology* 15(2): 214–43.

———. 1910. "Biblical Sociology, V." *American Journal of Sociology* 16(3): 392–419.

———. 1911a. "Biblical Sociology, VI." *American Journal of Sociology* 17(1): 61–76.

———. 1911b. "Biblical Sociology, VII." *American Journal of Sociology* 17(3): 329–50.

———. 1912. *The Sociology of the Bible.* Chicago: University of Chicago Press. Reprint of "Biblical Sociology, I–VII."

WALTERS, PAMELA BARNHOUSE. 2001. "Educational Access and the State: Historical Continuities and Discontinuities in Racial Inequality in American Education." Special issue. *Sociology of Education,* 35–49.

WARD, KATHERINE, J. GAST, and L. GRANT. 1992. "Visibility and Dissemination of Women's and Men's Scholarship." *Social Problems* 39(3): 291–98.

WARD, LESTER F. 1883/1968. *Dynamic Sociology.* 2 vols. New York: Appleton; New York: Johnson Reprint.

———. 1895a. "The Place of Sociology among the Sciences." *American Journal of Sociology* 1(1): 16–27.

———. 1895b. "Contributions to Social Philosophy. II. Sociology and Cosmology." *American Journal of Sociology* 1(2): 132–45.

———. 1895c. "Contributions to Social Philosophy. III. Sociology and Biology." *American Journal of Sociology* 1(3): 313–26.

———. 1896a. "Contributions to Social Philosophy. IV. Sociology and Anthropology." *American Journal of Sociology* 1(4): 426–33.

———. 1896b. "Contributions to Social Philosophy. V. Sociology and Psychology." *American Journal of Sociology* 1(5): 618-32.

———. 1896c. "Contributions to Social Philosophy. VI. The Data of Sociology." *American Journal of Sociology* 1(6): 738-52.

———. 1896d. "Contributions to Social Philosophy. VII. The Social Forces." *American Journal of Sociology* 2(1): 82-95.

———. 1896e. "Contributions to Social Philosophy. IX. The Purpose of Sociology." *American Journal of Sociology* 2(3): 446-60.

———. 1897. "Contributions to Social Philosophy. XI. Individual Telesis." *American Journal of Sociology* 2(5): 699-717.

———. 1900. "Review-Essay on Thorstein Veblen, *The Theory of the Leisure Class.*" *American Journal of Sociology* 5(6): 829-37.

———. 1902. "Contemporary Sociology, III." *American Journal of Sociology* 7(6): 749-62.

———. 1903. *Pure Sociology: A Treatise on the Origin and Spontaneous Development of Society.* New York: Macmillan.

———. 1907. "The Establishment of Sociology" [includes an excerpt from the first presidential address to the ASS, December 27, 1906]. *American Journal of Sociology* 12(5): 581-87.

———. 1909." Ludwig Gumplowicz." *American Journal of Sociology* 15(3): 410-13.

WARD, LESTER FRANK, and HENRY STEELE COMMAGER. 1967. *Lester Ward and the Welfare State.* Indianapolis: Bobbs-Merrill.

WARNER, AMOS. 1894/1989. *American Charities: A Study in Philanthropy and Economics.* New Brunswick, NJ: Transaction Publishers.

WARNER, R. STEPHEN. 1976. "Review of *Sociological Theory: Uses and Unities* and *The Structure of Sociological Theory.*" *Contemporary Sociology* 5:68-71.

WARNER, W. LLOYD, with the collaboration of WILFRID C. BAILEY and others. 1935. "Formal Education and the Social Structure." *Journal of Educational Sociology* 9:524-31.

———. 1943. "The Struggle for Status." *Journal of Educational Sociology* 16:336-40.

———. 1949. *Democracy in Jonesville: A Study in Quality and Inequality.* New York: Harper.

WARNER, W. LLOYD, ROBERT J. HAVINGHURST, and MARTIN B. LOEB. 1944. *Who Shall Be Educated? The Challenge of Unequal Opportunities.* New York: Harper and Brothers.

WARNER, W. LLOYD, ET AL. 1941, 1942, 1945, 1947, 1959. *Yankee City* (series). New Haven: Yale University Press.

WATERS, MALCOLM. 1996. *Daniel Bell.* New York: Routledge.

WATTS, W. DAVID, and ANN MARIE ELLIS. 1989. "Assessing Sociology Educational Outcomes: Occupational Status and Mobility of Graduates." *Teaching Sociology* 17:297-306.

WAX, ROSALIE H. 1971. *Doing Fieldwork: Warnings and Advice.* Chicago: University of Chicago Press.

WEBER, LYNN. 1998. "A Conceptual Framework for Understanding Race, Class, Gender, and Sexuality." *Psychology of Women Quarterly* 22:13–32.

WEBER, MAX. 1947. *The Theory of Social and Economic Organization*. Trans. Talcott Parsons. New York: Oxford University Press.

———. 1958. *The Protestant Ethic and the Spirit of Capitalism*. Trans. Talcott Parsons. New York: Scribner. Originally published in German in 1905.

WEBSTER, JOHN. 2000. *The Cambridge Companion to Karl Barth*. Cambridge: Cambridge University Press.

WEICK, KARL E. 1976. "Educational Organizations as Loosely Coupled Systems." *Administrative Science Quarterly* 21:1–19.

WEINER, ELAINE. 2005. "No (Wo)Man's Land: The Post-Socialist Purgatory of Czech Female Factory Workers" *Social Problems* 52(4): 572–92

WELLS, D. COLLIN. 1907. "Social Darwinism" [proceedings of the first ASS meeting]. *American Journal of Sociology* 12(5): 695–708; comments by Lester Ward, Carl Kelsey, William Allen, Charlotte Perkins Gilman, G. W. Cooke, and E. A. Ross, and response by Wells, 709–16.

WEST, CANDACE, and DON H. ZIMMERMAN. 1987. "Doing Gender." *Gender and Society* 1:125–51.

WEST, CORNEL. 1989. *The American Evasion of Philosophy: A Genealogy of Pragmatism*. Madison: University of Wisconsin Press.

WESTBROOK, R. 2004. *Why We Fought: Forging American Obligations in World War II*. Washington, DC: Smithsonian Books.

WESTIE, F. R. 1995. *Ash Wednesday '45*. Ann Arbor, MI: George Wahr Publishing.

WESTIE, M. L. 2004. "Obituary: Frank R. Westie." *ASA Footnotes* (May–June): 23.

WHITAKER, BRUCE E. 1972. "The Social Philosophy of Charles Ellwood." *North Carolina Historical Review* 49(2): n.p.

WHITE, LEONARD D. 1937. "New Opportunities for Economists and Statisticians in Federal Employment." *American Economic Review* 27 (supp.): 210–15.

WHITE, R. CLYDE. 1934. Contribution to "Questions for Sociology: An Informal Round Table Symposium." *Social Forces* 13: 170–77.

WHITEHURST, GROVER. 2003. "The Institute of Education Sciences: New Wine, New Bottles." Presentation at the annual meeting of the American Educational Research Association. April 22.

WHITFORD, JOSH. 2002. "Pragmatism and the Untenable Dualism of Means and Ends: Why Rational Choice Theory Does Not Deserve Paradigmatic Privilege." *Theory and Society* 31:325–63.

WHYTE, W. H. 1956. *The Organization Man*. New York: Simon and Schuster.

WHYTE, WILLIAM F. 1943/1955. *Street Corner Society: The Social Structure of an Italian Slum*. 2nd ed. Chicago: University of Chicago Press.

WIEDER, D. LAWRENCE. 1974. *Language and Social Reality: The Case of Telling the Convict Code*. The Hague, Netherlands: Mouton.

WIENER, N. 1950. *The Human Use of Human Beings*. New York: Houghton Mifflin.

WIESE, LEOPOLD VON. 1932. *Systematic Sociology.* New York: Wiley.

WIGGERSHAUS, ROLF. 1994. *The Frankfurt School: Its History, Theories, and Political Significance.* Trans. M. Robertson. Cambridge: MIT Press.

WILEY, NORBERT. 1979. "The Rise and Fall of Dominating Theories in American Sociology." In *Contemporary Issues in Theory and Research,* ed. William E. Snizek, Ellsworth R. Fuhrman, and Michael K. Miller, 47–83. Westport, CT: Greenwood.

——. 1994. *The Semiotic Self.* Chicago: University of Chicago Press.

WILKINSON, DORIS. 1975. "Review of *Black Sociologists: Historical and Contemporary Perspectives.*" *American Journal of Sociology* 81:461–62.

——. 1979. "A Report, Status of Women in Sociology, 1934–1977." *American Sociological Association Footnotes* 10:4–6.

WILLER, DAVID, and JUDITH WILLER. 1973. *Systematic Empiricism: Critique of a Pseudoscience.* Englewood Cliffs, NJ: Prentice Hall.

WILLEY, MALCOLM M. 1934. Contribution to "Questions for Sociology: An Informal Round Table Symposium." *Social Forces* 13:213–15.

WILLIAMS, CHRISTINE L. 1995. *Still a Man's World: Men Who Do "Women's Work."* Berkeley: University of California Press.

WILLIAMS, FRANK P. 1984. "The Demise of the Criminological Imagination: A Critique of Recent Criminology." *Justice Quarterly* 1:91–106.

WILLIAMS, JAMES MICKEL. 1933. *Human Aspect of Unemployment and Relief.* Chapel Hill: University of North Carolina Press.

WILLIAMS, RAYMOND. 1976. "Imperialism." In *Keywords: A Vocabulary of Culture and Society,* 159–60. New York: Oxford University Press.

WILNER, PATRICIA. 1985. "The Main Drift of Sociology between 1936 and 1982." *History of Sociology* 5(2): 1–19.

WILSHIRE, BRUCE W. 2002. *Fashionable Nihilism: A Critique of Analytic Philosophy.* Albany: State University of New York Press.

WILSON, JAMES Q. 1975. *Thinking about Crime.* New York: Basic Books.

WILSON, WILLIAM J. 1978. *The Declining Significance of Race: Blacks and Changing American Institutions.* Chicago: University of Chicago Press.

——. 1987. *The Truly Disadvantaged: The Inner City, the Underclass, and Public Policy.* Chicago: University of Chicago Press.

——. 1999. *The Bridge over the Racial Divide: Rising Inequality and Coalition Politics.* Berkeley: University of California Press.

WINANT, HOWARD. 1998. "It Was Just a Bad Dream. Everything's Fine Now, Dear. You Can Go Back to Sleep." Review of *America in Black and White: One Nation, Indivisible,* by Thernstrom and Thernstrom. *Contemporary Sociology* 27(6).

——. 2001. *The World Is a Ghetto: Race and Democracy since World War II.* New York: Basic Books.

WINKLER, A. M. 1978. *The Politics of Propaganda: The Office of War Information, 1942–1945.* New Haven: Yale University Press.

WIRTH, LOUIS. 1928. *The Ghetto.* Chicago: University of Chicago Press.

———. 1934/1935. "The Prospects of Regional Research in Relation to Social Planning." In *The Human Side of Social Planning*, ed. E. W. Burgess and Herbert Blumer, 107–14. Chicago: American Sociological Society.

———. 1947. "American Sociology, 1915–47." *American Journal of Sociology* [index to vols. 1–52, 1895–47] 52:273–81.

———. Papers. Regenstein Library, University of Chicago.

WISH, HARVEY, ed. 1960. *Antebellum Writings of George Fitzhugh and Hinton Rowan Helper on Slavery*. New York: Capricorn Books.

WITTGENSTEIN, LUDWIG. 1953/2001. *Philosophical Investigations*. 3rd ed. Trans. G. E. M. Anscombe. Malden, MA: Blackwell.

WOLFF, KURT H. 1959. "Sociology and History; Theory and Practice." *American Journal of Sociology* 65(1): 32–38

———. 1985. "A Sociological Approach to the History of Sociology." *Journal of the History of the Behavioral Sciences* 21 (October): 342–44.

WOLFGANG, MARVIN E. 1967. "Victim-Precipitated Criminal Homicide." In *Studies in Homicide*, ed. Marvin E. Wolfgang. New York: Harper and Row.

WOLFGANG, MARVIN E., and FRANCO FERRACUTI. 1967. *The Subculture of Violence: Towards an Integrated Theory in Criminology*. London: Tavistock.

WOLFGANG, MARVIN E., ROBERT M. FIGLIO, and THORSTEIN SELLIN. 1972. *Delinquency in a Birth Cohort*. Chicago: University of Chicago Press.

WOLFGANG, MARVIN E., TERENCE P. THORNBERRY, and ROBERT M. FIGLIO. 1987. *From Boy to Man, from Delinquency to Crime*. Chicago: University of Chicago Press.

WOOD, ARTHUR EVANS. 1930. "Charles Horton Cooley: An Appreciation." *American Journal of Sociology* 35(5): 707–17.

———. 1934. Contribution to "Questions for Sociology: An Informal Round Table Symposium." *Social Forces* 13:183–87.

WOODS, ROBERT A. 1923/1970. "The Neighborhood in Social Reconstruction" (1914). In *The Neighborhood in Nation-Building*, by Robert A. Woods, 147–63. Boston: Houghton Mifflin; New York: Arno Press.

WOODS, ROBERT A., and ALBERT A. KENNEDY, eds. 1911. *The Handbook of Settlements*. New York: Russell Sage Foundation.

WOODWARD, JULIAN L. 1884. "A History of Sociology at Cornell University." L. L. Bernard Papers, box 1, folder 5. University of Chicago Special Collections.

WORKS PROGRESS ADMINISTRATION (WPA). 1937. *Subject Index of Research Bulletins and Monographs Issued by Federal Emergency Relief Administration and Works Progress Administration, Division of Social Research*. Washington, DC.

———. 1938–39. *Index of Research Projects*. 3 vols. Washington, DC.

WORTHAM, ROBERT A. 2005. "The Early Sociological Legacy of W. E. B. Du Bois." In *Diverse Histories of American Sociology*, ed. Anthony Blasi. Leiden, Netherlands: Brill.

WRIGHT, CARROLL D. 1895. "Contributions of the United States Government to Social Science." *American Journal of Sociology* 1(3): 241–75.

WRIGHT II, EARL. 2002a. "The Atlanta Sociological Laboratory, 1896-1924: A Historical Account of the First American School of Sociology." *Western Journal of Black Studies* 26:3, 165-74.

——. 2002b. "Why Black People Tend to Shout! An Earnest Attempt to Explain the Sociological Negation of the Atlanta Sociological Laboratory Despite Its Possible Unpleasantness." *Sociological Spectrum* 22:335-61.

WRIGHT, ERIC OLIN. 2005. "Falling into Marxism; Choosing to Stay." In *A Disobedient Generation: Social Theorists in the Sixties*, ed. Alan Sica and Stephen Turner, 325-49. Chicago: University of Chicago Press.

WRIGHT, ERIK OLIN, and BILL MARTIN. 1987. "The Transformation of the American Class Structure, 1960-1980." *American Journal of Sociology* 93:1-29.

WRIGHT, JAMES. 1978. "Are Working Women *Really* More Satisfied?" *Journal of Marriage and the Family* 40:301-13.

WRONG, DENNIS H. 1971. "New Wine in Old Bottles-A Review of Two Books." *American Sociologist* 6:249-53.

——. 1999. "Digby Baltzell: Sociologist and Critical Celebrant of the Upper Class." *Sociological Theory* 17:112-16.

WYNN, NEIL A. 1976. *The Afro-American and the Second World War*. New York: Holmes and Meier.

YELLIN, JEAN FAGAN, and JOHN C. VAN HORNE, eds. 1994. *The Abolitionist Sisterhood*. Ithaca, NY: Cornell University Press.

YOUNG, DONALD. 1937. *Research Memorandum on Minority Peoples in the Depression*. New York: Social Science Research Council.

YOUNG, K. 1941. *Personality and Problems of Adjustment*. New York: F. S. Crofts.

YOUNG, ROBERT J. C. 1995. *Colonial Desire: Hybridity in Theory, Culture and Race*. New York: Routledge.

YU, HENRY. 2001. *Thinking Orientals: Migration, Contact, and Exoticism in Modern America*. Oxford: Oxford University Press.

ZAMIR, SHAMOON. 1995. *Dark Voices: W. E. B. DuBois and American Thought, 1888-1903*. Chicago: University of Chicago Press.

ZEISEL, HANS. 1947/1957. *Say It with Figures*. New York: Harper.

ZEITLIN, MAURICE. 1998. *The Civil Wars in Chile, or the Bourgeois Revolutions That Never Were*. Princeton: Princeton University Press.

ZETTERBERG, HANS LENNART. 1954/1965. *On Theory and Verification in Sociology*. Totowa, NJ: Bedminster Press.

——. 1956a. "A Guide to American Sociology, 1945-1955." In *Sociology in the United States of America*, 9-20. Paris: UNESCO.

——, ed. 1956b. *Sociology in the United States of America*. Paris: UNESCO.

ZHAO, DINXIN. 2004. *The Power of Tiananmen: State Society Relations and the 1989 Beijing Student Movement*. Chicago: University of Chicago Press.

ZIEGER, ROBERT H., and GILBERT J. GALL. 2002. *American Workers, American Unions: The Twentieth Century*. 3rd ed. Baltimore: Johns Hopkins University Press.

ZILBOORG, GREGORY. 1939. "Sociology and the Psychoanalytic Method." *American Journal of Sociology* 45(3): 341–55.

ZIMMERMAN, ANDREW. 2006. "Decolonizing Weber." Special issue, "Decolonizing German Theory," ed. George Steinmetz. *Postcolonial Studies* 9(1).

ZIMRING, FRANKLIN E., and GORDON HAWKINS. 1983. "Crime Commissions." In *Encyclopedia of Crime and Justice,* ed. Sanford H. Kadish, 353–57. New York: Free Press.

ZNANIECKI, FLORIAN. 1954. "Basic Problems of Contemporary Sociology" *American Sociological Review* 19:519–24.

ZORBAUGH, HARVEY. 1927. "Research in Educational Sociology." *Journal of Educational Sociology* 1:18–24.

———. 1929. *The Gold Coast and the Slum: A Sociological Study of Chicago's Near North Side.* Chicago: University of Chicago Press.

ZUBERI, TUKUFU. 2001. *Thicker Than Blood: How Racial Statistics Lie.* Minneapolis: University of Minnesota Press.

ZUBRZYCKI, GENEVIEVE. forthcoming. *Auschwitz with or without the Cross? Nationalism and Religion in Post-Communist Poland.* Chicago: University of Chicago Press.

ZUCKERMAN, PHIL, ed. 2004. *The Social Theory of W. E. B. Du Bois.* Thousand Oaks, CA: Pine Forge Press.

CONTRIBUTORS

ANDREW ABBOTT is the Gustavus F. and Ann M. Swift Distinguished Service Professor at the University of Chicago. He has written on occupations and professions, on social theory and methodology, on disciplines and knowledge, and on heuristics and inquiry. He is currently writing two books, one on general social theory and the other on the future of libraries.

DANIEL BRESLAU is an associate professor in the Department of Science, Technology, and Society at Virginia Tech. His research is on the sociology and social history of the social sciences, with a particular focus on sociology, economics, and statistics. His 1998 book, *In Search of the Unequivocal: The Political Economy of Knowledge in U.S. Labor Market Policy*, was given the Robert K. Merton Award by the American Sociological Association section Science, Knowledge, and Technology. Breslau's current research examines social networks in the field of game theory and the transmission of tacit knowledge in mathematics.

CRAIG CALHOUN is president of the Social Science Research Council and University Professor of Social Sciences at New York University. His most recent books include *Cosmopolitanism and Belonging* (Routledge, 2006), the edited collection *Lessons of Empire? Historical Contexts for Understanding America's Global Power* (with Frederick Cooper and Kevin Moore; New Press, 2006), and *The Roots of Radicalism* (University of Chicago Press, forthcoming).

CHARLES CAMIC is a professor of sociology at Northwestern University. His most recent books are *The Dialogical Turn* (edited with Hans Joas) and *Max Weber's "Economy and Society": A Critical Companion* (edited with Philip Gorski and David Trubek). He is currently writing two books, one on the early intellectual career of Thorstein Veblen and the other on the early intellectual career of Talcott Parsons.

MIGUEL A. CENTENO is professor of sociology and international affairs and director of the Princeton Institute for International and Regional Studies. From 1997 to 2004 he also served as master of Wilson College at Princeton. He has published nine books as author or editor. In 2000, he founded the Princeton University Preparatory Program, which provides intensive supplemental training for lower-income students at three local high schools.

PATRICIA HILL COLLINS is professor of sociology at the University of Maryland, College Park, and the Charles Phelps Taft Emeritus Professor of Sociology within the Department of African American Studies at the University of Cincinnati. She is author of the award-winning *Black Feminist Thought: Knowledge, Consciousness, and the Politics of Empowerment,* as well as *Race, Class, and Gender: An Anthology* (a reader used at more than two hundred colleges and universities), *Fighting Words: Black Women and the Search for Justice,* and *Black Sexual Politics: African Americans, Gender and the New Racism.*

MARJORIE L. DEVAULT is professor of sociology and a member of the Women's Studies Program at Syracuse University. Her research has explored the "invisible work" in women's household and family lives and in the historically female field of dietetics and nutrition education. Trained in the Chicago-school fieldwork tradition and deeply influenced by the feminism of the 1970s, she has written broadly on qualitative and feminist methodologies and has been a central participant in the development of a feminist institutional ethnography. She is author of *Feeding the Family: The Social Organization of Caring as Gendered Work* (1991) and *Liberating Method: Feminism and Social Research* (1999).

MYRA MARX FERREE is professor of sociology and director of the Center for German and European Studies at the University of Wisconsin–Madison. Among her recent books are *Shaping Abortion Discourse: Democracy and the Public Sphere in Germany and the United States* (Cambridge University Press, 2002) and *Global Feminism* (NYU Press, 2006). She is a former president of Sociologists for Women in Society and former vice president of the American Sociological Association.

NEIL GROSS is assistant professor of sociology at Harvard University. He is working on a book about Richard Rorty, written from the standpoint of the sociology of ideas. He is co-editor and cotranslator (with Robert Alun Jones) of *Durkheim's Philosophy Lectures: Notes from the Lycée de Sens Course, 1883–84.* His work has appeared in *American Sociological Review, Sociological Theory, Theory and Society, Annual Review of Sociology,* and other journals.

LORINE A. HUGHES is assistant professor of criminal justice at the University of Nebraska, Omaha. She has published in *Criminology,* the *Journal of Contemporary Criminal Justice,* and *Women and Crime,* and is a contributor and co-editor (with Jim Short) of *Studying Youth Gangs.*

MICHAEL D. KENNEDY is professor of sociology at the University of Michigan. He has served as that university's vice provost for international affairs and director of the International Institute, Center for European Studies, Center for Russian and East European Studies, and European Union Center. He has authored two monographs, *Cultural Formations of Postcommunism* (University of Minnesota Press, 2002) and *Professionals, Power and Solidarity in Poland* (Cambridge University Press, 1991), as well as edited and co-edited several collections, including the online publication "Responsibility in Crisis: Knowledge Politics and Global Publics."

SHAMUS RAHMAN KHAN is a doctoral candidate in the department of sociology at the University of Wisconsin–Madison. He has written on gender, deliberative processes, and modernist music. His dissertation, "The Production of Privilege," is an ethnographic study of an elite boarding school.

BARBARA LASLETT is professor emerita of sociology at the University of Minnesota. In addition to many articles and reviews, she edited, with Barrie Thorne, an original collection of autobiographical essays, *Feminist Sociology: Life Histories of a Movement* (1997), as well as several *Signs* readers during her term as editor of that journal (1990–95). In 2001 she was the winner of the Jessie Bernard Award given by the American Sociological Association. She is currently working on a volume, *Telling Stories: Personal Narratives in the Social Sciences and History*, with Mary Jo Maynes and Jennifer Pierce.

PATRICIA LENGERMANN is research professor of sociology at George Washington University. She is author of *Definitions of Sociology: A Historical Approach, Gender in America* (with Ruth Wallace) and *The Women Founders: Sociology and Social Theory, 1830–1930* (with Gillian Niebrugge). She is past chair of the ASA section on the History of Sociology. Her research focus is on the institutional dimensions of sociology's history.

DOUG MCADAM is professor of sociology at Stanford University and director emeritus of the Center for Advanced Study in the Behavioral Sciences. He is author or coauthor of eight books and more than fifty articles in the area of political sociology, with a special emphasis on the study of social movements and revolutions. Among his best-known works are *Political Process and the Development of Black Insurgency, 1930–1970*, a new edition of which was published in 1999 (University of Chicago Press), *Freedom Summer* (Oxford University Press, 1988), which was given the 1990 C. Wright Mills Award as well as being a finalist for the American Sociological Association's prize for best book of 1991, and *Dynamics of Contention* (Cambridge University Press, 2001) with Sid Tarrow and Charles Tilly. He was elected to membership in the American Academy of Arts and Sciences in 2003.

SHAUNA A. MORIMOTO is a doctoral candidate in sociology at the University of Wisconsin–Madison. Her dissertation is a comparative examination of the relationship between civic engagement and civic education in the United States. She recently coauthored a working paper for the Center for Information and Research on Civic Learning and Engagement.

ALDON D. MORRIS is professor of sociology and associate dean of faculty at Northwestern University. He has served as national president of the Association of Black Sociologists. Morris has written widely on race, social movements, and inequality. Among his publications is his award-winning book *The Origins of the Civil Rights Movement*. He is co-editor of *Frontiers in Social Movement Theory* and the *Subjective Roots of Social Protest*. He is currently working on a book about the sociology of W. E. B. DuBois.

GILLIAN NIEBRUGGE is scholar in residence at American University and has taught social theory at the University of Iowa, Gettysburg College, and the George Washington University. She is the founder of the ASA section on the History of Sociology and coauthor with Patricia Lengermann of *The Women Founders: Sociology and Social Theory, 1830–1930*. Her research focus is on the relation between sociology and the public.

ALTON PHILLIPS is a graduate student in the Department of Sociology at New York University. His current research includes field and network analyses of the development of sociology in the United States, as well as a social history of nevirapine and the provisioning of antiretroviral treatment in developing and transitional economies.

JAMES F. SHORT JR. is a former editor of the *American Sociological Review,* associate editor of the *Annual Review of Sociology,* and president of the Pacific and American Sociological Associations and the American Society of Criminology. His books include *Group Process and Gang Delinquency* and *Poverty, Ethnicity, and Violent Crime.* He is a recipient of the Edwin H. Sutherland, Bruce Smith, and Wolfgang awards as well as fellowships from the ASC, AAAS, Center for Advanced Study in the Behavioral Sciences, Institute of Criminology (Cambridge), Rockefeller's Bellagio Center, Centre for Socio-Legal Studies (Oxford), and John Simon Guggenheim Foundation.

ALAN SICA is professor of sociology and director of the Social Thought Program at Pennsylvania State University. He was formerly editor of *Sociological Theory,* and his latest books include *Social Thought: From the Enlightenment to the Present* (2004) and *The Disobedient Generation* (with Stephen Turner; University of Chicago Press, 2005).

JAMES T. SPARROW is assistant professor of U.S. history at the University of Chicago. He is currently completing *Americanism and Entitlement: Authorizing Big Government from the New Deal to the Cold War,* a history of the social politics of the American warfare state in its founding era.

GEORGE STEINMETZ is professor of sociology and German studies at the University of Michigan. He is author of *Regulating the Social: The Welfare State and Local Politics in Imperial Germany* (Princeton University Press, 1993) and *The Devil's Handwriting: Precoloniality and the German Colonial State in Qingdao, Samoa, and Southwest Africa* (University of Chicago Press, 2006), and he edited *State/Culture: State Formation after the Cultural Turn* (Cornell University Press, 1999), *The Politics of Method in the Human Sciences: Positivism and Its Epistemological Others* (Duke University Press, 2005), and a special issue of *Postcolonial Studies* on the topic "Decolonizing German Theory." He codirected the documentary film *Detroit; Ruin of a City* (DVD, Intellect Books, 2006) with Michael Chanan and is beginning work on a new historical documentary with Chanan (provisionally) titled *The Course of Empire in the 20th Century.*

STEPHEN TURNER is graduate research professor in the Department of Philosophy at the University of South Florida. His extensive writings on the history of American sociology include a disciplinary history, *The Impossible Science: An Institutional Analysis of American Sociology* (with Jonathan Turner, 1990), and articles and chapters on such topics as the program of the Rockefeller philanthropies for the social sciences, the Pittsburgh Survey, the origins of mainstream sociology, and early Columbia University sociology. His most recent book, edited with Alan Sica, *The Disobedient Generation: Social Theorists in the Sixties* (2005), collects autobiographies of a group of internationally known sociologists from the 1968 generation.

JONATHAN VANANTWERPEN is a PhD candidate in the Department of Sociology at the University of California, Berkeley, where he is writing a dissertation on transnational struggles over reconciliation in the aftermath of South Africa's Truth and Reconciliation Commission. He is co-editor (with Michael Burawoy) of an online volume titled *Producing Public Sociology* (2005, 2nd ed.); he is author of "Resisting Sociology's Seductive Name: Frederick J. Teggart and Sociology at Berkeley" in *Diverse Histories of American Sociology,* edited by Anthony J. Blasi (Brill, 2005), and "Critical Sociology and the Interdisciplinary Imagination" in *Thesis Eleven* (February 2006).

IMMANUEL WALLERSTEIN is senior research scholar at Yale University. He was president of the International Sociological Association in 1994–98 and chair of the international Gulbenkian Commission on the Restructuring of the Social Sciences in 1993–95. He is author of *The Modern World-System.*

PAMELA BARNHOUSE WALTERS is the James H. Rudy Professor of Sociology and director of the Center for Education and Society at Indiana University. She is a historical sociologist whose research focuses on social inequality in American education. Her work explores political debates over education equality, rights, and opportunities as well as political struggles over access to scarce education resources. With support from the Spencer Foundation, in collaboration with Jean Robinson and Julia Lamber, she is currently studying public and political debates since the 1970s about the meaning of equality with respect to Title IX, school vouchers, and school finance reform.

HOWARD WINANT is professor of sociology at the University of California, Santa Barbara, where he also directs the New Racial Studies Project. He is author of *The World Is a Ghetto: Race and Democracy since World War II, Racial Formation in the United States: From the 1960s to the 1990s* (coauthored with Michael Omi), and *The New Politics of Race: Globalism, Difference, Justice,* among other books.